DATE DUE			

The Hitting Habit

The Hitting Habit

Anger Control for Battering Couples

Jeanne P. Deschner

THE FREE PRESS
A Division of Macmillan, Inc.
NEW YORK

Collier Macmillan Publishers
LONDON

The Free Press
A Division of Macmillan, Inc.
866 Third Avenue, New York, N. Y. 10022

Collier Macmillan Canada, Inc.

Printed in the United States of America

printing number

1 2 3 4 5 6 7 8 9 10

Library of Congress Cataloging in Publication Data

Deschner, Jeanne P.
  The hitting habit.

  Bibliography: p.
  Includes index.
  1. Wife abuse—Treatment.   2. Family violence—
Treatment.   I. Title.
RC569.5.F3D47   1984   616.85′82   83–48413
ISBN 0–02–907780–X

Page 82: From *Overcoming Frustration and Anger*, by Paul
A. Hauck. Copyright © 1974 The Westminster Press (Philadelphia); Sheldon Press (London). Used by permission.

Contents

v

Preface

This book is an outgrowth of a need I have felt for ways to help women and men locked into battering relationships through improving those relationships, rather than dissolving them as the only route to safety. My own recognition of consort battering as a serious problem requiring special treatment strategies came only about six years ago, when I was invited to co-lead a group for battered women. There was as yet no shelter for such women in our city, but a telephone hotline had been organized at a women's center. Many abused women called for counseling help and were invited to gather on Wednesday evenings for a mutual support group. I had met victims of both consort battering and child battering from time to time among clients seeking help for other problems. Like most therapists I regarded the violence as just a symptom of something else which was the real difficulty. Suddenly I was faced with a room full of battered women, all telling of years of suffering pain, fear, isolation, and humiliation. The group offered a setting where the women could weep together and be indignant together, relieving the feelings of aloneness and helplessness that go with being battered. But the only solution we had to offer was to exhort and aid the women to escape and learn how to make it on their own. To the leaders' surprise, many of the women, even those with good independent incomes, resisted this well-meant suggestion.

When some of the women in that early group began asking me to provide therapy for their husbands, I was more than a little reluctant. Based on the women's own descriptions I had pictured the men as criminals or raging wild men who would intimidate me. However, several of the wives persuaded me to see their husbands and themselves for couples therapy. I made sure I was suitably buttressed by the presence of a large, strong male co-therapist.

The battering husbands were quite unlike what I had expected: They were anything but hostile monsters toward us authority figures. Each had his own story of pain, misunderstanding, and repeated humiliation, which went far to explain, though it did not excuse, their periodic violent outbursts. They tended to downplay the seriousness of that violence, and they were extremely easily provoked into aggressively hostile moods. In between angry moments most of them seemed distinctly subassertive. In short, battering men proved to be workable clients provided their anger problems could be dealt with by the therapist.

I doubted whether those counseling sessions were of much use to the couples involved. More of them separated permanently than reconciled as a result of the therapy, which may or may not be viewed as progress. At any rate, standard relationship counseling provided little help for the problem the couples most wanted resolved, which was how to keep from lapsing into rage and violence over and over again. Their unmet needs haunted me as I continued to work with more and more battered women along with their consorts and spouses. Eventually a treatment program was developed and field tested, without benefit of grant money, using the research and training facilities of the graduate school of social work where I teach and supervise graduate interns.

This book is a response to the many requests we have received to share the treatment methods in use at our clinic with others who wish to help battering couples eliminate the violence from their relationships. It contains both theoretical information about battering and violence and how-to guidelines for use in providing anger-control training. The theoretical information is intended as preparation for work with persons expressing periodic severe rages by providing the counselor with a thorough understanding of battering behaviors. The treatment suggestions are offered as a guide that may be followed exactly or adapted in part. Particularly, the group approach suggested in this book may be adapted by a counselor for use with one couple or one violence-prone individual.

Some battering couples or individuals will profit from reading the detailed presentations of both causative factors and treatments for violent behavior. Such reading should be a supplement to working with a counselor and not a substitute, because angry people have too little perspective to help themselves easily.

Most of the anger-control training methods are applicable with little change to groups of nonbattering but angry adults and adolescents. I am convinced that anyone who has difficulty with temper outbursts or with chronic hostile feelings will benefit from training in the five areas of anger management presented in this volume.

Undoubtedly further research by ourselves and others will lead to refinements and changes in anger-control training methods. I hope that the ideas outlined herein will provide readers with the guidance and inspiration to develop their own anger-control training programs so that they may be of better help to perpetrators and victims in their own localities in overcoming their hitting habits.

The help of a number of people who have generously given their time as co-therapists is gratefully acknowledged. They include Rosie Montgomery, Paul Maginnis, Carann Feazell, Paul Halvorson, Marcia Moore, Sue Mariani, Nancy Hart, and John McNeil.

JEANNE P. DESCHNER

The Hitting Habit

1 A Close Look at Battering

Definitions

Several years ago I appeared on a local television show as a member of a panel of "experts" on marital violence. The program featured call-in questions to be answered on the spot by the panel. One quivery-voiced caller began by saying, "I don't know whether I'm battered or not, but my husband hit me last night." The host of the show replied, "I don't know either, but has it ever happened before?" The caller described three other incidents spread over two years. While she talked, the host noticed the panelists behind him vigorously nodding heads, causing him to exclaim, "Lady, you're battered!"

The incident shows the need for a clear definition of the word "battered." The TV host's spontaneous question pointed to a distinction often made between "battering" and "abuse," which hinges on the number of times attacks have occurred. The following definition conveys the spirit of this growing specialization of the term, and will be used throughout this book:

Battering is a series of physically injurious attacks on an intimate or family member that form part of a repeated, habitual pattern.

Gayford (1978) and Moore (1979) defined battering in the same way. Walker (1979) also defined battering as repeated, coercive abuse but included emotional abuse, which our definition specifically excludes. Popular usage seems to favor the restriction of the term "battering" to physically injurious attacks. Verbal assaults are serious, but physical attacks have even more drastic effects that may include pain, permanent injuries, or death. In addition, a person's body remembers and cringes involuntarily when a situation arises that resembles a previous painful and threatening event. Only after a long time do involuntary panic reactions of this sort wear off. Battered women's continued fear reactions to their consorts damage the victims' mental health and their relationships with their men. Persons who suffer purely verbal and emotional blows are abused but usually not conditioned in quite the same way to experience panicky feelings.

Most important to the definition, battering is a repeated, habitual activity. "Habitual" is defined as occurring more than twice. It takes only a few successful repetitions, averaging about three, to establish a habit. There are exceptions: If the payoff is never rewarding, even many repetitions will not lead to firm habit acquisition. Occasionally people acquire a new habit after just one memorable experiment with a new behavior (e.g. "I always carry this rabbit's foot because I found $5.00 the day I got it."). One-time fights between intimates are serious, certainly, but relationships are more often warped and personalities damaged by the anger, fear, and despair aroused by habitual, recurring abuse.

The word "battering" also is turning into a specialized term for assaults against family members or intimates, so it excludes assaults on strangers. This is a useful distinction, for attackers of family members must somehow overcome their own natural caring for the victims before they attack. The caring usually returns some time later, but the battering event includes a temporary suspension of normal nurturant and supportive attitudes toward a loved one. Such attitudes may never exist toward strangers who are assaulted.

The above definition of battering applies whether the target is a spouse or a child. There are many similarities between consort- and child-battering events, which will be pointed out in later chapters. The primary focus of this book is on the treatment of men and women caught in consort battering relationships. Most of the specific treatment methods do apply to child battering as well as to spouse battering, but the overall program was developed for situations where the victim is another adult who is able to take part in a group treatment program.

One other special term will be used frequently in this book: "consort." This old-fashioned word for a sexual partner is neutral as to gender or legal status, so it makes an admirable substitute for all those awkward words we have had to use since the sexual revolution of the past decade, such as live-in, steady, fiancé, partner, girlfriend, boyfriend, or significant other. Violence can and does erupt between unmarried as well as married sexual partners. Since the legal status of the couple seems to make little if any difference to the pattern of battering, the term "consort battering" will be used instead of wife or spouse battering.

Incidence of Battering

Only a small minority of families ever fall into the cycle of repeated violence defined as battering. No one knows what the exact incidence really is. Even when methods for collecting national statistics have been perfected, data on battering will never be fully accurate, because many assaults within the home are never reported to anyone. Data from partial surveys are hard to compare, because different definitions for violence have been used. Gelles (1972) published an early estimate of the incidence of violence based on interviews with eighty families. Using a very inclusive definition of violence, he determined that/56 percent of the couples had at some time been violent, and 20 percent were violent repeatedly. The majority of the violent acts included were so mild as to cause no physical harm. However, in the absence of any other incidence data this study has often been cited as evidence that as many as half of American families practice battering. Battering is very serious and far more common than formerly believed, but the application of a violence rate that includes pushing and slapping in the definition to cover the rate of injurious battering is misleading.

A number of those who have written about battering have found other indications of the rate of occurrence, or at least the societal cost, in the high proportion of police and court effort devoted to family violence. Domestic disturbance calls are the largest single category of police calls (Parnas, 1967). One-fifth of police fatalities and

40 percent of police injuries occur on such calls, according to some researchers. Therefore many officers dislike handling them (Bard, 1971). Sometimes even the victim attacks the officer. These calls are also extremely frustrating because the victims so often drop charges later. Likewise, more than a third of all homicides are family affairs. Wolfgang and Ferracuti (1967) found that 25 percent of Philadelphia homicides were committed by close relatives, and 10 percent beyond that were committed by paramours. Lundsgaarde (1977) studied homicides in Houston. When the various categories of consort are combined his data shows that 19 percent of all murder victims were males killed by a female consort, and 15 percent were females killed by a male consort. Therefore 34 percent of all the murders happened between consorts, a figure remarkably close to Wolfgang and Ferracuti's 35 percent rate. Gelles and Straus (1979) cited even higher ratios of consort killings to other types of homicides in other nations. These statistics indicate what a serious societal problem battering is and how important preventive programs aimed at helping battering families would be in reducing assaults and homicides. However, the data only prove how common battering is when compared to other assaults and homicides, not how common it is compared to non-battering relationships.

Levinger (1974) examined 600 records of mandatory pretrial interviews of divorcing couples in Ohio. He found that 37 percent of the wives, but only 3 percent of the husbands, complained of physical abuse. Fields (1977) reported data showing that over 50 percent of New York City women listed physical violence as one of the grounds for seeking divorce. Since cruelty is one of the legal reasons for granting divorce, these figures may be inflated by the complainants' desire to make a good case. In contrast to these studies, which both relied on court allegations, a survey sent to a stratified random sample of 150 divorcing couples suggested a lower rate for battering (O'Brien, 1974). Only 8 percent mentioned violence. Half of these were one-time events and functioned like "behaviorally extreme, social exclamation points" that precipitated the divorce action. The other half were chronic violence patterns, which meant that 4 percent of the divorces involved battering couples.

Gaquin (1977–78) reported on findings of a National Crime Survey about victimization in 60,000 households over a period of three years. Data indicated that slightly more than five out of every thou-\ sand women who had ever married had experienced spouse abuse.

They had been assaulted an average of 2.4 times by the spouse or ex-spouse. The author speculated that spouse abuse was the most underreported of the victimization categories in the survey, because some respondents might not have considered it a crime. In addition, one wonders how safe some women felt in reporting it to a government interviewer with other family members possibly present. Gaquin did not indicate whether or not consort relationships were included. Ex-spouses were included, and the survey suggested that rates of battering increased after separation or divorce. Although the National Crime Survey may have underestimated battering, still the sampling method and the size of the sample were so impressive that the rate of 0.52 percent cannot be wholly disregarded.

Findings of two statewide marital violence surveys also show much lower rates for battering. Both surveys used large, randomized samples taken from the general population of the state. Each sought to determine how many women were assaulted by their consorts each year. Their figures differed slightly, perhaps because of differing definitions of "severe abuse" rather than regional differences, but both sets of estimates were much lower than those made by earlier writers using less adequate samples. A Harris poll (1979) found that a minimum of 4 percent of Kentucky women were seriously physically abused each year by a sexual partner. Stachura and Teske (1979) reported that a minimum of 2 percent annually of Texas women were abused severely by partners. Over 11 percent of Texas women and 2 percent of Texas men had been the target of at least a slap from a consort at least once.

Straus, Gelles, and Steinmetz (1980) conducted a nationwide survey of family violence, using a stratified sample of more than 2,100 families. They reported a 16 percent rate of consort violence for the prior year, and 28 percent of the partners had engaged in violence at some time during their relationship. Their definition of violence included eight kinds of events: throwing things; pushing or shoving; slapping; kicking, hitting or biting; hitting with an object or swinging and missing; beating up the consort; threatening with a knife or a gun; and using a knife or a gun. The commonest type of violence was pushing, slapping, or shoving, which had occurred between 14 percent of the couples in the prior year. The last five violence categories, from kicking onward, were grouped together as severe violence or wife- or husband-beating, because such actions carry the risk of doing severe injury. The rates for the five acts considered severe were much lower: 3.8 percent for wife-beating and 4.6 percent for husband-beating. About half in each category were part of a repeating pattern of attacks and so would qualify as battering, which gives a 1.9 percent rate for battered wives and, interestingly, a 2.3 percent rate for battered husbands.

Straus and his associates (1980) considered these figures to be severe underestimates. However, the 2.3 percent figure closely approximates the figures from the three other studies that used randomized sampling techniques and asked private citizens rather than depending on official statistics, which all suggest about a 2 percent to 4 percent rate of battering among couples. These are the two state surveys (Harris, 1979; Stachura and Teske, 1979) and O'Brien's randomized sample of divorcing couples. Now the National Crime Survey figure of 0.5 percent cited by Gaquin (1977–78) appears closer to the mark.

These same studies suggest that noninjurious force may be used by many more couples, so that the rates for noninjurious and injurious violence combined are somewhere between 11 and 28 percent of all couples during their entire relationship. Some of these slapping and shoving incidents doubtless occur during the buildup to a severe battering episode. Others may be isolated events, not producing the sequels of sustained terror, despair, depression, and remorse that follow repeated battering events. Therefore it would appear that about one out of four couples experience some violence. But this statement should not be changed to say "one out of four couples batter," for the battering rate is surely lower. The rock bottom minimum estimate is that two out of each hundred couples are caught up in repeated battering.

Even though a minimum rate of 2 percent does not sound like very much, it actually makes battering a very common problem. Picture a typical residential street with about fifty homes lining both sides. One of those houses probably hides a battering couple. Or visualize an apartment complex of one hundred units. There are likely to be at least two battering couples in residence there. Who are they? Is the pale, strained woman who hardly ever comes out a victim? How about the big, aggressive woman whose husband finally died of alcoholism—did they batter each other? Across the United States, even a 2 percent minimum figure for battering translates into nearly three million pairs habitually injuring, endangering, and also sometimes killing each other.

Meeting Battering Couples

When battered women feel it is safe to talk, they tell heart-wrenching stories of brutal, repeated abuse, which started early in the relationship, sometimes even before marriage. The ever present prospect of more abuse forces them into a life of fear, isolation, and feelings of helplessness. Yet the women hang on, with incredible will to survive, somehow making a semblance of family life for their children and spouse in spite of their own pain and terror.

> I left home after the last beating. My eye was swollen shut and my back was hurt. I still can't twist my body without pain. The mental abuse is as bad as the actual hitting. He tells me over and over, "Look what you made me do! You made me hit you!" until I believe it. My mother was married six times and was beaten by four of the husbands. Her present husband beats her and they are both alcoholic. The fourth one raped me. My husband is too rough with our little boy, too, and I admit I get too upset about that, too. Last night he visited us where we are staying since our last fight. They got to wrestling and I got a headache and welts all over my face just from watching.
>
> (Paula, age thirty-one)

> I have divorced my husband twice but it hasn't done any good. He finds me through the kids—we have seven at home—and keeps coming over. When he is drunk, he tries to kill me. On Halloween he came in and pushed me back against the sink till something popped in my back. When I slumped to the floor, he stomped on my stomach and ribs before he left. Luckily I was able to sort of scoot over to my neighbor's, who called the ambulance. I was in traction for a week.
>
> Sometimes I hide outside if he comes and listen to find out whether he is drunk or not. One time I got in the car to escape, but he blocked me with his truck and started bumping my car backwards, toward a cliff. Fortunately some teenagers called the police. He was arrested and stayed in jail one whole day.
>
> We got married at seventeen. He started getting drunk and hitting me two years later, after he was partly disabled in a farm accident. That was about the time the first baby came along. But he is a good father and never touches his children.

Eventually he will succeed in killing me, though, because there is no way for me to escape him.

(Mary, age thirty-seven)

Battering men, however, are not the full-time monsters one would expect just from hearing battered women exchange the details of their injuries. At least, those battering men who are enough in touch with the seriousness of their actions to come to counseling are quite reasonable and rational in their dealings with persons outside their families. Some seem even more needy and dependent than their wives, and alternate between submissiveness and aggressiveness when interacting with them. The smallest differences of opinion set off heated arguments between the pair, during which, more often than not, the battered wife scores the most verbal points.

ADA: I just wanted to have some happiness, so we took the whole day off and went to the fair. But he bought all the kids cotton candy and made them sick and then he was mad.

BOB: Now wait a minute! You're the one that wanted the candy. I got it when you said . . .

ADA: (*interrupting*) I wanted it for me but you got it for everyone. The kids are just too young to handle it. You just never use your head.

BOB: Yeah, yeah, yeah (*crosses arms and glares out the window*).

ADA: I wanted to have a peaceful time. But the kids were a mess and you were carrying on about it. Then no one could have fun. (*And on and on.*)

Certain kinds of couples seem more likely than others to acquire the habit of hitting each other. In the typical case two adolescents who each "need" very urgently to set up a home independent of their parents start living together, with or without formally marrying. Their needs may stem from poverty or unhappiness, but often they are trying to escape serious home problems, such as battering, incest, alcoholism, rejection by one or both parents, or forced labor as the parentified child running the family. In cases where the battering couple met when they were older, often one or both had left home for a previous consort by age seventeen or eighteen (Montgomery, Meraz, and Deschner, 1978).

My parents divorced when I was seven years old. When I was ten my father took over custody, as my mother was in the hospital and also on welfare.

I married two years ago when I was seventeen and she was sixteen. The only job I could find was out of town, helping my father-in-law fix trucks. Our baby was born there and we both felt pretty isolated. I drank a lot and hung out with my friends. Our physical fights started then.

My wife is with her parents now and they won't let me see my baby. You see, I kidnapped him for two weeks last Christmas. My stepmother, who was like a mother to me, had died the day before. I felt desperate to get my wife back, so I took the baby to try to get her to come back to me.

(Donald, age nineteen)

Some of my students surveyed almost one hundred women entering the local refuges for battered women, asking about the backgrounds of both the women and their consorts (Deschner et al., 1980). About half the battering men (54 percent) either were victims of child battering or else had mothers who had been battered. Often they had left school and family when they met and were quickly attracted to their wives. Many, about 72 percent, were abusing alcohol or drugs.

My mother had it in for me all my life. I was the oldest and the only boy and I guess I disappointed her. She could be nice to my little sisters. My dad was a drunkard, but really I liked him better. He never said anything at all. But I could tell by the look on his face that he was on my side and understood what I was going through.

Please understand, I very seldom hit my wife. Usually I just punch a hole in the wall with my fist or break something.

(Bill, age thirty)

He doesn't drink that much, but he is usually high on drugs. In fact he is now dealing in drugs and is out on bail. I used to try so hard to make everything perfect so he wouldn't be angry, but nothing was enough. Lately he has been hitting me every day for some little thing.

(Mary Ann, age twenty-three)

Less than a third (29 percent) of the battered women had experienced violence in their childhood. But half of them (57 percent) were oldest daughters in their families, and 49 percent fulfilled duties of a parentified child, substituting for an alcoholic, disturbed, or absent parent. Some were subjected to incest as part of the role switch.

> My earliest memory is of standing up at the kitchen sink on a wooden apple crate to make me tall enough, washing the dishes and weeping and crying for my mother. I was about four, and she was upstairs in bed having one of her crazy spells. She stayed in bed for a year that time. My father made me take care of the house, my mother, and my little brother, too. My father used to get in my pants, too. I got away at sixteen by marrying a man I didn't love.
>
> (Esther, age thirty-five)

> My mother worked nights when I was a kid. It was my job to keep my younger brothers quiet, which was hard to do. If they woke her up, then my father whipped me when he got home. Now my own wife works nights and when the baby cries while she's sleeping during the day, I just can't stand it.
>
> (Leon, age twenty-six)

These true cases give a glimpse of the pain endured by so many battering men and women as children, which drove them to initiate and then to persevere in unwise relationships, always hoping that need equals love and that their consorts would someday fulfill their dream for a happier life.

In other battering couples only one or neither partner fits the needy-adolescent pattern. Sometimes abuse of alcohol brings about the violence. Other times one or both of the partners is actually mentally ill and acts violently or else goads the consort into attacking by repeated crazy behavior. Some battering men seem to have learned habits of violence in military combat or some other high-violence environment, such as the criminal underworld or, sad to say, the police force.

> My parents never hit each other, or me. My dad did teach me to box, in self-defense. I joined the Marines at sixteen and when I got back from Vietnam, I was a very different person.

Nobody was going to get the jump on me. I would just explode.
My dad and I tried boxing again and I nearly killed him.

(Warren, age thirty-four)

Child Batterers

Since 1968 all states have required reporting of suspected cases of
child abuse. Therefore statistics are somewhat better for this category of family battering. Rates for child battering appear roughly
similar to those for consort battering. At least 4 percent of parents,
probably many more, use physical force on their children each year
(Straus, Gelles, and Steinmetz, 1980). Rates for severe child battering may be about 0.8 percent or about eight in a thousand children
under eighteen. This estimate is derived from 1980 census figures.
There are about 61,744,000 minor children in the United States and
500,000 abuse cases year year. According to Gil (1970) children under age three suffer 65 percent of the severe and fatal injuries. Gil's
figures were based on official reports of nearly 13,000 child abuse
cases.

Gil also found that half of all child abusers were mothers, and
one-third were single mothers. Many were very young women. About
40 percent were fathers or stepfathers, leaving only 10 percent of
child abusers in a nonparental relationship to the victim.

The relationship between consort battering and child abuse has
not been well documented, but most researchers find hints of a significant causal relation. The nature of the relationship will be examined in the next chapter on societal and personal factors that make
battering more likely. From one-quarter (Straus et al., 1980) to one-
third (Stacey and Shupe, 1983) of battering adults also abuse their
children at times. In turn these abused children tend to be very violent toward siblings and playmates, and even attack adults. Many
grow up to beat their own consorts and children. So battering behavior is passed on from generation to generation.

The most common or typical kind of child batterer comes from
a background similar to that of the typical consort batterer. Very
often they come from chaotic and deprived families (Oates, 1979)
and hasten to have children out of their intense need for someone
to love them. Episodes of unemployment are common and correlate
with increases in child abuse (Gil, 1970). Often one or both parents

grew up in a battering family. One may even have been placed in institutional or foster care as a result of abuse. When they become parents they are woefully ignorant of young children's developmental needs. They either consider it proper to discipline with injurious severity or are so beset by emotional problems that they easily go into an uncontrolled punitive rage against an irritating infant or child.

> My mother really rejected me. She had me put into a foster home when I was fourteen. By the time I was seventeen, I had run away to _____ and was into the drug scene and had a baby. I loved my little boy, but I couldn't take care of him right. The Welfare took him away from me after six months. They said I abused him. I let him be adopted. I hope it was for the best.
>
> (Penny, age thirty-one and battered)

> My four-year-old got into the car and released the brake, for the second time in a week. It was rolling slowly right at my baby daughter when I jumped in and stopped it. He could have killed her and so I just lost all control. I was choking him and really trying to kill him when they stopped me. But if he ever endangers her again I swear I will kill him. My own father? I never speak to him or write to him. He was very harsh towards me and I hate him.
>
> (Harold, age thirty-five)

The Cycle of Violence

The similarities between at least the typical cases of consort and child battering suggest that the phenomenon of family violence may be the same whether the target is an adult or a child. The greatest similarities occur in the acts of violence and the events building up to them. Participant accounts are the chief source for understanding the usual course of events. Reports from eyewitnesses would be more objective, but witnesses seldom see an entire battering episode. The only series of observational studies was on families with aggressive, acting-out offspring done in Oregon (Patterson, Reid, Jones, and Conger, 1975). Patterson and his co-workers made a unique contribution to the understanding of family violence by sending trained observers into troubled homes for two weeks of daily observations. The candid observations were permitted because the attackers were aggressive, out-of-control children and the victims often included parents as well as siblings. Their findings about violence between intimates appear to apply whatever the age or role status of the aggressor or victim.

First, some family member does something noxious to others. Another family member reacts to the unpleasant behavior by threatening punishing consequences, in hopes of coercing the first person into stopping. But if the threat is merely unpleasant rather than painful, the first person may increase the intensity of his or her negative acts too, trying as it were to outpunish the punisher. Patterson and Hops (1972) called these unpleasant scenes coercion spirals. They documented that some aggressive, out-of-control children frequently engage in coercion spirals with their parents. The child misbehaves, the parent threatens, the child behaves even more obnoxiously, the parent threatens harder, and so on, until finally the weary parent gives in in order to get some peace. If parents consistently give in, they eventually train up a little monster who will escalate tantrums, coercions, and even violence to any length in order to force the parent to stop demanding better behavior.

On the other hand, parents may resort to physical force in order to win out against the annoying or crying child. The child, being smaller and weaker, will have to submit to greater force in the end. Since the child is, in this instance, the one to give in consistently, the parent is the one trained to act like a monster. The parent, in fact, becomes a child abuser. Battered babies often unwittingly initiate a coercion spiral by refusing to be quickly comforted when crying. The abusive parent eventually shouts at, shakes or strikes the wailing infant in the effort to force it into obeying. The terrified infant may howl louder, causing the parent to strike harder, until finally the injured child loses consciousness.

The loser of the coercion spiral is rewarded too, in a negative way, because the winner also ceases for the time being to make coercive demands. Some victims admit that they may deliberately precipitate a battering incident "in order to get it over with" or "because he's always nicer afterwards."

Consort battering fits very well into the model of coercive exchanges building up to aggression by one party and forced submission by the other partner. The exchanges of nags and threats during the buildup phase clearly take the form of a coercion spiral. It hardly matters whether the husband or the wife initiated the first unpleasant event, for they both respond by trying to control the other person via escalation of negative remarks and threats, until one of them loses control and resorts to physical force to make the other one submit.

The spiral theory suggests that the pattern would not be repeated over and over unless each party was sometimes the victor, encouraging the hope that sufficient intensification of demands would coerce the other person into submission. Infants, children, and also consorts who never win coercion contests with a batterer eventually cease to make any demands at all. In cases of extreme child abuse, the young victim no longer cries or initiates any actions but stays still, in a state of "frozen watchfulness." Some very depressed, helpless, and submissive battered wives may be in a similar state. If an abused child still fusses or occasionally acts out, or a battered wife still resists or complains once in a while, it suggests that they still hope to win some of the coercive contests.

Based on several hundred interviews with battered women, Walker (1979) put together a graphic description of the cycle of consort violence, divided into three main phases: a tension-building phase, an acute violence stage, and a repentance phase. In the tension-building stage the batterer engages in minor threats and aggressions, and the victim attempts to cope either by trying to become more blameless, by counter-coercing, or both. Eventually violence breaks out, marked by uncontrolled and uncontrollable rage and primitive attack behaviors. The victim may fight back at first, but most victims soom learn that total passive submission is their best hope for getting the abuser to stop. This phase lasts from two to twenty- four hours, according to Walker. After the violence comes a repentance phase in which the batterer regrets and disavows the harm he has done and endeavors to win the victim back by generous gifts and voluntary submission to her wishes.

Battering accounts I have collected indicate that Patterson's and Walker's models should be combined. The result is a model of the battering cycle that goes through seven stages, whether the victim is a consort or a child:

1. *Mutual Dependency*

Two very needy individuals form a consort relationship, with expectations that all their own needs will be met by the other person. Many promises are exchanged, and passionate feelings generated, making for a very intensive and exciting, but isolated, relationship. The same sort of involvement frequently occurs between an abusive parent and a battered child. Both participants often are quite immature, in both consort battering and child battering dyads. The batterer may remain the subordinate person most of the time during the dependency stage. The battered woman often feels her consort is like an extra child that she must take care of and cannot abandon. The battered child may be required to try to satisfy all the emotional needs and some of the physical needs of the parent during dependency interludes.

2. *Noxious Event*

The victim-to-be does something unpleasant. A baby cries and refuses to stop crying despite the parent's efforts to hush him or her. A wife is away when her husband wants her attention. A husband buys liquor with the rent money and his wife complains. Often the noxious event seems incredibly trivial from the perspective of a few days later.

3. *Coercions Exchanged*

The abuser-to-be makes an attempt to stop the unpleasant behavior by means of verbal threats or denunciations. Sometimes it works, but often the consort just argues back or the baby cries harder. A spiral of escalating negative exchanges occurs.

4. *"Last Straw" Decision*

The climax comes when the potential abuser decides that the situation is intolerable. This is a key decision. If it is never made, violence is avoided. A prior history of verbally attacking and blaming the other party, and different cultural values about what is an intolerable affront, affect the speed with which this climax is reached.

5. *Primitive Rage*

Rage wells up in response to the preceding judgment. In their primitiveness, the rage behaviors of both consort and child abusers are very similar. Possessions in the house and even the walls and doors may be attacked indiscriminately. The batterer kicks, beats, bites, chokes, or even shoots the victim many more times than strictly necessary to win. Afterward many batterers have genuine trouble remembering what happened, as if their reasoning minds were switched off when rage took over.

Everyone has a repertory of aggressive behaviors, ranging from "humpf" for disapproval to lethal attacks. Their use depends on several factors, such as the amount of rage, threats made during the buildup that commit one's honor, resistance of the victim, and availability of weapons. Inhibitions against injuring a loved one disappear for the time being in a fog of primitive rage. In many battering families inhibitions already are low, since making frequent use of physical punishment for discipline seems to make violence easier to commit.

6. *Reinforcement for Battering*

Nearly all battered women agree that unless the victim is physically stronger, the best hope for surviving a rage attack is to submit as quietly as possible. Any struggling or resistance is likely to arouse further aggression. Unfortunately, this very lifesaving submissiveness functions to reinforce the battering behavior, because the target ceases doing whatever it was that displeased the attacker. This kind of reinforcement has a technical name, negative reinforcement. It is reinforcement because it maintains or even increases the preceding behavior, but it is negative because the reward comes from the cessation of some noxious stimulus. The batterer may want something much more positive like reassurance or proof of love. But the cessation of the victim's annoying behaviors is sufficient to reward his or her violent outbursts.

If not too badly injured, the victim may further reward the batterer by making placating gestures, such as taking all the blame on herself or trying harder to please him by providing food, housework, or sex. Battered children very often attempt to charm the battering parent soon after an abuse event, leading to the mistaken impression that they liked the abuse.

Even the victim finally gets some negative reinforcement for her submission, when at last the batterer ceases attacking. Placating gestures may earn further negative reinforcement by making the batterer's anger dissolve.

7. *Repentance Phase*

Both partners are deeply shocked by the final outbreak of violence. The victims withdraw to nurse their wounds. They may disappear completely by going to a hospital or a shelter. At the very least, they are too stunned to nurture their batterers in the usual manner. The attackers, because of partial amnesia, may hardly believe it was they who did such destructive things. Even if they can remember, they now feel so different that it seems the action of some other person. It is therefore easy for them to disown the violence and to swear sincerely that it could never happen again. Since the repentance and resolve to reform are so genuine, the victims more or less overcome their shock and fear and decide it is safe to continue to live with the contrite batterer, trying to believe their vows that it will never happen again. But unfortunately, submission during the rage phase has already made a recurrence of violence more likely by supplying negative reinforcement.

The net effect of the repentance phase is that batterers voluntarily abdicate the dominant position won by violent coercion. Protesting their neediness over and over, they pull their victims back into the mutual dependancy stage, which starts the whole battering cycle off again.

There is growing research evidence to support the cyclical model of battering, which also indicates that not all dyads go through all phases to come out at repentance and reconciliation. Stacey and Shupe (1983) reported that 49 percent of batterers felt the abuse was justified, 63 percent apologized to the victim, and 44 percent acted affectionately. Since these figures exceed 100 percent, the men evidently cycled through several reactions. But if the 63 percent figure for apologies is taken as the maximum number of men going through the full battering cycle, it suggests that slightly over one-third do not. Dobash and Dobash (1979) surveyed Scottish battered women and concluded that only about 30 percent of the men eventually expressed remorse after physical assaults. The other 70 percent continued to berate their wives verbally after attacking them or else just ignored the fact that the partner had been hurt and resumed business as usual. If they did refer later to the abuse incident, they either blamed the wives for causing all the trouble or belittled the extent of their injuries. The Dobashes' data indicated that the repentance phase was common in new relationships and dropped out after several years of violence. A survey of twenty-five battered women conducted by one of my students (Ballentine, 1983) revealed that 88 percent of couples went through the repentance phase the first time violence occurred, but only 32 percent of the batterers were still showing remorse by the time the victims fled to a shelter. The repentance phase dropped out of the cycle after an average of 2.25 years of battering.

One trouble with drawing conclusions about the prevalence of a repentance stage from the surveys cited is that the researchers made no distinctions between the out-of-control violence of the rage stage and the minor abuse incidents characteristic of the buildup phase. Couples spend a great deal more time conducting the skirmishes in the buildup than they do in raging fights. The British euphemism for battering is "thumping," and much of the violence occurring in the buildup phase could properly be called thumps. Such gestures are part of the exchange of coercive threats. Therefore, they do not evoke either fear or repentance but an escalation of anger on both sides. But after an uncontrolled outburst, when the victim is injured or is horrified enough to withdraw emotionally, the batterer generally must go through a semblance of contrition in order to get the victim back into a mutual dependancy relationship and restart the cycle.

Truncated Cycles

After many years of battering, the cycle may shorten to two stages: buildup and attack, buildup and attack. The batterer may abuse the victim every day, and the victim may stay full time in a frightened and submissive posture. Such victims struggle to please and placate the batterer and to avoid contact as much as possible. Their efforts can only temporarily postpone the routine of violence. The plight of such women and/or children is exactly like that of prisoners in a concentration camp. Some who escape from battering refer to their lives in just such terms.

> It was like living at the bottom of a very deep, dark well. He beat me nearly every day. He would get after me for any little thing. One night he made me stay up all night rewashing and reironing every one of his shirts, just because he had found a wrinkle in one of them. There were twenty-four in all, and it took me all night.
>
> (Mary Ann, age twenty-five)

> My father drank and was very abusive. I will not tell you the cruel things he did, but it was very rough for my mom and all of us kids. My mom went after us sometimes too. When I was fourteen I ran off and started working and living on my own.
>
> (Bert, age twenty-nine)

Victims who have felt imprisoned do not express the usual ambivalent desires to go back to the perpetrator once they have escaped. They experience no lingering love for their tormenters. For many it is as difficult to escape as it would be from an official prison and a return would be unthinkable. Mary Ann continued her story:

> He used to hide the car keys every night, but one night he forgot. I gathered up the baby and left and came to this shelter because it is in another city. I have filed for divorce and my lawyer will not tell him where I am and I never will. I left a beautiful home and furniture, but I only care about being free. I hope I never see him again.

Another truncated cyclical pattern may result from spouses periodically trading victim and persecutor roles. A classic form of this marital game was described by Satir (1972) as a victim-persecutor-rescuer triangle. Often three family members play this deadly game, frequently switching positions. Battering couples seem to play the game with only two participants taking turns at the three roles. The persecuting men switch at times to "rescuing" their wives by submerging themselves in a repentance phase. At other times the women leave off verbal persecutions (nagging) to rescue their spouses by caretaking. When neither will any longer play rescuer, the fighting pair simply alternate between giving and getting punishment. After a period of abuse the wife rises up and scolds her husband or else withdraws from him. After tolerating her negatives for a period, he rises up again in another act of violence. They never rescue each other by going into a stage of repentance and reconciliation. Such marriages, though not enjoyable, can be stable over a long period of time because each partner periodically enjoys the rewards of being on top.

> It has been the same way all thirty years we have been married. All she does is pester me; she never gives me a moment's peace except when I get rough. Truly I am afraid to retire and stay home with her all day. She will make me have a heart attack in a month. You can understand why I have to shut her up forcibly sometimes.
>
> (Al, age sixty-two)

Is the Cycle Theory Just a New Way to Blame the Victim?

Many explanatory theories concerning social problems seem to blame the victim for their own troubles. The unemployed are called shiftless and lazy, rape victims are labeled provocative or careless, and battered wives are called shrewish or masochistic. Such labels may fit a few cases, but the great majority of the victims in each of these categories did nothing to merit the magnitude of their suffering.

By entering into an entangled mutual dependency relationship and by actions at various points in the seven stages in the battering cycle, battering victims do make their own abuse more likely. In particular, they attempt to control their consort or parent during the buildup phase either by placating or by escalating the coercive statements, or by a mixture of both. In the acute stage they submit and inadvertantly reinforce violence. Finally, in the repentance stage they reconcile without ever enforcing a meaningful negative consequence for violent behaviors.

Making abuse more likely is not the same as causing it. Batterers still are responsible for allowing themselves to go out of control and behave as if a loved and needed person is a dire enemy. Attacks, even self-defensive attacks, are never justified inside the family. Except when a family member is truly intent on committing homicide, it is never a do-or-die situation inside one's own family, because alternative solutions are always available.

Batterers also are victims part of the time. Partly because they fear their own loss of self-control, many behave submissively and tolerate verbal complaints and minor abuse out of fear that if they resist at all their anger will carry them too far. Most battering men seem less skilled at verbal warfare than their wives, so they endure losses in numerous verbal confrontations. In addition they are prey to lonely feelings as their battered partners pull away from them emotionally. Finally, batterers are especially vulnerable to that most painful of human emotions, jealousy.

When physical violence breaks out, batterers may receive as well as inflict injuries. Victims-to-be may unwisely initiate the fighting or fight back in desperation. The official victim is the one who submits in the end, but both participants may receive painful wounds during the stage of primitive and violent aggression. Finally, some victims who decide they have had enough do murder their abusive consorts or parents.

An understanding of the variations in behavior of both attackers and victims during the seven stages of the violence cycle gives a very different perspective on the reasons battered women and children keep on loving their attackers and keep going back to them. Few battering consorts and parents are full-time monsters deserving long prison sentences. Most are needy human beings who are often lovable and even loving. They have acquired a grievous habit of accessing their own primitive violence in order to get their way with family members, and their victims have inadvertently reinforced their attacks by submitting. But between attacks most of them are capable of behaving quite differently toward the victim as well as behaving normally toward other family members, work associates, and others.

Why Do Women Stay?

According to information recently collected from women entering shelters in my own region (Stacey and Shupe, 1983), 75 percent of battered women tolerate abuse for more than one year before leaving and 26 percent tolerate it for over more than five years. The overall average length that abuse had occurred was 2.5 years. Only five years earlier, in 1978, prior to the opening of the first refuges in the area for battered women, I found that battered women calling a crisis hotline established at a women's center had been living with violence for an average of 6.6 years (Montgomery, Meraz, and Deschner, 1978). They had left home an average of 8.7 times, and several had divorced and then remarried the same man. No substantial changes in the laws have been accomplished between 1978 and 1982, and the economy has certainly worsened. The principal change has been the establishment of four small refuges in the greater metropolitan area. The finding that the average duration of a battering relationship has shortened from more than six years to less than three suggests that the refuges for battered women are having considerable success in helping their clients to leave battering relationships permanently.

Professionals have felt frustrated because when they have tried to help the women escape, the women either would not leave or would leave and soon return. Not too many years ago therapists labeled such women masochistic, secretly loving pain. Others have theorized that battered women have immature needs to be dependent on someone, or else they are using the neurotic defense tactic of identifying with their aggressor. Researchers have found that women who were abused as children tended to stay in battering relationships much more than women who were not (Gelles, 1976; Coleman and Weinman, 1978). This does not necessarily mean that they identify with the aggressor. More likely they have just learned resignation to such conditions. A few battered women even seem to go back to a dangerous consort again and again as if they were addicted to the soap opera–like excitement of the battering cycle.

> I have felt dead inside ever since I left him. I mean, I just can't feel anything, like I'm numb. But I contacted him last night, just to see if he still cared, and now I feel good again. I know you think I'm crazy to let him know where I am again, but I can't stand this feeling inside me, which he makes go away.
>
> (Ann, age twenty-three)

Battered children in care routinely show the same sort of illogical pull to return to their abusive parent, according to child welfare workers. Such children often worry, in the manner of a care-giver, about the parent's welfare or may romanticize about the parent's love as providing much more happiness than the foster family does. Only those whose parents have never cycled through repentance and mutual dependancy phases can easily give up their longing to return to a battering natural parent.

Since the typical battered woman left school to marry and bear children at a young age, she is faced with severe economic problems if she leaves a wage-earning consort to escape his battering. Rental of an apartment large enough to accommodate the children, plus child care costs, will consume most of what she can earn. Even if she worked and paid most of the bills before separation, credit cards and utility hookups were most probably in her consort's name, so she will have no credit rating to help her get started. If she stays home with the children instead of working, the welfare payments in some states will be insufficient for the family to survive. If she demands that her husband pay child support, he is quite likely not to remit it consistently and is even more likely to reenter her life. The director of a shelter for battered women summed it up: "If a woman leaves the shelter without having organized the four basic economic necessities, she will soon go back to the batterer. The four basics are a place to live, a source of income, child care arrangments, and transportation, which in our town means a car" (Tunnell, 1982).

Followup data on ex–shelter residents have been extremely hard to collect. Women who have just left a shelter often are too poor to afford a telephone or to stay put in one residence for very long. Shelter staff estimate that between 25 and 50 percent of their residents sooner or later return to their consorts, no matter what the danger of enduring further battering. Ballentine (1983) tracked the postshelter living arrangements of twenty-five battered women who had fled to area shelters, in order to learn what factors influenced their decision to return home or go on to independent living. Two-thirds were living apart from their consorts, and one-third had returned home. Success in making adequate new arrangements for housing and child care was the most significant influence on the women's decisions, with a judgment that their mate was a good father coming in second. Presence or absence of a repentance phase in the couple's battering cycle made a slight additional difference in the decision about where to go after leaving the shelter.

Economic considerations may have loomed so important in this study because the women who flee to shelters tend to have no financial resources at all of their own. Women with some money, including most employed and middle-class women, seem to resist leaving their abusive consorts or to go back after they do leave, more out of emotional than economic considerations. They are reluctant to separate even when they have adequate resources to manage as single parents. Many battered women seem to be unusually intensely involved with their consort relationships. That involvement, rather than reality-based legal and financial problems, often is the crucial element in their remaining with or going back to a clearly dangerous companion.

> I hate it when he hits me and yells at me. But I still love him and I want to live with him, but minus the violence.
>
> (Sara, age twenty-seven)

> I have been living with him for a year and he has been beating me for the past six months. He starts with maybe a shake, then it goes on to punching and choking. The last time was last weekend. He is not working and he was drunk. We are both living off my wages—I'm glad to get out of the apartment to work. But in a way I feel sorry for him. He is like a little boy, sort of weak and helpless. He had a terrible life as a child. I keep thinking that if I leave him he will sink right back down into the gutter where I found him.
>
> (Beth, age twenty)

Basically, battered women and children tend to return not because they love pain but because they hope and believe that life is mostly better with the batterer and his or her resources than without them, and that perhaps no more attacks will take place. As one veteran battered wife (Mary, with seven children and two divorces from their father) told a group of younger abused women, "As long as you have hope, you will be in danger."

Punishments Instead of Reinforcements for Battering

Not every episode of family violence leads to development of a chronic battering habit. Many first abuse events are never followed by second episodes. Some first assaults are followed by separation or divorce instead. Women who take care of themselves by separating for good after one fight never become battered wives. Children, of course, do not have the luxury of divorcing abusive parents. Some few attempt the same thing by running away. Many plunge into marriage as soon as anyone will have them, because marriage is their first opportunity to escape the abusive parent.

A very few women respond to chronic battering by mounting a superior counteroffensive. The punishment finally forces the men to learn how to stop themselves short of actual violence.

> He used to hit me, but he hasn't touched me for over two years, since I shot him in the thigh. He knows I keep my pistol, loaded, right here in my purse, and I always keep my purse right with me [pats the large handbag she always clutches in her lap].
>
> (Jean, age twenty-eight)

> My old man used to beat on me till one day I knocked him clean out the kitchen door and off the back porch. It plumb broke him of the habit.
>
> (Phoebe, age fifty-seven)

Hauck (1974) also described a battered wife who figured out a way to supply delayed punishment whenever she was forced to submit to violence. She waited until her husband was asleep, and then hit him on the head with the heel of a shoe. This woke him quite rudely and he beat her again, but she repeated the act whenever he fell asleep. After a few nights he began to suffer from insomnia. He stopped hitting her and confined himself to verbal arguments.

These strategies are not recommended for general imitation by battered wives. There is too much danger that the batterer will respond by escalating the violence up to the point of permanent injury or even murder. Nor do I recommend that the victim murder the family member who torments her, even though the homicide statistics indicate that many women and a few children do so. The outcome is likely to be a prison sentence, not necessarily an improvement in the battered person's situation.

A recent experiment conducted by the Police Foundation (Boffey, 1983) revealed that battering men arrested by police answering domestic disturbance calls had a lower recidivism rate than batterers to whom the officers administered advice or mediation, or who were ordered to leave the house for eight hours to cool off. Though the study, conducted in Minneapolis, has some flaws, it does suggest that prompt punishment by police authorities can make the commission of further battering seem unattractive to many individuals.

Victims of battering who have learned to use the anger-control strategies presented in this book also are able to cut down on and frequently eliminate violence from their relationships. Some have done so even though the batterer refused to take part in the training. Unless the batterer is truly psychotic, victims can learn to help themselves even if they choose not to leave.

2 Social and Personal Factors in Battering

Violence against wives and children is not just a product of modern urban society. The forceful subjugation of the weaker family members by the stronger is an ancient human tradition. Biology has something to do with destiny, in this instance at least. Not only are women generally not as strong and tall as men, but they have special needs for protection and assistance during pregnancy and early motherhood. The domination of men over women may also have derived from the extremely frequent ill health of women in societies with primitive obstetric practices, as a recent history of female health points out (Shorter, 1982).

At any rate, family violence has been legally recognized at least as long as written records have been kept by humans. The ancient Code of Hammurabi, the earliest known set of written laws, granted men the right to chastise their wives and children physically (May, 1978). In early patriarchal societies women and children were part of men's possessions, just like livestock. The natural corollary of possession was and is the use of whatever force is deemed necessary to keep control. The "right of chastisement" of wives seemed so proper that it continued to be a part of English common law until the early twentieth century. Not too many years ago children could expect to be beaten with sticks both at home and at school. The general cultural acceptance of a certain amount of violence among family members continues up to the present. The spread of the urban nuclear family pattern may actually encourage violence because of the privacy afforded to perpetrators (Gelles, 1978).

Cultural Factors in Battering

The Euro-American cultural atmosphere unwittingly helps promote battering through the traditional behavior repertories assigned to feminine and masculine roles. Parents and peers selectively reward aggressive behavior in boys and discourage aggressive acts in girls. Little girls receive the same modeling of aggression from their parents, peers, and television shows, but girls are not rewarded for imitating the aggressive models. Therefore girls learn to confine most of their aggressive actions to verbal bitchiness. Because they are smaller and weaker than so many potential foes, they practice physical aggression mainly in situations where they feel sure of victory, such as conflicts with younger siblings.

Furthermore, the traditional female vocational role of homemaker gives women little control over their own lives. Instead, their welfare and success depend on marrying a successful man. Walker (1977–78) and many other authors have noted that the more traditionally oriented women who believe strongly in marriage and homemaking have a much a harder time escaping from a battering relationship. Instead of believing themselves capable of finding a good life outside the abusive marriage, they struggle endlessly to make the marriage work.

Severe physical punishment for wives and children who get out of line is still the norm in some subcultures in our society. Toby (1974) concluded that the right to behave violently toward one's intimates lingers on as a clandestine masculine ideal in the subcultures where men achieve relatively little social power, as the one method by which they can affirm their masculinity. When the husband's educational or occupational status is lower than the wife's, he also has a greater tendency to use violence (O'Brien, 1971). Goode (1974) suggested that violence is a last-ditch resource used by such males to gain an area of dominance that society expects but has made it impossible to achieve in any other way. In addition, some particular groups seem to develop their own ways to punish family members. Densen-Gerber (1978) related how some groups in the New York City ghettos consider it proper parenting to punish a baby's lapses in toilet training by scalding the infant's bottom with hot water. British social workers report that some gypsy families routinely punish their children with cigarette burns. Social workers have found it quite difficult to persuade parents from such subgroups to cease their harsh practices and try less harmful methods of discipline. Children growing up in such cultures may not consider themselves battered. But the risk that occasional punishment episodes may turn into chronic battering is much greater among these families, because injurious attacks on family members are being practiced and reinforced.

In the United States the majority culture is remarkably encouraging of violence. Actually we live in quite an uncivilized civilization. The government, along with other governments, engages in wars and arms races in between wars with the potential of killing off all life on the earth. Cartoons, TV shows, movies, and the evening news all celebrate the fun and entertainment value as well as the political value of violence every day. In contrast, Asian families practice much less violence (Goode, 1974).

Researchers have found that although battering occurs in every ethnic and economic group, certain groups are decidely more at risk than others (Straus, Gelles, and Steinmetz, 1980). Numerous surveys have established the link between low economic status and battering. Gil (1970) found that nearly 60 percent of abusive families in a large sample had received public assistance funds in the prior year, and nearly half the fathers had been unemployed. Most abusers were poorly educated, and 60 percent belonged to minority ethnic groups. Nearly every survey of battering victims, including my own, yields similar findings.

The macho, male-dominant pattern associated with Hispanic family organization also pervades many anglo and black families with recent rural roots. Macho family patterns are rigidly hierarchical, with the male as unquestioned head, a system that legitimizes chastisement if not battering of wives and children.

Lack of financial resources severely stresses family members, especially the designated breadwinner, who experiences not only deprivation but the pleadings and scoldings of other family members. Poverty in itself does not lead to violence in a society where everyone is poor together. The lack of money in an affluent, money-dependent economy creates stress because of the greater expectations families have of obtaining the comforts they see others enjoy. The stress, and not the lack of money in itself, predisposes members of the family to acts of violence.

Middle-class and even upper-class families definitely do become involved in both consort and child battering, but not at the same rate. Not only do they have more money and goods, but also victims and potential victims can escape more easily. Women can afford divorces, couples can afford therapy, and abusive parents can afford housekeepers and summer camp to reduce the rate of stress-producing interactions with target children. So, because they experience less financial stress and have more ways to reduce contact with irritating family members, middle-class families engage in battering less often. It has been my observation that most middle-class families caught up in battering cycles have one or more members who are either drug or alcohol dependent, or otherwise severely emotionally disturbed. The behavior of such a person creates extreme interpersonal stress among all family members. Until more middle-class battering couples enter treatment it will not be possible to corroborate this observation.

An important aspect of a family's ability to withstand financial and interpersonal stress is its linkage to helpful support systems. This is especially important for families with young children. Battering families tend to be socially isolated, having few reliable relatives and few or no friends. Often they are new arrivals in a community. They are unaware of even the few existing community resources that could help them. The transient life of so many battering families also makes it difficult for social workers to provide early help, because many move away shortly after entering counseling. Incidentally, married battering mothers were found to be even more isolated than single mothers in one Swedish study (Parke and Lewis, 1981). Women living with husbands or consorts tend to use them as their primary support systems. If they try to reach out to some wider support network, they may have to contend with the partner's jealousy. If that one and only support system is unreliable, they have nowhere else to turn for aid in coping with a child who tempts them to uncontrolled rage and violence.

Alcohol and Drug Factors in Battering

Clearly, families with members who abuse alcohol or drugs are more at risk for battering. A survey of ninety-three battered women (Deschner, Geddes, Grimes, and Stancukas, 1980) indicated that alcohol or drug abuse was a cause of violence in about 72 percent of the cases. A larger survey of 452 battered women (Stacey and Shupe, 1983) found that alcohol or drug use was implicated in 70 percent of battering episodes. Ninety counselors operating programs for battering men reported that alcohol or drugs were involved in about 67 percent of battering relationships (Feazell, 1981). Usually the batterer is the problem drinker, but some spouse abuse is related to the victim's excessive use of alcohol. Either both husband and wife are drunk at the time of the battering, or the battering occurs when the wife is drunk and becomes particularly aversive to her partner.

May (1978) quoted a report dating from 1897 that ascribed one-half of the cases of child abuse to parental drunkenness. More recently, some researchers have pointed to excessive use of alcohol among some abusive parents (Young, 1964; Gil, 1970), but others have found very little alcohol abuse among their populations of abusive parents (Steele and Pollack, 1968; Smith, 1978). Perhaps alcohol does trigger less child abuse than consort abuse, because an adult is aware of how her partner's drinking is contributing to her suffering, and so she cannot refrain from attempting to reform him. Her attempts to get him to bring home at least part of his paycheck, for example, will repeatedly start the coercive spiral going that will eventually end in his beating her into silence. Young children may not be aware of the key role of alcohol in a parent's personality shifts or in the periodic lack of food in the house; even if they are aware, they usually try to stay out of the way rather than confront the drinking parent.

Since only (!) about 20 percent of adult American men are heavy drinkers (Calahan and Room, 1974) drinking and family violence appear to have an association that is far greater than chance. However, an association does not prove causation, and indeed batterers seldom indicate that they drink in order to become violent. Instead, evidence indicates that many heavy drinkers initiate their drinking in an effort to tolerate stressful situations that they feel helpless to correct (Marlatt, 1979). As several hours of drinking pass, the bad physical feelings may mingle with anxious thoughts about the wife's negative reaction when he returns, setting off anger and violence before the consort even knows there is a problem. Knowles and Middleton (1980) found that about 40 percent of the battering episodes studied seemed to have no clear precursor in the form of a quarrel. Sometimes the wife was even awakened in the middle of the night by a surprise attack. Such attacks were often very severe and injurious, and "almost always the assailant was drunk."

Densen-Gerber (1978) indicated that child abuse and child killing are far more common among drug addicts than among other parents. The mother's drug use exposes the unborn infant to risk of abnormality and handicap, factors which themselves increase risk of abuse by a frustrated parent. After birth the drug-taking impairs the caretaking parent's thinking. Drug users are particularly poor at thinking through the consequences of actions, so that they do not predict the results of such acts as hitting an infant, leaving it alone in the bathtub, permitting dangerous play, or forgetting to feed it. Mothers who heavily use prescription drugs also may become abusive. A British research team found that up to 90 percent of the abusive mothers being treated had at some time been on tranquilizers or antidepressants (Lynch, Lindsay, and Ounsted, 1975; Lynch, 1978). The medicines were usually prescribed by well-meaning doctors to combat the mothers' depression or anxiety, but apparently they had the side effect of lowering their inhibitions against acting out aggressively in response to their frustration and anxiety.

Family Factors in Battering

Women are socialized to earn rewards by acting nurturantly, a natural activity for women anyway. Some women, often those who have experienced the parentified-child role, are so fixated on nurturing others that they cannot assertively take care of themselves. They fear causing the other person pain, a condition that Richardson (1977) called "altruistic madness." Many battered women do seem to exhibit altruistic madness, for they disregard their own physical injuries and danger and stay because they worry about their consort's well-being. They are able to leave the man to fend for himself only when one of the children is finally included in the abuse, evoking a competing altruistic response.

A majority (64 percent) of battered women are eldest daughters, according to a survey of almost one hundred women in shelters conducted by a team of my students (Deschner et al., 1980). Most of the women had been pressed into service during childhood as the caretaker of siblings, household manager, and sometimes caregiver for an alcoholic, ill, or immature parent as well. Their "altruistic madness" enabled them to survive, for safety for a young parentified child lies in successfully caring for and restoring the incompetent parent to the role of resource provider. Such a role devolves most naturally on the eldest daughter, though some oldest or only sons and a few younger daughters also must assume responsibilities belonging to their parents.

In contrast, many battering men were younger sons. The most typical role played by participants in our batterers' groups in their families of origin was that of black sheep or scapegoat. They seldom acted as the surrogate parent. Instead they seemed to model themselves after the acting-out parent.

Child Abuse Factors in Battering

Slightly more than half (54 percent) of battering men either experienced abuse from a parent or witnessed their mother's battering, according to our survey of nearly one hundred battered women (Deschner et al. 1980). Stacey and Shupe (1983), who analyzed data from 452 battered women, found that 57 percent of the battering men were raised in violent families. Both surveys indicated that only about one-third of the battered women were raised in homes where physical violence occurred. Similar proportions were reported by Carlson (1977), who indicated that one-third of the battered women and one-half of the battering men came from families where battering of one kind or another had occurred.

A counselor who worked with battering husbands of women at the Chiswick Refuge in London reported that 70 percent of the men had been abused as children (Harper, 1979). Such a difference might be due to chance, or it may point to cultural differences between the two countries. In England there is less street violence, less police violence, less violence on television, adding up to less cultural inculcation of violence. This may mean that only 30 percent of abusive men picked up the habit from nonfamily experiences, in contrast to the nearly 50 percent of American men who apparently acquire models for violent behavior from nonfamily experiences.

The consistent finding of high rates of child abuse in the background of adult batterers indicates a relationship between child and consort battering. Both the modeling of excessive discipline methods and the emotional damage created by childhood victimization result in the frequent generational transfer of abuse. However, many abused children do not grow up to be batterers themselves. No studies have yet been done to indicate how many abused children are able to break the violence pattern. The statistics we do have suggest that more men than women pick up the tradition of violence from the previous generation. This may be another reflection of the greater cultural approval for male aggressive behaviors, or it may reflect women's tendency to submit rather than oppose stronger attackers.

Consort Battering as a Factor in Child Abuse

Another question is whether couples who batter each other also harm their children. All the child protective services workers I have interviewed indicate that many of the mothers among their cases are suffering from physical abuse along with the children. A survey of eighty-five families reported for child abuse (Johnson and Morse, 1968) revealed that 70 percent also were experiencing severe marital conflict, especially if the father was the parent abusing the child. Statistics gathered from the other side, at refuges for battered women, indicate that at least a third of the men who abuse their consorts also assault their children (Stacey and Shupe, 1983). Others have claimed that children are abused in fully 50 percent of the families of battering couples (Gayford, 1975; Roy 1977).

Sometimes battered women are too intimidated to do anything about attacks on the child or children. A few overly submissive mothers actually lose parental custody even though they themselves never abused or neglected a child, because they let a series of consorts abuse the children (Oates, 1979). Protective services workers have indicated that the majority of the failure-to-protect mothers were themselves abused as children and grew up to be battered again by their consorts. They exemplify the learned helplessness pattern in their despairing submissiveness.

The majority of battered wives do protect their children from attacks from their consorts, for they tend to leave when a child is included in the battering. Until then what we have called altruistic madness may cause them to endure years of battering, mainly for the sake of the affection and economic advantages the husband offers the children. A number of the battered wives I have spoken with stated that their consorts were "good fathers" who loved their children and never beat them. The pattern in such families may be similar to one often found in child-abusive families in which only one of the children, a sort of scapegoat, is ever attacked. Other family members play distractor, rescuer, or hero roles. Perhaps in some families the wife instead of one of the children fulfills the role of scapegoat and absorbs all of the batterer's wrath. Even the scapegoat wife herself may be helped to tolerate the abuse by the belief that she is helping keep her children safe by drawing all the father's wrath onto herself.

Emotional Damage in Battering Families

Battered women and children often receive permanent physical injuries, and some die as a result. But even if their injuries are temporary they still suffer for a long time from anger, terror, and a sense of worthlessness. The anger may be mostly repressed, except for nagging and the playing of psychological games. The fear is very prominent, expressed in many anxieties and avoidance behaviors. A conviction of worthlessness is common and nearly permanent even when actual abuse ceases. Some of the low self-regard may be due to "brainwashing," reflecting an acceptance of the batterer's oft-repeated negative comments that were part of the coercion spiral. More of the long-lasting sense of worthlessness probably comes from the experience of betrayal by a loved one and the realization of helplessness at a time of danger (Seligman and Rosellin, 1975).

Battering victims who have repeatedly tried and failed to avert injuries eventually stop attempting to cope or to end the battering. They sink into a despairing fatalism very like the "learned helplessness" shown by experimental animals who have found that they cannot escape being shocked and passively cower in their cages even when an escape route is offered.

Bystander children who only witness abuse also suffer from emotional damage, whether the victim is a mother or a sibling. Witnesses fear for the welfare of the victim and experience feelings of helplessness too. They also dread that their own turn may come soon, especially if they try to intervene. Sometimes witness children are kept up late to serve as buffers between the parents, especially if the abuser has some inhibitions about abusing the mother in front of the children. Their sleep patterns may be disturbed by sounds of fighting, by worry, and by frequent illnesses induced by stress. A natural result of all the stress and turmoil is that children from abusive families seldom achieve well in school and are frequently ill.

The children brought to refuges by battered women have created many problems because of their own violent behaviors (Renvoize, 1978). Many ape their parents' ways by striking siblings (60 percent) or even attacking their mothers (53 percent), according to one study of shelter children (Pfouts, Schopler, and Henley, 1981). Unfortunately, the critical lack of funds at most refuges has meant that the children can receive little more than custodial care while there. What programs there are for the children rely heavily on volunteers for staff. Because of the likelihood of generational transfer, these children should be receiving particularly concentrated help for as long as they remain accessible. Therapeutic work with the children accompanying battered women to shelters would be excellent primary prevention, helping to break the endless generational transfer of family violence patterns.

Marital Problems Among Child Abusers

Since battering usually occurs in privacy, the study of key family interactions will always be difficult. Little is known about the family system patterns in families tolerating consort battering year after year. The battered wife's emotional involvement with the child may inflame the consort in some cases. One research group described a young father who attacked his wife and newborn baby nursing at the breast, passionately crying, "Those are my breasts!" (Ounsted, Oppenheimer, and Lindsay, 1978). Most pregnant battered women report attacks by their consorts aimed particularly at their abdomens. The men may be motivated by a primitive jealousy of a rival who has supplanted their possession of the partner's body and has disrupted sexual gratification in addition. Attacks in the presence of older children may be motivated by jealousy of all the time and attention given to providing the children with nurture that the batterer wants for himself.

A cardinal tenet of structural family therapy holds that all habitual actions engaged in by one family member, such as battering behavior, must somehow be functional in maintaining the total system, or else other family members would not tolerate it (Haley, 1976). Perhaps the bystanders in the family tolerate battering in order to maintain relative peace for themselves, as the victim distracts the attacker from everyone else. Sometimes the bystanders are children who feel helpless to prevent a mother or even a sibling from being battered. In some families the victim also engages in very aversive behaviors; the periodic battering then has a payoff for everyone, because it keeps an unpleasant family member under control. Sometimes the bystander is a mother or a father who fails to prevent a difficult child or handicapped infant from being abused, because the extra care the child requires is very unwelcome. The bystander is colluding in the partner's use of coercion and violence to stop the child's demands for care.

A strained marital relationship seems to be one of the necessary preconditions for the occurrence of child abuse. Researchers have found that several weeks of unusual marital turbulence precede child abuse incidents (Bennie and Sclare, 1969), that abusive mothers react even more negatively to problems with husbands than to problems with children (Smith and Hanson, 1975), and that two-thirds of child abusers feel their marital relationship is really the main family problem (Reavely and Gilbert, 1979).

Even some single parent abuse falls in this category, because abuse often occurs in connection with the breakup of a relationship and consequent abandonment by the consort. The deserted and desperate parent feels so overwhelmed by nonstop child care, and so unfairly treated, that the child's normal demands seem to be attacks and are responded to by counterattack. If the single parent is a very young girl who utilizes her own mother to help raise her baby, the conflict may be between herself and her mother instead of with a male consort. As more and more unwed teen-age mothers elect to keep their babies rather than give them up for adoption, conflicts with the grandmother who acts as the second parent become a more common precipitating factor in child abuse.

> A 21-year-old woman who was convicted of murdering her 3-year-old child was sentenced Friday to 45 years in prison. She had pleaded innocent by reason of insanity to the charge of stabbing her sleeping daughter 17 times in the back on May 30. Prosecutors said she killed the child because she was tired of her mother telling her how to handle the girl [*Dallas Times-Herald*, November 10, 1982].

The consort can be in the home every day and still fail to give the caretaking parent the kind of support that would stop child battering once a parent has begun abuse. Typically the abusive parent feels a lack of support from the partner, in one way or another. Reavely and Gilbert (1978) noted four ways in which the nonabusive parent may precipitate abuse by failing to give support: (1) The nonabuser may refuse to recognize that the partner is having a problem.

(2) The nonabuser may take the opposite tack and scourge the abuser with withering criticism. (3) The nonabuser may usurp the child care role from the abuser, which is a form of damning criticism disguised as helpfulness. (4) The nonabusive parent may be so horrified that he or she withdraws and refuses to communicate with the abusive parent. None of these reactions spring from the nonabusive parent's approval of attacks on children, nor yet from fear of receiving abuse if attempts are made to intervene. They are attempts to deal with the problem of the other partner's outbursts against the child, in one way or another. But the strategies have in common a failure to take the abusive parent seriously as a person in need of help. Therefore all these reactions increase the battering parent's sense of isolation and desperation.

I worked with one battering mother who experienced severe panic attacks whenever she was left in charge of her two children. She would resolve her panic by attacking one of them. This would cause her husband to rush home and take over child care duties, with the result that her anxiety receded but always returned even more strongly. Part of her therapy was to keep a diary of child-caring events, which enabled her to discover the real sequence of feelings and events.

> First I get to feeling my husband doesn't pay me any attention, then right after that thought I feel I must not deserve his attention because I am worthless. Then I go right into a terrible panic since I am too worthless to be able to take care of the children. I want my husband to rescue me from the panic by taking over, so I just go ahead and hit one of them. My panic goes away when he comes home and takes care of them, but I feel more worthless than ever.
>
> (Madge, age twenty-eight)

Parke and Lewis (1981) suggested several more marital interaction patterns that sometimes lead to child abuse. A child made cranky by the inept or insensitive methods of one parent might then annoy the other parent to the point of abusive behavior. This pattern might prevail in homes where one is an inept child manager and the other parent cannot tolerate crying. In effect the abusive parent is joining a coercion spiral when it has already risen to a dangerous level.

Another kind of interaction is sometimes found in homes where both a consort and a child are battered. The child, as a conveniently weaker target, inherits the mother's wrath after a quarrel between consorts. Or the child is attacked in order to turn loss into victory, because the other spouse will submit in order to save the child. Quite a few batterers kidnap or hold their children hostage as a strategy to bring the spouse back when she has succeeded in separating from him.

Finally, the abusive parent may take the indifference or silence of the nonabusive consort as actual approval of child battering. Many nonabusive parents tell lies about the true origin of their child's injuries when they take them for emergency treatment. Such cover-up attempts result from fear that the authorities will remove the child and/or jail the abuser, so they are motivated by protective impulses rather than approval of abuse of a child. But the perpetrator can easily infer approval when he or she hears the consort lying about what happened. Whether the partner's approval is real or imagined, the belief that the partner approves encourages more frequent and more violent attacks.

Same or Different: Typologies of Batterers

If consort and child batterers are all basically similar, anger-control groups can be formed to treat batterers in general without consideration for the type of perpetrator or type of victim. But if consort and child batterers differ or contain subgroups of individuals who are substantially different, it may be necessary to design specialized treatment programs for them.

Studies attempting to differentiate among types of physically abusive parents—batterers—were reviewed in an article by Shorkey (1978). Though most authors concluded that child abusers are a very diverse lot, the early descriptions implied that all batterers exhibit the same personality characteristics. Shorkey said the evidence pointed to the existence of three clusters of personality variables among different sorts of child abusive parents: emotional immaturity, aggression stemming from low tolerance for frustration, and rigidity in thinking and behavior patterns.

Most people writing about consort batterers give a general description with a composite list of characteristics, as if all men who batter are alike. I have encountered just two therapists who have worked with enough consort batterers to discriminate some different types mong them. A male counselor working at the Chiswick shelter for women (Harper, 1979) suggested that there were two basic kinds of batterers: men who had been bullies or spoiled only sons and became intensely jealous as consorts, and men from subcultures approving the use of violence. Both kinds exhibited the mood swings of the violence cycle, with a pronounced repentance phase after an outburst. The men raised in homes or subcultural groups that taught them violence had often been abused as children. They lacked knowledge of any other way to relate to intimates than by coercing submission or else submitting themselves.

A forensic psychiatrist (Faulk, 1974) who had interviewed twenty-three men awaiting trial for murdering or injuring a wife or consort discerned five types of battering men. The five types were dependent and passive (nine men), dependent and suspicious (four), violent and bullying (one), successful but domineering (five), and some stable and normally affectionate men who went berserk during a depressive or psychotic episode (four). Just two-thirds of Faulk's group were chronic batterers. The other third had committed no previous crimes, according to police records. Faulk's categories are questionable because of the circumstances of the psychiatric interviews. No wives were present to tell their side of the story (one-third of the wives were dead), and the accused prisoners had a stake in representing themselves as blameless.

The most comprehensive and satisfactory typology was offered by Oates (1979), containing eight categories based on her experience in treating sixty clinical cases of child batterers. Her sample was unselected but not random. As a result it included fewer male batterers than would be expected from the population statistics, which indicate that just under half of all child batterers are male. The accuracy of the Oates typology has not yet been tested by other researchers, but it seems quite useful. The eight categories were:

1. Abuse specific to one child (7, mostly mothers)
2. Obsessional type (7, mothers)
3. Social chaos/deprivation type (19, either or both parents)
4. "Child parents" (8, either mother or father)
5. Disturbed deviants (14, usually male consorts)
6. Failure to protect type (3, mothers, with deviant consorts)
7. Multiple handicap type (1, mother, but could be either parent)
8. Mental illness type (1, a mother)

The following typological classification of batterers draws from the preceding theories, especially Oates, plus my own experience with cases. The categories provide a theoretical framework, which may prove useful in making diagnoses and treatment decisions. They should be looked on as tentative categories until research studies have tested their validity. Some battering men and women belong in more than one category, but the following major types seem distinguishable:

1. *Social Chaos/Deprivation Type*

This is the most common type of batterer, including most of the one-half of abusive consorts who experienced violence as children. According to Oates (1979), one-third of child abusers were of this type also, and included both abusive fathers and abusive mothers. Such parents and consorts come from the classic "problem families" so well known to social workers, who have been trapped in poverty and social chaos for generations. Numerous relatives have exhibited personality disorders and/or social malfunctioning such as crime or addiction to various drugs. The children either witness abuse or experience it themselves.

Young people growing up in such families tend to marry early in order to escape and to encounter severe survival problems out on their own. They bring their learned relationship styles with them and soon fall into a battering cycle. Such couples tend to ignore contraceptives. Soon too many children overwhelm the young couple with financial and personal stress. The children often are neglected as well as battered and suffer from frequent serious illnesses. The parents themselves often suffer from severe depression, stress illnesses, and phobic levels of anxiety. It should be no surprise that these individuals are strikingly unaware of their consorts' and their children's needs, so overwhelming are their own.

However, battering cannot be blamed on a chaotic/deprived upbringing alone. A number of researchers have compared nonabusive and abusive deprived parents and invariably found key differences in parenting styles. Abusive parents attempt to control their children more and respond to them less, even looking at them less as they play (Robison and Solomon, 1979). The abusive parents interrupt their children more, and the children, perhaps as a consequence, ignore their parents more often (Hyman, 1977). Observers also have found that battering families interact among each other less often than nonabusive families, and the interactions more often are negative exchanges. Even the adults comply less often with each other's requests (Burgess and Conger, 1978). The most significant difference, in terms of causing child abuse, may be the more aggressive methods that abusive parents use for dealing with irritating child behaviors (Disbrow, Doerr, and Caulfield, 1977).

Nonabusive parents from similarly deprived backgrounds are able to tune in to their children's signals and to guide their behavior without resorting to extreme punishments. They talk to their offspring more and teach them how to do things more often. They dispense more positive feedback to their children and to each other, making the reinforcement contingent on appropriate behavior, whereas battering families are indiscriminate, being as likely to reward deviant behavior by giving in to it as they are to reward good behavior (Reid and Taplin, 1977). It may be that a background of violence, as well as chaos and deprivation, makes for the lack of awareness of others because of preoccupation with one's own unmet needs. Or it may be that awareness of others' signals is a skill that is not passed on from generation to generation in abusive deprived families.

2. The "Child-Parent" Type

This type of batterer often overlaps with the preceding category. They are the very young consorts who unite as teenagers in order to escape unpleasant, often chaotic-deprived, families of origin. Often enough their early life included child abuse followed by foster care or periods of institutionalization. They have babies, several in quick succession, while they themselves are still children. They have very little idea of how to care for a baby but eagerly expect the infant to bring them the love and happiness they have missed. The baby may be normal and make only normal demands, but the immature and emotionally deprived parent is unprepared for the infant's unending neediness and relative unresponsiveness. Typically the abuse injuries are severe and indicate uncontrolled anger. Often a young baby is shaken, causing serious or even fatal brain injuries.

The theory that child abuse is caused by a role reversal, in which the needy young parent expects the infant to meet her or his needs and then becomes furious when the infant insists on demanding care itself, was popularized by the early leaders in child care treatment (Morris and Gould, 1963). For this reason Kempe and Helfer (1972), pediatricians who pioneered in developing sympathetic treatment for child batterers, believed that all perpetrators needed massive amounts of remothering care themselves and proposed that if the parents' needs were met, their child would be safe with them.

Several researchers have pointed out that battered children tend to be first or second born and that battering parents tend to be under twenty years of age at the birth of the first child. However, a large survey with random sampling techniques (Gil, 1970) did not find the battering parents to be unusually young. The contradictory findings support the notion of different types of batterers, with the extremely young and needy batterers as just one subgroup among others.

Something rather like the role reversal between a youthful parent and the infant occurs between immature battering consorts and their caretaking partners. The wife is expected to fulfill all needs and is attacked when she fails on some point, just as the baby becomes an enemy to attack when it fails to meet the parent's dire needs for love.

5. *Specific Scapegoat Type*

Some batterers seem to be adequate citizens and adequate fathers, so much so that hardly anyone will believe the wife's story of re-peated abuse. Some battering mothers attack only one child and do an adequate job of parenting other offspring. This kind of batterer may come from any social class, and there seem to be particular historical reasons for their poor relations with the one family member. A child victim often was born prematurely or is handicapped, abnormal, or severely ill, all conditions that require a mother to put forth more child care efforts with less results than usual. If the baby was normal, the mother was in an abnormal state at the time of birth, being so depressed, self-condemning, or otherwise stressed that she was unable to tolerate the child care requirements of even a nor-mal infant. Whether it was the infant or the mother who was the source of the stress, the mother failed to form affectional ties with the child in its early infancy. Therefore she cannot tolerate the ac-tivities of that particular child and easily loses her self-control and attacks him or her.

At least 20 percent of child abuse victims weighed less than five pounds at birth, twice the 10 percent prematurity rate in the general population. Parke and Lewis (1981) offered interesting theories about this phenomenon. The small and immature low-birth-weight baby looks unattractive, is relatively unresponsive, and has a unique high-pitched cry, which has been experimentally demonstrated to be more annoying than a normal-weight newborn's cry. Furthermore, the immature infants have more feeding problems and are slower to pass developmental milestones. So they are a great deal more trouble than normal infants and provide the mother with less reward.

Another possible cause of abuse of premature infants pointed out by many researchers may arise in the necessity to separate mother and infant for long periods while the infant stays in a hospital special care unit, which may interfere with the emotional bonding of mother and child. One researcher (De Chateau, 1979) increased the amount of mother–normal infant contact in the delivery room by just fifteen minutes and, amazingly, found differences one year later. The extra-contact mothers were more positive and comforting to their one-year-olds, and the toddlers were even ahead of the control children developmentally. Another research team included fathers in the extra contact and found that fathers receiving the opportunity for early contact with their newborn later participated more in the care of the infant at home (Kennel, Voos, and Klaus, 1978). This is a significant finding, since fathers are often the only people available to give the mother any relief.

3. *Obsessive-Compulsive Type*

Many middle-class batterers belong in this category. As a defense against anxiety they lead lives so rigid and compulsive that any little deviation enrages them. They store up memories of old grievances and exact revenge days or even years later. They are likely to be very successful in their careers and upstanding members of a church. A wife battered by an obsessive-compulsive may have an exceptionally hard time obtaining any help, because no one can believe her accusations about such a pillar of the community.

Most child batterers of the obsessive-compulsive type are female. The victim has grown beyond infancy to the messy toddler stage. The mother often is a successful career woman, with perfectionistic, unrealistic standards for herself and for her baby's performance. She particularly loathes messy excrement. She usually has a critical, undermining husband rather than a supportive partner. This kind of batterer seeks help early, often referring herself, and is able to stop battering with proper help.

4. *Abnormal Response to Crying and Loud Complaining*

Apparently inconsolable infant wailing arouses distorted and even delusional feelings in some parents, which lead to attacks on the infant as if he or she were an enemy. Reavely and Gilbert (1979) found this such a significant cause of child abuse that they always asked about reactions to crying. If a parent felt unable to cope with crying, the risk of child abuse was much greater. They gave as an example a mother who felt an uncontrollable wish to harm her baby when she cried. Kempe (1978) quoted a mother as saying, "When she cried it meant she didn't love me; so I hit her." Ounsted, Oppenheimer, and Lindsay (1978) interviewed an abusive mother who said, "His crying seemed to follow me around the house. I could not stop it. I could not escape." Sanders (1978) reported the case of a new father who felt that the wailing of his two-week-old son meant that "he was out to destroy me," a conviction which led to battering the infant.

Battering consorts often demonstrate a similar intolerance for the loud sound of their partners' shouted complaints.

> She likes to raise her voice so all the neighbors can hear us fight. When she starts up I go around the house closing all the windows. I can't stand her screaming going all over the neighborhood. Lots of times I stayed away and drank because I didn't want to go home and hear any more shouting. I don't know why she likes to set me off that way.
>
> (Pete, age thirty-six)

One may question the accuracy of Pete's understanding of his wife's motivation for yelling, but his statement clearly revealed his conditioned negative reaction to loud, demanding complaints, which would lead finally to his becoming violent.

About half of battering consorts hit only their partners, and the other half also attack the children from time to time. Those who specialize in victimizing their wives seem to relate to them as would a rejected and incessantly demanding child or a rebellious adoles-

cent. In other words, projections of an earlier parent–child antag-
onism seem to distort the consort relationship.

6. *Pathologically Jealous Type*

Perhaps as many as 70 percent of consort batterers periodically act
almost insane with jealousy (Feazell, 1981). Jealousy is triggered by
the possibility of losing the one who fulfills one's love needs. Battering men often experience the most acute anxiety about losing their
wives at the transition from the violence phase to the repentance
phase. At that time wives withdraw emotionally and sometimes literally to nurse their wounds, leaving the batterer bereft of the relationship on which he depends. The anxiety aroused turns easily to
jealousy as the victim recovers and threatens to leave him for someone who does not hit her.

Battering parents seldom feel the same dread of losing the victim-
partner that the battering consort so often experiences. However,
one type of child abuser who often exhibits pathological jealousy is
the incestuous parent. Incest is now recognized as a form of child
battering and a much more common phenomenon than was suspected a few years ago. In cases of incest, extreme jealousy on the
part of the parent is very common, starting when the victim becomes
old enough to begin attracting peers as sexual partners. The father's
pathological jealousy of all potential boyfriends and his coercive attempts to restrict his victim's freedom may be the first clear clues to
the existence of incestuous abuse.

7. *Mental Illness Type*

Battering occasionally is associated with outright psychosis. Most
psychotic child abusers are mothers. The injuries to the child are
severe and often fatal. The parent inflicts them because of distorted
and delusional thinking. For example, a recent newspaper account
of an infant killing told how the mother cut out her baby's heart "to
keep his heart from being stolen by the devil."

A few consort batterers also are insane. Such men generally abuse
any children as well as their partner and are dangerous most of the
time, not just during peaks in the violence cycle. Fortunately, psychotic batterers are rare. They may be manic-depressives who grow

agitated and irritable in the manic phase, paranoid schizophrenics suffering from delusions, or individuals with brain malfunctions resulting from alcohol-caused brain damage or, very infrequently, a growing brain tumor.

Faulk's report on homicidal batterers put about 20 percent into a psychotic category. Not many such persons would voluntarily enter an outpatient anger-control program. If such a person applies, he or she should be hospitalized, as a nonvoluntary patient if necessary, in order to protect the family, the counselors, and other group members.

8. *Mental Disturbance Type*

Though psychotic abusers are rare, many seem to suffer from severe personality disorders. Such persons cooperate poorly with treatment. They often have a long history of other crimes of violence. The battering incidents often are not rationally understandable in view of the situation. Instead the attacks seem to be committed on impulse or because of some unrelated irritation. Sometimes recurrent sadistic torture seems to be played as a game.

Alcoholic and drug-addicted batterers also experience some degree of thinking disorder. This can range from temporary loss of judgment about the long-range consequences of acts to permanent personality change through loss of brain cells.

Data about the sorts of personality disturbances batterers may suffer exists only for child batterers. S. M. Smith (1978) found that one-fourth of a group of abusive parents who took EEG tests showed abnormal brain wave patterns. All had serious personality disorders, generally severe depression with episodes of aggressive hostility. Reavely and Gilbert (1979) treated fifty-three cases, of whom 75 percent were depressed, 30 percent highly anxious, and 26 percent obsessional. They found, incidentally, that depressed abusive parents improved especially well with treatment.

Two researchers who have obtained physiological response data from samples of child abuser parents have made the same curious finding, namely that abusers do not respond differentially to positive and negative stimuli. Frodi and Lamb (1980) found that abusive parents' autonomic arousal in reaction to infant crying and infant smiling did not differ, whereas control subjects' responses did differ. Disbrow, Doerr, and Caulfield (1977) found that child abusers responded similarly to pleasant and unpleasant scenes, while control subjects showed more variability. Thus the lack of empathic responding may sometimes trace back to a perceptual defect or deviation, or at least to a learning deficit reflected in an organic response pattern. Some abusive parents may be under so much stress that they overreact not only to crying but to all the child's emotions.

Some people involved in consort battering may be what psychiatrists classify as borderline personalities. Borderline personalities are thought to occur when a person, in the toddler stage of development, attempts to develop an independent identity but cannot because the mother's need to cling to the infant as a part of herself is so intense. As the growing child continues to try for independence, the mother withdraws from the relationship in order to protect herself. So the child is rewarded for regressing back to infantile clinging and is abandoned whenever more mature independent behavior is attempted (Masterson, 1976). The grown-up borderline alternates between a pathological pursuit of pleasure in the effort to relieve feelings of subjugation and unrealistic convictions of abandonment. They lead very emotional, vivid lives, which exasperate those around them. In therapy they alternate between intensely loving and hating the therapist. They emotionally abuse their children, even if they do not always batter them physically.

I have met a number of women on the receiving end of battering who also should be diagnosed as suffering from borderline personality symptoms. I mention this observation with some misgiving, for it sounds like attacking or blaming the victim to say that some battered women are seriously disturbed emotionally. But a fair number fit the psychiatric description of borderline personality with eerie precision. Most of the battered women of the borderline type that I have met have been residents of shelters, where they are among the most difficult residents to handle, let alone help. Another therapist working with battering couples also recently noted the frequency of borderline types (Burgogne, 1983).

When borderline battered women come into counseling they seem to resist involving their consorts, whom they depict as brutal monsters, in therapy with them. As a result I have become acquainted with only one of their spouses. The one husband I did treat was a surprisingly stable, normal person who was very successful in his career and as a father. He stayed with his borderline wife partly because she was a fascinating woman who played continually on his emotions and partly because he feared she would get custody of the children. He rightly worried about their well-being if left wholly in her care. In many ways this husband was the battered one. He received frequent emotional abuse, responded with physical violence only once in a great while, and confined himself to attacking walls.

Battered Husbands

The case of the husband of the borderline woman leads into the topic of battered husbands. Many battered women do fight back or even start the hitting. But the men usually manage to inflict much greater damage in return. Only the very few men who never retaliate should qualify for the term "battered husband." Such pairs are very rare, but they do exist. I have worked with only a few pairs who reversed the attacker and victim roles. Straus, Gelles, and Steinmetz (1980) did not make this distinction when they cited the rate of 2.3 percent for battered husbands, but they did point out that the attacks made by the wives were less frequent and less severe.

The few truly battered men I have known have shown an incomplete reversal of roles, because men victims do not show the terrible fear that so characterizes women victims. Even though the men are receiving injuries, they seem to know they can be the ultimate winners any time they choose. Therefore not they, but their violent wives, walk about with terror as a daily companion, just like all their battered sisters who receive instead of inflict injuries.

The battering couples with reversed roles all had rather special childhood experiences that may help explain the phenomenon. All the men had been carefully trained to be nonviolent and caretaking by their affectionate but rather helpless mothers. In contrast, their battering wives had participated in violent fights with siblings, which they usually won. Sometimes the parent with whom the woman had identified as a child had abused the nonpreferred parent, thus becoming a role model of violence.

Conclusions

Further study is needed of batterers who come to the treatment programs beginning to be offered them, to learn whether different types of batterers profit more or less from anger-control training. So far chaotic-deprived, child-parent, and obsessive-compulsive types of batterers seem to respond with the most thorough and rapid improvements in anger control. The more disturbed and alcoholic or drug-addicted persons respond least well to training and relapse into violence if they resume drinking or abusing drugs.

Battering parents profit from the anger-control training, even when most of the group members are consort batterers. The abusive parents progress farther if their spouses also attend the groups because of the key function played by marital conflict in triggering child abuse. Reversed-role battering couples fit well into groups with "normal" battering couples, partly because the role reversal is incomplete as regards fear. Also, many battered women do readily admit that they fight back and sometimes start the violent phase first, so they can understand battering women, and the men can understand the victim role played by a battered husband.

3 Physiological Reactions Controlling Violence

The thesis of this book is that battering is a learned habit. However, the primitive rage reactions leading to aggression and battering are unlearned, instinctual patterns. Angry and aggressive responses are "wired" into every mammalian brain as a vital part of each individual's survival equipment. Battering couples habitually give way to their instinctual aggressive reactions. They need to acquire some understanding of the usually unconscious operations of their bodies under strong emotional stress in order to exert full cognitive control over their hitting habits. Therefore this chapter contains a detailed exposition of the physiological components of rage and aggresion patterns. Their adaptive and harmful roles will be examined. The next chapter focuses on the cognitive regulators of anger and aggression.

The Physiology of Angry Emotions

Emotions in general and anger and violent rage in particular are a fascinating topic for study. Batterers usually have a feeling of being possessed by a sudden, overwhelming force, which impels them into actions they would not normally undertake. For a short time they feel almost helpless to stop themselves, but in fact they do not want to stop, for the aggressive actions seem necessary and satisfying.

> Yes, hitting actually does make the tension go down. It's absolutely weird. You feel as if the top of your head is about to come off and you're losing sight of everything. I get to the point reality is disappearing and I gotta release this tension, this pressure. This lady in front of me is just in the wrong place at the wrong time.
>
> (Wallace, age thirty)

> My sense of compassion or wisdom used to black out and die in an explosion of frustration in the moment *before* the blow was struck, just as her compassion and wisdom must have died in the moment of final provocation.
>
> (Quoted in Pizzey, 1974, p. 89)

> Bite marks are present in roughly 15 percent of fatal battered child cases . . . . Bite marks are an undeniable indication of the extent of the primitive, regressive uncontrolled rages that grip the adult when he or she attacks the child [Densen-Gerber, 1978, p. 138].

The Limbic Home of Aggression

The current understanding of "instinctive" emotional reactions, such as rage, is that patterns of interlocking responses are stored in the form of brain circuitry and chemical hormonal links. Once activated by cognitive decisions, the patterns unfold in a stereotyped, automatic way that is roughly similar for all mammals and highly similar within a given species such as human beings (Schachter, 1971; Green and Green, 1979). Rage may be likened to a computer program, mobilizing a complex machine (the body) to carry out predetermined operations by means of a number of interlocking subroutines. The complex reactions called rage, and milder versions called anger, are the results of the action of the entire stored program. Visible emotions are analogous to program output typed out on the computer printer.

To continue the analogy, the "canned programs" for the emotions appear to be stored deep in the midbrain, in an area called the limbic system (MacLean, 1955). This particular brain structure evolved first in primitive mammals, which have little neocortex to enable them to make complex decisions. Perhaps this is why a part of the limbic system called the amygdala performs a crude decision function by evaluating incoming stimuli as either aversive or rewarding, according to their survival value for the species. Events leading to food or sex, for example, are evaluated as pleasant, while pain and threat are evaluated as aversive. The amygdala's decisions are emotional, not rational, and are only slowly influenced by experience. But they are useful in providing rapid decisions that activate potentially lifesaving response patterns (Leeper, 1968).

Unfortunately the amygdala is particularly sensitive to upsets such as epileptic seizures, which can trigger violent outbursts and uncontrollable murderous behavior in some individuals. A rather gruesome proof of the importance of the amygdala in triggering rage and violence is provided by instances of brain surgery that have successfully stopped pathological aggressive outbursts in disturbed children by destroying the amygdala (Fonberg, 1979).

Brain research on mammals indicates that different types of aggressive behaviors are stored in separate regions of another tiny limbic structure called the hypothalamus (Moyer, 1976). Researchers have electrically stimulated different spots in the hypothalamus and evoked predatory aggression from one location, fear-induced defensive aggression from another, and irritable rage from a third which partly overlaps the defensive area, a significant detail. The advantage of having such complex behavior sequences stored in the form of actual neural connections is that young individuals do not have to learn them. The whole sequence, highly adaptive, is instantly available at need. It is also available to enraged parents and spouses and doubtless accounts for the amazing similarity of battering incidents between different couples, despite the secretiveness and isolation of battering families.

The Sympathetic Nervous System

The anger program in the hypothalamus activates three main subroutines, with far-reaching effects throughout the body. The subroutines act on the sympathetic nervous system, the hormonal system, and the facial muscles. The sympathetic is the mid-division of the autonomic nervous system. Like all the autonomic system, its activities are normally outside of conscious control or awareness. The sympathetic nerves activate minute muscles all over the body with extreme rapidity, within one to three seconds after the appearance of a threatening stimulus (Schachter, 1957). Cannon (1920) and most researchers since have credited the origin of bodily changes accompanying emotion to the action of the sympathetic system and have found that these changes are precisely the same whether the individual is afraid, angry, or in pain. Evidently the purpose of sympathetic activity is to ready the individual for lifesaving effort at once, without taking time to decide which kind of effort is needed. Though the sympathetic responses are undifferentiated, they are capable of infinite and subtle gradations in strength, from changes barely perceptible to the most sensitive equipment to exceedingly strong and rapid reactions.

A great many reactions are triggered by the quick-acting neural messages zipping through the sympathetic nervous system. Most of the changes are adaptive for a fight-or-flight emergency. The pupils of the eyes dilate, the heart beats faster, and the breath catches. At the same time stomach contractions cease and secretions of digestive juices, including saliva, stop, resulting in a noticeably dry mouth. The minute muscles in the skin contract, resulting in erection of hair in furry animals, and sometimes goose bumps or a prickly sensation in humans. The contraction of these muscles also constricts the capillaries supplying blood to the skin. Therefore the face goes pale, and a bit of moisture or perspiration is squeezed out all over the body, which is noticed as clammy hands or a cold sweat.

The Adrenal Hormones

The second aggression subroutine activates the adrenal hormones. Hormones are chemical messengers that travel through the blood stream and activate other organs. Thus they function like chemical alternatives to the nerves, using blood vessels as their pathway. It is a slightly slower communication system, for adrenal hormone effects appear after ten to sixteen seconds, as against the sympathetic reaction time of one to three seconds. The adrenal hormones act powerfully to strengthen and prolong the emotional changes initiated by the sympathetic nerve action.

Investigators learned only thirty years ago that the adrenal medulla secreted not one but two related but different hormones, adrenalin or epinephrine and noradrenalin or norepinephrine. Opinions have gone back and forth since as to whether the two only augment each other's action or arouse different emotional responses.

All research so far shows that fear and epinephrine secretion are closely linked. Epinephrine makes the heart beat faster and harder, shown by increases in systolic blood pressure. It opens up the tiny airways in the lungs to increase oxygen uptake and releases a blood clotting substance into the bloodstream. Perhaps most important, epinephrine triggers the release of glycogen, or blood sugar, stored in the liver and muscles, so that a tremendous burst of effort is possible. Clearly, epinephrine finishes the job begun by the sympathetic nervous system, readying the whole body for a maximum lifesaving physical effort in a potentially damaging situation.

The emotional correlates of norepinephrine's actions are not as well understood. At first researchers considered that norepinephrine and anger were related (Ax, 1953; Funkenstein, 1955). Norepinephrine stimulates the heart to stronger rather than faster contractions and raises the diastolic rather than systolic blood pressure. The diastolic is the second, lower, number in a blood pressure reading. It indicates the pressure of the blood in the arteries in between heartbeats and therefore is the significant reading for diagnosis of high blood pressure. Norepinephrine raises the arterial pressure by constricting larger peripheral blood vessels, completing the process started when the sympathetic nervous system contracted the tiny capillaries in the skin.

One researcher (Vrij, 1956, cited by Arnold, 1968) reported that norepinephrine released stored blood sugar from the liver only, leaving the glycogen in the muscles untouched. This difference in the function of epinephrine and norepinephrine might account for the rapid onset of weakness and trembling under great fear and the sensation of increased strength that lasts for many minutes under the emotion of anger. This difference can be noticed in rush-hour traffic crises. A few seconds after a near-accident, one's heart pounds and arms tremble so that sometimes one must pull off the road to regain strength. But if another driver has deliberately cut in front of the car, one feels powerful anger and a reckless desire to pursue and challenge the offending automobile.

The effects of rage are well illustrated in a woman's recollection of a childhood battle:

Not bothering about obstacles I flew at Connie, bringing down the posts and tearing holes in the rotten netting. I punched her wherever I could find a landing-place for my fists, and finally grabbed a handful of her hair in each hand and battered her head against the ground. Fortunately, we were on the grass, so that I could do little actual damage, but I know that all I could see was a red mist, and all I wanted to do was to blot Connie out [Hitchman, 1960, pp. 136–37].

Schachter (1957) carried out an experiment that included not only fear and anger stimuli but pain as a third kind of stressful stimulus. He found that the pure norepinephrine reaction came in response to pain. Anger usually was associated with a mixture of norepinephrine and epinephrine. This is a most significant finding. It indicates that anger is not an opposite of fear, but a mix of fear and pain responses.

The Pain Element in Anger

The pain that contributes to anger usually is inflicted directly by the target of the anger. For example, Knowles and Middleton (1980) found that 10 percent of the battered women in their sample had hit their consorts first and then received a beating in return. A further 60 percent of their sample reported quarreling before the physical battering occurred. In arguments, cutting and derogatory remarks can create pain from within.

The pain also can originate from a source unrelated to the target of the batterer's violence. The battering man may experience deep psychic pain from deprivations associated with poverty, from unpleasant working conditions, or from an argument with a parent or even a child. Physical pain may be present from an unrelated source, such as a backache or tired feet. Even though the sufferer knows the true cause of the pain, the heightened state of arousal still makes anger against the consort more likely.

When the source of a low-grade, long-lasting pain is unclear, the sufferer feels truly irritated and irritable. The irritation may be experienced as a headache, an uneasy stomach, tiredness, or a feeling of nervousness, as epitomized in the common excuse, "My nerves are shot." The irritability seems to be free-floating, which puzzles sufferers and makes them look outside themselves for causes, which are found in the faulty behavior of others.

The primitive response to pain, as people who have handled injured animals know, is fierce counterattack. Biting is especially common. The primitive response to fear is flight, but when pain is also present, as when an animal is trapped, defensive aggression occurs (Fonberg, 1979). Many battering episodes begin as defensive aggression, if one believes the explanations given by the abusers themselves.

> I would try to walk away but she keeps insisting. I go to another room and she keeps following me, nagging me. Finally I have to hit her to make her shut up.
>
> (Wallace, age thirty)

> One day when the baby was crying loudly, Mr. A. felt "he was out to destroy me" and fractured several of his ribs. The second incident occurred when Billy was 3 months old. On this occasion Mr. A. became overwhelmed with anxiety; he felt the baby was "screaming on purpose" and broke Billy's arm [Sanders, 1978, p. 483].

If frustration and irritation, both milder degrees of the pain experience, are included, there is considerable experimental evidence of pain's relation to anger. For example, in a study of catharsis (Vantress and Williams, 1972) female subjects were frustrated, enough to raise their blood pressure, by the device of preventing them from completing a task for which they had been offered five dollars. Half the subjects could release their feelings by filling out a posttest evaluation, which allowed them to criticize the experimenter. But their elevated blood pressure readings dropped to normal only if the frustrating experimenter left the room too. Blood pressure then returned to normal within two minutes, whether or not subjects had engaged in supposedly cathartic counterattacks. This is a logical result in terms of the pain + fear = anger theory. Only when the experimenter left the room did all danger of further experimental frustrations cease, so that the threat of further pain stopped. Researchers studying animal aggression have found that defeated animals remain agitated for a long time, heal more slowly, and often suffer from additional stress illnesses (Fonberg, 1979). Victorious animals, in contrast, calm down quickly and enjoy rapid healing. Again, victory ends stressful anger because it ends the threat of further pain.

The brain site for irritable aggression, in animals at least, partly overlaps the site for defensive aggression. The two forms of aggression are differentiated mainly by the attempt to escape, which always precedes defensive attack (Moyer, 1976). Some attacks seem motivated by pure irritation. The goal is to remove some noxious stimulation, such as a wife's nagging or a child's misbehaving, or some frustrating barrier to a goal. But the irritation may also come from an internal source. Alcohol and drug abuse, frequently a factor in battering, result in highly unpleasant withdrawal symptoms. In other cases the chronic irritation comes from an external source, but one that is unrelated to the victim. Unemployment and/or severe financial problems are statistically correlated with battering. Lack of money blocks attainment of most goals in today's society, so poverty means frequent frustrations for those caught in its grip.

Alcohol and Sugar as Sources of Irritability

The most common causes of free-floating irritability are to be found in the substances sufferers deliberately ingest, especially alcohol, sugar, coffee, and tobacco. These substances are pleasant to consume, so the later irritability they cause seems unconnected to them. Studies cited in the previous chapter point to a strong link between alcohol abuse and battering in approximately two-thirds of cases where a consort is the victim and perhaps as many as half of cases where a child is battered.

The initial effect of alcohol brings the drinker increased euphoria and arousal—people do "get high." Unfortunately, the body's reaction to alcohol has a second stage marked by feelings of depression, fatigue, nausea, and general bad feelings. But one of the general rules of motivation points out that immediate rewards outcompete long-range punishments or rewards. So the heavy drinker chooses to drink for the sake of getting high right away and ignores the inevitable morning after. Prolonged binge drinking may be mostly an effort to postpone the unpleasant second phase of the body's reaction to alcohol.

Alcohol hangovers are a potent source of the irritability that can lead to rage and battering. Surprise attacks in the middle of the night by drunken consorts become more understandable in terms of the irritation created by the second stage of alcohol effects, coming after several hours of drinking. The bad physical feelings may mingle with anxious self-talk about the partner's negative reaction to come next day, setting off anger and violence before the victim even knows there is a problem.

Alcohol is a form of sugar, so it is no coincidence that the body's response to sugary foods or soft drinks also shows two phases. The immediate reaction is a sense of fresh energy and well-being. Ten minutes to half an hour later the surge of insulin released to take care of all the sugar entering the blood from the digestive system has metabolized not only the candy but all available blood sugars circulating as a result of previous meals. The blood sugar level now drops lower than it was before the sweets were consumed, causing an uncomfortable sensation of tiredness that often causes people to doze off after they finish a meal with a rich dessert. Because the brain cannot function well without a relatively high level of blood sugar, irritability is also pronounced. People suffering from severe drops in blood sugar level after consuming sweets are called hypoglycemics.

Wilder (1947) and many researchers since (Reed, 1983) have linked hypoglycemia to the commission of aggressive crimes. Bolton (1976) documented the same relationship in another culture, the Qolla Indian tribe in the high Andes Mountains. Qolla men were reputed even by the conquistadors to be exceptionally bad-tempered. They have poor diets, which include a lot of candy. Bolton arranged to test all the men of one village with the standard fasting test. The men with court records showing the most violence were moderately hypoglycemic but experienced a sharp drop in blood sugar level after just two hours of fasting. The severely hypoglycemic individuals, who became quite ill within two hours of the fast, had court records no worse than those who had no symptoms at all.

Bolton (1976) noted that some of the Indians said that fighting made them feel better. He linked this to the effect of the adrenal hormones releasing blood sugar stored in the liver, which would cure a moderate hypoglycemic irritable spell. Darwin (1872) also cited stories of men who deliberately invented imaginary offenses against them in order to combat excessive fatigue.

Nicotine and caffeine are both stimulants, raising the heart rate and giving a temporary feeling of a lift. They also increase insulin secretion, so they accentuate the swings in blood sugar levels with resulting irritable moods. These popular addictions have other side effects, which can increase stress, especially the respiratory malaise associated with heavy smoking and the hyperactivity and stomach problems from the caffeine in coffee and soft drinks.

Two different studies have found that more than 80 percent of criminals follow poor to atrocious diets, loaded with sugar and junk foods (Zucker, 1979). A significant proportion of these sugarholics have diabetic parents or grandparents also. A few correctional officials have begun programs for educating convicted persons about the links between diet and violence, with promising results. For example, the chief probation officer of an Ohio city developed a program of nutritional counseling for all persons on probation and lowered the annual recidivism rate to a low 11 percent (Reed, 1983).

Many men and women involved in marital violence indulge heavily in several of the four substances, sugar, alcohol, caffeine, and nicotine. Rather frequently batterers use other legal and illegal drugs as well, perhaps in part to counteract the unpleasant side effects of indulging in the first four drugs. Such people suffer frequently from internal irritable feelings but have no awareness that their "innocent" pleasures have made violence and criminal impulsivity much more likely.

> DON: Well, I eat breakfast. I like my coffee with two or three spoons of sugar in it and I eat some doughnuts or something. I guess I have a sweet tooth: I eat candy and stuff all day long, and lots of coffee with sugar.

> ART: The doctor put me on a hypoglycemic diet just six weeks ago. I mean it was drastic. I couldn't eat any sugar or any starches and I dropped off 30 pounds. But I feel so different now. It's like I'm just beginning to have emotions and to understand, as if my mind is clearing up.

Both men were in one of our groups for batterers. Art's hypoglycemia had been discovered just before he came to our group, and he preached so effectively to Don and the other men that the leaders needed to say little more.

The Fear Part of Anger

The fear component in anger has been observed by many writers. Darwin spoke of men who made themselves angry in order to overcome their terror or their fatigue. H. S. Sullivan, the psychoanalyst, claimed that people learn early in life to handle anxiety by becoming angry.

Battered women live with fear. Fear distorts their thinking and their behavior. During the buildup phase of the violence cycle, the victim-to-be frequently becomes afraid because of her consort's barrage of threats, control measures, minor slaps, and other attacks. Between the threats she tends to anticipate them, putting herself into a state of continual anxious tension. No wonder many battered women suffer from stress-related illnesses such as headaches, poor digestion, rashes, or even more serious illnesses. Some women even try to escape from their unbearable anxiety by deliberately precipitating the act of violence, just to "get it over with." A few battered women eat their way into obesity, perhaps because the act of eating comforts them and temporarily reduces anxiety. Several battered women have told me of gaining more than a hundred pounds at one period in their violent marriage and then losing all the extra weight at another point. These remarkable fluctuations again suggest a link between dietary disorders and violent outbursts.

Battering men also experience a great deal of anxiety. Some of the alcohol and drug abuses of violent men are attempts to relieve anxiety. The severe jealousy experienced by so many battering couples originates in fear of losing the partner. This topic will be covered more fully in the next chapter. The jealous monitoring of the consort's activities and even the threats and slaps are ways jealous partners use to try to relieve their anxieties about abandonment. Another potent source of anxiety comes from the financial problems that are so common in battering households. Nearly half of the couples we have treated in our own anger-control groups were between jobs and living hand-to-mouth. A further source of anxiety for the men comes from the reform attempts made by the women. The women attempt to change them by nagging and complaining, which seldom induces improvement but instead makes the men feel extra anxiety about their inability to change themselves.

After an outburst of violence, batterers are spurred into the repentance phase by overpowering anxiety and dread of losing the offended partner. Anger has vanished, and they are overwhelmed by their sense of acute need and fear of abandonment. Quite a few battering men threaten to commit suicide if their consorts should really leave. Some do commit suicide, evidently fearing death less than they fear living alone. A few make the newspapers by carrying out a murder-suicide. Battering parents whose children have been taken away by the courts very often get pregnant immediately in order to replace the lost children, because they cannot stand to be alone.

The Look of Anger

The third major subroutine in the brain's anger program creates changes in facial expression. Darwin (1872) collected descriptions of emotional reactions from observers around the world to determine whether emotional expressions are culturally determined or universally the same. He discovered that the major emotions, including anger, are expressed in the same ways among all human groups. Darwin described an angry person as erect and straight in posture with taut muscles, often including clenched fists or clenched jaws. Breathing changes are marked by a high, expanded chest and flared nostrils. The eyes are bright and sometimes grow bloodshot. There is usually a frown made by lowered eyebrows, but not always. Frequently an angry person retracts the lips at the corners of the jaw, which exposes the sharp canine teeth as if for biting. The result is an open mouth with a square shape, in contrast to the round "O" formed by the mouth of a surprised person. Darwin added that half-angry and defiant people often sneer by means of lifting just one side of the lip to expose one canine tooth. The same signal is often made by a dog growling at another dog to stay away from a prized bone.

A rather intriguing, though perhaps not vital, question is whether the face of an angry person grows red or white. Darwin noted reports of both colors. Cannon (1920) suggested that the pallor of rage would result from the constriction of the capillaries just under the skin, which is triggered by the sympathetic nervous system. When people become hot under the collar or red in the face with anger, sometimes even getting bloodshot eyes and literally "seeing red," it would mean that raised internal blood pressure has overcome the original constriction of the capillaries, through the action of norepinephrine. The conflicting reports of red and white faces may result from the successive actions of sympathetic and adrenal systems, or it may indicate that the mix of adrenal hormones varies from person to person, or even from moment to moment within the same person. Schachter (1957) did find that a few of his subjects had only one adrenal response pattern, either all epinephrine or all norepinephrine, no matter whether the stimulus was painful, frightening, or insulting.

Sex Differences

Regular variations in anger expression are associated with gender. Many of the differences in men's and women's emotional expression are doubtless due to cultural conditioning. Training of the young to conform to a cultural norm seems to be particularly strong in the area of anger responses. Even today most parents encourage their boys to "stand up for themselves" and remind their girls to "be nice."

The sexual differences may have some physiological basis as well, possibly having to do with the sex hormones. Males of many species of animals as well as humans do more fighting and attacking than do the females. Unfortunately, many human anger studies have used subjects of the same sex, so differences in such matters as norepinephrine secretion remain to be explored.

One group of researchers had both male and female subjects imagine happy, sad, angry, and fearful events, while EMG sensors were attached to various portions of their faces (Shwartz, Brown, and Ahern, 1980). The strongest finding was of a sex difference, with females experiencing more feelings overall and showing stronger responses in their facial muscles. The women showed anger chiefly by lowering their eyebrows; the men showed anger by clenching their jaws and only slightly lowering their brows. These differences are intriguing. Clenched jaws suggest that biting is being repressed. Eyebrows are also lowered, in a manner which Darwin thought duplicated the expression of anger, when a person is attempting to see in spite of bright sunshine that hurts the eyes. Is anger in women more of a defensive attempt to cope with pain, while anger in men is more of a rage-aggression response?

Another experiment that revealed interesting sex differences measured male and female college students' anger responses in terms of increases in blood pressure (Hokanson, Willers, and Koropsak, 1968). Subjects had the chance to make either a friendly or a hostile "shock" response in a sort of game played against a confederate of the experimenters, who was deliberately annoying. The men students gave out more shocks and experienced more dips in blood pressure after administering them; the women students made more concilia-tory responses and experienced more relief after these, as might be predicted.

The second phase of the experiment tried to reverse the effects of cultural conditioning. The confederate now rewarded the women (with a nonshock next move) if they had used a shock, and rewarded the men if they had not given a shock. The women did respond to the conditioning attempt by upping their rate of shocks, but their blood pressure became cumulatively higher and higher, as if the maintenance of higher rates of aggressive action was stressful to them. In contrast, the men's blood pressure showed they noticed the changed contingencies favoring friendly responses, for their blood pressure now fell rapidly whenever they made a friendly response. But their behavior did not change, for they still continued to respond mainly by pressing the shock button. Possibly the brief experiment was just not long enough to overcome a lifetime of training and cul-tural support for male aggressiveness and female nonaggressiveness. Or possibly the refusal of the men to change is further proof that anger is too much fun to give up easily—at least for men.

The Pleasure of Rage

The secret truth about anger is that it actually feels good. An angry person, strength pumped up by norepinephrine's release of stored sugars, feels powerful, brave, and assertive. The tinge of fear coming from epinephrine adds to a sense of excitement and tremendous aliveness. The powerful hormonal effects do not last long enough to cause stress damage if the anger brings victory and the end of danger. On top of all the exciting sense of powerfulness, victory brings its own further rewards through the submission of the loser and the capture of any available battle trophies.

Some may doubt that anger is pleasurable, but solid experimental evidence indicates that animals react to induced rage as if it were pleasant. Fonberg (1979) electrically stimulated several brain points in dogs to evoke their fear-flight, defensive attack, and rage-aggres-sion behaviors. First she sounded a warning tone so that the dogs could press a bar that prevented the brain stimulation if they disliked it. Soon the animals were avoiding the fear stimulation. Then they learned to avoid the defensive attack stimulation, but only one dog ever chose to prevent the rage. Time after time the dogs went willingly into the experimental box and produced rage responses with less and less stimulation, as if they found rage a pleasant experience.

A real reason for the popularity of the catharsis theory that anger must be released is that cathartic cursing and pounding does provide a bit of the fun of being angry, without the risks of serious aggression. However, a nonserious anger display seldom brings the payoffs that belong to a victor, or even the quick reduction in stressful arousal that comes when danger is ended. Even so, the indulgence in anger is pleasurable enough to make cathartic displays of anger a popular pastime for many people.

The Catharsis Myth

The catharsis theory depends on a conceptual model of anger as a fixed quantity which, once aroused, stays within a person causing all sorts of mischief in terms of psychosomatic disorders, depression, and other neurotic defense mechanisms. The battering husband Wallace, whose declaration was quoted at the beginning of this chapter, was typical of the many people who believe that anger, like steam in a pressure cooker on the stove, has to be released before it will go away. Tavris (1982) reviewed the evidence for this model and pointed out all the ways that research findings refute it. For example, one large long-term study on the East Coast sought links between personality type and later heart diease and found that high-risk Type A persons repressed their anger when it occurred. However, an even larger study on the West Coast found that Type A heart disease candidates expressed anger outward at a higher rate than other types of people. Experiments by Feshbach (1956) and others since all showed that aggressiveness increases, rather than dying down, when anger expression is encouraged. The studies are consistent in pointing out how the popular remedy for anger of ventilation or catharsis is really worse than useless. As Tavris commented, aggressive play and sarcastic jokes have no cathartic value at all. Even talking over one's anger with a sympathetic listener, brooding about it or expressing it directly to a target, does not decrease aggression but instead rehearses it and makes later violence more likely.

Expression of anger often does make the expressor feel better, but only when the outburst succeeds in changing a stressful situation. It so happened that Wallace, who found that battering relieved his tension, had a wife who reliably ceased making her jealous accusations when he hit her. No wonder violence made him feel better. Experimenters have shown that when violence is directed against someone in a position to retaliate and possibly defeat the aggressor, then expression of anger increases a person's stress. Much "cathartic" anger ventilation is directed deliberately at harmless targets for this reason. However, since the aggression is not a direct and serious attempt to vanquish the true opponent, cathartic attacks only accidentally bring the sweet rewards of victory.

Winning over an opponent is not the only way to dissolve anger. Experiments show that anger arousal also decreases when successful peacemaking gestures are made instead of expressions of wrath. Hokanson and colleagues' (1968) exploration of male and female responses to provocation shows these effects clearly.

A more accurate model of anger would depict it not as a constant quantity of steam but as a quicksilver reaction, as momentary as the rush of adrenal hormones that power it. The epinephrine and nor-epinephrine come seconds after an arousing event or thought and die away in a couple of minutes if the provocation disappears. If anger stays and stays and boils and boils, it is because the stress-provoking event is still present and remains unresolved, or else the angry person himself or herself is keeping up the adrenal secretions by holding the event mentally present and obsessing over it. This latter problem will be discussed in the next chapter.

Instrumental Aggression

Darwin's and Bolton's observations of the deliberate use of anger for the sake of its internal effects lead to a consideration of instrumental aggression. Animal researchers have identified a class of aggressive attacks that have no separate brain site or distinctive pattern. Instead such aggression has a distinctive history. Instrumental aggression is a learned response that is repeated because it is "instrumental" in gaining a desired reward. Predatory hunting attacks are at least partly learned performances, as are the "pecking order" attacks carried out by higher-status animals to preserve their dominance over the others. Instrumental aggression takes on a wide variety of behavioral expressions, depending entirely on whatever brought success previously. Even though severe injuries or death may be inflicted, the acts may be carried out with little emotion or planning, after the manner of any overlearned habit.

Some battering fits the description of instrumental aggression all too well, especially in a long-lasting battering relationship. Wives who have been beaten for many years report that their consorts strike them nearly every day with little show of emotion, suggesting that violence is no longer a primitive rage response but a habit engaged in for the sake of the rewarding effects.

> It used to be that after he beat me, he would be sorry. Now he totally denies that he has done it. . . Sometimes he beats me so badly I can barely walk. Once he beat my head against a wall until I had a concussion. He's so totally different when he's not drinking. But I've given up hope that he'll change.
>
> (Mary, age thirty-seven, married twenty years)

A person who has become a habitual, instrumental-type batterer of either a consort or child is not likely to give up the habit. Even though the abuse is no longer accompanied by an exciting rush of rage, the rewards in terms of the victim's suffering and submission are sufficient to keep the behavior going forever. Such a batterer will not experience sorrow or remorse but instead sees the violence as completely justified each and every time. My advice to women yoked to such a batterer is to leave, because attempts to involve him in therapy will be futile. Even if he should someday be forced by court order into coming to anger-control training, he would not be likely to give up violence, because it is so useful to him.

4 Cognitive Regulators of Violence

The previous chapter examined the instinctual anger and aggression patterns stored in the nervous and hormonal systems, rather like computer programs that automatically set off emergency actions when life is at risk. The instinctual responses to threat from an enemy are angry emotions and aggressive behaviors. Though the responses are preprogrammed, humans can still control them by a sort of manual override, because they are closely regulated, right up to the final moment of overwhelming physiological buildup, by interpretations and directives coming from the conscious mind. Aggression resembles sex in being a combination of learned and instinctual responses. The buildup for either activity can be terminated voluntarily at any moment short of the final point of inevitability, when the instinctual patterns take control.

Battering, the repeated escalation into rage and aggression against an intimate, is an acquired habit. It is learned when on some occasion a batterer-to-be lets himself or herself go into the primitive rage mode, physically abuses a consort or a child, and thereby gains some desired end such as the victim's submission. The attacker is more and more easily tempted to go into a rage each time such behavior pays. So he or she gradually becomes a batterer, unless something different happens that interrupts the anger-aggression-submission sequence. A section in Chapter 1 described some of the drastic and dangerous remedies used by a few determined women to stop battering sequences.

A better remedy is possible for many battering couples, namely, training in anger control. Anger-control procedures are largely cognitive, that is, they hinge on changing the mental perceptions and decisions that regulate the eruption of rage and violence. The first four sections of this chapter look at the manner in which human cognitive operations closely control the appearance of angry emotions, learned aggressive routines, and even instinctual violent rages. Later sections describe several anger-control methods, developed by cognitively oriented therapists, which have potential for use with battering consorts and parents. The treatment program described in the present book, beginning with Chapter 6, draws heavily on these cognitive-behavioral methods.

Cognitive Guardians of the Rage Program

Cognitive decisions closely regulate the timing, degree, and duration of all emotional behavior, including primitive aggressive outbursts, because the neocortex, the most highly developed part of the brain, must first determine that one is being attacked. The cognitive activities of the neocortex consist mainly of analyzing perceptions of external stimuli and/or internally produced stimuli coming from imagination or memory, plus the inner dialogue of self-statements that convey attitudes and decisions about the percepts. The particular cognitions that appear to control the appearance and abatement of anger and rage are described below.

Chapter 3 mentioned the research showing that incoming stimuli are evaluated by the amygdala for their life-threatening or life-enhancing potential. These primitive "good/bad" evaluations seem to control access to the anger programs in the hypothalamus. Fortunately, incoming stimuli must first be received and interpreted by the appropriate areas in the cerebral hemispheres specialized to handle sights, sounds, and so on. Therefore the amygdala passes judgment on stimuli that have first been filtered through the conscious parts of the mind, where all inputs are registered; compared with past memories, beliefs and expectations; and interpreted. This simple anatomical fact serves to screen the midbrain from the world and is the built-in basis for cognitive regulation of anger reactions.

Plutchik (1962) mentioned two early psychological studies that indicate the developmental growth of cognitive controls over rage reactions. J. B. Watson demonstrated that young infants reliably went into rages when an experimenter restrained them by holding down their legs. Then a subsequent study by Florence Goodenough showed that physical restraint had less and less effect as babies grew older. By the time they could talk, their reactions changed from raging to verbal complaints and protests. The neocortex is rather undeveloped in newborn babies and grows rapidly in size and complexity during the first three years of life. As it takes on the role of interpreting incoming stimuli it buffers the midbrain with its primitive emotional judgments and reaction patterns from the direct impact of the environment. To go back to the computer metaphor, the child's instinctual reactions are now stored on tape out of the active area, still quickly ready when needed, but requiring a cognitive "command" statement to access them.

Schachter and Singer (1962) performed a classic experiment to demonstrate the control of cognitions over emotions. First the researchers artificially created high arousal in their subjects by injecting them with epinephrine. Then subjects were left alone with an experimental confederate, who became either silly and playful or so angry that he walked out of the laboratory room. Subjects who were ignorant of the true nature of the injection tended to mimic the confederate's reactions, but those informed that they would feel arousal, or guessing that the injection was affecting them, displayed even less emotional response than the control subjects given a placebo injection. Many experiments since have supported this demonstration that cognitions override the effects of sheer arousal (Schachter, 1971). Cognitions also tend to override, or at least moderate, the effects of pain, frustration, fear, and sexual arousal in the same manner.

Dollard et al. (1939) theorized that aggression was a response to frustrated drives. Frustration is certainly related to anger arousal, but there is a cognitive element even in frustration, as Bandura (1973) pointed out, for frustrations can occur only when some sort of expectation has been disappointed. Expectations are cognitive, requiring memory and imagination. Furthermore, the frustrated person will not act aggressively unless the setting is perceived as appropriate for the expression of hostility. Thus soldiers attack enemy soldiers but submit quietly to frustrations imposed by their own officers. Husbands are more likely to attack wives in a culture that regards women as men's property. Persons whose own families practice violence have the most powerful role models of all to show them that aggression against frustrating loved ones is appropriate.

Furthermore, frustrating events may evoke fear, pain, or even grief reactions instead of anger. The critical cognition that seems to trigger anger is that the aversive event was committed deliberately. Children learn early to say, "It was an accident!" because it tends to prevent rage, whereas "You did that on purpose!" is guaranteed to arouse it. Averill (1981) asked forty subjects to keep diaries of real-life anger events. Without exception they reported anger arousal only when someone willfully committed some aversive act.

Deliberately inflicted pain or frustration carries a very different cognitive message from accidental damage, even though the harm done and pain experienced are exactly the same. The message is that an enemy is about and is on the attack, so that fear of further pain at the hands of this enemy combines with any already inflicted. The theory that pain + fear = anger was set forth in Chapter 3 on the basis of the effects of the two adrenal hormones, epinephrine and norepinephrine. Deliberately committed offenses evoke both fear and pain and so are tailor-made to inspire anger and the primitive rage-filled counterattack response.

It behooves people to be very careful about the way they think and talk to themselves about frustrations. Any of innumerable cognitions that even hint that an enemy has deliberately attacked can bring on a defensive rage. Even the word "angry" may be enough, since it contains an implicit prior judgment that an enemy has struck. To give a personal example, when I was a young mother I would sometimes try to cool down my misbehaving child by warning, "Stop it! I'm beginning to get angry!" The warning didn't work, because an instant after I uttered it I was furious and ready to punish, which allowed the child no time at all to reform. I used to think that I just wasn't sufficiently in touch with my feelings to give the warning in time. But more likely it was my unfortunate choice of the word "angry" in the warning that turned mild irritation into rage, because the strong word precipitated an emotional, amygdalal judgment of "An enemy is attacking!"

One of the amazing aspects of anger is the universal conviction of angry persons that they are 100 percent right and their opponents totally wrong.

> He would always make out it was my fault. If I hadn't said this or if I hadn't done that, it would never have happened. He always claimed that I provoked him. It was always I provoked him.
>
> (Quoted in Dobash and Dobash, 1979, p. 118)

This illogical, self-righteous certainty of innocence persists even while angry persons are meting out punishments far worse than the original transgression. But their conviction of rightness is logical to them because "bad" translates into "dangerous enemy" and "I'm right and you're wrong" means "I'm under attack and defending myself against you." The amygdala is making the judgments of right or wrong on the basis of fancied threats to life, not logic or fairness.

Cognitions That Stop Violence

Cognitions also help control the length and vigor of rage and violence. Very few attacks last until the victim is dead or the batterer exhausted. The intensity of the attack depends somewhat on the aggressor's skill and on cognitions about how much retaliation is deserved or needed, and on other factors described below.

Animal researchers have found that intermale conflicts, unlike predatory or defensive attacks, are regularly stopped by a submission signal from the vanquished male. Battered wives almost all try the strategy of signaling submission to their consort, in the hope of getting him to stop. Possibly submission signals from the loser indicate that the goal of the aggression, which is to stop some aversive behavior such as complaining, has been accomplished. This should stop all but the most enraged attackers, whose goal is not submission but retaliation by inflicting as much injury as possible.

> I found out the best way not to get him into a tirade would be not to cry out loud, do you know what I mean, not to cry out. I know it sounds silly, but if you can just think to yourself, "I'm going to get two or three and then he'll stop," that wasn't bad. He could just stop after two or three, but he wouldn't if you cried out or you protested.
>
> (Quoted in Dobash and Dobash, 1979, p. 109)

Pain signals are not as effective as submission signals in stopping violent attacks. Studies of real-life situations such as lynchings, gang attacks on strangers, and forced "pacification" of Vietnamese villagers all suggest that victims' pain signals may only arouse a group of attackers into greater violence (Fraczek, 1979). The cries of battered infants and wives may at times increase the aggression, especially if the batterer believes that the way to make people stop crying is to hit them. No wonder battered babies sometimes adopt a peculiar rigid, silent pose known as "frozen watchfulness." I have seen a battered wife adopt a similar rigid, nervously watching pose when in her husband's presence.

Reasonable explanations sometimes do stop aggression, as was shown in a study involving nine-year-old children (Mallick and McCandless, 1966). When the children were given a reasonable rationale for the insulting behavior of the experimental confederate they reduced their counteraggression.

Albert Ellis (1976), creator of Rational Emotive Therapy, has had a great deal to say about the cognitions' control of anger. He contends that rage always begins with absolutist and essentially irrational demands of one sort or another, usually having to do with getting one's own way. When people tell themselves such things as "He should have listened!" "She ought not to do that!" "I can't stand this!" or "You must obey me!" they are making absolutist demands. They draw a false conclusion that just because they want something very much and could theoretically obtain it, they ought to have it. On the other hand, if they say something more realistic and rational to themselves, such as, "It's unfortunate that this frustration happened, but the world is not arranged just to suit me," they will not go into a rage. Therefore they will have a chance to cope more effectively with the problem.

Hauck (1974) incorporated Ellis's ideas into a six-step model of the irrational decisions leading one to anger:

1. I want something.
2. I didn't get it and am frustrated.
3. It is awful and terrible not to get what I want.
4. You shouldn't frustrate me! I must have my way!
5. You're bad for frustrating me.
6. Bad people ought to be punished.

The decision about punishment gives one justification to counterattack. The blows struck do not seem like violence or battering; they are virtuous and righteous deeds, necessary for the preservation of life and the social order. Quite a few battering parents and consorts express self-righteous justifications like these for their violence. They even try to convince their victims of how much they needed and deserved to be battered.

Learned Helplessness

Battered women have been said to suffer from learned helplessness (Walker, 1979). They have tried so often to escape, never succeeding, that they finally give up even trying. Despairingly and numbly they continue to submit to unending abuse. Ellis pointed out that learned helplessness is also the result of unrealistic cognitions:

> You theoretically could have told yourself, "There goes crazy old Dad getting angry again, and about to punish me unjustly. Well, too bad; but I can survive his punishment and eventually, as I grow up, get away from him and live in a nonpunishing environment." You actually largely said to yourself, however, "I feel blameworthy for coming from such a crazy family and for having such weakness as to let the old buzzard take advantage of me." And with your first husband, you could have said to yourself, "Too bad: I made a mistake in marrying this individual who acts sadistically, but I feel strong enough to get away from him and leave him to his own crazy ways." But you again said: "I see myself as no good for making the terrible mistake of marrying this bastard; and now I remain too weak and idiotic to get away from him" [Ellis and Harper, 1979, p. 149].

This example illustrates two among several possible rational solutions for battering victims. One is to overcome irrational fear, self-hate and resentment so that the victim will feel more at peace with herself or himself. Another is to overcome irrational beliefs of helplessness and extract oneself from the abusive relationship.

Something akin to learned helplessness also afflicts some batterers, who avoid trying to get help for their violence because they believe the rages are too ingrained or too overwhelming ever to be controlled. Hauck (1974) confronted a batterer who believed he could not change a habit of violence that went back to his childhood. Hauck contended that even ingrained habits are carried forward into the present only by one's expectations and beliefs about them. The belief about helplessness, Hauck said, is really a way to avoid having to give up the short-term gains achieved by battering, such as the consort's submission. People will make the effort to change violent habits only when they are rationally convinced that the short-run gains are not worth the long-term losses through ruined relationships.

Jealousy

Pathologically severe jealousy seems to afflict about 60 percent of all batterers, according to the surveys I have conducted (Montgomery, Meraz, and Deschner, 1978; Feazell, 1981). Many battered women also experience jealousy, though the extent is not known. Jealousy appears to be a specialized form of anxiety over the possible loss of a valued love object. The anxiety may gain extra power from sexual drives and from urges toward intermale competition. Jealousy gathers so much power from its several energy sources that it can become a consuming obsession, occupying all waking thoughts.

> If there were only the two of us in the world we would have a wonderful life together. But it seems no matter what I do to assure him of my love he is insecure, so that any little thing convinces him I am unfaithful. I have to be careful about phone calls, even to my mother. Whenever I pay attention to another person in his presence he soon gets a look on his face and then I know I am in for it later. . . . Though he has never injured me seriously he is so strong that I am really afraid when he gets into one of those moods.
>
> (Toni, age thirty-two)

> He would always accuse me of having a lover. He told me he would catch me one day and kill me. Believe me, I didn't dare look at another man for fear of him. But the funny thing is, I know he was having affairs with the women he would meet in the bars, because he would brag about them to me.
>
> (Gail, age twenty-eight)

Jealousy has considerable social usefulness. Even the courts tend to be more lenient toward crimes committed in a passion of jealousy. On the individual level many persons accept jealousy as a natural part of love, perhaps the only proof of love where better evidence is scarce.

Oh yes, he's jealous of me. I guess that proves I'm still attractive.

(Betty, age twenty-five)

Psychoanalytic writers beginning with Freud have taken a strong interest in jealousy. They believe that pathological jealousy has little to do with the current partner and much to do with transference projections from insecurities in relation to the mother. A pair of psychiatrists wrote of treating three different jealous husbands who all, by coincidence, had happened upon their mothers in bed with a lover during their early adolescent years (Docherty and Ellis, 1976). Though maternal infidelity would threaten the stability of the family, which is distressing, it is not enough to create a serious emotional disturbance. However, boys' oedipal fantasies supposedly undergo a resurgence during early adolescence, and the mothers' affairs would make the boys second best to strange men, after already losing the first oedipal romance to their fathers.

Other commonalities in the three cases also were interesting. The fathers of all three men were passive, long-suffering, and more nurturant than the mothers. All three clients felt more affection for their wronged fathers than for their philandering mothers. This led the authors to postulate a subterranean homosexual element in their jealousy toward their spouses, as if the men were thinking, "I find men attractive, so I'll bet you do too!" The boys in all three cases kept their knowledge of their mothers' affair secret from the fathers. To keep their home together (and thus retain their fathers' presence) they had to bear the burden of duplicity for their mothers. Their mothers were demonstrating for all time how easy it is to conceal an affair and how vigilant men must be if they are to prevent their wives from cheating on them. Three case studies do not constitute proof of the origins of pathological jealousy, but they do suggest avenues that research on jealousy might pursue.

Incidentally, all three of the jealous husbands were also battering their wives, but the therapists barely mentioned this and did not view it as a problem in itself.

Jealousy also may become part of a game played by a couple to keep their relationship stable. Couples who fear the risks involved in real intimacy and who prefer not to resolve their conflicts one way or the other frequently maintain their relationship by including some third party in a triangular game (Haley, 1976). The marital pair can then relate through their common concern and/or conflict around the third entity, which holds them safely apart even as it holds them together. The third party often is a child whose problems are a never ending source of controversy. The triangle can also be over a behavior pattern of one of the spouses, such as alcoholism, ill health, or jealousy (Pinta, 1978). Jealous rages permit the partners to express their desire for closeness at the same time that they angrily stay apart.

Cognitive Anger-control Training

A survey of ninety agencies treating battering men (Feazell, 1981) is described in Chapter 5. Results indicated that the single most promising treatment for batterers is cognitive anger-control training, a procedure based on cognitive behavior therapy principles. The latter derive from behavior modification but take into account not only environmental stimuli but also humans' cognitive controls over their own behavior. A major part of treatment consists in teaching persons how to modify their own cognitive sets, often by using systematic methods such as thought stopping or mental rehearsal (Bandura, 1973; Meichenbaum, 1977; Mahoney, 1979). Reality therapy (Glasser, 1965; 1980) also is used frequently in treating batterers, according to the same survey. Reality therapy has been used successfully for the past decade by school counselors working with hostile and aggressive adolescents. Reality therapy also is a cognitive approach to anger control, since the stress is on taking responsibility for one's own life and using rational thinking and plan making in place of impulsive aggression.

Systematic Desensitization to Relieve Fears

A systematic method for helping people to cope with fears was introduced some twenty years ago by Joseph Wolpe (1958). He pointed out that anxieties of all degrees, from mild avoidance to crippling phobias, are all learned responses. The anxiety reactions are triggered by situations that resemble the setting in which severe fright was originally experienced. A new and more adaptive response in the anxiety-evoking situations can be learned by following the principle of associative learning, repeatedly pairing the old stimulus with a new response. Relaxation is the new response usually taught, since relaxation is pleasurable in itself and also directly counteracts the muscular tension that accompanies anxiety. A good description of the method, commonly called systematic desensitization, may be found in Wolpe's book *The Practice of Behavior Therapy* (1973), as well as numerous other works dealing with stress reduction. Systematic desensitization has amply proved its worth in reducing anxiety through both clinical use and formal experiments (Paul, 1969).

There are three elements in the systematic desensitization method: training in deep muscle relaxation, the systematic desensitization proper, and the *in vivo* application of calming procedures to stressful occasions in daily life.

1. *Relaxation*

Tension in the muscles to varying degrees is a normal accompaniment of the alert and awake state. The achievement of profound relaxation of all muscle groups while remaining awake requires making a deliberate decision to relax and the passage of a few minutes. Awake deep muscle relaxation is very akin to the hypnotic state, the meditation state, and the phase of brain activity characterized by alpha waves. These are all similar conditions, which people experience as highly pleasant, refreshing, and even restorative. There are many ways to help another person achieve deep relaxation, and the particular method used seems not to affect the rest of the systematic desensitization procedure. As with any other physical skill, repeated practice is necessary to be able to relax rapidly and efficiently.

2. *Visualization of an Anxiety Hierarchy*

The systematic part of systematic desensitization consists in a mental rehearsal of encounters with anxiety-provoking stimuli. Therapist and client first arrange a series of stressful scenes in a hierarchy, ranging from ones that barely disturb the client to those that produce all-out panic. The client relaxes and then practices visualizing the hierarchy scenes one by one, while deliberately maintaining the state of relaxation. Repeated mental rehearsals over a period of days or weeks have the effect of pairing the scenes, by means of associative learning, with calmness instead of tension. Therefore, when encountered in real life, these situations no longer automatically trigger un-manageable tension and anxiety.

3. In Vivo *Practice*

The third element in the systematic desensitization method, real life or *in vivo* practice, seems to be vital to a complete cure of a crippling fear. Therefore some therapists skip the relaxation training and mental rehearsals and immediately arrange for real-life practice with the coaching and support of the therapist (Thyer, 1983). The mental rehearsals are useful when *in vivo* practice is difficult to arrange. Since the events leading to a couple's engaging in violence are often impossible to simulate in a practice session, the alternative of mental rehearsals may be necessary. The real-life practice will happen when it will happen, and it is to be hoped that the partners will have practiced mentally well enough to be able to cope.

Systematic Desensitization to Relieve Anger

Only a few attempts have been made to use systematic desensitization in the treatment of anger problems. Rimm and colleagues (1971) tried using systematic desensitization methods with young men who admitted to becoming angry in various driving situations. After just one session the experimental group reported significantly less anger and showed less physiological arousal when imagining the frustrating driving events. The experimenters tried to explain their results by suggesting that anger is a self-generated way of coping with fear and that the desensitization procedures had helped subjects reduce the fear that preceded their anger. Their speculation accords well with our own theories about anger as a confluence of fear and pain feelings. Novaco (1979) included the teaching of relaxation as an element of his stress inoculation training for people with severe anger problems. The relaxation training was a minor part of his treatment program, described in a section below, because of his view that anger is a reaction to stress. Novaco noted that his anger clients were chronically tense people.

Feazell (1981) found that about 20 percent of the agencies treating batterers frequently included relaxation as a part of their treatment package for such clients. It was not clear whether relaxation was included just to relieve the general stress and tension of the battering men or whether it was taught as a part of systematic desensitization in order to treat their anxiety and jealousy.

How It Works

Goldfried (1977) took a fresh look at the theoretical explanations of how systematic desensitization works. He theorized that clients, far from undergoing a passive process of associative learning, learn an active coping procedure. They discover first that relaxation banishes anxiety. By learning to maintain relaxation while imagining hierarchy items, they master the skill of using relaxation to remove fear in various situations. Then in the *in vivo* situations they can lower their anxiety by relaxing enough to stay in the formerly dreaded situations and discover them to be survivable.

The reason that some anxiety becomes "neurotic," that is, totally resistant to extinction, is that the individuals feeling anxiety tend to develop patterns of behavior that enable them to avoid experiencing such an uncomfortable feeling. That is, the moment the first warning twinge of anxiety occurs, the stimulus that seemed to arouse it is somehow avoided. This brings such prompt relief that the avoidance pattern is reinforced. But since the stimulus is never faced and survived, the original dread is never proved to be unfounded. Extinction can occur only when a response repeatedly earns no reinforcement. Perhaps extinction of the fear response begins during systematic desensitization because the client has to stop avoiding the feared events, and instead repeatedly lives through them in imaginary form.

Total relaxation would be impossible and also downright bizarre in most real-life situations. The proper goal of systematic desensitization is coping, not relaxation. Therefore Goldfried modified the classic systematic procedures. He required the client to keep on imagining the feared event and to practice relaxing "as much as possible" in its presence, rather than strive for total relaxation. In this way the client practices keeping just calm enough to stay in the presence of the feared stimulus, which is what happens during *in vivo* practice. After some experiences of facing and surviving the avoided situation, people lose their anxiety and conclude that "it's not so bad after all."

Rational Emotive Therapy for Battering Couples

One of the earliest and most important of the cognitive therapy approaches is rational emotive therapy, or RET, developed by Albert Ellis. Ellis emphasized marital and sexual therapy, so his writings contain several case examples of the use of RET with battering couples (Ellis, 1976; Ellis and Harper, 1979). The first step in RET is called rational disputation, in which the counselor teaches the client how one's beliefs about external events, and not the events themselves, trigger emotional reactions such as anger. Victims of battering are prey to severe terror, since their bodies and very lives are endangered on a recurrent basis, not under their control. Great anger coalesces from all their fear and pain, though victims often try to suppress their wrath in order to avoid antagonizing the batterer. Batterers who were abused and victimized as children experienced the same sort of terror and suppressed rage over their treatment. They project those feelings into their consort relationship and spend much time feeling afraid and victimized, even though they themselves are now doing the attacking.

RET therapists identify and dispute battering clients' feelings of fear and resentment as dysfunctional because they work against their own best interests. For example, Ellis told a woman who had been battered by her father and her husband:

> First, your father abuses you, then you tell yourself that you can't do anything to stop his abuse, then you get terribly anxious, but, once you get anxious, and you only half-heartedly try to overcome anxiety, you start telling yourself you can't do anything about that. So you get anxious of getting, and of not feeling able to do anything about getting, anxious. . . . Then to take it one step further, you actually get so frightened and act so badly because of your fright, that you then get convinced of your original hypothesis. . . . And then, going one step further, you hate yourself for staying so weak and for having such a dire need for love; and you resent your present husband and daughters for not fulfilling your dire need to the exact extent you demand that they fill it—and for not making up for all the anger and punishment that your father and your first husband foisted on you. So that amounts to a goodly degree of resentment—which only tends to make you still more upset [Ellis and Harper, 1979, p. 152].

The irrational beliefs targeted for change by the RET therapist also are dysfunctional, because they cause people to act against their own best interests, which is much more important than whether the attitudes are rational or irrational. For example, Harper, Ellis's coauthor, treated a battering man (Ellis and Harper, 1979). The young man's mother had given in to him throughout his childhood whenever he made aggressive demands. Given this history of immediate payoffs, his belief in the merits of abusive behavior was more or less rational. Harper made the client review all his other relationships, in which aggressive behaviors had cost him friends and brought inner tension and loss of self-esteem, all long-term losses, even though it continued to bring him short-term gains through the submission of the other person.

Hauck (1974), another RET therapist, described a further step in the disputation of anger cognitions: Blaming others must be replaced by a more realistic assessment of their frailties. In treating a battered wife, Hauck insisted that she give up viewing her husband as "bad." People, he said, transgress against others not because they are deliberately evil or obnoxious, but for one of just three reasons: They are ignorant of what they are doing; they are stupid; or they are emotionally disturbed. One day this particular client was able to remember Hauck's counsel at the very moment her husband was provoking her to argue.

He had come home after work, started drinking, and was getting more foulmouthed with every passing minute. At first I tried to ignore it, and for some minutes that helped, but as he kept up his badgering I couldn't ignore him and then began to feel myself getting hotter and hotter under the collar. I was just about to answer one of his sarcastic remarks when I remembered some of the things you had been telling me. You know: no one can anger me but myself: why get angry with him when he's so fouled up, forgive him for his nastiness and I'll do myself a big favor, and so on. Well, what happened then was beautiful, a miracle. I felt the tension and anger simply drain from my body. I could hardly believe how good I felt. There he stood, getting redder and redder in the face, expecting me to fire back the same thing he was throwing at me. . . . He got madder and madder as I got calmer and calmer. Finally, he put on his hat and slamming the door behind him, went off to get drunk.

(Quoted in Hauck, 1974, pp. 13–14)

A year later this wife reported that even though her husband had not stopped drinking he had stopped fighting with her, "because I no longer play that game." This happened because victims who refuse to counterattack and play the escalation game make it very hard for the batterer to pump his or her rage up to the point where aggression is inevitable. The partner who neither submits nor counter-coerces can make a coercion spiral limp to a halt.

Finally, the learned helplessness of people caught in battering relationships must be disputed. The batterer feels just as helpless to stop his primitive rages as does the victim. The batterer must stop viewing it as terrible and unmanly to lose out on some immediate pleasure, and remember instead the long-term gains coming from self-control. Emotions will tend to change to be appropriate to the altered goal. Harper, Ellis's co- author, gave an example of disputing a batterer's learned helplessness:

> Just as you, partly as a rationalization for keeping your present goal of immediate gratification instead of longer-range goals, now keep telling yourself: "How can I ever expect to change, to lose my tantrum habit, when it goes back practically to birth and represents an inextricable part of my personality?" so you can tell youself, instead: "No matter how long I've had this childish habit, nor how many people I've cajoled into going along with it, I now defeat my own best ends, so I'd better work my backside off, against my habit and for myself, to behave differently" [Ellis and Harper, 1979, p. 173].

Where habits are strong, RET therapists recognize that rational disputation will not be enough to eradicate them. Clients must force themselves to try out new behaviors in real life, then consciously practice them for weeks until they become natural. Mental rehearsal of deliberately changing an angry response to a rational evaluation, in a procedure called rational-emotive imagery (Ellis and Harper, 1979), is helpful in shortening the time needed to establish new habits. This exercise resembles systematic desensitization but includes a preliminary step. As clients imagine an anger-provoking event, they first try deliberately to make themselves angry. Then they consciously change the anger to calmness. In the process of pumping their anger up and down, clients discover for themselves the irrational self-talk they are using to regulate their emotions.

Goldfried (1977) compared the effectiveness of rational restructuring, relaxation training, or assertiveness training in teaching clients to cope with anxiety. The three procedures seemed equally effective, but a long-term followup suggested that the effects of rational restructuring might last the longest and that a combination of all three kinds of training would be the most helpful treatment strategy of all.

Thought-stopping for Jealous Anxiety

Obsessive ruminating over black thoughts causes people to feel jealous, depressed, angry, and even murderous. Thought-stopping is a simple method for stopping the ruminations and the mischief that they cause. Let us take for an example a husband who wishes to overcome the jealousy that causes him to restrict his wife's activities. First he and his therapist should make a catalog of all the forms that his jealous thinking takes and attempt to eliminate all at the same time. As soon as one of the thoughts occurs, the jealous mate should shout to himself, *"Stop!"* as sharply as possible. Another good way to interrupt the obsessing is to snap a rubber band worn on the wrist for the purpose. The slight pain is very attention-getting and effectively chases the obsessive thought away for long enough to choose to replace it with a rational thought such as, "Probably she got caught in the traffic."

A daily tally of the number of thought stops should be kept on a handy card or envelope back. Within a very few days the count of jealous thoughts should drop steeply and eventually sink to zero. The tallying is useful as a distracting activity. The feedback from adding up the tallies for each day gives concrete evidence of progress toward breaking the power of the obsessive thought. If the count does not sink to zero in a week, additional procedures should be tried.

Further Treatment for Jealousy

Jealous reactions are severe anxiety reactions based on irrational assumptions about the duties of the loved one, one's own dire need for the beloved, and the loved one's untrustworthiness, according to Ellis (1977) and Hauck (1974). Jealousy should disappear when these beliefs are changed. The difficulty is that such beliefs are unconscious and taken for granted in most love relationships. Clients receiving rational emotive therapy are taught to "dispute" their own unconscious assumptions and replace them with more accurate statements which calm their jealous anxiety.

Assumption	*Rational Revision*
He should love me! (Because he promised once.)	I'd like it if he loves me.
She has to love me! (Or I'll die.)	I will be sad if she doesn't love me, but I will still be able to take care of myself.
If she looks at anyone else she'll dump me. (Because I'm really no good.)	I trust her to remember me and my needs because she loves me, even if she is somewhere else.

Ellis himself started his career as a psychoanalytic therapist. The irrational jealous beliefs in the list look like specific examples of the transference projections alluded to by the analytic writers. Learning rational thinking could be viewed as a systematic way of overcoming the projection of childish demands and fantasies onto adult relationships.

Since jealous consorts and spouses have given in to a great anxiety, they easily move on into rage. All they need is the addition of a little pain to the jealous fear and they are ready to commit "crimes of passion." Fortunately, jealous feelings respond well to treatments developed for other kinds of obsessive anxieties. Phillips (1978) used systematic desensitization and also thought-stopping very effectively with clients who were beset by jealous fears. Most importantly, the sufferer from jealousy must be willing to give up all checking-up activities. Though it may seem harmless and even reassuring to phone or drive by to check on a spouse's whereabouts, the act of giving in to a jealous urge reinforces and strengthens the fears that power it.

Novaco's Stress Inoculation for Anger Control

Novaco (1975; 1979) tailored the cognitive stress coping methods of Meichenbaum et al. (1975) specifically for persons troubled by anger outbursts. He called the procedures stress inoculation, as they were designed to help persons with anger problems to remain calm during stressful encounters. One main ingredient was a mental rehearsal of the self-talk people should use before, during, and after a confrontation in order to keep themselves calm and in control of themselves. Angry clients were taught to imagine a confrontation of the type that usually tripped off their rage responses, while reciting the self-instructions and picturing themselves coping with the situation. The repeated mental rehearsals came in the middle part of a three-phase training program consisting of cognitive preparation, skill acquisition, and application practice.

1. *Cognitive Preparation*

In this introductory phase Novaco taught clients about the nature and causes of anger and the general nature of the cognitive management techniques they would learn. The content resembled Ellis's rational disputations. Clients were told to begin keeping a diary of all experiences that aroused anger in order to learn more about what kinds of external events and internal self-talk set off hostile feelings.

2. *Skill Acquisition and Rehearsal*

Next, clients learned how to modify their anger-producing cognitions and appraisals by reciting self-instructions while visualizing an anger-evoking incident. Self-instructions were worked out for each of the four main stages of a stressful event: the preparation moments, impact or confrontation, the middle when stress is building, and thinking it over afterward. Novaco provided samples of helpful self-talk for each stage.

SELF-INSTRUCTIONS FOR REGULATING ANGER

Preparing for a Provocation
This could be a rough situation, but I know how to deal with it.
I can work out a plan to handle this. Easy does it.
Remember, stick to the issues and don't take it personally.
There won't be any need for an argument. I know what to do.

Impact and Confrontation
As long as I keep my cool, I'm in control of the situation.
You don't need to prove yourself. Don't make more out of this than you have to.
There is no point in getting mad. Think of what you have to do.
Look for positives and don't jump to conclusions.

Coping with Arousal
My muscles are getting tight. Relax and slow things down.
Time to take a deep breath. Let's take the issue point by point.
My anger is a signal of what I need to do. Time for problem solving.
He probably wants me to get angry, but I'm going to deal with it constructively.

Subsequent reflection

a. *Conflict unresolved*
Forget about the aggravation. Thinking about it only makes you upset.
Try to shake it off. Don't let it interfere with your job.
Remember relaxation. It's a lot better than anger.
Don't take it personally. It's probably not so serious.
b. *Conflict resolved*
I handled that one pretty well. That's doing a good job.
I could have gotten more upset than it was worth.
My pride can get me into trouble, but I'm doing better at this all the time.
I actually got through that without getting angry.*

The self-statements follow the same pattern at each stage of the confrontation. The first is a warning to keep the situation in proportion, for example, "This could be a rough situation, but I know how to deal with it." One statement reminds the person to keep arousal down, as in, "Time to take a deep breath. Easy does it." Another self-instruction reminds the person that he or she has the strength to cope with this situation, as in, "As long as I keep my cool, I'm in control of this situation," Another group of self-statements are reminders to focus on the problem, for example, "Remember to stick to the issues. Don't take it personally." The four basic ideas repeated over and over are really rational antidotes to dysfunctional beliefs that commonly trigger angry feelings. The four antidotes are: Though the situation is difficult it can be mastered; it should be viewed as a problem to be solved rather than as a personal

*Reprinted, with permission, from Raymond W. Novaco, "The Cognitive Control of Anger and Stress," in P. C. Kendall and S. D. Hollan (eds.), *Cognitive-Behavioral Interventions: Theory, Research, and Procedure* (New York: Academic Press, 1979), Table 8.1, p. 269.

affront; calmness is good and anger is unhelpful; and one is not help-less but has the ability to cope with the situation.

Like other cognitive-behavioral therapists, Novaco also gave his angry clients training in other skills along with the stress inoculation training. Since, as he noted, angry people are tense people, he in-cluded relaxation training. As they learned to counteract their ten-sion they were also learning that it is possible to control responses that seem automatic, like rage. Novaco also included assertion train-ing so that clients could learn how to state negative feelings to others without coercing them or antagonizing them. Finally, clients were taught to remain task-oriented and to apply problem-solving skills when under provocation.

3. *Application Training*

At first Novaco's clients practiced their emerging new skills in sim-ulated scenes during therapy. Imitating the therapist's model, they imagined an event which usually aroused their rage and practiced reciting self-instructions, asserting, and using problem-solving skills. Next, they role-played the same scene with the therapist acting as provocator. After this, they were encouraged to practice between ses-sions in actual provoking situations.

Novaco has carried out several studies, which indicate that his training program reduced the anger ratings made by clients, at least in role-play simulations of anger events. Novaco also reported on a study that compared the effects of stress inoculation training with social skills training (Atrops, 1978). Subjects were severely angry pa-tients at a hospital for the criminally insane. The cognitive stress inoculation taught patients to do better problem-solving and to speak more calmly under provocation; social skills training alone did not reduce their anger reactions at all. The subjects who received both kinds of training improved most in ability to control their anger.

Conclusion

The cognitive methods described in this chapter do not just keep anger under control but prevent severe anger from developing at all. Therefore the methods are at the heart of treatment for battering couples. When abusive persons succeed in realigning the cognitions that lead them to rage and aggression, they will be safe from committing further violence, no matter what provoking circumstances arise. The small amount of comparative research that has been done indicates that a combination of cognitive realignment with skill training, especially relaxation and assertiveness, works best of all in helping people with anger problems. Therefore the anger-control training program described in this book also combines several strands of training into one package for battering men and women.

5 Alternatives to Violent Behavior

Concerned people have been trying to stop abuse of family members for a long time. A complete history of the struggle to end family violence in the United States has yet to be written. The first four sections of this chapter attempt a chronological account, but many gaps remain. Some of the elements of the American history have been gathered from my own research and some from various books about battering (D. Martin, 1976; Davidson, 1978; Stacey and Shupe, 1983). A history of English reformers' efforts to outlaw battering (May, 1978) also provided information, since American cultural trends tend to follow a few years behind English and European ones.

History of Opposition to Battering

As early as the 1600s English reformers had challenged the ancient common law right of chastisement of wives, according to May's (1978) account. In the villages habitual battering husbands, and also the much rarer battering wives, were disciplined by mob action. Offenders were seized from their homes in the middle of the night and forced to ride through a jeering mob of neighbors while seated back-ward on a donkey. This vigilante type of action became less effective after the mass migrations into industrialized cities disrupted village community networks, from the early eighteenth century onward.

The British and other settlers who peopled the American colonies in the seventeenth and eighteenth centuries brought with them European attitudes about the supremacy of the male head of the family. Therefore chastisement of wives and children was accepted even when it was excessive. The Massachusetts Bay Colony was a notable exception; in 1655 wife battering was made illegal there (Stacey and Shupe, 1983).

In the mid-nineteenth century British Victorian reformers made a spirited attack on wife abuse, along with campaigns against cruelty to animals. John Stuart Mill, one of the most noted male authors of the time, published an essay on *The Subjection of Women* (Mill, 1869). The popular press took up the cause, featuring sensational battering cases. In 1853 parliament responded by passing an act aimed at punishing men who assaulted wives or children. The feminists continued their pressure, linking the rescue of battered wives with the crusade for women's suffrage. In the 1860s parliament modified the divorce laws so that some battered women could prosecute their husbands and obtain divorces. However, such women had to have enough money to hire an attorney, and they had to prove adultery as well as cruelty.

Unfortunately, then as now, most battered women were poor women. The lower classes were derisively nicknamed "the roughs," people to whom rough, violent behavior was natural. Social reformers, however, recognized that the violence of the poorer classes was due not to depravity but to the stresses of slum living conditions and extreme financial hardships (May, 1978). In the 1880s some legal relief was put within reach of battered women too poor to afford divorce lawyers in the form of legal separations and peace bonds to enforce the separations. Legal reforms in the American states one by one followed the British examples.

But reforming zeal was diverted from wife abuse to child abuse in the 1880s in both Britain and the United States, and child abuse proved to be a far more popular cause. Battered children are demonstrably innocent victims, attracting many effective male champions and more public and private funding than battered wives ever did. Laws prohibiting child abuse were gradually enacted throughout Great Britain, the United States, and most other countries. A social

service industry evolved to accomplish the tasks of identifying battered children and rescuing them by rearing them in institutions or
foster families. Only recently has research on the harmful effects of
removing children and also of institutional living in itself brought
home the message that such alternatives might be worse for many
children than leaving them with their sometimes abusive, sometimes
loving parents.

Meanwhile the more feminist-minded reformers turned from rescue of battered women to the great challenges of winning voting
rights for all women and of prohibiting the sale of alcohol. The violence that had aroused earlier reformers was all but forgotten. Consort battering was remembered only as comedy material for cartoons
and shows. Actresses depicted beaten women as funny instead of
tragic figures, and authors arranged plots so that the women brought
their punishment on themselves. Usually they were nagging and
domineering to the point that would drive anyone to revenge. The
moral of these highly popular comedy skits and cartoons was clear.
Women still belonged in a subordinate role and deserved their husband's chastisement if they forgot their true place.

A century passed before women, awakened by the renewed feminist movement of the 1970s, took up the cause of battered wives
once again. The first refuge for battered women was started almost
accidentally by a group of reform-minded women in Chiswick, a
western suburb of London, in 1971 (Pizzey, 1974). The women obtained an old building to serve as a community center, but their own
members began begging to stay there to escape daily abuse from their
violent husbands. Feminist writers like Pizzey and Del Martin (1976)
in the United States focused media attention once again on the tragic
plight of so many battered women. In a repetition of history, the
emerging women's rights movement adopted the issue of spouse
abuse as one of its main emphases.

Like any good idea long overdue, the impulse to establish refuges
just for battered women soon spread contagiously over the whole
civilized world. In the past ten years many local committees of
women (and a few concerned men) have worked against great odds
to procure enough funding to create a network of shelters in America, Great Britain, and other Western countries. A description of the
work of the shelters is beyond the scope of this book, because services are seldom offered to battering men. The interested reader may
want to read Renvoize's (1978) and Melville's (1978) descriptions of

British shelters and Stacey and Shupe's (1983) study of Texas shelter residents.

Most of the energy going into the struggle to end consort battering still is necessarily directed toward the survival of the refuges and modification of the many lingering legal impediments that make it difficult for battered women to escape even after they have decided to do so. A century ago the treatment of child abuse had already reached a similar level—institutions for the immediate rescue of victims existed, and some imperfect methods for detection and legal relief were available, but treatment of perpetrators was unknown.

Followup data on ex-shelter residents have been extremely hard to collect. The women are often too poor to afford a telephone or to stay put in one residence for very long. Shelter staff estimate that between 25 and 50 percent of their residents sooner or later return to their consorts, no matter what the danger of enduring further battering. For some women shelters provide a way to test out and compare independent living and reconciliations several times before finally making up their minds to leave for good. Other women learn at the shelter what they need to bring with them to make it alone, such as the children's birth certificates, then go back home to collect the essential items. But many go back home believing that things will be better and intending to stay in the relationship.

Beginning in the 1960s large amounts of federal research money were directed toward understanding and treating child abusers, with some fruitful results, some of which are mentioned in Chapter 9. Cuts in federal spending on social research have prevented any similar funding of experimental attempts to treat or prevent consort violence. However, some of the findings about helping child abusers appear relevant to consort-battering families. Also, much more is now known about how to treat marital problems and how to reduce angry and aggressive behaviors of juvenile delinquents and others. Therefore some practitioners have begun on their own to develop treatment programs for batterers. Their efforts will be described in detail in the next section.

Treatments for Batterers

Treatment programs for battering men have not spread with the speed of the women's shelter movement. Battering men do not attract popular champions, and the worldwide economic recession, while it has undoubtedly increased the prevalence of battering, has decreased the amount of money available for developing new social services. However, more and more experimental efforts to treat battering men have been reported. They seem to be arising as independent responses to the same social needs, with little or no communication among themselves.

One of the pioneering efforts to reach batterers was carried out by a specially trained unit of policemen in New York City (Bard, 1971). For two years they handled all family disturbance calls in their precinct, with the result that the number of arrests went down and the number of referrals to counseling agencies rose. Only one officer was slightly injured in the course of nearly 1,400 family disputes, which Bard attributed to the care the officers took not to "engage in degrading kinds of power displays which provoke the expected 'wild beast' response." Their basic techniques were to separate the disputants, eliminate the potential violence threats, and talk with each person separately and then together. Violence had occurred just before about half the calls, but the most common request made of the policemen was not to make an arrest but to arbitrate, mediate, or advise the callers, of whom fully 80 percent were consorts in conflict.

A cooperative project between police and a family service agency was carried out in Ontario (Knowles and Middleton, 1980). The police were trained in ways to be helpful on domestic disturbance calls and also were directed to ask families if they would like a counselor to call. When battering couples' requests for more help were followed up by a letter within three days and a home visit within a week by a trained pair of civilian counselors, 54 percent of them went on to avail themselves of some counseling services. This model of outreach seems preferable to attempts to substitute a social worker for a police officer at the time of the actual disturbance. Not only is the situation dangerous at such a time, but a visit by police emphasizes the fact that assaults on family members are crimes. Knowles and Middleton made a followup contact six months later with three-fourths of the families seen by a counselor. Sixty-three percent said violence had stopped, and 75 percent had not needed to call police again. Satisfaction with police handling of their problem rose from 39 percent two years earlier to 69 percent after the Frontenac program was instituted.

In 1976 the Chiswick Women's Aid group founded a Men's Aid House in London to provide refuge and basic support for battering men. An attempt was also made to start therapy groups for separated men and for couples. The house and the groups closed down after only two years because of lack of funds. Pizzey then found support for hiring a counselor for husbands, who still frequently came to the door of the women's refuge to ask for "front-porch therapy." Counselors report that most of the men who come to the refuge seem dependent and in need of care themselves. They tend to cry and to beg and plead as long as the counselor behaves in a way that is sympathetic and unafraid. The few who are belligerent are usually drunk. The police cooperate by quickly hauling such men off to sober up (Harper, 1979; Dunn, 1981).

The first counseling agency just for batterers, called Emerge, appears to be one begun in Boston in April 1977. Several women who were working at area shelters sought out interested and qualified men to counsel the partners of the shelter residents, because a number of men were requesting help and there was nowhere at all to send them. The volunteer counselors prepared, as much as possible, by attending a consciousness-raising group sponsored by the women, then began to see batterers individually and to form peer support groups among the men. Peer support groups have proved a popular treatment model, and a number of similar programs have been formed across the country.

A Survey of Programs for Battering Men

Carann Feazell and I carried out a survey in late 1980 of all known programs for battering men in order to learn how the men's programs were financed and staffed, which kinds of treatment approaches they were using, and what results they were obtaining (Feazell, 1981). The survey went out to 187 agency addresses, collected from several sources, from which we received 90 usable returns. Organizations attempting to provide treatment for battering men fell into two categories. A slight majority (50) had a special batterers' program, while the others (40) were absorbing batterers into regular caseloads of clients such as disturbed families or battered women.

Funds were extremely scarce everywhere. Many of the special programs were staffed by one paid worker, who was coordinating a group of trained volunteer counselors. The other programs were trying to begin working with batterers without a single specialized person. The specialist programs were seeing mostly men, using both group and individual treatment. The nonspecialized programs were seeing mostly women. When they did reach a battering man it was usually by means of individual therapy. Clearly, the specialist programs have so far been the most effective in engaging numbers of abusive consorts in treatment.

The survey form asked respondents to estimate how frequently they used different methods of therapy in treating batterers. Findings are shown in Table 5-1. The most popular treatment methods were cognitive stress management and assertion training, which were used "frequently" in about half of all the treatment programs. A variety of other treatment techniques were used by some agencies, as shown in the table below.

Some respondents mentioned other conditions they had found essential for successful treatment of a battering man: The man must really want help and commit himself to treatment, even though the original referral may not have been voluntary. Treatment must begin

Table 5-1.   Methods Frequently Used in Treating Batterers at Two Types of Agencies

Method	Special Programs for Batterers	Family or Women's Agencies
Cognitive anger-control training	52%	42%
Assertiveness training	49	53
Reality therapy	43	43
Peer counseling	37	43
Fair fight training	31	36
Transactional analysis	41	19
Rational emotive therapy	32	29
Gestalt	24	29
Relaxation training	22	19
Psychodrama	10	3
Family therapy	8	7
Psychoanalytic treatment	8	5
Behavior modification	8	0
Other	18	5

NOTE: Since most agencies used more than one method, percentages add up to more than 100.

promptly after referral, before the man has time to rationalize his guilt away. If the wife has left and stays away throughout the course of treatment, the man's motivation to stay in therapy remains much stronger. The intense mutual dependency of battering husband and battered wife must be replaced by mutual respect, greater independence, and less rigid sex-role expectations. The support of other men also struggling to overcome their violence is especially important in this regard. Finally, the men must learn new ways of expressing anger.

Ninety per cent of all the battering men in all the treatment programs reportedly refrained from any further violence throughout the period of treatment, according to the survey returns. Though this is a promising indication, it is also possible that the men who did not stop abusing their consorts were among the treatment dropouts. Respondents reported that from one-third to one-half of batterers dropped out of treatment after the first counseling session. The remainder stayed with treatment for an average of six weeks in group programs and three or four months when in individual therapy.

Only two programs were able to supply any formal data about their results. Apparently this field of treatment is still too new and unorganized for much data collection. The Women's Support Shelter in Tacoma, Washington, indicated that fifty-seven men had attended several group sessions and that 80 percent of them had stopped using physical violence. Project AMEND of Denver had conducted a one-year follow up survey. It reported that more than two- thirds of the men they had treated were still successful in avoiding hitting their marital partners one year later. As with shelter programs, long-term followup data on batterers is extremely hard to obtain because of the high mobility of battering couples. Nevertheless, such programs need to document their results more than they are apparently doing at present.

Treating Battering Men

Walker (1977; 1979) was one of the first clinicians to write about methods for treating battering husbands. She and her husband counseled a number of battering couples, always seeing each partner separately for the first several sessions. Standard couples therapy, Walker pointed out, teaches individuals to subordinate their needs partially, in order to make the relationship work. Battered wives already overuse subordinating and submitting when faced with their partners' hostility. Individual counseling strengthens the wife in her ability to take care of herself, so that she will not sabotage later couples therapy by submitting when she should not. Not only were the man and woman seen separately, but Walker preferred that they separate and live apart during the early part of treatment.

Walker found that the battering couples became very dependent on the therapy team for emotional support. It turned out to be too draining to have more than two battering couples in their caseload at a time. In part this may be attributed to their practice of having the couples call every day to report on events of the day, and in part to their seeing them individually instead of in a group. When treated in a group, battering consorts transfer a good deal of their emotional involvement to other group members instead of becoming so intensively involved with the therapists.

Saunders (1980) gave a detailed description of the format used for groups of men who battered their consorts. As with the Emerge groups, positive bonds among participants were formed by means of consciousness-raising about the harmfulness of the violence in their earlier lives, leading to a recognition of the harmfulness of their own current violence. The group training covered relaxation training, cognitive therapy, and assertion training, with some attention to the topics of jealousy and alcoholism. The program lasted twelve weeks. About 45 percent of the original members dropped out of the group, and attendance for the remainder averaged 65 percent, even for those who were under court orders to attend. Saunders did not have followup data on the rate of violence after treatment. He did indicate that those involved felt that twelve weeks had not been enough and that the program needed to be augmented with individual counseling, self-help groups, and couples counseling.

Geller and Walsh (1977–78) reported on the counseling program at the Victims Information Bureau of Suffolk County, New York. The majority of the battered women seeking help wanted to remain in their marriage but wanted the relationships to change, especially the violence. In those cases where the wife was not afraid to ask him and the husband was willing to come, both parties were involved in therapy. The authors reported that violence stopped between every couple who attended couples therapy for at least three weeks, which included two-thirds of those starting the program.

If the male partner was unwilling, or if the woman was too afraid even to let him know she was talking with a counselor, she was placed in a group with other women in a similar situation. The women worked on methods for surviving violence, since there was little hope of ending it. They were advised to fit one room with a lock on the inside of the door as a place of safety within the home and to keep a little money and a car key handy at all times.

Geller (1978) reported on an outreach effort by this same Suffolk County agency toward the batterers who did not enter couples therapy with their partners. The men were contacted by phone and invited to call for an appointment if they were interested in a ten-session "course" on family violence. The group was led by a male graduate student, using a largely unstructured group format. It seemed to follow the classic patterns of group development, though membership shifted from session to session at first. Geller noted that the men appeared normal in areas other than their marriages and that counseling just was not part of their cultural frame of reference. They were able to accept treatment because it was billed as a time-limited course focused on solving the one problem of violence, rather than as therapy. The group was significant because of the vigorous way in which resistant battering men were contacted and involved in treatment.

Ganley and Harris (1978) treated nine men who were battering their wives by keeping them for four weeks in a psychiatric unit of a veterans hospital. Some of the men experienced periodic depressions and suicidal ideas. Others abused alcohol or drugs. The men persistently belittled the extent of their battering activity. The staff found it essential for them to check on the men's stories by meeting weekly with other family members. No outcome data were presented concerning this project, which resembles some of the experiments in treating child abusive parents in hospitals. It may be that a period of compulsory hospitalization will prove to be the only way to reach alcoholic and drug-dependent battering men.

Behavioral Alternatives to Violence

The internal events reviewed in the previous two chapters, occurring inside the body and within the mind's cognitions, set the scene for the occurrence of rage and violence. But the immediate trigger for violence is almost always an external event occurring in the course of interactions with other people. Persons with poor interaction skills often get themselves and others into trouble, which leads to severe anger. Persons with the right interaction skills can generally overcome difficulties without going out of control. The control skills of most relevance for battering all have to do with clashes of interest and confrontations. Methods of handling events of this sort have never been widely taught in the way that work skills or even lovemaking skills have been. Instead, many people have been reared in families where some members handled disagreements with coercive escalations, or in opposite type families that totally avoided all unpleasant emotions. The remainder of this chapter gives details about a number of interaction skills that have proved relevant for managing clashes and confrontations without resort to violence.

Timeout Between Battling Adults

Many battering couples tell of trying to withdraw in order to avoid violence. The tactic usually fails because the other partner opposes the withdrawal and keeps the argument going. Abortive withdrawal attempts may be very common as the buildup phase peaks and one partner strives to keep matters from getting out of control. The angry consort may fall stonily silent, become deaf to anything but the show on television, or leave the house for a while. Stacey and Shupe (1983) found that 25 percent of battering men left home for a while to cool off after an abusive episode. They evidently were using withdrawal as a way to terminate violence. At other times the more frightened consort may seek safety by trying to go to another room. But the other partner reacts as if withdrawal were a fighting strategy that must be outfought. Crying out, "Don't you dare walk out on me!" the partner pursues and tries to physically restrain the departing person. Quite often the battered wife herself makes this mistake and touches off the acute violence phase by blocking her consort's exit from the room. Knowles and Middleton (1980) found that fully 60 percent of the violence between battering couples occurred as one angry partner followed the other through various rooms in the house.

Weiss and Birchler (1978) taught distressed marital pairs to take timeouts as a technique for defusing anger between them. They cautioned that timeouts should be used only when a time for getting back together had been established previously. Walker (1979) taught battering couples a special signal to use whenever one of them wanted to withdraw because tension was building to a dangerous level. One partner signaled the other by cupping the hand to make a little "C" and also uttered a neutral verbal signal, agreed on in advance. The signal chosen by most of the couples was "Walker-Flax," the names of Walker and her co-therapist husband. Both partners were supposed to stop all arguing for a half-hour to an hour to let their anger subside. Geller and Walsh (1977–78) advised women whose abusive consorts were unwilling to take part in therapy to use withdrawal to a locked room, or perhaps flight in the car, as their way to halt escalating confrontations.

Few experiments give clues as to how to conduct a timeout between angry adults. One group of researchers (Zillman, Katcher, and Milavsky, 1972) studied the effects of exercise on angry subjects. Mild exercise had no effect on later aggresiveness. Vigorous, arousing exercise had no effect on subjects who had been only mildly insulted, but increased the later aggressiveness of highly insulted and angry subjects. Another study (Konecni, 1975) showed that soothing music reduced the later aggressiveness of insulted and angry subjects to the same level as the noninsulted control group. These studies suggest that soothing rather than arousing activities are preferable during a timeout period. Walking may be better than running if one is trying to get over anger.

It is important that angry pairs get out of each other's physical presence and out of sight of one another during a timeout. Vantress and Williams (1972) aroused subjects' anger by using a confederate who behaved obnoxiously. After the confederate left, subjects' blood pressure returned to normal in a short time, averaging just two minutes. When the confederate stayed in the room, however, subjects' blood pressure remained high for a long time. This evidence supports the use of timeout periods, separating the noxious stimulus (the partner) from the angry person so that he or she can calm down. However, a much longer period of time usually is needed in the case of real marital conflicts. Perhaps more anger is stirred up, or perhaps ruminations about previous conflicts with the other person intrude and rearouse anger.

Timeout periods are already in common use in two different areas of life, the refereeing of competitive sports and the management of difficult children. In both instances an authority figure invokes and enforces the timeout for the purpose of controlling potential conflict. Sports referees call for timeout to prevent one side from taking advantage of the other while some procedural problem is overcome, such as changing pitchers or removing an injured player. A referee blows a whistle, calls "Time out!" and signals with a bold "T" sign made with hands at right angles. The moment the signal is made all players must stop and wait. Most American adults are already familiar with both the T signal and the obligatory waiting period, either through participation in school sports or through watching television sportscasts.

Fighting couples have no referee to invoke a timeout or enforce the "ceasefire" rules, unless someone has called the police. Officers dealing with domestic disturbances commonly take the man out for a walk around the block to help cool off the antagonists. In effect, the policemen are calling and refereeing a timeout. Sometimes the officers stay to help the couple negotiate their differences afterward; other times they assist the wife to leave for a shelter. Many of the women brought by police stay at a refuge for battered women for less than a day (Tunnell, 1982); they appear to use the trip to the shelter as just a longer form of timeout.

The timeout periods in child management have achieved wide use in educational settings but are not as well known by the general public. Timeout has proved to be a most effective and noninjurious way to deal with misbehaving children. Patterson, whose research on aggressive children has been referred to in earlier chapters (see Patterson et al., 1975b), treated the children by means of teaching their parent or parents how to modify their aggressive behaviors. Parents were taught how to target key behaviors, observe them, and change them by offering consistent positive rewards for desired changes. However, the children could not be cured of physical aggression by positive procedures alone, probably because aggression brings its own rewards whenever the victim submits. Therefore parents were taught how to apply a timeout procedure to punish aggressive acts.

First the parents explain their new timeout policy to the child: Whenever the child engages in an aggressive behavior such as hitting, he or she has to go into a timeout place (preferably a bare room) for a brief period of three to five minutes. The adult refrains from nagging or scolding, giving only a reminder such as, "You know our rule: You have to spend three minutes in timeout whenever you hit your sister." If the child is still yelling or resisting when the time is up the adult says, "You don't seem to be ready. You may come out after you have been quiet for three minutes."

Though acting-out children may have to be forced into the timeout room the first time the procedure is used, they soon learn to cooperate because they discover that taking a timeout is not painful, just dull. Theorists believe that the effect of temporary banishment from an arena where attention, even negative attention, is available feels mildly unpleasant. So the misbehavior is actually punished by the withdrawal of reinforcing attention. After only a few times children quiet down soon after entering the timeout area. The nonstressful environment of the room itself helps the child to calm down. Also the rules are arranged so that regaining self-control is consistently reinforced by release.

When used properly, that is, in connection with reinforcements for prosocial behavior at other times, use of timeout has repeatedly proved effective in stopping aggressive behaviors. Therefore many teachers, houseparents, and parents in private families have adopted timeout procedures for retraining difficult children. It should be noted that timeout is a coercive procedure and can be misused. Practitioners are gradually evolving guidelines for proper use in order to safeguard the rights of the children involved.

Glasser (1980), the creator of reality therapy, also recommended that parents and teachers impose a form of timeout on disruptive, noncompliant children. The adult requires the misbehaving child to go sit in a chair for a short time in some quiet, comfortable place. The chair time has two purposes: The child has an opportunity to calm down, and the child is assigned to the task of figuring out a plan for improved future behavior. When the adult ends the timeout period after a few minutes, he or she can help the child to devise a plan, provided the child is willing. If the child continues to fuss or refuses to work on a plan on how to do better, the parent or teacher may have to invoke several timeout periods in a row.

The slight difference between this system and Patterson's illustrates reality therapy's emphasis on the individual's taking responsibility for his or her own behavior, even if someone else has imposed a timeout. Patterson taught that the cue for ending a timeout should be a fixed period of time, like three minutes, plus the child's calm behavior. Glasser taught the adult to look for a different cue, the child's plan for future behavioral improvement. This is a more complex cue, but it may be a better one. The child receives a specific task to perform during the timeout, which helps distract the child from obsessing over the previous altercation. When the child has succeeded in devising a plan to do better, even if the plan is impractical, it signals the child's return to rationality. Although the requirement to "make a plan about how to follow the rules" implies that the child must surrender to the adult's superior force in order to get out of timeout, the child at the same time obtains a new area of freedom, one of planning and choosing just how to conform.

Carr (1981) has written an excellent review of the research showing the effectiveness of timeout periods in correcting all kinds of child behavior problems, especially severe aggression and violence. He also lists a series of twelve procedural guidelines to help the adult conduct a timeout with a minimum of fuss and a maximum of effect. However he cautioned against using timeout as a punisher in the very kind of situation in which this book is advocating its use, namely in the middle of a coercive escalation spiral. If the aggression was a response to some annoying demand made by the parent, then the child will welcome timeout, because it ends the parent's nagging too. Therefore timeout would actually increase the likelihood of the child's aggressing again in a similar situation.

A timeout between battering consorts is not for the purpose of punishment but only for cooling off so that the same discussion can be resumed, but more rationally. It is closer in spirit to the timeout of sports contests, which serve the same sort of function. The signal for ending timeout between battering couples, as with the reality therapy procedure, should be a cue that rational thinking has been resumed by both parties to the argument.

Timeout for battering couples is a very new method of anger control, in spite of the popularity of attempts to get away from each other. The particular procedure taught in the first session of the anger-control training, presented in the next chapter, is a new method undergoing its first testing through use. The technique appears promising, but much more research and field testing need to be done in order to refine the steps and understand better how they affect couples' interactions.

Assertive Versus Aggressive Interactions

One evening I was invited to explain the anger-control program to a small group of women who had founded a shelter in their city and kept it going for some eight years. They had done this as volunteers, almost by force of character alone, with never enough money for professional staff or an adequate building. When I began to describe the material in this chapter on assertion training, sparks flew. The young woman who lived at the shelter as its manager exclaimed,

"Aren't you betraying battered women by teaching assertiveness to their men? The women need to be more assertive, not the men!"

This reaction was based on a popular misconception of assertiveness as the midrange on a sort of continuum of self-expressive activity, going from submissiveness at one extreme to aggressiveness at the other pole, with assertiveness somewhere in the middle.

This simplistic model fails to represent what actually happens. When untrained subassertive people finally do express their feelings, they do not inch politely to the right and speak up assertively. Instead they erupt like volcanoes and scream and yell and hit at their foes. Likewise, when overly aggressive individuals restrain themselves they do not move over slightly into assertive action. They withdraw into submissiveness, perhaps with a surly manner, but submissive nonetheless. Submission and aggression seem to be as integrally related as two sides of the very same coin, and assertion is like the coin of another realm entirely.

A New Model of Assertive Behavior

The aggression/submission coin, if it were real, should have a motto stamped on its rim saying "control," for control of relationships is purchased with this coin, no matter which side is up (see Figure 5-1). Aggressive persons try to seize control and force compliance with their wishes, as if fearing to allow others to have a choice. Submissive persons encourage others to take control, as if fearing the

FIGURE 5–1.   Coinage for Citizens of the Realms of Distrust and of Trust

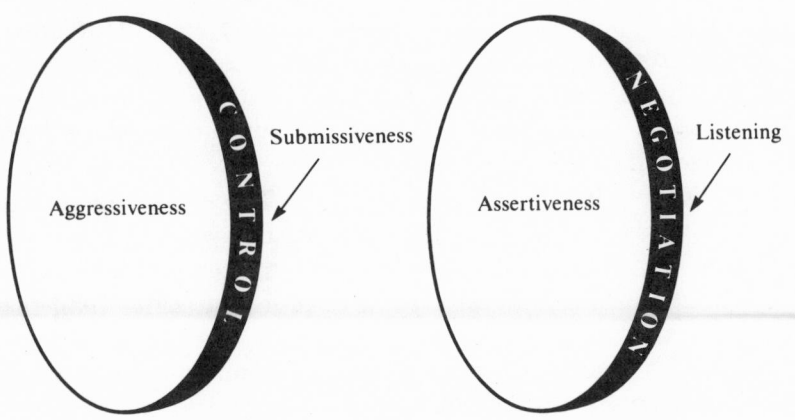

consequences of expressing their own wishes directly. Whether these fearful and distrustful individuals behave aggressively or submissively depends on the relative power relationships and the level of rage at the moment.

Assertiveness would belong on a different imaginary coin, the currency of realms where relationships are based on trust instead of distrust. Assertive persons trust that others will cooperate if they are informed of the asserter's own feelings and needs. Even if at times the other persons are not supportive of an assertion, they are still respected as having the right to make up their own minds. It is this basic trust and respect for others that gives asserters the courage to risk disclosing their feelings directly and expressing their wishes openly.

To keep the analogy going, what should go on the obverse side of the assertiveness coin? Submissiveness is a type of response behavior, so some sort of response activity belongs on the flip side of both coins. Sure enough, several types of listening responses are taught by assertion experts such as Smith (1976) and Bolton (1979). Responsive listening is the most fundamental and also the easiest of the assertive responses, so the word "listening" is appropriate for the back side of the assertion coin. The assertion/listening coin buys settlements achieved by negotiation instead of control, so the motto "negotiation" could be stamped on the rim. But this wonderful coin can be used as legal tender only by citizens of the Realm of Trust. Persons who maintain their citizenship in the Land of Distrust, and that includes most battering couples, have only Control type coinage available for purchases of desired goals in personal self-expression.

When I first began to meet battering men I expected them to act arrogant and domineering but found them to be nonassertive and even submissive, at least toward authority figures. They tended to withdraw into silence when they disagreed with anyone. Even toward their wives the battering men acted passive and subassertive most of the time. Some acted as dependent as children on their wives. Most of them had difficulty in expressing themselves in words, especially in comparison with their more verbal wives. The two-coin model predicts exactly this kind of behavior from persons who act aggressively toward weaker individuals when they encounter persons (such as therapists) whom they perceive to have more authority than themselves.

During those couples' sessions a single remark by a wife could instantly arouse the husband out of his passivity and into highly hostile aggressive talk. They seemed to have unusually low boiling points. Whether they were in the submissive or the aggressive mode, the men made frequent negative statements about their wives, clearly revealing their basic distrust.

The battered wives, when interacting with their partners, also fitted the two-coin model. They too made frequent negative statements to and about their husbands in their presence. All of them were surprisingly aggressive and domineering toward their men, considering their history as victims of these men's violence. But the women would flip quickly into silence or make submissive gestures whenever the men escalated their anger to a certain level. The particular level varied: Some women submitted after the first glare, while others continued to scrap spiritedly for some time. Presumably each woman was acting on the basis of her knowledge of her man's limits of self-control over his rage and violence.

Assertion Training

Assertion training courses have been popular for the past decade, the same decade in which women have struggled to achieve equal rights for themselves. Participants are, not by coincidence, mostly women. Most people taking assertion training want to learn how to stop being submissive or subassertive. They are troubled by their inability to take action to reach their goals, express their real feelings, or stand up for their rights without blowing up into an aggressive rage first. But only a few sign up for such courses with the hope of changing their aggressiveness. They think aggressive people already behave super-assertively, not realizing that assertive behaviors are entirely different from aggressive acts.

A number of leaders have published assertion training guides, and some have become bestselling paperbacks. Many people have improved their own assertive functioning by studying these self-help books. I particularly like two, *Don't Say Yes When You Want to Say No* by Fensterheim and Baer (1975) and *When I say No, I Feel Guilty* by Smith (1976). My current favorite assertion training manual is the less-well-known *People Skills* by Bolton (1979).

Groups for teaching assertion skills have been offered by workshop leaders in all sorts of settings, ranging from psychiatric hospitals to college continuing education classes. A few researchers have tried out assertion training for aggressive individuals. Rimm et al.

(1974) taught assertive skills to a group of aggressive young teenage boys, who reported reductions in their anger after training. Novaco (1975; 1979) included assertion skills in the comprehensive training program for angry adults, which has served as an inspiration for other practitioners, including myself.

Our survey of pioneer treatment projects for battering men (Feazell, 1981) showed that about half of these programs taught assertion skills to their battering men clients as a regular adjunct to the other treatment methods. In our own anger-control groups the men as well as the women have found the assertion skills extremely helpful. When assertion/listening is viewed as one kind of self-expression currency and aggression/submission as another kind of coin entirely, the reason for this consensus about its usefulness for batterers is clear.

When to Be Assertive

Bolton (1979) stressed the idea that assertions are appropriate only when there is some kind of tangible damage to a person's life space, which the assertion message attempts to change. "Concrete and tangible" effects are those which cost the asserter money, consume his or her time, harm possessions, cause extra work, or interfere with his or her job. Assertions made in the absence of some actual loss or interference usually stem from a desire to impose one's own values on another person, which is actually an aggressive intrusion into the other's life space. Assertive people trust others to maintain their own value systems and do not try to impose their own.

For example, a jealous husband often reacts to his wife's interactions with other people as if they indicated a lack of love for him. Even receiving a phone call from her mother may be branded as wrong. But taking such a phone call does not cost the husband anything tangible. His complaints are not assertions of his proper rights but attempts to impose his value system ("Pay attention only to me!") on his partner. Some battering husbands attempt to impose their values so often that their wives feel as if they were being brainwashed by some enemy captor. On the other hand, if the wife talks for a long time to her mother just when she and her husband were supposed to be going shopping together, the husband may legitimately assert that he is losing time.

The Assertion Message

Assertions are basically signals rather than actions (Smith, 1976). For example, infants assert by crying, a direct and persistent signal of the infant's needs, desires, and feelings. Since assertive behavior is signaling behavior, there are crucial nonverbal gestures or indicators, such as eye gaze and posture, which must accompany the spoken words if they are to be successful. The words only convey the details; the main message comes from the manner of the asserter. A significant part of assertion training consists in coaching people in how to look confident and assertive while they speak, instead of appearing submissive and expectant of failure.

Bolton (1979) stressed that successful assertion messages should contain three parts: a description of the other's behavior, one's own emotional reaction, and the reason that reaction has been aroused, stated in terms of tangible costs or effects as shown in Figure 5–2.

FIGURE 5-2. Three-part Assertion Message

Behavior Description	Disclosure of Feeling	Tangible Effect
"When you . . ."	"I feel . . ."	"because . . ."

1. *The Target Behavior*

By leading off with a brief description of the wanted or unwanted behavior—"When you . . ."—the asserter takes the mystery out of the discussion. If the declaration of a negative feeling is put first, as some assertion manuals recommend, the receiver endures extra anxiety while waiting to hear the accusation. The receiver may even imagine all sorts of untrue or exaggerated problems. In the telephone situation, which was a real problem with one battering couple, the husband should start his assertion by saying, "When you talk to your mother for an hour . . ."

"When you . . ." descriptions must be very specific to be effective, and they must delete all those colorful adjectives so satisfying to the irritated person, like "stupid" or "goddam," for these pass judgment on the other person's motives, character, industry, or canine parentage. Judgments arouse defensiveness in the receiver and so derail the assertion message. Lengthy descriptions must also be avoided, for lectures strike the receiver as verbal aggressive acts and arouse defensiveness instead of making their point. So the behavior description that initiates the assertion message must be only one phrase long, describing bare facts without any condemnatory adjectives. Though this kind of statement requires self-control and practice to learn, deviations from this rule generally get the result they deserve, a quarrel.

Finally, the assertion should be about the real issue and be made to the right person. Sometimes the real issue is a big one, like loneliness, but the speaker complains only about the wife's long phone chats with her mother. At other times the real issue is so small that the temptation is to "just let it go by," as one battering husband said whenever he and his wife disagreed. When he had let enough go by, his frustration became intolerable and he exploded in rage. Some assertions are deliberately made to the wrong person, as when a husband gripes to his wife about the noisy children or a victimized wife punishes her child for a minor disobedience. However, some assertions may be displaced unconsciously, usually because of severe anxiety about making a direct assertion. The assertion may be displaced to a substitute issue, a substitute recipient, or a different time. Assertions arising out of severe jealousy are generally displaced assertions that really concern fears of abandonment, as was described in an earlier chapter. Since the displacement is more or less unconscious, it is hard to control consciously. The asserter can usually avoid sending displaced messages, however, by confining the message to occasions on which the target receiver clearly caused a damaging effect by some specific action.

2. The Asserter's Feelings

Feelings are a vital part of an assertion message. The disclosure of the speaker's genuine distressed feeling underscores for the receiver the importance of the assertion message and makes the receiver more willing to make the effort to do something about the problem. But again, accurate expression of feelings is no easy task. Some people have practiced repressing unpleasant feelings for so long, considering them unsafe, that they are totally out of touch with their own moods. Others translate scary emotions into less scary ones, feeling depression when they are really angry or anger when they are really anxious. Sometimes the magnitude is shifted, and the person habitually calls a minor annoyance "fury" or, going in the opposite direction, passes off a panic attack as "nerves."

Expressing emotions in words is difficult in any case, and even more difficult when the feeling is negative. There is no doubt that expressing a negative feeling is more risky than repressing it, for the receiver may decide to retaliate. Or the receiver may be able to prove how wrong and silly the sender was to feel so upset. In such a case the asserter not only does not change the other person's behavior but may have to change his or her own behavior. However, when the asserter overcomes his or her anxiety and does take the risk of expressing some negative feeling honestly, the whole assertion message takes on such an urgency that the receiver cannot ignore it and must deal with it seriously.

Asserters often contaminate their "I feel . . ." statements with negative value judgments. People say "I feel abused," rather than "I'm afraid." Or they say, "I feel ignored," rather than "I feel lonely." It helps to be wary of feeling words that end in "ed." These are usually passive voice verbs. An action verb cast in the passive voice hides the actor and stresses the consequences of the action instead. For example the emotional declaration "I feel terrified," enables the utterer to gloss over the fact that someone invisible has been accused of acting in a way to create the terror. Use of the passive voice is one of the types of mind-confusing language identified by Bandler and Grinder (1979) in their linguistic approach to therapy. When people correct their mind-confusing language, which they use in private self-talk as well as spoken assertions, they can begin to analyze situations more accurately and act to solve the real problems.

3. *Tangible Effects*

The third and final part of a complete assertion statement begins with "Because . . ." It describes the tangible effect, in terms of harm or loss, caused by the offender's behavior, providing the rationale for making the assertive statement at all. If there is no good rationale in terms of tangible loss, harm, or interference, the assertion state-ment should not be made at all, because it will only start a quarrel.

Listening Reflectively to Assertions

The first response to an assertion message should be a paraphrase, which reflects back to the asserter what was understood by the re-ceiver. Such a statement has come to be known as "reflective listen-ing." The skill was emphasized by Rogerian counselors two decades ago and is now generally recognized as a crucial communication skill for everyone. For example, Gordon's well-known Parent Effective-ness Training course (Gordon, 1972) teaches parents to practice re-flective listening in order to improve relations with their own children. Guerney's (1977) course, called Relationship Enhancement for couples, teaches that the receiver of an assertion must learn to reply with a whole series of empathic reflections of the asserter's views, prior to reacting personally.

If the receiver is too surprised or anxious to think at first, he or she may be able only to repeat back the same words the asserter just used, as "You say I wasted our shopping time." However, a para-phrase into different language is more effective. Accurate reflections capture both the ideas and the emotional tone of the original. They can have a truly magical effect on the asserter. By translating the assertion into new words the receiver has conveyed, in a better way than saying it ever could, "I understand you; I respect your opin-ions." Such a tuned-in response cannot help but increase the as-serter's trust level, and his or her aggressiveness diminishes cor-respondingly. Even if the original asserter violated all the principles just described and made a long-winded judgmental attack for no good reason, a reflective listening response may in one stroke evap-orate his or her aggressive mood.

Dealing with Defensive Reactions to an Assertion

Unless the receiver also has taken assertion training, the most pre-dictable first responses to a three-part assertion are defensive denials or defensive counterattacks. Untrained or seriously angry receivers rarely manage such ideal behavior as reflective listening. They do not stop themselves long enough even to understand, let alone restate, an assertion directed at them. Instead they tune out most of the message and busy their minds with framing denials or counterattacks. One battering husband would lie on the bed and hold his ears when his wife began to assert (or, as he said, nag) about his faults. Eventually he would rise up and shout at her and sometimes hit her.

So a person who grows brave enough to send an assertion message, even a brief and perfect three-part one, must be prepared for defensive retaliations. Strangely enough, the first and possibly best response to a defensive reaction also is reflective listening. Bolton (1979) taught that after delivering the one-sentence assertion statement the asserter should stop, resisting the temptation to say anything more. The other person's response should be waited for silently, giving the receiver time to organize a reply. Whatever the reply is, the original asserter must paraphrase it back in a reflective listening statement, for example, "You feel I'm jealous of your relationship with your mother."

One reflection may not be enough to calm the defensive reactions of the original receiver. A whole series of reflections may be necessary, as new defensive reactions follow one after another. Perhaps only five or ten reflections later will the receiver have calmed down enough for the asserter to repeat the original assertion message. More defensive reactions may be triggered, to be neutralized by more reflections. But eventually the receiver will feel so well understood that he or she can take the risk of letting down the defenses and really listening to the asserter's request. Resolutions follow quickly. The whole process can be conceived of as a jagged line wobbling back and forth (Figure 5–3, p. 114). This diagram helps people realize that it normally takes both time and persistence to make a successful assertion. The diagram was inspired by one in Bolton's (1979) book.

Responding to Criticism

An extremely helpful anger containment skill is called "response to criticism." It should be used whenever powerful authority figures make confrontive, critical, or hostile statements, creating a situation where the natural urges to make self-defensive counterattacks would bring down consequences far worse than the original criticism. For example, persons are arrested for talking back aggressively to traffic policemen, which is far worse than getting a speeding ticket. Youths

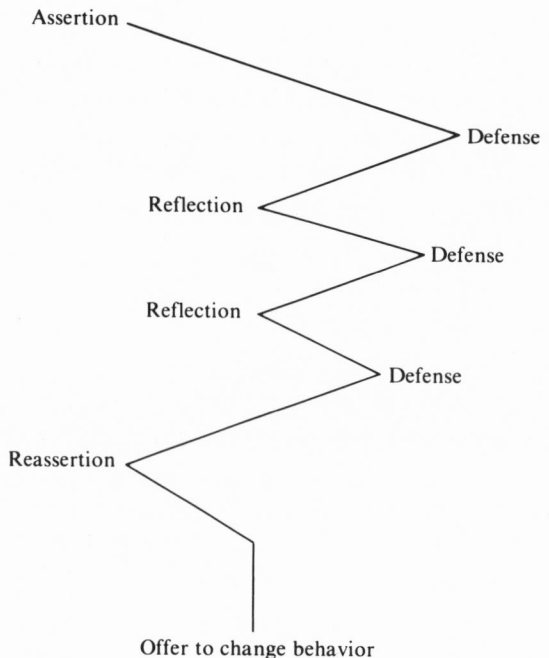

Assertion

Defense

Reflection

Defense

Reflection

Defense

Reassertion

Offer to change behavior

FIGURE 5–3. The Course of a Successful Assertion

are suspended for defying critical teachers; wives and children are beaten for arguing back at home. No matter how unjust the original criticism, backtalk is maladaptive because it invites much more severe reprisals. The four-step response to criticism was developed originally for aggressive juvenile delinquents in treatment at the well-known residential treatment home called Achievement Place (Phillips et al., 1974). Since such youths frequently get into trouble with authority figures by cursing or even fighting when a parent or teacher corrects them or a policeman questions them, this skill alone helps them to progress better at school, at home, and at jobs.

The four elements in a skillfull response to criticism are eye contact, verbal assent, behavioral compliance, and an absence of aggressive nonverbal gestures. The first and last elements are specific directions about the important nonverbal communications that should be sent back to an angry authority figure. Equals with nothing to hide look one another in the eye; therefore good eye contact is essential to convey the impression of honesty and equal rights between asserter and receiver. The last directive is to "clean up your act," by eliminating aggressive gestures. Aggressive nonverbal gestures, as has been mentioned before in this book, inflame both the self and the other person and therefore are a serious mistake in strategy. The verbal and behavioral compliance gestures in steps two and three of the response to criticism basically say, "OK, I'll cooperate." Persons being criticized by an authority figure should make this response whether they were wrong or not, because they cannot win by arguing at that moment in view of their inferior power position.

Postponing the Trial

Quite a few attacks made by authority figures are unfair. Phillips et al. (1974) taught adolescents that when they feel they are being unjustly "zapped," they should follow their four-step compliant response with a fifth, assertive step, which is to request another meeting later on to discuss the matter fully. The postponement will give all parties time to get over their anger and to think about solving the real issues.

> (TO A TEACHER): OK, I will write my name a hundred times now, but I'd like to come back after school and explain to you why I was talking. I'd like to bring Tom because he saw the whole thing.

> (TO A HUSBAND): OK, maybe I was complaining. I'll stop. But this weekend when you have time I want to see if we can figure out how to solve this problem.

The youth making such a response to a teacher avoided possible suspension by complying and has arranged for full discussion at a time when the teacher has calmed down and witnesses and supporting evidence can be used to help in the defense. The wife has stopped an escalation spiral, has avoided possible violence, and has arranged for another attempt to get her problem solved when her husband may be more cooperative.

Stuart (1974) recommended a similar technique for settling marital disputes. Couples were taught to set aside a twice-weekly Problem-solving Time and refer all disputes to that time. Rose (1977) particularly suggested that couples never try to solve disagreements at the scene of the crime. Since we have noted that even visualizing a stressful event tends to revive the original emotions, trying to solve a problem at the actual scene would be sure to revive so much angry affect that couples would have difficulty in reaching rational, negotiated agreements. The nonemotional atmosphere of a neutral place will aid significantly in the solution of a problem.

Correcting Others Diplomatically

For some years I have taught parents, teachers, and social workers a ten-step assertion procedure that I call Diplomatic Corrections. It consists of a three-part assertion message embedded in the middle of positive diplomacy statements, which greatly increase the probability of the message's acceptance by the receiver. In fact, there is usually no defensive response at all, just immediate cooperation. The procedure was developed by the originators of the Teaching-Family method for retraining delinquent youths. They analyzed what they did when they successfully corrected youths who were usually resistant and rebellious, and formalized it into the ten steps, which they called simply a "teaching interaction" (Phillips, et al., 1974). All group home staff practice the steps until they become second nature and have truly impressive success in teaching their young charges as a result. The ten steps shown below are a slight adaptation of the ten given by Phillips and his colleagues.

1. *Initial positive affirmation:*
   Have I told you lately that I love you, Honey? (*Hugs.*) (*or*)
   That salad you fixed was very tasty tonight. It was pretty, too.

2. *Description of inappropriate behavior:*
   When you cook the meat so long that it's turning black . . .

3. *Rationale—why it's inappropriate:*
   I don't like the taste. (*or*)
   It gets dry and tough to eat. The kids were giving it away to the dog.

4. *Description of appropriate behavior:*
   How about setting the timer when you put the meat in the broiler?

5. *Rationale—why the new behavior will be rewarding:*
   Then you can do other things, even answer the phone, and dinner will still be perfect.

6. *Offer of incentive:*
   If you'll do that I promise to fix that pot handle you wanted.

7. *Request for assent:*
   OK? (*or*)
   Does what I've said make sense to you? (*or*)
   Would you be willing to try that?

8. *Rehearsal of the appropriate behavior:*
   Why don't I find the timer while you look in the cookbook to see how long chops are really supposed to cook? (*or*)
   I'll go buy some more chops so we can try the new system tomorrow night, just for fun.

9. *Feedback during practice (catch 'em doing good!):*
   Is that the timer I hear clicking? Mmm, I'll bet this dinner will be a masterpiece. (*Gives a hug.*) (*or*)
   Jane, these chops are cooked just right. They taste great.

10. *Praise and reward:*
    Here is your pot, all repaired.
    I'm going to brag tomorrow at work about what a terrific cook you are. (*or*)
    Say, how about letting me do all the dishes by myself to reward you for cooking such a great supper?

Other Examples of Diplomatic Corrections

Some other practitioners have published strategies for correcting a resistant person about a matter of real importance. Guerney (1977) described a five-part "expressive mode" in couples communication. The first three parts were the same as the three-part assertion message, in a different order. The fourth part was a positive caring statement, and the fifth was a description of the alternative behavior desired by the asserter. Guerney stated that the last two elements were optional, depending on the touchiness of the situation. Our group participants were taught a similar principle: Use only a three-part assertion statement if that will suffice, but switch to a full ten-step diplomatic correction if the receiver is likely to react badly but it is very important to get across the assertive message nevertheless.

The other procedure, which embodies many of the steps of a diplomatic correction, was developed by Johnson (1980) as an "intervention" to persuade an alcoholic or chemically dependent person to enter treatment. The principal significant family members, employers, and friends of the addicted person all converge on him or her at the same time and recite prepared statements, one after another. Each and every statement begins with an expression of concern and caring. It goes on to describe in specific and gross detail the unacceptable behaviors observed by the speaker and to relate them to the chemical abuse. The speaker then reveals his or her personal feeling, which is especially touching when the speaker is a child, as in "and I wished you were not my daddy." Each individual statement closes with a second expression of concern. The impact of from five to twenty such personal confrontive statements is very powerful. The statements exactly parallel steps 1, 2, and 3 of a diplomatic correction.

At this point the designated leader of the intervention team reveals the arrangements the group has made to get the receiver into treatment. The arrangements must be specific and complete: bed space at a certain hospital beginning that night, airline tickets, even a packed bag. Since chemically dependent persons have lost most of their power to make decisions, the alternative behavior is spelled out in detail and the decision reduced to simply heading for the door with the designated chauffeur. These steps, of course, resemble steps 4, 5, and 7 of the diplomatic correction. Counselors trained in the Johnson intervention system claim a high success rate in getting chemically dependent persons into treatment (O'Neill and O'Neill, 1982). The method has been used by the families of some government officials and other prominent addicted persons to persuade them to enter treatment.

Conclusion

The various interactions skills described in this chapter all function to contain conflicts and set the scene for positive communication. In one way or another nearly all the skills have been included in the anger-control training we have been providing to battering couples, along with some specialized skills for conflicted couples. The next three chapters go into detail about the particular way we are teaching the anger-control skills. The teaching plans given are certainly not the only way to present the skills but are given to provide a model for others who might want to help battering families on their own caseloads to attain control of rages and violence.

6 Starting Anger-control Groups

This chapter begins with the organizational questions that must be addressed when planning anger-control groups for batterers. The middle section provides a rapid overview of the content of each of the five major units in the formal anger-control curriculum, plus a review and further concepts taught in later couples sessions. The final part of the chapter presents detailed lesson plans for the first group session. Clients' use of the timeout procedures taught in the very first session is crucial to their ability to refrain from further violence while in treatment and to their success with anger-control training in general. The particular steps taught differ in several ways from procedures for timeout advocated by other authors, so they are explained in considerable detail.

Separate or Together?

Battering, by definition, occurs only in interaction with some other family member. Therefore the treatment needs to include both family members involved, whenever possible. However, quite a few batterers and/or victims seek treatment only after their families have broken up. Others convince themselves that one partner has no need of therapy because the other partner bears 100 percent of the blame. Therefore a mixed lot of couples and individual men and women are likely to respond to announcements and advertisements offering anger-control groups for batterers. Applicants may differ widely in age, years of battering, and extent of participation in the violence. Some may abuse their children rather than or in addition to their consorts. Such differences do not seem to interfere with their relating to one another. It seems that consort batterers and child abusers have problems that are sufficiently similar, indeed, overlapping, for them to work well in the same group.

However, some kinds of applicants for anger-control training should not be placed in the same group with adult battering couples. Couples whose conflicts are entirely verbal and emotionally abusive usually are not appropriate for batterers' groups. They might begin to imitate their new friends in the group and take up physical violence! However, verbally abusive couples exhibit many of the same cycles and personality characteristics as physically abusive ones and would benefit from anger-control training in a group of people like themselves. Aggressive adolescents also should be taught anger control in their own groups, rather than exposing them to adults modeling consort violence. Teenage abusive mothers are something of a special case. Such girls definitely need the support provided by a peer therapy group. If not enough young single abusive mothers are available at once to make their own special group, their referral to adolescent or adult anger-control groups should be decided after assessing the maturity of each individual girl.

One of the first decisions to be made is whether to see batterers individually, in same-sex groups, or with their consorts. The survey of programs for batterers reported on in Chapter 5 indicated that most of the ninety existing programs for batterers are seeing them in mens' groups rather than individually or in couple dyads (Feazell, 1981). The support from male peers who are experiencing the same violence problem seems to be a very important part of the treatment. Similarly, battered women entering shelters have found that the support and understanding of other women in the same situation is extremely helpful. Battering couples often are overinvolved with one another and isolated from everyone else, so their needs for peer acceptance and support are especially great.

On the other hand there is abundant evidence that therapy with just one member of a family is less effective than treatment of the whole family, especially when the problem is an interactional one (Beck, 1976; Wellisch, Vincent, and Ro-Trock, 1976). When only one person undertakes therapy, that one may change but goes back home to an unchanged social environment, containing people who may covertly undermine or even actively oppose the changes. When only one member of a conflicted couple receives therapy, the likelihood of a marital breakup is increased, whereas if both members of the dyad participate the prospect for preserving their union increases. Preservation of the family unit is a major goal of anger-control training for batterers. If they can eliminate violence within their relationships they will not have to divorce each other in order to escape physical harm.

The configuration adopted for the anger-control groups conducted at our university counseling clinic combines the advantages of same-sex peer support groups and couples therapy. This is accomplished by scheduling five initial weeks of anger-control training in parallel male and female support groups. A similar system of parallel therapy groups has been used successfully by agencies treating families where the perpetrator is engaging in sexual abuse of a child (Giarretto, Giarretto, and Sgroi, 1978; McCarty, 1982). Then for the second five weeks all members of the parallel groups meet together for couples group therapy sessions. The advantage of this system is that both partners are able to enter therapy at the same time and learn the same anger-control strategies, yet receive the support of a sympathetic peer group with similar problems when they are first becoming involved in the program.

The main disadvantage of this system is that the parallel groups for men and women make more work for the leaders in the first five weeks. In a small program where only one or two workers are trained to teach anger control, those workers will have to lead the men's and women's groups on successive evenings. This format does have the extra benefit of eliminating babysitting problems for the couples and for the sponsoring agency. Larger programs, with enough meeting rooms and trained workers available, should consider offering all groups the same evening, with men and women meeting in separate rooms, in order to ease scheduling problems. Babysitting services should be provided in another room. If there are many children and infants, separate baby and child rooms may be needed.

Men's and Women's Support Groups

The same-sex sessions promote growth of participants' feelings of acceptance within groups of peers who are experiencing similar difficulties and have made a similar commitment to learn how to stop violence. Battering men or women arriving at the start of a new anger-control group are filled with both anxiety and hope. They hope that they will get help for violence, which has usually erupted very recently and motivated them to seek therapy. But they are afraid of being blamed, rejected, or intimidated by the leaders or other group members. The group leaders must help each person gain enough confidence in the group to risk self-disclosures and to lean on fellow group members for support.

No blame should be fixed on either the men or the women, no matter which one seems to start conflicts or which one inflicts the most injuries. Instead, the leaders show how consort battering and even child battering are always interaction events. Since both parties contribute to their disagreements, both parties must work on acquiring the skills to avert violence. Even abused infants contribute unwittingly to their own victimization by annoying their parents, and to some extent they can be taught less irritating alternative behaviors, though the parent must do most of the skill learning.

As participants arrive at each meeting they should fill in the one-page Weekly Anger Diary, shown in Figure 6–1. The leaders should move around the room as participants complete their diaries, noting any high anger ratings and talking briefly with participants while they fill out the forms. As they finish writing, the leaders can ask certain members to amplify their diary entries. This leads into a review of any disputes in the preceding week, their use of any anger-control methods, and examination of underlying problems between the couple. If new members have joined the group in this session, older members should be asked to explain and demonstrate the steps in the anger-control methods presented in earlier sessions, such as timeout. The review also benefits the older members, who solidify what they have learned by teaching it to others.

In this way the first part of each session quite naturally turns into a group sharing time. Unstructured sharing and problem solving should continue for about an hour and include all participants. The leaders need to have a working knowledge of the conduct of group therapy to guide this part of the session. It is a most important part

FIGURE 6-1. Weekly Anger Diary

Name_____Date_____

How many arguments did you have this week?_____

     Verbal_____ Rate your anger (0-10)_____
                     Rate your partner's anger_____
                     Rate your fear_____

     Physical_____ Rate your anger (0-10)_____
                     Rate your partner's anger_____
                     Rate your fear_____

What were your internal signals when trouble began?

What signals came from your partner?

How many times did you call for timeout?_____
How many times did your partner call time?_____

Which steps did you use? (Answer Yes or No)

T sign	_____	Exercise	_____
Return of T	_____	Error admitted	_____
Leave quietly	_____	Partner error	_____

How long did you stay apart in timeout?_____

What happened afterward?

What other anger-control methods did you use?

	Practiced	Used in real life
Relaxation	_____	_____
Cognitive Realignment	_____	_____
3-part assertion	_____	_____
Reflective listening	_____	_____
Diplomatic correction	_____	_____

Rate your happiness with this relationship if things go on just as they are (0-10)

Household responsibilities	_____	General happiness	_____
Rearing of children	_____	Communication	_____
Occupational progress	_____	Money	_____
Personal independence	_____	Sex	_____
Spouse's independence	_____	Social life	_____

of the evening, helping group members to bond together through intimate sharing and giving an opportunity for therapy with each person on their particular areas of difficulty.

We have found it helpful to schedule the same-sex sessions for three full hours, with a thirty-minute break in the middle. The break was originally designed for the sake of the smokers, since smoking was banned within the group room itself. However, spontaneous little subgroups formed over in the coffee room, which the leaders often joined. Other times a leader would use the break for a few minutes of individual work with one particular group member. So much important therapy has been accomplished in the new groups formed during the break that it has become a regular part of the program.

The postbreak half of each of the first five sessions contains the leaders' formally structured presentation of the lesson for the week. The same curriculum presented in the men's group is repeated each week for the women, so that both partners can learn the anger-control methods at the same time and can support one another's efforts to try out the new behaviors at home. The five major strategies for improving self-control over anger and aggression are presented and practiced in five successive units, briefly described below. Time must be allocated for role-play rehearsals of each new skill by every participant. Explanatory material is given out each week to serve as a reminder of the skills taught that session.

The Five Anger-control Session Units

Session 1

In the 1970s women's groups often began with "consciousness raising," which meant that participants got in touch with their experiences of discrimination and their feelings of inferiority as women. The discovery that other women felt the same way was instrumental in breaking participants' sense of isolation and despair. Groups of battering men and women also need to begin with a sort of consciousness raising by sharing with one another the experiences in their earlier lives that helped turn them into violence perpetrators or violence victims. Many will tell stories of childhood abuse or present-time joblessness and/or alcoholism. They are asked to describe the most recent event of violence and their own part in causing it. Since everyone has a similar problem, the group quickly unites in a common bond of suffering, sympathy, and a determination to find out how to stop the violence that is destroying their relationships.

After participants achieve a sense of closeness through sharing, they are asked to think about a recent violent scene and recall their internal feelings as they built toward the point of rage and physical aggression. The leaders should help each person identify some internal stress signal that could serve as a cue that rage is on the way, so that they can take a timeout well before their self-control vanishes under the onslaught of primitive emotions.

Next, the leaders should explain and demonstrate how to end an escalating quarrel by taking a timeout, following the procedures set forth in detail later in this chapter. Considerable time must be spent in guiding every participant through a role-play rehearsal of each step in the procedure. Then they are told to practice it at home by "finding an excuse to have a little argument." This is a paradoxical directive, prescribing the symptom behavior as the family's homework, which is a strategy often used by family therapists to reduce symptoms by taking advantage of people's inclination to defy good advice (Haley, 1976).

At the end of the session the leaders should distribute sheets with the timeout steps written out for participants to refer to at home. It is reproduced in Figure 6–2, page 126. A No-violence Pledge appears at the bottom of the sheet. All participants are asked to sign it at the end of the group meeting, signifying their personal commitment to trying to end the battering incidents that mar their lives.

Session 2

The leaders begin the second session by reviewing with the participants how they fared in the intervening week. Responses entered on the Weekly Anger Diaries form a natural point of departure for the group discussion. Some group members will probably tell of trying to use parts of the timeout procedure, giving the leaders an opportunity to do further coaching on how to carry out all the parts of this strategy. Other participants have to be urged for several weeks before they finally try to cut an argument short by taking timeout.

During the second half of the meeting the sources of physical stress in people's lives are reviewed, with particular attention to the effects of alcohol, drugs, and seemingly harmless substances like sugar and coffee. In most battering groups one or more persons will

STEPS IN TIMEOUT

When I feel my (or my partner's) anger rising I will give a "T" signal for timeout, and turn around and leave at once. I will not hit or kick at anything. I will not slam the door.

I will not return until I am no longer seriously angry. I will take a walk to use up the anger energy. I will think of something else that is pleasant.

I will choose to return when I am ready to start the conversation with, "I know I was partly wrong, as well as partly right," and describe a technical error I made.

If my spouse gives a "T" signal and leaves, I will return the sign and let my spouse go peacably, no matter what is going on. I will think of something else that is pleasant while my spouse is gone. When my spouse returns, I will start the conversation with, "I know I was partly wrong as well as partly right," and describe a technical error I made.

THE NO-VIOLENCE PLEDGE

I pledge never to allow my anger to go to the point where I forcefully touch another family member, no matter how right I feel I am.

I pledge to use timeout procedures instead, and to cooperate whenever my partner initiates timeout.

Name_____ Date _____

FIGURE 6-2. Handout for End of First Session

be discovered who suffer serious bouts of irritability as a consequence of heavy use of one or more of these substances.

The session concludes with twenty to thirty minutes of relaxation practice after the leader has explained the technique and its potential benefits in reducing stress. Lastly, individual appointments for further relaxation practice are arranged as the participants leave.

Session 3

Again, review of the Anger Diaries and group discussion takes up the first hour of the third men's and women's groups. In the second half the topic of cognitive realignment is presented. This is the control of angry feelings by changing the self-talk that arouses fury into more rational thoughts, which help one to stay calm and cope with the problem. Exercises and discussions should be conducted to help participants become aware of the controlling role of their usually ignored inner speech. A handout with examples of rational coping statements for anger-provoking events should be given to group members to take home. The session closes with participants practicing how to visualize themselves coping with a stressful scene by reciting the calming and rational phrases to themselves as the incident proceeds.

Session 4

After the initial group sharing time, assertion skills are presented. Leaders explain the three elements in assertion messages and have participants compose an assertion statement of their own on a worksheet. Then leaders demonstrate reflective listening as the way to respond to someone else's assertion. The group members practice asserting and responding to each other in pairs, while the leaders coach them.

Session 5

As usual, the fifth session begins with the Anger Diaries and discussion of group members' problems in carrying out any of the anger-control procedures taught so far. At the beginning of the didactic portion of the meeting, the asserting and reflecting skills should be reviewed. Then several further assertive ways to respond to angry people are demonstrated and practiced. Finally, the ten-step assertion method called Diplomatic Corrections is taught to participants for use when they need to institute a change successfully without instigating a fight.

Couples Groups

Beginning in the sixth week couples attend the same group together. By this time participants are very eager to meet one another's partners, about whom they have heard so many stories. Also some participants will have progressed faster than their consorts, making them feel the need to have leaders coach both parties at once. The couples sessions are an integral part of anger-control training. The skills just introduced require more time than five weeks to practice and master. Even after all violence has been controlled, persons who have been in battering relationships have other problems to work on, which may have contributed to the deterioration of the relationship in the first place. They find they are able to work on those problems once violence has subsided, so that the couples sessions come more and more to resemble "regular" marital group therapy.

Group members whose consorts or ex-consorts declined to join the anger-control training must of course continue to come alone. The solo members usually experience little difficulty in fitting into the couples group, since they already know some other participants well. But if enough single men and women have attended the first five sessions, a better strategy might be division into a couples group and a singles group for the remaining five anger-control sessions.

The couples groups follow the same basic format as the men's and women's groups. Each person continues to complete an Anger Diary upon arrival. General problem-solving discussion follows. Each week leaders review and conduct further practice in one or another of the five major anger-control strategies. This provides group members with a review of concepts and a second opportunity to practice, with both partners participating. Inadequacies in each one's procedures can be corrected by a leader. As the weeks go by other group members should be encouraged to gradually take over the refereeing and coaching functions of the leaders. In this way group members reinforce their own mastery of anger-control skills while they are helping each other. Typically at least one couple each session explodes into a highly emotional confrontation during the meeting. The exploding pair always seem to make unusually good progress during the following week.

Leaders may present additional communication skills at the couples meetings, when they perceive a need or interest within the group. Additional concepts we have presented during couples sessions include the eradication of jealousy, negotiation of conflicts, contracting for exchange of pleasing behaviors, and sensate focus exercises.

A part of the final session should be spent in listening to feedback from the participants about the impact of the anger- control training upon them. Not only are their comments valuable to the leaders for suggesting improvements to future anger-control groups, but the final review helps the group participants solidify their own learnings.

Individual Sessions

Individual interviews should be held with each participant before joining the anger-control groups in order to form a relationship, give some initial orientation, and collect pretreatment data. Individual followup interviews also are needed in order to assess changes after anger-control training and to make plans with the participant for continuation, referral, or termination of treatment.

After the second men's and women's meetings, which concludes with an explanation and demonstration of deep muscle relaxation, weekly individual appointments should be scheduled with every participant, if at all possible. These private interviews enable the counselor to guide the group participants individually in how to practice relaxation and other anger-control procedures. At our clinic we use biofeedback as an additional tool for teaching relaxation.

When the participants are able to relax themselves, their individual counselor guides them in stress-coping rehearsals in preparation for dealing with anger-provoking events, and systematic desensitization for jealousy and fears. Participants also use their individual hours as extra therapy time to work on an assortment of other problems. In effect they put themselves into a twice-a-week pattern of therapy. Many battering men and women are leading lives of such stress and turbulence that they urgently need the extra support offered by the more frequent sessions in order to manage at all, let alone make positive changes.

Sometimes a battering individual or couple very desirous of treatment simply cannot arrange to join an anger-control group, or else there is no such group available. In such cases we have taught the material intended for the group sessions to them in individual interviews. The main objection is that it is uneconomical of a leader's time to teach a five-part curriculum over and over to individuals instead of to a group. Also the group experience is probably more valuable to batterers than individual sessions covering the same topics, because participants learn so much from listening to and interacting with one another. However, if no anger-control groups are available, and an individual worker has the time, there is no reason why anger control should not be taught to one couple or one individual person at a time. Some may also benefit from reading the present book, even though it was written primarily for therapists rather than a client audience.

Session One: Sign Violence Away

"Aren't you worried about the safety of the women who will be coming to your group?" a newspaper reporter asked. She was interviewing me as part of an effort to attract more participants by publicizing the first pilot groups for battering couples. To tell the truth, I was worried. I knew that most battered women have received not only injuries but serious threats to their lives from enraged partners. Some couples who would otherwise end the violence by separating might stay together because of their faith in the efficacy of our program. If the treatment was actually ineffective they might end up more abused than if they had never heard of us. Even if the treatment was effective, but only after many sessions, participants would still be at risk during the early weeks.

Therefore the very first lesson in anger control offers new participants an emergency strategy for averting violence by taking a timeout. Timeout is a simple, standardized procedure to be used whenever either consort feels anger might go out of control. We have found that couples who follow the procedure are able to remain together, unharmed, even though they continue to have serious arguments. Since more advanced anger management skills take several weeks to teach, it is important to teach timeout in the first session, so that couples can work on their problems in somewhat more safety.

Steps in the Timeout Procedure

1. *Deciding When to Call Timeout*

Since there is no referee in a home, the battling participants themselves must learn the signals that mean they should initiate a cooling-off period. Persons with well-learned habits of violence go from hot anger to physical aggression so often that the sequence is nearly automatic. They can scarcely stop themselves from attacking something once they grow angry. Therefore battering couples need to call for timeout early, before either one has become really angry. They will need to heed small cues marking the onset of irritation or anxiety as the signal to take a timeout, well before the automatic anger-to-violence sequence starts.

Group members should discuss what they experience inside themselves during the buildup of an argument that ends in violence. They need to identify internal signs that their anger is reaching the level where violence could occur. Below are some examples of cues battering men in the groups have reported.

> You feel as if the top of your head is about to come off and you're losing sight of everything. I get to the point reality is disappearing and I gotta release this tension, this pressure. This lady in front of me is just in the wrong place at the wrong time.

> I just feel tight all over. Like a tight band across my chest. I'm cursing and swearing, too.

> I only get mad when I've been drinking. That's the only time I hit her.

> I feel my blood pressure going up. You know, like the pipes in my neck are swelling.

The women generally seem more adept at observing their partners' anger cues than their own. Inside themselves they tend to feel only anxiety, moving on to panic. Only after several weeks of treatment do the wives begin to get in touch with their own hostile feelings.

> I can just tell by the look on his face when things have gone too far.

> I get all scared feeling inside when he is really mad. That's how I can tell.

Most of the participants' descriptions of internal cues accord well with the research on physiological changes during anger, described in Chapter 3. The leader may wish to give participants information from that chapter during the discussion of anger cues. We have found that battering couples are interested in the theory that anger is composed of fear and pain responses, epinephrine and norepinephrine. They easily recognize the extra power released during anger and how irrationally and self-defensively angry people think.

By the end of this part of the session all participants should have identified some personal signal to serve as the early cue for starting the timeout process. Each week, in the course of filling out the Anger Diaries, they are asked to report any fresh discoveries about internal stress cues or clues in their partner's behavior that signal the onset of a confrontation.

2. *Making a T*

When one partner decides a timeout is needed, he or she must signal the other partner in a referee-like fashion before withdrawing. The initiator should make a T sign with both hands straight, one vertical and other horizontal atop it. If anything at all is said, it should be only the announcement, "Timeout!" The T sign has many merits in this kind of situation. The signer cannot make a fist or jab aggressively while forming a T. The crossed arms form a sort of protective screen. This can feel comforting, especially if the T is held high in front of the face.

The restrictions on expression of anger by either word or gesture are important. The automatic aggression sequence buried deep in the brain is triggered into action by cues that lifesaving self-defensive action is needed. Any angry or aggressive word or gesture gives the information that an enemy is about and is attackable. The hostile gestures that so many people indulge in, out of a belief that they relieve anger, actually escalate feelings and increase the likelihood of aggression. The T sign has the advantage of keeping the hands busy in a way that makes it impossible to make a fist or jab a finger. In the same way, the word "timeout" is neutral and therefore preferable to "I'm getting angry," or some similar warning, since the very word "angry" tends to arouse the automatic aggression sequence.

3. *Returning the T*

Either partner may initiate the timeout, but the other partner must cooperate if it is to succeed. The receiver's immediate task is to facilitate the signer's departure without violence or unnecessary increases in anger. The T sign should be acknowledged by an answering T and perhaps some brief statement such as, "OK, timeout." All other talking must cease at once, which calls for a real effort in self-control in order to suppress the tendency to have the last word. No touching should occur, because it might be taken as an act of aggression and trigger a battering episode.

It is far more difficult to respond properly upon receiving a T sign than it is to initiate a timeout sequence. The receiver may not feel that the situation is at all serious but must accept the sender's evaluation, without questioning it for the time being. The receiver of the T sign was very likely winning the argument at the moment the timeout is called, which makes it especially hard to stop. The sudden T sign from the consort may seem insulting.

The receiving party may be the angrier of the two, but still must stop everything and simply return the T sign. The decision must not be questioned at this point, even though a timeout may not be wanted or expected. The only words the receiver should say are, "OK, timeout!"

If the T sender is responding to anxiety cues because of the rising anger of the partner, then the receiver may have to exert heroic self-discipline to stop attacking and return the signal. Indeed, the proper execution of the responding T may be the hardest part of the whole procedure. The response may also be the most vital part, distinguishing timeouts from the abortive withdrawal attempts tried by so many couples, which only evoke pursuit and attack responses.

4. *Leaving Silently*

As soon as a T sign is exchanged, both parties must concentrate on helping one person to leave the scene properly. Usually the one who initiated the T sign should be the one to turn around and go out, saying nothing more. The departing one must take care not to stamp out aggressively and must take especial pains to close the door without slamming. This sounds simple but requires concentration to carry out when angered. Muscles tighten, blood pressure rises, and extra energy increases strength, all of which makes the body act upon the environment differently. The T signer who closes the door with the normal force will actually slam it because of the extra muscle tone. The loud sound reverberates like a hostile oath and increases everyone's anger. Concentrating on the task of leaving without banging the door helps to suppress the tendency to keep on arguing as well. Many withdrawal attempts also fail because someone fires off a verbal parting shot that escalates anger past the controllable point. A departure into timeout has been carried out successfully when no additional anger has been aroused in either party by unnecessary words, gestures or loud banging noises.

If possible, the angrier partner should be the one to leave in order to take advantage of outdoor exercise to drain off anger energy. Among most battering couples the man expresses the more overt anger and should take the walk, especially when his partner has initiated the timeout because of fear of his building anger. Besides, some neighborhoods are dangerous for women walking alone, especially late at night. Sometimes young children or cooking food cannot be left by one partner, usually the woman.

Instead of going out, couples may establish one room in the home as a refuge, possibly with an inside lock on the door. Both must agree not to follow a partner there or disturb him or her. This arrangement calls for more self-control, but some of our couples have used such a room successfully. The key element is to get out of one another's presence so that calming down will occur.

Before couples begin to use timeouts they need to discuss the procedural questions and agree about who is to go out. Then they will not have to debate about who must leave, in addition to the real issue in conflict at the moment.

5. *Taking a Walk*

After leaving, the T signer needs and wants vigorous physical action to work off all the anger-released energy. Activity feels good. Some people take a brisk walk, others like to jog for a while. Bicycle riding is also good exercise at this point. But certain activities are not recommended, including kicking trees, chopping wood, pounding a pillow, or bashing about with a soft foam bat. Such aggressive types of actions do not relieve angry feelings, despite widespread belief in them. They do not reduce pressure on some internal safety valve, because the metaphor of a boiling pot of anger somewhere inside is just a poetic image, not a reality. Instead, aggressive hitting activities tend to increase anger arousal, perhaps because the primitive anger center in the brain confuses them with actual combat. The so-called release of feelings only increases the minutes needed to cool off during a timeout.

While exercising, the T signer should deliberately try to stop the inner thoughts that go back over the incident again and again. These spontaneously recycling thoughts, called ruminations, do more to rearouse anger than to solve the problem. Thoughts diverted to almost anything else, so long as it is pleasant, seem to speed the process of calming down. Perhaps ruminating keeps the enemy in one's presence, in imagination, and that is why it postpones the calming down.

Unfortuantely, an angry person finds it positively pleasurable to think negative thoughts during a timeout. The mind just naturally revives the memory of every injustice the other person ever committed. There is enjoyment in thinking of sarcastic, wounding things to say. What is happening is a mental rehearsal of counterattack and victory. Anger is pleasant when it ends in victory. But the indulgence in such ruminations only prolongs a timeout. What could take two or three minutes stretches on and on, thanks to the obsessive rehearsal of encounters with the other person. People who keep their foes imaginarily present by thinking about them will need half an hour or even several hours to calm down, instead of a few minutes. Ruminating when angry is so natural and pleasurable that it takes a real act of self-discipline to stop. It helps to recall deliberately that the only way to get back home is to think of a technical error to use as a ticket of admission. Trying to spot one's own mistakes in strategy keeps the mind from obsessing over the other person's misdeeds.

The T signer may be tempted to drive a car and go somewhere during timeout, but it is unwise. In the first place the muscles of an angry person fairly cry out for exercise. About the only ways a person confined in the driver's seat can express energy are by driving too fast or taking dangerous risks. In the second place a person in a car has to go somewhere and is more likely to seek the solace of getting drunk, finding a sympathetic friend to take one's side, or both. Either drinking or telling the story of the argument to a sympathetic listener adds elements to a marital conflict that prolong it and escalate it. Therefore the T signer should stay on foot, stay alone, and concentrate only on cooling off.

6. *Deciding to Return*

The person who left for timeout should, ideally, return when both partners are no longer dangerously angry. The energy released by the adrenal hormones should have been expended and the blood pressure returned to normal. Rational thinking should be replacing primitive rage judgments. Drops in energy level or blood pressure are not easy for most people to notice, but they can easily learn to observe changes in thought patterns. Persons upset enough to take a timeout begin it convinced that they are entirely right and the other person totally wrong. This certainty of self-righteousness seems to be typical of the angry person for reasons given in Chapter 4. But after a while a novel idea of a particular type comes along: "Well, maybe at such and such a point I was a little bit at fault too!" "Maybe I also contributed to the preceding disagreeable situation by making a small strategic error (such as nagging or refusing to listen)." Group members nicknamed these partial confessions "One-percent-error" statements.

As soon as that kind of observation occurs, people notice that their anger has diminished, though it may not be gone. The notion of shared guilt is a logical and rational thought, because it truly does take two to make a quarrel. At least a little fault belongs on both sides. Rational thinking can operate only when anger has begun to die away, and so the emergence of the rational idea "Maybe I made a one percent error when I . . ." is a cue that anger is receding.

7. *Exchanging Technical Errors*

The time has come for the T signer to return when anger has diminished sufficiently to make violence unlikely. It will help if the returning partner leads off with the new rational idea, "I still think I'm mostly right, but I made a mistake when I said . . ."

If the person left behind has also cooled off, he or she finds it easy to reciprocate with a similar admission of some error in strategy. Suddenly anger seems very far away and inappropriate as warm feelings of reconciliation arise in both parties. It is not necessary and certainly not healthy for either party to take on all the blame for an incident. Admission of partial blame, which is more realistic, is sufficient to mend the relationship. If the returnee has come back too soon, giving the other partner insufficient time to calm down, it soon becomes obvious. The error admission will be met by a hostile comeback, such as, "Right, it was all your fault!"

When a returnee's error admission is not reciprocated, he or she should call a second timeout (or a third or a fourth), because it is a sign that the partner is still angry. Eventually the partner will recognize his or her own, perhaps small, share in creating the problem. When couples realize they can make a series of T signs, they no longer worry so much about when is the right time to come back, whether they will be taken advantage of if they admit to any guilt, or whether it is safe to bring up the contested topic again.

Reconciliation is the hidden payoff phase in the cycle of violence, as described in Chapter 1. The fear and pain are forgotten as feelings of closeness and caring for one another well up. When the T sign and timeout are used properly, reconciliation still occurs, but in a much healthier way. No one has been hurt or done anything that is later regretted. Nor has either party had to make peace by selling out all pride in an orgy of excessive self-blaming.

Permitting the Partner to Leave

Some spouses already use walking out in the midst of a quarrel as a fighting tactic. The walkout is a particularly effective weapon because the other person cannot score any more points while left alone. Sensing this, the one about to be left may exclaim, "Don't you dare leave me when I'm talking to you!" Sometimes the actual violence in a battering episode starts as an attempt to block the other person's exit.

The partner who is about to be left may panic if severe anxiety was experienced during previous walkout episodes. Left alone without any information, the deserted one worries about what the spouse might be doing. Has he or she left forever? Is he or she driving too fast? Getting drunk? Having an affair? Planning a terrible revenge on me? By ruminating over such possibilities the person left behind may suffer acutely. Next time the partner pleads with the one withdrawing not to leave, mostly in order to avoid a new dose of such anxiety.

But the only appropriate response is an answering T, which sets up an agreement to take timeout. After silently watching the T signer leave, the receiver also should carry out timeout procedures. Since he or she may not be able to leave the house because of children, exercise possibilities may be limited to sweeping the floor or washing dishes. The person should try diverting the mind to pleasant thoughts and avoid ruminating over the incident. The length of the timeout is not under this partner's control, but with luck it will last long enough for rational thoughts to arise about partial responsibility for causing the dispute.

Making the T Sign from Fear

The consort making the first T sign may not be the angrier one. The less angry one may become alarmed by the signs that the partner is about to lose control and invoke a timeout. But judging another person's inner world in this way is presumptuous and insulting and always invites an argument. Therefore a person should initiate timeouts based only on his or her own internal warning cues of stress or anxiety, which may be a response to the partner's signals of growing anger, but not on the partner's behavior per se. Since anger and fear are so interrelated that a person's mood can swing back and forth between the two feelings, it is entirely appropriate to base a timeout on anxiety feelings.

An angry person who receives a T from a partner experiencing fear has to show unusual self-control. The role of the receiver is to give up the initiative in the relationship for a period. The receiver must submit without debating the partner's judgment that a break is needed, and submission comes hard for an angry person. The receiver will be helped by remembering that T signs are cued by the other person's own feelings. Since no one else can judge the reality or intensity of those feelings, the sender's need for a timeout must be accepted at face value.

Rehearsal and Commitment Ceremonies

After describing all the steps in taking timeout, the leaders should model them in a role-play with each other. Then the leaders should conduct role-plays, with each participant individually, of a quarrel stopped by a timeout. The female leader might act the role of quarrelsome spouse for the men, while the male leader acts as coach. Roles can be exchanged for the women's group. In each role play the participants practice making the T sign as soon as they feel some anger, which helps individuals to discover their own early stress symptoms. Then each one must turn around silently and go out the door of the treatment room, taking care to close it without noise. Each person walks around briefly in the hallway, then comes back in. The returnee must finish by role-playing an admission of a one percent technical error made in the role-played argument.

Since receiving a real-life T sign is the most difficult step in the whole timeout procedure, participants should rehearse a second argument, playing the role of a receiver. One of the leaders again plays the role of angry spouse who escalates conflict for a while and then gives a T sign. The group member must respond correctly with a T before the "spouse" will go out. This role-play also ends with both partners making one-percent-error admissions. Group members playing the role of a partner left behind also experience the pressure to think of an error statement before the T signer comes popping back in the room.

The Written Pledge

At the end of the meeting each person is invited to sign a No-violence Pledge (see Figure 6–2), which includes a commitment to use timeout as an alternative to hitting. The main timeout steps are written out to serve as a memory aid.

It would be naive to assume that many battering couples would remember signing the pledge in the midst of some later fight and say, "Oops, sorry, can't hit you." However, the mass signing helps to unify both men's and wives' groups around the same goal of inhibiting violence. Moreover, group members are committing themselves to at least try out the novel timeout procedure as an aid in reaching the goal of nonviolence.

At-Home Practice

Participants should be urged to go home and deliberately practice the T at least once during the next week. They should use any trivial excuse to try it out, even making up a quarrel if necessary. The men especially are urged to try to take the easier role by making the T sign first, since it is usually more dangerous when the male consort becomes angry.

Some couples will start using timeouts immediately, and so early that one partner may even think the other one was just making a T-sign for fun. A too-early timeout does no harm, and it may, in fact, not be as premature as the other partner thinks.

He was trying to make our little boy finish his food. He was coming down heavy and I thought he might make a scene and hit him or something. I didn't want that in front of our friends. So I made a T sign but I did it kind of joking so he wouldn't get mad at me. It worked too. He thought it was a joke, but he went.

(Wilma, age twenty-six)

Other couples will wait till too late, when one consort already is angry enough to want to keep on fighting.

I made the T but she wouldn't return it. She just kept right on yelling.

(Lewis, age twenty-four)

Within a few weeks all participants should be using the T and taking timeout periods with all steps included. They gradually learn the value of timeouts for settling disputes without battering.

While I was running the dog around the yard, it came to me that it hadn't been very nice of me to wake him up at 1 A.M. to start a big discussion. I came back in and told him that was my one percent error. It was amazing: He said right away that he was sorry he had been too sleepy to talk to me. We sat down and talked for several hours right then. I feel we made some progress on a problem we've had for years, which is how he disciplines the children.

(Tania, age thirty-two)

Some couples learn to use timeouts but never do feel comfortable with the T sign.

We're not doing the actions, but we've come along in our talks to where one of us will get up and go to another room. So in essence I guess we are taking timeout, but we are not using the T sign.

(Eddie, age thirty-nine)

Other participants find that the T sign has real signaling value for them.

When he made the T and left, I really felt different. I have worried and worried, other times he has left, that he might never come back. The T was like a promise to me, "I will return! And you'd better be ready to talk when I do!" It was like we had made a contract to settle this as soon as we had calmed down.
(Judy, thirty-five)

Some battering couples seem to catch on immediately and carry out the entire routine successfully right away. Most will have to practice during several real-life quarrels. The commonest errors are refusal by the receiving party to return the T sign and stop arguing; returning too soon for the other partner to have cooled down; staying away too long or declining to talk after returning; and omitting the exchange of confessions about technical errors during the argument preceding.

Some couples have to be urged for weeks before they ever try to use a timeout to calm themselves down. It has been our observation that couples begin to make faster progress just as soon as they start using the full procedure. The reconciliation following the exchanges of error statements creates a better climate for negotiating differences. The batterers discover that they can control their anger by withdrawing into timeout, when their partners will cooperate with the procedure. Just as important, abused partners begin to lose the pervasive fear that interferes with the relationship and indeed warps their entire lives.

Conclusions

The formalized six-step timeout procedure introduced in the initial anger-control session is a new strategy, designed to give even unskilled new group members a way to avert violence at home. Evaluations are needed to prove its effectiveness in promoting anger control between battling couples. However, results so far show it to be an extremely promising technique, for no couple has yet battered after using as many as two of the six steps properly.

The timeout procedure also seems to be useful for cooling off angry parents and older children, teachers and students, roommates, and nonviolent spouses.

The usefulness of this kind of timeout is limited mainly by the fact that both parties in the conflict must know and basically agree to the same ground rules before the procedure will work. With young children the parent will have to decide on the timeout and then put the child in a quiet place out of sight till calm returns. A very young child or infant will not have the conceptual or verbal skills to talk about their own technical errors, so the parent may need to point out an error in strategy to the child, if appropriate. Procedures for using these timeouts as a child managment tool were discussed in Chapter 5.

7 Anger-control Sessions on Self-control Skills

This chapter comprises two major sections, which give the detailed teaching plans for the second and third units in the anger-control program. The timeout procedure taught in the first session is designed as an emergency strategy for battering couples to use while they are learning the more fundamental anger-control skills; sessions two and three begin the presentation of those skills. They cover two approaches, one seeking to manage the physiological ingredients of rage, and the other working to realign the cognitions that exacerbate anger.

About an hour of group time each evening is taken up by review and unstructured group process in order to meet the needs of participants experiencing frequent crises in their lives. The leaders may therefore find that they have to slow down the pace of presenting new material and spend two or more sessions on some units. If many new people join the group after it has begun to meet, it may be necessary to postpone introduction of new concepts and review the former lessons for them. An old member should be asked to explain and demonstrate the proper execution of all seven timeout steps. The new members must then practice the steps in a role-play and sign the No-Violence Pledge, as the others did in the first group session.

Session Two: Reduce Anger by Reducing Pain and Fear

The second unit is aimed at helping batterers and their family members reduce the strength of their anger by exerting control over its physiological sources, namely the adrenal hormones secreted when pain or fear is experienced. The pain or anxiety may seem unrelated to subsequent angry feelings, so people need to understand why the reduction of these stresses will help them to prevent aggressive rages. The leader should begin by explaining how pain or its mild form, irritation, is associated with one kind of adrenal hormone, norepinephrine. Fear and its milder forms such as anxiety are associated with release of another adrenal hormone, epinephrine, which has slightly different effects. As was described in Chapter 3, anger seems to be a compound reaction associated with both hormones together.

After this introduction, the group members should discuss their dietary habits and patterns of drug use, exploring the possibility that what they are innocently eating and drinking has a relationship to irritable feelings and outbursts of violence. Most groups contain several individuals whose free-floating irritability can be related to prior consumption of one or more of the substances discussed in Chapter 3. The leader should encourage group members to collect evidence of the connection for themselves by keeping daily records of substances ingested and rating any irritation, anxiety, or anger that occurs soon after. Group members who suspect that some substance such as sugar, caffeine, or alcohol is affecting their readiness for violence should be encouraged to check with a physician and also to try omitting the suspected substance from their diet for one month, "Just to see if it will help."

Other sources of irritability, such as headaches or high blood pressure, should not be overlooked. Leaders should be prepared to make medical referrals, since some serious untreated problems may be revealed. Leaders should be particularly prepared to make referrals for alcoholism treatment, if they are not trained in this area, and be willing to do some intensive work with the addicted person and his or her family to ensure that the person actually gets into treatment. Methods for accomplishing this were mentioned in Chapter 5.

Next, the group discussion should examine the fear-anxiety element in anger. Victims of battering experience moments of terror and many hours of dread and anxiety, as was discussed in some detail in the first several chapters. Most batterers also experience overwhelming anxieties, though not at the same points in the battering cycle as the victims. The leaders may want to introduce a description of the seven different stages in the typical battering cycle at this point to help participants understand the differences and similarities in feelings experienced by winners and losers at different points in the cycle.

Some men may not be able to own up to fear directly but may express anxiety by compulsive adherence to rules or by consuming jealousy. Most group participants are well aware of their fearful times and need little encouragement to share stories about their experiences of panic and of chronic anxious tension. The discussion should conclude with an explanation of deep muscle relaxation, the imaging exercise called systematic desensitization, and how the regular practice of relaxation and systematic desensitization acts to reduce even chronic, near-automatic anxiety responses. Since fear is an ingredient of anger, the reduction of the load of anxiety should help participants to experience less anger and less intensity of rage when they are angry. But even if treatment of battering couples' anxiety were ineffective in reducing their violence, it would still help them to function better personally. The group should end their discussion by thinking of possible scenes to include in their hierarchy of anxiety-arousing items for use in the systematic desensitization practice.

Relaxation Practice

The second session should close with a leader conducting a group practice in deep relaxation, lasting about twenty minutes. Some leaders have clients lie on the floor or perhaps in a reclining chair for relaxation practice. Others conduct the practice with everyone sitting in a chair. Since fewer participants drop off to sleep when sitting up, I prefer to have them stay in their chairs. If at all possible they should be seated in reasonably comfortable chairs with two supporting arms. Some people may not be able to achieve as deep a state of relaxation when sitting up, but they will relax enough to get the idea. They may practice at home in any posture they like, and most people do lie down at home. In fact the relaxation tape, played after getting into bed, is an excellent antidote for insomnia. However, a state of awake relaxation, not sleep, is the goal of a group demonstration of relaxation. The procedures participants need to follow daily at home are being modeled for them, so they need to observe as many details as possible.

How to Guide Relaxation

Good results may be obtained with a wide variety of relaxation methods. Even the particular script used does not matter much. However, some are notably quicker than others. Hypnotists can induce full relaxation in a subject in one or two minutes. In contrast, the classic Jacobson method of tension-relaxation of muscle group after muscle group takes more than thirty minutes to achieve total relaxation. The repeated command to tense a new muscle seems to undo the relaxation that has begun to spread throughout the body from the previous suggestions to relax.

However, deliberately tensing a muscle does help people get in touch with their own usually ignored kinesthetic feedback, so that they can better monitor their own growing state of relaxation. Therefore, it is useful to include one or two tense-relax commands near the beginning of an induction, especially with beginners. Novaco (1979) found that his clients, all of whom had anger problems, were very tense men who needed much training to get in touch with their own chronic muscle tightness. Therefore he used the full Jacobson script for teaching relaxation. So far I have not found battering men or women to be so tense that this was necessary.

There are three essential elements in all the various ways of inducing relaxation, including the Jacobson method. The explanations below include a description of the way I have incorporated the elements into the sample script given later in the chapter.

1. *Suggestions*

Repeating the suggestion that relaxation is deepening helps the client to relax further. The repeated suggestions must be paced far enough apart so that they can be carried out. I time the pauses more or less by my own breathing and find that a silence lasting for two or three breaths usually allows the client to carry out the suggestion and notice the results. Erickson, the noted hypnotherapist (see Bandler and Grinder, 1975), pointed out the importance of timing the relaxation suggestions so that they actually follow the client's experience even though the suggestions appear to lead it. For example, the therapist says "Your eyelids are growing heavy" only after noting that the client's eyelids are beginning to sag. As individuals progressively relax they display breathing changes, complete cessation of any finger twitching or body movements, and smooth, calm, untroubled faces. Even when there are many subjects, the leader can watch the group and pace instructions in tune with most, if not all, of their cues of relaxation.

Recital of a series of numbers is a useful way to deepen clients' relaxation, particularly when paired with a suggestion that each number means the person is entering deeper into some place of relaxation. I usually count from one to twenty, with many pauses and suggestions that "You are growing more and more relaxed, more relaxed than ever before."

2. *Distraction*

Any orienting response made to a new stimulus will revive some muscle tension. The easiest way to shut out all external stimuli is to divert clients' attention to their own internal physiological feedback. I generally begin a relaxation session by asking clients to focus only on their own breathing as I lead them through several deep inhalations and breath holds. Then I suggest that they continue to breath naturally, attending only to their breathing. I tell them to notice how their relaxation increases with every exhalation. Experienced subjects can become completely relaxed just by focusing on their breathing and need no further scripted suggestions.

Most people need more time, so I go on to focus attention on the kinesthetic feedback from the muscles. I generally ask them to tense and then relax one set of muscles, an arm and fist, in order to heighten awareness of barely perceptible feedback constantly coming back from the muscles. If the breathing exercise has already produced sufficient relaxation, I skip the tensing sequence, as it would merely disturb the relaxation already achieved in the arm. For the next few minutes I slowly recite a list of the major muscle groups, paired with suggestions to relax such as, "Pay attention to the way your neck muscles feel. . . . Relax you neck. . . . Feel the relaxation in those muscles increasing. . . ." The dots indicate pauses of from two to ten seconds.

Some leaders name muscle groups from the top of the head downward; others work their way up from the feet. It seems to make no difference at all. My personal preference is to work down, because I like to visualize relaxation as a sort of wave flowing down through the body. I used to believe that the mention of specific muscle groups paired with the command to relax led the clients to train their muscles to obey the key word "Relax!" by relaxing. However, I noticed that their relaxation often "got ahead" of my suggestions and had little relation to them. This may indicate that the real function of the muscle group recital is to distract the attention away from external stimuli, which would produce arousal and therefore tension.

3. *Decentering*

The usual thinking processes must also disengage, because internal thoughts are accompanied by organized brain wave patterns and some tension. Deep relaxation is accompanied by a less organized pattern called the alpha wave pattern. Alpha waves also occur during daydreaming, meditation, and hypnosis, proving the basic similarity of the three states. The alpha state for some unknown reason seems to be a highly enjoyable and refreshing experience for both brain and body, possibly providing even more refreshment than an equivalent amount of sleep. People do pass through the alpha state regularly at the threshold of sleep. However, sleep proper is different from the alpha state. For one thing, sleep is actually a complex event, including a recurring cycle of different brain wave patterns occurring at different times during a night of slumber.

About a decade ago, with the popularization of biofeedback, the deliberate induction of the alpha state became popular (Kamiya, 1968). As a result many people have learned how to induce the alpha state at will, but few have any clear idea of how they do it. Meditation teachers are of somewhat more help in verbalizing how to move the brain into the freewheeling alpha condition. But they tend to give paradoxical advice like "You must try not to try" or "Think about nothing at all," or to recommend staring at a single candle flame or repeating a single word or mantra over and over. Such techniques probably work because the mind, after receiving no novel inputs for a time, stops attending and therefore slips away into the alpha state. It is the absence of the more organized brain waves accompanying attending to stimuli that permits the underlyhing alpha pattern to appear. Therefore "trying not to try" contains profoundly true advice.

Vivid, transitory, daydreamlike images or scenes often occur during an alpha period, as if there were a linkage. At any rate, deliberately and vividly imaging a pleasant scene seems to help nudge the mind into alpha. Therefore the suggestion to visualize a pleasant scene has become a standard part of many relaxation scripts. The client should be directed to imagine how each of the senses would respond at the pleasant place, because recreating colors, sounds, and smells makes the scene much more vivid and seems to help induce more feelings and deeper relaxation. One researcher's analysis of the pleasant scenes selected by subjects yielded the fascinating fact that 75 percent chose scenes with water in them, such as by a lake, brook, or seaside (Bernstein and Borkovec, 1973). Out of curiosity I always ask clients about the pleasant scene they chose and have found that at least 95 percent imagine outdoor scenes containing water. Philosophers might wish to speculate on the reason for such a strong link between water and pleasant feeling.

Reciting the Relaxation Script

The complete relaxation script that follows is the one I generally use with an individual or group new to the art of relaxation. I have included it so that a leader who is unacquainted with teaching relaxation can do so by following the script from the book. A leader's reliance on a written script does not usually bother the persons who are trying to relax, perhaps because their eyes are shut anyway. Since the exact words used for an induction matter little, leaders with some experience should feel free to experiment with variations and to create their own scripts.

On the other hand, the correct pacing of instructions so as to synchronize with the clients' progress is quite important. Pacing is a skill that improves with practice. Pauses between statements should vary in length, lasting for about one or two breaths at some times, and ten or twenty seconds at other times. In the script that follows appropriate pauses are indicated by dots. At some of the places where a longer pause might occur, the number of breaths to wait is given.

There are numerous cassette tapes of relaxation instructions for sale commercially. These professionally made tapes are usually quite effective and are especially helpful in illustrating the correct pacing of statements.

I prefer to make my own tapes to give to clients for use at home. This is easily accomplished by switching on a tape recorder the first time relaxation is induced during a therapy session. Homemade tapes are much less expensive and are sure to be appropriate for each client. Best of all, clients hear their own counselor's reassuring, friendly voice every time the tape is used, thereby reinforcing the positive therapeutic relationship. After a client has acquired some skill at relaxing, descriptions of scenes chosen for that person's anxiety hierarchy can be dictated onto the end of the relaxation tape, which facilitates daily practice of the systematic desensitization method of anxiety reduction.

A Sample Relaxation Script

Sit in a comfortable chair, preferably one with arms. Make yourself as comfortable and as relaxed as you can. . . . . It is better to put both feet flat on the floor, rest your hands in your lap, and close your eyes. . . . . Take a deep breath and hold it. . . . . Now exhale. . . . . Take another breath. . . . hold. . . . . relax. . . . . Continue to breath naturally and pay attention to the way your body feels as you breathe. . . . . . . (*3 breaths silence*). . . . . Notice how your relaxation increases with each exhalation. . . . . More and more relaxed, as you let the air go. . . . . (*4 breaths*). . . .

Now as I name each body part, get in touch with the way it feels. Focus on that part only, then relax it when I give the command to relax. . . . . Make a fist with your right hand. . . . . Tense your arm until it trembles. . . . . Now relax! . . . . . Pay attention to the way your arm feels as you relax it. . . . . Feel the relaxation moving down your arm, more and more relaxed. . . . . The relaxation will deepen for several minutes as your arm grows warmer and heavier. . . . . more and more relaxed. . . . . . (*3 breaths*) . . . . .

Now focus on your forehead. . . . . Pay attention only to the way those muscles feel. . . . . Relax your forehead. . . . . smooth and relaxed. . . . (*2 breaths*) . . . . . Eyes . . . . . heavy and relaxed. . . . . Mouth . . . . . relaxed, teeth slightly apart, tongue resting comfortably against the back of your lower teeth . . . . . Neck muscles relaxed, letting your head balance comfortably. . . . . Chest . . . . . very relaxed. . . . . Arms relaxed. . . . . Hands, warm, heavy . . . . becoming too heavy to move . . . . . very comfortable. . . . . (*3 breaths*) . . . . . Stomach muscles . . . . . relaxed. . . . . Hips . . . . relaxed. . . . . Upper legs . . . . . knees . . . . calves of your legs,

all very warm and relaxed. . . . . Ankles, feet, toes . . . . all very relaxed . . . . .
warm and heavy and relaxed. . . . . (*3 breaths*) . . . . .

Now imagine a yardstick, one that measures relaxation. . . . . . The numbers
go along it from one to twenty. As I count up to twenty you are going deeper and
deeper into relaxation, measured by the yardstick. . . . . One . . . . . two . . . . .
three . . . . . four . . . . . deeper and deeper into the relaxation state . . . . . five .
. . . . six . . . . . seven . . . . . the yardstick is measuring . . . . . eight . . . . . nine
. . . . . ten . . . . . eleven . . . . . more relaxed . . . . . twelve . . . . . thirteen . . .
. . fourteen . . . . . deeply relaxed, hands very warm . . . . . fifteen . . . . . sixteen
. . . . . more relaxed than ever before . . . . . seventeen . . . . . feeling very good .
. . . . eighteen . . . . . nineteen . . . . . all the way, completely relaxed . . . . . twenty
. . . . just resting and enjoying the feeling of relaxation. . . . . (*5 or 6 breaths*)
. . . . .

Now imagine a pleasant scene . . . . . someplace you have been happy. . . . . .
Imagine the colors you could see there. . . . . What sounds would you hear? . . . .
. Try to actually smell a smell there . . . . . What does your skin feel there? . . . .
. Imagine someone you would like to be with you . . . . . (*3 breaths*) . . . . . Make
this pleasant scene your refuge. . . . . A place to go in your mind when you want
to experience calm and refreshment like you are feeling right now. . . . . (*3 breaths*).
. . . . .

*(Items from a systematic desensitization hierarchy may be visualized here, while
fully relaxed:*

You look at your watch and see that you will reach home late. . . . . Take a breath
and stay relaxed while you picture it. . . . . . Your wife does not speak to you when
you come into the house. . . . . Keeping calm, feeling relaxed while you visualize
it. . . . . . Your wife raises her voice, demanding that you change your ways. . . .
. Just picture the scene and stay calm, let yourself float. . . . She is screaming at
full voice. Her face is contorted with rage. . . . . . Remember to take a deep breath.
Just hold on to your calm. . .

*After the visualization of unpleasant scenes, the pleasant scene should be re-
visited for a few moments, in order to finish the relaxation session with calm,
pleasant feelings.)*

Now as I count from five to one backwards you will awaken, feeling very good,
very refreshed, and remembering all that you thought of while you were relaxed. .
. . . . Five . . . . . four . . . . . three . . . . . two . . . . . and one.

Lingering Effects

Relaxation bears a similarity to the hypnotic state in that relaxed
persons are vulnerable to suggestions of any sort made by others or

by themselves via self-talk. Therefore it is wise to end relaxation sessions with very positive suggestions about waking up feeling refreshed and remembering everything. These commands will counteract any negative suggestions that clients might give themselves while in relaxation, especially during the systematic desensitization scenes.

As clients stretch themselves and resume normal alertness, the leader should watch carefully in order to note any sign of lingering reactions. A brief discussion of clients' thoughts and feelings during relaxation will also uncover any posthypnotic effects. Clients enjoy discussing their experiences and solidify their learning by talking about them with each other.

Self-monitoring Relaxation

Persons can estimate their own relaxation level quite accurately without the aid of biofeedback equipment by noting their own bodily sensations during relaxation. The hands and feet really do feel warm and heavy if the person is fully relaxed. This is a reliable effect because the relaxation of tiny muscles in the skin permits the capillaries supplying blood to the surface of the extremities to expand, allowing an abundant blood supply. The temperature of the skin of the fingers may rise as much as seven or eight degrees after some minutes of deep relaxation practice. The heavy feeling may come from the extra weight of the increased amount of blood, or it may come from the lack of any muscular tension in the limbs. At any rate the limbs really do feel "heavy, too heavy to move," as is often suggested in a relaxation script. Another frequent body sensation is a floating feeling. Though the body feels heavy it also feels as if it were floating very comfortably on a cloud. The floating feeling probably derives from the lack of tension anywhere in the body.

Individual Relaxation and Biofeedback Training

Clients need to practice relaxation every day for several weeks in order to become effecient at reducing tension by commanding their bodies to relax. If at all possible each should be given a cassette tape to take home for private daily practice. The tape may be a recitation of the script given above, made by the leader, or some other script may be used. The taped script should last about fifteen minutes. If even this much use of electronic equipment is beyond the means of either the sponsoring agency or the client, the leader may give out written scripts instead. Clients will memorize them after a few days' use and be able to make the suggestions to themselves.

At the close of the second group meeting all participants should be scheduled for individual stress reduction sessions of thirty minutes per week at a time other than their group meeting time. About seven individual sessions can be fitted into a ten-week program. The purpose of the individual meetings is to help battering men and women to master relaxation thoroughly, and then to use systematic desensitization to reduce their stress responses to scenes that customarily arouse anxiety or anger. The participants complete their individual stress hierarchies with the help of their individual therapists. Hierarchy items are then recited one by one to the fully relaxed client during the relaxation session. They should be added to the client's relaxation tape at the indicated place in the script for further practice at home.

During the individual sessions at our clinic, biofeedback monitors registering muscle tension (EMG) were used as an additional training aid. The EMG feedback gives clients direct information about their own muscle tension in the form of crackling sounds whenever a muscle group contracts. When a client is fully relaxed the monitor can remain silent for considerable periods, punctuated by occasional single clicks indicating that a single muscle cell twitched. The quiet is in sharp contrast to the buzzing crackle that accompanies all states of normal alertness and the loud crescendo when a muscle is flexed. The biofeedback is especially helpful during systematic desensitization practice, for the sound from the monitor indicates when the client has mastered the skill of relaxing in the presence of each imagined scene. When the crackling slows or stops, the therapist then reads out the next hierarchy item.

A biofeedback machine is an inherently interesting gadget. Its use seems to motivate men especially to come regularly for the extra relaxation sessions. However, such costly equipment is not essential for good relaxation training; it is just a very nice extra frill, which we happened to be using to collect research data. Even without the direct confirmation provided by the EMG monitoring, a person can feel sure that deep relaxation is reached during a practice session if the limbs grow warm and heavy and a floating sensation is noticed.

Session Three: Cognitive Realignment

Internal cognitions play a key role in the appearance of anger and any subsequent violence, as was detailed in Chapter 4. Therefore the changing of battering clients' inner self-talk and beliefs is one of the most crucial elements in anger-control training. Session Three undertakes this cognitive realignment. The methods are based on procedures developed by Ellis (Ellis and Harper, 1979), Hauck (1974), and Novaco (1975, 1979), which were described in Chapter 5. They differ mainly in taking account of the theory that anger arises out of the coalescence of pain and fear reactions, set forth in Chapter 4.

It is called cognitive realignment because the modification of irrational cognitions that trigger anger seems rather like realigning the steering mechanism of an automobile. When the front wheels of a car are out of line it pulls constantly to one side of the road, increasing the danger of a wreck. When the wheels are realigned the driver can steer straight with less effort and much less hazard. Similarly, anger-generating self-talk tends to deflect people away from the goals they were pursuing and into angry collisions with others. Cognitive realignment enables them to stay on course even when they do encounter road hazards.

How to Observe Self-talk in Operation

Many people find it hard to believe that they themselves and not other people make them angry. They require much convincing to realize that their emotional reactions are controlled by their own self-talk and are not the automatic reactions to events that they seem to be. Yet everyone can relate instances when they did not react automatically but controlled their feelings instead, such as when provoked by an intimidatingly powerful person. Self-control in such a situation is accomplished by means of inner warnings, like "Oh, oh, better be careful with him!"

The leaders may wish to introduce the cognitive realignment session with an exercise that helps participants experience the connection between their inner speech and their feelings. It is based on the rational emotive imagery exercise described by Ellis and Harper

(1979). Group members close their eyes and relax for a moment. Then the leader says:

Picture to yourself just as vividly as you can the details of some unpleasant experience, where you got very angry, ... Lift a finger when you have thought of a particular event. . . . . Picture what happened and what was said. Let yourself feel the anger again. Get in touch with the feelings, the stress. Let yourself go for a moment, don't avoid it! Lift a finger when you can actually feel anger. . . . . .

Now make yourself change that feeling, so that you can stay in that scene and only feel disappointed—or perhaps challenged to solve a problem. Lift a finger when you have recreated the same event and felt something else instead of anger. . . . .

The dots in the script indicate rather lengthy pauses in order to allow participants time to fantasize vividly. The leader proceeds to the next statement when most of the participants have lifted a finger, which may take from thirty seconds to a couple of minutes. When fingers have been lifted for the third time, the leader asks participants to rate their anger for each scene, using the 0–10 rating scale familiar from the Weekly Anger Diaries.

Then a leader puts two columns on the blackboard entitled "Anger Up" and "Anger Down" and asks participants to share how they went about deliberately increasing and decreasing their feelings. Most people cannot recreate emotions just by visualing an event; they engage in self-talk in order to pump their feelings up or down. Therefore inner speech is a more obvious part of the fantasizing exercise than of a real happening. Participants should be able to furnish a number of good examples, which the leader enters in the appropriate column on the board. The Anger Up column will collect exclamations like "You idiot!" and "That's not fair!" The Anger Down column is likely to have "Calm down there," or "Oh well, it comes with the job." This exercise makes a convincing demonstration for participants of the way they actually regulate their anger through what they tell themselves.

The Road to Anger

The leader now puts on the board a list of five major intersections or choice points on the road to anger. Persons headed for anger have a choice at each fork in the road: If all the "right" turns are taken, raging anger and violence will surely be reached. But a different fork in the road leads away from anger at each choice point, illustrating that people actually have several opportunities to detour around anger even after they have been provoked (see Figure 7–1).

FIGURE 7–1.   The Road to Anger

HOW TO START: Pain or frustration occurs.

CHOICE POINT 2: Fear is added to the pain.

CHOICE POINT 3: Evil intent is assumed.

CHOICE POINT 4: Judgment is passed.

CHOICE POINT 5: Retaliation begins.

ARRIVAL AT PRIMITIVE RAGE: Violence seems good and necessary behavior.

After the leader illustrates the idea that persons actually choose several times over to make themselves angry, discussion should focus on placing the most appropriate calming self-talk at each choice point, from among those entered in the Anger Down column in the previous exercise. After group members have worked on creating their own coping statements for a time, the leader should distribute the worksheet shown in Figure 7–2. The sheet provides suggestions for rational, coping self-talk at each of the forks on the road to anger. Participants may want to inset their own phrases in the blank spaces.

FIGURE 7–2.   How to Turn Off the Road to Anger

HOW TO KEEP FROM STARTING: PAIN OR FRUSTRATION OCCURS

- This too shall pass. It's no big deal.
- When the going gets tough, the tough get going.
- Take a deep breath and relax. I can handle this easily.

CHOICE POINT 2: FEAR IS NOT ADDED

- Calm down, anyone can make a mistake.
- When I understand this problem I will find a solution.
- I don't control what other people do; but I am strong enough to handle it.

CHOICE POINT 3: EVIL INTENT IS NOT ASSUMED

- Look for reasons; everyone has a reason from their point of view.
- B is probably doing the best he/she can at this time.
- Most problems come from poor communication. Find the communication problem.

FIGURE 7–2. (*continued*)

CHOICE POINT 4: JUDGMENT IS NOT PASSED

- B made some errors and so did I. That's normal.
- Probably B lacks the skills to do any better. I can still like B as a person.
- What is B feeling? Reflecting feelings will help us both calm down.

CHOICE POINT 5: RETALIATION NEVER BEGINS

- Focus on the issues and try to solve them one by one.
- No one is to blame for a misunderstanding. Now, how can we solve it?
- I made it through all right. I'm controlling myself, and that's all that matters.

After the sheet has been discussed and participants have added their own ideas, the leader should teach them how to practice coping with provocation by using the detouring self-talk. Group members pick a specific provoking event to visualize, while the leader slowly recites the text on the worksheet. It is a good idea to begin at the very last choice point and work backward, so that participants are, in effect, imagining themselves diverting their anger earlier and earlier on the dangerous, irrational road to anger. The leader says:

First, visualize a situation which would make you really angry at someone, perhaps a member of your family. . . . . . . Lift a finger when you have picked the scene.

Imagine that this person has deliberately done something wrong. . . . Now *choose* not to punish that person. . . . Instead, say to yourself, "Focus on the issues here, and try to solve them. Take them one by one."

. . . .

Now imagine that this person has done something that has really caused you some trouble. . . . . . Now choose *not* to judge him or her. . . . . . "B made some errors, and so did I. That's normal."

. . . .

Now imagine yourself wondering if B did it on purpose. Turn away from that thought, and deliberately choose to say: "Look for reasons; everyone has a reason from their point of view."

. . . .

Picture to yourself that something unpleasant has happened and you are tempted to worry and catastrophize. . . . . Now *clear* your mind by reminding yourself: "Calm down, anyone can make a mistake."

. . . .

Now imagine the very first event on the road. You experience something painful or very frustrating. You *choose* to calm down by taking a deep breath and telling yourself: "This too shall pass. It's no big deal."

. . . .

Participants should take their completed sheets home for mental rehearsal of the rational self-talk. They should carry out a mental rehearsal of their chosen coping statements at least once a day during the next week. They may find it helpful to dictate the coping self-statements for each fork on the road to anger onto the tail-end of their relaxation tape to facilitate home practice.

Group members who really absorb the ideas and skills taught in Units 2 and 3 make remarkable progress in anger control. They seem inoculated, a term Novaco (1979) used, against any further lapses into violence and battering. Not only that, but other areas in their lives seem to go better after they have learned how to reduce irritation and stress on their bodies and to talk rationally in their heads, even when painful or fear-arousing events occur.

8 Anger-control Sessions on Interaction Skills

The first two sections of this chapter describe the fourth and fifth anger control sessions, which deal with the skills of making assertive requests, receiving assertions, dealing with others when they are angry, and correcting other people diplomatically. These topics conclude the series of skill-building units formally presented to the separate groups of battering men and women.

The third section of this chapter touches briefly on topics that may be added in the couples sessions. The main business of the five couples sessions is to practice and master the skills in the anger-control units already presented. However, several additional topics are briefly described in this section, because they often are of relevance for battering couples.

Session Four: Assert Effectively

The group leaders introduce assertion skills in the fourth unit, which may or may not be the fourth actual session, depending on the speed with which the particular group of participants has learned the skills taught in the preceding units. The three essential parts of a clear assertion message are presented first, using the discussion and examples to be found in Chapter 5. The three parts are a description of the targeted behavior, a disclosure of the asserter's feelings about the behavior, and a rationale for the wanted change in terms of its tangible effects. The leader should make three columns on a chalkboard with headings to indicate the three parts, as follows:

Behavior Description	Disclosure of Feeling	Tangible Effect
"When you . . ."	"I feel . . ."	"because . . ."

Group members are invited to think of assertions of their own that they would like to make, which are listed on the board. They begin by describing a specific "When you . . ." event. Most persons new to assertion training will need help from the leaders in making statements that are brief, factual, and uncontaminated by value judgments. For example, a participant is likely to say, "When you drink too much . . ." (by whose standards?) instead of the factual description, "When you drank two six-packs Saturday afternoon . . ."

The next part of the assertion statement, the "I feel . . ." message, is not as easy as it looks, especially for battering men and women nervous about setting off violent reactions by expressing negative feelings. Getting in touch with real feelings, angry, afraid, or otherwise, is a theme running through all the group sessions for anger control. In the very first meeting participants began to learn how to observe their own anger or anxiety symptoms. Now they are trying to get in touch with even smaller feelings of annoyance and to express them directly in an assertion message.

Next, group members practice adding "Because . . ." statements to their assertions. Usually some find they have to eliminate particular assertions, as their "because" is only a value judgment, like "Because I say so." "Because . . ." statements need to describe a tangible effect of harm or loss resulting from the other person's behavior if they are to carry enough power to convince that other person to heed the assertion message.

Below are some examples of participants' completed assertion messages. The first two were made up by women, and the latter two by men participants:

Behavior Description	Disclosure of Feeling	Tangible Effect
When you stayed out late	I felt angry	because I got no help with the kids.
When you got drunk	I was afraid	because you might hit me.
When you threaten to leave me	I get upset	because I need you.
When you talked an hour to your mom	it made me mad	because I want you to spend time with me.

Each group member is given a worksheet with three columns and headings as above and is asked to compose a three-part assertion message for delivery at home to their consort. The statement may be the same as one of those put on the blackboard during the group discussion, or it may be a new one. Leaders circulate while the participants work individually, assisting them in writing accurate, non-judgmental assertion messages.

Responding to an Assertion Message

Before participants practice their written messages with a role-play partner, the leaders must demonstrate the best way to respond to an assertive (or an aggressive) statement. The first response to an assertion message should be a reflection, a statement that paraphrases in the receiver's own words what was heard. For example, "You're angry because I called Mom instead of spending the evening with you" is a good reflection of the last assertion in the list given above. It conveys that the receiver has heard both the ideas and the emotional tone of the assertion. Whether the receiver agrees with the assertion or not, if he or she makes the effort to respond by a reflective listening statement, the likelihood of reaching a satisfactory solution will increase.

Leaders should now divide the group into pairs to let everyone rehearse the assertions they wrote down and practice reflecting back the other participant's assertion with a paraphrase. As they role-play, the leaders should circulate among pairs, pointing out any nonassertive or aggressive body language, especially defensive postures, tension, or flat tone of voice. Nonverbal signals (and also major bodily dysfunctions like migraine headaches or craving for alcohol) are sometimes the main clues a person who represses feelings has about his or her own powerful buried emotions. Nonverbals also communicate buried negative feelings quite clearly to the other person, which can spoil an otherwise correct assertion message or reflection.

Group members seem to enjoy assertion rehearsals very much. They exaggerate and make fun and laugh as well as practicing seriously. Nevertheless they take their papers home to try asserting to their real spouses with much foreboding about the results. Those who trust their partners enough, perhaps because they both have mastered timeout for use if someone fails to stay calm, do try assertions and reflections, sometimes with astonishing results. One husband came back the next week crowing, "For the first time in our marriage she understood me!"

Others wait for the safety of the couples sessions before trying out their three-part assertions on their partners. Harking back to the two-coin metaphor in Chapter 6, battering couples trying their first assertions are like travelers in a foreign land struggling with a strange currency. In the couples sessions, intensive coaching of both partners at once helps couples learn how to carry out transactions in the new Realm of Trust.

Session Five: Dealing with Others' Anger

According to my observations of battering couples, both partners deliver verbal attacks at a high rate. Indeed, for some couples "zaps" are the most common type of communication. Doubtless there are battered wives who are too frightened to utter a peep of protest at any time. Such women seldom invite their consorts into a treatment program designed for couples. They either submit like prisoners or get away and create a new life for themselves without the repressive relationship. So, almost by definition, couples entering a program for battering pairs contain two people who often verbally attack each other. Naturally they also endure many attacks from the other. Skills in responding to verbally expressed anger and aggression clearly are needed by both parties in a battering relationship.

The fifth session, the final one in which husbands and wives meet separately, teaches participants effective ways to deal with a partner's angry attacks or counterattacks when they initiate assertions. They also learn a longer but more diplomatic and detailed way to make an assertion, using ten steps, which often eliminates counterattacks before they start.

Reflective Listening—the First Response to Anger

The session begins with a review and another rehearsal of asserting and reflecting. The worksheet shown in Figure 8–1 is handed out. Group members should fill in the first box with an assertion they wish to make to their spouse, then practice it with a partner again. They should be reminded to pause after their three-part statement and to wait silently for the receiver's reply.

The best initial responses to assertions are reflections, but the most natural and usual responses are self-defensive. People defend themselves by rationalizing and giving excuses, by denying all allegations, or by counterattacking, unless they already are well-trained in paraphrasing and reflecting. Therefore asserters should be prepared to deal with angry, defensive rebuttals to their assertion message by taking on the reflective listening function themselves. Since the other person may continue to deny or to counterattack, a whole string of reflective responses may be necessary before the atmosphere is calm enough for a repetition of the original assertion statement.

For example, one couple arrived at a session already arguing. Ed had not called Dolores to tell her if he was coming home in time to eat before the group meeting. Dolores was ready to practice an assertion on this issue. Since Ed defended himself vigorously, leaders had an opportunity to coach Dolores in reflective listening and, later, other ways to deal with his hostile and defensive rejoinders to her assertion.

D. (*three-part assertion*): When you don't call to say when you're coming home, I feel frustrated because I don't know when to serve supper.

E. (*defending*): Damn it, woman, I did call and your office line was busy. I was at a pay phone too and I couldn't stop again.

FIGURE 8-1.   Dealing with the Anger of Others

1. ASSERTION (When you . . . , I feel . . . , because . . .)

"When you cook the meat   'cuz it tastes bad and
    so long it's black   I feel angry   the kids waste it."

2. REFLECTIVE LISTENING
"You feel angry because I accused you of ruining the supper."

3. NEGATIVE ASSERTION

"You're right, it was really stupid of me to speak up before I checked on the facts with the kids."

4. FOGGING

"Probably you're right; I'll have to check with the kids. I do get mixed up on the facts sometimes."

5. NEGATIVE INQUIRY

"Is there anything else I've been doing that bothers you?"

6. SET A TRIAL DATE

"I don't think we can discuss this now, till we've checked with the kids. So if it's all right with you I'd like to talk it over again after supper. OK?"

D. (*reflecting*): You say you did try and the phone was busy, and you weren't able to try again.

Smith (1976) described a similar strategy he called Broken Record, which is a variant of reflective listening. The asserter counters every retaliatory statement with a bit of reflecting, plus the reassertion of the original statement. I do not recommend that the battering couples use broken record reassertions, however. The continual reassertions are more provocative and therefore more dangerous than a series of pure reflective responses, punctuated only occasionally by reassertions. Also, pure reflective listening is a less complicated response, so that novice asserters will have less trouble remembering that this is their next move even amid the stress created by the counterattacks. Finally, the asserter who continually reasserts like a broken record cannot listen very seriously to the receiver's counterarguments. Sometimes the partner's rejoinders contain valuable new information, which can lead to a solution of the problem. Therefore I prefer Bolton's recommendation of pure reflective listening as the basic assertive response to defensiveness. Reassertions are made only at judicious intervals, for example, after every fourth reflection of the defensive person's feelings. This is often enough to keep the assertive initiative, while the intervening reflections help prepare the receiver to listen seriously to the assertion message.

After a brief time for the role-played review of asserting and reflecting, leaders should present four further ways of dealing with angry retorts. After each one is presented and demonstrated, participants should make up sample statements of each sort and write them in boxes on the worksheet. Each person should have the opportunity to carry out a role-play, with one leader acting as angry spouse and the other leader coaching the participant, as he or she attempts to use these new skills to deal with hostile or defensive responses. Considerable coaching may be needed before group members are able to make the various responses correctly when faced with an aggressive opponent.

How to Handle Being Wrong

Part of the risk in asserting one's own feelings and wishes is the possibility of finding out one is wrong and that those precious, long-nurtured feelings of anger or fear are unjustified. Many people would rather stay nonassertive and hang on to their emotional judgments. But it need not be devastating to one's self-respect to renounce a feeling or admit that some of one's actions were wrong. Smith (1976) taught three useful techniques for accepting being wrong while still maintaining the assertive initiative. They are called negative assertion, fogging, and negative inquiry.

Negative Assertion

The asserter accepts the counterattack's accuracy and assertively accepts being wrong. Most people react as if it would be terribly dangerous to be wrong. Someone might punish them or, even worse, they might punish themselves by calling themselves bad, stupid, insensitive, and so on. However, a calm admission of error deflates an attack, because there is no point in going on if a point is already made. Therefore a negative assertion powerfully protects one from further attacks by the other person.

> E.: Anyhow, you keep telling me not to call you at work, 'cuz you're too busy. So how am I supposed to let you know?

> D. (*negative assertion*): That's true, I did tell you not to call me during working hours. I've put you in a double bind, haven't I?

Fogging

If the retaliatory comment is untrue or only partly true, it can be dealt with by a technique Smith (1976) called fogging because of its power to confuse the opposition. Fogging is just like a negative assertion, except that the word "probably" is used.

> E.: I did try to call you but the phone was busy.

> D. (*fogging*): You're probably right. Sometimes the other clerk ties up the phone with her personal calls.

The "probably" postpones the decision about righteous or wrongness to some future time that is under the asserter's control. That makes it easier for the asserter to maintain self-respect than when making a negative assertion, which admits wrong at a time controlled by the other person.

Negative Inquiry

Smith's third technique for responding to telling counterattacks is the most daring and can be highly effective. The asserter deliberately asks for even more negative feedback.

> E.: That phone is always busy!
>
> D. (*negative inquiry*): You are right about the phone being busy a lot. Is there anything else wrong with my wanting to know when you are coming in for dinner?

Such an invitation bravely seizes the initiative. It models an attitude of openness to criticism, which may make it easier for the other person to open up to hearing the original assertive statement. Furthermore, if the quarrel was not on the real issue, the genuine problem may now surface. For example, Ed responded to the negative inquiry in a surprising way:

> E.: Yeah! I wasn't going over to see Sally and I don't like you implying that I was.

Ed had recently ended an affair with Sally—or had he? The presence of this issue just beneath the surface finally explained the strong feeling both husband and wife had expressed over the trivial matter of one phone call. After they worked out that Dolores's jealousy was groundless, on this day at least, the quarrel over phoning evaporated.

Reflective listening plus appropriate use of negative assertions, fogging, and negative inquiry are like shields that protect the one who wields them from angry and aggressive verbal attacks and counterattacks. The same defensive weapons will keep one from emotional harm when others assert or even aggressively attack, as well as when they respond angrily to one's own assertion. The person who uses the defensive assertion strategies finally will wear down even the most determined and angry opponent. The effect for the attacker is like trying to jump up and down on a soft pillow when one expects to bounce high on a trampoline. With no answering hostility to bounce back from, defensive counterattacks are soon extinguished. The asserter has been able to maintain self-respect and yet admit honestly to any and all accurate negative feedback.

So, armed with the above set of responses, a person can with much more confidence take on the battle stirred up by making direct and honest three-part assertions. The defensive techniques should not be overused. For maximum effectiveness, they should be interspersed periodically among more frequent reflective listening responses and restatements of the original assertion.

Setting a Later Trial Date

Even so, the asserter and the retaliator may not be able to find a quick solution. Arrangement for later examination of the issue greatly increases the probability of a resolution that will meet the needs of both parties. This strategy for dealing with another person's anger or defensiveness resembles the last step in a timeout. The asserter arranges for a later time to hold a calm and full discussion, rather than trying to settle the issue at that moment. A time period from half an hour to several hours may be suggested, depending on how much supporting evidence the asserter may want to organize and how angry the receiver seems. The postponement functions as a timeout, permitting the antagonists to calm down and think things over.

Couples should consider establishing a regular "Problem-solving Time" for themselves, which would occur once or twice a week at some unpressured hour. All disputes can be referred to that time for more complete discussion. In any case, the second discussion should not be held in the same physical location as the first controversy, because the angry emotions associated with that spot will more easily be revived there. Instead, the renewed discussion of the painful old topic in a spot with neutral or positive emotional associations will seem, to both partners, less charged with anger.

Diplomatic Corrections

The second half of the teaching session should present the ten-step method of correcting others, in which assertions are surrounded with so much skillful diplomacy that receivers change their behaviors instead of resisting and counterattacking. The worksheet below should be distributed, and the leaders should carry out a role-play modeling each step. Then participants should write down sample statements in each of the boxes, before practicing with a partner.

1. *Initial Positive Affirmation*

"Have I told you lately that I love you, Jane?" (*Hugs.*) (*or*) "That salad you fixed was really tasty tonight. It was pretty, too."

This first step is the most essential and the most easily forgotten in the heat of battle. Beginning an assertion with a positive affirmation makes an amazing difference to the attitude of both sender and receiver. The asserter reminds himself or herself that the other is a worthwhile human being, despite the current irritating behavior. The asserter's potential anger stays away as a result. Also, the receiver who hears a positive affirmation first is more inclined to listen to the rest of the message. The positive statement reassures the receiver that the asserter, even though critical at the moment, still values and respects the receiver. Instead of "turning off his hearing aid," the receiver listens to the critical message and begins to consider its merits. As the super-governess Mary Poppins sang to her young charges, "A little bit of sugar makes the medicine go down!"

The initial positive affirmation may be conveyed by a gesture of affection, a statement of caring, a praise statement related to the topic of the assertion to come, or a paraphrase of an assertion the intended receiver has just sent. All four ways reach out positively to affirm the value of the receiver. For many diplomatic corrections, just one of the four ways of expressing positive regard is a sufficient preparation. If the asserter wants to be extra careful, two or even all four ways of reaching out should be used.

2. *Description of Inappropriate Behavior*

"When you cook the meat so long that it's turning black . . ."

3. *Rationale—Why It's Inappropriate*

"I don't like the taste." (*or*)
"It gets dry and tough to eat. The kids were giving it away to the
  dog."

The assertion proper begins in the second step, which the reader will
recognize as a "When you . . ." statement. The third step is to give
a good reason why the target behavior should be changed. It contains
either an "I feel . . ." assertion, a "Because . . ." reason, or both.
The arousal of negative feelings in one's partner does constitute a
sufficient reason for a spouse to change a behavior, even if no more
objective reason exists. However, the demonstration of some tangible harm, loss, or inconvenience makes a rationale that is more
likely to earn compliance.

4. *Description of Appropriate Behavior*

"How about setting the timer when you put the meat in the
  broiler?"

5. *Rationale—Why the New Behavior Will Be Rewarding*

"Then you can do other things, even answer the phone, and dinner will still be perfect."

After describing the unwanted behavior (the criticism) the asserter makes a positive assertion in Steps 4 and 5 by describing a
desirable substitute behavior and giving a rationale that explains why
it is a better alternative. If the asserter cannot think of a specific
alternative behavior to list in Step 4, the receiver most likely will not
be able to think of one either. In such a case the assertion might
better be forgotten before it is ever uttered.

The pure three-part assertion does not include a suggestion for
an alternative behavior. Therefore the receiver has more freedom.
But the added freedom brings with it the risk that the desired behavior change may not be thought of for a long time. If the asserter
is more expert on the contested topic than the receiver, it is kinder
as well as quicker to specify the needed change. The rationale sup-

plied in Step 5 helps the receiver to choose to try the new alternative because it has merit, not because of coercion.

6. *Offer of Incentive*

"If you'll do that, I promise to fix that pot handle you wanted."

The sixth step, which is optional, is to offer the receiver an incentive to try the new behavior. Most people, when contemplating whether or not to try a new way, are inwardly calculating, "What's in it for me?" If the change promises to net some pleasant payoff, it is much more likely to be tried. Many times I have observed that the moment the asserter offers a reward for compliance, the receiver switches from defensive arguing to businesslike negotiating. The incentive offered should be chosen with care. Ideally it should have a natural relationship to the requested behavior change. Unrelated rewards may be perceived as manipulative control attempts. Also, the reward must not be inappropriately large, nor too small to be interesting. It must be something under the giver's control, so that it may take considerable ingenuity to think of a reward to offer. Therefore this step needs to be planned in advance of starting a diplomatic correction.

7. *Request for Assent*

"OK?" (*or*)
"Does what I've said make any sense to you?" (*or*)
"Would you be willing to try that?"

The seventh step is a request for assent, which conveys to the receiver that his or her right to make an independent decision is still respected. This step is easy to skip, but it is essential. I had occasion to use (as opposed to role-play) a Diplomatic Correction to correct one of the group participants in the midst of Session Five. Afterward she said, "You know, I didn't feel manipulated, because you asked me if I was willing to change. So I freely chose it." The request for agreement allows receivers to retain control of their own lives, so that their self-respect is not compromised by agreeing to try the new behavior. The assent or refusal, furthermore, commits the receiver to a course of action. The act of commitment makes it much more likely that the new behavior will be tried. Finally, if the receiver refuses to agree at this point, the asserter knows that further persuasive efforts must be made before completing the remaining steps in the diplomatic correction.

8. *Rehearsal of the Appropriate Behavior*

"Why don't I find the timer while you look in the cookbook to see how long chops are really supposed to cook?" (*or*)
"I'll go buy some more chops so we can try the new system tomorrow night, just for fun."

9. *Feedback During Practice (Catch 'Em Doing Good!)*

"Is that the timer I hear clicking? Mmm, I'll bet this dinner will be a masterpiece." (*Gives a hug.*) (*or*)
"Jane, these chops are cooked just right. They taste great."

The next two steps, the eighth and ninth, are optional. They can be skipped if the receiver is undertaking a simple or already learned behavior. But if the new, appropriate behavior calls for unfamiliar skills or is a correction of an overlearned habit, rehearsals with feedback are essential for success. The rehearsal can be a mental rehearsal, such as reading in a cookbook about how to cook pork chops, or it can be a role-play or a specially arranged behavioral rehearsal. Positive feedback for any approximation of the desired behavior must be given during and after the rehearsal. If needed, corrective feedback can also be given and a further rehearsal arranged.

10. *Praise and Reward*

"Here is your pot, all repaired." (*or*)
"I'm going to brag tomorrow at work about what a terrific cook you are." (*or*)
"Say, how about letting me do all the dishes by myself to reward you for cooking such a great supper?"

Finally, as a last step the asserter must commit himself or herself to watching for the first performance of the desired alternate behavior in the natural situation, and pouring out enthusiastic praise as soon as it happens. If an incentive reward was offered at Step 6, it must be awarded promptly, with as much public flourish as possible. If the receiver's attempt to use the new behavior goes unnoticed, he or she is quite likely never to try it again.

At times a short version of the diplomatic correction, containing the four most essential steps, will suffice. Which ones are the essential ones? Steps 1, 4, 6, and 10: initial praise, description of the appropriate behavior, request for assent, and a reward of praise only. The assertive request for a behavior change is surrounded by positive statements, and freedom of choice is explicitly preserved, making the receiver far more likely to comply without a struggle.

The worksheet in Figure 8–2 should be taken home by group members, after the role-play practice of the ten steps, to guide them as they try using it at home. Parents who need to correct rebellious teen-agers and employees who need to correct supervisors experiment very quickly with diplomatic corrections. Battering spouses need more encouragement to change their usual confrontational ways and try asserting to each other with skillful diplomacy. Those who do try discover that it is possible to get a partner to change without a verbal or physical fight.

I knew just what she was doing as soon as she praised me and then said, "but . . . ." The funny thing is, I went ahead and did what she was asking, anyway.

(Jeff, age twenty-six)

Session Six: Couples Assertion Practice

Many of the battering men and women will still expect noncooperation from their partners, even after mastering assertion and response skills. It is now time to bring the couples together for practice in interaction, under the direct coaching of the leaders.

Most of the first couples session should be devoted to review and practice of sending assertion messages and responding to them by reflective listening and the other techniques for assertively dealing with aggressive or defensive responses. At first participants practice

FIGURE 8–2.   Correcting Others Diplomatically

1. INITIAL POSITIVE AFFIRMATION

   "Have I told you lately that I love you, Jane?" (*Hugs.*) (*or*)
   "That salad you fixed was really tasty tonight. It was pretty, too."

   ┌───┐
   │   │
   │   │
   └───┘

2. DESCRIPTION OF INAPPROPRIATE BEHAVIOR
   "When you cook the meat so long that it's turning black . . . "

   ┌───┐
   │   │
   │   │
   └───┘

3. RATIONALE—WHY IT'S INAPPROPRIATE

   "I don't like the taste." (*or*)
   "It gets dry and tough to eat. The kids were giving it away to the dog."

   ┌───┐
   │   │
   │   │
   └───┘

4. DESCRIPTION OF APPROPRIATE BEHAVIOR

   "How about setting the timer when you put the meat in the broiler?"

   ┌───┐
   │   │
   │   │
   └───┘

5. RATIONALE—WHY THE NEW BEHAVIOR WILL BE REWARDING

   "Then you can do other things, even answer the phone, and dinner will still be perfect."

   ┌───┐
   │   │
   │   │
   └───┘

6. OFFER OF INCENTIVE

   "If you'll do that I promise to fix that pot handle you wanted."

   ┌───┐
   │   │
   │   │
   └───┘

FIGURE 8–2. *(continued)*

7. REQUEST FOR ASSENT

"OK?" *(or)*
"Does what I've said make any sense to you?" *(or)*
"Would you be willing to try that?"

[empty box]

8. REHEARSAL OF THE APPROPRIATE BEHAVIOR

"Why don't I find the timer while you look in the cookbook to see how long chops are really supposed to cook?" *(or)*
"I'll go buy some more chops so we can try the new system tomorrow night, just for fun."

[empty box]

9. FEEDBACK DURING PRACTICE (CATCH 'EM DOING GOOD!)

"Is that the timer I hear clicking? Mmm, I'll bet this dinner will be a masterpiece." *(Gives a hug.)* *(or)*
"Jane, these chops are cooked just right. They taste great."

[empty box]

10. PRAISE AND REWARD

"I'm going to brag tomorrow at work about what a terrific cook you are." *(or)*
"Say, how about letting me do all the dishes by myself to reward you for cooking such a great supper?"

[empty box]

with a person of the opposite sex who is not a spouse. Thus the rehearsal doubles as a group "mixer" by giving participants the opportunity to get acquainted with new people. If single persons whose consorts had left them have been attending the same-sex sessions, they will fit easily into exercises where marital partners are not paired together. Finally, participants find it less threatening to discuss and practice assertions about real problems with someone neutral at first.

After practicing their assertions with the neutral partner, each pair is asked to role-play the assertion again in front of the whole group. When appropriate the real consort, or someone else with the same problem, may be brought in to act as a double, feeding ideas to one or other of the participants in the role-play.

Sessions Seven to Ten: Couples' Communication Skills

Content of these sessions is more variable. Leaders need to plan specific topics in response to the needs of each particular set of participants. The chief focus should continue to be on improving couples' communication skills as each pair continues to bring up and work through the central issues over which they fight. When a participant grows so angry at a partner that he or she makes a T and takes a timeout in the middle of the group meeting, the event becomes a teaching opportunity for everyone. Part of the group should leave the room to work with the T-signer, and the other part should stay with the receiver. The other participants should try to help the angry pair to use timeout correctly: to cool down, stop ruminating over the other person's offenses, and think of their own "one percent" technical errors to confess at the end of timeout. The other participants absorb a good deal of vicarious learning as they help their friends through this process. For one thing, it is a great deal easier to see other people's technical errors than it is to observe one's own, and a great deal easier to suggest that the other person admit a certain mistake than to admit one's own. As the participants help each other, they are also rehearsing the procedures for themselves. The same principles apply to the stress reduction, cognitive realignment, assertion, and anger-fending skills presented in the other same-sex sessions. Sometimes one or another of these topics may need to be reviewed in some detail, either because some participants were absent the first time it was explained or because time was insufficient for a proper presentation.

New topics may also be presented in accord with the interests of the leaders or the group members. We have included such topics as jealousy eradication, contracting for pleasers, and negotiation skills, which are briefly described below.

The Eradication of Jealousy

Like many other aspects of the interactions of battering couples, each partner can easily identify all the jealous behavior of the spouse while denying his or her own jealousy. Therefore jealousy is best discussed in a couples session, where the partners can confront each other with the evidence and.force each other to admit to engaging in unfounded jealous reactions. Extreme and terrible jealousy is very common among battering men, as was discussed in Chapter 5; many battered women also are jealous. With both, jealousy is rooted in fear of losing the partner.

1. DECIDE JEALOUSY MUST GO

The first step, and the most important for the jealous person to take, is to decide that jealous feelings and behaviors are so unpleasant that they must be eliminated. In other words, the jealous one himself or herself must conclude that the jealousy's effects on both accuser and accused are even worse than the effects of the real or imagined infidelity.

2. CEASE ALL CHECKING UP

Often a consort of either sex may not realize that some actions, such as continual checking on a mate's activities, are really due to jealous anxiety rather than profound love. If the answer to the question "How would you feel if she (or he) wasn't where you expected when you checked?" is a reaction of suspicion rather than simple worry, then checking-up behavior is actually jealous monitoring. The partners need to help each other identify and describe all the seemingly harmless behaviors that are really monitoring and restricting of the other partner's freedom, so that all can be included in the basic decision to desist from jealous actions. If even one "innocent" checkup activity persists, like searching for unexplained phone numbers on a consort's calendar, then jealousy will fail to be cured.

The method for eliminating jealousy must not include or be contingent on the spouse's good behavior. Couple after couple have proved to their dismay that perfect devotion to the other person does not cure that other person's jealousy. Though jealousy is certainly related to unfaithfulness, real or imagined, it soon acquires an independent life of its own. Therefore the decision about jealousy should be stated as if it were just another exercise in cognitive realignment:

"I would like it if you were faithful to me, but whether you are or not, I resolve not to feel or act jealous, because it is too unpleasant for both of us."

3. THOUGHT STOPPING

This is a technique taught to clients who wish to eliminate recurring obsessive thoughts, sometimes called ruminations. It is amazingly effective for such a simple technique. As soon as the partner notices that one of those "innocent" jealous thoughts has come to mind, such as "Is he out picking someone up again?" "Is she dressing so nicely to get other men interested?" the thinker mentally shouts "Stop!" or "Get out!" Another way to interrupt the rumination is to wear a rubber band on the wrist and snap it vigorously whenever a jealous thought begins. The slight pain is very attention-getting and effectively interrupts ongoing thoughts long enough to exert deliberate control to change their course. After the jealous thought is stopped, it should be replaced with a rational thought, such as "He probably got caught in a traffic jam," "Women like to look pretty," or a pleasant new one like "What will the weather be like tomorrow?"

A daily tally of rubber band snaps or internal shouts should be kept on a card. Within a very few days the count of jealous thoughts should go down dramatically, which provides very helpful encouragement to a person striving to eliminate what was a devouring obsession. When the count has been zero for several days it is concrete evidence that a victory over jealousy has been won. If the number of jealous thoughts does not go down to zero after a week of thought stopping and abstinence from checking up, then it is time to apply additional methods to the problem.

4. SYSTEMATIC DESENSITIZATION

Since jealousy is a type of anxiety reaction, systematic desensitization treatment of the sort described in Chapter 4 can prove helpful. The jealous person begins by listing all the kinds of events that arouse anxiety about the partner. The scenes must be specific enough to be visualized. Client and therapist should rate them for anxiety-productiveness by giving each item a SUDS (Subjective Units of Disturbance) value, and then arrange them in hierarchical order.

Hierarchy of Jealous Anxiety

My wife talks to her ex-husband on the phone. She laughs at something he says. (5 SUDS)

She talks to Steve, her boss, on the phone at night. She speaks so softly I can't quite hear what she is saying. (20 SUDS)

My wife goes with her boss in his car to an evening business dinner. (40 SUDS)

She goes to happy hour at a singles bar with her girl friend. Men come to their table and she is flirting with them. (80 SUDS)

My wife goes to a motel room with another man. They go to bed. (95 SUDS)

While relaxed the jealous one imagines the first barely bothersome event, trying to maintain deep relaxation while visualizing it. After a few seconds the client should rest and return to the baseline level of relaxation. The same scene should be visualized several more times, with the goal of maintaining peace and calm in the presence of the anxiety-provoking stimulus. This is usually hardest to achieve with the first, lowest item in the hierarchy. Though the second scene provokes more anxiety, the client is beginning to figure out how to relax in the face of an imagined threat. As the skill is mastered, the client moves up one by one through the scenes in the hierarchy. It may take several sessions to be able to relax while visualizing the worst one, but eventually clients can maintain calm while imagining "my wife in bed with another man" or some similar maximally dreaded event.

Of course, imagining such an event is not the same as living through it. The systematic desensitization sessions provide practice for maintaining a calm emotional attitude. Like an actor reciting his lines to himself, the rehearsals increase the likelihood that the client will remember the desired behavior under stressful performance conditions. Instead of lines of script a new emotion is being learned, but the principle of repeated practice to the point of overlearning is the same.

How the Nonjealous Partner May Help

The directives in this section should be surrounded by cautions to the group members to use judgment and discretion. Men's jealous feelings can trigger extreme irrational violence. A woman's jealous attempts to restrict her husband can and do trigger violence as well. Both partners must first agree that one or both are acting jealous when they do such and such things, spelling these actions out specifically. They must agree that jealousy must go and that they should help each other, even if some of the remedies feel uncomfortable at first. Both the workers and the group participants should remember how many homicides and suicides are traceable to jealousy gone wild and proceed with earnestness but care.

If the four remedial actions to be taken by the jealous consort himself or herself seem not to eliminate jealousy, some suggestions may be made to the nonjealous partner. The first is to ignore jealous talk and attend only to nonjealous statements. This procedure can cause considerable friction if the jealous one has not owned up to having the problem and more or less agreed on what constitutes jealous behavior. For example, if the couple have agreed that checking up should be eliminated, the wife should ignore questions like, "Was that a man on the phone just now?"

A well-known family therapist who uses paradoxical directives to good effect once recommended that a standard ridiculous falsehood be used to counter checking-up behavior, such as "Yup, it was Burt Lancaster again" (Watzlawick, 1981). When either ignored or treated paradoxically, the jealous questions are no longer rewarded with information; in effect they are put on extinction and soon die away. It is very important not to relent and give truthful information to a jealous question, such as "It was only my sister," if using paradoxical falsehoods. Even occasional scraps of genuine information will reassure the jealous questioner and thus reinforce and perpetuate checking-up behavior.

Researchers have found that extinction works faster if an alternative behavior is reinforced at the same time. This method has become known as DRO, Differential Reinforcement for Other behavior. It has repeatedly proved a safe, rapidly effective method of retraining behavior (Whaley and Malott, 1968). In relations between mates, the alternative behaviors occur in endless variety, but the best are those which meet the same need as the behavior to be eliminated. That is, the alternative behavior to be reinforced should gratify in a direct manner the once-jealous partner's needs for attention and security. Below are a few examples of DRO for jealous behaviors. In each case the alternative behavior that is reinforced is a direct statement of a desire for attention, while the statement ignored is an attempt to get reassurance by checking up on the partner's faithfulness.

Ignore	*Respond to*
How long did the repairman stay here?	Which part was broken? The one I thought?
Who did you meet at your dinner?	Since we missed tonight, let's go out together tomorrow night.
Is anyone there working late with you?	I just called because I was lonesome.
Who was that calling?	Any messages for me?

Another action that the nonjealous partner may take, again only if the consort really agrees that jealousy must go, is to engage deliberately in formerly jealousy-evoking behaviors. Generally this would not include such acts as new sexual conquests, which few partners can tolerate. But many routine jealousy-producing actions, such as talking with ex-spouses about the children, socializing with opposite-sex co-workers, or going to parties while on business trips, should be in most couples' contracts for allowable activities. Time and again, in a futile attempt to stop jealous reprisals, accused spouses will curtail such activities to the point of social isolation for themselves.

This final, drastic but effective, treatment procedure requires the accused spouse to engage deliberately in formerly jealousy-arousing acts whenever desired. However, it is crucial that the nonjealous one soon after seek out the partner and arrange to give special attention. For example, right after a phone conversation with an opposite-sex co-worker, the nonjealous consort might fix a snack for the mate, sit down close to him or her, and inquire about the partner's day. By arranging a gift of pleasing attention right after the consort has tolerated a formerly anxiety-producing event, the nonjealous one will be reinforcing the jealous one's tolerance and at the same time weakening anxiety about possible loss of love.

Contracting for Pleasers

Even among nonviolent couples experiencing distress, negative behaviors are exchanged at a higher rate than pleasing actions (Birchler, Weiss, and Vincent, 1975). The simple-sounding procedure of increasing the number of pleasing behaviors exchanged will result within a few weeks in a changed perception of the relationship as more satisfying and worth preserving (Stuart, 1976). But it is not simple for battering couples to do nice things for one another during the buildup phase, when they are preoccupied with a coercive power struggle. The making of a formalized contract increases the possibility that some positive exchanges will begin.

For an initial mutual contracting experience, the goal should be for each consort to raise his or her rate of giving pleasers unilaterally, without regard to the other person's reciprocal actions. If they must compete rather than cooperate, the pair can sublimate their competition—each striving to give out the most pleasers—and still accomplish the contract goal. If the contract is set up to call for a reciprocal exchange, there is danger that if one of battering pair feels uncooperative the whole experiment will fail.

1. The leader explains the first step in contracting, which is the identification of a list of specific pleasing behaviors each group member would like to receive from his or her consort, and also a list of pleasers each would be willing to give. Each person takes a copy of the worksheet (Figure 8–3) into a brainstorming session for about fifteen minutes with another group member of the same sex. Leaders should circulate and may need to help some participants to think of at least one pleasing behavior of each kind for their lists.

2. Leaders now explain the second step in the contract, in which the consorts get together in pairs to share the ideas they have written on their two lists and give each other feedback. They may add to or amend their lists as a result of the partner's input, but the lists do not have to match. However, if one consort decides that a pleaser offered by the other would actually be displeasing to receive, it should be struck off the list. Requested pleasers that the potential giver feels would be too costly to give also should be deleted.

3. After the consort pairs have had ten to fifteen minutes to work on their lists together, the leaders explain the contract for one or more Caring Days (Stuart, 1976). The couple select a convenient day during the coming week for this event. They may decide to try several

FIGURE 8-3. Pleasers Contract Worksheet

PLEASERS			
PLEASERS I'D LIKE TO GET		PLEASERS I'M WILLING TO GIVE	
1.		1.	
2.		2.	
3.		3.	
4.		4.	
5.		5.	
6.		6.	
7.		7.	
8.		8.	
9.		9.	
10.		10.	

CARING DAYS

I agree that next _____ will be Caring Day(s). During each Caring Day I will strive to give my partner from 5–20 Pleasers. I will check off how many I give and how many I receive.

Signed_____

Date_____

days, but most should not attempt a whole week the first time they make this kind of contract. The Caring Days should be outstanding events whenever they occur, clearly calling for unusual efforts, rather like a Valentine's Day or a consort's birthday.

When Caring Day arrives, each consort strives to deliver from five to twenty pleasing behaviors to the partner, whether or not any pleasers come back in exchange. In effect, both consorts are expected to take the initiative and act first. Therefore if one is feeling totally noncooperative the efforts of the other partner are not sabotaged. The items on the list are intended as ideas; new pleasing behaviors can be performed on Caring Days as inspiration occurs. Consorts check off on their own list whenever they give a pleaser and also whenever they notice that their spouse has done something pleasing.

The couples should bring their lists back to the next session. The scores of each pair will be shared with the entire group. Discrepancies between the scores sometimes occur: One partner will indicate that pleasers were received that the partner did not even notice giving. Conversely some pleasers given may have gone unnoticed or may not have been checked because the receiver experienced them as actually displeasing. The group will give helpful feedback to the pair when disagreements have occurred. The leaders should make sure consorts give each other praise for all efforts made, even when results were not as successful as they hoped.

Sensate Focus Exercises

The sensate focus exercise developed by Masters and Johnson (Belliveau and Richter, 1970) might be termed tactile communications training. The exercise was originally designed to help emotionally compatible couples overcome sexual performance problems, especially impotence and frigidity. The couple practice together in privacy for a period of about two weeks, during which time all intercourse is banned in order to reduce performance anxiety. The pair practice giving each other sensate pleasure through stroking and massaging one another's nude bodies, at first avoiding genital areas. They must give one another feedback about what kinds of touching are pleasant and unpleasant so that the partners can improve in the skill of giving sensate pleasure.

Sensate focus practice can be very useful to battering couples, provided the violence has stopped and some genuinely pleasant reconciliations are occurring in between disagreements. Sex is often mis-used by batterers, quite a few of whom demand intercourse right after beating their consorts. For some, rage actually increases erotic desire. For other men, intercourse gives the illusion of loving rec-onciliation without their having to bother with repenting and re-forming to obtain the consort's forgiveness. When jealous anxiety precipitates the battering incident, sexual gratification may seem a vital reassurance about the consort's continued fidelity.

Few battered women enjoy sex right after being assaulted. It feels like just another forced submission to physically greater power and many women bitterly call such acts marital rape. Even when consorts do not demand sex right after acting violently, battering victims often acquire an aversion to all close contact with their attackers, which includes the close contact required for sex. The women are contin-ually nervous and on edge when the batterer is nearby, and nervous anxiety inhibits sexual desire. The wife's coldness in turn may ex-acerbate the man's jealousy and prompt more abuse, making the woman even more anxious when sex is a possibility, and so on and on in a vicious cycle.

Sensate focus teaches both partners to control their anxieties and their appetites in order to concentrate on how to give the other part-ner tactile pleasure. They learn that the way to get pleasure is to give pleasure, a most valuable discovery. If the woman has developed an aversion to being in the close vicinity of her partner, she may over-come her fears in the safety and pleasure of the daily sensate practice sessions.

Leaders should use judgment about when to assign this exercise. Our experience in trying it out with anger-control participants in-dicates that couples still at odds over serious unresolved issues re-lating to fear and anger will not carry out sensate focus assignments even after agreeing to try them at home. One or the other consort sabatoges the exercise either by refusing to receive pleasuring from the partner or by trying to break the ban on intercourse as soon as the partner touches their body in a friendly way for the sensate focus exercise. When couples have resolved the power and violence issues, the sensate focus exercise is significantly helpful.

Conflict Negotiation

The skills involved in reaching a mutual agreement need to be taught to battering couples, for they have settled past disagreements mostly by forced submission of one or the other person. These skills are ably described in various books on marital therapy and so will only be summarized briefly here. The essential steps for couples to take when trying to resolve a conflict formally were outlined by Guerney (1977). The steps on the worksheet presented as Figure 8–4 resemble Guerney's but include several skills that couples taking anger-control training have already mastered. Couples are given the worksheet and put to work in a dyad with their own consorts to fill in the blanks.

1. The first step in conflict negotiation is an assertion concerning the problem made by one partner and listened to and paraphrased reflectively by the other. The reflection should be followed by the other consort's assertion of the conflicting point of view.

2. The conflict should be translated into a relationship issue, if at all possible. Specific behavioral terminology should be used to describe the issue. For example, in a disagreement over disciplining a child the focus should be on "our disagreement" rather than on "that naughty child."

3. The next step will remind the anger-control trainees of the final part of the timeout procedure. Each partner must identify his or her own contribution to creating the conflict under consideration, such as, "I admit I sometimes don't follow up when I threaten to put him in his room." A consort's contribution to the problem may be only a small technical error, but the admission of it establishes a climate of cooperation instead of coercion. Negotiations move along more quickly after the partners hear each other admit to being slightly less than perfect. Perhaps it signals that even if one must make some painful changes to solve the problem, the other partner will also be making some changes to help bring about the solution.

4. Now the pair need to do some creative brainstorming in order to generate several alternative ideas about how to solve the problem. The requirement for several alternatives, even some far-fetched ones like "We could trade in this child for a new one," helps the pair to move beyond solving the problem by means of a rigid ultimatum imposed by one consort on the other. Also, the best solutions seem to come from new proposals, which generally meet the needs of both better than did either partner's original assertion. A list should be made of all alternatives suggested without stopping to judge the merits of any one of them. The idea at this point is quantity of ideas, not quality. On the worksheet the couple would fill out only the left-hand side at this time.

5. All the various alternatives are now evaluated by the couple as they fill in the next two columns. The solution with the most

FIGURE 8–4. Conflict Negotiations Worksheet

CONFLICT NEGOTIATION

ASSERTION BY A:

REFLECTED BY B? _____
ASSERTION BY B:

REFLECTED BY A? _____
OUR CONFLICT IS OVER:

I (A) CONTRIBUTED TO THIS PROBLEM BY:

I (B) CONTRIBUTED TO THIS PROBLEM BY:

POSSIBLE SOLUTIONS	PROS	CONS
1.		
2.		
3.		
4.		
5.		
6.		
7.		
8.		

WE AGREE TO TRY SOLUTION _____, TO _____

ON _____ AT _____ O'CLOCK WE BOTH WILL
  EVALUATE THE PROGRESS OF THIS SOLUTION. WE WILL
  KEEP ON, MODIFY, OR TRY ANOTHER SOLUTION AS
  NEEDED.

SIGNED_____

SIGNED_____

"pros" and the fewest "cons" or possible unpleasant side effects should be selected for a trial use. The sheet listing all the alternatives should be saved, for if the first-choice solution fails to resolve the problem, the next alternative should be tried.

6. A date for reviewing the status of the problem and the efficacy of the chosen solution must be set. This is a vital part of the conflict resolution process, for it creates a climate where solving the problem is not a matter of blind obedience to one person's commands but a joint experiment entered into in a scientific spirit. The scientific method calls for generating hypotheses and then putting them to an experimental test. Scientists do not worry if the experiment fails, for as much or more can be learned from a failure as from a success. In fact, research hypotheses are phrased as "null hypotheses," because more precise information is gained from observing that an intervention made no significant difference, that is, that it failed. The failure of one proposed solution just signals that it is time to try the next idea, not that someone is to be blamed or criticized.

Couples who eliminate their jealous feelings; create a more positive emotional climate by exchanging pleasers and practicing sensate focus exercises; and learn how to settle disputes by trying new options have acquired powerful new skills to use for improving their relationships. They need never again grow so stressed that they will escalate to the point of violence. They may need to remain in therapy for some time to come, as they work out their interpersonal difficulties, but they now can exist together free of the fear of battering.

9 Treatments for Child Batterers

The bulk of this book has been about consort battering and its treatment through anger-control training. This chapter looks at ways of adapting anger-control methods for use by parents who batter their children. Strategies similar to those proven effective in helping couples have been reported in the literature on behavioral treatments for abusive parents. The interested reader is referred to two excellent articles reviewing the treatment studies by Gambrill (1981) and by Schilling (1981).

Workability of Current Legal Procedures

Despite the laws requiring the reporting of suspected cases of child abuse, many instances of child battering go undetected. Most assaults made by parents take place in the privacy of the home, against children too small to defend themselves and too young to know how to obtain help. When the battered infant or child appears in public, obviously suspicious signs of injury may be ignored. Many cases are not investigated until tragically late, because teachers, social workers, and doctors join neighbors and family in failing to report what they observe. Unfortunately, when protective service agency workers' caseloads grow too large to manage, some of the cases reported may also go without action until too late to save the child.

Smith (1978) investigated 134 battered infants and children and found that 19 percent of their siblings had been abused previously, but only 1 percent of the parents had ever been charged with abuse. Densen-Gerber (1978) noted that 90 percent of the fatal child abuse cases in New York City were already known to one or more social institutions, all of which had failed to act to protect the child. She particularly blamed her fellow physicians, for they as a group had the most opportunity to observe battering injuries, yet had the lowest rate of case identification among the various helping professions. Even though battering parents tend to take their injured infants and children to new clinics each time in an attempt to avoid detection, the physician examining an injured child can easily see the pattern of healed and half-healed injuries distinctive to chronic abuse (Hull, 1974).

Mothers who batter an infant or child, or who permit a consort to batter the child, often suffer such severe depression that they seek medical treatment for themselves. Therefore finally physicians need to pay close attention to severely depressed women who are mothers. They should not just prescribe a tranquilizer and send them on their way without asking any questions or examining the child (Bentovin, 1974). The mother's depression may contribute to her giving way to rages and violence, or it may be a result of her feelings of guilt and helplessness to stop the outbursts. Either way, a young mother's complaint of severe depression should be a signal for a sympathetic investigation, not for a prescription of drugs that may make violence more likely.

Sometimes teachers and social workers ignore indications of child battering because they do not want to get involved, and sometimes they are trying to shield the parents from arrest and prosecution on the basis of mere suspicions. Police complain with some justification that their rates of case finding would be better if fellow professionals in contact with children were more willing to share what they suspect so that police could make an informed independent investigation (Renvoize, 1974).

Some experts feel that the process of indictment and court appearance can have a salutary effect on an abusive parent, because it enables the whole family to stop hiding from the reality of their troubled relationships and helps them expiate their guilt feelings. Furthermore, a sentence to probation with supervision can force the family to accept the counseling help they need to enable them to break the battering habit.

In contradiction, a team of social workers in Great Britain who accompanied abusive parents to court hearings found the parents severely stressed and shamed by the experience (Baher et al., 1976). The parents found waiting outside the chambers thoroughly intimidating, and made worse by the hallway reunion with their own frightened and bewildered child, brought in by a matron. They were put off by the legal formality of the proceedings and the way the judge had to make a ruling about their very lives on the basis of a few minutes' knowlege.

One of the most difficult aspects of the trial for parents and social worker alike is the ambigious dual role of the social worker as both supporter and informer. In order to obtain information and also to assess the parents' ability to improve with some guidance, the worker must make efforts to build a positive relationship. But at the time of the trial that same friendly worker has to testify against the parents, if she believes that the child is still at risk.

Current Treatment Methods

1. *Surveillance by a Case Worker*

The least drastic treatment for child batterers is to assign a social worker to the task of protecting the infant or child from further harm by supervising the family. This is an extraordinarily difficult assignment. Delays of more than a day in following up on reports of abuse seem to allow the parents to unify in resistance to any outside help (Baher et al, 1976). With the large caseloads most public agency case workers must carry, the needed speedy response to new reports of abuse may be impossible to achieve.

Nor can the assigned worker literally protect the battered child by being present in the home all the time. The only way the worker can protect the child is to help the batterer overcome the life crises that may have precipitated the abuse, recover from emotional breakdowns such as depression, and improve parenting and anger-control skills. Threats to remove the child are only partially effective, probably working best with parents who already have some skill at self-control.

In some agencies different workers handle intake and treatment functions to allow the parents to see their treatment case worker as a friend instead of an extension of the police force. But since the treatment worker must be responsible for ensuring the child's safety, the dual role remains. If she is effective, she almost becomes a temporary extended family for all the members of the battering family to rely on for help of various sorts. Yet she remains their potential foe in court, for if she finds fresh evidence of child abuse she may have to invoke another hearing.

2. Removal of the Child

When child abuse first became a popular cause in the nineteenth century, infants and children at risk were "rescued" by placing them in institutional care, alongside abandoned and orphaned children. Large institutions for the rearing of children were established all over the world under religious, charitable, and public auspices.

The popularity of institutional care for any kind of child decreased after revelations of distress and outright mental retardation suffered by children spending their formative years in large, impersonal groups with shifting, nonnurturing caretakers instead of parents (Spitz, 1945; Skeels, 1965; Bowlby, 1966). Efforts were redoubled to place all true orphans in permanent adoptive homes. Battered infants and children were placed with foster families whenever possible to avoid the harmful effects of institutionalization.

Unfortunately, evaluations of the effects of foster care indicate that some battered children end up worse off than if they had been left with the natural parents, for all their abusive tendencies. Foster parents are extremely ill-paid and usually untrained. They are expected to provide care twenty-four hours a day for a child who, if battered, routinely exhibits vexing emotional and behavioral problems. The child may act out as if inviting abuse or may be unresponsive and resistant to a new set of parents. Battered infants may be immobilized in a state of "frozen watchfulness." Just as the cyclical model of battering would predict, most abused children remain highly attached to their parents and may even run away from the foster home in order to return to the battering home. For any of the above reasons, many abused children suffer from a long series of shifts into new foster homes, alternating at times with trial periods with their natural parents. The result of having so many temporary parenting figures is a seriously maladjusted person (H. P. Martin, 1976).

Researchers are only beginning to consider the effect on the parents of removing their battered child from them. When the victim is taken out of the home only temporarily, many battering parents seem obsessed with getting the child back (Baher et al., 1976). Even a hospital convalescence seems to imply a condemnation of their parenting ability, which is intolerable. In retaliation they become highly critical of the care and the food in the hospital, even though they themselves show little empathy or affection for the child when visiting the children's ward. In the same way, when the child or children are removed permanently from battering parents they tend very often to replace the lost child by having a new baby at once and very possibly treating it the same way.

3. *Partial Placement for the Child*

In the last ten years some promising experimental programs have provided partial alternative care, leaving the battered child in the abusive home part of the time. Most such projects place the child in a therapeutic day nursery by day, which takes some of the pressure off the mothers and also provides positive nurturing experiences for the children. Generally staff attempt to involve the mothers in the program as well, so that they can receive emotional support and also training in parenting skills (Galdston, 1975).

4. *Residential Care for Parent–Child Pairs*

A few hospitals have tried bringing both the battering parent and injured child into a special hospital ward to stay together (Ounsted, Oppenheimer, and Lindsay, 1978). Mother as well as injured child receive total care and a great deal of nurturing. One such residential program for mother–child pairs was part of the Denver treatment center for four years (McBogg, McQuistion, and Alexander, 1979). The candid report of what happened raised some serious questions about a residential approach. The first wave of seven families stayed for six months. This proved too costly, so succeeding groups stayed for three months. They seemed to spend the first month adapting to the institutional environment, acting angry or anxious much of the time. Not until the second month did the young mothers adjust to institutional routines and form positive relationships. They then made considerable therapeutic progress. But in the third month the mothers were so beset by issues of separating from the institution as caregiver that much of their progress in therapy seemed to evaporate. It may be unwise and unkind to provide a short taste of reparenting care to deprived battering mothers, when economic realities mean that the care is too expensive to maintain.

5. *Nonprofessional Help for Battering Parents*

Parents Anonymous, a self-help organization modeled after Alcoholics Anonymous, has been organized in the past few years by abusive parents themselves. By means of group meetings and telephone networks, parents provide nurturance and emotional support for one another. The impact of such groups has yet to be assessed, but they appear promising.

A few communities have attempted to reduce the risk of child abuse by providing telephone hotlines for use by any parent experiencing difficulty with a child (Jackson, 1980). The phones are answered by nonabusive volunteer parents who have taken special training. Though evaluations of preventive programs like this are difficult to make, one review of a child abuse hotline's work in Australia indicated that it did reduce child abuse, and at a very reasonable cost.

6. *Intensive Treatment for the Battering Parent*

Efforts to treat battering parents, who usually are mothers, have followed two general strategies. Since so many abusive mothers fall into the chaotic/deprived, child-parent, and obsessive categories (Oates, 1979), they usually have traumatic experiences of rejection, neglect, and abuse in their own lives. One common strategy has been to try to "reparent" the abusive parents themselves. The theory is that the child will be all right if the mother is all right. Kempe and Helfer (1972) organized a team of paid, trained home visitors in Denver to go and see the mothers every day. The visitors were nurses and homemakers whose principal functions were to offer kindly friendship and practical help to the crisis-ridden mothers. Thus they modeled a nurturing parenting style for the abusive parents by actually providing needed nurturance.

Another Denver project featured supportive group therapy for battering parents (Johnston, 1978). The initial task of new members in any therapy group is to build relationships of trust with one another, overcoming their initial suspicion and isolation. Trust is exactly the attribute that abusive parents, almost by definition, most lack. Therefore the group method succeeded only because special efforts were made to reach out and overcome new members' isolation and suspicion. The therapists demonstrated caring by providing transportation to and from the weekly meetings and child care throughout the sessions, and especially by serving a complete meal to the group members at the beginning of each meeting. The partylike atmosphere helped the abusive parents make friends with each other. The co-therapists who provided the food became symbolic nurturant parents by this act, for they were showing concretely that they cared for the abusive parents and were available to meet physical and emotional needs. Though the extras made this group treatment more expensive than the usual kind of group therapy, it was still less expensive than providing residential treatment or foster homes for the children. The parents in the group were provided with an experience of reparenting just as in the home visitor programs, but their dependency was diffused among all the group members instead of concentrated on one or two paid professionals or paraprofessionals. McNeil and McBride (1979) led a therapy group for servicemen and their spouses who were abusing their children, and stopped their abusive behaviors. The favorable results of the professionaly led and the self-help groups for abusive parents indicate that group anger-control training should be fully as successful with groups of battering parents as it is with battering couples.

The partial care programs are, of course, far less expensive than the residential programs. Comparative studies of the effectiveness of the two kinds of care are needed before ruling out the most expensive kind of treatment, however. Comparisons should also be made of treating parents individually through home visits versus providing the extra inducements to make a group approach succeed.

The other therapeutic method that often has been employed for intensive treatment of battering parents is behavior therapy. A good many of the successful intensive treatments for battering parents have taught the parents behavioral and cognitive skills resembling various parts of the anger-control training presented in the preceding chapters (Tracy and Clark, 1974; Polakow and Peabody, 1975; Doctor and Singer, 1978). Surprisingly few have attempted a group treatment approach, considering how many well-developed parenting skills programs have been offered to nonabusive parents (Dangel and Polster, 1983). Some behavior therapists, such as Reavely and Gilbert (1979) in Great Britain, have now treated so many individual battering parents that they have published group outcome statistics. The results appear promising. No proper comparison studies of the effects of behavioral and other approaches for battering parents have yet been reported.

Adapting Anger-control Training for Child Abusers

The following sections contain suggestions for the adaptation of anger-control training for parents who batter their children instead of or in addition to battering each other. Many of the specific ideas are drawn from the published reports of behavioral treatments for abusive parents, which indicate ways the elements of anger-control training can be applied.

The Initial Contract

Behavioral treatments typically begin by specifying the target behaviors and the intervention methods to be used to change them. The No-violence Pledge described in Chapter 6, which is signed by battering couples at their first group session, is an example of such a contract. When working with individual abusive parents, workers may need to put into the contract details about the number of meetings for a given time period, such as six meetings in the next four weeks; fees, if any; and other agency operating rules.

An element that should be included in any contract between a court-appointed therapist and the client is a very specific set of criteria for earning favorable ratings on the report to the court. For example, the contracts made by one group of home visitors specified that if the parents' attendance was 90 percent or better, they would be rated as "participating on a regular basis," and if they completed 85 percent of their charting assignments and maintained a learning attitude they would be rated as "actively involved" (Doctor and

Singer, 1978). Such a clear grading system helps parents and workers deal with the workers' dual roles of support and surveillance. If the worker must send an adverse report, the parents know it was not a personal rejection by the worker but a failure of their own to measure up to known standards.

The initial contract between therapist and battering parents also must contain a no-violence commitment. Because such parents so easily go out of control, they should pledge themselves to abstain from all forms of physical punishment, even the mildest. If there are two parents in the home, both should sign even if only one has ever acted aggressively to a child. Doctor and Singer (1978) reported on results of pledges signed by thirty-five families receiving behavioral treatment. Some broke the pledge early in the treatment period by spanking or shaking a child but did not inflict damage in any case. As treatment continued and parents' skill with alternative management techniques increased, use of physical punishment sank to zero.

The initial contract is the foundation for later effective work. The process of negotiating the contract in the first interviews clarifies misunderstandings, the formal signing makes the clients accountable for their future behavior, and the written and specific criteria for progress give direction to the client's efforts and a way to evaluate even small amounts of progress. Later contracts are negotiated to give specific homework assignments to be carried out between visits by the parents.

Clients in treatment of any sort acquire new behaviors only when they themselves are committed to change, and not when society or a therapist tries to pressure them into change. Therefore the task of motivating the battering parent to want to change is of fundamental importance. Clients commit themselves to change only when three conditions occur: when they are convinced that the therapist values them as a person, when they have real hope for success, and when the rewards for changing look better than the reward for staying with the old set of behaviors. Battering parents should not be rushed into premature signing of behavioral contracts before these three conditions have been met.

Data Collection

After the initial contract is negotiated and the parents are ready for work, the usual first task is to collect data of some sort, so that an individualized intervention may be designed. For example, parents can be required to keep a diary of interactions with their children that are irritating or gratifying (Reavely and Gilbert, 1979; Doctor and Singer, 1978). Diary entires should briefly describe the event and the parent's own subjective reactions of anxiety or of enjoyment of the child at that time on a simple rating scale. Parents and workers alike learn a great deal from studying such diaries for a few weeks.

Many parents will find the data collection assignment very hard to carry out. Most people have little or no experience in making regular written records about anything, let alone behaviors of which they are ashamed. It may help to focus only on key high frequency events, such as "baby cries" or "anxiety when touching baby." The worker must help battering parents to learn how to keep records by providing simple forms for recording and getting the parent to practice recording some observations. Workers can easily devise custom-made forms if they carry a ruler and paper with them. A form similar to the one depicted here was created by a worker for a mother who abused her infant in a frantic effort to make her stop crying (Stephens, 1982). The worker should make a written note to herself of any assignment made. Otherwise it is easy to forget at the next meeting to reinforce the clients' efforts at data collection by reviewing their recording sheets.

If possible, client data should be supplemented and verified by the worker's own observations of parent–child interactions, preferably made in the home setting where the abuse occurs. The worker can choose to observe during a time when it is particularly difficult

Record of Baby's Crying					
Date, When, Where	Who Else Was There	Why She Cried	What I Did	Baby's Response	How I Felt: Anxiety: Pleasure (0–10)

for the abusive parent to cope, such as the child's mealtime or bedtime. Or the worker can ask parent and child to do something together while the worker records observations. If the observations must be made at the therapy office, practice play sessions between parent and child also provide useful information. Jeffery (1976) reported tape-recording fifteen-minute "talking sessions" between mother, child, and worker, and later measuring the amount of talk by mother and child and their rates of eliciting and maintaining communication with each other.

The process of teaching the parent to collect data, and then basing later work on the information gathered, enlists the parent as an active partner in the treatment. Because their contributions are taken seriously, the parents feel more important and more in control of their own destiny. Once preliminary data have been gathered, parents and workers agree on one or more intervention goals. Change efforts and data collection continue between sessions. The main goals and methods for working toward them are detailed in the following sections.

Timeouts for Battering Parents

When batterers enter treatment, their anger control gradually improves, but for some time the victim remains at risk in the home. Therefore timeout procedures have to be taught first, as an emergency way of stopping conflicts before they reach the point where the batterer loses self-control. The particular timeout procedure used by battering parents needs to be custom-designed by worker and client to fit the family's situation. The parent can and should teach any older children in the family to participate fully in the effort to stop physical abuse by carrying out the same steps, described in Chapter 6, that adult pairs use, beginning with an exchange of T-signs and ending with an exchange of error admissions. Since older abused children instigate at least some of the incidents that lead to battering, their participation in timeout routines will teach them self-control as well.

Young children, perhaps between the ages of two and eight years, should be removed from the parent's presence into a timeout place whenever the abusive parent feels the internal signals warning of impending anger. The procedure to be followed for this kind of timeout was described in detail in Chapter 5. The timeout place can be an uninteresting room such as the bathroom, or a quiet corner in a room, or a chair facing the wall and out of earshot of the TV. The parent must be able to supervise the child during the timeout but should not be able to see the child because the parent, too, needs to cool off.

As the parent is placing the child in the timeout location, he or she should reiterate the rule for ending the isolation. Here are some examples:

"You must stop crying. You may come out after you have been quiet for two minutes."

"You may come out as soon as you have figured out a way to play without hitting your sister."

"Whenever you are ready to take your bath you may come out and tell me."

Most timeouts are invoked by parents aroused by the child's non-compliance with some parental demand, or violation of some parental notion of acceptable behavior or noise level. When noncompliance precipitated the parent's anger, then the same demand must be made over again as soon as the child is released from timeout. If the child continues to refuse, a second timeout must immediately be invoked. The parent should be preparing herself or himself, during the quiet of the timeout, to assertively restate the original demand rather than to give in and comfort a teary-eyed child. However, the parent also should be searching for technical errors he or she might have made that helped to bring on the child's noncompliance. Perhaps the parent's assertion was too vague. Perhaps it interrupted a highly favored activity, or demanded a nonfavored activity. Perhaps the parent should have taken time to present the demand in the form of a ten-step diplomatic correction beginning with initial praise and ending with a reward for trying a difficult new behavior change, as was described in Chapter 8. The parent may or may not admit the technical error to the child returning from timeout, but the improved strategy should be tried when the renewed demand is given:

"I guess I wasn't being very understanding when I yelled at you just then, and I didn't say how much I liked the way you played with Joey all evening. But it is time for bed now, so you need to put up your toys and get yourself ready. As soon as you are ready let me know and I will come read you a story. OK?"

Many parents (and teachers, too) fear that they will lose their authority with a child if they admit to having made even a tiny one percent error in strategy, such as yelling, making a hasty judgment, or behaving inconsistently. The first time a battering parent admits such an error to a target child may be an occasion requiring considerable courage and even advance rehearsals. But parents, like battling consorts, who do try admitting to their technical errors at the close of a timeout discover that the exchange of honest admissions magically opens the way to settlment of conflicts. Their authority, far from being undermined, thus becomes more acceptable to the child to whom they have confessed their error.

All too many infants are attacked by their own parent or parent substitute. Very often the infant's crying is interpreted as rejection or defiance, and the parent reacts as if an older child had shouted, "No, I won't and you can't make me!" It is especially important to teach the parent who abuses a wailing infant how to take timeouts, since the infant is too young to cooperate and the parent must do all the work. Just as soon as the parent notices his or her own first internal stress signal, the infant must be left in a safe place such as a crib, and the parent must withdraw to another room. The parent must ignore what the infant is doing and concentrate on carrying out the calming procedures to be described in the next section. The timeout should last only a few minutes and should end as soon as the parent feels calm and in control, whether or not the infant has stopped fussing. Crying, after all, is a baby's only means of signaling its distress. Only a few babies cry because they are spoiled, that is, inadvertently trained by their caretakers that if they cry long enough they will always get their way. Those few spoiled babies may have to be left to cry themselves to sleep a few times to unspoil them; the rest should be tended to, not punished, when they assertively cry, "Tend to my distress!"

Many battering parents already have tried some sort of timeout strategy in their efforts to cope with overwhelming offspring. They generally carried out the timeout in an excessive and inappropriate manner, such as locking a young child away for hours at a time in a dark closet or running away themselves (Doctor and Singer, 1978). The worker should praise such parents for trying to avert violence by separating themselves from the target infant or child and then concentrate on developing timeout techniques that will be humane and effective in their particular situation.

An interesting survey of nonabusive mothers, which asked how they kept themselves from abusing their children, indicated that several anger-control techniques were practiced naturally by nonabusive parents when irritated by a child (Frude and Goss, 1979). Some mothers distracted themselves through activities such as doing housework, knitting, or making a cup of tea. Others distracted themselves mentally by thinking about happy holidays or people more rewarding than the misbehaving child. Some changed their appraisals of the noxious event by telling themselves the child knew no better, was weak and dependent on them, or was a child of God. Some mothers had even discovered ways to work directly on their arousal by counting to ten, using deep breathing and relaxation exercises learned for natural childbirth, or taking a nice warm bath. A few took a tranquilizer, not a method to be recommended no matter how overwhelmed the parent feels because of the research evidence cited at the beginning of this chapter.

Reduction of Anxiety

The fear level of battering parents often is abnormaly high. Reavely and Gilbert (1979) reported that 30 percent of the battering parents they had seen suffered from anxieties that reached panic intensities. Sanders (1978) published a case study of a young father who became unbearably anxious and then murderous when his infant son's crying did not stop quickly. This man also felt panic reactions in other stressful situations. The therapist used systematic desensitization to treat his fears. After treatment the father not only was able to tolerate crying without becoming anxious but also could permit himself to get normally angry at his son and punish him without losing self-control.

Procedures for systematic desensitization were described in Chapter 7. When applied to battering parents the therapist should emphasize learning quick calming procedures such as taking a deep breath, followed by recital of a set of coping statements already written out by parent and therapist together. These statements should be practiced several times a day during relaxation sessions and then recited aloud whenever the child's cries arouse anxiety (Gilbert, 1980). Below are a set of coping self-instructions for a mother panicked by her baby's crying.

1. Crying is Tim's way of saying he has a problem. What is it?
2. I will walk calmly over to him, taking a deep breath.
3. I will be able to handle it. I know how.

4. I am going to comfort him. He wants me to help him.
5. I will keep my voice soft to help him calm down.
6. I will not hit or shout. I can handle Tim calmly.
7. What is it I need to do for him right now?
8. While tending to him, I will talk softly to him.
9. I am coping with Tim's needs and I'll soon be done.
10. I did better this time. I stayed calm and Tim calmed down.
11. Now I should cuddle him and let us enjoy each other for a little while.

The severe depression so common among battering parents seems to be related to their feelings of helplessness and inability to cope with some feared situation or situations, and their condemnations of themselves for being so worthless and bad. These are not far from the desperate feelings of a cornered animal, so deep depression can easily transform into defensive rage and counterattack. Depression often is aggravated by obsessive ruminating over some particular self-condemning thought, such as "The baby acts like he hates me!" The more the irrational, stress-producing thoughts are engaged in, the more often they seem to recur. Such obsessing parents should be taught to use thought-stopping and deliberately replace depressing self-attacks with positive affirmations. First the parent shouts "Stop!" silently or snaps a rubber band to interrupt the judgmental ideas directed against the self or the child. Then by an act of will the parent should turn attention to the child's good points. Patterson et al. (1975b) described a mother who brooded for several hours a day over her troubles with managing her daughter, generally ending with condemnation of herself as a bad mother. She was taught to stop these painful ruminations and as a result decided she could cope with her daughter and did not need to send her away to a foster home.

Empathy Training

Several studies cited in Chapter 2 noted the lack of empathy for their offspring that characterizes many abusive parents. Increasing their empathy may be the most difficult treatment goal of all, but it is one of the most crucial. I worked with a seasoned child abuse worker to discover the intuitive criteria he used to decide when a formerly battered child was safe and the case could be terminated. He found that his conviction that a particular child was out of danger followed after the emergence in the mother of feelings of pleasure in her interactions with her child (Stephens, 1982).

Several strategies for increasing abusive parents' empathy have been tried with some success. The worker and the parent together should choose a method that seems most appropriate, after observing actual interactions and analyzing precisely which empathy skills the parent lacks. No controlled experiments have yet tried to compare the effects of different methods of training parents to experience empathy. The importance of focusing research on this area is evident, if empathy really differentiates abusive parents from merely inadequate ones.

Reavely and Gilbert (1978) noticed that many abusive mothers experienced no pleasure when handling the target child, even while cuddling a sleeping infant. Instead the parents were preoccupied by anxiety and fears of incompetence. Quite naturally the mothers were minimizing their contacts with the child. The parents were required to rate their anxiety and their pleasure every time they dealt with the child, trying to increase the latter. As their self-ratings of pleasure increased, the home visitors noticed that the mother–child pairs made more frequent positive approaches to each other.

Jeffery (1976) used the mother–child talk sessions mentioned earlier not only for observation, but to increase empathy. At each session mother and child played a game that involved trying to increase the number of attempts to elicit speech from the other person, and the number of responses to the other speaker, which are the two most basic verbal empathy skills.

Robison and Solomon (1979) found that when abusive mothers supervised their children at play, they seldom looked directly at their faces but instead hovered over them, frequently interfering with them. The researchers taught the mothers to attune themselves to the children by looking at them directly, watching for cues that the children were sending nonverbally as well as verbally and asking themselves, "What does he seem to want?"

Finally, the parent's failure to respond with empathy may occur principally when the parent is irritated, either by an unpleasant demand from the child or by the child's resistance to a parental demand. The anxiety, pain, and/or anger experienced by the parent makes him or her deaf to the child when a contest of wills occurs. The worker may introduce two methods to help overcome this common phenomenon of defensive tuning out, which I like to call "turning off the hearing aid." The first is to determine what labels the parent is applying to the child at that moment, looking for the natural tendency to dehumanize an opponent before attacking by applying a nonhuman label like "rat," "stinker," or worse. The therapist teaches the parent to stay with positive labels for their child, for these remind the parent that the child is still a valued person despite the conflict.

The second method is to teach the parent reflective listening, which is by definition the skill of empathic responding to another person's statement. Gordon (1972) considered this particular skill so important in improving parent–child relations that he made it the cornerstone of his highly popular parent effectiveness training. A parent can even reflectively respond to a young infant's wailing, saying things like, "Your crying is trying to tell me that you are hungry and you want me to feed you right now," instead of "Shut up, you little monster. I'll feed you when it's ready."

Assertive Child Management Skills

Parents of toddlers and older children usually are intending to discipline when they batter the child. Sometimes the excessive punishment is regarded as normal within the parents' subculture; sometimes it is an excuse for a pathologically hostile person to lash out yet again. But more often the injurious punishment is resorted to because the parent lacks the skills to control the child by lesser means. It is futile to expect such parents to give up physical punishment unless "more effective means of punishment" are taught as substitutes. The time-out is one substitute for physical punishment that is highly effective in bringing a child under control. Couching demands as diplomatic corrections is another way to decrease child resistance to the parent's control, and frequent use of reflective listening is a third proven method for reducing conflicts between parent and child.

Other basic child management skills may be missing from a battering parent's repertory. They may have to be taught how to specify the rules in advance of enforcing them, to give reasons for rules, and to punish promptly when the child breaks known rules. The parent should practice the skill of offering the child alternative activities when prohibiting something. Rewards and praise for the child when he or she behaves are very important encouragement, so parents need to learn how to offer positive reinforcers contingent on good behavior. Often the therapist will first have to overcome parents' objections to "bribing." Contracting to give positive reinforcers in exchange for good performance may seem wrong at first to people who have not received much positive feedback for their own efforts in the past. However, bribing is very different, for it always is an offer made outside of the usual channel of authority and is an attempt to persuade the recipient to do something illegal.

Marital Therapy

All child abuse researchers have noted that serious marital problems are present in homes where child battering occurs. How the other spouse responded to the abuse and how the abuser felt about that response can be crucial to understanding the pattern sustaining the battering. Examples of the way other family members may unwittingly help perpetuate the abusive behavior of the one family member were given in Chapter 2.

However, parents placed in treatment because of child abuse are often unwilling, at least at first, to admit to the need for help with the relationship between themselves. Their need for support from each other may be too great to take the risk of facing up to problems and attempting changes in their relationship. Janzen and Harris (1980) found that marital therapy could be conducted by means of focusing on how the other spouse behaved during the specific act of abuse for which referral was made. The treatment plan devised to avoid further abuse incidents also improved the marital relationship by moving the nonabusive spouse into a different role. For example, a nonabusive husband can be required to observe and praise his wife's practice sessions to increase her child care skills, rather than "rescuing" her by taking all responsibilities away from her. In this way he is maneuvered into the role of supporting instead of undermining his wife's confidence in herself.

Doctor and Singer's (1978) home interventionists found that marital crises erupted so often that it became part of the home visitor's duties to referee disputes. When the therapists taught the parents assertive skills, supposedly for the purpose of disciplining their children more effectively, the parents promptly put the assertive skills into practice in their confrontations with each other without any direct suggestions by the therapists. The teaching of the assertion skills described in this book should therefore be included in the "child management skills'' taught to abusive parents. Once again, the interlocking nature of child abuse and consort abuse is illustrated.

Conclusion

The writing of this book has been a work of love for me, dedicated to the battered women, damaged children, and unhappy men who have reached out for help. As my colleagues and I have led the anger-control groups week by week we were, in effect, trainees too. Our own skills at avoiding unnecessary conflicts and managing ourselves during those conflicts that do arise have improved right along with our clients' skills. There has been an unexpected personal benefit for me in all my relationships: As my anxiety about getting into confrontations that might go out of control has receded I have found that I am able to be more honest and more loving toward others. It is my hope that anger-control training will have this kind of liberating effect on many other people.

APPENDIX:
The Effects of
Anger-control Training

Several groups of battering men and women have gone through the anger-control training just described. All have been voluntary participants. Most were referred to the group by some other counselor who learned that the couple were engaging in battering. A few participants have referred themselves after reading a newspaper article or advertisement announcing a new anger-control group. The groups have been sponsored by the Community Service Clinic of the Graduate School of Social Work of the University of Texas at Arlington. Leadership was provided by the author and a series of co-leaders, most of whom were graduate social work students. The results about to be described relate to the first two groups treated at the Clinic.

Twelve persons, five couples referred because of recent battering and two men referred mainly for child abuse, attended the first series. Seventeen individuals, consisting of seven married couples and three divorcing men, took part in the second wave of anger-control training. All were involved in consort battering. Two of the men had also been reported for child abuse. The same curriculum was taught to both groups and the same data collection methods were used, so the second group was a replication of the first. The average age of all participants was thirty-two for the men and thirty-one for the women. All had taken part in consort violence at least twice.

Intake interviews were administered to a total of forty-six persons, of whom thirty-three actually attended one or more sessions. Four, one man and three women, dropped out after one meeting. The remaining twenty-nine, seventeen men and twelve women, became established group members. Of this number, seven completed only the first five sessions. Two couples moved away in search of employment, and three single men did not feel comfortable in coming to the couples sessions. Therefore complete data exist for twenty-two participants, who were treated as a single group for purposes of data analysis.

The following data were collected from each participant during individual intake interviews, and again in another individual session at the conclusion of the group training:

1. Participants completed a standard personality inventory, the Taylor–Johnson Temperament Analysis (1980). They answered "Yes," "No," or "Undecided" to 180 questions such as, "Are you inclined to tell people off?" Scoring stencils provided along with the administration manual (*Taylor-Johnson Temperament Analysis Manual,* 1980) yielded a profile for each respondent on nine bipolar personality traits: nervous/composed, depressive/light-hearted, quiet/active-social, inhibited/expressive-responsive, indifferent/sympathetic, subjective/objective, submissive/dominant, hostile/tolerant, and impulsive/self-disciplined. The test manual gives the mean scores for each trait for a large sample of normal people who were used as a standardization group, for high school students, and for hospitalized psychiatric patients.

2. After completing the personality inventory, each participant was introduced to the clinic biofeedback machine, the Tri-Mode Biofeedback Monitor (Advanced Electro Labs, Inc.). An EMG sensor was attached to the client's forehead, and the feedback tone was demonstrated so that the client could become accustomed to the equipment before proceeding. Next the examiner played a stimulus tape, which described a series of three scenes. The client was asked to imagine each one vividly as if it were really happening. The first scene was neutral-to-positive in emotional tone, being a description of a pleasant shopping trip. During this scene the subject's EMG level on the visual display was recorded by the examiner to serve as a baseline of that person's arousal level.

3. The second scene was designed to arouse feelings of stress and anger as the client listened to the tape and imagined the event actually happening. It described being wrongly accused by one's employer and then fired from a well- liked job. The EMG peak reading during the visualization was recorded by the examiner. After the scene was finished, the client was asked to rate on a 0–10 scale just how angry he or she would feel if the event had actually happened. The client also rated the desire to respond with verbal attacks or physical aggression and the likelihood of trying to stay calm and cope with the problem.

4. The final scene was set at home and was intended to depict a typical consort conflict. The voice on the tape told the subject to visualize:

> The house is in a terrible mess. You have to go out for a couple of hours. Your spouse promises to get things cleaned up while you are gone. You come home very tired and hot, after driving in rush-hour traffic. As soon as you open the door you can see the same messes all over the front room. Your spouse says, "Where have you been so long? Every time I need your help you're gone!"

The peak EMG level reached during visualization of the argument was recorded. After the scene participants again made four 0–10 ratings of the inclination they would feel in a similar situation in real life to react with anger, verbal attacks, physical aggression, or calmness.

The EMG readings posed some technical problems. Unfortunately, the biofeedback equipment available for testing subjects had visual and auditory displays of EMG levels but were not capable of making a permanent written record of the numerous transitory shifts in subjects' EMG arousal levels. The examiner was at times unable to catch very sudden brief jumps that seemed to come shortly after the subject thought of something disturbing.

The baseline EMG level reflected tension that the subjects brought into the testing situation from outside. Such arousal levels normally will vary from day to day in the same person. A new stimulus like the two visualized conflict-provoking scenes creates more arousal, which adds to or subtracts from the level already existing. Therefore change scores were calculated by subtracting each subject's baseline number from the peak level recorded for each anger scene. The change scores were used in the data analyses as the best indication

Table A-2. Mean Anger Ratings for Imagined Confrontations Before and After Anger-control Training

Measure	All Subjects (N = 19)			Men (N = 10)			Women (N = 9)		
	Pre	Post	Change	Pre	Post	Change	Pre	Post	Change
Provocation from Non-related Person									
Anger rating	5.9	3.7	−2.2*	5.8	3.5	−2.3	6.0	4.0	−2.0
Verbal aggression	5.8	2.7	−3.2**	6.5	2.4	−4.1**	5.1	3.0	−2.1
Physical aggression	2.6	1.0	−1.6*	4.1	.7	−3.3**	1.0	1.3	.3
Coping EMG	5.9	8.0	2.2**	5.3	8.0	2.7**	6.5	8.1	1.6
Arousal	3.3	.5	−2.8	.7	−.7	−1.4	5.9	1.8	−4.1
Provocation from Consort									
Anger rating	8.4	4.7	−3.8**	7.8	4.3	−3.4*	9.1	5.0	−4.1**
Verbal aggression	6.1	3.9	−2.2*	5.6	3.6	−2.0	6.7	4.3	−2.4
Physical aggression	5.0	2.2	−2.8**	4.1	1.7	−2.3*	5.8	2.6	−3.2
Coping EMG	5.0	6.4	1.4	4.6	7.1	2.4	5.4	5.8	.4
Arousal	10.9	−.5	−11.4*	4.4	.7	−3.7	18.1	−1.8	−19.9*

* p. < .05
** p. < .01

213

ment ratings were not obtained from three participants, so the total number of subjects was nineteen instead of twenty-two.

The top half of the table shows the changes in ratings from the imagined scene of provocation by a nonrelated person (an employer). Significant changes after treatment were registered by the whole group for the overall anger rating, a lessened tendency to engage in verbal or physical aggression, and a greater tendency to stay calm and try to cope with the problem. Favorable changes were significant on three of these variables for the men, but none were significant for women alone. The women did begin treatment already much less inclined toward physical aggression against an unrelated person than were their male consorts.

The bottom half of Table A-2 shows changes in self-ratings for the imagined scene of provocation by an irate consort. Again, the group as a whole showed anger ratings and tendencies toward verbal and physical aggression that were significantly lower, after taking part in an anger-control group. In addition the changes in arousal as measured by the EMG were significantly less after treatment. The women particularly had shown a strong jump in arousal, during the intake interview, when imagining a quarrel with their consort. At the end of the anger-control training they actually registered a slight drop in arousal, a highly significant change. Even though the self-ratings for trying to stay calm and cope with the provocation were not significantly higher, the EMG changes indicated that participants, especially the women, had at least learned how to make themselves calm when confronted by an angry consort.

In the case of hostility and self-discipline, the Taylor-Johnson Temperament Analysis and the four self-ratings made in response to imagined scenes measured the same things, but in different ways. The personality test tapped "traits," long-term attitude sets, while the self-ratings measured "states," momentary responses to the specific anger-provoking scenes visualized by the subjects. Trait scores should logically shift more slowly in response to therapy than state scores, as the long-term disposition to react in one way rather than another is the distillation of many specific reactions, along with their reinforcing consequences. When persons have successfully kept calm and coped with provoking events a number of times, then and only then do they begin to think of themselves as "self-disciplined."

Although hostility trait scores were not significantly lowered, the anger and verbal and physical aggression ratings all declined significantly. Likewise, although self-discipline trait scores did not increase to a significant degree, self-ratings of coping increased when confronted by a nonrelative, and stress responses as measured by the EMG were nearly erased when confronted by a consort. The only score that did not change in a favorable direction after treatment was the men's self-discipline score, which moved slightly in the direction of impulsivity after treatment. One wonders if this could be the fruit of the assertiveness training they received, or perhaps related to the general increase in dominance they reported. The Taylor–Johnson subscales also measured several other areas that were not explored through the self-ratings. Some were not relevant to the treatment program, such as social activeness, and showed little if any changes. Others were greatly affected by the anger-control training. The women especially became more calm and less nervous. This could be a direct benefit from the regular relaxation practice they undertook, or it could be a side effect of the reduction of violence and increase in peaceable resolution of marital problems. Both men and women became more light-hearted and less depressed. Depression was never directly treated, but the irrational feelings of helplessness that help trigger depression were a major focus of therapy. The women became more objective and less subjective in their thinking, another effect of the training in rational thinking.

The extensive training in assertion skills was reflected by greater expressiveness and less inhibition for both sexes. In addition, the men particularly became more dominant and less submissive.

The pattern of changes as a result of the anger control training is very consistently favorable, with the single exception of the men's score on self-discipline, which suggested that they had become slightly more impulsive rather than self-controlled as a result of the anger-control groups. However, some of the large mean changes were not statistically significant, for example, the women's 13.9-point drop in the hostility score, because of large standard deviations. These occur when a few subjects' scores vary a great deal from the rest. When analyzing results from a small sample, as in the present case, statistical tests are very stringent. All results are ruled out that could have been the product of the chance selection of those particular subjects, and only very consistent changes shown in much the same way by all subjects can be considered statistically significant, that is, the result of the treatment program.

Turning to changes shown in the self-ratings and EMG scores, the women evidently began treatment more inclined than the men to cope and less inclined to aggress, especially when provoked by an employer. After training the men's levels changed significantly and became equal to the women's when dealing with an employer. This is an example of a generalization effect, for the group sessions concentrated solely on family problems and did not deal with participants' relationships with employers.

When asked to imagine the argument with their consort, the women rated themselves more as more angry than the men, and more likely to aggress verbally and physically, too. The women also registered greater increases in EMG arousal. After training, both sexes grew less angry over the consort quarrel. The men were less likely to become violent, and the women, perhaps as a direct consequence, now showed a drop instead of an increase in EMG arousal when they imagined the event. In spite of this physiological change the women rated themselves as no better at coping with the consort quarrel than before, a puzzling result.

The participants' actual physical violence also declined during the period of treatment. All of the men had assaulted either a consort or a child shortly before entering treatment. They were assaulting a family member on the average of once a month, with the nonviolent intervals lasting anywhere from two weeks to two years. During the treatment period they continued to have quarrels and tense confrontations, but only once did a participant actually hit his wife a single blow. In addition, one wife hit her husband and one father who had been abusive to his child broke his promise not to spank the child. Since the treatment program was only two months long, it was impossible to know whether the rate had really declined, but certainly the severity and length of the battering incidents had dropped sharply. Only two couples have been reached who finished the anger-control training one year previously, and both couples have refrained from any battering incidents. Therefore it is too soon to say with certainty that ten weeks of anger-control training is sufficient to eliminate the violence from the relationships of battering couples, but results do appear promising.

Taken together, these results indicate that the anger-control training had a significant impact on the group participants. The general impressions gathered from face-to-face contact with the group members also indicated that they were improving in mental health and adaptive functioning. However, most of the couples needed further therapy after the groundwork laid by anger-control training in order to work on their other problems.

References

ATROPS, M. "Behavioral plus cognitive skills for coping with provocation in male offenders." Unpublished dissertation, Fuller Theological Seminary, Pasadena, CA, 1978.

AVERILL, J. "Studies on anger and aggression: Implications for theories of emotion." Paper presented at the American Psychological Association Annual Convention, Los Angeles, August 1981.

AX, A. F. "The physiological differentiation between fear and anger in humans." *Psychosomatic Medicine,* 15 (1953): 433–42.

BAHER, E.; C. HYMAN; C. JONES; R. JONES; A. KERR; and R. MITCHELL. *At Risk: An Account of the Work of the Battered Child Research Department, NSPCC.* London: Routledge & Kegan Paul, 1976.

BALLENTINE, S. A. "Economic and cultural factors influencing the post-shelter living arrangements of 25 battered women." Unpublished research practicum, University of Texas at Arlington, 1983.

BANDLER, R., and J. GRINDER. *Patterns of the Hypnotic Techniques of Milton H. Erickson, M.D.* Vol. 1. Cupertino, CA: Meta-Publications, 1975.

BANDURA, A. *Aggression: A Social Learning Analysis.* Englewood Cliffs, NJ: Prentice-Hall, 1973.

BARD, M. "The study and modification of intra-familial violence." In J. L. Singer (ed.), *The Control of Aggression and Violence*. New York: Academic Press, 1971.

BECK, D. F. "Research findings on the outcomes of marital counseling." In D. H. L. Olson (ed.), *Treating Relationships*. Lake Mills, IA: Graphic Publishing, 1976.

BELLIVEAU, F., and L. RICHTER. *Understanding Human Sexual Inadequacy*. Boston: Bantam Books, 1970.

BENNIE, E. H., and A. B. SCLARE. "The battered child syndrome." *American Journal of Psychiatry*, 125 (1969): 975–79.

BENTOVIN, A. "Treatment: A medical perspective." In J. Carter (ed.), *The Maltreated Child*. London: Priory Press, 1974.

BERNSTEIN, D. A., and T. D. BORKOVEC. *Progressive Relaxation Training: A Manual for the Helping Professions*. Champaign, IL: Research Press, 1973.

BIRCHLER, G. R.; R. L. WEISS; and J. P. VINCENT. "Multimethod analysis of social reinforcement exchange between maritally distressed and non-distressed spouse and stranger dyads." *Journal of Personality and Social Psychology*, 31 (1975): 349–60.

BOFFEY, P. M. "Domestic violence: Study favors arrest." *New York Times*, Tuesday, April 5, 1983, pp. C1, C4.

BOLTON, R. "Aggression and hypoglycemia among the Qolla: A study in psychological anthropology." In K. E. Moyer (ed.), *Physiology of Aggression and Implications for Control: An Anthology of Readings*. New York: Raven Press, 1976.

BOLTON, R. H. *People Skills: How to Assert Yourself, Listen to Others, and Resolve Conflicts*. Englewood Cliffs, NJ: Prentice-Hall, 1979.

BOWLBY, J. (ed.). *Maternal Care and Mental Health: II. Deprivation of Maternal Care*. New York: Schocken Books, 1966.

BURGESS, R. L., and R. D. CONGER. "Family interaction patterns related to child abuse and neglect: Some preliminary findings." *Child Abuse and Neglect*, 1 (1977): 269–77.

BURGOYNE, M. A. "The family violence connection: A treatment perspective." Paper presented at the National Conference on Social Welfare 110th Annual Forum, Houston, May 1983.

CALAHAN, D., and R. ROOM. *Problem Drinking Among American Men*. New Brunswick, NJ: Rutgers Center for Alcohol Studies, 1974.

CANNON, W. B. *Bodily Changes in Pain, Hunger, Fear and Rage*. New York: D. Appleton & Co., 1920.

CARLSON, B. E. "Battered women and their assailants." *Social Work*, 22 (1977): 455–60.

CARR, E. G. "Contingency management." In A. P. Goldstein, E. G. Carr, W. S. Davidson, and P. Wehr (eds.), *In Response to Aggression: Methods of Control and Prosocial Alternatives.* New York: Pergamon Press, 1981.

COLEMAN, K. H., and M. L. WEINMAN. *Conjugal Violence: A Comparative Study in a Psychiatric Setting.* Houston: Texas Research Institute of Mental Sciences, 1978 (duplicated).

DANGEL, R. F., and R. A. POLSTER. "Winning!" In R. F. Dangel and R. A. Polster (eds.), *Parent Training: Foundations of Research and Practice.* New York: Gilford, 1983.

DARWIN, C. *The Expression of Emotion in Man and Animals.* New York: D. Appleton & Co., 1915. Originally published in 1872.

DAVIDSON, T. *Conjugal Crime: Understanding and Changing the Wife-beating Problem.* New York: Hawthorn Books, 1978.

DE CHATEAU, P. "Parent–infant relationship after immediate post-partum contact." *Child Abuse and Neglect,* 3 (1979): 279–83.

DENSEN-GERBER, J. *We Mainline Dreams: The Odyssey House Story.* New York: Doubleday, 1973.

————. "The forensic pathology of drug-related child abuse." *Legal Medical Annual,* 1978, pp. 135–47.

DESCHNER, J. P., C. GEDDES; V. GRIMES; and E. STANCUKAS. *Battered Women: Factors Associated with Abuse.* Arlington: University of Texas at Arlington, Graduate School of Social Work, 1980 (duplicated).

DISBROW, M. A.; H. DOERR; and C. CAULFIELD. "Measuring the components of parents' potential for child abuse and neglect." *Child Abuse and Neglect,* 1 (1977) 279–96.

DOBASH, R. E., and R. DOBASH. *Violence Against Wives.* New York: Free Press, 1979.

DOCHERTY, J. P. and J. V. ELLIS. "A new concept and findings in morbid jealousy." *American Journal of Psychiatry,* 133 (1976): 679–83.

DOCTOR, R. M., and E. M. SINGER. "Behavioral intervention strategies with child abusive parents: A home intervention program." *Child Abuse and Neglect,* 2 (1978): 57–68.

DOLLARD, J.; L. W. DOOB; N. E. MILLER; O. H. MOWRER; and R. R. SEARS. *Frustration and Aggression.* New Haven: Yale University Press, 1939.

DUNN, M. "Working with batterers." Address delivered to the Bristol Family Therapy Association, Bristol, U.K., November 1981.

ELLIS, A. "Techniques of handling anger in marriage." *Journal of Marriage and Family Counseling,* 2 (1976): 305–15.

————. "Rational and irrational jealousy." In G. Clanton and L. G. Smith (eds.), *Jealousy.* Englewood Cliffs, NJ: Prentice-Hall, 1977.

ELLIS, A., and R. A. HARPER. *A New Guide to Rational Living*. North Hollywood, CA: Wilshire, 1979.

FAULK, M. "Men who assault their wives." *Medicine, Science and the Law,* 14 (1974): 180–83.

FEAZELL, C. S. "Status of services for men who batter their living partners with suggested implications for program development." Unpublished thesis, University of Texas at Arlington, April 1981.

FENSTERHEIM, H., and J. BAER. *Don't Say Yes When You Want to Say No*. New York: Dell Books, 1975.

FESHBACH, S. "The catharsis hypothesis and some consequences of interaction with aggressive and neutral play objects." *Journal of Personality,* 24 (1956): 449–62.

FIELDS, M. D. *Wife Beating: Facts and Figures*. New York: New York Bar Association, 1977 (duplicated).

FONBERG, E. "Physiological mechanisms of emotional and instrumental aggression." In S. Feshbach and A. Fraczek (eds.), *Aggression and Behavior Change: Biological and Social Processes*. New York: Praeger, 1979.

FRACZEK, A. "Functions of emotional and cognitive mechanisms in the regulation of aggressive behavior." In S. Feshbach and A. Fraczek (eds.), *Aggression and Behavior Change: Biological and Social Processes*. New York: Praeger, 1979.

FRODI, A., and M. LAMB. "Child abusers' responses to infant smiles and cries." *Child Development,* 51 (1980): 238–41.

FRUDE, N., and A. GOSS. "Parental anger: A general population survey." *Child Abuse and Neglect,* 3 (1979): 331–33.

FUNKENSTEIN, D. H. "The physiology of fear and anger." *Scientific American,* 192 (May 1955): 74–80.

GALDSTON, R. "Preventing the abuse of little children." *American Journal of Orthopsychiatry,* 45 (1975): 372–81.

GAMBRILL, E. "The use of behavioral procedures in cases of child abuse and neglect." *International Journal of Behavioral Social Work and Abstracts,* 1 (1981): 3–26.

GANLEY, A., and L. HARRIS. "Domestic violence: Issues in designing and implementing programs for male batterers." Paper presented at the American Psychological Association Annual Convention, Toronto, Ontario, August 1978.

GAQUIN, D. A. "Spouse abuse: Data from the National Crime Survey." *Victimology,* 2 (1977–78): 632–43.

GAYFORD, J. J. "Battered wives." *Medicine, Science, and the Law,* 15 (1975): 237–45.

_____."Battered wives." In J. P. Martin (ed.), *Violence and the Family.* New York: Wiley, 1978.

GELLER, J. A. "Reaching the battering husband." *Social Work with Groups,* 1 (1978): 27–37.

GELLER, J. A., and J. C. WALSH. "A treatment model for the abused spouse." *Victimology,* 2 (1977–78): 627–32.

GELLES, R. J. *The Violent Home: A Study of Physical Aggression Between Husbands and Wives.* Beverley Hills, CA: Sage, 1972.

GELLES, R. J. "Abused wives: Why do they stay?" *Journal of Marriage and the Family,* 38 (1976): 659–68.

_____. "Violence in the American Family." In J. P. Martin (ed.), *Violence and the Family.* New York: Wiley, 1978.

GELLES, R. J., and M. A. STRAUS. "Determinants of violence in the family: Toward a theoretical integration." In W. R. Burr, R. Hill, F. I. Nye, and J. L. Reiss (eds.), *Contemporary Theories About the Family.* Vol. 1. New York: Free Press, 1979.

GIARETTO, H.; A. GIARETTO; and S. M. SGROI. "Coordinated community treatment of incest." In A. W. Burgess, A. N. Groth, L. L. Holdstrom, and S. M. Sgroi (eds.), *Sexual Assault of Children and Adolescents.* Lexington, MA: Lexington Books, 1978.

GIL, D. G. *Violence Against Children: Physical Child Abuse in the United States.* Cambridge, MA: Harvard University Press, 1970.

GILBERT, M. T. "Child abuse: A behavioral approach." *Nursing,* 19 (1980): 828–31.

GLASSER, W. *Reality Therapy: A New Approach to Psychiatry.* New York: Harper & Row, 1965.

_____. "Reality therapy: An explanation of the steps of reality therapy." In N. Glasser (ed.), *What Are You Doing? How People Are Helped Through Reality Therapy.* New York: Harper & Row, 1980.

GOLDFRIED, M. R. "The use of relaxation and cognitive relabeling as coping skills." In R. B. Stuart (ed.), *Behavioral Self-management: Strategies, Techniques and Outcomes.* New York: Bruner/Mazel, 1977.

GOODE, W. J. "Force and violence in the family." In S. K. Steinmetz and M. A. Straus (eds.), *Violence in the Family.* New York: Harper & Row, 1974.

GORDON, T. *P.E.T.: Parent Effectiveness Training.* New York: Wyden, 1972.

GREEN, E., and A. GREEN. "General and specific applications of thermal feedback." In J. V. Basmajian (ed.), *Biofeedback: Principles and Practice for Clinicians.* Baltimore: Williams & Wilkins, 1979.

GUERNEY, B. G., Jr. *Relationship Enhancement.* San Francisco: Jossey-Bass, 1977.

HALEY, J. *Problem-solving Therapy.* New York: Harper & Row, 1976.

HARPER, S. "Violent men and fathers." Paper presented at the Conference on Battered Women: Learning How to Help, University of Texas at Arlington, May 1979.

HARRIS, L., and ASSOCIATES, Inc. *A Survey of Spousal Violence Against Women in Kentucky.* Louisville: Kentucky Commission on Women, Study No. 792701, 1979.

HAUCK, P. A. *Overcoming Frustration and Anger.* Philadelphia: Westminster Press, 1974.

HITCHMAN, J. *The King of the Barbareens: The Autobiography of an Orphan.* London: Putnam, 1960.

HOKANSON, J. E.; K. R. WILLERS; and E. KOROPSAK. "The modification of autonomic responses during aggressive interchange." *Journal of Personality,* 36 (1968): 386–404.

HULL, D. "Medical diagnosis." In J. Carter (ed.), *The Maltreated Child.* London: Priory Press, 1974.

HYMAN, C. A. "Preliminary study of mother/infant interaction." *Child Abuse and Neglect,* 1 (1977): 315–20.

JACKSON, B. *National Children's Centre: Quinquennial Report 1980.* Longroyd Bridge, Huddersfield, Yorkshire: National Children's Centre, 1980.

JANZEN, C., and D. HARRIS. *Family Treatment in Social Work Practice.* Itasca, IL: Peacock, 1980.

JEFFERY, M. "Practical ways to change parent–child interaction in families of children at risk." In R. E. Helfer and C. H. Kempe (eds.), *Child Abuse and Neglect.* Cambridge, MA: Ballinger, 1976.

JOHNSON, B., and N. MORSE. "Injured children and their parents." *Children,* 15 (1968): 147–52.

JOHNSON, V. *I'll Quit Tomorrow.* Rev. ed. New York: Harper & Row, 1980.

JOHNSTON, M. S. K. "Practical advice for beginning a therapeutic group for abusive parents." *Child Abuse and Neglect,* 2 (1978): 223–32.

KAMIYA, J. "Conscious control of brain waves." *Psychology Today,* 1 (1968): 56–60.

KEMPE, C. H. "Paediatric implications of the battered baby syndrome." In C. M. Lee (ed.), *Child Abuse: A Reader and Sourcebook.* Milton Keynes, U.K.: The Open University Press, 1978.

KEMPE, C. H., and R. E. HELFER. "Innovative therapeutic approaches." In C. H. Kempe and R. E. Helfer (eds.), *Helping the Battered Child and His Family.* Philadelphia: Lippincott, 1972.

————. *Child Abuse and Neglect.* Cambridge, MA: Ballinger, 1976.

KENNELL, J.; D. VOOS; and M. KLAUS. "Parent-infant bonding." In C. M. Lee (ed.), *Child Abuse: A Reader and Sourcebook*. Milton Keynes, U.K.: The Open University Press, 1978.

KNOWLES, M., and D. MIDDLETON. *Violent Couples*. Kingston, Ont.: Frontenac Family Referral Services, 1980 (duplicated).

KONECNI, V. J. "The mediators of aggressive behavior: Arousal level vs. anger and cognitive labeling." *Journal of Personality and Social Psychology,* 32 (1975): 706–12.

LEEPER, R. W. "The motivational theory of emotion." In M. B. Arnold (ed.), *The Nature of Emotion*. Baltimore: Penguin, 1968.

LEVINGER, G. "Physical abuse among applicants for divorce." In S. K. Steinmetz and M. A. Straus (eds.), *Violence in the Family*. New York: Harper & Row, 1974.

LUNDSGAARDE, H. P. *Murder in Space City: A Cultural Analysis of Houston Homicide Patterns*. New York: Oxford University Press, 1977.

LYNCH, M. A. "The critical path." In C. M. Lee (ed.), *Child Abuse: A Reader and Sourcebook*. Milton Keynes, U.K.: The Open University Press, 1978.

LYNCH, M. A.; J. LINDSAY; and C. OUNSTED. "Tranquillisers causing aggression." *British Medical Journal,* 1 (1975): 266.

MACLEAN, P. D. "The limbic system." *Psychosomatic Medicine,* 17 (1955): 355.

MAHONEY, M. J. *Self-change: Strategies for Solving Personal Problems*. New York: W. W. Norton, 1979.

MALLICK, S. K., and B. R. MCCANDLESS, "A study of catharsis of aggression." *Journal of Personality and Social Psychology,* 4 (1966): 591–96.

MARLATT, G. A. "Alcohol use and problem drinking: A cognitive- behavioral analysis." In P. C. Kendall and S. D. Hollan (eds.), *Cognitive-behavioral Interventions: Theory, Research and Procedures*. New York: Academic Press, 1979.

MARTIN, D. *Battered Wives*. San Francisco: Glide Publications, 1976.

MARTIN, H. P. *The Abused Child: A Multidisciplinary Approach to Developmental Issues and Treatment*. Cambridge, MA: Ballinger, 1976.

MASTERSON, J. F. *Psychotherapy of the Borderline Adult: A Developmental Approach*. New York: Bruner/Mazel, 1976.

MAY, M. "Violence in the family: An historical perspective." In J. P. Martin (ed.), *Violence and the Family*. New York: Wiley, 1978.

MCBOGG, P.; M. MCQUISTION; and H. ALEXANDER. "Circle House residential treatment program." *Child Abuse and Neglect,* 3 (1979): 863–67.

MCCARTY, L. "Incest: The victim and the family." Paper presented at the

North Texas Conference on Parenting, University of Texas at Arlington, Graduate School of Social Work, December 1982.

MCNEIL, J. S., and M. L. MCBRIDE. "Group therapy with abusive parents." *Social Casework,* 60 (1979): 36–42.

MEICHENBAUM, D. *Cognitive-Behavior Modification: An Integrative Approach.* New York: Plenum Press, 1977.

MEICHENBAUM, D.; D. TURK; and S. BURSTEIN. "The nature of coping with stress." In I. G. Sarason and C. D. Spielberger (eds.), *Stress and Anxiety.* Vol. 2. New York: Wiley, Hemisphere Publishing, 1975.

MELVILLE, J. "Women in refuges." In J. P. Martin (ed.), *Violence and the Family.* New York: Wiley, 1978.

MILL, J. S. *The Subjection of Women.* Cambridge, MA: MIT Press, 1970. Originally published in 1869.

MONTGOMERY, R.; M. MERAZ; and J. DESCHNER. *A Survey of Battered and Non-battered Clients.* Dallas: Women's Center of Dallas, 1978 (duplicated).

MOORE, D. M. (ed.). *Battered Women.* Beverly Hills: Sage. 1979.

MORRIS, M. G., and R. W. GOULD. "Role reversal: A concept in dealing with the neglected/battered-child syndrome." In *The Neglected Battered-Child Syndrome.* New York: Child Welfare League of America, 1963.

MOYER, K. E. "Kinds of aggression and their physiological basis." In K. E. Moyer (ed.), *Physiology of Aggression and Implications for Control: An Anthology of Readings.* New York: Raven, 1976.

NOVACO, R. W. *Anger Control: The Development and Evaluation of an Experimental Treatment.* Lexington, MA: Lexington Books, 1975.

————. "The cognitive regulation of anger and stress." In P. C. Kendall and S. D. Hollan (eds.), *Cognitive-Behavioral Interventions: Theory, Research and Procedures.* New York: Academic Press, 1979.

OATES, M. R. "A classification of child abuse and its relation to treatment and prognosis." *Child Abuse and Neglect,* 3 (1979): 907–15.

O'BRIEN, J. "Violence in divorce-prone families." *Journal of Marriage and the Family,* 33 (1971): 692–98.

O'NEILL, J., and P. O'NEILL. *Intervention: A Powerful Answer for the Suffering Family.* Austin, TX: Creative Assistance, Inc., 1982 (duplicated).

OUNSTED, C.; R. OPPENHEIMER; and J. LINDSAY. "Aspects of bonding failure." In C. M. Lee (ed.), *Child Abuse: A Reader and Sourcebook.* Milton Keynes, U.K.: The Open University Press, 1978.

PARKE, R. D. and N. G. LEWIS. "The family in context: A multilevel interactional analysis of child abuse." In R. W. Henderson (ed.), *Parent-*

Child Interaction: Theory, Research and Prospects. New York: Academic Press, 1981.

PARNAS, R. I. "The police response to domestic disturbance." *Wisconsin Law Review,* 1967, 914–60.

PATTERSON, G. R., and H. HOPS. "Coercion, a game for two: Intervention techniques for marital conflict." In R. E. Ulrich and P. T. Mountjoy (eds.), *The Experimental Analysis of Social Behavior.* New York: Appleton-Century-Crofts, 1972.

PATTERSON, G. R.; H. HOPS; and R. L. WEISS. "Interpersonal skills for couples in early stages of conflict." *The Journal of Marriage and the Family,* 37 (1975a): 295–303.

PATTERSON, G. R.; J. B. REID; R. R. JONES: and R. E. CONGOR. *Families with Aggressive Children.* Eugene, OR: Castalia Publishing, 1975b.

PAUL, G. L. "Outcome of systematic desensitization." In C. M. Franks (ed.), *Behavior Therapy: Appraisal and Status.* New York: McGraw-Hill, 1969.

PFOUTS, J. H.; J. H. SCHOPLER; and H. C. HENLEY. "Forgotten victims of violence." *Social Work,* 27 (1982): 367–68.

PHILLIPS, D. *How to Fall Out of Love.* Boston: Houghton, Mifflin, 1978.

PHILLIPS, E. L.; E. A. PHILLIPS; D. L. FIXSEN; and M. M. WOLF. *The Teaching-Family Handbook.* Rev. ed. Lawrence: Bureau of Child Research, University of Kansas, 1974.

PINTA, E. R. "Pathological tolerance." *American Journal of Psychiatry,* 135 (1978): 698–701.

PIZZEY, E. *Scream Quietly or the Neighbors Will Hear.* Short Hills, NJ: Ridley Enslow, 1974.

PLUTCHIK, R. *The Emotions.* New York: Random House, 1962.

POLAKOW, R. L., and D. L. PEABODY. "Behavioral treatment of child abuse." *International Journal of Offender Therapy and Comparative Criminology,* 19 (1975): 100–103.

REAVELY, W., and M. T. GILBERT. "The behavioral treatment approach to potential child abuse." In C. M. Lee (ed.), *Child Abuse: A Reader and Sourcebook.* Milton Keynes, U.K.: The Open University Press, 1978.

———. "The analysis and treatment of child abuse by behavioral psychotherapy." *Child Abuse and Neglect,* 3 (1979): 509–14.

REED, B. *Food, Teens and Behavior.* Manitowoc, WI: Natural Press, 1983.

REID, J. B., and P. S. TAPLIN. *A Social Interactional Approach to the Treatment of Abusive Children.* Eugene: University of Oregon, 1977 (duplicated).

RENVOIZE, J. *Web of Violence.* London: Routledge & Kegan Paul, 1978.

RICHARDSON, L. A. "Women and altruistic madness: A study of sex-based vulnerability." Paper presented at the American Sociological Association Annual Meeting, Chicago, 1977.

RIMM, D. C.; J. C. DeGROOT; P. BOORD; J. HEIMAN; and P. V. DILLOW. "Systematic desensitization of an anger response." *Behavior Research and Therapy,* 9 (1971): 273–80.

RIMM, D. C.; G. A. HILL; N. N. BROWN; and J. E. STUART. "Group-assertive training in treatment of expression of inappropriate anger." *Psychological Reports,* 34 (1974): 791–98.

ROBISON, E., and E. SOLOMON. "Some further findings on the treatment of the mother–child dyad in child abuse." *Child Abuse and Neglect,* 3 (1979): 247–51.

ROSE, S. D. *Group Therapy: A Behavioral Approach.* Englewood Cliffs, NJ: Prentice-Hall, 1977.

ROY, M. *Battered Women: A Psychosociological Study of Domestic Violence.* New York: Van Nostrand Reinhold, 1977.

SANDERS, R. W. "Systematic desensitization in the treatment of child abuse." *American Journal of Psychiatry,* 135 (1978): 483–84.

SAUNDERS, D. G. "A model for the structured group treatment of male-to-female violence." *Behavior Group Therapy,* 2 (1980): 2–9.

SATIR, V. *Peoplemaking.* Palo Alto, CA: Science and Behavior Books, 1972.

SCHACHTER J. "Pain, fear, and anger in hypertensives and normotensives." *Psychosomatic Medicine,* 19 (1957): 17–29.

SCHACHTER, S. *Emotion, Obesity, and Crime.* New York: Academic Press, 1971.

SCHACHTER, S., and S. E. SINGER. "Cognitive, social, and physiological determinants of emotional state." *Psychological Review,* 69 (1962): 379–99.

SCHILLING, R. F., II. "Treatment of child abuse." In S. P. Schinke (ed.), *Behavioral Methods in Social Welfare: Helping Children, Adults and Families in Community Settings.* Chicago: Aldine, 1981.

SCHWARTZ, G. E.; S. L. BROWN; and G. L. AHERN. "Facial muscle patterning and subjective experience during effective imagery: Sex differences." *Psychophysiology* 17 (1980): 75–82.

SELIGMAN, M. E., and R. A. ROSELLIN. "Frustration and learned helplessness." *Journal of Experimental Psychology,* 104 (1975): 149–57.

SHORKEY, C. T. "Psychological characteristics of child abusers: Speculation and the need for research." *Child Abuse and Neglect,* 2 (1978): 69–76.

SHORTER, E. *A History of Women's Bodies.* New York: Basic Books, 1982.

SKEELS, H. M. "Adult status of children with contrasting early life experiences." *Monographs of the Society for Research in Child Development,* 31, No. 3 (1965): 1–65.

SMITH, M. *When I Say No, I Feel Guilty.* New York: Bantam Books, 1976.

SMITH S., and R. HANSON. "Interpersonal relationships and child rearing practices in 214 parents of battered children." *British Journal of Psychiatry,* 127 (1975): 513–25.

SMITH, S. M. "Psychiatric characteristics of abusing parents." In C. M. Lee (ed.), *Child Abuse: A Reader and Sourcebook.* Milton Keynes, U.K.: The Open University Press, 1978.

SPITZ, R. "Hospitalism." *The Psychoanalytic Study of the Child,* 1 (1945): 53–74.

STACEY, W., and A. SHUPE. *The Family Secret: Domestic Violence in America.* Boston: Beacon Press, 1983.

STACHURA, J. S., and R. H. C. TESKE. *A Special Report on Spouse Abuse in Texas.* Huntsville, TX: Criminal Justice Center, Sam Houston State University, March 1979.

STEELE, B. V., and C. B. POLLACK. "A psychiatric study of parents who abuse infants and small children." In R. E. Helfer and C. H. Kempe (eds.), *The Battered Child.* Chicago: University of Chicago Press, 1968.

STEPHENS, L. "Evaluation methods for behavioral interventions with abusive parents." Unpublished paper, University of Bristol, Department of Social Work, 1982.

STRAUS, M. A.; R. J. GELLES; and S. K. STEINMETZ. *Behind Closed Doors: Violence in the American Family.* Garden City, NY: Doubleday, 1980.

STUART, R. B. "Behavioral remedies for marital ills: A guide to the use of operant-interpersonal techniques." In A. S. Gurman and D. G. Rice (eds.), *Couples in Conflict: New Directions in Marital Therapy.* New York: Aronson, 1974.

————. "An operant interpersonal program for couples." In D. H. L. Olson (ed.), *Treating Relationships.* Lake Mills, IA: Graphic Publishing, 1976.

TAVRIS, C. "Anger defused." *Psychology Today,* 16, No. 11 (1982): 25–35.

Taylor–Johnson Temperament Analysis Manual. 1980 edition. Los Angeles: Psychological Publications, 1980.

THYER, B. A. "Treating anxiety disorders with exposure therapy." *Social Casework,* 64, No. 2 (1983): 77–82.

TOBY, J. "Violence and the masculine ideal: Some qualitative data." In S. K. Steinmetz and M. A. Straus (eds.), *Violence in the Family.* New York: Harper & Row, 1974.

TRACY, J. J., and E. H. CLARK. "Treatment for child abusers." *Social Work,* 19 (1974): 338–42.

TUNNELL, J. Personal communication, 1982. Arlington Women's Shelter, Arlington, TX.

VANTRESS, F. E., and C. B. WILLIAMS "The effect of the presence of the provocator and the opportunity to counteraggress on systolic blood pressure." *The Journal of General Psychology,* 86 (1972): 63–68.

VRIJ, J. *Acta Physiolog. Pharm. Nurl,* 4 (1956): 524–31. Cited in M. B. Arnold, *The Nature of Emotion.* Baltimore: Penguin Books, 1968, p. 357.

WALKER, L. E. "Battered women and learned helplessness." *Victimology,* 2 (1977–78): 525–34.

————. *The Battered Woman.* New York: Harper & Row, 1979.

WATZALAWICK, P. "Brief family therapy." Workshop presented at Southwest Family Institute, Dallas, February 1981.

WEISS, R. L., and G. R. BIRCHLER. "Adults with marital dysfunction." In M. Herson and A. S. Bellack (eds.), *Behavior Therapy in the Psychiatric Setting.* Baltimore: Williams & Wilkins, 1978.

WELLISCH, D. K.; J. VINCENT; and G. K. RO-TROCK. "Family therapy versus individual therapy: A study of adolescents and their parents." In D. H. L. Olson (ed.), *Treating Relationships.* Lake Mills, IA: Graphic Publishing, 1976.

WHALEY, D. L., and R. W. MALOTT. *Elementary Principles of Behavior.* Englewood Cliffs, NJ: Prentice-Hall, 1968.

WILDER, J. "Sugar metabolism in its relation to criminology." In R. M. Lindner and R. V. Seliger (eds.), *Handbook of Correctional Psychology.* New York: Philosophical Library, 1947.

WOLFGANG, M. E., and F. FERRACUTI. *The Subculture of Violence.* London: Tavistock Publications, 1967.

WOLPE, J. *Psychotherapy by Reciprocal Inhibition.* Standford, CA: Standford University Press, 1958.

————. *The Practice of Behavior Therapy.* 2d ed. New York: Pergamon, 1973.

YOUNG, L. *Wednesday's Children: A Study of Child Neglect and Abuse.* New York: McGraw-Hill, 1964.

ZILLMAN, D.; A. H. KATCHER; and B. MILAVSKY. "Excitation transfer from physical exercise to subsequent aggressive behavior." *Journal of Experimental Social Psychology,* 8 (1972): 247–59.

ZUCKER, M. "Crime and diet." *Let's Live,* May 1979, pp. 57–62.

Index

The International
Transmission of Inflation

A National Bureau
of Economic Research
Monograph

The International
Transmission
of Inflation

Michael R. Darby
James R. Lothian
and
Arthur E. Gandolfi
Anna J. Schwartz
Alan C. Stockman

 The University of Chicago Press
Chicago and London

The University of Chicago Press, Chicago 60637
The University of Chicago Press, Ltd., London

Library of Congress Cataloging in Publication Data
Main entry under title:

The International transmission of inflation.

(A National Bureau of Economic Research monograph)
Includes indexes.
1. Inflation (Finance)—Addresses, essays, lectures.
2. International finance—Addresses, essays, lectures.
3. Inflation (Finance)—Mathematical models—Addresses,
essays, lectures.   4. International finance—Mathematical
models—Addresses, essays, lectures.   I. Darby, Michael R.
II. Series.
HG229.I63   1983   332.4'1   83-5785
ISBN 0-226-13641-8 (cloth)   0-226-13642-6 (paper)

To Jaye, Judy, Anna,
Isaac, and Cindy

Contents

Preface

In the spring of 1975 the industrialized world was in the midst of its second consecutive year of double-digit inflation, for most countries the highest rates of price increase at any time during the post–World War II period. Anna Schwartz and Michael Darby, dissatisfied with many of the explanations then being advanced for this increase in inflation and with the dearth of hard empirical evidence to support them, decided to organize a project to study the international inflation process. At the time both were at the National Bureau of Economic Research, then at its old location in New York. Darby, however, was slated to return to UCLA the coming fall. Two research teams were therefore to be formed: one based at the Bureau in New York, the other at UCLA. Jim Lothian joined the first effort; Ben Klein, the second.

In autumn 1976, the project began; close to five years later it ended when the final draft of this volume was completed in spring 1981. During that interval, two important developments occurred in personnel. The composition of the researchers in the group changed: Klein completed work on central bank reaction functions and decided to direct his research to other areas of economics; Alan Stockman, then at UCLA, took his place; and Arthur Gandolfi, of Citibank, came on in New York. In addition, the graduate students who started out as research assistants on the project matured intellectually and went on to make their own independent contributions to research on the international inflation topic. Besides the papers by Daniel Laskar, Dan Lee, and Mike Melvin, all derived from doctoral dissertations at UCLA and included in this volume, the project gave rise to dissertations by four other individuals: John Price at UCLA, Anthony Cassese and Nurhan Helvacian at the Graduate Center of the City University of New York, and Robert Greenfield at Rutgers University. We consider their successes no small part of the benefits of the project and take some pride of our own in their accomplishments.

As originally conceived, the project was to accomplish two goals: the construction of a consistent and temporally comprehensive data base for the eight major industrial countries we wished to study; and estimation of a theoretically sound simultaneous model that we could use to test and otherwise evaluate competing hypotheses about the genesis and spread of inflation internationally.

The project accomplished both goals. The four chapters that describe the work done in these areas, however, make up less than a quarter of the volume. Excluding the introductory and concluding chapters, there are eleven additional chapters that complement the core of the study, both in the range of issues covered and in the methods of investigation employed. Given this complementarity and the corroborative nature of much of the resultant evidence we feel that the study is of considerably greater value than it would have been had we and our colleagues stuck to our original plan. We trust that the readers will therefore be better able to calibrate their own internal probability calculators when evaluating our conclusions.

Before closing we wish to acknowledge those individuals and organizations that in one way or another assisted the project. Were we to list all of them here, the litany would seem virtually endless. Many individuals, however, have already been cited both in the individual chapters and in the Data Appendix.

The major source of direct funding for the project was the National Science Foundation. Scaife Family Charitable Trust, the Alex C. Walker Educational and Charitable Foundation, and the Relm Foundation also generously supported our efforts. In addition, Citibank, N.A., in an arrangement that to our knowledge is unique, donated one day per week of Lothian's time for the full period of the project's life and one day a week of Gandolfi's time during the period of his involvement. Leif H. Olsen, Harold van B. Cleveland, and Peter H. Crawford, who initiated and supported this arrangement, deserve special thanks.

We also are grateful to our adivsory panel. The members of this panel at various times during the life of the project were Sven Arndt, Michael Hamburger, Robert Heller, Donald Matthieson, Paul Craig Roberts, Guy Stevens, Henry Wallich, and Robert Weintraub. The role of this group was to counsel us on the relevant questions to be investigated and to receive and comment critically on our interim results. The members of the panel have performed these functions exceedingly well. Their approval of, or concurrence in, our results or conclusions, however, ought not be supposed. Indeed some members of the board have been frank in their sharp disagreement with certain of our methods and inferences.

We owe a special debt to the secretaries and research assistants who helped both of us in the course of our compiling various papers into a coherent whole and seeing the final manuscript through publication. Donna Bettini in New York and Henrietta Reason and Carole Wilbur did excellent jobs of typing a particularly difficult manuscript. Cornelia McCarthy did and does provide excellent research assistance in New York. Linda Dunn and Laura Nowak also were of great assistance before going into business and completing the Ph.D. degree, respectively. Andrew A. Vogel was a tower of strength in completing the Mark III and Mark IV estimations and simulations and is currently pursuing his doctoral studies. M. Holly Crawford did much of the preliminary work on these models before being lured away from economics by the astonishingly greener pastures of a successful career as an artist. Marilou J. Uy prepared the index. The project could never have been finished without such congenial co-workers.

Michael R. Darby and James R. Lothian

I Preliminaries

1   Introduction and Summary

Michael R. Darby and James R. Lothian

Inflation became the dominant economic, social, and political problem of the industrialized West during the 1970s. This book is about how the inflation came to pass and what can be done about it. To answer these questions, we must first discover the nature of the economic linkages which apparently transmitted inflation from country to country like a contagious disease. To accomplish this is a very tall order, but the interrelated and mutually supporting empirical studies reported in this volume go a long way toward filling it. This brave boast can be substantiated only by the studies themselves, but first we provide in this chapter an overview of our results and how we obtained them.

Our major conclusions can be summarized briefly. As to channels of transmission, both goods and assets are substitutable internationally but neither is perfectly so. The balance of payments has had no discernible effect on the American money supply, and at least partial sterilization has been a universal practice among nonreserve central banks although lagged adjustments of their money supplies to the balance of payments are noted. Currency substitution and the traditional absorption channel provide at most weak linkages, and the main transmission occurs via the balance-of-payments effects of goods and assets substitutability. Our empirical results thus offer support for the assumptions characterizing the portfolio-balance approach.

The major cause of the world inflation of the early 1970s was an upward trend in American monetary growth goals. As illustrated in table 1.1, the American inflation rate increased in the latter half of the 1960s but sterilization policies delayed the impact on the nonreserve countries until the beginning of the 1970s.[1] While the upward trend in American money

---

1. The initial resistance to the increased U.S. inflation may explain the larger increase in nonreserve inflation during 1971–75. On a decade-average basis, U.S. inflation increased by

Table 1.1   **Average Continuously Compounded Inflation Rates 1956–75**

Period[1]	United States[2]	Nonreserve Countries[3]	All Eight Countries[4]	Adjusted for Exchange-Rate Changes[5]	
				Nonreserve Countries	All Eight Countries
Quinquennia					
1956–60	2.28%	3.25%	2.74%	2.26%	2.27%
1961–65	1.66%	3.96%	2.74%	3.96%	2.74%
1966–70	4.32%	4.25%	4.29%	4.01%	4.18%
1971–75	6.74%	9.22%	7.90%	11.84%	9.13%
Decades					
1956–65	1.97%	3.60%	2.74%	3.11%	2.50%
1966–75	5.53%	6.74%	6.10%	7.92%	6.66%
Others					
1956–70	2.75%	3.82%	3.26%	3.41%	3.06%
1971–73I	4.50%	6.46%	5.41%	13.50%	8.71%
1973II–75	8.57%	11.48%	9.94%	10.48%	9.47%
1956–75	3.75%	5.17%	4.42%	5.52%	4.58%

1. All inflation rates are computed from the quarter preceding the indicated period to the quarter which ends the period (e.g. average logarithmic change from fourth quarter 1955 to fourth quarter 1960).

2. The basic price index is the GNP deflator.

3. The seven nonreserve countries are Canada, France, Germany, Italy, Japan, the Netherlands, and the United Kingdom. The deflators used are detailed in table 6.20 below. The seven-country price index is geometrically weighted by nominal income weights (see table 5.7 below).

4. The eight-country price index is geometrically weighted by nominal income weights (see table 5.7 below).

5. In these indexes, all nonreserve deflators were divided by the exchange rate (domestic currency/U.S. dollar) before the geometrically weighted average was computed.

growth cannot be definitely attributed to any particular factor, it does not appear to be responsive in any significant way to international variables. The major increases in oil prices occurring during 1973II–74I played a supporting role to money growth in explaining the more rapid inflation in the second half of 1971–75, but coincidental removal of general price controls in the United States and abroad may have been even more important. In the latter half of the 1970s, domestic inflation was determined by the monetary policy of each central bank and cannot be attributed directly to the United States except as the foreign central banks

3.56 percentage points from 1.97% for 1956–65 to 5.53% for 1966–75 while nonreserve inflation increased by 3.14 percentage points from 3.60% to 6.74%, respectively. Thus, the 1971–75 burst of nonreserve inflation may be a partial "catch-up" of the sort emphasized in Darby (1979): a lagged initial movement in the growth rate compensated for by subsequent overshooting. The last two columns of table 1.1 demonstrate that these patterns are despite—not due to—changes in exchange rates.

were reluctant to bear the costs of reducing the previously established inflation rate.

This evidence points to two policy conclusions. One has to do with the international monetary system; the other, which partially embraces the first, with the control of inflation. As we see it, a necessary and sufficient condition for a country to reduce its trend rate of inflation is a reduction in the trend rate of growth of its nominal stock of money. Our evidence indicates that the myriad of other palliatives that have been proposed in recent years and continue to be advocated in the popular press as well as in scholarly circles are beside the point.

The problem with the Bretton Woods system was that over time increases in monetary growth in the United States tended to spill over to other countries. Those countries that were more averse to inflation than the United States therefore abandoned pegged rates for floating. Those that wanted to inflate at an even faster pace did the same. Floating exchange rates are thus an integral part of an anti-inflation program in a nonreserve country confronted by inflationary policies abroad. And in our view they are the only viable longer-term alternative in a world in which domestic policy goals differ.

We see no effective means for any country to eliminate inflation without the political consensus to enforce a monetary constitution, be it de jure or de facto, that limits the ability of the central bank to print money. Our preference is for a fiat monetary standard with fixed money-supply growth, but a gold standard would also serve to provide long-run (if not short-run) stability. A third monetary constitution open to countries other than the United States would be to rigidly fix their exchange rates with a country constrained by an effective monetary constitution.

The strong empirical results summarized at the beginning of this chapter could be achieved only because of the creation of a major new data bank providing consistent quarterly series from 1955 through 1976 for the United States, the United Kingdom, Canada, France, Germany, Italy, Japan, and the Netherlands. James Lothian, who was responsible for its creation, describes this data bank in chapter 3. Complete documentation and listing are provided in the Data Appendix to this volume. The major advantages of the data bank are longer coverage and somewhat higher quality than the International Monetary Fund data which are the best alternative.

Two other chapters complete the preliminary part of this volume. In the earlier of these Anna Schwartz describes the historical evolution of—and revolutions in—the international monetary system. Even the expert practitioner will benefit from this review, particularly as it reminds us of events which appeared trivial at the time they happened but ultimately proved to have major consequences. The second remaining chapter of part I, by Anthony Cassese and James Lothian, concludes the preliminaries by beginning the empirical analysis.

Cassese and Lothian apply Granger-causality tests to a number of pairs of variables. This provides a direct method for eliminating a number of popular hypotheses from consideration and thus serves as a basis for the more structural approaches which follow it. Their tests of domestic money and prices, for example, effectively reject the hypothesis that prices adjust instantaneously via goods arbitrage and then money supplies adjust with a lag; in general the timing relation is just the reverse. The general lack of support for prices causing money is also contrary to the hypothesis that independent movements in wages or other costs have been accommodated by passive central banks. Comparison of nonreserve country prices with either American prices or an index of foreign prices provides little evidence of causality running in either direction. The strongest evidence for international transmission occurs in the asset markets, but even here nonreserve interest rates generally adjust over time rather than instantaneously to changes in American interest rates. There is some evidence of sterilization of reserve flows by offsetting changes in domestic credit, but the mostly contemporaneous nature of this issue is ill suited to the Granger tests.

The second part of the book reports the results of a major effort to build a medium-scale structural model which would permit the data to choose among the monetary, portfolio-balance, and Keynesian approaches.[2] Michael Darby and Alan Stockman in chapters 5 and 6 report on the specification and estimation of the Mark III International Transmission Model. In chapter 7, Darby uses a simplified simulation version of this model to draw out its implications for monetary and fiscal policy in the United States and the nonreserve countries. He uses the same model in chapter 8 to simulate the effect of the 1973–74 increase in the real price of oil. Chapter 9 is an extended digression on the Lucas-Barro real income equation used in the model with mixed success.

The Mark III International Transmission Model is specified and estimated in two versions, one corresponding to pegged and the other to floating exchange rates. There are sixty-seven behavioral equations in the former and seventy-four in the latter, with a nearly equal number of identities used to close each model. Each country is described by a

2. We use the term "monetary approach" to refer to the class of models in which goods, assets, or both are perfectly substitutable internationally so that the money supply adjusts under pegged exchange rates to equal the quantity demanded at the international parity values. The Keynesian approach refers to those that assume price and interest-rate linkages are negligible and concentrate instead on the absorption channel (increased foreign income implying increased domestic exports and vice versa). In between these extremes lies the portfolio-balance approach, which incorporates substantial but not perfect price and interest-rate linkages so that both foreign and domestic influences simultaneously determine a nonreserve country's money supply, prices, and interest rates.

domestic macroeconomic subsector and an international subsector. The domestic sector uses a rational-expectations/natural-rate approach to determine real income, the price level, and interest rates given exogenous real government spending and endogenous nominal money and exports. Nominal money is determined within the subsector by central bank reaction functions which are responsive to inflation, unemployment or transitory income, unexpected government spending, and (for the non-reserve countries only) the scaled balance of payments. The international subsector determines exports, imports, import prices, capital flows, the balance of payments, and (for the nonreserve countries in the floating version) the exchange rate. The model is specified so that goods or capital flows may overwhelm any attempt at independent nonreserve monetary policy, but whether this is so depends on the estimated values of various parameters. Other potential international linkages include a currency substitution channel in the money-demand functions, the traditional Keynesian absorption channel, and direct effects of the real price of oil.

The estimation of the Mark III International Transmission Model yielded some surprising results which can be summarized by the statement that linkages among countries joined by pegged exchange rates appear to be much looser or more elusive than has been assumed in many previous studies. In particular, substantial or complete sterilization of the contemporaneous balance of payments appears to be a universal practice among central banks so that domestic credit is properly treated as an endogenous variable. Sterilization policies increase these central banks' control of their domestic money supplies, which is made possible by the relatively weak substitutability of goods and assets as estimated in the trade and capital flows equations, respectively. Currency substitution does not appear to provide much of a link either: Foreign interest rates are statistically significant only in the British and Japanese money-demand functions, and the coefficients are very small in absolute magnitude.

The slow and weak international transmission estimated in the Mark III Model was explored further in a series of simulation experiments reported in chapter 7. First, a simplified simulation version, the Mark IV International Simulation Model, was created by dropping insignificant variables and combining terms where a priori hypotheses on equality of coefficients were not rejected by the data. The pegged version of the Mark IV Model is dynamically stable and appears to track the actual values of the variables well throughout the eight-year feasible simulation period. Unfortunately dynamic instabilities become important in the floating version after only seven quarters; this apparently reflects the impossibility of adequately eliminating simultaneous equation bias with the short sample available for some of the floating equations.

Two types of simulation experiments were designed to illustrate the model's implications for monetary and fiscal policy. Care was taken that the experiments were consistent with the actual evolution of nominal money and real government spending in the sample period: The money experiments involved a one-quarter increase in the disturbance of a given country's money-supply reaction function, and the government spending experiments considered a one-quarter increase in unexpected real government spending. The less reliable data for France, Italy, and Japan yielded mutually inconsistent results here as in a number of other instances reported in this volume. Accordingly, the discussion centers on the other five countries.

Under pegged exchange rates, only the German simulations indicated an immediate if partial movement in the money supply in response to the American money-supply shock. The Netherlands money supply also adjusted but with a lag, while the British and Canadian money supplies seemed unaffected by American monetary policy. These results reflect the weakness of both the estimated international linkages among countries and the liquidity effect on domestic interest rates. British and German money-supply shock experiments both indicated considerable control of their respective domestic money supplies at least for the first several years.

The instability of the floating version model precluded much substantive discussion, but the American money shock experiment was reported to illustrate a possibly perverse effect of the estimated J curves in import demand equations. Because short-run price elasticity of import demand is much smaller than in the long run, the immediate effect of a depreciation is to increase the value of imports and so worsen the balance of trade. In the simulations reported, this J-curve phenomenon in a general equilibrium setting implied that some other currencies initially *depreci*ated in response to an unexpected increase in the American money supply.

The experiments involving shocks to government spending indicated the largest temporary effects for the American case where the shock implied a permanent increase in the level of real government spending and an induced increase in the money supply. The total multiplier amounted to about 1.5 in the quarter of maximum impact. In the British case, government spending was permanently increased by only about half of the initial shock and even using this small base the peak multiplier is only about 0.75 because of perverse effects of induced money-supply changes. No significant effects were estimated in the German case. Only the American fiscal shock had significant international repercussions, and those seemed to be due as much to the increased American money supply as to the induced increases in foreign exports.

In chapter 8 Darby attempts to assess the role of oil price increases in the 1970s world inflation. A formal analysis focuses on the two channels by which an effect on the price level might occur: induced decreases in the real quantity of money demanded and induced increases in the nominal quantity of money supplied. The major result is that the theoretical, estimated, and simulated results are not at all robust to changes in specification: The effect on the price *level* could be as little as 0 or as much as 5%; in terms of inflationary trends over say four years, this implies only a range of 0 to 1¼% effect on the average inflation rate. Reference to table 1.1 will illustrate the sense in which this range implies that the oil price shock played at most a supporting role in explaining the 1971–75 increase in the world inflation rate.

The main reason for the ambiguity in the estimated and simulated price-level effect of the oil price shock is the coincidental removal of general price controls in a number of countries. On the whole, those countries which removed price controls during 1973–74 are also those for which we obtain a significant decrease in real income (and so real money demand) as a result of the 1973–74 oil price increase. Only future research can unravel whether these estimated oil price effects are real or a statistical illusion due to overstatement of measured real income and understatement of the increased price level due to price controls.[3]

A disturbing feature of the Mark III Model was the relatively poor explanatory power of the real-income equation for nonreserve countries. This equation explains the growth rate of real income by lagged logarithmic transitory income and current and lagged values of the shocks (innovations) in nominal money, real government spending, and real exports. It is thus an extended version of Barro's approach to solving a standard aggregate demand curve in conjunction with the Lucas aggregate supply function. Experiments reported in this chapter show that distributed lags on the actual rather than unexpected value of the aggregate demand variables do no better for the nonreserve countries and worse for the United States. While the relatively poor nonreserve country results may be due to greater measurement problems, these results do suggest a cautious approach toward application of the Barro-Lucas equation.

The third part of this volume continues examination of the degree to which national economies are linked in statistical environments other than the Mark III and IV Models. The authors of these four chapters either apply a relatively model-free approach or else use smaller-scale models so that the results are more simply interpreted. Darby and Laskar in chapters 10 and 11, respectively, both test for the exercise of monetary control by nonreserve central banks under pegged exchange rates. They

---

3. As price controls are removed and hidden price increases measured, removal of understatement in the deflators would cause a decrease in reported real output and an increase in the reported price level.

show that previous tests were biased by failure to control for sterilization and that monetary control was in fact exercised by these central banks. The implied ability of sterilized intervention to affect floating exchange rates is developed by Dan Lee in a dynamic portfolio-balance model. In chapter 13, Michael Melvin provides further empirical evidence for the portfolio-balance approach by introducing exchange-rate risk covariance measures implied by the international-asset-pricing model.

In chapter 10, Darby develops a convenient expositional model which includes as special cases variants of the monetary approach both with and without sterilization. This framework makes domestic credit, which is endogenous with sterilization, a superfluous concept. The analysis illustrates two points: (1) Factors (other than the current balance of payments) appearing in the nominal-money reaction function will be uncorrelated with actual growth in nominal money if either variant of the monetary approach holds. (2) Expectational instability may imply a limited feasible range within which monetary control can be exercised.

The first of these two conclusions underlies Darby's empirical test of the null hypothesis that the nonreserve countries did not exercise control over their domestic money supplies. This hypothesis could be rejected at the 5% level or better for six of the seven countries, the exception being the Netherlands.

Laskar specifies a set of small-scale models to test whether offsetting capital flows defeat attempts by partially sterilizing central banks to exercise monetary control. The "offset coefficient" is significantly less than the no-control value for six countries at the 5% level and for Canada at the 10% level. Laskar goes further to measure the fraction of a shift in the money-supply reaction function which will actually be reflected in money growth when account is taken of the extent (always significant) to which the central bank sterilizes the induced capital flows. He finds that this fraction is always significantly greater than 0 and in no case significantly less than 1.

Because of dynamic instabilities, the floating version of the Mark IV International Simulation Model is relatively uninformative on the effects of nonreserve monetary and exchange policy. Dan Lee provides a theoretical analysis of the effects of foreign exchange and open market operations consistent with imperfect substitutability of assets and strong expectational effects on interest rates. He reconciles long-run neutrality with differential short-run effects on exchange rates and interest rates of the two means of creating money. Of particular interest is his analysis of the lack of overshooting in the exchange rate if rational inflation expectations cause the nominal interest rate to rise during the adjustment to an unexpected increase in the money supply.

Michael Melvin demonstrates that it is feasible to specify proxies for exchange-rate risk which are consistent with standard finance theory and also contribute significantly to the explanatory power of net-capital-flow equations in the partial adjustment formulation. His attempts to replace the capital-flows equations in the Mark III Model with his own formulation proved unsuccessful, however, as a consequence of the absence of a satisfactory correlation between the risk variables and the instrument variables. When Melvin uses an alternative data set covering 1973–78, the empirical dominance of his formulation improves over standard formulations. His results thus provide single-equation estimation results supportive of the empirical value of the portfolio approach.

Part IV addresses the question of what were the causes of the inflation of the late 1960s and the 1970s in the United States and our other seven industrialized countries. In chapter 14, Gandolfi and Lothian use a reduced-form price equation derived along the lines of Barro (1978) to assess the relative roles of domestic money, international price and monetary developments, and oil price changes. Next Darby shows that purchasing-power parity can be a useful paradigm for understanding the harmonization of inflationary trends even though the predictability of the purchasing-power ratio deteriorates over time. The same analysis explains why monetary growth variations may explain nearly all variations in trend inflation rates despite random permanent shifts in the money-demand function such as reported by Gandolfi and Lothian. In chapter 16, Darby confirms their findings that American money-supply growth has evolved independently of foreign influences and goes further to show that variations in American money growth explain practically all variations in American inflation trends. Thus an exogenous rise in American inflationary trends operating primarily via monetary channels to maintain purchasing-power-parity growth trends is found to be the dominant source of the inflation which infected the industrialized West in the early 1970s.

Specifically, in chapter 14 Gandolfi and Lothian combine a Lucas aggregate supply function and a conventional money-demand function to obtain a reduced-form price equation in nominal money, permanent income, the long-term interest rate, and a distributed lag on money-supply shocks. International factors enter these basic equations only indirectly through expected money supply as lagged scaled balances of payments or American money growth are found significant as predictors of current money growth. The authors tried adding foreign variables which might shift the aggregate supply function directly into their basic price equations: the real price of oil, a world commodity price index, the American price deflator, and a rest-of-world price index. These variables were generally insignificant although the oil price was significant in nearly all of the cases examined. The estimated fraction of total inflation attributable to oil price increases had a median value of only 15% for 1973–74, or 9% over the longer period of 1973–76.[4] In summary Gandolfi and Lothian's results indicate that domestic monetary developments rather than foreign price movements were the dominant *proximate* determinant of price behavior with at most a supporting role for the oil price increase even during 1973–74.

In chapter 15, Darby focuses on the statistical paradox that the variance of average growth rate of the purchasing-power ratio goes to 0 as the prediction interval increases while the variance of the *level* of the same ratio goes to infinity. He uses data from 1971 through 1978 to illustrate that substantial variations in the level of the purchasing-power ratio may occur even though the (exchange-rate converted) reserve country inflation rate adequately explains the domestic inflation rates in the nonreserve countries. The point is to illustrate the dominance of systematic factors in trend inflation despite the presence of significant random-walk elements moving other price levels relative to that of the United States.

Darby elaborates this theme further in chapter 16. First, he shows that world inflation trends are determined exogenously under pegged exchange rates within the reserve-currency country if both its nominal money-supply growth and its real money-demand growth are unresponsive to foreign influences. The American money-supply reaction function is explored at length in search of a response to either gold flows or the balance of payments on a official reserves settlement basis. Since only insignificant and generally perverse effects of these variables are estimated, the conclusion is that American nominal money growth is indeed exogenous with respect to foreign influences. Finally, Darby turns to the question of whether or not the foreign influences on American real money demand detected with quarterly data have any significant influence on its trend growth rate. While a substantial fraction (40 to 20%) of the variance of inflation cannot be explained by nominal money growth using quarterly, annual, or biennial observations, this fraction drops to only 3% for quadrennial observations. Thus factors—domestic or foreign—other than nominal money growth variations play no appreciable role in explaining variations in either the growth rate of the real quantity of money demanded or the American inflation rate.

We conclude that American inflation caused by the Federal Reserve System was an exogenous source of world inflationary trends. Because of the unwillingness of their central banks to appreciate or float their currencies until in extremis, the nonreserve countries too caught the American disease. The lag of the nonreserve countries behind the American lead noted previously in table 1.1 reflects the operation of a slower specie-flow

---

4. These numbers are for the estimates made with a second-order autoregressive correction.

mechanism rather than the smooth contemporaneous adjustment posited by the monetary approach. This mechanism may have accentuated the variability of the nonreserve inflation rates during the catch-up period of the early 1970s as increasing balance-of-payments surpluses finally induced very rapid money-supply growth.

We opened this chapter with a summary of the conclusions that we have drawn from the research reported both in this volume and by others. Those conclusions and the reasons for them are presented in detail in the final chapter. If the research reported here has gone a long way toward answering basic questions about linkages among countries and the causes and cures of the recent inflation, it is only because there was so much to do. More remains to be done, and we close by outlining a program of promising areas for future research.

Acknowledgments

The authors have benefited in drafting this chapter from conversations with the other contributors to this volume but are solely responsible for any opinions expressed here.

References

Barro, R. J. 1978. Unanticipated money, output, and the price level in the United States. *Journal of Political Economy* 86 (August): 549–80.

Darby, M. R. 1979. *Intermediate macroeconomics*. New York: McGraw-Hill.

2 The Postwar Institutional Evolution of the International Monetary System

Anna J. Schwartz

The international monetary system that was designed at the Bretton Woods Conference in 1944 reflected professional views on the defects of the arrangements that had prevailed in the 1930s. Protectionist trade policies, exchange controls, and competitive currency depreciations[1] of the pre–World War II period were the cautionary experiences to be avoided by the postwar world. Removal of controls on trade and payments under a system of fixed exchange rates, with adjustment of parities limited to "fundamental" disequilibrium in the balance of payments, accordingly were the goals of the system created by the delegates to the conference. Exchange rates were to be pegged within narrow margins to the dollar. Countries would buy or sell dollars in the foreign exchange market to keep their currencies from appreciating or depreciating more than 1% from parity. The United States in turn would undertake to convert dollars into gold or the reverse at a fixed price of $35 an ounce. The International Monetary Fund, to which each member subscribed 25% of its quota in gold or 10% of its net official reserves of gold and dollars, whichever was smaller, was established by the terms of the Bretton Woods charter. It was expected that lending facilities of the Fund would be available to supplement the members' gold and foreign exchange reserves to provide them liquidity when their balances-of-payments were temporarily in deficit on current account.

The establishment of par values for currencies was an important item on the Fund's agenda. Of our sample of countries, Canada, France, the Netherlands, the United Kingdom, and the United States declared their par values in December 1946, Germany and Japan in 1953, and Italy not until 1960. Some of these parities were short-lived. An abortive attempt

1. We share the view of Harry G. Johnson (1978) expressed in *Exchange Rate Flexibility*: "It is not clear, actually, that there was much competitive devaluation even in the 1930's."

at convertibility of sterling in 1947 ended in September 1949, when the pound was devalued. The Netherlands thereupon devalued the guilder, and France, which had had separate rates for financial and commercial transactions, unified them, depreciating the franc vis-à-vis sterling.

The pegged exchange-rate system that was created collapsed in 1971.[2] Following futile efforts to restore it, in 1973 governments reluctantly turned to managed floating exchange rates. In both regimes, the United States served as the reserve-currency country, other countries primarily holding dollar assets among their international reserves.

Discussion of the institutions of the international monetary system is instructive for all the theoretical channels of international transmission of price change. One of these is completely monetary in nature and is therefore directly affected by the character of the international monetary system; the other three are nonmonetary, or in one instance only partially monetary, and hence may be only indirectly affected. The four channels are (1) international money flows as a result of international payments imbalances that affect the growth of national money supplies and eventually rates of price change; (2) direct effects on national prices and interest rates through international arbitrage of prices of goods and services or of interest rates as a result either of changes in the world quantity of money and prices or of cost factors independent of monetary conditions; (3) shifts in foreign demand for a country's output that affect its prices; (4) effects on prices of changes in international basic commodity supplies. Some comments on each of the channels follow.

1. The money-flow channel was undoubtedly available during the postwar period. For the moment consider only the non-reserve-currency countries in the international monetary system.

Under a pegged exchange-rate system, central banks must buy from or sell to their nationals foreign exchange, according as countries face a surplus or a deficit in the balance of payments. Central banks may also choose to do so under a managed floating exchange-rate regime. Whenever a central bank buys foreign exchange, it issues newly created high-powered money—usable as reserves by banks or currency by the public—just as if it had purchased government securities in an open market operation or bankers' promissory notes through discounting. Conversely, a sale of foreign exchange destroys high-powered money just as does a reduction in the central bank's portfolio of securities or discounts. For this reason, a balance-of-payments surplus is a source of increase, a balance-of-payments deficit a source of decrease in high-powered money in a strictly arithmetic, or accounting, sense. If, however, the central bank offsets (sterilizes) the effect of a bal-

---

2. Foreshadowing that breakdown were the revaluations of the deutsche mark in October 1969 and the return to floating, albeit of a heavily manged sort, of the Canadian dollar in May 1970.

ance-of-payments surplus by reducing its portfolio of domestic securities and discounts, or increasing it less than it otherwise would, there is no effect on the growth rate of high-powered money. The sources of growth in high-powered money then are flows of international reserves and domestic credit creation by the central bank. It was thus possible for a non-reserve-currency country either to accept imported inflation or deflation, or for a time to resist such an outcome by sterilizing under pegged exchange rates.[3] Under floating rates, the country had the additional option of varying its exchange rate to protect its price level.

For the U.S., the reserve-currency country, the effect of deficits in its balance of payments had no necessary contractionary effect on Federal Reserve policies under either exchange system. The acquisition of dollars by foreign central banks did not reduce U.S. high-powered money. Dollars were either credited to the balance of those banks at Federal Reserve banks or else committed to the purchase of U.S. Treasury debt. Until March 1968, the gold requirement to which Federal Reserve notes were subject may have served as a constraint, but once abolished there was no legal limitation on the creation of high-powered money or money-supply growth, even after the 1970s, when the Federal Reserve system began specifying targets for growth rates of money.

Until U.S. monetary policy shifted to an inflationary course in the mid-1960s, deficits in the U.S. balance of payments provided the rest of the world with desired dollars. After the shift occurred, the defense of sterilizing undesired additions to dollar holdings as the U.S. balance of payments deteriorated was eventually overwhelmed by the magnitude of the required operation. Given the commitment to pegged exchange rates that surplus countries were reluctant to break by revaluing, dollars increased their high-powered money stocks and inflation rates. In the absence of such a commitment and the adoption of flexible exchange rates, short-run independence of national high-powered money stocks is increased.[4]

2. The operation of the arbitrage channels of transmission requires a high degree of, and in the extreme perfect, substitutability of goods and financial assets among countries.[5] Applied to the goods markets, the perfect-substitutability view is usually described as the "law of one price level." Another approach stresses the effects of changes in wages, exter-

3. Laskar in chapter 11 provides a particularly thorough econometric investigation of this sterilization question. Cassese and Lothian in chapter 4 and Darby and Stockman in chapter 6 also present evidence relevant to this issue.

4. Some, however, view currency substitution and asset substitution as limiting national monetary independence even under floating exchange rates. See, for instance, Miles (1978) and Brittain (1981). The Darby and Stockman investigation of this question in chapter 6, however, lends considerably less support to these propositions.

5. See section 17.2 for a summary of the evidence on the arbitrage channel contained in various papers in this volume.

nal prices, and productivity on the two sectors of tradable versus nontradable goods which characterize open economies. The law of one price level, or the "goods arbitrage approach," emphasizes the impact of world monetary growth on the rise in prices; the second approach emphasizes "structural" factors that allow no such role for monetary conditions. Restrictions on international trade and capital flows obviously block the operation of this channel, which denies the degree of autonomy to individual countries attributed to them by the first channel under fixed exchange rates. Even if international equalizing of tradable goods prices is assumed, inflation rates can differ between countries if relative prices of traded and nontraded goods vary. Under flexible exchange rates, transmission of a different sort may occur because an immediate change in the foreign exchange value of domestic money, as a result of expectations of future domestic monetary policy, will affect domestic money prices of imports and tradable goods and thus the domestic inflation rate.[6] For the alternative approach, exchange-rate changes may provide a signal to price and wage setters of changes in economic conditions.

3. Monetary growth plays no direct role in the operation of this or the following channel. Downward shifts in foreign demand for a country's output lead to declines in prices, output, and incomes, through a contractionary multiplier effect; upward shifts, to increases in prices, output, and incomes, through an expansionary multiplier effect.[7] This channel may be important under fixed exchange rates for particular countries, for example, the effects of U.S. real income changes on the demand for Canadian exports, or of German real income changes on the demand for Austrian exports, but not necessarily so for the transmission from the U.S. to European countries. Floating exchange rates may decrease the magnitude of the effects through this channel.

4. Transmission through this channel occurs because the rise in prices of basic commodities is viewed as entering either as supply components of products initially unaffected and raising their prices also or by pulling up the prices of substitute domestic inputs. Prices in all countries are affected, the effect depending on the input weights of these commodities in each economy. Some proponents of the importance of this channel also view exchange-rate changes as affecting export and import prices of basic commodities.

Although thus far only the pegged and managed floating exchange-rate regimes have been mentioned, it is useful to distinguish four subperiods in the evolution of the international monetary system from 1955 to date: (1) the preconvertibility phase for nondollar currencies, 1955–58; (2) the

---

6. Frenkel and Mussa (1981) discuss this and other channels.
7. The deterioration in the U.S. current account in 1971 has been identified by Harry G. Johnson (1972) as a source of increased demand by U.S. residents for foreign goods and services that raised their prices.

heyday of the Bretton Woods dollar-exchange standard, 1959–67; (3) the weakening and ensuing collapse of the Bretton Woods arrangements, 1968–73; (4) the managed floating exchange-rate phase, 1973 to date.

For each of the subperiods we shall summarize developments that relate to the channels of international transmission of price change.

2.1 Preconvertibility, 1955–58

In 1955, when our data begin, postwar recovery in Europe was well under way. Wartime destruction and disruption in Europe and Asia left the countries there with limited productive capacity and swelled the immediate postwar demand for U.S. exports. Restrictions against dollar transactions were widespread, and multiple exchange rates were not unusual. In the postwar years before 1955, important steps had been taken to develop a system of multilateral trade and payments for Western European countries. Of these, the most significant was the establishment in the summer of 1950, with U.S. support, of the European Payments Union (EPU). Before 1950, the conduct of trade and payments among members of the EPU as well as with non-European countries was on a bilateral basis. By contrast, under the EPU, every month the multilateral net debtor-creditor position of each member with respect to other members was determined. The dollar served as the unit of account, and each European currency was pegged at a fixed dollar parity with no band of admissible variation. Receipts and payments were expressed as claims against the clearing union, debtors paying a gradually increasing fraction of their deficits in gold or dollars, with creditor countries extending the balance as a loan to the EPU. Maximum credit lines for debtor countries were imposed, so that creditor countries were assured of eventual payment in gold or dollars.

Paralleling the adoption of the clearing union, a trade liberalization program among members advanced. In trade with the United States, however, European countries applied discriminatory tariff and quota restrictions, which the United States did not protest, in order to enable them to accumulate gold and dollar assets. It was expected that the dollar gap problem, which in 1955 was widely regarded as a long-term one, would thereby be mitigated.

In private gold markets until 1953, the price of gold was at a premium, but the IMF required monetary authorities to refrain from selling gold at premium prices. In March 1954, several months after the premium had been eliminated, reflecting balance of supply and demand, the London gold market reopened. For the rest of the decade the price of gold in private markets remained at $35 an ounce.

Faced with deficits in its current account in 1957–58, France imposed import restrictions, devalued at the end of 1958, and borrowed mainly from the United States, supplemented by EPU and IMF credits, which were conditioned on a ceiling on public expenditures and the budget deficit, as well as restrictive monetary policy by the Banque de France.

Until 1958, all foreign exchange transactions required the approval of central banks, which were the agents under the EPU for arranging settlements. They were thus well positioned to maintain exchange controls and payments restrictions. With the dissolution of the EPU on 24 December 1958, fifteen Western European countries (including the five in our sample) made their currencies convertible for current transactions. It was not until 1961, however, that restrictions against U.S. exports were removed. Most countries maintained strict controls against capital outflows. Only Germany in 1957 authorized its residents to export capital in any form anywhere in the world and permitted nonresidents to convert the proceeds of capital transactions in D-marks into any other currency.

Japan's recovery from the war was less rapid than that of the Western European countries. Its current account remained in deficit until the mid-1960s, and it continued exchange and capital flow restrictions until 1964.

Canada enjoyed special status in the international system. Although the IMF, in line with the prevailing U.S. view, set fixed exchange rates as the monetary regime par excellence, it tolerated the decision made by Canada in 1950 to float its dollar. Canada did not revert to a fixed rate until 1962. The reason for floating was to resist the inflationary effects that U.S. capital inflows produced under fixed exchange rates.[8]

2.2   The Heyday of the Bretton Woods Dollar-Exchange Standard, 1959–67

With the return of many European currencies to convertibility in 1958, the achievement of the Bretton Woods conception of international monetary normalcy seemed only a matter of time. The outflow of dollars in U.S. official aid, military spending, and private investment, and economic recovery in Europe and Japan had enabled foreigners to add to their holdings of dollars and gold. Apart from the 1950–51 Korean War upsurge, U.S. prices were generally stable until the middle of the 1960s, and their rate of rise generally lower than in the rest of the world (table 2.1). Money supplies in the rest of the world (except in the U.K.) grew at a faster rate than in the U.S. (table 2.2).

Part of the difference between this generally faster monetary growth in the rest of the world than in the United States was not reflected in a difference in inflation rates. Real income growth in general was much more rapid in Europe and Japan, which were still recovering from the

---

8. See Paul Wonnacott (1965) for a discussion of the Canadian float during this period.

Table 2.1   Quarterly Rates of Change of Consumer Prices at Annual Rates (percent per year)

Period[†]	CA[§]	FR	GE	IT	JA	NE	UK	US
1955I–58IV	2.02	5.37	2.05	2.01	0.88	3.32	3.75	2.04
1958IV–67IV	2.07	3.54	2.41	3.61	4.99	3.32	2.86	1.73
1967IV–73I	4.13	5.57	4.45	4.58	5.87	6.17	6.86	4.58
1973I–76IV	8.85	10.68	4.89	16.09	13.19	8.92	16.36	7.95

[†]All rates are computed from the first quarter of each period to the quarter which ends the period. Periods mark changes in international monetary institutions.

[§]Throughout this volume the following country mnemonics are used:

CA	Canada	JA	Japan
FR	France	NE	Netherlands
GE	Germany	UK	United Kingdom
IT	Italy	US	United States

Table 2.2   Quarterly Rates of Change of Money[†] at Annual Rates (percent per year)

Period[§]	CA	FR	GE	IT	JA	NE	UK	US
1955I–58IV	5.67	8.74	10.52	11.96	17.11	5.27	−0.46	3.34
1958IV–67IV	6.79	12.15	8.01	13.26	17.41	7.90	6.00	5.83
1967IV–73I	10.97	9.40	12.75	14.02	18.11	11.98	11.09	8.09
1973I–76IV	16.21	12.99	5.07	19.29	13.16	15.01	11.52	8.62

[†]Money is defined as currency plus adjusted demand and time deposits held by the public.

[§]All rates of change computed from the first quarter of each subperiod to the quarter which ends the subperiod.

war. Furthermore in some of these countries at least the income elasticity of demand for money was higher than in the U.S. (See Gandolfi and Lothian, chapter 14, for estimates.) That some difference in inflation was actually maintained over long periods without devaluations may be due to changes in the relative prices of tradable to nontradable goods in these more rapidly growing economies. Differences over shorter periods, particularly during the early 1970s, are explainable in terms of lags in the operation of U.S. reserve flows on monetary growth in the nonreserve countries.

The dollar's status as the reserve currency of the international economy seemed impregnable during these years. Commercial banks and private firms could make foreign payments in their convertible currencies without the approval of central banks. Tariff and quota restrictions on commodity trade among the industrialized countries were eased, and foreign trade grew at a rapid rate during the period. International transfers of capital grew, with New York at the center of the flows and the dollar as the vehicle currency in which the borrowers obtained capital and the investors lent their savings.

The successful operation of the system depended on foreign central banks intervening with their own currencies against the dollar to maintain par values and the United States standing ready to buy or sell gold at $35 per ounce in transactions with foreign monetary authorities. The U.S. balance of payments accordingly was determined by the exchange parities other countries established. In general, other countries desired surpluses that would add to their dollar reserves, and the system tended to produce a steadily weakening U.S. balance of payments and growing doubts about the sustainability of the U.S. gold convertibility commitment.

2.2.1   Gold and the Dollar

A portent of the troubled future of the system was that 1960 was the first year in which U.S. gold reserves declined below the level of its total liquid liabilities to all foreign holders of assets denominated in dollars (table 2.3).

Until March 1961, the U.S. intervened to maintain the price of gold by selling and buying dollars. Concern over the continuing conversion of dollars into gold led the Treasury to activate the Exchange Stabilization Fund. In its initial operations on 13 March 1961, acting through the Federal Reserve Bank of New York as its agent, the Fund sold forward D-marks to reduce the premium on that currency.[9] On 13 February 1962 the bank was also authorized to buy or sell foreign currencies on behalf of the Federal Open Market Committee in both spot and forward markets. For this purpose a stock of foreign currencies in addition to those acquired from the Stabilization Fund was needed. The Federal Reserve therefore negotiated a network of swap facilities with the central banks of other countries. The swap provided a specified amount of foreign currency in exchange for an equivalent dollar credit for the foreign central bank, with each party protected against loss from a change in the par value of the other party's currency. Invested balances of both parties earned the same rate of interest, foreign balances in special U.S. Treasury certificates, Federal Reserve balances in interest-earning deposits abroad. Balances were available for payments to the other party or for foreign exchange market transactions. The swap was a credit line, usually for three-month periods, renewable at maturity. By drawing on the credit, both parties initially raised their gross reserves. The Federal Reserve normally used the proceeds of a swap to absorb foreign official dollar holdings; these transactions in effect provided forward cover to foreign official dollarholders, reducing their incentive to convert dollars into gold.

---

9. See "Treasury and Federal Reserve Foreign Exchange Operations," in the September 1962 *Federal Reserve Bulletin* (pp. 1138–53), for a discussion of the system's role in the gold market during this period.

Table 2.3   **United States Monetary Gold Stock**
             and Liquid Liabilities to Foreigners
             (millions of dollars)

End of Year (1)	Total Monetary Gold Stock[†] (2)	Total Liquid Liabilities to All Foreigners[‡] (3)
1954	21,793	12,454
1955	21,753	13,524
1956	22,058	15,291
1957	22,857	15,825
1958	20,582	16,845
1959	19,507	19,428
1960	17,804	⎰20,994 ⎱21,027
1961	16,947	⎰22,853 ⎱22,936
1962	16,057	24,068
1963	15,596	⎰26,361 ⎱26,322
1964	15,471	⎰28,951 ⎱29,002
1965	13,806[§]	29,115
1966	13,235	⎰29,904 ⎱29,779
1967	12,065	⎰33,271 ⎱33,119
1968	10,892	⎰33,828 ⎱33,614
1969	11,859	⎰41,735 ⎱41,894
1970	11,072	⎰43,291 ⎱43,242
1971	10,206	⎰64,166 ⎱64,223
1972	10,487[#]	78,680
1973	11,652[††]	87,620
1974	11,652	120,325[§§]
1975	11,599	127,432[§§]
1976	11,598	152,468[§§]

Sources:

Col. (2), *Treasury Bulletin*, December 1965, IFS-1; July 1975, IFS-1; February 1982, IFS-1.

Col. (3), *Treasury Bulletin*, July 1975, IFS-2; February 1982, IFS-2.

[†]The stock includes gold sold to the U.S. by the IMF with the right of repurchase, and gold deposited by the IMF to mitigate the impact on the U.S. of foreign purchases for the purpose of making gold subscriptions to the IMF under quota increases.

[§]The figure excludes $259 million gold subscription to the IMF in June 1965 for a U.S. quota increase that became effective 23 February 1966.

Repayments of short-term swap credits meant a corresponding decline in gross reserves. For the U.S. this could entail a loss of gold. To deter this eventuality, the U.S. began issuing nonmarketable bonds, with maturities of fifteen months to two years, denominated in the holder's currency, to fund outstanding swap debt. The bonds were, however, convertible into Treasury bills on demand.[10]

A further indication of U.S. concern about gold was the prohibition after mid-1961 on the holding of gold outside the U.S. by U.S. firms and households, and on 3 March 1965 the abolition of gold reserve requirements against Federal Reserve deposits.

A focus of pressure on the U.S. dollar was the London gold market. In March 1960, the price rose above $35 an ounce, as European central banks and private investors bought gold for dollars. The Bank of England sold gold to stabilize the price, but the U.S. Treasury initially was not willing to restore the bank's holdings. Hence, when a rise in the price of gold occurred in October, the bank did not intervene. On 27 October, with the price reaching $40 an ounce, the Treasury agreed to sell gold to the bank, reserving for the bank the decision on intervention in the market. European central banks soon after agreed to refrain from buying gold in the London market for monetary purposes whenever the price rose above $35.20, the U.S. price plus shipping costs. When the price fell below that level in 1961, the central banks returned to the market. However, in October 1961, when the price again was reacting to heightened demand, an agreement to create a "gold pool" was reached among the U.S. and seven European governments. Each member undertook to supply an agreed portion of net gold sales to stabilize the market, as the Bank of England as agent of the group determined to be appropriate. The members of the pool subsequently agreed not to buy gold individually on the market, but to give the Bank of England the right to buy on their joint account when gold supply exceeded demand, the amount purchased to be distributed in proportion to each country's contribution to the pool. The

---

10. In addition, the United States issued nonmarketable bonds, starting in 1963.

---

‡The total includes small amounts due to the IMF arising from gold transactions, amounts due to official institutions, commercial banks abroad, to other foreigners, and to nonmonetary and regional organizations. Nonliquid liabilities to official institutions included in the source beginning 1962 through 1973 have been deducted. Years for which two entries are shown show differences because of changes in reporting coverage. Figures on the first line are comparable to figures for preceding dates; figures on the second line are comparable to those for the following dates.

#Change in par value of dollar on 8 May 1972 increased the value of the total gold stock by $822 million.

††Change in par value of dollar on 18 October 1973 increased the value of the gold stock by $1,165 million.

§§Includes categories of liabilities previously classified as nonliquid.

pool functioned until the end of 1967, when a surge of buying led to the suspension of the agreement in March 1968. During the period of the pool's operation, the participants sold a net of $2.5 billion of gold on the London market, of which $1.6 billion was provided by the United States.

2.2.2   The Dollar's Performance

A key development for the international monetary system that was not perceived as such at the time was the acceleration of the U.S. monetary growth rate and the subsequent acceleration of the U.S. inflation rate in the final years of this subperiod. What was perceived was the cumulative growth of deficits in the U.S. balance of payments. Assets denominated in dollars grew in excess of the demand for them by the rest of the world. Their conversion into gold, by shrinking U.S. gold reserves, threatened one of the basic underpinnings of the Bretton Woods structure, namely, convertibility of dollars into gold.

One measure the U.S. authorities might have taken was a raise in the dollar price of gold, thus increasing the value of the stock and the flow of reserve assets. If other countries did not follow suit by adopting a proportional increase in the price of gold in their currencies, the U.S. in this way might have obtained a devaluation of the dollar that the Bretton Woods system otherwise ruled out. Had the price of gold risen, the gold demands of other countries might have been satisfied without the rundown in U.S. reserve assets. Some countries might also have revalued because of the inflationary consequences of their payments surplus, given the gold-based increase in their asset holdings.

The U.S., however, resolutely opposed a change in the monetary price of gold. Such action would have required an Act of Congress which would have produced a long and unsettling debate in the two Houses, during which time the foreign exchange markets would have been disturbed. Moreover, there was no assurance that other countries would not make corresponding changes in their own par values, and it was feared that confidence in the stability of the monetary system would be seriously impaired by a change in the official dollar price of gold. Given the fixed price of gold when national price levels were rising, gold became an undervalued asset with a resulting gold shortage.

The Bretton Woods system might have been able to survive an end of gold convertibility. It could not survive inflationary monetary policy in the center country that characterized the decade from the mid-1960s on. Crisis management by the IMF and the central banks of the leading industrialized countries became the hallmark of the international monetary system during the heyday of Bretton Woods.[11] The chief currency

11. Margaret de Vries (1976).

under pressure, apart from the dollar, was sterling. Persistent or recurring U.K. balance-of-payments deficits impaired the credibility of sterling's external value, already insecure by reason of the size of sterling balances held worldwide relative to U.K. gold and foreign exchange reserves. Private agents displayed lack of confidence in the dollar and sterling by shifting to currencies whose external values were regarded as stable or likely to appreciate (during this period, the D-mark and guilder). Repeated rescue operations to support the exchange value of sterling were overwhelmed in November 1967. Sterling, however, was a sideshow. The main act was the dollar's performance.

A variety of measures, adopted in countries with over- or undervalued currencies to stave off devaluation or revaluation, affected the channels of international transmission of price change.[12] Surplus countries tried to avoid price increases, deficit countries price declines, both as external consequences of their balance-of-payments positions. Intermittently, depending on cyclical conditions, countries in both categories took steps to right payments imbalances.

2.2.3 Growth of World Foreign Reserves

Since palliatives to improve the balance of payments proved ineffective, deficits had to be financed either by drawing down reserves or seeking external credit or borrowing facilities, while surpluses obviously increased net reserve accumulations. During the heyday of the Bretton Woods system, despite the growth of dollar assets, the adequacy of international liquidity, in the sense of the quantity of international monetary reserves, was widely debated. Discussions during this period growing out of misplaced concern for the supply of reserves ultimately led to the creation of SDRs by the IMF, but that development belongs in the account of the breakdown of the system.[13] Until the end of 1967, international reserves were limited to gold, convertible foreign exchange, and reserve positions in the IMF.

Contrary to the design of Bretton Woods, financing of payments imbalances for the most part was arranged through credits governments extended on a bilateral basis and through international borrowing and lending activities of commercial banks. Thus, to restore depleted reserves of countries with persistent deficits, facilities for borrowing were created in addition to drawings from the IMF.

Official dollar reserves of the surplus countries were augmented at times by actions those countries took in the Eurodollar market. Dollars

---

12. For a description of the controls that were imposed, see the various editions of the IMF *Annual Report on Exchange Restrictions*.

13. Underlying the emphasis upon international liquidity during this period and the subsequent introduction of SDRs, as Lance Girton (1974) has pointed out, was the real-bills doctrine, in this instance applied to the international realm rather than to its preferred habitat, the domestic.

acquired by their central banks and deposited in the Eurodollar market either directly or through the Bank for International Settlements would usually be re-lent to private borrowers who could resell the dollars to the central banks.

With the exception of the U.K. and the U.S., all the countries in our sample increased their holdings of international reserves. In sum, world reserves grew during the period, leaving greater scope for the direct monetary channel of transmission of inflation to operate (table 2.4).

2.3   Weakening and Collapse of Bretton Woods, 1968–73

The devaluation of sterling in November 1967 was not regarded as the prelude to changes in the par values of other currencies, the devaluation of the dollar in terms of gold, the realignment of exchange-rate relations among the major currencies, and the substitution of a short-lived regime of central rates for the par value system—all of which took place between November 1967 and December 1971. Instead, it was hoped that balance in the U.S. and U.K. external payments was finally on the point of achievement, and that the creation of a special drawing rights facility in the IMF would replace reserve assets that dollar and sterling deficits had provided.

The hope was belied. The pattern of deficits and surpluses persisted and worsened in 1970 and 1971. The U.S. current account surplus dwindled, and the U.S. capital account deficit grew dramatically, producing current account surpluses and capital inflows in other countries. The activation of SDRs in 1970–72 provided additions to already massive acquisitions of dollar reserve assets.[14]

As in the heyday of the Bretton Woods system, disbelief of market participants in the pegged external values of currencies precipitated eruptions of turbulence in foreign exchange and gold markets, but the heart of the problem affecting the international monetary system was the performance of the dollar. The failure of the U.S. to maintain price stability led to institutional change in 1968, repegging in 1971, and finally the total collapse of fixed exchange-rate parities in 1973.

2.3.1   Foreign Exchange Turbulence

In May 1968, student riots in France touched off strikes and lockouts throughout the country. The settlement raised hourly wage rates by 11%, shortened the work week, and provoked a flight of capital, primarily into D-marks but also into gold. Rumors of a revaluation of the mark encour-

---

14. By the end of the fourth quarter of 1972, the value of SDRs was slightly over $9.4 billion, or 6% of total world international reserves as reported by the IMF (*International Financial Statistics*, July 1974).

Table 2.4 Average Quarterly Change at Annual Rates and Variance in the Level of International Reserves (millions of U.S. dollars)

	CA	FR	GE	IT	JA	NE	UK	US
1953–58IV	8	−301	797	307	−45	56	163	−297
	(9)	(824)	(831)	(126)	(238)	(92)	(522)	(1,879)
1958IV–67IV	40	766	219	199	102	90	−26	−694
	(325)	(265)	(1,471)	(364)	(118)	(76)	(936)	(1,100)
1967IV–73I	477	619	4,504	323	3,059	538	366	−339
	(1,026)	(11,638)	(68,212)	(1,359)	(22,856)	(826)	(4,642)	(13,719)
1973I–76IV	−248	−563	195	1,202	−664	406	118	537
	(638)	(20,341)	(152,624)	(44,234)	(2,005)	(743)	(3,647)	(1,523)

Note. Variances are shown in parentheses beneath the change figures.

aged further shifts of funds. France imposed tighter price controls, re-stricted imports and some external payments, introduced subsidies for exports, and imposed exchange controls. These measures were revoked in September, and credit restrictions substituted. In November, the flight from francs to marks intensified, and on 20 November, major European exchange markets were shut down. Between April and November 1968, official French foreign exchange reserves declined by $2.9 billion. France resisted advice to devalue, Germany advice to revalue. Germany im-posed a temporary export tax and an import subsidy, and in December a 100% reserve requirement on increases in nonresident deposits in Ger-man banks, but almost immediately relaxed the measure as funds flowed out. France in turn restored exchange and credit controls, the former having only been fully relaxed a year earlier, cut public spending and increased indirect taxes, and imposed ceilings on commercial bank lend-ing and raised interest rates.

The deficit in the French current account grew in the first two quarters of 1969, and capital that flowed to Germany not only from France but also from the U.K. and other countries totaled $4.4 billion in May. Again, Germany adopted measures to deter the inflow: a 50% reserve require-ment for nonresident deposits received before 15 April and 15% on resident deposits. The French tightened restrictions on bank credit and raised minimum requirements for hire purchase. In July funds for public investment programs were frozen. When the drain on French reserves continued and short-term debts of $2.3 billion had been incurred, France finally gave in and devalued by 11.11% as of 10 August. Currencies linked to the French franc followed suit.

Thanks to increased monetary growth in the U.S. and the resultant higher balance-of-payments deficit, France rapidly moved from $1.7 billion deficit on current account in 1969 to a small surplus in 1970, an overall balance-of-payments surplus of $2 billion in that year and of $3.4 billion in 1971. Official reserves grew correspondingly.

The perception that the D-mark was undervalued in relation to the dollar, now that the French franc had been devalued, led to a further flow of funds to Germany. A few days before German elections in October 1969, the Bundesbank closed the exchange market, and a day after reopening it, permitted the D-mark to float. The spot rate against the dollar appreciated, and on 26 October, a revaluation of 9.29% was announced. Although there was a capital outflow in the last quarter of 1969, by 1970 there were large inflows of foreign funds and official reserves increased substantially. Domestic inflation in Germany was thereby eventually worsened.

The persistent outflow of funds from the U.S. overwhelmed foreign exchange markets in the first few days of May 1971. On 5 May seven European countries closed their foreign exchange markets, and five other countries on several continents withdrew their support for the dollar and suspended dealings in D-marks, guilders, and Swiss francs. On 9 May, both Germany and the Netherlands announced that their currencies would float, since they could not maintain exchange rates within the established margins.

2.3.2   Gold and the Dollar

The gold market was the second market in which participants expressed lack of confidence in the dollar-based international monetary system. After the devaluation of sterling in November 1967, the vulnerability of the dollar took center stage. In the winter of 1967–68, a surge of demand for gold threatened both the London Gold Pool and the statutory backing for Federal Reserve notes that then amounted to $10 billion. On 12 March 1968 the U.S. gold reserve requirement was abolished. Ostensibly, the gold stock was then available for conversion of dollars held by foreign central banks. On 17 March, however, the London gold market was closed to avoid further U.S. gold losses. The members of the gold pool announced that they would no longer supply gold to the London or any other gold market or buy gold from the market. Official transactions between central banks were to be conducted at the unchanged official price of $35 an ounce, but the gold price for private transactions was to be determined in the market. Central banks were still free de jure to buy U.S. Treasury gold for dollars but in fact refrained from doing so. Germany had explicitly forsworn converting its dollar holdings into gold in May 1967.

In March 1971, before the panic of the foreign exchange market, there was a request from several European countries for conversion of officially held dollars into gold to enable them to pay for an increase in their IMF quotas. The payout reduced the U.S. gold stock to the lowest level since 1936. The dollar outflow meanwhile accelerated, leading, as noted, to the floating of European currencies. The devaluation of the dollar vis-à-vis the D-mark as the result of the float left unsolved the dollar's exchange rate vis-à-vis the yen. Japan's capital controls were proof against the dollar flows that inundated European foreign exchange markets, but not against the large deficit in U.S. trade with Japan. That bilateral trade imbalance was a provocation, over and above the imbalance between U.S. reserves and outstanding dollar liabilities, for the changes the U.S. introduced on 15 August 1971 to achieve a dollar devaluation. Chief among them (besides a price and wage freeze, tax increases, and federal government spending cuts) was a 10% import surcharge on 50% of total U.S. imports. The convertibility of the dollar into gold was formally suspended, as was the use of the swap network through which dollars could be exchanged with central banks for other currencies. The effect was to oblige other countries to hold dollars or to trade them for a price determined in the market and so to revalue their currencies. Foreign exchange markets abroad, except in Japan, shut down. The Japanese initial attempt to maintain the pegged rate of the yen compelled them to purchase $4 billion in the two weeks after 15 August. The yen was then freed to float upward; other currencies floated when exchange markets were reopened on 23 August. France introduced a dual exchange market, with trade and government exchange dealings based on the par value, financial exchange dealings at a floating rate. Restoration of a repegged system of exchange rates, however, remained the goal of the U.S. and its partners.

After much negotiation, a readjustment of currency parities was arranged at a meeting at the Smithsonian Institution in Washington on 17–18 December 1971. In return the U.S. agreed to withdraw the import surcharge. The currencies of six of the countries in our sample (plus those of nonsample ones) were revalued by percentages ranging from 2¾% (the Netherlands) to 7.7% (Japan) with the proviso that 2¼% margins of fluctuation (replacing the former 1% margin) above and below the so-called central exchange rates were permissible. The Canadian dollar continued to float. The Smithsonian agreement also specified that the official dollar price of gold would henceforth be $38, a concession by the U.S. for appearance' sake only, since the dollar remained inconvertible. The new price of gold implied a depreciation of 7.9% of the gold value of the dollar rather than an appreciation of the dollar value of other currencies.

2.3.3   European Economic Community Snake

The notion of a European monetary union had been the subject of discussion for years. Implementing the notion had been scheduled for a start in June 1971. The floating of the D-mark in May delayed the introduction of the plan to keep fluctuations between EEC–country currencies within narrower limits than those vis-à-vis the dollar. The activation of the snake came in April 1972 in response to the 2¼% margin above and below the central rate that the Smithsonian agreement set. In relation to the dollar a European currency could fluctuate by 4½% from floor to ceiling, but in relation to another European currency the relative fluctuation could be as much as 9% if one rose from floor to ceiling and the other fell from ceiling to floor. The motivation for the snake was to narrow margins of fluctuation between EEC currencies by a convergence of economic and monetary policies so that exchange parities among them would be fixed.

Operationally, if an EEC currency premium over its central rate plus the discount on the central rate of another EEC currency reached 2¼% (half the amount permitted by the Smithsonian agreement), the weak currency was to be bought by the strong currency. The purchase could be made by the weak-currency country, by the strong-currency country, or by both. A monthly settlement was provided, so the creditor country could exchange the weak currency acquired for a desired reserve asset and obtain repayment for its short-term credit facility if it had lent its currency to the debtor. Debtors were to make settlement in a prescribed mix of reserve assets.

Six countries (France, Germany, Italy, Belgium, Luxemburg, the Netherlands) originally joined the snake; three others joined in May 1972 but left in June (U.K., Denmark, Eire). Denmark rejoined in October 1972, Italy left in December 1972. France left in January 1974, rejoined in July 1975, and left again in March 1976. Sweden and Norway, non–EEC countries, joined in May 1972. Sweden left in August 1977.[15]

The feasibility of the snake was dubious in the absence of consensus by the national governments to yield to the union direct monetary autonomy and control over exchange-rate changes, and to seek convergence of economic policies.

2.3.4   The End of the Sterling Area

Within weeks after joining the snake, sterling came under pressure in foreign exchange markets. The central banks of the EEC countries supported sterling, but on the next settlement day the U.K. would have had to repay them. On 22 June 1972 the bank rate was raised by 1%, and on the following day the exchange rate was floated. The float marked the end of the sterling area. Capital flows to overseas sterling areas were made subject to the same exchange controls as other areas, and Bank of England approval was required for official foreign exchange for direct investment in the overseas sterling area. Only a few small countries of the sixty-five that had formerly pegged their currencies on sterling continued to do so after sterling floated.

2.3.5   The End of the Convertible Dollar Standard

The central rates established at the Smithsonian meeting crumbled during the nine months following the floating of sterling. Once again, the disbelief of market participants in those rates was revealed in the gold and foreign exchange markets. The London free market price of gold rose with few reversals. Money growth and inflation rates continued to rise in the U.S., and both the balance of trade and the U.S. balance-of-payments deficit soared, with a corresponding surge in dollar holdings of

15. Many changes in exchange rates within the snake were made. On four occasions between March 1973 and October 1978, the mark was revalued within the system. The guilder and the Norwegian krone were each revalued once. Countries other than Germany devalued in October 1976. The Swedish krona was subsequently devalued again, as was the Danish krone, and the Norwegian krone several times. For a table on these changes, see Major (1979, pp. 212–13).

the industrialized European countries and Japan. Capital controls were imposed in 1972 by the Netherlands and Japan before sterling was floated, and Germany followed suit afterward. On 10 February 1973 Japan closed its foreign exchange market and suspended support of the dollar. New central values were set in a hurried round of negotiations, although the lira, yen, Canadian dollar, U.K. and Irish pounds, and Swiss franc all floated. Again, the official price of gold was raised (this time to $42.22), leaving unchanged the gold value of other currencies. The new central rates did not staunch the flow of dollars abroad, and a further crisis erupted in March 1973. This time the major industrial countries discontinued pegging their exchange rates to the dollar. The EEC countries in the snake plus Sweden and Norway agreed to a joint float, with Germany revaluing by 3% (in terms of SDRs) in relation to the other members. Canada, Japan, and Switzerland floated individually, as did a handful of other countries. Though a large group of nonindustrialized countries pegged to the dollar, the dollar currency area worldwide contracted; smaller groups of countries pegged to the French franc or to the pound.

Market forces had triumphed.

2.4 Managed Floating Exchange Rates

When pegged rates were abandoned in March 1973, it was initially assumed that floating was a temporary expedient to be succeeded by a reformed par value system. The U.S. took the lead in opposing the return to such a system. The dispersion of inflation rates among the industrialized countries and the higher variability of rates of inflation since the late 1960s enforced more frequent changes of exchange rates. Under the earlier system, changes in par values were delayed until foreign exchange market crises were provoked. The lesson since the shift in March 1973 was that floating provided more flexibility. The U.S. view prevailed. With the suspension of official gold convertibility, and widespread departures from the IMF's par value provisions, negotiations were held to codify, in the form of amendments to the IMF Articles, the international monetary arrangements that had evolved in practice.

Under the amendments to the IMF Articles agreed on in early 1976 and implemented in April 1978, gold was formally removed from its previous central role in the IMF and IMF par value obligations were eliminated. The official IMF gold price was abolished, as were also gold convertibility and maintenance of gold value obligations. Gold was eliminated as a significant instrument in IMF transactions with members, and the IMF was empowered to dispose of its large gold holdings. Although the amended IMF Articles provide for the future possibility of establishing a system of stable but adjustable par values, such a decision by the Fund would require an 85% affirmative vote by the members, thus giving the United States an effective veto. The provisions in the amended IMF Articles relating to the establishment of par values specify that the common denominator of the system shall not be gold or a currency.

It is useful to examine the manner in which various aspects of the international monetary system have been affected by the shift from the pegged to the managed floating exchange-rate system. These aspects include (a) the role of reserve assets and of dollar assets; (b) the role of gold; (c) the role of central bank intervention in foreign exchange markets; (d) the variability of exchange rates; (e) the role of monetary policy.

2.4.1   Role of Reserve Assets and of Dollar Assets

It was widely believed that the stock of reserve assets would contract in a world of floating exchange rates compared to a world of pegged rates. In fact, (nominal) official holdings of reserve assets have increased every year since the float. From 1950 to 1969, on average, world reserves including gold rose by less than 3% per year, the foreign exchange component by 5% per year. From the end of 1969 to the end of 1972, the average annual rate of increase of foreign currency reserves was 43%. Since 1973, the average annual rate of increase has been 15%. The main source of growth of foreign currency reserves since 1973, as in earlier years, has been in the form of dollars.[16] The demand for reserves has increased even under floating rates because the system is substantially managed.[17]

A significant change in the distribution of foreign exchange reserves has occurred since October 1973 as a result of the rise in the price of oil. Total foreign exchange reserves of industrial oil-importing countries have increased at a slightly slower pace than reserves of all countries, which sextupled since 1970, but the major oil-exporting countries, which in 1970 held only about 8% of total world foreign exchange reserves, by the end of the decade held about one-quarter of the total. The motivations of oil-exporting countries for holding foreign-currency denominated assets are, however, clearly quite different from those of industrial countries.

Although other currencies have increased their role as reserve currencies in recent years, the dollar has continued to serve as the main reserve currency, accounting for about 80% of the world's official foreign exchange reserves. To the extent of intervention, as under pegged rates, the

16. Although in December 1978 the IMF resumed the allocation of SDRs to member countries at a rate of 4 billion SDR per year (to be continued for a period of three years), the action had no immediate effect on the growth of reserves. The reason is that an increase in quotas, of which one-fourth was payable in SDRs, took effect in 1979, Accordingly, about 5 billion SDRs reverted to the IMF in that year.

17. Frenkel (1978), using time series of cross section data, provides evidence of substantial similarities in the demand for international reserves between exchange-rate regimes.

U.S. has settled its payments deficits in dollars, which foreigners willingly add to their asset holdings and use in payments to other countries. The dollar also remains the main official intervention currency in foreign exchange markets and serves as a common vehicle currency in the inter-bank market for foreign exchange. In effect, the world has adopted an inconvertible dollar standard.

One change in the international reserve profile was the creation on 13 March 1979 of the European Monetary System—replacing the "smaller" size European joint float—by nine European countries (Belgium, Denmark, France, Germany, Eire, Italy, Luxembourg, and the Netherlands; the U.K. is a member but does not participate in intervention arrangements). The center of the system is the European Currency Unit (a basket of all nine currencies), issued by the European Monetary Cooperation Fund in an amount equal to a deposit of 20% of gold and dollar reserves of participating countries, to be used for settlement of intervention debts (see below). ECUs now included in foreign exchange holdings of the participating countries, except for revaluation changes, do not increase world monetary reserves.[18]

With gold valued at market price, gold reserves at the end of 1979 were larger than foreign exchange reserves. The U.S., however, values its own gold assets at the official price of $42.22 per ounce, despite the abolition of an official IMF price for gold.

If a high rate of growth of world foreign exchange reserves provides evidence of an international transmission process at work, it is apparent that no change in behavior in the aggregate has occurred in that regard since 1973.

2.4.2   The Role of Gold

After the float, the U.S. took the position that gold should be demonetized. An opposing view was promoted principally by France. Developments reflect the extent to which one or the other dominated international decisions. At issue was the use of gold in official transactions at the free market price, and the substitution of gold for the dollar in inter–central bank settlements at a fixed but higher official price.

The prescription against official transactions in the gold market that had been adopted in March 1968 was terminated in November 1973, but the official price of $42.22 posted in February 1973 was so far below the private market price that central banks were unwilling to buy and sell gold among themselves at the official price. The central banks were equally reluctant to sell gold on the private market in view of the possible

18. The ECUs issued value gold on the basis of either the average market price of the six preceding months or the average market price on the day before issue, whichever was lower.

depressive effect of sales on the market price or in anticipation of the opportunity to sell in the future at a higher price. In December 1973 the IMF terminated arrangements made four years earlier, under which it had been prepared to purchase gold from South Africa.

In June 1974 countries in the Group of Ten (the U.S., the U.K., Germany, France, Italy, Japan, Canada, the Netherlands, Belgium, and Sweden) agreed that gold could be used as collateral for intercentral bank loans at a price other than the official gold price, and in September Italy obtained a loan from Germany on the pledge of Italian gold valued at a mutually agreed price. In December the U.S. and France agreed that central banks were at liberty in valuing gold holdings for balance sheet purposes to use the market price, which the Bank of France proceeded to do.

Early in 1975 the countries in the Group of Ten and Switzerland agreed for a two-year period not to increase the sum of their and the IMF's gold holdings and to contribute no support to the price of gold in the free market. In August 1975 agreement was reached by an IMF committee that[19]
- the official price of gold would be abolished;
- members would not be obliged to use gold in transactions with the Fund;
- a part of the Fund's gold holdings would be sold at auction for the benefit of developing countries, and another part would be returned to member countries in proportion to their quotas.

The first public auction of part of the Fund's gold holdings was held in June 1976. A four-year sales program was scheduled. In the first two years, sixteen auctions were held approximately every six weeks, with aggregate sales of 12.5 million ounces. The balance of 12.5 million ounces was sold mainly in twenty-four auction lots through May 1980, and a small amount in noncompetitive sales. Restitution of 25 million ounces to member countries over a four-year period was completed in December 1979/January 1980.

The U.S. repealed the prohibition against gold holding by U.S. residents as of 31 December 1974 and empowered the Treasury to offset any increase in market price as a result of this increment to private demand by offering gold at auction. The first auctions were held in January and June 1975, when the Treasury disposed of 13 million ounces. No auctions were held in 1976 and 1977. They were resumed in 1978 and 1979, when the Treasury sold 4.0 and 11.8 million ounces, respectively, motivated both by the desire to reduce the U.S. balance-of-payments deficit on current account and by the belief "that neither gold nor any other commodity

19. IMF *Annual Report*, 1975, p. 44.

provides a suitable base for monetary arrangements."[20] Since 1979 the Treasury has sold no gold bullion.[21]

Members no longer define the exchange value of their currency in terms of gold and trade in and account for gold at any price consistent with their domestic laws. Gold is no longer the *numéraire* of the international monetary system. The introduction of SDRs (valued in terms of a basket of national currencies, as of July 1974, rather than in terms of gold) was intended to replace both the dollar and gold in the international monetary system.

The market price of gold has increased more rapidly since the float than the prices of most other durable assets.[22] The future role of gold in the international monetary system as a reserve asset and as a determinant of the world's price level may depend on the performance of the dollar. If the performance of the dollar improves, gold may be dethroned even if its use as a reserve asset continues. Failure of the dollar to perform in a stable fashion in the future leaves open the possibility of a restoration of a significant role for gold.

2.4.3   Role of Central Bank Intervention

Direct official intervention to maintain the open market price of currencies within narrow limits has not lessened under floating rates compared with the pegged parity system. Intervention in some countries is assigned to nationalized industries that borrow foreign currency in order to buy their own currency on the foreign exchange market, in Italy and the U.K. with government provision of insurance against foreign exchange loss, in France with no such provision. In Japan and sometimes in France, dollar deposits held by the government at commercial banks are used for intervention. Italian and French commercial banks intervene at the government's behest. Central bank intervention may thus be conducted by a variety of institutions at the direction of the monetary authorities.

20. See *Annual Report of the Secretary of the Treasury on the State of the Finances*, 1979, p. 491, Exhibit 60, a press release on the increase in the amount of gold sales, announced 22 August 1978 ("The sales will make an important contribution toward reducing the U.S. balance of payments deficit on current account"), and Exhibit 61, a statement by Assistant Secretary Bergsten before the Senate Committee on Banking, Housing, and Urban Affairs, in which the quotation in the text appears.

21. The Reagan administration announced that its position on the proper role of gold in the international monetary system would not be formulated until the congressionally mandated gold commission issued its report in March 1982. Testimony of Beryl W. Sprinkel, under secretary for monetary affairs, Treasury Department, at hearings of the Joint Economic Committee, 4 May 1981.

22. The price of gold from the end of 1973 to the end of 1980 increased at an average annual rate of 20.7%. By comparison the total returns on common stock and on long-term government bonds (computed according to Ibbotson and Sinquefield 1977) increased at average annual rates of 7.2% and 4.0%, respectively. The U.S. CPI over this period increased at a rate of 7.8% per year on average, and the *London Economist*'s world commodity price index in dollars at a 9.5% rate.

The pattern of intervention since the float by the U.S. and its trading partners is to buy dollars both when the dollar depreciates relative to a particular foreign currency and when one foreign currency appreciates relative to another. Countries with weak currencies sell dollars. When the supply of dollars increases in foreign exchange markets, managed floaters may buy up some of the additional dollars or may permit the price of dollars to fall in terms of their own currencies. Buying up dollars has negative consequences for domestic monetary control; permitting the price of dollars to rise can have negative consequences for oil-importing countries.

There was apparently little intervention during the four months following the float in February 1973. The progressive decline in the weighted exchange rate of the dollar between February and July 1973 vis-à-vis a group of major currencies led to a decision by the governors of the central banks of the Group of Ten to support the dollar. In July 1973 the Federal Reserve Bank of New York began to intervene in the New York spot exchange market to avoid "disorderly market conditions." Intervention was effected with the Federal Reserve's own small holdings of foreign currency or by activating the much larger total of foreign currency loans through swap agreements.

Concerted exchange intervention was agreed to by the Federal Reserve, the Bundesbank, and the Swiss National Bank in May 1974, after several months of dollar depreciation. The dollar strengthened until September, when renewed weakness developed through March 1975. The explanation given by the Board of Governors was:[23]

Contributing to this decline in the dollar's exchange value was the asymmetry in intervention policies between countries with weaker currencies and those with strengthening currencies. Intervention sales of dollars by countries supporting weaker currencies exceeded purchases of dollars by countries resisting the appreciation of their currencies. The net effect of these operations was to add to the market supply of dollars, depressing the dollar's average exchange rate.

Explicit approval of management of floating exchange rates was expressed by the IMF in six guidelines it issued in June 1974.[24] Acceptance

23. Board of Governors of the Federal Reserve System, *61st Annual Report*, 1974, pp. 65–66.
24. The first guideline stated: "A member with a floating exchange rate should intervene on the foreign exchange market as necessary to prevent or moderate sharp and disruptive fluctuations from day to day and from week to week in the exchange value of the currency." A second guideline encouraged intervention to moderate movements from month to month and quarter to quarter "where factors recognized to be temporary are at work." A third guideline suggested consultation with the Fund if a country sought to move its exchange rate "to some target zone of rates." A fourth guideline dealt with the size of a country's reserve relative to planned intervention; a fifth, with avoiding restrictions for balance-of-payments purposes; a sixth, with the interests of other countries than the intervening one. IMF *Annual Report*, 1974, pp. 112–16.

of intervention as desirable policy was reiterated in a November 1975 meeting that preceded the revision of the IMF's Articles of Agreement in 1976.

The dollar showed little weakness in 1976, and the Federal Reserve intervened to sell dollars on behalf of other currencies. In January the Italian lira came under pressure. The decline in its exchange value weakened the French franc within the European currency snake, leading to substantial French intervention. Massive intervention to support sterling, which declined from $2.00 in March to $1.77 in mid-September, was provided by a $5.3 billion stand-by credit arranged by the Group of Ten countries, Switzerland, and the Bank for International Settlements. Sterling's further decline later in the year led to an IMF drawing, further borrowing, and a facility to reduce official sterling balances. Interventions were also engaged in to moderate appreciations of the D-mark, the Swiss franc, and the yen.

Renewed weakness of the dollar in early 1977 was masked by large intervention purchases of dollars by the Bank of England and the Bank of Italy undertaken to limit the appreciation of their currencies and to rebuild their reserve positions. The Federal Reserve intervened only occasionally during the first three quarters. When the Bank of England ended its large purchases of dollars, the dollar dropped sharply. The Federal Reserve increased the scale of intervention and in January 1978 was joined by the U.S. Treasury Exchange Stabilization Fund, which negotiated a new swap facility with the Bundesbank.

The decline in the weighted average exchange value of the dollar accelerated in 1978 through the end of October.[25] An anti-inflation program announced on 24 October (contractionary fiscal and monetary policy, voluntary wage and price standards, and a reduction in the cost of regulatory actions) had no effect on the exchange market. On 1 November, the administration and the Federal Reserve took further action. A $30 billion intervention package was arranged with Germany, Japan, and Switzerland. The Federal Reserve raised the discount rate from 8½% to 9½% and imposed a 2% supplementary reserve requirement on large time deposits. During the last two months of 1978, U.S. support operations for the dollar totaled $6.7 billion, including sales of Treasury securities denominated in foreign currencies and significant purchases of dollars by Germany, Japan, and Switzerland. By June 1979 the dollar's value (measured on a trade-weighted basis) had risen from its 1978 low by about 10%, and U.S. authorities had repurchased a greater sum of foreign currency than had been sold in the last two months of 1978. The

25. The index of weighted average exchange values of the dollar against the Group of Ten countries plus Switzerland (March 1973 = 100) declined at an average annual rate of 9.3% between January and November 1978. From January 1976 to January 1978 it had declined at a 3.3% annual rate.

dollar then began to weaken, and U.S. intervention sales of foreign currencies, chiefly D-marks, resumed. Gross sales amounted to $9½ billion equivalent between mid-June and early October. In addition, the Federal Reserve raised the discount rate to 11% in September.

On 6 October 1979 the Federal Reserve announced a wide-ranging set of measures to tighten monetary control (a shift in operating procedures to place less emphasis upon control of the Federal Funds rate and more emphasis upon control of bank reserves; an increase in the discount rate to 12%; a marginal reserve requirement on banks' managed liabilities), and the dollar began to appreciate. After April 1980, however, the dollar began to decline, a movement that was reversed in September. From October 1979 on, the U.S. intervened frequently, operating on both sides of the market. When the dollar was in demand, it acquired foreign currencies in the market and from correspondents to repay earlier debt and to build up balances. The Federal Reserve was a buyer from February to March. From late March to early April and beyond, it sold D-marks, Swiss francs, and French francs. By the end of July, the U.S. was again accumulating currencies. Both the Treasury and the Federal Reserve Trading Desk made net purchases of D-marks and lesser amounts of Swiss francs and French francs on days when the dollar was strong, selling on days when the dollar weakened. By the end of 1980, the U.S. was intervening in the foreign exchange markets virtually on a day-to-day basis. For 1980 as a whole, U.S. authorities were net buyers of foreign currencies in an amount of $8.7 billion equivalent.

The Reagan administration soon after taking office announced its intention to reduce the scale of intervention, to discontinue the policy of building up currency reserves, and to cut back its short-term swap arrangements with foreign countries. The reason for the shift in policy is the administration's view that intervention is both costly and ineffectual and that the way to restore exchange-rate stability is by the creation of more stable domestic economic conditions. Many foreign central banks do not share the Reagan administration's views and continue to intervene to affect the exchange value of their currencies. This raises a question whether the degree of control U.S. authorities can exercise over the effective exchange rate for the dollar under a floating rate system is any greater than under a pegged exchange-rate system.

The rationale for central bank intervention under floating rates is that the market does not move exchange rates smoothly to equilibrium levels, produces "disorderly conditions," and sets rates at variance with underlying economic conditions. It is assumed that central banks can determine better than markets the correct level of exchange rates and the proper degree of variability. A policy of leaning against the wind is justified by advocates of intervention as slowing the movement of exchange rates in either direction.

To stabilize foreign exchange markets central banks should buy their currencies when prices are low to drive them up and sell their currencies when prices are high to drive them down. Such operations should net the central banks a profit. Buying at high but falling prices and selling at low but rising prices are defended as needed to achieve "orderly" markets. By resisting a gradual movement in exchange rates, central banks lose reserves and money until they abandon the support operation, with a resulting sudden large movement in exchange rates.

If the purpose of intervention were to reduce deviations of the market exchange rate from the equilibrium exchange rate, central bank operations would net profits but might not reduce the variance of exchange-rate movements. If the equilibrium exchange rate shifts as a result of an economic shock, leaning against the wind may lower the variance of the exchange rate but will increase the size of the deviation of the exchange rate from its equilibrium level. In addition, the central bank will lose money on the operation. If there is no intervention, the variance will be larger, the central bank will not lose money, and the exchange rate will reflect the new equilibrium value sooner, thus allowing the rate to transmit undistorted information.

The central banks as a group have not been conducting a profitable exercise by intervening in foreign exchange markets. An estimate for nine countries puts the loss for central bank intervention since the beginning of the float at $10 to $12 billion, far in excess of losses sustained by nationalized industries although for selected time periods a country may record a profit.[26] The evidence is that central banks have been suffering from an anachronistic behavior, resisting exchange-rate changes under nominally floating rates much as they did under pegged rates. Central banks have no way of knowing when there is a change in the fundamental equilibrium level of exchange rates.[27] By assuming the absence of a change in the equilibrium exchange rate and intervening to hold the exchange rate, they lose substantial amounts of money and ultimately have no choice but to permit the exchange rate to move.

2.4.4 Variability of Exchange Rates

One major change since the float has been the increased variability of exchange rates of the major industrial countries (table 2.5). Critics of the floating regime argue that the variability has been excessive. Much of the movement, it is said, is unrelated to underlying economic and financial conditions which are not themselves likely to undergo rapid changes.

26. For the source of the estimate on losses and an illuminating discussion of intervention, see Taylor (1982).
27. Darby in chapter 15 of this volume presents evidence relevant to this issue. He shows that growth rates of the dollar exchange rates of the countries in our sample tend on average to a purchasing-power parity relation but that the levels of exchange rates become unpredictable.

Table 2.5   Average Quarterly Change at Annual Rates and the Variance of the Exchange Rate

	CA	FR	GE	IT	JA	NE	UK
1955I–58IV	−.21	6.30	−.14	−.01	0	−.19	−.16
	(1.58)	(2.27)	(.39)	(.001)	(0)	(1.68)	(1.82)
1958IV–67IV	1.18	1.12	−.54	−.03	.07	−.51	1.12
	(1.31)	(.46)	(9.18)	(0.27)	(1.42)	(7.58)	(39.26)
1967IV–73I	−1.45	−.43	−6.54	−.144	−4.96	−3.17	.66
	(16.41)	(121.49)	(161.53)	(13.90)	(89.18)	(55.04)	(87.44)
1973I–76IV	−.13	1.05	−4.53	10.69	1.40	−5.15	10.59
	(33.)	(499.)	(560)	(413)	(141)	(403)	(401)

Notes. The table understates the variability of exchange rates for individual countries before 1973I. For a correct measure for the individual countries, the subperiods would be chosen for each country to correspond with dates for stable or changing exchange rates. Variances are shown in parentheses beneath the change figures.

Injury to international trade through exchange-rate fluctuation is claimed. The exchange rate is regarded as contributing to inflation, strong currencies not experiencing a reduction in exports as a result of appreciation, and weak currencies not experiencing a reduction in imports as a result of depreciation. The widening of bid-ask spreads or increase of transactions costs and the failure of forward rates to predict future spot prices as well in the 1970s as in the 1960s are offered as evidence that speculators destabilize foreign exchange markets. The impact of floating rates is said to increase uncertainty.

The negative assessment of the behavior of exchange rates since the float omits a crucial factor: the market's expectations with respect to inflation rates, monetary and fiscal policy, and general economic conditions. Unstable domestic policies contribute to unstable exchange rates.[28] Exchange-rate changes are dominated by speculation about these underlying economic factors. If, despite appreciation, strong-currency countries experience growth in exports and, despite depreciation, weak-currency countries experience growth in imports, the explanation is that costs of production in the former remain favorable if policies in the latter permit inflationary expansion of demand, wage hikes, and increase in strike activity. It is uncertainty about domestic policies that produces higher transactions costs in foreign exchange markets. With respect to the failure of forward rates to predict future spot rates, the predictions have not been biased. Despite the volatility of exchange rates, no major disruptions to trade and capital flows have occurred since the float. In fact, floating exchange rates permitted the elimination of some capital controls. Capital controls introduced since the float are associated with the snake, where rates of exchange among the bloc were relatively fixed and moved in relation to one another only within relatively narrow bands.[29] The balance-of-payments motive for tariffs is also defused by floating rates. If protectionism is perceived as on the rise since the float, it is related to stagflation rather than exchange-rate developments.

A final point with respect to exchange rates relates to experience within the European Monetary System. The initial year after the activation of the exchange-rate mechanism of the European Monetary System in 1979 reduced the range of movements of the participant currencies against the D-mark compared to the range in the preceding year. Nevertheless, two realignments of exchange rates were required as a result of divergencies in economic performance and in inflation exprience (Germany, September 1979; Denmark, November 1979). Large-scale interventions were undertaken to preserve the former exchange rates but to no avail. The continued existence of large inflation differentials among the countries in

28. Frenkel and Mussa (1980) present a particularly concise statement of this position.
29. The D-mark was revalued by 5½% relative to other snake currencies on 20 June 1973, and simultaneously controls on capital inflow were tightened to defend the new rate.

the EMS suggests the fragility of the arrangement is not less than it was for the predecessor snake. Countries that inflate at a faster rate than their trading partners cannot avoid depreciation of their currencies. As markets have become more insistent on allowing for expected future price movements in setting nominal interest rates, wider swings in interest-rate differentials among countries are also likely to contribute to exchange-rate instability.

2.4.5   Role of Monetary Policy

The Bretton Woods system broke down essentially because non-reserve-currency countries were unwilling as a group to adopt the policy of inflationary monetary growth the reserve-currency country was pursuing. To achieve independent monetary policy, the only workable exchange-rate system was floating. It was hoped that flexible exchange rates would permit a country to choose its desired long-run trend rate of monetary growth and of inflation, independent of other countries' choices.

Even when autonomy exists, monetary policy may perform badly. It is in this context that the movement in a number of countries during the 1970s toward the improvement of monetary control must be viewed.

Central banks have typically used short-term interest rates as the instruments to control monetary growth. Under noninflationary conditions, this conduct produced a procyclical movement in monetary growth. Under the gathering inflationary conditions since the mid-1960s, the inflation premium that became embedded in interest rates made the instrument unreliable as an indicator of restriction or ease. Reliance on it contributed to a secular rise in the rate of monetary growth. Central banks in a number of countries, some more willingly than others, in the 1970s adopted targets for monetary growth without necessarily abandoning their desire to hold down interest rates or exchange rates, so that successful targeting has not invariably been the result. If it was hoped that public announcement of targets for monetary growth would itself reduce expectations of inflation, the failure time after time to achieve the targets has diluted any possible effect on the formation of expectations.

2.5   Summary

By the end of 1958, the idealized Bretton Woods regime of exchange rates pegged within relatively narrow bounds seemed on the point of achievement. Problems arose in the 1960s when individual countries resorted to restrictions on trade and commodities in order to contain balance-of-payments deficits which would have otherwise required lower rates of monetary growth and inflation. The United States, the reserve-currency country, was the prime destabilizer of the system. Because countries were unwilling to subordinate domestic monetary policies to the requirements of a fixed exchange-rate system, recurring financial crises led to occasionally large devaluations and to some revaluations of individual currencies. In the end, the system broke down and countries were free after 1973 to float their currencies or to adopt regional pegged currency schemes that floated against the dollar. Since the float has been a managed system, with substantial official intervention to prevent or slow exchange-rate movements, countries have continued to hold foreign exchange reserves and internal monetary policy independence has not invariably produced noninflationary monetary growth.

References

Board of Governors of the Federal Reserve System. 1974. *61st Annual Report.*
————. 1976–80. *Federal Reserve Bulletin.*
Brittain, B. 1981. International currency substitution and the apparent instability of velocity in some Western European economies and in the United States. *Journal of Money, Credit and Banking* 13, no. 2 (May): 135–55.
de Vries, M. G. 1976. *The International Monetary Fund, 1966–71: The system under stress*, vol. 1. Washington: International Monetary Fund.
Frenkel, J. A. 1978. International reserves: Pegged exchange rates and managed float. In K. Brunner and A. H. Meltzer, eds., *Public policies in open economies*, vol. 9. Carnegie-Rochester Conference Series on Public Policy, and Supplementary Series to the *Journal of Monetary Economics*, pp. 111–40.
Frenkel, J. A., and M. L. Mussa. 1980. The efficiency of foreign exchange markets and measures of turbulence. *American Economic Review* 70 (May): 374–81.
————. 1981. Monetary and fiscal policies in an open economy. *American Economic Review* 71 (May): 253–58.
Girton, L. 1974. SDR creation and the real-bills doctrine. *Southern Economic Journal* 43 (January): 57–61.
Ibbotson, R. G., and R. A. Sinquefield. 1977. *Stocks, bonds, bills and inflation: The past (1926–1976) and the future (1977–2000)*. Financial Analysts Research Foundation, Charlottesville, Va.
International Monetary Fund, 1974–75. *Annual Report.*
————. 1970–80. *Annual Report on Exchange Restrictions.*
Johnson, H. G. 1972. The Bretton Woods system, key currencies, and the dollar crisis of 1971. *Three Banks Review*, June, pp. 17–18.
————. 1978. Commentaries: Evaluation of the performance of the floating exchange rate regime. In J. S. Dreyer, G. Haberler, and T. D.

Willet, eds., *Exchange rate flexibility*. Washington: American Enterprise Institute For Public Policy Research.

Major, R., ed. 1979. *Britain's trade and exchange rate policy*. NIESR Economic Policy Papers 3. London: Heinemann Educational Books.

Miles, M. A. 1978. Currency substitution, flexible exchange rates, and monetary independence. *American Economic Review* 68, no. 3 (June): 428–36.

Sprinkel, B. W. 1981. Testimony at hearings of the Joint Economic Committee, 4 May.

Taylor, D. 1982. Official intervention in the foreign exchange market or bet against the central bank. *Journal of Political Economy* 90 (April): 356–68.

United States Department of the Treasury. 1979. *Annual Report of the Secretary of the Treasury on the Finances*.

Wonnacott, P. 1965. *The Canadian dollar, 1948–1962*. Toronto: University of Toronto Press.

3 The International Data Base: An Introductory Overview

James R. Lothian

The authors of most studies of foreign economic phenomena have adopted one or the other of two quite different approaches to the data. Foreign economists investigating experience in their own countries have usually gone directly to primary sources—bulletins of the central bank, publications of the government statistical office and the like—in compiling their data. In almost all respects, this is the preferred technique. On the other hand, economists who are not nationals of these countries as well as economists analyzing economic behavior in a group of countries have usually lacked the expertise necessary to compile data from the original sources. Accordingly, they generally have relied on secondary source material—publications of the IMF, the OECD, and other international agencies.

Given this situation, both comparison of existing studies and replication of experiments become more difficult than usual. Not only are the data themselves apt to differ substantially among studies but so also are the sample periods. The reason is that series given in primary sources generally cover longer periods and are accompanied by better explanatory material than those in secondary sources.

Problems of another sort arise, however, for researchers who try to extend data bases derived by other scholars from primary publication. Such data usually remain relatively inaccessible and lack the documentation necessary for them to be updated or backdated easily.

For these reasons we have made a major effort to construct a data base from primary sources for the United States and the seven foreign countries we are studying that is of reasonably long duration (1955I–76IV), is as homogenous as possible among countries, and is accompanied by sufficient documentation to be used by other scholars.[1]

1. The data used in the studies that are detailed in the subsequent chapters are available on the TROLL system.

The remainder of this chapter first outlines our basic approach. We then discuss some of the major problems encountered and our solutions to them—both the relatively successful and the relatively unsuccessful—in order to provide future users with the flavor of the data (section 3.2). We then consider the reliability of our data across countries and concepts and relative to the IMF data (section 3.3). The Data Appendix to this volume provides more complete documentation of the individual series along with the series themselves.

3.1 Basic Approach

For both economic and statistical reasons we chose to begin our series with the first quarter of 1955. For one thing, we wanted to have data for as long a period as possible, in particular, one that encompassed as many business cycles as possible. Beginning in 1955 and even allowing for lags we would have a sample that included the U.S. and foreign recessions of 1958. At the same time (1955 or thereabouts) sources for many important series became more readily available in the various countries. By that time, moreover, wartime price controls had been removed in all countries and international trade had begun to be liberalized.

At the outset we decided that wherever possible we would collect the data on a monthly, non–seasonally adjusted basis. We would then transform these underlying series to the quarterly seasonally adjusted series to be used in our subsequent statistical analyses, and we would make both the seasonally adjusted and the unadjusted quarterly data available to other researchers. Doing this seemed to us to have two advantages. It would allow future users of the data to obtain a homogeneous updated series more easily; they would not be constrained by lack of readily accessible published historical data in country sources when seasonal factors were reestimated. Furthermore, it would impose some regularity on the seasonal adjustment techniques among countries.[2]

Our starting point in the selection of series for the foreign countries was to find out which series other economists customarily used in their analyses of these countries. To do so, we consulted economists from abroad who then were undertaking or had recently completed statistical studies of their own countries that were similar to ours as well as economists engaged in commenting on current economic developments in these countries. Two groups provided extremely valuable assistance in this regard: the academic and government economists assembled by Karl Brunner and Allan Meltzer for a conference on inflation at the University of Rochester and colleagues of mine in the international section of the

---

2. We used the standard U.S. Census X11 procedure for these adjustments. When the data were consistently positive, we used the X11 multiplicative option; when a series took on nonpositive values, we used the additive adjustment option.

Economics Department at Citibank. In virtually all instances, the series used by the two groups corresponded. Where discrepancies arose, we chose the series we deemed appropriate, usually on the basis of our ability to obtain reasonably homogeneous past data.

After making these initial choices of data, we traced each series back in time in the individual country sources to see if the data were available on a completely comparable basis for the entire sample period on at least a quarterly and, preferable, a monthly basis. In a considerable number of instances they were not. Many series were discontinuous. Others simply contained missing observations, usually for the earlier part of the sample period and in the version of the series reported in the most recent editions of the country sources.

In each of these instances, we made a considerable effort to identify the cause of the problem. We turned first to earlier editions of the country data source. In most cases, these contained at least a cursory description of the problem along with an earlier version of the series in question for some overlap period. In some cases, however, no such data were given in the sources. When that happened or if we had prior knowledge of the problem, we searched for alternative data for the earlier period that were reasonably comparable to the data for the later period.

Depending upon the length of the period of overlap, we then used one or the other of a variety of interpolation techniques.[3] Where the period was exceedingly short—one or only a few months or quarters of overlapping observations—we used the mean of the ratios of the new to the old series during the period to adjust the old series to the new basis. Where we had several years of monthly or quarterly observations for both series, we used ordinary least squares regression of the new on the old series as a method of interpolation. In both instances we worked in logarithmic terms when the series appeared to be trended, in arithmetic terms otherwise.

Missing observations were also dealt with in a variety of ways. When there was a single observation missing, we used linear interpolation, again, depending on the nature of the series, either of the logarithmic or of the arithmetic values of the adjacent observations to estimate the intervening one. When there were a number of observations missing, due usually to a change in the periodicity of the data, we tried to take account of other information to improve on the simple linear interpolation or interpolation by a single related series.[4]

When these various data problems were specific to components of an aggregate series, such as the currency component of $M1$, we disaggre-

3. The basic guide in our interpolation procedures was Milton Friedman's (1962) monograph on the subject. Friedman and Schwartz (1970) contains a concise restatement of these principles together with numerous examples of their practical application.

4. These included articles on various aspects of international data, series compiled by international agencies and past statistical studies utilizing the series in question.

gated the data, adjusted the component in question separately, and then reaggregated. Insofar as possible, we tried to work with seasonally adjusted data when we were performing the interpolation.[5] Often, however, this was impossible. In many instances a series contained so many breaks that the resulting subseries were of too short a duration for us to obtain estimates of seasonal factors. In these cases we constructed a non–seasonally adjusted series for the full period and seasonally adjusted it.

3.2   Data Problems and Their Resolution

To illustrate some of the problems we encountered in compiling the data as well as in obtaining our solutions to them, we think it would be useful to discuss several examples. The three we have chosen are the narrow money supply ($M1$) in the United Kingdom, the official settlements balance in the United States, and consumer prices in France. We view the first two as successful and relatively important contributions. In both instances there were no official published series for earlier parts of our sample period. Using other data, we were able to derive series for these earlier periods that appear to be reasonably homogeneous with the later.

In the third case, the French data, we were again successful, but in retrospect the overall contribution seems to us to have been relatively minor. A simpler approach than ours would likely have produced nearly identical results.

3.2.1   British M1

Officially published British money data for years prior to 1963 are available only on an annual basis. The end-of-quarter series begin with the observation for the first quarter of 1963; the mid-month series begin in late 1971. Both sets of data moreover contain a considerable number of breaks. However, for observations prior to 1963 there are monthly data for some of the major components of M1 and M2: currency held by the public and some bank deposits. The latter consist of data on both current accounts (demand deposits) and deposit accounts (time deposits) in three major classes of domestic banks (London Clearing, Scottish, and Northern Irish). Since these data ended before the official mid-month series began, we worked with the official quarterly series, extending it back in time.

As a first step, we derived monthly figures for current account deposits adjusted for float for all three categories of banks for the period 1955I to 1969 IV. To estimate float for the London Clearing banks, we used the

5. In the instances in which we used seasonally adjusted component series in our compilation of the final series, we did not reconstruct an unadjusted final series.

estimate implicit in the official figures for total deposits of this set of banks; i.e. adjusted current accounts equal gross current accounts less the difference between total gross deposits and total net (adjusted) deposits. For the Scottish Banks similar estimates of float are available only from October 1960 on; for the Northern Irish there are no net figures. Hence, to estimate float for the period prior to October 1960 for the Scottish banks, we assumed that the ratio of float to current accounts was the same for Scottish and London Clearing Banks; for the Northern Irish we assumed that the ratio was the same throughout as for the Scottish.

To the sum of the monthly adjusted current accounts of all three classes of banks we added the official monthly estimates of currency. We then took quarterly averages of the seasonally adjusted monthly figures centered in the last month of each quarter to arrive at a proxy series for M1. We then regressed the official on the proxy M1 series over the period of overlap 1963I to 1969IV. Using this relation and the proxy series, we extended the official series back to 1955.

Prior to interpolating via regression, we adjusted the official series for the breaks in it after 1963: in 1967 IV, 1972I, and 1973I due to inclusion of additional banks and in 1971IV and 1975II due to changes in reporting techniques. In each instance the official sources contained figures compiled on both the old and new basis for each quarter in which a break occurred. We used the ratio of the new to the old figures during these quarters to adjust earlier data for the various discontinuities.

3.2.2   United States Balance of Payments

The components of the American official settlements balance are only available from the Department of Commerce beginning in 1960. Prior to 1960, there are data on net transactions in U.S. official reserve assets but no data on other U.S. government liabilities to foreign official agencies.

The Treasury Department, however, does publish data for total (government and nongovernment) liquid liabilities to foreign official agencies as reported by commercial banks. Therefore, for 1955–59, we estimated the official portion of liquid liabilities by first regressing U.S. liquid liabilities to foreign official agencies on bank-reported short-term liabilities to foreign official agencies for the period 1960I to 1975IV. We then estimated the official portion of U.S liquid liabilities on the basis of the bank-reported data reported by banks for 1955I to 1959IV.

The only quarterly data for nonliquid liabilities to foreign official agencies that were available for the years 1955–59 were for a component of that total. Annual data, however, indicated that the total itself was only a small fraction of the official settlements balance during this period. Accordingly, we used the subseries without further adjustment as a proxy for the full series. We then added these estimates to our estimates of liquid liabilities and to net transactions in U.S. official reserve assets to obtain the official settlements balance for 1955–59.

3.2.3 French Consumer Prices

Before 1962, published data for consumer prices for France as a whole exist only on an annual basis. Throughout our sample period, however, there are monthly data for a Paris CPI. For the period 1957–61, there are end-of-quarter data for an urban provincial CPI, and yearly data are available for both prior to 1957. Using a variety of interpolation techniques, we were able to obtain monthly CPI data for the whole of France for the full sample period. Doing so involved the following three steps.

To construct a monthly index for the period through 1957, we estimated the relation between the yearly provincial and Parisian indexes for the years 1949–56 and used this relation, together with the monthly Parisian index, to obtain a monthly provincial index.

For the period 1957–63, we estimated the relation between the quarter provincial index and the Parisian index for the last month of the quarter and used it, together with the monthly Parisian index, to estimate the monthly provincial index.

Using equal weights, we combined the monthly Parisian and estimated monthly provincial index for each period. That gave us two separate national indexes: a 1949-based series for the period through 1957 and a 1956/58-based index for the period 1957–63. We linked these indexes and the two published indexes for all of France, the 1962-based index for 1962–70 and the 1970-based index for 1970–76, by multiplying by the means of the ratios of overlapping observations in the relevant overlapping year. The result was a continuous 1970-based monthly series, which we then converted to a quarterly.

Examining these data graphically and comparing the behavior of French inflation with inflation in other countries has, however, raised doubts in our minds about the accuracy of the underlying data. The relatively smooth pattern of French inflation throughout most of the sample period—even the part in which we made no adjustments—suggests that either interpolation played a major role in the generation of the original data or they are based largely upon (controlled) list prices rather than actual transactions prices.

3.3 Reliability of the Data

The experience with the French CPI data is not unique. In a number of instances—French monetary aggregates, Canadian currency, French industrial production, the balance of payments for a number of countries—we made a considerable effort to ascertain the nature of the data deficiencies, the cause of breaks, for instance, or to collect more suitable series than commonly used. Many of these attempts resulted in "dry holes." In some cases data did not exist in any usable form. In others, simpler methods of adjustment, such as linking the totals by the ratio of overlapping observation rather than adjusting individual components separately on the basis of related data, probably would have led to few appreciable differences in the final product. Hindsight in these instances, however, is better than foresight, or, to return to the earlier metaphor, one cannot simply eliminate the dry holes and be left with the gushers.

Two additional sets of data problems are worth some discussion: the homogeneity of particular series, or groups of series, among countries, and the accuracy of one country's data relative to those of other countries. Let us consider these two issues in order.

Prior experience in working with some of the foreign data, as well as a perusal of the literature comparing particular types of data internationally, convinced us that in most instances about the best we could do would be to obtain data that were consistent over time for each country but that differed to varying and, in most instances, somewhat unknown degrees among countries.

The major exception is the monetary data—M1, M2, and especially high-powered money. The components necessary to derive these three totals are available for most countries. Moreover, there appears to be at least a broad consensus among economists on which subtotals to use for each country. Accordingly, we view these data as the most homogeneous, at least from an accounting standpoint.[6]

Next best, we suspect, are the series on interest rates. These data differ somewhat with respect to the maturity of the instruments within each of the two categories and also with respect to the issuer—government versus private sector. Neither set of differences, however, seems likely to create major difficulties. The one problem that may be of some importance is the tendency of some countries more than others to exercise direct control over rates during some part of our sample period.[7]

Most of the remaining data—income, price and industrial production indexes, balance-of-payments statistics, and government accounts—suffer from well-known difficulties such as differences in samples among countries, (e.g. price indexes), differences in concept (e.g. GNP as opposed to GDP or the French *produit intérieur brut*), and differences in

6. Differences in financial development as well as in the legal restrictions imposed upon banks—reserve requirements, interest ceilings, and the like—conceivably could cause the deposit data to differ in economic meaning among countries, as Friedman and Schwartz (1970, pp. 137–46) and Lothian (1976) point out.

7. In Japan, for instance, this appears to be a problem up until at least the early 1970s. In Italy, there are no quarterly data for short-term rates prior to that time. The major reason appears to be a desire by banks to avoid involvement with the regulatory authorities.

types of data available (e.g. national income versus other methods of reporting government expenditures).[8]

How severe these problems are and what magnitude of measurement error they induce in the data for the various countries is, however, mostly a matter of conjecture. One rough cross-country index is the amount of effort we had to expend deriving the series for each country. By this criterion, France, Italy, and the U.K. would score lowest in terms of data reliability. Japan and the Netherlands would come next. Canada, Germany, and the U.S. would rank highest. The obvious problems with using that index, however, is that it suggests that our own adjustments to the data of some countries made after the fact are inferior to the adjustments made beforehand by government statistical offices of others.

An alternative index of data reliability, which is not without its own faults but that does not suffer from this problem, is differences among countries in the goodness of fit of some of the behavioral equations reported elsewhere in this volume. One such set of equations is the real income equations reported by Darby in chapter 9. Darby, in fact, cites measurement errors for the poorer performance of the equations in some countries than in others. He demonstrates that the existence of such errors is consistent with the pattern of coefficients estimated for several foreign countries. Grouping the countries on the basis of Darby's results, we would rank France, Italy, and Japan as having the least reliable data; Canada, Germany, and the Netherlands would be given the middle ground. The United Kingdom and the United States we would judge to be the best.

The exact ranking based on several other equations we have examined would be different. However, a broad pattern of differences among countries in data quality is evident. The simple nominal income equations in the next section of this chapter, for example, perform relatively poorly for the United Kingdom, France, and Italy—high standard errors as a percentage of the mean of the dependent variable—while those for the United States perform relatively well. The results for Canada, Japan, Germany, and the Netherlands lie in between.

The one reasonably firm inference that can be drawn from all of this is that France and the United States very likely occupy the two extremes in data quality. In addition, Italy—and perhaps Japan and the United Kingdom—seems to be on the low side of the mean while Canada, Germany, and the Netherlands seem to be on the high side.

---

8. International agencies such as the United Nations Statistical Office, the IMF, and the OECD attempt to reconstruct some of these series on a common basis. For the most part, however, the resultant data are unavailable on a quarterly basis for anything other than exceedingly short periods. See, for example, the discussion of balance-of-payments data by Erwin Veil (1975) and of consumer price data by Charlotte Vannereau (1975) in the OECD's *Occasional Studies*.

3.3.1   Comparison with the IMF Data

Publications of the International Monetary Fund, in particular its *International Financial Statistics* and their companion tapes, have been a standard source for a wide variety of international data. For that reason we thought it would be useful to compare our data with comparable series available from the IMF.

Table 3.1 provides summary data on relative temporal coverage. The individual entries in the table are means of the ratios of the number of quarters spanned by the IMF series to the number of quarters spanned by our series. We calculate these two ways: as the mean across all eight countries for each of the series and as the mean across all series for each of the eight countries. This comparison is for fourteen of the basic eighteen series available for each country in our data bank. We have omitted population and unemployment altogether, and only listed the official settlements balance or a proxy thereof instead of its separate current account and capital account components.

Let us consider the country means first. Here the distribution is bimodal. For four of the countries, Canada, France, Italy and the Netherlands, the ratio of the IMF coverage to ours is approximately 0.75. For the remaining four, it is roughly 10 percentage points higher.

The series by series breakdown reveals a somewhat different distribution. Approximately half the series on the IMF tapes cover 80% or more of the quarters covered by our series. The coverage of the remainder, however, is widely dispersed, ranging from roughly 43% for the overall

Table 3.1	Temporal Coverage of the IMF as a Percentage of the NBER Quarterly Data		
	a) Country Means		
Canada	.765	Japan	.851
France	.761	Netherlands	.728
Germany	.854	U.K.	.849
Italy	.741	U.S.	.832
	b) Series Means		
M1	.910	Real GNP/GDP	.688
M2	.865	Industrial production	.889
High-powered money	.910	CPI/cost of living	.910
Official reserves	.910	Exchange rate	.910
Short-term interest rate	.813	Balance of payments	.428
Long-term interest rate	.848	Government expenditures	.738
Nominal GNP/GDP	.551	Government deficit	.800
	c) Grand Mean = .798		

balance of payments to approximately 74% for government expenditures. In no instance, moreover, do the IMF data cover our full sample period.

Not only are the IMF data available only for shorter periods, but they also appear to contain a sizable number of breaks of one sort or another. On the tapes themselves, these breaks usually are not indicated. The *International Financial Statistics Yearbook*, though, currently provides annual data for a twenty-nine-year period. A cross-check of the *1980 Yearbook* reveals an average of 3.7 breaks per country. No country has fewer than two breaks, and three, Germany, Japan, and the U.K., each has four or more. Since the difficulties involved in compiling quarterly figures for some of the series are liable to be greater than the difficulties in compiling the yearly, these figures are likely to provide lower limits on the number of breaks in the quarterly data.

To get some indication of the relative accuracy of our data and those available on the IMF tapes for the seven foreign countries, we ran a series of simple nominal income and price equations of the form

$$(3.1) \qquad \Delta \log X_t = a + \sum_{i=0}^{n} b_i \, \Delta \log \mathrm{M1}_{t-i},$$

where X was nominal income (or a proxy thereof) in one set of equations, the consumer price index in the other; M1 was the narrowly defined money supply; and n took the alternative values of 4 and 8. For the countries lacking nominal income data on the IMF tapes, we used the same proxy other researchers have used: the algebraic sum of the changes in the logarithms of the CPI and industrial production. In the comparisons of nominal income equations, the sample period that we used was determined by the availability of the IMF data. In the comparisons of price equations, we faced no such data constraint; hence we used the same sample period for all countries (1959II to 1976IV). In general the regressions with the longer lag fitted better in both instances. Judging these on the basis of either R^2 or standard error of the estimate, we found that for four of the seven foreign countries the nominal income results were clearly superior with our data, the results for two were approximately the same regardless of the data used, and the results for one, France, were in both instances too poor to be considered for comparison.

The price equations on the whole were less satisfactory than the nominal income equations in terms of goodness of fit. Our data did, however, tend to perform marginally better. Viewed in terms of R^2, three of the foreign countries were superior with our data, three with the IMF; viewed in terms of standard error of estimates, five were superior with our data, one was the same with both. Again, France was equally poor with both data sets.

3.4 Conclusions

As we see it, our construction of an international data base from an original source has two major benefits. Data of tolerable comparability among countries and substantial homogeneity over time are now readily available for a longer time period than previously. In addition, the pedigree of these data—both their merits and their limitations—is well enough documented that future researchers need not themselves go through the same arduous process that we have. As data for new time periods become available, they can in most instances simply be linked to our series.

The data nevertheless are still far from ideal. The dubious quality of some series is one problem. We doubt, however, that it can be greatly mitigated by additional manipulation of the underlying data by private researchers. Government statistical offices and central banks will have to take the lead. Intercountry heterogeneity of certain other series is a second problem. Its resolution unfortunately is far from simple. In each instance a cooperative effort by official agencies in all of the various countries would be necessary.

How fruitful our efforts have been can perhaps be best judged in terms of the studies to which these data have given rise. The wide range of successful empirical investigations reported in this volume provides the best check on the data in general just as the research underlying their construction has provided a check in detail.

Acknowledgments

A considerable number of individuals played a role in the construction and documentation of the international data base. At the NBER, Anthony Cassese, in particular, deserves a substantial share of the credit for whatever success was achieved. Cassese not only contributed extremely competent research assistance but also made a number of independent analytical contributions. In addition, he and Anna Schwartz, whose own involvement in every phase of the project requires special mention, provided the editorial skills that turned an, at times, haphazard rambling series of notes on the data into a concise and readable whole. Laura Nowak provided able assistance throughout. Linda Dunn and Robert Greenfield also aided in the compilation of some of the series. Connie McCarthy rechecked all of the data after the studies were completed and did a truly excellent job updating them.

At Citibank, N.A., David Devlin, Thomas Huertas, Robert Leftwich, Werner Chilton, and Ryuji Tahara—on leave from the Sanwa Bank—provided advice and assistance. In addition, there were a number of private and government economists from the United States and abroad who graciously supplied us with data and patiently answered our questions. In particular, we wish to thank Jack Bame, Andre Fourçans, Charles Freedman, Michele Fratianni, Pieter Korteweg, Richard Levich, Jacques Melitz, Manfred Neumann, and Vincenzo Siesto.

References

France, Institut National de la Statistique et des Etudes Economiques. 1962–76. *Bulletin Mensuel des Statistiques*.

Friedman, M. 1962. The interpolation of time series by related series. NBER Technical Paper, no. 16.

Friedman, M., and A. J. Schwartz. 1970. *Monetary statistics of the United States: Estimates, sources, and methods*. New York: Columbia University Press.

International Monetary Fund. 1957–76. *International Financial Statistics*.

Lothian, J. R. 1976. The demand for high-powered money. *American Economic Review* 66 (March): 56–68.

United Kingdom, Bank of England. 1970 and 1975. *Statistical Abstract I and II*.

―――. 1963–76. *Quarterly Bulletin*.

United States, Department of Commerce. 1955–76. *Survey of Current Business*.

Vannereau, C. 1975. Comparability of consumer price indices in OECD countries. *OECD Economic Outlook: Occasional Studies*, July, pp. 35–45.

Veil, E. 1975. Surpluses and deficits in the balance of payments: Definition and significance of alternative concepts. *OECD Economic Outlook: Occasional Studies*, July, pp. 23–34.

4 The Timing of Monetary and Price Changes and the International Transmission of Inflation

Anthony Cassese and James R. Lothian

4.1 Introduction

Our aim in this chapter is to present evidence on two issues: the relative contributions to inflation in each of these countries of domestic and of international factors, and the relative importance of the channels through which the international factors have operated.

The difficulty that arises in investigating these issues is that most, if not all, of the foreign countries we consider seem to have been neither fully open nor fully closed. Exchange rates in a number of notable instances during the Bretton Woods era underwent substantial changes; the various domestic monetary authorities often seemed to pursue policies different from those of the world at large, and the propensity of government of some of these countries to tinker with markets for international goods and capital ran high. Nevertheless, all seven foreign countries experienced the same general pattern of inflation as the United States, the reserve-currency country, for close to half the sample period.

One solution to the problem would be to estimate more general models that relax some of the simplifying assumptions of the polar-case open- and closed-economy models.[1] Darby and Stockman in chapter 5 and Gandolfi and Lothian in chapter 14 adopt that approach. Our approach, in contrast, is to conduct a series of tests of Granger-causality for each country for a number of relations, some between domestic variables alone, others between domestic and foreign variables.

Anthony Cassese is a financial economist and portfolio strategist at Citibank, N.A.

An earlier version of this chapter appeared in the *Journal of Monetary Economics* 10 (August 1982): 1–23.

1. Blejer (1977), Cross and Laidler (1976), Jonson (1976), and Laidler (1978) are all examples of earlier work in this area.

The merit in this approach is that it avoids the problem of the structure of the model limiting the range of investigation. Indeed, the tests we apply are intended to provide evidence that will permit us to rule out some previous model-identifying restrictions. It therefore not only serves as a convenient point of departure for constructing and estimating more general models but provides a way of reevaluating some of the models that have been already estimated. The drawback, of course, is that the simple bivariate relations underlying our tests may themselves give rise to specification bias caused by the omission of other important variables.

4.2   Theoretical Consideration

To derive a set of testable hypotheses about the international transmission of inflation based on timing relations among variables, we first review the model underlying the simple monetary approach to the balance of payments (MABP).[2] We present expressions for the rates of inflation and of monetary growth in a small open economy and point out the model's implications for both. In so doing, we point out what we believe is a popular misconception surrounding the MABP: the view that, in the context of the most basic model, changes in monetary growth will follow rather than precede changes in inflation.[3] We then relax some of the simplifying assumptions of the model and state the timing implications of these modifications for questions of international transmission.

4.2.1   The Monetary Approach

The simplest expositions of the MABP start with a money demand function of the standard form, a purchasing power parity relation, and a money market equilibrium condition. Ignoring interest rates, we can write the first as

$$(4.1) \qquad \log (M/P)^d_t = k \log y_{pt},$$

where M is the nominal stock of domestic money, P the domestic price level, y_p permanent income, and k the income elasticity of demand. The purchasing power parity or, if the exchange rate is assumed perfectly rigid, price arbitrage relation is simply

$$(4.2) \qquad P_t = \pi P'_t,$$

where P' is the rest-of-world price level and π the (constant) exchange

---

2. Johnson (1976) is the classic statement of the monetary approach.

3. Swoboda (1977), in discussing the monetary approach to the transmission of inflation, states that the monetary approach may be distinguished from others in that "causation for a small open economy runs from income to the stock of money" (p. 15). For a contrasting view, see Branson (1977).

rate. The equilibrium condition relates the nominal stock of money supplied to the nominal stock demanded,

(4.3) $$M_t = M_t^d.$$

Taking logarithms of (4.2) and (4.3), differencing the results along with equation (4.1), and making the appropriate substitutions, we arrive at the standard expressions for the domestic rate of inflation

(4.4) $$\dot{P}_t = \dot{P}_t'$$

and monetary growth

(4.5) $$\dot{M}_t = \dot{P}_t' + k\dot{y}_{pt},$$

where a dot over a variable indicates a logarithmic first difference.

Equations (4.4) and (4.5) are equilibrium relations that describe the long-run growth paths of domestic money and domestic prices. This is readily apparent from the assumption of instantaneous adjustment of money demand to supply. In much of the literature, however, these dynamic relations are thought to do more: to have implications also for the time path of the adjustment to equilibrium. As the authors of one recent study using the simple MABP model have put it, "there is a clear presumption to [the] existence and direction" of the leads and lags between domestic money, prices, and nominal income in a small open economy under a fixed exchange-rate regime (Putnam and Wilford 1978).

4.2.2   Extensions of the Basic Model

What the authors of the statement seem to have in mind is something like the following. Consider a position of dynamic equilibrium in which the reserve-currency country's money stock and prices and the domestic money stock and prices are growing at constant rates, for simplicity all assumed to be equal. Now let monetary growth in the reserve-currency country increase. Its rate of inflation will eventually follow suit. The increase in inflation will, via arbitrage, be transmitted as an instantaneous and equal increase in inflation in non-reserve-currency countries. The new rate of inflation, in turn, will mean that domestic real cash balances are now growing more slowly than desired. The rate of hoarding, the inflow of foreign reserves, will increase as a result. Therefore, after the fact, so will the rate of growth of the domestic money supply.

The problem is, however, that this sequence of events does not follow directly from the model presented above. In the model everything takes place within a single period. For the reserve inflow to follow the equalization of inflation rates, the growth rates of the actual and desired nominal stocks of money would have to differ. That can be effected within the model fairly simply, but it requires replacing equation (4.3) with some form of stock adjustment relation like

(4.6a)
$$\log M_t - \log M_{t-1} = \beta(\log M_t^d - \log M_{t-1}),$$

or, equivalently,

(4.6b)
$$\log M_t = \beta(\log M_t^d) + (1 - \beta)\log M_{t-1}.$$

Using (4.1), substituting successively for the lagged actual stock of money and differencing the result, we would then arrive at a new equation in which the current period's monetary growth would be a distributed lag, with geometrically declining weights of inflation in the reserve-currency country and of growth in permanent income:

(4.7)
$$\dot{M}_t = \beta \sum_{i=0}^{\infty} (1 - \beta)^i (k\dot{y}_{pt-i} + \dot{P}'_{t-i}).$$

Extending the model in this way also seems reasonable from an empirical standpoint since most demand-for-money studies have uncovered lags of several quarters or more in the adjustment process linking actual and desired money balances. To derive alternative testable hypotheses about the international transmission mechanism, one might also want to relax some of the other strong assumptions of the simple MABP model. Three possible modifications of the simple model are to relax the assumptions of instantaneous price arbitrage, equilibrium in the money market of the reserve-currency country, and full employment. Later we consider the implications of permitting short-run sterilization policies.

First, let us consider the question of price arbitrage. Here the empirical evidence to date is inconsistent with convergence of overall rates of inflation within a quarter and perhaps even within a period of several years.[4] One reason often given is the existence of sizable nontradable goods sectors. In this instance, even if prices of tradable goods adjust quickly, prices of nontradable goods may adjust only with a substantial lag. If that is the case, then the domestic inflation equation, (4.4), and the domestic money growth equation, (4.5) or (4.7), would have to be rewritten to take account of the differences in speeds of adjustment of prices between tradable and nontradable goods across countries.[5] The end result is that the timing relation between domestic monetary growth and overall inflation becomes less easy to determine. Given a sufficiently slow adjustment of prices of nontradable goods, domestic inflation might not be observed to lead domestic monetary growth.

The next logical step would be to relax the implicit assumption that prices in the reserve-currency country adjust fully and instantaneously to monetary changes. For example, consider the monetary transmission mechanism Friedman and Schwartz (1963a) outline for a closed econ-

---

4. Kravis and Lipsey (1978), among others, present evidence counter to the arbitrage hypothesis.
5. See Blejer (1977) for a model in which the slower adjustment of prices of nontradable than of tradable goods plays a crucial role.

omy. The key element in their view is the series of portfolio adjustments that an unanticipated change in monetary growth engenders.[6]

To illustrate, suppose monetary growth in a closed economy suddenly increases. Initially, market yields on financial assets and equities, and then a whole host of implicit yields on consumer goods of every degree of durability, temporarily fall as money holders desire to rid themselves of excess cash balances and as the adjustment proceeds from one sector to another. Spending in all of these areas therefore increases, and output and prices begin to rise more rapidly. Eventually stock equilibrium is reestablished; holdings of real cash balances are lower, and inflation is higher than before the increase in money growth.

Suppose we now open that model to the international realm. Consider, for instance, what happens to the small country in a world of fixed exchange rates when monetary growth in the reserve-currency country undergoes an unanticipated increase.[7] Initially, this excess supply of money in the reserve-currency country reflects itself in an excess demand for alternative assets denominated in both the reserve currency and foreign currencies. The prices of those assets rise, and their yields fall. The fall in interest rates produces an excess demand for money in the small country which, in part, is satisfied by the inflow of reserves as residents of the reserve-currency country reduce their excess holdings of money and then increase their expenditures on bonds and equities. Eventually the process spreads to the markets for consumption and investment goods in both the reserve- and non-reserve-currency countries. As expenditures on these goods increase, their prices and the overall price levels in both countries begin to rise more rapidly. At the same time, interest rates on bonds and on equities begin to rise and approach their initial levels.

The final equilibrium position is one in which monetary growth, inflation, and the nominal interest rate on bonds, both in the reserve- and non-reserve-currency countries, are all higher; holdings of real cash balances are lower; and international payments positions are altered. The reserve-currency country now has a greater balance-of-payments deficit, and foreign countries have greater balance-of-payments surpluses or smaller deficits. If the asset approach is a reasonable expression of the adjustment mechanism, then we have a further reason to suppose that domestic monetary changes in a small open economy would *not* lag price-level changes.

6. If the monetary change were fully anticipated, the price-level response would be immediate. The information set used to form anticipations therefore has a crucial bearing on the exact timing relation.

7. The papers by Frenkel and Rodriguez (1975) and by Girton and Henderson (1976) describe models of this general sort. In both, however, the authors confine their analysis to organized asset markets.

We could also relax the implicit assumption in the MABP of full employment; then the transmission mechanism operating through portfolio adjustment provides a further rationale for small-country monetary growth actually leading its rate of inflation. For example, suppose an unanticipated increase in monetary growth in the reserve-currency country induced the portfolio adjustments described above. This would be followed by increased expenditures by residents of the reserve-currency country on foreign goods, which would lead to a balance-of-payments surplus and expansion of aggregate demand and output in the small economy. At the same time, the accumulation of reserves by the small economy's central bank would lead to an expansion of its high-powered money and overall money supply. Initially the bulk of the increase in the nominal income of the small economy would be reflected in output. Only after some time had elapsed would the effect be manifest upon the price level alone.

In conclusion, the lead or lag of money over prices, in what appears to be an open economy, is an uncertain guide to settling questions of causation and more importantly the international transmission of inflation. We would view a lead of prices over money and to a lesser extent a coincidence in movements as prima facie evidence of the importance of foreign influences. But a lag of prices behind money is consistent with either domestic or foreign monetary forces being the causative factor.

4.2.3   Other Implications of the Alternative Models

Fortunately these modifications of the simple model have other empirical implications that can help us differentiate among alternative hypotheses about the international inflation process. One testable hypothesis, of course, is derived from the presumed operation of price arbitrage. For a small open economy, if arbitrage were not instantaneous, we would expect prices in the rest of the world to lead domestic prices.

Similarly, if assets markets provide another linkage among countries we would expect there to be a relation among interest rates in one country and those in the rest of the world during periods of fixed exchange rates. Again, assuming that the effects are not instantaneously felt, we would expect changes in interest rates in the rest of the world, or in the reserve-currency country, to precede those in a small open economy.

Analyzing the timing relations between high-powered money and its counterparts on the asset side of the central bank's balance sheet—foreign reserves and domestic assets (domestic credit)—and between those two asset components themselves can also help to clear up some of the ambiguities that surround the timing relation between money and prices. Let us consider three cases: the reserve-currency country, a completely open small economy, and an intermediate case.

In the reserve-currency country, the U.S., the increase in monetary expansion underlying an increase in its inflation and ultimately that of the rest of the world is the result of credit expansion by the reserve-currency country's central bank. Accordingly, its domestic assets will be positively related to, and either lead or be coincident with, its high-powered money. Indeed, the foreign component of the reserve-currency country's high-powered money is of minor importance for that country. Changes in its balance of payments will be a result rather than a cause of variations in the growth of the reserve-currency country's high-powered money. High-powered money therefore will be negatively related, and either lead or be coincident with, the balance of payments of a reserve-currency country.

In a completely open small economy, movements in its domestic assets are unimportant as an effective source of monetary change. An overexpansion of domestic assets of the central bank ultimately will be nullified by reserve outflows, underexpansion by reserve inflows. Changes in foreign reserve holdings of the central bank are the channel through which monetary expansion occurs. Therefore foreign reserves will bear a positive and either coincident or leading relation to high-powered money. Changes in domestic assets will be unrelated to high-powered money growth but bear a negative and either coincident or leading relation to foreign reserve changes for a non-reserve-currency country.

The intermediate case is the most difficult to handle. Changes in domestic assets and foreign reserves are both potential sources of monetary changes. Some sterilization of balance-of-payments movements is likely, and at the same time some feedback of domestic credit expansion on foreign reserves flows will be observed. We would expect therefore to see changes in both foreign reserves and domestic assets to bear a leading, or perhaps coincident, positive relation to high-powered money growth and a negative and bidirectional relation to each other. Both foreign reserves and domestic asset movements can influence high-powered money growth in the intermediate case.

4.3   Testing Timing Relations

In this section we describe the technique we use to test timing relations. We define such relations as relations that exhibit a temporal precedence of one or more variables over another. In this paper we concentrate on bivariate timing relations. We believe these tests are useful for discriminating between relations which are postulated to be fundamentally different in various versions of the monetary model of transmission discussed in the previous section.

To examine timing relations, we use the incremental prediction criterion introduced by Granger (1969) and developed further by Sims (1977). Granger defines a causal relation, e.g. between X and Y, on the basis of the usefulness of information on the characterization (probability laws) of one stochastic process, say X_t, for the description of the joint stochastic process, $\{Y_t, X_s\}$. This is usually stated as: series X (Granger) causes series Y if we can better predict Y by utilizing past values of Y *and* X than by using merely past Y alone. The criterion Granger suggests for making this assessment is a comparison of conditional mean squared errors contingent upon the information sets inclusive and exclusive of series X. Thus, if X helps to predict Y, in the sense of reducing the mean squared prediction error for Y, then X Granger-causes Y.

Sims proves two theorems on (stationary) stochastic processes which are relevant in this context. Sims's analysis begins by recognizing that the stationary processes Y and X can be represented as

(4.8) $$Y_t = A(L)u_t + B(L)\epsilon_t,$$

(4.9) $$X_t = C(L)u_t + D(L)\epsilon_t,$$

where u_t and ϵ_t are uncorrelated stationary processes and $A(L)$, $B(L)$, $C(L)$, and $D(L)$ are polynomials in the lag operator L. According to Sims's first theorem, a necessary and sufficient condition for Y *not* causing X is that either $C(L)$ or $D(L)$ be identically zero. For example, Y would not cause X if, and only if, equation (4.9) could be written as

(4.10) $$X_t = D(L)\epsilon_t.$$

His second theorem states that the failure of Y to Granger-cause X is a necessary and sufficient condition for treating X as strictly econometrically exogenous with respect to Y.

The import of these two theorems is that once we establish the existence of a particular representation between two variables (or, more accurately, once we establish that we cannot refute the existence of one) we have good reason to treat one variable as exogenous. Of course, one variable, which may be exogenous with respect to another variable in the framework of a bivariate system, may be endogenous with respect to a third variable. Nevertheless, the treatment of certain variables as exogenous lends structure to our economic models. The implied structure permits us to choose a better model from among classes of models each of which has a structure with a particular set of exogenous variables.

To conduct the causality tests, we ran regressions of the general form[8]

(4.11) $$Y_t = \alpha_0 + \sum_{i=1}^{m} \beta_i Y_{t-i} + \sum_{j=1}^{n} \gamma_j X_{t-j} + U_t,$$

as well as the corollary regressions in which we constrained the γ_j to be identically zero,

(4.12) $$Y_t = \alpha_0 + \sum_{i=1}^{m} \beta_i Y_{t-i} + U_t.$$

8. Sargent (1976) contains a discussion of this form of the test.

By comparing the improvement in the explanation of Y obtained from
(4.11) with that derived from the companion regression (4.12), we can
determine whether series X contains information useful in explaining
series Y. Then, by reversing the roles of X and Y in regressions (4.11) and
(4.12), we can establish whether an empirical representation of Y and X
implies that one of the series is exogenous. Thus, if we can demonstrate
within reasonable statistical limits that the following representation is
plausible,

$$(4.13) \qquad Y_t = a_1 + \sum_{i=1}^{m} b_i Y_{t-i} + \sum_{j=1}^{n} c_i X_{t-i}$$

and

$$(4.14) \qquad X_t = a_2 + \sum_{i=1}^{m} d_i X_{t-i},$$

then, according to Sims's theorems, Y does not cause X or, alternatively,
X is exogenous.

This is the regression test suggested by Granger; our interpretation of it
is, however, somewhat looser than the conventional one. For the most
part, we eschew using the word "cause" and instead speak in terms of
timing. The reason, which should be clear from the theoretical presentation in section 4.2, is that in at least one of the areas in which we deal—the
money-price relations—leads and lags are a poor guide to the question of
causation in economies that have an unknown degree of openness. In
terms of the debate over "measurement versus theory" that has recently
been rekindled (see Sims 1977) our approach can perhaps best be described as "measurement with some theory."

A related point about methodology that bears mentioning is the potential bias inherent in this type of testing procedure. Commonality of
movements in the series being analyzed may be captured in the autoregressive terms; this is implicitly disregarded by the method we use. As
several others have pointed out (e.g. Zellner 1977), this can lead to
accepting the null hypothesis of no relations between the two series
when, in fact, one actually exists. In defense of the methodology, we
should point out that this bias can also be a blessing. The simple fact of the
matter is that in most industrial contries inflation and monetary growth
over our sample period rose dramatically and at much the same time.
Analyzing innovations in the time series may be the only way to separate
the influence of one factor from another.

In almost all instances, we transform the data for the purpose of
rendering the series stationary. In general, we use natural logs of the
levels to reduce the problem of heteroscedasticity. We then difference
the log levels, usually once but in some experiments twice. This procedure is intended to eliminate the trend in the mean of a series which is
often encountered in aggregate economic time series. This procedure has

the advantage of simply and symmetrically "prefiltering" the data without the substantial time costs and lost degrees of freedom one typically incurs when applying Box-Jenkins techniques. Moreover, it is not subject to the criticism that too much has been removed since nearly all aggregate economic time series regression analysis must consider the transformation we apply in order to come to terms with the estimation-efficiency question. The one exception to the general transformation procedure was the (net) domestic asset versus (net) foreign asset relations for certain of the countries for which the net positions took on a negative value. In these exceptional instances, we used arithmetic values of the levels and arithmetic first differences scaled by high-powered money.

4.4 Empirical Results

Our discussion of empirical results is divided into several parts: domestic money and prices, price and interest-rate arbitrage, asset components of high-powered money, and sources of monetary change. In our analysis, we cover periods beginning in 1958II and experiment with a variety of lag structures.

4.4.1 Domestic Money and Prices

We summarize the money-price results in tables 4.1 and 4.2. There we report the F statistics for the Granger tests of the relations between three monetary aggregates, high-powered money, M1 and M2, and two measures of prices, the GNP or GDP deflator (table 4.1) and the consumer or other similar retail price index (table 4.2), for the eight countries in our sample.[9]

Except for France and Italy, a significant effect of lagged money on prices exists for at least one domestic monetary aggregate and both price variables for all three periods. In the case of France, the only significant effects for all periods were for high-powered money growth on consumer price inflation. In the case of Italy, the significance of the money-price relation varies among the combinations of monetary and price variables from period to period. In most countries, however, we find a more pervasive influence than appears in either the French or Italian case; the majority of the relations prove significant for both definitions of the price level.

The reverse influence (prices on money) is considerably less visible. A significant effect of prices on money without feedback only appears in Italy and the U.K. in two instances, each with high-powered money, and in France in two instances with M2. Significant bidirectional influences appear in relatively few instances. Moreover, only in the case of the U.K.

---

9. The data we use were compiled from individual country sources by the NBER Project on the International Transmission of Inflation.

Table 4.1   **Money and Price Deflator**

$$Y_t = \alpha_0 + \sum_{i=1}^{m} \beta_i Y_{t-i} + \sum_{j=1}^{n} \gamma_j X_{t-j}$$

F Statistics for Lags (m, n) and Period Ending:[§]

Country	Variable[†] Y	Variable[†] X	1971III $m=6$ $n=3$	1971III $m=8$ $n=8$	1973IV $m=6$ $n=3$	1973IV $m=8$ $n=8$	1976IV $m=6$ $n=3$	1976IV $m=8$ $n=8$
CA	PD	H	5.0857##	2.8006#	4.2300##	2.2937#	2.3145‡	2.3198#
	PD	M1	1.2176	1.0800	1.9479	1.9383‡	3.3748#	3.2819##
	PD	M2	2.6210‡	3.3309##	3.3975#	2.9488##	1.6940	2.1065
	H	PD	0.9001	0.9920	0.3877	0.7326	0.7274	0.8209
	M1	PD	0.9338	1.2448	0.5172	0.8475	0.8610	1.4687
	M2	PD	1.2395	1.5719	2.7234#	1.9840‡	2.3919‡	1.2493
FR	PD	H	4.7019##	1.7986	4.6467##	1.7584	0.8354	0.7941
	PD	M1	0.5858	0.9226	0.3987	1.0925	0.1559	0.4114
	PD	M2	0.1516	0.6431	0.3631	0.2317	0.6683	0.5199
	H	PD	1.0110	2.6440#	1.0153	1.5907	0.7415	1.2736
	M1	PD	1.1399	0.8372	1.1634	1.0560	0.5488	0.8831
	M2	PD	2.4164‡	1.6700	2.4090‡	1.2625	0.4447	0.4643
GE	PD	H	3.5186#	1.0623	2.4042‡	1.0295	0.6435	2.4534#
	PD	M1	0.4479	0.3952	0.4683	0.2100	1.1187	1.3269
	PD	M2	1.7745	1.2036	2.0504‡	1.2604	0.9762	0.6737
	H	PD	1.5316	1.0373	1.1161	0.4482	0.2838	0.1091
	M1	PD	0.7794	0.7514	0.9441	0.6567	2.1476‡	1.2652
	M2	PD	0.0693	0.2920	0.2636	0.6659	0.4931	1.0815

IT	PD	H	1.1682	1.1094	1.3511	0.8454	0.9918	0.7573
	PD	M1	1.9426	1.2206	3.0492#	2.0289‡	1.7427	1.3796
	PD	M2	0.6455	0.7834	2.2500‡	2.3987#	1.0636	1.3427
	H	PD	1.8111	0.7057	2.7941#	1.2006	8.7666##	3.4494##
	M1	PD	0.9739	0.5882	0.5743	0.4037	1.2931	0.8135
	M2	PD	0.5978	0.2149	0.4895	0.2453	2.6562‡	1.1188
JA	PD	H	3.8405#	1.9646‡	6.0414##	2.4172#	3.2189#	1.3024
	PD	M1	2.2473‡	1.6163	2.2842‡	1.8310‡	0.9347	1.7369‡
	PD	M2	1.1656	1.5835	2.2754‡	1.8709‡	1.6225	1.4317
	H	PD	1.5237	1.0461	1.3528	0.8219	0.6845	1.0836
	M1	PD	3.0488#	1.2816	1.0183	0.9410	1.8314	1.5997
	M2	PD	1.3220	0.9918	1.4421	0.7172	4.2628##	1.4727
NE	PD	H	0.7663	0.6710	0.1439	0.5099	0.2313	0.7476
	PD	M1	2.8542#	2.8115#	3.4698#	2.2073#	1.1498	0.7352
	PD	M2	2.9346#	2.1987#	2.8755#	2.0128‡	3.2533#	1.4874
	H	PD	0.1041	0.7291	0.3436	1.1746	0.4657	1.3963
	M1	PD	0.9419	1.0318	0.8451	1.3412	1.7868	1.3853
	M2	PD	0.1341	0.9253	0.8393	1.6698	0.7360	0.9330

Table 4.1 (continued)

Country	Variable[†] Y	X	1971III $m=6$ $n=3$	1971III $m=8$ $n=8$	1973IV $m=6$ $n=3$	1973IV $m=8$ $n=8$	1976IV $m=6$ $n=3$	1976IV $m=8$ $n=8$
UK	PD	H	1.1017	0.9244	1.3687	1.0933	0.2929	1.9991‡
	PD	M1	3.5272#	3.6844##	4.2292##	4.1970##	2.1304‡	3.9948##
	PD	M2	3.3290#	4.0148##	3.4599#	4.8635##	1.0124	2.3725#
	H	PD	5.9046##	2.3159##	4.2821##	2.8633##	0.6952	1.4133
	M1	PD	0.4415	1.2775	1.5263	1.6117	2.8020#	2.0691#
	M2	PD	0.2520	1.6050	2.2744‡	4.1369##	3.3308#	1.4786
US	PD	H	3.0960#	1.2327	1.1244	0.8451	2.1612‡	0.7881
	PD	M1	7.1747##	3.2115##	3.9259#	2.3341#	3.6139#	2.6592##
	PD	M2	5.0927##	2.0143‡	2.2580‡	1.8163‡	2.5727‡	2.6491##
	H	PD	1.9995	2.1232‡	2.4702‡	2.5302#	1.6230	3.6927##
	M1	PD	0.6292	0.3813	0.7209	0.8829	1.0213	0.4108
	M2	PD	0.5870	0.2438	1.3583	0.6631	0.4676	0.5512

[†] All variables are first differences of the natural log; PD is the GNP or GDP deflator, H is high-powered money, M1 is currency plus demand deposits, and M2 is currency plus the sum of demand and time deposits.

[§] All regressions start in 1958II. The null hypothesis is that the γ_j are as a group equal to zero.

‡ Reject null hypothesis at $\alpha = 0.10$.

Reject null hypothesis at $\alpha = 0.05$.

Reject null hypothesis at $\alpha = 0.01$.

Table 4.2   **Money and Consumer Price Index**

$$Y_t = \alpha_0 + \sum_{i=1}^{m} \beta_i Y_{t-i} + \sum_{j=1}^{n} \gamma_j X_{t-j}$$

F Statistics for Lags (m, n) and Period Ending:[§]

Country	Variable[†] Y	Variable[†] X	1971III m=6 n=3	1971III m=8 n=8	1973IV m=6 n=3	1973IV m=8 n=8	1976IV m=6 n=3	1976IV m=8 n=8
CA	PC	H	1.7304	2.0398‡	2.8630#	3.4068##	2.4287‡	3.3497##
	PC	M1	0.9011	1.3335	2.3543‡	2.6750#	0.9549	1.8960‡
	PC	M2	1.8998	2.3211#	2.1980‡	2.4818#	1.7972	1.7089‡
	H	PC	0.4004	0.9647	0.7010	0.7435	1.8513	1.0520
	M1	PC	0.7429	1.2814	0.6568	0.7356	1.1255	0.9205
	M2	PC	1.9417	1.2898	4.0227##	2.0999##	3.1621#	1.6265
FR	PC	H	3.0838#	1.6784	5.9429##	2.1667#	2.1861‡	1.1267
	PC	M1	0.9035	0.4313	0.8488	0.9236	0.9707	0.7959
	PC	M2	0.9320	0.8640	1.5080	0.6122	1.2368	0.5168
	H	PC	1.0301	1.1479	0.6391	0.8123	1.1896	0.9482
	M1	PC	0.1366	0.7419	0.0794	0.8701	0.0667	1.0880
	M2	PC	0.0472	1.1412	0.4648	1.0315	0.4843	0.8597
GE	PC	H	0.3373	0.6452	0.7065	0.6828	0.6488	0.7574
	PC	M1	3.6700#	2.0091‡	2.2902‡	1.1840	0.8899	0.4544
	PC	M2	2.0487	0.9324	3.6316#	1.4334	2.0873‡	1.0248
	H	PC	1.3580	1.5144	0.7117	0.6157	0.1522	0.3870
	M1	PC	0.1615	0.5855	0.2980	0.2447	0.3265	0.1900
	M2	PC	0.0639	0.5631	0.1868	0.6004	0.2075	0.7861

Table 4.2 (continued)

Country	Variable[+]		1971III		1973IV		1976IV	
	Y	X	$m=6$ $n=3$	$m=8$ $n=8$	$m=6$ $n=3$	$m=8$ $n=8$	$m=6$ $n=3$	$m=8$ $n=8$
IT	PC	H	2.0895	1.7326	2.2146‡	1.4969	0.4835	0.5277
	PC	M1	0.7485	1.1998	0.6685	1.2960	2.5815‡	1.4106
	PC	M2	0.0562	1.4058	0.5205	1.9588‡	2.6051‡	1.9020‡
	H	PC	1.6496	1.5617	2.3577‡	2.0966‡	6.1068##	2.6657##
	M1	PC	1.2290	0.9196	1.0196	0.9489	2.7236#	1.1030
	M2	PC	0.8907	0.4999	1.3936	0.9262	5.1792##	2.2908#
JA	PC	H	2.5529‡	2.2855#	5.5676##	2.7080#	3.8263##	2.8386##
	PC	M1	0.8923	1.3026	1.3859	2.6490#	0.1656	1.6207‡
	PC	M2	1.2829	0.4988	1.7822	0.1308	1.7505	0.5856
	H	PC	1.0003	0.5991	0.5468	0.3308	1.3736	0.9399
	M1	PC	1.2112	1.6718	0.8157	0.9009	1.6885	1.2710
	M2	PC	0.3674	0.5470	0.1371	0.7524	1.8995	1.7773‡
NE	PC	H	1.4213	0.7616	0.9301	0.6842	0.7642	0.5470
	PC	M1	5.4306##	3.5512##	6.8611##	3.6791##	1.8408	1.1385
	PC	M2	3.7966#	2.5407#	4.5943##	2.9069##	3.8946#	2.6756##
	H	PC	0.7038	0.6883	0.3858	0.6059	0.6452	0.7099
	M1	PC	1.9109	0.9570	1.8164	0.8057	1.8521‡	0.9979
	M2	PC	0.4137	0.8526	1.5806	1.5429	2.1967‡	1.5192

_F_ Statistics for Lags (m, n) and Period Ending:§

UK	PC	H	4.9425##	2.2847#	5.6819##	2.6542#	3.2730#	4.0026##
	PC	M1	1.3392	0.9494	1.6227	1.1369	0.7719	1.8216‡
	PC	M2	0.4981	1.1294	2.3374‡	1.7292	1.6433	2.4200#
	H	PC	1.0225	0.7083	0.5323	1.1533	1.2367	2.1754#
	M1	PC	3.2914#	1.8360	4.4124##	2.9159##	5.7665##	2.5341#
	M2	PC	3.7181#	1.7491	5.1800##	2.8629##	1.0491	0.7693
US	PC	H	3.3590#	1.6969	1.3730	1.1135	2.3505‡	1.2689
	PC	M1	4.5219##	5.0305##	6.6044##	3.9097##	8.6231##	4.2129##
	PC	M2	0.5545	2.8073#	1.3136	3.1041##	2.4869‡	3.2708##
	H	PC	0.1369	0.3614	0.4343	0.3393	0.2956	0.4610
	M1	PC	2.4532‡	1.8937‡	2.6349‡	2.2025#	1.8309	1.5376
	M2	PC	0.9170	1.9163‡	1.2794	2.2896#	0.8068	1.9386‡

† All variables are first differences of the natural log; PC is the consumer price index, H is high-powered money, M1 currency plus demand deposits, and M2 is currency plus the sum of demand and time deposits.

§ All regressions start 1958II. The null hypothesis is that the γ_j are as a group equal to zero.

‡ Reject null hypothesis at $\alpha = 0.10$.

Reject null hypothesis at $\alpha = 0.05$.

Reject null hypothesis at $\alpha = 0.01$.

do these reverse influences show any consistency with regard to the monetary aggregate employed.[10] These results therefore suggest that the rate of inflation is not necessarily exogenous in monetary models regardless of the degree to which prices are equalized via arbitrage.[11]

One problem with the results is that in several of the countries the relations differ markedly depending upon which price variable is used. Britain is the prime example. Using the GDP deflator, we find no influence from lagged high-powered money to prices in Britain and a significant influence, in two of the three periods, running the other way. Using the retail price index, we find almost exactly the opposite. A similar inconsistency exists using M1 and M2.[12] In the regressions with the GDP deflator, both monetary aggregates have a significant influence on prices with little relation the other way; in the regressions with the retail price index, prices more often influence money. For the other countries, the results are more consistent between price-level measures.

The data therefore establish a pattern that on the whole is consistent with monetary explanations of the inflation process. They fail, however, to corroborate the popular interpretation of the MABP, in which prices adjust instantaneously but money supply adjusts only with a lag. Either domestic monetary forces by themselves or international forces operating via some combination of a reserve-flow mechanism and central bank reaction function (or some combination of the two) were important.

4.4.2   Price and Interest-Rate Arbitrage

In table 4.3 we report test results derived from two sets of international price relations. In one we compare movements in the domestic price levels in each of the eight countries with movements in an index of price levels in the remaining seven countries. In the other we compare movements in the price level in each of the seven non-reserve-currency countries with movements in the price level in the U.S. Both sets of results are for the period through 1971III, since after that time most countries experienced substantial changes in their dollar exchange rate. In all instances we included six lagged values of the dependent variable in the equation and three of the independent variable.

For the comparisons of domestic and rest-of-world inflation, the results are mixed. We find some influence from lagged rest-of-world to domestic prices for the period ending 1971III in two countries, France and Japan. When we included the contemporaneous value of the world price index in

10. British results from much longer-term time series consistent with these findings are reported in Huffman and Lothian (1980) and for the postwar period in Williams, Goodhart, and Gowland (1976).

11. This same result was obtained for a broad range of Latin American countries in Cassese (1979, chapter 6).

12. In the U.K. what we call M2 is what the Bank of England calls sterling M3, but unlike their series it excludes government deposits and certificates of deposit.

Table 4.3   **Price Arbitrage**

$$Y_t = \alpha_0 + \sum_{i=1}^{m} \beta_i Y_{t-i} + \sum_{j=1}^{n} \gamma_j X_{t-j}$$

	Variable[†]		F Statistic[§] $m=6$ $n=3$	Variable		F Statistic $m=6$ $n=3$
Country	Y	X		Y	X	
CA	PD	PDw	1.6741	PD	PDus	1.6765
	PDw	PD	3.4386[#]	PDus	PD	0.5394
FR	PD	PDw	3.0056[#]	PD	PDus	0.9744
	PDw	PD	3.9842[##]	PDus	PD	0.4912
GE	PD	PDw	0.2701	PD	PDus	3.9752[#]
	PDw	PD	0.8389	PDus	PD	1.1123
IT	PD	PDw	1.1179	PD	PDus	0.3129
	PDw	PD	1.3534	PDus	PD	1.1805
JA	PD	PDw	2.3618[‡]	PD	PDus	0.6907
	PDw	PD	0.6436	PDus	PD	1.4863
NE	PD	PDw	1.2523	PD	PDus	1.3365
	PDw	PD	0.9483	PDus	PD	0.3511
UK	PD	PDw	0.3151	PD	PDus	2.0759[‡]
	PDw	PD	0.3744	PDus	PD	0.4319
US	PD	PDw	1.4831			
	PDw	PD	2.4181[‡]			

[†]All variables are first differences of the natural log. PD is the GNP or GDP deflator, PDw is the rest-of-world deflator, and PDus is the GNP deflator for the United States.

[§]All regressions 1958II to 1971III. The null hypothesis is that the γ_j as a group are equal to zero.

[‡]Reject null hypothesis at $\alpha = 0.10$.

[#]Reject null hypothesis at $\alpha = 0.05$.

[##]Reject null hypothesis at $\alpha = 0.01$.

the equations, there was a significant relation for Canada also. For the U.S., the relation ran in the opposite direction. Somewhat anomalously, we uncovered a statistically significant reverse influence for Canada and France.

The U.S. versus individual foreign country price comparisons showed significant effects of lagged U.S. prices on German and British prices only and a borderline relation for Canada, which again became significant when we included the contemporaneous value of U.S. prices. France and Japan, the countries that exhibited the strongest response to rest-of-world prices, showed no relation with the U.S.

We summarize the U.S. versus foreign interest rate relations in table 4.4. With the exception of Italy for which we could obtain only a long-term rate, these comparisons are for three-month U.S. Treasury bills and a similar short-term foreign rate. Of all of the arbitrage relations, these

Table 4.4   **Interest Arbitrage**

$$Y_t = \alpha_0 + \sum_{i=1}^{m} \beta_i Y_{t-i} + \sum_{j=1}^{n} \gamma_j X_{t-j}$$

| | Variable[†] | | F Statistic[§] $m = 6$ |
Country	Y	X	$m = 3$
CA	IS	ISus	3.3243[#]
	ISus	IS	1.6404
FR	IS	ISus	2.7322[#]
	ISus	IS	0.8850
GE	IS	ISus	3.6046[#]
	ISus	IS	4.9406[##]
IT	IL	ILus	3.9248[#]
	ILus	IL	1.4547
JA	IS	ISus	0.2948
	ISus	IS	1.4438
NE	IS	ISus	5.9041[##]
	ISus	IS	1.0401
UK	IS	ISus	3.8546[#]
	ISus	IS	0.8776

[†]The interest rates are in first difference form. IS is the short-term interest rate for each country except Italy, for which the long-term interest rate is used. ISus is the short-term interest rate for the United States.

[§]All regressions 1958II to 1971III. The null hypothesis is that the γ_j as a group are equal to zero.

[‡]Reject null hypothesis at $\alpha = 0.10$.

[#]Reject null hypothesis at $\alpha = 0.05$.

[##]Reject null hypothesis at $\alpha = 0.01$.

show the most consistency among countries. For all the foreign countries other than Japan, lagged U.S. interest rates have a significant effect. And in most instances—Canada especially—both the magnitude and significance of the effect increase when we include the contemporaneous value of the U.S. rate along with the lagged. For Germany, however, we also uncovered a reverse influence. For Japan, our failure to find any relation may be largely the result of the nature of the Japanese capital market over much of this period, the fact that the Japanese government exercised substantial direct control over interest rates.

4.4.3   Central Bank Behavior and the Balance of Payments

In table 4.5 we report the results of the Granger tests of the relations between changes in foreign reserves and in domestic assets of the monetary authorities of the seven foreign countries.[13] For the U.S., since it is

13. Blejer (1979) presents results of similar tests for four of the countries in our sample—France, Germany, Italy, and the U.K.—and for Sweden. He, however, finds considerably less evidence of sterilization.

Table 4.5   **Domestic Credit and the Balance of Payments**

$$Y_t = \alpha_0 + \sum_{i=1}^{m} \beta_i Y_{t-i} + \sum_{j=1}^{n} \gamma_j X_{t-j}$$

Country	Variable[†] Y	Variable[†] X	F Statistics for Lags (m, n) and Period Ending:[§] 1971III $m = 3$ $n = 3$	F Statistics for Lags (m, n) and Period Ending:[§] 1973IV $m = 3$ $n = 3$	F Statistics for Lags (m, n) and Period Ending:[§] 1976IV $m = 3$ $n = 3$
CA	FH	DH	1.2185	1.4081	1.6945
	DH	FH	0.8582	1.0134	1.0938
FR	FH	DH	0.1140	0.4690	0.1017
	DH	FH	3.8398[##]	2.7887[#]	2.4045[‡]
GE	FH	DH	0.2463	0.6432	0.4089
	DH	FH	2.2295[‡]	3.3784[#]	3.9930[##]
IT	FH	DH	0.1142	0.4898	1.0168
	DH	FH	0.8010	1.0569	2.2833[‡]
JA	FH	DH	0.8563	1.9006[‡]	1.5299
	DH	FH	2.4706[‡]	2.9194[#]	1.9233[‡]
NE	FH	DH	0.9079	2.7864[#]	2.7909[#]
	DH	FH	4.6111[##]	4.3709[##]	6.0623[##]
UK	FH	DH	0.3949	0.8334	1.4041
	DH	FH	0.1568	2.4819[‡]	2.5390[‡]
US	BP	H	0.5770	2.0949[‡]	2.6524[‡]
	H	BP	1.2728	1.1110	1.0156

[†]The variables for Canada, Germany, Italy, and Japan are first differences of the natural log. The variables for France, the Netherlands, the U.K., and the U.S. are arithmetic first differences scaled by high-powered money. FH is official reserve assets, DH is domestic credit, BP is the U.S. official settlements balance, and H is high-powered money.

[§]All regressions start in 1958II. The null hypothesis is that the γ_j are as a group equal to zero.

[‡]Reject null hypothesis at $\alpha = 0.10$.

[#]Reject null hypothesis at $\alpha = 0.05$.

[##]Reject null hypothesis at $\alpha = 0.01$.

the reserve-currency country, we report results based on the relation between the balance of payments, on an official settlements basis and scaled by high-powered money, and changes in total high-powered money.

By far, the more consistent relation for the foreign countries is from changes in foreign reserves to changes in domestic credit. France, Germany, Japan, the Netherlands, the U.K., and, to a lesser extent, Italy all show a significant and negative effect of foreign reserves on domestic assets. In Canada, the sums of the coefficients are positive but not statistically significant at the lag lengths reported in the table. However, when we extended the lag to six periods for the independent variable, the coefficients became significant and their sum remained positive.

The relations running in the other direction, somewhat surprisingly, are less well defined. Among the foreign countries, Japan is the only country for which there is a significant and negative influence of domestic on foreign assets. In the Netherlands, the relation is significantly different from zero in two instances but the sum of the coefficients is positive.

In the U.S., in two of the periods we find a significant relation running from high-powered money to the official settlements balance and no effect in the opposite direction.

In all of the foreign countries, therefore, some type of central bank reaction function seems to have existed over the sample period. The monetary authorities, in countries other than Canada, apparently tried to offset the effects of balance-of-payments movements on their domestic money stocks. The Bank of Canada, in contrast, seems to have done the opposite. Desirous perhaps of maintaining a stable exchange rate with the U.S. dollar, the Canadians appear to have reacted to balance-of-payments inflows by engaging in some monetary expansion of their own.

The Federal Reserve's actions—and the results are hardly at variance with what one could expect for the central bank of a reserve-currency country—appears to have paid little attention to the balance of payments in conducting policy. That policy, however, seems to have been the source of the sometimes sizable U.S. balance-of-payments deficits during this period.

4.4.4   Sources of Monetary Change

We ran two other series of regressions and performed the associated Granger tests to analyze the sources of monetary growth in the seven foreign countries in the sample from two slightly different perspectives.[14] In one, we compared movements in the three domestic monetary aggregates in each of the countries with the movements of their counterparts in the U.S. In the other, we compared the movements in each of the domestic aggregates with movements in foreign and domestic assets of that country's monetary authorities. For the sake of brevity, we do not report these results.

The first set of results was not terribly satisfactory. Only in the Canadian and German regressions were there significant positive relations between the lagged U.S. aggregate and the comparable domestic aggregate. In both countries, moreover, there were somewhat implausible significant reverse influences in several instances.

The foreign asset and domestic asset versus domestic monetary aggregate tests were slightly better. For all the non-reserve-currency countries except the U.K., movements in lagged foreign assets made a statistically

---

14. The results that we discuss in this section are for the period ending 1971III only. Results for the longer period during which exchange rates were more variable were considerably less satisfactory.

significant contribution to the explanation of movements in at least one of the monetary aggregates. The results for domestic assets were a mixed lot. For three of the countries—Canada, Italy, and the U.K.—domestic assets had no perceptible influence on any of the three monetary aggregates. For the others—France, Germany, Japan, and the Netherlands—domestic assets had a statistically significant, but negative, effect.

These latter results are difficult to rationalize as reflections of central bank behavior. They could arise because of either spurious correlation or the existence of a more intricate relation between foreign assets of the central banks of the reserve-currency and non-reserve-currency countries.

4.5   Summary and Conclusions

Our purpose in this chapter has been to investigate the channels through which inflation has been transmitted internationally. To do so we have focused upon five areas that featured prominently in our theoretical discussion: the relation between domestic money and prices, the influence of foreign prices on domestic prices, the influence of foreign interest rates on domestic interest rates, the behavior of the central bank, and the relation between the components of high-powered money and the monetary aggregates.

The results we have obtained have several major implications. Let us consider the money-price relation first. In all countries our tests showed a significant effect of lagged domestic money growth on domestic inflation, which appears to be fairly robust across the specifications we tried. The strength of these relations suggests that one-shot and transitory phenomena, such as shifts in money demand, are unlikely to have been the major causative factors behind inflation. Similarly, given the absence of a consistent reverse relation from inflation to money growth for most countries, an explanation of inflation that attributes it primarily to cost-push accommodated by domestic monetary growth appears doubtful for most, if not all, of the countries in the sample.

What at first glance appears surprising about these results is the similarity in the timing relations among countries. According to one somewhat popular notion, they ought to differ: changes in monetary growth occurring before changes in inflation in the United States, the reserve-currency country, and occurring afterward in the seven foreign countries. As we have pointed out, however, there is no necessary correspondence between openness and the direction of Granger-causation.

Our results are consistent with the seven foreign economies being independent of the U.S. or, alternatively, with a chain of transmission running from U.S. money via the balance of payments to foreign money and thence to foreign prices. They are inconsistent with an adjustment mechanism that operates exclusively via price arbitrage.

Further evidence on the question of price arbitrage comes from the two sets of price comparisons we have made. They provide no evidence of a strong price arbitrage relation and thus do not suggest that domestic money was purely passive or that foreign central banks were purely silent partners of the U.S. monetary authorities. They imply that some potential existed for a number of the non-reserve-currency countries to operate an independent monetary policy, at least in the short run.

To the extent that there was an international transmission process, it appears to have worked through asset markets. In all countries but Japan, some evidence of interest arbitrage was uncovered. Additionally, in all but the U.K., changes in foreign reserves had a statistically significant effect on at least one of the three monetary aggregates. Furthermore, in Canada and Germany—the countries that both had very similar inflation experiences to that of the U.S. in the period prior to 1972—U.S. monetary variables had a significant effect on the domestic monetary variables. Thus, when we combine the inflation comparison results with the interest arbitrage and the foreign reserve–domestic credit results, we obtain a picture of the operation of a self-regulating mechanism preventing long-run monetary independence but allowing some scope for short-term domestic monetary control.

Another set of implications stems from what we have learned from analyses of changes in the asset components of the central banks' portfolios and of their relations with changes in high-powered money and the two broader monetary aggregates. These are, however, somewhat tenuous. In a number of countries—France, Germany, Japan, the Netherlands, and to some extent Italy and the U.K.—we find evidence of some sterilization of reserve inflows. For Canada, we found a significant positive effect of reserve inflows on domestic assets.

On the whole, these are a priori appealing results that appear to explain some of the differences among countries: low- and moderate-inflation countries trying to avoid importing inflation from the U.S. and being at least partially successful; Canada seeking to stabilize its price level and exchange rate vis-à-vis the U.S. dollar; and Italy and the U.K.—the higher-inflation countries—acquiescing in the face of reserve inflows and perhaps, though the data are mostly moot on this point, going the U.S. one step better in the way of monetary expansion.[15]

15. The general thrust of these conclusions is similar to that of Connolly and Taylor (1979). Tullio (1979) contains a model of the U.S. balance of payments that is also consistent with our results. His finding of an initial overshooting in the U.S. balance of payments following an increase in U.S. domestic credit is suggestive of a chain of causation similar to the one we have outlined: from U.S. monetary policy via the balance of payments to foreign money and then to foreign prices.

Acknowledgments

The authors would like to acknowledge the able research assistance of Connie McCarthy and the helpful comments of the other members of the NBER Project on the International Transmission of Inflation, Anna J. Schwartz, Alan Stockman, and, in particular, Michael R. Darby and Arthur Gandolfi. The suggestions received from members of the Macroeconomics Workshop at New York University were also helpful, especially those of Michael Hamburger.

References

Blejer, M. I. 1977. Short-run dynamics of prices and the balance of payments. *American Economic Review* 67 (June): 419–28.
———. 1979. On causality and the monetary approach to the balance of payments—the European experience. *European Economic Review* 12: 289–96.
Branson, W. H. 1977. A "Keynesian" approach to worldwide inflation. In L. R. Krause, and W. S. Salant, eds., *Worldwide inflation*, pp. 63–92. Washington: Brookings Institution.
Cassese, A. 1979. Money, the dynamics of inflation, and the balance of payments in Latin America. Ph.D. dissertation, City University of New York.
Connolly, M., and D. Taylor. 1979. Exchange rate changes and neutralization: A test of the monetary approach applied to developed and developing countries. *Economica* 46 (August): 281–94.
Cross, R. J., and D. Laidler. 1976. Inflation, excess demand, and expectations in fixed exchange rate open economies: Some preliminary results. In J. M. Parkin, and G. Zis, eds., *Inflation in the world economy*, pp. 221–55. Manchester: Manchester University Press.
Darby, M. R. 1980. The monetary approach to the balance of payments: Two specious assumptions. *Economic Inquiry* 18 (April): 321–26.
Darby, M. R., and A. C. Stockman. 1983. The Mark III international transmission model. Chapter 5 in this volume.
Frenkel, J. A., and C. Rodriguez. 1975. Portfolio equilibrium and the balance of payments: A monetary approach. *American Economic Review* 64, no. 4: 674–88.
Friedman, M., and A. J. Schwartz. 1963a. Money and business cycles. *Review of Economics and Statistics* 45, supplement (February): 32–64.
———. 1963b. *A monetary history of the United States, 1867–1960.* Princeton: Princeton University Press.

Gandolfi, A. E., and J. R. Lothian. 1983. International price behavior and the demand for money. Chapter 14 in this volume.

Girton, L., and D. W. Henderson. 1976. Financial capital movements and central bank behavior in a two-country, short-run portfolio balance model. *Journal of Monetary Economics* 2, no. 1: 33–61.

Granger, C. W. J. 1969. Investigating causal relations by econometric models and cross-spectral methods. *Econometrica* 37 (July): 424–38.

Huffman, W. E., and J. R. Lothian. 1980. Money in the U.K., 1833–1880. *Journal of Money, Credit and Banking*, vol. 12, no. 2.

Johnson, H. G. 1976. Towards a general theory of the balance of payments. In J. A. Frenkel and H. G. Johnson, eds. *The Monetary approach to the balance of payments*, pp. 46–63. Toronto and Buffalo: University of Toronto Press.

Jonson, P. D. 1976. Monetary and economic activity in the open economy: The United Kingdom, 1880–1970. *Journal of Political Economy* 84 (October): 979–1012.

Kravis, I. B., and R. E. Lipsey. 1978. Price behavior in the light of balance of payments theories. *Journal of International Economics* 8 (May): 193–246.

Laidler, D. 1978. A monetarist viewpoint. In M. Posner, ed., *Demand management*, pp. 35–65. London: London National Institute of Economic and Social Research.

Putnam, B. H., and D. S. Wilford. 1978. Money, income, and causality in the United States and the United Kingdom: A theoretical explanation of different findings. *American Economic Review* 68 (June): 423–27.

Sargent, T. J. 1976. A classical macroeconomic model for the United States. *Journal of Political Economy* 84, no. 2: 207–37.

Sims, C. 1977. Exogeneity and causal ordering in macroeconomic models. In C. Sims, ed., *New methods in business cycle research: Proceedings from a conference*, pp. 23–43. Minneapolis: Federal Reserve Bank of Minneapolis.

Swoboda, A. K. 1977. Monetary approaches to worldwide inflation. In L. R. Krause, and W. S. Salant, eds., *Worldwide inflation*, pp. 9–50. Washington: Brookings Institution.

Tullio, G. 1979. Monetary equilibrium and balance of payments adjustment: An empirical test of the U.S. balance of payments, 1951–73. *Journal of Money, Credit and Banking* 11 (February): 68–79.

Williams, D.; C. A. E. Goodhart; and D. H. Gowland. 1976. Money, income, and causality: The U.K. experience. *American Economic Review* 66, no. 3: 417–23.

Zellner, A. 1977. Comments on time series analysis and causal concepts in business cycle research. In C. Sims, ed., *New methods in business cycle research: Proceedings from a conference*, pp. 167–74. Minneapolis: Federal Reserve Bank of Minneapolis.

II

The Mark III International Transmission Model

Whenever we know enough, the preferred procedure for answering one or more empirical questions is to specify an econometric model with as much structure as our knowledge and data permit and then estimate the model—and simulate it, if necessary—to answer these questions. Our efforts to follow this methodology are reported in the five chapters which make up this part. It is always possible to criticize such an effort on the grounds that we do not really know the appropriate structure. While we try to test for indications of specification error here, we must ultimately appeal to conformity of the results reported in this part with the relatively model-free results of parts III and IV which follow.

Darby and Stockman in chapters 5 and 6 specify and estimate pegged and floating exchange-rate versions of the Mark III International Transmission Model. This is a medium-scale structural model designed to test the existence and estimate the strength of various channels for international transmission. The estimates of the model indicate that linkages among countries joined by pegged exchange rates appear to be much looser or more elusive than has been assumed in many previous studies. The universal practice of sterilization by nonreserve central banks increased their control over their domestic money supplies—a control made possible by the imperfect substitutability of goods and assets. Nor are other international linkages found to be very strong. The dual of these findings for floating exchange-rate systems is that sterilized intervention in the foreign exchange market can move the exchange rate.

In chapter 7 Darby uses a simplified Mark IV International Simulation Model to illustrate the implications of the structural model for the efficacy of monetary and fiscal policy. Under pegged exchange rates, the simulated results depend on the particular country, with Germany most closely approaching the openness idealized by the monetary approach and Canada and the United Kingdom very nearly closed aside from the Keynesian absorption channel. The flexible version of the Mark IV Model is less successful but does illustrate a potentially perverse short-run effect by which unexpected money-supply increases may temporarily appreciate the currency.

In chapter 8 Darby presents a general framework to discuss the effect of the 1973–74 real oil price increase on the price level. When this analysis is applied within the structure of the Mark III and Mark IV models, the estimated and simulated effects on the price *level* range from 0 to 5 percentage points. This ambiguity results from the coincidental removal of general price controls in 1973–74 in a number of our countries since a significant effect is found only in those countries. The difficulty arises because of potential biases in reported price levels and hence real output as a side effect of evasions of the general price controls.

This part is closed with an analysis of the Lucas-Barro real income equation included in the Mark III Model. Although the distinction between unanticipated and actual changes in aggregate demand variables is fruitful for the United States, it adds little if anything in the case of the nonreserve countries.

These five chapters provide a structural assessment of the international linkages among our eight industrialized countries. While linkages are indeed found, they are not nearly so strong as suggested by much of the recent international literature.

5 The Mark III International Transmission Model: Specification

Michael R. Darby and Alan C. Stockman

The Mark III International Transmission Model provides a convenient framework for testing a variety of hypotheses about the workings of and linkages among individual macroeconomics. It is a quarterly macroeconometric model of the United States, the United Kingdom, Canada, France, Germany, Italy, Japan, and the Netherlands estimated for 1957 through 1976.[1] A number of hypotheses are incorporated in the structure of the model so that the data can determine their empirical relevance; test results for those hypotheses will be reported in the next chapter. More complex alternative hypotheses involving the impact of anticipated changes in aggregate demand variables and the channels of influence of the real oil price are examined in chapters 8 and 9. Simulation experiments with a simplified version of the model are reported in chapter 7. Both the full model as specified here and the simulation (Mark IV) model are available to other researchers via the TROLL system upon arrangement with the authors.

The Mark III Model has been constructed to test the existence of various channels by which inflation can be transmitted from country to country and to quantify the relative importance of those channels. We have attempted to include all the major channels emphasized in the international literature to determine their empirical relevance. We have been very parsimonious in our choice of exogenous variables lest a possible transmission channel be assumed away.[2]

Briefly, the model consists of two sorts of submodels: the reserve country (U.S.) submodel and the nonreserve country submodels. In turn,

---

1. This is the period covered by the basic project data bank (see chapter 4) after loss of initial observations due to lagged values appearing in the model proper and in the definitions of expected values.
2. The model is identified by a large number of lagged endogenous variables.

the latter submodels exist in two forms, pegged and floating, according to whether the exchange rate is taken as exogenous or an exchange intervention reaction function is specified. Each submodel contains eight to ten behavioral equations and about the same number of identities. Each submodel can be conveniently divided into two main groups of behavioral equations, domestic and international. The specification of the domestic equations is presented in section 5.1, and the international equations and identities follow. Section 5.3 discusses the formation of expectations in the model. The chapter concludes with a review of the international transmission channels contained in the model.

5.1 The Domestic Subsectors

These subsectors consist of four or five stochastic equations which can be identified by the variable upon which we have normalized for simultaneous estimation. They are the real-income, price-level, unemployment-rate, nominal money, and interest-rate equations. Since these equations are nearly identical for all the different submodels, it is simplest to go through them equation by equation. Note that for easy reference, notation and the model equations are collected in tables 5.1 through 5.7 at the end of this chapter.

5.1.1 Real Income—Equations (R1) and (N1)

The real-income equation is similar to that of Barro (1978), except that it is specified in growth-rate form and it includes real-government-spending and scaled-export shocks (innovations) in addition to nominal money shocks. The most easily accessible form of the equation is

$$(5.1) \qquad \Delta \log y_j = \alpha_{j1} - \alpha_{j2}(\log y_{j,t-1} - \log y_{j,t-1}^P)$$
$$+ \sum_{i=0}^{3} \alpha_{j,3+i} \hat{M}_{j,t-i} + \sum_{i=0}^{3} \alpha_{j,7+i} \hat{g}_{j,t-i}$$
$$+ \sum_{i=0}^{3} \alpha_{j,11+i} \hat{x}_{j,t-i} + \epsilon_{j1}.$$

This form allows the money, government-spending, and export shocks ($\hat{M}_j$, $\hat{g}_j$, and $\hat{x}_j$) to have an impact in the first four quarters, but thereafter the same exponential decay at the rate α_{j2} is imposed however the logarithmic transitory income ($\log y_j - \log y_j^P$) is achieved. This allows considerable freedom without estimating a great many coefficients.[3] Note that if real income initially equals permanent income and no shocks (including the disturbance ϵ_{j1}) occur, real income grows at the trend rate of α_{j1} per quarter. The estimating equations (R1) for the reserve sub-

---

3. Inclusion of actual values of money, government spending, and scaled exports is explored in chapter 9 below. A detailed derivation of the equation is presented there in section 9.1.

model and (N1) for the nonreserve submodels are the same as (5.1) except for shifting $\log y_{j,t-1}$ from the left to the right side. (See tables 5.2, 5.3, and 5.4.)

5.1.2   Price Level—Equations (R2) and (N2)

The price-level equation is obtained by equating nominal money supply and demand and solving for the price level. The demand for money function used is generalized from that of Carr and Darby (1981). The Carr-Darby function allows for different adjustment processes depending on whether a change in nominal money is anticipated or unanticipated. The logarithm of real money demand is assumed to be a function of logarithmic permanent and transitory income, the domestic interest rate R_j, the foreign interest rate adjusted for expected depreciation, the lagged logarithm of real money, and a four-quarter distributed lag on the money shocks.[4] Thus a typical nonreserve money demand function would be

$$
\begin{aligned}
(5.2) \qquad \log M_j^D - \log P_j = {} & \chi_1 + \chi_2 \log y_j^P + \chi_3 (\log y_j - \log y_j^P) \\
& + \chi_4 R_j + \chi_5 [R_1 + (4\Delta \log E_{j,t+1})^*] \\
& + \chi_6 (\log M_{j,t-1} - \log P_{j,t-1}) \\
& + \sum_{i=0}^{3} \chi_{7+i} \hat{M}_{j,t-i} - \epsilon_{j2}.
\end{aligned}
$$

The coefficients χ_2 and χ_3 are expected to have positive signs, χ_4 and χ_5 are supposed to be negative, and the partial adjustment parameter χ_6 should lie between 0 and 1. The impact effect χ_7 of a money demand shock should also lie between 0 and 1 and indicates the shock-absorber increase in money demand. The values χ_8 through χ_{10} allow for lagged shock-absorber demand effects.

The price-level equation is obtained by substituting the money market equilibrium condition that nominal money supply $\log M$ equals nominal money demand $\log M^D$ and normalizing on $\log P_j$:

$$
\begin{aligned}
(N2) \qquad \log P_j = {} & \log M_j + \beta_{j1} + \beta_{j2}\log y_j^P + \beta_{j3}(\log y_j - \log y_j^P) \\
& + \beta_{j4} R_j + \beta_{j5}[R_1 + (4\Delta \log E_{j,t+1})^*] \\
& + \beta_{j6}(\log M_{j,t-1} - \log P_{j,t-1}) \\
& + \sum_{i=0}^{3} \beta_{j,7+i} \hat{M}_{j,t-i} + \epsilon_{j2}.
\end{aligned}
$$

Obviously the β_{ji} are simply the negative of the corresponding χ_i. Thus the expected parameter values are

---

4. The foreign interest rate is included at the suggestion of Don Mathieson and Michael Hamburger to test for the substitutability of foreign bonds for domestic money. The U.S. interest rate R_1 is used for the nonreserve countries, and the U.K. interest rate is used for the United States. Carr and Darby (1981) entered only the current money shock, but our distributed lag permits the data to determine a more complicated adjustment process.

$$\beta_{j2}, \beta_{j3} < 0 \qquad 0 \ge \beta_{j6}, \beta_{j7} \ge -1$$
$$\beta_{j4}, \beta_{j5} > 0.$$

The reserve-country equation is practically the same except that the U.K. interest rate and expected depreciation are used instead of the U.S. variables for the foreign interest rate. Thus

(R2)
$$\log P_1 = \log M_1 + \beta_{11} + \beta_{12}\log y_1^P$$
$$+ \beta_{13}(\log y_1 - \log y_1^P) + \beta_{14}R_1$$
$$+ \beta_{15}[R_2 - (4\Delta \log E_{2,t+1})^*]$$
$$+ \beta_{16}(\log M_{1,t-1} - \log P_{1,t-1})$$
$$+ \sum_{i=0}^{3} \beta_{1,7+i}\hat{M}_{1,t-i} + \epsilon_{12}.$$

Note that we subtract the expected depreciation of the foreign currency $(\Delta \log E_{2,t+1})^*$ here while we add the expected depreciation of the domestic currency in equations (N2). The expected parameter values for β_{12} through β_{17} are as indicated above.

5.1.3   Unemployment Rate—Equations (R3) and (N3)

This is a dynamic form of Okun's law which allows for an eight-quarter distributed lag effect of real income growth on changes in the unemployment rate. It is included only in the U.S., U.K., and French submodels. The other countries in the model have unemployment rates which are uncorrelated with present and past changes in real income. For those countries, logarithmic transitory real income replaces the unemployment rate in the nominal money reaction functions.

5.1.4   Nominal Money—Equations (R4) and (N4)

A standard nominal money reaction function (N4) has been adopted for the nonreserve countries. We have specified a form with sufficient generality to allow for varying lags in acquisition and utilization of information by the various monetary authorities.[5] The reaction functions explain the nominal money growth rate by the current and appropriately lagged scaled balance of payments, the lagged unemployment rate or transitory real income, lagged inflation rates, and current and lagged innovations in real government spending. Semiannual observations were used for lagged values to reduce the number of fitted coefficients except for the unemployment-rate or transitory-income variable, for which preliminary experimentation suggested a complicated lag pattern. Since

---

5. Preliminary investigation uncovered substantial variation in how quickly different countries responded to the various determinants. In the exploratory Mark II version of the model, money reaction functions were tailored to the individual countries (see Darby 1979). Experience with that approach indicated both difficulties in cross-country comparisons and difficulties with understated standard errors.

under floating exchange rates more attention can be paid to inflation goals and less to balance-of-payments equilibrium, we used a floating dummy variable to estimate shifts in the inflation and balance-of-payments coefficients during the floating period. This equation is

$$
\begin{aligned}
\text{(N4)} \qquad \Delta \log M_j = \; & \eta_{j1} + \eta_{j2}t + \eta_{j3}\hat{g}_j + \eta_{j4}(\hat{g}_{j,t-1} + \hat{g}_{j,t-2}) \\
& + \eta_{j5}(\hat{g}_{j,t-3} + \hat{g}_{j,t-4}) \\
& + \eta_{j6}(\log P_{j,t-1} \log P_{j,t-3}) \\
& + \eta_{j7}[DF_j(\log P_{j,t-1} - \log P_{j,t-3})] \\
& + \eta_{j8}(\log P_{j,t-3} - \log P_{j,t-5}) \\
& + \eta_{j9}[DF_j(\log P_{j,t-3} - \log P_{j,t-5})] \\
& + \eta_{j,10}u_{j,t-1} + \eta_{j,11}u_{j,t-2} + \eta_{j,12}u_{j,t-3} \\
& + \eta_{j,13}u_{j,t-4} + \eta_{j,14}(B/Y)_j \\
& + \eta_{j,15}[DF_j(B/Y)_j] \\
& + \eta_{j,16}[(B/Y)_{j,t-1} + (B/Y)_{j,t-2}] \\
& + \eta_{j,17}\{DF_j[(B/Y)_{j,t-1} + (B/Y)_{j,t-2}]\} \\
& + \eta_{j,18}[(B/Y)_{j,t-3} + (B/Y)_{j,t-4}] \\
& + \eta_{j,19}\{DF_j[(B/Y)_{j,t-3} + (B/Y)_{j,t-4}]\} \\
& + \epsilon_{j4},
\end{aligned}
$$

where minus logarithmic transitory income $(\log y_j^P - \log y_j)$ is substituted for u in the equations for Canada, Germany, Italy, Japan, and the Netherlands.

The real-government-spending shocks are included to allow for monetization of unusual deficits.[6] If this occurs, then the coefficients should be positive at least initially with negative lagged coefficients possible if the central bank reverses its even-keeling operations. Inflation coefficients η_{j6} and η_{j8} should be negative. The additional coefficients η_{j7} and η_{j9} during the floating period should also be negative if the central bank shifts weight from the balance of payments to fighting inflation.[7] Some of the coefficients $\eta_{j,10}$ through $\eta_{j,13}$ should be positive so that higher levels of unemployment or lower levels of transitory income are associated with higher nominal-money growth rates. In preliminary experiments, it was noted that the data seemed to indicate it was the change rather than the level that entered.[8] Given the problems with unemployment-rate data, in five of our countries negative logarithmic transitory income $(\log y_j^P - \log y_j)$ was substituted for u_j. While the expected signs are thus preserved, the coefficients should be lower by a factor of 3 to 4 than in the unemployment-rate countries.

---

6. We experimented with changes in interest rates to model even keeling directly, but simultaneity was too severe to obtain usable estimates.

7. At least some countries may have ceased worry about either the balance of payments or inflation once the commitment to a pegged exchange rate was dropped.

8. That is, the sum of the coefficients was often zero with a positive coefficient followed by an offsetting negative coefficient.

The balance of payments is scaled here (to avoid nonlinearities in the model) by nominal income rather than nominal high-powered money as is common in the monetary approach literature. Since the ratio of nominal high-powered money to nominal income H/Y is reasonably stable in our sample period, conversions are straightforward from one scaling to the other. If the coefficient on the contemporaneous scaled balance of payments[9] equals Y/H, this indicates the absence of sterilization since the proportional increase in the money supply equals the ratio of the balance-of-payments surplus to high-powered money. The remainder of the nominal-money reaction function could be thought of as determining money growth due to domestic credit as in the monetary approach literature. If the coefficient of $(B/Y)_j$ is less than Y/H, then some sterilization is being practiced, regardless of whether monetary control is being exercised.[10] The lagged response of money growth to the balance of payments is important to the stability of a pegged exchange-rate system if monetary control is exercised through short-run sterilization. Both impact and cumulative effects of the balance of payments will be discussed in some detail in chapter 6.

The nominal-money reaction function (R4) for the reserve-currency country differs from the nonreserve equations in (a) omitting all terms involving the balance of payments and the floating dummy and (b) including two lagged dependent variables in response to a seemingly complicated adjustment process and indicated by earlier work. The first of these differences is consistent with the unique role of the reserve country stressed in Darby (1980). For the most part, the balance of payments consists of purchases and sales of U.S.–dollar denominated interest-bearing securities and deposits which have no effect on U.S. high-powered money. Any intervention undertaken by the U.S. monetary authorities can be sterilized so that the U.S. controls its nominal money supply and implicitly determines the world price level under pegged exchange rates. Empirical work reported in Darby (1981) supports the absence of balance-of-payments effects on U.S. nominal money growth. In fact, as reported there, whenever the current and two lagged semiannual scaled balance-of-payments terms were added to equation (R4) or variants thereof, their estimated coefficients were trivial in magnitude, insignificantly different from zero, and generally perverse in sign. Thus the balance-of-payments link is severed, and international influences affect the U.S. money supply only indirectly via the lagged inflation and unemployment rates.

---

9. This is $\eta_{j,14}$ during the pegged period and $\eta_{j,14} + \eta_{j,15}$ during the floating period.
10. This question is discussed at length in part III (especially chapters 10 and 11).

5.1.5   Interest Rate—Equations (R5) and (N5)

The real interest-rate equation is based on a goods market equilibrium condition, but problems were encountered in specifying a dynamic investment function. As a result, we explain the real interest rate by the lagged expected inflation rate, time, the lagged interest rate, and four-quarter distributed lags on innovations in nominal money, real government spending, and real net exports. The nominal interest rate is therefore explained by these terms and by the expected inflation rate. Thus the interest-rate and real-income equations can be interpreted as reflecting the outcome of a short-period IS-LM model which shifts around long-run equilibrium in response to current and lagged innovations in the demand variables. Persistent effects on the real interest rate are possible via the lagged expected-inflation and interest rates.

To be precise, the equations estimated are of the form

(R5) &
(N5)
$$R_j = \delta_{j1} + \delta_{j2}t + \delta_{j3}(4\Delta \log P_{j,t+1})^* + \delta_{j4}R_{j,t-1}$$
$$+ \delta_{j5}(4\Delta \log P_j)^* + \sum_{i=0}^{3} \delta_{j,6+i}\hat{M}_{j,t-i}$$
$$+ \sum_{i=0}^{3} \delta_{j,10+i}\hat{g}_{j,t-i} + \sum_{i=0}^{3} \delta_{j,14+i}\hat{x}_{j,t-i} + \epsilon_{j5}.$$

As with the real-income equations, the last twelve RHS terms capture the effects of innovations in aggregate demand variables on the interest rate. The first five terms specify a normal level[11] of the interest rate and a rather free partial adjustment process. If there is partial adjustment of the real interest rate but instantaneous adjustment to changes in inflation expectations, then it can be shown that $\delta_{j5} = -\delta_{j3}\delta_{j4}$, where δ_{j3} is the full impact of expected inflation on the nominal interest rate.[12] If a partial adjustment process applies to the nominal rate, then δ_{j5} goes to zero and δ_{j3} goes to the long-run impact times $(1 - \delta_{j4})$.

5.2   The International Subsectors

The international subsectors consist of an import demand equation, an import supply equation, an export equilibrium equation, a net-capital-outflows equation, and, for floating nonreserve submodels only, an exchange-rate intervention reaction function. As explained below, different normalizations are used for the import demand and supply equations under floating exchange rates to correspond to the exchange intervention reaction function.

---

11. The normal level of the interest rate may be growing via the time trend term $\delta_{j2}t$.
12. Because of income taxation, this need not be unity as in the classic Fisher equation; see Darby (1975).

5.2.1   Import Demand—Equations (R7), (N7P), and (N7F)

The basic form of the import demand equation is used for the reserve and pegged nonreserve submodels. The dependent variable is imports as a fraction of income.[13] The standard explanatory variables are the lagged dependent variable, permanent income, and distributed lags on the relative price of imports and domestic logarithmic transitory income:

(R7) &
(N7P)

$$(I/Y)_j = \lambda_{j1} + \lambda_{j2}(I/Y)_{j,t-1} + \lambda_{j3}\log y_j^P$$

$$+ \sum_{i=0}^{1} \lambda_{j,4+i}(\log y_{j,t-i} - \log y_{j,t-i}^P)$$

$$+ \sum_{i=0}^{3} \lambda_{j,6+i} Z_{j,t-i} + \epsilon_{j7}.$$

If a partial adjustment process is operative here, λ_{j2} should fall between 0 and 1. The sign λ_{j3} depends on whether the long-run income elasticity of imports is greater or less than unity. The coefficients λ_{j4} and λ_{j5} are similarly ambiguous in sign since they indicate whether transitory income increases imports more of less than in proportion to income. The relative price of imports variable Z_j is the logarithm of import prices less the logarithm of the domestic price level. Whether the coefficients λ_{j6} through λ_{j9} are positive or negative depends on the relative price elasticity of imports since the dependent variable is the scaled *value* of imports. The traditional literature has suggested a so-called *J*-curve phenomenon in which the short-run price elasticity is much smaller than in the long run. This would be reflected in a positive λ_{j6} offset by negative values of λ_{j7} through λ_{j9}.

For the floating nonreserve submodel, the import demand equation is renormalized by solving for the current relative price of imports:

(N7F)

$$Z_j = \frac{-\lambda_{j1}}{\lambda_{j6}} + \frac{1}{\lambda_{j6}}(I/Y)_j - \frac{\lambda_{j2}}{\lambda_{j6}}(I/Y)_{j,t-1} - \frac{\lambda_{j3}}{\lambda_{j6}}\log y_j^P$$

$$- \sum_{i=0}^{1} \frac{\lambda_{j,4+i}}{\lambda_{j6}}(\log y_{j,t-i} - \log y_{j,t-i}^P)$$

$$- \sum_{i=1}^{3} \frac{\lambda_{j,6+i}}{\lambda_{j6}} Z_{j,t-i} - \frac{\epsilon_{j7}}{\lambda_{j6}}.$$

Under floating rates, scaled imports are given by the balance-of-payments identity.

5.2.2   Import Supply—Equations (R8), (N8P), and (N8F)

The import supply equation is used to determine the logarithm of import prices in the reserve and pegged nonreserve submodels. It was

---

13. We similarly measure exports and capital flows as a fraction of income so that a balance of payments scaled as a fraction of income results from imposition of the identity to assure asset market equilibrium.

necessary to first-difference the equation to obtain stationary residuals. The equation explains the change in the logarithm of import prices by a constant and the first differences of the logarithm of the real oil price, the scaled import variable, the logarithm of foreign real income, the logarithm of the foreign price level, the logarithm of the exchange rate, and also the lagged dependent variable.

(R8) &
(N8P)

$$\log P_j^I = \log P_{j,t-1}^I + \mu_{j1} + \mu_{j2}\Delta \log P_{j,t-1}^I$$
$$+ \mu_{j3}\Delta \log P^{RO} + \mu_{j4}\Delta \log y_j^R + \mu_{j5}\Delta(I/Y)_j$$
$$+ \mu_{j6}\Delta \log P_j^R + \mu_{j7}\Delta \log E_j + \epsilon_{j8}.$$

The coefficient μ_{j2} should lie between 0 and 1 if there is a partial adjustment process for import prices, perhaps due to shipping and contracting lags. The real price of oil is included as an exogenous variable shifting the import supply curve since no OPEC country is included directly in the model; so μ_{j3} should be positive. Rest-of-world real income proxies foreign capacity, and so μ_{j4} is expected to be positive. The supply curve may be either flat or upward sloping depending on the country and its importance in the world demand for its imports; so $\mu_{j5} \geq 0$. Both μ_{j6} and μ_{j7} should be positive since $\log P_j^R + \log E_j$ is the logarithm of rest-of-world prices converted into domestic currency units. The equality constraint is not imposed a priori on μ_{j6} and μ_{j7} since at least under pegged rates changes in $\log E_j$ may be associated with offsetting movements in tariffs and other barriers.

The import supply equation is renormalized to solve for the exchange rate in the floating nonreserve submodels:

(N8F)

$$\log E_j = \log E_{j,t-1} - \frac{\mu_{j1}}{\mu_{j7}} + \frac{1}{\mu_7}\Delta \log P_j^I$$

$$- \frac{\mu_{j2}}{\mu_{j7}}\Delta \log P_{j,t-1}^I - \frac{\mu_{j3}}{\mu_{j7}}\Delta \log P^{RO}$$

$$- \frac{\mu_{j4}}{\mu_{j7}}\Delta \log y_j^R - \frac{\mu_{j5}}{\mu_{j7}}\Delta(I/Y)_j$$

$$- \frac{\theta_{j6}}{\mu_{j7}}\Delta \log P_j^R - \frac{\epsilon_{j8}}{\mu_{j7}}.$$

Of course in a simultaneous model, no single equation can be said to determine the exchange rate or any other endogenous variable.

5.2.3 Exports—Equations (R6) and (N6)

No acceptable price series were generally available for exports, so we specified an equilibrium equation in the form

(R6) &
(N6)

$$(X/Y)_j = \theta_{j1} + \theta_{j2}t + \theta_{j3}\log P^{RO} + \theta_{j4}(\log y_j - \log y_j^P)$$

$$+ \sum_{i=0}^{1} \theta_{j,5+i}(X/Y)_{j,t-1-i} + \sum_{i=0}^{1} \theta_{j,7+i}\log y_{j,t-i}^R$$

$$+ \sum_{i=0}^{1} \theta_{j,9+i}\log P_{j,t-i} + \sum_{i=0}^{1} \theta_{j,11+i}\log P_{j,t-i}^R$$

$$+ \sum_{i=0}^{1} \theta_{j,13+i}\log E_{j,t-i}$$

$$+ \sum_{i=0}^{1} \theta_{j,15+i}DF_{j,t-i}\log E_{j,t-i} + \epsilon_{j6}.$$

Time (in lieu of an index of permanent incomes) and the two foreign real-income variables shift foreign demand, so θ_{j7} and θ_{j8} should be positive. The real price of oil indicates increased wealth of OPEC export demanders, so θ_{j3} should be positive. Domestic transitory income has a negative effect since X is scaled by Y but a positive effect as a capacity measure, so θ_{j4} has an ambiguous sign. Two lagged dependent variables were included to allow for partial adjustment processes in both export supply and demand similar to those allowed for imports; θ_{j5} and θ_{j6} should lie between 0 and 1. The price variables enter because a decrease in the logarithm of the domestic price level relative to the exchange-rate-converted foreign price level (i.e. $\log P_j - \log P_j^R - \log E_j$) should encourage domestic tradables production generally and the sale of exports in particular. Thus θ_{j9} and $\theta_{j,10}$ should be negative while $\theta_{j,11}$ through $\theta_{j,14}$ should be positive. The coefficients $\theta_{j,15}$ and $\theta_{j,16}$ allow for differential effects of exchange-rate changes under floating exchange rates. For the reserve country, the exchange rate is identically 1 and all foreign prices are converted into dollars in computing $\log P^R$; thus the terms involving $\theta_{j,13}$ through $\theta_{j,16}$ are omitted in (R6).

5.2.4   Net Capital Outflows—Equations (R9) and (N9)

These equations are specified along traditional portfolio adjustment lines. An alternative approach is explored by Melvin in chapter 13 below. It should be noted that both the levels and changes of the components of the interest-rate differential appear: As is well known, changes in the interest differential will cause flows necessary to adjust the portfolio to a new equilibrium. The levels also appear because the interest-rate differential affects the optimal portfolio and hence capital flows in the context of real growth. Our dependent variable is measured to avoid counting most spurious nominal capital flows due to high levels of nominal interest rates, but if a country increases its accumulation of *nominal* dollar reserves when U.S. inflation and interest rates are high, then its scaled private capital outflows are decreased and U.S. capital outflows correspondingly increased.

The equation used is

(R9) &
(N9)

$$(C/Y)_j = \xi_{j1} + \xi_{j2}t + \xi_{j3}\log P^{RO} + \xi_{j4}R_j$$
$$+ \xi_{j5}(4\Delta \log E_{j,t+1})^* + \xi_{j6}R_1$$
$$+ \xi_{j7}[(X/Y)_j - (I/Y)_j]$$
$$+ \xi_{j8}(\log y_j - \log y_j^P) + \xi_{j9}\Delta \log y_j$$
$$+ \xi_{j,10}\Delta \log y_j^R$$
$$+ \sum_{i=0}^{2} \xi_{j,11+i}\Delta R_{j,t-i} + \sum_{i=0}^{2} \xi_{j,14+i}\Delta R_{1,t-i}$$
$$+ \sum_{i=0}^{2} \xi_{j,17+i}\Delta(4\Delta \log E_{j,t+1-i})^* + \epsilon_{j9}.$$

Domestic transitory income is included because of the use of Y as a scaling variable; so ξ_{j8} would be negative. Time and the change in domestic and foreign real income capture trend and cyclical movements in wealth. The sign of ξ_{j2} is indeterminant, but ξ_{j9} should be positive and $\xi_{j,10}$ negative on the view that they measure increases in the scale of the domestic and foreign portfolios. However, if booms attract foreign investment while recessions deter it, just the opposite signs would be anticipated.[14] Similarly the creation of OPEC as captured by log P^{RO} increases the potential wealth of foreign investors but may also deter foreign investment via increased uncertainty. Finally, increases in the scaled trade balance $(X/Y)_j - (I/Y)_j$ is widely supposed to induce an increase in trade credit so that ξ_{j7} is positive.

As to the interest variables, we have the domestic interest rate R_j, the foreign interest rate R_1, and the corresponding expected depreciation of the exchange rate $(4\Delta \lambda o\gamma E_{j,t+1})^*$.[15] Generally the increase in the differential $R_j - (4\Delta \log E_{j,t+1})^* - R_1$ will decrease net capital outflows in long-run equilibrium and particularly during a transitional portfolio adjustment period. Therefore the coefficients should be generally negative on the level and changes in R_j but positive for the levels and changes in $(4\Delta \log E_{j,t+1})^*$ and R_1. The implicit constraints were not imposed because of varying quality of data on each component of the differential, and because of the problems inherent in measuring the balances of payments in nominal terms.

5.2.5 Balance of Payments—Equations (N10F)

In the nonreserve floating submodel, a tenth behavioral equation is added to complete the model since the logarithm of the exchange rate becomes an endogenous variable. This is our exchange intervention equation which explains the scaled balance of payments by the lagged

14. Branson (1968) and Prachowny (1969) have other explanations for ambiguity of the income signs.

15. For the U.S. equation (R9), the British interest rate R_2 is used as the foreign interest rate and the corresponding expected depreciation is $-(4\Delta \log E_{2,t+1})^*$.

dependent variable and the log change in the exchange rate as compared to the same log change lagged one-quarter and to the lagged differential between the domestic and U.S. inflation rates:

(N10F) $\qquad (B/Y)_j = \psi_{j1} + \psi_{j2}(B/Y)_{j,t-1} + \psi_{j3}\Delta \log E_j$
$$+ \psi_{j4}\Delta \log E_{j,t-1}$$
$$+ \psi_{j5}(\Delta \log P_{j,t-1} - \Delta \log P_{1,t-1}) + \epsilon_{j,10}.$$

The coefficient ψ_{j2} could be positive or negative depending on whether intervention is persistent or self-reversing. If the authorities resist depreciations of the exchange rate at a faster rate than recently or than indicated by the fundamentals (differential inflation), then ψ_{j3} should be negative and ψ_{j4} and ψ_{j5} positive.

5.2.6   Identities—Equations (R11)–(R19) and (N11)–(N19)

Logarithmic permanent income is defined in identities (R11) and (N11).[16] Identities (R12) and (N12P) determine the scaled balance of payments; this is solved instead for scaled imports in the floating (N12F). Money and export shocks are defined in identities (R13), (R14), (N13), and (N14). Identities (R15) and (N15P) define the relative price of imports; in the floating case, this is solved for import prices as in (N15F). The expectational identities (R16), (R17), (N16), and (N17) are for expectations of next period's prices and exchange rate based on current information. Their specification is discussed in section 5.3. Nominal-income-weighted geometric averages of the other seven countries' real income and prices are defined by identities (R18), (R19), (N18), and (N19). The weights W_j are the ratios of country j's total nominal income (converted by E_j into dollars) for 1955I–76IV to the total for all eight countries. The parameters base y_j and base P_j set the indices y_j^R and P_j^R to 1 for 1970 and are listed with the W_j in table 5.7. Although these variables are endogenous for the whole model, they are treated somewhat differently in the simultaneous equation estimation method discussed in chapter 6.

5.3   Expected Values

There are four explicit plus one implicit expectational variables in the model: The explicit variables are $(4\Delta \log E_j)^*$, $(4\Delta \log P_j)^*$, $(\log M_j)^*$, and $(X/Y)_j^*$; $(\log g_j)^*$ also must be estimated in creating the exogenous variable $\hat{g}_j$. The first two of these variables appear in the model with leads

---

16. The weight ϕ_{j2} of current income in permanent income is taken as 0.025 following Darby (1977–78); this is equivalent to a real yield on all (human and nonhuman) wealth of about 10% per annum. The trend quarterly growth rate ϕ_{j3} was estimated, together with the initial value of $\log y_j^P$, by fitting the regression $\log y_j = \log y_j^P + \phi_{j3}t$; therefore $\phi_{j1} \equiv \phi_{j3}(1 - \phi_{j2})$.

so that they are based on current information. Therefore we treat them as endogenous for purposes of estimation.[17] The other three expected values are based only on lagged information and are therefore treated as predetermined for purposes of estimation.

The three predetermined expectational variables are all based on optimal univariate ARIMA processes. We also tried defining $(\log M_j)^*$ in terms of a transfer function based on the money-supply reaction functions (R4) and (N4), but the univariate process worked somewhat better both in terms of explanatory power and in terms of meeting our prior notions regarding the values of coefficients.[18] Since we are treating real government spending as exogenous, it was appropriate to model $(\log g_j)^*$ by a univariate ARIMA process. Because of the short lags in the export equations and the relatively minor role of export shocks in the model as estimated, we did not attempt a full-scale transfer function approach for $(X/Y)_j^*$.

For the expected inflation rate $(4\Delta \log P_j)^*$ we adopted a transfer function based on the price-level equations (R2) and (N2) with information lags imposed. As detailed in table 5.5, the expected inflation rate $(4\Delta \log P_{j,t+1})^*$ is the systematic part of a transfer function which has as input series $(\log M_j)^*$, two lags of $\log M_j$, $\Delta \log y_{j,t-1}$, R_j, $R_{j,t-1}$, current and lagged exchange-rate-adjusted foreign interest rate, two lags of $\log P_j$, and three lagged money shocks. Note that since this expected inflation rate appears in the interest-rate equation, it is appropriate to assume that the information set includes current interest rates.

Finally, expected growth in the exchange rate $(4\Delta \log E_{j,t+1})^*$ differs by period and country. In general we do not wish to use the forward rate for this expectation because (1) this would require an additional equation for each nonreserve country to explain endogenously the forward rate's movements relative to movements in the expected growth in the exchange rate, and especially (2) the forward rate data are incomplete. For the floating period, we fitted regressions explaining $E_{j,t+1}$ by the current values of the variables appearing in the exchange-rate equation (N8F) and the lagged dependent variable. No significant autocorrelation appeared in the residuals. The predicted value of these regressions is used as $(4\Delta \log E_{j,t+1})^*$. Details are in part (a) of table 5.6. For the pegged period, we use a transfer function which has input series useful to predict both a revaluation and movements occurring in the absence of a revaluation. The expected change due to a revaluation is assumed to vary with the level of the scaled balance of payments and with this level times its

17. See identities (R16), (R17), (N16), and (N17).
18. This is understandable if the acquisition and processing of information is costly. See Darby (1976) and Feige and Pearce (1976). Some results on the sensitivity of estimates to alternative definitions of $(\log M_j)^*$ are reported in chapter 9.

absolute value.[19] Movements occurring in the absence of a revaluation are captured by the current growth rate and the logarithmic difference between the actual and pegged values of E_j. The latter variable may serve as well in predicting revaluations. Finally, lagged revaluation dummies are included because of the different meaning of the variables in the quarter immediately following a revaluation. Details are given in table 5.6, part (*b*).

5.4   International Linkages

Before turning to estimates in chapter 6 and simulations in chapter 7, let us summarize the manner in which alternative channels for the international transmission of inflation are specified in the model. The goal of estimation is to assess the relative empirical magnitudes of these channels.

First, changes in foreign prices affect domestic prices through a Humean price-specie-flow mechanism, which can occur either within a quarter or more slowly over time. Imports and exports are affected, in the model, by current and lagged changes in domestic prices. Unless this change in the balance of trade is exactly offset by a change in net capital outflows, it affects the balance of payments. But current and lagged levels of the balance of payments can affect nominal money growth (and the model permits this effect to differ under pegged and flexible exchange rates)— and hence inflation. (For a direct entry of the foreign price level into the domestic price equation, see Darby 1979.)

Second, changes in the expected foreign inflation rate (and hence interest rate) may affect the demand for domestic money through a currency substitution channel. Thus a permanent change in foreign inflation may have a temporary effect on domestic inflation through this channel.

Third, variables affecting international capital flows affect domestic inflation through their effect on the balance of payments and hence the nominal money supply. These effects may operate in the model either within the quarter or with lags. Since changes in the domestic money supply may induce changes in interest rates, real income, and the domestic price level, it may induce capital flows that have subsequent effects on the nominal money supply through the balance of payments. Thus the model permits the possibility that massive capital flows would frustrate any attempts at an independent monetary policy by a non-reserve-currency country. Another possibility permitted in the model is that such monetary policy may have short-run effects, but lead to offsetting capital flows after a lag.

19. This formulation closely approximates an expectation based on a Tobit analysis in which both the probability of a change and the size of the change varies with the balance of payments.

Fourth, changes in foreign real income may affect the domestic price level through an "absorption" channel: changes in income may affect the balance of payments and hence the money supply and price level by affecting either the balance of trade or capital flows. Furthermore, export shocks may affect domestic real income and, through the demand for money, the domestic price level.

Finally, changes in the real price of oil may affect domestic variables through effects on the trade balance, import prices, and international capital flows. Chapter 8 reports tests of whether there is an additional direct effect of this (or some other) kind of international supply shock on real income and the price level, or whether the effect can operate mainly through the effects on the trade balance and capital flows. It should be noted that both the balance of trade and the capital account may operate either separately or simultaneously in the model to transmit inflation internationally through the channels discussed here.

Estimates of the model are presented in chapter 6.

Acknowledgments

The other contributors to this volume have made innumerable contributions to the specification and estimation of the model reported in this chapter and the next. The authors acknowledge the able research assistance of Daniel M. Laskar, Michael T. Melvin, M. Holly Crawford, and Andrew A. Vogel and helpful suggestions from members of the project Advisory Board and the UCLA Monetary Economics Workshop. An exploratory version of the model was reported in Darby (1979).

References

Barro, R. J. 1978. Unanticipated money, output, and the price level in the United States. *Journal of Political Economy* 86 (August): 549–80.

Branson, W. H. 1968. *Financial capital flows in the U.S. balance of payments.* Amsterdam: North-Holland.

Carr, J., and M. R. Darby. 1981. The role of money supply shocks in the short-run demand for money. *Journal of Monetary Economics* 8 (September): 183–99.

Darby, M. R. 1975. The financial and tax effects of monetary policy on interest rates. *Economic Inquiry* 13 (June): 266–76.

————. 1976. Rational expectations under conditions of costly information. *Journal of Finance* 31 (June): 889–95.

————. 1977–78. The consumer expenditure function. *Explorations in Economic Research* 4 (Winter–Spring): 645–74.

———. 1979. The NBER international transmission model: The Mark II disequilibrium version, estimates and lessons. In *Proceedings of 1978 West Coast Academic/Federal Reserve Economic Research Seminar*. San Francisco: Federal Reserve Bank of San Francisco.

———. 1980. The monetary approach to the balance of payments: Two specious assumptions. *Economic Inquiry* 18 (April): 321–26.

———. 1981. The international economy as a source of and restraint on United States inflation. In W. A. Gale, ed., *Inflation: Causes, consequents, and control*. Cambridge, Mass.: Oelgeschlager, Gunn & Hain, Publishers.

Feige, E. L., and D. K. Pearce. 1976. Economically rational expectations: Are innovations in the rate of inflation independent of innovations in measures of monetary and fiscal policy? *Journal of Political Economy* 84 (June): 499–522.

Prachowny, M. F. J. 1969. *A structural model of the U.S. balance of payments*. Amsterdam: North-Holland.

Table 5.1   **Symbols Used in Mark III Model**

baseP_j	Base to set mean value of log p_j^R to 0 for 1970 (i.e. P_j^R has geometric mean 1 for 1970). See table 5.7.
basey_j	Base to set mean value of log y_j^R to 0 for 1970 (i.e. y_j^R has geometric mean 1 for 1970). See table 5.7.
$(B/Y)_j$	Balance of payments as a fraction of GNP. (GDP is substituted if GNP is unavailable. The balance of payments is on the official reserve settlement basis at quarterly rates where possible and otherwise is the quarterly change in official reserves.)
$(C/Y)_j$	Net capital outflows as a fraction of GNP (measured as $(X/Y)_j - (I/Y)_j - 4(B/Y)_j$).
DF_j	Dummy variable equal to 1 for floating exchange-rate period; 0 otherwise.
E_j	Exchange rate in domestic currency units (DCUs) per U.S. dollar ($E_1 \equiv 1$).
g_j	Real government spending.
$\hat{g}_j$	Innovation in real government spending, log $g_j - (\log g_j)^*$.
$(I/Y)_j$	Imports as a fraction of GNP.

Table 5.1 (continued)

M_j	Money stock in billions of DCUs.
$\hat{M}_j$	Innovation in money, $\log M_j - (\log M_j)^*$.
P_j	Price deflator for GNP (or GDP) in DCUs per base-year DCU $(1970 = 1.000)$.
P_j^I	Import price index $(1970 = 1.000)$.
P_j^R	Index of foreign prices converted by exchange rates into U.S. dollars per base-year U.S. dollar.
P^{RO}	Real price of oil (dollar price of barrel of Venezuelan oil divided by P_1).
R_j	Short-term nominal interest rate in decimal per annum form (three-month treasury bill yield where available).
t	Time index (1955I $= 1$, 1955II $= 2$, etc.).
u_j	Unemployment rate in decimal form.
W_j	Nominal income weight; share of country j in total sample nominal income. See table 5.7.
$(X/Y)_j$	Exports as a fraction of GNP.
$\hat{x}_j$	Innovation in exports, $(X/Y)_j - (X/Y)_j^*$.
y_j	Real GNP (or GDP if GNP unavailable) in billions of base-year DCUs.
y_j^P	Permanent income in billions of base-year DCUs.
y_j^R	Index of foreign real income $(1970 = 1.000)$.
Z_j	Relative price of imports, $\log P_j^I - \log P_j$.
$*$	Indicates expected value based on information up through previous quarter, with exception noted in section 5.3.

Country indices:

1	United States	5	Germany
2	United Kingdom	6	Italy
3	Canada	7	Japan
4	France	8	Netherlands

Table 5.2 **Reserve Country (U.S.) Submodel**

EQUATIONS

(R1) $\log y_1 = \alpha_{11} + \alpha_{12}\log y_{1,t-1}^P + (1 - \alpha_{12})\log y_{1,t-1} + \sum_{i=0}^{3} \alpha_{1,3+i}\hat{M}_{1,t-i}$

$+ \sum_{i=0}^{3} \alpha_{1,7+i}\hat{g}_{1,t-i} + \sum_{i=0}^{3} \alpha_{1,11+i}\hat{x}_{1,t-i} + \epsilon_{11}$

(R2) $\log P_1 = \log M_1 + \beta_{11} + \beta_{12}\log y_1^P + \beta_{13}(\log y_1 - \log y_1^P) + \beta_{14}R_1$

$+ \beta_{15}[R_2 - (4\Delta \log E_{2,t+1})^*] + \beta_{16}(\log M_{1,t-1} - \log P_{1,t-1})$

$+ \sum_{i=0}^{3} \beta_{1,7+i}\hat{M}_{1,t-i} + \epsilon_{12}$

(R3) $u_1 = u_{1,t-1} + \gamma_{11} + \sum_{i=0}^{7} \gamma_{1,2+i}\Delta \log y_{1,t-i} + \epsilon_{13}$

(R4) $\Delta \log M_1 = \eta_{11} + \eta_{12}t + \eta_{13}\hat{g}_1 + \eta_{14}(\hat{g}_{1,t-1} + \hat{g}_{1,t-2})$

$+ \eta_{15}(\hat{g}_{1,t-3} + \hat{g}_{1,t-4}) + \eta_{16}(\log P_{1,t-1} - \log P_{1,t-3})$

$+ \eta_{18}(\log P_{1,t-3} - \log P_{1,t-5}) + \eta_{1,10}u_{1,t-1} + \eta_{1,11}u_{1,t-2}$

$+ \eta_{1,12}u_{1,t-3} + \eta_{1,13}u_{1,t-4} + \eta_{1,20}\Delta \log M_{1,t-1}$

$+ \eta_{1,21}\Delta \log M_{1,t-2} + \epsilon_{14}$

(R5) $R_1 = \delta_{11} + \delta_{12}t + \delta_{13}(4\Delta \log P_{1,t+1})^* + \delta_{14}R_{1,t-1} + \delta_{15}(4\Delta \log P_1)^*$

$+ \sum_{i=0}^{3} \delta_{1,6+i}\hat{M}_{1,t-i} + \sum_{i=0}^{3} \delta_{1,10+i}\hat{g}_{1,t-i} + \sum_{i=0}^{3} \delta_{1,14+i}\hat{x}_{1,t-i}$

$+ \epsilon_{15}$

(R6) $(X/Y)_1 = \theta_{11} + \theta_{12}t + \theta_{13}\log P^{RO} + \theta_{14}(\log y_1 - \log y_1^P)$

$+ \sum_{i=0}^{1} \theta_{1,5+i}(X/Y)_{1,t-1-i} + \sum_{i=0}^{1} \theta_{1,7+i}\log y_{1,t-i}^R$

$+ \sum_{i=0}^{1} \theta_{1,9+i}\log P_{1,t-i} + \sum_{i=0}^{1} \theta_{11+i}\log P_{1,t-i}^R + \epsilon_{16}$

(R7) $(I/Y)_1 = \lambda_{11} + \lambda_{12}(I/Y)_{1,t-1} + \lambda_{13}\log y_1^P$

$+ \sum_{i=0}^{1} \lambda_{1,4+i}\log y_{1,t-i} - \log y_{1,t-i}^P)$

$+ \sum_{i=0}^{3} \lambda_{1,6+i}Z_{1,t-i} + \epsilon_{17}$

(R8) $\log P_1^I = \log P_{1,t-1}^I + \mu_{11} + \mu_{12}\Delta \log P_{1,t-1}^I$

$+ \mu_{13}\Delta \log P^{RO} + \mu_{14}\Delta \log y_1^R + \mu_{15}\Delta(I/Y)_1$

$+ \mu_{16}\Delta \log P_1^R + \epsilon_{18}$

(R9)[†] $(C/Y)_1 = \xi_{11} + \xi_{12}t + \xi_{13}\log P^{RO} + \xi_{14}R_1$

$- \xi_{15}(4\Delta \log E_{2,t+1})^* + \xi_{16}R_2$

$+ \xi_{17}[(X/Y)_1 - (I/Y)_1] + \xi_{18}(\log y_1 - \log y_1^P)$

$+ \xi_{19}\Delta \log y_1 + \xi_{1,10}\Delta \log y_1^R + \sum_{i=0}^{2} \xi_{1,11+i}\Delta R_{1,t-i}$

$+ \sum_{i=0}^{2} \xi_{1,14+i}\Delta R_{2,t-i} - \sum_{i=0}^{2} \xi_{1,17+i}\Delta(4\Delta \log E_{2,t+1-i})^* + \epsilon_{19}$

(R10) No equation ($E_1 \equiv 1$).

Table 5.2 (continued)

IDENTITIES

(R11) $\log y_1^P \equiv \phi_{11} + \phi_{12}\log y_1 + (1 - \phi_{12})\log y_{1,t-1}^P$

(R12) $(B/Y)_1 \equiv [(X/Y)_1 - (I/Y)_1 - (C/Y)_1]/4$

(R13) $\hat{M}_1 \equiv \log M_1 - (\log M_1)^*$

(R14) $\hat{x}_1 \equiv (X/Y)_1 - (X/Y)_1^*$

(R15) $Z_1 \equiv \log P_1^I - \log P_1$

(R16) $(4\Delta \log P_{1,t+1})^*$: See table 5.5 for a complete listing.

(R17) $(4\Delta \log E_{2,t+1})^*$: See table 5.6 for a complete listing.

(R18) $\log y_1^R \equiv \dfrac{1}{1 - W_1} \sum\limits_{i=2}^{8} W_i \log y_i - \text{base}\,y_1$

(R19) $\log P_1^R \equiv \dfrac{1}{1 - W_1} \sum\limits_{i=2}^{8} W_i(\log P_i - \log E_i) - \text{base}\,P_1$

ENDOGENOUS VARIABLES

$\log y_1$, $\log P_1$, u_1, $\log M_1$, R_1, $(X/Y)_1$, $(I/Y)_1$, $\log P_1^I$, $(C/Y)_1$;
$\log y_1^P$, $(B/Y)_1$, $\hat{M}_1$, $\hat{x}_1$, Z_1, $(4\Delta \log P_{1,t+1})^*$, $(4\Delta \log E_{2,t+1})^*$

PREDETERMINED VARIABLES

Exogenous Variables
$\hat{g}_1$, $\hat{g}_{1,t-1}$, $\hat{g}_{1,t-2}$, $\hat{g}_{1,t-3}$, $\hat{g}_{1,t-4}$, $\log P^{RO}$, $\log P_{t-1}^{RO}$, t

Expected Values Based on Prior Information
$(\log M_1)^*$, $(X/Y)_1^*$

Lagged Endogenous Variables
$(4\Delta \log E_2)^*$, $(4\Delta \log E_{2,t-1})^*$, $(4\Delta \log E_{2,t-2})^*$, $(I/Y)_{1,t-1}$, $\log M_{1,t-1}$,
$\log M_{1,t-2}$, $\log M_{1,t-3}$, $\hat{M}_{1,t-1}$, $\hat{M}_{1,t-2}$, $\hat{M}_{1,t-3}$, $\log P_{1,t-1}$, $\log P_{1,t-2}$,
$\log P_{1,t-3}$, $\log P_{1,t-4}$, $\log P_{1,t-5}$, $\log P_{t-1}^I$, $\log P_{t-2}^I$, $R_{1,t-1}$, $R_{1,t-2}$,
$R_{1,t-3}$, $u_{1,t-1}$, $u_{1,t-2}$, $u_{1,t-3}$, $u_{1,t-4}$, $(X/Y)_{1,t-1}$, $(X/Y)_{1,t-2}$, $\hat{x}_{1,t-1}$,
$\hat{x}_{1,t-2}$, $\hat{x}_{1,t-3}$, $\log y_{1,t-1}$, $\log y_{1,t-2}$, $\log y_{1,t-3}$, $\log y_{1,t-4}$, $\log y_{1,t-5}$,
$\log y_{1,t-6}$, $\log y_{1,t-7}$, $\log y_{1,t-8}$, $\log y_{1,t-1}^P$, $Z_{1,t-1}$, $Z_{1,t-2}$, $Z_{1,t-3}$

Foreign Variables (endogenous in full model)§
$\log E_2$, $\log P_I^R$, R_2, $\log y_1^R$

Lagged Foreign Variables
$\log E_{2,t-1}$, $\log E_{2,t-2}$, $\log E_{2,t-3}$, $\log P_{1,t-1}^R$, $R_{2,t-1}$, $R_{2,t-2}$, $R_{2,t-3}$, $\log y_{1,t-1}^R$

---

†The United Kingdom (index 2) is used as the best alternative capital market in estimating the U.S. capital flows equation. Note that this equation is irrelevant to the previous equations since the balance of payments does not affect the U.S. money supply.

§In estimating the submodels by principal-components 2SLS, we include in our instrument list fitted values for these foreign variables based on the foreign countries' domestic predetermined variables. See chapter 6 for details.

Table 5.3   **Nonreserve Country Submodel: Pegged Exchange Rate Periods**

EQUATIONS

(N1) $\log y_j = \alpha_{j1} + \alpha_{j2}\log y_{j,t-1}^P + (1 - \alpha_{j2})\log y_{j,t-1} + \sum_{i=0}^{3} \alpha_{j,3+i}\hat{M}_{j,t-i}$

$\qquad\qquad + \sum_{i=0}^{3} \alpha_{j,7+i}\hat{g}_{j,t-i} + \sum_{i=0}^{3} \alpha_{j,11+i}\hat{x}_{j,t-i} + \epsilon_{j1}$

(N2) $\log P_j = \log M_j + \beta_{j1} + \beta_{j2}\log y_j^P + \beta_{j3}(\log y_j - \log y_j^P) + \beta_{j4}R_j$

$\qquad\qquad + \beta_{j5}[R_1 + (4\Delta \log E_{j,t+1})^*] + \beta_{j6}(\log M_{j,t-1} - \log P_{j,t-1})$

$\qquad\qquad + \sum_{i=0}^{3} \beta_{j,7+i}\hat{M}_{j,t-i} + \epsilon_{j2}$

(N3)† $u_j = u_{j,t-1} + \gamma_{j1} + \sum_{i=0}^{7} \gamma_{j,2+i}\Delta \log y_{j,t-i} + \epsilon_{j3}$

(N4)§ $\Delta \log M_j = \eta_{j1} + \eta_{j2}t + \eta_{j3}\hat{g}_j + \eta_{j4}(\hat{g}_{j,t-1} + \hat{g}_{j,t-2})$

$\qquad\qquad + \eta_{j5}(\hat{g}_{j,t-3} + \hat{g}_{j,t-4}) + \eta_{j6}(\log P_{j,t-1} - \log P_{j,t-3})$

$\qquad\qquad + \eta_{j7}[DF_j(\log P_{j,t-1} - \log P_{j,t-3})]$

$\qquad\qquad + \eta_{j8}(\log P_{j,t-3} - \log P_{j,t-5}) + \eta_{j9}[DF_j(\log P_{j,t-3} - \log P_{j,t-5})]$

$\qquad\qquad + \eta_{j,10}u_{j,t-1} + \eta_{j,11}u_{j,t-2} + \eta_{j,12}u_{j,t-3} + \eta_{j,13}u_{j,t-4}$

$\qquad\qquad + \eta_{j,14}(B/Y)_j + \eta_{j,15}[DF_j(B/Y)_j] + \eta_{j,16}[(B/Y)_{j,t-1} + (B/Y)_{j,t-2}]$

$\qquad\qquad + \eta_{j,17}\{DF_j[(B/Y)_{j,t-1} + (B/Y)_{j,t-2}]\} + \eta_{j,18}[(B/Y)_{j,t-3} + (B/Y)_{j,t-4}]$

$\qquad\qquad + \eta_{j,19}\{DF_j[(B/Y)_{j,t-3} + (B/Y)_{j,t-4}]\} + \epsilon_{j4}$

(N5) $R_j = \delta_{j1} + \delta_{j2}t + \delta_{j3}(4\Delta \log P_{j,t+1})^* + \delta_{j4}R_{j,t-1} + \delta_{j5}(4\Delta \log P_j)^*$

$\qquad\qquad + \sum_{i=0}^{3} \delta_{j,6+i}\hat{M}_{j,t-i} + \sum_{i=0}^{3} \delta_{j,10+i}\hat{g}_{j,t-i} + \sum_{i=0}^{3} \delta_{j,14+i}\hat{x}_{j,t-i} + \epsilon_{j5}$

(N6) $(X/Y)_j = \theta_{j1} + \theta_{j2}t + \theta_{j3}\log P^{RO} + \theta_{j4}(\log y_j - \log y_j^P)$

$\qquad\qquad + \sum_{i=0}^{1} \theta_{j,5+i}(X/Y)_{j,t-1-i} + \sum_{i=0}^{1} \theta_{j,7+i}\log y_{j,t-i}^R$

$\qquad\qquad + \sum_{i=0}^{1} \theta_{j,9+i}\log P_{j,t-i} + \sum_{i=0}^{1} \theta_{j,11+i}\log P_{j,t-i}^R$

$\qquad\qquad + \sum_{i=0}^{1} \theta_{j,13+i}\log E_{j,t-i} + \sum_{i=0}^{1} \theta_{j,15+i}DF_{j,t-i}\log E_{j,t-i} + \epsilon_{j6}$

(N7P) $(I/Y)_j = \lambda_{j1} + \lambda_{j2}(I/Y)_{j,t-1} + \lambda_{j3}\log y_j^P$

$\qquad\qquad + \sum_{i=0}^{1} \lambda_{j,4+i}(\log y_{j,t-i} - \log y_{j,t-i}^P)$

$\qquad\qquad + \sum_{i=0}^{3} \lambda_{j,6+i} Z_{j,t-i} + \epsilon_{j7}$

(N8P) $\log P_j^I = \log P_{j,t-1}^I + \mu_{j1} + \mu_{j2}\Delta \log P_{j,t-1}^I$

$\qquad\qquad + \mu_{j3}\Delta \log P^{RO} + \mu_{j4}\Delta \log y_j^R + \mu_{j5}\Delta(I/Y)_j$

$\qquad\qquad + \mu_{j6}\Delta \log P_j^R + \mu_{j7}\Delta \log E_j + \epsilon_{j8}$

(N9) $(C/Y)_j = \xi_{j1} + \xi_{j2}t + \xi_{j3}\log P^{RO} + \xi_{j4}R_j$

$\qquad\qquad + \xi_{j5}(4\Delta \log E_{j,t+1})^* + \xi_{j6}R_1 + \xi_{j7}[(X/Y)_j - (I/Y)_j]$

$\qquad\qquad + \xi_{j8}(\log y_j - \log y_j^P) + \xi_{j9}\Delta \log y_j + \xi_{j10}\Delta \log y_j^R$

$\qquad\qquad + \sum_{i=0}^{2} \xi_{j,11+i}\Delta R_{j,t-i} + \sum_{i=0}^{2} \xi_{j,14+i}\Delta R_{1,t-i}$

$\qquad\qquad + \sum_{i=0}^{2} \xi_{j,17+i}\Delta(4\Delta \log E_{j,t+1-i})^* + \epsilon_{j9}$

(N10)   No equation for pegged rate periods.

Table 5.3 (continued)

IDENTITIES

(N11) $\log y_j^P \equiv \theta_{j1} + \theta_{j2}\log y_j + (1 - \theta_{j2})\log y_{j,t-1}^P$

(N12P) $(B/Y)_j \equiv [(X/Y)_j - (I/Y)_j - (C/Y)_j]/4$

(N13) $\hat{M}_j \equiv \log M_j - (\log M_j)^*$

(N14) $\hat{x}_j \equiv (X/Y)_j - (X/Y)_j^*$

(N15P) $Z_j \equiv \log P_j^I - \log P_j$

(N16) $(4\Delta \log P_{j,t+1})^*$: Varies according to country. See table 5.5 for a complete listing.

(N17) $(4\Delta \log E_{j,t+1})^*$: Varies according to country. See table 5.6 for a complete listing.

(N18) $\log y_j^R \equiv \dfrac{1}{1 - W_j} \displaystyle\sum_{\substack{i=1 \\ i \neq j}}^{8} W_i \log y_i - \text{base}\,y_j$

(N19) $\log P_j^R \equiv \dfrac{1}{1 - W_j} \displaystyle\sum_{\substack{i=1 \\ i \neq j}}^{8} W_i (\log P_i - \log E_i) - \text{base}\,P_j$

ENDOGENOUS VARIABLES

$\log y_j$, $\log P_j$, u_j, $\log M_j$, R_j, $(X/Y)_j$, $(I/Y)_j$, $\log P_j^I$, $(C/Y)_j$;
$\log y_j^P$, $(B/Y)_j$, $\hat{M}_j$, $\hat{x}_j$, Z_j, $(4\Delta \log P_{j,t+1})^*$, $(4\Delta \log E_{j,t+1})^*$

PREDETERMINED VARIABLES

Exogenous Variables
DF_j, $DF_{j,t-1}$, $\log E_j$, $\log E_{j,t-1}$, $\log E_{j,t-2}$, $\log E_{j,t-3}$, $\hat{g}_j$, $\hat{g}_{j,t-1}$,
$\hat{g}_{j,t-2}$, $\hat{g}_{j,t-3}$, $\hat{g}_{j,t-4}$, $\log P^{RO}$, $\log P_{t-1}^{RO}$, t

Expected Values Based on Prior Information
$(\log M_j)^*$, $(X/Y)_j^*$

Lagged Endogenous Variables
$(4\Delta \log E_j)^*$, $(4\Delta \log E_{j,t-1})^*$, $(4\Delta \log E_{j,t-2})^*$, $(I/Y)_{j,t-1}$, $\log M_{j,t-1}$, $\hat{M}_{j,t-1}$,
$\hat{M}_{j,t-2}$, $\hat{M}_{j,t-3}$, $\log P_{j,t-1}$, $\log P_{j,t-3}$, $\log P_{j,t-5}$, $\log P_{j,t-1}^I$, $\log P_{j,t-2}^I$,
$R_{j,t-1}$, $R_{j,t-2}$, $R_{j,t-3}$, $(X/Y)_{j,t-1}$, $(X/Y)_{j,t-2}$, $\hat{x}_{j,t-1}$, $\hat{x}_{j,t-2}$, $\hat{x}_{j,t-3}$,
$(B/Y)_{j,t-1}$, $(B/Y)_{j,t-2}$, $(B/Y)_{j,t-3}$, $(B/Y)_{j,t-4}$, $\log y_{j,t-1}$, $\log y_{j,t-1}^P$,
$Z_{j,t-1}$, $Z_{j,t-2}$, $Z_{j,t-3}$, $\{u_{j,t-1}$, $\log y_{j,t-2}$, $\log y_{j,t-3}$, $\log y_{j,t-4}$,
$\log y_{j,t-5}$, $\log y_{j,t-6}$, $\log y_{j,t-7}$, $\log y_{j,t-8}\}^\ddagger$; plus any other lagged endogenous
variables appearing in (N4.j).

Foreign Variables (endogenous in full model)[#] $\log P_j^R$, R_1, $\log y_j^R$

Lagged Foreign Variables $\log P_{j,t-1}^R$, $R_{1,t-1}$, $R_{1,t-2}$, $R_{1,t-3}$, $\log y_{j,t-1}^R$

[†]The unemployment equation appears only in the submodels for France and the United Kingdom.

[§]For the submodels other than France and the United Kingdom, the unemployment rate variables u_j are replaced with negative logarithmic transitory income $\log y_j^P - \log y_j$.

[‡]The variables in braces appear only in the submodels for France and the United Kingdom; see note † above.

[#]In estimating the submodels by principal-components 2SLS, we include in our instrument list fitted values for these foreign variables based on the foreign countries' domestic predetermined variables. See chapter 6 for details.

Table 5.4   **Nonreserve Country Submodel: Floating Exchange-Rate Periods**

EQUATIONS

(N1) $\log y_j = \alpha_{j1} + \alpha_{j2} \log y_{j,t-1}^P + (1 - \alpha_{j2}) \log y_{j,t-1} + \sum_{i=0}^{3} \alpha_{j,3+i} \hat{M}_{j,t-i}$

$+ \sum_{i=0}^{3} \alpha_{j,7+i} \hat{g}_{j,t-i} + \sum_{i=0}^{3} \alpha_{j,11+i} \hat{x}_{j,t-i} + \epsilon_{j1}$

(N2) $\log P_j = \log M_j + \beta_{j1} + \beta_{j2} \log y_j^P + \beta_{j3} (\log y_j - \log y_j^P)$

$+ \beta_{j4} R_j + \beta_{j5} [R_1 + (4\Delta \log E_{j,t+1})^*] + \beta_{j6} (\log M_{j,t-1} - \log P_{j,t-1})$

$+ \sum_{i=0}^{3} \beta_{j,7+i} \hat{M}_{j,t-i} + \epsilon_{j2}$

(N3)† $u_j = u_{j,t-1} + \gamma_{j1} + \sum_{i=0}^{7} \gamma_{j,2+i} \Delta \log y_{j,t-i} + \epsilon_{j3}$

(N4)§ $\Delta \log M_j = \eta_{j1} + \eta_{j2}t + \eta_{j3}\hat{g}_j + \eta_{j4}(\hat{g}_{j,t-1} + \hat{g}_{j,t-2})$

$+ \eta_{j5}(\hat{g}_{j,t-3} + \hat{g}_{j,t-4}) + \eta_{j6}(\log P_{j,t-1} - \log P_{j,t-3})$

$+ \eta_{j7}[DF_j(\log P_{j,t-1} - \log P_{j,t-3})]$

$+ \eta_{j8}(\log P_{j,t-3} - \log P_{j,t-5}) + \eta_{j9}[DF_j(\log P_{j,t-3} - \log P_{j,t-5})]$

$+ \eta_{j,10}u_{j,t-1} + \eta_{j,11}u_{j,t-2} + \eta_{j,12}u_{j,t-3} + \eta_{j,13}u_{j,t-4}$

$+ \eta_{j,14}(B/Y)_j + \eta_{j,15}[DF_j(B/Y)_j] + \eta_{j,16}[(B/Y)_{j,t-1} + (B/Y)_{j,t-2}]$

$+ \eta_{j,17}\{DF_j[(B/Y)_{j,t-1} + (B/Y)_{j,t-2}]\} + \eta_{j,18}[(B/Y)_{j,t-3} + (B/Y)_{j,t-4}]$

$+ \eta_{j,19}\{DF_j[(B/Y)_{j,t-3} + (B/Y)_{j,t-4}]\} + \epsilon_{j4}$

(N5) $R_j = \delta_{j1} + \delta_{j2}t + \delta_{j3}(4\Delta \log P_{j,t+1})^* + \delta_{j4}R_{j,t-1} + \delta_{j5}(4\Delta \log P_j)^*$

$+ \sum_{i=0}^{3} \delta_{j,6+i} \hat{M}_{j,t-i} + \sum_{i=0}^{3} \delta_{j,10+i} \hat{g}_{j,t-i} + \sum_{i=0}^{3} \delta_{j,14+i} \hat{x}_{j,t-i} + \epsilon_{j5}$

(N6) $(X/Y)_j = \theta_{j1} + \theta_{j2}t + \theta_{j3} \log P^{RO} + \theta_{j4} (\log y_j - \log y_j^P)$

$+ \sum_{i=0}^{1} \theta_{j,5+i} (X/Y)_{j,t-1-i} + \sum_{i=0}^{1} \theta_{j,7+i} \log y_{j,t-i}^R$

$+ \sum_{i=0}^{1} \theta_{j,9+i} \log P_{j,t-1} + \sum_{i=0}^{1} \theta_{j,11+i} \log P_{j,t-i}^R$

$+ \sum_{i=0}^{1} \theta_{j,13+i} \log E_{j,t-i} + \sum_{i=0}^{1} \theta_{j,15+i} DF_{j,t-i} \log E_{j,t-i} + \epsilon_{j6}$

(N7F) $Z_j = \dfrac{-\lambda_{j1}}{\lambda_{j6}} + \dfrac{1}{\lambda_{j6}}(I/Y)_j - \dfrac{\lambda_{j2}}{\lambda_{j6}}(I/Y)_{j,t-1} - \dfrac{\lambda_{j3}}{\lambda_{j6}} \log y_j^P$

$- \sum_{i=0}^{1} \dfrac{\lambda_{j,4+i}}{\lambda_{j6}} (\log y_{j,t-i} - \log y_{j,t-i}^P)$

$- \sum_{i=1}^{3} \dfrac{\lambda_{j,6+i}}{\lambda_{j6}} Z_{j,t-i} - \dfrac{\epsilon_{j7}}{\lambda_{j6}}$

(N8F) $\log E_j = \log E_{j,t-1} - \dfrac{\mu_{j1}}{\mu_{j7}} + \dfrac{1}{\mu_7}\Delta \log P_j^I - \dfrac{\mu_{j2}}{\mu_{j7}}\Delta \log P_{j,t-1}^I$

$- \dfrac{\mu_{j3}}{\mu_{j7}}\Delta \log P^{RO} - \dfrac{\mu_{j4}}{\mu_{j7}}\Delta \log y_j^R - \dfrac{\mu_{j5}}{\mu_{j7}}\Delta (I/Y)_j$

$- \dfrac{\mu_{j6}}{\mu_{j7}}\Delta \log P_j^R - \dfrac{\epsilon_{j8}}{\mu_{j7}}$

Table 5.4 (continued)

(N9) $(C/Y)_j = \xi_{j1} + \xi_{j2}t + \xi_{j3}\log P^{RO} + \xi_{j4}R_j + \xi_{j5}(4\Delta\log E_{j,t+1})^*$

$+ \xi_{j6}R_1 + \xi_{j7}\left[(X/Y)_j - (I/Y)_j\right] + \xi_{j8}(\log y_j - \log y_j^P)$

$+ \xi_{j9}\Delta\log y_j + \xi_{j10}\Delta\log y_j^R + \sum_{i=0}^{2}\xi_{j,11+t}\Delta R_{j,t-i}$

$+ \sum_{i=0}^{2}\xi_{j,14+i}\Delta R_{1,t-i} + \sum_{i=0}^{2}\xi_{j,17+i}\Delta(4\Delta\log E_{j,t+1-i})^* + \epsilon_{j9}$

(N10F) $(B/Y)_j = \psi_{j1} + \psi_{j2}(B/Y)_{j,t-1} + \psi_{j3}\Delta\log E_j + \psi_{j4}\Delta\log E_{j,t-1}$

$+ \psi_{j5}(\Delta\log P_{j,t-1} - \Delta\log P_{1,t-1}) + \epsilon_{j,10}$

IDENTITIES

(N11) $\log y_j^P \equiv \theta_{j1} + \theta_{j2}\log y_j + (1-\theta_{j2})\log y_{j,t-1}^P$

(N12F) $(I/Y)_j \equiv (X/Y)_j - 4(B/Y)_j - (C/Y)_j$

(N13) $\hat{M}_j \equiv \log M_j - (\log M_j)^*$

(N14) $\hat{x}_j \equiv (X/Y)_j - (X/Y)_j^*$

(N15F) $\log P_j^I \equiv \log P_j + Z_j$

(N16) $(4\Delta\log P_{j,t+1})^*$: Varies according to country. See table 5.5 for a complete listing.

(N17) $(4\Delta\log E_{j,t+1})^*$: Varies according to country. See table 5.6 for a complete listing.

(N18) $\log y_j^R \equiv \dfrac{1}{1-W_j}\displaystyle\sum_{\substack{i=1\\i\neq j}}^{8} W_i\log y_i - \text{base}\,y_j$

(N19) $\log P_j^R \equiv \dfrac{1}{1-W_j}\displaystyle\sum_{\substack{i=1\\i\neq j}}^{8} W_i(\log P_i - \log E_i) - \text{base}\,P_j$

ENDOGENOUS VARIABLES

$\log y_j$, $\log P_j$, u_j, $\log M_j$, R_j, $(X/Y)_j$, Z_j, $\log E_j$, $(C/Y)_j$, $(B/Y)_j$;
$\log y_j^P$, $(I/Y)_j$, $\hat{M}_j$, $\hat{x}_j$, $\log P_j^I$, $(4\Delta\log P_{j,t+1})^*$, $(4\Delta\log E_{j,t+1})^*$

PREDETERMINED VARIABLES

Exogenous Variables
DF_j, $DF_{j,t-1}$, $\hat{g}_j$, $\hat{g}_{j,t-1}$, $\hat{g}_{j,t-2}$, $\hat{g}_{j,t-3}$, $\hat{g}_{j,t-4}$, $\log P^{RO}$, $\log P_{t-1}^{RO}$, t

Expected Values Based on Prior Information
$(\log M_j)^*$, $(X/Y)_j^{\ddagger}$

Lagged Endogenous Variables
$\log E_{j,t-1}$, $\log E_{j,t-2}$, $\log E_{j,t-3}$, $(4\Delta\log E_j)^*$, $(4\Delta\log E_{j,t-1})^*$,
$(4\Delta\log E_{j,t-2})^*$, $(I/Y)_{j,t-1}$, $\log M_{j,t-1}$, $\hat{M}_{j,t-1}$, $\hat{M}_{j,t-2}$, $\hat{M}_{j,t-3}$, $\log P_{j,t-1}$,
$\log P_{j,t-2}$, $\log P_{j,t-3}$, $\log P_{j,t-5}$, $\log P_{j,t-1}^I$, $\log P_{j,t-2}^I$, $R_{j,t-1}$, $R_{j,t-2}$,
$R_{j,t-3}$, $(X/Y)_{j,t-1}$, $(X/Y)_{j,t-2}$, $(B/Y)_{j,t-1}$, $(B/Y)_{j,t-2}$, $(B/Y)_{j,t-3}$, $(B/Y)_{j,t-4}$,
$\hat{x}_{j,t-1}$, $\hat{x}_{j,t-2}$, $\hat{x}_{j,t-3}$, $\log y_{j,t-1}$, $\log y_{j,t-1}^P$, $Z_{j,t-1}$, $Z_{j,t-2}$, $Z_{j,t-3}$,
$\{u_{j,t-1}$, $\log y_{j,t-2}$, $\log y_{j,t-3}$, $\log y_{j,t-4}$, $\log y_{j,t-5}$, $\log y_{j,t-6}$,
$\log y_{j,t-7}$, $\log y_{j,t-8}\}^{\ddagger}$; plus and other lagged endogenous variables appearing
in (N4.j).

Table 5.4 (continued)

Foreign Variables (endogenous in full model)[#]
$\log P_j^R$, R_1, $\log y_j^R$

Lagged Foreign Variables
$\log P_{1,t-1}$, $\log P_{1,t-2}$, $\log P_{j,t-1}^R$, $R_{1,t-1}$, $R_{1,t-2}$, $R_{1,t-3}$, $\log y_{j,t-1}^R$

[†]The unemployment equation appears only in the submodel for France and the United Kingdom.

[§]For the submodels other than France and the United Kingdom, the unemployment-rate variables u_j are replaced with negative logarithmic transitory income $\log y_j^P - \log y_j$.

[‡]The variables in braces appear only in the submodels for France and the United Kingdom; see note † above.

[#]In estimating the submodels by principal-components 2SLS, we include in our instrument list fitted values for these foreign variables based on the foreign countries' domestic predetermined variables. See chapter 6 for details.

Table 5.5   **Expected-Inflation Transfer Functions**

(R16) $(\Delta \log P_{1,t+1})^* \equiv -\ 0.754\ -\ 1.704(\log M_1)^* + 1.001 \log M_{1,t-1}$
$+\ 0.850 \log M_{1,t-2}\ -\ 0.063\Delta \log y_{1,t-1}$
$+\ 0.248 R_1\ -\ 0.038 R_{1,t-1}\ +\ 0.008[R_2\ -\ (4\Delta \log E_{2,t+1})^*]$
$-\ 0.009[R_{2,t-1}\ -\ (4\Delta \log E_2)^*] + 0.158 \log P_{1,t-1}$
$-\ 0.279 \log P_{1,t-2}\ +\ 1.711 \hat{M}_{1,t-1}\ +\ 0.222 \hat{M}_{1,t-2}$
$+\ 0.020 \hat{M}_{1,t-3}\ +\ 0.160 \epsilon_{1,16,t-1}\ -\ 0.230 \epsilon_{1,16,t-2}$

(N16.2) $(\Delta \log P_{2,t+1})^* \equiv -\ 0.09655\ +\ 2.315(\log M_2)^*\ -\ 4.655 \log M_{2,t-1}$
$+\ 2.382\log M_{2,t-2}\ +\ 0.186\Delta \log y_{2,t-1}\ +\ 0.030 R_2$
$+\ 0.146 R_{2,t-1}\ +\ 0.043[R_1\ +\ (4\Delta \log E_{2,t+1})^*]$
$-\ 0.035[R_{1,t-1}\ +\ (4\Delta \log E_2)^*] + 0.385 \log P_{2,t-1}$
$-\ 0.408 \log P_{2,t-2}\ +\ 2.052 \hat{M}_{2,t-1}\ -\ 0.407 \hat{M}_{2,t-2}$
$+\ 0.284 \hat{M}_{2,t-3}\ -\ 0.238 \epsilon_{2,16,t-1}\ +\ 0.416 \epsilon_{2,16,t-2}$

(N16.3) $(\Delta \log P_{3,t+1})^* \equiv -\ 0.060\ -\ 1.002(\log M_3)^*\ +\ 1.053 \log M_{3,t-1}$
$-\ 0.008 \log M_{3,t-2}\ +\ 0.065\Delta \log y_{3,t-1}\ +\ 0.301 R_3$
$-\ 0.460 R_{3,t-1}\ +\ 0.012[R_1\ +\ (4\Delta \log E_{3,t-1})^*]$
$-\ 0.033[R_{1,t-1}\ +\ (4\Delta \log E_3)^*] + 0.433 \log P_{3,t-1}$
$-\ 0.459 \log P_{3,t-2}\ +\ 0.434 \hat{M}_{3,t-1}\ -\ 0.162 \hat{M}_{3,t-2}$
$-\ 0.019 \hat{M}_{3,t-3}\ -\ 0.618 \epsilon_{3,16,t-1}\ -\ 0.382 \epsilon_{3,16,t-2}$

(N16.4) $(\Delta \log P_{4,t+1})^* \equiv -\ 0.023\ +\ 0.095(\log M_4)^*\ +\ 0.250 \log M_{4,t-1}$
$-\ 0.344 \log M_{4,t-2}\ +\ 0.003\Delta \log y_{4,t-1}\ +\ 0.055 R_4$
$+\ 0.214 R_{4,t-1}\ +\ 0.003[R_1\ +\ (4\Delta \log E_{4,t+1})^*]$
$+\ 0.011[R_{1,t-1}\ +\ (4\Delta \log E_4)^*] + 0.102 \log P_{4,t-1}$
$-\ 0.110 \log P_{4,t-2}\ -\ 0.287 \hat{M}_{4,t-1}$
$-\ 0.042 \hat{M}_{4,t-2}\ -\ 0.073 \hat{M}_{4,t-3}\ +\ 0.545 e_{4,t-1}$
$-\ 0.164 e_{4,16,t-2}$

(N16.5) $(\Delta \log P_{5,t+1})^* \equiv 1.727\ -\ 79.865(\log M_5)^*\ +\ 79.905 \log M_{5,t-1}$
$-\ 0.022 \log M_{5,t-2}\ +\ 0.132\Delta \log y_{5,t-1}\ -\ 0.012 R_5$
$+\ 0.075 R_{5,t-1}\ +\ 0.019[R_1\ +\ (4\Delta \log E_{5,t+1})^*]$
$+\ 0.014[R_{1,t-1}\ +\ (4\Delta \log E_5)^*] + 0.027 \log P_{5,t-1}$
$-\ 0.056 \log P_{5,t-2}\ +\ 8.540 \hat{M}_{5,t-1}\ +\ 21.966 \hat{M}_{5,t-2}$
$+\ 28.536 \hat{M}_{5,t-3}\ +\ 0.187 \epsilon_{5,16,t-1}\ +\ 0.555 \epsilon_{5,16,t-2}$

Table 5.5 (continued)

(N16.6) $(\Delta \log P_{6,t+1})^* \equiv 1.858 - 75.036(\log M_6)^* + 85.887 \log M_{6,t-1}$
$- 10.820 \log M_{6,t-2} - 0.103\Delta \log y_{6,t-1} + 0.069 R_6$
$+ 0.154 R_{6,t-1} - 0.031[R_1 + (4\Delta \log E_{6,t-1})^*]$
$- 0.018[R_{1,t-1} + (4\Delta \log E_6)^*] - 0.218 \log P_{6,t-1}$
$+ 0.165 \log P_{6,t-2} + 0.974 \hat{M}_{6,t-1} + 27.169 \hat{M}_{6,t-2}$
$+ 8.456 \hat{M}_{6,t-3} + 0.133 \epsilon_{6,16,t-1} + 0.640 \epsilon_{6,16,t-2}$

(N16.7) $(\Delta \log P_{7,t+1})^* \equiv 0.131 - 0.281(\log M_7)^* + 0.455 \log M_{7,t-1}$
$- 0.180 \log M_{7,t-2} - 0.026\Delta \log y_{7,t-1} + 1.658 R_7$
$- 2.219 R_{7,t-1} + 0.044[R_1 + (4\Delta \log E_{7,t-1})^*]$
$+ 0.004[R_{1,t-1} + (4\Delta \log E_7)^*] + 0.092 \log P_{7,t-1}$
$- 0.060 \log P_{7,t-2} + 0.107 \hat{M}_{7,t-1} + 0.153 \hat{M}_{7,t-2}$
$+ 0.034 \hat{M}_{7,t-3} + 0.131 \epsilon_{7,16,t-1}$

(N16.8) $(\Delta \log P_{8,t+1})^* \equiv - 0.641 + 10.564(\log M_8)^* - 5.440 \log M_{8,t-1}$
$- 5.046 \log M_{8,t-2} + 0.244\Delta \log y_{8,t-1} - 0.050 R_8$
$+ 0.180 R_{8,t-1} - 0.039[R_1 + (4\Delta \log E_{8,t+1})^*]$
$- 0.027[R_{1,t-1} + (4\Delta \log E_8)^*] - 0.234 \log P_{8,t-1}$
$+ 0.116 \log P_{8,t-2} - 8.937 \hat{M}_{8,t-1} - 7.000 \hat{M}_{8,t-2}$
$- 5.788 \hat{M}_{8,t-3} - 0.343 \epsilon_{8,16,t-1} + 0.248 \epsilon_{8,16,t-2}$

Notes. These identities are for expected inflation rates per quarter; the rates per annum in the model are simply $(4\Delta \log P_j)^* \equiv 4(\Delta \log P_j)^*$.

$e_{j,16} \equiv (\Delta \log P_{j,t+1}) - (\Delta \log P_{j,t+1})^*$
$\epsilon_{1,16} \equiv e_{1,16} - .160 \epsilon_{1,16,t-1} + .230 \epsilon_{1,16,t-2}$
$\epsilon_{2,16} \equiv e_{2,16} + .238 \epsilon_{2,16,t-1} - .416 \epsilon_{2,16,t-2}$
$\epsilon_{3,16} \equiv e_{3,16} + .618 \epsilon_{3,16,t-1} + .382 \epsilon_{3,16,t-2}$
$\epsilon_{5,16} \equiv e_{5,16} - .187 \epsilon_{5,16,t-1} - .555 \epsilon_{5,16,t-2}$
$\epsilon_{6,16} \equiv e_{6,16} - .133 \epsilon_{6,16,t-1} - .640 \epsilon_{6,16,t-2}$
$\epsilon_{7,16} \equiv e_{7,16} - .131 \epsilon_{7,16,t-1}$
$\epsilon_{8,16} \equiv e_{8,16} + .343 \epsilon_{8,16,t-1} - .248 \epsilon_{8,16,t-2}$

The fitted ARMA error processes by country are:
1 (0,2)   5 (0,2)
2 (0,2)   6 (0,2)
3 (0,2)   7 (0,1)
4 (2,0)   8 (0,2)

Table 5.6 Expected Exchange-Rate Growth

$(4\Delta \log E_j)^* \equiv 4(\Delta \log E_j)^*$

a) Floating Exchange-Rate Periods

(N17F) $(\Delta \log E_{j,t+1})^* \equiv \omega_{j1} + \omega_{j2}\Delta \log P_j^I + \omega_{j3}\Delta \log P^{RO} + \omega_{j4}\Delta \log y_j^R + \omega_{j5}\Delta (I/Y)_j + \omega_{j6}\Delta \log P_j^R + \omega_{j7}\Delta \log E_j$

The parameters (estimated by OLS) are:

Country	ω_{j1}	ω_{j2}	ω_{j3}	ω_{j4}	ω_{j5}	ω_{j6}	ω_{j7}	Floating Periods
2, UK	.00597	.80037	−.02808	1.20971	−2.03867	−.98978	−.20116	1971III–76IV
3, CA	−.00314	.05183	−.00683	.07509	−.30121	.18038	.31538	1956I–62III, 1970II–76IV
4, FR	.06315	.13361	−.06955	−1.13931	1.42566	−3.15593	−.39385	1971III–76IV
5, GE	.00064	−.95133	.05737	−.73465	2.98731	−.13434	.18685	1971II–76IV
6, IT	.02320	−.08897	−.02900	.76727	.15530	−.35833	.15115	1971III–76IV
7, JA	.00323	−.03233	−.03956	−.87177	3.92447	−.02198	.20401	1971III–76IV
8, NE	.02739	.11611	−.07818	−.66181	−.10364	−1.97462	−.35813	1971II–76IV

Note. The first $(\Delta \log E_j)^*$ defined as above is for the second quarter in each floating period. The previous quarter value is defined by the pegged rate period.

b) Pegged Exchange-Rate Periods

(N17P.2) $(\Delta \log E_{2,t+1})^* \equiv 0.0014 - 0.5398(B/Y)_2 + 29.8764[(B/Y)_2|(B/Y)_2|] + 0.1369(\log E_2 - \log \bar{E}_2) + 0.5283\Delta \log E_2 - 0.0197 DR_{2,t-1}$

(N17P.3) $(\Delta \log E_{3,t+1})^* \equiv -0.0002 - 0.4222(B/Y)_3 + 33.9022[(B/Y)_3|(B/Y)_3|] - 0.0089(\log E_3 - \log \bar{E}_3) + 0.3183\Delta \log E_3 - \epsilon_{3,17,t-1}$

(N17P.4) $(\Delta \log E_{4,t+1})^* \equiv 0.0058 - 1.1289(B/Y)_4 + 131.5500[(B/Y)_4|(B/Y)_4|] + 0.6546(\log E_4 - \log \bar{E}_4) + 0.7406\Delta \log E_4 - 0.0384 DR_{4,t-1}$
$\qquad - 0.65\epsilon_{4,17,t-1} - 0.35\epsilon_{4,17,t-2}$

(N17P.5) $(\Delta \log E_{5,t+1})^* \equiv -0.0026 + 0.9585(B/Y)_5 - 116.8350[(B/Y)_5|(B/Y)_5|] - 0.2109(\log E_5 - \log \bar{E}_5) + 0.4755\Delta \log E_5 + 0.0106 DR1_{5,t-1}$
$\qquad - 0.0086 DR2_{5,t-1}$

(N17P.6) $(\Delta \log E_{6,t+1})^* \equiv -0.0001 + 0.0660(B/Y)_6 - 9.7561[(B/Y)_6|(B/Y)_6|] - 0.0321(\log E_6 - \log \bar{E}_6) + 0.9541\Delta \log E_6 - \epsilon_{6,17,t-1}$

(N17P.7) $(\Delta \log E_{7,t+1})^* \equiv -0.0013 + 1.9035(B/Y)_7 - 405.337[(B/Y)_7|(B/Y)_7|] + 0.2366(\log E_7 - \log \bar{E}_7) + 0.2636\Delta \log E_7 - 0.5\epsilon_{7,17,t-1}$
$\qquad - 0.5\epsilon_{7,17,t-2}$

(N17P.8) $(\Delta \log E_{8,t+1})^* \equiv -0.0014 - 0.1362(B/Y)_8 + 10.9493[(B/Y)_8|(B/Y)_8|] - 0.2170(\log E_8 - \log \bar{E}_8) + 0.6339\Delta \log E_8 + 0.0253 DR_{8,t-1}$

Notes. $\bar{E}_j$ is the official parity value. For France only this is set equal to E_j through 1958IV, when a fixed official parity value was established. DR_j, $DR1_5$, and $DR2_5$ are revaluation dummies with value of 1 in the indicated quarter and 0 otherwise:

DR_2	1967IV	$DR1_5$	1961I
DR_4	1969III	$DR2_5$	1969IV
		DR_8	1961I

$e_{j,17} \equiv (\Delta \log E_{j,t+1}) - (\Delta \log E_{j,t+1})^*$ for all j

$\epsilon_{3,17} \equiv e_{3,17} + \epsilon_{3,17,t-1}$

$\epsilon_{4,17} \equiv e_{4,17} + .65\epsilon_{4,17,t-1} + .35\epsilon_{4,17,t-2}$

$\epsilon_{6,17} \equiv e_{6,17} + \epsilon_{6,17,t-1}$

$\epsilon_{7,17} \equiv e_{7,17} + .5\epsilon_{7,17,t-1} + .5\epsilon_{7,17,t-2}$

The fitted ARMA error processes by country are:

3 (0,1)	6 (0,1)
4 (0,2)	7 (0,2)

Table 5.7   **Parameter Values for Foreign Real Income
and Foreign Price Index Identities** (R18), (R19), (N18), **and** (N19)

Country	j	$W_j^\dagger$	base $y_j^\S$	base $P_j^\S$
US	1	0.531464	7.40946	-2.53058
UK	2	0.063287	7.36068	-1.32478
CA	3	0.046296	7.26361	-1.24117
FR	4	0.077221	7.18014	-1.14182
GE	5	0.107001	7.20584	-1.17274
IT	6	0.048061	6.93985	-0.920318
JA	7	0.107898	6.64583	-0.617771
NE	8	0.018771	7.17908	-1.183800

$\dagger$Nominal income shares are computed as follows, where the time summation is from 1955I–76IV:

$$W_j = \frac{\sum\limits_t (Y/E)_{j,t}}{\sum\limits_{i=1}^{8} \sum (Y/E)_{i,t}}$$

$\S$The values of base y_j and base P_j are such that the mean values of the logarithmic indices are 0 for our base year 1970. This is equivalent to the 1970 geometric means being 1.

6 The Mark III International Transmission Model: Estimates

Michael R. Darby and Alan C. Stockman

The simultaneous estimation of the Mark III International Transmission Model produced some surprising results. The major implications of the model estimates are: (1) Countries linked by pegged exchange rates appear to have much more national independence than generally supposed. (2) Substantial or complete sterilization of the contemporaneous effects of the balance of payments on nominal money appears to be a universal practice of nonreserve central banks. (3) Quantities such as international trade flows are not well explained by observed prices, exchange rates, and interest rates. (4) Explaining real income by innovations in aggregate demand variables works well for U.S. real income but does not transfer easily to other countries.

Our estimation method is explained in section 6.1 before the results are reported and interpreted in section 6.2. A detailed summary concludes the chapter.

6.1 Estimation Methods

If a simultaneously determined model such as ours is estimated by ordinary least squares (OLS), simultaneous equation bias occurs. This arises because the endogenous variables respond to each other so that the random disturbance in any one behavioral equation may be reflected in movements of all the other endogenous variables. As a result, when some endogenous variables are used to explain the behavior of another endogenous variable, their values are potentially correlated with the random disturbance in the equation. Their OLS coefficients will reflect not only their effect on the variable being explained but also the effect of its residual on them. Simultaneous equation methods are used to remove this spurious correlation that is due to reverse causality.

113

The most popular simultaneous equation methods are two-stage and three-stage least squares (2SLS and 3SLS, respectively.)[1] Unfortunately, neither exists for our model. This is because the first stage of each approach involves obtaining fitted values of each of the endogenous variables which are uncorrelated with the other endogenous variables. This is done by fitting OLS regressions for each endogenous variable as a function of all the predetermined variables (exogenous and lagged endogenous). In large samples, these fitted values are uncorrelated with the residuals in the behavioral equations and, when substituted for the actual values in OLS estimates of the behavioral equations, give unbiased estimates of the coefficients. Unfortunately, when the number of predetermined variables equals or exceeds the number of observations, the first-stage regressions can perfectly reproduce the actual values of the endogenous variables and no simultaneous equation bias is removed.

We reduce the number of predetermined variables relative to the number of observations in two ways: (1) For each country we use as predetermined variables only domestic variables for that country plus fitted values of only those foreign variables which enter that country's submodel. The fitted foreign variables are obtained by fitting interest rates, income, and prices on each foreign country's own domestic variables and then forming indexes (where necessary as indicated by identities (R18), (R19), (N18), and (N19)) of these fitted foreign variables. (2) Using this reduced set of predetermined variables,[2] we take sufficient principal components to explain over 99.95% of their variance. (Variables were initially standardized so that the principal components are not affected by their scale.) Usually this involves thirty to thirty-five components (indicating thirty to thirty-five independent sources of variation in the instrument list). However, in estimating certain equations for short subperiods[3] it is necessary to limit the number of principal components to half the number of observations in the subperiod. In either case these principal components are used as our matrix for obtaining fitted values of the endogenous variables in the first stage of our 2SLS regressions.

In summary, the model is estimated by the principal-components 2SLS method where (a) the basic instrument list for each country consists of domestic predetermined variables plus fitted values of those foreign variables which appear in the model based on foreign predetermined variables, and (b) this basic instrument list is spanned by a number of components either equal to half the observations being used or sufficient to explain over 99.95% of the variance in the basic instrument list, whichever is smaller.

1. Other, more complicated methods exist but could not be entertained for such a large model as ours because of software and computing budget limitations.

2. The actual lists of predetermined variables for each country are presented in table 6.1.

3. That is, for the floating period for all nonreserve countries except Canada and the pegged period for Canada.

6.2 Estimation Results

The estimated model is reported in tables 6.2 through 6.16. We first discuss the estimates equation by equation in this section and then check the cross-correlations of the residuals for evidence of omitted channels of transmission. We draw our general conclusions in section 6.3. The period of estimation is 1957I–76IV except, as indicated, where the model differs during pegged and flexible rate periods. Details on the data used are contained in the appendix to this chapter.

6.2.1 Real-Income Equations (R1) and (N1)—Table 6.2

For the United States, there appear to be substantial effects from money shocks and weak or nonexistent effects from both real-government spending and export shocks. For the nonreserve countries, a few apparently significant monetary shocks enter, but we generally cannot reject the hypothesis that all the money shock coefficients are zero. This is shown in table 6.3, where only Canada and Italy among the nonreserve countries reach even the 10% level of significance. The apparent impotence of monetary policy in the nonreserve countries may be real, or it may reflect either a greater measurement error in defining the money shocks or a stable monetary policy, which would also reduce the signal-to-noise ratio in the $\hat{M}_j$ data.[4]

The other demand shock variables, with occasional exceptions, also seem to have little systematic effect on the nonreserve countries' real incomes. The sensitivity of these results to alternative definitions of demand shocks and to effects of anticipated variables is examined in chapter 9.

6.2.2 Price-Level Equations (R2) and (N2)—Table 6.4

The price-level equations have the difficulties usually encountered in the stock-adjustment formulation: a tendency for autocorrelation in the residuals to bias the coefficient of the lagged dependent variable toward 1 and the long-run demand variables toward zero.[5] We have included three lagged money shocks in addition to the current one suggested by Carr and Darby (1981). These serve to explain current movements in demand variables in what are nearly first difference in $(\log P - \log M)$ equations.

---

4. If, for example, the nonreserve central banks smoothed out the Federal Reserve System's erratic growth-rate changes via an effective sterilization policy, the actual variation in money shocks might be too small to estimate a significant coefficient even though a substantial monetary shock, if it were ever attempted, would have a substantial effect on real income. Although such effective sterilization appears consistent with results reported below, the authors are not agreed on its existence.

5. The long-run parameter estimates are more stable, of course. For example, five of the long-run permanent income elasticities lie between 0.5 and 1.5, with 0.2 for the United Kingdom and 3.0 for France as the extreme values.

Software difficulties prevented us from trying a correction for autocorrelation.[6]

The fact that current money shocks enter with a coefficient near -1 indicates, since $\log M_j - \hat{M}_j = (\log M_j)^*$, that expected rather than actual money enters in the price-level equation. With a coefficient of -1, money shocks affect the current price level only via indirect interest-rate or real-income effects. The shock-absorber adjustment process suggested by Carr and Darby is thus supported by the data.

The foreign interest-rate channel (β_{j5}) is both significant and of the right sign only for the United Kingdom and Japan. Further, if we recall that interest rates are measured as decimal fractions, we see that both elasticities are very small in absolute value and compared to the elasticity of money demand with respect to the domestic interest rate. Nonetheless we are able to detect some asset substitution in two of our eight countries.

6.2.3   Unemployment-Rate Equations (R3) and (N3)—Table 6.5

The unemployment-rate equations indicate conformity to a dynamic version of Okun's law for the United States, United Kingdom, and France. For the other countries there was no significant correlation between changes in the unemployment rate and past and present changes in real income. As the equation was not required for the model, it was dropped for those countries.

6.2.4   Nominal-Money Equations (R4) and (N4)—Tables 6.6 and 6.7

The U.S. reaction function (R4) reported in table 6.6 indicates a negative impact of lagged inflation on nominal money growth, surprisingly weak (though) positive effects from unexpected real government spending, and a stimulative effect from a two-quarter lagged change in unemployment rate. The time trend term is extremely potent: For plausible steady-state values it increases the growth rate of nominal money from 0.2% per annum in 1956 to 5.9% per annum in 1976. Indeed a constant and time trend alone would explain approximately 31% of the variance of the growth rate of nominal money, with all the other variables together accounting for only another 25%.

Darby (1981) reports on experiments testing other variables which might explain U.S. money growth. The balance of payments entered with coefficients which were trivial, insignificant, and of the wrong sign. The joint test of all coefficients being 0 yielded an $F(3/64)$ statistic of only 0.26 compared to a 95% critical value of 2.75. So the U.S. appears to have determined its monetary policy without regard to its balance of payments (as is appropriate for a fiat reserve country).[7] Although financing the

---

6. The current TROLL system regression package has a program defect when 2SLS and correction for autocorrelation are used simultaneously. France, Germany, Italy, and Japan appear to have significant positive autocorrelation judging from Durbin's h statistic.

7. See Darby (1980) and chapter 16.

Vietnamese War is a popular explanation of the onset of the inflationary process, neither the fraction of the total labor force in the military nor the number of troops in Vietnam entered the reaction function (R4) at all significantly.[8] So the Vietnamese War apparently had no more effect than any similar sequence of unexpected increases in government spending.

A number of factors have been suggested to explain the gradually rising target level of inflation implicit in the U.S. reaction function. Most—such as the increasing influence of Keynesian economics on politicians—appear unquantifiable and untestable. It may well be that the upward trend reflects acceptance of whatever has been our recent experience, so that the government spending shocks of the Vietnamese War began a dynamic process which has since fed upon itself.

The results for the nonreserve countries are reported in table 6.7. The key element for international transmission is the effect of the balance of payments on the money supply. Table 6.8 indicates what fraction of the balance of payments is not sterilized by the central bank—a value of 1 indicates no sterilization and a value of 0 indicates complete sterilization. During the pegged period, sterilization appears to have been a universal practice, although there was a substantial impact effect of the balance of payments on the German and Japanese nominal money supply. When we take account of lagged adjustments, the money supplies of all countries except Italy appear to respond, albeit partially, to the balance of payments. In principle a lagged adjustment may be sufficient to maintain a pegged exchange-rate system.[9] The continued impact of the balance of payments on nominal money during the floating period is consistent with a joint policy of exchange intervention and monetary adjustments in response to exchange-rate pressures.

6.2.5   Interest-Rate Equations (R5) and (N5)—Table 6.9

The interest-rate equations are somewhat puzzling: A partial adjustment process appears to operate with nominal rather than real interest rates. A partial adjustment process for real interest rates is not ruled out by efficient capital markets, but a partial adjustment process for nominal rates is harder to rationalize. One possibility is that this result reflects an expectational process in the adjustment formulation along lines suggested by Waud (1968). The money shocks and export shocks generally have the expected signs on their impact coefficients (negative and positive, respectively), but real-government-spending shocks generally have a negative impact effect on interest rates. We suspect the solution to these puzzles may lie in the formation of expectations, but leave this as an area for future research.

---

8. Distributed lags of the military variables alone or in combination with the balance-of-payments variables also failed to enter.

9. The implications of sterilization (and hence endogenous domestic credit) are examined in chapters 10 and 11.

6.2.6   Export Equations (R6) and (N6)—Table 6.10

The export equations indicate that measured price influences are not very strong. An increased real oil price enters as a proxy for increased real income of the rest of the world and has the expected positive sign except for Japan. Foreign real income has much weaker positive impact than would be expected from the absorption approach. The sum of the current and lagged domestic price level is negative for all countries except the U.S. and Canada, but the effects are universally weak. Similarly, foreign prices and the exchange rate generally have weak positive effects.

6.2.7   Import Equations (R7) and (N7P)—Table 6.11

The import demand equations display a *J*-curve type of effect. An increase in relative import prices initially (except for Germany and Italy) increases the nominal value of imports relative to nominal income. Lagged quantity adjustment, indicated by negative coefficients on lagged relative import prices, gradually offsets the initial increase. While the price effects are somewhat stronger here than for exports,[10] there is no evidence of a "law of one price level" operating strongly in the current period.

6.2.8   Relative-Price-of-Imports Equations (N7F)—Table 6.12

During the floating period, we solve the import demand equation for the relative price of imports. The implied parameter estimates are frequently quite different from those in table 6.11. This may be due to biases from the (different) lagged dependent variable which appears in each equation.

6.2.9   Import-Price Equations (R8) and (N8P)—Table 6.13

The import supply equations indicate that increases in foreign prices increase import prices, although the coefficients are insignificant for the United States and Canada. Changes in exchange rates are significantly positive for the four countries which changed their peg during the period of estimation, but not for Canada, Italy, or Japan. Oil prices are important only for the U.S. and perhaps Italy and the Netherlands.

6.2.10   Exchange-Rate Equations (N8F)—Table 6.14

The inverted import supply equations are used to explain exchange-rate movement during the floating period. Although it is somewhat

---

10. This may be because with relatively reliable import price data we can estimate separate import demand and supply equations while the export equation is a market equilibrium equation in which the exchange rate and foreign price level enter directly. That is, an increase in the relative price of imports—for given quantities of imports—increases the ratio of the value of imports to nominal income. An increase in the price level, ceteris paribus, increases the value of exports and nominal income proportionately.

arbitrary in a simultaneous model which one is declared *the* exchange-rate equation, this one was chosen because exchange rates entered most directly and strongly here. The approach clearly worked well for France, Japan, and the Netherlands and not so well for the United Kingdom, Canada, Germany, and Italy. Why this is so is puzzling to us.

6.2.11   Capital-Flows Equations (R9) and (N9)—Table 6.15

The capital-flows equations worked poorly for the United Kingdom and Japan, perhaps reflecting the effectiveness of their capital controls. For the other countries, net capital outflows generally were negatively related (albeit weakly so) either to the exchange-rate adjusted interest differential $[R_j - (4\Delta \log E_{j,t+1})^* - R_1]$ or to changes in this differential, judging from the coefficients estimated on its component parts. But the estimated coefficients are neither large nor precisely estimated as would be suggested by discussions of "interest arbitrage" in the asset approach. Apparently foreign and domestic securities are treated as imperfect substitutes in the portfolio. Alternatively, movements in the differential may reflect changes in the equilibrium value with no flows resulting. These issues are further investigated in chapters 10 and 11.

6.2.12   Balance-of-Payments Equations (N10F)—Table 6.16

These equations attempt to model intervention in the floating exchange-rate markets and include the variables popularly discussed: movements in the exchange rate relative to recent movements or lagged relative inflation rates and the lagged dependent variable. These variables appear to have some explanatory power for intervention except in the French and Dutch cases.

6.2.13   A Check for Omitted Channels

A useful check of model adequacy is to examine cross-correlations of the residuals.[11] A pattern of significant residuals would indicate where we had failed to include important channels of influence. Here we report checks for two classes of residual cross-correlation: (1) within the country submodel and (2) U.S. nominal money, real income, and price level versus all residuals in the foreign submodels.[12] If the model is inadequate, evidence should certainly show up here.

Tables 6.17 and 6.18 report all the significant cross-correlation coefficients obtained for the pegged and floating periods, respectively. The entry "$\rho(\log P_1, R_1) = -0.348^*$" in table 6.17, for example, indicates that the residuals of the U.S. price-level and interest-rate equations (R2)

---

11. We are indebted to Robert P. Flood, Jr., for suggesting this check.
12. These 923 cross-correlations are the main potential dangers for omitted channels. Given the relatively clean bill of health reported below for these, we did not compute the other 3,989 cross-correlation coefficients.

and (R5), respectively, were negatively correlated during the pegged period; the asterisk indicates that the correlation was significant at the 0.01 level or better. We might infer that our treatment of inflationary expectations was wrong if we focused on this coefficient alone. However, when we look at a large number of residual correlation coefficients, some should appear significant even if all the residuals are drawn from independent white noise processes.

The evidence suggests that we have not missed significant channels of transmission, particularly international channels of transmission. Of the 923 cross-correlation coefficients computed, only 7.8% are significant at the 5% level or better. Among these we have 3.1% of the total significant at the 1% level or better. Further, these small excesses of observed over nominal frequencies are almost entirely due to within-country cross-correlations as detailed in table 6.19. Thus, to the small extent that our simple model has missed significant relations among variables, these omissions appear to be within rather than across countries. Further, as indicated in the notes to tables 6.17 and 6.18, in no case were the same cross-correlations significant in more than two countries;[13] so no pattern of missed channels is indicated. If we wish to consider models comparable across countries, this is about as clean a result as we could hope for. In summary, there appear to be no significant channels of transmission either within or across countries which we have failed to incorporate in the model.

6.3   Conclusions and Areas for Future Research

Our main empirical results can be summarized by the statement that linkages among countries joined by pegged exchange rates appear to be much looser or more elusive than has been assumed in many previous studies, particularly those associated with the monetary approach to the balance of payments. In particular, substantial or complete sterilization of the effects of *contemporaneous* reserve flows on the money supply appears to be a universal practice. This implies, among other things, that domestic credit cannot be properly treated as an exogenous variable and that central banks may have influenced their nominal money supplies despite pegged exchange rates. Much of the remainder of this volume is devoted to further investigation of these issues and their implications.

The estimates reported in this chapter indicate that:

1. The link between countries provided by the price-specie-flow mechanism is not strong and operates only with a lag. There are two reasons for this. First, relative price effects on the balance of trade are not

---

13. In only one case—$\rho(\log y_j, \log P_1)$ for the United Kingdom and Netherlands in the pegged period—were there even two significant cross-correlations of the same type involving cross-country comparisons.

large, although they increase over time. Second, the effect of the balance of payments on the domestic money supply and hence domestic prices is small and operates with a lag. This reflects the apparent practice of sterilization of contemporaneous reserve flows mentioned above.

2. Currency substitution does not seem to provide a significant link between countries. Evidence of currency substitution was found only in the British and Japanese cases, and its magnitudes even there were small.

3. International capital flows do not appear to be very well related to interest differentials (adjusted for expected depreciation). One possible explanation is that we only observe changes in the equilibrium interest-rate differential consistent with risk differences, controls, and the like. The role of capital flows in the transmission of inflation would be small in any case due to sterilization of the effects of reserve flows on the money supply.

4. A J-curve phenomena was observed for imports, so that the short-run and long-run effects of variables affecting domestic inflation through the balance of trade (the absorption channel) may differ. This weakens the short-run link between countries on pegged exchange rates relative to the long-run link.

5. The effects of money shocks on real income are much weaker in the countries other than the United States.

6. Money seems to play a shock-absorber role, as emphasized by Carr and Darby, in all of the countries. Innovations in nominal money have little effect on contemporaneous inflation, although there are small contemporaneous effects on real income and interest rates.

These results raise serious questions about a number of popular hypotheses and some widely used assumptions in models of open economies.

Acknowledgments

The other contributors to this volume have made innumerable helpful suggestions in regard to the estimates and their interpretation. Daniel M. Laskar, Michael T. Melvin, M. Holly Crawford, and Andrew A. Vogel performed the calculations using the TROLL system and Charles Nelson's Box-Jenkins routines at MIT.

Appendix

The variables described in table 5.1 of the previous chapter generally either are drawn directly from the project data bank (see chapter 3 and the Data Appendix to this volume) or are transformations of such variables. In a few cases minor revisions have been made in the data bank series subsequent to the date in which we placed the variable in the model data set, but in no case were the changes sufficiently substantial to justify reestimation and resimulation of the model.[14] The specific basic data series are summarized in tables 6.20 and 6.21.

References

Carr, J., and M. R. Darby. 1981. The role of money supply shocks in the short-run demand for money. *Journal of Monetary Economics* 8 (September): 183–99.

Darby, M. R. 1980. The monetary approach to the balance of payments: Two specious assumptions. *Economic Inquiry* 18 (April): 321–26.

———. 1981. The international economy as a source of and restraint on United States inflation. In W. A. Gale, ed., *Inflation: Causes, consequents, and control.* Cambridge, Mass.: Oelgeschlager, Gunn & Hain, Publishers.

Waud, R. N. 1968. Misspecification in the "partial adjustment" and "adaptive expectations" models. *International Economic Review* 9 (June): 204–17.

14. In some cases, the data series names in the Data Appendix will differ slightly from those used here as an indication of such revisions; the correspondence will be obvious from the descriptions. We based our judgment of whether or not to reestimate the whole model on an examination of changes in reestimated regressions of only those equations in which the revised data or their transformations appeared. The only remaining differences are ones that passed this check.

Table 6.1   **Basic Instrument Lists for Computation of Principal Components**[†]

a) United States

Domestic Instruments

$\hat{g}_1$, $\hat{g}_{1,t-1}$, $\hat{g}_{1,t-2}$, $\hat{g}_{1,t-3}$, $\hat{g}_{1,t-4}$, $\log P^{RO}$, $\log P^{RO}_{t-1}$, $(X/Y)^*_1$, $(I/Y)_{1,t-1}$, $\log M_{1,t-1}$, $\hat{M}_{1,t-1}$, $\hat{M}_{1,t-2}$, $\hat{M}_{1,t-3}$, $\log P_{1,t-1}$, $(\log P_{1,t-1} - \log P_{1,t-3})$, $(\log P_{1,t-3} - \log P_{1,t-5})$, $\log P^I_{1,t-1}$, $R_{1,t-1}$, $R_{1,t-2}$, $R_{1,t-3}$, $u_{1,t-1}$, $u_{1,t-2}$, $u_{1,t-3}$, $u_{1,t-4}$, $(X/Y)_{1,t-1}$, $(X/Y)_{1,t-2}$, $\hat{x}_{1,t-1}$, $\hat{x}_{1,t-2}$, $\hat{x}_{1,t-3}$, $\log y_{1,t-1}$, $Z_{1,t-2}$

Fitted Foreign Instruments[§]

$(\log P^R_1)^{\text{FIT}}$, $(\log P^R_{1,t-1})^{\text{FIT}}$, $(\log y^R_1)^{\text{FIT}}$, $(\log y^R_{1,t-1})^{\text{FIT}}$, $(R_2)^{\text{FIT}}$, $(R_{2,t-1})^{\text{FIT}}$, $(R_{2,t-2})^{\text{FIT}}$, $(R_{2,t-3})^{\text{FIT}}$,

b) Nonreserve Countries

Domestic Instruments

$[DF_j, DF_{j,t-1}]$,[‡] $\hat{g}_j$, $\hat{g}_{j,t-1}$, $\hat{g}_{j,t-2}$, $\hat{g}_{j,t-3}$, $\hat{g}_{j,t-4}$, $\log P^{RO}$, $\log P^{RO}_{t-1}$, $(X/Y)^*_j$, $(I/Y)_{j,t-1}$, $\log M_{j,t-1}$, $\hat{M}_{j,t-1}$, $\hat{M}_{j,t-2}$, $\hat{M}_{j,t-3}$, $\log P_{j,t-1}$, $(\log P_{j,t-1} - \log P_{j,t-3})$, $(\log P_{j,t-3} - \log P_{j,t-5})$, $\log P^I_{j,t-1}$, $R_{1,t-1}$, $R_{1,t-2}$, $R_{1,t-3}$, $(X/Y)_{j,t-1}$, $(X/Y)_{j,t-2}$, $\hat{x}_{j,t-1}$, $\hat{x}_{j,t-2}$, $\hat{x}_{j,t-3}$, $(B/Y)_{j,t-1}$, $(B/Y)_{j,t-2}$, $[(B/Y)_{j,t-3} + (B/Y)_{j,t-4}]$, $\log y_{j,t-1}$, $Z_{j,t-2}$, $[u_{j,t-1}, u_{j,t-2}, u_{j,t-3}, u_{j,t-4}]$[#]

Fitted Foreign Instruments[§]

$(\log P^R_j)^{\text{FIT}}$, $(\log P^R_{j,t-1})^{\text{FIT}}$, $(\log y^R_j)^{\text{FIT}}$, $(\log y^R_{j,t-1})^{\text{FIT}}$, $(R_1)^{\text{FIT}}$, $(R_{1,t-1})^{\text{FIT}}$, $(R_{1,t-2})^{\text{FIT}}$, $(R_{1,t-3})^{\text{FIT}}$

[†]Certain variables listed as predetermined are not listed here because of extreme multicollinearity with listed variables or because they are not predetermined generally for the whole sample period.

[§]Fitted foreign instruments (indicated by superscript [FIT]) are obtained by fitting $\log y_j$, $\log P_j$, and R_j on the domestic instruments for country j for $j = 1, \ldots, 8$. The indices $(\log y^R_j)^{\text{FIT}}$ and $(\log P^R_j)^{\text{FIT}}$ are obtained by applying (R18), (R19), (N18), and (N19) using the weights in table 5.7.

[‡]The DF_j variables are included only for estimates spanning the entire period; i.e. they are omitted in estimates made for only the pegged or floating period.

[#]For nonreserve countries other than the United Kingdom and France, $\log y_j - \log y^P_j$ is substituted for u_j.

Table 6.2 Real-Income Equations (R1) and (N1)

$$\log y_j = \alpha_{j1} + \alpha_{j2}\log y_{j,t-1} + (1-\alpha_{j2})\log y_{j,t-1}^P + \sum_{i=0}^{3}\alpha_{j,3+i}\hat{M}_{j,t-i} + \sum_{i=0}^{3}\alpha_{j,7+i}\hat{g}_{j,t-i} - \sum_{i=0}^{3}\alpha_{j,11+i}\hat{x}_{j,t-i} + \epsilon_{j1}$$

Coefficients	US	UK	CA	FR	GE	IT	JA	NE
α_{j1}	.0079	.0056	.0108	.0125	.0108	.0114	.0204	.0100
	(.0010)	(.0016)	(.0014)	(.0020)	(.0015)	(.0015)	(.0017)	(.0015)
	8.082	3.533	7.845	6.219	7.233	7.636	11.710	6.591
α_{j2}	.0747	.2259	.1376	.0833	.0457	.0275	-.0178	.0756
	(.0352)	(.0867)	(.0613)	(.0695)	(.0425)	(.0447)	(.0351)	(.0547)
	2.124	2.605	2.245	1.198	1.076	.615	-.508	1.381
α_{j3}	.7784	-.1974	.3020	-.2651	.3515	.0939	.1427	.3078
	(.3116)	(.1418)	(.1644)	(.3130)	(.1571)	(.1401)	(.1725)	(.1496)
	2.498	-1.392	1.837	-.847	2.238	.670	.827	2.058
α_{j4}	.5902	.0404	.2068	.0688	.0694	.0791	.1083	.1988
	(.2208)	(.1008)	(.1052)	(.1848)	(.1107)	(.0993)	(.1148)	(.1237)
	2.673	.401	1.966	.372	.627	.796	.944	1.607
α_{j5}	-.0470	-.0262	.1044	.1001	-.0173	.2768	.1856	.0352
	(.2305)	(.0954)	(.1057)	(.1823)	(.1094)	(.1033)	(.1141)	(.1221)
	-.204	-.275	.988	.549	-.158	2.680	1.627	.288
α_{j6}	.8172	-.1269	.1943	-.0552	.0408	-.0176	.0884	.0237
	(.2326)	(.0930)	(.1022)	(.1776)	(.1105)	(.1100)	(.1140)	(.1115)
	3.513	-1.365	1.901	-.311	.369	-.160	.775	.212
α_{j7}	-.0345	.1831	-.0049	.0447	-.0349	-.0014	.0443	.0352
	(.0545)	(.0540)	(.0554)	(.0411)	(.0275)	(.0105)	(.0362)	(.0366)
	-.632	3.395	-.088	1.089	-1.273	-.129	1.223	.962

α_{j8}	.1128	.0274	-.1641	.0075	.0286	.0006	-.0196	-.0586
	(.0573)	(.0603)	(.0604)	(.0415)	(.0276)	(.0102)	(.0371)	(.0385)
	1.969	.454	-2.714	.180	1.033	.058	-.527	-1.520
α_{j9}	.0547	.1069	-.0283	.0518	-.0076	-.0016	.0450	-.0014
	(.0545)	(.0575)	(.0536)	(.0409)	(.0271)	(.0100)	(.0361)	(.0373)
	1.002	1.860	-.528	1.265	-.281	.163	1.247	-.036
α_{j10}	.0837	-.0240	-.0135	.0164	.0139	.0274	-.0393	.0180
	(.0563)	(.0571)	(.0547)	(.0403)	(.0273)	(.0102)	(.0366)	(.0378)
	1.489	-.420	-.247	.408	.510	2.700	-1.074	.477
α_{j11}	.7428	.1897	.6833	.3427	.2780	-.3343	-2.0920	-.1159
	(.4943)	(.2348)	(.3606)	(.4893)	(.2648)	(.2931)	(1.0645)	(.1312)
	1.503	.808	1.895	.700	1.050	-1.141	-1.965	-.884
α_{j12}	.4548	.4127	.1648	-.7154	-.2451	-.0443	.3499	-.1186
	(.4148)	(.1799)	(.2401)	(.3847)	(.2215)	(.1897)	(.9034)	(.0961)
	1.097	2.293	.687	-1.860	-1.107	-.233	.387	-1.235
α_{j13}	-.0415	-.2129	-.0287	.0153	-.3293	-.2277	-1.7648	.0943
	(.4282)	(.1886)	(.2358)	(.3919)	(.2339)	(.1967)	(.9331)	(.0884)
	-.097	-1.129	-.122	.039	-1.408	-1.158	-1.891	1.066
α_{j14}	-.9251	.0069	.5699	.1215	-.5084	-.4655	-.7337	-.1334
	(.4255)	(.1916)	(.2495)	(.4069)	(.2268)	(.1995)	(.9308)	(.0847)
	-2.174	.036	2.284	.299	-2.242	-2.333	-.788	-1.575
$\bar{R}^2$	.9982	.9923	.9982	.9969	.9974	.9978	.9992	.9977
S.E.E.	.0087	.0140	.0122	.0180	.0133	.0131	.0155	.0134
D-W	1.81	1.91	2.42	2.13	1.94	2.22	1.97	1.71

Note. Period: 1957I–74IV. Standard errors are in parentheses below coefficient estimates; t statistics are below the standard errors.

Table 6.3   *F* **Statistics for Groups of Demand Shock Variables for Estimates in Table 6.2**

Country	$\hat{M}$ Variables	$\hat{g}$ Variables	$\hat{x}$ Variables
US	7.128	1.820	2.188
UK	1.164	3.531	1.763
CA	2.315	3.191	1.858
FR	0.341	0.783	1.006
GE	1.473	0.748	2.353
IT	2.201	2.004	1.766
JA	1.152	1.141	1.660
NE	1.530	1.137	1.675

F(4/66) Statistics

Notes. The reported *F* statistics are appropriate for testing the joint hypothesis that all four of the demand shock variables of the type indicated have a coefficient of zero. Such a test is conditional upon the other variables entering in the equation.

For $F(4/66)$, the 10% significance level is 2.04, the 5% significance level is 2.52, and the 1% significance level is 3.63.

Table 6.4 Price Level Equations (R2) and (N2)

$$\log P_j = \log M_j + \beta_{j1} + \beta_{j2}\log y_j^P + \beta_{j3}(\log y_j - \log y_i^P) + \beta_{j4}R_j + \beta_{j5}[R_1 + (4\Delta \log E_{j,t+1})^*]^\dagger + \beta_{j6}(\log M_{j,t-1} - \log P_{j,t-1})$$
$$+ \sum_{i=0}^{3} \beta_{j;7+i}\dot{M}_{j,t-i} + \epsilon_{j2}$$

	US	UK	CA	FR	GE	IT	JA	NE
Coefficients								
β_{j1}	.0851	−.2409	.1175	−.0692	.0818	.1672	.4466	−.0057
	(.1067)	(.1361)	(.0421)	(.0554)	(.0517)	(.2679)	(.1109)	(.0417)
	.798	−1.770	2.789	1.248	1.583	.624	4.026	−.136
β_{j2}	−.0224	−.0313	−.2196	−.0247	−.0662	−.0648	−.2017	−.0796
	(.0058)	(.0282)	(.0368)	(.0250)	(.0228)	(.0480)	(.0363)	(.0332)
	−3.863	−1.113	−5.967	−.987	−2.900	−1.349	−5.562	−2.397
β_{j3}	−.0915	−.3687	−.1519	−.0189	−.0062	−.0430	−.0621	.0938
	(.0199)	(.1490)	(.0678)	(.0576)	(.0255)	(.0781)	(.0421)	(.0526)
	−4.601	−2.476	−2.242	−.328	−.245	−.550	−1.474	1.785
β_{j4}	.3489	.4405	.2487	.4813	.0227	.1183	.9316	.0227
	(.0685)	(.1694)	(.1372)	(.0852)	(.0448)	(.1588)	(.4464)	(.0945)
	5.094	2.601	1.813	5.647	.506	.745	2.087	.241
β_{j5}	−.0011	.0815	−.0209	.0239	−.0089	−.0378	.0873	−.0397
	(.0117)	(.0355)	(.0981)	(.0196)	(.0168)	(.0397)	(.0376)	(.0288)
	−.097	2.295	−.213	1.216	−.527	−.951	2.322	−1.380

Table 6.4 (continued)

	US	UK	CA	FR	GE	IT	JA	NE
β_{j6}	-.9907	-.8571	-.6260	-.9918	-.9335	-.9485	-.8273	-.8941
	(.0248)	(.0548)	(.0606)	(.0203)	(.0200)	(.0255)	(.0296)	(.0347)
	-39.974	-15.646	-10.329	-48.824	-46.760	-37.190	-27.963	-25.750
β_{j7}	-.7145	-.7401	-1.0824	-.7633	-1.0874	-1.2105	-1.0066	-1.0174
	(.1503)	(.1734)	(.1504)	(.1927)	(.0774)	(.1280)	(.1165)	(.1271)
	-4.754	-4.269	-7.199	-3.962	-14.049	-9.456	-8.640	-8.008
β_{j8}	-.3961	.0374	-.2690	-.2414	-.1448	-.1738	-.3656	-.4761
	(.0924)	(.1065)	(.1080)	(.1111)	(.0518)	(.0900)	(.0839)	(.0866)
	-4.288	.351	-2.491	-2.172	-2.798	-1.932	-4.358	-5.497
β_{j9}	.1655	-.1519	-.2761	.0248	-.3170	-.3615	-.3207	-.6534
	(.0914)	(.1009)	(.1046)	(.1059)	(.0521)	(.0925)	(.0849)	(.0889)
	1.810	-1.506	-2.641	.234	-6.084	-3.909	-3.779	-7.352
β_{j10}	.0164	-.1675	-.6435	.0494	-.3196	-.1435	-.3017	-.2813
	(.1028)	(.0996)	(.1051)	(.1045)	(.0571)	(.0951)	(.0876)	(.0868)
	.160	-1.681	-6.212	.473	-5.601	-1.509	-3.445	-3.243
$\bar{R}^2$	.9997	.9983	.9978	.9987	.9993	.9988	.9987	.9989
S.E.E.	.0035	.0147	.0116	.0105	.0063	.0117	.0119	.0109
h [D-W]§	1.69	.66	-1.64	3.57	2.85	[1.54]	2.67	-1.92

Note. Period: 1957I–76IV. Standard errors are in parentheses below coefficient estimates; t statistics are below the standard errors.

†For the United States, the foreign interest rate is $R_2 - (4\Delta \log E_{2,t+1})^*$.

§The biased Durbin-Watson statistic is reported in square brackets in those cases in which Durbin's h cannot be computed (is imaginary).

Table 6.5   **Unemployment-Rate Equations** (R3) and (N3)

$$u_j = u_{j,t-1} + \gamma_{j1} + \sum_{i=0}^{7} \gamma_{j,2+i}\Delta \log y_{j,t-i} + \epsilon_{j3}$$

	US	UK	FR
Coeffi- cients			
γ_{j1}	.0046 (.0004) 11.183	.0023 (.0003) 7.031	.0019 (.0003) 6.648
γ_{j2}	−.1952 (.0277) −7.055	−.0849 (.0162) −5.252	−.0339 (.0077) −4.385
γ_{j3}	−.1876 (.0241) −7.802	−.0327 (.0125) −2.616	−.0360 (.0058) −6.202
γ_{j4}	−.0528 (.0235) −2.248	−.0660 (.0122) −5.407	−.0240 (.0060) −4.010
γ_{j5}	−.0624 (.0232) −2.691	−.0556 (.0125) −4.437	−.0125 (.0059) −2.116
γ_{j6}	.0529 (.0234) 2.257	−.0415 (.0126) −3.300	−.0037 (.0059) −.628
γ_{j7}	.0177 (.0237) .746	−.0165 (.0126) −1.311	−.0116 (.0060) −1.944
γ_{j8}	−.0349 (.0244) −1.431	−.0057 (.0129) −.444	.0005 (.0060) .079
γ_{j9}	−.0602 (.0226) −2.668	.0004 (.0126) .028	.0074 (.0058) 1.285
$\bar{R}^2$	.8089	.4428	.4492
S.E.E.	.0019	.0016	.0009
D-W	1.36	1.26	1.40

Note. Period: 1957I–76IV. Standard errors are in parentheses below coefficient estimates; t statistics are below the standard errors.

Table 6.6   **Reserve-Country Nominal-Money Equation (R4)**

$$\Delta \log M_1 = 0.4612 \Delta \log M_{1,t-1} - 0.2295 \Delta \log M_{1,t-2} + 0.0044 + 0.0003t$$
$$ (0.1158) \qquad\qquad\quad (0.1159) \qquad\qquad (0.0028)\ (0.0000)$$
$$ 3.984 \qquad\qquad\qquad\ -1.981 \qquad\qquad\ \ 1.587 \quad\ 5.057$$

$$+ 0.0040 \hat{g}_1 + 0.0016(\hat{g}_{1,t-1} + \hat{g}_{1,t-2}) + 0.0293(\hat{g}_{1,t-3} + \hat{g}_{1,t-4})$$
$$ (0.0286) \quad (0.0205) \qquad\qquad\qquad (0.0200)$$
$$ 0.141 \qquad\ \ 0.076 \qquad\qquad\qquad\ \ 1.465$$

$$- 0.0576(\log P_{1,t-1} - \log P_{1,t-3}) - 0.2372(\log P_{1,t-3} - \log P_{1,t-5}) - 0.1167 u_{1,t-1}$$
$$ (0.0905) \qquad\qquad\qquad\qquad (0.0996) \qquad\qquad\qquad\qquad (0.1930)$$
$$ -0.636 \qquad\qquad\qquad\qquad\ -2.381 \qquad\qquad\qquad\qquad\ -0.604$$

$$+ 0.5393 u_{1,t-2} - 0.4316 u_{1,t-3} - 0.0546 u_{1,t-4}$$
$$ (0.3627) \qquad (0.3670) \qquad (0.1950)$$
$$ 1.487 \qquad\ -1.176 \qquad\ -0.280$$

$$\bar{R}^2 = 0.5624, \quad \text{S.E.E.} = 0.0046, \quad [\text{D-W} = 2.05]^{\dagger}$$

Note. Period: 1957I–76IV. Standard errors are in parentheses below coefficient estimates; t statistics are below the standard errors.
†The biased Durbin-Watson statistic is reported in square brackets because Durbin's h cannot be computed (is imaginary).

Table 6.7 Nonreserve-Country Nominal-Money Equations (N4)

$$\Delta \log M_j = \eta_{j1} + \eta_{j2}t + \eta_{j3}\hat{g}_j + \eta_{j4}(\hat{g}_{j,t-1} + \hat{g}_{j,t-2}) + \eta_{j5}(\hat{g}_{j,t-3} + \hat{g}_{j,t-4}) + \eta_{j6}(\log P_{j,t-1} - \log P_{j,t-3}) + \eta_{j7}[DF_j(\log P_{j,t-1} - \log P_{j,t-3})]$$
$$- \log P_{j,t-3})] + \eta_{j8}(\log P_{j,t-3} - \log P_{j,t-5}) + \eta_{j9}[DF_j(\log P_{j,t-3} - \log P_{j,t-5})] + \eta_{j,10}u_{j,t-1} + \eta_{j,11}u_{j,t-2}$$
$$+ \eta_{j,12}u_{j,t-3} + \eta_{j,13}u_{j,t-4} + \eta_{j,14}(B/Y)_j + \eta_{j,15}[DF_j(B/Y)_j] + \eta_{j,16}[(B/Y)_{j,t-1} + (B/Y)_{j,t-2}] + \eta_{j,17}\{DF_j[(B/Y)_{j,t-1}$$
$$+ (B/Y)_{j,t-2}]\} + \eta_{j,18}[(B/Y)_{j,t-3} + (B/Y)_{j,t-4}] + \eta_{j,19}\{DF_j[(B/Y)_{j,t-3} + (B/Y)_{j,t-4}]\} + \epsilon_{j4}$$

Coefficients	UK	CA	FR	GE	IT	JA	NE
η_{j1}	-.0058	.0101	.0354	.0160	.0167	.0540	.0097
	(.0103)	(.0055)	(.0051)	(.0090)	(.0117)	(.0067)	(.0070)
	-.561	1.841	6.936	1.793	1.434	8.026	1.375
η_{j2}	-.0000	.0002	-.0003	-.0001	.0004	-.0000	-.0003
	(.0002)	(.0002)	(.0001)	(.0001)	(.0002)	(.0001)	(.0001)
	-.003	1.001	-2.517	-.586	2.363	-.149	2.151
η_{j3}	.0874	.1156	.0030	.0363	-.0145	-.0219	.0641
	(.0656)	(.0760)	(.0254)	(.0305)	(.0232)	(.0422)	(.0405)
	1.333	1.521	.119	1.192	-.622	-.518	1.582
η_{j4}	.1540	.1849	.0307	-.0149	-.0342	.0317	-.0395
	(.0562)	(.0613)	(.0221)	(.0232)	(.0208)	(.0426)	(.0307)
	2.741	3.018	1.387	-.644	-1.647	.744	-1.286
η_{j5}	.0299	-.0035	-.0178	-.0225	-.0317	.0262	-.0397
	(.0661)	(.0655)	(.0228)	(.0227)	(.0222)	(.0388)	(.0312)
	.452	-.054	-.781	-.993	-1.430	.676	-1.274

Table 6.7 (continued)

	UK	CA	FR	GE	IT	JA	NE
η_{j6}	.0771 (.2107) .366	−.1972 (.5889) −.334	−.0859 (.0989) −.868	.0977 (.2470) .395	−.0956 (−.2764) −.346	−.5453 (.1811) −3.011	−.2390 (.1639) −1.458
η_{j7}	.0242 (.2218) .109	.2649 (.5583) .474	.5748 (.3598) 1.597	−.8816 (.3516) −2.507	.0372 (.3573) .1041	.4078 (.2181) 1.870	.3620 (.2675) 1.353
η_{j8}	.1567 (.2396) .654	−.1133 (.6025) −.188	−.0535 (.0972) −.551	−.4020 (.2971) −1.353	.2625 (.2601) 1.009	−.2006 (.1490) −1.346	.0566 (.1628) .348
η_{j9}	−.0748 (.2727) −.274	−.0016 (.5691) −.003	−.3655 (.4059) −.900	.6823 (.4041) 1.688	−.1297 (.4102) −.316	.0145 (.2135) .068	.0622 (.2397) .260
η_{j10}	1.2313 (1.5107) .815	−.1548 (.1785) −.867	1.5859 (1.8373) .863	.0364 (.1331) .274	−.1055 (.2265) −.466	−.0059 (.1410) −.042	−.0338 (.1589) −.213
η_{j11}	−3.4256 (2.3092) −1.483	.0546 (.2149) .254	−4.0365 (3.2469) −1.243	−.1024 (.1684) −.608	.1264 (.2788) .453	.0221 (.1697) .130	−.3617 (.2141) −1.690
η_{j12}	7.0718 (2.5266) 2.799	.0777 (.2193) .354	7.8250 (3.3058) 2.367	.1912 (.1734) 1.103	−.1260 (.2759) −.457	.1636 (.1724) .949	.3568 (.2104) 1.696

	(1)	(2)	(3)	(4)	(5)	(6)	(7)
$\eta_{1j,13}$	-4.2754 (1.7219) -2.483	.0413 (.2003) .206	-5.0553 (2.1008) -2.406	-.0848 (.1297) -.653	.3273 (.2263) 1.446	-.3035 (.1343) -2.260	.0288 (.1524) .189
$\eta_{1j,14}$	-.5155 (.5838) -.883	-.1068 (1.2418) -.086	-.4060 (.6601) -.615	1.6489 (.5769) 2.858	-5.7268 (2.5394) -2.255	2.2503 (1.2800) 1.758	.4210 (.8439) .499
$\eta_{1j,15}$	2.1291 (1.0068) 2.115	3.3238 (2.3210) 1.432	.1031 (1.1007) .094	.0196 (.8884) .022	6.5592 (3.0475) 2.152	-.5742 (1.5246) -.377	.7008 (1.4222) .493
$\eta_{1j,16}$	.4856 (.2139) 2.270	.8225 (.5970) 1.378	.3233 (.3260) .992	.0938 (.2371) .395	2.5421 (1.1070) 2.296	1.5380 (.6816) 2.256	.3972 (.3402) 1.168
$\eta_{1j,17}$	-.5212 (.3625) -1.438	-3.2249 (1.2196) -2.644	-.1322 (.5630) -.235	.3328 (.4828) .689	-.6868 (1.0566) -.650	-2.5332 (.8004) -3.165	-1.1151 (.6231) -1.790
$\eta_{1j,18}$	.3309 (.2078) 1.592	.2862 (.6238) .459	.7214 (.2587) 2.788	.5458 (.2864) 1.906	-.3723 (.7726) -.482	1.8032 (.7378) 2.444	.0915 (.2997) .305
$\eta_{1j,19}$	-.2042 (.3388) -.603	1.4646 (1.1676) 1.254	.0605 (.5414) .112	.0399 (.4740) .084	.8100 (1.0940) .740	-1.8875 (.8633) -2.186	-.9712 (.5983) -1.623
$\bar{R}^2$	.2888	.1540	.3474	.2765	-.6681	.4160	.2950
S.E.E.	.0170	.0163	.0118	.0133	.0224	.0155	.0148
D-W	1.95	1.88	1.78	2.30	2.11	1.65	1.87

Note. Period: 1957I–76IV. Standard errors are in parentheses below coefficient estimates; t statistics are below the standard errors.

Table 6.8   Interpretation of $(B/Y)_j$ Coefficients in Table 6.7

Country	Pegged Period		Floating Period		Mean Value of $(H/Y)_j$[‡]
	Impact Money Effect[†]	Cumulative Money Effect[§]	Impact Money Effect[†]	Cumulative Money Effect[§]	
UK	−0.058	0.125	0.181	0.201	0.1122
CA	−0.007	0.138	0.210	0.125	0.0652
FR	−0.057	0.235	−0.042	0.229	0.1394
GE	0.158	0.280	0.160	0.353	0.0957
IT	−0.926	−0.224	0.135	0.876	0.1617
JA	0.165	0.656	0.123	−0.035	0.0734
NE	0.045	0.150	0.121	−0.223	0.1076

[†]This is the fraction of the current effect of the balance of payments on nominal money which is *not* sterilized by the central bank; computed as $(\partial \Delta \log M_j)/[\partial(B/H)_j] \approx$ [coefficient of $(B/Y)_j$] × [mean value of $(H/Y)_j$], where H_j is high-powered money.

[§]This is the total effect including lagged adjustments by the central bank; computed as $(\partial \Delta \log M_j)/[\partial(B/H)_j] \approx [\Sigma_i$ coefficients of $(B/Y)_{j,t-i}]$ × [mean value of $(H/Y)_j$].

[‡]Sample mean for 1957I–76IV.

Table 6.9 Interest-Rate Equations (R5) and (N5)

$$R_j = \delta_{j1} + \delta_{j2}t + \delta_{j3}(4\Delta \log P_{j,t+1})^* + \delta_{j4}R_{j,t-1} + \delta_{j5}(4\Delta \log P_j)^* + \sum_{i=0}^{3}\delta_{j,6+i}\hat{M}_{j,t-i} + \sum_{i=0}^{3}\delta_{j,10+i}\hat{g}_{j,t-i} + \sum_{i=0}^{3}\delta_{j,14+i}\hat{x}_{j,t-i} + \epsilon_{j5}$$

Coefficients	US	UK	CA	FR	GE	IT	JA	NE
δ_{j1}	.0059	.0016	.0037	.0049	.0003	-.0031	-.0019	.0059
	(.0023)	(.0061)	(.0023)	(.0033)	(.0042)	(.0020)	(.0021)	(.0035)
	2.584	.262	1.622	1.481	.068	-1.523	-.907	1.708
δ_{j2}	.0000	.0002	-.0001	.0002	.0000	.0000	-.0001	.0001
	(.0000)	(.0001)	(.0001)	(.0001)	(.0001)	(.0000)	(.0000)	(.0001)
	.455	1.985	-1.599	2.767	.440	.406	-6.182	1.422
δ_{j3}	.2085	.0018	.0949	.1369	.2868	.0246	.0393	-.1238
	(.1035)	(.0449)	(.0320)	(.0680)	(.1703)	(.0280)	(.0107)	(.0716)
	2.015	.041	2.963	2.012	1.684	.878	3.674	-1.727
δ_{j4}	.7577	.8761	.9951	.6435	.7940	1.0404	1.0043	.7998
	(.0991)	(.1277)	(.0854)	(.1050)	(.0929)	(.0370)	(.0249)	(.0740)
	7.649	.861	11.651	6.117	8.545	28.086	40.282	10.813
δ_{j5}	-.1046	-.0223	.0060	.0124	-.0695	-.0200	.0333	.0451
	(.0865)	(.0287)	(.0215)	(.0663)	(.1215)	(.0229)	(.0076)	(.0547)
	-1.210	-.776	.278	.187	-.572	-.872	4.406	.826
δ_{j6}	-.3230	-.3059	-.0782	-.4602	.1307	-.0204	-.0100	.0784
	(.2031)	(.0866)	(.1056)	(.1576)	(.1349)	(.0492)	(.0101)	(.1192)
	-1.590	-3.533	-.741	-2.920	.969	-.415	-.988	.658

Table 6.9 (continued)

	US	UK	CA	FR	GE	IT	JA	NE
δ_{j7}	.3091 (.1334) 2.317	.0254 (.0692) .367	.0153 (.0662) .231	-.1887 (.0938) -2.012	.0757 (.0961) .788	.0046 (.0345) .134	-.0276 (.0086) -3.202	-.1676 (.0949) -1.766
δ_{j8}	.0917 (.1256) .730	.0365 (.0586) .622	.1491 (.0671) 2.223	-.0914 (.1011) -.904	.1094 (.1052) 1.040	.0479 (.0328) 1.464	-.0380 (.0080) -4.734	.1154 (.0941) 1.226
δ_{j9}	.1624 (.1186) 1.369	.0851 (.0557) 1.527	.1540 (.0606) 2.543	.0367 (.1018) .361	.0585 (.1017) .575	.0274 (.0340) .807	-.0194 (.0071) -2.737	.0062 (.0810) .077
δ_{j10}	-.0205 (.0294) -.696	-.0524 (.0309) -1.694	-.0614 (.0282) -2.175	-.0278 (.0215) -1.290	-.0239 (.0237) -1.010	-.0053 (.0032) -1.663	.0005 (.0022) .220	-.0024 (.0270) .088
δ_{j11}	.0189 (.0304) .622	.0229 (.0325) .703	-.0020 (.0308) -.065	.0167 (.0208) .804	.0028 (.0235) .118	-.0059 (.0031) -1.915	.0029 (.0023) 1.266	.0004 (.0271) .015
δ_{j12}	.0229 (.0288) .797	.0142 (.0307) .462	.0556 (.0296) 1.878	-.0161 (.0217) -.743	-.0128 (.0242) -.529	-.008 (.0035) -.218	.0009 (.0025) .359	.0066 (.0256) .259
δ_{j13}	.0154 (.0302) .509	.0015 (.0316) .046	.0307 (.0282) 1.088	-.0079 (.0207) -.384	.0167 (.0260) .641	-.0033 (.0033) -1.005	.0006 (.0024) .257	.0161 (.0263) .611

	(1)	(2)	(3)	(4)	(5)	(6)	(7)	(8)
δ_{j14}	.6220	.1849	−.0079	.2001	.2022	.2097	.0074	.1605
	(.2585)	(.1683)	(.1792)	(.2551)	(.2741)	(.0945)	(.0709)	(.0920)
	2.407	1.099	−.044	.784	.738	2.220	.104	1.744
δ_{j15}	.3002	.0184	.0373	.1224	−.2416	.1516	−.0252	.0721
	(.2448)	(.1366)	(.1262)	(.2146)	(.2058)	(.0601)	(.0549)	(.0678)
	1.226	.135	.295	.570	−1.174	2.521	−.459	1.064
δ_{j16}	.5449	−.0039	−.0140	.3068	.0877	.0547	.0257	.0338
	(.2549)	(.1278)	(.1182)	(.2033)	(.2014)	(.0627)	(.0573)	(.0622)
	2.138	−.031	−.118	1.509	.435	.871	.448	.544
δ_{j17}	−.2137	.1883	−.0327	.0768	−.2494	−.0098	.0023	−.0736
	(.2339)	(.1174)	(.1330)	(.2116)	(.1937)	(.0633)	(.0581)	(.0599)
	−.914	1.603	−.246	.363	−1.288	−.154	.039	1.229
$\bar{R}^2$	.9267	.9109	.8996	.8764	.8120	.9586	.9782	.7489
S.E.E.	.0046	.0078	.0060	.0089	.011	.0040	.0009	.0091
h [D-W]†	−.28	[1.82]	1.84	[1.63]	[1.67]	[1.70]	2.28	[1.67]

Note. Period: 1957I–76IV. Standard errors are in parentheses below coefficient estimates; t statistics are below the standard errors.
†The biased Durbin-Watson statistic is reported in square brackets in those cases in which Durbin's h cannot be computed (is imaginary).

Table 6.10   **Export Equations (R6) and (N6)**

$$(X/Y)_j = \theta_{j1} + \theta_{j2}t + \theta_{j3}\log P^{RO} + \theta_{j4}(\log y_j - \log y_j^P) + \sum_{i=0}^{1}\theta_{j,5+i}(X/Y)_{j,t-1-i} + \sum_{i=0}^{1}\theta_{j,7+i}\log y_{j,t-i}^R + \sum_{i=0}^{1}\theta_{j,9+i}\log P_{j,t-i}$$

$$+ \sum_{i=0}^{1}\theta_{j,11+i}\log P_{j,t-i}^R + \left[\sum_{i=0}^{1}\theta_{j,13+i}\log E_{j,t-i} + \sum_{i=0}^{1}\theta_{j,15+i}DF_{j,t-i}\log E_{j,t-i}\right]^{\dagger} + \epsilon_{j6}$$

Coefficients	US	UK	CA	FR	GE	IT	JA	NE
θ_{j1}	.0976	.6132	.2497	.1831	.1097	−.8423	−.0395	.2820
	(.0189)	(.0805)	(.0884)	(.0657)	(.0523)	(.1945)	(.0820)	(.1430)
	5.169	7.618	2.826	2.785	2.099	−4.331	−.482	1.972
θ_{j2}	−.0012	−.0035	−.0025	−.0052	−.0010	−.0017	−.0002	−.0026
	(.0003)	(.0010)	(.0013)	(.0011)	(.0011)	(.0010)	(.0003)	(.0026)
	−4.356	−3.511	−1.863	−4.890	−.938	−1.625	−.616	−1.009
θ_{j3}	.0138	.0148	.0089	.0139	.0296	.0188	−.0028	.0321
	(.0026)	(.0064)	(.0072)	(.0049)	(.0053)	(.0075)	(.0034)	(.0150)
	5.356	2.325	1.234	2.846	5.616	2.502	−.826	2.146
θ_{j4}	.0299	−.0384	−.0688	.0111	.0435	−.0962	−.0405	.1931
	(.0161)	(.0695)	(.0790)	(.0448)	(.0426)	(.0726)	(.0139)	(.1629)
	1.855	−.553	−.871	.248	1.021	−1.335	−2.919	1.186
θ_{j5}	.5326	.1784	.2876	.1989	.3689	.2681	.2783	.4754
	(.1193)	(.1276)	(.1277)	(.1119)	(.1216)	(.1213)	(.1064)	(.1250)
	4.466	1.398	2.251	1.778	3.034	2.211	2.615	3.802

θ_{j6}	.0723 (.1077) .671	.1021 (.1025) .996	.3141 (.1146) 2.742	.2406 (.0967) 2.488	.1134 (.1285) .883	.2652 (.1214) 2.185	.1423 (.1095) 1.300	.0819 (.1281) .639
θ_{j7}	.0586 (.0312) 1.881	-.0101 (.1152) -.088	.1090 (.1030) 1.058	.2338 (.1027) 2.276	.1931 (.1066) 1.811	.0555 (.1703) .326	-.0967 (.0452) -2.140	.6712 (.2613) 2.569
θ_{j8}	.0184 (.0343) .535	.1624 (.1178) 1.379	.1337 (.1131) 1.182	.0542 (.1030) .526	-.0217 (.0898) -.241	.1797 (.1438) 1.250	.1139 (.0404) 2.821	-.3902 (.2586) -1.509
θ_{j9}	.0083 (.0354) .234	-.1545 (.0787) -1.962	.0855 (.0682) 1.254	-.0215 (.0689) -.312	-.0665 (.1252) -.531	.0559 (.0909) .616	.0311 (.0364) .854	-.5752 (.2051) -2.804
θ_{j10}	.0114 (.0348) .327	-.0952 (.0726) -1.312	-.0416 (.0644) -.646	-.0539 (.0650) -.829	-.1939 (.1426) -1.360	-.1409 (.0833) -1.690	-.0330 (.0281) -1.176	.1862 (.1940) .960
θ_{j11}	.0102 (.0207) .491	.1635 (.1105) 1.480	.0251 (.0940) .267	.0103 (.0738) .139	.1815 (.1102) 1.648	-.0713 (.1096) -.651	.0617 (.0365) 1.692	.8770 (.2853) 3.074
θ_{j12}	-.0085 (.0201) -.423	.3009 (.0955) 3.151	-.0552 (.0890) -.621	.2875 (.0812) 3.543	.0446 (.0881) .506	.1265 (.0960) 1.318	-.0487 (.0332) -1.465	-.4179 (.2952) -1.415

Table 6.10 (continued)

	US	UK	CA	FR	GE	IT	JA	NE
θ_{j13}	—	.0572 (.0380) 1.508	-.1529 (.0921) -1.661	.0657 (.0198) 3.315	.0408 (.0305) 1.340	-.0186 (.0450) -.412	.0250 (.0206) 1.216	.1332 (.0932) 1.429
θ_{j14}	—	.1432 (.0424) 3.382	.1425 (.0960) 1.483	.0670 (.0258) 2.594	.0099 (.0272) .364	.1804 (.0474) 3.804	-.0129 (.0176) -.732	-.0657 (.1155) -.568
θ_{j15}	—	-.0069 (.0086) -.799	.0852 (.0741) 1.150	-.0007 (.0033) -.197	-.0013 (.0051) -.261	.0011 (.0014) .805	.0003 (.0004) .674	-.0034 (.0130) -.260
θ_{j16}	—	.0173 (.0099) 1.747	-.0838 (.0702) -1.195	-.0038 (.0034) -1.111	.0031 (.0057) .556	-.0005 (.0013) -.386	-.0004 (.0005) -.865	.0002 (.0143) .0173
$\bar{R}^2$	.9799	.9647	.9500	.9685	.9696	.9727	.7767	.8568
S.E.E.	.0023	.0069	.0062	.0050	.0058	.0071	.0121	.0149
h [D-W]§	[2.06]	[1.96]	[2.05]	-6.42	[1.65]	[2.14]	-.55	[1.49]

Note. Period: 1957I–76IV. Standard errors are in parentheses below coefficient estimates; t statistics are below the standard errors.

†The exchange-rate terms do not appear in the U.S. equation (R6).

§The biased Durbin-Watson statistic is reported in square brackets in those cases in which Durbin's h cannot be computed (is imaginary).

Table 6.11   **Import Equations (R7) and (N7P)†**

$$(I/Y)_j = \lambda_{j1} + \lambda_{j2}(I/Y)_{j,t-1} + \lambda_{j3}\log y_j^P + \sum_{i=0}^{1} \lambda_{j,4+i}(\log y_{j,t-i} - \log y_{j,t-i}^P) + \sum_{i=0}^{3} \lambda_{j,6+i}Z_{j,t-i} + \epsilon_{j7}$$

	US	UK	CA	FR	GE	IT	JA	NE
Coefficients								
λ_{j1}	-.1034	-.3300	-.3403	-.0497	-.3324	-.3432	-.0296	-.9957
	(.0388)	(.0935)	(.2160)	(.0506)	(.1296)	(.2732)	(.0421)	(.7004)
	-2.662	-3.529	-1.576	-.982	-2.566	-1.257	-.703	-1.422
λ_{j2}	.6667	.3540	.2796	.8132	.3815	.7865	.7148	.3908
	(.1128)	(.1405)	(.2134)	(.0918)	(.1505)	(.0919)	(.0945)	(.1504)
	5.910	2.520	1.310	8.858	2.535	8.554	7.561	2.598
λ_{j3}	.0178	.1358	.1164	.0114	.0708	.0350	.0035	.2773
	(.0066)	(.0339)	(.0483)	(.0089)	(.0235)	(.0259)	(.0039)	(.1600)
	2.714	4.004	2.409	1.281	3.015	1.353	.880	1.734
λ_{j4}	.0808	-.1075	-.0179	.0710	.0634	.0927	.0137	.1427
	(.0421)	(.1141)	(.1643)	(.0347)	(.0765)	(.1158)	(.0221)	(.2757)
	1.921	-.942	-.109	2.045	.828	.800	.619	.518
λ_{j5}	-.0644	.0348	.1806	-.0677	.0146	-.0139	-.0003	.0428
	(.0368)	(.1026)	(.1252)	(.0306)	(.0653)	(.1098)	(.0202)	(.2168)
	-1.751	.339	1.442	-2.216	.224	-.127	.016	.197

Table 6.11 (continued)

	US	UK	CA	FR	GE	IT	JA	NE
λ_{j6}	.0366	.1425	.1882	.0500	-.0077	-.0401	.0101	.5824
	(.0188)	(.0583)	(.1146)	(.0234)	(.0570)	(.0697)	(.0204)	(.1957)
	1.953	2.446	1.643	2.135	-.135	-.575	.497	2.975
λ_{j7}	.0545	.0890	-.0756	-.0189	.0336	.1494	.0438	-.1574
	(.0349)	(.0628)	(.1167)	(.0253)	(.0660)	(.0812)	(.0250)	(.1955)
	1.562	1.416	-.647	-.747	.510	1.841	1.754	-.805
λ_{j8}	-.0753	-.0320	-.0556	-.0481	.0536	-.1032	-.0001	-.0741
	(.0401)	(.0617)	(.1158)	(.0239)	(.0705)	(.0897)	(.0225)	(.1670)
	-1.877	-.518	-.481	-2.016	.760	-1.151	-.004	-.444
λ_{j9}	.0044	.0145	.0661	.0181	-.0289	.0162	-.0412	-.0417
	(.0230)	(.0471)	(.0910)	(.0186)	(.0485)	(.0621)	(.0161)	(.1344)
	.191	.308	.726	.976	-.595	.260	-2.556	-.310
$\bar{R}^2$	.9746	.8174	.8977	.9383	.9082	.8885	.8612	.7034
S.E.	.0027	.0070	.0045	.0033	.0047	.0077	.0017	.0143
h [D-W][§]	[1.97]	[1.83]	[1.75]	-1.08	[1.88]	[1.88]	1.80	[1.96]

Note. Standard errors are in parentheses below coefficient estimates; t statistics are below the standard errors.

[†]For the nonreserve countries, these regressions are estimated over only the pegged portion of 1957I–76IV (excludes floating periods listed in part a of table 5.6).

[§]The biased Durbin-Watson statistic is reported in square brackets in those cases in which Durbin's h cannot be computed (is imaginary).

Table 6.12 **Relative-Price-of-Imports Equations (N7F)**

$$Z_j = \frac{-\lambda_{j1}}{\lambda_{j6}} + \frac{1}{\lambda_{j6}}(I/Y)_j - \frac{\lambda_{j2}}{\lambda_{j6}}(I/Y)_{j,t-1} - \frac{\lambda_{j3}}{\lambda_{j6}}\log y_j^P - \sum_{i=0}^{1}\frac{\lambda_{j,4+i}}{\lambda_{j6}}(\log y_{j,t-i} - \log y_{j,t-i}^P) - \sum_{i=1}^{3}\frac{\lambda_{j,6+i}}{\lambda_{j6}}Z_{j,t-i} - \frac{\epsilon_{j7}}{\lambda_{j6}}$$

	UK	CA	FR	GE	IT	JA	NE
Coefficients							
$-\lambda_{j1}/\lambda_{j6}$	-.7098	.3108	4.0912	-2.8389	-10.5063	.4408	-.5967
	(1.0135)	(.0990)	(2.5134)	(3.3782)	(11.0556)	(2.4054)	(1.0728)
	-.700	3.141	1.628	-.866	-.950	.183	-.556
$1/\lambda_{j6}$	1.9019	1.3247	4.3304	2.2772	1.6392	11.5779	1.3619
	(.3771)	(.5007)	(1.2205)	(2.2405)	(1.4812)	(3.9031)	(.5171)
	5.044	2.645	3.548	1.016	1.107	2.966	2.634
$-\lambda_{j2}/\lambda_{j6}$	-.1897	-.4200	-.4294	-1.7447	-.8465	-1.5938	-.2921
	(.6476)	(.5098)	(1.1609)	(1.7221)	(.9947)	(5.2844)	(.4519)
	-.293	-.824	-.370	-1.013	-.851	-.302	-.646
$-\lambda_{j3}/\lambda_{j6}$	.0489	-.1201	-.7055	.4096	.9383	-.0654	.0047
	(.2656)	(.0349)	(.3942)	(.5436)	(1.0244)	(.2069)	(.1917)
	.184	-3.439	-1.790	.753	.916	-.316	.024
$-\lambda_{j4}/\lambda_{j6}$	-.1153	-.0508	.1843	.6405	1.0612	-.5164	1.2541
	(.4699)	(.2953)	(1.0028)	(1.2641)	(1.2402)	(1.0151)	(1.1212)
	-.245	-.172	.184	.507	.856	-.509	1.119

Table 6.12 (continued)

	UK	CA	FR	GE	IT	JA	NE
$-\lambda_{f5}/\lambda_{f6}$	-.3631	-.3419	.1800	-.0096	.5556	-.3701	-1.1448
	(.2864)	(.2542)	(.5645)	(.8593)	(1.2274)	(.8033)	(.7698)
	-1.268	-1.345	.319	-.011	.453	-.382	-1.487
$-\lambda_{f7}/\lambda_{f6}$	.6335	.8510	.1853	.8729	.6988	.4583	.6319
	(.2782)	(.1563)	(.1723)	(.3690)	(.2831)	(.3703)	(.3738)
	2.277	5.445	1.075	2.365	2.469	1.238	1.691
$-\lambda_{f8}/\lambda_{f6}$	-.2346	-.1488	.1247	-.2489	-.0300	-.1189	-.0552
	(.2588)	(.1810)	(.2363)	(.3266)	(.3213)	(.3002)	(.3680)
	-.906	-.822	.528	-.762	-.093	-.396	-.150
$-\lambda_{f9}/\lambda_{f6}$	.0585	-.0821	.2125	.1413	.1455	-.0560	.0680
	(.1555)	(.1252)	(.2145)	(.3371)	(.2968)	(.2319)	(.3114)
	.376	-.656	.991	.419	.490	.242	.219
$\bar{R}^2$	.9865	.9353	.9570	.8534	.9475	.9718	.8818
S.E.E.	.0188	.0184	.0225	.0349	.0543	.0303	.0297
h [D-W]†	[1.50]	[2.20]	3.25	[2.14]	[2.56]	[2.29]	[2.99]

Note. These regressions are for the floating periods listed in part a of table 5.6. Standard errors are in parentheses below coefficient estimates; t statistics are below the standard errors.

†The biased Durbin-Watson statistic is reported in square brackets in those cases in which Durbin's h cannot be computed (is imaginary).

Table 6.13 **Import Price Equations (R8) and (N8P)†**

$$\log P^I_j = \log P^I_{j,t-1} + \mu_{j1} + \mu_{j2}\Delta \log P^I_{j,t-1} + \mu_{j3}\Delta \log P^{RO} + \mu_{j4}\Delta \log y^R_j + \mu_{j5}\Delta(I/Y)_j + \mu_{j6}\Delta \log P^R_j + [\mu_{j7}\Delta \log E_j]^\S + \epsilon_{j8}$$

	US	UK	CA	FR	GE	IT	JA	NE
Coefficients								
μ_{j1}	-.0017	-.0151	-.0030	-.0070	-.0107	-.0069	-.0193	-.0012
	(.0038)	(.0076)	(.0083)	(.0105)	(.0045)	(.0088)	(.0057)	(.0057)
	-.446	-1.993	-.357	-.673	-2.380	-.786	-3.392	-.208
μ_{j2}	-.6420	-.0020	-.0538	-.0994	.2422	.0728	.1248	.2289
	(.0850)	(.1319)	(.2077)	(.1115)	(.1150)	(.1588)	(.1422)	(.1196)
	7.557	-.015	-.259	-.891	2.107	.458	.877	1.914
μ_{j3}	.0717	-.0403	-.2454	.0522	.0070	.1656	-.0717	.0999
	(.0160)	(.0901)	(.5708)	(.1115)	(.0613)	(.1008)	(.0655)	(.0644)
	4.483	-.448	-.430	.468	.113	1.644	-1.095	1.550
μ_{j4}	.1522	.6483	.2795	-.0267	.2902	-.1488	.8201	-.2553
	(.2428)	(.4400)	(.4498)	(.5936)	(.2723)	(.4512)	(.3479)	(.3150)
	.627	1.473	.621	-.045	1.066	-.330	2.358	-.810

Table 6.13 (continued)

	US	UK	CA	FR	GE	IT	JA	NE
μ_{j5}	1.9255 (.9474) 2.032	.1900 (.3909) .486	.7223 (.3940) 1.833	1.9406 (1.0139) 1.914	−.3779 (.3335) −1.133	−.2210 (.4550) −.497	3.0762 (1.2324) 2.496	.1692 (.1091) 1.550
μ_{j6}	.1424 (.1420) 1.003	1.3714 (.5919) 2.317	.2029 (.8294) .245	1.2349 (.7141) 1.729	1.2003 (.3822) 3.140	1.2481 (.7171) 1.741	1.3652 (.4252) 3.211	.8842 (.4491) 1.969
μ_{j7}	—	.5061 (.1568) 3.229	.0214 (.5412) .040	.6364 (.1086) 5.861	.4684 (.1312) 3.570	−1.1264 (1.3049) −.863	.6959 (.6067) 1.147	.8225 (.2579) 3.189
$\bar{R}^2$	.9964	.9734	.9347	.9468	.9108	.9194	.9410	.9135
S.E.E.	.0129	.0159	.0084	.0197	.0106	.0170	.0117	.0110
h [D-W]‡	−4.48	−23.57	[1.86]	−1.05	−.22	[2.13]	[2.10]	.59

Note. Standard errors are in parentheses below coefficient estimates; t statistics are below the standard errors.

†For the nonreserve countries, these regressions are estimated over only the pegged portion of 1957I–76IV (excludes floating periods listed in part a of table 5.6).

§The exchange-rate term does not appear in the U.S. equation (R8).

‡The biased Durbin-Watson statistic is reported in square brackets in those cases in which Durbin's h cannot be computed (is imaginary).

Table 6.14 **Exchange-Rate Equations (N8F)**

$$\log E_j = \log E_{j,t-1} - \frac{\mu_{j1}}{\mu_{j7}} + \frac{1}{\mu_{j7}} \Delta \log P^I_j - \frac{\mu_{j2}}{\mu_{j7}} \Delta \log P^I_{j,t-1} - \frac{\mu_{j3}}{\mu_{j7}} \Delta \log P^{RO} - \frac{\mu_{j4}}{\mu_{j7}} \Delta \log y^R_j - \frac{\mu_{j5}}{\mu_{j7}} \Delta(I/Y)_j - \frac{\mu_{j6}}{\mu_{j7}} \Delta \log P^R_j - \frac{\epsilon_{j8}}{\mu_{j7}}$$

	UK	CA	FR	GE	IT	JA	NE
Coefficients							
$-\mu_{j1}/\mu_{j7}$	.0490	-.0040	.0507	.0174	.0283	.0508	.0162
	(.0368)	(.0055)	(.0257)	(.0363)	(.0402)	(.0212)	(.0202)
	1.333	-.727	1.976	.480	.704	2.393	.803
$1/\mu_{j7}$	.3454	.2732	-.0635	.3949	.8467	.1140	.3805
	(.8276)	(.2211)	(.5233)	(.5426)	(.4179)	(.2468)	(.4575)
	.417	1.236	-.121	.728	2.026	.462	.832
$-\mu_{j2}/\mu_{j7}$	.2291	.0273	.2030	-.6752	-.2330	-.2069	-.2598
	(.4163)	(.1829)	(.2485)	(.3770)	(.2445)	(.1554)	(.2703)
	.550	.149	.817	-1.791	-.953	-1.331	-.961
$-\mu_{j3}/\mu_{j7}$	-.0018	-.0202	.0518	-.0775	-.0045	-.0078	.0367
	(.0582)	(.0144)	(.0493)	(.0651)	(.0732)	(.0332)	(.0406)
	-.032	-1.401	1.050	-1.190	-.061	-.236	.903

Table 6.14 (continued)

	UK	CA	FR	GE	IT	JA	NE
$-\mu_{j4}/\mu_{j7}$	.9776	.2732	-.9932	-1.4449	.5851	-2.8944	-.2758
	(1.3640)	(.3320)	(1.2940)	(1.3021)	(1.4865)	(.8975)	(.6667)
	.717	.823	-.768	-1.110	.394	-3.225	-.414
$-\mu_{j5}/\mu_{j7}$	-1.3030	-.3851	1.7303	4.7085	-2.2140	7.0538	-.5083
	(1.3132)	(.4451)	(2.1846)	(3.6567)	(1.8783)	(4.9008)	(.4632)
	-.992	-.865	.792	1.288	-1.179	1.439	-1.097
$-\mu_{j6}/\mu_{j7}$	-2.8498	-.0676	-2.9759	-1.4430	-1.8682	-1.9986	-1.6610
	(.9892)	(.2367)	(.8646)	(1.4249)	(1.4868)	(.6666)	(.6668)
	-2.881	-.286	-3.442	-1.013	-1.256	-2.998	-2.491
$\bar{R}^2$	.1213	.0007	.6551	.1563	-.6624	.3304	.5852
S.E.E.	.0443	.0135	.0291	.0493	.0590	.0283	.0275
D-W	2.76	1.38	2.45	2.40	3.12	2.04	1.94

Note. These regressions are for the floating periods listed in part *a* of table 5.6. Standard errors are in parentheses below coefficient estimates; *t* statistics are below the standard errors.

Table 6.15   **Capital-Flows Equations (R9) and (N9)**

$$(C/Y)_j = \xi_{j1} + \xi_{j2}t + \xi_{j3}\log P^{RO} + \xi_{j4}R_1 + [\xi_{j5}(4\Delta\log E_{j,t+1})^* + \xi_{j6}R_1]^\dagger + \xi_{j7}[(X/Y)_j - (I/Y)_j] + \xi_{j8}(\log y_j - \log y_i^P)]$$
$$+ \xi_{j9}\Delta\log y_j + \xi_{j10}\Delta\log y_j^R + \sum_{i=0}^{2}\xi_{j,11+i}\Delta R_{j,t-i} + \left[\sum_{i=0}^{2}\xi_{j,14+i}\Delta R_{1,t-i} + \sum_{i=0}^{2}\xi_{j,17+i}\Delta(4\Delta\log E_{j,t+1-i})^*\right]^\dagger + \epsilon_{j9}$$

	US	UK	CA	FR	GE	IT	JA	NE
Coefficients								
ξ_{j1}	.0077	.0198	−.0211	−.0159	.0008	.0249	.1931	.0009
	(.0053)	(.0206)	(.0128)	(.0114)	(.0227)	(.0237)	(.1136)	(.0149)
	1.455	.965	−1.642	−1.396	.034	1.052	1.700	.060
ξ_{j2}	.0004	−.0003	−.0001	−.0001	−.0000	.0002	−.0005	.0004
	(.0001)	(.0004)	(.0002)	(.0002)	(.0004)	(.0002)	(.0005)	(.0002)
	3.142	−.716	−.474	−.472	−.010	.641	−1.134	1.747
ξ_{j3}	−.0013	−.0760	.0075	.0134	.0044	.0002	.0134	.0162
	(.0082)	(.0269)	(.0090)	(.0124)	(.0123)	(.0098)	(.0301)	(.0099)
	−.164	−2.820	.480	1.085	.358	.019	1.042	1.638
ξ_{j4}	−.1007	.7525	−.2095	−.6406	−.3022	−.6437	−2.4553	−.5028
	(.1849)	(.5526)	(.2558)	(.2298)	(.3641)	(.3542)	(1.3871)	(.3246)
	−.545	1.362	−.819	−2.788	−.830	−1.817	−1.770	−1.549
ξ_{j5}	.0348	.4443	.3993	.1171	.0971	.1421	.0645	.2198
	(.0534)	(.1535)	(.2398)	(.0493)	(.1478)	(.1020)	(.0876)	(.1079)
	.651	2.895	1.665	2.373	.657	1.393	.736	2.036

Table 6.15 (continued)

	US	UK	CA	FR	GE	IT	JA	NE
ξ_{j6}	-.2098 (.1402) -1.496	-.9278 (.6580) -1.410	.5253 (.3505) 1.499	1.0231 (.3579) 2.859	.2431 (.6019) .404	.1986 (.3294) .603	.3620 (.3415) 1.060	-.0984 (.4612) -.213
ξ_{j7}	.7666 (.2568) 2.986	-.8730 (.4839) -1.804	.7222 (.2698) 2.677	.7770 (.3074) 2.528	.5354 (.5225) 1.025	.5817 (.1277) 4.556	-.2125 (.6198) -.343	.7699 (.1968) 3.911
ξ_{j8}	-.0535 (.0681) -.786	-.4390 (.3257) -1.348	.1017 (.1219) .835	.0609 (.1693) .360	-.0654 (.1639) -.399	-.0065 (.1297) -.050	.0441 (.1487) .296	.2249 (.1612) 1.395
ξ_{j9}	-.1069 (.1890) -.566	.4491 (.3905) 1.150	-.4494 (.2863) -1.570	-.2608 (.2020) -1.291	.3244 (.4095) .792	-.1259 (.1908) -.660	-.3308 (.1824) -1.814	-.0454 (.3549) -.128
$\xi_{j,10}$	.0550 (.1612) .341	.0804 (.8828) .091	.8661 (.4604) 1.881	.5558 (.4806) 1.156	-1.0229 (.7941) -1.288	-.2624 (.5041) -.521	.0348 (.4485) .078	-.4544 (.7418) -.612
$\xi_{j,11}$	-.2997 (.4298) -.697	.7571 (.6444) 1.175	-.5176 (.4238) -1.221	.6364 (.3094) 2.057	.0952 (.5455) .714	1.3828 (.9374) 1.475	-.6103 (3.1056) -.197	.6962 (.4190) 1.661
$\xi_{j,12}$	.3474 (.2492) 1.394	-.8290 (.5917) -1.401	-.2984 (.3544) -.842	.2588 (.2594) .998	-.4225 (.3424) -1.234	.4430 (.6100) .726	-1.1426 (2.3290) -.491	-.6873 (.3728) -1.844
$\xi_{j,13}$	-.6649 (.3729) -1.783	-.8227 (.5648) -1.457	.1658 (.3765) .440	.9085 (.2729) 3.330	.4053 (.4166) .973	.3617 (.6552) .552	-.3466 (2.0206) -.172	.3636 (.4770) .762

$\xi_{j,14}$	.0076	.3171	.1848	−.6548	1.6290	−.1722	−.8260	.9836
	(.1695)	(1.3718)	(.5837)	(.7819)	(.9686)	(.5950)	(.6718)	(.7686)
	.045	.231	.317	−.837	1.682	−.289	−1.230	1.280
$\xi_{j,15}$	.0345	−.5770	.2139	−.9947	.1326	−.3523	−.0918	.1718
	(.1314)	(.9802)	(.4590)	(.4586)	(.7422)	(.4126)	(.3850)	(.5909)
	.262	−.589	.466	−2.169	.179	−.854	−.238	.291
$\xi_{j,16}$	.2389	.9616	−.1944	.3867	.5469	−.0210	−.2326	.9798
	(.1300)	(1.0101)	(.4392)	(.4544)	(.6142)	(.3988)	(.4311)	(.6156)
	1.838	.952	−.443	.851	.891	−.053	−.540	1.592
$\xi_{j,17}$	.0033	−.3424	−.3006	−.0023	.0029	−.0451	.0383	−.0866
	(.0404)	(.1224)	(.2497)	(.0589)	(.1142)	(.0698)	(.0808)	(.0867)
	.082	−2.797	−1.204	−.038	.025	−.646	.474	−.999
$\xi_{j,18}$	−.0040	−.0765	−.0482	.0007	.0469	.0380	.0331	−.0515
	(.0119)	(.0607)	(.0860)	(.0231)	(.0448)	(.0414)	(.0516)	(.0370)
	−.332	−1.261	−.561	.029	1.049	.917	.640	−1.392
$\xi_{j,19}$	.0019	−.0117	−.0687	−.0173	.0516	.0711	.0236	.0468
	(.0116)	(.0542)	(.0880)	(.0217)	(.0455)	(.0379)	(.0487)	(.0349)
	.167	.215	−.781	−.798	1.134	1.875	.485	1.341
$\bar{R}^2$	.1968	−.0965	.2811	.1908	.1568	.3486	−.1952	.4587
S.E.E.	.0072	.0291	.0133	−.0419	.0228	.0137	.0135	.0189
D-W	1.87	1.98	1.69	1.72	2.30	1.20	1.65	1.84

Note. Period: 1957I–76IV. Standard errors are in parentheses below coefficient estimates; t statistics are below the standard errors.
$^{+}$For the U.S. equation only, for "$(4\Delta \log E_j \ldots$" read "$-(4\Delta \log E_2 \ldots$," and for "$R_1$" read "$R_2$" (see equation (R9)).

Table 6.16 **Balance-of-Payments Equations (N10F)**

$$(B/Y)_j = \psi_{j1} + \psi_{j2}(B/Y)_{j,t-1} + \psi_{j3}\Delta \log E_j + \psi_{j4}\Delta \log E_{j,t-1} + \psi_{j5}(\Delta \log P_{j,t-1} - \Delta \log P_{1,t-1}) + \epsilon_{j,10}$$

Country	ψ_{j1}	ψ_{j2}	ψ_{j3}	ψ_{j4}	ψ_{j5}	$\bar{R}^2$	S.E.E.	h [D-W][†]
UK	0.0002	0.4170	0.0191	-0.0346	-0.1007	0.1710	0.0074	0.05
	(0.0023)	(0.1889)	(0.0518)	(0.0371)	(0.0896)			
	0.095	2.208	0.368	-0.931	-1.125			
CA	0.0003	0.2975	-0.0927	0.0403	-0.0109	0.0943	0.0018	[1.89]
	(0.0003)	(0.1704)	(0.0328)	(0.0223)	(0.0147)			
	1.005	1.746	-2.824	1.802	-0.738			
FR	0.0004	0.1640	-0.0304	0.0124	0.0332	-0.1965	0.0047	[1.82]
	(0.0015)	(0.2494)	(0.0333)	(0.0220)	(0.2015)			
	0.241	0.658	-0.912	0.564	0.165			
GE	0.0052	-0.0723	-0.1020	0.0025	0.0766	0.0606	0.0053	[1.98]
	(0.0021)	(0.2621)	(0.0332)	(0.0267)	(0.1649)			
	2.471	-0.276	-3.073	0.094	0.464			
IT	-0.0022	0.1758	-0.0465	-0.0232	0.0411	0.1731	0.0046	[1.51]
	(0.0016)	(0.2351)	(0.0247)	(0.0268)	(0.0922)			
	-1.412	0.748	-1.884	-0.865	0.446			
JA	0.0007	0.7929	0.0397	0.0244	-0.0193	0.4109	0.0038	1.01
	(0.0010)	(0.2136)	(0.0392)	(0.0276)	(0.0633)			
	0.652	3.712	1.014	0.883	-0.305			
NE	0.0021	-0.2072	-0.0078	-0.0295	0.0196	-0.1179	0.0063	[2.09]
	(0.0019)	(0.2557)	(0.0529)	(0.0333)	(0.1303)			
	1.144	-0.810	-0.147	-0.885	0.150			

Note. These regressions are for the floating periods listed in part a of table 5.6. Standard errors are in parentheses below coefficient estimates; t statistics are below the standard errors.

[†] The biased Durbin-Watson statistic is reported in square brackets in those cases in which Durbin's h cannot be computed (is imaginary).

Table 6.17   **Significant Cross-Correlation Coefficients for Residuals within Countries and with U.S. Money, Income, and Prices: 0.05 Level or Better**
Pegged Period: 1957II–71I (1962IV–70I Canada)

Country	Significant Correlations within Country	Significant Correlations with U.S. Variables
US	$\rho(\log P_1, R_1) = -0.348^*$ $\rho(\log P_1, (X/Y)_1) = -0.310$ $\rho(\log P_1, (C/Y)_1) = 0.327$ $\rho(\log y_1, (I/Y)_1) = -0.490^*$ $\rho(\log y_1, (C/Y)_1) = 0.358^*$ $\rho(u_1, R_1) = -0.275$ $\rho(\log P_1^I, (X/Y)_1) = -0.286$	N.A.
UK	$\rho(\log P_2, \log P_2^I) = -0.325$ $\rho(\log P_2, (I/Y)_2) = -0.274$ $\rho(\log y_2, u_2) = 0.272$ $\rho(\log y_2, \log M_2) = 0.274$ $\rho(u_2, (X/Y)_2) = 0.279$ $\rho((I/Y)_2, (C/Y)_2) = -0.336$	$\rho(\log y_2, \log P_1) = -0.350^*$ $\rho(\log M_2, \log M_1) = 0.327$ $\rho(\log P_2^I, \log y_1) = -0.314$ $\rho((X/Y)_2, \log y_1) = 0.372^*$
CA	$\rho(\log P_3, \log M_3) = 0.521^*$ $\rho(\log y_3, (X/Y)_3) = -0.396$ $\rho(\log y_3, (C/Y)_3) = 0.427$ $\rho(\log M_3, R_3) = -0.473^*$ $\rho(\log M_3, (C/Y)_3) = -0.366$	None
FR	$\rho(\log P_4, R_4) = -0.320$ $\rho(\log y_4, u_4) = 0.500^*$ $\rho(\log y_4, P_4^I) = -0.311$ $\rho(\log y_4, (X/Y)_4) = 0.307$ $\rho(\log M_4, R_4) = 0.349^*$ $\rho(\log P_4^I, (I/Y)_4) = -0.367^*$ $\rho(\log P_4^I, (C/Y)_4) = -0.334$	$\rho(R_4, \log M_1) = 0.272$

Table 6.17 (continued)

Country	Significant Correlations within Country	Significant Correlations with U.S. Variables
GE	None	None
IT	$\rho(\log M_6, (C/Y)_6) = -0.599^*$	$\rho((I/Y)_6, \log y_1) = 0.300$
	$\rho(R_6, (I/Y)_6) = 0.393^*$	
	$\rho(I/Y)_6, (X/Y)_6) = 0.380^*$	
JA	$\rho(\log M_7, \log P_7^I) = 0.299$	
	$\rho(R_7, (I/Y)_7) = -0.455^*$	
NE	$\rho(\log M_8, (I/Y)_8) = -0.521^*$	$\rho(\log P_8, \log M_1) = 0.303$
	$\rho(R_8, (X/Y)_8) = -0.348^*$	$\rho(\log y_8, \log P_1) = -0.278$
		$\rho(\log P_8^I, \log P_1) = -0.402^*$

Notes. Correlations marked with an asterisk are significant at the 0.01 level or better. The critical values for the correlation coefficients are ± 0.265 (± 0.361 for Canada) at the 0.05 level and ± 0.342 (± 0.463 for Canada) at the 0.01 level.

For each country, correlation coefficients were computed for all possible combinations of the residuals to all the equations (R1) through (R9) or (N1) through (N9) for the pegged period. In addition for the nonreserve countries, correlation coefficients were computed for the residuals of the U.S. equations (R1), (R2), and (R4) (i.e. the $\log y_1$, $\log P_1$, and $\Delta \log M_1$ equations) with the residuals of each of the equations (N1) through (N9). Since equation (N3) is estimated only in the cases of the United Kingdom and France, the total number of correlation coefficients examined varies by country as follows:

Country	Domestic ρ	International ρ
United States	36	0
U.K., France	36 each	27 each
Other 5 countries	28 each	24 each
TOTAL ALL COUNTRIES	248	174

The following correlation pairs were significant for more than one country:
($\log P_j, R_j$): United States*, France
($\log y_j, (C/Y)_j$): United States*, Canada
($\log y_j, u_j$): United Kingdom, France
($\log y_j, (X/Y)_j$): Canada, France
($\log M_j, R_j$): Canada, France*
($R_j, (I/Y)_j$): Italy*, Japan
($\log y_j, \log P_1$): United Kingdom*, Netherlands

Table 6.18   **Significant Cross-Correlation Coefficients for Residuals within Countries and with U.S. Money, Income, and Prices: 0.05 Level or Better**
Floating Period: 1971III–76III

Country	Significant Correlations within Country	Significant Correlations with U.S. Variables
US	$\rho(\log P_1, R_1) = -0.452$ $\rho(R_1, (I/Y)_1) = -0.482$	N.A.
UK	$\rho(\log P_2, u_2) = 0.488$ $\rho(\log M_2, (C/Y)_2) = 0.489$ $\rho(\log M_2, (B/Y)_2) = -0.536$ $\rho(R_2, \log Z_2) = -0.505$	None
CA	$\rho(\log P_3, \log y_3) = -0.513$ $\rho(\log P_3, \log Z_3) = -0.677^*$ $\rho(\log Z_3, (C/Y)_3) = 0.443$	$\rho(\log Z_3, \log y_1) = -0.553^*$
FR	$\rho(\log P_4, \log M_4) = -0.621^*$ $\rho(\log P_4, R_4) = -0.557^*$ $\rho(\log Y_4, u_4) = -0.434$ $\rho(\log E_4, (B/Y)_4) = 0.469$	$\rho(u_4, \log M_1) = 0.466$
GE	$\rho(\log E_5, (X/Y)_5) = -0.535$ $\rho(\log Z_5, (C/Y)_5) = 0.532$	$\rho((B/Y)_5, \log y_1) = 0.660^*$
IT	$\rho(\log E_6, \log Z_6) = -0.573^*$ $\rho(\log E_6, (B/Y)_6) = 0.485$	None
JA	$\rho(\log y_7, R_7) = -0.659^*$ $\rho(\log y_7, (X/Y)_7) = 0.486$ $\rho(R_7, \log E_7) = -0.587^*$ $\rho(R_7, \log Z_7) = 0.455$ $\rho((C/Y)_7, (B/Y)_7) = -0.710^*$	$\rho((B/Y)_7, \log P_1) = -0.459$

Table 6.18 (continued)

Country	Significant Correlations within Country	Significant Correlations with U.S. Variables
NE	$\rho(\log y_8, (C/Y)_8) = -0.575^*$ $\rho(\log M_8, R_8) = 0.467$ $\rho(R_8, (B/Y)_8) = -0.512$ $\rho((C/Y)_8, (B/Y)_8) = -0.588^*$	$\rho(R_8, \log M_1) = -0.563^*$

Notes. Correlations marked with an asterisk are significant at the 0.01 level (exceed 0.549 in absolute value). The critical values at the 0.05 level are ± 0.433.

For each country, correlation coefficients were computed for all possible combinations of the residuals to all the equations (R1) through (R9) and (N1) through (N10F) for the floating period. In addition for the nonreserve countries, correlation coefficients were computed for the residuals of the U.S. equations (R1), (R2), and (R4) (i.e. the $\log y_1$, $\log P_1$, and $\Delta\log M_1$ equations) with the residuals of each of the equations (N1) through (N10F). Since equation (N3) is estimated only in the cases of the United Kingdom and France, the total number of correlation coefficients examined varies by country as follows:

Country	Domestic ρ	International ρ
United States	36	0
U.K., France	45 each	30 each
Other 5 countries	36 each	27 each
TOTAL ALL COUNTRIES	306	195

The following correlation pairs were significant for more than one country:
(log P_j, R_j): United States, France*
(R_j, log Z_j): United Kingdom, Japan
(log Z_j, $(C/Y)_j$): Canada, Germany
(log E_j, $(B/Y)_j$): France, Italy
$((C/Y)_j, (B/Y)_j)$: Japan,* Netherlands*

Table 6.19   **Frequency of Significant Cross-Correlation Coefficients for Residuals by Type and Period**

	Within Country	With U.S. Variables
	5% Level or Better	
Pegged period	12.9%	5.2%
Floating period	8.5%	2.6%
	1% Level or Better	
Pegged period	5.6%	1.7%
Floating period	2.9%	1.5%

Table 6.20   Data Sources for the Mark III Model

$(B/Y)_j$	Numerators $[B_j]$	
	USBPQSDR	Nominal balance of payments, official reserve settlement basis, SA,QR
	UKBPQSCF	Nominal balance of payments, official reserve settlement basis, SA,QR
	CABPQSCC	Quarterly change in nominal official reserves, SA,QR
	FRBPQSFF	Quarterly change in nominal net official reserves, SA,QR
	GEBPQSDR	Nominal balance of payments, official reserve settlement basis, SA,QR
	ITBPQSVL	Quarterly change in nominal official reserves, SA,QR
	JABPQSJJ	Quarterly change in nominal official reserves, SA,QR
	NEBPQSSB	Nominal balance of payments, official reserve settlement basis, SA,QR

Denominators $[Y_j]$

	USYNQSGN	Nominal gross national product, SA, AR
	UKYNQSGD	Nominal gross domestic product, SA,AR
	CAYNQSCA	Nominal gross national product, SA,AR
	FRYNQSFF	Nominal *produit intérieur brut* (PIB),SA,AR
	GEYNQSGN	Nominal gross national product, SA,AR
	ITYNQSGD	Nominal gross domestic product, SA,AR
	JAYNQSJJ	Nominal gross national product, SA,AR
	NEYNQSNP	Nominal gross national product, SA,AR

$(C/Y)_j$ Calculated as: $(C/Y)_j \equiv (X/Y)_j - (I/Y)_j - 4(B/Y)_j$. Note that $(C/Y)_j$, $(X/Y)_j$, and $(I/Y)_j$ are at annual rates; $(B/Y)_j$ is at quarterly rates.

DF_j Floating dummy; is 1 except in the following (pegged) quarters, when it is 0:

UK	1955I–71II	IT	1955I–71II
CA	1962III–70I	JA	1955I–71II
FR	1955I–71II	NE	1955I–71I
GE	1955I–71I		

E_j	US $\equiv$ 1	
	UKXRQNLB	Spot exchange rate (London exchange), QAEM
	CAXRQNSP	Exchange rate (Canadian interbank), QAD
	FRXRQNFF	Spot exchange rate (IMF), QAD
	GEXRQNDM	Spot exchange rate (Frankfurt exchange), LMAD
	ITXRQNLR	Spot exchange rate (Rome and Milan exchanges), QAD
	JAXRQNSP	Exchange rate (interbank), QAEM
	NEXRQNGL	Spot exchange rate (Amsterdam exchange), QAW

g_j	G_j/P_j, where P_j is defined below and G_j is:	
	USGXQSFD	Nominal federal government expenditure, SA,AR
	UKGXQSCG	Nominal central government expenditure, SA,AR
	CAGXQSEX	Nominal federal government expenditure, SA,AR
	FRGXQSFF	Nominal central government expenditure, SA,AR

Table 6.20 (continued)

	GEGXQSFG	Nominal federal government expenditure, SA,AR
	ITGXQSFD	Nominal federal government expenditure, SA,AR
	JAGXQSEX	Nominal treasury payments (QAM),SA,AR
	NEGXQSFD	Nominal central government payments, SA,AR

$\hat{g}_j$ Residuals from ARIMA (p, d, q) processes fitted to log g_j. The (p, d, q) values of the fitted processes are:[†]

US	(0,1,0)	GE	(0,1,1)
UK	(2,1,0)	IT	(0,1,1)
CA	(0,1,1)	JA	(0,1,6) $[\theta_2 = \theta_4 = \theta_5 = 0]$
FR	(0,1,1)	NE	(0,1,4) $[\theta_2 = \theta_3 = 0]$

$(I/Y)_j$ Numerators $[I_j]$:

	USIMQSTL	Nominal total imports, SA,AR
	UKIMQSCA	Nominal total imports, SA,AR
	CAIMQSTL	Nominal total imports, SA,AR
	FRIMQSFF	Nominal merchandise imports, SA,AR
	GEIMQSTL	Nominal total imports, SA,AR
	ITIMQSTL	Nominal total imports, SA,AR
	JAIMQSJJ	Nominal merchandise imports (customs basis), SA,AR
	NEIMQSTL	Nominal total imports, SA,AR

Denominators $[Y_j]$ as defined at $(B/Y)_j$ above.

M_j

	USM1QSAE	Nominal narrow money stock, SA,QAD
	UKM1QSDR	Nominal narrow money stock, SA,QAM
	CAM1QSCC	Nominal narrow money stock, SA,QAW
	FRM2QSFF	Nominal broader money stock, SA,QAM
	GEM2QSDR	Nominal broader money stock, SA,EQ
	ITM1QSDR	Nominal narrow money stock, centered on EQ
	JAM1QSJJ	Nominal narrow money stock, SA,QAM
	NEM2QSDR	Nominal broader money stock, SA, EQ

$\hat{M}_j$ Residuals from ARIMA (p, d, q) processes fitted to log M_j. The (p, d, q) values of the fitted processes are:[†]

US	(1,2,2) $[\theta_1 = 0]$
UK	(2,1,0)
CA	(2,2,4) $[\theta_1 = \theta_2 = 0]$
FR	(1,1,6) $[\theta_1 = \theta_2 = \theta_3 = \theta_4 = \theta_5 = 0]$
GE	(0,1,3)
IT	(1,1,3) $[\theta_1 = 0]$
JA	(2,1,4) $[\theta_1 = \theta_2 = \theta_3 = 0]$
NE	(2,1,4) $[\theta_1 = \theta_2 = \theta_3 = 0]$

P_j

	USPDQSN0	GNP implicit price deflator (1970 = 1.00), SA
	UKPDQSD7	GDP implicit price deflator (1970 = 1.00), SA
	CAPDQS70	GNP implicit price deflator (1970 = 1.00), SA
	FRPDQS70	PIB implicit price deflator (1970 = 1.00), SA
	GEPDQSN7	GNP implicit price deflator (1970 = 1.00), SA
	ITPDQS70	GDP implicit price deflator (1970 = 1.00), SA
	JAPDQSJJ	GNP implicit price deflator (1970 = 1.00), SA
	NEPDQSN7	GNP implicit price deflator (1970 = 1.00), SA

Table 6.20 (continued)

P_j^I	USPIQS70/100	Index of unit value of imports (1970 = 100, IFS series 75), SA
	UKPIQS70/100	Index of total imports unit value (1970 = 100, IFS series 75), SA
	CAPIQS70/100	Index of import prices (1970 = 100, IFS series 75), SA
	FRPIQS70/100	Index of import prices (1970 = 100, IFS series 75), SA
	GEPIQS70/100	Index of purchase prices of foreign goods (1970 = 100, IFS series 75.x), SA
	ITPIQS70/100	index of import prices (1970 = 100, IFS series 75), SA
	JAPIQS70/100	Index of contract prices of importers (1970 = 100, IFS series 75.x), SA
	NEPIQS70/100	Index of unit value of imports (1970 = 100, IFS series 75), SA

P_j^R See identities (R19) and (N19) and table 5.7.

P^{RO} Computed as VPOIL/(100 · P_1), where VPIOL is the dollar price index of Venezuelan crude oil (1970 = 100) described in table 6.21.

R_j	USRSQN3T	Three-month treasury bill yield, QAD
	UKRSQN3T	Three-month treasury bill yield, QAEM
	CARSQNTB	Three-month treasury bill yield, QAEM
	FRRSQNST	Short-term money market rate on private bills, QAD
	GERSQN3M	Three-month money market rate, pre-1967 LMAW, post-1966 LMAD
	ITRLQNGU	Market yield on long-term corporate bonds, QAM
	JARSQNLD	Average contracted interest rate on bank loans, QAW
	NERSQN3T	Three-month treasury paper yield to maturity, QAD

t Time index (1955I = 1, 1955II = 2, etc.)

u_j	USURQSCV	Unemployment rate, SA,QAM
	UKURQSDR	Unemployment rate, SA,QAM
	FRURQSFF	Unemployment rate, SA,EQ

For experiments discussed in text (these do not appear in the model):

	CAURQS14	Unemployment rate, SA
	GEURQSDR	Unemployment rate, SA
	ITURQSDR	Unemployment rate, SA
	JAURQSUR	Unemployment rate, SA,QAM
	NEURQSSE	Unemployment rate, SA

$(X/Y)_j$	Numerators $[X_j]$:	
	USEXQSTL	Nominal total exports, SA,AR
	UKEXQSCA	Nominal total exports, SA,AR
	CAEXQSTL	Nominal total exports, SA,AR
	FREXQSFF	Nominal merchandise exports, SA,AR
	GEEXQSTL	Nominal total exports, SA,AR
	ITEXQSTL	Nominal total exports, SA,AR
	JAEXQSJJ	Nominal merchandise exports (customs basis), SA,AR
	NEEXQSTL	Nominal total exports, SA,AR

Denominators $[Y_j]$ as defined at $(B/Y)_j$ above.

Table 6.20 (continued)

$\hat{x}_j$	Residuals from ARIMA (p, d, q) processes fitted to $(X/Y)_j$. The (p, d, q) values of the fitted processes are:[†]

US $(0,1,3)$ $[\theta_1 = 0]$
UK $(0,1,7)$ $[\theta_1 = \theta_3 = \theta_5 = \theta_6 = 0]$
CA $(1,1,8)$ $[\theta_1 = \theta_2 = \theta_3 = \theta_4 = \theta_5 = \theta_6 = \theta_7 = 0]$
FR $(1,1,4)$ $[\theta_1 = \theta_3 = 0]$
GE $(0,1,4)$ $[\theta_1 = \theta_2 = \theta_3 = 0]$
IT $(2,1,11)$ $[\theta_1 = \theta_2 = \theta_3 = \theta_4 = \theta_5 = \theta_6 = \theta_7 = \theta_9 = \theta_{10} = 0]$
JA $(2,2,9)$ $[\theta_1 = \theta_2 = \theta_3 = \theta_5 = \theta_6 = \theta_7 = \theta_8 = 0]$
NE $(0,1,9)$ $[\theta_2 = \theta_3 = \theta_4 = \theta_5 = \theta_6 = \theta_7 = \theta_8 = 0]$

y_j	USYRQSN0	Real gross national product, SA,AR
	UKYRQSD7	Real gross domestic product, SA,AR
	CAYRQS70	Real gross national product, SA,AR
	FRYRQS70	Real *produit intérieur brut*, SA,AR
	GEYRQSN7	Real gross national product, SA,AR
	ITYRQSD7	Real gross domestic product, SA,AR
	JAYRQS70	Real gross national product, SA,AR
	NEYRQSN7	Real gross national product, SA,AR

y_j^P See identities (R11) and (N11). All $\phi_{j2} \equiv 0.025$; other parameters are:

Country	$\phi_{j3} \equiv \phi_{j1}/0.975$	$\log y_{j,[1954\text{IV}]}^P$
US	0.00866	6.34717
UK	0.00670	3.34166
CA	0.01200	3.70432
FR	0.01379	5.68231
GE	0.01143	5.76526
IT	0.01218	10.15820
JA	0.02280	9.65613
NE	0.01161	3.97958

y_j^R See identities (R18) and (N18) table 5.7.

Notes. "Nominal" implies billions of domestic currency units (DCUs). "Real" implies billions of 1970 DCUs. The nature of each series is indicated following its description by SA if it is seasonally adjusted and any of the following which (generally) apply:

AR   flows at annual rates
EQ   end of quarter data
LMAD   average of daily data for last month of quarter
LMAW   average of weekly data for last month of quarter
QAD   quarterly average of daily data
QAEM   quarterly average of end-of-month data
QAM   quarterly average of monthly data
QAW   quarterly average of weekly data

[†]The q in the descriptions of the ARIMA processes for $\hat{g}_j$, $\hat{M}_j$, and $\hat{x}_j$ indicates the highest-order moving average term which was fitted; some θ_i (indicated in square brackets) were, however, constrained to equal 0 in the estimation.

Table 6.21   **Dollar Price Index of Venezuelan Crude Oil**
(VPOIL; 1970 = 100)

| Year | Quarters | | | |
	1	2	3	4
1955	105.015	105.015	105.015	103.052
1956	103.052	104.034	103.052	102.071
1957	106.978	107.959	107.959	107.959
1958	107.959	107.959	107.959	110.904
1959	105.015	99.1264	99.1264	99.1264
1960	100.	100.	100.	100.
1961	100.	100.	100.	100.
1962	100.	100.	100.	100.
1963	100.	100.	100.	100.
1964	100.	100.	100.	100.
1965	100.	100.	100.	100.
1966	100.	100.	100.	100.
1967	100.	100.	100.	100.
1968	100.	100.	100.	100.
1969	100.	100.	100.	100.
1970	100.	100.	100.	100.
1971	117.	126.	121.	127.
1972	137.	122.	132.	131.
1973	142.	215.	215.	215.
1974	550.	550.	550.	572.
1975	587.	587.	587.	633.
1976	633.	608.	614.	632.
1977	683.	683.	683.	

Sources

Basic data from *International Financial Statistics*.

1955–59 data (base 1953 = 100): February 1958–62 issues, respectively.

1960–65 data (base 1958 = 100): February 1963–68 issues, respectively.

1966–67 data (base 1963 = 100): February 1970–71 issues, respectively.

1968–70 data (base 1963 = 100): February 1972 issue.

1971–72 data (base 1971 = 100): February 1975 issue.

1973–74 data (base 1971 = 100): February 1977 issue.

1975–77 data (base 1971 = 100): December 1977 issue.

All of the above observations were rebased to 1970 = 100 by repeated applications of the ratio method.

7 International Transmission of Monetary and Fiscal Shocks under Pegged and Floating Exchange Rates: Simulation Experiments

Michael R. Darby

The estimates of the Mark III Model reported in chapter 6 indicated surprisingly slow and weak transmission from country to country. Moreover, substantial sterilization policies appeared to be universal and, given these weak linkages, capable of ensuring a degree of short-run monetary control under pegged exchange rates. This chapter continues the investigation of these findings by presenting the results of monetary and fiscal policy experiments with a simulation version of the Mark III International Transmission Model.

The results here generally support the earlier findings of weak transmission under pegged exchange rates. Monetary linkages with the United States appear strongest for Germany, moderate for the Netherlands, and practically nonexistent for the United Kingdom and Canada although absorption-type channels are operative for the latter two countries. While monetary shocks in nonreserve countries have sensible domestic effects, international transmission is trivial. Similarly the domestic effects of real-government-spending shocks are too small to have an appreciable foreign impact in any case examined. These results force us to question the standard assumptions which imply strong channels for international transmissions since those channels are not obvious in the data.

Unlike the pegged case, the floating simulations display dynamic instabilities. This difference is attributable to the relatively short sample period. The simulations do indicate how a J-curve phenomenon due to short-run inelasticity of import demand can affect the adjustment process.

The Mark IV Model is outlined in section 7.1 and the appendix to this chapter. Section 7.2 discusses the simulation results for the United States money-shock experiments. The third section illustrates the results of nonreserve-country money-shock experiments and of real-government shock experiments. The final section presents conclusions and suggestions for future research.

7.1 The Simulation Model

The Mark III Model was designed to test a number of popular hypotheses about the transmission of inflation while allowing for a variety of lag patterns across countries. Unfortunately the large number of insignificant coefficients and collinear endogenous variables makes the model unusable for simulation purposes. A special simulation version to the model (the Mark IV) has been created by dropping insignificant variables and combining terms[1] except where variables are left in to permit transmission or for strong a priori reasons (such as the interest-rate terms in the money-demand or price-level equation). The resulting model thus includes the significant relationships of the Mark III Model but is sufficiently simplified for the reasonable calculation of simulation results. Given the way in which the model was derived, classical statistical statements cannot be made with respect to the Mark IV. Its purpose instead is to illustrate the implications of the relations found significant in the Mark III Model.

The Mark IV Model exists in two versions. The pegged-exchange-rate version (Mark IV–PEG) combines the reserve-country (U.S.) submodel with the pegged-rate submodels for the seven nonreserve countries. Floating-rate nonreserve submodels are used instead in the floating-exchange-rate version (Mark IV–FLT). This section summarizes the models while the chapter appendix lists the actual computer model together with the estimated coefficients.

The basic structure of the Mark IV Model is the same as the Mark III: The reserve-country submodel of the Mark IV consists of nine behavioral equations and thirteen identities.[2] The behavioral equations determine a skeletal macroeconomic model (real income, price level, unemployment rate, nominal money, and interest rate) together with a bit more detailed international sector (exports, imports, import prices, and capital flows).

---

1. Collinearity is reduced where the coefficients of various lagged levels of a variable indicate that either a sum or first difference is the appropriate variable. Similarly a number of hypotheses implying equality of coefficients permitted combining terms into simple logarithmic sums or differences. In one case (Germany in the Mark IV–PEG), this made the whole equation for the logarithm of import prices and the associated identity for relative import prices redundant; so they were dropped.

2. This is four more identities than listed in chapter 5 for the Mark III Model: Two of these define expected money and exports based on last period's information; these series are predetermined for purposes of estimation but endogenous in a dynamic simulation. A third identity defines logarithmic transitory income which was written explicitly in the Mark III. The fourth defines a lagged prediction error term needed for dynamic simulation. Similar identities were added to all the other submodels to obtain consistent dynamic simulations.

The pegged-exchange-rate nonreserve submodels are basically the same as the reserve submodel with the important exception that the balance of payments enters the nonreserve (but not the reserve) countries' money-supply reaction functions.[3] The floating nonreserve submodels differ only in their international sectors: To make the seven domestic-currency-per-dollar exchange rates endogenous, an exchange-intervention reaction function is added to determine the balance of payments previously determined by an identity. The sector is then renormalized to solve for the exchange rate.[4]

Let us first examine the skeletal macroeconometric model included in each of the submodels. Real income and the (nominal) interest rate are determined by shocks (innovations) in the money supply, real government spending, and real exports, and, for the interest-rate equation only, the expected inflation rate.[5] Thus real income and the *real* interest rate are affected by the factors which unexpectedly shift aggregate demand relative to aggregate supply. The price-level equations simply equate short-run money demand to money supply.[6] Nominal money supply is determined by a reaction function in response to lagged inflation and unemployment rates, to current and lagged government spending shocks, and, for nonreserve countries, to current and lagged balances of payments. The unemployment rate is determined by a dynamic version of Okun's law for the United States, United Kingdom, and France. Changes in measured unemployment and real income were uncorrelated for the other countries; so for them the unemployment equation is deleted and logarithmic transitory income used instead in the money-supply reaction function.

The included channels by which international shocks can be transmitted to these basic macroeconomic variables are three in number: (1) For the nonreserve countries, the current and lagged balances of payments affect the nominal money supply. The estimates indicated very substantial if not total sterilization of the *current* balance of payments in every case, however. This is consistent with the central banks' pursuing money-growth or interest-rate goals set at least partially in response to past data

3. As is appropriate for a reserve country, the balance of payments was found to have no influence on the U.S. money supply. See Darby (1980, 1981) and chapter 16.

4. The equations are solved for exports, relative price of imports, exchange rate, net capital outflows, and the balance of payments.

5. Variables such as real income, prices, and money are measured in logarithms. The interest rates and unemployment rates are decimal fractions. Exports, imports, net capital outflows, and the balance of payments are all scaled by dividing by nominal income. Shocks are deviations of actual values from optimal ARIMA predictions of the variables.

6. The short-run money-demand function is adapted from Carr and Darby (1981). It allows money-supply shocks to affect money demand. In the Mark III Model a foreign interest rate adjusted for expected depreciation was included to test for asset substitution, but this was significant only for the United Kingdom and Japan and (at only a 15% significance level) France.

on the balance of payments. (2) Export shocks affect both real income and the interest rate along standard Keynesian absorption lines. (3) An asset substitution channel exists by which foreign interest rates adjusted by expected depreciation can affect money demand and the price level in the United Kingdom, France, and Japan. The real oil price does not enter in this sector but in the international sector and influences the domestic economy through these three channels.[7]

The reserve and pegged nonreserve international sectors will be discussed next. The export equation depends on foreign real income, the real price of oil, the domestic and foreign price levels, and the exchange rate. Imports are explained by a demand equation including domestic real income and current and lagged import prices relative to the price level. Import prices in turn depend on import supply variables such as the size of imports, foreign price levels, and the exchange rate. The capital-flows equations allow for interest-rate and expected depreciation effects, foreign and domestic real income effects, and trade-deficit financing. In the floating nonreserve models the import demand and supply equations are renormalized to relative-import-price and exchange-rate equations, respectively. The added balance-of-payments or intervention equation relates the balance to changes in exchange rates relative to lagged changes and lagged changes in relative purchasing power.

One check of model adequacy which might uncover omitted channels of transmission was suggested by Bob Flood. Omitted channels will show up as correlations of the residuals of the model's equations. As reported in chapter 6, these correlations were checked for the Mark III Model both within each country and for U.S. nominal money, real income, and price level versus all foreign variables. Few more than the expected number of correlations were significant at the 5% level for either the pegged or floating period, and no pair of correlations was significant in more than two cases. Therefore it was concluded that the model adequately represented the channels apparent in the data.

The international sector thus incorporates a variety of potential channels of transmission. For example, as suggested by the monetary approach, either trade or capital flows might cause huge movements in the balance of payments (and hence money) if domestic prices or interest rates were to begin to differ from international parity values. This did not appear likely from the small estimated coefficients, but only simulations can determine this definitely.

In preparation for such simulation experiments and as a check on the simulation models, we first obtained a base dynamic simulation for each version of the model.[8] For the Mark IV–PEG this base simulation was

7. See, however, chapter 8 below for tests of direct oil influences.
8. In a dynamic simulation, the input series are the exogenous variables plus the initial conditions (endogenous variables before the beginning of simulation). The values of

computed for 1962III through 1970I, which was the entire period that all nonreserve countries were maintaining firm pegged exchange rates with the dollar. The corresponding period for the Mark IV–FLT would be 1971III through 1976IV, but dynamic instabilities in the model became important after seven quarters (1973I), so the base simulation covers only this shorter period for which the simulations might be informative. The dynamic instability of the Mark IV–FLT should be sufficient warning that the results of the floating period simulations must be read with considerable skepticism.[9]

Table 7.1 compares the standard errors of estimate for each behavioral equation with the root mean square errors (RMSEs) of the simulated values of the dependent variables both for the first year and for the entire period of the simulation. The standard errors reported here are generally lower than those reported for the corresponding equations in the Mark III International Transmission Model because of the deletion of insignificant variables and the imposition of constraints discussed above.[10] The first-year RMSEs appear to be generally reasonable, but errors do accumulate over the entire simulation period, especially for the international sectors and for the floating model even though the simulation period is much shorter. On this basis, the first-year simulations appear to be most informative, with longer periods at most suggestive of general tendencies.

7.2   U.S. Money-Shock Experiments

As is well known,[11] a common problem with policy studies based on econometric models is that the policy experiment is often inconsistent with the policy regime for which the model is estimated. As a result, the

---

endogenous variables within the simulation period are assigned their predicted values. Especially for a large model with few exogenous variables, the cumulative errors in the endogenous variables eventually may take the simulation off track even if the model is dynamically stable.

9. The dynamic instability does not seem to depend on when we begin the simulation. It apparently results from our inability to do much to eliminate simultaneous equation bias with such a short sample. Three pieces of evidence besides experience with other models point to this conclusion: (1) The instability appears to arise in the renormalized international sector equations which are estimated over the short sample period. (2) The pegged model is estimated over a longer sample period but with the same basic structure and is rather stable. (The instability in the Mark IV–FLT remains even if we artificially constrain the exchange rates to equal their actual values as in the Mark IV–PEG, where they are exogenous.) (3) Only for Canada—which has the short pegged period—is there a hint of instability in the pegged veriosn of the model.

10. These standard errors will thus be on the optimistic side. The few cases of increase apparently reflect deletion of variables which individually appear insignificant but are jointly significant with other deleted variables. The only important increases occur in the exchange-rate equations, where it was necessary to impose a constraint generally ruled out by the data for reasons discussed in section 7.2 below.

11. See Lucas (1976).

Table 7.1   Standard Errors of Estimate Compared with Base Simulation Root Mean Square Errors: Mark IV–PEG and Mark IV–FLT

Variables[†]	Statistics	Countries							
		US	UK	CA	FR	GE	IT	JA	NE
Logarithm of real output $\log y_j \equiv$ LNYR**	Mark IV–PEG:								
	S.E.E.	.0089	.0136	.0118	.0177	.0129	.0132	.0152	.0130
	4 qtr. RMSE	.0063	.0116	.0059	.0153	.0230	.0076	.0118	.0148
	31 qtr. RMSE	.0321	.0241	.0399	.0372	.0246	.0206	.0902	.0316
	Mark IV–FLT:								
	S.E.E.	.0089	.0136	.0118	.0177	.0129	.0132	.0152	.0130
	4 qtr. RMSE	.0084	.0078	.0176	.0080	.0339	.0131	.0148	.0102
	7 qtr. RMSE	.0256	.0199	.0233	.0068	.0448	.0187	.0129	.0124
Logarithm of price level $\log P_j \equiv$ LNP**	Mark IV–PEG:								
	S.E.E.	.0035	.0148	.0115	.0103	.0062	.0115	.0121	.0109
	4 qtr. RMSE	.0025	.0213	.0062	.0183	.0047	.0191	.0167	.0143
	31 qtr. RMSE	.0110	.1115	.0388	.0960	.0311	.0496	.0998	.0168
	Mark IV–FLT:								
	S.E.E.	.0035	.0148	.0115	.0103	.0062	.0115	.0121	.0109
	4 qtr. RMSE	.0135	.0224	.0070	.0215	.0078	.0241	.0103	.0212
	7 qtr. RMSE	.0207	.0310	.0170	.0192	.0093	.0437	.0242	.0262
Unemployment rate $u_j \equiv$ UN**	Mark IV–PEG:								
	S.E.E.	.0018	.0015	NA	.0009	NA	NA	NA	NA
	4 qtr. RMSE	.0028	.0012		.0004				
	31 qtr. RMSE	.0067	.0057		.0036				
	Mark IV–FLT:								
	S.E.E.	.0018	.0015		.0009				
	4 qtr. RMSE	.0017	.0023		.0010				
	7 qtr. RMSE	.0071	.0033		.0009				

Table 7.1 (continued)

Variables†	Statistics	Countries							
		US	UK	CA	FR	GE	IT	JA	NE
Logarithm of nominal money	Mark IV–PEG:								
log $M_j \equiv$ LMN**	S.E.E.	.0045	.0160	.0156	.0118	.0126	.0188	.0148	.0153
	4 qtr. RMSE	.0074	.0438	.0321	.0339	.0118	.0584	.0728	.0132
	31 qtr. RMSE	.0082	.1253	.0556	.1088	.0313	.0574	.1219	.0217
	Mark IV–FLT:								
	S.E.E.	.0045	.0160	.0156	.0118	.0126	.0188	.0148	.0153
	4 qtr. RMSE	.0057	.0240	.0112	.0065	.0356	.0207	.0171	.0163
	7 qtr. RMSE	.0166	.0259	.0200	.0200	.0454	.0163	.0269	.0220
Short-term interest rate	Mark IV–PEG:								
$R_j \equiv$ R**	S.E.E.	.0043	.0074	.0063	.0090	.0109	.0038	.0011	.0090
	4 qtr. RMSE	.0008	.0060	.0053	.0081	.0042	.0051	.0013	.0075
	31 qtr. RMSE	.0095	.0106	.0131	.0173	.0166	.0076	.0067	.0111
	Mark IV–FLT:								
	S.E.E.	.0043	.0074	.0063	.0090	.0109	.0038	.0011	.0090
	4 qtr. RMSE	.0162	.0239	.0053	.0130	.0182	.0078	.0023	.0194
	7 qtr. RMSE	.0137	.0218	.0094	.0273	.0166	.0137	.0056	.0323
Ratio of nominal exports to nominal output	Mark IV–PEG:								
$(X/Y)_j \equiv$ XTOY**	S.E.E.	.0022	.0069	.0062	.0049	.0056	.0067	.0022	.0141
	4 qtr. RMSE	.0018	.0056	.0016	.0053	.0042	.0045	.0017	.0074
	31 qtr. RMSE	.0054	.0255	.0198	.0202	.0107	.0091	.0030	.0180
	Mark IV–FLT:								
	S.E.E.	.0022	.0069	.0062	.0049	.0056	.0067	.0022	.0141
	4 qtr. RMSE	.0046	.0330	.0059	.0154	.0140	.0031	.0014	.0394
	7 qtr. RMSE	.0040	.0521	.0095	.0384	.0295	.0129	.0022	.0560

Ratio of nominal imports to nominal output $(I/Y)_j$ = ITOY**								
Mark IV–PEG:								
S.E.E.	.0027	.0069	.0044	.0033	.0048	.0074	.0017	.0146
4 qtr. RMSE	.0026	.0059	.0061	.0053	.0023	.0125	.0017	.0166
31 qtr. RMSE	.0049	.0344	.0060	.0060	.0066	.0123	.0111	.0295
Logarithm of relative price of imports§ Z_j = LNQIM**								
Mark IV–FLT:								
S.E.E.	.0027	.0179	.0178	.0221	.0393	.0477	.0245	.0247
4 qtr. RMSE	.0063	.1138	.0748	.1700	.2982	.0683	.0784	.0773
7 qtr. RMSE	.0078	.1700	.2568	.2891	.4776	.1109	.0739	.1695
Logarithm of import price index $\log P^f_j$ = LNPIM**								
Mark IV–PEG:								
S.E.E.	.0129	.0157	.0076	.0194	NA	.0165	.0118	.0111
4 qtr. RMSE	.0187	.0179	.0198	.0150		.0148	.0233	.0067
31 qtr. RMSE	.0565	.0322	.0224	.0521		.0520	.0871	.0501
Logarithm of exchange rate‡ $\log E_j$ = LNE**								
Mark IV–FLT:								
S.E.E.	.0129	.0482	.0129	.0340	.0436	.0340	.0285	.0387
4 qtr. RMSE	.0300	.0957	.0196	.0781	.2670	.0484	.0276	.0278
7 qtr. RMSE	.0436	.0999	.0484	.1400	.4146	.0869	.0613	.0359
Ratio of nominal net capital outflows to nominal output $(C/Y)_j$ = CTOY**								
Mark IV–PEG:								
S.E.E.	.0074	.0291	.0103	.0159	.0246	.0138	.0125	.0198
4 qtr. RMSE	.0062	.0122	.0383	.0094	.0105	.0077	.0049	.0262
31 qtr. RMSE	.0059	.0314	.0235	.0160	.0284	.0124	.0064	.0220
Mark IV–FLT:								
S.E.E.	.0074	.0291	.0103	.0159	.0246	.0138	.0125	.0198
4 qtr. RMSE	.0159	.0409	.0788	.0203	.1586	.0160	.0284	.0166
7 qtr. RMSE	.0144	.0327	.3483	.0211	.1891	.0128	.0238	.0359
Ratio of nominal balance of payments to nominal output $(B/Y)_j$ = BTOY**								
Mark IV–FLT:								
S.E.E.	NA	.0071	.0017	.0044	.0049	.0044	.0038	.0063
4 qtr. RMSE		.0109	.0027	.0061	.0117	.0039	.0064	.0059
7 qtr. RMSE		.0084	.0051	.0049	.0234	.0034	.0054	.0069

† The mnemonics are given first in the notation of chapter 5 and then in the computer code described in the appendix to this chapter.

§ For the United States only, this equation is not renormalized and the reported statistics are for $(I/Y)_1$ = ITOYUS.

‡ For the United States only, this equation is not renormalized and the reported statistics are for $\log P^f_1$ = LNPIMUS.

simulated behavior may be irrational under the alternative policy regime. Thus one must choose a policy experiment which is consistent with the estimated model. The consistent policy experiment chosen is a 0.01 increase in the disturbance term of the U.S. nominal-money-supply reaction function for one quarter. Thereafter the money supply develops according to the endogenous structure of the model.

This experiment was performed for both the pegged and floating versions of the Mark IV Model. The main results for the pegged simulation are summarized in the six panels of figure 7.1. This figure shows the difference between the simulated values of the major variables given the 1% money shock and the values in the corresponding base simulation without the money shock. Note that the vertical scales are adjusted to the simulated variations so that similar movements may be for much different magnitudes. Examining first the results for the United States, we note that nominal money (panel a) initially increases by 1% (100 basis points) and then fluctuates between 150 and 75 basis points for the first five years, eventually tailing down to about 50 basis points at the end of the simulation period. The price-level effect builds up gradually, reaching 1% some three and a half years after the initial shock and peaking at almost 140 basis points some three years after that. There is a transitory increase in real output (peaking at 160 basis points in the fourth quarter) which is all but eliminated after seven quarters and even turns negative later as money persistently falls.[12] The interest rate displays a small, brief liquidity effect, but this is quickly dominated by income and expectations effects.[13] Imports (not displayed here) do rise slightly initially, but the trivial export variation in panel e of figure 7.1 suggests that feedback from foreign effects is negligible for the United States. Aside from oscillations, the balance-of-payments behavior is also consistent with standard lore at least initially when deficits dominate; the small (0 to 3 basis points) surpluses later can be rationalized by declining nominal money.[14]

Figure 7.1 also displays the results of the same experiment for the United Kingdom, Canada, Germany, and the Netherlands.[15] Looking again at panel a, only for Germany do we see a large initial increase in nominal money suggested by the classical presentations of the monetary approach to the balance of payments, and this percentage increase is less than a third of that in the reserve country. The Netherlands displays a

12. The negative real income in the latter part of the adjustment is thus a result (artifact?) of basing expected nominal money on a univariate expectations function rather than full rational expectations.

13. The oscillations in the indicated adjustment process would appear to be spurious.

14. These oscillations apparently reflect the interaction of the expected depreciation and capital-flows equations.

15. The simulation results for France, Japan, and Italy were so erratic as to be inexplicable. The peculiar estimated coefficients—which we attribute to severe data problems for these countries—appear to be the problem. See chapter 6.

more gradual adjustment of nominal money while Canadian money never rises significantly and British money rises only after five years.[16] Thus Germany provides the sole example in panel f of the sharp initial balance-of-payments surplus due to capital flows so much emphasized in the recent literature. Considering the other variables for Germany alone, we see an attenuated version of the U.S. pattern aside from the absence of an initial liquidity effect on the interest rate. In the Netherlands, the induced increase in exports is initially important for both real income and the interest rate, with both money and prices rising more gradually. This pattern seems consistent with a Humean specie-flow process in which monetary transmission is more gradual and there are significant short-run effects on trade flows through both absorption (real income) and relative price channels. For the United Kingdom and Canada, however, there is no sign of monetary transmission—unless the U.K. increase after four years is taken seriously. There is evidence of real income (and for the United Kingdom interest rate) effects, but these seem to derive from absorption-type effects of increases in exports. The Canadian price level even falls slightly at first due to income effects increasing the real quantity of money demanded.

Summing up, under pegged exchange rates the simulation results vary from the monetary approach paradigm (Germany), through the Humean lagged monetary adjustment paradigm (Netherlands), to the simple Keynesian absorption in which prices and interest rates are irrelevant (the United Kingdom and Canada). Clearly the results are partially puzzling whatever view of transmission one might hold. The construction of the Mark III Model had attempted to allow the data to determine which transmission patterns are important; at least that attempt appears to have been successful.

The floating-period results summarized in figure 7.2 are problematical in that the initial effect (if any) of the U.S. money-supply increase is to depreciate the foreign currencies.[17] This result may reflect a structural problem in the Mark IV Model. Only in the import supply equation were strong, consistent exchange-rate effects obtained in the pegged period. This equation was solved for the logarithmic change in the exchange rate in the floating period. (An intervention equation was also added to explain the balance of payments.) In initial unconstrained estimates for the floating period, the logarithmic change in import prices entered with a coefficient of between 0.3 and 0.5 while the change in the dollar-denominated rest-of-world price index entered with coefficients of -1.5 to -3. In theory, these coefficients should be of equal magnitude and

16. The initial decline in British money is due to the perverse (negative) balance-of-payments coefficients.

17. The exchange rates are measured in domestic currency units per dollar, so an increase is a depreciation of the domestic currency.

X 10^{-2}

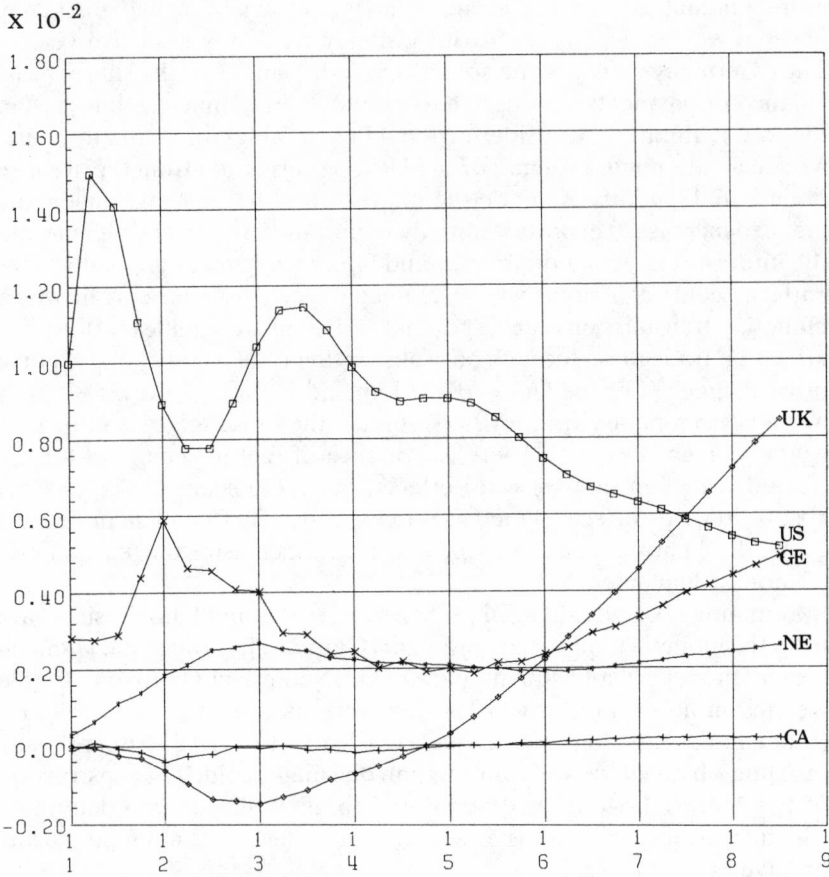

Fig. 7.1   Deviations of key variables from base simulation, American money-shock experiment, pegged period.

a) Nominal money—log M_i

X 10^{-2}

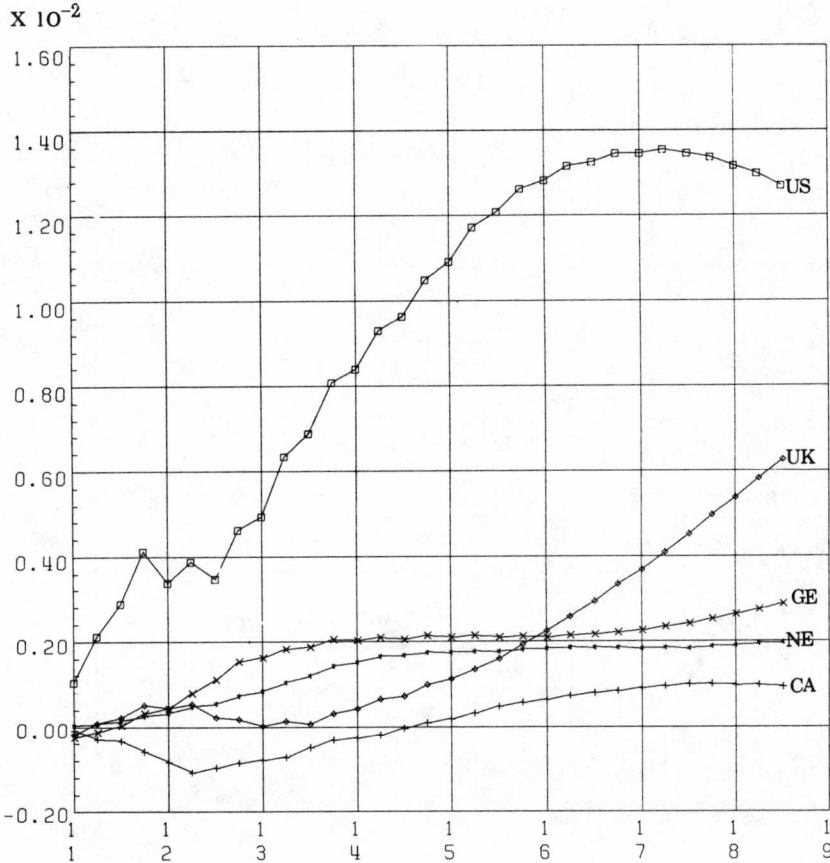

Fig. 7.1 (continued)

   b) Price level—log P_i

X 10^{-2}

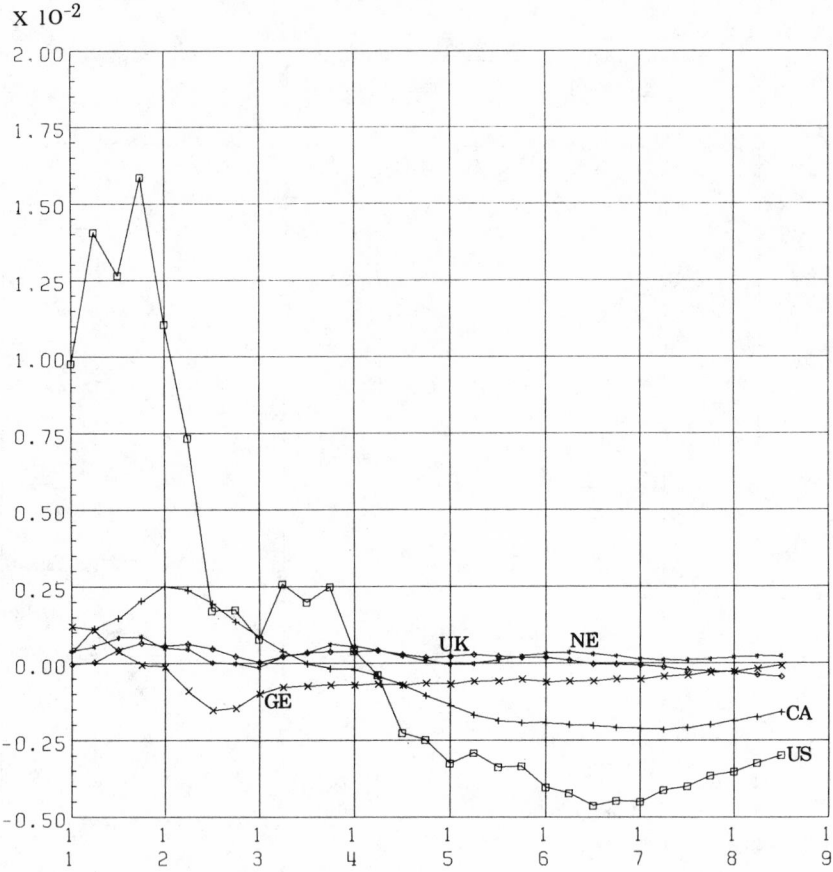

Fig. 7.1 (continued)

c) Real income—log y_i

X 10^{-3}

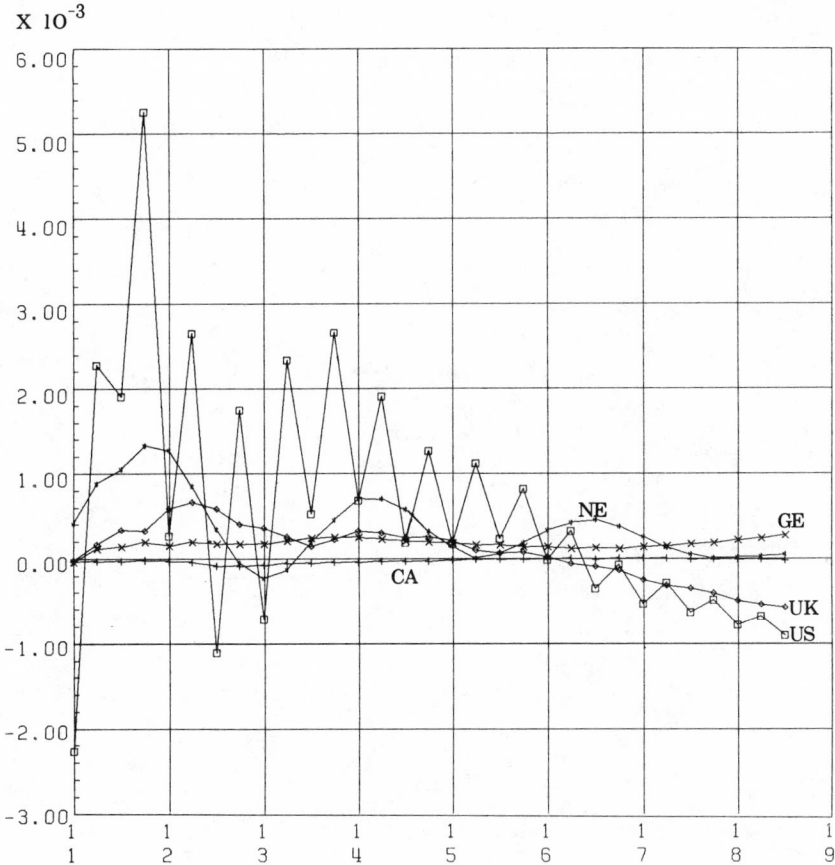

Fig. 7.1 (continued)

d) Short-term interest rate—R_i

X 10^{-3}

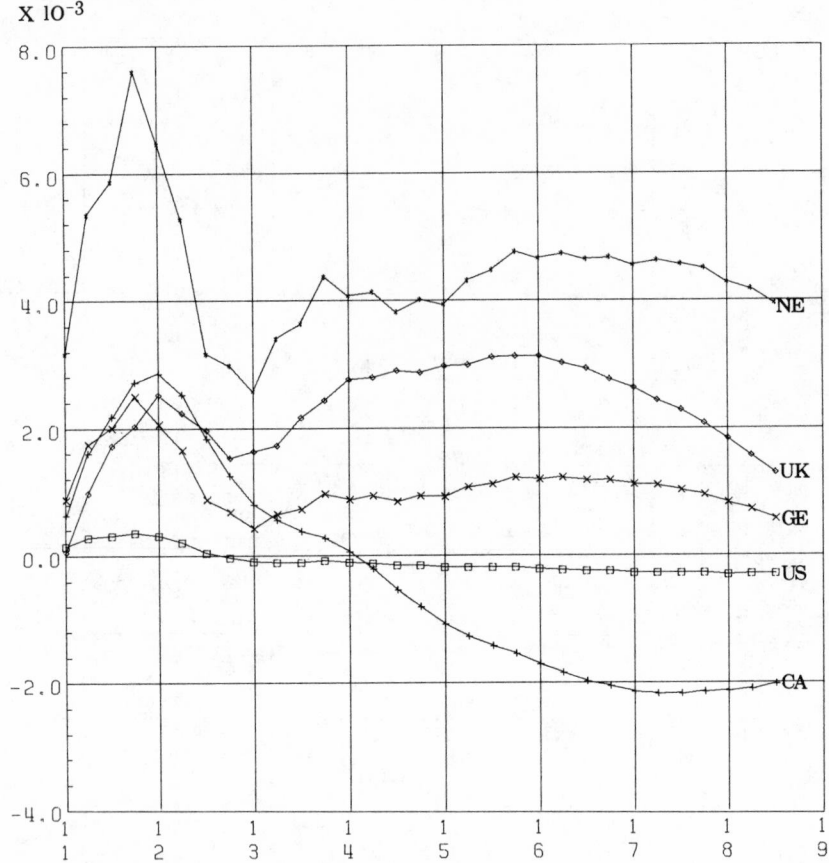

Fig. 7.1 (continued)

  e) Scaled exports—$(X/Y)_i$

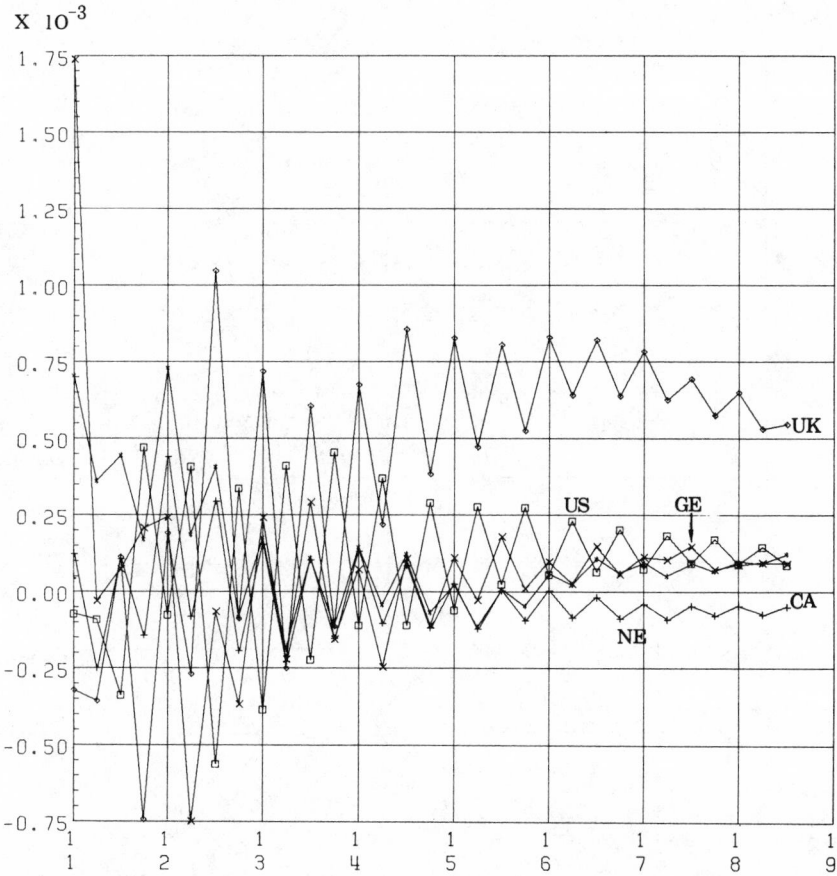

Fig. 7.1 (continued)

f) Scaled balance of payments—$(B/Y)_i$

X 10^{-2}

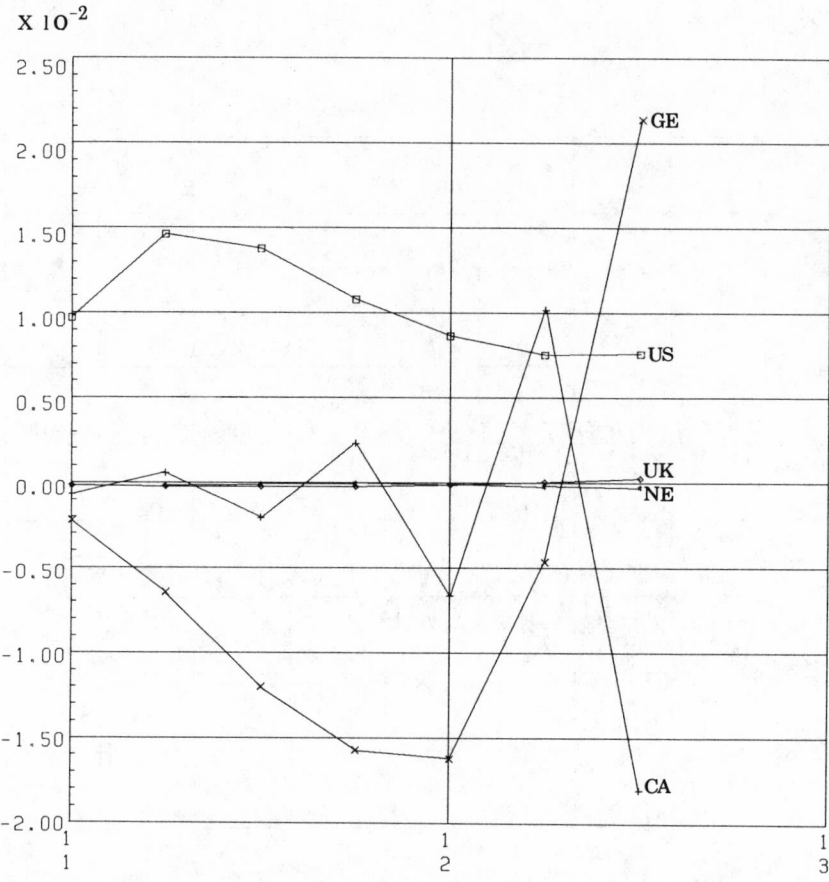

Fig. 7.2   Deviations of key variables from base simulation, American money-shock experiment, floating period.

a) Nominal money—log M_i

X 10^{-2}

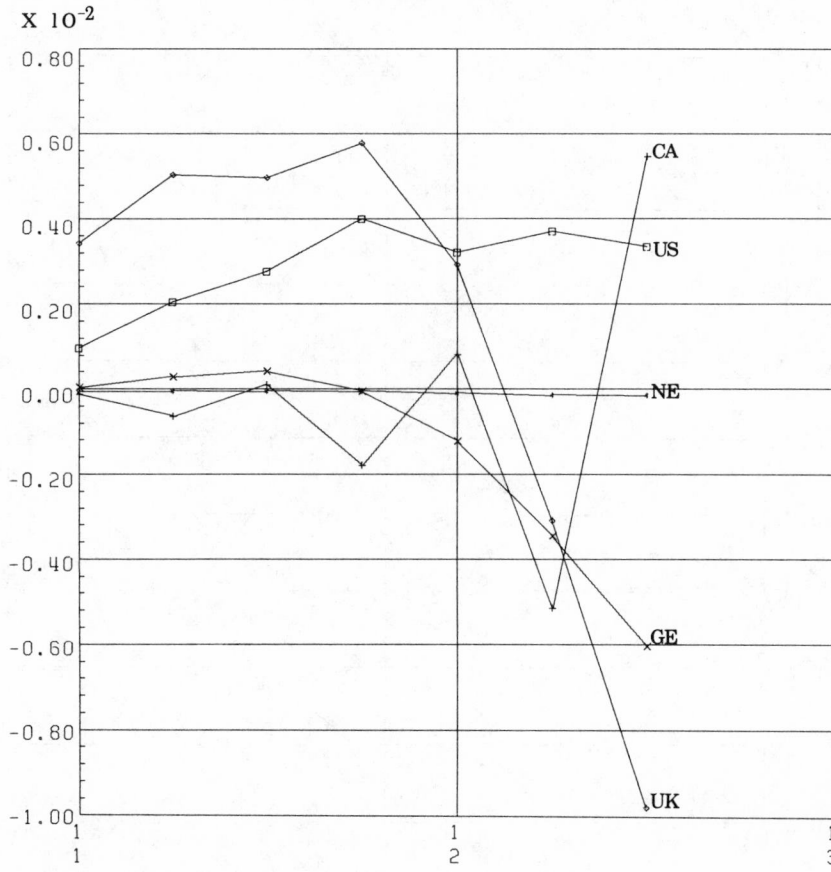

Fig. 7.2 (continued)

        b) Price level—log P_i

X 10^{-2}

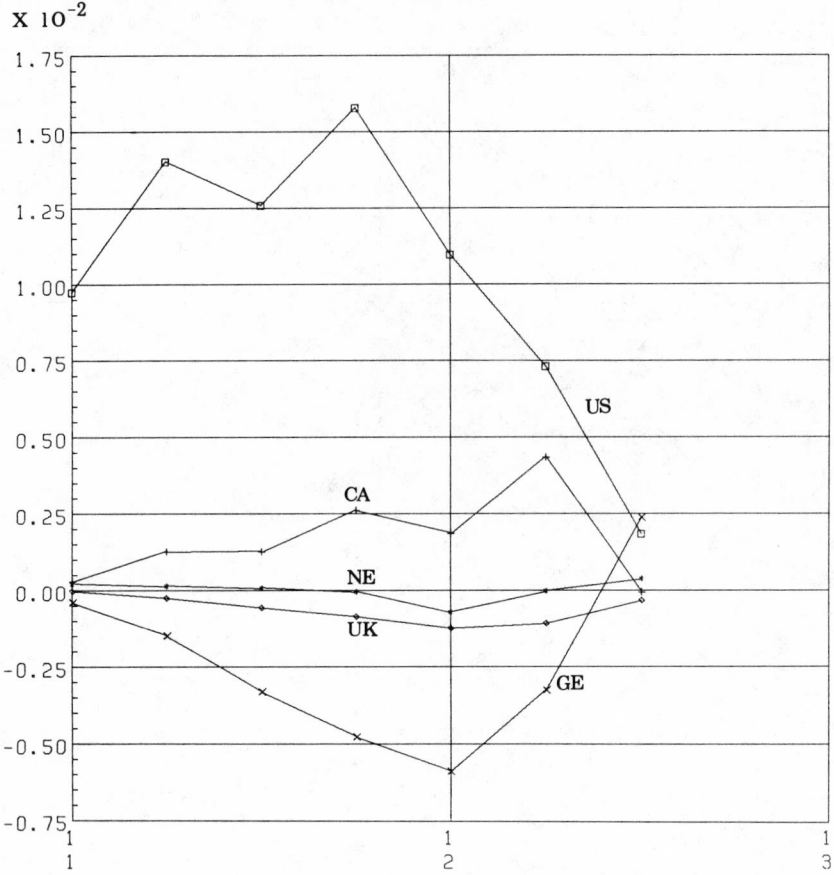

Fig. 7.2 (continued)

c) Real income—log y_i

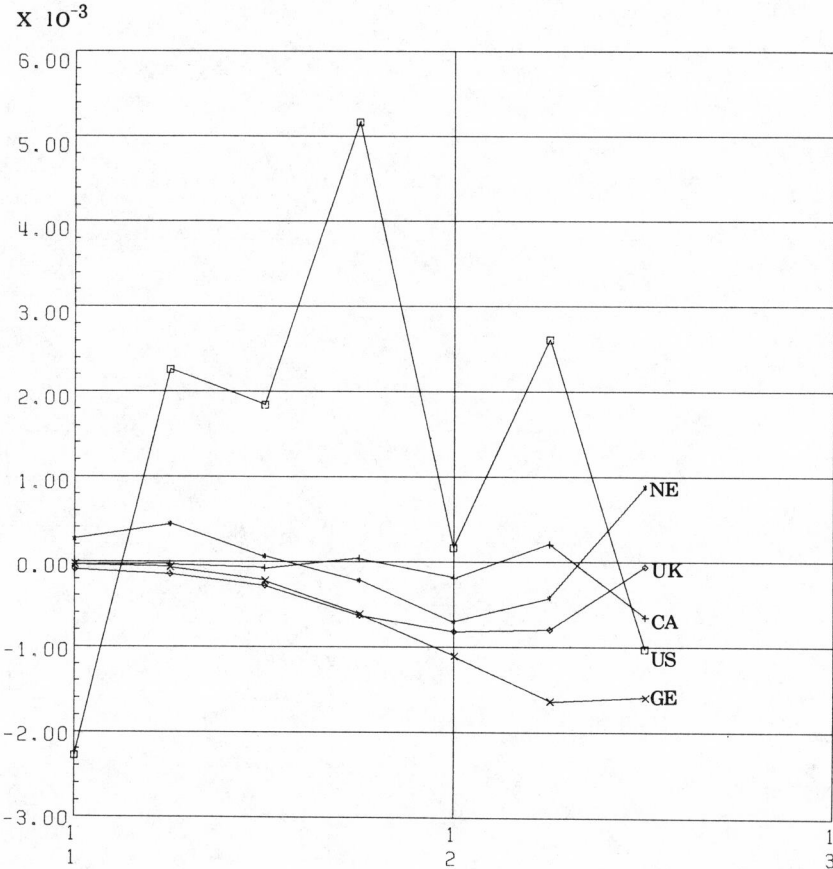

Fig. 7.2 (continued)

d) Short-term interest rate—R_i

X 10^{-2}

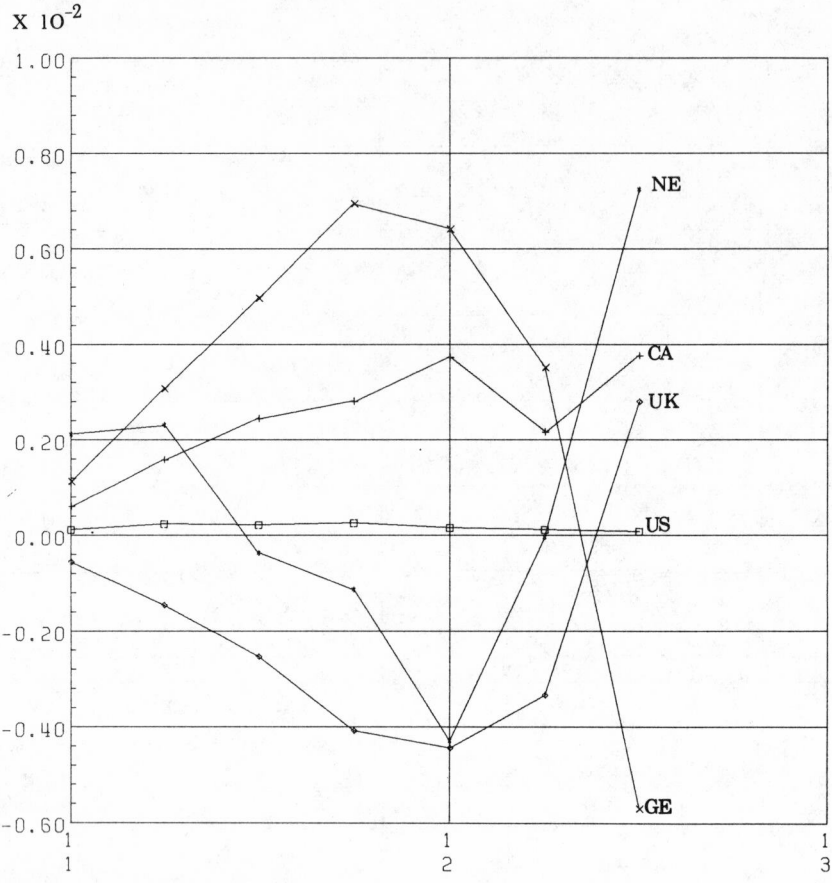

Fig. 7.2 (continued)

     e) Scaled exports—$(X/Y)_i$

X 10^{-2}

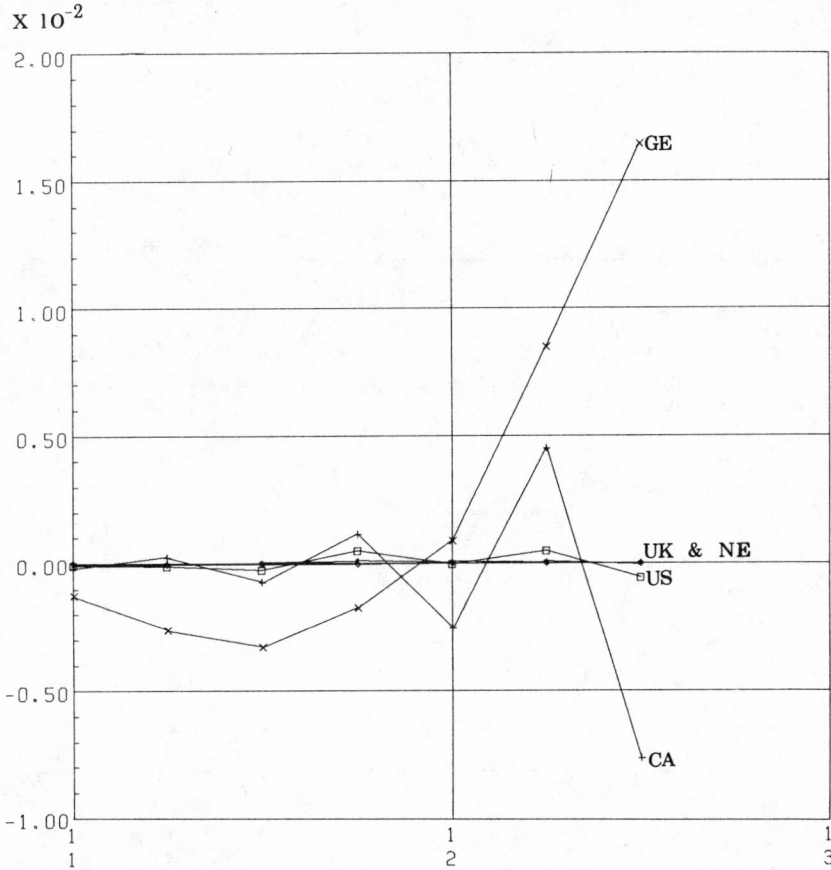

Fig. 7.2 (continued)

f) Scaled balance of payments—$(B/Y)_i$

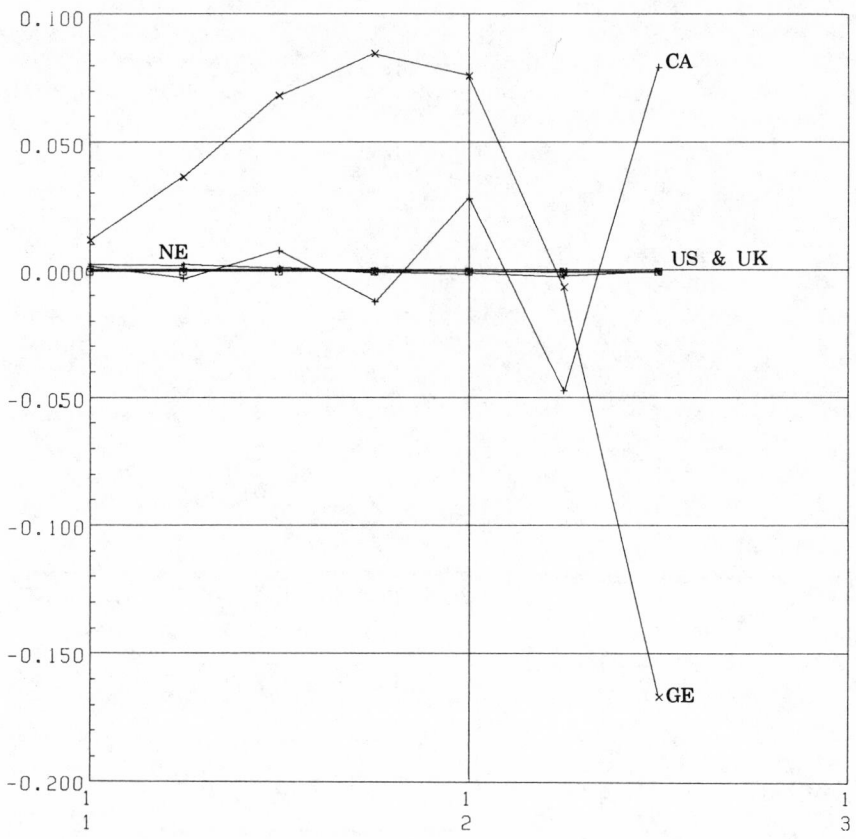

Fig. 7.2 (continued)

g) Exchange rate—log E_i

opposite sign; this theory is consistent with the pegged period estimates. Unfortunately the floating period estimates appear to be dominated by common movements in exchange rates against the dollar. Simulations using the unconstrained, inconsistent coefficients resulted not only in greater dynamic instability in the base simulations but also in nearly universal initial exchange-rate appreciations of 2% which grew much larger over time with no corresponding movements in interest rates or price levels in the experiment at hand. For this reason, the constraint of a single coefficient on the logarithmic change in the ratio of import to rest-of-world prices was imposed. When the constraint is imposed, however, the surprising initial depreciation results. These results are reported since, as explained immediately below, some sense can be made of them and they do illustrate the potentially perverse effects of a J-curve phenomenon.

First, note that the simulated effects within the United States are nearly identical to those for the first seven quarters of the pegged experiment so that discussion need not be repeated here. Given an initial exchange-rate depreciation, the German monetary authorities intervene to support the mark and the money supply falls. Prices and income follow the monetary movements. The initial movement in the German exchange rate occurs in the simulation because of an estimated J-curve pattern in the import demand (relative-price-of-imports) equation. Since exports rise with the rise in U.S. income and capital outflows fall with the fall in the U.S. interest rate, imports plus the balance-of-payments surplus has to rise given the identity. The balance of payments (intervention) is not very responsive under floating rates, so the dominant movement is an increase in the value of imports. Since the demand curve is somewhat inelastic in the short run, the increase in value requires a substantial increase in the domestic-currency price of imports. The more rapid growth in import prices than dollar-denominated rest-of-world prices leads to a higher (depreciated) exchange rate.

The other countries display less exaggerated simulated effects than does Germany: For the Netherlands all the effects are trivial except for the export effect, and that is much smaller than in the pegged case. The exchange rate initially depreciates and then appreciates, but the range of movement is from 2 to −5 basis points. The United Kingdom displays few effects other than those associated with a perverse decrease in exports. For Canada instability is so severe as to preclude any characterization.

In contrast to the Mark IV–PEG, the Mark IV–FLT Model appears to be so unstable as to provide little information about the international transmission of shocks under floating exchange rates. The main fruit of this exercise appears to be identification of the perverse results which might occur if a J-curve pehnomenon is present in import demand.

Further development of the Mark IV–FLT Model must await extension of the data bank to cover a longer floating period.

7.3 Other Experiments

The implications of the Mark IV–PEG model were further explored in five additional experiments. Two of these compare the effects under pegged exchange rates of one-quarter money shocks (as described in section 7.2) in Germany and the United Kingdom. The other three involve a one-quarter increase of 0.01 (1% of government spending) in the government spending shock in the United States, Germany, and the United Kingdom, respectively.

The domestic effects of the German and British money-shock experiments are contrasted in figure 7.3. Examining first the German case, we see that nominal money is in fact increased by almost 1% throughout the first year. The initial increase is less than the amount of the shock to the money-supply reaction function because of the partially offsetting effects of the induced balance-of-payments deficit (see panel f). Nonetheless, a remarkably high degree of monetary control is exhibited and the deficits are never large: Nominal money does not start falling until after the first year (largely as a result of the induced increases in inflation and real income) and even after two years a 75 basis point increase in nominal money remains; it takes some four years for the initial increase in the nominal money supply to drop to 20 basis points. The real income, price level, and export effects are predictable given the movements in the nominal money supply. But unlike the United States, no noticeable transmission to any other countries is detected in the simulations (or graphed here): None of these six major variables in any of the other four countries in any quarter deviates from the base simulation by as much as 10 basis points, and *peak* effects on the order of 1 basis point or less are the rule.

The simulated effects of the British money-shock experiment are also plotted in figure 7.3. Not only is the one-quarter shock to the British nominal-money growth rate never offset but indeed British nominal money displays a slight tendency to rise further over time. Domestic prices rise and exports fall as a result, but the simulated balance-of-payments deficits never become unmanageable. The only remarkable result is the (incredible) negative impact of a money shock on British real income.[18] Again there was no noticeable transmission to other countries (on the 10-basis-point-peak criterion) to report.

These two nonreserve money-shock experiments confirm the impres-

---

18. The negative coefficients on money shocks were not jointly significant in the Mark III Model, but were retained in the reestimation of the Mark IV Model so that this channel was not foreclosed.

sion gained from the U.S. money-shock experiment: The German monetary authorities displayed the tendencies suggested by the monetary approach, although those tendencies are attenuated in magnitude and here slow in effect. For Britain, in contrast, monetary transmission appears to be essentially nil, with policy conducted as if the United Kingdom were a closed economy.

The next set of experiments involves one-quarter increases of 100 basis points in unexpected real government spending. This sort of government-spending shift is consistent with the policy regime for which the model was estimated. However, the implications of this shock for the actual level of real government spending differ according to the actual process observed to govern the evolution of real government spending in each country. Because the logarithm of U.S. real government spending appears to follow a random walk with drift, the 100 basis point increase in real government spending is implicitly a permanent one. The corresponding German variable follows a first-order moving average process, which implies that the level of real government spending is increased by 100 basis points in the initial quarter but by only 25 basis points thereafter. For the United Kingdom the pattern is more complicated due to a second-order autoregressive process, but the effect on the level of real government spending is very nearly approximated by an initial 100 basis point increase and a 57 basis point increase thereafter.[19]

The domestic results of these three experiments are summarized in figure 7.4. The peak effect on U.S. real income is about 27 basis points. Given that real government expenditures average about one-sixth of real income, this implies a peak multiplier of about 1.5. Although on the high end of recent estimates of the bond-financed government-spending multiplier, a value of 1.5 is not surprising since it reflects as well reinforcing effects of a small, lagged induced increase in nominal money. Since the simulated effect of real income in increasing money demand initially dominates interest-rate effects and the small nominal money increase, the price level first falls and then rises as the real income effects die out. As might be supposed from the small size of the home country effects, simulated transmission to other countries is too small to merit discussion.[20]

19. To be precise, the implied increase in U.K. real government spending compared to the base run for the first nine quarters is 100, 56, 44, 63, 59, 55, 58, 58, and 57 basis points, respectively.

20. It is not strictly true that there are no effects greater than 10 basis points, however. As would be inferred from the previous money-shock experiment, a sympathetic variation in German nominal money was simulated, peaking at 12 basis points after two years. Also, British nominal money drifted down passing -10 basis points after four and one-half years and troughing at -19 basis points during the seventh year. An induced decline in the British price level to -14 basis points after seven years completes the list of exceptions to the 10 basis point criterion.

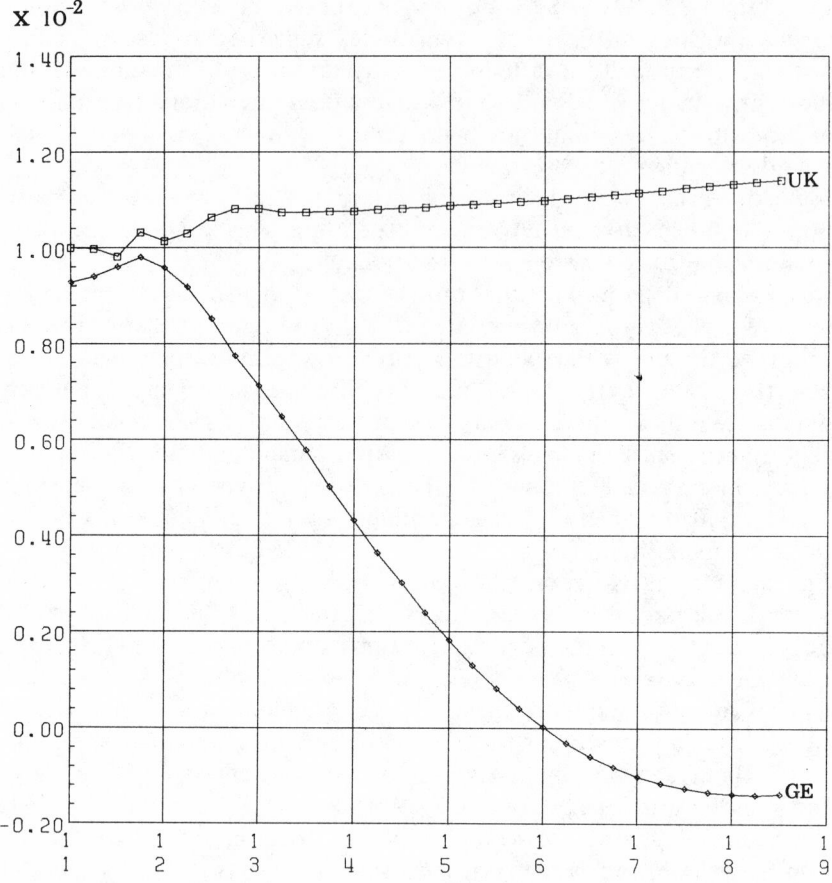

Fig. 7.3   Deviations of key domestic variables from base simulation, British and German money-shock experiments, pegged period.

a) Nominal money—log M_i

X 10^{-2}

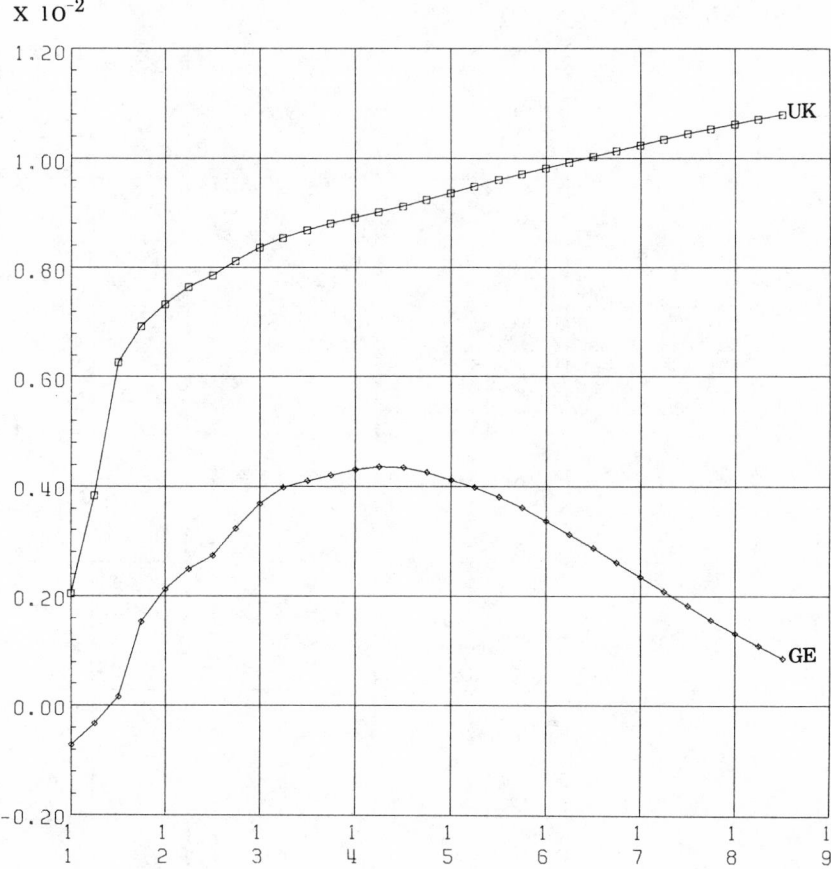

Fig. 7.3 (continued)

> *b*) Price level—log P_i

X 10^{-3}

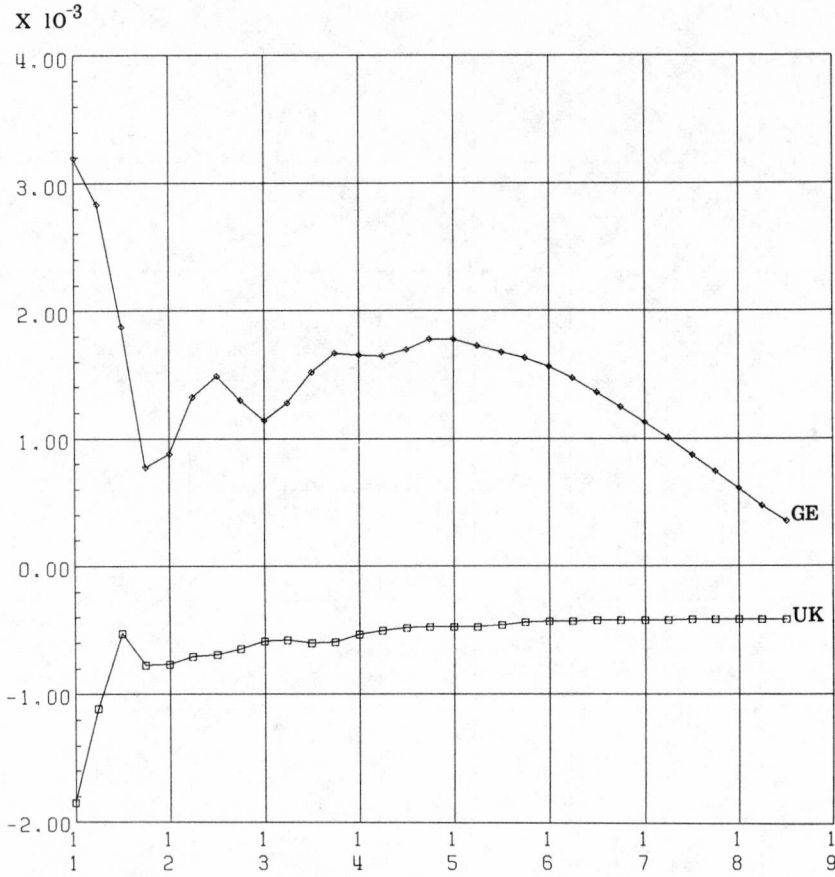

Fig. 7.3 (continued)

c) Real income—log y_i

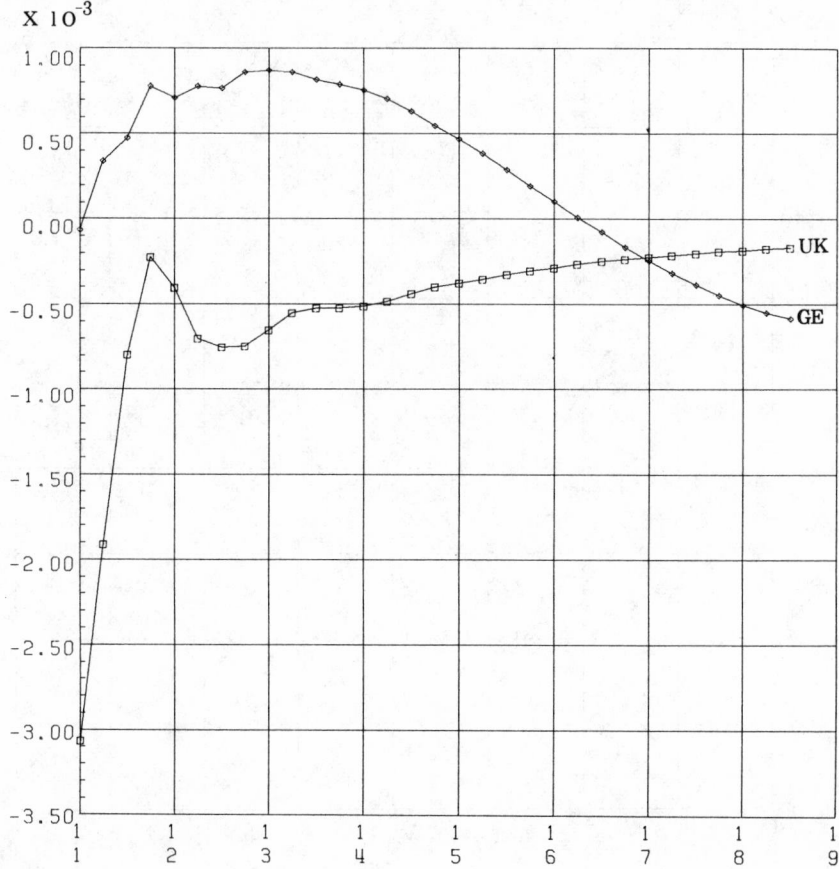

Fig. 7.3 (continued)

d) Short-term interest rate—R_i

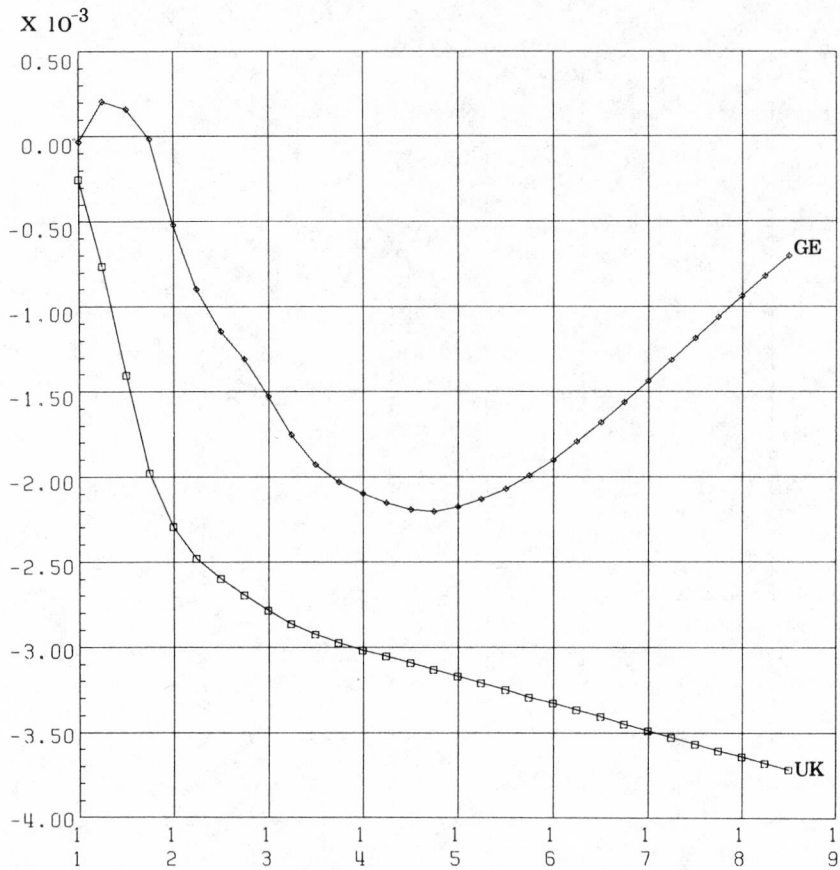

Fig. 7.3 (continued)

e) Scaled exports—$(X/Y)_i$

X 10^{-4}

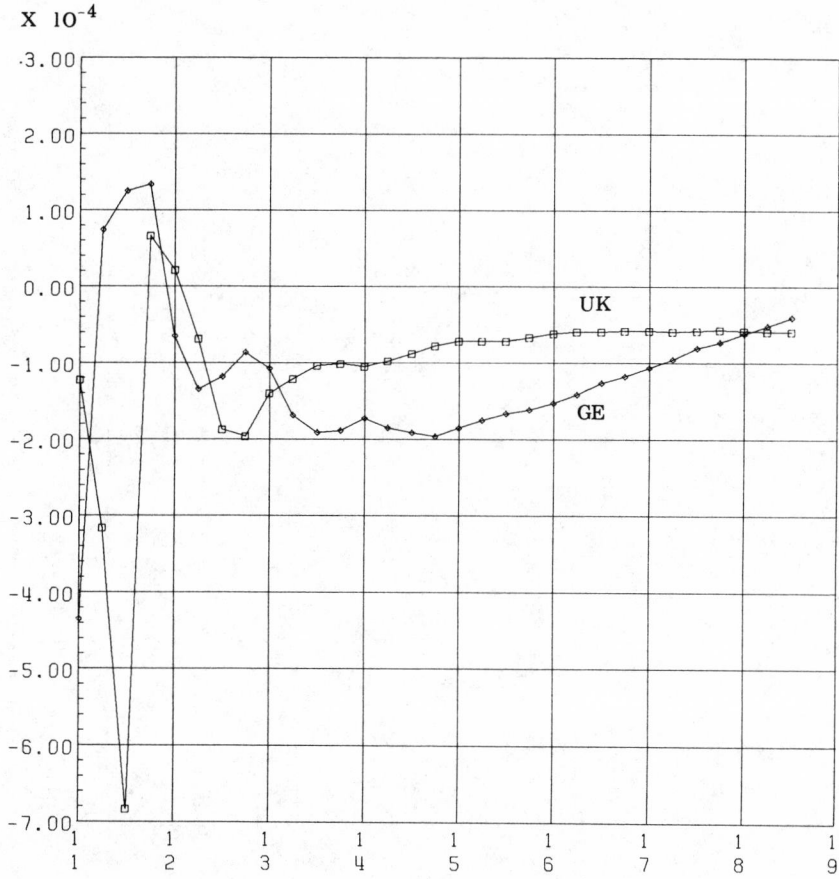

Fig. 7.3 (continued)

f) Scaled balance of payments—$(B/Y)_i$

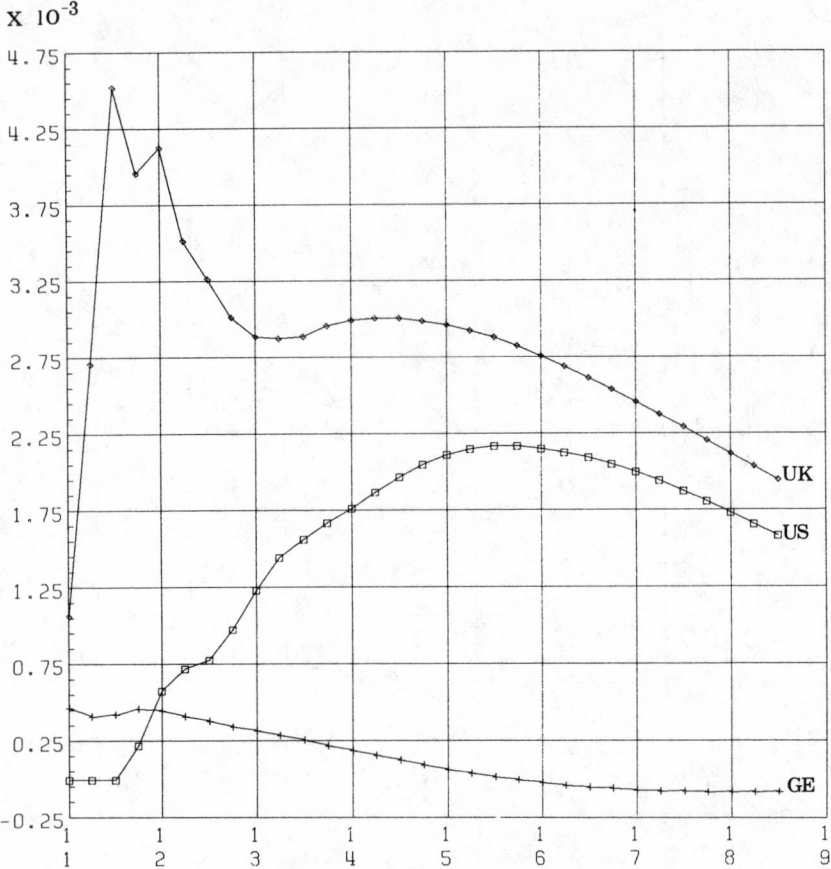

Fig. 7.4   Deviations of key domestic variables from base simulation, American, British, and German government-spending-shock experiments, pegged period.

a) Nominal money—log M_i

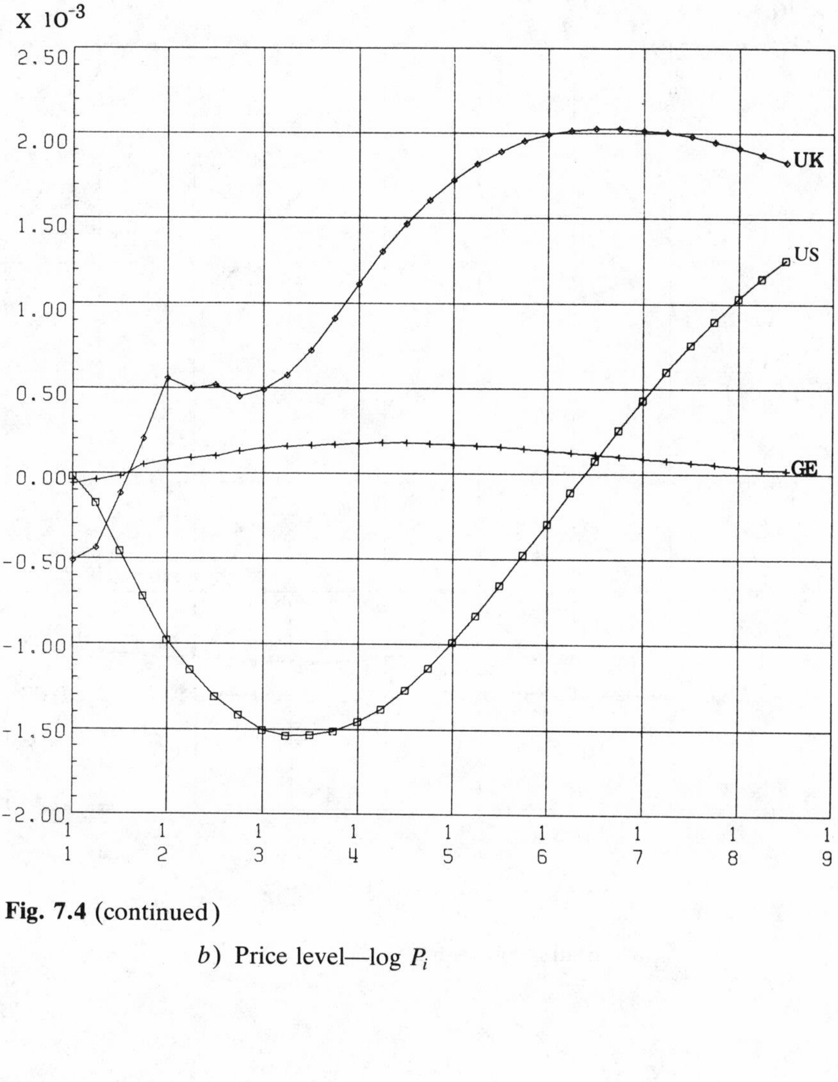

X 10^{-3}

Fig. 7.4 (continued)

b) Price level—log P_i

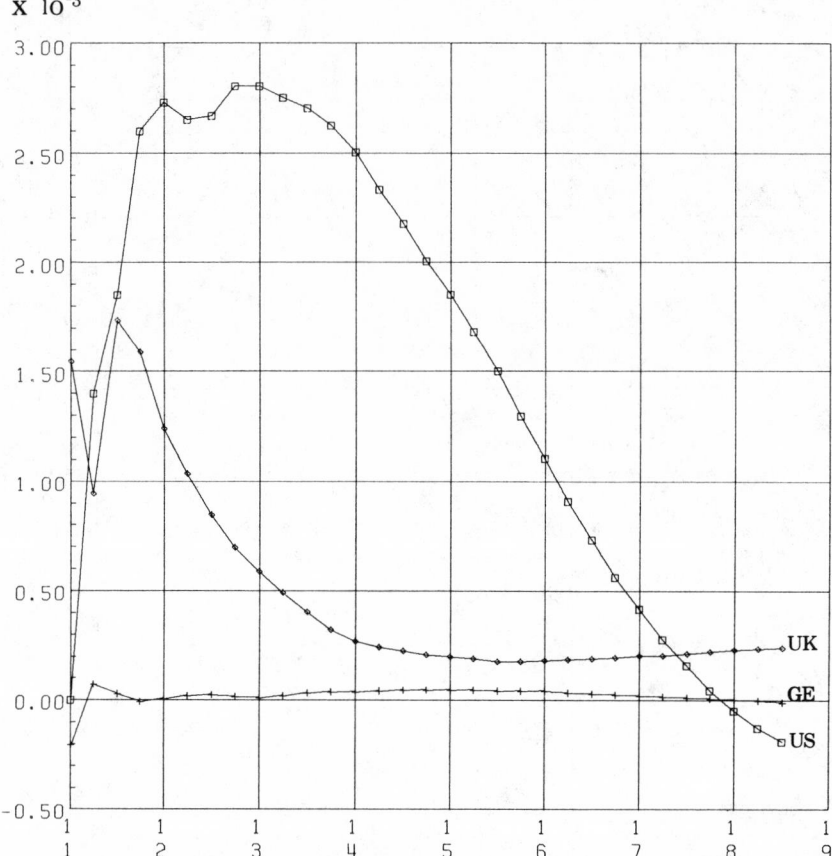

Fig. 7.4 (continued)

c) Real income—log y_i

X 10⁻³

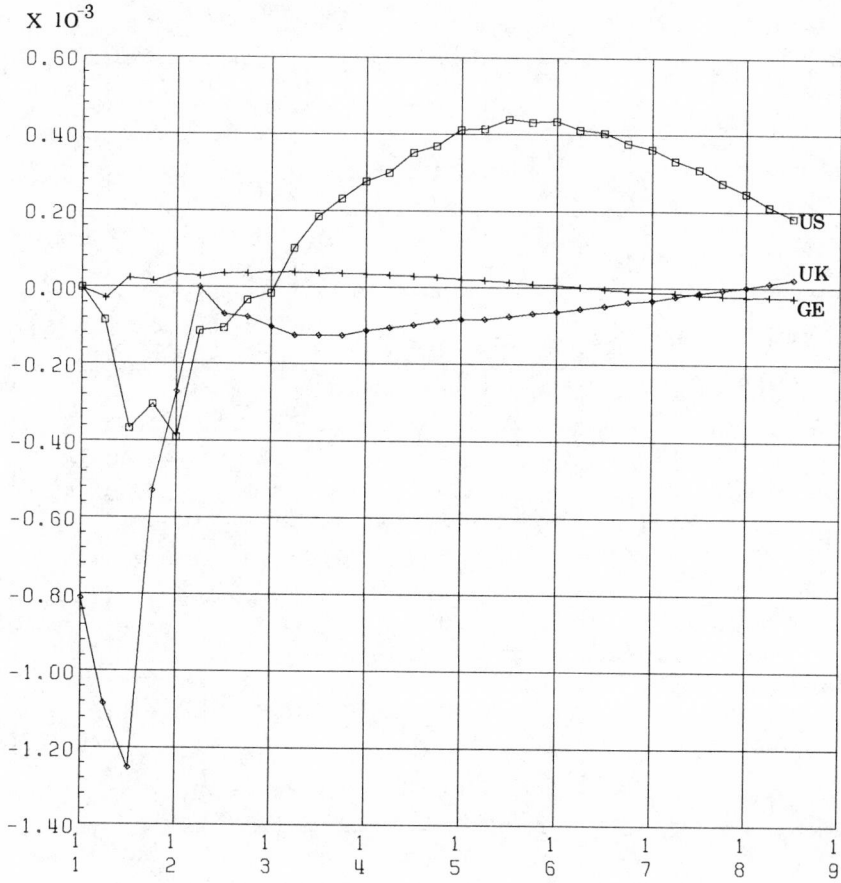

Fig. 7.4 (continued)

d) Short-term interest rate—R_i

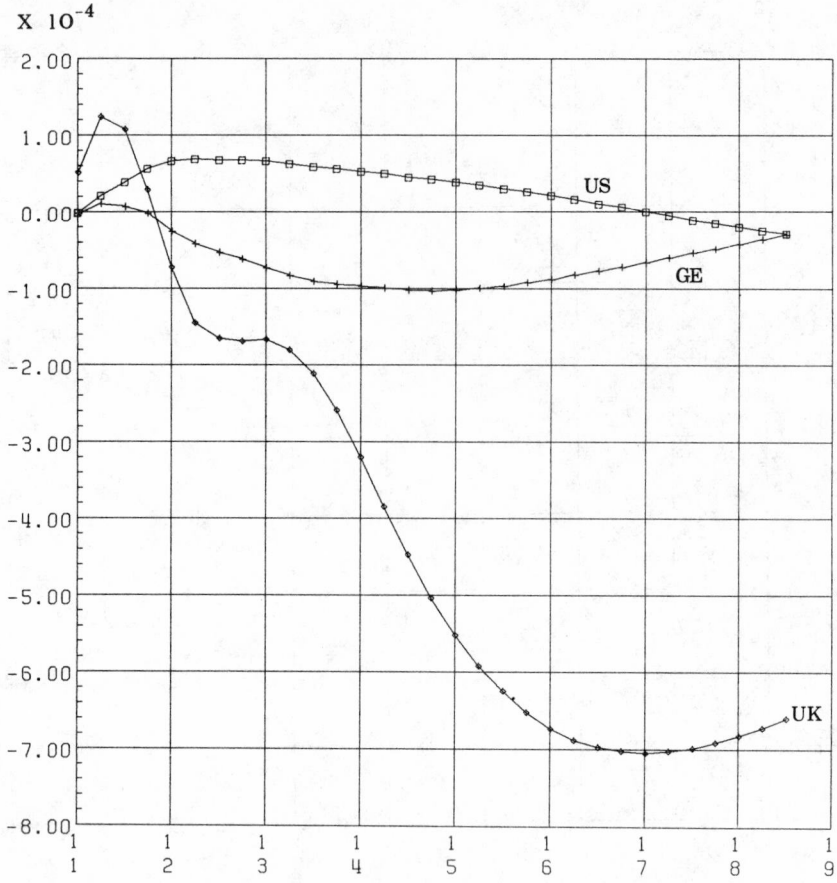

Fig. 7.4 (continued)

e) Scaled exports—$(X/Y)_i$

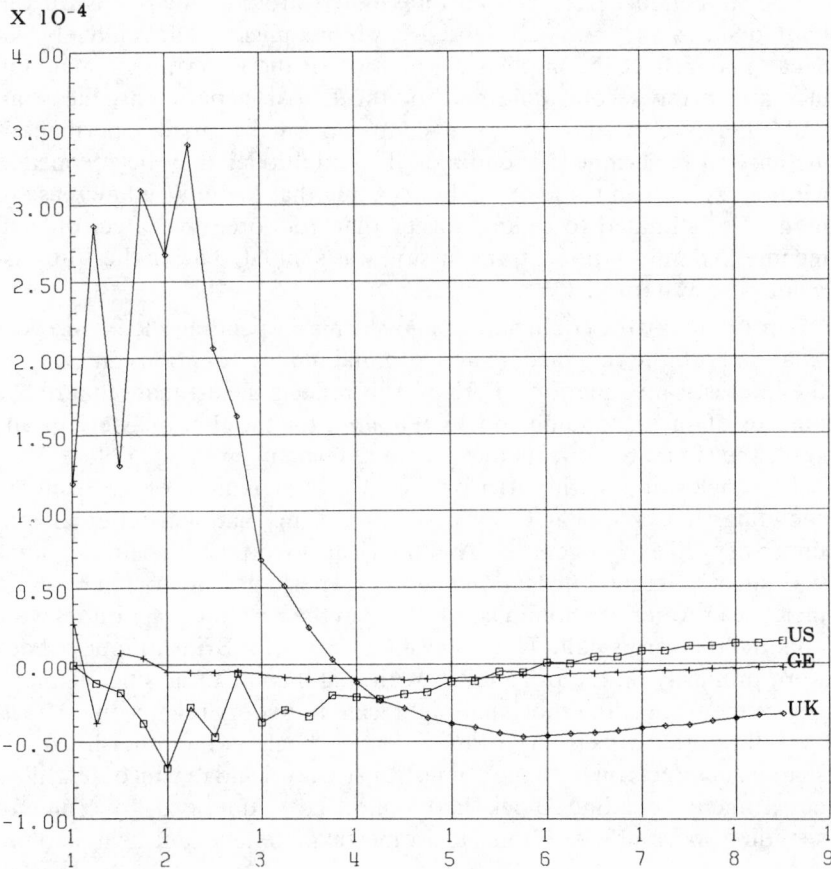

Fig. 7.4 (continued)

f) Scaled balance of payments—$(B/Y)_i$

The simulated British real income effects are not as large as for the United States, but both occur and decay more quickly. The relatively fast decay may reflect the implicit elimination of the government spending increase in the second quarter. For the British experiment, the peak multiplier is only about 0.75, even based on the smaller permanent increase in government spending.[21] This multiplier may be reconciled with the American value of 1.5 by recalling that the induced increase in money is estimated to reduce rather than reinforce the effect on real income. No international transmission was simulated using the 10-basis-point-peak criterion.

For Germany the coefficients of government spending shocks are very small in both the real income and nominal money equations and zero in the interest-rate equations. Perhaps this reflects the estimate that only a quarter of such spending shocks remain after the first quarter. In any case, the simulated effects even within Germany are negligible.

In conclusion, neither British nor German money or government spending shocks appear to have significant international repercussions under pegged exchange rates. An American government-spending shock had slightly larger international effects—perhaps due to the induced increase in American nominal money—but the absolute magnitudes were nonetheless very small. The domestic effects of a British money shock were primarily on the price level, with real income effects negligible; a government spending shock had significant transitory real income effects as well as price effects. A German money shock on the other hand had significant effects on both the domestic price level and real income while a government spending shock had none. The American government-spending shock affected both the domestic price level and real income.

7.4   Conclusion and Implications for Future Research

Simulation experiments help us to understand the workings of a large model in which the simultaneous and dynamic relations are too complicated to consider analytically. The results of the experiments tell us something about how the world would operate for a given model specification and coefficient values which are not inconsistent with a set of data. The results may tell us something about the way the world works, but they surely tell us more about just what simplifications in our *simple* models may lead to erroneous results.

Consider, for example, standard models in which an increased domestic money supply leads to lower domestic relative to foreign interest rates and a resulting adjustment process. This implicitly assumes that the

---

21. That is, the 100 basis point increase in government spending is implicitly a 57 basis point permanent increase. Government spending averages about 40% of total income in Britain, so this increase is .4 × 57, or 0.228%, of real income.

liquidity effect dominates any inflationary expectations effect on interest rates during the relevant adjustment period. With relatively weak liquidity effects and strong expectations effects as estimated here, the transmission and adjustment process does not follow standard lines.[22]

The simulations confirm the apparent implications of the Mark III estimates: International transmission of inflation through money flows is a weak and slow process even under pegged exchange rates, with nonreserve countries exercising considerable short-run control over their money supplies. Of the four nonreserve countries examined, only Germany appeared to quickly—if partially—adjust its money supply to a U.S. monetary shock while for the United Kingdom and Canada the only simulated transmission was via absorption effects. Further, when a German monetary supply shock was simulated, overwhelming balance-of-payments flows were not simulated so that substantial money, real income, and price effects were observed. These simulations certainly do not disprove the usefulness of the monetary approach to the balance of payments in the short run, but they do contribute to a growing body of literature which raises questions about its short-run usefulness.

The floating results were too unstable to be of much use. At best they suggest that the implications of short-run inelasticity of import demand (*J*-curves) should be investigated further. If the world, like the Mark IV Model, is characterized by imperfect international substitutability among goods and assets, *J*-curves may play a significant role in the adjustment and transmission process.

The nonreserve money-shock experiments revealed no significant international transmission under either pegged or floating rates. Some monetary approach writers[23] have argued that an increase in these countries' domestic credit would result in a generalized increase in the world money supply, but this is incorrect for a system such as Bretton Woods tied to a fiat reserve currency with reserves being dollar-denominated bonds.[24] Since monetary transmission is nil under either pegged or floating rates, only the very small increase in world export demand is operative and this is trivial in magnitude for a money shock in any one of these nonreserve countries.

The government spending shocks were generally too weak in their domestic effects to have any appreciable impact abroad. The largest

22. Dan Lee demonstrates in chapter 12 below that Dornbusch's (1976) famous overshooting result for floating exchange rates follows from allowing participants in the financial markets to have rational expectations with respect to exchange rates but not prices: Recall that Dornbusch argued that lower home interest rates after a money-shock increase must be balanced by (rational) expectations of an appreciating currency and this implies an initial overdepreciation. If the interest rate instead rises with (rational) inflationary expectations, then expectations of depreciation are appropriate and the overshooting argument falls.

23. See, for example, Swoboda (1976), Meiselman and Laffer (1975), and Parkin and Zis (1976a, b).

24. This point is developed at length in Darby (1980) and chapter 16.

simulated effect was in the United States, with a peak government spending multiplier of about 1.5 *inclusive* of the reinforcing effects of an induced nominal money increase. However, the initial 1% increase in real government spending is implicitly permanent in the United States, half permanent in the United Kingdom, and one-quarter permanent in Germany.

In conclusion, the simulation results suggest a great deal of national economic independence under pegged and—by implication—floating exchange rates. These results, although surprising, are consistent with the evidence reported elsewhere in this volume. A first order for research in international macroeconomics is to explain why the data fail to disclose the strong transmission channels we customarily assume.

Acknowledgments

The good counsel of Arthur Gandolfi, Dan Lee, James Lothian, and Michael Melvin made this paper possible, but they are not to be implicated in the results. Other valuable comments were received from Anthony Cassese, Robert P. Flood, Jr., and especially Anna J. Schwartz and participants in the UCLA Money Workshop and the NBER Summer Institute. The calculations were performed by Michael Melvin and Andrew Vogel on the TROLL system at MIT. An earlier version of this paper is to be found in Bhandari and Putnam (1982).

Appendix
The Mark IV International Transmission Simulation Model

This appendix lists the Mark IV Model. Table 7.2 defines the variables used. Table 7.3 lists the Mark IV–PEG used for simulations in the pegged period. Table 7.4 lists the Mark IV–FLT used for simulations in the floating period. Note that the "Coefficient and Parameter Values" at the ends of tables 7.3 and 7.4 contain a number of extraneous coefficients which are irrelevant to the Mark IV Model. The model is resident in the TROLL system at MIT. The Mark IV is a simplified version of the Mark III Model described in chapters 5 and 6.

A few notes on TROLL's modeling language are in order: An asterisk indicates multiplication. A negative number in parentheses immediately following a variable denotes that the variable is lagged that many quarters: $X(-1) \equiv X_{-1}$. The first difference operator is $DEL(1: X) \equiv X - X(-1)$. Double equal signs (= =) are used for identities with the exception of permanent income identities.

Table 7.2   **Definitions of Variables and Parameters in the Mark IV Model**

Country mnemonics are indicated in the listing below by double asterisks (**). The mnemonics are:

CA	Canada	JA	Japan
FR	France	NE	Netherlands
GE	Germany	UK	United Kingdom
IT	Italy	US	United States

BTOY**	Balance of payments divided by GNP (or GDP if GNP is unavailable.) The balance of payments is on the official reserve settlements basis.
CTOY**	Net capital outflows as a fraction of GNP (measured as CTOY** = XTOY** − ITOY** − BTOY**).
DMY611 DMY674 DMY693	Revaluation dummies with 0 everywhere except 1961I, 1967IV, or 1969III, respectively.
DV**	Nominal income weight; share of country ** in total sample nominal income.
ER**1L ER**2L	Error terms for ARIMA process of exchange-rate expectation formation as defined in model.
GRE**X11 GRE**X21	Expected annualized growth rate of the exchange rate from present quarter to next quarter.
GRPX1**1 GRPX1**2	Expected annualized growth rate of the price level from present quarter to next quarter.
ITOY**	Imports as a fraction of GNP.
LNE**	Logarithm of the exchange rate measured in domestic currency units (DCUs) per U.S. dollar (LNEUS ≡ 1).
LNG**U	Innovation in the logarithm of real government spending based on a univariate ARIMA process.
LNM**U	Innovation in money; LNMN** − LNMN**EX.
LNMN**	Logarithm of money stock measured in billions of DCUs.
LNMN**EX	Expected value of LNMN** based on a univariate ARIMA process.
LNP**	Logarithm of the price deflator for GNP (or GDP). These deflators are measured in DCUs per 1970 DCU; so LNP** = 0 for 1970.
LNPIM**	Logarithm of import price index (LNPIM** = 0 for 1970).
LNPR**	Logarithm of an index of foreign prices converted by exchange rates into U.S. dollars per 1970 U.S. dollar (LNPR** = 0 for 1970).
LNQIM**	Logarithm of relative price of imports; LNPIM** − LNP**.
LNRPOIL	Logarithm of an index the real price of oil based on deflating the dollar price of Venezuelan oil by the U.S. deflator. (LNRPOIL = 0 for 1970).
LNYR**	Logarithm of real GNP (or GDP if GNP is unavailable) measured in billions of 1970 DCUs.
LNYR**P	Logarithm of permanent income measured in billions of 1970 DCUs.

Table 7.2 (continued)

LNYRR**	Logarithm of an index of foreign real income (LNYRR** = 0 for 1970).
LNYRT**	Logarithmic transitory income; LNYR** − LNYR**P.
PEGDIF**	Logarithmic difference between actual and parity value of the exchange rate.
R**	Short-term nominal interest rate in decimal per annum form. (Three-months treasury bill yield where available; but a long-term government bond yield had to be used for Italy.)
SGRPX1*1 SGRPX1*2	Variables used to simulate the expected-inflation-rate transfer functions.
T	Time index (1955I = 1, 1955II = 2, etc.).
UN**	Unemployment rate in decimal form.
XP**	Trend quarterly growth rate of real income used in computing logarithmic permanent income.
XTOY**	Exports as a fraction of GNP.
XTOY**EX	Expected value of XTOY** based on a univariate ARIMA process.
XTOY**U	Innovation in scaled exports; XTOY** − XTOY**EX.
Z1**1 Z1**1L Z1**2 Z2**1	Variables used to simulate the expected-inflation-rate transfer functions.
ZP**	Weight of current income in forming logarithmic permanent income (taken as 0.025 in all cases).

Table 7.3   **The Pegged Period Model: Mark IV–PEG**

SYMBOL DECLARATIONS

ENDOGENOUS:
```
BTOYCA  BTOYFR  BTOYGE  BTOYIT  BTOYJA  BTOYNE  BTOYUK  BTOYUS  CTOYCA
CTOYFR  CTOYGE  CTOYIT  CTOYJA  CTOYNE  CTOYUK  CTOYUS  ERCA1L  ERFR1L
ERıTıL  ERJA2L  GRECAX11  GREFRX11  GREGEX21  GREITX11  GREJAX21  GRENEX11
GREUKX11  GRPX1CA1  GRPX1FR1  GRPX1GE1  GRPX1IT1  GRPX1JA2  GRPX1NE1
GRPX1UK1  GRPX1US1  ITOYCA  ITOYFR  ITOYGE  ITOYIT  ITOYJA  ITOYNE  ITOYUK
ITOYUS  LNMCAU  LNMFRU  LNMGEU  LNMITU  LNMJAU  LNMNCA  LNMNCAEX  LNMNEU
LNMNFR  LNMNFREX  LNMNGE  LNMNGEEX  LNMNIT  LNMNITEX  LNMNJA  LNMNJAEX
LNMNNE  LNMNNEEX  LNMNUK  LNMNUKEX  LNMNUS  LNMNUSEX  LNMUKU  LNMUSU  LNPCA
LNPFR  LNPGE  LNPIMCA  LNPIMFR  LNPIMIT  LNPIMJA  LNPIMNE  LNPIMUK  LNPIMUS
LNPIT  LNPJA  LNPNE  LNPRCA  LNPRFR  LNPRGE  LNPRIT  LNPRJA  LNPRNE  LNPRUK
LNPRUS  LNPUK  LNPUS  LNQIMCA  LNQIMFR  LNQIMIT  LNQIMJA  LNQIMNE  LNQIMUK
LNQIMUS  LNYRCA  LNYRCAP  LNYRFR  LNYRFRP  LNYRGE  LNYRGEP  LNYRIT  LNYRITP
LNYRJA  LNYRJAP  LNYRNE  LNYRNEP  LNYRRCA  LNYRRFR  LNYRRGE  LNYRRIT  LNYRRJA
LNYRRNE  LNYRRUK  LNYRRUS  LNYRTCA  LNYRTFR  LNYRTGE  LNYRTIT  LNYRTJA
LNYRTNE  LNYRTUK  LNYRTUS  LNYRUK  LNYRUKP  LNYRUS  LNYRUSP  RCA  RFR  RGE
RIT  RJA  RNE  RUK  RUS  SGRPX1C1  SGRPX1F1  SGRPX1I1  SGRPX1J2  UNFR  UNUK
UNUS  XTOYCA  XTOYCAEX  XTOYCAU  XTOYFR  XTOYFREX  XTOYFRU  XTOYGE  XTOYGEEX
XTOYGEU  XTOYIT  XTOYITEX  XTOYITU  XTOYJA  XTOYJAEX  XTOYJAU  XTOYNE
XTOYNEEX  XTOYNEU  XTOYUK  XTOYUKEX  XTOYUKU  XTOYUS  XTOYUSEX  XTOYUSU
Z1CA1L  Z1GE1L  Z1IT1  Z1JA2  Z1NE1L  Z1UK1L  Z1US1L  Z2FR1
```

EXOGENOUS:
```
DMY611  DMY674  DMY693  LNECA  LNEFR  LNEGE  LNEIT  LNEJA  LNENE  LNEUK
LNEUS  LNGCAU  LNGFRU  LNGGEU  LNGITU  LNGJAU  LNGNEU  LNGUKU  LNGUSU
LNRPOIL  PEGDIFIT  PEGDIFJA  PEGDIFNE  T
```

COEFFICIENT:
```
A1CA  A1FR  A1GE  A1IT  A1JA  A1NE  A1UK  A1US  A10IT  A10JA  A10NE  A10US
A11CA  A11FR  A11GE  A11IT  A11JA  A11NE  A11US  A12GE  A12NE  A12UK  A12US
A13GE  A13IT  A13JA  A13NE  A14CA  A14GE  A14JA  A14NE  A2CA  A2FR  A2GE
A2IT  A2JA  A2NE  A2UK  A2US  A3CA  A3FR  A3GE  A3NE  A3UK  A3US  A4CA  A4NE
A4US  A5CA  A5IT  A5JA  A5NE  A6CA  A6NE  A6US  A7FR  A7GE  A7NE  A7UK  A8CA
A8GE  A8NE  A8US  A9FR  A9NE  A9UK  A9US  B1CA  B1FR  B1GE  B1IT  B1JA  B1NE
B1UK  B1US  B10FR  B10JA  B10NE  B10UK  B2CA  B2FR  B2GE  B2IT  B2JA  B2NE
B2UK  B2US  B3CA  B3JA  B3NE  B3UK  B3US  B4CA  B4FR  B4GE  B4IT  B4JA  B4NE
B4UK  B4US  B5CA  B5FR  B5GE  B5IT  B5JA  B5NE  B5UK  B5US  B6CA  B6FR  B6GE
B6IT  B6JA  B6NE  B6UK  B6US  B7CA  B7FR  B7GE  B7IT  B7JA  B7NE  B7US  B8CA
B8GE  B8IT  B8JA  B8NE  B8US  B9CA  B9GE  B9IT  B9JA  B9NE  C1FR  C1UK  C1US
C20FR  C20UK  C20US  C21FR  C21UK  C21US  C22FR  C22UK  C22US  C23FR  C23UK
C23US  C24UK  C24US  C25FR  C25UK  C26US  C27FR  C27US  D0CA  D0FR  D0GE
D0IT  D0JA  D0NE  D0UK  D0US  D1CA  D1FR  D1GE  D1IT  D1JA  D1NE  D1UK  D1US
D10IT  D10NE  D10UK  D10US  D11IT  D11NE  D11US  D12FR  D12US  D13NE  D13UK
D14CA  D14FR  D14GE  D14IT  D14JA  D14NE  D14UK  D14US  D15CA  D15FR  D15JA
D15NE  D15UK  D15US  D16JA  D16US  D2FR  D2JA  D2UK  D2US  D3FR  D3JA  D3NE
D3US  D4CA  D4IT  D4JA  D4NE  D5CA  D5JA  D5UK  D5US  D6CA  D6FR  D6UK  D7IT
D7JA  D8CA  D9CA  E1CA  E1FR  E1GE  E1IT  E1JA  E1NE  E1UK  E1US  E10CA
E11FR  E11NE  E11UK  E11US  E12FR  E12JA  E12NE  E12UK  E12US  E13FR  E13IT
E13JA  E13UK  E14CA  E14FR  E14GE  E14IT  E14JA  E14NE  E14UK  E15CA  E15IT
E15UK  E16CA  E16FR  E16IT  E16JA  E16NE  E16UK  E17CA  E17JA  E17NE  E18FR
E18GE  E18JA  E18UK  E19CA  E19JA  E2CA  E2FR  E2IT  E2NE  E2US  E20US  E21US
E3CA  E3GE  E3NE  E3UK  E4CA  E4FR  E4IT  E4NE  E4UK  E5IT  E5NE  E5US  E6FR
E6IT  E6JA  E6NE  E7GE  E7JA  E7NE  E8FR  E8GE  E8JA  E8US  E9FR  E9GE  F0CA
F0FR  F0IT  F0JA  F0NE  F0UK  F0US  F10NE  F10US  F20IT  F20NE  F20US  F30JA
F30UK  F40CA  F40FR  F40JA  F40NE  F40US  F50CA  F50FR  F50IT  F50JA  F50NE
F50UK  F50US  F60FR  F60JA  F60NE  F60UK  G0CA  G0FR  G0GE  G0IT  G0JA  G0NE
G0UK  G0US  G1JA  G1NE  G1US  G10CA  G10GE  G12UK  G12US  G2NE  G2UK  G20CA
G20GE  G22UK  G22US  G3FR  G3IT  G3JA  G3NE  G30CA  G30GE  G32UK  G32US  G4FR
G4IT  G4JA  G4NE  G5FR  G5IT  G5JA  G5NE  G6CA  G6FR  G6GE  G6IT  G6NE  G6UK
G6US  G7NE  G7UK  G8CA  G8FR  G8GE  G8JA  G8UK  G9CA  G9FR  G9GE  H0CA  H0FR
H0GE  H0IT  H0JA  H0NE  H0UK  H0US  H1FR  H1GE  H1JA  H1NE  H1UK  H1US  H10GE
H10JA  H10NE  H10UK  H11CA  H11FR  H11IT  H11UK  H12CA  H12FR  H12GE  H12JA
H12NE  H13CA  H13IT  H13NE  H13UK  H14JA  H14NE  H14UK  H15CA  H15FR
H15GE  H15IT  H15UK  H2US  H3CA  H3FR  H3IT  H3UK  H3US  H4CA  H4UK  H4US
H5CA  H5FR  H5GE  H5IT  H5JA  H5NE  H5UK  H6IT  H6JA  H6NE  H7CA  H7FR  H7IT
H7JA  H7NE  H7UK  H8CA  H8FR  H8GE  H8IT  H8JA  H8NE  H8US  H9CA  H9FR  H9FR
H9IT  H9JA  I0CA  I0FR  I0GE  I0IT  I0JA  I0NE  I0UK  I0US  I1CA  I1FR  I1GE
I1IT  I1JA  I1NE  I1UK  I1US  I2CA  I2FR  I2GE  I2IT  I2JA  I2NE  I2UK  I2US
I3FR  I3GE  I3IT  I3JA  I3NE  I3UK  I3US  I4CA  I4FR  I4US  I5CA  I5FR  I5NE
I5US  I5US  I6IT  I6JA  I6UK  I6US  I7FR  I7IT  I7US  I8JA  K0CA  K0FR  K0GE
```

Table 7.3 (continued)

```
KOIT   KOJA   KONE   KOUK   KOUS   K1GE   K1NE   K1UK   K10CA  K10UK  K10US  K11FR
K11IT  K11NE  K11UK  K11US  K12IT  K13CA  K13IT  K14FR  K14IT  K14JA  K14NE
K14UK  K14US  K15FR  K15IT  K15JA  K15NE  K15UK  K15US  K2CA   K2FR   K2IT
K2JA   K2NE   K2UK   K2US   K3CA   K3UK   K3US   K4GE   K4IT   K4NE   K4UK   K4US   K5CA
K5JA   K5US   K6CA   K6FR   K6GE   K6IT   K6JA   K6NE   K7JA   K7UK   K8UK   K9CA   K9FR
K9GE   K9IT   K9JA   K9NE   K9UK   K9US   L0CA   L0FR   L0GE   L0IT   L0JA   L0NE   L0UK
L1CA   L1FR   L1GE   L1JA   L3IT   L3JA   L3NE   L4CA   L4FR   L4GE   L4IT   L4JA   L4NE
L4UK   L5CA   L5FR   L5IT   L5JA   L5NE   L5UK   L6FR   L6JA   L7FR
```

PARAMETER:
```
DVCA   DVFR   DVGE   DVIT   DVJA   DVNE   DVUK   DVUS   XPCA   XPFR   XPGE   XPIT   XPJA
XPNE   XPUK   XPUS   ZPCA   ZPFR   ZPGE   ZPIT   ZPJA   ZPNE   ZPUK   ZPUS
```

EQUATIONS

1: $LNYRUSP = (1-ZPUS)*XPUS+ZPUS*LNYRUS+(1-ZPUS)*LNYRUSP(-1)$

2: $4*BTOYUS == XTOYUS-ITOYUS-CTOYUS$

3: $LNQIMUS == LNPIMUS-LNPUS$

4: $LNMUSU == LNMNUS-LNMNUSEX$

5: $LNMNUSEX == 2*LNMNUS(-1)-LNMNUS(-2)-0.44937*(DEL(1 : LNMNUS(-1))-$
    $DEL(1 : LNMNUS(-2)))+0.00021-0.80994*LNMUSU(-2)$

6: $XTOYUSU == XTOYUS-XTOYUSEX$

7: $XTOYUSEX == XTOYUS(-1)+0.35462*XTOYUSU(-2)+0.20228*XTOYUSU(-3)+$
    0.00053

8: $LNYRTUS == LNYRUS-LNYRUSP$

9: $LNYRRUS == (DVUK*LNYRUK+DVCA*LNYRCA+DVFR*LNYRFR+DVGE*LNYRGE+DVIT*$
    $LNYRIT+DVJA*LNYRJA+DVNE*LNYRNE)*1/(1-DVUS)-7.40946$

10: $LNPRUS == (DVUK*(LNPUK-LNEUK)+DVCA*(LNPCA-LNECA)+DVFR*(LNPFR-LNEFR$
    $)+DVGE*(LNPGE-LNEGE)+DVIT*(LNPIT-LNEIT)+DVJA*(LNPJA-LNEJA)+DVNE*($
    $LNPNE-LNENE))*1/(1-DVUS)+2.53058$

11: $GREUKX11 == 4*(L0UK+L4UK*DEL(1 : LNEUK)+L5UK*DMY674(-1))$

12: $Z1US1L == 4*DEL(1 : LNPUS)-GRPX1US1(-1)$

13: $GRPX1US1 == 4*(K0US+K2US*LNMNUS(-1)+K3US*LNMNUS(-2)+K4US*DEL(1 :$
    $LNYRUS(-1))+K5US*RUS+K9US*LNPUS(-1)+K10US*LNPUS(-2)+K11US*LNMUSU($
    $-1))+K14US*Z1US1L+K15US*Z1US1L(-1))$

14: $LNPUS = B1US+LNMNUS+B2US*LNYRUSP+B3US*LNYRTUS+B4US*RUS+B5US*($
    $LNMNUS(-1)-LNPUS(-1))+B6US*LNMUSU+B7US*LNMUSU(-1)+B8US*LNMUSU(-2)+$
    $0*LNMUSU(-3)$

15: $LNYRUS = A1US+A2US*LNYRUSP(-1)+(1-A2US)*LNYRUS(-1)+A3US*LNMUSU+$
    $A4US*LNMUSU(-1)+0*LNMUSU(-2)+A6US*LNMUSU(-3)+0*LNGUSU+A8US*LNGUSU($
    $-1)+A9US*LNGUSU(-2)+A10US*LNGUSU(-3)+A11US*XTOYUSU+A12US*XTOYUSU($
    $-1)+0*XTOYUSU(-2)+0*XTOYUSU(-3)$

16: $DEL(1 : UNUS) = C1US+C20US*DEL(1 : LNYRUS)+C21US*DEL(1 : LNYRUS(-1$
    $))+C22US*DEL(1 : LNYRUS(-2))+C23US*DEL(1 : LNYRUS(-3))+C24US*DEL(1$
    $: LNYRUS(-4))+C26US*DEL(1 : LNYRUS(-6))+C27US*DEL(1 : LNYRUS(-7))$

17: $DEL(1 : LNMNUS) = E1US+E2US*T+0*LNGUSU+E5US*(LNGUSU(-3)+LNGUSU(-4)$
    $)+E8US*(LNPUS(-3)-LNPUS(-5))+0*UNUS(-1)+E11US*UNUS(-2)+E12US*UNUS($
    $-3)+0*UNUS(-4)+E20US*DEL(1 : LNMNUS(-1))+E21US*DEL(1 : LNMNUS(-2))$

18: $RUS = D0US+D1US*GRPX1US1+D14US*RUS(-1)+D16US*GRPX1US1(-1)+D15US*T+$
    $D2US*LNMNUS+D3US*LNMUSU(-1)+0*LNMUSU(-2)+D5US*LNMUSU(-3)+0*LNGUSU+$
    $0*LNGUSU(-1)+0*LNGUSU(-2)+0*LNGUSU(-3)+D10US*XTOYUSU+D11US*XTOYUSU$
    $(-1)+D12US*XTOYUSU(-2)+0*XTOYUSU(-3)$

19: $LNPIMUS = LNPIMUS(-1)+F0US+F10US*DEL(1 : LNPIMUS(-1))+F20US*DEL(1$
    $: LNRPOIL)+0*DEL(1 : LNYRRUS)+F40US*DEL(1 : ITOYUS)+F50US*DEL(1$
    $: LNPRUS)$

20: $ITOYUS = I0US+I1US*ITOYUS(-1)+I2US*LNYRUSP+I3US*LNYRTUS+I4US*$
    $LNYRTUS(-1)+I5US*LNQIMUS+I6US*LNQIMUS(-1)+I7US*LNQIMUS(-2)+0*$
    $LNQIMUS(-3)$

21: $XTOYUS = H0US+H1US*LNRPOIL+H2US*LNYRTUS+H3US*T+H4US*XTOYUS(-1)+0*$
    $XTOYUS(-2)+0*LNPRUS+0*LNPRUS(-1)+H8US*LNYRRUS+0*LNYRRUS(-1)+0*$
    $LNPUS+0*LNPUS(-1)$

Table 7.3 (continued)

22: CTOYUS = G0US+G1US*T+0*LNRPOIL+0*RUS+0*GREUKX11+0*RUK+G6US*(XTOYUS
-ITOYUS)+0*LNYRTUS+0*DEL(1 : LNYRUS)+0*DEL(1 : LNYRRUS)+0*DEL(1 :
RUS)+0*DEL(1 : RUS(-1))+G12US*DEL(1 : RUS(-2))+0*DEL(1 : RUK)+0*
DEL(1 : RUK(-1))+G22US*DEL(1 : RUK(-2))+0*DEL(1 : GREUKX11)+0*DEL(
1 : GREUKX11(-1))+G32US*DEL(1 : GREUKX11(-2))

23: LNYRUKP = (1-ZPUK)*XPUK+ZPUK*LNYRUK+(1-ZPUK)*LNYRUKP(-1)

24: LNQIMUK == LNPIMUK-LNPUK

25: LNMUKU == LNMNUK-LNMNUKEX

26: LNMNUKEX == LNMNUK(-1)+0.21096*(LNMNUK(-1)-LNMNUK(-2))+0.28454*(
LNMNUK(-2)-LNMNUK(-3))+0.00627

27: XTOYUKU == XTOYUK-XTOYUKEX

28: XTOYUKEX == XTOYUK(-1)+0.2491*XTOYUKU(-2)-0.14272*XTOYUKU(-4)-
0.37838*XTOYUKU(-7)+0.00084

29: 4*BTOYUK == XTOYUK-ITOYUK-CTOYUK

30: LNYRTUK == LNYRUK-LNYRUKP

31: LNYRRUK == (DVUS*LNYRUS+DVCA*LNYRCA+DVFR*LNYRFR+DVGE*LNYRGE+DVIT*
LNYRIT+DVJA*LNYRJA+DVNE*LNYRNE)*1/(1-DVUK)-7.36068

32: LNPRUK == (DVUS*(LNPUS-LNEUS)+DVCA*(LNPCA-LNECA)+DVFR*(LNPFR-LNEFR
)+DVGE*(LNPGE-LNEGE)+DVIT*(LNPIT-LNEIT)+DVJA*(LNPJA-LNEJA)+DVNE*(
LNPNE-LNENE))*1/(1-DVUK)+1.32478

33: Z1UK1L == 4*DEL(1 : LNPUK)-GRPX1UK1(-1)

34: GRPX1UK1 == 4*(K0UK+K1UK*LNMNUKEX+K2UK*LNMNUK(-1)+K3UK*LNMNUK(-2)+
K4UK*DEL(1 : LNYRUK(-1))+0*RUK+0*RUK(-1)+K7UK*(RUS+GREUKX11)+K8UK*
(RUS(-1)+GREUKX11(-1))+K9UK*LNPUK(-1)+K10UK*LNPUK(-2)+K11UK*LNMUKU
(-1)+0*LNMUKU(-2)+0*LNMUKU(-3)+K14UK*Z1UK1L+K15UK*Z1UK1L(-1)

35: LNPUK = B1UK+LNMNUK+B2UK*LNYRUKP+B3UK*LNYRTUK+B4UK*RUK+B10UK*(RUS+
GREUKX11)+B5UK*(LNMNUK(-1)-LNPUK(-1))+B6UK*LNMUKU+0*LNMUKU(-1)+0*
LNMUKU(-2)+0*LNMUKU(-3)

36: LNYRUK = A1UK+A2UK*LNYRUKP(-1)+(1-A2UK)*LNYRUK(-1)+A3UK*LNMUKU+0*
LNMUKU(-1)+0*LNMUKU(-2)+0*LNMUKU(-3)+A7UK*LNGUKU+0*LNGUKU(-1)+A9UK
*LNGUKU(-2)+0*LNGUKU(-3)+0*XTOYUKU+A12UK*XTOYUKU(-1)+0*XTOYUKU(-2)
+0*XTOYUKU(-3)

37: DEL(1 : UNUK) = C1UK+C20UK*DEL(1 : LNYRUK)+C21UK*DEL(1 : LNYRUK(-1
))+C22UK*DEL(1 : LNYRUK(-2))+C23UK*DEL(1 : LNYRUK(-3))+C24UK*DEL(1
: LNYRUK(-4))+C25UK*DEL(1 : LNYRUK(-5))

38: DEL(1 : LNMNUK) = E1UK+0*T+E3UK*LNGUKU+E4UK*(LNGUKU(-1)+LNGUKU(-2)
)+E11UK*UNUK(-2)+E12UK*UNUK(-3)+E13UK*UNUK(-4)+E14UK*BTOYUK+E15UK*
0*BTOYUK+E16UK*(BTOYUK(-1)+BTOYUK(-2))+E18UK*(BTOYUK(-3)+BTOYUK(-4
))

39: RUK = D0UK+D1UK*GRPX1UK1+D14UK*RUK(-1)+0*GRPX1UK1(-1)+D15UK*T+D2UK
*LNMUKU+0*LNMUKU(-1)+0*LNMUKU(-2)+D5UK*LNMUKU(-3)+D6UK*LNGUKU+0*
LNGUKU(-1)+0*LNGUKU(-2)+0*LNGUKU(-3)+D10UK*XTOYUKU+0*XTOYUKU(-1)+0
*XTOYUKU(-2)+D13UK*XTOYUKU(-3)

40: LNPIMUK = LNPIMUK(-1)+F0UK+F30UK*DEL(1 : LNYRRUK)+F50UK*DEL(1 :
LNPRUK)+F60UK*DEL(1 : LNEUK)

41: ITOYUK = I0UK+I1UK*ITOYUK(-1)+I2UK*LNYRUKP+I3UK*LNYRTUK+0*LNYRTUK(
-1)+I5UK*LNQIMUK+I6UK*LNQIMUK(-1)+0*LNQIMUK(-2)+0*LNQIMUK(-3)

42: XTOYUK = H0UK+H1UK*LNEUK+(H3UK+H4UK*0)*LNEUK(-1)+H5UK*LNRPOIL+0*
LNYRTUK+H7UK*T+H8UK*XTOYUK(-1)+0*XTOYUK(-2)+H10UK*LNPRUK+H11UK*
LNPRUK(-1)+0*LNYRRUK+H13UK*LNYRRUK(-1)+H14UK*LNPUK+H15UK*LNPUK(-1)

43: CTOYUK = G0UK+G2UK*LNRPOIL+G6UK*(XTOYUK-ITOYUK)+G7UK*LNYRTUK+G8UK*
DEL(1 : LNYRUK)+G12UK*DEL(1 : RUK(-2))+G22UK*DEL(1 : RUS(-2))+
G32UK*DEL(1 : GREUKX11(-2))

44: LNYRCAP = (1-ZPCA)*XPCA+ZPCA*LNYRCA+(1-ZPCA)*LNYRCAP(-1)

45: LNQIMCA == LNPIMCA-LNPCA

46: LNMCAU == LNMNCA-LNMNCAEX

47: XTOYCAU == XTOYCA-XTOYCAEX

Table 7.3 (continued)

```
48:     XTOYCAEX == XTOYCA(-1)-0.20227*(XTOYCA(-1)-XTOYCA(-2))+0.00075-
        0.30644*XTOYCAU(-8)

49:     LNMNCAEX == 2*LNMNCA(-1)-LNMNCA(-2)-0.64605*(DEL(1 : LNMNCA(-1))-
        DEL(1 : LNMNCA(-2)))-0.65993*(DEL(1 : LNMNCA(-2))-DEL(1 : LNMNCA(
        -3)))+0.0004-0.46226*LNMCAU(-3)-0.58997*LNMCAU(-4)

50:     4*BTOYCA == XTOYCA-ITOYCA-CTOYCA

51:     LNYRTCA == LNYRCA-LNYRCAP

52:     LNYRRCA == (DVUS*LNYRUS+DVUK*LNYRUK+DVFR*LNYRFR+DVGE*LNYRGE+DVIT*
        LNYRIT+DVJA*LNYRJA+DVNE*LNYRNE)*1/(1-DVCA)-7.26361

53:     LNPRCA == (DVUS*(LNPUS-LNEUS)+DVUK*(LNPUK-LNEUK)+DVFR*(LNPFR-LNEFR
        )+DVGE*(LNPGE-LNEGE)+DVIT*(LNPIT-LNEIT)+DVJA*(LNPJA-LNEJA)+DVNE*(
        LNPNE-LNENE))*1/(1-DVCA)+1.24117

54:     Z1CA1L == 4*DEL(1 : LNPCA)-SGRPX1C1(-1)

55:     SGRPX1C1 == 4*(K0CA+K2CA*LNMNCA(-1)+K3CA*LNMNCA(-2)+K5CA*RCA+K6CA*
        RCA(-1)+K9CA*LNPCA(-1)+K10CA*LNPCA(-2)+K13CA*LNMCAU(-3))

56:     GRPX1CA1 == SGRPX1C1-0.64968*Z1CA1L(-1)

57:     ERCA1L == 4*DEL(1 : LNECA)-GRECAX11(-1)

58:     GRECAX11 == 4*(L0CA+L1CA*BTOYCA+L4CA*DEL(1 : LNECA))+L5CA*ERCA1L

59:     LNPCA = B1CA+LNMNCA+B2CA*LNYRCAP+B3CA*LNYRTCA+B4CA*RCA+B5CA*(
        LNMNCA(-1)-LNPCA(-1))+B6CA*LNMCAU+B7CA*LNMCAU(-1)+B8CA*LNMCAU(-2)+
        B9CA*LNMCAU(-3)

60:     LNYRCA = A1CA+A2CA*LNYRCAP(-1)+(1-A2CA)*LNYRCA(-1)+A3CA*LNMCAU+
        A4CA*LNMCAU(-1)+A5CA*LNMCAU(-2)+A6CA*LNMCAU(-3)+A8CA*LNGCAU(-1)+
        A11CA*XTOYCAU+A14CA*XTOYCAU(-2)

61:     DEL(1 : LNMNCA) = E1CA+E2CA*T+E3CA*LNGCAU+E4CA*(LNGCAU(-1)+LNGCAU(
        -2))+E10CA*LNYRTCA(-1)+E14CA*BTOYCA+E15CA*0*BTOYCA+E16CA*(BTOYCA(
        -1)+BTOYCA(-2))+E17CA*(0*(BTOYCA(-1)+BTOYCA(-2)))+E19CA*(0*(BTOYCA
        (-3)+BTOYCA(-4)))

62:     RCA = D0CA+D1CA*GRPX1CA1+D14CA*RCA(-1)+D15CA*T+D4CA*LNMCAU(-2)+
        D5CA*LNMCAU(-3)+D6CA*LNGCAU+D8CA*LNGCAU(-2)+D9CA*LNGCAU(-3)

63:     LNPIMCA = LNPIMCA(-1)+F0CA+F40CA*DEL(1 : ITOYCA)+F50CA*DEL(1 :
        LNPRCA)

64:     ITOYCA = I0CA+I1CA*ITOYCA(-1)+I2CA*LNYRCAP+I4CA*LNYRTCA(-1)+I5CA*
        LNQIMCA

65:     XTOYCA = H0CA+(H3CA+H4CA*0)*LNECA(-1)+H5CA*LNRPOIL+0*LNYRTCA+H7CA*
        T+H8CA*XTOYCA(-1)+H9CA*XTOYCA(-2)+0*LNPRCA+H11CA*LNPRCA(-1)+H12CA*
        LNYRRCA+H13CA*LNYRRCA(-1)+0*LNPCA+H15CA*LNPCA(-1)

66:     CTOYCA = G0CA+G6CA*(XTOYCA-ITOYCA)+G8CA*DEL(1 : LNYRCA)+G9CA*DEL(1
        : LNYRRCA)+G10CA*DEL(1 : RCA)+G20CA*DEL(1 : RUS)+G30CA*DEL(1 :
        GRECAX11)

67:     LNYRFRP = (1-ZPFR)*XPFR+ZPFR*LNYRFR+(1-ZPFR)*LNYRFRP(-1)

68:     LNQIMFR == LNPIMFR-LNPFR

69:     LNMFRU == LNMNFR-LNMNFREX

70:     LNMNFREX == LNMNFR(-1)+0.54204*(LNMNFR(-1)-LNMNFR(-2))+0.01294+
        0.45793*LNMFRU(-6)

71:     XTOYFRU == XTOYFR-XTOYFREX

72:     XTOYFREX == XTOYFR(-1)-0.23545*(XTOYFR(-1)-XTOYFR(-2))+0.26219*
        XTOYFRU(-2)-0.36552*XTOYFRU(-4)+0.00131

73:     4*BTOYFR == XTOYFR-ITOYFR-CTOYFR

74:     LNYRTFR == LNYRFR-LNYRFRP

75:     LNYRRFR == (DVUS*LNYRUS+DVUK*LNYRUK+DVCA*LNYRCA+DVGE*LNYRGE+DVIT*
        LNYRIT+DVJA*LNYRJA+DVNE*LNYRNE)*1/(1-DVFR)-7.18014

76:     LNPRFR == (DVUS*(LNPUS-LNEUS)+DVUK*(LNPUK-LNEUK)+DVCA*(LNPCA-LNECA
        )+DVGE*(LNPGE-LNEGE)+DVIT*(LNPIT-LNEIT)+DVJA*(LNPJA-LNEJA)+DVNE*(
        LNPNE-LNENE))*1/(1-DVFR)+1.14182
```

Table 7.3 (continued)

```
77:     Z2FR1 == 4*DEL(1 : LNPFR)-SGRPX1F1(-1)

78:     SGRPX1F1 == 4*(K0FR+K2FR*DEL(1 : LNMNFR(-1))+K6FR*RFR(-1)+K9FR*DEL
        (1 : LNPFR(-1))+K11FR*LNMFRU(-1))

79:     GRPX1FR1 == SGRPX1F1+K14FR*Z2FR1+K15FR*Z2FR1(-1)

80:     ERFR1L == 4*DEL(1 : LNEFR)-GREFRX11(-1)

81:     GREFRX11 = 4*(L0FR+L1FR*BTOYFR+L4FR*DEL(1 : LNEFR)+L5FR*DMY693(-1)
        )+L6FR*ERFR1L+L7FR*ERFR1L(-1)

82:     LNPFR = B1FR+LNMNFR+B2FR*LNYRFRP+0*LNYRTFR+B4FR*RFR+B10FR*(RUS+
        GREFRX11)+B5FR*(LNMNFR(-1)-LNPFR(-1))+B6FR*LNMFRU+B7FR*LNMFRU(-1)+
        0*LNMFRU(-2)+0*LNMFRU(-3)

83:     LNYRFR = A1FR+A2FR*LNYRFRP(-1)+(1-A2FR)*LNYRFR(-1)+A3FR*LNMFRU+
        A7FR*LNGFRU+A9FR*LNGFRU(-2)+A11FR*XTOYFRU

84:     DEL(1 : UNFR) = C1FR+C20FR*DEL(1 : LNYRFR)+C21FR*DEL(1 : LNYRFR(-1
        ))+C22FR*DEL(1 : LNYRFR(-2))+C23FR*DEL(1 : LNYRFR(-3))+C25FR*DEL(1
        : LNYRFR(-5))+C27FR*DEL(1 : LNYRFR(-7))

85:     DEL(1 : LNMNFR) = E1FR+E2FR*T+E4FR*(LNGFRU(-1)+LNGFRU(-2))+E6FR*(
        LNPFR(-1)-LNPFR(-3))+E8FR*(LNPFR(-3)-LNPFR(-5))+E9FR*(0*(LNPFR(-3)
        -LNPFR(-5)))+E11FR*UNFR(-2)+E12FR*UNFR(-3)+E13FR*UNFR(-4)+E14FR*
        BTOYFR+E16FR*(BTOYFR(-1)+BTOYFR(-2))+E18FR*(BTOYFR(-3)+BTOYFR(-4))

86:     RFR = D0FR+D1FR*GRPX1FR1+D14FR*RFR(-1)+D15FR*T+D2FR*LNMFRU+D3FR*
        LNMFRU(-1)+D6FR*LNGFRU+D12FR*XTOYFRU(-2)

87:     LNPIMFR = LNPIMFR(-1)+F0FR+F40FR*DEL(1 : ITOYFR)+F50FR*DEL(1 :
        LNPRFR)+F60FR*DEL(1 : LNEFR)

88:     ITOYFR = I0FR+I1FR*ITOYFR(-1)+I2FR*LNYRFRP+I3FR*LNYRTFR+I4FR*
        LNYRTFR(-1)+I5FR*LNQIMFR+0*LNQIMFR(-1)+I7FR*LNQIMFR(-2)+0*LNQIMFR(
        -3)

89:     XTOYFR = H0FR+H1FR*LNEFR+H3FR*LNEFR(-1)+H5FR*LNRPOIL+H7FR*T+H8FR*
        XTOYFR(-1)+H9FR*XTOYFR(-2)+H11FR*LNPRFR(-1)+H12FR*LNYRRFR+H15FR*
        LNPFR(-1)

90:     CTOYFR = G0FR+G3FR*RFR+G4FR*GREFRX11+G5FR*RUS+G6FR*(XTOYFR-ITOYFR)
        +G8FR*DEL(1 : LNYRFR)+G9FR*DEL(1 : LNYRRFR)

91:     LNYRGEP = (1-ZPGE)*XPGE+ZPGE*LNYRGE+(1-ZPGE)*LNYRGEP(-1)

92:     LNMGEU == LNMNGE-LNMNGEEX

93:     LNMNGEEX == LNMNGE(-1)+0.02266+0.1074*LNMGEU(-1)+0.27425*LNMGEU(-2
        )+0.35616*LNMGEU(-3)

94:     XTOYGEU == XTOYGE-XTOYGEEX

95:     4*BTOYGE == XTOYGE-ITOYGE-CTOYGE

96:     XTOYGEEX == XTOYGE(-1)-0.42012*XTOYGEU(-4)+0.00141

97:     LNYRTGE == LNYRGE-LNYRGEP

98:     LNYRRGE == (DVUS*LNYRUS+DVUK*LNYRUK+DVCA*LNYRCA+DVFR*LNYRFR+DVIT*
        LNYRIT+DVJA*LNYRJA+DVNE*LNYRNE)*1/(1-DVGE)-7.20584

99:     LNPRGE == (DVUS*(LNPUS-LNEUS)+DVUK*(LNPUK-LNEUK)+DVCA*(LNPCA-LNECA
        )+DVFR*(LNPFR-LNEFR)+DVIT*(LNPIT-LNEIT)+DVJA*(LNPJA-LNEJA)+DVNE*(
        LNPNE-LNENE))*1/(1-DVGE)+1.17274

100:    Z1GE1L == 4*DEL(1 : LNPGE)-GRPX1GE1(-1)

101:    GRPX1GE1 == 4*(K0GE+K1GE*(LNMNGEEX-LNMNGE(-1))+K4GE*DEL(1 : LNYRGE
        (-1))+K6GE*RGE(-1)+K9GE*(LNPGE(-1)-LNPGE(-2)))+0.0475*Z1GE1L-
        0.4236*Z1GE1L(-1)

102:    GREGEX21 == 4*(L0GE+L1GE*BTOYGE+L4GE*DEL(1 : LNEGE))

103:    LNPGE = B1GE+LNMNGE+B2GE*LNYRGEP+0*LNYRTGE+B4GE*RGE+0*(RUS+
        GREGEX21)+B5GE*(LNMNGE(-1)-LNPGE(-1))+B6GE*LNMGEU+B7GE*LNMGEU(-1)+
        B8GE*LNMGEU(-2)+B9GE*LNMGEU(-3)

104:    LNYRGE = A1GE+A2GE*LNYRGEP(-1)+(1-A2GE)*LNYRGE(-1)+A3GE*LNMGEU+0*
        LNMGEU(-1)+0*LNMGEU(-2)+0*LNMGEU(-3)+A7GE*LNGGEU+A8GE*LNGGEU(-1)+0
        *LNGGEU(-2)+0*LNGGEU(-3)+A11GE*XTOYGEU+A12GE*XTOYGEU(-1)+A13GE*
        XTOYGEU(-2)+A14GE*XTOYGEU(-3)
```

Table 7.3 (continued)

105:
```
DEL(1 : LNMNGE) = E1GE+0*T+E3GE*LNGGEU+E7GE*(0*(LNPGE(-1)-LNPGE(-3
)))+E8GE*(LNPGE(-3)-LNPGE(-5))+E9GE*(0*(LNPGE(-3)-LNPGE(-5)))+0*
LNYRTGE(-1)+0*LNYRTGE(-2)+0*LNYRTGE(-3)+0*LNYRTGE(-4)+E14GE*BTOYGE
+0*0*BTOYGE+E18GE*(BTOYGE(-3)+BTOYGE(-4)))
```

106:
```
RGE = D0GE+D1GE*GRPX1GE1+D14GE*RGE(-1)+0*GRPX1GE1(-1)+0*T+0*LNMGEU
+0*LNMGEU(-1)+0*LNMGEU(-2)+0*LNMGEU(-3)+0*LNGGEU+0*LNGGEU(-1)+0*
LNGGEU(-2)+0*LNGGEU(-3)+0*XTOYGEU+0*XTOYGEU(-1)+0*XTOYGEU(-2)+0*
XTOYGEU(-3)
```

107:
```
ITOYGE = I0GE+I1GE*ITOYGE(-1)+I2GE*LNYRGEP+I3GE*LNYRTGE+0*LNYRTGE(
-1)
```

108:
```
XTOYGE = H0GE+H1GE*LNEGE+0*LNEGE(-1)+H5GE*LNRPOIL+0*LNYRTGE+0*T+
H8GE*XTOYGE(-1)+0*XTOYGE(-2)+H10GE*LNPRGE+0*LNPRGE(-1)+H12GE*
LNYRRGE+0*LNYRRGE(-1)+0*LNPGE+H15GE*LNPGE(-1)
```

109:
```
CTOYGE = G0GE+0*T+0*LNRPOIL+0*RGE+0*GREGEX21+0*RUS+G6GE*(XTOYGE-
ITOYGE)+0*LNYRTGE+G8GE*DEL(1 : LNYRGE)+G9GE*DEL(1 : LNYRRGE)+G10GE
*DEL(1 : RGE)+0*DEL(1 : RGE(-1))+0*DEL(1 : RGE(-2))+G20GE*DEL(1 :
RUS)+0*DEL(1 : RUS(-1))+0*DEL(1 : RUS(-2))+G30GE*DEL(1 : GREGEX21)
+0*DEL(1 : GREGEX21(-1))+0*DEL(1 : GREGEX21(-2))
```

110:
```
LNYRITP = (1-ZPIT)*XPIT+ZPIT*LNYRIT+(1-ZPIT)*LNYRITP(-1)
```

111:
```
LNQIMIT == LNPIMIT-LNPIT
```

112:
```
LNMITU == LNMNIT-LNMNITEX
```

113:
```
LNMNITEX == LNMNIT(-1)+0.15625*(LNMNIT(-1)-LNMNIT(-2))+0.02829+
0.35998*LNMITU(-2)+0.10908*LNMITU(-3)
```

114:
```
XTOYITU == XTOYIT-XTOYITEX
```

115:
```
XTOYITEX == XTOYIT(-1)-0.15095*(XTOYIT(-1)-XTOYIT(-2))+0.19592*(
XTOYIT(-2)-XTOYIT(-3))-0.14307*XTOYIT(-8)+0.29814*XTOYITU(-11)+
0.00221
```

116:
```
4*BTOYIT == XTOYIT-ITOYIT-CTOYIT
```

117:
```
LNYRTIT == LNYRIT-LNYRITP
```

118:
```
LNYRRIT == (DVUS*LNYRUS+DVUK*LNYRUK+DVCA*LNYRCA+DVFR*LNYRFR+DVGE*
LNYRGE+DVJA*LNYRJA+DVNE*LNYRNE)*1/(1-DVIT)-6.93985
```

119:
```
LNPRIT == (DVUS*(LNPUS-LNEUS)+DVUK*(LNPUK-LNEUK)+DVCA*(LNPCA-LNECA
)+DVFR*(LNPFR-LNEFR)+DVGE*(LNPGE-LNEGE)+DVJA*(LNPJA-LNEJA)+DVNE*(
LNPNE-LNENE))*1/(1-DVIT)+0.920318
```

120:
```
Z1IT1 == 4*DEL(1 : LNPIT)-SGRPX1I1(-1)
```

121:
```
SGRPX1I1 == 4*(K0IT+K2IT*DEL(1 : LNMNIT(-1))+K4IT*DEL(1 : LNYRIT(
-1))+K9IT*DEL(1 : LNPIT(-1))+K11IT*LNMITU(-1)+K12IT*LNMITU(-2)+
K13IT*LNMITU(-3))
```

122:
```
GRPX1IT1 == SGRPX1I1+K14IT*Z1IT1+K15IT*Z1IT1(-1)
```

123:
```
ERIT1L == 4*DEL(1 : LNEIT)-GREITX11(-1)
```

124:
```
GREITX11 == 4*(L0IT+L3IT*PEGDIFIT+L4IT*DEL(1 : LNEIT))+L5IT*ERIT1L
```

125:
```
LNPIT == B1IT+LNMNIT+B2IT*LNYRITP+0*LNYRTIT+B4IT*RIT+B5IT*(LNMNIT(
-1)-LNMNIT(-1))+B6IT*LNMITU+B7IT*LNMITU(-1)+B8IT*LNMITU(-2)+B9IT*
LNMITU(-3)
```

126:
```
LNYRIT = A1IT+A2IT*LNYRITP(-1)+(1-A2IT)*LNYRIT(-1)+A5IT*LNMITU(-2)
+A10IT*LNGITU(-3)+A11IT*XTOYITU+A13IT*XTOYITU(-2)
```

127:
```
DEL(1 : LNMNIT) = E1IT+E2IT*T+E4IT*(LNGITU(-1)+LNGITU(-2))+E5IT*(
LNGITU(-3)+LNGITU(-4))+E6IT*(LNPIT(-1)-LNPIT(-3))+E13IT*LNYRTIT(-4
)+E14IT*BTOYIT+E15IT*0*BTOYIT+E16IT*(BTOYIT(-1)+BTOYIT(-2))
```

128:
```
RIT = D0IT+D1IT*GRPX1IT1+D14IT*RIT(-1)+D4IT*LNMITU(-2)+K6IT*LNGITU
+D7IT*LNGITU(-1)+D10IT*XTOYITU+D11IT*XTOYITU(-1)
```

129:
```
LNPIMIT = LNPIMIT(-1)+F0IT+F20IT*DEL(1 : LNRPOIL)+F50IT*DEL(1 :
LNPRIT)
```

130:
```
ITOYIT = I0IT+I1IT*ITOYIT(-1)+I2IT*LNYRITP+I3IT*LNYRTIT+0*LNYRTIT(
-1)+0*LNQIMIT+I6IT*LNQIMIT(-1)+I7IT*LNQIMIT(-2)+0*LNQIMIT(-3)
```

Table 7.3 (continued)

```
131:    XTOYIT = H0IT+H3IT*LNEIT(-1)+H5IT*LNRPOIL+H6IT*LNYRTIT+H7IT*T+H8IT
        *XTOYIT(-1)+H9IT*XTOYIT(-2)+H11IT*LNPRIT(-1)+H13IT*LNYRRIT(-1)+
        H15IT*LNPIT(-1)

132:    CTOYIT = G0IT+G3IT*RIT+G4IT*GREITX11+G5IT*RUS+G6IT*(XTOYIT-ITOYIT)

133:    LNYRJAP = (1-ZPJA)*XPJA+ZPJA*LNYRJA+(1-ZPJA)*LNYRJAP(-1)

134:    LNQIMJA == LNPIMJA-LNPJA

135:    LNMJAU == LNMNJA-LNMNJAEX

136:    LNMNJAEX == LNMNJA(-1)+0.45216*(LNMNJA(-1)-LNMNJA(-2))+0.18984*(
        LNMNJA(-2)-LNMNJA(-3))+0.01423-0.41074*LNMJAU(-4)

137:    XTOYJAU == XTOYJA-XTOYJAEX

138:    XTOYJAEX == 2*XTOYJA(-1)-XTOYJA(-2)-1.1134*(DEL(1 : XTOYJA(-1))-
        DEL(1 : XTOYJA(-2))-0.38594*(DEL(1 : XTOYJA(-2))-DEL(1 : XTOYJA(
        -3))-0.60316*XTOYJAU(-4)+0.36554*XTOYJAU(-9)+5.000000E-05

139:    4*BTOYJA == XTOYJA-ITOYJA-CTOYJA

140:    LNYRTJA == LNYRJA-LNYRJAP

141:    LNYRRJA == (DVUS*LNYRUS+DVUK*LNYRUK+DVCA*LNYRCA+DVFR*LNYRFR+DVGE*
        LNYRGE+DVIT*LNYRIT+DVNE*LNYRNE)*1/(1-DVJA)-6.64583

142:    LNPRJA == (DVUS*(LNPUS-LNEUS)+DVUK*(LNPUK-LNEUK)+DVCA*(LNPCA-LNECA
        )+DVFR*(LNPFR-LNEFR)+DVGE*(LNPGE-LNEGE)+DVIT*(LNPIT-LNEIT)+DVNE*(
        LNPNE-LNENE))*1/(1-DVJA)+0.617771

143:    Z1JA2 == 4*DEL(1 : LNPJA)-SGRPX1J2(-1)

144:    SGRPX1J2 == 4*(K0JA+K2JA*DEL(1 : LNMNJA(-1))+K5JA*RJA+K6JA*RJA(-1)
        +K7JA*(RUS+GREJAX21)+K9JA*DEL(1 : LNPJA(-1)))

145:    GRPX1JA2 == SGRPX1J2+K14JA*Z1JA2+K15JA*Z1JA2(-1)

146:    ERJA2L == 4*DEL(1 : LNEJA)-GREJAX21(-1)

147:    GREJAX21 == 4*(L0JA+L1JA*BTOYJA+L3JA*PEGDIFJA+L4JA*DEL(1 : LNEJA))
        +L5JA*ERJA2L+L6JA*ERJA2L(-1)

148:    LNPJA = B1JA+LNMNJA+B2JA*LNYRJAP+B3JA*LNYRTJA+B4JA*RJA+B10JA*(RUS+
        GREJAX21)+B5JA*(LNMNJA(-1)-LNPJA(-1))+B6JA*LNMJAU+B7JA*LNMJAU(-1)+
        B8JA*LNMJAU(-2)+B9JA*LNMJAU(-3)

149:    LNYRJA = A1JA+A2JA*LNYRJAP(-1)+(1-A2JA)*LNYRJA(-1)+A5JA*LNMJAU(-2)
        +A10JA*LNGJAU(-3)+A11JA*XTOYJAU+A13JA*XTOYJAU(-2)+A14JA*XTOYJAU(-3
        )

150:    DEL(1 : LNMNJA) = E1JA+E6JA*(LNPJA(-1)-LNPJA(-3))+E7JA*(0*(LNPJA(
        -1)-LNPJA(-3)))+E8JA*(LNPJA(-3)-LNPJA(-5))+E12JA*LNYRTJA(-3)+E13JA
        *LNYRTJA(-4)+E14JA*BTOYJA+E16JA*(BTOYJA(-1)+BTOYJA(-2))+E17JA*(0*(
        BTOYJA(-1)+BTOYJA(-2)))+E18JA*(BTOYJA(-3)+BTOYJA(-4))+E19JA*(0*(
        BTOYJA(-3)+BTOYJA(-4)))

151:    RJA = D0JA+D1JA*GRPX1JA2+D14JA*RJA(-1)+D16JA*GRPX1JA2(-1)+D15JA*T+
        D2JA*LNMJAU+D3JA*LNMJAU(-1)+D4JA*LNMJAU(-2)+D5JA*LNMJAU(-3)+0*
        LNGJAU+D7JA*LNGJAU(-1)

152:    LNPIMJA = LNPIMJA(-1)+F0JA+F30JA*DEL(1 : LNYRRJA)+F40JA*DEL(1 :
        ITOYJA)+F50JA*DEL(1 : LNPRJA)+F60JA*DEL(1 : LNEJA)

153:    ITOYJA = I0JA+I1JA*ITOYJA(-1)+I2JA*LNYRJAP+I3JA*LNYRTJA+0*LNYRTJA(
        -1)+0*LNQIMJA+I6JA*LNQIMJA(-1)+0*LNQIMJA(-2)+I8JA*LNQIMJA(-3)

154:    XTOYJA = H0JA+H1JA*LNEJA+H5JA*LNRPOIL+H6JA*LNYRTJA+H7JA*T+H8JA*
        XTOYJA(-1)+H9JA*XTOYJA(-2)+H10JA*LNPRJA+H12JA*LNYRRJA+H13JA*
        LNYRRJA(-1)+H14JA*LNPJA

155:    CTOYJA = G0JA+G1JA*T+G3JA*RJA+G4JA*GREJAX21+G5JA*RUS+G8JA*DEL(1 :
        LNYRJA)

156:    LNYRNEP = (1-ZPNE)*XPNE+ZPNE*LNYRNE+(1-ZPNE)*LNYRNEP(-1)

157:    LNQIMNE == LNPIMNE-LNPNE

158:    LNMNEU == LNMNNE-LNMNNEEX

159:    LNMNNEEX == LNMNNE(-1)+0.34717*(LNMNNE(-1)-LNMNNE(-2))+0.37492*(
        LNMNNE(-2)-LNMNNE(-3))-0.43951*LNMNEU(-4)+0.00681
```

Table 7.3 (continued)

```
160:    XTOYNEU == XTOYNE-XTOYNEEX

161:    XTOYNEEX == XTOYNE(-1)-0.31379*XTOYNEU(-1)-0.33862*XTOYNEU(-9)+
        0.00094

162:    4*BTOYNE == XTOYNE-ITOYNE-CTOYNE

163:    LNYRTNE == LNYRNE-LNYRNEP

164:    LNYRRNE == (DVUS*LNYRUS+DVUK*LNYRUK+DVCA*LNYRCA+DVFR*LNYRFR+DVGE*
        LNYRGE+DVIT*LNYRIT+DVJA*LNYRJA)*1/(1-DVNE)-7.17908

165:    LNPRNE == (DVUS*(LNPUS-LNEUS)+DVUK*(LNPUK-LNEUK)+DVCA*(LNPCA-LNECA
        )+DVFR*(LNPFR-LNEFR)+DVGE*(LNPGE-LNEGE)+DVIT*(LNPIT-LNEIT)+DVJA*(
        LNPJA-LNEJA))*1/(1-DVNE)+1.1838

166:    Z1NE1L == 4*DEL(1 : LNPNE)-GRPX1NE1(-1)

167:    GRPX1NE1 == 4*(K0NE+K1NE*LNMNNEEX+K2NE*LNMNNE(-1)+K4NE*DEL(1 :
        LNYRNE(-1))+K6NE*RNE(-1)+K9NE*DEL(1 : LNPNE(-1))+K11NE*LNMNEU(-1))
        +K14NE*Z1NE1L+K15NE*Z1NE1L(-1)

168:    GRENEX11 == 4*(L0NE+L3NE*PEGDIFNE+L4NE*DEL(1 : LNENE)+L5NE*DMY611(
        -1))

169:    LNPNE = B1NE+LNMNNE+B2NE*LNYRNEP+B3NE*LNYRTNE+B4NE*RNE+B10NE*(RUS+
        GRENEX11)+B5NE*(LNMNNE(-1)-LNPNE(-1))+B6NE*LNMNEU+B7NE*LNMNEU(-1)+
        B8NE*LNMNEU(-2)+B9NE*LNMNEU(-3)

170:    LNYRNE = A1NE+A2NE*LNYRNEP(-1)+(1-A2NE)*LNYRNE(-1)+A3NE*LNMNEU+
        A4NE*LNMNEU(-1)+A5NE*LNMNEU(-2)+A6NE*LNMNEU(-3)+A7NE*LNGNEU+A8NE*
        LNGNEU(-1)+A9NE*LNGNEU(-2)+A10NE*LNGNEU(-3)+A11NE*XTOYNEU+A12NE*
        XTOYNEU(-1)+A13NE*XTOYNEU(-2)+A14NE*XTOYNEU(-3)

171:    DEL(1 : LNMNNE) = E1NE+E2NE*T+E3NE*LNGNEU+E4NE*(LNGNEU(-1)+LNGNEU(
        -2))+E5NE*(LNGNEU(-3)+LNGNEU(-4))+E6NE*(LNPNE(-1)-LNPNE(-3))+E7NE*
        (0*(LNPNE(-1)-LNPNE(-3)))+E11NE*LNYRTNE(-2)+E12NE*LNYRTNE(-1)+
        E14NE*BTOYNE+E16NE*(BTOYNE(-1)+BTOYNE(-2))+E17NE*(0*(BTOYNE(-1)+
        BTOYNE(-2)))

172:    RNE = D0NE+D1NE*GRPX1NE1+D14NE*RNE(-1)+D15NE*T+D3NE*LNMNEU(-1)+
        D4NE*LNMNEU(-2)+D10NE*XTOYNEU(-1)+D11NE*XTOYNEU(-1)+D13NE*XTOYNEU(-3)

173:    LNPIMNE = LNPIMNE(-1)+F0NE+F10NE*DEL(1 : LNPIMNE(-1))+F20NE*DEL(1
        : LNRPOIL)+F40NE*DEL(1 : ITOYNE)+F50NE*DEL(1 : LNPRNE)+F60NE*DEL(
        1 : LNENE)

174:    ITOYNE = I0NE+I1NE*ITOYNE(-1)+I2NE*LNYRNEP+I3NE*LNYRTNE+I5NE*
        LNQIMNE

175:    XTOYNE = H0NE+H1NE*LNENE+H5NE*LNRPOIL+H6NE*LNYRTNE+H7NE*T+H8NE*
        XTOYNE(-1)+H10NE*LNPRNE+H12NE*LNYRRNE+H13NE*LNYRRNE(-1)+H14NE*
        LNPNE

176:    CTOYNE = G0NE+G1NE*T+G2NE*LNRPOIL+G3NE*RNE+G4NE*GRENEX11+G5NE*RUS+
        G6NE*(XTOYNE-ITOYNE)+G7NE*LNYRTNE
```

COEFFICIENT AND PARAMETER VALUES (CONST_MARK4PEG)

A1CA	0.010803	A1FR	0.012619	A1GE	0.010821
A1IT	0.011699	A1JA	0.020614	A1NE	0.009964
A1UK	0.005561	A1US	0.007884	A10CA	-0.01349
A10FR	0.016439	A10GE	0.013896	A10IT	0.025164
A10JA	-0.026697	A10NE	0.035157	A10UK	-0.023974
A10US	0.067441	A11CA	0.679057	A11FR	0.213191
A11GE	0.296236	A11IT	-0.383459	A11JA	-1.91914
A11NE	0.097619	A11UK	0.189683	A11US	0.717539
A12CA	0.164836	A12FR	-0.715374	A12GE	-0.23778
A12IT	-0.044277	A12JA	0.349852	A12NE	-0.064686
A12UK	0.42402	A12US	0.532314	A13CA	-0.028676
A13FR	0.015316	A13GE	-0.333226	A13IT	-0.227114
A13JA	-1.15516	A13NE	0.104741	A13UK	-0.21287
A13US	-0.0415	A14CA	0.544787	A14FR	0.121494
A14GE	-0.514582	A14IT	-0.465483	A14JA	-1.09256
A14NE	-0.113143	A14UK	0.006859	A14US	-0.925131
A2CA	0.134071	A2FR	0.102126	A2GE	0.04147
A2IT	0.02481	A2JA	-0.038396	A2NE	0.090174
A2UK	0.240655	A2US	0.088859	A3CA	0.244862
A3FR	-0.264118	A3GE	0.344867	A3IT	0.093876
A3JA	0.142673	A3NE	0.241184	A3UK	-0.18449

Table 7.3 (continued)

A3US	0.967393	A4CA	0.177733	A4FR	0.068796
A4GE	0.069415	A4IT	0.079064	A4JA	0.1083
A4NE	0.094424	A4UK	0.040359	A4US	0.548935
A5CA	0.075535	A5FR	0.10011	A5GE	-0.01725
A5IT	0.266542	A5JA	0.211515	A5NE	-0.03886
A5UK	-0.026207	A5US	-0.04704	A6CA	0.193415
A6FR	-0.055212	A6GE	0.04078	A6IT	-0.01757
A6JA	0.088371	A6NE	0.006819	A6UK	-0.126895
A6US	0.935403	A7CA	-0.004872	A7FR	0.072732
A7GE	-0.036326	A7IT	-0.001348	A7JA	0.044268
A7NE	0.037422	A7UK	0.174624	A7US	-0.034466
A8CA	-0.149956	A8FR	0.007462	A8GE	0.030281
A8IT	0.000596	A8JA	-0.019563	A8NE	-0.031181
A8UK	0.027366	A8US	0.138711	A9CA	-0.02829
A9FR	0.049895	A9GE	-0.00762	A9IT	-0.001628
A9JA	0.044973	A9NE	0.016572	A9UK	0.118697
A9US	0.05507	B1CA	0.119397	B1FR	0.05478
B1GE	0.073547	B1IT	0.206264	B1JA	0.448139
B1NE	-0.005675	B1UK	-0.151938	B1US	0.083905
B10CA	-0.056102	B10FR	0.029941	B10GE	-0.008847
B10IT	-0.037786	B10JA	0.080375	B10NE	0.000617
B10UK	0.078828	B10US	-0.001131	B2CA	-0.218794
B2FR	-0.018392	B2GE	-0.063613	B2IT	-0.069682
B2JA	-0.201664	B2NE	-0.081835	B2UK	-0.046894
B2US	-0.022227	B3CA	-0.152691	B3FR	-0.018886
B3GE	-0.006227	B3IT	-0.042952	B3JA	-0.065941
B3NE	0.107645	B3UK	-0.276035	B3US	-0.09072
B4CA	0.244962	B4FR	0.462903	B4GE	0.023618
B4IT	0.160445	B4JA	0.95586	B4NE	-0.013744
B4UK	0.504004	B4US	0.346502	B5CA	-0.628784
B5FR	-0.996486	B5GE	-0.935252	B5IT	-0.947684
B5JA	-0.827685	B5NE	-0.890964	B5UK	-0.872932
B5US	-0.9906	B6CA	-1.07886	B6FR	-0.724769
B6GE	-1.07676	B6IT	-1.24523	B6JA	-0.988582
B6NE	-0.977966	B6UK	-0.689923	B6US	-0.725851
B7CA	-0.267171	B7FR	-0.237026	B7GE	-0.141736
B7IT	-0.191914	B7JA	-0.356822	B7NE	-0.451249
B7UK	0.037385	B7US	-0.393195	B8CA	-0.271711
B8FR	0.024827	B8GE	-0.311723	B8IT	-0.378815
B8JA	-0.312743	B8NE	-0.621455	B8UK	-0.151933
B8US	0.169832	B9CA	-0.635726	B9FR	0.04942
B9GE	-0.308631	B9IT	-0.151063	B9JA	-0.289714
B9NE	-0.309134	B9UK	-0.167466	B9US	0.016405
C1FR	0.001842	C1UK	0.002293	C1US	0.004693
C20FR	-0.033332	C20UK	-0.087536	C20US	-0.198491
C21FR	-0.036075	C21UK	-0.032481	C21US	-0.187741
C22FR	-0.024205	C22UK	-0.064932	C22US	-0.050647
C23FR	-0.011601	C23UK	-0.054861	C23US	-0.063531
C24FR	-0.003691	C24UK	-0.041132	C24US	0.059092
C25FR	-0.010717	C25UK	-0.01505	C25US	0.017716
C26FR	0.000474	C26UK	-0.005727	C26US	-0.027592
C27FR	0.0072	C27UK	0.000353	C27US	-0.061705
DVCA	0.046296	DVFR	0.077221	DVGE	0.107001
DVIT	0.048061	DVJA	0.107898	DVNE	0.018771
DVUK	0.063287	DVUS	0.531464	D0CA	0.002086
D0FR	0.003366	D0GE	0.003628	D0IT	-0.002471
D0JA	-0.000932	D0NE	0.003585	D0UK	0.003081
D0US	0.010089	D1CA	0.049893	D1FR	0.073674
D1GE	0.231726	D1IT	0.027008	D1JA	0.027117
D1NE	-0.043995	D1UK	0.009035	D1US	0.434367
D10CA	-0.007863	D10FR	0.20013	D10GE	0.20221
D10IT	0.239529	D10JA	0.007364	D10NE	0.137002
D10UK	0.192508	D10US	0.508074	D11CA	0.037268
D11FR	0.12238	D11GE	-0.24158	D11IT	0.161757
D11JA	-0.025161	D11NE	0.06167	D11UK	0.018407
D11US	0.23597	D12CA	-0.013955	D12FR	0.194568
D12GE	0.0877	D12IT	0.054745	D12JA	0.025661
D12NE	0.03381	D12UK	-0.003938	D12US	0.544253
D13CA	-0.032712	D13FR	0.07675	D13GE	-0.24942
D13IT	-0.009773	D13JA	0.002267	D13NE	0.048054
D13UK	0.213998	D13US	-0.213716	D14CA	0.961863
D14FR	0.763452	D14GE	0.76264	D14IT	1.02768
D14JA	0.983108	D14NE	0.799926	D14UK	0.825858
D14US	0.539202	D15CA	-3.498167E-05	D15FR	0.000154
D15GE	3.845550E-05	D15IT	1.960370E-05	D15JA	-2.144426E-05
D15NE	0.000151	D15UK	0.000183	D15US	-6.091796E-06
D16CA	0.005978	D16FR	0.0124	D16GE	-0.06953
D16IT	-0.019956	D16JA	0.030428	D16NE	0.04514
D16UK	-0.022298	D16US	-0.154852	D2CA	-0.078202
D2FR	-0.49829	D2GE	0.1307	D2IT	-0.020386
D2JA	-0.006893	D2NE	0.07838	D2UK	-0.299766
D2US	-0.230722	D3CA	0.015319	D3FR	-0.154023
D3GE	0.07571	D3IT	0.004611	D3JA	-0.021473

Table 7.3 (continued)

D3NE	-0.162029	D3UK	0.025404	D3US	0.163077
D4CA	0.092836	D4FR	-0.09139	D4GE	0.10942
D4IT	0.037063	D4JA	-0.032911	D4NE	0.06593
D4UK	0.036448	D4US	0.091665	D5CA	0.116664
D5FR	0.03674	D5GE	0.05852	D5IT	0.02739
D5JA	-0.016782	D5NE	0.00622	D5UK	0.077159
D5US	0.103347	D6CA	-0.073145	D6FR	-0.034926
D6GE	-0.02391	D6IT	-0.005287	D6JA	0.000489
D6NE	0.00239	D6UK	-0.050417	D6US	-0.020453
D7CA	-0.001992	D7FR	0.01672	D7GE	0.00277
D7IT	-0.004384	D7JA	0.001793	D7NE	0.00041
D7UK	0.022854	D7US	0.01894	D8CA	0.032561
D8FR	-0.01609	D8GE	-0.0128	D8IT	-0.000764
D8JA	0.000889	D8NE	0.00664	D8UK	0.014188
D8US	0.02294	D9CA	0.017438	D9FR	-0.00794
D9GE	0.01666	D9IT	-0.003281	D9JA	0.000607
D9NE	0.01609	D9UK	0.001453	D9US	0.015392
E1CA	0.007281	E1FR	0.03332	E1GE	0.013288
E1IT	0.019544	E1JA	0.054274	E1NE	0.010131
E1UK	-0.00433	E1US	0.00329	E10CA	-0.034398
E10FR	1.58587	E10GE	-0.036416	E10IT	0.105504
E10JA	0.005894	E10NE	0.033838	E10UK	1.23133
E10US	-0.116645	E11CA	-0.054589	E11FR	-1.02545
E11GE	0.102443	E11IT	-0.126347	E11JA	-0.022105
E11NE	0.004899	E11UK	-0.550499	E11US	0.426361
E12CA	-0.077664	E12FR	4.39695	E12GE	-0.191149
E12IT	0.126007	E12JA	-0.158405	E12NE	0.019509
E12UK	5.57298	E12US	-0.468037	E13CA	-0.041273
E13FR	-3.24907	E13GE	0.084755	E13IT	-0.151066
E13JA	0.284267	E13NE	-0.028792	E13UK	-4.2394
E13US	-0.054576	E14CA	-0.396027	E14FR	0.10534
E14GE	1.628	E14IT	-3.88655	E14JA	1.95052
E14NE	0.403001	E14UK	-0.068485	E15CA	3.68752
E15FR	0.103117	E15GE	0.019635	E15IT	4.10458
E15JA	-0.574234	E15NE	0.700825	E15UK	0.596763
E16CA	0.670052	E16FR	0.108524	E16GE	0.09378
E16IT	1.57536	E16JA	1.83261	E16NE	0.292781
E16UK	0.282168	E17CA	-2.84711	E17FR	-0.132219
E17GE	0.332797	E17IT	-0.686828	E17JA	-2.53069
E17NE	-0.892653	E17UK	-0.521172	E18CA	0.286188
E18FR	0.761771	E18GE	0.625931	E18IT	-0.372264
E18JA	1.71901	E18NE	0.091526	E18UK	0.187571
E19CA	2.14929	E19FR	0.060458	E19GE	0.039871
E19IT	0.810022	E19JA	-1.78208	E19NE	-0.971241
E19US	-0.204191	E2CA	0.000184	E2FR	-0.000192
E2GE	-8.064001E-05	E2IT	0.000454	E2JA	-1.888251E-05
E2NE	0.000421	E2UK	-6.443714E-07	E2US	0.000243
E20US	0.496825	E21US	-0.248602	E3CA	0.10149
E3FR	0.00301	E3GE	0.043045	E3IT	-0.014448
E3JA	-0.021866	E3NE	0.058633	E3UK	0.107434
E3US	0.004036	E4CA	0.138066	E4FR	0.011217
E4GE	-0.014921	E4IT	-0.03104	E4JA	0.031742
E4NE	-0.027174	E4UK	0.163098	E4US	0.001552
E5CA	-0.003532	E5FR	-0.017824	E5GE	-0.0225
E5IT	-0.023132	E5JA	0.026185	E5NE	-0.040335
E5UK	0.02989	E5US	0.033956	E6CA	-0.197234
E6FR	-0.057298	E6GE	0.097666	E6IT	-0.09435
E6JA	-0.564806	E6NE	-0.316001	E6UK	0.07705
E6US	-0.057597	E7CA	0.264871	E7FR	0.574765
E7GE	-0.763707	E7IT	0.037192	E7JA	0.415324
E7NE	0.206985	E7UK	0.024239	E8CA	-0.113296
E8FR	-0.0748	E8GE	-0.343714	E8IT	0.262491
E8JA	-0.226858	E8NE	0.05664	E8UK	0.156708
E8US	-0.286081	E9CA	-0.001604	E9FR	0.28364
E9GE	0.700672	E9IT	-0.129687	E9JA	0.014509
E9NE	0.062226	E9UK	-0.074746	F0CA	0.001455
F0FR	-0.00816	F0GE	-0.010675	F0IT	-0.009255
F0JA	-0.018463	F0NE	-0.004765	F0UK	-0.015403
F0US	0.000225	F10CA	-0.053768	F10FR	-0.099353
F10GE	0.242206	F10IT	0.072819	F10JA	0.124816
F10NE	0.223077	F10UK	-0.002007	F10US	0.616185
F20CA	-0.245403	F20FR	0.052207	F20GE	0.006946
F20IT	0.176537	F20JA	-0.07173	F20NE	0.09354
F20UK	-0.040341	F20US	0.067515	F30CA	0.279496
F30FR	-0.026652	F30GE	0.290149	F30IT	-0.14876
F30JA	0.804933	F30NE	-0.255302	F30UK	0.740935
F30US	0.15222	F40CA	0.784069	F40FR	1.76086
F40GE	-0.377934	F40IT	-0.221008	F40JA	3.84313
F40NE	0.138543	F40UK	0.189983	F40US	2.25319
F50CA	0.270787	F50FR	1.25097	F50GE	1.20028
F50IT	1.31648	F50JA	1.30657	F50NE	0.968503
F50UK	1.28695	F50US	0.153811	F60CA	0.02143
F60FR	0.612717	F60GE	0.468396	F60IT	-1.1264

Table 7.3 (continued)

F60JA	0.710113	F60NE	0.799582	F60UK	0.533112
G0CA	-0.003648	G0FR	-0.001236	G0GE	-0.012056
G0IT	-0.003179	G0JA	0.045769	G0NE	-0.008552
G0UK	0.013468	G0US	0.004428	G1CA	-0.000105
G1FR	-9.407155E-05	G1GE	-3.927120E-06	G1IT	0.000155
G1JA	-3.658464E-05	G1NE	2.173991E-05	G1UK	-0.000265
G1US	5.279754E-05	G10CA	-0.050435	G10FR	0.636369
G10GE	-0.002451	G10IT	1.38277	G10JA	-0.610265
G10NE	0.696158	G10UK	0.757122	G10US	-0.299741
G11CA	-0.298437	G11FR	0.258753	G11GE	-0.422543
G11IT	0.442983	G11JA	-1.14262	G11NE	-0.687287
G11UK	-0.828963	G11US	0.347438	G12CA	0.16578
G12FR	0.908516	G12GE	0.405291	G12IT	0.361741
G12JA	-0.346612	G12NE	0.363585	G12UK	-0.680074
G12US	-0.480483	G2CA	0.007542	G2FR	0.013437
G2GE	0.0044	G2IT	0.000184	G2JA	0.031405
G2NE	0.015183	G2UK	-0.046579	G2US	-0.001341
G20CA	0.259146	G20FR	-0.654758	G20GE	0.621408
G20IT	-0.172217	G20JA	-0.826017	G20NE	0.983567
G20UK	0.317069	G20US	0.007598	G21CA	0.213911
G21FR	-0.994672	G21GE	0.132577	G21IT	-0.352289
G21JA	-0.091766	G21NE	0.171835	G21UK	-0.576976
G21US	0.034483	G22CA	-0.194408	G22FR	0.386726
G22GE	0.546939	G22IT	-0.02103	G22JA	-0.232578
G22NE	0.979523	G22UK	0.525568	G22US	0.111434
G3CA	-0.209463	G3FR	-0.249651	G3GE	-0.3022
G3IT	-0.204769	G3JA	-0.583978	G3NE	-0.679193
G3UK	0.752483	G3US	-0.100705	G30CA	0.04415
G30FR	-0.002254	G30GE	0.052299	G30IT	-0.045144
G30JA	0.038284	G30NE	-0.086553	G30UK	-0.342353
G30US	-0.003303	G31CA	-0.048232	G31FR	0.000667
G31GE	0.046935	G31IT	0.037957	G31JA	0.033051
G31NE	-0.051527	G31UK	-0.076486	G31US	0.003961
G32CA	-0.06872	G32FR	-0.017283	G32GE	0.051619
G32IT	0.071145	G32JA	0.023627	G32NE	0.04683
G32UK	0.016799	G32US	-0.004193	G4CA	0.399296
G4FR	0.073793	G4GE	0.097097	G4IT	0.071244
G4JA	0.05497	G4NE	0.024806	G4UK	0.444298
G4US	-0.034747	G5CA	0.525327	G5FR	0.332204
G5GE	0.243101	G5IT	0.328725	G5JA	0.064557
G5NE	0.543858	G5UK	-0.927833	G5US	-0.209762
G6CA	0.854509	G6FR	0.184551	G6GE	0.679257
G6IT	0.4522	G6JA	-0.212536	G6NE	0.53443
G6UK	-1.08654	G6US	0.571938	G7CA	0.101733
G7FR	0.060923	G7GE	-0.065372	G7IT	-0.006446
G7JA	0.04405	G7NE	0.077908	G7UK	-0.696908
G7US	-0.053545	G8CA	-0.115046	G8FR	0.076835
G8GE	0.516343	G8IT	-0.125914	G8JA	-0.219103
G8NE	-0.045435	G8UK	0.51128	G8US	-0.106903
G9CA	0.037359	G9FR	-0.195855	G9GE	-0.940238
G9IT	-0.262394	G9JA	0.034766	G9NE	-0.454351
G9UK	0.080414	G9US	0.05499	H0CA	0.203896
H0FR	0.129624	H0GE	0.089664	H0IT	-0.878539
H0JA	-0.060943	H0NE	0.253769	H0UK	0.548739
H0US	0.077502	H1CA	-0.152912	H1FR	0.073406
H1GE	0.040487	H1IT	-0.018547	H1JA	0.016673
H1NE	0.12252	H1UK	0.051451	H1US	0.014957
H10CA	0.025102	H10FR	0.010249	H10GE	0.247567
H10IT	-0.071293	H10JA	0.018682	H10NE	0.586296
H10UK	0.091918	H10US	0.00826	H11CA	-0.049448
H11FR	0.239274	H11GE	0.044574	H11IT	0.081144
H11JA	-0.048667	H11NE	-0.41788	H11UK	0.306618
H11US	0.01138	H12CA	0.113463	H12FR	0.248513
H12GE	0.1238	H12IT	0.05552	H12JA	-0.119308
H12NE	0.500342	H12UK	-0.010101	H13CA	0.08955
H13FR	0.054154	H13GE	-0.021665	H13IT	0.201372
H13JA	0.149767	H13NE	-0.165191	H13UK	0.113126
H14CA	0.085483	H14FR	-0.021497	H14GE	-0.066495
H14IT	0.055937	H14JA	-0.010149	H14NE	-0.499385
H14UK	-0.103932	H15CA	0.035674	H15FR	-0.077889
H15GE	-0.326702	H15IT	-0.109401	H15JA	-0.03302
H15NE	0.186242	H15UK	-0.124118	H2CA	0.085196
H2FR	-0.000659	H2GE	-0.001326	H2IT	0.001095
H2JA	0.000277	H2NE	-0.003371	H2UK	-0.006863
H2US	0.01107	H3CA	-0.038753	H3FR	0.049731
H3GE	0.009901	H3IT	0.164379	H3JA	-0.012907
H3NE	-0.065659	H3UK	0.148371	H3US	-0.00087
H4CA	0.053718	H4FR	-0.003771	H4GE	0.003139
H4IT	-0.000501	H4JA	-0.000414	H4NE	0.000248
H4UK	0.003317	H4US	0.610356	H5CA	0.012595
H5FR	0.01573	H5GE	0.028759	H5IT	0.018264
H5JA	-0.000268	H5NE	0.032386	H5UK	0.014503

Table 7.3 (continued)

H5US	0.072265	H6CA	-0.068748	H6FR	0.011124
H6GE	0.043488	H6IT	-0.116616	H6JA	-0.030858
H6NE	0.154034	H6UK	-0.038433	H6US	0.010184
H7CA	-0.001767	H7FR	-0.00426	H7GE	-0.001028
H7IT	-0.001111	H7JA	-0.000251	H7NE	-0.002796
H7UK	-0.002765	H7US	-0.008498	H8CA	0.342569
H8FR	0.234953	H8GE	0.347365	H8IT	0.235021
H8JA	0.292216	H8NE	0.51165	H8UK	0.329246
H8US	0.067992	H9CA	0.272154	H9FR	0.250369
H9GE	0.113401	H9IT	0.229865	H9JA	0.123404
H9NE	0.081916	H9UK	0.102093	H9US	0.018369
I0CA	-0.372035	I0FR	-0.040159	I0GE	-0.113784
I0IT	-0.361626	I0JA	-0.023309	I0NE	-1.37868
I0UK	-0.334918	I0US	-0.104698	I1CA	0.202255
I1FR	0.795262	I1GE	0.545657	I1IT	0.772121
I1JA	0.720108	I1NE	0.326505	I1UK	0.346076
I1US	0.661462	I2CA	0.127849	I2FR	0.010317
I2GE	0.032126	I2IT	0.036875	I2JA	0.002864
I2NE	0.364942	I2UK	0.13774	I2US	0.018057
I3CA	-0.017921	I3FR	0.062886	I3GE	0.032967
I3IT	0.093963	I3JA	0.013094	I3NE	0.277274
I3UK	-0.08037	I3US	0.082842	I4CA	0.179301
I4FR	-0.059963	I4GE	0.014642	I4IT	-0.013925
I4JA	0.00033	I4NE	0.042767	I4UK	0.034769
I4US	-0.066497	I5CA	0.131179	I5FR	0.037033
I5GE	-0.007693	I5IT	-0.040057	I5JA	0.010134
I5NE	0.406705	I5UK	0.129456	I5US	0.036839
I6CA	-0.075556	I6FR	-0.018874	I6GE	0.033623
I6IT	0.117275	I6JA	0.053008	I6NE	-0.157412
I6UK	0.085876	I6US	0.052165	I7CA	-0.055634
I7FR	-0.041407	I7GE	0.053553	I7IT	-0.091501
I7JA	-8.886478E-05	I7NE	-0.074126	I7UK	-0.031961
I7US	-0.068607	I8CA	0.066109	I8FR	0.018122
I8GE	-0.028847	I8IT	0.016146	I8JA	-0.041865
I8NE	-0.04174	I8UK	0.014522	I8US	0.004386
K0CA	-0.03672	K0FR	-0.007933	K0GE	-0.004188
K0IT	0.030647	K0JA	0.066137	K0NE	-0.019439
K0UK	-0.08629	K0US	-0.118647	K1CA	-1.00189
K1FR	0.09518	K1GE	0.084483	K1IT	-70.1123
K1JA	-0.28134	K1NE	0.074312	K1UK	-0.21725
K1US	-1.704	K10CA	-0.50794	K10FR	-0.10998
K10GE	-0.05558	K10IT	0.1779	K10JA	-0.05976
K10NE	0.11578	K10UK	-0.36774	K10US	-0.266557
K11CA	0.43356	K11FR	-0.205692	K11GE	8.54003
K11IT	0.510238	K11JA	0.10676	K11NE	-0.120811
K11UK	0.7103	K11US	-0.011724	K12CA	-0.16197
K12FR	-0.04162	K12GE	21.9658	K12IT	0.196408
K12JA	0.15317	K12NE	-7.00023	K12UK	-0.40683
K12US	0.222	K13CA	-0.19053	K13FR	-0.07258
K13GE	28.5363	K13IT	0.182301	K13JA	0.0343
K13NE	-5.78759	K13UK	0.28402	K13US	0.02
K14CA	-0.2753	K14FR	0.6105	K14GE	0.1874
K14IT	0.36478	K14JA	0.2194	K14NE	-0.2528
K14UK	-0.21338	K14US	0.2778	K15CA	-0.6962
K15FR	-0.1698	K15GE	0.5547	K15IT	0.42363
K15JA	0.4259	K15NE	0.5438	K15UK	0.5093
K15US	-0.1317	K2CA	-0.04238	K2FR	0.275907
K2GE	79.9045	K2IT	-0.372853	K2JA	0.14682
K2NE	-0.064781	K2UK	-0.29567	K2US	0.087633
K3CA	0.06676	K3FR	-0.34383	K3GE	-0.02164
K3IT	-10.1092	K3JA	-0.18028	K3NE	-5.04602
K3UK	0.56026	K3US	-0.065193	K4CA	0.06475
K4FR	0.0028	K4GE	0.138669	K4IT	-0.185426
K4JA	-0.02574	K4NE	0.243743	K4UK	0.13262
K4US	-0.055842	K5CA	0.34558	K5FR	0.05509
K5GE	-0.01241	K5IT	0.07162	K5JA	1.33237
K5NE	-0.04987	K5UK	0.02992	K5US	0.140337
K6CA	-0.51519	K6FR	0.216151	K6GE	0.089455
K6IT	-0.004496	K6JA	-2.03841	K6NE	0.108302
K6UK	0.14599	K6US	-0.038	K7CA	0.01197
K7FR	0.00344	K7GE	0.01888	K7IT	-0.03065
K7JA	0.056447	K7NE	-0.03923	K7UK	0.04164
K7US	0.008	K8CA	-0.0327	K8FR	0.01106
K8GE	0.01352	K8IT	-0.01914	K8JA	0.00436
K8NE	-0.02741	K8UK	-0.02842	K8US	-0.009
K9CA	0.49477	K9FR	0.11732	K9GE	0.579013
K9IT	-0.15663	K9JA	-0.212914	K9NE	-0.392292
K9UK	0.35337	K9US	0.246549	L0CA	-0.000111
L0FR	0.001753	L0GE	0.001334	L0IT	-0.000106
L0JA	-0.000313	L0NE	-0.001407	L0UK	0.001221
L1CA	-0.044797	L1FR	-0.736738	L1GE	-0.672213
L1IT	-0.2118	L1JA	-0.579833	L1NE	-0.1362
L1UK	-0.5398	L2CA	33.9022	L2FR	131.55

Table 7.3 (continued)

L2GE	-113.957	L2IT	17.655	L2JA	-405.337
L2NE	10.9493	L2UK	29.8764	L3CA	-0.0089
L3FR	0.6546	L3GE	-0.2109	L3IT	-0.032609
L3JA	0.076104	L3NE	-0.192914	L3UK	0.1369
L4CA	0.510603	L4FR	0.916987	L4GE	0.238757
L4IT	0.970475	L4JA	0.142382	L4NE	0.624358
L4UK	0.564549	L5CA	-1.	L5FR	-0.036492
L5GE	0.0106	L5IT	-1.	L5JA	-0.0779
L5NE	0.024793	L5UK	-0.023716	L6FR	-0.65
L6GE	-0.0086	L6JA	-0.3398	L7FR	-0.35
M0CA	-0.00314	M0FR	0.06315	M0GE	0.00064
M0IT	0.0232	M0JA	0.00323	M0NE	0.02739
M0UK	0.00597	M1CA	0.05183	M1FR	0.13361
M1GE	-0.95133	M1IT	-0.08897	M1JA	-0.03233
M1NE	0.11611	M1UK	0.80037	M2CA	-0.00683
M2FR	-0.06955	M2GE	0.05737	M2IT	-0.029
M2JA	-0.03956	M2NE	-0.07818	M2UK	-0.02808
M3CA	0.07509	M3FR	-1.13931	M3GE	-0.73465
M3IT	0.76727	M3JA	-0.87177	M3NE	-0.66181
M3UK	1.20971	M4CA	-0.30121	M4FR	1.42566
M4GE	2.98731	M4IT	0.1553	M4JA	3.92447
M4NE	-0.10364	M4UK	-2.03867	M5CA	0.18038
M5FR	-3.15593	M5GE	-0.13434	M5IT	-0.35833
M5JA	-0.02198	M5NE	-1.97462	M5UK	-0.98978
M6CA	0.31538	M6FR	-0.39385	M6GE	0.18685
M6IT	0.15115	M6JA	0.20401	M6NE	-0.35813
M6UK	-0.20116	P	4.	XPCA	0.012
XPFR	0.01379	XPGE	0.01143	XPIT	0.01218
XPJA	0.0228	XPNE	0.01161	XPUK	0.0067
XPUS	0.00866	ZPCA	0.025	ZPFR	0.025
ZPGE	0.025	ZPIT	0.025	ZPJA	0.025
ZPNE	0.025	ZPUK	0.025	ZPUS	0.025

Table 7.4   **The Floating Period Model: Mark IV–FLT**

SYMBOL DECLARATIONS

ENDOGENOUS:
```
BTOYCA  BTOYFR  BTOYGE  BTOYIT  BTOYJA  BTOYNE  BTOYUK  BTOYUS  CTOYCA
CTOYFR  CTOYGE  CTOYIT  CTOYJA  CTOYNE  CTOYUK  CTOYUS  GRECAX11 GREFRX11
GREGEX21 GREITX11 GREJAX21 GRENEX11 GREUKX11 GRPX1CA1 GRPX1FR1
GRPX1GE1 GRPX1IT1 GRPX1JA2 GRPX1NE1 GRPX1UK1 GRPX1US1 ITOYCA  ITOYFR
ITOYGE  ITOYIT  ITOYJA  ITOYNE  ITOYUK  ITOYUS  LNECA  LNEFR  LNEGE  LNEIT
LNEJA  LNENE  LNEUK  LNMCAU  LNMFRU  LNMGEU  LNMITU  LNMJAU  LNMNCA  LNMNCAEX
LNMNEU  LNMNFR  LNMNFREX  LNMNGE  LNMNGEEX  LNMNIT  LNMNITEX  LNMNJA
LNMNJAEX  LNMNNE  LNMNNEEX  LNMNUK  LNMNUKEX  LNMNUS  LNMNUSEX  LNMUKU
LNMUSU  LNPCA  LNPFR  LNPGE  LNPIMCA  LNPIMFR  LNPIMGE  LNPIMIT  LNPIMJA
LNPIMNE  LNPIMUK  LNPIMUS  LNPIT  LNPJA  LNPNE  LNPRCA  LNPRFR  LNPRGE
LNPRIT  LNPRJA  LNPRNE  LNPRUK  LNPRUS  LNPUK  LNPUS  LNQIMCA  LNQIMFR
LNQIMGE  LNQIMIT  LNQIMJA  LNQIMNE  LNQIMUK  LNQIMUS  LNYRCA  LNYRCAP  LNYRFR
LNYRFRP  LNYRGE  LNYRGEP  LNYRIT  LNYRITP  LNYRJA  LNYRJAP  LNYRNE  LNYRNEP
LNYRRCA  LNYRRFR  LNYRRGE  LNYRRIT  LNYRRJA  LNYRRNE  LNYRRUK  LNYRRUS
LNYRTCA  LNYRTFR  LNYRTGE  LNYRTIT  LNYRTJA  LNYRTNE  LNYRTUK  LNYRTUS
LNYRUK  LNYRUKP  LNYRUS  LNYRUSP  RCA  RFR  RGE  RIT  RJA  RNE  RUK  RUS
SGRPX1C1  SGRPX1F1  SGRPX1I1  SGRPX1J2  UNFR  UNUK  UNUS  XTOYCA  XTOYCAEX
XTOYCAU  XTOYFR  XTOYFREX  XTOYFRU  XTOYGE  XTOYGEEX  XTOYGEU  XTOYIT
XTOYITEX  XTOYITU  XTOYJA  XTOYJAEX  XTOYJAU  XTOYNE  XTOYNEEX  XTOYNEU
XTOYUK  XTOYUKEX  XTOYUKU  XTOYUS  XTOYUSEX  XTOYUSU  Z1CA1L  Z1GE1L  Z1IT1
Z1JA2  Z1NE1L  Z1UK1L  Z1US1L  Z2FR1
```

EXOGENOUS:
```
LNEUS  LNGCAU  LNGFRU  LNGGEU  LNGITU  LNGJAU  LNGNEU  LNGUKU  LNGUSU
LNRPOIL  T
```

COEFFICIENT:
```
A1CA  A1FR  A1GE  A1IT  A1JA  A1NE  A1UK  A1US  A10IT  A10JA  A10NE  A10US
A11CA  A11FR  A11GE  A11IT  A11JA  A11NE  A11US  A12GE  A12NE  A12UK  A12US
A13GE  A13IT  A13JA  A13NE  A14CA  A14GE  A14JA  A14NE  A2CA  A2FR  A2GE
A2IT  A2JA  A2NE  A2UK  A2US  A3CA  A3FR  A3GE  A3NE  A3UK  A3US  A4CA  A4NE
A4US  A5CA  A5IT  A5JA  A5NE  A6CA  A6NE  A6US  A7FR  A7GE  A7NE  A7UK  A8CA
A8GE  A8NE  A8US  A9FR  A9NE  A9UK  A9US  B1CA  B1FR  B1GE  B1IT  B1JA  B1NE
B1UK  B1US  B10FR  B10JA  B10NE  B10UK  B2CA  B2FR  B2GE  B2IT  B2JA  B2NE
B2UK  B2US  B3CA  B3JA  B3NE  B3UK  B3US  B4CA  B4FR  B4GE  B4IT  B4JA  B4NE
B4UK  B4US  B5CA  B5FR  B5GE  B5IT  B5JA  B5NE  B5UK  B5US  B6CA  B6FR  B6GE
B6IT  B6JA  B6NE  B6UK  B6US  B7CA  B7FR  B7GE  B7IT  B7JA  B7NE  B7US  B8CA
B8GE  B8IT  B8JA  B8NE  B8US  B9CA  B9GE  B9IT  B9JA  B9NE  C1FR  C1UK  C1US
C20FR  C20UK  C20US  C21FR  C21UK  C21US  C22FR  C22UK  C22US  C23FR  C23UK
C23US  C24UK  C24US  C25FR  C25UK  C26US  C27FR  C27US  D0CA  D0FR  D0GE
D0IT  D0JA  D0NE  D0UK  D0US  D1CA  D1FR  D1GE  D1IT  D1JA  D1NE  D1UK  D1US
D10IT  D10NE  D10UK  D10US  D11IT  D11NE  D11US  D12FR  D12US  D13NE  D13UK
D14CA  D14FR  D14GE  D14IT  D14JA  D14NE  D14UK  D14US  D15CA  D15FR  D15JA
D15NE  D15UK  D15US  D16JA  D16US  D2FR  D2JA  D2UK  D2US  D3FR  D3JA  D3NE
D3US  D4CA  D4IT  D4JA  D4NE  D5CA  D5JA  D5UK  D5US  D6CA  D6FR  D6UK  D7IT
D7JA  D8CA  D9CA  E1CA  E1FR  E1GE  E1IT  E1JA  E1NE  E1UK  E1US  E10CA
E11FR  E11NE  E11UK  E11US  E12FR  E12JA  E12NE  E12UK  E12US  E13FR  E13IT
E13JA  E13UK  E14CA  E14FR  E14GE  E14IT  E14JA  E14NE  E14UK  E15CA  E15IT
E15UK  E16CA  E16FR  E16IT  E16JA  E16NE  E16UK  E17CA  E17JA  E17NE  E17UK
E18FR  E18GE  E18JA  E18UK  E19CA  E19JA  E2CA  E2FR  E2IT  E2NE  E2US  E20US
E21US  E3CA  E3GE  E3NE  E3UK  E4CA  E4FR  E4IT  E4NE  E4UK  E5IT  E5NE  E5US
E6FR  E61T  E6JA  E6NE  E7GE  E7JA  E7NE  E8FR  E8GE  E8JA  E8US  E9FR  E9GE
F0CA  F0FR  F0GE  F0IT  F0JA  F0NE  F0UK  F0US  F1CA  F1FR  F1GE  F1IT  F1JA
F1NE  F1UK  F10US  F2FR  F20US  F3CA  F3FR  F3GE  F4GE  F4JA  F40US  F50US
F6CA  F6FR  F6GE  F6IT  F6JA  F6NE  F6UK  G0CA  G0FR  G0GE  G0IT  G0JA  G0NE
G0UK  G0US  G1JA  G1NE  G1US  G10CA  G10GE  G12UK  G12US  G2NE  G2UK  G20CA
G20GE  G22UK  G22US  G3FR  G3IT  G3JA  G3NE  G30CA  G30GE  G32UK  G32US  G4FR
G4IT  G4JA  G4NE  G5FR  G5IT  G5JA  G5NE  G6CA  G6FR  G6GE  G6IT  G6UK  G6US
G6US  G7NE  G7UK  G8CA  G8FR  G8GE  G8JA  G8UK  G9CA  G9FR  G9GE  H0CA  H0FR
H0GE  H0IT  H0JA  H0NE  H0UK  H0US  H1FR  H1GE  H1JA  H1NE  H1UK  H1US  H10GE
H10JA  H10NE  H10UK  H11CA  H11FR  H11IT  H11UK  H12CA  H12FR  H12GE  H12JA
H12NE  H13CA  H13IT  H13JA  H13NE  H13UK  H14JA  H14NE  H14UK  H15CA  H15FR
H15GE  H15IT  H15UK  H2US  H3CA  H3FR  H3IT  H3UK  H3US  H4CA  H4UK  H4US
H5CA  H5FR  H5GE  H5IT  H5JA  H5NE  H5UK  H6IT  H6JA  H6NE  H7CA  H7FR  H7IT
H7JA  H7NE  H7UK  H8CA  H8FR  H8GE  H8IT  H8JA  H8NE  H8UK  H8US  H9CA  H9FR
H9IT  H9JA  I0CA  I0FR  I0GE  I0IT  I0JA  I0NE  I0UK  I0US  I1CA  I1FR  I1GE
I1IT  I1JA  I1NE  I1UK  I1US  I2US  I3CA  I3FR  I3US  I4FR  I4IT  I4JA  I4US
I5CA  I5NE  I5UK  I5US  I6CA  I6FR  I6GE  I6IT  I6JA  I6NE  I6UK  I6US  I7US
J0CA  J0FR  J0GE  J0IT  J0JA  J0NE  J0UK  J1CA  J1JA  J1UK  J2CA  J2FR  J2GE
```

Table 7.4 (continued)

```
J2IT   J2NE   J3IT   J3NE   J3UK   J4GE   K0CA   K0FR   K0GE   K0IT   K0JA   K0NE   K0UK
K0US   K1GE   K1NE   K1UK   K10CA  K10UK  K10US  K11FR  K11IT  K11NE  K11UK
K11US  K12IT  K13CA  K13IT  K14FR  K14IT  K14JA  K14NE  K14UK  K14US  K15FR
K15IT  K15JA  K15NE  K15UK  K15US  K2CA   K2FR   K2IT   K2JA   K2NE   K2UK   K2US
K3CA   K3UK   K3US   K4GE   K4IT   K4NE   K4UK   K4US   K5CA   K5JA   K5US   K6CA   K6FR
K6GE   K6IT   K6JA   K6NE   K7JA   K7UK   K8UK   K9CA   K9FR   K9GE   K9IT   K9JA   K9NE
K9UK   K9US   M0CA   M0FR   M0GE   M0IT   M0JA   M0NE   M0UK   M1CA   M1FR   M1GE   M1IT
M1JA   M1NE   M1UK   M2CA   M2FR   M2GE   M2IT   M2JA   M2NE   M2UK   M3CA   M3FR   M3GE
M3IT   M3JA   M3NE   M3UK   M4CA   M4FR   M4GE   M4IT   M4JA   M4NE   M4UK   M5CA   M5FR
M5GE   M5IT   M5JA   M5NE   M5UK   M6CA   M6FR   M6GE   M6IT   M6JA   M6NE   M6UK
```

PARAMETER:
```
DVCA   DVFR   DVGE   DVIT   DVJA   DVNE   DVUK   DVUS   XPCA   XPFR   XPGE   XPIT   XPJA
XPNE   XPUK   XPUS   ZPCA   ZPFR   ZPGE   ZPIT   ZPJA   ZPNE   ZPUK   ZPUS
```

EQUATIONS

1: $\text{LNYRUSP} = (1-\text{ZPUS})*\text{XPUS}+\text{ZPUS}*\text{LNYRUS}+(1-\text{ZPUS})*\text{LNYRUSP}(-1)$

2: $4*\text{BTOYUS} == \text{XTOYUS}-\text{ITOYUS}-\text{CTOYUS}$

3: $\text{LNQIMUS} == \text{LNPIMUS}-\text{LNPUS}$

4: $\text{LNMUSU} == \text{LNMNUS}-\text{LNMNUSEX}$

5: $\text{LNMNUSEX} == 2*\text{LNMNUS}(-1)-\text{LNMNUS}(-2)-0.44937*(\text{DEL}(1 : \text{LNMNUS}(-1))-\text{DEL}(1 : \text{LNMNUS}(-2)))+0.00021-0.80994*\text{LNMUSU}(-2)$

6: $\text{XTOYUSU} == \text{XTOYUS}-\text{XTOYUSEX}$

7: $\text{XTOYUSEX} == \text{XTOYUS}(-1)+0.35462*\text{XTOYUSU}(-2)+0.20228*\text{XTOYUSU}(-3)+0.00053$

8: $\text{LNYRTUS} == \text{LNYRUS}-\text{LNYRUSP}$

9: $\text{LNYRRUS} == (\text{DVUK}*\text{LNYRUK}+\text{DVCA}*\text{LNYRCA}+\text{DVFR}*\text{LNYRFR}+\text{DVGE}*\text{LNYRGE}+\text{DVIT}*\text{LNYRIT}+\text{DVJA}*\text{LNYRJA}+\text{DVNE}*\text{LNYRNE})*1/(1-\text{DVUS})-7.40946$

10: $\text{LNPRUS} == (\text{DVUK}*(\text{LNPUK}-\text{LNEUK})+\text{DVCA}*(\text{LNPCA}-\text{LNECA})+\text{DVFR}*(\text{LNPFR}-\text{LNEFR})+\text{DVGE}*(\text{LNPGE}-\text{LNEGE})+\text{DVIT}*(\text{LNPIT}-\text{LNEIT})+\text{DVJA}*(\text{LNPJA}-\text{LNEJA})+\text{DVNE}*(\text{LNPNE}-\text{LNENE}))*1/(1-\text{DVUS})+2.53058$

11: $\text{GREUKXX11} == 4*(1*(\text{M0UK}+\text{M1UK}*\text{DEL}(1 : \text{LNPIMUK})+\text{M2UK}*\text{DEL}(1 : \text{LNRPOIL})+\text{M3UK}*\text{DEL}(1 : \text{LNYRRUK})+\text{M4UK}*\text{DEL}(1 : \text{ITOYUK})+\text{M5UK}*\text{DEL}(1 : \text{LNPRUK})+\text{M6UK}*\text{DEL}(1 : \text{LNEUK})))$

12: $\text{Z1US1L} == 4*\text{DEL}(1 : \text{LNPUS})-\text{GRPX1US1}(-1)$

13: $\text{GRPX1US1} == 4*(\text{K0US}+\text{K2US}*\text{LNMNUS}(-1)+\text{K3US}*\text{LNMNUS}(-2)+\text{K4US}*\text{DEL}(1 : \text{LNYRUS}(-1))+\text{K5US}*\text{RUS}+\text{K9US}*\text{LNPUS}(-1)+\text{K10US}*\text{LNPUS}(-2)+\text{K11US}*\text{LNMUSU}(-1))+\text{K14US}*\text{Z1US1L}+\text{K15US}*\text{Z1US1L}(-1))$

14: $\text{LNPUS} = \text{B1US}+\text{LNMNUS}+\text{B2US}*\text{LNYRUSP}+\text{B3US}*\text{LNYRTUS}+\text{B4US}*\text{RUS}+\text{B5US}*(\text{LNMNUS}(-1)-\text{LNPUS}(-1))+\text{B6US}*\text{LNMUSU}+\text{B7US}*\text{LNMUSU}(-1)+\text{B8US}*\text{LNMUSU}(-2)+0*\text{LNMUSU}(-3)$

15: $\text{LNYRUS} = \text{A1US}+\text{A2US}*\text{LNYRUSP}(-1)+(1-\text{A2US})*\text{LNYRUS}(-1)+\text{A3US}*\text{LNMUSU}+\text{A4US}*\text{LNMUSU}(-1)+0*\text{LNMUSU}(-2)+\text{A6US}*\text{LNMUSU}(-3)+0*\text{LNGUSU}+\text{A8US}*\text{LNGUSU}(-1)+\text{A9US}*\text{LNGUSU}(-2)+\text{A10US}*\text{LNGUSU}(-3)+\text{A11US}*\text{XTOYUSU}+\text{A12US}*\text{XTOYUSU}(-1)+0*\text{XTOYUSU}(-2)+0*\text{XTOYUSU}(-3)$

16: $\text{DEL}(1 : \text{UNUS}) = \text{C1US}+\text{C20US}*\text{DEL}(1 : \text{LNYRUS})+\text{C21US}*\text{DEL}(1 : \text{LNYRUS}(-1))+\text{C22US}*\text{DEL}(1 : \text{LNYRUS}(-2))+\text{C23US}*\text{DEL}(1 : \text{LNYRUS}(-3))+\text{C24US}*\text{DEL}(1 : \text{LNYRUS}(-4))+\text{C26US}*\text{DEL}(1 : \text{LNYRUS}(-6))+\text{C27US}*\text{DEL}(1 : \text{LNYRUS}(-7))$

17: $\text{DEL}(1 : \text{LNMNUS}) = \text{E1US}+\text{E2US}*\text{T}+0*\text{LNGUSU}+\text{E5US}*(\text{LNGUSU}(-3)+\text{LNGUSU}(-4))+\text{E8US}*(\text{LNPUS}(-3)-\text{LNPUS}(-5))+0*\text{UNUS}(-1)+\text{E11US}*\text{UNUS}(-2)+\text{E12US}*\text{UNUS}(-3)+0*\text{UNUS}(-4)+\text{E20US}*\text{DEL}(1 : \text{LNMNUS}(-1))+\text{E21US}*\text{DEL}(1 : \text{LNMNUS}(-2))$

18: $\text{RUS} = \text{D0US}+\text{D1US}*\text{GRPX1US1}+\text{D14US}*\text{RUS}(-1)+\text{D16US}*\text{GRPX1US1}(-1)+\text{D15US}*\text{T}+\text{D2US}*\text{LNMUSU}+\text{D3US}*\text{LNMUSU}(-1)+0*\text{LNMUSU}(-2)+\text{D5US}*\text{LNMUSU}(-3)+0*\text{LNGUSU}+0*\text{LNGUSU}(-1)+0*\text{LNGUSU}(-2)+0*\text{LNGUSU}(-3)+\text{D10US}*\text{XTOYUSU}+\text{D11US}*\text{XTOYUSU}(-1)+\text{D12US}*\text{XTOYUSU}(-2)+0*\text{XTOYUSU}(-3)$

19: $\text{LNPIMUS} = \text{LNPIMUS}(-1)+\text{F0US}+\text{F10US}*\text{DEL}(1 : \text{LNPIMUS}(-1))+\text{F20US}*\text{DEL}(1 : \text{LNRPOIL})+0*\text{DEL}(1 : \text{LNYRRUS})+\text{F40US}*\text{DEL}(1 : \text{ITOYUS})+\text{F50US}*\text{DEL}(1 : \text{LNPRUS})$

20: $\text{ITOYUS} = \text{I0US}+\text{I1US}*\text{ITOYUS}(-1)+\text{I2US}*\text{LNYRUSP}+\text{I3US}*\text{LNYRTUS}+\text{I4US}*\text{LNYRTUS}(-1)+\text{I5US}*\text{LNQIMUS}+\text{I6US}*\text{LNQIMUS}(-1)+\text{I7US}*\text{LNQIMUS}(-2)+0*\text{LNQIMUS}(-3)$

Table 7.4 (continued)

```
21:    XTOYUS = H0US+H1US*LNRPOIL+H2US*LNYRTUS+H3US*T+H4US*XTOYUS(-1)+
       H8US*LNYRRUS

22:    CTOYUS = G0US+G1US*T+0*LNRPOIL+0*RUS+0*GREUKX11+0*RUK+G6US*(XTOYUS
       -ITOYUS)+0*LNYRTUS+0*DEL(1 : LNYRUS)+0*DEL(1 : LNYRRUS)+0*DEL(1 :
       RUS)+0*DEL(1 : RUS(-1))+G12US*DEL(1 : RUS(-2))+0*DEL(1 : RUK)+0*
       DEL(1 : RUK(-1))+G22US*DEL(1 : RUK(-2))+0*DEL(1 : GREUKX11)+0*DEL(
       1 : GREUKX11(-1))+G32US*DEL(1 : GREUKX11(-2))

23:    LNYRUKP = (1-ZPUK)*XPUK+ZPUK*LNYRUK+(1-ZPUK)*LNYRUKP(-1)

24:    LNPIMUK == LNQIMUK+LNPUK

25:    LNMUKU == LNMNUK-LNMNUKEX

26:    LNMNUKEX == LNMNUK(-1)+0.21096*(LNMNUK(-1)-LNMNUK(-2))+0.28454*(
       LNMNUK(-2)-LNMNUK(-3))+0.00627

27:    XTOYUKU == XTOYUK-XTOYUKEX

28:    XTOYUKEX == XTOYUK(-1)+0.2491*XTOYUKU(-2)-0.14272*XTOYUKU(-4)-
       0.37838*XTOYUKU(-7)+0.00084

29:    ITOYUK == XTOYUK-4*BTOYUK-CTOYUK

30:    LNYRTUK == LNYRUK-LNYRUKP

31:    LNYRRUK == (DVUS*LNYRUS+DVCA*LNYRCA+DVFR*LNYRFR+DVGE*LNYRGE+DVIT*
       LNYRIT+DVJA*LNYRJA+DVNE*LNYRNE)*1/(1-DVUK)-7.36068

32:    LNPRUK == (DVUS*(LNPUS-LNEUS)+DVCA*(LNPCA-LNECA)+DVFR*(LNPFR-LNEFR
       )+DVGE*(LNPGE-LNEGE)+DVIT*(LNPIT-LNEIT)+DVJA*(LNPJA-LNEJA)+DVNE*(
       LNPNE-LNENE))*1/(1-DVUK)+1.32478

33:    Z1UK1L == 4*DEL(1 : LNPUK)-GRPX1UK1(-1)

34:    GRPX1UK1 == 4*(K0UK+K1UK*LNMNUKEX+K2UK*LNMNUK(-1)+K3UK*LNMNUK(-2)+
       K4UK*DEL(1 : LNYRUK(-1))+0*RUK+0*RUK(-1)+K7UK*(RUS+GREUKX11)+K8UK*
       (RUS(-1)+GREUKX11(-1))+K9UK*LNPUK(-1)+K10UK*LNPUK(-2)+K11UK*LNMUKU
       (-1)+0*LNMUKU(-2)+0*LNMUKU(-3))+K14UK*Z1UK1L+K15UK*Z1UK1L(-1))

35:    LNPUK = B1UK+LNMNUK+B2UK*LNYRUKP+B3UK*LNYRTUK+B4UK*RUK+B10UK*(RUS+
       GREUKX11)+B5UK*(LNMNUK(-1)-LNPUK(-1))+B6UK*LNMUKU+0*LNMUKU(-1)+0*
       LNMUKU(-2)+0*LNMUKU(-3)

36:    LNYRUK = A1UK+A2UK*LNYRUKP(-1)+(1-A2UK)*LNYRUK(-1)+A3UK*LNMUKU+0*
       LNMUKU(-1)+0*LNMUKU(-2)+0*LNMUKU(-3)+A7UK*LNGUKU+0*LNGUKU(-1)+A9UK
       *LNGUKU(-2)+0*LNGUKU(-3)+0*XTOYUKU+A12UK*XTOYUKU(-1)+0*XTOYUKU(-2)
       +0*XTOYUKU(-3)

37:    DEL(1 : UNUK) = C1UK+C20UK*DEL(1 : LNYRUK)+C21UK*DEL(1 : LNYRUK(-1
       ))+C22UK*DEL(1 : LNYRUK(-2))+C23UK*DEL(1 : LNYRUK(-3))+C24UK*DEL(1
       : LNYRUK(-4))+C25UK*DEL(1 : LNYRUK(-5))

38:    DEL(1 : LNMNUK) = E1UK+0*T+E3UK*LNGUKU+E4UK*(LNGUKU(-1)+LNGUKU(-2)
       )+E11UK*UNUK(-2)+E12UK*UNUK(-3)+E13UK*UNUK(-4)+E14UK*BTOYUK+E15UK*
       1*BTOYUK+E16UK*(BTOYUK(-1)+BTOYUK(-2))+E17UK*(1*(BTOYUK(-1)+BTOYUK
       (-2)))+E18UK*(BTOYUK(-3)+BTOYUK(-4))

39:    RUK = D0UK+D1UK*GRPX1UK1+D14UK*RUK(-1)+0*GRPX1UK1(-1)+D15UK*T+D2UK
       *LNMUKU+0*LNMUKU(-1)+0*LNMUKU(-2)+D5UK*LNMUKU(-3)+D6UK*LNGUKU+0*
       LNGUKU(-1)+0*LNGUKU(-2)+0*LNGUKU(-3)+D10UK*XTOYUKU+0*XTOYUKU(-1)+0
       *XTOYUKU(-2)+D13UK*XTOYUKU(-3)

40:    DEL(1 : LNEUK) = F0UK+F1UK*DEL(1 : LNPIMUK)-F1UK*DEL(1 : LNPRUK)

41:    LNQIMUK = I0UK+I1UK*ITOYUK+I5UK*LNYRTUK(-1)+I6UK*LNQIMUK(-1)

42:    BTOYUK = J0UK+J1UK*BTOYUK(-1)+J3UK*DEL(1 : LNEUK(-1))

43:    XTOYUK = H0UK+H1UK*LNEUK+(H3UK+H4UK*0)*LNEUK(-1)+H5UK*LNRPOIL+0*
       LNYRTUK+H7UK*T+H8UK*XTOYUK(-1)+0*XTOYUK(-2)+H10UK*LNPRUK+H11UK*
       LNPRUK(-1)+0*LNYRRUK+H13UK*LNYRRUK(-1)+H14UK*LNPUK+H15UK*LNPUK(-1)

44:    CTOYUK = G0UK+G2UK*LNRPOIL+G6UK*(XTOYUK-ITOYUK)+G7UK*LNYRTUK+G8UK*
       DEL(1 : LNYRUK)+G12UK*DEL(1 : RUK(-2))+G22UK*DEL(1 : RUS(-2))+
       G32UK*DEL(1 : GREUKX11(-2))

45:    LNYRCAP = (1-ZPCA)*XPCA+ZPCA*LNYRCA+(1-ZPCA)*LNYRCAP(-1)

46:    LNPIMCA == LNQIMCA+LNPCA
```

Table 7.4 (continued)

47: LNMCAU == LNMNCA-LNMNCAEX

48: XTOYCAU == XTOYCA-XTOYCAEX

49: XTOYCAEX == XTOYCA(-1)-0.20227*(XTOYCA(-1)-XTOYCA(-2))+0.00075-
     0.30644*XTOYCAU(-8)

50: LNMNCAEX == 2*LNMNCA(-1)-LNMNCA(-2)-0.64605*(DEL(1 : LNMNCA(-1))-
     DEL(1 : LNMNCA(-2)))-0.65993*(DEL(1 : LNMNCA(-2))-DEL(1 : LNMNCA(
     -3)))+0.0004-0.46226*LNMCAU(-3)-0.58997*LNMCAU(-4)

51: ITOYCA == XTOYCA-4*BTOYCA-CTOYCA

52: LNYRTCA == LNYRCA-LNYRCAP

53: LNYRRCA == (DVUS*LNYRUS+DVUK*LNYRUK+DVFR*LNYRFR+DVGE*LNYRGE+DVIT*
     LNYRIT+DVJA*LNYRJA+DVNE*LNYRNE)*1/(1-DVCA)-7.26361

54: LNPRCA == (DVUS*(LNPUS-LNEUS)+DVUK*(LNPUK-LNEUK)+DVFR*(LNPFR-LNEFR
)+DVGE*(LNPGE-LNEGE)+DVIT*(LNPIT-LNEIT)+DVJA*(LNPJA-LNEJA)+DVNE*(
     LNPNE-LNENE))*1/(1-DVCA)+1.24117

55: Z1CA1L == 4*DEL(1 : LNPCA)-SGRPX1C1(-1)

56: SGRPX1C1 == 4*(K0CA+K2CA*LNMNCA(-1)+K3CA*LNMNCA(-2)+K5CA*RCA+K6CA*
     RCA(-1)+K9CA*LNPCA(-1)+K10CA*LNPCA(-2)+K13CA*LNMCAU(-3))

57: GRPX1CA1 == SGRPX1C1-0.64968*Z1CA1L(-1)

58: GRECAX11 == 4*(1*(M0CA+M1CA*DEL(1 : LNPIMCA)+M2CA*DEL(1 : LNRPOIL)
     +M3CA*DEL(1 : LNYRRCA)+M4CA*DEL(1 : ITOYCA)+M5CA*DEL(1 : LNPRCA)+
     M6CA*DEL(1 : LNECA)))

59: LNPCA = B1CA+LNMNCA+B2CA*LNYRCAP+B3CA*LNYRTCA+B4CA*RCA+B5CA*(
     LNMNCA(-1)-LNPCA(-1))+B6CA*LNMCAU+B7CA*LNMCAU(-1)+B8CA*LNMCAU(-2)+
     B9CA*LNMCAU(-3)

60: LNYRCA = A1CA+A2CA*LNYRCAP(-1)+(1-A2CA)*LNYRCA(-1)+A3CA*LNMCAU+
     A4CA*LNMCAU(-1)+A5CA*LNMCAU(-2)+A6CA*LNMCAU(-3)+A8CA*LNGCAU(-1)+
     A11CA*XTOYCAU+A14CA*XTOYCAU(-3)

61: DEL(1 : LNMNCA) = E1CA+E2CA*T+E3CA*LNGCAU+E4CA*(LNGCAU(-1)+LNGCAU(
     -2))+E10CA*LNYRTCA(-1)+E14CA*BTOYCA+E15CA*1*BTOYCA(-1)+E16CA*(BTOYCA(
     -1)+BTOYCA(-2))+E17CA*(1*(BTOYCA(-1)+BTOYCA(-2)))+E19CA*(1*(BTOYCA
     (-3)+BTOYCA(-4)))

62: RCA = D0CA+D1CA*GRPX1CA1+D14CA*RCA(-1)+D15CA*T+D4CA*LNMCAU(-2)+
     D5CA*LNMCAU(-3)+D6CA*LNGCAU+D8CA*LNGCAU(-2)+D9CA*LNGCAU(-3)

63: DEL(1 : LNECA) = F0CA+F1CA*DEL(1 : LNPIMCA)+F3CA*DEL(1 : LNRPOIL)-
     F1CA*DEL(1 : LNPRCA)

64: LNQIMCA = I0CA+I1CA*ITOYCA+I3CA*LNYRCAP+I5CA*LNYRTCA(-1)+I6CA*
     LNQIMCA(-1)

65: BTOYCA = J0CA+J1CA*BTOYCA(-1)+J2CA*DEL(1 : LNECA)

66: XTOYCA = H0CA+H3CA*LNECA(-1)+H5CA*LNRPOIL+H7CA*T+H8CA*XTOYCA(-1)+
     H9CA*XTOYCA(-2)+H11CA*LNPRCA(-1)+H12CA*LNYRRCA+H13CA*LNYRRCA(-1)+
     H15CA*LNPCA(-1)

67: CTOYCA = G0CA+G6CA*(XTOYCA-ITOYCA)+G8CA*DEL(1 : LNYRCA)+G9CA*DEL(1
     : LNYRRCA)+G10CA*DEL(1 : RCA)+G20CA*DEL(1 : RUS)+G30CA*DEL(1 :
     GRECAX11)

68: LNYRFRP = (1-ZPFR)*XPFR+ZPFR*LNYRFR+(1-ZPFR)*LNYRFRP(-1)

69: LNPIMFR == LNQIMFR+LNPFR

70: LNMFRU == LNMNFR-LNMNFREX

71: LNMNFREX == LNMNFR(-1)+0.54204*(LNMNFR(-1)-LNMNFR(-2))+0.01294+
     0.45793*LNMFRU(-6)

72: XTOYFRU == XTOYFR-XTOYFREX

73: XTOYFREX == XTOYFR(-1)-0.23545*(XTOYFR(-1)-XTOYFR(-2))+0.26219*
     XTOYFRU(-2)-0.36552*XTOYFRU(-4)+0.00131

74: ITOYFR == XTOYFR-4*BTOYFR-CTOYFR

75: LNYRTFR == LNYRFR-LNYRFRP

Table 7.4 (continued)

76:
```
LNYRRFR == (DVUS*LNYRUS+DVUK*LNYRUK+DVCA*LNYRCA+DVGE*LNYRGE+DVIT*
LNYRIT+DVJA*LNYRJA+DVNE*LNYRNE)*1/(1-DVFR)-7.18014
```

77:
```
LNPRFR == (DVUS*(LNPUS-LNEUS)+DVUK*(LNPUK-LNEUK)+DVCA*(LNPCA-LNECA
)+DVGE*(LNPGE-LNEGE)+DVIT*(LNPIT-LNEIT)+DVJA*(LNPJA-LNEJA)+DVNE*(
LNPNE-LNENE))*1/(1-DVFR)+1.14182
```

78:
```
Z2FR1 == 4*DEL(1 : LNPFR)-SGRPX1F1(-1)
```

79:
```
SGRPX1F1 == 4*(K0FR+K2FR*DEL(1 : LNMNFR(-1))+K6FR*RFR(-1)+K9FR*DEL
(1 : LNPFR(-1))+K11FR*LNMFRU(-1))
```

80:
```
GRPX1FR1 == SGRPX1F1+K14FR*Z2FR1+K15FR*Z2FR1(-1)
```

81:
```
GREFRX11 == 4*(1*(M0FR+M1FR*DEL(1 : LNPIMFR)+M2FR*DEL(1 : LNRPOIL)
+M3FR*DEL(1 : LNYRRFR)+M4FR*DEL(1 : ITOYFR)+M5FR*DEL(1 : LNPRFR)+
M6FR*DEL(1 : LNEFR)))
```

82:
```
LNPFR = B1FR+LNMNFR+B2FR*LNYRFRP+0*LNYRTFR+B4FR*RFR+B10FR*(RUS+
GREFRX11)+B5FR*(LNMNFR(-1)-LNPFR(-1))+B6FR*LNMFRU+B7FR*LNMFRU(-1)+
0*LNMFRU(-2)+0*LNMFRU(-3)
```

83:
```
LNYRRFR = A1FR+A2FR*LNYRFRP(-1)+(1-A2FR)*LNYRRFR(-1)+A3FR*LNMFRU+
A7FR*LNGFRU+A9FR*LNGFRU(-2)+A11FR*XTOYFRU
```

84:
```
DEL(1 : UNFR) = C1FR+C20FR*DEL(1 : LNYRRFR)+C21FR*DEL(1 : LNYRFR(-1
))+C22FR*DEL(1 : LNYRFR(-2))+C23FR*DEL(1 : LNYRFR(-3))+C25FR*DEL(1
: LNYRFR(-5))+C27FR*DEL(1 : LNYRFR(-7))
```

85:
```
DEL(1 : LNMNFR) = E1FR+E2FR*T+E4FR*(LNGFRU(-1)+LNGFRU(-2))+E6FR*(
LNPFR(-1)-LNPFR(-3))+E8FR*(LNPFR(-3)-LNPFR(-5))+E9FR*(1*(LNPFR(-3)
-LNPFR(-5)))+E11FR*UNFR(-2)+E12FR*UNFR(-3)+E13FR*UNFR(-4)+E14FR*
BTOYFR+E16FR*(BTOYFR(-1)+BTOYFR(-2))+E18FR*(BTOYFR(-3)+BTOYFR(-4))
```

86:
```
RFR = D0FR+D1FR*GRPX1FR1+D14FR*RFR(-1)+D15FR*T+D2FR*LNMFRU+D3FR*
LNMFRU(-1)+D6FR*LNGFRU+D12FR*XTOYFRU(-2)
```

87:
```
DEL(1 : LNEFR) = F0FR+F1FR*DEL(1 : LNPIMFR)+F3FR*DEL(1 : LNRPOIL)-
F1FR*DEL(1 : LNPRFR)
```

88:
```
LNQIMFR = I0FR+I1FR*ITOYFR+I3FR*LNYRFRP+I4FR*LNYRTFR+I6FR*LNQIMFR(
-1)
```

89:
```
BTOYFR = J0FR+J2FR*DEL(1 : LNEFR)
```

90:
```
XTOYFR = H0FR+H1FR*LNEFR+H3FR*LNEFR(-1)+H5FR*LNRPOIL+H7FR*T+H8FR*
XTOYFR(-1)+H9FR*XTOYFR(-2)+H11FR*LNPRFR(-1)+H12FR*LNYRRFR+H15FR*
LNPFR(-1)
```

91:
```
CTOYFR = G0FR+G3FR*RFR+G4FR*GREFRX11+G5FR*RUS+G6FR*(XTOYFR-ITOYFR)
+G8FR*DEL(1 : LNYRFR)+G9FR*DEL(1 : LNYRRFR)
```

92:
```
LNYRGEP = (1-ZPGE)*XPGE+ZPGE*LNYRGE+(1-ZPGE)*LNYRGEP(-1)
```

93:
```
LNPIMGE == LNQIMGE+LNPGE
```

94:
```
LNMGEU == LNMNGE-LNMNGEEX
```

95:
```
LNMNGEEX == LNMNGE(-1)+0.02266+0.1074*LNMGEU(-1)+0.27425*LNMGEU(-2
)+0.35616*LNMGEU(-3)
```

96:
```
XTOYGEU == XTOYGE-XTOYGEEX
```

97:
```
ITOYGE == XTOYGE-4*BTOYGE-CTOYGE
```

98:
```
XTOYGEEX == XTOYGE(-1)-0.42012*XTOYGEU(-4)+0.00141
```

99:
```
LNYRTGE == LNYRGE-LNYRGEP
```

100:
```
LNYRRGE == (DVUS*LNYRUS+DVUK*LNYRUK+DVCA*LNYRCA+DVFR*LNYRFR+DVIT*
LNYRIT+DVJA*LNYRJA+DVNE*LNYRNE)*1/(1-DVGE)-7.20584
```

101:
```
LNPRGE == (DVUS*(LNPUS-LNEUS)+DVUK*(LNPUK-LNEUK)+DVCA*(LNPCA-LNECA
)+DVFR*(LNPFR-LNEFR)+DVIT*(LNPIT-LNEIT)+DVJA*(LNPJA-LNEJA)+DVNE*(
LNPNE-LNENE))*1/(1-DVGE)+1.17274
```

102:
```
Z1GE1L == 4*DEL(1 : LNPGE)-GRPX1GE1(-1)
```

103:
```
GRPX1GE1 == 4*(K0GE+K1GE*(LNMNGEEX-LNMNGE(-1))+K4GE*DEL(1 : LNYRGE
(-1))+K6GE*RGE(-1)+K9GE*(LNPGE(-1)-LNPGE(-2)))+0.0475*Z1GE1L-
0.4236*Z1GE1L(-1)
```

Table 7.4 (continued)

104: GREGEX21 == 4*(1*(M0GE+M1GE*DEL(1 : LNPIMGE)+M2GE*DEL(1 : LNRPOIL)
+M3GE*DEL(1 : LNYRRGE)+M4GE*DEL(1 : ITOYGE)+M5GE*DEL(1 : LNPRGE)+
M6GE*DEL(1 : LNEGE)))

105: LNPGE = B1GE+LNMNGE+B2GE*LNYRGEP+0*LNYRTGE+B4GE*RGE+0*(RUS+
GREGEX21)+B5GE*(LNMNGE(-1)-LNPGE(-1))+B6GE*LNMGEU+B7GE*LNMGEU(-1)+
B8GE*LNMGEU(-2)+B9GE*LNMGEU(-3)

106: LNYRGE = A1GE+A2GE*LNYRGEP(-1)+(1-A2GE)*LNYRGE(-1)+A3GE*LNMGEU+0*
LNMGEU(-1)+0*LNMGEU(-2)+0*LNMGEU(-3)+A7GE*LNGGEU+A8GE*LNGGEU(-1)+0
*LNGGEU(-2)+0*LNGGEU(-3)+A11GE*XTOYGEU+A12GE*XTOYGEU(-1)+A13GE*
XTOYGEU(-2)+A14GE*XTOYGEU(-3)

107: DEL(1 : LNMNGE) = E1GE+0*T+E3GE*LNGGEU+E7GE*(1*(LNPGE(-1)-LNPGE(-3
)))+E8GE*(LNPGE(-3)-LNPGE(-5))+E9GE*(1*(LNPGE(-3)-LNPGE(-5)))+0*
LNYRTGE(-1)+0*LNYRTGE(-2)+0*LNYRTGE(-3)+0*LNYRTGE(-4)+E14GE*BTOYGE
+0*0*BTOYGE+E18GE*(BTOYGE(-3)+BTOYGE(-4)))

108: RGE = D0GE+D1GE*GRPX1GE1+D14GE*RGE(-1)+0*GRPX1GE1(-1)+0*T+0*LNMGEU
+0*LNMGEU(-1)+0*LNMGEU(-2)+0*LNMGEU(-3)+0*LNGGEU+0*LNGGEU(-1)+0*
LNGGEU(-2)+0*LNGGEU(-3)+0*XTOYGEU+0*XTOYGEU(-1)+0*XTOYGEU(-2)+0*
XTOYGEU(-3)

109: DEL(1 : LNEGE) = F0GE+F1GE*DEL(1 : LNPIMGE)+F3GE*DEL(1 : LNRPOIL)+
F4GE*DEL(1 : LNYRRGE)-F1GE*DEL(1 : LNPRGE)

110: LNQIMGE = I0GE+I1GE*ITOYGE+I6GE*LNQIMGE(-1)

111: BTOYGE = J0GE+J2GE*DEL(1 : LNEGE)+J4GE*DEL(1 : LNPGE(-1))

112: XTOYGE = H0GE+H1GE*LNEGE+H5GE*LNRPOIL+H8GE*XTOYGE(-1)+H10GE*LNPRGE
+H12GE*LNYRRGE+H15GE*LNPGE(-1)

113: CTOYGE = G0GE+0*T+0*LNRPOIL+0*RGE+0*GREGEX21+0*RUS+G6GE*(XTOYGE-
ITOYGE)+0*LNYRTGE+G8GE*DEL(1 : LNYRGE)+G9GE*DEL(1 : LNYRRGE)+G10GE
*DEL(1 : RGE)+0*DEL(1 : RGE(-1))+0*DEL(1 : RGE(-2))+G20GE*DEL(1 :
RUS)+0*DEL(1 : RUS(-1))+0*DEL(1 : RUS(-2))+G30GE*DEL(1 : GREGEX21)
+0*DEL(1 : GREGEX21(-1))+0*DEL(1 : GREGEX21(-2))

114: LNYRITP = (1-ZPIT)*XPIT+ZPIT*LNYRIT+(1-ZPIT)*LNYRITP(-1)

115: LNPIMIT == LNQIMIT+LNPIT

116: LNMITU == LNMNIT-LNMNITEX

117: LNMNITEX == LNMNIT(-1)+0.15625*(LNMNIT(-1)-LNMNIT(-2))+0.02829+
0.35998*LNMITU(-2)+0.10908*LNMITU(-3)

118: XTOYITU == XTOYIT-XTOYITEX

119: XTOYITEX == XTOYIT(-1)-0.15095*(XTOYIT(-1)-XTOYIT(-2))+0.19592*(
XTOYIT(-2)-XTOYIT(-3))-0.14307*XTOYITU(-8)+0.29814*XTOYITU(-11)+
0.00221

120: ITOYIT == XTOYIT-4*BTOYIT-CTOYIT

121: LNYRTIT == LNYRIT-LNYRITP

122: LNYRRIT == (DVUS*LNYRUS+DVUK*LNYRUK+DVCA*LNYRCA+DVFR*LNYRFR+DVGE*
LNYRGE+DVJA*LNYRJA+DVNE*LNYRNE)*1/(1-DVIT)-6.93985

123: LNPRIT == (DVUS*(LNPUS-LNEUS)+DVUK*(LNPUK-LNEUK)+DVCA*(LNPCA-LNECA
)+DVFR*(LNPFR-LNEFR)+DVGE*(LNPGE-LNEGE)+DVJA*(LNPJA-LNEJA)+DVNE*(
LNPNE-LNENE))*1/(1-DVIT)+0.920318

124: Z1IT1 == 4*DEL(1 : LNPIT)-SGRPX1I1(-1)

125: SGRPX1I1 == 4*(K0IT+K2IT*DEL(1 : LNMNIT(-1))+K4IT*DEL(1 : LNYRIT(
-1))+K9IT*DEL(1 : LNPIT(-1))+K11IT*LNMITU(-1)+K12IT*LNMITU(-2)+
K13IT*LNMITU(-3))

126: GRPX1IT1 == SGRPX1I1+K14IT*Z1IT1+K15IT*Z1IT1(-1)

127: GREITX11 == 4*(1*(M0IT+M1IT*DEL(1 : LNPIMIT)+M2IT*DEL(1 : LNRPOIL)
+M3IT*DEL(1 : LNYRRIT)+M4IT*DEL(1 : ITOYIT)+M5IT*DEL(1 : LNPRIT)+
M6IT*DEL(1 : LNEIT)))

128: LNPIT = B1IT+LNMNIT+B2IT*LNYRITP+0*LNYRTIT+B4IT*RIT+B5IT*(LNMNIT(
-1)-LNPIT(-1))+B6IT*LNMITU+B7IT*LNMITU(-1)+B8IT*LNMITU(-2)+B9IT*
LNMITU(-3)

Table 7.4 (continued)

```
129:    LNYRIT = A1IT+A2IT*LNYRITP(-1)+(1-A2IT)*LNYRIT(-1)+A5IT*LNMITU(-2)
        +A10IT*LNGITU(-3)+A11IT*XTOYITU(-3)+A13IT*XTOYITU(-2)

130:    DEL(1 : LNMNIT) = E1IT+E2IT*T+E4IT*(LNGITU(-1)+LNGITU(-2))+E5IT*(
        LNGITU(-3)+LNGITU(-4))+E6IT*(LNPIT(-1)-LNPIT(-3))+E13IT*LNYRTIT(-4
        )+E14IT*BTOYIT+E15IT*1*BTOYIT+E16IT*(BTOYIT(-1)+BTOYIT(-2))

131:    RIT = D0IT+D1IT*GRPX1IT1+D14IT*RIT(-1)+D4IT*LNMITU(-2)+K6IT*LNGITU
        +D7IT*LNGITU(-1)+D10IT*XTOYITU+D11IT*XTOYITU(-1)

132:    DEL(1 : LNEIT) = F0IT+F1IT*DEL(1 : LNPIMIT)-F1IT*DEL(1 : LNPRIT)

133:    LNQIMIT = I0IT+I1IT*ITOYIT+I4IT*LNYRTIT+I6IT*LNQIMIT(-1)

134:    BTOYIT = J0IT+J2IT*DEL(1 : LNEIT)+J3IT*DEL(1 : LNEIT(-1))

135:    XTOYIT = H0IT+H3IT*LNEIT(-1)+H5IT*LNRPOIL+H6IT*LNYRTIT+H7IT*T+H8IT
        *XTOYIT(-1)+H9IT*XTOYIT(-2)+H11IT*LNPRIT(-1)+H13IT*LNYRRIT(-1)+
        H15IT*LNPIT(-1)

136:    CTOYIT = G0IT+G3IT*RIT+G4IT*GREITX11+G5IT*RUS+G6IT*(XTOYIT-ITOYIT)

137:    LNYRJAP = (1-ZPJA)*XPJA+ZPJA*LNYRJA+(1-ZPJA)*LNYRJAP(-1)

138:    LNPIMJA == LNQIMJA+LNPJA

139:    LNMJAU == LNMNJA-LNMNJAEX

140:    LNMNJAEX == LNMNJA(-1)+0.45216*(LNMNJA(-1)-LNMNJA(-2))+0.18984*(
        LNMNJA(-2)-LNMNJA(-3))+0.01423-0.41074*LNMJAU(-4)

141:    XTOYJAU == XTOYJA-XTOYJAEX

142:    XTOYJAEX == 2*XTOYJA(-1)-XTOYJA(-2)-1.1134*(DEL(1 : XTOYJA(-1))-
        DEL(1 : XTOYJA(-2)))-0.38594*(DEL(1 : XTOYJA(-2))-DEL(1 : XTOYJA(
        -3)))-0.60316*XTOYJAU(-4)+0.36554*XTOYJAU(-9)+5.000000E-05

143:    ITOYJA == XTOYJA-4*BTOYJA-CTOYJA

144:    LNYRTJA == LNYRJA-LNYRJAP

145:    LNYRRJA == (DVUS*LNYRUS+DVUK*LNYRUK+DVCA*LNYRCA+DVFR*LNYRFR+DVGE*
        LNYRGE+DVIT*LNYRIT+DVNE*LNYRNE)*1/(1-DVJA)-6.64583

146:    LNPRJA == (DVUS*(LNPUS-LNEUS)+DVUK*(LNPUK-LNEUK)+DVCA*(LNPCA-LNECA
        )+DVFR*(LNPFR-LNEFR)+DVGE*(LNPGE-LNEGE)+DVIT*(LNPIT-LNEIT)+DVNE*(
        LNPNE-LNENE))*1/(1-DVJA)+0.617771

147:    Z1JA2 == 4*DEL(1 : LNPJA)-SGRPX1J2(-1)

148:    SGRPX1J2 == 4*(K0JA+K2JA*DEL(1 : LNMNJA(-1))+K5JA*RJA+K6JA*RJA(-1)
        +K7JA*(RUS+GREJAX21)+K9JA*DEL(1 : LNPJA(-1)))

149:    GRPX1JA2 == SGRPX1J2+K14JA*Z1JA2+K15JA*Z1JA2(-1)

150:    GREJAX21 == 4*(1*(M0JA+M1JA*DEL(1 : LNPIMJA)+M2JA*DEL(1 : LNRPOIL)
        +M3JA*DEL(1 : LNYRRJA)+M4JA*DEL(1 : ITOYJA)+M5JA*DEL(1 : LNPRJA)+
        M6JA*DEL(1 : LNEJA)))

151:    LNPJA = B1JA+LNMNJA+B2JA*LNYRJAP+B3JA*LNYRTJA+B4JA*RJA+B10JA*(RUS+
        GREJAX21)+B5JA*(LNMNJA(-1)-LNPJA(-1))+B6JA*LNMJAU+B7JA*LNMJAU(-1)+
        B8JA*LNMJAU(-2)+B9JA*LNMJAU(-3)

152:    LNYRJA = A1JA+A2JA*LNYRJAP(-1)+(1-A2JA)*LNYRJA(-1)+A5JA*LNMJAU(-2)
        +A10JA*LNGJAU(-3)+A11JA*XTOYJAU+A13JA*XTOYJAU(-2)+A14JA*XTOYJAU(-3
        )

153:    DEL(1 : LNMNJA) = E1JA+E6JA*(LNPJA(-1)-LNPJA(-3))+E7JA*(1*(LNPJA(
        -1)-LNPJA(-3)))+E8JA*(LNPJA(-3)-LNPJA(-5))+E12JA*LNYRTJA(-3)+E13JA
        *LNYRTJA(-4)+E14JA*BTOYJA+E16JA*(BTOYJA(-1)+BTOYJA(-2))+E17JA*(1*(
        BTOYJA(-1)+BTOYJA(-2)))+E18JA*(BTOYJA(-3)+BTOYJA(-4))+E19JA*(1*(
        BTOYJA(-3)+BTOYJA(-4)))

154:    RJA = D0JA+D1JA*GRPX1JA2+D14JA*RJA(-1)+D16JA*GRPX1JA2(-1)+D15JA*T+
        D2JA*LNMJAU+D3JA*LNMJAU(-1)+D4JA*LNMJAU(-2)+D5JA*LNMJAU(-3)+0*
        LNGJAU+D7JA*LNGJAU(-1)

155:    DEL(1 : LNEJA) = F0JA+F1JA*DEL(1 : LNPIMJA)+F4JA*DEL(1 : LNYRRJA)-
        F1JA*DEL(1 : LNPRJA)

156:    LNQIMJA = I0JA+I1JA*ITOYJA+I4JA*LNYRTJA+I6JA*LNQIMJA(-1)
```

Table 7.4 (continued)

```
157:    BTOYJA = J0JA+J1JA*BTOYJA(-1)

158:    XTOYJA = H0JA+H1JA*LNEJA+H5JA*LNRPOIL+H6JA*LNYRTJA+H7JA*T+H8JA*
        XTOYJA(-1)+H9JA*XTOYJA(-2)+H10JA*LNPRJA+H12JA*LNYRRJA+H13JA*
        LNYRRJA(-1)+H14JA*LNPJA

159:    CTOYJA = G0JA+G1JA*T+G3JA*RJA+G4JA*GREJAX21+G5JA*RUS+G8JA*DEL(1 :
        LNYRJA)

160:    LNYRNEP = (1-ZPNE)*XPNE+ZPNE*LNYRNE+(1-ZPNE)*LNYRNEP(-1)

161:    LNPIMNE == LNQIMNE+LNPNE

162:    LNMNEU == LNMNNE-LNMNNEEX

163:    LNMNNEEX == LNMNNE(-1)+0.34717*(LNMNNE(-1)-LNMNNE(-2))+0.37492*(
        LNMNNE(-2)-LNMNNE(-3))-0.43951*LNMNEU(-4)+0.00681

164:    XTOYNEU == XTOYNE-XTOYNEEX

165:    XTOYNEEX == XTOYNE(-1)-0.31379*XTOYNEU(-1)-0.33862*XTOYNEU(-9)+
        0.00094

166:    ITOYNE == XTOYNE-4*BTOYNE-CTOYNE

167:    LNYRTNE == LNYRNE-LNYRNEP

168:    LNYRRNE == (DVUS*LNYRUS+DVUK*LNYRUK+DVCA*LNYRCA+DVFR*LNYRFR+DVGE*
        LNYRGE+DVIT*LNYRIT+DVJA*LNYRJA)*1/(1-DVNE)-7.17908

169:    LNPRNE == (DVUS*(LNPUS-LNEUS)+DVUK*(LNPUK-LNEUK)+DVCA*(LNPCA-LNECA
        )+DVFR*(LNPFR-LNEFR)+DVGE*(LNPGE-LNEGE)+DVIT*(LNPIT-LNEIT)+DVJA*(
        LNPJA-LNEJA))*1/(1-DVNE)+1.1838

170:    Z1NE1L == 4*DEL(1 : LNPNE)-GRPX1NE1(-1)

171:    GRPX1NE1 == 4*(K0NE+K1NE*LNMNNEEX+K2NE*LNMNNE(-1)+K4NE*DEL(1 :
        LNYRNE(-1))+K6NE*RNE(-1)+K9NE*DEL(1 : LNPNE(-1))+K11NE*LNMNEU(-1))
        +K14NE*Z1NE1L+K15NE*Z1NE1L(-1)

172:    GRENEX11 == 4*(1*(M0NE+M1NE*DEL(1 : LNPIMNE)+M2NE*DEL(1 : LNRPOIL)
        +M3NE*DEL(1 : LNYRRNE)+M4NE*DEL(1 : ITOYNE)+M5NE*DEL(1 : LNPRNE)+
        M6NE*DEL(1 : LNENE)))

173:    LNPNE = B1NE+LNMNNE+B2NE*LNYRNEP+B3NE*LNYRTNE+B4NE*RNE+B10NE*(RUS+
        GRENEX11)+B5NE*(LNMNNE(-1)-LNPNE(-1))+B6NE*LNMNEU+B7NE*LNMNEU(-1)+
        B8NE*LNMNEU(-2)+B9NE*LNMNEU(-3)

174:    LNYRNE = A1NE+A2NE*LNYRNEP(-1)+(1-A2NE)*LNYRNE(-1)+A3NE*LNMNEU+
        A4NE*LNMNEU(-1)+A5NE*LNMNEU(-2)+A6NE*LNMNEU(-3)+A7NE*LNGNEU+A8NE*
        LNGNEU(-1)+A9NE*LNGNEU(-2)+A10NE*LNGNEU(-3)+A11NE*XTOYNEU+A12NE*
        XTOYNEU(-1)+A13NE*XTOYNEU(-2)+A14NE*XTOYNEU(-3)

175:    DEL(1 : LNMNNE) = E1NE+E2NE*T+E3NE*LNGNEU+E4NE*(LNGNEU(-1)+LNGNEU(
        -2))+E5NE*(LNGNEU(-3)+LNGNEU(-4))+E6NE*(LNPNE(-1)-LNPNE(-3))+E7NE*
        (1*(LNPNE(-1)-LNPNE(-3)))+E11NE*LNYRTNE(-2)+E12NE*LNYRTNE(-1)+
        E14NE*BTOYNE+E16NE*(BTOYNE(-1)+BTOYNE(-2))+E17NE*(1*(BTOYNE(-1)+
        BTOYNE(-2)))

176:    RNE = D0NE+D1NE*GRPX1NE1+D14NE*RNE(-1)+D15NE*T+D3NE*LNMNEU(-1)+
        D4NE*LNMNEU(-2)+D10NE*XTOYNEU+D11NE*XTOYNEU(-1)+D13NE*XTOYNEU(-3)

177:    DEL(1 : LNENE) = F0NE+F1NE*DEL(1 : LNPIMNE)-F1NE*DEL(1 : LNPRNE)

178:    LNQIMNE = I0NE+I1NE*ITOYNE+I5NE*LNYRTNE(-1)+I6NE*LNQIMNE(-1)

179:    BTOYNE = J0NE+J2NE*DEL(1 : LNENE)+J3NE*DEL(1 : LNENE(-1))

180:    XTOYNE = H0NE+H1NE*LNENE+H5NE*LNRPOIL+H6NE*LNYRTNE+H7NE*T+H8NE*
        XTOYNE(-1)+H10NE*LNPRNE+H12NE*LNYRRNE+H13NE*LNYRRNE(-1)+H14NE*
        LNPNE

181:    CTOYNE = G0NE+G1NE*T+G2NE*LNRPOIL+G3NE*RNE+G4NE*GRENEX11+G5NE*RUS+
        G6NE*(XTOYNE-ITOYNE)+G7NE*LNYRTNE
```

Table 7.4 (continued)

COEFFICIENT AND PARAMETER VALUES (CONST_MARK4FLT)

A1CA	0.010803	A1FR	0.012619	A1GE	0.010821
A1IT	0.011699	A1JA	0.020614	A1NE	0.009964
A1UK	0.005561	A1US	0.007884	A10CA	-0.01349
A10FR	0.016439	A10GE	0.013896	A10IT	0.025164
A10JA	-0.026697	A10NE	0.035157	A10UK	-0.023974
A10US	0.067441	A11CA	0.679057	A11FR	0.213191
A11GE	0.296236	A11IT	-0.383459	A11JA	-1.91914
A11NE	0.097619	A11UK	0.189683	A11US	0.717539
A12CA	0.164836	A12FR	-0.715374	A12GE	-0.23778
A12IT	-0.044277	A12JA	0.349852	A12NE	-0.064686
A12UK	0.42402	A12US	0.532314	A13CA	-0.028676
A13FR	0.015316	A13GE	-0.333226	A13IT	-0.227114
A13JA	-1.15516	A13NE	0.104741	A13UK	-0.21287
A13US	-0.0415	A14CA	0.544787	A14FR	0.121494
A14GE	-0.514582	A14IT	-0.465483	A14JA	-1.09256
A14NE	-0.113143	A14UK	0.006859	A14US	-0.925131
A2CA	0.134071	A2FR	0.102126	A2GE	0.04147
A2IT	0.02481	A2JA	-0.038396	A2NE	0.090174
A2UK	0.240655	A2US	0.088859	A3CA	0.244862
A3FR	-0.264118	A3GE	0.344867	A3IT	0.093876
A3JA	0.142673	A3NE	0.241184	A3UK	-0.18449
A3US	0.967393	A4CA	0.177733	A4FR	0.068796
A4GE	0.069415	A4IT	0.079064	A4JA	0.1083
A4NE	0.094424	A4UK	0.040359	A4US	0.548935
A5CA	0.075535	A5FR	0.10011	A5GE	-0.01725
A5IT	0.266542	A5JA	0.211515	A5NE	-0.03886
A5UK	-0.026207	A5US	-0.04704	A6CA	0.193415
A6FR	-0.055212	A6GE	0.04078	A6IT	-0.01757
A6JA	0.088371	A6NE	0.006819	A6UK	-0.126895
A6US	0.935403	A7CA	-0.004872	A7FR	0.072732
A7GE	-0.036326	A7IT	-0.001348	A7JA	0.044268
A7NE	0.037422	A7UK	0.174624	A7US	-0.034466
A8CA	-0.149956	A8FR	0.007462	A8GE	0.030281
A8IT	0.000596	A8JA	-0.019563	A8NE	-0.031181
A8UK	0.027366	A8US	0.138711	A9CA	-0.02829
A9FR	0.049895	A9GE	-0.00762	A9IT	-0.001628
A9JA	0.044973	A9NE	0.016572	A9UK	0.118697
A9US	0.05507	B1CA	0.119397	B1FR	0.05478
B1GE	0.073547	B1IT	0.206264	B1JA	0.448139
B1NE	-0.005675	B1UK	-0.151938	B1US	0.083905
B10CA	-0.056102	B10FR	0.029941	B10GE	-0.008847
B10IT	-0.037786	B10JA	0.080375	B10NE	0.000617
B10UK	0.078828	B10US	-0.001131	B2CA	-0.218794
B2FR	-0.018392	B2GE	-0.063613	B2IT	-0.069682
B2JA	-0.201664	B2NE	-0.081835	B2UK	-0.046894
B2US	-0.022227	B3CA	-0.152691	B3FR	-0.018886
B3GE	-0.006227	B3IT	-0.042952	B3JA	-0.065941
B3NE	0.107645	B3UK	-0.276035	B3US	-0.09072
B4CA	0.244962	B4FR	0.462903	B4GE	0.023618
B4IT	0.160445	B4JA	0.95586	B4NE	-0.013744
B4UK	0.504004	B4US	0.346502	B5CA	-0.628784
B5FR	-0.996486	B5GE	-0.935252	B5IT	-0.947684
B5JA	-0.827685	B5NE	-0.890964	B5UK	-0.872932
B5US	-0.9906	B6CA	-1.07886	B6FR	-0.724769
B6GE	-1.07676	B6IT	-1.24523	B6JA	-0.988582
B6NE	-0.977966	B6UK	-0.689923	B6US	-0.725851
B7CA	-0.267171	B7FR	-0.237026	B7GE	-0.141736
B7IT	-0.191914	B7JA	-0.356822	B7NE	-0.451249
B7UK	0.037385	B7US	-0.393195	B8CA	-0.271711
B8FR	0.024827	B8GE	-0.311723	B8IT	-0.378815
B8JA	-0.312743	B8NE	-0.621455	B8UK	-0.151933
B8US	0.169832	B9CA	-0.635726	B9FR	0.04942
B9GE	-0.308631	B9IT	-0.151063	B9JA	-0.289714
B9NE	-0.309134	B9UK	-0.167466	B9US	0.016405
C1FR	0.001842	C1UK	0.002293	C1US	0.004693
C20FR	-0.033332	C20UK	-0.087536	C20US	-0.198491
C21FR	-0.036075	C21UK	-0.032481	C21US	-0.187741
C22FR	-0.024205	C22UK	-0.064932	C22US	-0.050647
C23FR	-0.011601	C23UK	-0.054861	C23US	-0.063531
C24FR	-0.003691	C24UK	-0.041132	C24US	0.059092
C25FR	-0.010717	C25UK	-0.01505	C25US	0.017716
C26FR	0.000474	C26UK	-0.005727	C26US	-0.027592
C27FR	0.0072	C27UK	0.000353	C27US	-0.061705
DVCA	0.046296	DVFR	0.077221	DVGE	0.107001
DVIT	0.048061	DVJA	0.107898	DVNE	0.018270
DVUK	0.063287	DVUS	0.531464	D0CA	0.002086
D0FR	0.003366	D0GE	0.003628	D0IT	-0.002471
D0JA	-0.000932	D0NE	0.003585	D0UK	0.003081
D0US	0.010089	D1CA	0.049893	D1FR	0.073674
D1GE	0.231726	D1IT	0.027008	D1JA	0.027117

Table 7.4 (continued)

D1NE	-0.043995	D1UK	0.009035	D1US	0.434367
D10CA	-0.007863	D10FR	0.20013	D10GE	0.20221
D10IT	0.239529	D10JA	0.007364	D10NE	0.137002
D10UK	0.192508	D10US	0.508074	D11CA	0.037268
D11FR	0.12238	D11GE	-0.24158	D11IT	0.161757
D11JA	-0.025161	D11NE	0.06167	D11UK	0.018407
D11US	0.23597	D12CA	-0.013955	D12FR	0.194568
D12GE	0.0877	D12IT	0.054745	D12JA	0.025661
D12NE	0.03381	D12UK	-0.003938	D12US	0.544253
D13CA	-0.032712	D13FR	0.07675	D13GE	-0.24942
D13IT	-0.009773	D13JA	0.002267	D13NE	0.048054
D13UK	0.213998	D13US	-0.213716	D14CA	0.961863
D14FR	0.763452	D14GE	0.76264	D14IT	1.02768
D14JA	0.983108	D14NE	0.799926	D14UK	0.825858
D14US	0.539202	D15CA	-3.498167E-05	D15FR	0.000154
D15GE	3.845550E-05	D15IT	1.960370E-05	D15JA	-2.144426E-05
D15NE	0.000151	D15UK	0.000183	D15US	-6.091796E-06
D16CA	0.005978	D16FR	0.0124	D16GE	-0.06953
D16IT	-0.019956	D16JA	0.030428	D16NE	0.04514
D16UK	-0.022298	D16US	-0.154852	D2CA	-0.078202
D2FR	-0.49829	D2GE	0.1307	D2IT	-0.020386
D2JA	-0.006893	D2NE	0.07838	D2UK	-0.299766
D2US	-0.230722	D3CA	0.015319	D3FR	-0.154023
D3GE	0.07571	D3IT	0.004611	D3JA	-0.021473
D3NE	-0.162029	D3UK	0.025404	D3US	0.163077
D4CA	0.092836	D4FR	-0.09139	D4GE	0.10942
D4IT	0.037063	D4JA	-0.032911	D4NE	0.06593
D4UK	0.036448	D4US	0.091665	D5CA	0.116664
D5FR	0.03674	D5GE	0.05852	D5IT	0.02739
D5JA	-0.016782	D5NE	0.00622	D5UK	0.077159
D5US	0.103347	D6CA	-0.073145	D6FR	-0.034926
D6GE	-0.02391	D6IT	-0.005287	D6JA	0.000489
D6NE	0.00239	D6UK	-0.050417	D6US	-0.020453
D7CA	-0.001992	D7FR	0.01672	D7GE	0.00277
D7IT	-0.004384	D7JA	0.001793	D7NE	0.00041
D7UK	0.022854	D7US	0.01894	D8CA	0.032561
D8FR	-0.01609	D8GE	-0.0128	D8IT	-0.000764
D8JA	0.000889	D8NE	0.00664	D8UK	0.014188
D8US	0.02294	D9CA	0.017438	D9FR	-0.00794
D9GE	0.01666	D9IT	-0.003281	D9JA	0.000607
D9NE	0.01609	D9UK	0.001453	D9US	0.015392
E1CA	0.007281	E1FR	0.03332	E1GE	0.013288
E1IT	0.019544	E1JA	0.054274	E1NE	0.010131
E1UK	-0.00433	E1US	0.00329	E10CA	-0.034398
E10FR	1.58587	E10GE	-0.036416	E10IT	0.105504
E10JA	0.005894	E10NE	0.033838	E10UK	1.23133
E10US	-0.116645	E11CA	-0.054589	E11FR	-1.02545
E11GE	0.102443	E11IT	-0.126347	E11JA	-0.022105
E11NE	0.004899	E11UK	-0.550499	E11US	0.426361
E12CA	-0.077664	E12FR	4.39695	E12GE	-0.191149
E12IT	0.126007	E12JA	-0.158405	E12NE	0.019509
E12UK	5.57298	E12US	-0.468037	E13CA	-0.041273
E13FR	-3.24907	E13GE	0.084755	E13IT	-0.151066
E13JA	0.284267	E13NE	-0.028792	E13UK	-4.2394
E13US	-0.054576	E14CA	-0.396027	E14FR	0.10534
E14GE	1.628	E14IT	-3.88655	E14JA	1.95052
E14NE	0.403001	E14UK	-0.068485	E15CA	3.68752
E15FR	0.103117	E15GE	0.019635	E15IT	4.10458
E15JA	-0.574234	E15NE	0.700825	E15UK	0.596763
E16CA	0.670052	E16FR	0.108524	E16GE	0.09378
E16IT	1.57536	E16JA	1.83261	E16NE	0.292781
E16UK	0.282168	E17CA	-2.84711	E17FR	-0.132219
E17GE	0.332797	E17IT	-0.686828	E17JA	-2.53069
E17NE	-0.892653	E17UK	-0.521172	E18CA	0.286188
E18FR	0.761771	E18GE	0.625931	E18IT	-0.372264
E18JA	1.71901	E18NE	0.091526	E18UK	0.187571
E19CA	2.14929	E19FR	0.060458	E19GE	0.039871
E19IT	0.810022	E19JA	-1.78208	E19NE	-0.971241
E19UK	-0.204191	E2CA	0.000184	E2FR	-0.000192
E2GE	-8.064001E-05	E2IT	0.000454	E2JA	-1.888251E-05
E2NE	0.000421	E2UK	-6.443714E-07	E2US	0.000243
E20US	0.496825	E21US	-0.248602	E3CA	0.10149
E3FR	0.00301	E3GE	0.043045	E3IT	-0.014448
E3JA	-0.021866	E3NE	0.058633	E3UK	0.107434
E3US	0.004036	E4CA	0.138066	E4FR	0.011217
E4GE	-0.014921	E4IT	-0.03104	E4JA	0.031742
E4NE	-0.027174	E4UK	0.163098	E4US	0.001552
E5CA	-0.003532	E5FR	-0.017824	E5GE	-0.0225
E5IT	-0.023132	E5JA	0.026185	E5NE	-0.040335
E5UK	0.02989	E5US	0.033956	E6CA	-0.197234
E6FR	-0.057298	E6GE	0.097666	E6IT	-0.09435
E6JA	-0.564806	E6NE	-0.316001	E6UK	0.07705
E6US	-0.057597	E7CA	0.264871	E7FR	0.574765

Table 7.4 (continued)

E7GE	-0.763707	E7IT	0.037192	E7JA	0.415324
E7NE	0.206985	E7UK	0.024239	E8CA	-0.113296
E8FR	-0.0748	E8GE	-0.343714	E8IT	0.262491
E8JA	-0.226858	E8NE	0.05664	E8UK	0.156708
E8US	-0.286081	E9CA	-0.001604	E9FR	0.28364
E9GE	0.700672	E9IT	-0.129687	E9JA	0.014509
E9NE	0.062226	E9UK	-0.074746	F0CA	0.001373
F0FR	-0.009077	F0GE	-0.004262	F0IT	0.001751
F0JA	-0.008808	F0NE	-0.01574	F0UK	0.016768
F0US	0.000225	F1CA	0.179737	F1FR	0.573409
F1GE	0.822682	F1IT	0.409235	F1JA	0.319091
F1NE	0.28658	F1UK	0.024094	F10CA	-0.053768
F10FR	-0.099353	F10GE	0.242206	F10IT	0.072819
F10JA	0.124816	F10NE	0.223077	F10UK	-0.002007
F10US	0.616185	F2FR	0.418867	F20CA	-0.245403
F20FR	0.052207	F20GE	0.006946	F20IT	0.176537
F20JA	-0.07173	F20NE	0.09354	F20UK	-0.040341
F20US	0.067515	F3CA	-0.020791	F3FR	-0.001183
F3GE	-0.120761	F30CA	0.279496	F30FR	-0.026652
F30GE	0.290149	F30IT	-0.14876	F30JA	0.804933
F30NE	-0.255302	F30UK	0.740935	F30US	0.15222
F4GE	-0.731788	F4JA	-0.66905	F40CA	0.784069
F40FR	1.76086	F40GE	-0.377934	F40IT	-0.221008
F40JA	3.84313	F40NE	0.138543	F40UK	0.189983
F40US	2.25319	F50CA	0.270787	F50FR	1.25097
F50GE	1.20028	F50IT	1.31648	F50JA	1.30657
F50NE	0.968503	F50UK	1.28695	F50US	0.153811
F6CA	-0.095084	F6FR	-3.23475	F6GE	-1.95928
F6IT	-1.85255	F6JA	-2.01446	F6NE	-1.9384
F6UK	-2.2736	F60CA	0.02143	F60FR	0.617717
F60GE	0.468396	F60IT	-1.1264	F60JA	0.710113
F60NE	0.799582	F60UK	0.533112	G0CA	-0.003648
G0FR	-0.001236	G0GE	-0.012056	G0IT	-0.003179
G0JA	0.045769	G0NE	-0.008552	G0UK	0.013468
G0US	0.004428	G1CA	-0.000105	G1FR	-9.407155E-05
G1GE	-3.927120E-06	G1IT	0.000155	G1JA	-3.658464E-05
G1NE	2.173991E-05	G1UK	-0.000265	G1US	5.279754E-05
G10CA	-0.050435	G10FR	0.636369	G10GE	-0.002451
G10IT	1.38277	G10JA	-0.610265	G10NE	0.696158
G10UK	0.757122	G10US	-0.299741	G11CA	-0.298437
G11FR	0.258753	G11GE	-0.422543	G11IT	0.442983
G11JA	-1.14262	G11NE	-0.687287	G11UK	-0.828963
G11US	0.347438	G12CA	0.16578	G12FR	0.908516
G12GE	0.405291	G12IT	0.361741	G12JA	-0.346612
G12NE	0.363585	G12UK	-0.680074	G12US	-0.480483
G2CA	0.007542	G2FR	0.013437	G2GE	0.0044
G2IT	0.000184	G2JA	0.031405	G2NE	0.015183
G2UK	-0.046579	G2US	-0.001341	G20CA	0.259146
G20FR	-0.654758	G20GE	0.621408	G20IT	-0.172217
G20JA	-0.826017	G20NE	0.983567	G20UK	0.317069
G20US	0.007398	G21CA	0.213911	G21FR	-0.994672
G21GE	0.132577	G21IT	-0.352289	G21JA	-0.091766
G21NE	0.171835	G21UK	-0.576976	G21US	0.034483
G22CA	-0.194408	G22FR	0.386726	G22GE	0.546939
G22IT	-0.02103	G22JA	-0.232578	G22NE	0.979839
G22UK	0.525568	G22US	0.111434	G3CA	-0.209463
G3FR	-0.249651	G3GE	-0.3022	G3IT	-0.204769
G3JA	-0.583978	G3NE	-0.679193	G3UK	0.752483
G3US	-0.100705	G30CA	0.04415	G30FR	-0.002254
G30GE	0.052299	G30IT	-0.045144	G30JA	0.038284
G30NE	-0.086553	G30UK	-0.342353	G30US	-0.003303
G31CA	-0.048232	G31FR	0.000667	G31GE	0.046935
G31IT	0.037957	G31JA	0.033051	G31NE	-0.051527
G31UK	-0.076486	G31US	0.003961	G32CA	-0.06872
G32FR	-0.017283	G32GE	0.051619	G32IT	0.071145
G32JA	0.023627	G32NE	0.04683	G32UK	0.016799
G32US	-0.004193	G4CA	0.399296	G4FR	0.073793
G4GE	0.097097	G4IT	0.071244	G4JA	0.05497
G4NE	0.024806	G4UK	0.444298	G4US	-0.034747
G5CA	0.525327	G5FR	0.332204	G5GE	0.243101
G5IT	0.328725	G5JA	0.064557	G5NE	0.543858
G5UK	-0.927833	G5US	-0.209762	G6CA	0.854509
G6FR	0.184551	G6GE	0.679257	G6IT	0.4522
G6JA	-0.212536	G6NE	0.53443	G6UK	-1.08654
G6US	0.571938	G7CA	0.101733	G7FR	0.060923
G7GE	-0.065372	G7IT	-0.006446	G7JA	0.04405
G7NE	0.077908	G7UK	-0.696908	G7US	-0.053545
G8CA	-0.115046	G8FR	0.076835	G8GE	0.516343
G8IT	-0.125914	G8JA	-0.219103	G8NE	-0.045435
G8UK	0.51128	G8US	-0.106903	G9CA	0.037359
G9FR	-0.195855	G9GE	-0.940238	G9IT	-0.262394
G9JA	0.034766	G9NE	-0.454351	G9UK	0.080414
G9US	0.05499	H0CA	0.203896	H0FR	0.129624

Table 7.4 (continued)

H0GE	0.089664	H0IT	-0.878539	H0JA	-0.060943
H0NE	0.253769	H0UK	0.548739	H0US	0.077502
H1CA	-0.152912	H1FR	0.073406	H1GE	0.040487
H1IT	-0.018547	H1JA	0.016673	H1NE	0.12252
H1UK	0.051451	H1US	0.014957	H10CA	0.025102
H10FR	0.010249	H10GE	0.247567	H10IT	-0.071293
H10JA	0.018682	H10NE	0.586296	H10UK	0.091918
H10US	0.00826	H11CA	-0.049448	H11FR	0.239274
H11GE	0.044574	H11IT	0.081144	H11JA	-0.048667
H11NE	-0.41788	H11UK	0.306618	H11US	0.01138
H12CA	0.113463	H12FR	0.248513	H12GE	0.1238
H12IT	0.05552	H12JA	-0.119308	H12NE	0.500342
H12UK	-0.010101	H13CA	0.08955	H13FR	0.054154
H13GE	-0.021665	H13IT	0.201372	H13JA	0.149767
H13NE	-0.165191	H13UK	0.113126	H14CA	0.085483
H14FR	-0.021497	H14GE	-0.066495	H14IT	0.055937
H14JA	-0.010149	H14NE	-0.499385	H14UK	-0.103932
H15CA	0.035674	H15FR	-0.077889	H15GE	-0.326702
H15IT	-0.109401	H15JA	-0.03302	H15NE	0.186242
H15UK	-0.124118	H2CA	0.085196	H2FR	-0.000659
H2GE	-0.001326	H2IT	0.001095	H2JA	0.000277
H2NE	-0.003371	H2UK	-0.006863	H2US	0.01107
H3CA	-0.038753	H3FR	0.049731	H3GE	0.009901
H3IT	0.164379	H3JA	-0.012907	H3NE	-0.065659
H3UK	0.148371	H3US	-0.00087	H4CA	0.053718
H4FR	-0.003771	H4GE	0.003139	H4IT	-0.000501
H4JA	-0.000414	H4NE	0.000248	H4UK	0.003317
H4US	0.610356	H5CA	0.012595	H5FR	0.01573
H5GE	0.028759	H5IT	0.018264	H5JA	-0.000268
H5NE	0.032386	H5UK	0.014503	H5US	0.072265
H6CA	-0.068748	H6FR	0.011124	H6GE	0.043488
H6IT	-0.116616	H6JA	-0.030858	H6NE	0.154034
H6UK	-0.038433	H6US	0.010184	H7CA	-0.001767
H7FR	-0.00426	H7GE	-0.001028	H7IT	-0.001111
H7JA	-0.000251	H7NE	-0.002796	H7UK	-0.002765
H7US	-0.008498	H8CA	0.342569	H8FR	0.234953
H8GE	0.347365	H8IT	0.235021	H8JA	0.292216
H8NE	0.51165	H8UK	0.329246	H8US	0.067992
H9CA	0.272154	H9FR	0.250369	H9GE	0.113401
H9IT	0.229865	H9JA	0.123404	H9NE	0.081916
H9UK	0.102093	H9US	0.018369	I0CA	0.302888
I0FR	4.16517	I0GE	-0.265758	I0IT	-0.491863
I0JA	-0.358942	I0NE	-0.570559	I0UK	-0.621571
I0US	-0.104698	I1CA	1.00269	I1FR	4.01
I1GE	1.09201	I1IT	2.3297	I1JA	11.8281
I1NE	1.04947	I1UK	2.04017	I1US	0.661462
I2CA	0.127849	I2FR	0.010317	I2GE	0.032126
I2IT	0.036875	I2JA	0.002864	I2NE	0.364942
I2UK	0.13774	I2US	0.018057	I3CA	-0.123952
I3FR	-0.715105	I3GE	0.032967	I3IT	0.093963
I3JA	0.013094	I3NE	0.277274	I3UK	-0.08037
I3US	0.082842	I4CA	0.179301	I4FR	-0.494583
I4GE	0.014642	I4IT	0.295977	I4JA	-0.531693
I4NE	0.042767	I4UK	0.034769	I4US	-0.066497
I5CA	-0.332617	I5FR	0.037033	I5GE	-0.007693
I5IT	-0.040057	I5JA	0.010134	I5NE	-0.228264
I5UK	-0.53198	I5US	0.036839	I6CA	0.640689
I6FR	0.348802	I6GE	0.615658	I6IT	0.655782
I6JA	0.29103	I6NE	0.49757	I6UK	0.374063
I6US	0.052165	I7CA	-0.055634	I7FR	-0.041407
I7GE	0.053553	I7IT	-0.091501	I7JA	-8.886478E-05
I7NE	-0.074126	I7UK	-0.031961	I7US	-0.068607
I8CA	0.066109	I8FR	0.018122	I8GE	-0.028847
I8IT	0.016146	I8JA	-0.041865	I8NE	-0.04174
I8UK	0.014522	I8US	0.004386	J0CA	0.00023
J0FR	0.000654	J0GE	0.005948	J0IT	-0.002227
J0JA	0.000194	J0NE	0.001483	J0UK	-0.001317
J1CA	0.280069	J1JA	0.636045	J1UK	0.404612
J2CA	-0.069894	J2FR	-0.028109	J2GE	-0.101694
J2IT	-0.046984	J2NE	-0.028487	J3IT	-0.030714
J3NE	-0.027252	J3UK	-0.037745	J4GE	-0.092671
K0CA	-0.03672	K0FR	-0.007933	K0GE	-0.004188
K0IT	0.030647	K0JA	0.066137	K0NE	-0.019439
K0UK	-0.08629	K0US	-0.118647	K1CA	-1.00189
K1FR	0.09518	K1GE	0.084483	K1IT	-70.1123
K1JA	-0.28134	K1NE	0.074312	K1UK	-0.21725
K1US	-1.704	K10CA	-0.50794	K10FR	-0.10998
K10GE	-0.05558	K10IT	0.1779	K10JA	-0.05976
K10NE	0.11578	K10UK	-0.36774	K10US	-0.266557
K11CA	0.43356	K11FR	-0.205692	K11GE	8.54003
K11IT	0.510238	K11JA	0.10676	K11NE	-0.120811
K11UK	0.7103	K11US	-0.011724	K12CA	-0.16197

Table 7.4 (continued)

K12FR	-0.04162	K12GE	21.9658	K12IT	0.196408
K12JA	0.15317	K12NE	-7.00023	K12UK	-0.40683
K12US	0.222	K13CA	-0.19053	K13FR	-0.07258
K13GE	28.5363	K13IT	0.182301	K13JA	0.0343
K13NE	-5.78759	K13UK	0.28402	K13US	0.02
K14CA	-0.2753	K14FR	0.6105	K14GE	0.1874
K14IT	0.36478	K14JA	0.2194	K14NE	-0.2528
K14UK	-0.21338	K14US	0.2778	K15CA	-0.6962
K15FR	-0.1698	K15GE	0.5547	K15IT	0.42363
K15JA	0.4259	K15NE	0.5438	K15UK	0.5093
K15US	-0.1317	K2CA	-0.04238	K2FR	0.275907
K2GE	79.9045	K2IT	-0.372853	K2JA	0.14682
K2NE	-0.064781	K2UK	-0.29567	K2US	0.087633
K3CA	0.06676	K3FR	-0.34383	K3GE	-0.02164
K3IT	-10.1092	K3JA	-0.18028	K3NE	-5.04602
K3UK	0.56026	K3US	-0.065193	K4CA	0.06475
K4FR	0.0028	K4GE	0.138669	K4IT	-0.185426
K4JA	-0.02574	K4NE	0.243743	K4UK	0.13262
K4US	-0.055842	K5CA	0.34558	K5FR	0.05509
K5GE	-0.01241	K5IT	0.07162	K5JA	1.33237
K5NE	-0.04987	K5UK	0.02992	K5US	0.140337
K6CA	-0.51519	K6FR	0.216151	K6GE	0.089455
K6IT	-0.004496	K6JA	-2.03841	K6NE	0.108302
K6UK	0.14599	K6US	-0.038	K7CA	0.01197
K7FR	0.00344	K7GE	0.01888	K7IT	-0.03065
K7JA	0.056447	K7NE	-0.03923	K7UK	0.04161
K7US	0.008	K8CA	-0.0327	K8FR	0.01106
K8GE	0.01352	K8IT	-0.01914	K8JA	0.00436
K8NE	-0.02741	K8UK	-0.02842	K8US	-0.009
K9CA	0.49477	K9FR	0.11732	K9GE	0.579013
K9IT	-0.15663	K9JA	-0.212914	K9NE	-0.392292
K9UK	0.35337	K9US	0.246549	L0CA	-0.000111
L0FR	0.001753	L0GE	0.001334	L0IT	-0.000106
L0JA	-0.000313	L0NE	-0.001407	L0UK	0.001221
L1CA	-0.044797	L1FR	-0.736738	L1GE	-0.672213
L1IT	-0.2118	L1JA	-0.579833	L1NE	-0.1362
L1UK	-0.5398	L2CA	33.9022	L2FR	131.55
L2GE	-113.957	L2IT	17.655	L2JA	-405.337
L2NE	10.9493	L2UK	29.8764	L3CA	-0.0089
L3FR	0.6546	L3GE	-0.2109	L3IT	-0.032609
L3JA	0.076104	L3NE	-0.192914	L3UK	0.1369
L4CA	0.510603	L4FR	0.916987	L4GE	0.238757
L4IT	0.970475	L4JA	0.142382	L4NE	0.624358
L4UK	0.564549	L5CA	-1.	L5FR	-0.036492
L5GE	0.0106	L5IT	-1.	L5JA	-0.0779
L5NE	0.024793	L5UK	-0.023716	L6FR	-0.65
L6GE	-0.0086	L6JA	-0.3398	L7FR	-0.35
M0CA	-0.00314	M0FR	0.06315	M0GE	0.00064
M0IT	0.0232	M0JA	0.00323	M0NE	0.02739
M0UK	0.00597	M1CA	0.05183	M1FR	0.13361
M1GE	-0.95133	M1IT	-0.08897	M1JA	-0.03233
M1NE	0.11611	M1UK	0.80037	M2CA	-0.00683
M2FR	-0.06955	M2GE	0.05737	M2IT	-0.029
M2JA	-0.03956	M2NE	-0.07818	M2UK	-0.02808
M3CA	0.07509	M3FR	-1.13931	M3GE	-0.73465
M3IT	0.76727	M3JA	-0.87177	M3NE	-0.66181
M3UK	1.20971	M4CA	-0.30121	M4FR	1.42566
M4GE	2.98731	M4IT	0.1553	M4JA	3.92447
M4NE	-0.10364	M4UK	-2.03867	M5CA	0.18038
M5FR	-3.15593	M5GE	-0.13434	M5IT	-0.35833
M5JA	-0.02198	M5NE	-1.97462	M5UK	-0.98978
M6CA	0.31538	M6FR	-0.39385	M6GE	0.18685
M6IT	0.15115	M6JA	0.20401	M6NE	-0.35813
M6UK	-0.20116	P	4.	XPCA	0.012
XPFR	0.01379	XPGE	0.01143	XPIT	0.01218
XPJA	0.0228	XPNE	0.01161	XPUK	0.0067
XPUS	0.00866	ZPCA	0.025	ZPFR	0.025
ZPGE	0.025	ZPIT	0.025	ZPJA	0.025
ZPNE	0.025	ZPUK	0.025	ZPUS	0.025

References

Bhandari, J. S., and B. Putnam. 1982. *Economic interdependence and flexible exchange rates*. Cambridge: MIT Press.

Carr, J., and M. R. Darby. 1981. The role of money supply shocks in the short-run demand for money. *Journal of Monetary Economics* 8 (September): 183–99.

Darby, M. R. 1980. The monetary approach to the balance of payments: Two specious assumptions. *Economic Inquiry* 18 (April): 321–26.

———. 1981. The international economy as a source of and restraint on United States inflation. In W. A. Gale, ed., *Inflation: Causes, consequents, and control*. Cambridge: Oelgeschlager, Gunn & Hain, Publishers.

Dornbusch, R. 1976. Expectations and exchange rate dynamics. *Journal of Political Economy* 84 (December): 1161–76.

Lucas, R. E., Jr. 1976. Econometric policy evaluation: A critique. In K. Brunner and A. H. Meltzer, eds., *The Phillips curve and labor markets*, Carnegie-Rochester Conference Series on Public Policy, vol. 1. Amsterdam: North-Holland.

Meiselman, D. I., and A. B. Laffer. 1975. *The phenomenon of worldwide inflation*. Washington: American Enterprise Institute.

Parkin, M., and G. Zis. 1976a. *Inflation in the world economy*. Toronto: University of Toronto Press.

———. 1976b. *Inflation in open economies*. Toronto: University of Toronto Press.

Swoboda, A. K. 1976. Monetary policy under fixed exchange rates: Effectiveness, the speed of adjustment, and proper use. In J. A. Frenkel and H. G. Johnson, eds., *The monetary approach to the balance of payments*. Toronto: University of Toronto Press.

8   The Importance of Oil Price Changes in the 1970s World Inflation

Michael R. Darby

The increase in the real price of oil during 1973–74 is widely believed to have been a major cause of inflation in the United States and abroad. In part, this belief is based on a partial equilibrium (or adding-up) approach which explains the inflation rate as the weighted sum of the inflation rates of individual goods and services without making due allowance for the general equilibrium effects on factor prices of an increase in the relative price of an imported factor. But arguments acceptable theoretically can be made which attribute inflation—or at least an upward price-level shift—to factors decreasing the real quantity of money demanded or increasing the nominal quantity of money supplied by the central banks. This chapter reports an empirical investigation of the magnitude of these possible effects consistent with general equilibrium.

First, a theoretical analysis of the long-run and short-run effects of an oil price change is presented in section 8.1. It is seen there that the long-run effect on real income and the real quantity of money demanded may be quite small, if not negligible, particularly when real income is measured in terms of real GNP and money is deflated by the corresponding implicit deflator. While this result may be due to the use of a three-factor Cobb-Douglas production function in the context of a neoclassical growth model, it certainly illustrates that a long-run reduction of real GNP of even 1 or 2% is very much an empirical question. Short-run effects on real income and prices associated with shifts in aggregate demand and supply appear to be similar in magnitude to those for the long run. Central banks' reaction to the short-run real-income and inflation effects may offset or reinforce these effects once monetary policy is allowed to be endogenous.

Tests of significance of oil price variables in an extended Lucas-Barro real income equation are reported in section 8.2. The results are mixed and confounded by price control and decontrol programs which were widespread at nearly the same time as the 1973–74 oil price change. Much future work is required to disentangle the effects of these two factors definitively.

Section 8.3 reports simulation experiments on the effects of the 1973–74 oil price change. These experiments are conducted using the Mark IV–FLT Simulation Model presented in chapter 7 above. This model—a simplified version of the Mark III International Transmission Model[1]—is a quarterly macroeconomic model of the United States, United Kingdom, Canada, France, Germany, Italy, Japan, and the Netherlands. In addition to the basic Mark IV–FLT Model, an extended Mark IV–Oil Model is used which incorporates oil price variables in the real-income equations for those five countries for which the variables were found to be significant in section 8.2. Using the basic model, some notable effects are found as a result of induced movements in exports, exchange rates, money supplies, and the like. Stronger effects are simulated using the Mark IV–Oil Model, but the price-control caveat of section 8.2 again applies.

The concluding section summarizes the results of this chapter and suggests areas for future research as international data on the effects of the 1979–80 oil price increase become available.

8.1 Theory

The price level, measured in dollars per basket of goods, is the inverse of the price of money, goods per dollar. So it is convenient to classify the forces determining the price level according to whether they influence the supply of or demand for money.

A standard (long-run) money-demand function explains the real quantity of money demanded m^d by real income y and the nominal interest rate R. The nominal quantity demanded M^d is the product of this real demand and the price level:

(8.1) $$M^d = m^d(y, R) \cdot P.$$

Equating money supply M^s to money demand and solving for the price level,

(8.2) $$P = \frac{M^s}{m^d(y, R)}.$$

That is, the price level equals the ratio of the nominal quantity of money supplied to the real quantity of money demanded.

---

1. See Chapters 5 and 6 for details.

Although the inflationary impact of an oil price change is generally analyzed given an exogenously determined nominal money supply, this may be misleading or at least counterfactual. That is, to the extent that the oil price change increases the price level and unemployment (at least temporarily) and decreases real income for a given nominal money supply, the inflationary effect would induce central banks to reduce M^s while the recessionary effect tends to increase M^s. Which effect is dominant would depend on the relative weights the individual central bank puts on inflation and unemployment. In addition, other factors—discussed below—may influence central bank policy response to an oil price change. With this warning, let us proceed for now to analyze the effects of an oil price change for an exogenous monetary policy.

8.1.1 Long-Run (Full Employment) Effects

Consider first the long-run effects of an oil price change on real output. For illustrative purposes suppose real output y is produced according to a three-factor Cobb-Douglas production function using domestic capital k, labor ℓ, and imported petroleum ϕ:[2]

$$(8.3) \qquad y = k^\alpha \ell^\beta \phi^\gamma,$$

$$(8.4) \qquad \alpha + \beta + \gamma = 1.$$

Let us assume that output is produced by competitors who treat all prices as parametric including in particular the real price of oil θ.[3] In equilib-

---

2. A fuller specification would include a factor $e^{\delta + \tau t}$ on the right-hand side, but it simplifies the notation without loss to choose labor units such that the e^δ is eliminated and to incorporate technical progress τ into our measurement of labor in efficiency units. The basic results (8.8) and (8.12) below are stated in Tatom (1979a, pp. 10–11) and Rasche and Tatom (1980) starting from the same production function (8.3). Their longest-run results (8.12), however, are derived from the simple assertion that the marginal product of capital is fixed in the long run by supply conditions rather than as the result of a growth analysis as is done below. Their assertion—although it is correct in this case—is generally false. They erroneously interpret the gross "rental price of capital" which is equated to the marginal product of capital as the "relative price of capital" (e.g. Tatom 1979a, pp. 10–11) and argue that this will equal its fixed supply price in the long run. In the appendix to Rasche and Tatom (1980), they instead have attempted to relate changes in output to changes in capacity of individual firms, but this seems to ignore the fact that the number of firms is not fixed.

In the main body of the paper, they present evidence supportive of the usage of a Cobb-Douglas production function of this form (8.3). Kopcke (1980) argues that it is improper to include energy as an argument in the aggregate production function since energy is itself an intermediate product produced by capital and labor. This objection does not apply to imported petroleum, which is produced by foreign labor and capital. Care must be taken, as seen below, however, in going from the domestic output concept appropriate to the production function (8.3) to the value-added concept of real GNP. Unfortunately this last step has not been made in the three-factor analyses of the effects of oil price changes.

3. This assumption is arguable also. For example, Phelps (1978) treated the quantity of imported oil ϕ as determined erogenously; the nominal price of oil is assumed fixed by Mork and Hall (1979) and by Berner et al. (1977) in their multicountry model. Rasche and Tatom (1980) argue persuasively that neither of these representations captures the meaning of OPEC's ability to set an optimal real price of oil.

rium, one of the first-order conditions requires that the marginal product of petroleum be equated to its real price:

(8.5) $\dfrac{dy}{d\phi} = \gamma k^{\alpha} \ell^{\beta} \phi^{1-\gamma} = \theta$.

It is straightforward to solve for the equilibrium usage of petroleum as a function of θ, k, and ℓ:

(8.6) $\phi = \left(\dfrac{\gamma}{\theta}\right)^{[1/(\alpha+\beta)]} k^{[\alpha/(\alpha+\beta)]} \ell^{[\beta/(\alpha+\beta)]}$

If we now substitute this equilibrium ϕ into the production function (8.3), we obtain equilibrium real output as a function of the real price of oil and given, fully employed resources of capital and labor:

(8.7) $y = \left(\dfrac{\gamma}{\theta}\right)^{[\gamma/(\alpha+\beta)]} k^{[\alpha/(\alpha+\beta)]} \ell^{[\beta/(\alpha+\beta)]}$

Taking logarithms and differentiating, we find the elasticity of equilibrium output with respect to the real oil price for given capital and labor resources:

(8.8) $\left.\dfrac{d \log y}{d \log \theta}\right|_{k,\ell} = -\dfrac{\gamma}{\alpha+\beta} \equiv -\dfrac{\gamma}{1-\gamma}$.

If, for example, γ were on the order of 0.01, a 1% increase in the real oil price would decrease real output by only 0.01% (1 basis point) for given resources and given the assumptions of this illustration.[4]

The full, long-run equilibrium effect would be slightly larger due to a reduction in the steady-state capital-labor ratio for a given growth path of labor. To see this, suppose that saving and investment $\dot{k}$ is a constant fraction σ of domestic factor income:

(8.9) $\dot{k} = \sigma(y - \theta\phi)$.

Dividing both sides of (8.9) by k and noting that $y - \theta\phi = (\alpha+\beta)y$,

(8.10) $\dfrac{\dot{k}}{k} = \sigma(\alpha+\beta)\dfrac{y}{k}$.

Thus the growth rate of capital is a fixed proportion of the output-capital ratio. In view of (8.7), this latter ratio is

---

4. The value of γ is discussed at some length below. To the extent that capital is in the form of existing machines which cannot be readily modified and which require fixed petroleum inputs, the quasi rents of existing machines will fall without any reduction in output or petroleum usage. A possibly offsetting factor would be the premature obsolescence of machines on which the quasi rents fall below zero. Neither of these factors is operative in full long-run equilibrium discussed immediately below, and the two factors are taken as negligible on net here.

(8.11)
$$\frac{y}{k} = \left(\frac{\gamma}{\theta}\right)^{[\gamma/(\alpha+\beta)]} \left(\frac{\ell}{k}\right)^{[\beta/(\alpha+\beta)]}$$

The simple neoclassical growth model can therefore be applied, which, after tedious manipulations, yields the result that

(8.12)
$$\frac{d \log y}{d \log \theta} = -\frac{\gamma}{\beta}.$$

This effect, which allows for the (proportionate) reduction in the capital stock, would be about a third larger than that in (8.8) for given resources and a labor share equal to three-quarters of value added. We should note that since income and capital fall proportionately in full steady-state equilibrium, there is no long-run effect on the real interest rate.[5]

A curiosity of national income accounting proves important in applying the analysis to empirical data. Gross national product is a value-added concept so that imported inputs are subtracted from total output to obtain GNP. This works fine for nominal GNP or Q:

(8.13)
$$Q = Py - (P\theta)\phi = P(1 - \gamma)y.$$

So nominal GNP is simply the price of output P times real domestic factor income $(1 - \gamma)y$. However, in computing real GNP or q, imported inputs are valued at *base-year* relative prices $\bar{\theta}$:

(8.14)
$$q = y - \bar{\theta}\phi = \left(1 - \frac{\bar{\theta}}{\theta}\gamma\right)y.$$

Thus measured real GNP rises relative to factor income $(1 - \gamma)y$ when the real oil price θ is increased. *Nominal* aggregate demand as measured by nominal GNP is not affected since there is an offsetting measurement error in the measured GNP deflator D:

$$D = \frac{Q}{q} = \frac{P(1 - \gamma)y}{\left(1 - \dfrac{\bar{\theta}}{\theta}\gamma\right)y},$$

(8.15)
$$D = \frac{1 - \gamma}{1 - \dfrac{\bar{\theta}}{\theta}\gamma} P,$$

We can differentiate (8.14) to find the elasticity of real GNP with respect to the real oil price as

(8.16)
$$\frac{d \log q}{d \log \theta} = \frac{\gamma\bar{\theta}}{\theta - \gamma\bar{\theta}} + \frac{d \log y}{d \log \theta}.$$

5. Before capital adjusts, but with resources fully employed, the marginal product of capital $\alpha k^{\alpha-1}\ell^{\beta}\phi^{\gamma}$ falls (slightly) with ϕ and hence so does the real interest rate.

For small changes in θ before the capital stock adjusts,[6]

(8.17)
$$\left.\frac{d \log q}{d \log \theta}\right|_{k,\ell,\theta \simeq \overline{\theta}} = \frac{\gamma}{1-\gamma} - \frac{\gamma}{1-\gamma} = 0.$$

Thus we see that in the neighborhood of the original oil price, the output effect is completely masked in measured GNP. However, for large changes in θ relative to $\overline{\theta}$ such as those occurring in 1973–74, there would be a negative effect on measured real GNP.[7] Using Δ for the change relative to base-year prices we have

(8.18)
$$\Delta \log q = \log\left(\frac{1 - \dfrac{\overline{\theta}}{\theta}\gamma}{1-\gamma}\right) + \frac{d \log y}{d \log \theta} \log(\theta/\overline{\theta}),$$

where

$$\frac{d \log y}{d \log \theta}$$

is from (8.8) or (8.12) depending on whether or not the capital stock is presumed to have adjusted.[8] Note that the deflator is decreased relative to the price of output by

$$\log\left(\frac{1 - \dfrac{\overline{\theta}}{\theta}\gamma}{1-\gamma}\right)$$

just as real GNP is increased relative to real factor incomes.

In summary, an increase in the real price of oil is predicted to decrease real output by the logarithmic change times $\gamma/(1-\gamma)$ before capital adjusts or times γ/β when capital is fully adjusted. However, such an oil price change will cause a partially offsetting overstatement of measured real GNP (and understatement of the GNP deflator).

Obviously the values of γ and β are of considerable interest. For current illustrative purposes, only petroleum imports will be considered.[9] To the extent that petroleum imports are for resale to consumers rather than used in production, they have no effect on output or measured GNP (real or nominal). Thus the ratio of the value of petroleum imports to GNP serves as an upper limit on γ. If we use prechange U.S. data, this

---

6. That is, $\theta \simeq \overline{\theta}$ so that $\gamma\overline{\theta}/(\theta - \gamma\theta) \simeq \gamma/(1-\gamma)$.

7. Although $(d \log q)/(d \log \theta) = 0$ initially as seen in (8.17), as θ increases, the positive RHS term in (8.16) decreases while the negative RHS is unchanged. The negative effect is yet greater if capital is allowed to adjust.

8. Note that the first RHS term in (8.18) is approximately equal (for small γ) to $\gamma(1 - (\overline{\theta}/\theta))$, which illustrates that as θ becomes large the adjustment for imported inputs in measured GNP becomes trivial and all output is included in measured GNP.

9. It is possible to apply the analysis to energy more generally, but the increase in γ is largely offset by a reduced logarithmic change in θ.

upper limit would be about 0.003 for 1970. In 1976, this share had risen to 0.02. This rise in the share could indicate inelastic consumer demand for imported petroleum products, a problem with the Cobb-Douglas production function, or both. So while 0.003 should be an upper limit for γ if the Cobb-Douglas function is correct, 0.02 will also be considered as an upper-upper limit. Finally suppose that $\alpha/(\alpha + \beta)$ and $\beta/(\alpha + \beta)$ have their traditionally estimated values of ¼ and ¾. Then the multiplier $-\gamma/(1 - \gamma)$ is -0.003 or -0.020 depending on γ. The corresponding multipliers allowing for capital stock change are -0.004 and -0.027. The real price of a barrel of crude oil increased some 3.57fold from 1973I to 1974I (a logarithmic increase of 1.273). This is surely an upper limit on $\theta/\bar{\theta}$ for all petroleum products. Table 8.1 presents estimates of the maximum effects on output and measured real GNP. We see that the maximum full adjustment effects on real output range from a decrease of 0.5 to 3.5% according to whether one takes a prechange or postchange estimate of γ. For measured real GNP the corresponding decreases are only 0.3 to 2.0%. Even smaller changes correspond to the intermediate period corresponding to full employment of resources but no adjustment of the capital stock.

Rasche and Tatom have long argued for much larger real-income effects of the oil price change. They rely upon regression estimates of the quasi-production function (8.7) and find much larger values of γ than considered here. Part of that difference is illusory: They use a much broader energy price index which has a logarithmic increase of only 0.408 from 1972 to 1974[10] compared to the 1.273 increase for a barrel of oil used here; so the larger elasticity is offset by a lower value of $\log(\theta/\bar{\theta})$. Further they do not take account of the biases in reported real GNP so that their estimates may refer to the output effect rather than the GNP effect. Finally, in their (1980) paper, they report an equation (6) in which they estimate the production function (8.3) directly (after taking logs) and also add $\log \theta$ separately. The estimated γ is 0.05 while the coefficient on $\log \theta$ is -0.07. Using $\gamma = 0.05$, $\beta = 0.70$ (as reported), and $\log(\theta/\bar{\theta}) = 0.408$, we get an output change of -0.0215 with no capital adjustment and of -0.0291 with capital adjustment, which is in the same ball park as the figures in table 8.1. It is the things other than in the production function— captured in the $\log \theta$ coefficient of -0.07—which permit such big estimates. These other things may have to do with cyclical factors, induced monetary policy, or fortuitous removal of price controls at roughly the same time as discussed below. Further the 0.05 estimate of γ may be biased upward if energy usage (relative to capital and labor) serves as an indicator of whether the economy is in a boom or recession. Thus the Rasche and Tatom conclusions may have weak empirical foundations.

---

10. Rasche and Tatom (1980, table 6).

Table 8.1   **Illustrative Calculations of Maximum Long-Run Effect of 1973–74 Real Oil Price Increase**

	No Capital Adjustment		Full Capital Adjustment	
	$\gamma = 0.003$	$\gamma = 0.02$	$\gamma = 0.003$	$\gamma = 0.02$
Change in log output ($\Delta \log y$)	-0.0038	-0.0260	-0.0051	-0.0346
Change in measured real GNP ($\Delta \log q$)	-0.0017	-0.0114	-0.0029	-0.0200
Difference ($\Delta \log q - \Delta \log y \equiv \Delta \log P - \Delta \log D$)	0.0022	0.0146	0.0022	0.0146

This exercise has shown that even a huge change in the real price of oil such as in 1973–74 may result in very small if not negligible effects on real output and especially upon measured real GNP. Different assumptions would result in different results, but the model used is surely a standard one in practice. Thus it would appear to be an empirical question as to whether the oil price change had any significant long-run effect on measured real GNP.

We can now return to our original question of the long-run effect of the oil price change on the real quantity of money demanded and hence, given the nominal money supply, on the price level. First, we note that in long-run equilibrium real income is reduced by a constant fraction but the growth rate of real income is reduced only temporarily during the transitional period. Second, we note that the real interest rate is unchanged. Under these conditions, in long-run equilibrium the real and nominal interest rate will be unchanged and the real quantity of money demanded will behave similarly to real income—a downward parallel shift in its growth path. The logarithmic downward shift will equal the elasticity of real money demand with respect to real income times the logarithmic shift in real income. Thus, if this income elasticity is around 1, there will be a long-run increase in the price level equal to the long-run decrease in real income.[11] If during the early part of the adjustment period the price-level effect exceeds this long-run effect, then the inflation rate must be reduced (ceteris paribus) below what it would otherwise be to reach long-run equilibrium.

Two problems may arise in econometric work based on real GNP as

---

11. A formal solution to this problem is presented in Darby (1979, chapter 5).

measured in the national income accounts. First, the reduction in measured real GNP will understate the output reduction which actually occurs. A second problem arises only if the income elasticity of the demand for money differs significantly from unity: Then the offsetting measurement errors in real GNP and the GNP deflator would cause an apparent shift in the money-demand function equal to the product of the measurement error and the difference of the elasticity from 1. This latter problem is a second-order matter which will not be pursued further in this chapter.

8.1.2   Short-Run Effects

Short-run effects of the 1973–74 oil price shock have been analyzed in terms of induced shifts in aggregate demand and aggregate supply curves under the assumption that nominal wages are predetermined (or at least sticky) in the short run. As with the long-run analysis, the analysis of the short-run effects proceeds on the assumption that the government's monetary and fiscal policy is unaffected by the unexpected oil price increase.

The aggregate demand effects of an oil price shock can be viewed as analogous to that of an increase in taxes.[12] Assume for simplicity that in the short run both producer and consumer demands for imported petroleum are perfectly inelastic. For producers, this means that higher import prices will be paid out of reduced quasi rents, reducing private income. For consumers, higher oil prices would directly reduce expenditures on *other* consumption goods for given private income and these expenditures would be further reduced by the reduction of private income.[13] Thus, at initial levels of real income and interest rates, aggregate expenditures would fall *unless* increased demand for exports by oil exporters equals or exceeds the induced reduction in consumption. When we allow for some elasticity of demand for imported oil and for increased exports of goods to oil producers, the plausible magnitude of these basically distributional effects is sharply reduced and could even be reversed.[14] In what follows, we shall nonetheless consider the possibility of a small decrease in aggregate demand.

The aggregate supply effect would appear more substantial and has been analyzed on varying assumptions by Bruno and Sachs (1979), Hud-

12. This tax analysis is given little if any weight in recent analyses. Rasche and Tatom (1980), for example, term it the "1974 view," and the belief that aggregate demand shifts were important appears to have been an ephemeral phenomenon. It is included here for the sake of completeness.

13. The exact amount of these reductions depends on consumer expectations, but the direction is unambiguous.

14. There is no long-run effect on output or interest rates via this channel unless differences between foreign and domestic propensities to save cause a shift in the domestic investment-output ratio.

son and Jorgenson (1978), Mork and Hall (1979), Norsworthy, Harper, and Kunze (1979), Phelps (1978), and Rasche and Tatom (1977a, 1980). Following the latter authors, suppose that the short-run conditions underlying the aggregate supply curve are fixity of the capital stock, the nominal wage W, and the real price of oil. Using the aggregate production function (8.3), one can readily derive output as

$$(8.19) \qquad y = \left(\frac{\gamma}{\theta}\right)^{\gamma/\alpha} \left(\frac{\beta P}{W}\right)^{\beta/\alpha} k .$$

On comparing (8.19) and (8.7), we note that for a given price level there is a much greater output effect with nominal wages fixed than when labor is assumed to be at its natural unemployment rate. Specifically

$$(8.20) \qquad \left.\frac{d \log y}{d \log \theta}\right|_{k,W} = -\frac{\gamma}{\alpha} + \frac{\beta}{\alpha} \frac{d \log P}{d \log \theta} .$$

Note that the elasticity of the aggregate supply curve is

$$(8.21) \qquad \frac{d \log y}{d \log P} = \frac{\beta}{\alpha} .$$

It is convenient to plot aggregate supply and demand curves in terms of log y and log P so that slopes and elasticities have a simple correspondence. The logarithmic aggregate supply curve corresponding to equation (8.19) is

$$(8.22) \qquad \log y = \left[\frac{\beta}{\alpha}\log(\beta/W) + \frac{\gamma}{\alpha}\log \gamma + \log k\right]$$

$$- \frac{\gamma}{\alpha}\log \theta + \frac{\beta}{\alpha}\log P .$$

This is plotted as S in figure 8.1 for given values of k, W, and the base-year relative price of oil $\bar{\theta}$. The slope of S is the inverse (α/β) of the elasticity of aggregate supply. An aggregate demand curve D is also drawn to determine short-run output and the price level, $\bar{y}$ and $\bar{P}$.[15]

As can be seen in equation (8.22) an increase in the real price of oil shifts the aggregate supply curve horizontally by $-(\gamma/\alpha) \log(\theta/\bar{\theta})$, as illustrated in figure 8.2.[16] This can alternatively be described as an upward shift equal to minus the slope of S times the horizontal shift:

$$(8.23) \qquad \left(-\frac{\alpha}{\beta}\right)\left(-\frac{\gamma}{\alpha}\log (\theta/\bar{\theta})\right) = \frac{\gamma}{\beta}\log(\theta/\bar{\theta}) .$$

---

15. The aggregate demand curve is derived by solving the IS relation for R and substituting in equation (8.2).

16. A negative sign indicates a shift to the left.

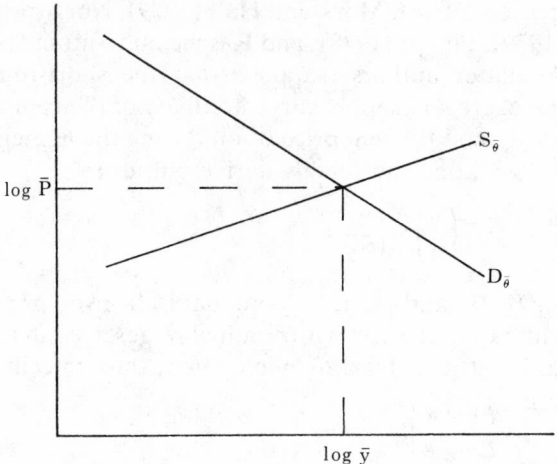

Fig. 8.1   Determination of base output and price level.

If any shift in the aggregate demand curve is negligible, the new equilibrium output and price level are y and P. The short-run displacement in output from that corresponding to the base real oil price $\bar{\theta}$ is

$$(8.24) \qquad \Delta \log y = \frac{-1}{\dfrac{\alpha}{\beta} - \dfrac{1}{\eta_D}} \frac{\gamma}{\beta} \log(\theta/\bar{\theta}),$$

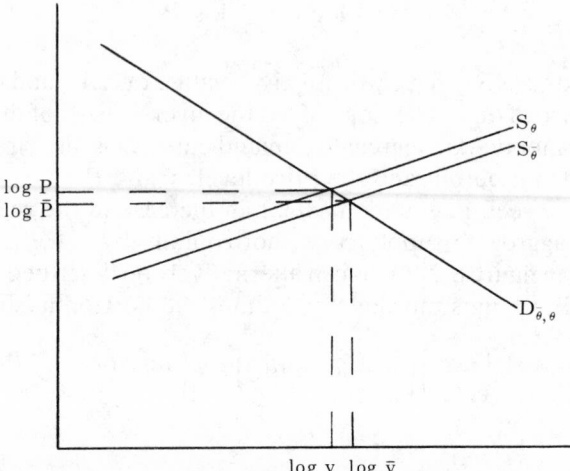

Fig. 8.2   Determination of changes in output and price level from base values with no aggregate-demand shift.

where η_D is the elasticity of the aggregate demand curve so that α/β and $1/\eta_D$ are the slopes of the aggregate supply and demand curves, respectively. Suppose that the aggregate demand curve is unit elastic ($\eta_D = -1$); then

$$(8.25) \qquad \Delta \log y = - \frac{\gamma}{1-\gamma} \log(\theta/\overline{\theta}),$$

which is identical to the long-run effect implied by (8.8) before the capital stock adjusts. The increase in the price level,

$$(8.26) \qquad \Delta \log P = \frac{1}{\eta_D} \Delta \log y = \frac{\gamma}{1-\gamma} \log(\theta/\overline{\theta}),$$

reduces real wages just sufficiently to maintain employment at the natural level. Thus, in the absence of a shift in the aggregate demand curve, employment rises or falls (and output is greater or less than the given-capital long-run level indicated by (8.25)) according to whether the elasticity of aggregate demand is smaller or greater than 1 in absolute value. If aggregate demand were inelastic, increased employment would lessen the short-run decline in output. In Darby (1976c, pp. 161–63) I argued that short-run and hence transitory movements in output will induce much less than proportionate movements in money demand, which suggests that the short-run aggregate demand curve is in fact elastic.[17] This would imply a short-run reduction in employment, which would accentuate the initial fall in output predicted by the full-employment analysis.[18] Once expected nominal wages are reduced, this

17. Purvis (1975) displays the correct formula for η_D, which is

$$\eta_D = \frac{-1}{\dfrac{\partial \log m^d}{\partial \log y} + \psi \dfrac{\partial \log m^d}{\partial \log R}},$$

where ψ is $(d \log R)/(d \log y)$ or the elasticity of the interest rate with respect to output on the IS curve. For a normal negatively sloped IS curve, $\psi(\partial \log m^d)/(\partial \log R)$ will be positive but insufficient to bring the denominator of η_D up to 1 if short-run interest elasticity of money demand is small and the IS curve is rather flat as argued by Hall (1977).

Rasche and Tatom (1980) make a convoluted version of Gamb's error (which Purvis corrected) to conclude that the aggregate demand curve was inelastic. Rather than accept the implication of increased employment, they repeat their (1977a) assumption that nominal wages rise freely once the natural unemployment rate is reached. I can see no justification for this appendage to a basic search view of the labor market. It is of course irrelevant if $\eta_D < -1$ or the aggregate demand curve shifts to the left sufficiently to reduce employment despite an inelastic aggregate demand curve.

18. If the elasticity of aggregate demand is less than -1 but greater than $-\beta/(\beta - \alpha)$ (about -1.5), the short-run effect will be greater than the full-employment effect for a given capital stock but less than the long-run effect allowing for capital adjustment. That is, in the absence of significant shifts in aggregate demand, the long-run effects with full capital adjustment such as calculated in table 8.1 exceed the short-run effects unless $\eta_D < -\beta/(\beta - \alpha) \approx -1.5$.

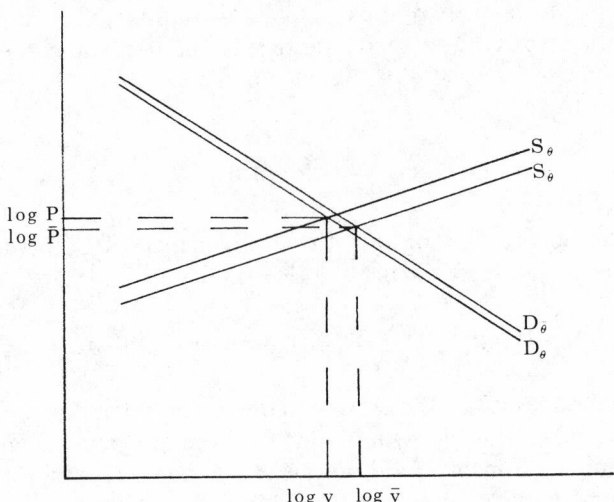

Fig. 8.3   Determination of changes in output and price level from base values with shift in aggregate demand.

difference would disappear. In addition, the aggregate demand curve may shift to the left as previously argued if there is a distributional effect due to faster decreases in consumer spending than increases in oil-exporter spending; this is illustrated in figure 8.3.

Again it must be emphasized that these calculations are only illustrative of the sort of effects which might be expected. If, for example, we assumed partial adjustment of nominal wages to their equilibrium values, the aggregate supply curve would be less elastic and the output change would be more closely tied to the change in the given-capital long-run level of output.[19]

The aggregate demand curve is derived using our price-level equation (8.2) so the short-run price-level effect

$$(8.27) \qquad \Delta \log P = \frac{1}{\eta_D} \Delta \log y$$

is valid for the short-run period in which IS-LM analysis is applicable. If $-1/\eta_D$ is less than the long-run elasticity of demand for money with respect to output, the short-run increase in the price level would be less than that associated with an equal long-run decrease in output.

Note that the same accounting problem in relating output and the price level to real GNP and the deflator apply in the short run as in the long run.

---

19. More wage flexibility implies less employment variation, so output would be lower than indicated by equation (8.24) if $\eta_D > -1$ and less if $\eta_D < -1$.

8.1.3   Endogenous Monetary Policy

The time has now come to consider effects of the oil shock upon monetary policy. Suppose that we can write the money supply reaction function of the monetary authorities as

(8.28) $$\log M = \log M^* + h_y \log(y/y^*)$$
$$+ h_p \log(P/P^*) + \epsilon_M .$$

In logarithms, actual money equals expected money as predicted by lagged variables systematically affecting central bank behavior plus negative coefficients times the innovations in output and the price level and a random disturbance.[20] Write the semireduced forms for output and the price level as

(8.29) $$y = f(k, W, \theta, M, M^*, \epsilon_y),$$

(8.30) $$P = \pi(k, W, \theta, M, M^*, \epsilon_p).$$

Denote the real-oil-price and money elasticities of these equations by f_θ, f_M, π_θ, and π_M. Then taking the log changes in equations (8.28) through (8.30) and solving for $\Delta \log M$ yields

(8.31) $$\Delta \log M = \frac{h_y f_\theta + h_p \pi_\theta}{1 - h_y f_M - h_p \pi_M} \Delta \log \theta .$$

We have seen above that f_θ is negative and π_θ is positive while h_y and h_p are both negative. Whether money is increased, decreased, or left unchanged by the central bank depends both on the relative sizes of the output and price effects and on the relative aversion of the central bank to recession and inflation. The denominator of (8.31) allows for attenuation of money changes to the extent that there are within-period (positive) responses in output and prices. Finally, the price-level effect is obtained by substituting (8.31) into the log-change form of (8.30):

(8.32) $$\Delta \log P = \left(\pi_\theta + \frac{(h_y f_\theta + h_p \pi_\theta)\pi_M}{1 - h_y f_M - h_p \pi_M} \right) \Delta \log \theta .$$

Here π_θ is the value of $(\Delta \log P)/(\Delta \log \theta)$ such as is computed in (8.27) for a given nominal money supply and the ratio term is the additional (ambiguously signed) effect due to endogenous nominal money supply changes.

---

20. The lack of a term in the balance of payments implies that we are dealing with either a reserve country (the U.S.), a freely floating country, or a country which can and does sterilize balance-of-payments effects in the relevant period; see chapter 10. By the time of the first oil shock (1973–74) this is probably a reasonable characterization although current balance-of-payments effects will also be present for some countries in the simulations reported in section 8.3 below.

Simulation experiments which allow for such endogenous movements in the nominal money supply are reported below in section 8.3. It is perhaps understandable why most analyses assume that the ambiguously signed change in nominal money must be negligible and proceed on that basis. One can at least explain the effect if the central bank were to hold money supply unchanged.

8.1.4   Conclusions from Theory

Considering first the results of our analysis conditional upon a given monetary policy, with resources at their natural employment levels, the output elasticity with respect to the real price of oil is $-\gamma/(1-\gamma)$ before capital adjusts and $-\gamma/\beta$ with full capital adjustment. The parameter γ, the value share of oil imports used in producing domestic output, may be quite small, certainly less than 0.02 for the United States, for example. The labor share β is on the order of 0.7 to 0.8, so the long-run elasticities vary from about γ to 1.3γ or 1.4γ. In the short run, unemployment will increase slightly (if aggregate demand is elastic), but the short-run output elasticity seems to lie in the same range as for the long run. The price level is shifted up in the long run by the long-run income elasticity of money demand (around 1) times the output elasticity. In the short run the price level shifts less than in proportion to output since the short-run aggregate demand curve is elastic.

These shifts in the levels of output and prices affect their growth rates only during the transitional period. They may be reinforced or offset by endogenous money supply reactions of the central bank. These reactions depend on the relative aversion of the central bank to decreases in output and increases in prices and so are ambiguous in sign a priori.

Biases in the calculation of real value added imply smaller elasticities in absolute value for real GNP and the implicit price deflator than for real output and the price level. Indeed, an increase in the real oil price of the size which occurred in 1973–74 implies that the logarithmic change in real GNP would be less than half that for output.

8.2   Tests for Structural Change in the Real-Income Equation

The behavior of the real price of oil is dominated by a downward secular trend from the 1950s until the early 1970s as illustrated for the United States in figure 8.4. There was a small upward movement in 1971–72, but the major increase occurred in the second quarter of 1973 and especially the first quarter of 1974. Widespread recessions in 1973–75 provide the major empirical evidence in support of a large real-income effect of oil price increases. However, several alternative hypotheses focus on other major events occurring roughly coincidentally.

The first of these alternative hypotheses points to the final breakdown

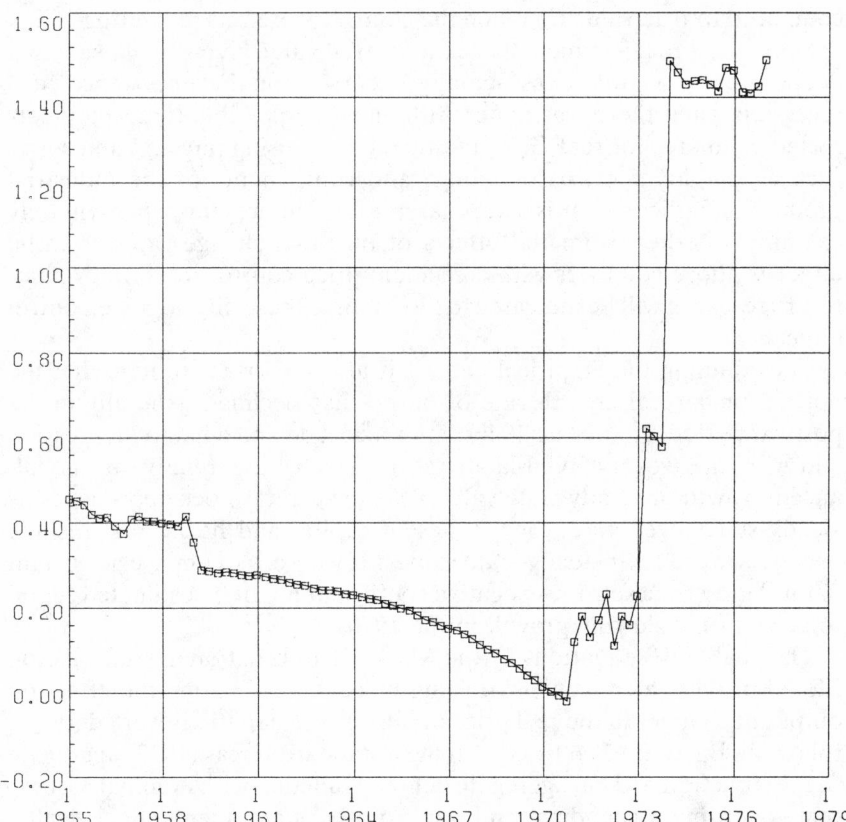

Fig. 8.4   The logarithm of the United States real price of imported oil.
                      Source: The dollar price index of Venezuelan crude oil is taken
                      from various issues of *International Financial Statistics* and
                      rebased to 1.00 in 1970. This is then deflated by the U.S. GNP
                      deflator (1970 = 1.00) to obtain θ (θ_{1970} = 1.00).

of pegged exchange rates in 1973 which permitted (previously) nonreserve countries to regain control of their money supplies and to stop the
inflation imported from the United States. In the United States, meanwhile, the Fed reduced money supply growth in mid-1973 and again in
mid-1974. The average reduction in the growth rate of the money supply
in the eight countries in our sample exceeded 5 percentage points.
Obviously any estimate of the effect of oil price changes must account for
the effect of these restrictive monetary shocks.

   A second alternative hypothesis points to the widespread adoption of
price controls, following the U.S. lead in August 1971, and their subsequent dismantling in the period 1973–75. Such controls may have caused
overstatement of real GNP (and understatement of the GNP deflator)

compared to true values.[21] When the controls were relaxed during 1973–75, *measured* real income fell back to its true value giving an illusion of a deeper recession than was actually occurring or the occurrence of a recession when there was none. Although it is possible to develop corrected estimates for real GNP and the deflator using physical unit series such as employment, car-loadings, and components of the industrial production indices, that is a very large job. The present paper will only examine whether estimated effects of oil price changes appear to be larger in those countries with coincident price-control relaxation. If so, future research will be indicated to disentangle these oil and price-control effects.

In examining the empirical data, it is also important to note that the normal or natural growth rate of output has declined generally in the postwar period. In the late 1940s, after a decade and a half of depression and war, the world capital-labor ratio was very low relative to its balanced-growth or steady-state value.[22] As the capital stock approaches its steady-state level, the growth rates of capital and hence real income decline toward their steady-state values. If we were to impose a constant natural growth, a spurious negative coefficient might be estimated for oil to account for slowing growth in the 1970s.

The real GNP equations of the Mark III International Transmission Model provide a convenient starting place for estimating the effect on output of changes in the real price of oil.[23] These equations were derived, following Barro (1978), by combining a standard Lucas (1973) aggregate supply function with an aggregate demand function with nominal money, real government spending, and real exports as arguments. Specifically, they express the rational-expectation/natural-rate approach as

$$(8.33) \qquad \log y_t - \log y_{t-1} = a_1 - a_2(\log y_{t-1} - \log \overline{y}_{t-1})$$
$$+ \sum_{i=0}^{3} a_{3+i}\hat{M}_{t-i}$$
$$+ \sum_{i=0}^{3} a_{7+i}\hat{g}_{t-i}$$
$$+ \sum_{i=0}^{3} a_{11+i}\hat{x}_{t-i} + \epsilon_t,$$

where the time subscripts are made explicit, $\overline{y}_t$ is the natural-employment level of real output in quarter t, and $\hat{M}_t$, $\hat{g}_t$, and $\hat{x}_t$ are the innovations in the aggregate demand variables $\log M_t$, logarithm of real government

---

21. See Darby (1976*a*, *b*).

22. Even for the relatively unscathed United States, capital grew by only about 0.4% per annum from 1929 through 1948 compared to a normal growth rate of 3.2%; see Christensen and Jorgenson (1978, p. 56). This implies that by 1948 the actual U.S. capital stock was less than 60% of the steady-state capital stock.

23. See chapters 5 and 6 above for a description of the model and chapter 9 below for a detailed analysis of the real-income equations.

expenditures for goods and services, and exports divided by GNP, respectively.[24] Thus, in the absence of innovations or stochastic disturbance ϵ_t, log y_t adjusts toward its natural level at the rate a_2 per quarter. Innovations in the determinants of aggregate demand affect log y_t with an unconstrained four-quarter distributed lag to allow for any inventory adjustment lags.

To estimate the effect of the real oil price, it remains to specify log $\bar{y}_t$ appropriately. A form which allows for both declining natural output growth as just discussed and for an oil price effect is

(8.34) $\log \bar{y}_t = b_1 + b_2 t + b_3 t^2 + b_4 \log \theta_t .$

A positive b_2 and negative b_3 implies a declining natural growth rate. The parameter b_4 estimates the full long-run value of $(d \log y)/(d \log \theta)$. If the expression (8.34) were simply substituted in equation (8.34), an oil price change would implicitly be assumed to have no immediate effect and then a partial adjustment effect at the rate a_2 per quarter. This is inconsistent with the analysis of section 8.1 in which it was shown that the short-run effect is similar in magnitude to the long-run effect.[25] So, as with the aggregate demand variables, a four-quarter distributed lag on the first difference of log θ is included to capture a rapid short-run adjustment process.

Substituting equation (8.34) in (8.33) and adding the short-run adjustment process yields the estimating equation

(8.35)
$$\begin{aligned}
\log y_t = {} & a_1 + a_2(b_1 - b_2) + (1 - a_2)\log y_{t-1} \\
& + a_2 b_2 t + a_2 b_3 (t-1)^2 \\
& + a_2 b_4 \log \theta_{t-1} + \sum_{i=0}^{3} a_{3+i}\hat{M}_{t-i} \\
& + \sum_{i=0}^{3} a_{7+i}\hat{g}_{t-i} + \sum_{i=0}^{3} a_{11+i}\hat{X}_{t-i} \\
& + \sum_{i=1}^{4} c_i(\log \theta_{t+1-i} - \log \theta_{t-i}) + \epsilon_t .
\end{aligned}$$

This equation has been estimated using the 1957–76 quarterly data set and instruments for the eight countries in the Mark III International Transmission Model. The regressions are based on the two-stage least-squares principal-components (2SLSPC) technique because of the large

24. The scaling of exports as a fraction of income rather than in logarithmic terms was done to permit application of the balance-of-payments identity in the model. In the results reported here all the innovations are defined as residuals from optimal ARIMA processes applied to log M_t, log g_t, and $(X/Y)_t$, respectively.

25. Immediately after an increase in the real oil price, the capital stock is greater than in full long-run equilibrium while labor utilization is less. The net effect depends on the elasticity η_D of the aggregate demand curve, but approximates the full long-run effect on plausible assumptions.

number of predetermined variables in the model.[26] The coefficients of the aggregate demand variables, not at issue here, are substantially the same as those discussed in chapter 6 above, and so are omitted for the sake of brevity from the present discussion.[27]

The regression results are summarized in table 8.2. The coefficient of $\log \theta_t$ is negative in every case although only four of the t statistics meet conventional levels of significance. The implicit estimate of the long-run oil effect is reported in the ninth row as ranging from a 2 basis point decrease in real income per percentage point increase in the real price of oil for the U.S. to 19 basis points for Japan. Table 8.3 indicates the implied long-run reduction in real income for the eight contries based on the 1973I–76IV increase in the real price of oil. Rasche and Tatom (1980, table 7) prepared similar estimates for their model (discussed in section 8.1) on the basis of 1973–77 energy price increases, and those estimates are reported for comparison. Despite some differences in detail, the calculations here tell broadly the same story as those of Rasche and Tatom. However, this strong story does not do so well under closer examination.

Let us first consider the possibility that the share of imported oil in total output is so small that any effects are in fact negligible. This is tested by computing the F statistic for the hypothesis that all the oil coefficients are zero (H_0: $a_2 b_4 = c_1 = c_2 = c_3 = c_4 = 0$). As reported in table 8.2, only five of the countries have any statistically significant oil effect at the 5% level[28] and for one of these (the United States) the significant response is due to short-run movements which might be related to various panic policy responses, briefly adopted here and abroad, to the temporary OPEC embargo at the end of 1973. Further, the significant French effects imply that French income was higher throughout 1973 as a result of rising oil prices and so does not really support the hypothesis.

Since experience indicates that the French, Italian, and Japanese data may be quite unreliable,[29] let us focus on the results for the United States, the United Kingdom, Canada, Germany, and the Netherlands. Of these five, the F statistic is insignificant for Canada and Germany and significant for the United States, United Kingdom, and the Netherlands. In-

---

26. The only current endogenous variables in equation (8.35) are $\hat{M}_t$, $\hat{x}_t$, and $\log \theta_t$. Time t and government spending shocks are exogenous in the model, but $\hat{M}_t$ and $\hat{x}_t$ are endogenous. The price of oil in base-year dollars is exogenous, so $\log \theta_t$ is exogenous for the U.S. For the other seven countries endogenous movements in the purchasing power ratio make the real price of oil in base-year domestic currency units endogenous, but they are dominated by movements in the U.S. real price.

27. To the extent that these aggregate demand variables were correlated with any significant oil variables added here, their numerical values were of course affected. However, the general pattern and conclusions remained unaltered from those in chapter 6. See also the simulation equation coefficients in section 8.3 below.

28. Only France is significant at the 1% level.

29. See discussions in chapters 3, 6, and 7 above.

terestingly, these three countries with significant F statistics all removed general price controls coincidentally with the 1973–74 oil price increase while Canada and Germany had no price controls during the relevant period.[30] If, as I have argued elsewhere (1976a, b), the decontrol process results in the elimination of overstatement of real GNP built up during the control period, then the spurious drop in reported real GNP relative to true GNP will be captured as part (or all!) of the effect of the coincidental increase in real oil prices. Certainly the pattern of significant oil effects only where simultaneous decontrol occurred strongly indicates the value of research to formulate real GNP estimates unbiased by price-control evasions which overstate quantities and understate prices.

In summary, these empirical results give a rather ambiguous answer to the question of whether a large increase in the real price of oil will reduce real income significantly for given nominal money supplies, real government spending, and real exports. Such a reduction is estimated for half the cases, but this may be a spurious result due to the simultaneous removal of price controls in those countries.

8.3 Simulation Experiments

To assess the effects of the 1973–74 oil price increase on real income—and ultimately the price level—we must allow for induced changes in nominal money supplies and real exports aside from any possible direct effects such as examined in section 8.2. To take account of these indirect effects, one must resort to a simulation model of some sort, and this section reports results from the Mark IV Simulation Model described in chapter 7 above.[31] The results of any one simulation model cannot be

---

30. The United States took the lead in imposing price controls in August 1971, which Darby (1976a, b) argues led to an increasing overstatement of real GNP (and understatement of the deflator) through the first quarter of 1973. Controls were then relaxed in phases through the third quarter of 1974 with progressive elimination of overstatement in real GNP. That is, real-income *growth* was overstated from 1971III through 1973I and then understated from 1973II through 1974IV. According to Parkin in Shenoy (1978, pp. 150–51), the United Kingdom followed a similar pattern: controls instituted with a freeze in November 1972 peaked in their effect on the data with the end of stage II in August 1973 and eventually were abandoned entirely after the Conservative loss of February 1974. Shenoy (1978, pp. 132–35) reports a similar albeit more complex pattern for the Netherlands beginning also with a 1972 price freeze. Carr (1976, p. 40) points out that Canada was free of general price controls until October 1975, too late to cause any biases in the oil price coefficients. West Germany imposed no price controls on the ground that such policies distract attention from the real problems (Shenoy 1978, pp. 138–41).

31. The Mark IV Simulation Model is a simplified simulation version of the Mark III International Transmission Model described in chapters 5 and 6 above. The main simplifications involve (1) deletion of insignificant variables except where they are required a priori to permit international transmission and (2) combining variables to reduce multicollinearity where a priori hypotheses on equality of coefficients were not rejected by the data. The resulting model is thus both consistent with the data and tractable for simulation. The Mark IV Model exists in versions corresponding to pegged and floating exchange rates, but only the latter (Mark IV–FLT) is used in this paper since we are concerned with 1973–74.

Table 8.2   2SLSPC Regression Estimates of Oil Price Effects in Real-Income Equation (8.35)

	US	UK	CA	FR	GE	IT	JA	NE
Adjustment coefficient (a_2)	0.180	0.448	0.171	0.613	0.176	0.260	0.206	0.334
	(0.049)	(0.112)	(0.070)	(0.120)	(0.080)	(0.083)	(0.082)	(0.087)
	3.656	3.985	2.446	5.089	2.205	3.127	2.529	3.850
Coefficient of:								
t	0.00196	0.00284	0.00203	0.00892	0.00236	0.00404	0.00485	0.00284
	(0.00058)	(0.00095)	(0.00080)	(0.00173)	(0.00116)	(0.00145)	(0.00179)	(0.00083)
	3.349	2.978	2.529	5.163	2.035	2.785	2.711	3.418
$(t-1)^2 \times 10^{-6}$†	-3.215	2.449	1.293	-1.977	-5.581	-11.474	-2.244	11.646
	(3.389)	(6.089)	(5.283)	(7.316)	(6.748)	(6.440)	(6.043)	(7.465)
	-0.949	0.402	0.245	-0.270	-0.827	-1.782	-0.371	1.560
$\log \theta_{t-1}$	-0.0038	-0.0253	-0.0081	-0.0581	-0.0068	-0.0092	-0.0393	-0.0394
	(0.0052)	(0.0093)	(0.0073)	(0.0168)	(0.015)	(0.0073)	(0.0178)	(0.0138)
	-0.732	-2.717	-1.097	-3.455	-0.456	-1.252	-2.205	-2.862
$\Delta \log \theta_t$	-0.021	-0.047	-0.005	0.038	0.002	0.010	-0.048	-0.027
	(0.011)	(0.018)	(0.016)	(0.021)	(0.026)	(0.014)	(0.018)	(0.016)
	-1.897	-2.602	-0.304	1.823	0.074	0.749	-2.711	-1.672

	(1)	(2)	(3)	(4)	(5)	(6)	(7)	(8)
$\Delta \log \theta_{t-1}$	−0.022	0.025	0.004	0.083	0.013	0.005	0.007	0.035
	(0.011)	(0.017)	(0.015)	(0.026)	(0.020)	(0.015)	(0.020)	(0.019)
	−2.074	1.489	0.273	3.167	0.678	0.333	0.345	1.839
$\Delta \log \theta_{t-2}$	−0.009	0.019	−0.010	0.062	0.022	0.010	0.014	0.018
	(0.010)	(0.016)	(0.015)	(0.024)	(0.019)	(0.015)	(0.018)	(0.018)
	−0.092	1.127	−0.642	2.576	1.187	0.617	0.788	0.967
$\Delta \log \theta_{t-3}$	−0.018	0.007	−0.004	0.009	−0.010	0.001	0.010	0.009
	(0.011)	(0.017)	(0.016)	(0.023)	(0.020)	(0.014)	(0.018)	(0.017)
	−1.650	0.433	−0.260	0.373	−0.492	0.073	0.562	0.534
Long-run oil effect $(a_2 b_4/a_2)^{\S}$	−0.021	−0.057	−0.047	−0.095	−0.039	−0.035	−0.191	−0.118
$F(5,59)$ statistic§	2.54‡	3.32‡	0.49	4.40#	0.56	0.54	2.27‡	2.38‡
$\bar{R}^2$	0.9984	0.9943	0.9982	0.9976	0.9975	0.9982	0.9994	0.9981
S.E.E.	0.0082	0.0120	0.0121	0.0159	0.0131	0.0120	0.0135	0.0122
h [D-W]††	−0.53	1.10	−3.40	[2.33]	0.26	−2.02	−1.74	1.59

Note. Period: 1971I–76IV. Standard errors are reported in parentheses below coefficient estimates; t statistics are below standard errors. Coefficient estimates for the constant and the aggregate demand shocks $(a_3, \ldots, a_{14})$ are not reported for brevity's sake.

†Note that the coefficients and standard errors in the third row are a multiple 10^6 of those for $(t-1)^2$.

§The $F(5,59)$ statistic is for the test of the hypothesis that $a_2 b_4 = c_1 = c_2 = c_3 = c_4 = 0$. The 0.05 significance level (indicated by ‡) requires $F > 2.23$. The 0.01 significance level (indicated by #) requires $F > 3.34$.

††The biased Durbin-Watson statistic is reported in square brackets in those cases in which Durbin's h cannot be computed (is imaginary).

Table 8.3   Implied Estimates of Long-Run Decrease in Real GNP
due to 1973I–76IV Increases in Real Price of Oil

Country	$\dfrac{d \log q^{\dagger}}{d \log \theta}$	$\log \theta_{1976\text{IV}}$ $- \log \theta_{1973\text{I}}$	Long-Run Decrease in $q^{\S}$	Rasche-Tatom Long-Run Estimate[‡]
US	−0.021	1.2119	−2.5%	−7.0%
UK	−0.057	1.2749	−7.3%	−3.5%
CA	−0.047	1.1045	−5.2%	−4.4%
FR	−0.095	1.1477	−10.9%	−4.1%
GE	−0.039	1.1101	−4.3%	−1.9%
IT	−0.035	1.3995	−4.9%	NA
JA	−0.191	1.1402	−21.8%	−17.1%
NE	−0.118	0.9856	−11.6%	NA

[†]This is the ratio of the estimated values of $a_2 b_4$ to a_2 from table 8.2.

[§]Product of the previous two columns.

[‡]From Rasche and Tatom (1980, table 7 for 1973–77 energy-price increases.

taken too seriously except as they illustrate the possible importance of channels not inconsistent with the data which might otherwise be overlooked. So, with a spirit of healthy skepticism, let us turn to the specific experiments.

To assess the effects of the oil price increase, we compare the results from simulating the model in one case with the actual real price of oil and in another case with the real price of oil held constant at the 1973I price. The assumed difference in the logarithm of the real price of oil ($\log (\theta/\bar{\theta})$) is plotted in figure 8.5. The dynamic simulations begin in 1973II and continue for six quarters thereafter.[32]

In view of the mixed evidence for direct oil price effects on real income as reported in section 8.2, the basic Mark IV Model does not incorporate such effects. An alternative simulation model, the Mark IV–Oil, was therefore estimated. It differs from the basic Mark IV Model only in two ways: (a) The variables listed in table 8.2 for those five countries for which the oil variables were significant (United States, United Kingdom, France, Japan, and the Netherlands) are added to the real income equations. These five countries are listed with their estimated coefficients in table 8.4. (b) Corresponding identities are added to define the logarithm of the domestic price of oil as the sum of the logarithms of the dollar price and the purchasing power ratio.

32. In a dynamic simulation, the input series are the exogenous variables plus the initial conditions (endogenous variables at the beginning of the simulation). The values of endogenous variables within the simulation period are assigned their predicted values. Dynamic instabilities become important in the Mark IV–FLT Model after seven quarters as discussed in chapter 7. These instabilities apparently arise from our inability to eliminate simultaneous equation bias in the short estimation period. Therefore the previous caveat that these results are only illustrative must be reemphasized.

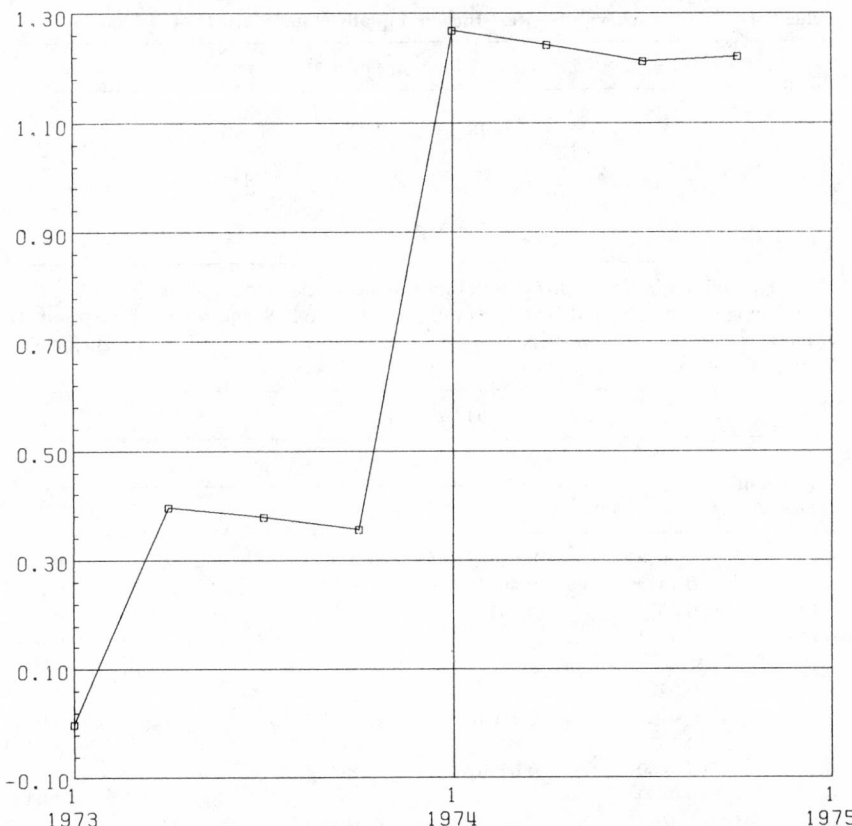

Fig. 8.5   Logarithmic increase in U.S. real price of oil from 1973I.

Figures 8.6 and 8.7 illustrate the simulation results for the five countries with reliable data. The basic Mark IV Model is used to simulate the effects of the oil price increase as displayed in figure 8.6 for six major macroeconomic variables for each country. The effect is estimated as the difference between the simulation values based on the actual real price of oil and the values based on a constant post-1973I price. Figure 8.7 displays the corresponding simulated effects when the Mark IV–Oil Model is used to perform the basic simulations.

Figure 8.6 illustrates that in the basic model without direct real income effects, real income (panel *a*) generally rises due to increases in export demand (panel *e*). Whether this raises or lowers the price level depends on the simulated movements in interest rates (and so the net change in real money demand) and in the nominal money supply.[33] The money

33. Recall that $P = M^s/m^a(y,R)$. Increases in real income tend to raise m^a and hence lower the price level, other things equal. Increases in M^s or in R, on the other hand, tend by themselves to raise the price level.

Table 8.4   **Alternative Real-Income Equations for Mark IV–Oil Model**

a) Equation Form

$$\log y_j = \alpha_{j1} + \alpha_{j2}\log y^P_{j,t-1} + (1 - \alpha_{j2})\log y_{j,t-1} + \sum_{i=0}^{3} \alpha_{j,3+i}\hat{M}_{t,t-i}$$

$$+ \sum_{i=0}^{3} \alpha_{j,7+i}\hat{g}_{j,t-i} + \sum_{i=0}^{3} \alpha_{j,11+i}\hat{x}_{j,t-i} + \alpha_{j,20}t + \alpha_{j,21}(t-1)^2$$

$$+ \alpha_{j,22}\log \theta_{j,t-1} + \sum_{i=0}^{3} \alpha_{j,23+i}\log(\theta_{j,t-i}/\theta_{j,j-i-1}) + \epsilon_j$$

Note. The country index is j, $\log y^P_j$ is permanent income, and $\log \theta_j \equiv \log P^{RO} + \log P_1 + \log E_j - \log P_j$, where P_1 and P_j are the price levels for the U.S. and country j, respectively, E_j is the exchange rate, and P^{RO} is the index of the real price of a barrel of Venezuelan oil in 1970 U.S. dollars.

b) Coefficients

Coefficient Name	Values by Country (j)				
	US	UK	FR	JA	NE
α_{j1}	− 0.0016	− 0.0148	0.0843	0.2338	0.0668
α_{j2}	0.1472	0.4631	0.5351	0.2122	0.2869
α_{j3}	0.8335	− 0.1410	− 0.2414	—	0.1542
α_{j4}	0.4271	—	—	—	0.0679
α_{j5}	—	—	—	0.2152	− 0.0676
α_{j6}	0.9220	—	—	—	− 0.1044
α_{j7}	—	0.1464	0.0487	—	0.0625
α_{j8}	0.1320	—	—	—	− 0.0239
α_{j9}	0.0960	0.0959	0.0531	—	0.0222
$\alpha_{j,10}$	0.0852	—	—	− 0.0522	0.0398
$\alpha_{j,11}$	1.4624	—	− 0.1536	− 0.8308	0.0352
$\alpha_{j,12}$	1.0743	0.5147	—	—	− 0.0231
$\alpha_{j,13}$	—	—	—	− 0.6263	0.1660
$\alpha_{j,14}$	—	—	—	− 0.8518	− 0.0236
$\alpha_{j,20}$	0.0005	0.0005	0.0007	0.0006	− 0.0004
$\alpha_{j,21}$	− 0.0000	− 0.0000	− 0.0000	− 0.0000	+ 0.0000
$\alpha_{j,22}$	0.0003	− 0.0188	− 0.0447	− 0.0351	− 0.0307
$\alpha_{j,23}$	− 0.0187	− 0.0294	0.0089	− 0.0481	− 0.0269
$\alpha_{j,24}$	− 0.0231	0.0236	0.0500	0.0024	0.0257
$\alpha_{j,25}$	− 0.0064	0.0213	0.0402	0.0105	0.0096
$\alpha_{j,26}$	− 0.0200	0.0073	0.0084	0.0022	0.0032

Notes. The Mark IV–Oil Model replaces the real-income equations in the Mark IV–FLT Simulation Model with these five equations. The only other changes are the addition of identities for the United Kingdom, France, Japan, and the Netherlands defining their domestic real price of oil as

$$\log \theta_j \equiv \log P^{RO} + \log P_1 + \log E_j - \log P_j.$$

A coefficient for a suppressed variable (t statistic less than 1 in absolute value; α_{j3} through $\alpha_{j,14}$ only) is indicated by dash.

X 10⁻²

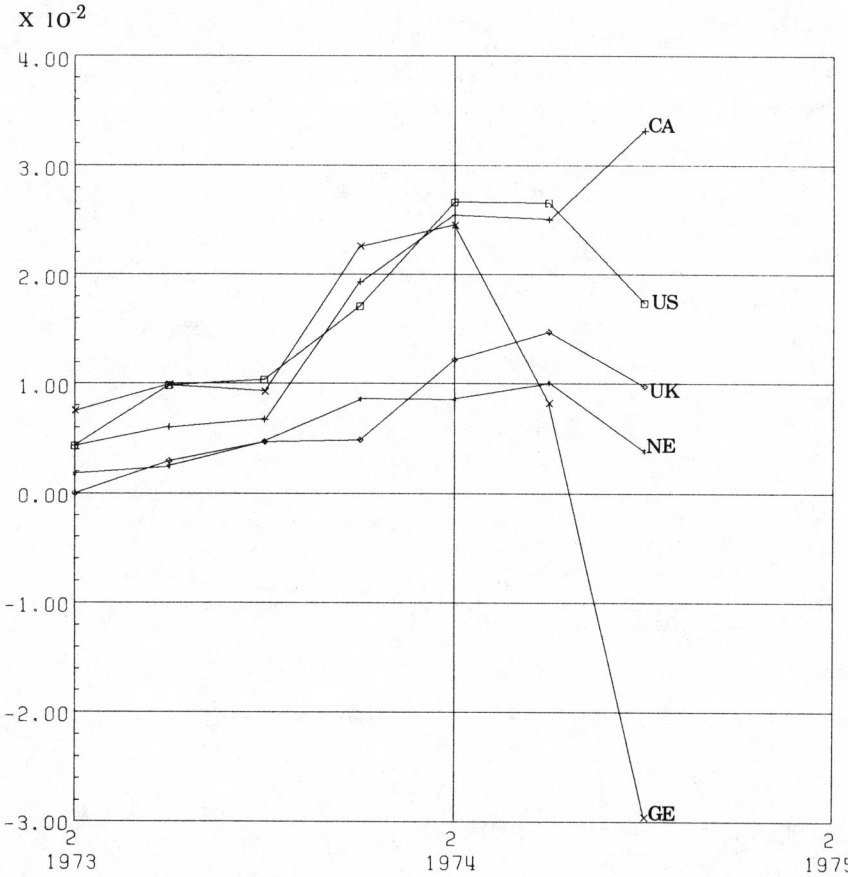

Fig. 8.6   Simulated effects of the 1973–74 increase in the real price of oil using basic Mark IV model.

a) Real income—log y_i

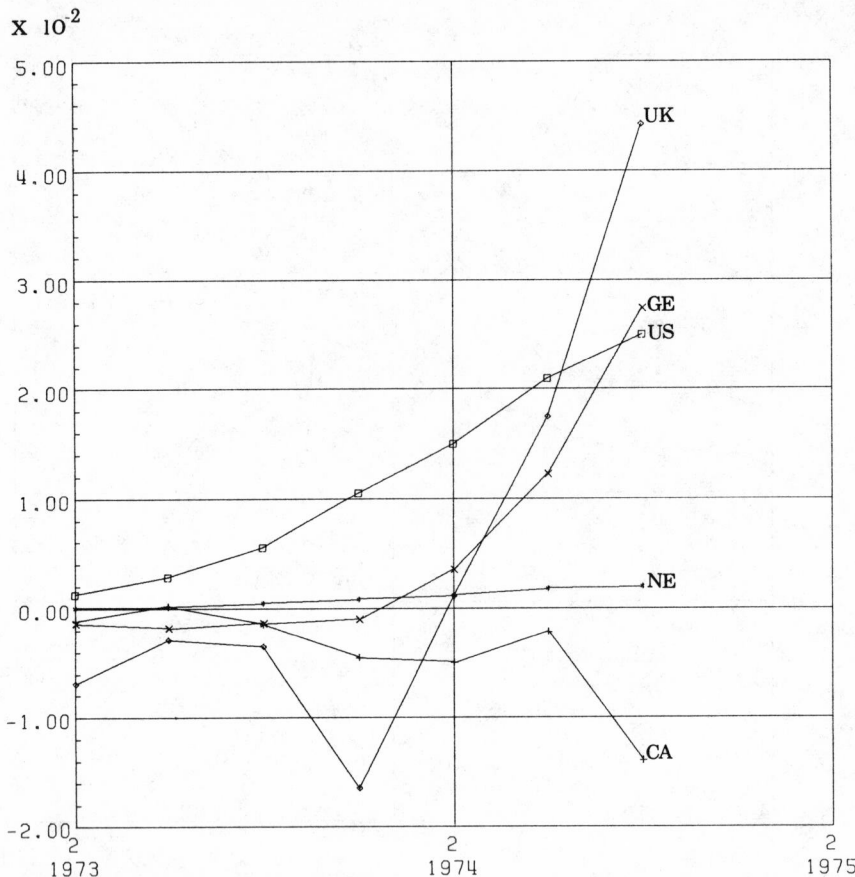

Fig. 8.6 (continued)

b) Price level—log P_i

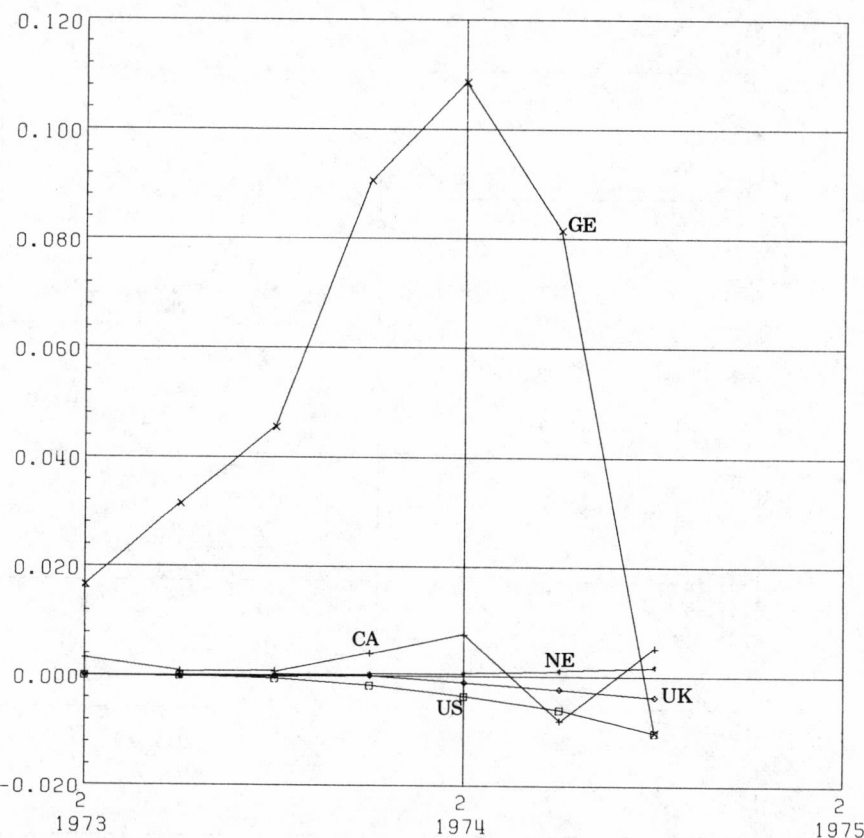

Fig. 8.6 (continued)

c) Nominal money—log M_i

X 10⁻²

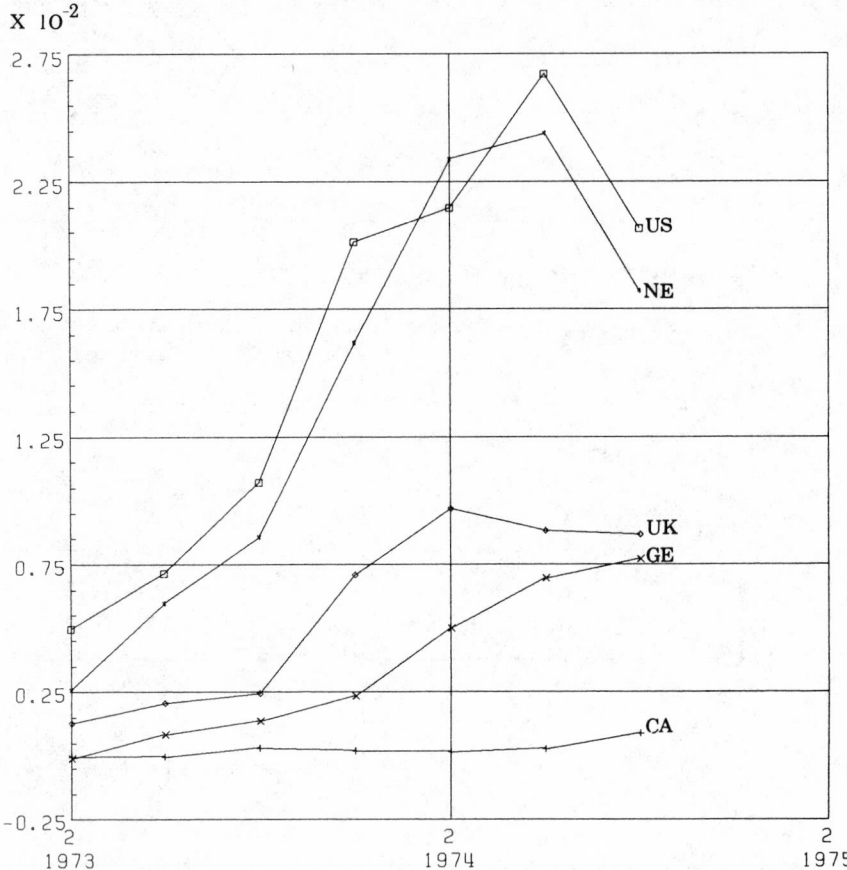

Fig. 8.6 (continued)

d) Short-term interest rate—R_i

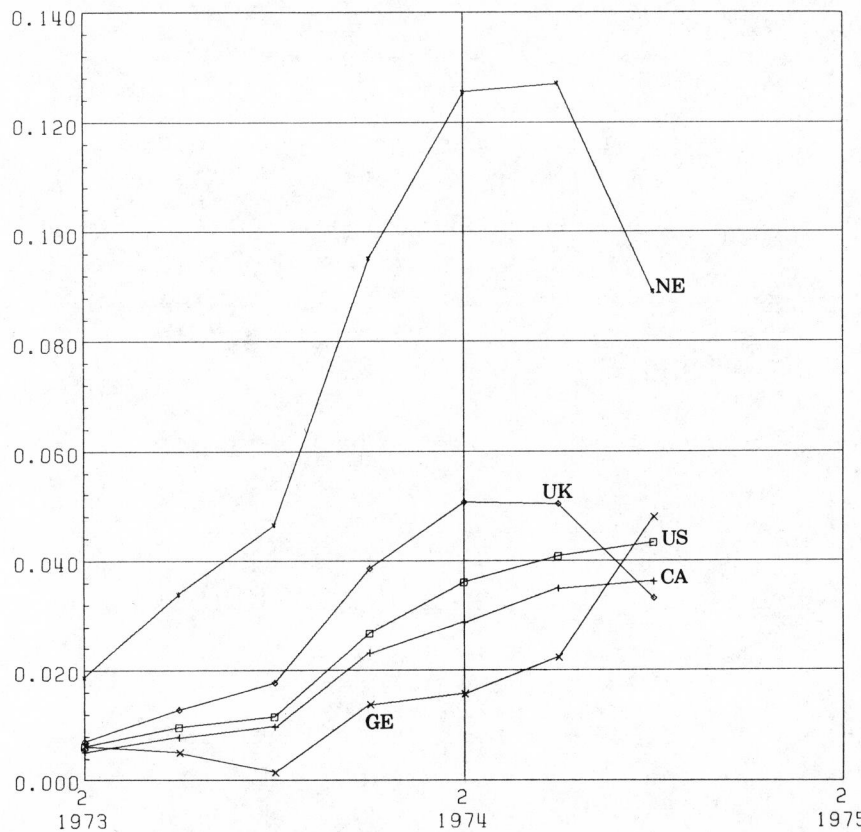

Fig. 8.6 (continued)

e) Scaled exports—$(X/Y)_i$

X 10^{-2}

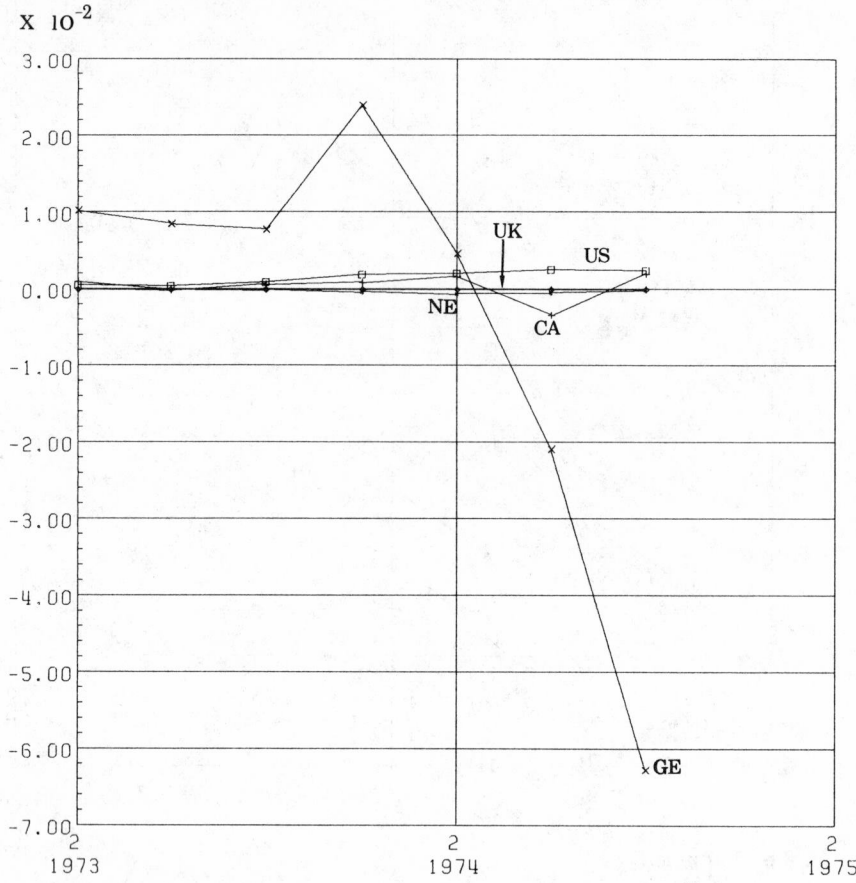

Fig. 8.6 (continued)

f) Scaled balance of payments—$(B/Y)_i$

X 10^{-2}

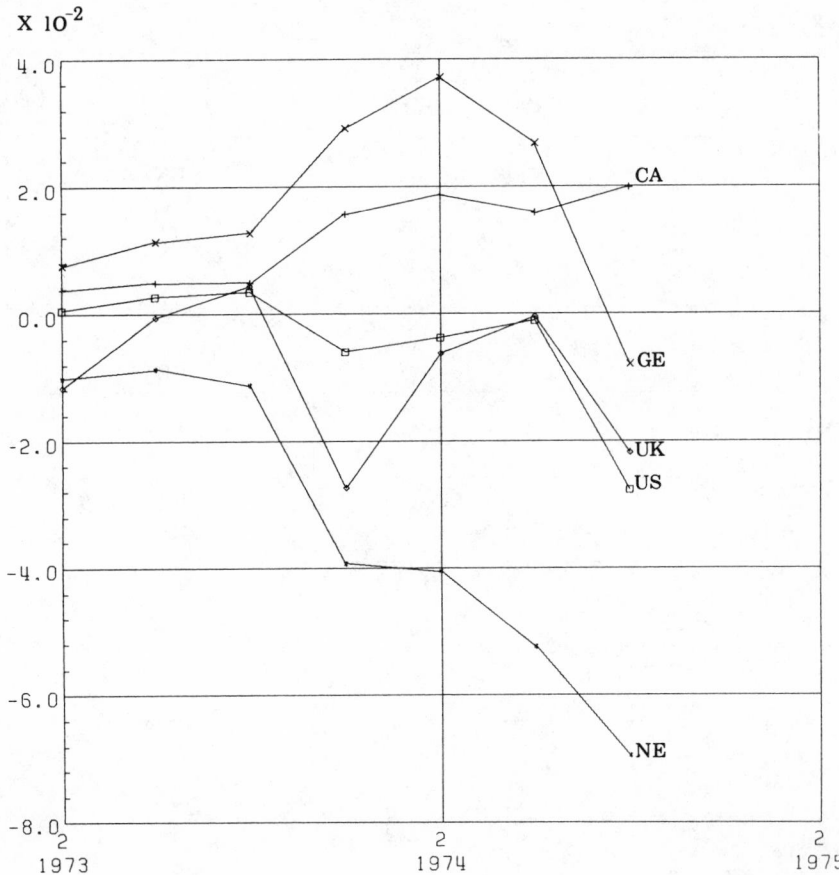

Fig. 8.7   Simulated effects of the 1973–74 increase in the real price of oil using Mark IV oil model.

a) Real income—log y_i

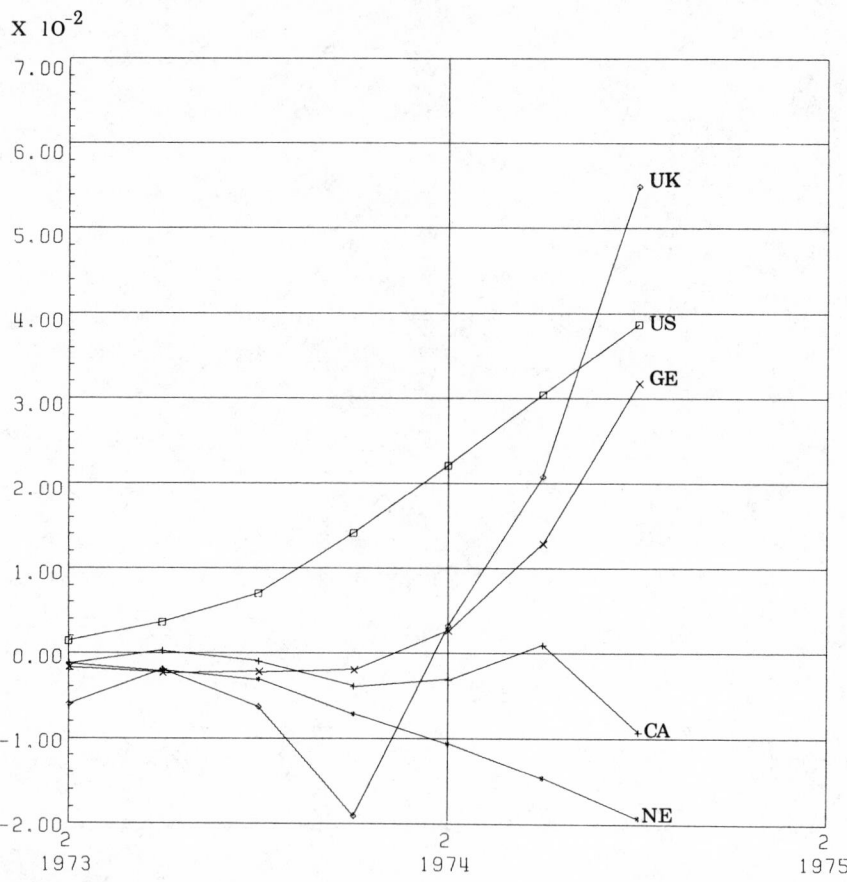

Fig. 8.7 (continued)

b) Price level—log P_i

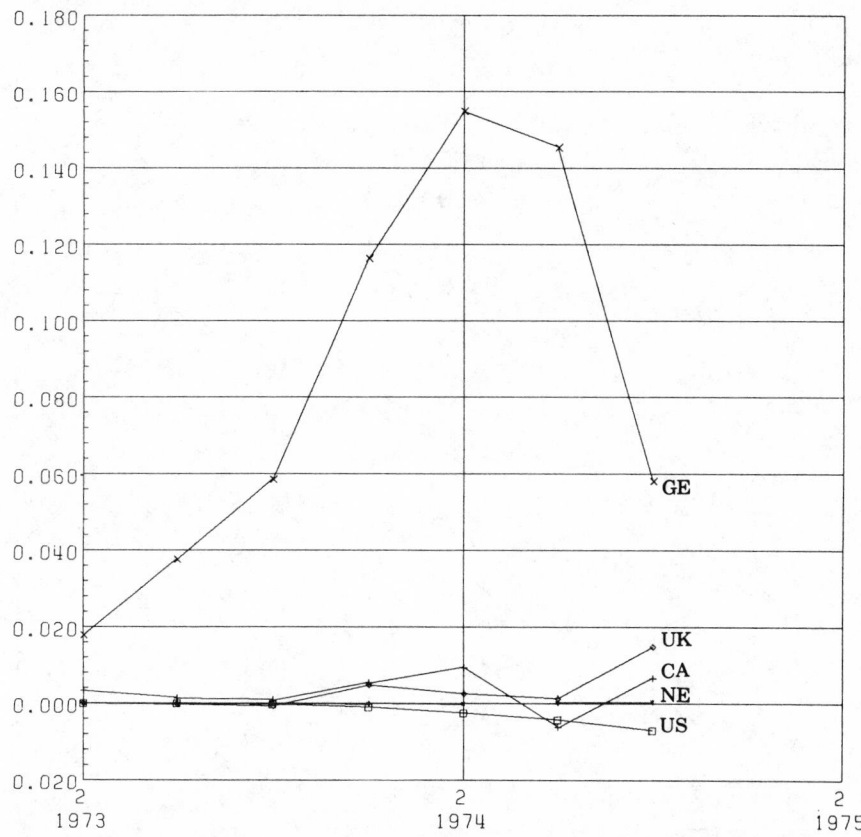

Fig. 8.7 (continued)

c) Nominal money—log M_i

X 10^{-2}

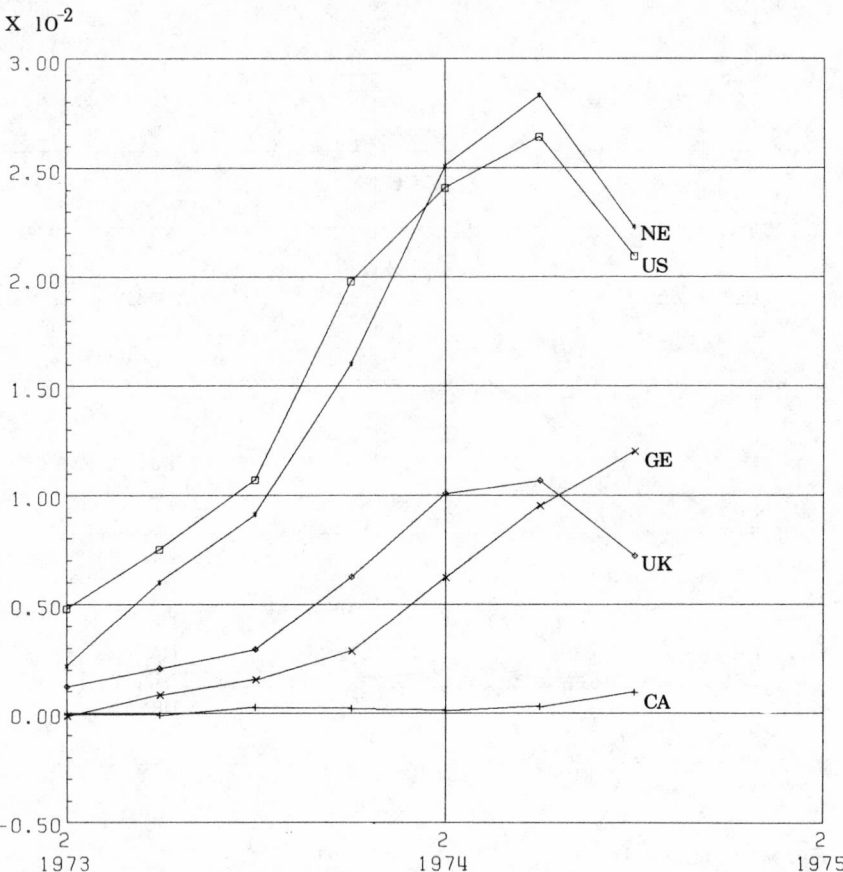

Fig. 8.7 (continued)

d) Short-term interest rate—R_i

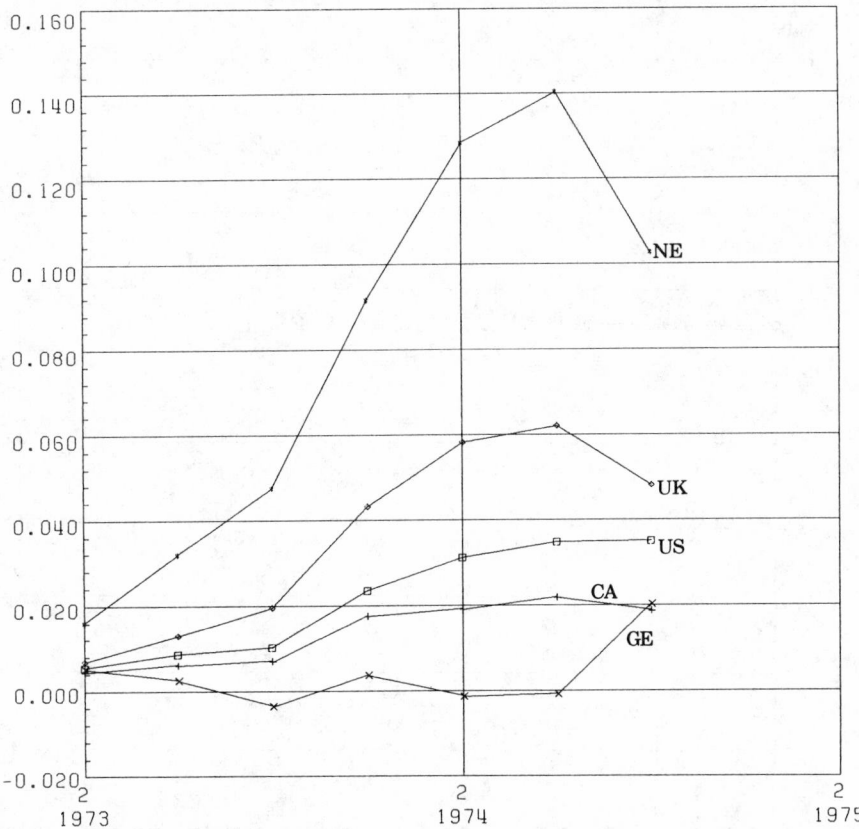

Fig. 8.7 (continued)

e) Scaled exports—$(X/Y)_i$

X 10^{-2}

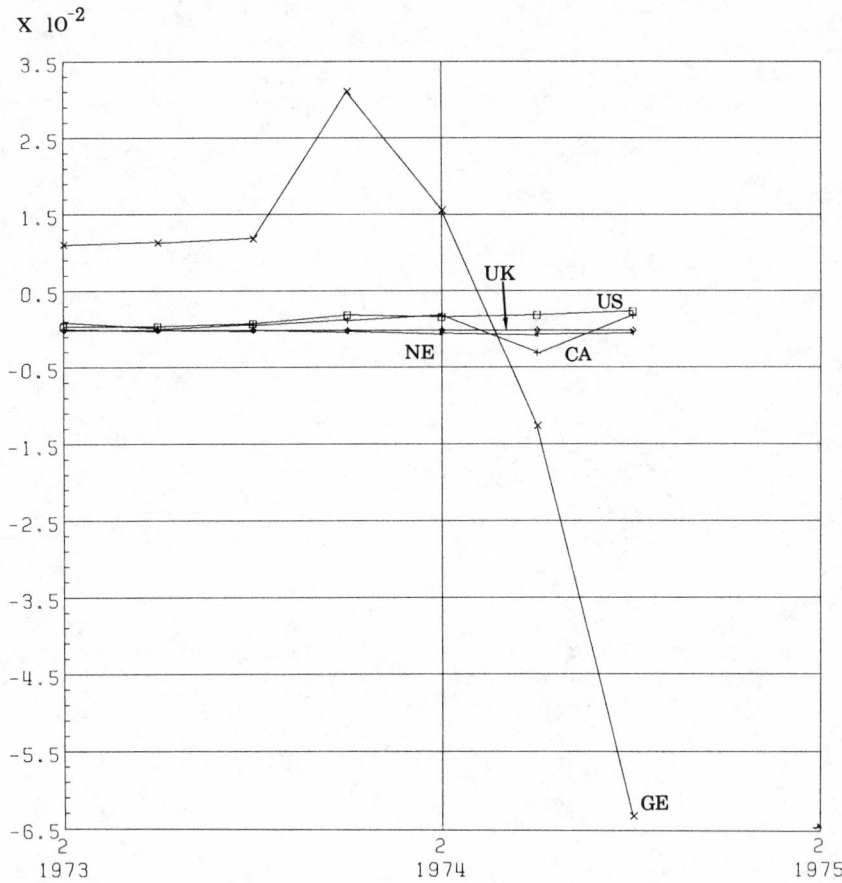

Fig. 8.7 (continued)

f) Scaled balance of payments—$(B/Y)_i$

supply movements are generally small except in Germany where strong simulated balance-of-payments effects cause a sharp but temporary increase in nominal money.

Figure 8.7 illustrates just how sensitive the results are to the inclusion of direct real-income effects. Notice in panel *a* the considerable real-income declines which occur in the three countries (the United States, the United Kingdom, and the Netherlands) with direct real-income effects included. For the United States and the United Kingdom, the price level rises due to the lower real income and hence real money demand and, for the U.K. only, due to a rise in nominal money.[34] The anomalous fall in the Dutch price level occurs because of a perverse, statistically insignificant negative coefficient on transitory income in the money-demand equation. For Canada and Germany the results differ little from the basic Mark IV simulations.

These simulation results illustrate the large difference it makes whether or not we take at face value the estimated real-oil-price effects in the real-income equations: Real-income effects vary from slightly positive to as much as -7% by the end of 1974. A smaller variation in simulated price-level effects also occurs in the alternative simulations. It is both the sorrow and challenge of our nonexperimental science that other things were not held constant when the oil price change occurred. One factor which may explain the estimated real-income effects in 1973–74 was identified in section 8.2: the coincidental removal of price controls in those countries for which real effects were found. Only much further research can show whether the large simulated effects in the Mark IV–Oil Model have a basis in reality or are the result of other changes—such as price decontrol—occurring in the same period.

8.4 Conclusions

The effects on real income and the price level of the 1973–74 increases in the real price of oil are subject of strongly held but diverse opinions.[35] Unfortunately the results of this paper indicate that a wide range of opinions is indeed consistent with the data. Perhaps we should not be surprised that with effectively one degree of freedom it is difficult to have much confidence in estimates of both an oil price coefficient and its standard error.

The oil price shock of 1979–80 will provide us data on a second major

34. There is a significant rise in British money because only unemployment and not inflation is important. In the American case these factors are offsetting.

35. Taking two of the best studies for the long-run U.S. real-income effect as examples, Norsworthy, Harper, and Kunze (1979, p. 412) report an average reduction in productivity growth of 0.18% per annum for 1973–78, which implies a total reduction in real income of 0.9%, while Rasche and Tatom (1980), in contrast, as reported in table 8.3, estimate a 7.0% long-run effect.

move in the real price of oil.[36] But these data are unlikely to resolve the empirical question. It seems to me that a more fruitful avenue may be to develop quantitative measures of the biases in official real output data due to price controls and then to see what oil price effects are estimated using these corrected data. This approach is feasible because price controls were generally imposed much before the oil price change. Thus historical relations between labor input, electricity production, carloadings, and other physical unit series can be used to estimate the biases up to the oil price change.

If this chapter has demonstrated that the effects of the real-oil-price increases in 1973–74 remain an open question and thus stimulates research toward answering it, then I will be amply recompensed for having to report such inconclusive conclusions.

Acknowledgments

The author acknowledges helpful comments received at a seminar at the International Monetary Fund and the able research assistance of Michael T. Melvin and Andrew A. Vogel. The calculations were performed on the TROLL system at MIT. The bulk of the empirical results appeared with additional evidence in Darby (1982).

References

Barro, R. J. 1978. Unanticipated money, output, and the price level in the United States. *Journal of Political Economy* 86 (August): 549–80.

Berner, R.; P. Clark; E. Hernández-Catá; H. Howe; S. Kwack; and G. Stevens. 1977. A multi-country model of the international influences on the U.S. economy: Preliminary results. International Finance Discussion Papers, no. 115, Board of Governors of the Federal Reserve System, December.

Bruno, M., and J. Sachs. 1979. Supply versus demand approaches to the problem of stagflation. NBER Working Paper, no. 382, August.

Carr, J. 1976. Wage and price controls: Panacea for inflation or prescription for disaster. In M. Walker, ed., *The illusion of wage and price control*. Vancouver: Fraser Institute.

Christensen, L. R., and D. W. Jorgenson. 1978. U.S. input, output, saving, and wealth, 1929–1969. Unpublished paper, Harvard Institute of Economic Research, December.

Darby, M. R. 1976a. "Price and wage controls: The first two years" and "Further evidence." In K. Brunner and A. H. Meltzer, eds, *The

36. When these data for the United States alone were used in Darby (1982), no statistically significant effects of oil prices on real GNP were detected in regressions which also included labor force and price-control variables.

economics of price and wage controls. Carnegie-Rochester Conference Series on Public Policy, vol. 2, supplement to the *Journal of Monetary Economics*, April 1976.

———. 1976b. The U.S. economic stabilization program of 1971–1974. In M. Walker, ed., *The illusion of wage and price control*. Vancouver: Fraser Institute.

———.1976c. *Macroeconomics: The theory of income, employment, and the price level*. New York: McGraw-Hill.

———. 1979. *Intermediate macroeconomics*. New York: McGraw-Hill.

———. 1982. The price of oil and world inflation and recession. *American Economic Review* 82 (September): 738–51.

Hall, R. E. 1977(1). Investment, interest rates, and the effects of stabilization policies. *Brookings Papers on Economic Activity*, pp. 61–103.

Hudson, E. A., and D. W. Jorgenson. 1978. Energy prices and the U.S. economy, 1972–1976. *Natural Resources Journal* 18 (October): 877–97.

Kopcke, R. 1980. Potential growth, productivity, and capital accumulation. *New England Economic Review*, May/June, pp. 22–41.

Lucas, R. E., Jr. 1973. Some international evidence on output-inflation tradeoffs. *American Economic Review* 63 (June): 326–34.

Mork, K. A., and R. E. Hall. 1979. Energy prices, inflation, and recession, 1974–1975. NBER Working Paper, no. 369, July.

Norsworthy, J. R.; M. J. Harper; and K. Kunze. 1979(2). The slowdown in productivity growth: Analysis of some contributing factors. *Brookings Papers on Economic Activity*, pp. 387–421.

Perloff, J. M., and M. L. Wachter. 1979. A production function—nonaccelerating inflation approach to potential output: Is measured potential output too high? In K. Brunner and A. H. Meltzer, eds., *Three aspects of policy and policymaking*, Carnegie-Rochester Conference Series in Public Policy, vol. 10, supplement to the *Journal of Monetary Economics*.

Phelps, E. S. 1978. Commodity-supply shock and full-employment monetary policy. *Journal of Money, Credit and Banking* 10 (May): 206–21.

Purvis, D. D. 1975. A comment on "The use of the aggregate demand curve." *Journal of Economic Literature* 13 (June): 474.

Rasche, R. H., and J. A. Tatom. 1979a. The effects of the new energy regime on economic capacity, production, and prices. *Federal Reserve Bank of St. Louis Review* 59, no. 5 (May): 2–12.

———. 1977. Energy resources and potential GNP. *Federal Reserve Bank of St. Louis Review* 59, no. 6 (June): 10–24.

———. 1980. Energy price shocks, aggregate supply, and monetary policy: The theory and the international evidence. Paper presented at the Carnegie-Rochester Conference Series on Public Policy, April.

Selden, R. T. 1980. The inflationary seventies: Comparisons among selected high-income countries. Paper presented at Conference on Inflation through the Ages, Brooklyn College CUNY, 10–12, March.

Shenoy, S. R., ed. 1978. *Wage-price control: Myth and reality*. Turra-murra, Australia: Centre for Independent Studies.

Tatom, J. A. 1979a. Energy prices and capital formation: 1972–1977. *Federal Reserve Bank of St. Louis Review* 61, no. 5 (May): 2–11.

———. 1979b. The productivity problem. *Federal Reserve Bank of St. Louis Review* 61, no. 9 (September): 3–16.

9   Actual versus Unanticipated Changes in Aggregate Demand Variables: A Sensitivity Analysis of the Real-Income Equation

Michael R. Darby

A large, if not dominant, body of recent research in macroeconomics incorporates the Barro (1977, 1978) variant of the Lucas supply function. The analytical convenience of this approach is well known. For empirical work it has considerable attraction as well: It imposes restrictions upon how changes in money affect real income, and it may be stable despite a change in the monetary regime governing the money supply process.[1] In particular, an empirical investigator can define expected money growth by an ARIMA process, a transfer function, or other parsimonious means and then include in the real-income equation only a few money shocks (innovations)—the difference between actual and expected money growth. Thus a great saving in parameters estimated is to be achieved compared to estimating a long distributed lag on actual money growth rates as would be required to obtain effectively the same equation.[2]

This paper investigates whether the Barro restriction that only money shocks (not anticipated money growth) affect real income is supported by the data for other countries and for two other factors affecting aggregate demand: real government spending and real exports. The empirical

An earlier version of this chapter, entitled "Unanticipated and Actual Changes in Aggregate Demand Variables: A Cross-Country Analysis," was published in the *Proceedings of Fourth West Coast Academic/Federal Reserve Economic Research Seminar, October 1980*, the November 1981 Conference Supplement to the *Federal Reserve Bank of San Francisco Economic Review*, pp. 160–89.

1. If a change in monetary regime does not alter the predictability of the future money supply, then the coefficients on money-supply innovations (or shocks) in the Barro variant would apparently remain unchanged.

2. See Sargent (1976) on the equivalence of these two approaches in the absence of identifying information in a money-supply transfer function which is not present in the real-income equation. See also McCallum (1979) on testing for the validity of the Barro variant even in the absence of such a priori identifying information on a change in monetary regime.

results suggest that the data are not inconsistent with the Barro restrictions. However, except for the United States, it makes very little difference whether one-year distributed lags on unanticipated or actual changes in aggregate demand variables are used in the real-income regressions. Certainly the results would not suggest use of the unanticipated variables in the absence of a priori preference. While these results can be rationalized by greater measurement errors in the foreign data—no real-income regression explains much—they are sufficiently surprising to warrant further investigation and cautious application of Barro's approach.

The Mark III International Transmission Model's real-income equations (R1) and (N1) are derived in section 9.1 as a generalization of the familiar Barro real-income equation. These equations are subjected to a sensitivity analysis in research reported in section 9.2. A summary and suggestions for future research conclude the chapter.

9.1   A Generalized Barro Real-Income Equation

The real-income equation is derived by combining a Lucas supply function with a standard aggregate demand function to obtain real income as a function of lagged transitory real income and shocks in nominal money, real government spending, and real exports.[3] Other aggregate demand variables such as taxes are not included because of lack of adequate international data.[4]

The aggregate supply function is of the Lucas (1973) form:

$$(9.1) \qquad \Delta \log y = a_1 - a_2 \log(y_{-1}/y^p_{-1}) + a_3 \hat{P} + \epsilon,$$

where country subscripts are omitted for simplicity, y is real income, y^p is the natural-employment or permanent value of real income, a_1 is the periodic growth rate of y^p, ϵ is a white noise disturbance, and $\hat{P}$ is the price-level shock:

$$(9.2) \qquad \hat{P} = \log P - (\log P)^*,$$

where P is the price level and an asterisk denotes expectations based upon the previous period's information set.

The aggregate demand function is assumed semi-log linear:

$$(9.3) \qquad \log y = b_1 + b_2 \log(M/P) + b_3 \log g \\ + b_4 x + v,$$

3. For similar derivations, see McCallum (1978), Korteweg (1978), and Horrigan (1980).

4. No bias will result from including the effects of these variables in the error term unless their innovations are correlated with the innovations in the included variables. Were this the case, the expected values of estimated coefficients would be augmented by the product of the omitted coefficients and the regression coefficients of the omitted variables on the included variables. See Theil (1971, pp. 548–56).

where M is the nominal money supply, g is real government spending, x is exports divided by income,[5] and v is another white noise disturbance uncorrelated with ϵ. Familiar manipulations yield the semi-reduced-form real-income equation

(9.4)
$$\Delta \log y = a_1 - a_2 \log(y_{-1}/y^P_{-1})$$
$$+ \frac{1}{1 + \frac{b_2}{a_3}}\left(b_2 \hat{M} + b_3 \hat{g} + b_4 \hat{x} + \left(\frac{b_2}{a_3}\epsilon + v\right)\right),$$

where $\hat{M}$, $\hat{g}$, and $\hat{x}$ are the differences between the actual and expected values of $\log M$, $\log g$, and x, respectively. It is generally argued that inventory fluctuations will lead to some lags in the adjustment of output (as opposed to final sales) so that some short distributed lags on $\hat{M}$, $\hat{g}$, and $\hat{x}$ are permitted as well as the contemporaneous terms.[6] For example, using quarterly data and assuming any inventory lags are corrected within a year,

(9.5)
$$\Delta \log y = a_1 - a_2 \log(y_{-1}/y^P_{-1})$$
$$+ \sum_{i=0}^{3} c_{1+i}\hat{M}_{-i} + \sum_{i=0}^{3} c_{5+i}\hat{g}_{-i}$$
$$+ \sum_{i=0}^{3} c_{9+i}\hat{x}_{-i} + e,$$

where e is the combined residual disturbance.

This is the form of the real-income equation used in the Mark III International Transmission Model[7] and investigated in section 9.2 below. The empirical basis for including only innovations in money and not anticipated changes in money is by now well known, but it is perhaps worthwhile to comment briefly here on the corresponding basis for real government spending and exports.

The real-income equation (9.5)—assuming positive short-run effects—implies that unexpected increases in government spending or exports cause a short-run increase in real income, but this short-run increase is eliminated over time. That is, there is complete long-run *real* crowding out. I have argued elsewhere (1979, pp. 225–27) that this pattern represents a rough consensus of empirical results for the United States. As with money growth, however, alternative anticipated levels of real government spending and of real exports may imply different steady-state values of the capital-labor ratio so that their anticipated levels may belong in the

5. Recall from chapter 5 above that exports are scaled by dividing by income instead of by taking logarithms because in the Mark III International Transmission Model a balance-of-payments identity involving sometimes negative numbers is imposed. This should only cause an offsetting change in the magnitude but not the significance of the estimated export coefficients.

6. See particularly Haraf (1979).

7. The lagged value of $\log y$ is moved from the left to right side in the Mark III Model, but this has no effect on estimated coefficients and standard errors.

real-income equation even though they do not affect the natural-employment level of labor input. Further, there may be incentive effects on labor supply and efficiency effects associated with different sizes of government, but again empirical evidence is lacking to date. As specified, the real-income equation (9.5) embodies a hypothesis that the effects of anticipated M, g, and x on y via capital or otherwise are negligible.

9.2 Empirical Results

Our empirical investigation is based upon the 1955–76 quarterly data bank described in chapter 3 and the Data Appendix to this volume. Data are available for the United States, the United Kingdom, Canada, France, Germany, Italy, Japan, and the Netherlands. Two years are lost due to lagged variables which appear in the real-income equation (9.5) and in the definitions of expected values, so all estimations are for the eighty quarters from 1957I through 1976IV.

Table 9.1 reports ordinary least squares (OLS) estimates of equation (9.5), where $\hat{M}$, $\hat{g}$, and $\hat{x}$ are defined as the residuals on univariate ARIMA processes fitted according to the methods of Box and Jenkins (1976) using the programs described in Nelson (1973). As reported in chapter 6 above, these equations were also fitted by the two-stage least-squares method using principal components (2SLSPC) to take account of the endogeneity in the Mark III Model of the current money and export shocks $\hat{M}$ and $\hat{x}$. The results reported here differ little from those 2SLSPC results, and certain bugs in the TROLL system make them more useful for sensitivity analyses.[8]

Examining the results in table 9.1, we can first observe that, with the exception of the United States, the explanatory powers of the regressions are very weak: Only 10 to 20% of the residual variance around the mean growth rate of real income is explained for five countries, and for France and Japan less than 10% is explained.[9] While some of the individual t statistics would be quite significant given the maintained hypothesis that all the other variables belong in the regression, this is less true for groups of coefficients. Table 9.2 reports F statistics for the null hypothesis that all the coefficients applied to a particular shock variable are zero;[10] these are reproduced from the 2SLSPC estimates reported in chapter 6. Only the

---

8. The basic problem is that it is impossible to recover in TROLL the sum of squared residuals based on the fitted values of the endogenous variables. Work is under way to correct this.

9. The $F(13/66)$ value of 1.634 for France is right at the border of the critical region for rejecting the null hypothesis $a_2 = c_1 = c_2 = \ldots = c_{12} = 0$ at the 0.10 significance level, while the F value of 1.491 for Japan fails even this test. For all the other countries, this null hypothesis can be rejected at the 0.05 significance level or better. It should be noted that data reliability is a particular problem for France, Italy, and Japan.

10. That is, the F for $\hat{M}$ variables is for testing the null hypothesis $c_1 = c_2 = c_3 = c_4 = 0$.

U.S. money shock variables as a group reach significance at the 0.01 level or better. In addition, British and Canadian government spending shocks reach significance at the 0.05 level while Canadian and Italian money shocks and American and German export shocks are significant at better than the 0.10 level. I conclude that in an absolute sense the explanatory power of the generalized Barro real-income equation is weak other than for the United States.

One question is whether the use of only unanticipated changes in the aggregate demand variables is consistent with the data. Table 9.3 reports the standard errors of estimate for regressions in which actual changes are substituted for unanticipated changes for each group of aggregate demand variables.[11] The form of the regression is indicated by a combination of three U's and/or A's, where U represents unanticipated and A represents actual changes and the ordering is M, g, x. Thus a UAA specification has unanticipated changes in log M for the $c_1, \ldots, c_4$ terms and actual changes in log g and x for the $c_5, \ldots, c_{12}$ terms. The main message of table 9.3 appears to be that except for the United States it makes very little difference whether one uses actual or unanticipated changes in the real-income equation specified. If we examine the minimal-sum-of-squared-residuals regression for each country, half of the cases involve money shocks, another, partially overlapping set of four have government spending shocks, and only two have export shocks. While tests on nonnested models are difficult, it is clear from the small or no increase in the SSRs for the UUU regression form as opposed to the best alternative that a null hypothesis that UUU is the correct form is not inconsistent with the data.

Since the addition of insignificant variables may increase the standard error of estimate and reduce the (corrected) $\bar{R}^2$, the real-income regressions were also run with money shocks only as suggested by Barro.[12] The results reported in table 9.4 show that the explanatory powers of all the regressions, in fact, deteriorate slightly. The last row of the table gives the $F(4/74)$ statistic for the null hypothesis $c_1 = c_2 = c_3 = c_4 = 0$; the U.S. money shocks as a group are still significant at the 1% level and the Italian at the 10% level, but now the German and Dutch money shocks are significant at the 5% level and the Canadian money shocks not at all. If these regressions are slightly encouraging for the money shock approach, the results of replacing the money shocks with the actual changes as

---

11. The alternative procedure of adding additional terms for anticipated changes and testing whether they belong is not feasible in this case because the estimated ARIMA processes frequently imply extreme multicollinearity. Only variables known a priori to determine anticipated money but not to belong in the real-income equation would make this alternative approach usable.

12. That is, with coefficients $c_5, \ldots, c_{12}$ in equation (5) all set equal to 0. This would follow if b_3 and b_4 were 0 in the aggregate demand equation (3) due to short-run demand-side real crowding out.

Table 9.1   Generalized Barro Real-Income Equation (9.5)

$$\Delta \log y = a_1 - a_2\log(y_{-1}/y^p_{-1}) + \sum_{i=0}^{3} c_{1+i}\dot{M}_{-i} + \sum_{i=0}^{3} c_{5+i}\hat{g}_{-i} + \sum_{i=0}^{3} c_{9+i}\hat{x}_{-i} + e$$

Coefficients	US	UK	CA	FR	GE	IT	JA	NE
a_1	.0079	.0056	.0109	.0125	.0108	.0114	.0204	.0100
	(.0010)	(.0016)	(.0013)	(.0020)	(.0015)	(.0015)	(.0017)	(.0015)
	8.206	3.539	8.075	6.334	7.245	7.658	11.791	6.762
$-a_2$	-.0662	-.2165	-.1262	-.0590	-.0437	-.0182	.0219	-.0880
	(.0341)	(.0826)	(.0584)	(.0660)	(.0423)	(.0435)	(.0342)	(.0527)
	-1.940	-2.621	-2.160	-.893	-1.031	-.418	.641	-1.672
c_1	.6354	-.1321	.1450	-.0180	.3476	.0972	.0322	.2522
	(.2127)	(.0923)	(.1073)	(.1829)	(.1129)	(.0966)	(.1140)	(.1037)
	2.987	-1.431	1.351	-.098	3.078	1.006	.283	2.431
c_2	.6338	.0439	.1842	.1263	.0689	.0853	.1060	.1098
	(.2145)	(.0986)	(.1014)	(.1763)	(.1105)	(.0981)	(.1138)	(.1109)
	2.955	.446	1.816	.716	.623	.870	.932	.990
c_3	-.0210	-.0281	.1128	.0923	-.0187	.2630	.1883	-.0278
	(.2254)	(.0947)	(.1020)	(.1736)	(.1092)	(.1001)	(.1131)	(.1130)
	-.093	-.296	1.106	.531	-.172	2.627	1.665	-.246
c_4	.7679	-.1249	.1670	-.0900	.0387	-.0358	.0759	.0093
	(.2247)	(.0914)	(.0980)	(.1707)	(.1099)	(.1044)	(.1118)	(.1076)
	3.417	-1.366	1.704	-.527	.353	-.342	.679	.086
c_5	-.0255	.1788	.0194	.0367	-.0361	-.0019	.0489	.0370
	(.0535)	(.0528)	(.0517)	(.0396)	(.0272)	(.0103)	(.0350)	(.0348)
	-.476	3.388	.375	.925	-1.326	-.189	1.399	1.064

	1	2	3	4	5	6	7	8
c_6	.1045 (.0551) 1.898	.0138 (.0563) .245	-.1572 (.0549) -2.864	.0064 (.0397) .160	.0289 (.0273) 1.059	.0010 (.0102) .100	-.0114 (.0356) -.319	-.0352 (.0354) -.992
c_7	.0388 (.0531) .732	.1003 (.0555) 1.807	-.0303 (.0522) -.581	.0466 (.0392) 1.189	-.0073 (.0270) -.272	-.0013 (.0100) -.125	.0480 (.0357) 1.347	.0139 (.0353) .395
c_8	.0742 (.0544) 1.363	-.0224 (.0564) -.398	-.0112 (.0529) -.212	.0293 (.0372) .788	.0133 (.0271) .491	.0271 (.0100) 2.700	-.0369 (.0362) -1.020	.0327 (.0358) .912
c_9	.2766 (.3815) .725	.1476 (.1870) .789	.3557 (.2225) 1.599	.8552 (.3571) 2.395	.3643 (.2225) 1.637	-.2336 (.1953) -1.196	-2.0498 (.8332) -2.460	.0666 (.0884) .754
c_{10}	.3674 (.3933) .934	.4153 (.1791) 2.319	.1001 (.2260) .443	-.7501 (.3730) -2.011	-.2456 (.2202) -1.115	-.0368 (.1890) -.195	.5237 (.8636) .606	-.0727 (.0899) -.809
c_{11}	-.0021 (.4131) -.005	-.2149 (.1861) -1.155	.0190 (.2264) .084	.0095 (.3798) .025	-.3378 (.2279) -1.483	-.2348 (.1938) -1.212	-1.7616 (.9134) -1.929	.1031 (.0853) 1.208
c_{12}	-.9809 (.4119) -2.381	.0067 (.1900) .035	.4470 (.2298) 1.945	-.0383 (.3864) -.099	-.5199 (.2258) -2.302	-.4591 (.1979) -2.320	-.7920 (.9213) .860	-.1160 (.0811) -1.431
$\bar{R}^2$	.3694	.1867	.1297	.0944	.1409	.1273	.0748	.1339
S.E.E.	.0086	.0140	.0119	.0175	.0133	.0131	.0153	.0130
D-W	1.72	1.95	2.41	2.13	1.94	2.23	1.99	1.67

Note. Period: 1957I–76IV. Standard errors are in parentheses below coefficient estimates; t statistics are below the standard errors.

Table 9.2   *F* Statistics for Groups of Demand Shock Variables
                   for 2SLSPC Estimates

		$F(4/66)$ Statistics		
	Country	$\hat{M}$ Variables	$\hat{g}$ Variables	$\hat{x}$ Variables
	US	7.128	1.820	2.188
	UK	1.164	3.531	1.763
	CA	2.315	3.191	1.858
	FR	0.341	0.783	1.006
	GE	1.473	0.748	2.353
	IT	2.201	2.004	1.766
	JA	1.152	1.141	1.660
	NE	1.530	1.137	1.675

Notes. The reported *F* statistics are appropriate for testing the joint hypothesis that all four of the demand shock variables of the type indicated have a coefficient of zero. Such a test is conditional upon the other variables entering in the equation.

For $F(4/66)$, the 10% significance level is 2.04, the 5% significance level is 2.52, and the 1% significance level is 3.63.

reported in table 9.5 are not. Again, only for the United States is there a dramatic fall in $\bar{R}^2$ or rise in S.E.E. when actual changes are substituted for unanticipated changes. Among the other seven countries it makes little difference whether actual or unanticipated changes are used, but the $\bar{R}^2$ is higher for four countries when actual changes are used. So the money-only-matters equations tell essentially the same agnostic story as the generalized Barro real-income equations.

Errors in the independent variables are an obvious explanation for the poor explanatory power of the money and other shocks. These errors might arise from the fact that the shocks are based on constructed expectations series or from the apparent fact that the data for the other seven countries have larger measurement errors than are present in the United States data.

Table 9.3   Standard Errors of Estimate for Alternative
                   Real-Income Equation Specifications

Coun-try	Specification of Aggregate Demand Variables							
	UUU	AUU	UAA	AAA	UAU	AAU	UUA	AUA
US	0.0086	0.0098	0.0083	0.0091	0.0086	0.0098	0.0083	0.0091
UK	0.0140	0.0141	0.0133	0.0134	0.0138	0.0139	0.0134	0.0136
CA	0.0119	0.0117	0.0118	0.0116	0.0119	0.0117	0.0119	0.0116
FR	0.0175	0.0175	0.0176	0.0175	0.0174	0.0174	0.0176	0.0176
GE	0.0133	0.0133	0.0133	0.0134	0.0133	0.0133	0.0133	0.0134
IT	0.0131	0.0130	0.0132	0.0131	0.0132	0.0131	0.0131	0.0130
JA	0.0153	0.0153	0.0151	0.0150	0.0154	0.0153	0.0150	0.0149
NE	0.0130	0.0131	0.0126	0.0126	0.0128	0.0129	0.0127	0.0126

Table 9.4   **Basic Barro Real-Income Equation**

$$\Delta \log y = a_1 - a_2\log(y_{-1}/y^P_{-1}) + \sum_{i=0}^{3} c_{1+i}\hat{M}_{-i} + e$$

	US	UK	CA	FR	GE	IT	JA	NE
Coefficients								
a_1	.0080	.0061	.0107	.0125	.0108	.0114	.0208	.0101
	(.0010)	(.0017)	(.0014)	(.0021)	(.0015)	(.0015)	(.0018)	(.0015)
	7.906	3.554	7.608	6.010	6.988	7.385	11.767	6.813
$-a_2$	-.0756	-.1946	-.1307	-.0918	-.0213	-.0151	.0120	-.1010
	(.0330)	(.0757)	(.0574)	(.0692)	(.0403)	(.0420)	(.0341)	(.0515)
	-2.286	-2.569	-2.276	-1.328	-.527	-.360	.353	-1.961
c_1	.7694	-.0629	.0131	-.1204	.3534	.1627	.1022	.3095
	(.2034)	(.0911)	(.0977)	(.1828)	(.1117)	(.0966)	(.1081)	(.0972)
	3.782	-.690	.134	-.659	3.163	1.685	.946	3.184
c_2	.6413	-.0057	.0960	.1194	.1024	.1305	.0843	.0812
	(.2026)	(.0936)	(.0961)	(.1817)	(.1107)	(.0964)	(.1060)	(.0946)
	3.165	-.061	.999	.657	.925	1.353	.795	.859
c_3	.1868	-.0321	.0768	.0862	-.0470	.2132	.2033	.0114
	(.2138)	(.0934)	(.0962)	(.1785)	(.1107)	(.0966)	(.1055)	(.0955)
	.874	-.343	.798	.483	-.424	2.206	1.927	.120
c_4	.7213	-.1376	.1181	-.0278	.0448	-.0557	.0773	.0045
	(.2261)	(.0931)	(.0967)	(.1775)	(.1121)	(.0974)	(.1084)	(.0938)
	3.190	-1.478	1.221	-.156	.400	-.572	.713	.048
$\bar{R}^2$	.3048	.0414	.0391	-.0215	.0749	.0567	.0234	.1111
S.E.E.	.0090	.0151	.0125	.0186	.0138	.0136	.0158	.0132
D-W	1.53	1.97	2.35	2.36	1.89	2.01	1.99	1.73
$F_{(4/74)}$[†]	9.82	.68	.77	.28	2.83	2.39	1.40	2.67

Note. Period 1957I–76IV. Standard errors are in parentheses below coefficient estimates; t statistics are below the standard errors.

[†] The $F_{(4/74)}$ statistic tests the null hypothesis that $c_1 = c_2 = c_3 = c_4 = 0$. Critical values are 2.03 (10% significance level), 2.43 (5%), and 3.61 (1%).

Table 9.5   **Actual Money Growth Real-Income Equation**

$$\Delta \log y = a_1 - a_2 \log(y_{-1}/y^P_{-1}) + \sum_{i=0}^{3} c_{1+i} \Delta \log M_{-i} + e$$

	US	UK	CA	FR	GE	IT	JA	NE
Coefficients								
a_1	.0026	.0070	.0068	.0095	.0057	.0049	.0100	.0061
	(.0026)	(.0025)	(.0024)	(.0059)	(.0040)	(.0047)	(.0058)	(.0032)
	.998	2.789	2.829	1.612	1.441	1.039	1.716	1.897
$-a_2$	−.0356	−.1836	−.1404	−.0813	−.0175	−.0058	.0106	−.1013
	(.0389)	(.0768)	(.0569)	(.0688)	(.0414)	(.0422)	(.0350)	(.0514)
	−.916	−2.391	−2.467	−1.181	−.421	−.137	.303	−1.969
c_1	.4805	−.0629	−.0370	−.0198	.3431	.1925	.1084	.3032
	(.2291)	(.0923)	(.0839)	(.1700)	(.1111)	(.0944)	(.1064)	(.0930)
	2.097	−.681	−.441	−.116	3.090	2.039	1.019	3.261
c_2	.0555	.0079	.1442	.1712	.0708	.1119	.0767	−.0373
	(.2836)	(.0961)	(.0864)	(.1745)	(.1048)	(.0943)	(.1136)	(.0915)
	.196	.082	1.669	.981	.676	1.186	.675	−.408
c_3	.0329	.0400	.0272	−.0068	−.1166	.0978	.1247	−.0828
	(.2851)	(.0963)	(.0868)	(.1738)	(.1049)	(.0947)	(.1121)	(.0926)
	.115	.415	.313	−.039	−1.112	1.033	1.112	−.893
c_4	−.0560	−.0665	.0919	−.0354	−.0726	−.2112	−.0347	−.0251
	(.2402)	(.0941)	(.0831)	(.1646)	(.1147)	(.0948)	(.1067)	(.0905)
	−.233	−.707	1.105	−.215	−.633	−2.227	−.325	−.278
$\bar{R}^2$	.0505	.0192	.0734	−.0218	.0699	.0790	.0366	.1120
S.E.E.	.0105	.0153	.0123	.0186	.0138	.0134	.0157	.0132
D-W	1.21	2.00	2.32	2.38	1.89	2.08	2.02	1.73
$F(4/74)^{\dagger}$	2.24	.25	1.48	.28	2.72	2.89	1.68	2.69

Note. Period 1957I–76IV. Standard errors are in parentheses below coefficient estimates; t statistics are below the standard errors.

$\dagger$The $F(4/74)$ statistic tests the null hypothesis that $c_1 = c_2 = c_3 = c_4 = 0$. Critical values are 2.03 (10% significance level), 2.43 (5%), and 3.61 (1%).

Consider first the extremely limited information set (past values of the variable only) used to divide $\log M$, $\log g$, and x into expected and unanticipated components. If the true expectations are based on a broader information set, the actual change might be as good as or a better measure of the unanticipated change than our ARIMA innovation. To investigate this question, I constructed transfer function estimates of expected money using Nelson's TRANSEST program applied to the variables appearing in the Mark III Model's money supply reaction function: the inflation rate, $\log(y/y^p)$ or unemployment rate, $\hat{g}$, and, except for the U.S., the scaled balance of payments. However, in six cases out of eight, the univariate ARIMA processes resulted in lower SSRs that these transfer estimates.[13] Further, chapter 6 reports on checks of correlations (among others) of the residuals of the real-income equations with the residuals of all the other domestic equations and of the reserve-country (U.S.) nominal money, real-income, and price-level equations. There was no apparent pattern of significant correlations which might suggest other variables for expectations transfer functions; so the approach was not pursued. It may be rational for individuals not to use costly information even if it has some predictive value (see Darby 1976 and Feige and Pearce 1976), but this may constitute some evidence against the costless-information interpretation of rational expectations.

Appeals to measurement error, like appeals to patriotism, have a deserved reputation as a last resort of scoundrels. Nonetheless, in any particular case they may be correct. Measurement error in the dependent variables ($\Delta \log y$) could account for the generally low explanatory power of the regressions and significance levels of the explanatory variables.[14] There may be greater danger of measurement error in the independent variables in general and in money in particular. Table 9.6 presents the standard deviations around the mean of each of the shock variables plus the dependent variable. For each of the independent variables, the U.S. standard deviation is only about one-third of the average standard deviations for the seven countries, but for the dependent variable the U.S. standard deviation is about three-quarters of the mean for the other countries.

Now there are good reasons why money shocks in nonreserve countries

13. The six out of eight dominance of univariate expectations occurred in the UUU regressions; in one case (France) the use of transfer expectations shifted the minimum-SSR regression from the AAU to the UAU form.

14. Measurement error in the dependent variable if it is uncorrelated with measurement error in the independent variables does not bias the coefficients but does increase s^2 (the S.E.E.). It might be that measurement error due to deflation would cause a spurious positive relation to appear between $\Delta \log y$ and $\hat{g}$ while measurement error in nominal income might create a spurious negative relation between $\Delta \log y$ and $\hat{x}$. Such a hypothesis would find some support in the estimates reported in table 9.1.

Table 9.6   **Standard Deviations of Real-Income Growth and Shock Variables**

| Country | Standard Deviation of | | | |
	$\hat{M}$	$\hat{g}$	$\hat{x}$	$\Delta \log y$
US	0.0052	0.0197	0.0028	0.0108
UK	0.0188	0.0329	0.0090	0.0155
CA	0.0146	0.0283	0.0066	0.0128
FR	0.0119	0.0566	0.0059	0.0184
GE	0.0139	0.0562	0.0070	0.0143
IT	0.0159	0.1583	0.0083	0.0140
JA	0.0168	0.0537	0.0023	0.0159
NE	0.0155	0.0448	0.0196	0.0140

would be greater than in the reserve country.[15] Suppose that nonetheless we assume that all of the difference between the standard deviations of $\hat{M}$ for the United States and the average of the other countries is accounted for by a normally distributed error component. Table 9.7 illustrates for ten drawings what such a measurement error does to the summary statistics and money shock F statistic for the regression estimates of equation (9.5).[16] Certainly the range of reported summary statistics is similar to that for the other countries appearing in tables 9.1 and 9.2. The means of the ten drawings are very similar to the means for the other seven countries noted at the bottom of table 9.7.[17] Thus an assumption that all the differences in the standard deviations of $\hat{M}$ across countries are due to measurement error is sufficient to account for the weak results observed for countries other than the United States. Doubtless other more reasonable assumptions as to measurement errors would do likewise. While this is no proof that measurement errors are the reason for the weak results outside the United States, it is evidence that measure-

15. For example, under the strictest version of the monetary approach to the balance of payments and under the assumption of independence of the sources of shocks, the variance of a nonreserve country's money shocks would equal the sum of the variance of the reserve country's money shocks, the variance of changes in the purchasing power parity, and the variance of the disturbance term to the money-demand equation.

16. That is, table 9.7 reports regressions for the United States where $\hat{M}$ is replaced with $\tilde{M} = \hat{M} + N$ where N is a computer-generated normal deviate with mean 0 and standard deviation 0.014389. To explore sampling variation, ten different drawings of N were made with the regressions computed for each one. Alternatively, an analytical examination of biases based on an assumed variance-covariance matrix of the errors might be pursued as suggested by Garber and Klepper (1980).

17. This similarity is also apparent in the (unreported) individual coefficients and t statistics. Note that the two mean S.E.E.'s are in the same ratio as the standard deviations of $\Delta \log y$ for the U.S. and the other countries. The hint of negative autocorrelation implicit in the nonreserve countries' mean Durbin-Watson statistic of 2.29 is consistent with greater measurement error in the *level* of $\log y$ which would induce negative autocorrelation in $\Delta \log y$. By construction, autocorrelation due to measurement error is removed from the shock variables.

Table 9.7 **Summary Statistics for United States Generalized Barro Real-Income Equation with Artificial Money Shock Measurement Error**

Drawing Number	$\bar{R}^2$	S.E.E.	D-W	$F(4/66)^{\dagger}$	Std. Dev. of $\hat{M}$
1	0.1613	0.0099	1.60	1.885	0.0152
2	0.1265	0.0101	1.60	1.153	0.0146
3	0.1744	0.0098	1.63	2.176	0.0130
4	0.1153	0.0102	1.52	0.928	0.0149
5	0.1397	0.0100	1.46	1.423	0.0154
6	0.1879	0.0097	1.44	2.406	0.0152
7	0.1105	0.0102	1.49	0.835	0.0149
8	0.1874	0.0097	1.61	2.474	0.0143
9	0.0827	0.0104	1.49	0.309	0.0142
10	0.1366	0.0100	1.59	1.358	0.0152
Mean	0.1422	0.0100	1.54	1.495	0.0147
Mean of other 7 countries	0.1268	0.0140	2.29	1.453	0.0153

Note. The first ten sets of summary statistics are for the U.S. equation (9.5) with $\hat{M}$ replaced by $\hat{M} = \hat{M} + N$, where N is normally distributed with mean 0 and standard deviation 0.014389. The next line is the mean of the first ten lines, and the final line is the mean of the corresponding values from tables 9.1 and 9.2 for countries other than the United States.
†The $F(4/66)$ statistic is for the test of the null hypothesis $c_1 = c_2 = c_3 = c_4 = 0$. The critical values are 2.04 for the 10% significance level, 2.52 for 5%, and 3.63 for 1%.

ment error in the basic data[18] is a tenable defense for those who believe that the Barro approach is a correct description of the real world.

An alternative structural argument based on Lucas (1973) could be made: Countries which have larger prediction variances will be characterized by steeper aggregate supply curves. As a_3 in equation (9.1) approaches 0 so do the coefficients of $\hat{M}$, $\hat{g}$, and $\hat{x}$ as seen in equation (9.4) above. However, Lucas required huge variations in nominal income variance to detect this effect, so it would not appear to be a viable defense for the current results.

In sum, the empirical estimates indicate that, with the exception of the United States, actual and unanticipated changes in aggregate demand variables do about equally poorly as explanations of real-income growth. While these poor results may be due to measurement errors in both the dependent and independent variables, they are disappointing to support-

18. If the measurement error is not in the basic data but is instead due to the inadequacy of the expectations functions as representations of the true market expectations, then the Barro approach will not be useful even if the Lucas supply function is a true description of the economy. Leiderman (1980) reports that the rational-expectations approach to specifying expectations works for the United States. Figlewski and Wachtel (1981) and Urich and Wachtel (1980) report mixed results in reconciling survey data with rational-expectations proxies.

ers of the Barro approach to modeling the joint hypothesis of the natural-unemployment rate and rational expectations.

9.3 Implications for Economic Policymaking

In the 1960s the analytical and empirical elegance of the Phillips curve gave it wide currency as a tool for both evaluation and formulation of macroeconomic policy. It was not realized generally until the beginning of the 1970s that despite its aesthetic appeal, the Phillips curve did not work. The Lucas supply curve—particularly in the Barro reduced form—has similarly become a major tool for policy formulation and evaluation largely on the basis of a priori appeal rather than a solid foundation of empirical work. Needless to say, both the theoretical appeal and preliminary empirical work suggest that this approach is a good bet. But the results of this chapter suggest that there is less reason to adopt the approach when we examine data sets other than the one used to formulate the hypothesis. Thus policy prescriptions or evaluations which rely on the Lucas-Barro approach should be clearly labeled "Unproved; use at your own risk."

Surprising or anomalous results are our best clues to promising areas for future research. Other results casting doubt on the empirical robustness of the Lucas-Barro approach have been reported by Pigott (1978), Barro and Hercowitz (1980), and Boschen and Grossman (1980). Further research is required so that we can either use the approach with confidence or proceed to a more workable analysis.

Acknowledgments

The author acknowledges helpful comments from David Friedman, Milton Friedman, Dean Taylor, and members of the UCLA Money Workshop and from his colleagues Arthur Gandolfi, James Lothian, Anna Schwartz, and Alan Stockman. Michael T. Melvin and Andrew A. Vogel provided able research assistance.

References

Barro, R. J. 1977. Unanticipated money growth and unemployment in the United States. *American Economic Review* 67 (March): 101–15.

———. 1978. Unanticipated money, output, and the price level in the United States. *Journal of Political Economy* 86 (August): 549–80.

Barro, R. J., and Z. Hercowitz. 1980. Money shock revisions and unanticipated money growth. *Journal of Monetary Economics* 6 (April): 257–67.

Boschen, J. F., and H. I. Grossman. 1980. Tests of equilibrium macroeconomics using contemporaneous monetary data. NBER Working Paper, no. 558, October.

Box. G. E. P., and G. M. Jenkins. 1976. *Time series analysis: Forecasting and control*. Rev. ed. San Francisco: Holden-Day.

Darby, M. R. 1976. Rational expectations under conditions of costly information. *Journal of Finance* 31 (June): 889–95.

———. 1979. *Intermediate macroeconomics*. New York: McGraw-Hill.

Feige, E. L., and D. K. Pearce. 1976. Economically rational expectations: Are innovations in the rate of inflation independent of innovations in measures of money and fiscal policy? *Journal of Political Economy* 84 (June): 499–522.

Figlewski, S., and P. Wachtel. 1981. The formation of inflationary expectations. *Review of Economics and Statistics* 63 (February): 1–10.

Garber, S., and S. Klepper. 1980. Extending the classical normal errors-in-variable model. *Econometrica* 48 (September): 1541–46.

Haraf, W. S. 1979. Inventories, orders, and the persistent effects of monetary shocks. *Proceedings of 1978 West Coast Academic/Federal Reserve Economic Research Seminar*. San Francisco: Federal Reserve Bank of San Francisco.

Horrigan, B. R. 1980. An estimation and test of the Brunner-Meltzer model of inflation and output fluctuations. Ph.D. dissertation, Department of Economics, UCLA.

Korteweg, P. 1978. The economics of inflation and output fluctuations in the Netherlands, 1954–1975: A test of some implications of the dominant impulse-cum-rational expectations hypothesis. In K. Brunner and A. H. Meltzer, eds., *The problem of inflation*. Carnegie Rochester Conference Series on Public Policy, vol. 8.

Leiderman, L. 1980. Macroeconometric testing of the rational expectations and structural neutrality hypotheses for the United States. *Journal of Monetary Economics* 6 (January): 69–82.

Lucas, R. E., Jr. 1973. Some international evidence on output-inflation tradeoffs. *American Economic Review* 63 (June): 326–34.

McCallum, B. T. 1978. Price level adjustments and the rational expectations approach to macroeconomic and stabilization policy. *Journal of Money, Credit and Banking* 10 (November): 418–36.

———. 1979. On the observational inequivalence of classical and Keynesian models. *Journal of Political Economy* 87 (April): 395–402.

Nelson, C. R. 1973. *Applied time series analysis for managerial forecasting*. San Francisco: Holden-Day.

Pigott, C. 1978. Rational expectations and counter-cyclical monetary policy: The Japanese experience. *Federal Reserve Bank of San Francisco Economic Review*, Summer, pp. 6–22.

Sargent, T. J. 1976. The observational equivalence of natural and unnatural rate theories of macroeconomics. *Journal of Political Economy* 84 (June): 631–40.

Theil, H. 1971. *Principles of econometrics*. New York: Wiley.

Urich, T., and P. Wachtel. 1980. Market response to the weekly money supply announcements in the 1970s. Unpublished paper, New York University, July.

III

Capital Flows, Sterilization, Monetary Policy, and Exchange Intervention

The central issue in understanding the international transmission of inflation is whether or not national borders make a real difference: Is the world economy an aggregate of individually perfectly open economies, or is it an aggregate of linked, but partially independent economies?

Channels of transmission among countries were examined within the context of the Mark III International Transmission Model in part II. There the channels were found to be surprisingly weak, but, as with any large-scale model, these results might be an artifact of some unknown peculiarity in the model's specification. So the research on the openness question reported in chapters 10 through 13 is either relatively model free or at least based on alternative, smaller-scale models. Thus the reader can assess these results without substantial investment in evaluating the model.

Darby and Laskar in chapters 10 and 11, respectively, test for perfect openness by examining its implication that nonreserve central banks under pegged exchange rates have no control over their individual domestic money supplies. They argue that previous analysts, with a few notable exceptions, have not adequately dealt with the sterilization activities of the nonreserve central banks and, as a result, have performed tests which have little power to distinguish an alternative hypothesis of monetary control from a null hypothesis of no control. New tests are presented which confirm the exercise of monetary control by nonreserve central banks during the Bretton-Woods era.

Nonreserve monetary control under pegged exchange rates implies that a pure foreign exchange operation can influence the country's floating exchange rate. Dan Lee develops a dynamic portfolio-balance model in chapter 12 and uses it to contrast the effects of a central-bank exchange of domestic bonds for foreign bonds with those of an exchange for domestic money.

Many economists—including perhaps most persuasively William Branson—have used a portfolio-balance approach to argue that international assets are not perfect substitutes. Since perfect substitutability of assets is the most popular assumption leading to perfect openness, the issue is an important one. In chapter 13, Michael Melvin advances the portfolio-balance approach by introducing with some success the exchange-rate risk covariance measures implied by the international-asset-pricing model into the capital flows equation. This analysis provides an alternative to the capital-flows specification presented in chapter 5 and used in the Mark III International Transmission Model.

Thus part III supplements the results of part II by first presenting alternative and more formal tests of monetary control under pegged exchange rates. The implications under floating exchange rates of the lack of perfect openness are then examined. Finally, an empirical advance is made in the implementation of the portfolio-balance approach—the underlying theoretical explanation for the observed imperfect substitutability of international assets.

10 Sterilization and Monetary Control: Concepts, Issues, and a Reduced-Form Test

Michael R. Darby

Monetary-approach models characteristically assume that goods, assets, or both are perfect substitutes internationally. For a nonreserve country maintaining pegged exchange rates, this implies that the central bank has no control over or influence on the country's money supply but only determines how the demand-determined quantity is supplied by reserve flows and domestic credit creation. The successful exercise of monetary control under pegged exchange rates therefore contradicts the monetary approach and the assumption that goods, assets, or both are perfect substitutes internationally.

The above argument provides the basis for this chapter's tests of the monetary approach to the balance of payments.[1] Before proceeding to the empirical tests, it is necessary to formulate a general model which is consistent with the possible exercise of monetary control but which subsumes the monetary approach as a special case. Because the observed negative correlation between reserve flows and domestic-credit changes can be explained by sterilization policies as well as the monetary-approach channels, it is important that the general model allow for sterilization policies whether or not monetary control is present.

Standard monetary-approach discussions assume that no sterilization operations are attempted by the central banks of nonreserve countries.[2] Although a number of authors have noted that sterilization policies may

1. These tests supplement—and confirm—the empirical results from the Mark III International Transmission Model. As reported in part II of this volume, direct structural estimates indicated that neither goods nor assets were perfect substitutes internationally. Thus, contrary to the monetary approach, nonreserve central banks exercised a degree of monetary control within the quarter.

2. To cite the locus classicus, see, for example, Frenkel and Johnson (1976, passim, esp. pp. 152–53). An important recent exception is a theoretical analysis by Boyer (1979) which uses a portfolio-balance approach.

bias empirical tests of the monetary approach,[3] adherents of the approach have argued that sterilization is neither significant in magnitude nor an important source of bias.[4] Other authors are less sanguine about the impossibility and insignificance of sterilization.[5] In particular, the estimates of the Mark III International Transmission Model, reported in chapter 6 above, indicate that the direct effects on national money supplies are very largely sterilized by offsetting transactions in domestic credit instruments.

Since the no-sterilization (or exogenous-domestic-credit) assumption is both factually untrue and controversial, it appears to be an obfuscating rather than simplifying assumption. It will be shown in section 10.1 below that a simple monetary-approach model can be presented without any reliance on this assumption or the ancillary concept of domestic credit. Only if sterilization is complete can one infer anything about the presence or absence of monetary control.

Section 10.1 outlines the general model incorporating sterilization which encompasses as a special case a modified version of the monetary approach in which both reserve flows and domestic-credit flows are endogenous variables. Generally, nonreserve central banks can exercise control over their domestic money supply in the short run unless certain conditions which imply validity of the monetary approach are met. In this monetary-approach special case, central bank attempts to exercise monetary control are futile and instead simply induce exaggerated reserve flows.

Section 10.2 presents a simple direct test of whether determinants of monetary policy other than the current balance of payments influenced the nominal money supply given foreign variables determining money demand. For quarterly data of seven countries in our sample (Canada, France, Germany, Italy, Japan, the Netherlands, and the United Kingdom), all but the Netherlands showed clear evidence that monetary control was, in fact, exercised under the Bretton Woods system of pegged exchange rates. This evidence is strongly inconsistent with the validity of

3. See, for example, Argy and Kouri (1974), Magee (1976), Maddala (1977, p. 253), and Darby (1980).

4. I can find no substantial basis for the denigration of the existence of substantial sterilization policies (implicit in money growth or interest-rate goals) beyond the assertion that they are impotent and therefore irrational (see, for example, quotations in footnotes 7 and 9). In much cited pieces, Argy and Kouri (1974) and Genberg (1976) used rudimentary reaction functions and quarterly data to obtain significant estimates of sterilization, but this did not lead to substantial changes in the relevant monetary-approach coefficients. Connolly and Taylor (1979) came to similar conclusions using both annual and biennial observations. Stockman (1979) used a sophisticated reaction function, but again came to the same conclusion. The basic flaw in these tests is discussed below in footnote 16.

5. For example, from their review of the earlier literature on sterilization and monetary control, Sweeney and Willett (1976, p. 444) conclude that "there is little evidence that such autonomy is impossible in the short-run, and considerable evidence it is possible." See especially the careful work of Herring and Marston (1977) on Germany.

the monetary approach to the balance of payments in either its standard or its modified form for analysis of quarterly data. Thus there is a relevant "short run" within which central banks can and have exercised monetary control under pegged exchange rates.

10.1 Analysis

The analysis proceeds in four steps: First, sterilization is formally defined in terms of the money supply reaction function of the central bank. Next, a modified monetary approach is presented which is consistent with partial sterilization. Then a more general model is developed in which the central bank may control its domestic money supply; if this control is not present, the model reduces to the modified monetary approach. Finally, the conditions for monetary control are interpreted in terms of responsiveness of capital flows, trade flows, and the expected depreciation of the exchange rate.

10.1.1 Sterilization and the Money Supply Reaction Function

The central bank of a nonreserve country will resist an incipient appreciation (for example) of its exchange rate by buying some foreign reserves with its domestic base money.[6] This new base money increases the domestic money supply. Standard central bank procedure involves offsetting sales of domestic assets (for example, government bonds) for base money. These offsetting transactions are said to sterilize the effect of the balance of payments on the money supply.

In the standard monetary approach, the construct of domestic credit (base money less reserves) or its change has been assumed exogenous. This assumption is unwarranted if monetary authorities sterilize the balance of payments in whole or in part so that a balance-of-payments surplus induces a decrease in domestic credit. But, of course, the immediate sterilization might be reversed so rapidly that for all practical purposes no sterilization occurred over a period of observation such as a quarter. Then the exogenous-domestic-credit assumption would be acceptable for analysis of quarterly data.

A money supply reaction function provides a formal statement of the behavior of the monetary authorities working through the banking system. The existence and extent of sterilization are measured by the coefficient of the contemporaneous scaled balance of payments in the reaction function. A general form of this reaction function is

$$(10.1) \qquad \Delta \log M = \alpha \frac{B}{H} + X\beta + u,$$

6. The analysis is properly applied only to nonreserve countries if the reserve country (such as the United States) is on a fiat standard as discussed in Darby (1980).

where M is the nominal money supply, B the balance-of-payments surplus, H nominal base or high-powered money, and X a vector containing all other variables which systematically affect the monetary authority's behavior. Note in particular that lagged balances of payments may appear in X since the issue of ultimate concern is monetary control within the period of observation. If α is 1, then there is no sterilization since the balance of payments leads to a proportionate increase in the money supply. If α is zero, then complete sterilization is practiced. Values of α between 0 and 1 indicate partial sterilization. By way of information, the Mark III estimates reported in table 6.8 above suggest that α lies in the range from 0 to 0.2.

The meaning of equation (10.1) may be clarified by restating it in terms of domestic credit D. Assuming a constant money multiplier, we have

$$\Delta \log M \equiv \Delta \log H$$

$$(10.2) \qquad \Delta \log M \approx \frac{B}{H} + \frac{\Delta D}{H}$$

Substituting into equation (10.1), we have

$$(10.3) \qquad \frac{\Delta D}{H} = (\alpha - 1)\frac{B}{H} + X\beta + u$$

Thus we see that if $\alpha = 1$ (no sterilization), then the reaction function determines domestic credit exogenously with respect to the balance of payments. If $\alpha < 1$, then the central bank adjusts domestic credit in whole ($\alpha = 0$) or part ($0 < \alpha < 1$) to offset the effects of the balance of payments on money growth. In what follows, it will be seen that domestic credit is not a useful concept if the central bank is concerned with money growth or the level of interest rates (that is, if $\alpha < 1$).

10.1.2   A Modified Monetary Approach

While the received monetary approach has been based on the assumption that nonreserve countries do not sterilize in whole or part, this assumption is in no sense essential to the theoretical approach.[7] The really essential idea is that the domestic money supply is demand determined given the exchange-rate-converted foreign price level and foreign

7. Harry Johnson (1976, pp. 152–53) noted that the monetary approach "assumes—in some cases, asserts—that these monetary inflows or outflows associated with surpluses or deficits are not sterilized—or cannot be, within a period relevant to policy analysis—but instead influence the domestic money supply." But Mussa (1976, p. 192) rightly observes that this assumption is unnecessary: "If the monetary authorities sterilize the balance-of-payments surplus created by, say, the imposition of a tariff, then the monetary approach predicts that there will be a further surplus, equal to the reduction in the domestic source component of the base which is implied by sterilization, and so on, until the sterilization operations cease." This subsection merely works out the analytical framework sketched by Mussa.

interest rate. Any attempt of monetary authorities to vary the quantity of money from this demand-determined growth $\overline{\Delta \log M}$ will induce massive capital flows, trade flows, or both until the money supply is equated to the parity value $\overline{\Delta \log M}$.

To illustrate, suppose that the demand-determined change in money is given by

(10.4) $\qquad \overline{\Delta \log M} = Z\delta + \epsilon$.

If the balance of payments is indeed infinitely elastic with respect to incipient deviations from $\overline{\Delta \log M}$, then

(10.5) $\qquad \dfrac{B}{H} = \theta(\Delta \log M - Z\delta - \epsilon)$,

where θ is negative infinity. That is, any attempt by the central bank to increase (decrease) money relative to $\overline{\Delta \log M}$ results in an unbounded balance-of-payments deficit (surplus). So equation (5) implies, given $\theta = -\infty$, that

(10.6) $\qquad \Delta \log M = Z\delta + \epsilon$.

Equation (10.6) and the money supply reaction function (10.1) form a recursive system in which the change in money is determined by demand and this, plus the "domestic policy" portion $(X\beta + u)$ of monetary policy, determines the balance of payments:

(10.7) $\qquad \dfrac{B}{H} = \dfrac{1}{\alpha}(Z\delta + \epsilon - X\beta - u)$.

The balance of payments is the inverse of the sterilization parameter times the difference between the demand-determined money growth and the domestic-policy money growth.

The modified monetary approach is illustrated graphically in figure 10.1. The vertical line indicates the infinite elasticity of the balance of payments with respect to incipient deviations of money supply growth from its demand-determined level. The positively sloped line is the money supply reaction function.[8] Their intersection determines the equilibrium balance of payments $(B/H)^{\text{eq}}$. Note that an increase in unemployment which shifted the reaction function to the right (more money growth for a given balance of payments) results in a substantial decrease in the balance of payments which just balances the desire for more money growth.

Figure 10.2 illustrates the impotence of monetary policy under the

---

8. If this line were vertical $(\alpha = 0)$, there would generally be no equilibrium in the modified-monetary-approach case. A negative slope $(\alpha < 0)$ implies an unstable equilibrium.

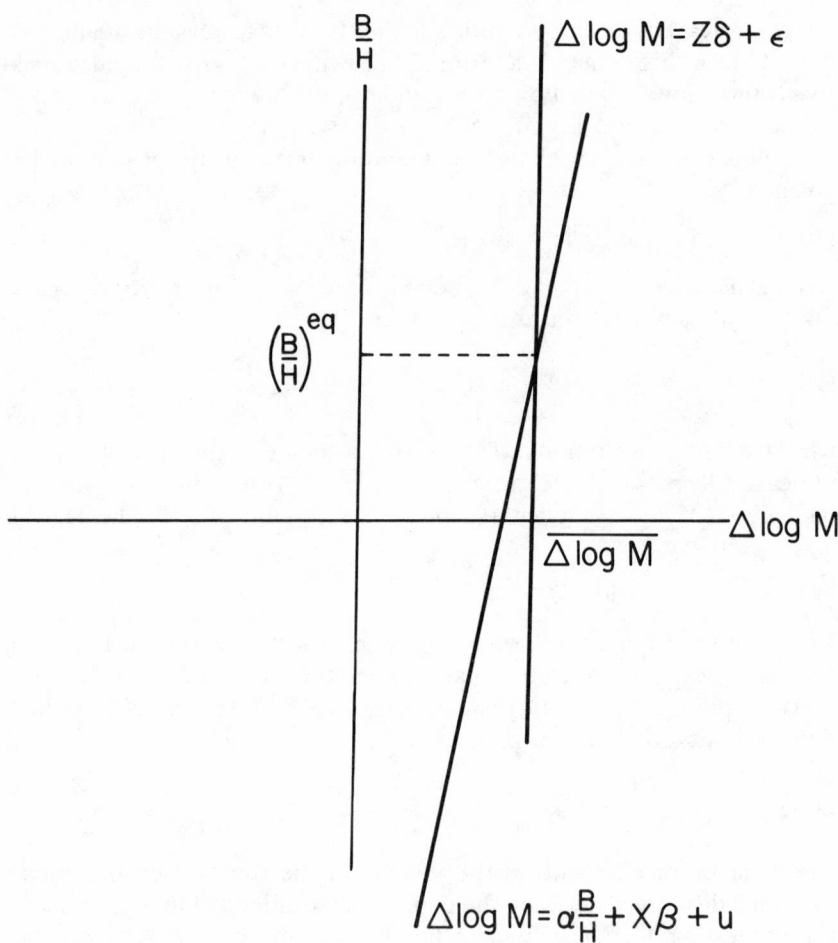

Fig. 10.1   Determination of balance of payments in the modified monetary approach.

modified monetary approach. Consider two vectors of domestic policy
variables X_0 and X_1: Suppose that they differ only in the unemployment
rate which is higher in case 1 so that the central bank desires a higher
money growth rate, other things (i.e. B/H) being equal: $X_1\beta > X_0\beta$. In
the standard monetary approach, in which domestic credit is determined
without regard to the current balance of payments ($\alpha = 1$), the scaled
balance of payments would fall in case 1 relative to case 0 by $X_1\beta - X_0\beta$
to maintain money growth at $\overline{\Delta \log M}$. In the modified approach with
partial sterilization, the scaled balance of payments falls by much more:

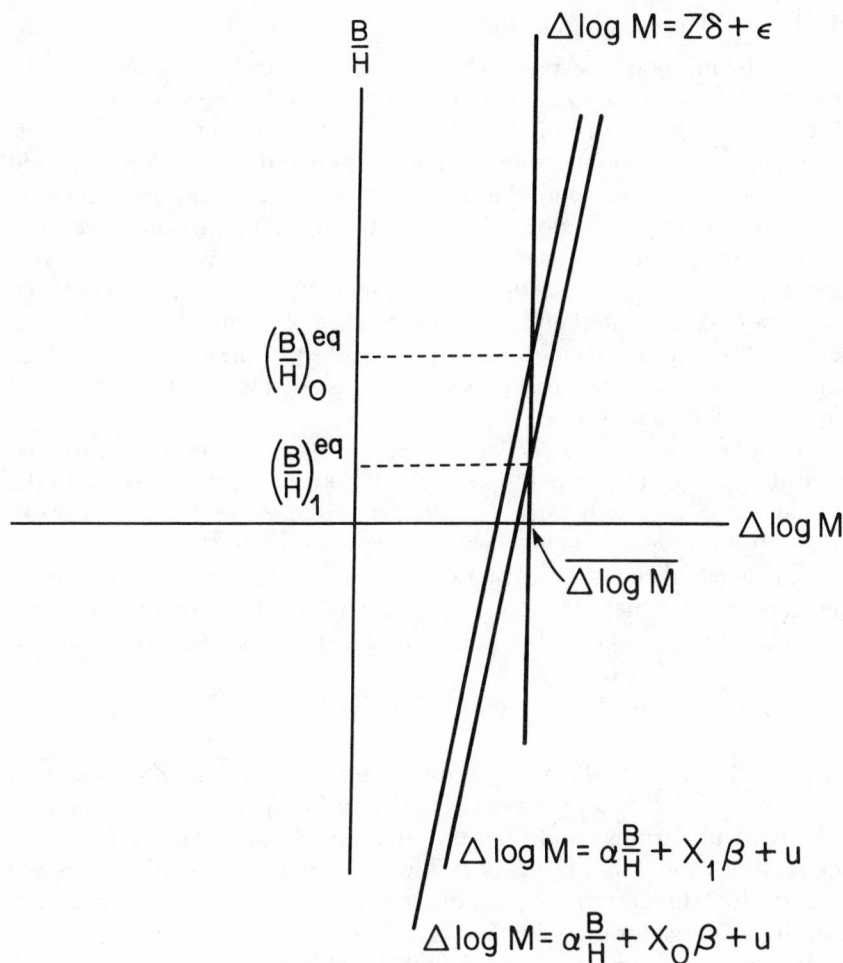

Fig. 10.2   Effect of shift in domestic policy goals in the modified monetary approach.

$$(10.8) \qquad \left(\frac{B}{H}\right)_1^{\text{eq}} - \left(\frac{B}{H}\right)_0^{\text{eq}} = -\frac{X_1\beta - X_0\beta}{\alpha}.$$

That is, the balance-of-payments multiplier is $-1/\alpha$ times the change in the domestic-policy portion of monetary policy.

In conclusion, the existence of partial sterilization does not imply any monetary control by a nonreserve central bank under pegged exchange rates. It may just result in accentuated balance-of-payments movements.

10.1.3   A More General Model

The assumption of exogenous determination of the arguments of the money demand function is deeply ingrained in the monetary-approach literature. Indeed, it is this assumption which allows one easily to transform statements about monetary equilibrium and money supply conditions into statements about the balance of payments.[9] If instead monetary and fiscal actions can move the domestic interest rate and price level relative to the foreign variables (not to mention any effect on real income), then monetary actions will cause movements in money demand with more complicated effects on the balance of payments. The remainder of this section considers such nonmonetary-approach models which are nonetheless characterized by continuous equality of money supplied and money demanded.

If neither goods nor assets are perfect substitutes, it no longer follows that the balance of payments will be infinitely elastic with respect to the money supply growth rate. The domestic interest and price level can move from the parity values which determine $\overline{\Delta \log M} = Z\delta + \epsilon$. Other factors (such as those appearing in trade supply and demand equations) represented by the vector S will also play a role in determining the balance of payments so that equation (10.5) is expanded to

$$(10.5')\qquad \frac{B}{H} = \theta\,(\Delta \log M - Z\delta - \epsilon) + S\lambda,$$

where $0 > \theta > -\infty$. If money growth were greater than $Z\delta + \epsilon$ so that interest rates fell and prices rose relative to foreign values, the balance-of-payments surplus would fall through movements along noninfinitely elastic net-capital and net-export flow schedules. The empirical tests in section 10.2 do not require a list of the elements in S so that we need not specify a full general equilibrium model here.[10]

Solving equation (10.5') for $\Delta \log M$ yields

$$(10.9)\qquad \Delta \log M = \frac{1}{\theta}\left(\frac{B}{H} - S\lambda\right) + Z\delta + \epsilon.$$

---

9. In a particularly relevant example, Genberg (1976, p. 322) argues that a sterilization policy "is implausible for several reasons. Firstly it implies an extraordinary stability of the central bank's behaviour with respect to policy formation. Secondly it implies that the sterilization is always of a magnitude consistent with the demand for money, *since with prices, interest rates and output determined by exogenous forces, the money market must be equilibrated through either reserve flows or domestic credit creation*" (emphasis added). We have already seen that Genberg errs in supposing any difficulty in reconciling sterilization to lack of monetary control. But note the absolute certainty that the arguments of the money demand function are exogenously determined.

10. One particular version of equation (10.5') or (10.9) would be the semireduced form obtained by solving for B/H and $\Delta \log M$ in the non-reaction-function equations in a country submodel in the Mark III International Transmission Model. Since those results have met monetary-approach skepticism, a less model-dependent approach is followed here. In chapter 11 below, Daniel Laskar specifies a smaller-scale model and obtains similar results.

When equation (10.9) is combined with the reaction function (10.1), we obtain a truly simultaneous system determining $\Delta \log M$ and B/H together. The (reduced-form) solutions for the equilibrium values are

$$(10.10) \qquad \Delta \log M = \frac{1}{1-\alpha\theta} X\beta + \frac{\alpha}{1-\alpha\theta} S\lambda + \frac{\alpha\theta}{\alpha\theta - 1} Z\delta$$

$$+ \frac{1}{1-\alpha\theta} u + \frac{\alpha\theta}{\alpha\theta - 1} \epsilon,$$

$$(10.11) \qquad \frac{B}{H} = \frac{\theta}{1-\alpha\theta} X\beta + \frac{1}{1-\alpha\theta} S\lambda + \frac{\theta}{\alpha\theta - 1} Z\delta$$

$$+ \frac{\theta}{1-\alpha\theta} u + \frac{\theta}{\alpha\theta - 1} \epsilon.$$

It can be readily verified that as the balance-of-payments elasticity goes to negative infinity, the solutions (10.10) and (10.11) go to the modified-monetary-approach solutions (10.6) and (10.7). Thus the modified monetary approach is, indeed, a special case (for $\theta = -\infty$) of this more general model.

The more general model is illustrated by figure 10.3. The vertical line of figure 10.1 is replaced with a negatively sloped line relating the balance of payments to money growth, the trade factors $S\lambda$, and the demand variables $Z\delta + \epsilon$. The intersection of this line with the reaction function determines both the balance of payments and money supply growth. In this case, as seen in figure 10.4, a desire to increase money growth (due to increased unemployment, say) in fact does increase money growth as well as decrease the balance of payments. The relative size of the two effects of course depends on the slopes of the two equations. But unlike the modified-monetary-approach case, there will be a correlation between movements in the domestic policy goals ($X\beta + u$) and changes in the money supply.

Note that our model deletes the concept of domestic credit entirely. One can derive the equilibrium value of the scaled change in domestic credit from equations (10.10) and (10.11)—or (10.6) and (10.7) in the modified-monetary-approach special case—and the usual identity (10.2). Trivial manipulations yield a domestic-credit equation, but only if it is exogenously determined ($\alpha = 1$) does domestic credit have causal or analytical significance. As an endogenous variable it adds nothing to the exposition. As will be discussed further in section 10.2, the negative correlation between the scaled change in domestic credit and the scaled balance of payments makes for easy confusion in empirical analysis.

10.1.4   Conditions for Monetary Control

Unless the balance of payments is infinitely elastic with respect to money growth, the central bank of a nonreserve country does exercise a

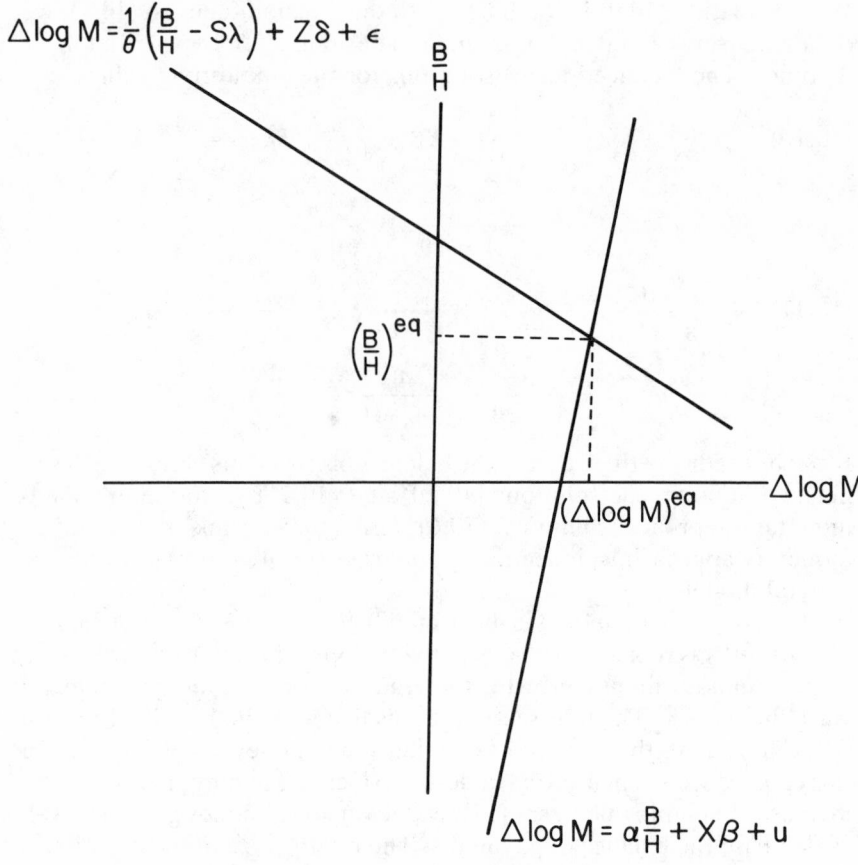

Fig. 10.3   Simultaneous determination of balance of payments and nominal money in the more general model.

degree of monetary control. This control is not absolute (if $\alpha > 0$) in the sense that the balance-of-payments effects will enter the bank's choice of money growth, but neither will these effects completely overwhelm all other influences such as domestic unemployment or inflation goals. Since lagged balances of payments may be counted among those other influences, the pegged system may be quite stable dynamically via specie-flow types of adjustments, but this is a different process than envisioned by the monetary approach. This subsection examines in more detail the crucial parameter

$$\theta = \frac{d\,(B/H)}{d\,\Delta\,\log\,M}.$$

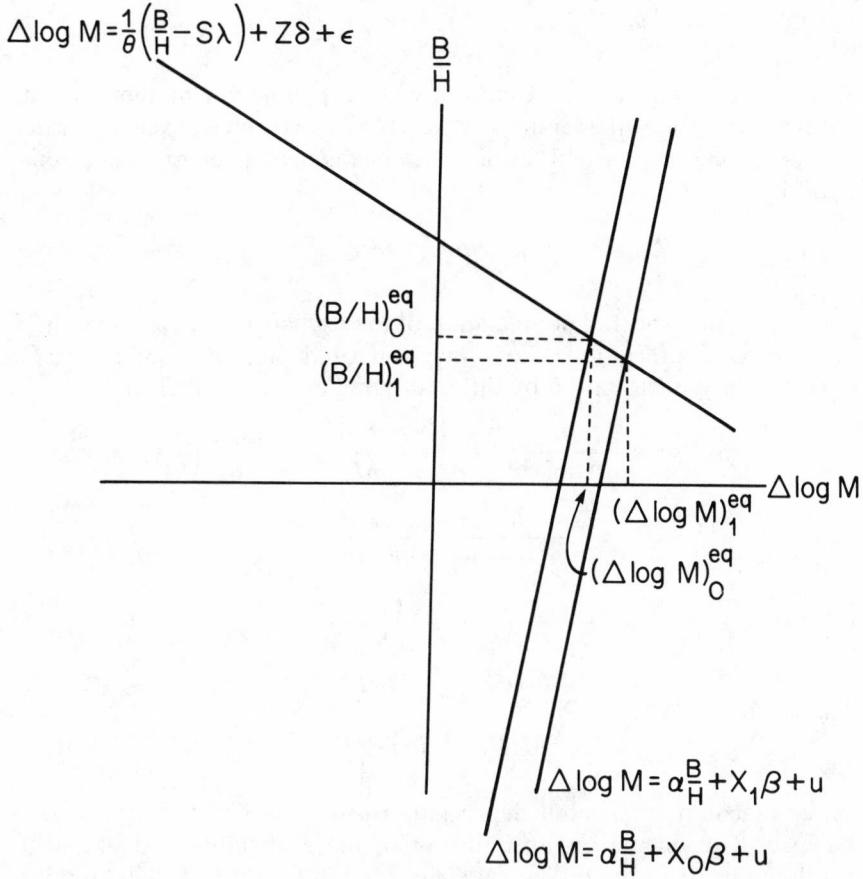

Fig. 10.4   Effect of shift in domestic policy goals in the more general model.

Whether θ is negative infinity has generally been addressed in terms of either assets or goods being perfect substitutes internationally. If assets are perfect substitutes and the derivatives of the interest rate R with respect to money growth is negative due to a liquidity effect, then overwhelming net private capital flows will force the domestic interest rate to its parity value. Similarly if goods are perfect substitutes and the derivative of the contemporaneous price level P with respect to money growth is positive, overwhelming trade flows will force the domestic price level to its parity value. Either of these cases is sufficient, but it is not necessary for either or both to hold in order to obtain $\theta = -\infty$.

To see this, write the scaled balance of payments as the difference between the scaled balance of trade and the scaled net private capital outflows:

(10.12) $$\frac{B}{H} \equiv \frac{T}{H} - \frac{C}{H}$$

Scaled net private capital outflows will be a function of the current covered interest differential (adjusted for expected exchange-rate changes) and other variables which may be taken as given for the current period:[11]

(10.13) $$\frac{C}{H} = f(R - \rho - R^F),$$

where ρ is the expected depreciation of the exchange rate ($\rho < 0$ implies an expected appreciation), R^F is the given foreign interest rate, and so f' is negative. We can find θ by differentiating equation (10.12):

$$\theta \equiv \frac{d(B/H)}{d\Delta \log M} = \frac{d(T/H)}{d\Delta \log M} - f' \frac{dR}{d\Delta \log M}$$

$$+ f' \frac{d\rho}{d(B/H)} \frac{d(B/H)}{d\Delta \log M},$$

(10.14) $$\theta = \frac{1}{1 - f' \dfrac{d\rho}{d(B/H)}} \left(\frac{d(T/H)}{d\Delta \log M} - f' \frac{dR}{d\Delta \log M} \right).$$

The multiplier

$$1 / \left(1 - f' \frac{d\rho}{d(B/H)} \right)$$

states that if the expected depreciation ρ responds to the size of the balance of payments (as an indicator of the probability and size of a revaluation), then the direct trade and capital-flows effects will be reinforced by induced "speculative" capital flows. These induced speculative capital flows will be overwhelming unless

(10.15) $$f' \frac{d\rho}{d(B/H)} < 1.$$

Therefore, instead of the standard two, there are three conditions required for a $\theta > -\infty$: (1) Trade flows must not be overwhelming.[12] (2) The

---

11. Among these other variables are, of course, the lagged covered interest differential since *changes* in the differential will cause portfolio revisions and hence net capital flows. These other variables are predetermined within the period and so implicit in the function $f(\ )$. Dooley and Isard (1980) provide a convenient recent exposition of the role of political risk in allowing $R - \rho - R^F$ to differ from 0 when the interest rates refer to domestic rates rather than Eurorates.

12. Formally,

$$\frac{\partial(T/H)}{\partial \log P} \frac{d \log P}{d \Delta \log M} > -\infty.$$

direct effect on capital flows must not be overwhelming.[13] (3) Speculative capital flows must not be overwhelming (condition (10.15) must be met). Note that with costs of adjustment and lags in information these three conditions may be met for certain periods of observation but not for longer periods. With longer periods, lagged values of B/H which are included in $X\beta$ in the short-period analysis would instead be included in the contemporaneous value of B/H.

Obviously it is an empirical question whether these three conditions for monetary control are met for any relevant observation length, and we shall turn to some empirical evidence shortly in section 10.2. But first, the third condition (10.15) raises an interesting possibility. Suppose that the probability of a revaluation increases with the absolute value of the scaled balance of payments and the expected (signed) magnitude of the revaluation varies with the value of the scaled balance of payments. Then the expected depreciation might be determined by a function like

$$(10.16) \qquad \rho = g\left(\left|\frac{B}{H}\right| \cdot \frac{B}{H}\right),$$

where g' is, of course, negative. The derivative of interest is

$$(10.17) \qquad \frac{d\rho}{d(B/H)} = 2g'\left|\frac{B}{H}\right|,$$

which increases in absolute value with the absolute value of B/H. Thus there is some reason to suppose that condition (10.15) might hold for "small" absolute values of the scaled balance of payments but fail if the central bank attempted a policy which were "too" inconsistent with international conditions. This is illustrated in figure 10.5. The central bank exercises a degree of monetary control so long as it stays in the negatively sloped portion of the international balance curve. If it shifts into the vertical range, however, overwhelming speculative capital flows result.[14]

10.2 Empirical Results

Blejer (1979) applied the Granger-Sims causality test to quarterly data for France, Germany, Italy, Sweden, and the United Kingdom and found that scaled changes in domestic credit "cause" scaled reserve flows in all five (albeit as part of a two-way feedback structure for Sweden and the

---

13. Formally,

$$f' \frac{dR}{d \Delta \log M} < \infty.$$

14. This provides another basis for Niehans's (1974) idea that nonreserve countries can exercise monetary control within a limited range.

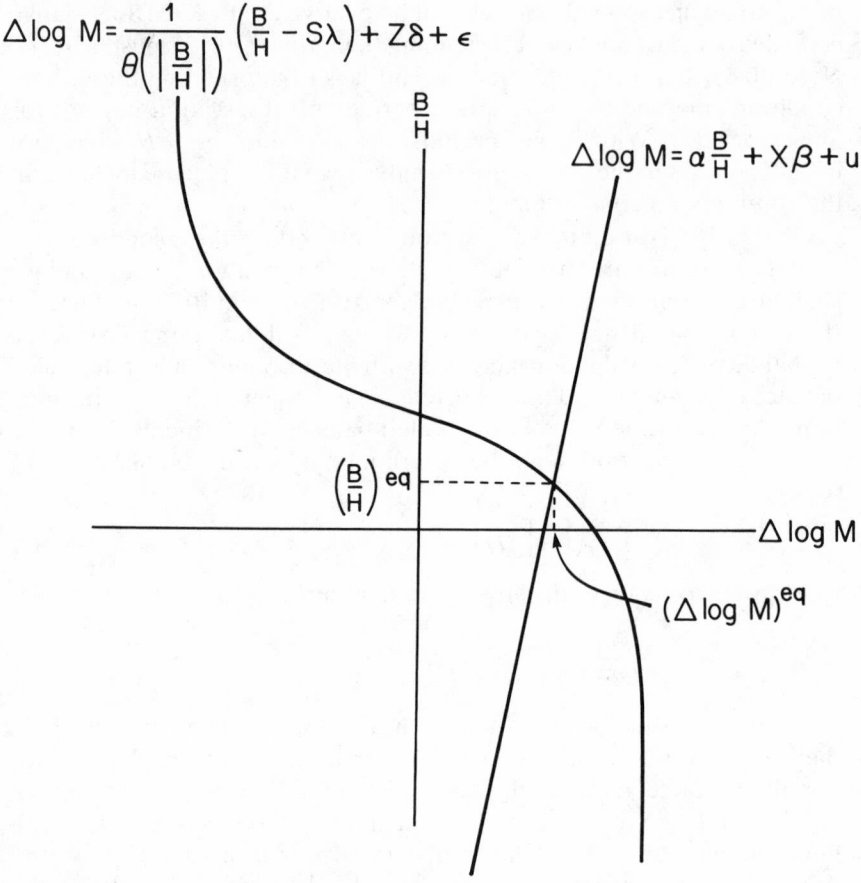

$$\Delta \log M = \frac{1}{\theta\left(\left|\frac{B}{H}\right|\right)} \left(\frac{B}{H} - S\lambda\right) + Z\delta + \epsilon$$

$$\Delta \log M = \alpha \frac{B}{H} + X\beta + u$$

Fig. 10.5   Simultaneous determination of balance of payments and money where potential unstable speculation limits monetary control.

United Kingdom). Blejer erroneously claimed that this supports the monetary approach, but it in fact suggests short-run monetary control since the test shows that *past* changes in domestic credit affect current reserve flows. This evidence for short-run monetary control is not conclusive, however, since past changes in domestic credit might have been induced by reserve-country actions which have current effects on foreign prices and hence reserve flows.[15] It is simply not appropriate to apply an exogeneity test to two endogenous variables.

The analysis of section 10.1 suggest two research strategies which focus directly on the issue of monetary control: The first is to fully specify the more general model and estimate equations (10.1) and (10.9) by a simul-

15. See Cassese and Lothian (chapter 4 above) for this point.

taneous system method to test whether $1/\theta$ is, indeed, zero. This method is pursued in the Mark III International Transmission Model and is beyond the scope of the present chapter.[16] The second approach is to proceed on the assumption that the *null hypothesis of no monetary control* is true and perform some classical hypothesis tests. Following this second path allows us to avoid the difficulty of fully specifying the variables which belong in S.

These hypothesis tests rely on the difference between the reduced forms for $\Delta \log M$ under the null hypothesis and the alternative hypothesis. Let us rewrite the reduced forms here for comparison:

$$(10.6) \qquad \Delta \log M = Z\delta + \epsilon,$$

$$(10.10) \qquad \Delta \log M = \frac{1}{1 - \alpha\theta} X\beta + \frac{\alpha}{1 - \alpha\theta} S\lambda + \frac{\alpha\theta}{\alpha\theta - 1} Z\delta$$
$$+ \frac{1}{1 - \alpha\theta} u + \frac{\alpha\theta}{\alpha\theta - 1} \epsilon.$$

Note that neither $X\beta$ nor $S\lambda$ enters in the reduced form if the null hypothesis is true. *One* test of the null hypothesis is to add the domestic variables $X\beta$ to the reduced form (10.6) and test whether they fail to enter as required by the null hypothesis. That is, the null hypothesis implies $\phi = 0$ in

$$(10.18) \qquad \Delta \log M = \phi X\beta + Z\delta + \epsilon.$$

A more powerful test would also include $S\lambda$, but this requires a full specification of the alternative hypothesis as noted above.

The empirical tests are based on the quarterly data bank and the money supply reaction functions in the Mark III Model, discussed above in chapters 3 and 5, respectively. We must first specify which variables appear in the vector Z. Stockman (1979) follows the standard practice of explaining the first difference of money demand as the first difference of a Cagan or long-run money-demand function:

$$(10.19) \qquad \Delta \log M = \delta_1 + \delta_2 \Delta \log y + \delta_3 \Delta R + \delta_4 \Delta \log P + \eta.$$

The further assumption is made that the change in domestic real income $\Delta \log y$ is exogenous and that the domestic interest rate R and price level

---

16. See chapters 5 and 6 above. Equation (10.9) can be thought of as a semireduced form of all the non-reaction-function equations in the model. Stockman (1979) dealt with this problem by implicitly assuming $S\lambda = 0$ in equation (10.9) and estimating transformations of equations (10.1) and (10.9) by two-stage least squares. Since $S\lambda \neq 0$ if the alternative hypothesis is true, his estimates of $1/\theta$ are inconsistent and likely biased toward zero. In view of this specification error, his failure to find evidence of monetary control does not seem very informative. This and other criticisms apply to Argy and Kouri (1974), Genberg (1976), and Connolly and Taylor (1979). If one is to use a simultaneous-equation approach, the general model must be fully specified. See Laskar (1980) for a formal analysis of the biases in the tests of Stockman et al.

P are exogenously determined by the foreign interest rate R_U and the exchange-rate-converted foreign price level EP_F:[17]

(10.20) $$\Delta R = \Delta R_U + \omega,$$

(10.21) $$\Delta \log P = \Delta \log(EP_F) + \psi.$$

The disturbances ω and ψ permit *exogenous* shifts in the interest and purchasing-power parities and would have variance 0 in the most extreme versions of the monetary approach. Thus the Stockman version of the reduced form (10.6) is

(10.22) $$\Delta \log M = \delta_1 + \delta_2 \Delta \log y + \delta_3 \Delta R_U$$
$$+ \delta_4 \Delta \log (EP_F) + \epsilon,$$

where $\epsilon = \eta + \delta_3 \omega + \delta_4 \psi$.[18] Table 10.1 reports estimates of the reduced-form (and structural) equation (10.6) for $\Delta \log M$ on this specification of Z for all seven nonreserve countries in the data bank. The pegged periods used in the estimates are indicated in the table. These regressions seem very poor compared to standard monetary-approach results. The reason is that standard estimates move domestic credit to the right-hand side on the erroneous assumption that it is exogenous. This provides a spuriously high R^2. Direct estimates (not tabulated here) of equation (10.19) with domestic variables are also insignificant for three of the countries; so the specification (10.19) is somewhat suspect.

Following Genberg (1976), we can improve the fit of the regressions by using the short-run money-demand function introduced by Chow (1966). This amounts to adding the change in the logarithm of lagged real money or $\Delta \log (M/P)_{-1}$ to the vector Z. Table 10.2 reports the results obtained using the Chow specification. These results are rather more favorable to the monetary approach although the $\bar{R}^2$ are not very impressive in an absolute sense.[19] There is some evidence of residual autocorrelation for Japan and the Netherlands, but this disappears in the more correctly specified test equations. Let us now proceed to the reduced-form tests.

17. As pointed out by Magee (1976), the assumption that $\Delta \log y$ is exogenous may unduly favor the monetary approach. The foreign interest rate R_U is the U.S. three-month treasury bill rate. Also, following Stockman (1979), P_F is an income-weighted index of foreign prices. All tables in this chapter were also computed using the exchange-rate-converted U.S. price index EP_U instead of EP_F. The standard errors were generally a bit lower for the form reported here, but the basic results were qualitatively the same. The alternate tables are available upon request from the author.

18. Obviously the estimated coefficients will be biased estimates of the values in equation (10.19) if there are exogenous shifts in the parities; this does not affect the validity of the tests conducted so long as those shifts are unrelated to the variables in X as discussed below.

19. Generally the $\bar{R}^2$ values are better when domestic variables are substituted for the foreign variables. For Italy, however, only a poor measure of the domestic interest rate is available and it does notably worse; indeed, Italy is the only regression not significant at the 10% or better level using domestic variables.

Table 10.1   **Estimates of Modified-Monetary-Approach Equation: Long-Run Money Demand Version**

$$\Delta \log M = \delta_1 + \delta_2 \Delta \log y + \delta_3 \Delta R_U + \delta_4 \Delta \log (EP_F) + \epsilon$$

Country	Period	Coefficients				S.E.E.	$\bar{R}^2$	D-W
		δ_1	δ_2	δ_3	δ_4			
UK	1957I–71II	0.008	0.108	0.084	0.065	0.018	−0.045	1.46
		(0.003)	(0.202)	(0.481)	(0.160)			
		2.520	0.535	0.174	0.406			
CA	1962II–70I	0.025	−0.207	−1.640	−0.608	0.011	0.188**	1.93
		(0.007)	(0.257)	(0.606)	(0.520)			
		3.794	−0.806	−2.707	−1.170			
FR	1958I–71II	0.028	0.067	−0.271	−0.218	0.013	0.094**	0.68
		(0.003)	(0.092)	(0.351)	(0.092)			
		10.664	0.720	−0.772	−2.355			
GE	1957I–71I	0.018	0.323	−0.188	0.269	0.011	0.169**	1.44
		(0.002)	(0.102)	(0.283)	(0.118)			
		8.860	3.169	−0.664	2.278			
IT	1957I–71II	0.028	0.097	−0.450	0.497	0.014	0.014	1.37
		(0.004)	(0.147)	(0.371)	(0.369)			
		7.111	0.657	−1.213	1.348			
JA	1957I–71II	0.030	0.153	0.466	0.753	0.020	0.013	0.99
		(0.006)	(0.177)	(0.527)	(0.515)			
		5.117	0.867	0.884	1.462			
NE	1957I–71I	0.017	0.369	−0.118	−0.043	0.014	0.060*	1.92
		(0.003)	(0.146)	(0.358)	(0.235)			
		6.069	2.522	−0.329	−0.183			

Notes. Standard errors appear in parentheses below the coefficient estimates; t statistics are below the standard errors. One asterisk after the $\bar{R}^2$ indicates rejection of the hypothesis $\delta_2 = \delta_3 = \delta_4 = 0$ at better than 0.10 level, two asterisks at better than 0.05 level.

Table 10.2 Estimates of Modified-Monetary-Approach Equation: Chow Money Demand Version

$$\Delta \log M = \delta_1 + \delta_2 \Delta \log y + \delta_3 \Delta R_U + \delta_4 \Delta \log (EP_F) + \delta_5 \Delta \log (M/P)_{-1} + \epsilon$$

Country	Coefficients					S.E.E.	$\bar{R}^2$	Durbin's h [D-W]†
	δ_1	δ_2	δ_3	δ_4	δ_5			
UK	0.008	0.047	0.123	0.023	0.279	0.018	0.012	[1.95]
	(0.003)	(0.198)	(0.469)	(0.157)	(0.137)			
	2.691	0.240	0.263	0.150	2.032			
CA	0.025	−0.211	−1.667	−0.598	−0.052	0.012	0.160*	1.10
	(0.007)	(0.262)	(0.622)	(0.529)	(0.163)			
	3.731	−0.805	−2.680	−1.130	−0.316			
FR	0.015	0.050	−0.415	−0.078	0.617	0.009	0.568**	1.50
	(0.003)	(0.064)	(0.243)	(0.067)	(0.083)			
	6.137	0.776	−1.705	−1.166	7.465			
GE	0.015	0.326	−0.201	0.311	0.197	0.011	0.196**	1.05
	(0.003)	(0.100)	(0.278)	(0.119)	(0.118)			
	5.036	3.254	−0.721	2.613	1.663			
IT	0.022	0.073	−0.323	0.346	0.292	0.014	0.074*	[1.98]
	(0.005)	(0.143)	(0.364)	(0.365)	(0.138)			
	4.692	0.514	−0.887	0.950	2.116			
JA	0.021	0.032	0.128	0.320	0.486	0.018	0.219**	2.26
	(0.006)	(0.160)	(0.477)	(0.472)	(0.125)			
	3.638	0.198	0.269	0.680	3.896			
NE	0.015	0.336	−0.136	0.009	.0157	0.014	0.074*	−2.10
	(0.003)	(0.148)	(0.355)	(0.236)	(0.117)			
	4.808	2.278	−0.384	0.037	1.341			

Notes. Standard errors appear in parentheses below the coefficient estimates; t statistics are below the standard errors.
One asterisk after the $\bar{R}^2$ indicates rejection of the hypothesis $\delta_2 = \delta_3 = \delta_4 = 0$ at better than 0.10 level, two asterisks at better than 0.05 level.
† In those cases in which Durbin's h cannot be calculated (is imaginary), the (biased) Durbin-Watson statistic is reported instead in square brackets.

The reaction functions in the Mark III Model are very general in form to allow for cross-country differences in timing of response. For the pegged period, included variables, other than a scaled balance-of-payments term, are a time trend, current and lagged unexpected real government spending, lagged semiannual inflation rates, lagged unemployment rates or logarithmic transitory incomes, and lagged scaled balance of payments. When all these variables (except the current B/H) are added to the regressions reported in tables 10.1 and 10.2, we can do the joint test of whether the coefficients of the additional variables are all zero as implied by the null hypothesis. The results of these F tests are reported in table 10.3. For the Chow money demand function the modified monetary approach (no monetary control) is rejected stongly for the United Kingdom, France, and Japan and at the 10% significance level for Canada and Germany. Similar, though more erratic, results are obtained for the long-run money demand function. Consider the tests, however:

Table 10.3 F **Tests for Unconstrained Addition of Domestic-Policy Reaction Function Variables**

	F Statistics	
Country	Chow Money Demand Function	Long-Run Money Demand Function
UK	2.241 (12, 41) $[0.025>p>0.01]$	2.731 (12, 42) $[0.01>p>0.005]$
CA	2.085 (12, 14) $[0.10>p>0.05]$	1.495 (12, 15) $[p>0.10]$
FR	2.658 (12, 37) $[0.025>p>0.01]$	4.040 (12, 38) $[0.001>p]$
GE	1.929 (12, 40) $[0.10>p>0.05]$	2.239 (12, 41) $[0.05>p>0.025]$
IT	1.250 (12, 41) $[p>0.10]$	1.651 (12, 42) $[p>0.10]$
JA	2.643 (12, 41) $[0.025>p>0.01]$	4.287 (12, 42) $[0.001>p]$
NE	1.372 (12, 40) $[p>0.10]$	1.571 (12, 41) $[p>0.10]$

Notes. Each F statistic is followed in parentheses by the associated degree of freedom. Significance levels are indicated in brackets below the F statistics.

The significance levels refer to the level at which we would just reject the null hypothesis that the coefficients on all reaction function variables equal zero. The twelve reaction function variables are t, $\hat{g}$, $(\hat{g}_{t-1} + \hat{g}_{t-2})$, $(\hat{g}_{t-3} + \hat{g}_{t-4})$, $(\log P_{t-1} - \log P_{t-3})$, $(\log P_{t-3} - \log P_{t-5})$, u_{t-1}, u_{t-2}, u_{t-3}, u_{t-4}, $[(B/H)_{t-1} + (B/H)_{t-2}]$, and $[(B/H)_{t-3} + (B/H)_{t-4}]$, where t is time, $\hat{g}$ the innovation in real government spending, P the GNP deflator, and u either the unemployment rate (for the U.K. and France) or logarithmic transitory income.

They ask whether all the additional variables reduce the sum of squared residuals by significantly more than would be expected for such a number of unrelated random variables. Since not all of these variables enter any given reaction function, this is a low-power test (it is hard to reject the null hypothesis).

A sharper test would include only those variables which actually enter the reaction functions for each country. The Mark IV Simulation Model described in chapter 7 above is a simplified simulation version of the Mark III International Transmission Model. Its specification of X in equation (10.1) dropped all variables with t statistics less than unity. Table 10.4 reports results of the F tests based upon these country-specific money supply reaction functions. We see that only the Netherlands (the smallest and most open country in the sample) fails to exhibit significant correlation between money growth and the money supply variables. Thus these reduced-form tests generally confirm the results obtained using structural models by Herring and Marston (1977), Darby and Stockman (chapter 6 above), and Laskar (1980): Nonreserve countries exercised a significant degree of control over their domestic money supplies within a quarter. Thus even the modified monetary approach is unacceptable for analysis of quarterly data.

Table 10.4   **F Tests for Addition of Mark IV Model Domestic-Policy Reaction Function Variables**

Country	Chow Money Demand Function	Long-Run Money Demand Function
	F Statistics	
UK	4.071 (7, 46) [0.005>p>0.001]	4.999 (7, 47) [0.001>p]
CA	3.312 (5, 21) [0.025>p>0.01]	1.958 (5, 22) [p>0.10]
FR	3.413 (9, 40) [0.005>p>0.001]	4.869 (9, 41) [0.001>p]
GE	3.205 (3, 49) [0.05>p>0.025]	3.658 (3, 50) [0.025>p>0.01]
IT	2.401 (6, 47) [0.05>p>0.025]	3.082 (6, 48) [0.025>p>0.01]
JA	4.463 (6, 47) [0.005>p>0.001]	7.021 (6, 48) [0.001>p]
NE	1.432 (8, 44) [p>0.10]	1.705 (8, 45) [p>0.10]

Note. Each F statistic is followed in parentheses by the associated degrees of freedom. Significance levels are indicated in brackets below the F statistics.

Two reservations should be noted: (1) The money supply demand functions do not fit very well by U.S. standards and may be misspecified. However, since they are the standard forms in the literature and a stable, *known* money demand function is essential to the monetary approach, this provides little comfort to adherents of the monetary approach. (2) The variables in X might enter because they are correlated with the exogenous parity shifts ω and ψ. This could conceivably be the case, but an examination of the list in the notes to table 10.3 provides no obvious or, to this writer, even plausible candidates.

10.3 Summary and Conclusions

Recent empirical research on sterilization had demonstrated that standard monetary-approach models which assume domestic credit exogenous are invalid. This paper presents a modified-monetary-approach model which retains the message of central bank impotence despite extensive sterilization activities. A more general model was also sketched under which the central bank's policy objectives do influence the change in the money supply. Whether a nonreserve central bank can determine its domestic money supply in the short run was shown to depend on whether one or more of the conditions are met: goods are perfect substitutes, assets are perfect substitutes, or expected depreciation is too responsive to changes in the balance of payments. The responsiveness in this new third condition may depend on the size of the balance of payments so that central bank monetary control is feasible only within a limited range.

The reduced-form tests showed strong evidence of the exercise of monetary control within the quarter for the United Kingdom, Canada, France, Germany, Italy, and Japan. Only for the Netherlands could we not reject the restriction on the more general model which implies the applicability of the modified monetary approach. These results confirm in a relatively model-free manner earlier findings based on specific structural models. They therefore answer suggestions that those earlier results are due to peculiarities in the structural model. There is no reason for predetermined money supply reaction function variables to be correlated with realized money growth unless the nonreserve central bank could and did exercise a degree of monetary control.

These results need not indicate any long-run monetary control; indeed, even short-run monetary control may be feasible only between the limits at which overwhelming speculative capital flows are induced. But the strong implications of the monetary approach (in standard or modified form) no longer appear tenable for use with quarterly data. Instead, more general macroeconomic models must be specified and tested to explain the *simultaneous* determination of nominal money and the balance of payments under pegged exchange rates.

Acknowledgments

Valuable comments on earlier drafts were received from Anthony Cassese, Michael Connolly, Robert Engel, Daniel Friedman, Clive Granger, Dan Lee, James Lothian, Michael Melvin, Jürg Niehans, Anna Schwartz, Alan Stockman, Dean Taylor, and Mark Watson, and in seminars at the Claremont Colleges, Emory University, the NBER–New York, University of California, San Diego, and UCLA. The calculations were performed on the TROLL system at MIT by Michael Melvin and Andrew Vogel.

References

Argy, V., and P. J. K. Kouri. 1974. Sterilization policies and the volatility in international reserves. In R. Z. Aliber, ed., *National monetary policies and the international financial system.* Chicago: University of Chicago Press.

Blejer, M. I. 1979. On causality and the monetary approach to the balance of payments: The European experience. *European Economic Review* 12 (July): 289–96.

Boyer, R. S. 1979. Sterilization and the monetary approach to balance of payments analysis. *Journal of Monetary Economics* 5 (April): 295–300.

Chow, G. C. 1966. On the long-run and short-run demand for money. *Journal of Political Economy* 74 (April): 111–31.

Connolly, M., and D. Taylor. 1979. Exchange rate changes and neutralization: A test of the monetary approach applied to developed and developing countries. *Economica* 46 (August): 281–94.

Darby, M. R. 1980. The monetary approach to the balance of payments: Two specious assumptions. *Economic Inquiry* 18 (April): 321–26.

Dooley, M. P., and P. Isard. 1980. Capital controls, political risk, and deviations from interest-rate parity. *Journal of Political Economy* 88 (April): 370–84.

Frenkel, J. A., and H. G. Johnson, eds. 1976. *The monetary approach to the balance of payments.* Toronto: University of Toronto Press.

Genberg, A. H. 1976. Aspects of the monetary approach to balance-of-payments theory: An empirical study of Sweden. In J. A. Frenkel and H. G. Johnson, eds., *The monetary approach to the balance of payments.* Toronto: University of Toronto Press.

Herring, R. J., and R. C. Marston. 1977. *National monetary policies and international financial markets.* Amsterdam: North-Holland.

Johnson, H. G. 1976. The monetary approach to balance-of-payments theory. In J. A. Frenkel and H. G. Johnson, eds., *The monetary approach to the balance of payments*. Toronto: University of Toronto Press.

Laskar, D. 1980. Sterilization behavior and independence of monetary policy under a pegged-exchange-rates system: An econometric approach. Ph.D. thesis, UCLA Department of Economics.

Maddala, G. S. 1977. *Econometrics*. New York: McGraw-Hill.

Magee, S. P. 1976. The empirical evidence on the monetary approach to the balance of payments and exchange rates. *American Economic Review, Papers and Proceedings* 66 (May): 163–70.

Mussa, M. 1976. Tarrifs and the balance of payments: A monetary approach. In J. A. Frenkel and H. G. Johnson, eds., *The monetary approach to the balance of payments*. Toronto: University of Toronto Press.

Niehans. J. 1974. Reserve composition as a source of independence for national monetary policies. In R. Z. Aliber, ed., *National monetary policies and the international financial system*. Chicago: University of Chicago Press.

Stockman, A. C. 1979. Monetary control and sterilization under pegged exchange rates. Unpublished paper, University of Rochester, Department of Economics, August.

Sweeney, R. J., and T. D. Willett. 1976. The international transmission of inflation: Mechanisms, issues, and evidence. In M. Fratianni and K. Tavernier, eds., *Bank credit, money, and inflation in open economics*, supplement to *Kredit und Kapital*, Heft 3, pp. 441–517.

11 Short-Run Independence of Monetary Policy under a Pegged Exchange-Rates System: An Econometric Approach

Daniel M. Laskar

The extent to which a pegged exchange-rates system undermines the independence of an open economy's monetary policy has not been satisfactorily examined. Current empirical literature on the subject presents conclusions that are often contradictory and difficult to compare. In this paper we reevaluate the relevant empirical data and reestimate the degree of independence of monetary policy within the period of a quarter.

The literature presents three different views relevant to the independence of monetary policy under pegged exchange rates. The empirical literature on the monetary approach to the balance of payments (MABP) emphasizes the extreme situation in which the prices of goods and securities are dictated by the international market. Then the demand for money is given exogenously, and the money stock cannot be changed. Under such circumstances, monetary policy can determine only the level of international reserves. The MABP position consequently implies that no independence of monetary policy is possible. On the other hand, literature analyzing the sterilization behavior of the central bank finds that sterilization is important, suggesting that some monetary control exists.[1] Finally, the literature on capital flows argues that these flows are determined mainly by interest-rate differentials. As Z. Hodjera (1976) noted, the estimated interest-rate elasticities are small, which indicates that some independence of monetary policy is possible.

Daniel Laskar is with CEPREMAP, Paris, France.

An earlier version of this chapter appeared in the *Journal of International Money and Finance* 1 (April 1982): 57–79.

1. The empirical study of sterilization behavior was first analyzed without any formal model by Nurske (1944) and Michaely (1971). Then reaction functions of the central banks were estimated (see Price 1978) for a survey and an empirical study of reaction functions for six main industrialized countries).

A number of authors, however, have questioned the single-equation context of these analyses. Kouri and Porter (1974) pointed out that the estimates of the interest-rate coefficient in capital-flow equations are negatively biased because of the effect, emphasized by the MABP, of capital flows on the money supply. Consequently, they estimated a "reduced-form" capital-flows equation that showed the amount of offsetting capital flows generated by a change in domestic credit and estimated this "offset coefficient." Their approach tries to synthesize the MABP literature and the capital-flows literature.[2] H. Genberg (1976), V. Argy and P. J. Kouri (1974), G. L. Murray (1978), and A. C. Stockman (1979) integrated the MABP or Kouri and Porter type of analysis with that of sterilization behavior. In their studies the reserve flow equation and the central bank reaction function are simultaneously estimated.

Unfortunately, no clear picture of the independence of monetary policy emerges from this literature.[3] There are two main reasons why: none of the authors estimate a simultaneous-equations structural model, and all treat expectations of exchange rates unsatisfactorily.[4] When variables to reflect exchange-rate expectations variables are left out of the analysis, the degree of independence of monetary policy is apt to be underestimated. The cause of this problem is downward bias in the coefficient of change in domestic credit in an MABP or Kouri-Porter type of equation in the presence of sterilization. If a structural model were estimated, however, it would appear that interest-rate elasticities of capital flows are not actually as large as the biased estimates of the offset coefficient have suggested. Because the exchange-rate expectations variables are correlated with the instruments, the use of 2SLS cannot eliminate this bias.

Recently, scholars have attempted to address these two difficulties. Herring and Marston (1977a) estimated a structural model of the financial sector of Germany. However, they developed such an analysis only for that country. For other European countries they used an interest-rate reduced-form equation. S. W. Kohlagen (1977), using endogenous expectations, estimated a Kouri and Porter type of capital-flow equation, also only for Germany. M. R. Darby (1980) made two separate contributions which were based on studies of seven main industrial countries. First, on a theoretical level, he emphasized the possible loss of monetary control which could occur because of some effect on exchange-rate expectations. In particular, he showed that outside some range, monetary policy can cause overwhelming capital flows. Second, he derived a

---

2. Other empirical studies using the same approach are Porter (1972), Kouri (1975), and Neumann (1978).

3. A detailed critical review may be found in Laskar (1981).

4. Usually authors introduce dummy variables for "speculative episodes"; Argy and Kouri (1974) take a purchasing power parity equation.

money stock equation typical of those that can be obtained from a general structural model. Using such an equation, he showed that monetary objectives do have an effect on the money stock, and hence he rejected the strict MABP hypothesis that monetary policy has no independence.

This chapter will attempt to resolve some of these issues with respect to the short-run independence of monetary policy under pegged exchange rates. To do so, we will first specify an appropriate structural model, which we will then estimate for seven industrial countries during the period of pegged exchange rates. This model will then be used to analyze the (partial) loss of monetary control due to the substitutability of domestic and foreign assets, when exchange-rate expectations are taken as given. We will then evaluate how the imperfection of knowledge about exchange-rates expectations affects the issues we have posed, consequently examining how sensitive our results may be to different treatments of exchange-rate expectations.

The model will be estimated both with and without exchange-rate expectations variables. Then, since the measurements of exchange-rate expectations we use are likely to be faulty, we will try to determine how much their inaccuracy affects the correctness of our results. Because estimates about the independence of monetary policy may be biased differently depending on whether we use the structural equations estimates, the Kouri and Porter type of equations estimates,[5] or the reduced-form money stock estimate, we will estimate all three types of equations. Finally, because estimates of sterilization behavior may be sensitive to the specification of the money supply reaction function, we will consider alternative specifications. Section 11.1 will present the model, derive three alternative estimates of independence of monetary policy, and analyze biases in these estimates when speculative variables are left out. Each of the two subsequent sections will consider one side of the issue: section 11.2 studies offsetting capital flows, and section 11.3 analyzes sterilization behavior of the central bank. Finally, section 11.4 synthesizes and presents new conclusions about the independence of monetary policy.

11.1   Presentation of the Model and Alternative Estimates of Independence of Monetary Policy

Independence of monetary policy will be taken as the possibility of the central bank's objective to affect the money supply in the short run. In this section we present our model, more precisely define and interpret what we mean by independence of monetary policy, and give three ways

5. Hodjera (1976) pointed out that, if we use OLS, the simultaneous equation biases of estimates are likely to be in opposite directions in these two kinds of equations. He also tried to compare the two approaches to capital flows but did not obtain very significant results.

of estimating the coefficient which is an indicator of such an independence.

For that, first we will present the basic structural model. The estimation of such a model will give a first estimate of our coefficient. In the next subsections we will derive two other equations. One is a semireduced-form capital-flows equation like that used in the Kouri and Porter approach. The other one is the money stock reduced form of our model. The purpose is twofold. First, we will make explicit the reasons why monetary policy may not be fully realized in an open economy. Second, we will thus obtain two other alternative estimates of our coefficient. An interesting feature of the three estimates we obtain comes from the fact that they are differently biased when exchange-rate expectation variables are left out. Therefore the last subsection analyzes these biases.

11.1.1 Basic Model

The model we are presenting contains three structural equations: a money demand equation, a capital-flows equation, and a money supply reaction function of the central bank. The money demand equation is the first difference of the short-run money demand function introduced by Chow (1966):

$$(11.1) \qquad \Delta \log\left(\frac{M}{P}\right) = a_0 + a_1 \Delta r + a_2 \Delta \log y$$
$$+ a_3 \Delta \log\left(\frac{M}{P}\right)_{-1} + e_1.$$

In this equation, r is the interest rate, y is real income, M is the money stock, P is the price level, and e_1 is the residual.

Capital flows are created by the portfolio choices of residents and foreigners who consider domestic and foreign bonds as imperfect substitutes. The composition of their portfolios depends on domestic and foreign interest rates, real income, and the expected exchange-rate change. The portfolio adjustment is supposed to be completely realized within the period. Capital flows are then a function of the variation of these variables. The capital-flows variable is scaled by high-powered money,[6] and the equation is

$$(11.2) \qquad \frac{\text{CF}}{H_{-1}} = b_0 + b_1 \Delta r + b_1^* \Delta r^* + b_2 \Delta \log y + b_2^* \Delta \log y^*$$
$$+ b_3 \Delta (\log E - \log E^e) + e_2.$$

---

6. This may not be the best deflator if the portfolio choice model of a stock of assets B for residents is $B/W = f(r,r^*,y)$, where W is wealth. Some (foreign or domestic) wealth variable may have been better. But apart from the fact that these variables are difficult to introduce, the error made is probably comparatively small, because the main observed variations of CF/H_{-1} are due to variations in CF and not to variations in H_{-1}. Furthermore, as the coefficient of r_{-1} is let free in the estimation, the error may be partially corrected if the ratio of high-powered money to wealth is explained by the interest rate.

CF are capital inflows, H is high-powered money, E is the exchange rate (value of one dollar in terms of domestic currency), r^* is the world interest rate, y^* is foreign real income, and E^e is the expected exchange rate of next period. In this equation the coefficients b_1, $(-b_1^*)$ and b_3 might be seen as equal. However, due to some lack of homogeneity in the quality of data,[7] these coefficients will not be constrained. Estimates of the coefficients may also be biased differently under some specification error, such as when a speculative variable is excluded. Furthermore, in order to account for any flow effect,[8] we are eliminating constraints on the coefficients of r, r^*, and $\log E - \log E^e$ which would require that they be equal to the opposite of the coefficients of the lagged variables. The equation can thus be rewritten as

$$(11.3) \qquad \frac{\text{CF}}{H_{-1}} = b_0 + b_1 r + b_1' r_{-1} + b_1^* r^* + b_1^{*\prime} r_{-1}^*$$
$$+ b_2 \Delta \log y + b_2^* \Delta \log y^* + b_3 (\log E - \log E^e)$$
$$+ b_3' (\log E - \log E^e)_{-1} + e_2 .$$

The specification for the money supply reaction function is close[9] to that used by Darby and Stockman in the Mark III Model of chapters 5 and 6. According to this specification, the money supply responds to domestic variables such as past rates of inflation, past rates of unemployment or past values of transitory real income, depending on the country, and current and past real-government-spending shocks. It also responds to balance-of-payments variables such as the current balance of payments scaled by high-powered money BP/H_{-1}, the level of reserves over high-powered money of the last period $(R/H)_{-1}$, and past changes in the balance of payments also scaled by high-powered money $(\text{BP}/H_{-1})_{-i}$, $i = 1, \ldots, k$. Because we introduce the level of reserves $(R/H)_{-1}$, we allow all the past values of the balance-of-payments variables to have an effect on the money supply. However, as the past changes of these variables $(\text{BP}/H_{-1})_{-i}$ also enter the equation, the effect of the more recent values is allowed to be different. When past values of variables

---

7. All rates of interest are short-term rates except the rate of Italy, which is a long-term rate. For five among the six countries, the short-term interest rates used are three-month treasury bill or money market rates. The rate of Japan is a bank-loan rate which is higher and has a much lower variance than the others.

8. If $B/W = f(r, r^*, y)$, then $dB = f(r, r^*, y)dW + W\, df(r, r^*, y)$. The first term gives rise to the flow effect while the second corresponds to the stock effect which was previously discussed. Also, because we are mainly interested in the estimation of the coefficients of interest rates and of $\log E - \log E^e$, and because the effect of y and y^* is probably small, the flow effect due to y and y^* is neglected in the analysis. That is the reason why only $\Delta \log y$ and $\Delta \log y^*$ enter equation (11.3).

9. The main difference between the two specifications lies in the introduction, here, of the variable $(R/H)_{-1}$, where R is the level of reserves. Thus we may account for the balance-of-payments effects for more than four quarters. Also, the deflator of the balance of payments is different: H_{-1} is used instead of nominal income. Finally, for some countries (Germany and the Netherlands), unemployment rates are used instead of real income.

enter our analysis, four lags have been taken. To reduce the number of explanatory variables, the lagged values, except for the unemployment rate or real income, have been aggregated two by two: $(x_{-1} + x_{-2})$ and $(x_{-3} + x_{-4})$. A time trend has also been introduced.[10] The resulting equation is

$$(11.4) \qquad \Delta \log M = C_0 + k \frac{BP}{H_{-1}} + C_1 \left(\frac{R}{H} \right)_{-1} + C_2 LBP1$$
$$+ C_3 LBP3 + C_4 t + C_5 \hat{g} + C_6 Lg1 + C_7 Lg3$$
$$+ C_8 LP1 + C_9 LP3 + C_{10} u_{-1} + C_{11} u_{-2}$$
$$+ C_{12} u_{-3} + C_{13} u_{-4} + e_3,$$

where $LBP1 = (BP/H_{-1})_{-1} + (BP/H_{-1})_{-2}$ and $LBP3 = LBP1_{-2}$. Lg1, Lg3, LP1, LP3 are defined in the same way and correspond to government spending shocks $\hat{g}$ and rates of inflation. As in the Mark III, u is the unemployment rate, though log y' or transitory income is substituted for u in the cases of Italy, Japan, and Canada.

The equation can also be written more completely:

$$(11.4') \qquad \Delta \log M = k \frac{BP}{H_{-1}} + G_3 + e_3.$$

In order to introduce the domestic component of the money supply in the model and define the sterilization coefficient, we consider the following two identities:

$$(11.5) \qquad \Delta D + BP \equiv \Delta H,$$

$$(11.6) \qquad \Delta \log H + \Delta \log \mu \equiv \Delta \log M.$$

The first identity comes from the central bank balance sheet; D is "domestic credit." The second identity defines the money multiplier μ. Then we define the variable DDM in the following way:

$$(11.7) \qquad DDM \equiv \frac{\Delta D}{H_{-1}} + \Delta \log \mu.$$

With this definition of DDM, the previous identities imply that

$$(11.8) \qquad DDM + \frac{BP}{H_{-1}} \equiv \Delta \log M.$$

DDM is the domestic component of the money supply growth rate. We are presuming that the monetary authorities can control DDM. In an open economy, however, they may not have a similar control of $\Delta \log M$ because they create money when they intervene in the foreign exchange market, in order to peg the exchange rate. Using (11.8), the money supply reaction function (11.4') can also be written as

10. In the equation of France, the lagged dependent variable is also introduced.

(11.9) $$\mathrm{DDM} = -(1 - k)\frac{\mathrm{BP}}{H_{-1}} + G_3 + e_3.$$

The *sterilization coefficient* (c) is the coefficient of BP/H_{-1} in this equation. Therefore we have

(11.10) $$c = -(1 - k).$$

If $0 \le k \le 1$, then $-1 \le c \le 0$. A strictly negative value for c indicates that the central bank has tried to get more control on the money supply by sterilizing reserve flows. If sterilization is complete ($c = -1$), full control of the money supply is realized.

The model is completed by adding the identity

(11.11) $$\mathrm{CF} + \mathrm{BT} \equiv \mathrm{BP},$$

where BT is the balance of trade. The system of five equations given by the three equations of the model (11.1, 11.3, 11.4) and the two identities (11.8) and (11.11) determine the five unknowns ($\Delta \log M$, r, CF/H_{-1}, BP/H_{-1}, DDM). This means that in our model contemporaneous variables BT/H_{-1}, $\Delta \log y$, $\Delta \log p$, and ($\log E - \log E^e$) are regarded as givens. As we explained in the introduction, we are focusing on the pure substitutability of domestic and foreign assets effects and are not considering, for example, the channel which goes through exchange-rate expectations. However, in the *estimation procedure* of the model, the four contemporaneous variables (BT/H_{-1}, $\Delta \log y$, $\Delta \log p$, and ($\log E - \log E^e$)) will be considered as *endogenous*. Therefore some exogenous variables used to explain these variables more fully are added to the set of instruments. These instruments are explained in more detail in appendix 1. The three equations (11.1), (11.3), and (11.4) can be written more compactly:

(11.1') $$\Delta \log\left(\frac{M}{P}\right) = a_1 r + a_2 \Delta \log y + G_1 + e_1,$$

(11.3') $$\frac{\mathrm{CF}}{H_{-1}} = b_1 r + b_2 \Delta \log y + b_3 (\log E - \log E^e) + G_2 + e_2,$$

(11.4') $$\Delta \log M = k \frac{\mathrm{BP}}{H_{-1}} + G_3 + e_3.$$

All the variables contained in G_1, G_2, and G_3 are exogenous in the estimation.

As we mentioned at the beginning of this section, independence of monetary policy is taken as the possibility of the central bank's objective to affect the money supply in the short run. In our model an indicator of this independence is given by the coefficient, say A, of the objective G_3 in the money stock reduced-form equation. Such an equation and the exact meaning of coefficient A are presented in detail in subsection 11.1.3 below. For the moment we can just note that coefficient A is a function of the three structural parameters a_1, b_1, and k (or c). From (11.16) below, it is equal to $-a_1/(b_1 k - a_1)$. Therefore if $\hat{a}_1, \hat{b}_1$, and $\hat{k}$ are estimates of these coefficients, we can take $-\hat{a}_1/(\hat{b}_1 \hat{k} - \hat{a}_1)$ as an estimate of A.

11.1.2 Semireduced-Form Capital-Flows Equation

We can also obtain an estimate of A by first considering a semireduced-form capital-flows equation of the Kouri and Porter type. To arrive at such an equation, we eliminate r from (11.1') and (11.3'). Then we use identities (11.8) and (11.11) and we obtain the semireduced-form equation

$$(11.12) \qquad \frac{CF}{H_{-1}} = -\frac{b_1}{b_1 - a_1}\left(DDM + \frac{BT}{H_{-1}} - \Delta \log p\right)$$

$$+ \frac{b_1 a_2 - a_1 b_2}{b_1 - a_1} \Delta \log y$$

$$- \frac{a_1}{b_1 - a_1} b_3(\log E - \log E^e) + \frac{b_1}{b_1 - a_1} G_1$$

$$- \frac{a_1}{b_1 - a_1} G_2 + \frac{b_1}{b_1 - a_1} e_1 - \frac{a_1}{b_1 - a_1} e_2.$$

Equation (11.12) is an equation of the Kouri and Porter type. The *offset coefficient* is a, where

$$(1.13) \qquad a = -\frac{b_1}{b_1 - a_1}.$$

Since $a_1 \leq 0$ and $b_1 \geq 0$, then $-1 \leq a \leq 0$. Using identities (11.8) and (11.11), equation (11.12) implies

$$(11.14) \qquad \Delta \log M = (1 + a)\left(DDM + \frac{BT}{H_{-1}}\right)$$

$$- a\Delta \log p + \dots \qquad \text{(as in (11.12))}.$$

When $a = -1$ or $a = 0$, we confront two extreme situations. The first case ($a = -1$) occurs if domestic and foreign assets are perfect substitutes, making b_1 infinite. It also occurs if money demand is insensitive to the domestic interest rate, making $a_1 = 0$. Under such circumstances, as (11.14) indicates, there is no possibility for an effective monetary policy because DDM cannot affect the money supply unless it can also affect the current variables $\Delta \log p$, $\Delta \log y$, or ($\log E - \log E^e$). Note that BT/H_{-1} has no influence. The second case ($a = 0$) occurs when there is no substitutability between domestic and foreign assets, making $b_1 = 0$. It also occurs if there is an infinite interest elasticity of money demand, making a_1 infinite. In this situation, unless the current variables BT/H_{-1}, $\Delta \log y$, or $(\log E - \log E^e)$ are changed by DDM, we would observe a variation $\Delta \log M$ equal to DDM, without any induced capital flow. Capital flows do not depend on the current monetary policy. In that case, BT/H_{-1}, $\Delta \log y$, or $(\log E - \log E^e)$ may influence the money stock because they affect BP/H_{-1}; therefore, if sterilization of reserve flow is incomplete, $\Delta \log M$ will respond to them. Note that $\Delta \log p$ has no effect.

As shown below in subsection 11.1.3, coefficient A, our indicator of independence of monetary policy, can actually be expressed as a function of only two parameters: the offset coefficient a and the sterilization coefficient c. We have $A = (1 + a)/(1 - ac)$. Therefore, if we estimate equation (11.12) and get an estimate a, we obtain $(1 + \hat{a})/(1 - \hat{a}\hat{c})$ as a second estimate of A. In fact, the first estimate we gave in the previous subsection is equivalent to the estimate $(1 + \hat{a}^*)/(1 - \hat{a}^*\hat{c})$ where $\hat{a}^*$ is not directly estimated from (11.12) but calculated from the structural parameters estimates: $\hat{a}^* = -\hat{b}_1/(\hat{b}_1 - \hat{a}_1)$.

11.1.3   Money Stock Reduced Form

A third estimate $\hat{A}$ of coefficient A can also be obtained by directly regressing the money stock reduced-form equation. Such an equation may be obtained from (11.12), (11.4′), and the two identities (11.8) and (11.11). We get the equation

$$(11.15) \qquad \Delta \log M = \frac{-a_1}{b_1k - a_1} G_3 + \frac{-a_1k}{b_1k - a_1} \frac{BT}{H_{-1}}$$

$$+ k\frac{b_1a_2 - a_1b_2}{b_1k - a_1} \Delta \log y$$

$$- \frac{a_1k}{b_1k - a_1} b_3(\log E - \log E^e)$$

$$+ \frac{b_1k}{b_1k - a_1}(G_1 + \Delta \log p) + \frac{-a_1k}{b_1k - a_1} G_2$$

$$+ \frac{b_1k}{b_1k - a_1} e_1 - \frac{a_1k}{b_1k - a_1} e_2 - \frac{a_1}{b_1k - a_1} e_3.$$

We define

$$(11.16) \qquad A = \frac{-a_1}{b_1k - a_1}.$$

We also have

$$A = \frac{1 + a}{1 - ac}.$$

If both a and c are between -1 and 0, then $0 \le A \le 1$. Coefficient A

decreases with $|a|$ and increases with $|c|$. We get the estimate $\hat{A}$ from the regression of (11.15) by taking the estimated coefficient of $\hat{G}_3$, where $\hat{G}_3$ is given by the estimation of the money supply reaction function.

Now we will examine why monetary objectives may not be realized. Equation (11.15) can be rewritten

$$(11.17) \qquad \Delta \log M = A(G_3 + e_3)$$
$$+ (1 - A)(G_1 + a_2 \Delta \log y + \Delta \log p + e_1)$$
$$+ kA\left[\frac{BT}{H_{-1}} + G_2 + b_2 \Delta \log y\right.$$
$$\left. + b_3(\log E - \log E^e) + e_2\right].$$

Now consider the case when domestic and foreign assets are perfect substitutes and the interest-rate parity relation holds:

$$(11.18) \qquad r = r^* - (\log E - \log E^e).$$

Then, substituting into the money demand equation (11.1), we obtain

$$\Delta \log M = (\Delta \log M)^\zeta,$$

where

$$(11.19) \qquad (\Delta \log M)^\zeta = \Delta \log p + a_0 + a_1 \Delta r^*$$
$$+ a_2 \Delta \log y + a_3 \Delta \log \left(\frac{M}{P}\right)_{-1}$$
$$- a_1 \Delta(\log E - \log E^e).$$

In that case the money demand is determined independently of the monetary objective, and we have the MABP version.[11] We can introduce this value $(\Delta \log M)^\zeta$ in the more general reduced-form money stock equation (11.17), and we get

$$(11.20) \qquad \Delta \log M = A(G_3 + e_3) + (1 - A)(\Delta \log M)^\zeta + kA\Lambda,$$

where

$$(11.21) \qquad \Lambda = \frac{BT}{H_{-1}} + G_2 + b_2 \Delta \log y$$
$$+ b_3(\log E - \log E^e) + e_2 + b_1 r_{-1}$$
$$+ b_1 \Delta r^* - b_1 \Delta(\log E - \log E^e).$$

---

11. Our term $(\Delta \log M)^\zeta$ is very similar to the term $\overline{\Delta \log M}$ used in Darby (1980). However, they differ in two respects. First, because we take it as given in our analysis, the domestic price level enters $(\Delta \log M)^\zeta$, while the foreign one enters $\overline{\Delta \log M}$. Second, the exchange-rate expectation change $\Delta(\log E - \log E^e)$ is included in $(\Delta \log M)^\zeta$ but not in $\overline{\Delta \log M}$. The reason is that we also take the exchange-rate expectations as given in our analysis. Furthermore, as we explained earlier, in most of the MABP literature, exchange-rate expectations are either omitted or treated in a very crude way. Therefore the term $\overline{\Delta \log M}$ may be more representative of the standard MABP literature than our $(\Delta \log M)^\zeta$.

The gap between the money stock realized rate of growth $\Delta \log M$ and the objective $(G_3 + e_3)$ is given by

(11.22) $\qquad \Delta \log M - (G_3 + e_3) = -(1 - A)[(G_3 + e_3)$
$$- (\Delta \log M)^\zeta] + kA\Lambda.$$

From this last equation, we can see two reasons why monetary objectives may not be realized. First, monetary objectives may differ from $(\Delta \log M)^\zeta$. Second, some variables, contained in Λ, have an effect on the balance of payments,[12] and consequently affect the money supply if sterilization is incomplete. The first effect arises because there are offsetting capital flows which are not completely sterilized: it disappears if the offsetting coefficient a is equal to zero or if sterilization is complete (in both cases $A = 1$). On the contrary, the second effect vanishes if there is complete offsetting ($a = 1$ and therefore $A = 0$), because, in that case, the variables contained in Λ actually have no effect on the balance of payments. Note, that, even if no offsetting occurs ($a = 0$ and therefore $A = 1$), the monetary objective may not be realized if sterilization is incomplete, for the second term $kA\Lambda$ may not be equal to zero. Both effects decrease and go to zero when sterilization increases and becomes complete. Here we will focus on the first effect, which is the only one related to the monetary objective itself. As mentioned, *coefficient A* defined in (11.16) will be taken as an *indicator of independence of monetary policy within the period*.

11.1.4 Biases Due to Omission of Speculative Variables

If the model is not correctly specified, these three estimates of A may be asymptotically biased, but the direction and amount of the biases will not be the same and will depend on the nature of exchange-rate expectations. Call SP $= (\log E - \log E^e)$ a speculative variable. To simplify the discussion further, suppose $b_3' = -b_3$. We can then consider the three following cases. First, we can have white noise expectations. If $\Delta SP = \epsilon$, where ϵ is white noise, a model without speculative variables would give consistent estimates. Second, we can examine "exogenous" expectations. Suppose that ΔSP is correlated with the instruments but is not a function of any of the five variables which are solutions of the model. We

---

12. Using the definition of G_2 and noting that, at a theoretical level, we can take $b_1 = -b_1^* = b_3$ and $b_1' = -b_1^{*'} = b_3'$, we obtain from (11.21)

$$\Lambda = \frac{BT}{H_{-1}} + b_0 + b_2 \Delta \log y + b_2^* \Delta \log y^*$$
$$+ (b_1 + b_1')[r_{-1} - (r_{-1}^* - (\log E - \log E^e))]$$

The variables entering Λ are the balance of trade and variables entering the capital-flows equation: domestic and foreign real income, and the possible flow effect, which occurs if $b_1 \neq -b_1'$.

should add, however, that ΔSP may be statistically endogenous for the estimation if it is a function of BT/H_{-1}, $\Delta \log y$, or $\Delta \log p$. In this case, a model without speculative variables may not give consistent estimates, even when 2SLS are used.[13] But if this inconsistency results, then, as appendix 2 demonstrates, it is likely that the bias of $\hat{b}_1$ is negative and decreases with sterilization. Consequently, the corresponding estimate will overestimate the independence of monetary policy. On the other hand, it is also likely that the bias of $\hat{a}$ is negative and increases with sterilization. Consequently, the corresponding estimate will underestimate the independence of monetary policy. It is also likely that $\hat{A}$ will not be biased. Finally, the third case concerns "endogenous" expectations. In this situation ΔSP is a function of the variables which are solutions of the model. Take the case

$$(11.23) \qquad SP = d_0 + d_1 \frac{BP}{H_{-1}}, \qquad d_1 \geq 0,$$

$$= d_0 + d_1 \frac{CF}{H_{-1}} + d_1 \frac{BT}{H_{-1}}.$$

If we substitute in equation (11.3), all the coefficients of this equation are divided by $(1 - b_3 d_1)$ and the variables $(b_3 d_1 (BT/H_{-1}))$ and $(-b_3 d_1 (BP/H_{-1})_{-1})$ are added. The model without speculative variables can then be considered as a structural model wherein all coefficients of equation (11.3) are higher in absolute value (we suppose $0 < 1 - b_3 d_1 < 1$), and where the variables $(b_3 d_1 (BT/H_{-1}))$ and $(-b_3 d_1 (BP/H_{-1})_{-1})$ are left out. Two kinds of biases will result. First, all estimates will tend to underestimate the independence of monetary policy. Second, because of the omitted variables, we will also have biases similar to those resulting from omitted exogenous variables. The two biases work in opposite directions for $\hat{b}_1$.

In order to measure exchange-rate expectations, we have taken into account the possibility that exchange-rate expectations might be endogenous and have used the balance of payments as an explanatory variable. For countries which did not devalue or revalue, the forward premium is regressed on the current balance of payments (scaled by nominal income). For countries which had a change in the value of the peg, a Tobit procedure is used in which both the probability of a change and the size of the change vary with the balance of payments. The exchange-rate expectation arrived at by the Tobit procedure is approximated by a linear

---

13. The problem may arise partly because we are not using an infinite sample size. Then, as in the white noise case, ΔSP may not be asymptotically correlated with the instrument set. However, for our finite sample size, there may be some correlation because the number of observations is not much larger than the number of instruments. The argument is indeed true for any residual of the system, but we consider that the variance of the capital-flows equation may be greatly increased if we leave out speculative variables.

function of both the level and the square of the value of the balance of payments (scaled by nominal income).[14]

11.2 Offsetting Capital Flows

Our model is estimated using quarterly data. Unless specified otherwise, the periods of estimation are 1957I–71II for the United Kingdom, France, Italy, and Japan; 1957I–71I for Germany and the Netherlands; and 1962III–70I for Canada. Estimation is by 2SLS. The endogenous variables are $\Delta \log M$, r, CF/H_{-1}, BP/H_{-1}, DDM, BT/H_{-1}, $\Delta \log y$, $\Delta \log p$, and $(\log E - \log E^e)$. Details on the instrument list and data are given in appendix 1.

In this section we will estimate the offset coefficient a. The two estimates presented are consistent if there are no specification errors. The first estimate is derived from the structural coefficients estimates. Using (11.13), the estimate is $-\hat{b}_1/(\hat{b}_1 - \hat{a}_1)$, where, as defined in section 1, $\hat{b}_1$ is the coefficient of the domestic rate of interest in the structural capital-flow equation and where $\hat{a}_1$ is the coefficient of the (domestic) interest rate in the money demand equation. The second estimate is obtained by regressing the semireduced-form equation (11.12) and taking the estimate $\hat{a}$ of the coefficient of the variable $(DDM + (BT/H_{-1}) - \Delta \log p)$. Two alternative specifications of the model have been examined. In the first model, speculative variables are excluded while in the second model, these speculative variables are introduced in the capital-flow equations. We will present the results for the money demand equation, structural capital-flow equation, and semireduced-form capital-flow equation.

The money demand equation is presented in table 11.1.[15] In this equation, the interest-rate coefficient has the right sign and in most cases is significantly different from zero at the 5% or 10% level. The lowest t statistic occurs in the equation for Italy, maybe because it was the only country for which a long-term interest rate was used. For four countries, the absolute values of these estimates fall between 0.35 and 0.7. The estimates for Canada and the Netherlands are a little higher at 1.5. Japan stands out as an exceptional case with a coefficient close to -12. The peculiar kind of interest rate used in Japan probably accounts for this

14. In these countries numerous and important "speculative episodes" occurred. By introducing the square of the value of the balance of payments, we can reduce the weight of these observations. Therefore such exchange-rate expectations variables could also be justified even if expectations were "exogenous."

The countries which devalued or revalued are the U.K., France, Germany, and the Netherlands. These expectation functions were preliminary versions of those described in chapter 5 for the Mark III International Transmission Model. They differ, however, from the ones finally used in the estimation of the Mark III Model. One difference consists in the use in these last series of $|BP/Y|(BP/Y)$, instead of $(BP/Y)^2$, which is more correct if the sign of the balance of payments changed during the period.

15. In table 11.1, the variable $(\log E - \log E^e)_{-1}$ does not belong to the instrumental variables. When we included this variable, we obtained almost identical results.

Table 11.1   Money Demand Equation

	Constant	$\Delta \log \left(\frac{M}{P}\right)_{-1}$	Δr	$\Delta \log y$	S.E.E.	$\bar{R}^2$	D-W
UK	-0.001	0.069	-0.685	0.146	0.0213	0.043	2.11
	(0.003)	(0.140)	(0.530)	(0.292)			
	-0.246	0.494	-1.292	0.500			
CA	0.003	0.141	-1.462	0.231	0.0105	0.331	1.76
	(0.004)	(0.162)	(0.374)	(0.241)			
	0.891	0.873	-3.910	0.958			
FR	0.005	0.735	-0.455	-0.074	0.0122	0.536	2.04
	(0.002)	(0.091)	(0.242)	(0.103)			
	2.123	8.048	-1.879	-0.721			
GE	0.006	0.193	-0.421	0.484	0.0119	0.191	2.30
	(0.003)	(0.118)	(0.226)	(0.151)			
	1.978	1.626	-1.861	3.217			
IT	0.016	0.142	-0.355	0.372	0.0163	0.045	1.94
	(0.004)	(0.131)	(0.807)	(0.218)			
	3.521	1.085	-0.440	1.708			
JA	0.024	0.195	-12.070	-0.071	0.0171	0.321	1.74
	(0.005)	(0.144)	(3.514)	(0.210)			
	4.28	1.354	-3.435	-0.339			
NE	0.001	-0.002	-1.446	0.724	0.0173	0.136	1.96
	(0.004)	(0.138)	(0.709)	(0.232)			
	0.357	-0.013	-2.041	3.124			

Note. In all tables we give the estimate of the coefficient, its standard error (in parentheses), and the t statistic.

unusual figure. Instead of the three-month treasury bill or money market rate we used for five other countries, for Japan we used a short-term bank-loan rate. This rate is much less volatile, and consequently a small change here may be comparable to larger swings in the rates used for other countries.[16]

In this money demand equation, real income is found to be significant and of the right sign in three cases. Its elasticity is less than 1. Since the equation is run in the first difference form, we can consider that the constant is a proxy for the variation of permanent income and that therefore the coefficient of $\Delta \log y$ is a transitory income elasticity. The lagged value of the dependent variable is not significant, except in the equation for France. The overall fit is not very high, and for some countries it is low. But the regressions are in the first difference form. In levels the R^2 would have been much higher.[17]

When no speculative variables are introduced, results of the capital-flow equations are on the whole unsatisfactory. Overall fits of structural capital-flow equations are very poor for most countries. For three countries, the United Kingdom, France, and Japan, the $\hat{b}_1$ coefficients of the current interest-rate variable have the wrong sign, significantly so in the case of the United Kingdom and France, as seen in table 11.2. Consequently, for these countries, the structural estimates of the offset coefficient do not fall between -1 and 0 (see table 11.2). Also, as table 11.2 shows, there is a large difference between the structural estimates and the reduced-form estimates of the offset coefficients. While reduced-form estimates indicate an almost complete offsetting, structural estimates give a lower degree of offsetting or no offsetting at all. This result is consistent with the analysis of left out speculative variables of section 1. This emphasizes the error we can make if, in that case, we only consider one type of estimates.

---

16. If we multiply these values by the mean values of the interest rates during the periods of estimation, we can interpret these coefficients in terms of elasticities. We obtain -0.037 for the United Kingdom, -0.073 for Canada, -0.024 for France, -0.020 for Germany, -0.021 for Italy, -0.950 for Japan, and -0.052 for the Netherlands. The Japanese elasticity is by far the highest. However, as we mentioned (footnote 7), the standard deviation of the Japanese interest rate is the smallest (0.0038) and the mean is the largest (0.0787). Therefore the ratio (mean/standard deviation) of the Japanese interest rate is much higher than are those for any of the other countries: for Japan, this ratio is 20.7; for the other countries, the standard deviations are around 0.016, except for Italy, and the means are around 0.05, which gives a ratio of 3.1. (The variance of the Italian interest rate is smaller (0.008), and the corresponding ratio is 7.1.) Then, if we multiply the Japanese elasticity by (3.1/20.7), we obtain a value of -0.142. This interest-rate elasticity is still high in absolute value, but it is not so far afield of those of the other countries.

17. Also, in the MABP equation the $\bar{R}^2$ is quite high. This equation is actually a money demand equation, where the variable on the left-hand side is $\Delta R/H_{-1}$ and where, on the right-hand side, we have $\Delta D/H_{-1}$, $\Delta \log p$, and the money demand variables. But, as explained in Laskar (1981), the quality of the fit of this equation has no immediate interpretation.

Table 11.2   **Offset Coefficients**

	$\hat{a}_1$	$\hat{b}_1$	$\hat{b}_1^s$	$-\hat{b}_1(\hat{b}_1-\hat{a}_1)$	$-\hat{b}_1^s(\hat{b}_1^s-\hat{a}_1)$	$\hat{a}$	$\hat{a}^s$
UK	-0.685	-4.483	0.176	-1.180	-0.204	-0.892	-0.346
	(0.530)	(1.546)	(0.941)			(0.069)	(0.124)
	-1.292	-2.900	0.187			-12.994	-2.794
CA	-1.462	7.489	7.439	-0.837	-0.836	-0.936	-0.910
	(0.374)	(2.146)	(2.763)			(0.050)	(0.056)
	-3.910	3.489	2.692			-18.796	-16.340
FR	-0.455	-1.197	0.382	0.764	-0.456	-0.886	-0.673
	(0.242)	(0.619)	(0.419)			(0.064)	(0.082)
	-1.879	-1.933	0.913			-13.934	-8.191
GE	-0.421	3.064	3.377	-0.879	-0.889	-0.990	-0.880
	(0.226)	(1.810)	(1.246)			(0.040)	(0.051)
	-1.861	1.693	2.710			-24.585	-17.346
IT	-0.355	2.155	2.293	-0.859	-0.866	-0.635	-0.618
	(0.807)	(1.217)	(1.074)			(0.120)	(0.105)
	-0.440	1.770	2.134			-5.304	-5.866
JA	-12.070	-1.979	9.573	0.196	-0.442	-0.811	-0.518
	(3.514)	(6.341)	(3.188)			(0.114)	(0.082)
	-3.435	-0.312	3.002			-7.095	-6.292
NE	-1.446	5.560	5.151	-0.794	-0.781	-0.879	-0.782
	(0.709)	(2.294)	(1.946)			(0.067)	(0.058)
	-2.041	2.424	2.647			-13.195	-13.394

Note. The index s indicates that the coefficients are estimated in a model in which speculative variables are introduced.

The model with speculative variables is more satisfactory, and the full results are given in tables 11.3 and 11.4. Overall fits of structural capital-flow equations are improved. Most interest-rate coefficients have the right sign. All coefficients of the current interest rate are positive,[18] and except those of the United Kingdom and France, they are all significant. In the case of four countries, the United Kingdom, France, Germany, and Japan, the current speculative variable enters significantly and with the right sign. For the other countries the speculative variables do not enter in a meaningful way and, especially for the Netherlands, they even enter significantly with the wrong sign. For this last country the expectation variable we take may be inadequate. However, for these three countries results were quite satisfactory in the model without speculative variables, as table 11.2 indicates. Actually, these results are not much changed when we add our speculative variables, which, as noted, do not enter in a meaningful way. Finally, note that for most countries the coefficient of the current interest-rate variable has a higher absolute value than the coefficient of the lagged variable, which suggests that a flow effect exists.

The semireduced-form capital-flow equations are presented in table 11.4. As can be seen, the absolute values of the offset coefficient are lower than those obtained in the model without speculative variables. The difference is quite large for the U.K.: 0.346 instead of 0.892. For each country except Canada, the offset coefficient is significantly different from -1, at the 5% level. The pattern of the speculative variables coefficients is the same as that of the structural equation, but, as expected, they are smaller because in equation (11.12) they are multiplied by $(-a_1/(b_1 - a_1))$.

A comparison of the offset coefficients obtained can be seen in table 11.2. When the speculative variables are added, all coefficients $\hat{b}_1$ are positive. Therefore the corresponding offset coefficients have values between (-1) and 0 (see column 5). For all countries except Italy and Germany, these offset coefficients $(-(\hat{b}_1^s/(\hat{b}_1^s - \hat{a}_1)))$ are still lower than the ones we get from the semireduced form $(\hat{a}^s)$. However, the difference between them is not large. Especially in the cases of the four countries for which the speculative variables entered significantly, the United Kingdom, France, Germany, and Japan, the difference is actually much smaller than the one we observed in the model without speculative variables. There are two reasons for this finding. First, the coefficients $\hat{b}_1$

18. In the interpretation of the magnitude of the domestic interest-rate coefficients of the equation of Japan, we should have in mind the peculiar rate of interest used for this country (see footnote 16 above). The value of the coefficient of r is large (9.5), but, in fact, the implied capital mobility may not be high: if we try to "correct" this value, multiplying it by the ratio of the standard deviation of the Japanese interest rate divided by the standard deviation of the other countries' interest rates (0.0038/0.016) (see footnote 16 above), then we obtain a value of 2.26.

are higher, especially for Japan and the United Kingdom. Consequently, a greater amount of offsetting is implied. Second, the offset coefficients estimated from the semireduced form are smaller in absolute value for all countries but more importantly for these four countries. Again, these results are consistent with the analysis of biases due to speculative variables of section 11.1.

The estimates of the offset coefficients we obtain indicate that capital flows do not completely offset any change in the domestic component of the money supply. Actually, using the reduced-form estimates, the hypothesis of complete offsetting is rejected at the 5% level for six of the countries and at the 10% level for Canada. The highest offset coefficients in absolute value are those for Canada and Germany, which are around -0.9. The coefficient of the Netherlands is also high in absolute value, around -0.8. The offset coefficient for France is between -0.67 and -0.45, for Japan between -0.50 and -0.40. The offset coefficient of the United Kingdom seems comparatively quite low in absolute value, between -0.35 and -0.20.[19] Italy presents a special case. The offset coefficient calculated from the structural estimates is lower than the estimate given by the semireduced form, even in the model without speculative variables. The values are -0.86 and -0.63, respectively. The use of a long-term interest rate may have caused this peculiar finding. We can note that these intercountry differences make sense because France and Japan seemed to rely more on capital controls than Canada or Germany did.

Even if the offset coefficients are different from -1, their absolute values may still be thought to be "high," especially for some countries. However, a value of the offset coefficient which is not equal to zero actually means that some monetary policy has a cost in terms of undesired reserves. Therefore, in order to interpret the magnitude of the offset coefficient, we should consider this cost. To illustrate the point, suppose that we start from an equilibrium situation where all countries have the same rate of inflation as the U.S., say 6%. Now suppose that one of these countries wants to decrease its inflation rate to 4%. If the offset coefficient of this country is equal to -0.5, which may be the case for France or Japan, then there would be an implied gain of reserves equal to 0.5% of high-powered money within the quarter.[20] However, if the offset

19. However, the coefficient of the U.S. interest-rate variables in the structural capital-flow equation might suggest a higher absolute value for the offset coefficient of the U.K. The coefficients of r^{US} and r^{US}_{-1} are -1.56 and 1.65, respectively. They are both significantly different from 0 at the 5% level. If we take a value of 1.6 for b_1 (this may be justified because the U.K. and U.S. interest rates used are quite homogenous in their definitions), then the implied offset coefficient is -0.70. I do not see an explanation of the discrepancy between this value and the other lower values found.

20. From (11.14) the variation in domestic credit required to produce a variation δ in the money supply growth rate is equal to $\delta/(1 + a)$. Therefore the variation in reserves is equal to $[a/(1 + a)]\delta$. Here $\delta = \pm0.5\%$ ($\pm2\%$ at an annual rate).

Table 11.3   Structural Capital-Flow Equation (Speculative Variables Added)

	UK	CA	FR	GE	IT	JA	NE
Coefficients							
Constant	.081	.129	−.010	−.046	−.017	−.003	−.010
	(.017)	(.046)	(.009)	(.026)	(.026)	(.089)	(.023)
	4.72	2.830	−1.073	−1.722	−.669	−.031	−.421
r	.176	7.439	.382	3.377	2.293	9.573	5.151
	(.941)	(2.763)	(.419)	(1.246)	(1.074)	(3.188)	(1.946)
	.187	2.692	.913	2.710	2.134	3.002	2.647
r_{-1}	.037	−2.979	−.046	−1.204	−1.119	−9.341	−3.226
	(.697)	(2.136)	(.374)	(1.050)	(1.083)	(3.313)	(1.757)
	.053	−1.395	−.122	−1.147	−1.033	−2.820	−1.836
r^{US}	−1.557	−7.689	−.001	−5.118	−.789	−.355	−3.757
	(.688)	(3.163)	(.496)	(1.538)	(.537)	(.459)	(1.243)
	−2.263	−2.004	−.002	−3.328	−1.468	−.772	−3.024
r^{US}_{-1}	1.652	1.843	.351	2.833	−.629	−.363	3.219
	(.771)	(3.163)	(.541)	(1.626)	(.535)	(.448)	(1.294)
	2.143	.583	.650	1.742	−1.175	−.810	2.487

$\Delta \log y$	.162	1.088	−.333	.276	−.196	.131	−.729
	(.323)	(1.189)	(.222)	(.637)	(.255)	(.208)	(.654)
	.502	.916	−1.499	.432	−.768	.629	−1.115
$\Delta \log y^R$	.694	−3.697	.134	2.185	−.415	−.044	1.377
	(.492)	(1.922)	(.379)	(1.064)	(.379)	(.360)	(.944)
	1.409	−1.923	.354	2.054	1.094	−.122	1.459
$4(\log E - \log E^e)$	10.850	−.659	.683	2.227	−.634	4.203	−17.864
	(1.269)	(.703)	(.127)	(.565)	(.227)	(.449)	(4.941)
	8.550	−.938	5.386	3.939	−2.790	9.536	−3.615
$4(\log E_{-1} - \log E^e_{-1})$	1.019	.126	.036	−1.791	−.254	−.221	3.718
	(1.131)	(.777)	(.090)	(.417)	(.206)	(.441)	(4.308)
	.901	.163	.406	−4.292	−1.232	−.500	.863
S.E.E.	.0228	.0435	.0167	.0470	.0172	.0155	.0377
$\bar{R}^2$	.843	.289	.650	.550	.587	.795	.499
D-W	1.65	1.39	1.47	1.87	1.92	1.45	1.45

Table 11.4 Semireduced-Form Capital-Flow Equation (Speculative Variables Added)

	UK	CA	FR	GE	IT	JA	NE
Coefficient							
Constant	.060	.013	.001	.014	.017	−.009	.016
	(.015)	(.016)	(.007)	(.009)	(.021)	(.065)	(.009)
	4.015	.779	.141	1.691	.837	−.131	1.824
$DDM+BT/H_{-1}-$ $\Delta \log P$	−.346	−.910	−.673	−.880	−.618	−.518	−.782
	(.124)	(.056)	(.082)	(.051)	(.105)	(.082)	(.058)
	−2.794	−16.340	−8.191	−17.346	−5.866	−6.292	−13.394
$\Delta \log\left(\dfrac{M}{P}\right)_{-1}$	−.057	.042	.404	−.045	.015	.155	−.128
	(.134)	(.216)	(.114)	(.171)	(.119)	(.090)	(.115)
	−.428	.194	3.558	−.264	.124	1.711	−1.112
r_{-1}	−.176	.491	.022	−.045	.134	.299	.424
	(.323)	(.464)	(.136)	(.170)	(.345)	(.726)	(.230)
	−.546	1.059	.162	−.266	.389	.411	1.843
r^{US}	−.828	−1.269	−.201	−.521	−.192	−.274	−.061
	(.574)	(.634)	(.283)	(.407)	(.381)	(.334)	(.431)
	−1.442	−2.004	−.710	−1.281	−.503	−.819	−.119

	(1)	(2)	(3)	(4)	(5)	(6)	(7)
r^{US}_{-1}	1.122	.593	.339	.319	-.136	-.034	-.082
	(.596)	(.749)	(.307)	(.444)	(.425)	(.325)	(.507)
	1.881	.792	1.106	.719	-.320	-.104	-.161
$\Delta \log y$	.124	-.040	-.134	.486	.186	-.013	.502
	(.237)	(.325)	(.129)	(.171)	(.200)	(.157)	(.257)
	.521	-.123	-1.043	2.840	.929	-.086	1.952
$\Delta \log yR$	.612	.399	.483	.122	-.047	-.108	.017
	(.357)	(.608)	(.219)	(.298)	(.283)	(.254)	(.364)
	1.716	.655	2.205	.422	-.167	-.423	.048
$4(\log E - \log E^e)$	7.153	-.285	.198	.597	-.478	2.353	-7.079
	(1.604)	(.187)	(.089)	(.195)	(.173)	(.416)	(1.997)
	4.458	-1.519	2.220	3.068	-2.755	5.661	-3.545
$4(\log E_{-1} - \log E^e_{-1})$	.724	-.103	.075	-.367	-.246	.110	-.890
	(.723)	(.186)	(.051)	(.127)	(.154)	(.343)	(1.997)
	1.002	-.556	1.467	-2.895	-1.596	.322	-.542
S.E.E.	.0170	.0115	.0095	.0125	.0127	.0112	.0135
$\bar{R}^2$	.913	.950	.887	.968	.774	.892	.935
D-W	1.85	1.60	1.86	2.07	2.10	1.67	2.13

coefficient were equal to -0.9, as in Canada or Germany, then the gain in reserves would be equal to 4.5% of high-powered money. We would have the opposite loss of reserves if the desired inflation rate were equal to 8%. These illustrative numbers may explain why countries like France, Japan, and the United Kingdom were able to have inflation rates which were different from that of the U.S., while Canada and Germany seemed to have inflation rates similar to that of the U.S. However, in order to be able to interpret what happened, we must also take into account the weight the central banks attribute to undesired losses or gains of reserves. Sterilization behavior takes this aspect into account.

11.3 Sterilization Behavior

In this section we focus on the estimation of the sterilization coefficient. As defined in section 11.1, equation (11.10), the sterilization coefficient is $c = -(1 - k)$, where k is the coefficient of the current balance-of-payments variable BP/H_{-1} in the money supply reaction function. Here we will estimate the money supply reaction function (11.4) and then briefly consider alternative specifications.

The estimates[21] of the coefficients of the balance-of-payments variables of the money supply reaction function are given in table 11.5. Contemporaneous sterilization is high for all countries, and the hypothesis of no sterilization is always rejected at the 5% level. All the sterilization coefficients are close to -1 and only in two cases, Germany and the Netherlands, does money supply respond to the current balance-of-payments variable BP/H_{-1} in a significant way. But even in these cases, almost 90% of the effect of the balance of payments on the money supply is sterilized.[22]

Money supply seems to respond more significantly to past changes of the balance of payments. The coefficient of the level of reserves over high-powered money of the last quarter $(R/H)_{-1}$ is positive for all countries except France, where it is negative but not significant. For Italy, Japan, and the Netherlands, this positive response is significant at the 5% level. The value of the coefficient is around 0.1 for Italy and the Netherlands and 0.2 for Japan. Individual coefficients of the lagged balance-of-payments variables are not significantly different from zero at the 5% level except the coefficient of the lagged variable by 3 or 4 in the German equation. At a lower level of significance (20%), these variables produce a positive effect in the equations for France and the United Kingdom, and

---

21. Here, the instruments used for the 2SLS estimation contain the lagged speculative variable $(\log E - \log E^e)_{-1}$.

22. For Canada, France, and Italy the estimates indicate a slight oversterilization, which may be unlikely; the sterilization coefficient is, however, not significantly different from -1.

Table 11.5   **Money Supply Reaction Function Equation (Coefficients of Balance-of-Payments Variables Only)**
Dependent Variable = $\Delta \log M$

	BP/H_{-1}	$(R/H)_{-1}$	LBP1	LBP3	S.E.E.	$\bar{R}^2$	D-W
UK	0.040 (0.062) 0.650	0.079 (0.073) 1.082	0.018 (0.027) 0.681	0.038 (0.023) 1.628	0.0161	0.180	2.07
CA	-0.103 (0.207) -0.500	-0.0233 (0.125) -0.187	0.077 (0.045) 1.704	0.013 (0.052) 0.252	0.0131	-0.063	2.58
FR	-0.014 (0.080) -0.179	0.015 (0.030) 0.494	0.057 (0.037) 1.547	0.005 (0.044) 0.116	0.0086	0.599	1.99
GE	0.113 (0.030) 3.758	0.033 (0.023) 1.422	-0.004 (0.015) -0.290	0.054 (0.019) 2.781	0.0077	0.565	2.14
IT	-0.234 (0.205) -1.137	0.093 (0.045) 2.063	0.099 (0.100) 0.984	-0.052 (0.093) -0.555	0.0141	0.038	1.95
JA	0.127 (0.098) 1.294	0.196 (0.066) 2.957	-0.019 (0.065) -0.295	0.008 (0.050) 0.159	0.0129	0.588	1.72
NE	0.152 (0.063) 2.404	0.106 (0.039) 2.685	-0.060 (0.034) -1.753	-0.054 (0.040) -1.753	0.0118	0.297	2.60

a negative effect for the Netherlands. The fits of the equations for Canada and Italy are very poor, and that for the United Kingdom is also quite poor. Other equations show a better fit.

The sterilization coefficient may be sensitive to alternative specifications of the reaction function, especially when these alternative specifications concern the balance-of-payments variables. Therefore we experimented with a variety of such reaction function specifications.[23] The results indicate that we have to modify our previous findings for three countries: Japan, Italy, and the Netherlands. The corresponding reaction functions are given in table 11.6. For Japan, the distinction between surpluses and deficits is found to be relevant. For Italy and the Netherlands, the current and lagged balance-of-trade variables are substituted for the lagged balance-of-payments variables.

Clearly, contemporaneous sterilization of reserve flows exists and is important in all the countries studied. However, the behavior of each country is different. In the United Kingdom, Canada, and France, sterilization appears to be complete. The hypothesis of full sterilization is not rejected, and the estimates of the sterilization coefficient are very close to -1. In Germany, 89% of reserve flows are sterilized. In Japan, sterilization behavior toward deficits is not the same as toward surpluses. Only 50% of deficits are sterilized while sterilization of surpluses is complete. For the Netherlands, several specifications are acceptable. However, the values of the estimates are not the same in these alternative specifications. The values found for this coefficient range from -0.85 to -0.95. Although most specifications indicate that Italy's reserve flows are completely sterilized, the best fit obtained shows that only 66% of them are sterilized. Although the estimate is somewhat imprecise, it allows us to reject the hypothesis of full sterilization at the 10% level.

11.4 Independence of Monetary Policy

In this section, we present estimates of coefficient A, which was defined in section 11.1, equation (11.16). This coefficient is regarded as an

---

23. The results of these experimentations are presented in detail in Laskar (1981). One of the findings is that three countries, the United Kingdom, Canada, and France, let their money supply respond to speculative capital flows, while they completely sterilized the other components of the balance of payments. Note that this finding eliminates some inconsistencies in our results. Otherwise, the complete sterilization of reserve flows in France, and almost complete one in the United Kingdom, that we found in this section would have been inconsistent with the findings of section 11.3. There, we found that left-out speculative variables produced a negative bias in the estimates b_1. But, theoretically, at least under the assumptions explicated in appendix 2, such a bias cannot exist if sterilization is complete. Finally, we note that sterilization of speculative capital flows is irrelevant for the issue of independence of monetary policy considered here, because we take exchange-rate expectations as given in the analysis.

Table 11.6   **Other Specifications of the Reaction Function:**
Equations of Japan, Italy, and the Netherlands

a) Equations of Japan

$$1) \left(\frac{BP}{H_{-1}}\right)^{-} \text{ added } \left(\frac{BP}{H_{-1}}\right)^{-} = \frac{BP}{H_{-1}} \text{ if } \frac{BP}{H_{-1}} < 0 \text{ and } 0 \text{ otherwise}$$

$\left(\dfrac{BP}{H_{-1}}\right)^{-}$	$\dfrac{BP}{H_{-1}}$	$\left(\dfrac{R}{H}\right)_{-1}$	LBP1	LBP3
0.767	−0.159	0.363	−0.072	−0.033
(0.240)	(0.128)	(0.081)	(0.063)	(0.048)
3.193	−1.243	4.494	−1.144	−0.689

S.E.E. = 0.0120 $\bar{R}^2$ = 0.644   D-W = 248

$$2) \left(\frac{BP}{H_{-1}}\right)^{-} \quad \begin{array}{c}\text{and lagged values} \\ \text{LBPM1 and LBPM3 added}\end{array} \quad \left(\text{LBPM1} = \left(\frac{BP}{H_{-1}}\right)^{-}_{-1} + \left(\frac{BP}{H_{-1}}\right)^{-}_{-2}\right)$$

$\left(\dfrac{BP}{H_{-1}}\right)^{-}$	$\dfrac{BP}{H_{-1}}$	$\left(\dfrac{R}{H}\right)_{-1}$	LBPM1	LBPM3	LBP1	LBP3
0.447	−0.021	0.310	0.020	0.139	−0.055	−0.100
(0.174)	(0.106)	(0.068)	(0.103)	(0.107)	(0.085)	(0.077)
2.577	−0.200	4.566	0.199	1.298	−0.644	−1.292

S.E.E. = 0.0117 $\bar{R}^2$ = 0.665   D-W = 2.35
(OLS estimates)

b) Equations of Italy and the Netherlands

	$\dfrac{BP}{H_{-1}}$	$\dfrac{R}{H_{-1}}$	$\dfrac{BT}{H_{-1}}$	LBT1	LBT3	S.E.E.	$\bar{R}^2$	D-W
IT	0.344	0.018	−0.102	−0.072	0.302	0.0119	0.311	2.06
	(0.192)	(0.038)	(0.208)	(0.116)	(0.104)			
	1.795	0.472	−0.493	−0.623	2.908			
NE	0.045	0.025	0.167	−0.051	0.017	0.0106	0.439	2.40
	(0.050)	(0.033)	(0.079)	(0.035)	(0.035)			
	0.896	0.742	2.119	−1.459	0.488			

indicator of the independence of monetary policy within the period. Its value should be between 0 and 1. A value equal to 0 indicates that no independence of monetary policy exists, while complete independence is obtained when its value is equal to 1. From equation (11.16), we have $A = (1 + a)/(1 - ac)$. Therefore, with the results obtained in the previous two chapters, we can give estimates of this coefficient. Alternatively, we can also regress the money stock reduced-form equation (11.15) and take the estimated coefficient $\hat{A}$ of the variable $\hat{G}_3$, the estimated objective of monetary policy obtained from the regression of the money supply reaction function.[24] The results obtained when the standard specification of the model is used appear in table 11.7. We consider both cases in which speculative variables are introduced and cases in which they are added to the model.[25]

The results found for the estimates $\hat{A}$ show the existence of a large degree of independence in monetary policy. At the 5% level, all coefficients are significantly different from zero and none is significantly different from 1. We can compare the estimates $\hat{A}$ with the estimates of the first two columns. According to our findings about the biases caused by omitted speculative variables, values in columns 1 and 2 are likely to be higher and lower, respectively, than the values of column 3, especially in the model without speculative variables. In the model with speculative variables the three estimates should be close.[26] This is verified in the cases of the United Kingdom, Canada, France, and Japan. For the first three countries, the estimates $\hat{A}$ are close to 1, which is consistent with the results of complete sterilization found for these countries.[27] For Japan, all these estimates in the model with speculative variables indicate a value of 0.9 for coefficient A. However, we do not find the expected pattern for these three estimates in the other three countries. In the case of Italy, the estimated coefficient $\hat{A}$ has a value around 0.7, although in the standard specification sterilization is estimated to be complete. For the Netherlands and Germany, the $\hat{A}$ estimates are higher than the other two estimates.

It is important to evaluate how the results obtained from other specifications of the reaction function in section 11.3 modify our previous findings. Then, for Italy and the Netherlands, we find estimates which are not far from the values of the estimates of $\hat{A}$.[28] For Italy, if we use the

24. This regression bears some resemblance to the one considered by Darby (1980). But some differences exist. First, we can take the domestic price as given; second, we specify an alternative model. Therefore we add the "other factors" which "also play a role in determining the balance of payments" (p. 6) under the alternative model considered here. Darby's purpose was to see whether he could reject the null hypothesis of no independence of monetary policy implied by the MABP rather than to estimate a coefficient which would measure this independence.

25. According to the previous findings, the model with speculative variables should give more correct results for the United Kingdom, France, Germany, and Japan, while the model without speculative variables may give satisfactory results for Canada and the Netherlands. For Italy, no model seems to work really well.

26. These statements assume that there are no other specification errors than left-out speculative variables. Therefore these statements may not be verified if the money supply reaction function is incorrectly specified.

27. For the United Kingdom the estimated coefficient $\hat{c}$ is slightly less than 1 in absolute value (-0.96). Also, we saw in section 11.2, footnote 19, that in the model with a speculative variable the offset coefficient may be higher in absolute value (-0.7) than the one given by $\hat{b}_1/(\hat{a}_1 - \hat{b}_1)$ or $\hat{a}$. Taking the same sterilization coefficient as before (-0.96), the implied value for A is 0.91, which is still high.

28. However, if that new specification is correct, the values of A in the tables may not be good estimators because $\hat{G}_3$ is not the same.

Table 11.7 **Estimates of the Independence of Monetary Policy**

	Model without Speculative Variable			Model with Speculative Variable		
	Structural Estimate (1)	Semireduced-Form Estimate (2)	$\hat{A}$ (3)	Structural Estimate (1)	Semireduced-Form Estimate (2)	$\hat{A}$ (3)
UK	1	0.752	0.946 (0.192) 4.920	0.990	0.979	1.040 (0.227) 4.591
CA	1	1	0.983 (0.368) 2.671	1	1	1.083 (0.381) 2.843
FR	1	1	0.984 (0.298) 3.303	1	1	1.405 (0.351) 4.001
GE	0.549	0.082	0.760 (0.217) 3.503	0.525	0.547	0.920 (0.193) 4.771
IT	1	1	0.720 (0.187) 3.857	1	1	0.666 (0.255) 2.610
JA	1	0.647	0.876 (0.213) 4.103	0.909	0.880	0.890 (0.214) 4.162
NE	0.631	0.475	0.879 (0.217) 0.043	0.648	0.647	0.987 (0.221) 4.476

Note. A value equal to 1 has been put in columns 1 and 2 whenever the sterilization coefficient is more than 1 in absolute value or when coefficient b_1 is negative. Then full independence of monetary policy is obtained because either sterilization is complete or offsetting capital flows do not exist.

estimate $\hat{c}$, which is equal to -0.656, given by the improved specification, we obtain other estimates of A in columns 1 and 2 of the tables. In the model with speculative variables these values are 0.310 and 0.642, respectively. Therefore, in Italy, the independence of monetary policy may not be vary large, although the results are imprecise and questionable. For the Netherlands, the higher degree of sterilization given by the estimate of table 11.6 ($\hat{c} = -0.955$) implies an estimate of A equal to 0.85 (for that we use an offset coefficient equal to -0.8, given by the empirical analysis of section 11.2). From this value we can conclude that even in a small open economy like the Netherlands, monetary policy may have a large independence. Finally, we found that the money supply of Japan does not respond to surpluses but strongly reacts to deficits. Consequently, we have to distinguish between an expansionary and a restrictive monetary policy. The objective of a restrictive policy is realized but not that of an expansionary policy. With an offsetting coefficient[29] equal to -0.45 and a sterilization coefficient of deficits equal to -0.5, the estimated value for A is 0.71.

The estimates show that a high degree of independence exists in monetary policy during the quarter. With the exception of Italy, where the imprecisions in the estimates of both the offset coefficient and the sterilization coefficient allow a range from 30% to 100%, the countries realize at least 50% of their objectives. In Canada, France, and the United Kingdom, more than 90% of control is obtained. In the Netherlands, from 65% to 85% of the objectives are realized. In Germany, the situation is less clear. Although the offset coefficient and the sterilization coefficient estimates indicate that a control of only 50% exists, the money stock reduced-form estimate suggests a control of 90%. In Japan, on the "average," 90% of the objectives are realized, but, while a restrictive policy may be completely under control, only 70% of an expansionary one may be controlled. The main reasons for these findings are that the almost complete sterilization of reserve flows implies an almost full control for Canada, France, and the United Kingdom. The importance of offsetting capital flows explains the possible comparatively low independence found for Germany.[30] The high "average" degree of independence of Japan is explained by the small amount of offsetting capital flows. Although the estimates concerning the independence of an expansionary

29. However, if such a large difference in sterilization behavior exists, another difference in capital controls might also exist. Consequently the offset coefficient for an expansionary monetary policy might be lower and therefore the independence of an expansionary monetary policy might be higher than the value we give here.

30. In their study of Germany, Herring and Marston (1977a, b) found an offset coefficient equal to -0.78 and a sterilization coefficient equal to -0.913. The implied value for coefficient A is 0.746. There are no differences between their results and ours concerning the estimates of the sterilization coefficient: the value they find is close to the one we take (-0.868) for the estimation of A. However, our estimate of the offset coefficient (-0.88) has a greater absolute value.

monetary policy for the Netherlands and Japan are both around 70%, the two countries are actually very different. In the case of the Netherlands, both offsetting capital flows and sterilization are important. For Japan, both are low.

Our analysis indicates that the substitutability of domestic and foreign assets has not been an insurmountable obstacle to the central banks of the countries we studied. This possibility of short-run independence may explain why inflation rates differed among countries. In that respect most intercountry differences we found make sense. For as we already mentioned in section 11.2, Germany had an inflation rate more like that of the U.S. than France, the U.K., or Japan had. Also, the Netherlands seemed to differ more from the U.S. than Germany did. On the other hand, however, the result of the almost complete independence we obtained for Canada does not seem to be reflected in its observed rate of inflation, because this country had a similar experience to the one of the U.S. Several explanations may account for this discrepancy. First, we must keep in mind the partial and short-run nature of our analysis. Second, the Canadian reaction function is the least satisfactory one we found. It has a negative $\bar{R}^2$ in the standard specification. Therefore the result of complete sterilization may appear doubtful. As the offset coefficient has a high absolute value, the highest one with Germany, even a small response of the money supply to the balance of payments may considerably decrease the independence of monetary policy. Third, relative inflation rates between countries also depend on the monetary objectives of these countries. Because of some other similarities, the monetary objective of Canada may be close to the one of the U.S.

Acknowledgments

The author received valuable suggestions and encouragement from Michael R. Darby during this work. James R. Lothian also made helpful comments on a previous draft of this chapter.

Appendix 1
Instrument List and Data

Instrument List

The instrument set contains all the exogenous variables of the model and some variables used to explain $\log y$, $\log p$, and BT/H_{-1}, which are treated as endogenous variables for the estimation. These variables are

$$\log y_{-1}, \hat{M}_{-1}, \Delta \log p^{\text{US}}, \Delta \log p_{-1},$$

$$\left(\frac{X}{Y}\right)_{-1}, \left(\frac{I}{Y}\right)_{-1}, \log\left(\frac{P_I}{P}\right)_{-1},$$

where $\hat{M}$ is a money innovation $\log M - \log M^e$, X exports, I imports, P_I the import price, and Y nominal income. For five countries, when no speculative variable is included, we have twenty-six variables in the instrument set. For France, we have two more variables: the lagged money stock $\Delta \log M_{-1}$, which is added to the reaction function; and a dummy for 1968II, because of May–June 1968 events. In fact, this last variable never entered significantly in the model. Canada is apart: because of the small number of observations (thirty-five), the balance of trade is treated as exogenous and then the number of instruments is equal to twenty-four. This is actually still high; therefore, for this country, the 2SLS estimates may indeed not be very satisfactory. In the model with speculative variables, one variable, $(\log E - \log E^e)_{-1}$, is added to the instrument list.

Data

The foreign interest rate is the U.S. three-month treasury bill interest rate. The foreign real income is a nominal income weighted average of other countries' real income. In this calculation the U.S. is added to the set of countries considered here. The balance-of-payments definition is the official settlement one. The variation of domestic credit ΔD is defined as $\Delta D = \Delta H - \text{BP}$. Capital flows are defined as $\text{CF} = \text{BP} - \text{BT}$. The money stock is M_1 for the United Kingdom, Canada, Italy, and Japan, and M_2 for France, Germany, and the Netherlands. All data come from the files of the Mark III Model described in chapter 6 or from the basic data bank described in the Data Appendix.

Appendix 2

Biases in Case of Left-out "Exogenous" Speculative Variables

Since we suppose $b_3' = -b_3$, suppose also $b_1' = -b_1$. Then, define G_1' and G_2' such that

$$G_2 = G_2' - b_3\text{SP}_{-1} - b_1 r_{-1},$$
$$G_1 = G_1' - a_1 r_{-1}.$$

Therefore

$$G_1' = a_0 + a_3 \Delta \log\left(\frac{M}{P}\right)_{-1},$$

$$G_2' = b_0 + b_1^* r^* + b_1^{*\prime} r_{-1}^*$$
$$+ b_2 \Delta \log y + b_2^* \Delta \log y^*.$$

Then (11.1) can be written

(11.24) $$\Delta \log\left(\frac{M}{P}\right) = a_1 \Delta r + a_2 \Delta \log y + G_1' + e_1.$$

As we assumed here that $b_1 = -b_1'$ and $b_3 = -b_3'$, equation (11.3) can be written

(11.25) $$\frac{\text{CF}}{H_{-1}} = b_1 \Delta r + b_2 \Delta \log y + b_2 \Delta \text{SP} + G_2' + e_2.$$

Then, eliminating Δr, we obtain the same semireduced-form capital-flows equations as (11.12), where, however, ΔSP is substituted for $(\log E - \log E^e)$, and where G_1' and G_2' have replaced G_1 and G_2, respectively. Then, using the definition of a, we can write

(11.26) $$\frac{\text{CF}}{H_{-1}} = a\left(\text{DDM} + \frac{\text{BT}}{H_{-1}} - \Delta \log p\right) + \alpha \Delta \log y$$
$$+ (1 + a)b_3 \Delta \text{SP} - aG_1' + (1 + a)G_2' + v_1.$$

where $\alpha = (b_1 a_2 - a_1 b_2)/(b_1 - a_1)$ and v_1 is a residual.

Now suppose that, although correlated with the instrument set, ΔSP is not correlated with G_1', G_2', or $\Delta \log y$. Then the direction of the 2SLS asymptotic biases of $\hat{b}_1$ when we estimate the structural capital-flows equation and the direction of $\hat{a}$ when we estimate the semireduced-form one are given by $\text{cov}((\Delta r)^\psi, b_3 \Delta \text{SP})$ and $\text{cov}((\text{DDM})^\psi + (\text{BT}/H_{-1})^\psi) - (\Delta \log p)^\psi, (1 + a)b_3 \Delta \text{SP})$, respectively ($\text{cov}(x, y)$ denotes the covariance of the variables x and y, and $(x)^\psi$ denotes the projection on the instrument set). We can compute these covariances from the reduced forms for Δr and DDM. To obtain the reduced form for Δr, first invert the money demand equation (11.24):

(11.27) $$\Delta r = \frac{1}{a_1} \Delta \log M - \frac{1}{a_1} \Delta \log p$$
$$- \frac{a_2}{a_1} \Delta \log y - \frac{G_1'}{a_1} - \frac{e_1}{a_1}.$$

Then substitute the reduced form for $\Delta \log M$, which is given by equation (11.15). Again, under the assumptions considered here, this equation can be written with ΔSP, G_1', and G_2' substituted for $(\log E - \log E^e)$, G_1 and G_2, respectively. This gives

$$(11.28) \qquad \Delta r = \frac{-1}{b_1 k - a_1} G_3 - \frac{k}{b_1 k - a_1} \frac{BT}{H_{-1}} + \frac{a_2 - kb_2}{b_1 k - a_1} \Delta \log y$$

$$- \frac{k}{b_1 k - a_1} b_3 \Delta SP + \frac{1}{b_1 k - a_1} (G_1' + \Delta \log p)$$

$$- \frac{k}{b_1 k - a_1} G_2 + w_1,$$

where w_1 is a residual. In order to find the reduced form for DDM, write the money supply reaction function under the form

$$(11.29) \qquad DDM = c \frac{CF}{H_{-1}} + c \frac{BT}{H_{-1}} + G_3 + e_3.$$

Then consider $\{(11.26), (11.29)\}$ and, eliminating CF/H_{-1}, solve for DDM:

$$(11.30) \qquad DDM = \frac{a(1 + c)}{1 - ac} \frac{BT}{H_{-1}} + \frac{1}{1 - ac} G_3 - \frac{ac}{1 - ac} \Delta \log p$$

$$+ \frac{ac}{1 - ac} \Delta \log y + \frac{(1 + a)c}{1 - ac} b_3 \Delta SP$$

$$- \frac{ac}{1 - ac} G_1' + \frac{(1 + a)c}{1 - ac} G_2' + w_2.$$

Now, if we consider the special case where ΔSP is not correlated with BT/H_{-1}, $\Delta \log p$ and G_3, then we have, from (11.28):

$$(11.31) \qquad \text{cov}\Big((\Delta r)^\psi, b_3 \Delta SP\Big) = - \frac{k}{b_1 k - a_1} \text{var}\big(b_3 (\Delta SP)^\psi\big).$$

This is negative and is equal to 0 if $k = 0$ (complete sterilization). The coefficient of the interest rate in the structural capital-flow equation will therefore be biased negatively if sterilization is incomplete. The absolute value of the bias increases when sterilization decreases and when the explanatory power of the speculative variable increases. Using the estimate $\hat{b}_1$, we will overestimate the amount of independence of monetary policy.

From (11.30) we have:

$$(11.32) \qquad \text{cov}\Big((DDM)^\psi + \Big(\frac{BT}{H_{-1}}\Big)^\psi - (\Delta \log p)^\psi, (1 + a)b_3 \Delta SP\Big)$$

$$= \frac{(1 + a)^2 c}{1 - ac} \text{var}(b_3 (\Delta SP)^\psi).$$

The covariance is negative. It is 0 if $c = 0$ or $a = -1$. Its absolute value increases when sterilization increases or when the explanatory power of the speculative variable increases.[31] We will therefore overestimate the amount of offsetting capital flows and underestimate monetary control if we use the estimate from the semireduced-form capital-flow equation (11.12). Finally, under the hypothesis there will be no bias in $\hat{A}$ when we estimate the money stock reduced form (11.15)[32] because the left-out variables are not correlated with the variables on the right-hand side.

References

Argy, V., and P. J. K. Kouri. 1974. Sterilization policies and the volatility in international reserves. In R. Z. Aliber, ed., *National monetary policies and the international monetary system*. Chicago: University of Chicago Press.

Chow, G. C. 1966. On the long-run and short-run demand for money. *Journal of Political Economy* 74 (April): 111–31.

Darby, M. R. 1980. Sterilization and monetary control under pegged exchange rates: Theory and evidence. NBER Working Paper, no. 449, February. (Preliminary version of chapter 10.)

Frenkel, J. A., and H. G. Johnson. 1976. *The monetary approach to the balance of payments*. Toronto: University of Toronto Press.

Genberg, A. H. 1976. Aspects of the monetary approach to balance-of-payments theory: An empirical study of Sweden. In J. A. Frenkel and H. G. Johnson, *The monetary approach to the balance of payments*.

Herring, R. J., and R. C. Marston. 1977a. *National monetary policies and international financial markets*. Amsterdam: North-Holland.

———. 1977b. Sterilization policy: The trade off between monetary autonomy and control over foreign exchange reserves. *European Economic Review* 10: 325–43.

Hodjera, Z. 1976. Alternative approaches in the analysis of international

---

31. If we wanted to find the bias, we should multiply by $\text{plim}[(\hat{X}'\hat{X}/T)^{-1}]_{11}$, where X is the right-hand side variables matrix. Note that if $a = 0$, $c = -1$, and $V(b_3(\Delta\text{SP})^\psi)$ is large, $V(\text{DDM}/H_{-1})$ is almost equal to $V(b_3(\Delta\text{SP})^\psi)$. Therefore $\text{plim}[(X'X/T)^{-1}]_{11}$ is almost equal to the inverse of the variance of this variable and the bias is almost equal to -1. Then the true value of a is 0, but $\hat{a}$ is equal to -1.

32. This special case may seem plausible if most of the correlation of ΔSP with the instrument set is due to the small sample size, as noted in footnote 13 above. In that case it may seem reasonable to assume that the correlation of ΔSP with only six variables $(G_1', G_2', G_3, \Delta \log p, \Delta \log y, \text{BT}/H_{-1})$ is not far from zero.

If we consider a more general case where $\text{cov}(\text{BT}/H_{-1}, \Delta\text{SP}) > 0$, $\text{cov}(\text{BT}/H_{-1}, \Delta\text{SP}) > 0$, and $\text{cov}(G_3, \Delta\text{SP}) < 0$, then the negative bias of $\hat{b}_1$ is increased, the one of $\hat{a}$ is reduced (and may even become positive), and the reduced-form money stock estimate $\hat{A}$ is positively biased (more details may be found in Laskar 1981).

Note that when we consider the case of endogenous expectations and examine the bias due to the left-out variables BT/H_{-1} and $(\text{BP}/H_{-1})_{-1}$, we cannot suppose they are not correlated with BT/H_{-1}.

capital movements: A case study of Austria and France. *International Monetary Fund Staff Papers*, vol. 23, no. 3, November.

Kohlagen, S. W. 1977. "Rational" and "endogenous" exchange rate expectations and speculative capital flows in Germany. *Welwirtsch. Arch.* 113(4).

Kouri, P. J. K. 1975. The hypothesis of offsetting capital flows: A case study of Germany. *Journal of Monetary Economics* 1: 21–39.

Kouri, P. J. K., and M. G. Porter. 1974. International capital flows and portfolio equilibrium. *Journal of Political Economy*, May/June.

Laskar, D. M. 1981. Sterilization behavior and independence of monetary policy under a pegged exchange rates system: An econometric approach. Ph.D. dissertation, UCLA.

Magee, S. P. 1976. The empirical evidence on the monetary approach to the balance of payments and exchange rates. *American Economic Review*, May.

Michaely, M. 1971. *The responsiveness of demand policies to balance of payments: Postwar patterns*. New York and London: Columbia University Press for the National Bureau of Economic Research.

Murray, G. L. 1978. Monetary policy and capital inflow. *Economic Record*, August.

Neumann, M. J. M. 1978. Offsetting capital flows: A re-examination of the German case. *Journal of Monetary Economics* 4: 131–42.

Nurske, R. 1944. *International currency experience*. Montreal: League of Nations.

Porter, M. G. 1972. Capital flows as an offset to monetary policy: The German exprience. *IMF Staff Papers*, no. 19 (July), pp. 395–424.

Price, J. W. 1978. Time series analysis of money supply reaction functions: International evidence. Ph.D. dissertation, UCLA.

Stockman, A. C. 1979. Monetary control and sterilization under pegged exchange rates. Unpublished paper, University of Rochester, August.

12 Effects of Open Market Operations and Foreign Exchange Market Operations under Flexible Exchange Rates

Dan Lee

During the period of pegged exchange rates under the Bretton Woods Agreement, attention was directed to the problems of capital and reserve flows in the literature of international monetary economics. One relevant question was whether an individual country can conduct an independent monetary policy under fixed exchange rates. After the collapse of this system in the early seventies, attention was diverted to the determination of exchange rates and the workings of the flexible exchange-rate system. At least in theory, it seems that we finally have independent monetary policies.

This chapter examines one of the topics in this still developing field, namely the relative effects of the two alternative instruments, open market operations (OMO) and foreign exchange market operations (FXO), in a small open economy. This topic is of great importance to policymakers who are faced with various policy targets and have two alternative instruments. For example, when the objective is to stabilize exchange rates in the short run, they have to decide which instrument to use. To do this, they need a theory and empirical evidence that supports the use of one instrument or the other for the purpose at hand.

The issue of the relative use of domestic and foreign assets in the conduct of monetary policy under flexible exchange rates was first raised by Jürg Niehans (1976). In discussing the problems of the international monetary mechanism after the collapse of the Bretton Woods system, he conjectured that an OMO would have more influence on domestic demand and a FXO on foreign exchange rates, although the two operations affect domestic demand and foreign exchange rates in the same direction. If this conjecture were correct, he argues, then Mundell's assignment

Dan Lee is an economist with the International Monetary Fund.

principle could be used and the policy implication is clear. It says that an OMO should be used for domestic stabilization and a FXO for foreign exchange-rate stabilization. However, Niehans did not elaborate his argument or give any empirical evidence to support his conjecture. He just stopped at raising the question.

There have been largely two main strands of literature on international monetary economics in recent years. One is the monetary approach (MA), and the other is the portfolio balance approach (PBA). They are both "asset market approaches," in the sense that the balance-of-payments or exchange-rate fluctuations are caused basically by asset disequilibrium. However, there are some major differences.

In MA, it is implicitly (e.g. most of the articles in Frenkel and Johnson 1978) or explicitly (e.g. Frenkel and Rodriguez 1975) assumed that the asset holdings can be classified under two categories: money and non-money assets. Under such an assumption, one needs to look at only one of the two assets, money in this case. In this sense, MA may be regarded as a special case of PBA. In a portfolio balance model with three assets, money, domestic assets, and foreign assets, if the latter two are perfect substitutes, one ends up with a MA model. And this is the usual justification of MA. MA proponents believe that interest parity holds given an appropriate risk premium, and therefore domestic assets and foreign assets can be regarded as perfect substitutes. In this case, there is no need to distinguish between OMOs and FXOs, because any operation that changes money supply by an equal amount is identical. This is the result of most MA models (e.g. Girton and Roper 1977; Dornbusch 1976a, b; Bilson 1978) or portfolio balance models in MA spirit, i.e. with two assets (e.g. Frenkel and Rodriguez 1975; Kouri 1976).[1]

But in portfolio balance models (e.g. Henderson 1976; Girton and Henderson 1977), there usually are three assets, money, domestic assets and foreign assets, which are strictly gross substitutes. Since domestic and foreign assets are not perfect substitutes, the interest parity condition does not hold and each asset demand depends on the rate of return from each asset holding, i.e. domestic interest rate and foreign interest rate adjusted for forward premium, and asset prices. Operations on different assets are expected to have different effects on macroeconomic variables, because they imply different changes in asset composition and therefore in domestic and foreign interest rates adjusted for forward premiums. It is not surprising that the first attempt to distinguish the effects of OMOs and FXOs used a portfolio balance framework.

So far, there have been very few studies of this subject that compare in

1. Some portfolio balance models, constructed in MA spirit, use only two assets and reach the same general conclusions as in a typical MA model. For example, Frenkel and Rodriguez (1975) use money and real capital (domestic and foreign equities are assumed to be perfect substitutes), and Kouri (1976) has money and foreign assets.

a systematic way the effects of OMO and FXO. None of them are either satisfactory or complete.[2]

The specific questions that are asked in this study are: (1) What are the dynamic effects (i.e. not only the impact effects, but also the short-run and long-run effects) of OMO and FXO on major macroeconomic variables such as interest rate, exchange rate, price level, and real income in a small open economy under flexible exchange rates? Are they identical? If different, how? (2) What are the policy implications? Is it possible to have an assignment principle which tells us which policy instrument to use for the purpose at hand?

The objective of this chapter is to provide theoretical answers to these questions. Specifically, the objectives are (1) to develop a satisfactory theoretical framework which overcomes some common problems in existing models, and in which the dynamic analysis of OMOs and FXOs can be conducted systematically, and (2) to provide a dynamic theory about the effects of OMOs and FXOs on major macroeconomic variables.

The existing models of small open economies under flexible exchange rates are critically discussed in section 12.1. In section 12.2, a macroeconomic model in which OMOs and FXOs can be discussed in a nontrivial way is constructed. In section 12.3, a nonmathematical analysis of OMOs and FXOs is conducted using the model developed in section 12.2. In section 12.4, the results of the analysis are summarized and the policy implications are discussed.

12.1 Problems in Existing Open Macromodels

In this section, some common problems in the existing models of open economies under flexible exchange rates are discussed with a view to avoiding these problems in developing a model in the following section.

12.1.1 Purchasing Power Parity

In the typical MA model, purchasing power parity (PPP) serves the crucial role of representing the relative price of two monies by an exchange rate. MA models are usually concerned with the long-run equilibrium with the notable exception of Dornbusch (1976*a*, *b*), and the PPP is a plausible long-run hypothesis. In many cases, however (e.g. the papers in Frenkel and Johnson 1978; Barro 1978), the PPP is assumed to hold even in the short run. Although the PPP assumption is very convenient in that it makes any model much simpler than otherwise, there seem to be

---

2. For example, both Henderson (1976) and Girton and Henderson (1977) deal with this subject directly, but because they limit their analyses to the impact effects and ignore the real sector reactions and the short-run dynamics, they are not really satisfactory or complete. There is another study by Henderson (1979), which considers short-run dynamics and real sector reactions, but it is about a FXO only and does not compare OMOs and FXOs.

some problems in using it, especially in the determination of exchange rates in the short run.[3]

In contrast, in portfolio balance literature, the PPP is completely ignored (e.g. Girton and Henderson 1977) or reserved for the long run as in Dornbusch (1975). For short-run analyses, it is usually assumed that exchange-rate determination is completely dominated by asset markets and that goods market arbitrage is ineffective.

In a paper which was otherwise written in the vein of MA, Dornbusch (1976*a*) takes this position and allows short-run deviations from PPP, which holds in the long run when all the asset markets and the goods market are in equilibrium. In this chapter I will follow Dornbusch in doing without the PPP in the short run, because I believe the evidence for short-run validity of PPP is rather weak so far and there is an important role for the short-run deviations from PPP to perform in the model.

12.1.2   Real Sector

In the asset market approach in general, the price level, which is determined in the real sector, is assumed to adjust very slowly, if at all, so that it can be ignored for the purpose of a short-run analysis. Although this assumption is usually adopted without much persuasive theoretical argument, the facts seem to point in this direction, and realistic results that resemble actual movements of exchange rates in the short run are obtained by using this assumption. However, the emphasis on the short-run asset markets appears to have resulted in neglecting the linkage with the real sector until recently.

In MA literature full employment is generally assumed (e.g. Barro 1978), which can be justified by limiting the analysis to the long run, or real income is included as an exogenous variable. Consequently the possibility of interaction between the asset and real sector is precluded. A satisfactory treatment of the real sector in MA literature can be found in Bilson (1978). In introducing rational expectations in MA, Bilson used a reduced-form variant of a Lucas-Barro type of short-run Phillips curve relation. His transitory income consists of three elements, a first-order autoregressive term, a term that represents a short-run output response to an unexpected money shock, and a term for exogenous real income shock. Although this treatment of the real sector certainly makes the rational expectations model easier to solve and test than it would be otherwise, we know that, by treating the real sector this way, we are missing many of the interesting and revealing structural aspects of the

---

3. See Frenkel (1976) for the use of the PPP in both the short-run and the long-run determination of exchange rates. See Roll (1978) for a critical view on the use of the PPP in the short run.

short-run behavior of macrovariables such as consumption, investment, and international trade. Frenkel and Rodriguez (1975) provide a rigorous theory about the dynamics of the interactions between capital stock, investment, and the balance of payments. A fairly good treatment of the real sector can also be found in Dornbusch (1976b). However, his model's real output is strictly demand-determined, and consequently he misses the aspect of Lucas-type aggregate supply responses.

12.1.3   Expectations

When general attention shifted from the fixed exchange-rate regime to the flexible one, the forward exchange rate naturally emerged as the critical variable. The forward premium or discount, which is the expected rate of depreciation or appreciation adjusted for risks, is part of the returns from holding foreign assets, and therefore an opportunity cost of holding other assets. It is a crucial variable in any asset market approach, regardless of whether domestic and foreign assets are perfect substitutes.

For example, in Dornbusch (1976b) an increase in the money supply tends to reduce the interest rate because the price level is assumed fixed in the short run ("short-run liquidity effect"). Then, because of the interest parity condition, the foreign interest rate adjusted for the forward premium must fall. Because the foreign interest rate is assumed to be fixed by foreign central banks, it is the forward premium that must adjust downward. Given the adaptive expectations mechanism in which the forward premium is proportional to the difference between the current and the long-run exchange rates, the current rate must overshoot the long-run rate, which has been revised following the money shock, to have the forward premium fall. Dornbusch later considers a perfect foresight path, which he calls a rational expectations path, by imposing the condition that the expectations about future exchange rates derived by using the adaptive expectations mechanism are always correct.

Although Dornbusch's contribution is significant and a step in the right direction, there is a problem regarding the price expectations. Dornbusch (and most writers) ignores the possibility of changes in price expectations during the adjustment period after a shock. When the PPP is abandoned in the short run as in Dornbusch, we no longer have the automatic link between the forward exchange rate and the expected rate of inflation as in MA models. When the whole adjustment process takes place with great speed, we might not need to specify a separate expectations mechanism for the expected rate of inflation, assuming the inflationary expectations stay constant during the adjustment period. However, when the process takes considerable time, as some empirical studies suggest it does, inflationary expectations are likely to change during the adjustment period, and a separate formula must be specified for the inflationary expectations.[4] Furthermore, when Dornbusch implicitly assumes that the private sector immediately realizes the new long-run level of exchange rates after the money shock, it is hard to understand why the same information should not cause the same private sector to do the same thing about the long-run price level.

Dornbusch, like all other writers, ignores this possibility altogether and implicitly assumes a constant expected rate of inflation. In the model to be developed in the following section, inflationary expectations are explicitly specified. This enables us to distinguish between the real and the nominal interest rate, which becomes very important when there is investment in the real sector which depends on the real interest rate.

12.1.4   Long-Run Neutrality

The long-run neutrality of money is intuitively appealing, because it is consistent with such well-established long-run hypotheses as the PPP. And such long-run results can serve as relatively simple reference time paths in dynamic analysis. In general, the sufficient conditions for long-run neutrality with respect to a change in a nominal variable are: (1) The model is homogenous of degree 0 in all nominal variables. (2) The nominal variable that is being changed is the only exogenous nominal variable. In MA, the usual specification of the asset sector, which allows only one exogenous nominal variable, money, guarantees the long-run neutrality of money. In MA, money is the only nominal variable and therefore a doubling of money would result in the doubling of the price level, which leaves real variables unchanged in the long run. However, the PBA models in general are not concerned with a long-run analysis and do not exhibit long-run neutrality of money except for those with only two assets and only one nominal variable (e.g. Frenkel and Rodriguez 1975). Consider a portfolio balance model which has three assets—money, domestic bonds with fixed nominal value, and foreign assets. There are three nominal variables—money, nominally fixed domestic bonds, and the price level. The first two variables are exogenous, and the third is endogenous. Therefore, when the stock of money is doubled, the doubling of price level would not leave the real variables, for example real interest rates, unchanged. The real value of domestic bond holdings will be reduced to one-half, and this will obviously affect the interest rate. The model is therefore not long-run-neutral with respect to changes in money stock.

It is possible to make a portfolio balance model long-run-neutral with respect to changes in money by assuming that all the domestic assets are real claims. However, this does not automatically guarantee a long-run neutrality with respect to OMOs or FXOs because these operations

---

4. For example, Barro's (1978) empirical study suggests that it takes more than two years for the effects of a monetary shock to abate completely.

involve changes in one of the other assets as well as in money. If we want to retain the long-run virtues of MA such as the long-run PPP in discussing the effects of OMOs and FXOs, we need the long-run neutrality of the model with respect to OMOs and FXOs as well.

One way to avoid this problem is to assume that the government is fully "internalized" by the private sector; i.e. the private sector regards the government as nothing more than its agent and therefore government transactions on assets do not constitute changes in the perceived composition of the asset holdings by the private sector. With this assumption, OMOs and FXOs are identical to simple changes in the money stock by unilateral transfer payments in their effect on macrovariables. The model is then long-run-neutral with respect to any kind of changes in money. This position was recently taken by Stockman (1979).

Despite its obvious advantage in making a model simpler and despite its intuitive appeal, this "internalized" government assumption seems to be inconsistent with the common observation about the private sector. It is unrealistic to expect the private sector of a small open economy to be completely indifferent to government purchases and sales of assets. Therefore such an assumption will not be adopted in this study. Instead, in the following section a model which exhibits asymptotic neutrality with respect to OMOs and FXOs will be developed.

12.2 The Basic Model

In this section a model of a small open economy under flexible exchange rates is developed.[5] In doing so, an attempt is made to reduce the shortcomings of the existing models as discussed in the preceding section. Also, efforts are made to simplify the model as much as possible at various stages for the sake of tractability and practicality.

12.2.1   The Building Blocks

It is assumed that the "public"[6] holds three assets—domestic money (M), domestic nonmoney assets (B_p), and foreign bonds (F_p)—which are

5. The advantage of a small-country assumption is obvious when one is concerned with domestic monetary policy alone, ceteris paribus. This advantage is analogous to that of a partial equilibrium analysis over a general equilibrium analysis.

6. The term "public" is used here instead of "domestic residents" because the wealth constraint here is for all those whose holdings of domestic money are included in the money stock, some of whom are presumably foreigners or foreign residents. If we want to make OMOs and FXOs affect money stock by the full amounts of the operations regardless of whether the transactions are with domestic or foreign residents, there must be corresponding changes in other asset holdings. In this sense, the relevant wealth constraint should include asset holdings by those foreign residents and foreigners who hold domestic assets or money. In some studies, transactions with foreigners affect the money supply, but not other asset holdings by "domestic residents," which seems to be erroneous and a clear violation of the wealth constraint, regardless of how it is defined.

strictly gross substitutes. The last two are interest-bearing with the interest rates of i and i^*, respectively.

The domestic economy is small in the sense that it is a price taker in the international markets of goods and assets. Foreign interest rates are assumed to be kept at a constant level by foreign monetary authorities.

Assume that domestic nonmoney assets are all equities, i.e. claims to real capital. Also, assume that capital goods do not depreciate.

The domestic economy produces an internationally traded single output according to a neoclassical production function. Because the domestic economy is assumed to be a price taker, the prices of its product and foreign products on the international market are not affected by the domestic economy. The output can be used for either consumption or investment. Only the private sector is engaged in the production and investment activities. The private sector invests and increases its capital stock according to a nontrivial investment function with increasing marginal cost.

The role of government is limited to that of a simple supplier of money. It is assumed that the government increases the money stock at a constant rate continuously in the steady state, by printing and spending. The government is not "internalized" by the private sector, and therefore government transactions on assets with the private sector do imply changes in the private sector's asset composition. The government does not save and increase its capital stock.

Consider an economy in which everything grows at a constant rate that is given by the exogenous growth rate of the labor force g_l, in accordance with the neoclassical growth model. It is well known that in a neoclassical steady state, real income, wealth, real money balance, and capital stock grow at the rate g_l, which is equal to the marginal product of capital, assuming that the economy is in the Golden Rule situation.

12.2.2 Asset Sector

There are four basic equations for the asset sector:

(12.1) $$(M/P)_t^d = m(r_t, \pi_t^e, \overline{i}^* + \epsilon_j, y_t/w_t)w_t$$
$$m_1 < 0,\ m_2 < 0,\ m_3 < 0,\ m_4 > 0,$$

(12.2) $$(B_p)_t^d = (P_k)_t (K_p)_t = (\rho_t/r_t)(K_p)_t$$
$$= b(r_t, \pi_t^e, \overline{i}^* + \epsilon_t, y_t/w_t)w_t = (P_k)_t(K - K_g)$$
$$b_1 > 0,\ b_2 > 0,\ b_3 < 0,\ b_4 < 0,$$

(12.3) $$(eF_p/P)_t^d = f(r_t, \pi_t^e, \overline{i}^* + \epsilon_t, y_t/w_t)w_t$$
$$f_1 < 0,\ f_2 > 0,\ f_3 > 0,\ f_4 < 0,$$

(12.4) $$m + b + f = 1,$$

where
M = nominal stock of money,
P = price of domestic output,
w = real value of financial wealth in terms of consumption goods,
B_p = nominal value of private equity holdings,
B_g = nominal value of government equity holdings,
K_p = real value of private equity holdings in units of capital goods,
P_k = price of capital goods in terms of consumption goods,
K_g = real value of government equity holdings in units of capital goods,
K = real value of the total capital stock in the economy,
F_p = value of private holdings of foreign bonds in foreign currency units,
F_g = value of government holdings of foreign bonds in foreign currency units,
r = domestic real interest rate,
π^e = expected rate of domestic inflation,
$\bar{i}^*$ = foreign nominal rate of interest, which is assumed constant,
y = real output = real income,
ϵ = forward premium on future exchange rate,
ρ = marginal product of capital,
e = foreign exchange rate = number of domestic currency units per unit of foreign currency,

$$m = \frac{(M/P)}{w}$$ = share of real money balance in the total real wealth,

$$b = \frac{P_k \cdot K_p}{w}$$ = share of domestic bond holdings in the total real wealth,

$$f = \frac{(eF_p/P)}{w}$$ = share of foreign assets in the total wealth.

Equations (12.1), (12.2), and (12.3) are asset demand equations and (12.4) is the wealth constraint. Because of the wealth constraint equation (12.4), we have the relation between elasticities

(12.5) $m \cdot m_i + b \cdot b_i + f \cdot f_i = 0$,

where m_i, b_i, and f_i are the elasticities of asset demands with respect to the variables in parentheses in equations (12.1), (12.2), and (12.3). Equation (12.5) makes one of the three asset demand equations linearly dependent on the other two.

In the asset demand equations, the nominal interest rate i is divided into the real interest rate r and the expected rate of interest π^e. The distinction between r and π^e is very important in discussing investment, and π^e is likely to change when the economy is subjected to a shock. It seems that when r and π^e change in opposite directions leaving i constant, K_p^d presumably changes, suggesting different coefficients for r and π^e. However, assuming an identical coefficient for both r and π^e would not seem to change the results much.

In the money demand equation, it is assumed that the relevant price variable is the price of domestic output. Of course, we can use a weighted sum of the prices of domestic output and imports as the relevant price level, but this does not seem to change the results significantly.

In equation (12.2), P_k is defined as ρ/r such that in the long-run steady-state equilibrium, P_k, which is the price of capital goods, in terms of consumption goods, is equal to unity; i.e. using an overbar to denote a steady-state value, $\bar{P}_k = 1$ and therefore $\bar{\rho} = \bar{r}$.

The term y/w is the transactions demand term. The real income y is divided by wealth, w, because m presumably would not increase when y and w both increase proportionately. When y increases alone, m would increase. This specification implies unit elasticity of money demand with respect to permanent income, because a change in permanent income implies proportionate changes in y and w, leaving y/w unchanged.

Before going any further, let us investigate the long-run properties of the asset sector, especially long-run neutrality. In the steady state, real values of assets grow at the rate g_l in the absence of disturbances. This is because the relative shares are constant, while the total value of assets grows at the rate g_l. Assume at this point that the money stock is increased at a constant rate by a continuous process of printing and random distribution by the government, not by continuous open market purchases and foreign exchange purchases. With the assumption that all the domestic bonds are equities, the model is long-run-neutral with respect to changes in either the level or growth rate of the money supply, because it is the only nominal exogenous variable in the model. For example, if the money supply is doubled without accompanying any other changes, it will be exactly offset by a doubling of price level in the long run without affecting the real variables such as capital stock. The model is long-run-neutral also with respect to FXOs because the steady-state level of foreign asset holdings can be restored through accumulation of current account balances.

However, the model does not seem to be long-run-neutral with respect to disturbances in domestic asset holdings. For example, an open market purchase of domestic assets raises P_k through a decline in r. Investment by the private sector continues until $P_k = 1$, given the type of investment function used here. This investment by the private sector over and above the steady-state level will eventually restore its holdings of domestic assets to the steady-state level, making the total stock of capital in the economy K, which is equal to $K_p + K_g$, lie above the steady-state path. As long as we do not assume a fixed capital-labor ratio, this implies a drop in the marginal product of capital, and therefore a drop in the interest rate. This drop in the real rate of interest would change the steady-state paths of the real money balance and foreign assets, as well as the real output.

However, in a neoclassical steady state in which asset holdings grow at a constant rate, including domestic capital, the effect of this one-time level shock on the steady-state path of the economy's capital stock by a one-time purchase of capital by the government would decline in terms of percentage deviations from the original steady-state path. In other words, the level shock would decline over time in log scale. In this sense, we have an asymptotic long-run neutrality with respect to OMO in the model.[7] This neutrality will never be an exact one, but if we consider that the magnitude of an OMO would probably be very small compared to the total capital stock in the economy, such neutrality would make more sense.

In the short-run dynamic analysis in the following section, we will conduct our analysis as if we had an exact long-run neutrality. The fact that what we actually have is not an exact long-run neutrality, but instead an asymptotic one does not change the results qualitatively.

12.2.3   Real Sector

There are three basic equations in the real sector:

$$(12.6) \qquad y_t^d = C(w_t - \bar{w}_t, y_t) + I(P_{kt}, t) + X(e_t P_t^*/P_t, y_t, \bar{y}_t^*)^{8}$$
$$C_1 > 0,\ C_2 > 0,\ I_1 > 0,\ X_1 > 0,\ X_2 < 0,\ X_3 > 0,$$

---

7. The assumption that the government increases the money stock at a constant rate by printing and transfer payments in the steady-state is crucial here. If it were assumed that the money supply is increased by continuous open market purchases and foreign exchange market purchases, we might not get this asymptotic long-run neutrality, depending on the specific assumptions about the situation.

8. Some readers might wonder about the absence of any variable that is associated with the inflationary finance in the steady state, because it was assumed that the government increases the money supply at a constant rate in the steady state by printing and transfer payments. However, this absence can be justified in the following way.

The disposable income can be expressed as

$$y_t^{\text{dis}} = y_t + \tau_t = y_t + \frac{g_M \cdot M_t}{P_t},$$

where τ is the transfer payments financed by printing money, ignoring taxes and government spending, and g_M the growth rate of nominal money.

This should be equal to the expenditure, i.e.

$$y_t^{\text{dis}} = C_t + I_t + \frac{e_t}{P_t} \Delta F_{p,t} + \frac{\Delta M_t^d}{P_t},$$

where the last three terms represent additions to each asset holding.

We know that in the steady-state equilibrium,

(12.7) $y_t^s = g(P_t/\tilde{P}_t)\bar{y}_t^s, \qquad g' > 0,$

(12.8) $y_t^d = y_t^s,$

where C = real consumption,
$\quad I$ = real investment,
$\quad X$ = value of net exports in domestic output = exports $-$ imports,
$\quad \tilde{P}_t$ = expected price level in time t as expected in time $t-1$,
$\quad y_t^d$ = aggregate demand for real output,
$\quad y_t^s$ = aggregate supply of real output,
$\quad \bar{y}_t^s$ = planned output for time t with price expectation of P_t which is assumed to be equal to $\bar{y}_t$, the long-run steady-state output level,
$\quad P_t^*$ = foreign price level = price of imports in foreign currency units,
$\quad \bar{y}_t^*$ = foreign steady-state level of real income at time t,
$\quad \bar{w}_t$ = steady-state level of real wealth that would otherwise have prevailed at time t,
$\quad e_t$ = exchange rate.

Consumption is a function of the deviation of the real wealth from its steady-state path and the real income which grows at the rate g_l. It is assumed that C is unit-elastic with respect to the permanent income in the steady state, so that C grows at the same rate as real income in the steady state.

It is essential in building a macroeconomic model to have a nontrivial investment function. The investment part of equation (12.6) is derived as follows. Recall that the economy produces a single type of output which can be used for either consumption or investment. Also, assume that capital does not depreciate. Let us distinguish investment from capital formation. The former can be regarded as the input requirement for the latter in terms of consumption goods. Assume that the marginal cost of capital formation above the steady-state level $g_l \bar{K}_t$ is an increasing function of the input requirement, i.e.

$$\frac{1}{P_t} g_M M_t^s = \frac{1}{P_t} \Delta M_t^d,$$

i.e. government cannot force the private sector to hold a real balance larger than desired, and

$$\frac{e_t}{P_t} \Delta_{p,t} = X_t.$$

Therefore, by equating the income with the expenditure, we get

$$y_t = C_t + I_t + X_t,$$

which is equation (12.6).

$$\frac{\Delta K_t}{\Delta t} - g_I \bar{K}_t = k(I_t - \bar{I}_t), \qquad k' > 0,\ k'' < 0,\ k'(0) = 1,$$

where $\bar{I}$ is the steady-state level of investment.

Profit maximization implies that the marginal cost of capital formation k' is equal to the price of capital in terms of consumption of goods P_k. Then the level of capital formation over and above the steady-state level becomes a function of P_k, and

$$I_t - \bar{I}_t = k^{-1}\left(\frac{\Delta K_t}{\Delta t} - g_I \bar{K}_t\right)$$

$$= h(P_k), \qquad h' > 0,\ h(1) = 0;$$

i.e. investment over and above the steady-state level is a positive function of the price of capital in terms of consumption goods.

Recall that the steady-state price of capital in terms of consumption goods was assumed to be equal to unity. This implies a horizontal long-run stock supply curve in a (P_k, K) diagram. In this diagram, the steady-state growth of capital stock would be represented by continuous outward shifts of the stock demand curve for the capital stock.

Now, because only the private sector invests, the resulting investment function would actually look like

(12.9) $$I_t = \frac{\Delta K_{pt}}{\Delta t} = I(P_{kt} - 1) + \bar{g}_k \bar{K}_{pt},$$

where $\bar{g}_I$ is the long-run steady-state growth rate of private capital stock and $\bar{K}_{pt}$ the steady-state level of private capital stock at time t. Investment is a positive function of the deviation of P_k from unity plus the long-run growth of the capital stock. And it can be readily seen from equation (12.9) that I grows at the same rate as capital stock g_k. This investment function specifies investment as an adjustment to the stock disequilibrium.

Net exports are a function of the terms of trade and real income. Income elasticities of net exports with respect to domestic and foreign incomes are assumed to be identical. However, there is a specific role for net exports to play in the model. Because foreigners are not assumed to hold domestic money and vice versa, the only way to alter domestic holdings of foreign bonds is to accumulate current account balances over time. The current account balance in terms of domestic output is

(12.10) $$CA_t = (e_t/P_t)\frac{\Delta F_{pt} + \Delta F_{gt}}{\Delta t} = X_t$$

$$+ i^*(F_{p,t-1} + F_{g,t-1})(e_t/P_t);$$

i.e. it is the sum of the trade account balance (net exports) and service account balance.

If we assume that the domestic steady-state real interest rate is equal to that of the rest of the world, i.e. $\bar{r} = \bar{r}^* = g_l$, and that the government lets its foreign bond holdings increase by the interest income and any capital gains,[9] it can be shown that, in the steady state, the service account surplus is just enough to meet the steady-state growth requirement of demand for foreign assets, i.e. $\bar{i}^* \bar{F}(\bar{e}/\bar{P}) = \Delta(\overline{eF/P})^d$, and therefore $\bar{X}$, the steady-state level of net exports, is equal to 0.[10] These assumptions and the resulting implications for X not only simplify the model but also are intuitively plausible. Therefore we adopt this assumption here. The sufficient condition for X to be on its steady-state path, i.e. $\bar{X} = 0$ in equation (12.6), is that the purchasing power ratio is equal to the steady-state value (purchasing power parity), which is a constant, and that the domestic and foreign real incomes are on their steady-state paths.

Equation (12.7) is an aggregate supply function in the spirit of Lucas-type rational expectations.[11] According to this type of aggregate supply function, the supply reacts (deviates from its steady-state path in this model) to price changes only if the changes are unexpected. This specification seems to be superior to the usual specification in MA that assumes real output is constant at the full-employment level or that in which output is strictly demand-determined as in Dornbusch (1976b), simply because it seems to be a more accurate description of the real world.

12.2.4 Expectations

In this model, we have two expectations, one for the forward exchange rate and the other for the expected rate of inflation.

$$\epsilon_t = E(e_{t+1}) - e_t^{[12]},$$

$$\pi_t^e = E(P_{t+1}) - P_t.$$

9. The question is what the government does with the interest income from asset holdings. If the government spends its foreign interest income on foreign goods, the steady-state trade balance will be a negative constant in real terms, which will not change the substance of the model; we can simply replace the zero with a constant for the steady-state trade account balance.

10. By definition, $\bar{i}^* = \bar{r}^* + \bar{\pi}^{e*}$. The steady-state growth rate of the domestic value of foreign assets in terms of domestic output is equal to g_l, which is equal to $\bar{r}$ in the Golden Rule situation; i.e.

$$\overline{(eF_p/P)}^d = g_l = \bar{r} = \dot{\bar{e}} - \dot{\bar{P}} + \dot{\bar{F}}_p^d = -\bar{\pi}^* + \dot{\bar{F}}_p^d,$$

because $\dot{\bar{e}} = \bar{\pi} - \bar{\pi}^*$, where an overdot denotes the percentage growth rate. From this we get $\dot{\bar{F}}_p^d = \bar{r} + \bar{\pi}^* = \bar{r}^* + \bar{\pi}^* = \bar{i}^*$. Assuming that the government lets its foreign asset holdings grow by the interest payments, i.e. $\dot{\bar{F}}_g^d = \bar{i}^*$, and substituting these into (12.10), we get $\bar{X} = 0$.

11. See R. E. Lucas (1973) for an explanation of this type of supply function.

12. Forward premium is actually the expected rate of depreciation plus risk premium. However, following Stockman (1978), the risk premium is assumed to be a constant and is ignored here. This contrasts with Dooly and Isard (1979), where the risk premium is crucial in the determination of asset composition between domestic and foreign assets.

This is different from existing models, which usually have expectation mechanisms for only forward exchange rates (e.g. Dornbusch 1976a, b). But as discussed previously, when the adjustment period is sufficiently long, as some empirical studies show, π^e is likely to be revised temporarily during the period of adjustment.[13]

An adaptive expectations mechanism is adopted here which has been widely used in open macroeconomic models by Dornbusch and others. The forward premium is given by

$$(12.11) \qquad \epsilon_t = \frac{-\theta}{\bar{e}_t}(e_t - \bar{e}_t) + \bar{\pi}^e - \bar{\pi}^{e*},$$

where overbars denote steady-state values of variables and the asterisk denotes foreign variables. According to this type of specification, the private sector knows what the new long-run steady-state paths will be as soon as a government action takes place. The private sector revises its expectations according to the discrepancy between the actual and the new steady-state value which would have prevailed otherwise at the time, on the presumption that the value will eventually return to its steady-state path but not immediately. It is usually assumed that the revision is a constant fraction of the discrepancy between the actual and the steady-state value, and therefore the resulting expectation is not necessarily correct.

Equation (12.11) is similar to the equation used in Dornbusch (1976b). It is a version modified for use in the present model in which domestic and foreign price levels continue to rise instead of being stagnant as in Dornbusch. In the steady state, the real demand for money grows at the rate g_l, and $\bar{\pi}_t^i = g_M - g_l$, where $\bar{g}_M$ is the steady-state growth rate of nominal money supply. And the same is true for the rest of the world. Because PPP holds in the long run in this model, the exchange rate depreciates at the constant rate of $\bar{\pi}^e - \bar{\pi}^{e*}$ in the steady state.

The adaptive expectations mechanism like equation (12.11) gives the well-publicized result of overshooting (e.g. Dornbusch 1976a, b). When the forward premium must change in response to asset market disturbances, (12.11) implies a change in the exchange rate that is larger than the shifts in the long-run steady-state exchange-rate path.

By extending the same expectations mechanism as in equation (12.11) to expectations about future inflations, the expected rate of inflation between this period and the next would be

$$(12.12) \qquad \pi_t^e = -\frac{\lambda}{\bar{P}_t}(P_t - \bar{P}_t) + \bar{\pi}^{e14},$$

13. See, for example, Barro (1978).
14. The apparent inconsistency between equation (11.12), in which the current price level seems to be known to everybody, and equation (11.7), in which producers do not seem to observe it, can be resolved by assuming a discrepancy in the information available to

where $\bar{P}_t$ is the steady-state price level that would have prevailed otherwise according to the new steady-state time path of P.

12.2.5   Summary of the Model

We have nine basic equations in the model.

(12.1)
$$(M/P)_t^d = m(r_t, \pi_t^e, \bar{i}^* + \epsilon_t, y_t/w_t)w_t$$
$$m_1 < 0, \ m_2 < 0, \ m_3 < 0, \ m_4 > 0,$$

(12.2)
$$(B_p)_t^d = (P_k)_t(K_p)_t = (\rho_t/r_t)(K_p)_t$$
$$= b(r_t, \pi_t^e, \bar{i}^* + \epsilon_t, y_t/w_t)w_t$$
$$= (P_k)_t(K - K_g)$$
$$b_1 > 0, b_2 > 0, \ b_3 < 0, \ b_4 < 0,$$

(12.3)
$$(eF_p/P)_t^d = f(r_t, \pi_t^e, \bar{i}^* + \epsilon_t, y_t/w_t)w_t$$
$$f_1 < 0, \ f_2 > 0, \ f_3 > 0, \ f_4 < 0,$$

(12.4)
$$m + b + f = 1,$$

(12.6)
$$y_t^d = C(w_t - \bar{w}_t, y_t) + I(P_{k,t}, t)$$
$$+ X(e_t P_t^*/P_t, y_t, \bar{y}_t^*)$$
$$C_1 > 0, \ C_2 > 0, \ I_1 > 0,$$
$$X_1 > 0, \ X_2 < 0, \ X_3 > 0,$$

(12.7)
$$y_t^s = g(P_t/\tilde{P}_t)\bar{y}_t^s, \qquad g' > 0,$$

(12.8)
$$y_t^d = y_t^s,$$

(12.11)
$$\epsilon_t = -\frac{\theta}{\bar{e}_t}(e_t - \bar{e}_t) + \bar{\pi}^e - \bar{\pi}^{e*},$$

(12.12)
$$\pi_t^e = -\frac{\lambda}{\bar{P}_t}(P_t - \bar{P}_t) + \bar{\pi}^e.$$

Note that one of equations (12.1), (12.2), and (12.3) is linearly dependent on the other two, and we really have eight independent equations. We can eliminate ϵ_t and π_t^e by using expectations (12.11) and (12.12). And because of equation (12.8), in the end we only have one independent equation in the real sector. We end up with four independent equations

producers and that available to the participants in the financial market. In this paper, producers are assumed to have expectations only about the current price level, based on the past values of the prices of their output and other relevant variables. Any price higher than this expectation is interpreted as a genuine increase in the relative price and the production is increased. However, the people in the financial market, who determine the nominal interest rate, are assumed to have a better information set, which includes the current price level as well as those pieces of information available to producers.

and four unknowns—r, P, y, and e—which we can solve for the unknowns.[15]

12.2.6   Steady-State Properties

In the steady state, every asset grows at a constant rate; i.e.

$$\dot{K}_p = \overline{(\dot{M/P})} = \overline{(\dot{eF_p/P})} = \dot{w} = g_l,$$

where the overdot denotes the growth rate of a variable. Also, real output and its components grow at the same rate; i.e.

$$\dot{y} = \dot{C} = \dot{I} = g_l.$$

The steady-state rate of inflation is determined by the relative growth of money supply and real money demand, which is identical to the expected rate of inflation; i.e.

$$\bar{\pi} = \bar{\pi}^e = \bar{g}_M - \overline{(\dot{M/P})}^d = \bar{g}_M - g_l.$$

The long-run PPP is assumed to hold, which is consistent with the steady-state specification of X; i.e.

$$\overline{(eP^*/P)} = \alpha, \qquad X = X(\alpha, \bar{y}, \bar{y}^*) = 0,$$

where the overbar denotes a long-run steady-state PPP ratio, and $\bar{y}$ and $\bar{y}^*$ are the steady-state levels of domestic and foreign real income.

Therefore the steady-state level of the forward premium, ignoring the risk premium, is equal to the difference between the domestic and foreign steady-state rate of inflation; i.e.

$$\bar{\epsilon} = \bar{\pi} - \bar{\pi}^*,$$

where $\bar{\pi}^* = \bar{g}_M^* - g_l^*$ ($\bar{g}_M^*$ is the fixed growth rate of foreign money stock, and g_l^* is the natural growth rate of foreign labor).

12.3   Effects of OMO and FXO

In this section, using a diagram and without using mathematics, a simple analysis of OMOs and FXOs is conducted.[16] In discussing dynamics, it will be assumed that the dynamics are stable.

---

15. Using appropriate functional forms, the model can be solved for the levels of the four endogenous variables—r, P, y, and e. There could be problems in doing this, but it can be done by assuming linear asset demand functions and a linear aggregate demand function. However, the level solutions are not important in the present context, because we are interested mainly in the short-run dynamics. For present purposes, it is sufficient to know that there exists a set of level solutions for the steady state. See Henderson (1979) for the level solutions using linear functions.

16. For mathematical analysis of the short-run dynamics, see Lee (1980). It is omitted here because of its length. This section is a nonmathematical summary of the analysis.

12.3.1   Definitions of OMOs and FXOs

An OMO is defined as a once-and-for-all exchange of domestic money for domestic bonds between the government and the private sector. This implies a permanent parallel shift in the time path of $\ln M$, because the government is assumed to continue increasing the money supply at a constant rate after the one time level shock in money stock by an OMO. The analysis of OMOs will be concentrated on open market purchases, because the results for open market sales can be obtained simply by reversing the signs.

An FXO is similarly defined as a once-and-for-all exchange of domestic money for foreign assets between the government and the private sector.[17] It implies a permanent parallel shift in the time path of $\ln M$ and a temporary deviation of F_p from its steady-state path. Here also, the analysis of an FXO is concentrated on the foreign exchange market purchase, because the results for foreign exchange market sales can be obtained simply by reversing the signs.

In terms of notations, an OMO is represented by

$$\Delta B_g = -\Delta B_p = \Delta M$$

and an FXO by

$$(e + \Delta e)\Delta F_g = -(e + \Delta e)\Delta F_p = \Delta M .$$

12.3.2   Long-Run Effects

Long-run effects of an OMO are easy to see given the asymptotic long-run neutrality discussed previously. The condition for the long-run steady-state equilibrium is that all the real variables M/P, $P_k K_p$, eF_p/P, y, C, and I grow at the constant rate g_l. After an OMO, which is a permanent level shock in M, proportional shifts in the time paths of the endogenous nominal variables p and e are consistent with all the real variables on their original steady-state paths, given the asymptotic long-run neutrality. The long-run effects of an FXO are identical to the above results for an OMO, except that the neutrality is an exact, not an asymptotic one.

Therefore we have a typical MA result here for the long-run effects. As in an MA model, regardless of the asset on which the government operates to increase the money supply, the results are identical in the long run. That is, money is neutral regardless of the method of changing it in the long run.

---

17. This specification of FXO may seem too restrictive because there can be other types of FXO, such as exchange of domestic money for foreign monies, etc. However, in this model it is the only type of FXO that is allowed because foreign bonds are the only type of foreign assets held by the private sector. This seems to be the most representative case of FXO.

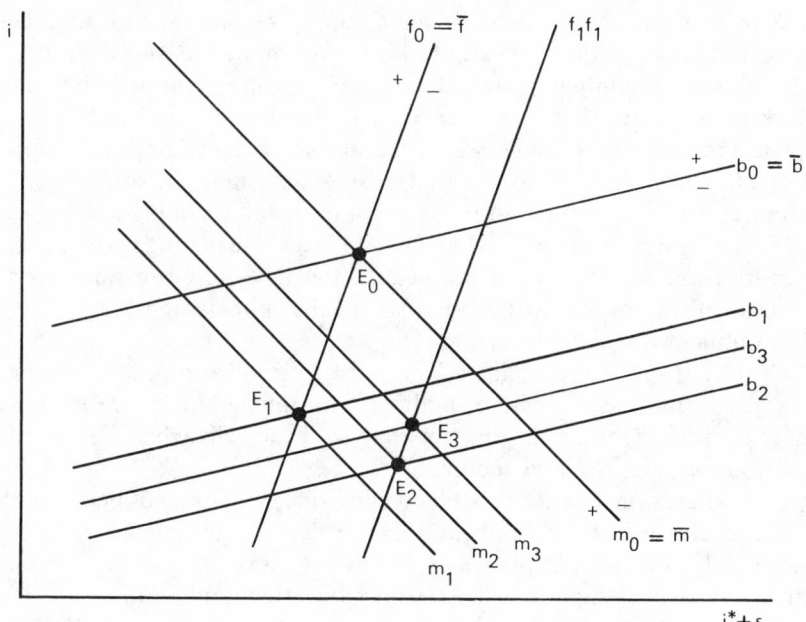

Fig. 12.1

12.3.3   Open Market Operation

Given the historic level of wealth, and assuming that demands for domestic and foreign assets are more elastic with respect to their own returns, and that the partial derivatives for r and π^e are identical, the whole asset market (equations (12.1), (12.2), (12.3)) can be represented in a single diagram as in figure 12.1.[18] Each curve represents the combination of i $(= r + \pi^e)$ and $i^* + \epsilon$ that will hold the shares of assets, money (m), domestic assets (b), and foreign assets (f) at constant levels. Curve m is negatively sloped because when i rises, it must be compensated for by lower values of $i^* + \epsilon$ to keep m from declining. Both b and f are positively sloped because when i rises, it must be compensated for by an increase in $i^* + \epsilon$ to keep b and f from increasing and decreasing, respectively. Curve f is steeper than curve b, because it is assumed that an asset demand is more elastic with respect to its own returns than to returns from other assets. Also, it is clear that one of the three is redundant; i.e. we need only two curves to get equilibrium values of i and ϵ. And because i^* is assumed to be fixed, it is ϵ that adjusts when $i^* + \epsilon$ must adjust.

An open market purchase of domestic assets with money shifts b and m downward to b_1 and m_1 in figure 12.1 because it implies a reduction in b

18. A diagram similar to this was first used by Girtón and Henderson (1977).

and an increase in m, i.e. an excess supply of money and an excess demand for domestic assets at old levels of i and ϵ. As shown in figure 12.1, this will unambiguously reduce i, but it is ambiguous whether ϵ will increase or decrease, because excess supply of domestic bonds implies upward pressure on ϵ while excess demand for money implies the opposite. However, if we assume that f stays constant, b_1 and m_1 must intersect on the f curve and therefore ϵ must fall unambiguously.

With adaptive expectations like (12.11), a decline in ϵ means more than a proportionate increase in e, because the new long-run rate has increased in proportion to the increase in the money stock. This is the well-publicized result of overshooting.

Usually in portfolio balance literature (e.g. Girton and Henderson 1977), the analysis ends here, making it an impact analysis. Obviously there is more to it than this impact analysis, especially when we consider the relation with the real sector.

First, there is an effect of the change in e on asset demands because of a higher exchange rate (e) implies a higher value of a given stock of foreign assets, which in turn implies a higher wealth level, triggering a wealth effect on asset demands. This revaluation effects raises f, creating an excess supply situation and shifting the f curve downward to f_1 in figure 12.1. However, the increase in wealth in this case involves an actual decrease in m and b, because f increases through revaluation, implying a strengthening of the excess demand for domestic assets and a reduction in excess supply of money. The reduction in the transactions demand term y/w that results from the revaluation effect would further strengthen the excess demand for domestic assets and the excess supply of money. Therefore the net effect of this wealth increase on the excess supply of money is not certain. In figure 12.1, this wealth effect on money and domestic assets is shown by the movement of the m curve from m_1 to m_2 (assuming that the effect through the transactions term is relatively small), and that of the b curve from b_1 to b_2. It might seem possible that ϵ could even increase if the downward shift of the f curve were large enough, but it is impossible because it was the reduction in ϵ that caused e to increase and the f curve to shift downward in the first place. The net result of this revaluation effect is that it dampens the effect of an OMO on ϵ and e, but never reverses the sign.[19]

Second, there are interactions with the real sector:

i) An increase in wealth will increase consumption directly through a conventional wealth effect.

ii) A decrease in the real interest rate, which means higher P_k ($= \rho/r$), increases investment.

---

19. This revaluation effect hinges upon the relative increase in e and p. The above analysis depends on the implicit assumption that the price level does not change. When the price level is allowed to change, it is possible that the value of foreign asset holdings (eF/P) might even fall if the percentage increase in P is larger than that in e.

iii) A depreciated exchange rate, given a constant price level, implies an improvement in the trade balance, i.e. an increase in X, through a change in the terms of trade.

iv) Now (i), (ii), and (iii) above imply higher demand for real output, as can be seen from equation (12.6). This in turn implies a higher price level, as can be seen from equations (12.6) and (12.7).

v) These increases in output and the price level affect asset demands, and a new chain of reactions described in (i), (ii), (iii), and (iv) follows. Increases in the price level and output reduce the original excess supply of money by reducing the real increase in the money supply through increase in P, and by increasing the transactions demand through the increase in real income. They reduce the original excess demand for domestic assets through the increase in the transactions demand for money, which implies a reduction in demand for domestic assets. As for foreign assets, the net effect is not clear because a price increase tends to reduce the value of foreign asset holdings in terms of domestic consumption while the increase in the transactions demand for money tends to reduce the demand for foreign assets. In terms of figure 12.1, all these imply a further reduction in the impact effects of an OMO on ϵ (and therefore on e) and i, by upward shifts of b and m curves to b_3 and m_3, assuming that the f curve does not shift. If the income effect is large enough, i.e. if the shift of the m curve is large enough, it is possible that an open market purchase will cause appreciation as Henderson conjectured.

These real sector reactions will be further strengthened because the increase in the price level will raise π^e, reducing r for a given decline in i and therefore increasing investment and aggregate demand further, as can be seen from equation (12.12). This would be true even if a more general form of rational expectations mechanism were assumed instead of the adaptive expectations.

Over time, the whole system moves toward the new long-run equilibrium steady state, as shown in figure 12.2. First, the price level continues to approach the new long-run path after the initial level shock in the nominal stock of money is gone and the money supply resumes its normal growth rate $\bar{g}_M$.[20] As long as there remain deviations in asset holdings from their steady-state paths, there will be residual effects on aggregate demand through r and ϵ (and therefore through I and X) that are lower than the long-run steady-state levels. It is even possible for the real output and price level to overshoot their new long-run paths in approaching them, as depicted in figures 12.2b and 12.2f.[21] Eventually,

20. At the time of OMO, $M = g + \mu$, where μ represents the once-and-for-all level shock.

21. This is because when price level and real output approach their new long-run paths for the first time after a shock, depending on the speed of investment the capital stock may still be below its long-run path and require more investment, therefore requiring a level of consumption lower than, and a level of net exports higher than, the respective steady-state levels.

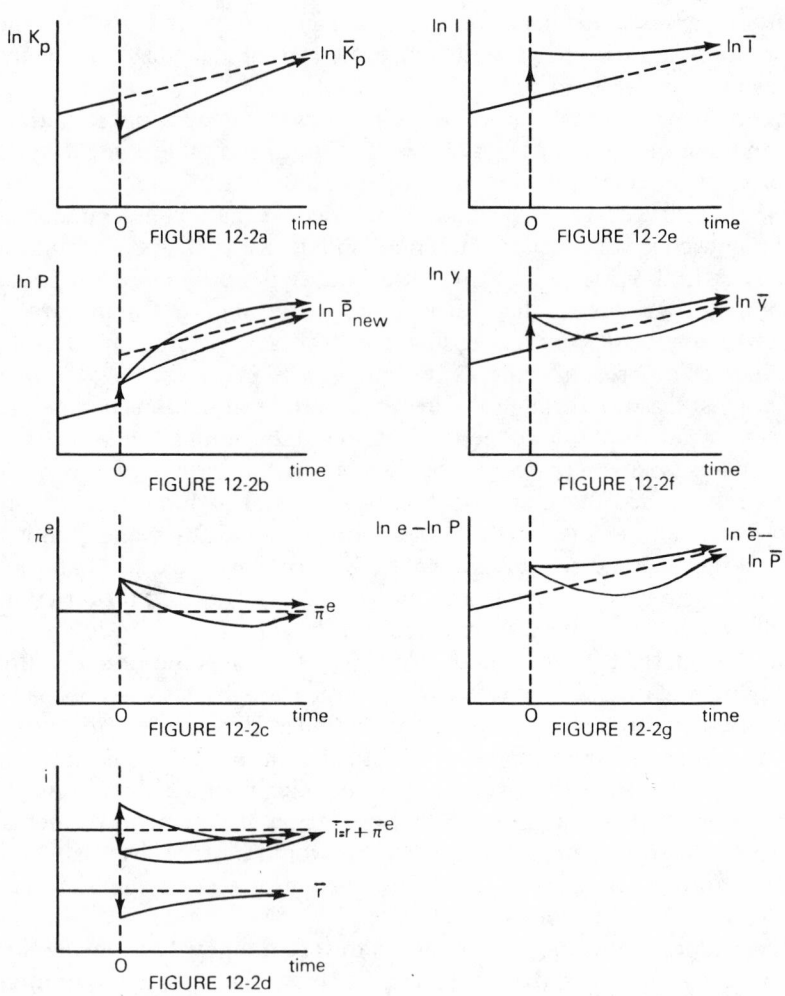

Fig. 12.2   Dynamic effects of an OMP.

however, when asset markets return to the long-run steady state, r (approximately) and ϵ will return to the original long-run steady-state values.

The time paths of π^e corresponding to those of the price level are shown in figure 12.2c. Given any rational or adaptive expectations mechanism such as equation (12.12), there will be a temporary deviation of π^e from its long-run steady-state level, which is given by the steady-state growth rate of the nominal money supply $\bar{g}_M$ minus the steady-state growth rate of the real demand for money g_l.

As long as there is a deviation from the long-run steady-state path in domestic asset holdings and therefore $P_k \neq 1$, there will be a flow adjustment in the form of investment. Given the asymptotic long-run neutrality with respect to OMO discussed in the previous section, the real interest rate r will approach its old long-run level over time, as K_p approaches its long-run steady-state level. This is depicted in figure 12.2d. And given an investment function such as equation (12.9), investment will gradually decrease over time until it reaches the steady-state level, as depicted in figure 12.2e.

Under the simplifying assumption that the partial derivatives of r and π^e in asset demand equations are identical, the nominal interest rate must fall after an open market purchase. Given that the real interest rate approaches its long-run level monotonically and π^e follows the time path shown in figure 12.2c, paths a and b in figure 12.2d are possible for the nominal interest rate. However, if we drop the assumption that the partial derivatives with respect to r and π^e are identical, the nominal interest rate will not necessarily decline after an open market purchase. It is possible that the increase in π^e will be large enough to offset the decline in r, such that i will increase after an open market purchase as depicted by path c in figure 12.2d.

The time path of K_p implied by the above analysis is shown in figure 12.2a. The actual domestic asset holdings of the private sector approach the long-run steady-state path over time. As discussed earlier, the effect of OMO on r will eventually be washed out (in the sense that r approaches its long-run level asymptotically), because the one-time increase in K ($= K_p + K_g$) diminishes as a proportion of the total K, as K grows over time.

The effects of an open market purchase on the foreign asset market are not clear-cut. However, it is obvious that when the long-run PPP holds and e/P is restored to its original level in the long run, F_p must be restored to its long-run path. In other words, if the current account turns to surplus first, increasing F_p for a while, it must be followed by a period of deficit or lower-than-normal surplus to restore F_p to its long-run path. And the opposite is true if F_p first decreases.

Given the net export function implicit in equation (12.6),

(12.13) $X = X(eP^*/P, y)$,

it is ambiguous whether X would increase or decrease after an open market purchase. Given the initial overshooting of e and the undershooting of P, the terms of trade (eP^*/P) should initially increase and would be followed by a monotonic decrease as they approach the long-run path, implying a continuous but declining pressure toward trade surplus. However, there is an offsetting pressure from the increase in y, making the net effect on the trade account ambiguous. The time path of X might be one with an initial increase and a subsequent monotonic decrease followed by a period of negative X, keeping the foreign bond holdings on the long-run path in the long run.[22]

Given the dynamic time paths of I, C, and X as discussed above, the real income y would follow the time path shown in figure 12.2f.

12.3.4   Foreign Exchange Market Operation

Using the same diagram as in figure 12.1, we can analyze the effect of a FXO in asset markets. Consider a foreign exchange market purchase, in which the central bank purchases foreign assets with domestic money. This means an excess demand for foreign assets at the old levels of r and ϵ, shifting the f curve upward to f_1, and an excess supply of money, shifting m downward to m_1 in figure 12.3. These lower ϵ unambiguously and probably i too, assuming b stays constant. Note that in this case the effect on i is smaller and that on ϵ is larger than in the case of an OMO of the same size.

Now a chain reaction similar to the case of OMO follows, but with different relative magnitudes for different variables. First, a decline in ϵ would imply an increase in e (an overshooting given the adaptive expectation in equation (12.11)). This increases the value of the remaining foreign asset holdings of the private sector and causes a revaluation effect. In the present context, this means downward shifts of f and b curves to f_2 and b_2 in figure 12.3 and an upward shift of the m curve to m_2, which results in dampening the original impact effect on ϵ. Again, this revaluation effect hinges on the relative strength of rises in ϵ and P.

In the real sector, the increase in P_k, due to lower r and higher e, tends to increase investment and net exports, resulting in a higher aggregate demand for the real output. Now the price level and output increase. Whether the increase in output and the price level caused by a foreign exchange market purchase is larger or smaller than that caused by an open market purchase of the same size depends partly on the relative strengths of the effects of P_k and e on investment and net exports, because a FXO works mainly through its effect on e and an OMO through its effect on P_k. It might seem that the effect of a FXO on the real sector is smaller than that of an OMO of the same magnitude because there is an offsetting pressure on X resulting from the increase in y. However, it is

---

22. Sometimes it is argued that an increase in the money supply would deteriorate the trade balance because of the resulting increase in real income which raises import demands. In the present context, this means that the income effect dominates the substitution effect, i.e. improvement in the terms of trade.

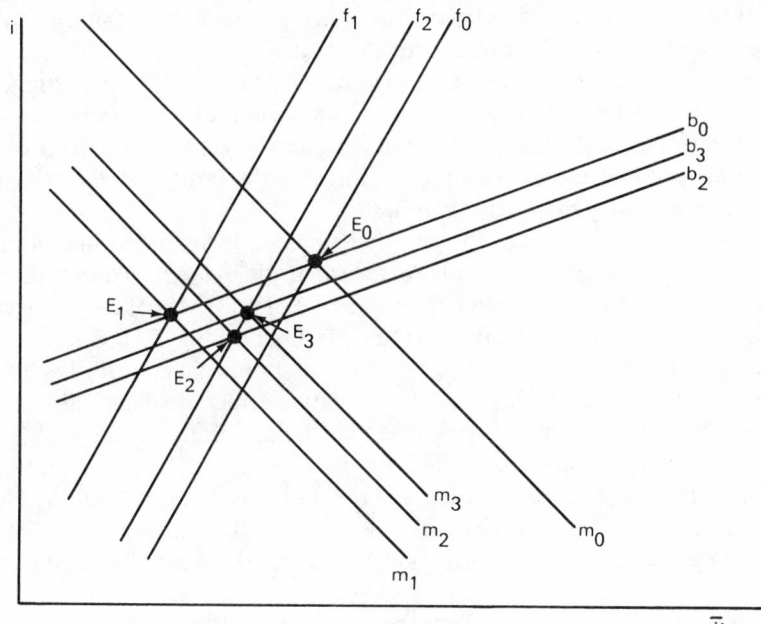

Fig. 12.3

still possible that the terms of trade effect dominates the income effect so that a FXO is more effective than an OMO in influencing the real sector. Also important is the relative speed of the reactions to OMOs and FXOs in this regard. These are basically empirical questions because there is no a priori reason to believe one or the other.

Whatever the sizes of the initial increases in output and the price level are, they will reduce the excess supply of money through a reduction in the real money supply and through increases in the transactions demand for money, and probably create an excess supply of domestic bonds by the negative transactions demand. The latter makes it possible for i to even increase, because this means an upward shift of the b curve, contrary to what is generally believed. However, even in this case, r is likely to decline because π^e would be adjusted upward. When r does increase, we must assume that the increase in X dominates the resulting decline in investment in order to have an increase in real output and price level in the first place. In that case, it is less likely that a FXO is more effective than an OMO in influencing the real sector.

The effect of increases in output and price level on the foreign asset market is ambiguous because the former reduces the demand for foreign assets by increasing the transactions demand for money and the latter reduces the value of foreign asset holdings in terms of domestic output.

Over time, all the variables would adjust in a way that is similar to the case of an OMO in general, except that this time the main disturbance is in the foreign asset market and in e rather than in the domestic asset market and in P_k. Although it is ambiguous whether the effect on output and the price level is larger or smaller than the case of an OMO of the same magnitude, the long-run effect must be the same; i.e. they must be on the same long-run path eventually.

Now, let us investigate the implied time paths of individual components of the aggregate demand. As for the trade balance, a larger drop in ϵ implies a larger increase in e than the case of an OMO of the same size. Again, given the overshooting e and undershooting P, the temporary change in the terms of trade in favor of the domestic country is guaranteed, as shown in figure 12.4e. If the negative effect of an increase in y on X is sufficiently strong, it is possible that the net effect on X by a foreign exchange market purchase will be negative, making the dynamics unstable, because y could still increase through increases in C and I. However, this is unlikely, because the wealth effect on C, through the revaluation effect, and the fall in r are likely to be relatively small (r could even rise).

It is also possible to have something like the well-publicized J curve, in a different context. If, due to rigid contracts, it takes a considerable length of time to change the effective terms of trade, it is possible for X to be negative for a while after a foreign exchange market purchase, dominated by the income effect until the effect of the change in the terms of trade materializes.

In the normal case in which the effect of a change in the terms of trade outweighs that of an increase in real income, the time paths of X and F_p are as shown in figures 12.4f and 12.4a.

As for the I and K_p, because the reduction in the real interest rate would be small and could even be positive when the increase in the transactions demand for money is strong enough, the effects on I and K_p are likely to be negligible. In any case, r could take one of the time paths depicted in figure 12.4g. The important thing here is that a period of above (below) the steady-state real interest rate must be followed by a period of below (above) the steady-state rate to make the capital stock (K_p) return to the long-run path.

12.3.5   OMO versus FXO

One way to compare the relative strengths of an OMO and a FXO in influencing the economy is to combine an OMO with a FXO of the opposite direction. Consider an open market purchase combined with foreign exchange market sales of the same magnitude, which is equivalent to the purchase of domestic assets with foreign assets leaving the

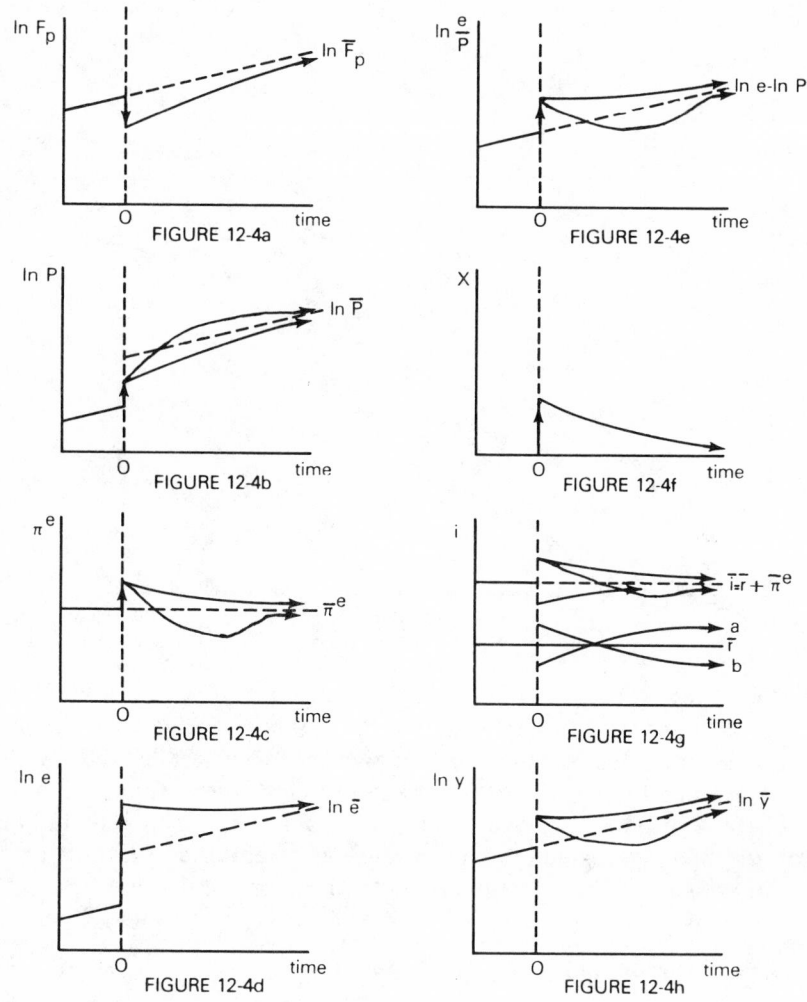

Fig. 12.4   Dynamic effects of a FXP.

money supply constant. This implies an excess demand situation for domestic assets, shifting the b curve in figure 12.5 downward, and an excess supply situation for foreign assets, shifting the f curve downward also. Assuming that the m curve does not shift, this would lower i and raise ϵ, which implies a fall in given e. Lowering i increases investment

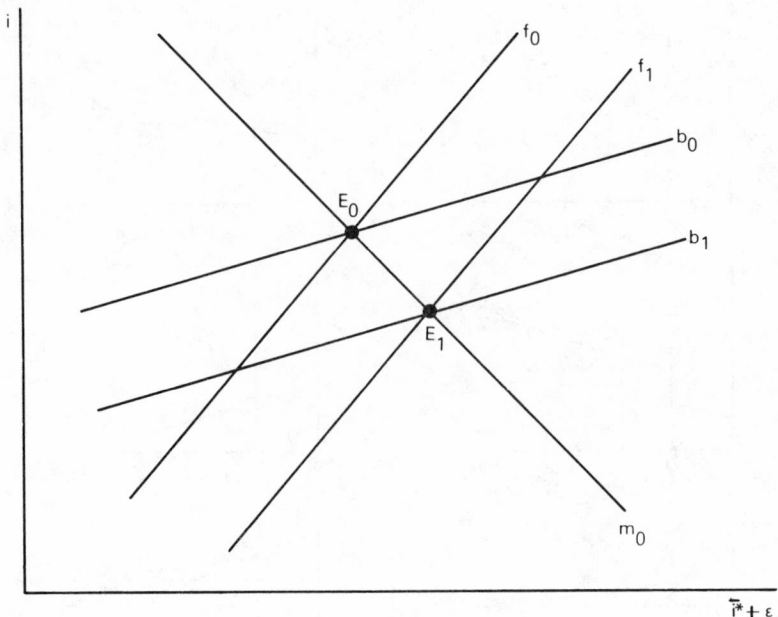

Fig. 12.5

and lowering e decreases net exports, making the net effect on aggregate demand ambiguous. As mentioned above, the net effect depends on the relative strength and speed of the effects of an increase in I and a decrease in X. If the response of investment is faster and stronger than that of net exports, then aggregate demand would increase; i.e. an OMO is more effective than a FXO in affecting the real sector in this case.

12.4 Conclusion and Policy Implications

In this chapter, effects of the two alternative instruments in the conduct of monetary policy, OMOs and FXOs, were discussed using a portfolio balance framework with a real sector in the context of a small open economy, for the short run and the long run.

i) Regardless of the short-run effects, both OMO and FXO have (asymptotically) identical long-run effects under the steady-state assumption. In the long run, all the variables except the price level and the exchange rate return to their original steady-state paths. The long-run PPP holds, and the changes in the exchange rate and the price level, which are proportional to the monetary shock, take care of all the disturbances in the long run.

ii) In the short run, it is true that an OMO exercises greater influence on the interest rate than a FXO of identical size and a FXO exercises greater influence on the exchange rate than an OMO. Therefore the short-run response to an OMO in the real sector occurs mainly through changes in investment, while that to a FXO occurs through changes in the trade balance.

iii) The relative strengths of effects of OMO and FXO on output and price in the short run are ambiguous. If the response of the trade balance to changes in the terms of trade is relatively slower and weaker than that of investment to interest-rate changes, we might be able to say that the immediate short-run effect of an OMO is stronger than a FXO. Or, if the foreign sector is relatively large and responsive, we might be able to say the opposite. All these are basically empirical questions, because there is no a priori reason to believe one thing or the other.

iv) Given our inability to resolve the question posed in (iii) without satisfactory empirical evidence,[23] the choice between OMOs and FXOs is at present a choice between short-run investment and short-run trade balance, as conjectured by Niehans.

v) When we assume a stationary state in which long-run stock values are constant rather than growing at a constant rate, the asymptotic long-run neutrality with respect to an OMO disappears. In this case, an OMO leaves a permanent mark on the capital stock, the relative importance of which does not diminish over time, and therefore on the real interest rate and real income as long as the public does not fully "internalize" the government. A FXO poses no such problem, because foreign assets can be replenished by the private sector at constant prices. Although the short-run relative effects of an OMO and a FXO may be ambiguous, the long-run relative effects are obviously different. An OMO, which is equivalent to a financing of domestic investments by the central bank, raises the capital stock permanently, while a FXO, which is equivalent to a financing of foreign investment, does not leave any permanent mark on the domestic economy under the small-country assumption.

Acknowledgments

This chapter was written when the author was a graduate student at UCLA. The author wishes to thank Professor Michael Darby for helpful comments. The views expressed here do not necessarily reflect those of the IMF.

---

23. See Darby (1980), for example, for an international study of balance of payments and exchange rates. Also see Lee (1980) for some preliminary empirical evidence regarding the hypotheses derived here.

References

Barro, R. J. 1978. A stochastic equilibrium model of open economy under flexible exchange rates. *Quarterly Journal of Economics*, February, pp. 149–64.

Baumol, W. J. 1970. *Economic dynamics*, 3d ed. London: Macmillan.

Bilson, J. F. O. 1978. Rational expectations and the exchange rates. In J. A. Frenkel and H. Johnson, eds., *The economics of exchange rates*. Reading, Mass.: Addison-Wesley.

Darby, M. R. 1980. Sterilization and monetary control under pegged exchange rates: Theory and evidence. NBER Working Paper, no. 449.

Dooly, M. F., and P. Isard. 1979. The portfolio-balance model of exchange rates. International Finance Division Papers, no. 141, Federal Reserve Board.

Dornbusch, R. 1975. A portfolio balance model of the open economy. *Journal of Monetary Economics* 1: 3–20.

———. 1976a. The theory of flexible exchange rate regimes and macroeconomic policy. *Scandinavian Journal of Economics* 78: 255–75.

———. 1976b. Expectations and exchange rate dynamics. *Journal of Political Economy* 84: 1161–76.

Frenkel, J. A. 1976. A monetary approach to the exchange rate: Doctrinal aspects of empirical evidence. *Scandinavian Journal of Economics* 78: 280–304.

Frenkel, J. A., and H. Johnson, eds. 1978. *The economics of exchange rates*. Reading, Mass.: Addison-Wesley.

Frenkel, J. A., and C. Rodriguez. 1975. Portfolio equilibrium and the balance of payments: A monetary approach. *American Economic Review* 65: 674–88.

Girton, L., and D. Henderson. 1977. Central bank operations in foreign and domestic assets under fixed and flexible exchange rates. In P. Clark, D. Logue, and R. Sweeny, eds., *The effects of exchange rate changes*. Washington.

Girton, L., and D. Roper. 1977. A monetary model of exchange market pressure applied to the postwar Canadian experience. *American Economic Review* 67: 537–48.

Henderson, D. 1976. Modeling the interdependence of national money and capital markets. *American Economic Review* 66: 190–99.

———. 1979. The dynamic effects of exchange market intervention policy: Two views and a synthesis. International Finance Division Papers, no. 142.

Kouri, P. 1976. The exchange rate and the balance of payments in the short run and in the long run: A monetary approach. *Scandinavian Journal of Economics* 78: 280–304.

Lee, D. 1980. Effects of open market operations and foreign exchange market operations under flexible exchange rates: A dynamic theory and some empirical evidence. Ph. D. dissertation, UCLA.

Lucas, R. E. 1973. Some international evidence on output-inflation trade-offs. *American Economic Review* 63: 326–34.

Niehans, J. 1976. How to fill an empty shell. *American Economic Review* 66: 181.

Roll, R. 1978. Violations of the law of one price and their implications for differentially denominated assets. Mimeographed paper, UCLA.

Stockman, A. 1978. Risk, information, and forward exchange rates. In J. A. Frenkel and H. Johnson, eds., *The economics of exchange rates*. Reading, Mass.: Addison-Wesley.

————. 1979. Monetary control and sterilization under pegged exchange rates. Discussion paper, UCLA.

13   An Alternative Approach to International Capital Flows

Michael Melvin

Since the mid-1960s, the standard literature on international capital flows has been characterized by the use of the Tobin-Markowitz type of portfolio choice models to determine the portfolio shares devoted to foreign and domestic assets. In this framework, the stocks of assets held depend on risk and return measures associated with alternative assets. Thus the change in the stocks, the capital flows, will depend on changes in the risk and return measures. This stock-adjustment approach is generally considered an advance beyond the earlier studies that related capital flows to *levels* of return measures. However, the newer models, with their theoretical frameworks including risk terms, have created new problems that have yet to be adequately dealt with. While the risk terms are included in the theoretical models and it is generally recognized that risk reduction through portfolio diversification provides an incentive for capital flows,[1] the empirical treatment of risk has been the low point of the literature to date. One aim of this chapter is to incorporate in a capital-flows equation a measure of risk suggested by a standard finance model.

Besides the introduction of an explicit risk proxy, this chapter will also derive and estimate a theoretically consistent functional form for the capital-flows equation. The existing literature has in many cases not even considered the matter of proper functional form, but instead assumed a simple model where all variables enter in an additive fashion.

The approach taken here will differ from most of the previous studies in two additional ways besides the treatment of risk: (1) net capital flows will be the variable of interest, whereas other studies have estimated the

Michael Melvin is an assistant professor of economics at Arizona State University.

1. See Grubel (1968). Even with constant return differentials there would be capital flows to maintain the optimal portfolio shares.

domestic demand for foreign assets separately from the foreign demand for domestic assets (and have usually disaggregated the capital account into components yielding the best empirical fit); (2) the capital-flows equation will be placed in the framework of an eight-country macromodel allowing for simultaneous equation estimation techniques.[2]

13.1   Empirical Predecessors

The leading literature on capital flows generally develops a portfolio model where capital flows are a function of interest rates, wealth, and risk. For example, Miller and Whitman (1970) have a model where long-term portfolio foreign investment is determined in part by the variance of returns on domestic and foreign assets. Since these variances are unobservable, they examine the likely determinants of each, concluding that the variance of domestic returns moves inversely with domestic transitory income. So they use national income and time to proxy for the unobservable transitory income and we have one unobservable proxying for another unobservable with the result that observed income and time are supposed to represent the variance of domestic returns. Likewise foreign return variability should be a function of foreign transitory income, but they also argue for including domestic income and dummy variables for U.S. capital controls and European currency convertibility. Then, by assuming that U.S. and foreign income generally move together, they have the variance of foreign returns represented by U.S. income, time, and the dummy variable. One could easily argue that these variables in a demand for foreign assets function will more likely represent the portfolio scale variable than the determinants of the variances of the domestic and foreign returns. In such a case, the fact that the variables entered significantly should not be surprising, even if they in no way represent variability of returns.

Kouri and Porter (1974), in an oft-cited article, developed a portfolio approach model where capital flows were viewed as equating money demand and money supply. The model included a measure of risk which was supposed to derive from a Markowitz-Tobin formulation, but rather than develop some measure of variability of returns, Kouri and Porter assume that in their model the risk variable should measure changes in exchange-rate expectations. Facing the difficult problem of measuring

2. Most of the existing studies have assumed interest rates and exchange rates exogenous and so used OLS. Since the focus here is on one equation of some larger model, a suitable set of simultaneous equations is provided by the NBER International Transmission of Inflation Model (see part II of this volume). The NBER model contains a capital-flows equation, so the proposed equation may be inserted in place of the existing model equation as no new endogenous variables are introduced and only the exogenous risk terms are added. Note that three of the countries in the NBER Model are not investgated here (France, Japan, and the Netherlands), due to poor quality or unavailability of some data.

exchange-rate expectations in the fixed-rate period, they decide to use dummy variables for "periods when there were definite expectations of parity changes" (Kouri and Porter, p. 452).

In an early application of the portfolio approach to capital flows, Lee (1969) developed a theoretical model based on mean and variance and then in the empirical section estimated a regression where portfolio shares are run on interest differentials letting the estimated coefficients represent the risk terms (which assumes the risk is constant).

In most instances, while risk is mentioned in the theoretical arguments, it is ignored in the empirics. Bryant and Hendershott (1970) dismissed the problem by saying,

> In actual practice, researchers never have adequate information (if they have any at all) about the probability distributions economic units associate with various returns and costs . . . As a result we have not developed proxies for . . . the risk associated with each of the expected costs and returns. (p. 27)

Branson (1968), in what is considered a pioneering effort, developed the application of the portfolio approach to capital flows. His theoretical analysis incorporates risk, but then he ignores the problem in the empirical section. In a follow-up article, Branson and Hill (1971) mention that they are assuming risk to be constant throughout the analysis.

In the more recent literature it is apparent that authors are increasingly concerned over the shortcomings of their empirical work. Hodgson and Holmes (1977) stated

> Recent critics of empirical work have complained that the risk variables are wrongfully ignored when moving from theory to specific estimating equations and applying them to data. While this is true, our market rates of return are unadjusted for risk premia, due to the practical difficulty in obtaining quantified risk data. (p. 267)

While the problems of incorporating a "good" measure of risk in the capital-flows literature are considerable, it appears that even in the most highly regarded articles, the authors have chosen to reach for simple ad hoc formulations that are often hard to relate to the cited portfolio choice theory. As Bryant (1975) has pointed out in an excellent critique of the literature, there appears to be a large gap between the theory and the equations actually estimated.

The failure to develop better risk proxies is rather surprising considering the wide-scale use of ad hoc proxies permeating all the applied econometrics literature. Rather than use time trends and dummy variables to "explain" our ignorance, in the next section we will explicitly enter proxies to attempt to capture the measures of risk discussed in the literature.

13.2   The Traditional Framework

Following the standard framework of studies based on a portfolio selection approach (see Branson and Hill 1971 for instance), we can write the portfolio share devoted to foreign assets as a function of risk and return variables:

$$(13.1) \qquad F/W = f(R_d, R_f, E),$$

where F is foreign assets, W is domestic wealth, R_d and R_f are domestic and foreign interest rates, and E is the risk attached to F relative to domestic assets. Multiplying (13.1) through by W, we get the desired stock of foreign assets:

$$(13.2) \qquad F = W \cdot f(R_d, R_f, E).$$

The (f) function is then assumed to be linear, and we have our estimating equation:

$$(13.3) \qquad F = b_1 W R_d + b_2 W R_f + b_3 W E + b_4 W,$$

where the b_4 term represents a constant added to equation (13.2). The stock of domestic liabilities to foreigners is similarly written so that we may write net foreign asset holdings of country i as

$$N_i = b_1 W_i R_i + b_2 W_i R_f + b_3 W_i E_i + b_4 W_i$$
$$- b_5 W_f R_i - b_6 W_f R_f - b_7 W_f E_f - b_8 W_f,$$

or by assuming that it is the return differential that matters, we can write[3]

$$(13.4) \qquad N_i = b_1 W_i (R_i - R_f) + b_3 W_i E_i + b_4 W_i$$
$$- b_5 W_f (R_i - R_f) - b_7 W_f E_f - b_8 W_f.$$

Differencing (13.4) gives us the net capital-flow equation:

$$(13.5) \qquad \Delta N_i = b_1 \Delta(W_i(R_i - R_f)) + b_3 \Delta(W_i E_i) + b_4 \Delta W_i$$
$$- b_5 \Delta(W_f(R_i - R_f)) - b_7 \Delta(W_f E_f) - b_8 \Delta W_f,$$

where ΔN_i represents net capital outflows from country i ($\Delta N_i > 0$ is a net capital outflow from i). The foreign return variable has often been an interest rate unadjusted by expected exchange-rate changes. We should, however, consider the return on a foreign security to be the interest rate plus the expected change in the exchange rate. Theoretically, of course, all return and risk variables in the portfolio belong in the equation, but there are practical constraints that would caution against such practice. Besides the obvious problem of few degrees of freedom for the flexible exchange-rate period, there is also the problem of collinearity among the

---

3. The imposition of such a reasonable restriction seems desirable given the limited degrees of freedom available for the flexible exchange-rate period.

variables. Usually researchers just include one alternative return variable and proceed as if they had a two-country world. While such a solution is theoretically inappropriate and really doesn't "cure" the multicollinearity problem in that theory suggests all assets be represented, it is the "traditional" solution, and is therefore consistent with the spirit of this section (for $i \neq$ U.S., the U.S. interest rate will be the foreign rate, while the Canadian rate will serve as the foreign rate for the U.S.).

The risk variable (E) is the missing link between theory and empirics. Measures of variance are the risk proxies discussed in papers like Miller and Whitman (1970) and Lee (1969), yet such risk measures are hardly consistent with the finance models cited by the authors (we shouldn't care about the variance of a portfolio asset, but rather the contribution of that asset to the overall portfolio variance). In order to preserve the spirit of the capital-flows literature (we will abandon this approach shortly), equation (13.5) will be estimated using the concept of variance of returns as the risk proxy.[4]

The domestic and foreign wealth measures are, respectively, real domestic permanent income and a nominal income weighted average of foreign real income.[5] The interest rates are represented by the ninety-day treasury bill rate for the U.S., and a similar short-term rate elsewhere. The expected change in the exchange rate is taken from the exchange-rate equation of the NBER model, and is defined as the systematic part of a regression of the change in the exchange rate on lagged values of the exchange rate, the change in import prices, the prices of foreign oil, rest-of-world income, imports, rest-of-world prices, and the current change in the exchange rate. An alternative to using observed interest rates and the expected change in the exchange rate is to calculate the "risk premium" in the forward rate. Such an approach will be used below.

Defining the correct risk proxy is not strictly an empirical question, but making the simplifying assumption that the nominal return in each currency is certain so that only the exchange-rate uncertainty is important,

4. There are other kinds of risks besides the market risk considered here, such as default risk, but in keeping with the "traditional" approach, only the variability of return risk will be considered here.

5. For a further description of this and other series see the Data Appendix at the end of this volume. The model includes eight countries with the following i subscript assignment: 1. U.S., 2. U.K., 3. Canada, 4. France, 5. Germany, 6. Italy, 7. Japan, 8. Netherlands. We should note that the data for each country are in terms of domestic currency, so that the estimated coefficient magnitudes reported below tend to reflect the differences in currencies as measuring devices. For instance, Italian capital flows, measured in lira, have a larger numerical magnitude than U.S. capital flows measured in dollars. Since the income series in the NBER model (used in the simultaneous estimation) are in logs, the wealth measures used in the present paper will also be logs.

A weighted average of foreign permanent income was also tried, but since the results did not improve, it was decided to use the real income weighted average, as this series appears in the NBER model.

we can estimate equation (13.5) using the variability of the expected exchange-rate change as the relevant risk measure. This proxy is created as the standard deviation of the expected change in the exchange rate, where the standard deviations are computed over the last eight quarters.

Table 13.1A presents the estimates of (13.5) omitting the risk proxies, and table 13.1B gives the results with the risk terms included. The overall explanatory power of the regressions is generally poor in terms of R^2 when compared to the earlier literature. However, the equations estimated here differ from the earlier literature in that net capital flows are the dependent variable, whereas earlier works generally looked at the foreign holdings of domestic liabilities apart from domestic holdings of foreign liabilities. More important, however, is the fact that the present study looks at the entire capital account—current account minus official settlements balance of payments. Previous researchers have found that by eliminating certain components of the capital account they could improve the fit of their equations.

An exception to these generalities is provided by Branson and Hill (1971), who used disaggregated capital account data for the U.S. but net capital-flows data for the U.K., Canada, France, Germany, Italy, and Japan.[6] While their study is conducted over the fixed rate period excluding certain "crisis" quarters and departs from a strict portfolio distribution approach by including trade balance and "monetary indicator" variables such as velocity, their results might serve as a crude standard. Comparing unadjusted R^2 (since this is what they report), we find the following:

	B and H	Table 13.1B
U.K.	.78	.50
Canada	.55	.93
Germany	.79	.79
Italy	.74	.41

Given the amount of experimentation carried out by Branson and Hill, we may consider their R^2 measures as an upper bound on the explanatory power of capital-flows equations run over the fixed rate period. With similar ad hoc searching, the flexible period results in table 13.1B, which in some cases compare favorably already, could perhaps run a close race

---

6. Herring (1973) used the net capital account for the U.S. plus the same countries used by Branson and Hill (1971). In his study, very high R^2 values were achieved by including an additional variable, "unusual capital movements." These "unusual" movements he first identified, and then, by normalizing all of the estimates on the largest estimated movement, he created a dummy series of relative magnitudes of unusual capital movements. While this is most definitely a way to explain much of the variability in capital movements, it represents no theory and essentially states that capital movements are "explained" primarily by random shocks. Since the goal of the current paper is to estimate a systematic component of capital flows, such approaches are not very useful.

Table 13.1A   **Equation (13.5) without Risk Variables**

	US	UK	CA	GE	IT
Coefficients					
b_0	63.58	7.22	−44.72	64.90	−2657
	(2.95)	(2.41)	(−13.29)	(2.10)	(−.97)
b_1	17.64	−4.00	−4.83	18.13	618
	(.46)	(−1.73)	(−1.13)	(.96)	(.99)
b_4	−6318	−1284	3516	−5340	124538
	(−2.30)	(−2.74)	(12.58)	(−1.81)	(.50)
b_5	−270	−114.0	−106.79	730.00	32015
	(−.15)	(−1.75)	(−.65)	(.79)	(.65)
b_8	−319	−95.09	4.20	1048	−51271
	(−1.29)	(−3.01)	(.27)	(3.06)	(−1.82)
Error process	AR2 −.00, −.20	AR2 .38, −.54	AR2 .31, −.72	AR1 −.21	AR2 .88, −.15
S.E.E.	11.63	1.70	.96	19.45	993
$\bar{R}^2$	.15	.40	.88	.40	.02
D-W	1.99	2.36	2.36	1.90	2.05

with the Branson and Hill findings. Because of the few degrees of freedom available, equation (13.5) remains a basic portfolio distribution approach, as I have refrained from further ad hoc experimentation.

Given the disclaimers above, the variables of interest are the risk terms. While the traditional approach leads to an estimating equation like (13.5), actual estimation using proxies for E has not been carried out by past authors. The usual procedure is to estimate an equation omitting the risk proxies as reported in table 13.1A. When the risk proxies are included, the results are somewhat mixed as reported in table 13.1B. In four of the five countries the fit (in terms of standard error of estimate) is improved when the risk terms are included, and six of the individual risk coefficients enter significantly at the 10% level of significance. In terms of a joint F test of the hypothesis $b_3 = b_7 = 0$, only for the U.S and Italy are both b_3 and b_7 significant.

Regarding the signs of the various coefficients, we must remember that wealth enters interactively with both risk and return. Thus, to determine the sign of any individual effect, we must evaluate the partial derivative of the function with respect to the particular argument. Interaction terms also have implications for hypothesis testing. The test that a variable has no effect on capital flows would involve an F test of the hypothesis that all regressors involving that variable have coefficients that are jointly zero.

Table 13.1B   **Equation (13.5) with Risk Variables**

	US	UK	CA	GE	IT
Coefficients					
b_0	75.13	8.06	−45.93	28.04	−1780
	(4.76)	(2.33)	(−14.43)	(1.15)	(−.70)
b_1	36.63	−5.29	−5.56	24.90	297
	(1.14)	(−1.92)	(−1.27)	(1.29)	(.50)
b_3	6297	55.82	−32.95	−1095	37802
	(3.47)	(.83)	(−.13)	(−2.81)	(1.87)
b_4	−8157	−1456	3622	−1188	21116
	(−4.00)	(−2.61)	(13.63)	(−.49)	(−.09)
b_5	607	−145	−157	917	−3730
	(.38)	(−1.89)	(−.89)	(1.01)	(−.08)
b_7	2.6×10^5	1001	1701	−37798	3862830
	(3.38)	(.59)	(.22)	(−2.20)	(2.18)
b_8	−2248	−126	1.58	2169	−140277
	(−3.77)	(−2.28)	(.03)	(4.49)	(−3.07)
Error process	AR2 .11, −.62	AR2 .45, −.54	AR2 .34, −.85	AR2 −.67, −.13	AR2 .83, −.07
S.E.E.	9.87	1.77	.95	17.87	908
$\bar{R}^2$	.49	.32	.90	.71	.19
D-W	2.60	2.28	2.50	1.74	1.97

b_0 Constant
b_1 Δ(Product of domestic wealth and return differential)
b_3 Δ(Product of domestic wealth and risk)
b_4 Δ(Domestic wealth)
b_5 Δ(Product of foreign wealth and return differential)
b_7 Δ(Product of foreign wealth and risk)
b_8 Δ(Foreign wealth)
AR1 First-order autoregressive process
AR2 Second-order autoregressive process
Estimation period 1971II to 1976IV
t statistics in parentheses

Analyzing the various derivatives in table 13.1B we have

$$\delta\Delta N_i/\delta E = b_3 W_{it} - b_7 W_{ft},$$
$$\delta\Delta N_i/\delta(R_i - R_f) = b_1 W_{it} - b_5 W_{ft},$$
$$\delta\Delta N_i/\delta W_i = b_1(R_{it} - R_{ft}) + b_3 E_{it} + b_4,$$
$$\delta\Delta N_i/\delta W_f = -b_5(R_{it} - R_{ft}) - b_7 E_{ft} - b_8.$$

Considering first the risk variable (E), in each equation this variable appears twice, as the risk proxy enters in both the domestic demand for foreign securities and the foreign demand for domestic securities. Under the theory considered in this section, the net effect of an increase in E is uncertain. As the risk associated with foreign assets increases, the domestic demand for foreign assets falls as does the foreign demand for domestic assets so that the net effect could go either way. Thus, ceteris paribus, the effect of greater exchange-rate variability would be to reduce the overall level of activity with no clear effect on the net capital flows of any country. Analyzing the partial $\delta \Delta N_i / \delta E$, at each point in the sample space we find mixed results. For the U.S., the U.K., and Germany the sign is positive, but for Canada and Italy the effect is negative. While intuition is of little use in determining the expected sign of the risk term, on the basis of the joint F test mentioned above we assert that this variable can be important in explaining capital flows along the lines of the traditional approach.

For the return differentials, we would clearly expect a negative effect as we are measuring the return on a country i security minus the return on a foreign security. As this differential increases, ceteris paribus, capital outflows should fall. Examining the derivative $\delta \Delta N_i / \delta (R_i - R_f)$ at each point in the sample space indicates that only for Canada is the sign overwhelmingly negative while for the U.K. approximately half the signs are negative. However, the individual t statistics on b_1 and b_5 suggest that the estimated coefficients are insignificantly different from zero.

Finally, for the domestic and foreign wealth terms we expect positive and negative signs respectively according to the portfolio theory, as increases in the portfolio scale lead to asset purchases. Thus an increase in domestic wealth would increase capital outflows while an increase in foreign wealth would lead to increased capital inflows. Examining the derivatives with respect to domestic wealth, only for Canada and Italy are the signs positive while the U.S., the U.K., and Germany have surprisingly negative signs. An examination of the derivatives with respect to foreign wealth reveals negative signs for Canada and Germany and positive signs for the U.S., the U.K., and Italy. Thus in each case only two of the five countries have the sign expected by the portfolio theory.

Previous authors have told stories about wealth entering with signs opposite to what would be expected from a portfolio theory. Prachowny (1969) has suggested that capital flows should be a function of the growth rates of domestic and foreign income in that the demand for foreign assets is related to the general level of economic activity. In his analysis, higher domestic income and lower foreign income are associated with capital inflows. Branson's (1968) analysis allows for wealth effects to go either direction as the portfolio effect of increasing the demand for foreign securities could be offset by an increase in the domestic supply of securities via a wealth effect on the desired stock of liabilities. Kreicher (1981), in a study using the Branson approach, found that in his sample the sign of the wealth effect did indeed vary across countries.

Taken together, the results presented in table 13.1B are interpreted as offering promise with regard to specifying empirical proxies for risk as defined in the traditional capital-flows literature. Had we just examined the results for the U.S., Germany, and Italy, we would have made a much more impressive case. But considering a wider application of the approach allows us to draw more useful conclusions. First, we know that specifying a proxy variable for risk involves a great deal of arbitrariness. No doubt what works well in some countries won't work in others so that a persistent searcher could probably find more significant risk proxies. A second point regards the theoretical consideration of portfolio risk. As mentioned above, the capital-flows literature has generally spoken of risk in terms of the variance of returns on individual assets. This is certainly not the risk discussed in the modern finance models where the risk of an individual asset is a function of not only its own variance, but also the covariances with other assets. So we see that the inclusion of proxies like the standard deviations included here may not provide a useful test other than to illustrate the naive notion of risk portrayed by the earlier literature. The next section attempts to develop an alternative proxy consistent with a well-known finance model.

Before proceeding to the next section, we should reconsider the return differential used above, as this same variable will be of interest throughout the analysis. In specifying appropriate interest rates to be used in international comparisons, we always run into the problem of finding comparable rates. The author has no a priori confidence in comparing U.S. and U.K. treasury bill rates, for instance, but uses such rates on the basis of their availability. Rather than be forced into specifying domestic interest rates for each country in order to create a return differential, we could instead construct a series for the "risk premium" contained in the forward rate. In order to proceed along these lines we need the preliminary assumption that interest parity holds.

In equation (13.5), the return differential was written as $(R_i - R_f)$, where R_i was the domestic interest rate, and R_f the foreign rate. Now let's explicitly write $R_f = R_j + \mu_{ji}$, where R_j is the interest rate in foreign country j and μ_{ji} is the expected change in the exchange rate, or

$$\mu_{ji} = \frac{E(S_{ji,t+1}) - S_{ji,t}}{S_{ji,t}},$$

where S_{ji} is units of i's currency per unit of j's. The investor in country i can then earn $(1 + R_i)$ at home by investing 1 unit of currency i or $[(1 + R_j)F_{ji}/S_{ji}]$ by investing the unit of i currency in country j securities (F_{ji} is the relevant forward rate at which the j currency earnings are sold).

Arbitrage results in the following:

$$1 + R_i = \frac{(1 + R_j)F_{ji}}{S_{ji}},$$

or

$$\frac{1 + R_i}{1 + R_j} = \frac{F_{ji}}{S_{ji}},$$

subtracting one from both sides, we get

$$\frac{R_i - R_j}{1 + R_j} = \frac{F_{ji} - S_{ji}}{S_{ji}},$$

which is usually approximated as

$$R_i - R_j = \frac{F_{ji} - S_{ji}}{S_{ji}}.$$

Since the relevant return differential is $(R_i - R_j - \mu_{ji})$, by subtracting μ_{ji} from each side of the above equation we get

$$R_i - R_j - \mu_{ji} = \frac{F_{ji} - E(S_{ji, t+1})}{S_{ji}}.$$

Thus, if interest-rate parity holds (and careful studies seem to indicate that it does), we can write the return differential strictly in terms of the risk premium in the foreign exchange market.

Note that there exists some controversy over the very existence of this risk premium. The controversy stems from a debate centering on whether the forward rate is an unbiased predictor of the future spot rate. The question is considered in detail elsewhere (Melvin 1981), but this author feels that the evidence is not yet overwhelming on either side, as there exists empirical support both for the existence of a risk premium and for no premium.

The risk premium series was created from spot and forward rate data provided by Richard Levich to the NBER international model effort (the data are originally from Harris Bank). Assuming efficient markets, the realized future spot rate should only differ from the expected future rate by an additive error term, so the realized rate was used as a proxy for the expected rate. Then the risk premium series was used in place of the return differential in reestimating tables 13.1A and 13.1B as shown in tables 13.1C and 13.1D respectively.

---

7. No doubt there is measurement error involved here. If the risk premiums alone were measured incorrectly, then their coefficients would be biased downward. However, if some other variables involved measurement error, then the effect on the risk premium coefficients would not necessarily be downward.

There is a striking similarity between table 13.1A and table 13.1C. Just as the return differentials were insignificant in explaining capital flows in 13.1A, so are the risk premiums insignificant in 13.1C.[7] The other coefficients remain just about the same in 13.1C as they were in 13.1A. Comparing table 13.1B to 13.1D, we find that the results are generally alike here also. The similarity of the results seems to bode well both for the domestic rates chosen for the original return differential and for the assumption of interest parity holding for these particular rates. Since the results are so similar (there certainly is no reason to prefer the risk premiums over the return differentials), the analysis will proceed in terms of the return differential rather than the risk premium, as the NBER model to be used for simultaneous equation estimation contains the interest rates. The novel approach to capital-flows estimation to be developed in the next section will also be phrased in terms of the return differential.

So far the period of analysis has conformed to the data base used in the NBER model. Alternative results estimated through 1978 using IMF *International Financial Statistics* data are presented in section 13.4.

13.3 An Alternative Framework

This section will develop an estimating equation consistent with the utility-maximizing behavior of individuals. Previous studies have started with a general notation as in equation (13.1), asserting that theory suggests that capital flows are some function of returns and risks. With such a beginning, the author declares the hunting season open for the "proper" fuctional form. Usually the assumption of linearity is made. As Branson and Hill (1971) say after writing down their general form, "Since we have, at this point, no particular *a priori* information on the form of the portfolio distribution function $f(\cdot)$, we may assume it is linear" (p. 7). It is my contention that the estimating equation derived from the portfolio theory will in general have variables not entering in a strictly additive fashion. Rather than merely assert that portfolio theory suggests capital flows are *some* function of risks and returns, it would be preferable to derive the functional form suggested by the theory. Then, if the researcher proceeds to move away from this form, it is clear that the estimating equation is not exactly consistent with the underlying theory. After developing what I believe to be a theoretically consistent estimating equation, I will investigate its empirical possibilities.

A measure of risk more consistent with theory than that of the previous section may be found in Solnik's international asset pricing model. Solnik (1973) developed an "international asset pricing model" (IAPM) by extending Merton (1973) to encompass international portfolio diversification. Included in the model are demand functions for foreign assets.

Table 13.1C   **Equation (13.5) without Risk Variables, with Risk Premium**

Coeffi-cients	US	UK	CA	GE	IT
b_0	63.71	6.74	−44.97	72.29	−2757
	(1.86)	(2.22)	(−12.56)	(3.01)	(−.96)
b_1	8.62	11.28	1.54	−29.69	−1666
	(.12)	(1.20)	(.24)	(−.44)	(−1.23)
b_4	−6403	−1223	3534	−5887	1.4×10^5
	(−1.49)	(−2.59)	(11.90)	(−2.56)	(.54)
b_5	879	279	18.48	−428	1.0×10^5
	(.34)	(1.29)	(.10)	(−.14)	(−1.14)
b_8	−423	−103	2.42	1299	−45037
	(−1.48)	(−3.23)	(.15)	(4.63)	(−1.74)
Error process	MA2 −.24, −.26	AR2 .36, −.57	AR2 .37, −.79	AR2 −.19, −.29	AR2 .88, −.16
S.E.E.	11.85	1.75	1.01	18.12	1000
$\bar{R}^2$	−.004	.39	.87	.61	−.004
D-W	2.01	2.34	2.03	1.93	2.05

Rather than reproduce the entire derivation (which is lengthy and published elsewhere), I will begin from one of the optimality conditions (Solnik, p. 22) keeping all of Solnik's assumptions except for his initial assumption that the expected change in exchange rates is zero. In my version I will assume that the expected return from holding foreign assets is equal to the foreign rate of interest plus the expected change in the exchange rate. The optimality condition is then

(13.6) $$(R_i + \mu_{ik} - R_k) = -\frac{W^k J_{ww}^k}{J_w^k} [\Sigma_{j \neq k} Y_j^k \phi_{ij}^k],$$

where R_i = the risk-free interest rate in country i;

   μ_{ik} = the expected change in the exchange rate, in units of k's currency per unit of i's: $(S_{ik,t+1}^* - S_{ik,t})/S_{ik,t}$;

   W^k = the wealth of k;

   J^k = the utility of wealth function, where J_{ww}^k and J_w^k are second and first derivatives respectively so that $-J_{ww}^k/J_w^k$ represents absolute risk aversion for k investors;

   Y_j^k = the proportion of k's wealth invested in j's liabilities;

   ϕ_{ij}^k = the elements of the covariance matrix of exchange rates for country k; for instance, $||\phi_{ij}^k||_{n-1 \times n-1}$,

Table 13.1D   **Equation (13.5) with Risk Variables and Risk Premium**

	US	UK	CA	GE	IT
Coefficients					
b_0	72.08	4.73	−45.55	37.17	−2669
	(3.34)	(1.44)	(−13.21)	(1.61)	(−.97)
b_1	5.12	19.66	3.69	39.49	−650
	(.09)	(1.85)	(.60)	(.46)	(−.41)
b_3	6025	−30.03	−107	−1038	35515
	(3.12)	(−.55)	(−.47)	(−2.33)	(1.60)
b_4	7822	−940	3591	−2144	1.2×10^5
	(2.83)	(−1.83)	(12.50)	(−.94)	(.46)
b_5	352	511	102	2552	−27716
	(.16)	(1.99)	(.56)	(.65)	(−.26)
b_7	2.4×10^5	−1926	−649	−39307	3.4×10^6
	(3.00)	(−1.24)	(−.09)	(−1.89)	(1.72)
b_8	−2193	−76.05	14.88	2264	$−1.1 \times 10^5$
	(−3.29)	(−1.67)	(.29)	(4.38)	(−2.52)
Error Process	AR2 .30, −.48	AR2 .34, −.58	AR2 .41, −.92	AR2 −.65, −.40	AR1 .75
S.E.E.	11.09	1.72	1.00	17.62	986
$\bar{R}^2$	.29	.42	.89	.77	.07
D-W	2.45	2.28	2.07	1.88	1.93

b_0 Constant
b_1 Δ(Product of domestic wealth and risk premium)
b_3 Δ(Product of domestic wealth and risk)
b_4 Δ(Domestic wealth)
b_5 Δ(Product of foreign wealth and risk premium)
b_7 Δ(Product of foreign wealth and risk)
b_8 Δ(Foreign wealth)
MA2 Second-order moving average process
AR1 First-order autoregressive process
AR2 Second-order autoregressive process
Estimation period 1971II to 1976IV
t statistics in parentheses

where ϕ_{ij}^k is the covariance of the change of i's and j's exchange rate where both are stated relative to k.

Since Y_j^k is equal to the proportion of k's wealth invested in j's liabilities, or $Y_j^k = e_j^k / W^k$, where e_j^k is the demand for j's liabilities by k, we can use (13.6) to solve for the asset demand. Rewriting (13.6) in matrix form,

$$||R_i + \mu_{ik} - R_k|| = \phi^k Y^k A^k,$$

where

$$A^k = -\frac{W^k J^k_{ww}}{J^k_w}.$$

We can solve for Y^k by matrix inversion:

(13.7) $$Y^k = (\phi^k)^{-1}||R_i + \mu_{ik} - R_k||(A^k)^{-1},$$

or, for illustrative purposes (assuming k is the nth country),

$$
\begin{bmatrix} Y^n_1 \\ Y^n_2 \\ \cdot \\ \cdot \\ \cdot \\ Y^n_{n-1} \end{bmatrix}
=
\begin{bmatrix} \phi^n_{11} & \phi^n_{12} \ldots \phi^n_{1,n-1} \\ \phi^n_{21} & \phi^n_{22} \ldots \\ \cdot & \ldots \\ \cdot & \ldots \\ \cdot & \ldots \\ \phi^n_{n-1,1} & \ldots \phi^n_{n-1,n-1} \end{bmatrix}^{-1}
\begin{bmatrix} R_1 + \mu_{1n} - R_n \\ R_2 + \mu_{2n} - R_n \\ \cdot \\ \cdot \\ \cdot \\ R_{n-1} + \mu_{n-1,n} - R_n \end{bmatrix}
(A^k)^{-1}
$$

Writing (13.7) in summation notation and multiplying through by W^k, we get the demand for i's liabilities by k:

(13.8) $$e^k_i = B^k W^i \Sigma_{j \neq k} \eta^k_{ij}(R_j + \mu_{jk} - R_k)$$
$$+ B_0 W^k,$$

where the η^k_{ij} are elements of the $(\phi^k)^{-1}$ matrix, $B^k = -[J^k_w/W^k J^k_{ww}]$, and B_0 represents a constant term inserted in (13.7).[8]

The total demand for foreign assets by K is found by summing (13.8) over i. The total foreign demand for i's liabilities is found by summing over k. Thus net holdings of foreign assets by i can be found as total foreign assets minus total liabilities to foreigners:

(13.9) $$N_i = \Sigma_{k \neq i} e^i_k - \Sigma_{k \neq i} e^k_i$$

or by substituting

(13.10) $$N_i = B_i W^i \sum_k \Sigma_{j \neq i} \eta^i_{kj}(R_j + \mu_{ji} - R_i)$$
$$+ B^i_0 W^i - \Sigma_{k \neq i} B_k W^i \Sigma_{j \neq k} \eta^k_{ij}$$
$$(R_j + \mu_{jk} - R_k) - B^k_0 W^k.$$

---

8. The constant is inserted in recognition of the fact that we are dealing with the entire capital account of a nation. The portfolio theory presented here determines the portfolio shares for individual investors. But the capital account data include flows besides portfolio assets (for instance, foreign direct investment and errors and omissions) so that we would expect to observe flows not explained by the theory. It should be noted, however, that in correspondence with the author, John Makin indicated that his recent work has led him to believe that "errors and omissions" are in fact capital flows.

N_i gives the total net demand for foreign assets by i. The change in N_i would represent i's capital flows. If $dN_i > 0$, we have a net capital outflow from i; if $dN_i < 0$, then there is a net capital inflow to i. Differencing (13.10) would give us net capital outflows as a function of changes in the covariances of exchange-rate changes and return differentials (treating the risk aversion terms as parameters) as well as changes in wealth.

There are some obvious differences between equation (13.10) and the "traditional" approach outlined earlier. Besides the different measure of risk, we also note that in contrast to the previous section, the theory suggests that the covariances and return differentials enter in a multiplicative form so that we are creating indexes of return differentials (the price of risk) weighted by covariances of exchange-rate changes (the measure of risk).

Since asset pricing models produce static equilibrium relations, wealth or portfolio scale is assumed constant. Then, holding wealth constant, the demand for any particular asset is given by its return and risk characteristics. While the equilibrium relation given by equation (13.10) is assumed to hold at each period, to use the model in a time series framework we must place the equation in a model that can explain changes in variables which the static framework takes as given. The NBER Mark III International Transmission Model discussed earlier will serve this purpose.

Differencing (13.10) gives a capital-flows equation of the form

(13.11) $$\Delta N_i = \beta_i \Delta [W^i \sum_k \Sigma_{j \neq i} \, \eta^i_{kj} (R_j + \mu_{ji} - R_i)]$$
$$+ \beta^i_0 \Delta W^i - \Sigma_{k \neq i} \beta_k \Delta [W^k \Sigma_{j \neq k} \, \eta^k_{ij}$$
$$(R_j + \mu_{jk} - R_k)] - \beta^k_0 \Delta W^k .$$

The η variable is the explicit risk proxy. As discussed above, the η^k_{ij} are elements of the inverted matrix of covariances of exchange-rate changes. The proxies for the η^k_{ij} will be formed, using monthly exchange-rate data, by taking the pairwise covariances over the past eighteen months. Thus the covariance matrix at period t is created by computing the covariance over monthly data corresponding to the previous six quarters, $t - 1$ to $t - 6$. The resulting matrix is a standard symmetric matrix with the variances of the exchange-rate changes along the main diagonal and the various pairwise covariances in the off-diagonal elements as illustrated by the matrix above. In the eight-country world under consideration, for each country k, the other seven currencies are stated in terms of currency k and then a 7×7 covariance matrix is formed using these other seven currencies. A 7×7 matrix of covariances for each period is then inverted to give the η^k_{ij} for that period (for country k). The process is then repeated for each country and period.

As before, we have the problem of collinearity, only this time it involves the various covariance weighted return differentials. Since the theory suggests that all the covariance weighted return differentials belong in the equation, we cannot "cure" the multicollinearity problem unless we have strong prior convictions that a subset of the variables will capture the relevant phenomena. Suppose we begin our estimation procedure by taking the familiar approach of choosing one foreign country as proxying for the foreign sector. Following the approach of the previous section, we will let the U.S. represent the foreign sector for each country (Canada represents the foreign sector for the U.S.), so we can estimate (13.11) as an equation with five parameters if we include a constant.

At first glance it may seem improper to use the observed nominal interest rates in the return differential $(R_j + \mu_{ji} - R_i)$ as the IAPM is phrased in terms of certain real returns in each country. However, it must be remembered that the variable of interest is the return differential, and when the investor deflates both domestic and foreign returns by his domestic price, the price effects cancel out so that writing $(R_j + \mu_{ji} - R_i)$ in terms of observed rates is consistent with the underlying theory.

The estimation results are presented in table 13.2. Comparing this table with table 13.1B, we see that the standard error of the regression was lowered in only one of the five countries so that equation (13.11) cannot be said to do a "better" job in explaining net capital flows over this period. Only four of the risk-return coefficients enter significantly at the 10% level in table 13.2.[9] In evaluating the effect of the wealth terms, we must look at the partial derivatives in equation (13.11):

$$\delta \Delta N_i / \delta W^i = \beta_i \sum_k \sum_{j \neq i} \eta^i_{kj}(R_j + \mu_{ji} - R_i) + \beta^i_0,$$

$$\delta \Delta N_i / \delta W^k = -\beta_k \sum_{j \neq k} \eta^k_{ij}(R_j + \mu_{jk} - R_k) - \beta^k_0.$$

Evaluating these derivatives at each point in the sample space, we find results similar to those of table 13.1B. Domestic wealth has a positive effect on net capital outflows in Canada and Italy while foreign wealth has a negative effect only for Canada and Germany. Thus, as before, only for Canada do the wealth effects seem consistent with the portfolio approach while for the other countries the results seem to fall in line with the Prachowny (1969) or Branson (1968) arguments.

One might question whether (13.11) is properly specified when applied to the aggregate net capital account. In particular, there may be an important omitted variable since many researchers over the fixed rate period found the balance of trade to be a significant proxy for the "trade

9. While relative risk aversion is theoretically a positive value, I don't really care to test either the sign or magnitude of β, just that it differs significantly from zero. I'm interested in testing for the effect of the risk and return variables on capital flows. β is a convenient parameter that arises from the theory.

financing" motive for capital flows.[10] However, when country i's balance of trade was added to equation (13.11), only in the U.K. equation did it seem important, and even then the sign was wrong.

So far we have been assuming that actual capital flows equal desired capital flows as the market attains equilibrium each period. Yet it is well known that many countries place restrictions on international capital flows. Thus, besides the usual macroeconomic assumption of adjustment costs due to some nonspecified causes, in the international monetary literature we also have government regulation providing a specific barrier to complete adjustment. Bryant (1975) has argued that the existing capital-flows literature (with the exception of Bryant and Hendershott 1970) has failed to incorporate the effects of governmental restrictions on capital flows (Bryant, p. 339). Yet without specific knowledge of the effects of controls we are constrained to use such approaches as dummy variables or partial adjustments. If we assume that $\Delta N_i = \alpha_i(N_i^* - N_{i,t-1})$, where N_i^* is the desired level, then as Bryant points out we should model α as changing with changes in capital controls. Lacking degrees of freedom and knowledge of how controls affected market participants in different countries, I am willing to assume a constant effect across the recent flexible rate period and specify α as a constant.

Writing the desired net asset holdings in the form of (13.10), we have

$$\Delta N_i = N_i - N_{i,t-1} = \alpha_i(N_i^* - N_{i,t-1}) \text{ or}$$

(13.12)
$$N_i = \alpha_i[\beta_i W^i \sum_k \sum_{j \neq i} \eta_{kj}^i (R_j + \mu_{ji} - R_i)$$
$$+ \beta_0^i W^i - \sum_{k \neq i} \beta_k W^k$$
$$\sum_{j \neq k} \eta_{ij}^k (R_j + \mu_{jk} - R_k) - \beta_0^k W^k]$$
$$+ (1 - \alpha_i)N_{i,t-1}.$$

Differencing (13.12) gives us the partial adjustment capital-flows model:

(13.13)
$$\Delta N_i = \alpha_i \beta_i \Delta[W^i \sum_k \sum_{j \neq i} \eta_{kj}^i (R_j + \mu_{ji} - R_i)] + \alpha_i \beta_0^i \Delta W^i$$
$$- \alpha_i \sum_{k \neq i} \beta_k \Delta[W^k \sum_{j \neq k} \eta_{ij}^k (R_j + \mu_{jk} - R_k)$$
$$- \alpha_i \beta_0^k \Delta W^k] + (1 - \alpha_i)\Delta N_{i,t-1}.$$

---

10. Leamer and Stern (1970) argue that "the primary variable for explaining trade financing should be expressed in terms of *changes* in sales rather than levels. The reason for this is that rapid growth in sales that reflects favorable profit opportunities will engender increases in trade credit. When sales and profit opportunities level off, there will be a tendency for firms to rely more on internal financing and domestic credit sources. The result will be a leveling off and perhaps even a decline in the use of foreign credits" (p. 96). It is interesting to note that Branson and Hill (1971) found the change in the trade balance to be an important explanatory variable over the fixed rate period for the net capital account of the U.K. and Canada.

Table 13.2   Equation (13.11)

	US	UK	CA	GE	IT
Coefficients					
b_0	57.18 (2.79)	6.84 (2.39)	−44.28 (−12.38)	73.12 (2.94)	−3216 (−1.13)
b_1	−.0001 (−2.44)	8.6×10^{-7} (.23)	1.5×10^{-6} (.71)	-3×10^{-6} (−.13)	-5×10^{-4} (−.75)
b_2	.003 (2.41)	7.7×10^{-4} (3.50)	-1.9×10^{-4} (−.83)	.011 (1.93)	.31 (1.49)
b_3	−5434 (−2.09)	−1237 (−2.75)	3477 (11.67)	−6151 (−2.56)	203248 (.79)
b_4	−256 (−1.24)	−96.04 (−2.97)	5.44 (.31)	1043 (3.37)	−8273 (−.33)
Error process	—	AR2 .69, −.72	AR2 .51, −.86	AR2 −.17, −.38	AR2 1.09, −.36
S.E.E.	9.88	1.51	1.00	19.00	1000
$\bar{R}^2$	.36	.51	.86	.61	.01
D-W	1.91	2.34	2.21	1.95	2.19

Table 13.3   Equation (13.13)

	US	UK	CA	GE	IT
Coefficients					
αb_0	30.88 (2.96)	6.81 (2.44)	−29.31 (−4.55)	1.22 (.06)	−2524 (−1.17)

αb_1	-2.2×10^{-4} (−3.86)	3.2×10^{-6} (.69)	-9.7×10^{-7} (−.54)	-1.7×10^{-5} (−1.23)	-3.7×10^{-4} (−.53)
αb_2	.001 (1.12)	8.8×10^{-4} (3.10)	-2.9×10^{-4} (−.92)	.010 (2.02)	.684 (2.01)
αb_3	−2888 (−2.33)	−1209 (−2.73)	2295 (4.46)	247.58 (.12)	2.1×10^{-5} (1.03)
αb_4	−48.20 (−.41)	−79.18 (−2.11)	−14.00 (−.88)	357.95 (1.43)	−7183 (−.29)
$(1-\alpha)$	.439 (3.91)	.201 (.99)	.374 (2.63)	.715 (4.28)	.793 (3.33)
Error process	AR2 −.79, −.64	AR2 .56, −.67	AR2 .03, −.59	AR2 −.97, −.56	AR2 .25, .25
S.E.E.	8.89	1.53	.95	16.88	927
$\bar{R}^2$	.77	.51	.90	.85	.40
h [D-W]	−.10	−3.99	−1.31	.24	[1.92]

b_0 Constant

b_1 Δ(Product of domestic wealth, inverse of covariance matrix, and return differential)

b_2 Δ(Product of foreign wealth, inverse of covariance matrix, and return differential)

b_3 Δ(Domestic wealth)

b_4 Δ(Foreign wealth)

α Partial adjustment coefficient

AR2 Second-order autoregressive process

h Durbin's "h" statistic; when h can't be computed (this occurs when the product of the sample size and the estimated variance of $(1-\alpha)$ exceeds one), the D-W statistic is reported

Estimation period 1971II to 1976IV

t statistics in parentheses

Table 13.3 presents estimates of (13.13). Only for the U.K. could we not reject the hypothesis that α equals one. Implied values of α range from .80 for the U.K. to .21 for Italy. Compared to table 13.2, the standard error of the regression falls for all but the U.K. Those familiar with the work on net capital flows will recognize that these results would not compare unfavorably with the previous work, especially if we were to compare unadjusted R^2, the statistic reported by many previous authors.

It is interesting to note the sensitivity of the results to the error process estimated. The TROLL system allows the estimation of first- and second-order autoregressive and moving average processes. The process that minimized the sum of squared errors (and therefore the standard error of the regression) was chosen. If the empirical race was to be run on the basis of $\bar{R}^2$, then in certain instances different processes would have been chosen as the quasi-differencing induced by an assumed error process results in a different dependent variable series with sometimes less variation to be explained by the regression (the TROLL package computes $\bar{R}^2$ using the quasi-differenced equations). For instance, the standard error and $\bar{R}^2$ for Italy in table 13.3 are 927 and .40 respectively, based on fitting a second-order autoregressive process. In contrast, the OLS estimate for Italy produces a standard error and $\bar{R}^2$ of 949 and .44. Since much of the older literature does not include fitted error processes (even though there is often evidence of at least first-order autocorrelation from the Durbin-Watson statistic), the informativeness of the reported diagnostic statistics is somewhat suspect and not exactly comparable to the current results.

As discussed earlier, there is no a priori expected sign on b_1 or b_2. Also, we now see in table 13.3 that the estimated scale coefficients have the positive sign consistent with the portfolio theory only for Germany. The remaining negative coefficients again seem counter to the notion that the income terms represent portfolio scale variables and seem more consistent with Prachowny's or Branson's approach.

13.4   A Simultaneous Equation Approach

A recurring problem in the capital-flows literature is the failure to acknowledge the presence of simultaneity problems. As shown in the previous chapter, interest rates and wealth terms are included on the right-hand side of these equations, and it is unreasonable to expect these terms to be exogenous variables.

The NBER International Transmission of Inflation Model provides a ready-made general equilibrium setting into which the present capital-flows equations may be inserted. The choice of variables and time span for estimation has been made consistent with the model. As the new capital-flows equations add no new endogenous variables, they can simply replace the similar equations existing in the model (the model includes a capital-flows equation for each country).

As discussed in part II of this volume, the problem in using two-stage least-squares (2SLS) estimation with the model is that the number of predetermined variables exceeds the number of observations. Thus the standard econometric solution of taking the leading principal components of the predetermined variables is used. The first-stage regression is then done using the principal components rather than the actual predetermined variables. Given the short sample for the floating exchange-rate period, the number of components taken was constrained to be equal to half the number of observations (if the number of predetermined variables in the first-stage regression equals the number of observations, then the actual values of the endogenous variables are perfectly reproduced and no simultaneous equation bias is removed). By taking the first eleven principal components, however, it was possible in each case to explain at least 95% of the variance of the instrument list.

The 2SLS estimates of equation (13.5) without and with the risk proxies are given in tables 13.4A and 13.4B respectively. When compared to the single-equation estimates, the results, in particular the standard errors of the regressions (SEE), have deteriorated with the simultaneous estimation. Note that the R^2 values are reported, but of course they have a different meaning in a simultaneous setting and can range from minus infinity to one.[11]

Why do the results of the simultaneous estimations look poorer? The problem lies in the first-stage regressions. If the R^2 in the first stage is close to one, then the results in the second stage will be very close to OLS estimates, as the fitted values of the endogenous variables are very close to their actual values. If the first-stage R^2 values are close to zero, then the fitted values of the endogenous variables will in no way resemble the actual endogenous variables and the second-stage regression is nonsense. Unfortunately, the first-stage R^2 values for all but the wealth terms are quite low, and the results presented in tables 13.4A and 13.4B are therefore not very useful.

The 2SLS estimates of equations (13.11) and (13.13) are presented in tables 13.5 and 13.6 respectively; once again the problem of low first-stage R^2 values is present so that the estimated regressions are not

---

11. If the structural equation to be estimated is $Y_1 = Y_2\beta + X\delta + u$ and Y_1 and Y_2 are endogenous while X is exogenous, then we regress Y_2 on instruments in the first stage and use the fitted values $\hat{Y}_2$ in the second-state regression: $Y_1 = \hat{Y}_2\beta + X\delta + e$. One can then construct a measure of R^2 as $R^2_{2SLS} = 1 - [\hat{v}'\hat{v}/\hat{Y}_1'\hat{Y}_1]$, where $\hat{Y}_1$ has the mean removed and $\hat{v}$ is given as $\hat{v} = Y_1 - Y_2\hat{\beta} - X\hat{\delta}$, where the true Y_2, not the fitted value, is used. Thus R^2_{2SLS} cannot exceed one, but could be negative, and is not the measure of the percentage of variance explained that appears in an OLS regression.

Table 13.4A   2SLS Estimate of Equation (13.5) without Risk Variables

	US	UK	CA	GE	IT
Coefficients					
b_0	60.02	2.31	−39.68	49.88	−3717
	(2.19)	(.62)	(−8.73)	(1.01)	(−1.44)
b_1	−8.81	−1.61	.319	94.16	−156
	(−.12)	(−.36)	(.04)	(1.11)	(−.15)
b_4	−5773	−463	3094	−3623	2.4×10^5
	(−1.63)	(−.78)	(8.20)	(−.76)	(.98)
b_5	−1464	−49.58	170	3825	−24231
	(−.48)	(−.49)	(.65)	(1.11)	(−.30)
b_8	−268	−22.66	−14.16	1353	−48472
	(−.73)	(−.37)	(−.70)	(2.27)	(−1.37)
Error process	MA1	MA1	MA1	AR1	AR1
	.01	−.77	.10	−.15	.82
S.E.E.	11.92	1.93	1.13	28.95	1040
$\bar{R}^2$	.07	−.04	.76	−.38	−.04
D-W	1.70	2.28	1.40	2.45	2.07

particularly informative. While some of the parameters estimated in tables 13.5 and 13.6 are close to their OLS counterparts, we also observe some rather strange results such as an implied adjustment coefficient in the partial adjustment equation for Germany that is greater than one in table 13.6.

As stated in Intriligator (1978, p. 392), "the method of two-stage least squares works poorly if the R^2 values in the first stage are 'too small,' i.e., close to zero" and "it is only in the case of 'intermediate' values of R^2 in the first stage that the 2SLS estimators make sense." While statements like "too small" and "too close to zero" are open to subjective evaluation, I believe that the results displayed in tables 13.4A through 13.6 are indeed the product of such phenomena. It is small comfort to know that others have also experienced difficulty in applying 2SLS to a net capital-flows equation. Herring (1973) attempted to estimate a Canadian capital-flows equation using 2SLS but given the bizarre behavior of his second-stage estimates is "forced to rely on the results of the ordinary least squares estimation" (p. 73).

Thus it is not clear at all that 2SLS is a useful approach in terms of the current data set under consideration. While OLS is generally biased in a simultaneous setting, we are venturing into somewhat unknown territory with small sample applications of 2SLS, as 2SLS is unbiased and *asymptotically* efficient. It may well be the case that in a small sample the biased

Table 13.4B **2SLS Estimate of Equation (13.5) with Risk Variables**

	US	UK	CA	GE	IT
Coefficients					
b_0	40.96	3.45	−38.47	12.23	−3124
	(2.29)	(.65)	(−6.04)	(.35)	(−1.22)
b_1	21.76	−10.88	−3.67	83.13	−453
	(.37)	(−1.49)	(−.39)	(1.10)	(−.40)
b_3	6522	222	965	−1250	76489
	(2.79)	(1.05)	(1.40)	(−1.50)	(1.72)
b_4	−3785	−840	2962	485	98852
	(−1.60)	(−.98)	(5.48)	(.14)	(.39)
b_5	−345	−290	15.56	3432	−66818
	(−.13)	(−1.51)	(.05)	(1.11)	(−.68)
b_7	2.6×10^5	4621	28715	−44109	6.2×10^6
	(2.64)	(.92)	(1.46)	(−1.23)	(1.79)
b_8	−2098	−170	−229	2428	$−2.0 \times 10^5$
	(2.69)	(−1.00)	(−1.52)	(2.70)	(−2.51)
Error process	AR2 .30, −.55	AR1 .70	MA1 .04	AR1 −.43	AR2 .43, .39
S.E.E.	11.59	2.25	1.32	23.60	1060
$\bar{R}^2$	.25	−.24	.64	.28	.15
D-W	2.19	1.82	2.21	2.13	1.71

b_0 Constant
b_1 Δ(Product of domestic wealth and return differential)
b_3 Δ(Product of domestic wealth and risk)
b_4 Δ(Domestic wealth)
b_5 Δ(Product of foreign wealth and return differential)
b_7 Δ(Product of foreign wealth and risk)
b_8 Δ(Foreign wealth)
MA1 First-order moving average process
AR1 First-order autoregressive process
AR2 Second-order autoregressive process
Estimation period 1971II to 1976IV
t statistics in parentheses

OLS estimate may "make up" for the bias in terms of smaller variance so that the mean square error of the OLS estimates is less than that of an unbiased, asymptotically efficient 2SLS estimate. At any rate, as Intriligator suggests (p. 420), "OLS may be appropriate if the first-state R^2 values are either 'too small' or 'too large,'" and so I conclude that the OLS regressions are more informative than the 2SLS.

Table 13.5   **2SLS Estimate of Equation (13.11)**

	US	UK	CA	GE	IT
Coefficients					
b_0	58.69 (2.04)	5.39 (1.26)	−35.89 (−5.77)	33.85 (.69)	−4194 (−1.51)
b_1	−.0003 (−2.08)	7.6×10^{-6} (.82)	-2.1×10^{-6} (−.57)	2.7×10^{-5} (.26)	−.0007 (−.59)
b_2	.0042 (1.89)	.0008 (.82)	.0004 (.65)	.0125 (1.54)	.0469 (.09)
b_3	−5714 (−1.54)	−984 (−1.46)	2782 (5.38)	−2661 (−.57)	2.9×10^{5} (1.10)
b_4	−353 (−.91)	−31.86 (−.58)	−14.99 (−.53)	984 (1.27)	−54933 (−1.32)
Error process	MA1 −.13	AR1 .43	AR1 .10	MA1 −.37	AR1 .81
S.E.E.	11.79	1.93	1.27	21.20	1100
$\bar{R}^2$	.05	.04	.58	.23	−.16
D-W	2.06	1.39	1.53	2.29	1.87

Table 13.6   **2SLS Estimate of Equation (13.13)**

	US	UK	CA	GE	IT
Coefficients					
αb_0	12.89 (.99)	4.09 (.96)	−23.14 (−2.62)	53.49 (1.43)	−1700 (−.77)

αb_1	-.0001 (-1.00)	1.2×10^{-5} (1.24)	7.0×10^{-7} (.24)	4.0×10^{-5} (.47)	-1.1×10^{-5} (-.01)
αb_2	.0029 (1.54)	.0008 (1.04)	.0004 (.66)	.0126 (1.13)	.6430 (1.01)
αb_3	-757 (-.48)	-773 (-1.13)	1793 (2.53)	-4239 (-1.22)	95114 (.48)
αb_4	48.57 (.23)	-20.75 (-.36)	-15.74 (-.79)	1371 (1.89)	-25853 (-.56)
$(1-\alpha)$	.5679 (3.68)	.1688 (.67)	.4405 (2.35)	-.1168 (-.45)	.4716 (1.65)
Error process	AR1 -.59	MA1 -.57	MA1 .10	AR2 .25, -.43	AR1 .37
S.E.E.	9.93	1.90	1.03	21.47	1010
$\bar{R}^2$	.59	.03	.80	.44	.29
h [D-W]	-.82	(1.84)	-1.37	(1.97)	(1.87)

b_0 Constant

b_1 Δ(Product of domestic wealth, inverse of covariance matrix, and return differential)

b_2 Δ(Product of foreign wealth, inverse of covariance matrix, and return differential)

b_3 Δ(Domestic wealth)

b_4 Δ(Foreign wealth)

α Partial adjustment coefficient

MA1 First-order moving average process

AR1 First-order autoregressive process

AR2 Second-order autoregressive process

Estimation period 1971II to 1976IV

t statistics in parentheses

h Durbin's "h" statistic; when h can't be computed (this occurs when the product of the sample size and the estimated variance of $(1 - \alpha)$ exceeds one), the D-W statistic is reported

13.5   Estimation with an Alternative Data Set

The empirical work described above used the data set created for the NBER International Transmission of Inflation Model. Unfortunately this data set only runs through 1976, so to provide more recent data it was necessary to use the IMF *International Financial Statistics* data base. After identifying and collecting the appropriate IFS counterparts to the NBER data set, it was possible to estimate equations (13.5) and (13.11) through 1978IV (see the data appendix to this chapter for a list of IFS variables chosen and a discussion of the data set construction).[12]

The results for equation (13.5) without risk variables are presented in table 13.1A' while table 13.1B' presents the estimates with the risk variables included. In two of the four countries the fit (in terms of standard error of estimate) is improved when the risk terms are included, and two of the individual risk coefficients enter significantly at the 10% level of significance. In terms of a joint F test, only for Germany are both b_3 and b_7 significant. The evidence of promise with regard to specifying risk proxies as defined in the traditional capital-flows literature is weaker for this time period. By just including the results for Germany we could have made a stronger case. Unfortunately any single specification of the period over which the standard deviations are calculated will not work well for all countries. Experimentation did reveal that one could tailor the choice for individual countries and find risk proxies that entered more significantly for certain countries than the evidence presented here. Those researchers predisposed to ad hoc searching may take comfort in knowing that choosing the period over which the standard deviation is to be taken is like most other empirical specifications: if you beat the data long enough, it will confess.

To determine the sign of the effects of the various coefficients, we must again evaluate the various derivatives. A priori, the reasoning presented in section 13.2 applies here. The net effect of an increase in the risk variable is a priori uncertain. Evaluating the partial derivative, $\delta \Delta N_i / \delta E$, at each point in the sample space we generally find a positive sign for the U.S., Germany, and Italy and a negative sign for Canada. For the return differentials, we expect a negative effect as net capital outflows fall with increases in the differential. Examining the derivative $\delta \Delta N_i / \delta (R_i - R_f)$, we find negative signs for the U.S. and Italy and positive signs for Canada and Germany. Looking at the t statistics on the individual coefficients, it is difficult to believe that the return differentials contain much explanatory power for capital flows.

Finally, for the wealth terms, we expect a positive sign for domestic wealth and a negative sign for foreign wealth according to the portfolio

---

12. Note that the U.K. results are excluded from the extended data set. The IFS tape obtained did not contain a complete data series for the U.K.

theory. However, only for Canada is the derivative with respect to domestic wealth positive while the derivative with respect to foreign wealth is negative for Canada, Germany, and Italy.

Comparing these results to those reported for the earlier period in section 13.2, we see that once again there is some evidence supporting the usefulness of empirical risk proxies, once again the return differentials do not seem to be very useful in explaining capital flows, the wealth terms perform somewhat better than before for foreign wealth (in terms of consistency with the portfolio theory), while domestic wealth again gives support to a Branson (1968) or Prachowny (1969) approach.

With the availability of the extended data set it became possible to consider the question of the appropriate starting period. Although there was quite clearly a break from fixed exchange rates in 1971, generalized floating did not begin until early 1973. Therefore one might rightly question how sensitive the results would be if begun in 1973. Equation (13.5) was reestimated over the 1973–78 period. The results without risk variables are presented in table 13.1A″, while the results with risk variables are shown in table 13.1B″. Over this time period we see that two of the four countries have an improved fit (in terms of standard error of estimate) when the risk proxies are included. The sign of the effect of the risk proxy changes for the U.S. and Germany (although the risk proxies don't seem to carry much explanatory power in any case over this sample period). The sign of the return differential changes for the U.S. so that only Italy is left with the expected negative sign (overall the return differentials still don't explain much). The wealth effects have maintained the same signs as before. As for supporting an argument in favor of the "traditional" risk proxies, the 1973–78 estimation results do poorly.

Turning now to the IAPM formulation of the capital-flows equation, we find quite interesting results. Table 13.2′ presents the estimates of equation (13.11) over the 1971–78 period. Compared to table 13.1B′ we find that the SEE (standard error of estimate) fell in only two of the cases. Table 13.2″ gives the estimation results over the period 1973–78. Compared to table 13.1B″, we find that the SEE falls in two of the cases. Note that 13.2′ only moderately improves the explanatory power of a few countries (compared to 13.1B′) while 13.2″ improves the explanatory power for the U.S. and Canadian equations considerably. While individual risk return coefficients don't enter significantly in table 13.2′, in 13.2″ we find four significant coefficients. Evaluating the derivatives of the wealth terms, we find for both periods that domestic wealth has a positive effect on net capital outflows for Canada only, while foreign wealth has a negative effect for Germany and Italy. Thus the wealth effects are similar whichever functional form is chosen (equation (13.5) or (13.11)).

Finally, if we estimate the partial adjustment equation (13.13) over the

Table 13.1A′   Equation (13.5) without Risk Variables

	US	CA	GE	IT
Coeffi-cients				
b_0	51.98	−22.11	63.11	19635
	(1.49)	(−1.94)	(1.67)	(2.60)
b_1	−.63	2.40	4.00	−210
	(−.24)	(1.74)	(1.78)	(−.84)
b_4	−7157	1827	−8079	-2.8×10^6
	(−1.51)	(1.74)	(−1.30)	(−2.72)
b_5	119	150	124	−32785
	(.58)	(1.38)	(.34)	(−.43)
b_8	−84.19	23.29	1499	37652
	(−.41)	(.52)	(4.54)	(.61)
Error process	AR2 .85, −.14	AR2 −.14,.66	MA2 .18,.08	AR2 .08,.35
S.E.E.	7.13	2.25	19.76	2920
$\bar{R}^2$	−.05	.06	.43	.13
D-W	1.93	1.79	1.94	1.95

two periods, we find results as presented in tables 13.3′ and 13.3″. The differences here are striking. Over the 1971–78 period, the adjustment coefficient is significantly different from unity in all cases and implies values of α ranging from .19 for Italy to .45 for Germany. For the 1973–78 period, the adjustment coefficient differs significantly from unity only for Italy. In the context of the discussion underlying the development of equation (13.13) in section 13.3, we would infer that the differences between tables 13.3′ and 13.3″ are due to lower costs of adjusting capital flows to desired levels over more recent periods. The dismantling of exchange and capital controls and the refinement and expansion of the international money market through the 1970s would lead to actual and desired capital flows converging.

While the "traditional approach" equations do not fare too well over the more recent estimation periods, the "alternative approach" equations do quite well. Comparing the estimation results for the 1971–78 and 1973–78 periods, we see that the starting period does make a difference and allows us to infer that actual capital flows are closer to desired levels for more recent periods.

13.6   Conclusions

The "portfolio approach" to capital flows that has been popular since the mid-1960s has advanced the state of the art. Unfortunately the

Table 13.1B′   **Equation (13.5) with Risk Variables**

	US	CA	GE	IT
Coefficients				
b_0	60.66	−22.85	75.53	23601
	(1.65)	(−2.06)	(1.39)	(2.91)
b_1	−.81	2.32	3.50	−36.11
	(−.30)	(1.61)	(2.07)	(−.15)
b_3	14.62	−21.66	81.38	21597
	(.19)	(−.49)	(.78)	(1.94)
b_4	−8383	1905	−10056	-3.4×10^6
	(−1.67)	(1.86)	(−1.09)	(−3.03)
b_5	151	181	187	3382
	(.70)	(1.58)	(.64)	(.05)
b_7	8141	−3255	−17619	1.1×10^6
	(.96)	(−1.24)	(−2.02)	(.95)
b_8	212	65.23	2005	146
	(−.87)	(1.12)	(2.92)	(.00)
Error process	AR2	AR2	AR2	AR2
	.87, −.15	−.17,.60	−.12,.22	.22,.35
S.E.E.	7.28	2.27	17.15	2780
$\bar{R}^2$	−.10	.07	.44	.18
D-W	1.92	1.87	1.96	1.90

b_0 Constant
b_1 Δ(Product of domestic wealth and return differential)
b_3 Δ(Product of domestic wealth and risk)
b_4 Δ(Domestic wealth)
b_5 Δ(Product of foreign wealth and return differential)
b_7 Δ(Product of foreign wealth and risk)
b_8 Δ(Foreign wealth)
MA2 Second-order moving average process
AR2 Second-order autoregressive process
Estimation period 1971II to 1976IV
t statistics in parentheses

empirical work done in this area has not been particularly faithful to the theory cited. In the second section an ad hoc formulation of the portfolio approach is represented as being characteristic of the approach taken by past authors. This ad hoc approach contained one glaring omission in practice in that while the specification included risk variables, the empirical approach of past authors was to throw risk out. We know that such equations are misspecified by leaving out the risk terms, but a priori we

Table 13.1A″   Equation (13.5) without Risk Variables

	US	CA	GE	IT
Coefficients				
b_0	54.10	−31.64	60.58	19175
	(1.29)	(−3.75)	(1.88)	(2.22)
b_1	3.12	3.25	6.58	−166
	(.73)	(1.46)	(2.85)	(−.52)
b_4	−7393	2668	−7142	-2.8×10^6
	(−1.31)	(3.48)	(−1.35)	(−2.40)
b_5	475	515	417	−15071
	(1.14)	(3.24)	(1.01)	(−.15)
b_8	−166	49.67	1514	51449
	(−.70)	(.99)	(4.96)	(.72)
Error process	AR2 .95, −.22	AR2 −.04, −.11	AR2 .01, −.68	MA2 .06, −.42
S.E.E.	7.86	2.31	19.30	3200
$\bar{R}^2$	−.04	.50	.59	.09
D-W	1.98	1.91	1.96	1.84

don't know how important the omitted variables are. It is shown that it is possible to specify proxies for risk that can add significant explanatory power to the ad hoc formulations.

In the third section, the functional form of the estimating equation is derived from the underlying portfolio theory. In contrast to the ad hoc approach, risk and return now enter interactively and the concept of risk involves covariances with all the exchange rates in the model rather than just the variance of one exchange rate. Of course as in all empirical work, one's evaluation of the estimation results depends on the questions one has in mind. The "traditional" approach in most cases performs better in terms of standard error than the theoretically consistent estimating equation, but they are generally close. Thus, in terms of an ability to "explain" capital flows, the theoretically consistent equation cannot be said to outperform the ad hoc approach. This is not a very surprising result. If economists believed that developing their estimating equations rigorously from theory would allow an improvement in their ability to "explain" the world, we would not see the volume of ad hoc applied work that we observe. Still, when a partial adjustment approach is added to the theoretically consistent estimating equation, the results generally improve relative to the ad hoc approach. Those familiar with the work on net capital flows will recognize that these improved results would not

Table 13.1B″   **Equation (13.5) with Risk Variables**

	US	CA	GE	IT
Coefficients				
b_0	60.51	−30.71	61.36	27026
	(1.26)	(−3.34)	(.79)	(2.65)
b_1	3.06	3.22	4.38	−50.34
	(.66)	(1.41)	(2.31)	(−.17)
b_3	−12.55	−3.13	−14.87	20195
	(−.08)	(−.03)	(−.09)	(1.41)
b_4	−8294	2585	−6644	-3.8×10^6
	(−1.28)	(3.08)	(−.49)	(−2.77)
b_5	565	503	30.30	−4033
	(1.23)	(3.03)	(.10)	(−.04)
b_7	8374	−2109	−23776	8.0×10^5
	(.44)	(−.44)	(−1.61)	(.53)
b_8	−251	72.64	2773	33590
	(−.76)	(.95)	(2.63)	(.38)
Error process	AR2	AR2	AR2	AR2
	.95, −.21	−.06, −.08	.28, −.27	.24, .42
S.E.E.	8.20	2.39	17.15	3160
$\bar{R}^2$	−.13	.44	.59	.15
D-W	1.97	1.93	1.90	1.85

b_0 Constant
b_1 Δ(Product of domestic wealth and return differential)
b_3 Δ(Product of domestic wealth and risk)
b_4 Δ(Domestic wealth)
b_5 Δ(Product of foreign wealth and return differential)
b_7 Δ(Product of foreign wealth and risk)
b_8 Δ(Foreign wealth)
MA2 Second-order moving average process
AR2 Second-order autoregressive process
Estimation period 1973II to 1978IV
t statistics in parentheses

compare unfavorably with previous work, especially if we were to compare unadjusted R^2, the statistic reported by many previous authors.

In section 13.4, the capital-flows equations are estimated in a simultaneous equation framework but with little success. Due to small first-stage R^2 values for many of the proxies used, it was concluded that the OLS estimates are more informative than the 2SLS estimates.

Finally, in section 13.5 an alternative data set is used which goes

Table 13.2'   **Equation (13.11)**

	US	CA	GE	IT
Coefficients				
b_0	50.51	−14.97	56.96	20404
	(1.44)	(−1.18)	(1.45)	(2.74)
b_1	-3.1×10^{-4}	-6.9×10^{-5}	-2.8×10^{-4}	.10
	(−.14)	(−.42)	(−.26)	(1.48)
b_2	−.10	.19	−.22	−213
	(−.53)	(1.14)	(−.23)	(−1.21)
b_3	−6977	1143	−7296	-3.0×10^6
	(−1.46)	(.98)	(−1.13)	(−2.86)
b_4	−115	−11.55	1362	39999
	(−.60)	(−.28)	(4.00)	(.73)
Error process	AR2	AR2	AR2	MA2
	.86, −.15	−.09,.71	−.28, −.02	.01, −.54
S.E.E.	7.15	2.34	20.72	2770
$\bar{R}^2$	−.06	−.03	.35	.16
D-W	1.89	1.94	1.93	1.83

through 1978. The ad hoc approach generally deteriorates over the most recent estimation period while the theoretically consistent approach works quite well. Regressions over the 1973–78 period allow us to infer that lags in adjusting actual capital flows to desired levels have decreased over the recent floating exchange-rate period.

Regarding the effects of individual variables, it was found that the portfolio scale variables and risk proxies often had considerable explanatory power while return differentials did not. This latter finding should not be surprising to some. Black (1979), for instance, has argued that we should observe no particular correlation between asset flows and rates of return, as the flows will probably occur before the rates change in anticipation of their change. With perfect markets we would expect the flows to be instantaneous in response to return differentials so that no (risk adjusted) differentials are ever observed. Considering the real world, the financial news often explains capital flows in terms of interest-rate changes. So while capital flows appear to be related in some plausible fashion to interest rates, the response is likely to be fast so that in the absence of barriers to capital movements we should not expect to see any long-term average relation between capital flows and return differentials. The old capital-flows literature assumed that we would observe a correlation between interest rates and capital flows, and usually a significant

Table 13.3′   **Equation (13.13)**

	US	CA	GE	IT
Coeffi- cients				
αb_0	26.08 (1.11)	−12.60 (−2.40)	−1.42 (−.05)	15137 (4.77)
αb_1	.003 (.79)	4.0×10^{-5} (.26)	-6.3×10^{-4} (−.73)	.04 (.61)
αb_2	−.02 (−.99)	.13 (.65)	.07 (.07)	−414 (−1.77)
αb_3	−3417 (−1.05)	1141 (2.27)	1535 (.34)	-2.0×10^6 (−4.61)
αb_4	95.94 (.55)	−37.69 (−1.57)	846 (2.84)	1.1×10^5 (3.21)
$(1-\alpha)$	.56 (3.42)	.71 (5.56)	.55 (3.29)	.81 (7.35)
Error process	AR2 .14,.37	AR2 −.97, −.09	AR2 −.87, −.36	AR2 −.89, −.20
S.E.E.	7.09	2.12	19.98	2500
$\bar{R}^2$	.32	.73	.70	.81
h [D-W]	.34	−.02	.32	.29

b_0 Constant
b_1 Δ(Product of domestic wealth, inverse of covariance matrix, and return differential)
b_2 Δ(Product of foreign wealth, inverse of covariance matrix, and return differential)
b_3 Δ(Domestic wealth)
b_4 Δ(Foreign wealth)
α Partial adjustment coefficient
MA2 Second-order moving average process
AR2 Second-order autoregressive process
h Durbin's "h" statistic; when h can't be computed (this occurs when the product of the sample size and the estimated variance of $(1-\alpha)$ exceeds one), the D-W statistic is reported
Estimation period 1971II to 1978IV
t statistics in parentheses

relation was in fact found. While there is nothing wrong with assuming capital flows respond to yield differentials (after all, the flows are the mechanism that keeps the differentials constant), the empirical findings of the early researchers are called into question by the present study. It is shown in the present paper that capital flows do not appear to be systematically and significantly related to return differentials when the estimating equation is faithful to the underlying theory. The fact that early researchers included various extraneous variables in order to "improve

Table 13.2″   **Equation (13.11)**

	US	CA	GE	IT
Coefficients				
b_0	75.69	-41.11	63.18	18819
	(2.31)	(-3.61)	(1.45)	(2.04)
b_1	.01	4.1×10^{-4}	$-.03$	.13
	(3.06)	(.36)	(-4.23)	(.13)
b_2	2.23	2.38	-1.46	-310
	(5.10)	(5.73)	$(-.88)$	$(-.84)$
b_3	-10169	3481	-8122	-2.8×10^6
	(-2.30)	(3.34)	(-1.13)	(-2.2)
b_4	-27.45	-58.52	1254	45467
	$(-.19)$	(-1.15)	(3.73)	(.68)
Error	AR2	AR2	AR2	MA2
process	$1.29, -.51$	$.45, -.12$	$.50, -.68$	$.01, -.49$
S.E.E.	5.58	2.07	18.10	3160
$\bar{R}^2$	.53	.63	.64	.07
D-W	2.15	1.98	1.98	1.83

the fit" casts doubt on any hypothesis testing done for interest-rate coefficients in the context of such "portfolio approach" models. Those who claim that the capital-flows literature casts doubt on Black's assertions may not have very strong evidence.

The findings of the current study suggest that while wealth and risk proxies do have some explanatory power in capital-flows regressions, the overall explanatory power of these regressions is not in general high (in terms of $\bar{R}^2$). The failure to find a strong systematic component of capital flows indicates that much of observed capital flows reflects the behavior of profit maximizers responding to new events and opportunities.

The contribution of this paper has been to (1) incorporate a risk proxy in an equation based on the existing capital-flows literature, and (2) rigorously derive and estimate an alternative functional form for capital flows using the underlying portfolio theory. The goal is to bring the empirical work closer to the underlying theory.

Acknowledgments

This research was partially funded by the NBER Project on the International Transmission of Inflation through the World Monetary System, the Foundation for Research in Economics and Education, and the

Table 13.3″   **Equation (13.13)**

	US	CA	GE	IT
Coefficients				
αb_0	75.88	−47.63	114	15399
	(2.21)	(−3.45)	(1.59)	(4.28)
αb_1	.01	4.1×10^{-4}	−.01	.31
	(2.91)	(.42)	(−.71)	(.27)
αb_2	2.25	1.96	−1.53	−576
	(4.17)	(3.31)	(−1.15)	(−1.47)
αb_3	−10190	4007	−16697	-2.1×10^6
	(−2.21)	(3.19)	(−1.43)	(−4.13)
αb_4	−25.68	−56.63	1011	1.3×10^5
	(−.17)	(−1.08)	(2.65)	(3.36)
$(1-\alpha)$	.01	−.34	−.35	.82
	(.05)	(−1.38)	(−1.15)	(6.48)
Error process	AR2 1.28, −.50	AR2 .70, −.28	AR2 .79, −.49	AR2 −.97, −.23
S.E.E.	5.73	2.07	18.30	2710
$\bar{R}^2$	.51	.71	.63	.79
h [D-W]	−1.74	[1.99]	[2.17]	−.64

b_0 Constant
b_1 Δ(Product of domestic wealth, inverse of covariance matrix, and return differential)
b_2 Δ(Product of foreign wealth, inverse of covariance matrix, and return differential)
b_3 Δ(Domestic wealth)
b_4 Δ(Foreign wealth)
α Partial adjustment coefficient
MA2 Second-order moving average process
AR2 Second-order autoregressive process
h Durbin's "h" statistic; when h can't be computed (this occurs when the product of the sample size and the estimated variance of $(1-\alpha)$ exceeds one), the D-W statistic is reported
Estimation period 1973II to 1978IV
t statistics in parentheses

Eisenhower Foundation. The author acknowledges the helpful comments of Brad Cornell, Robert Jones, Richard Roll, and particularly Michael Darby. The author alone is responsible for any errors.

Data Appendix
(IFS data for extending sample)

Dependent Variable: ΔN_i, measured as current account minus change in reserves. Referring to IFS line number, capital flows are found as

$$77\text{aad} + 77\text{acd} + 77\text{abd} + 77\text{add} + 77\text{aed}$$
$$+ 77\text{agd} - 79\text{kd}.$$

Variables were converted to billions of domestic currency units, and seasonally adjusted before summing.

Exchange Rates: Average of noon buying rates in New York for cable transfers as reported in the *Federal Reserve Bulletin*.

Interest Rates: IFS line 60c.

Wealth and Foreign Wealth: Created as in the NBER model using real income from line 99ar.

References

Black, F. 1979. The ins and outs of foreign investment. In D. Lessard, ed., *International financial management*. Boston and New York: Warren, Gorham, & Lamont.

Branson, W. H. 1968. *Financial capital flows in the U.S. balance of payments*. Amsterdam: North-Holland.

Branson, W. H., and R. D. Hill. 1971. Capital movements in the OECD area. *OECD Economic Outlook, Occasional Studies*. December.

Bryant, R. C. 1975. Empirical research on financial capital flows. In P. Kenen, ed., *International trade and finance: Frontiers for research*. New York: Cambridge University Press.

Bryant, R. C., and P. H. Hendershott. 1970. *Financial capital flows in the balance of payments of the United States: An exploratory empirical study*. Princeton Studies in International Finance, no. 25.

Grubel, H. G. 1968. Internationally diversified portfolios: Welfare gains and capital flows. *American Economic Review* 58: 1299–1314.

Herring, R. J. 1973. International financial integration: Capital flows and interest rate relationships among six industrial nations. Ph.D. dissertation, Princeton University.

Hodgson, J.S., and A. B. Holmes. 1977. Structural stability of international capital mobility: An analysis of short-term U.S.–Canadian bank claims. *Review of Economics and Statistics* 59: 465–73.

Intriligator, M. D. 1978. *Econometric models, techniques, and applications*. Englewood Cliffs, N.J.: Prentice-Hall.

Kouri, P. J. K., and M. G. Porter. 1974. International capital flows and portfolio equilibrium. *Journal of Political Economy* 82: 443–67.

Kreicher, L. L. 1981. International portfolio capital flows and real rates of interest. *Review of Economics and Statistics* 63: 20–28.

Leamer, E. E., and R. M. Stern. 1970. *Quantitative international economics*. Boston: Allyn & Bacon.

Lee, C. H. 1969. A stock-adjustment analysis of capital movements: The United States–Canadian case. *Journal of Political Economy* 77: 512–33.

Melvin, M. 1981. Foreign exchange risk and the risk premium: Myth or reality. Arizona State University. Mimeographed.

Merton, R. C. 1973. An intertemporal capital asset pricing model. *Econometrica* 41: 867–87.

Miller, N. C., and M. v. N. Whitman. 1970. A mean-variance analysis of United States long-term portfolio foreign investment. *Quarterly Journal of Economics* 84: 175–96.

Prachowny, M. F. J. 1969. *A structural model of the U.S. balance of payments*. Amsterdam: North-Holland.

Solnik, B. H. 1973. *European capital markets: Towards a general theory of international investment*. Lexington, Mass.: Lexington Books.

IV International Price Movements

What was the cause or causes of the international burst of inflation in the early 1970s? In this part we address that question directly. A number of suspects are popular in the literature: American money growth, international reserve growth, oil price increases, other commodity price increases, and increased union greed. The latter is supposed to be validated by accommodative monetary policy and was shown to be inconsistent with the data in chapter 4 above. So this part attempts to sort the remaining factors into categories of dominant cause, supporting cause, and symptom of the world inflation. We find that American money growth was the dominant factor with oil price increases playing at most a supporting role in the evolution of international inflationary trends. International reserve growth and other commodity price increases are symptoms of the inflation and its international transmission.

Gandolfi and Lothian derive a reduced-form price equation from a Lucas-aggregate supply function and a standard money demand equation. They then test whether international factors enter this equation directly via shifting the aggregate supply function or only indirectly via rational expectations of money growth. The four international factors tested (the real price of oil, a world commodity price index, the American price deflator, and a rest-of-world price index) were generally insignificant except that the price of oil is statistically significant in nearly half of the cases. Even taking the point estimates at face value, oil price changes were estimated to account for only about 15% of total inflation even in 1973–74. The dominant factor determining inflation in each country was the evolution of the domestic money supply.

The evidence in parts II and III strongly indicates that purchasing-power parity is not a rigid condition established by goods arbitrage. In chapter 15, Darby shows that even though substantial shifts in the level of the purchasing-power ratio may occur and cumulate over time, the purchasing-power-parity approach may still be useful in explaining international trends: Almost any reasonable level effects will average out sufficiently over a number of years so that the average inflation rates are approximately harmonized.

In the concluding chapter of this part, Darby demonstrates that the United States would be the exogenous source of world inflation under pegged exchange rates if two conditions are met: if U.S. nominal-money-supply and real-money-demand growth trends are independent of foreign influences. Neither gold flows nor the balance of payments (or any other foreign variable) was found to enter significantly in the American money supply reaction function, so the first condition is met. Although there is considerable variation in real-money-demand growth in the short run from nonmonetary sources (both domestic and foreign), these effects are largely self-reversing so that there is essentially no effect on average growth over periods of four years or more.

Accelerated American money growth was thus the dominant and independent cause of the world inflation of the early 1970s. Unfortunately, it remains for future research to explain why American money growth goals accelerated gently throughout the period 1957–76: An important trend factor in the U.S. reaction function only labels this refractory area of ignorance.

14 International Price Behavior and the Demand for Money

Arthur E. Gandolfi and James R. Lothian

Oil prices, commodity prices, and American monetary policy, the last operating through a variety of channels, have all figured prominently in explanations of the international inflation process in the late 1960s and early 1970s. In this chapter, we test these various hypotheses within the context of a reduced-form rational expectations price equation that we have estimated for the United States and the seven other industrial countries in our sample.[1]

A key concern in the estimation of this model was the properties of the demand for money function. Unlike many studies using post–World War II time-series data that rely on the stock adjustment model, we obtain what we regard as reasonable estimates of the parameters of the long-run demand for money function—particularly the income elasticity—without having to posit unacceptably slow speeds of adjustment. The adjustment mechanism implicit in the estimated equation, in fact, is quite different from the standard formulation.

For all eight countries we find evidence of second-order serial correlation that is consistent with the existence of two types of error processes: permanent stochastic shifts that follow a random walk and other types of disturbances that, unlike the first sort, are transitory in nature. Hence a shock that alters the equilibrium *rate of change* of prices will gradually be eliminated, but the *level* of prices will not necessarily return to its original path.

With respect to the causes of inflation internationally, our results are consistent with those reported elsewhere in this volume. They suggest

An earlier, abbreviated version of this chapter was published in *Economic Inquiry*, the journal of the Western Economics Association, vol. 21, no. 3 (July 1983).

1. See chapter 3 for a description of the data.

that domestic money supplies played the crucial role in the process. In the seven foreign countries, the increases in monetary growth underlying the increases in inflation came in response to both foreign monetary pressures and domestic factors. In the U.S., the reserve-currency country, domestic factors alone were important. Direct price arbitrage appears to have little additional effect in most countries. Oil price shocks, however, may have made some contribution to the increases in U.S. and most foreign price levels, but relative to domestic money they were clearly of secondary importance.[2]

14.1 The Structural and Reduced-Form Price Equation

Three equations make up the basic model: a money demand function, an aggregate supply function, and an expected money equation.

The money demand function takes the fairly conventional form

$$(14.1) \qquad (M/P)_t = \alpha + \beta_1 y_t^p + \beta_2 y_t^t + \beta_3 r_t,$$

where M/P is the log of real per capita cash balances, y^p is the log of real per capita permanent income, y^t is transitory income—defined as the difference between the logs of measured and permanent real income— and r is the log of the interest rate.[3]

The aggregate supply function is of the form used by Lucas (1973):

$$(14.2) \qquad y_t^t = \lambda y_{t-1}^t + \phi(P_t - P_t^*),$$

where P and P^* are the logs of the actual and expected levels of prices, respectively.

Expected prices in this framework represent the cost of production. An increase in actual over expected price fools producers into believing that there has been a rise in the relative price of their product and induces an increase in output. The autocorrelation that is apparent in movements in real output has been rationalized by Blinder and Fischer (1978) as the result of using inventories to stabilize production. A positive price shock leads suppliers to increase their sales partially from increased production and partially from drawing down stocks of inventories. The shock will have a delayed effect on output as inventories are replaced slowly over time.

By solving for real transitory income in equation (14.1), substituting it into equation (14.2), and taking expected values of the variables, we derive the following equation for expected prices:

2. See chapter 3, by Cassese and Lothian, using Granger causality tests, and chapter 5 by Darby and Stockman, using a simultaneous model, for corroborative evidence for these countries over this period. The study by Dewald and Marchon (1978) and various papers in the conference volume edited by Brunner and Meltzer (1978) also contain findings that are largely consistent with ours.

3. In the empirical work reported below, we use a long-term bond rate as the interest-rate variable to reduce problems of simultaneity.

(14.3) $p_t^* = M_t^* - \alpha - \beta_1 y_t^p - \lambda\beta_2 y_{t-1}^t - \beta_3 r_t,$

where the asterisk denotes expected values. Substituting this expression into the aggregate supply equation (14.2) and rearranging terms yields the reduced-form price equation:

(14.4) $P_t = -\alpha + M_t - \beta_1 y_t^p - \beta_2 \lambda y_{t-1}^t$

$$- \beta_3 r_t - \frac{\phi\beta_2}{1 + \phi\beta_2}(M - M^*)_t.$$

Given the equations for P and P^*, we can also derive a reduced-form real output relation:

(14.5) $y_t^t = \lambda y_{t-1}^t + \dfrac{\phi}{1 + \beta_2\phi}(M_t - M_t^*).$

Using (14.5), we can then substitute for y_{t-1}^t in the price equation (14.4) to arrive at the alternative form:[4]

(14.6) $P_t = M_t - \alpha - \beta_1 y_t^p - \beta_3 r_t$

$$- \sum_{i=0}^{\infty} \frac{\lambda^i \beta_2\phi}{1 + \beta_2\phi}(M - M^*)_{t-i}.$$

The last term on the right-hand sides of (14.4) and of (14.6) is the monetary shock—the difference between the actual and the expected values of the nominal stock of money. The latter we determined empirically, from a variety of equations of the general form

(14.7) $M_t = f(L(M_t), X),$

where L is a lag operator and X is a vector of variables that enter the monetary authority's reaction function.

14.2   Estimates of the Price Equation

In table 14.1 we report the estimates of equation (14.6) using M2 as the definition of money, the GNP or GDP deflator as the price variable, and Friedman's weighting scheme for our proxies for real permanent income.[5] We constrained the coefficient for actual per capita nominal money balances to unity, so the dependent variable was $\log(P/M2N)$, the

---

4. The final form of our price equation is similar to the equation estimated by Barro (1978) with annual data for the United States.

5. Of the three monetary variables we tried, M1, M2, and high-powered money, M2 performed the best. The estimated coefficients were more consistent among countries and closer to what we regard as plausible magnitudes.

We derived the permanent income series using a logarithmic version of the method outlined in Darby (1972). The choice of weights was largely arbitrary. We wanted to use an a priori scheme and the two most likely—Darby's (0.10 annual weight) and Friedman's (0.33 annual weight)—produced no appreciable differences in the estimates.

Table 14.1 Price Equation with Dependent Variable log PD − log(M2/N), 1957III to 1976IV (absolute value of t statistic in parentheses)

Coefficient	CA	FR	GE	IT	JA	NE	UK	US
Constant	3.096 (3.977)	0.678 (0.620)	4.121 (7.480)	11.733 (15.676)	3.540 (7.323)	0.614 (0.525)	−1.948 (1.217)	−0.684 (2.459)
ResM2$_t$	−0.508 (2.931)	−0.936 (9.717)	−0.927 (12.507)	−0.845 (5.387)	−0.910 (5.347)	−0.879 (8.549)	−1.021 (9.726)	−0.904 (10.071)
ResM2$_{t-1}$	−1.099 (4.813)	−1.044 (6.006)	−0.686 (5.049)	−0.645 (2.537)	−1.078 (4.024)	−0.846 (6.207)	−0.842 (5.215)	−1.571 (9.683)
ResM2$_{t-2}$	−0.860 (3.675)	−0.842 (4.001)	−0.561 (3.157)	−0.523 (1.675)	−1.096 (3.911)	−0.837 (5.773)	−0.771 (4.031)	−1.592 (7.592)
ResM2$_{t-3}$	−0.897 (4.210)	−0.581 (2.552)	−0.600 (3.080)	−0.292 (0.892)	−1.002 (3.934)	−0.620 (4.293)	−0.941 (4.853)	−1.276 (5.840)
ResM2$_{t-4}$	−0.731 (3.150)	−0.441 (1.984)	−0.404 (2.178)	−0.104 (0.335)	−0.863 (3.146)	−0.523 (3.317)	−0.745 (3.826)	−0.809 (3.880)

ResM2$_{t-5}$	−0.973 (4.367)	−0.205 (1.060)	−0.221 (1.473)	−0.127 (0.502)	−0.373 (1.488)	−0.333 (2.259)	−0.591 (3.433)	−0.533 (3.215)
ResM2$_{t-6}$	−0.339 (2.044)	−0.087 (0.831)	−0.171 (1.945)	0.079 (0.532)	−0.154 (0.960)	−0.287 (2.620)	−0.265 (2.187)	−0.285 (3.023)
log$(y^P/N)_{t-1}$	−1.224 (14.303)	−0.941 (8.154)	−1.288 (21.808)	−1.817 (35.171)	−1.182 (35.569)	−0.938 (7.378)	−0.577 (2.529)	−0.818 (26.666)
log R_L	0.079 (1.907)	0.076 (2.423)	0.002 (0.110)	0.068 (2.206)	0.303 (4.391)	0.009 (0.257)	−0.030 (0.535)	−0.005 (0.456)
log y^t_{t-7}	0.058 (0.424)	0.022 (0.540)	0.057 (0.866)	0.172 (1.449)	0.122 (1.907)	0.134 (1.034)	−0.0001 (0.001)	−0.039 (0.757)
Rho1	1.0383	1.8667	1.7176	1.4123	1.4245	1.1737	1.3967	1.6667
Rho2	−0.1492	−0.8929	−0.7971	−0.5274	−0.4694	−0.2092	−0.4666	−0.7890
$\bar{R}^2$	0.835	0.784	0.908	0.955	0.950	0.667	0.661	0.945
S.E.E.	0.0147	0.0086	0.0085	0.0124	0.0086	0.0136	0.0176	0.0040
D-W	2.04	1.93	2.68	2.26	2.16	2.06	2.48	2.44

Note. ResM2 is the residual from the expected money function (see table 14.2), PD is the GNP/GDP deflator, y^P/N is real per capita permanent income, R_L is the long-term bond rate, and y^t is transitory income.

log of the reciprocal of real per capita money balances rather than simply log P.[6]

In table 14.2 we present the estimates of the expected money equations that we used to construct the monetary shocks. Before discussing the price equations themselves, let us briefly describe these results.

The final form of the expected money equation relates the current quarter's change in the log of M2 to lagged values of itself, lagged transitory income, lagged values of the balance of payments scaled by high-powered money, and the change in the lagged log of U.S. M2.

For all countries at least one autoregressive money term (and usually more) is statistically significant. Transitory income has the hypothesized negative sign in all except Japan and the U.K. It is significant at the 5% level in two of the countries, Italy and the U.S., and at the 10% level in one other, the Netherlands. The balance of payments, though again of the correct sign in seven of eight cases, is significant at the 5% level in only two, Japan and the U.K., and at the 10% level in two others, France and Italy. The lagged U.S. monetary variable is significant at the 5% level in Canada and Germany and the 10% level in France, the Netherlands, and the U.K. Tests for serial correlation of the residuals of these equations revealed no significant serial correlation in any of the eight equations.

Now let us turn to the price equations themselves. Since we found evidence of both first- and second-order autocorrelation in the price equations for all eight countries, we used GLS with a second-order correction to estimate the equations. The OLS estimates and GLS estimates based on a first-order correction are given in the appendix to this chapter. The reason for the autocorrelation is a topic we return to in the next section.[7]

In general, these equations fit the data reasonably well. The standard errors, other than those for the U.S. and the U.K. (40 and 176 basis points, respectively), tend to be around 100 basis points. Moreover, the coefficients are fairly consistent with prior expectations.

The coefficients of permanent income and the interest rate in these equations are both well identified, being opposite in sign from those in the money demand function. The coefficients on the lagged monetary shocks, however, are underidentified. They are a composite of the coefficient on transitory income β_2 from the money demand function, the price elasticity from the supply equation ϕ, and, in the case of the lagged shock terms, the autocorrelation coefficient from the supply equation λ.

---

6. As Laidler (1980) has pointed out, having actual money on the right-hand side of the equation may lead to bias. Reestimating our equations with expected rather than actual money, however, produced virtually the same results.

7. The estimated equations also include transitory income lagged seven quarters, which is one more quarter than the maximum lag on the monetary shocks. In no instance is this term significant. This is consistent with the assumption implicit in our derivation of the price equation that the monetary shocks account for movements in transitory income.

Table 14.2 Expected Money Function with Dependent Variable log $\dot{M}2$, 1956I to 1976IV (absolute value of t statistic in parentheses)

Coefficient	CA	FR	GE	IT	JA	NE	UK	US
Constant	0.004 (1.283)	0.012 (3.570)	0.002 (0.395)	0.018 (3.560)	0.016 (3.654)	0.005 (1.194)	0.001 (0.239)	0.005 (3.549)
log $\dot{M}2_{t-1}$	0.411 (3.629)	0.349 (3.785)	0.040 (0.340)	0.054 (0.497)	0.515 (4.286)	0.276 (2.393)	0.077 (0.685)	0.880 (7.871)
log $\dot{M}2_{t-2}$	...	...	0.183 (1.743)	0.201 (1.940)	0.094 (0.822)	0.249 (2.186)	0.206 (1.953)	−0.352 (2.419)
log $\dot{M}2_{t-3}$	...	...	0.352 (3.233)	0.212 (1.955)	...	0.010 (0.086)	0.251 (2.424)	0.172 (1.583)
$(BP/MH)_{t-1}$	0.023 (0.665)	...	0.012 (0.431)	...	0.036 (2.027)	−0.057 (1.511)	0.060 (2.120)	
$(BP/MH)_{t-2}$	...	0.164 (4.131)	...	0.066 (1.765)	...	...	...	
log y^t_{t-1}	−0.041 (0.919)	...	−0.028 (0.403)	−0.154 (3.553)	0.008 (0.695)	−0.137 (1.815)	0.026 (0.231)	−0.050 (2.602)
log $\dot{M}2US_{t-1}$	0.628 (2.847)	0.276 (1.733)	0.379 (1.966)	...	...	0.403 (1.699)	0.540 (1.763)	
$\bar{R}^2$	0.522	0.351	0.162	0.275	0.433	0.211	0.257	0.617
S.E.E.	0.0115	0.0118	0.0143	0.0099	0.0070	0.0167	0.0191	0.0052
D-W	1.92	2.15	1.91	1.88	1.90	1.98	2.00	1.91

Note. BP is the official settlements balance, MH is high-powered money, and y^t is transitory income. A dot above a variable signifies a first difference.

Still, we can say something about the size and sign of the shock variables. Since λ should be positive and less than or equal to unity and since β_2 and ϕ are greater than or equal to zero, the coefficient on the contemporaneous shock variable should be negative and between zero and minus one. The lagged terms should also be negative and declining in absolute value by an exponential of λ.

In broad outline, the estimates we obtain conform to this pattern. All of the monetary shock variables have the correct sign. In every country other than Italy, the great majority are significant and they display a general tendency to decline over time. The decline, however, is not monotonic and a number of the coefficients are greater than unity—three significantly so. In addition, for each of the eight countries, tests indicated we could reject the hypothesis of a geometrically declining pattern for the coefficients of the shock terms taken as a group.[8]

For the most part, our estimate of the parameters of the money demand functions appear reasonable. The income elasticities—with the exception of the estimate for Italy of 1.82—cluster about unity, ranging from a low of approximately .60 for the U.K. to a high of approximately 1.3 for Germany. The Italian income elasticity, moreover, we have reason to suspect, is biased upward by measurement error in the income series. According to Antonio Martino (1980), tax evasion has led to a systematic understatement of the rate of growth as well as the level of Italian income during this period. This downward bias in income growth, in turn, would lead to an upward bias in the income elasticity. In Britain, the introduction of Competition and Credit Controls in 1971 could conceivably produce a bias of the opposite sort. It led to the payment of more competitive rates of interest on certificates of deposit and hence a substitution into CDs from other types of commercial bank deposits. Our inability to account for this change may mean that our estimated income elasticities are therefore less than the true values.

The interest elasticities are a more mixed lot than the income elasticities. For two countries—the U.K. and the U.S.—these estimates, which are opposite in sign from the coefficients themselves, are positive. Those for the remaining six, though negative and similar in magnitude, are significantly different from zero at the .10 level or better in only four instances.

---

8. Our initial reaction was that these departures of our empirical estimates from the theoretical pattern reflected model misspecification due to omission of foreign price shocks from the reduced-form price equations. Misspecification of this sort might also account for the rather short lags on the shock terms we observe. In regressions reported below in which we include foreign price variables the patterns of money-shock coefficients, however, show little change. Something other than foreign prices must therefore account for these problems.

14.3 Implications for Money Demand

Our estimates of the price equations provide new and reasonably consistent cross-country evidence on what we regard as two of the important unresolved questions of money demand. One is the magnitude of the parameters of the long-run money demand function, in particular, the income elasticity. The other is the speed with which the monetary sector reaches equilibrium. Studies with recent time-series data provide a disconcertingly broad range of estimates of both. Many of these, moreover, differ from what we would have expected to find a priori. Comparison of two recent papers using multicountry quarterly data samples similar to ours illustrates the problem.

In one, Samir Al-Khuri and Saleh M. Nsouli (1978) estimated money demand functions of the simple stock-adjustment genre for M1 and M2 for six of our eight countries over a sample period slightly shorter than ours. As their paper's title implies, their chief concern lay in estimating the speed of adjustment between actual and desired cash balances. Most of these estimates appear plausible: an adjustment of 30% or greater per quarter in seventeen of twenty-four instances and, for at least one formulation for each country, an adjustment in the 40–60% range. The problem is that their estimates of long-run income elasticities make almost no sense at all. In each of their four formulations, the average of the individual-country elasticities is 0.3 or lower and the range is from slightly negative to a high of less than 0.6.

James Boughton's (1979) study of the demand for money in seven of our eight countries (he excludes the Netherlands) produces results at the opposite end of the spectrum. His estimates of long-run income elasticities, also derived from a simple stock-adjustment model and based upon data for the period 1960–77, are a good deal higher than those of Al-Khuri and Nsouli. The mean of the elasticities for M1 is 1.27 and for M2 is 1.52. Furthermore, in only four instances, M1 in the U.S., M2 in the U.K., for which no estimate could be obtained (the coefficient on the lagged dependent variable being greater than unity) and both M1 and M2 in Italy, for which the estimated elasticities are both over 2.5, are there great divergences from those averages. The difficulty is that the adjustment coefficients for all of these countries are exeedingly low—most falling below 0.15 per quarter and none being much above 0.20.

The problem therefore is that statistically there apears to be a trade-off between the estimated values of the speed of adjustment and of the income elasticity in the simple stock-adjustment formulation. Relatively rapid speeds of adjustment can be obtained, but at the expense of extremely low income elasticities; higher income elasticities can be had but only with much slower adjustments. That trade-off, moreover, seems to be a common result with postwar data not just a peculiarity of these two studies.

Our own belief is that the short-run adjustment is fairly rapid and the income elasticity of demand for money fairly high—close to unity, perhaps above, in these countries. Stock-adjustment speeds of between 5% and 10% per quarter, in contrast, imply that it takes somewhere between five and eleven years for 90% of the gap between money demand and money supply to be closed. In a world in which there are other financial assets, the existence of disequilibrium for that length of time is incongruous. Similarly, other bodies of data almost universally yield estimates of income elasticities considerably higher than those often obtained with postwar data. Long-term time series for the U.S. and U.K. cross-state data for the U.S., and cross-country data are all examples. In each of these instances, the estimated income elasticities range from slightly below unity to considerably above for various monetary assets.[9]

The results we have reported conform closely with these prior beliefs. They thus stand in sharp contrast to the standard findings of studies using post–World War II time-series data. We suspect that the source of these differences is the manner in which various studies treat the adjustment process whereby actual and desired money balances are equated.

The usual way of handling the adjustment process is to specify a stock-adjustment model that entails including a lagged-dependent variable in the final estimating equation. But, as Griliches (1961) has pointed out, even if the lagged-dependent variable is appropriate, the presence of positive autocorrelation will bias the coefficient on the lagged-dependent variable upward, thus leading to the conclusion that the adjustment process is slower than it actually is. A further problem is that the lagged-dependent variable may "improve" an equation when the true structure does not include such an adjustment process if the autocorrelation of the residuals is due to some other misspecification.

Normally the stock-adjustment process is modeled as follows:

$$(14.8) \qquad M_t = M_{t-1} + \rho(M_t^d - M_{t-1}) + \epsilon_t.$$

If M_t is not a stationary series but rather is trend dominated, actual money balances will consistently and unrealistically lag behind desired.

As an alternative to the conventional stock-adjustment process we initially chose to define one of the following form:

$$(14.9) \qquad M_t = M_t^d + \rho(M_{t-1} - M_{t-1}^d) + \epsilon_t.$$

This is equivalent to a standard first-order autoregressive process:

$$(14.10) \qquad M_t = M_t^d + u_t$$

9. Laidler (1977) contains a summary of the long-term time-series evidence. More recent studies include Huffman and Lothian (1980), which estimates demand functions for high-powered money for the U.K. for the years 1833–1968, and Friedman and Schwartz (1982), which presents estimates for M2 for both the U.K. and U.S. for the years 1874–1975. Gandolfi and Lothian (1976) contains estimates from time series of cross-state data for the period 1929–68, and Lothian (1976) estimates from time series of cross-country data.

and

(14.11) $u_t = \rho u_{t-1} + \epsilon_t.$

The GLS estimates of the price equation based on this model, however, were unsatisfactory. The Durbin-Watson statistics on average were exceedingly low, suggesting a more complicated structure for the errors. For this reason we used a second-order model of the errors in the estimates we report in table 14.1. From the standpoint of the Durbin-Watson statistics these equations are much more acceptable, though there is some evidence of mild negative serial correlation remaining.

The problem with these estimates is that the autoregressive pattern for the price equation appears to follow not only a second-order process but one which entails an overadjustment to last period's error and then an offsetting adjustment to this error in the next period.

The weights associated with the lagged errors in table 14.1 provide a clue as to the possible nature of the adjustment process. Since the autocorrelation correction is equivalent to a series of quasi-differencing operations on all the variables, the fact that the coefficient on the first lagged error term is equal to one plus the absolute value of the coefficient on the second lagged term suggests that the proper specification of the price equation entails a first-order correction of the first difference of the dependent and independent variables,

(14.12) $X_t - (1 + \rho)X_{t-1} + \rho X_{t-2},$

which in turn equals

(14.12a) $(X_t - X_{t-1}) - \rho(X_{t-1} - X_{t-2}).$

What possible arguments could justify such a specification? The most obvious is that there are two types of error processes involved in our estimation. First, there are stochastic shifts that follow an essentially random walk process, for example, a shift in "tastes" or some error in measurement that affects the intercept in a once and for all fashion:

(14.13) $\alpha_t = \alpha_{t-1} + v_t,$

where α is the intercept and v is the error term, which may or may not be serially correlated. There is no reason for this type of error to be adjusted away in subsequent periods. This drift means that a disturbance from level equilibrium need never be eliminated and the level of desired real money balances or correspondingly the price level will be subject to the same sort of random walk.[10]

---

10. The papers by Coats (1979) and by Hafer and Hein (1980) present results for money demand functions estimated with quarterly U.S. data that are consistent with this explanation. The authors of both papers claim that a first-differenced version of the equation is warranted. Gordon's (1980) study of longer-term U.S. inflation is similarly consistent with our findings.

Our results also suggest that in addition to the random walk process there are other types of disturbances which are not permanent but which are autocorrelated. Thus, if there is a shock which alters the equilibrium *rate of change* or prices, it will gradually be eliminated, but the *level* of prices need not return to its original path.

For example, if the error term of equation (14.13) which describes the behavior of the intercept term of the price equation were autocorrelated and accounted for all the stochastic behavior of prices, we could write

(14.14) $P_t = \alpha_t + \beta X_t,$

(14.15) $\alpha_t = \alpha_{t-1} + v_t,$

(14.16) $v_t = \rho v_{t-1} + \epsilon_t,$

where ϵ is normally distributed, not serially correlated with mean zero, and βX_t represents all explanatory variables. In this case, we could solve this series of equations and estimate the following:

(14.17) $$(P_t - P_{t-1}) - \rho(P_{t-1} - P_{t-2}) = \beta[(X_t - X_{t-1}) - \rho(X_{t-1} - X_{t-2})].$$

If our interpretation of the error term is correct, the extremely large coefficients on the lagged-dependent variable and hence extremely long periods of adjustment in equations estimated in level form are the result of confusing the shorter-term adjustment process with longer-term shifts. Similarly, the very low estimated income elasticities obtained in other studies like that of Al-Khuri and Nsouli, who use a first-differenced equation and include both a lagged-dependent variable and a correction for first-order serial correlation of the disturbances in that differenced equation, also appear suspect. We conjecture that the use of both the lagged-dependent variable and the first-order autoregressive transformation is affecting both the estimates of the adjustment process and the income coefficient.

14.4   Foreign Shocks

The way in which international factors operate in the price equations that we have presented is through the public's expected money function. For almost all countries we have uncovered some evidence of an effect of the balance of payments or of U.S. money—sometimes both—on the domestic nominal stock of money. An international transmission mechanism of this sort is consistent with theoretical models of the specie-flow type. It is not, however, consistent with the adjustment mechanism posited in the early literature of the monetary approach to the balance of payments or with the mechanisms implicit in various discussions of international inflation that emphasize the role played by commodity and oil price shocks.

In the early monetary approach literature, the "law of one price" and international price arbitrage were key areas of emphasis. Viewed from that perspective, our price equations are misspecified.

The way in which inflation is transmitted internationally in the simplest models of this type is via price arbitrage. An increase in the inflation in the rest of the world leads to a near-instantaneous increase in domestic inflation in the small open economy subject to a regime of fixed exchange rates. This, in turn, leads to an excess demand for money in the small economy, a balance-of-payments surplus, and an increase in the domestic nominal stock of money, in that order.

One way to test whether such effects are empirically important in the context of our model is to add foreign price variables to our basic equations. If price arbitrage does provide an international link, and unless adjustment of the domestic nominal stock of money to an incipient excess supply of, or demand for, money produced by increases in price levels abroad were completed within the quarter, then these foreign price variables should enter the equations positively and significantly.

To the extent that the domestic monetary authorities prevent the adjustment of the domestic nominal supply of money to eliminate the excess supply of or demand for money, real output will vary. If the coefficients on transitory income in the demand for money function were close to unity, the addition of foreign price variables might prove to be insignificant even though they were responsible for the change in the price level and the opposite and equal change in real income. In this case, the change in real transitory income would be sufficient to offset the change in real balances due to the price shock. In our model we avoid this simultaneity problem by making transitory income endogenous and replacing its current and lagged values with current and lagged values of the monetary shock variable.[11]

Table 14.3 summarizes the results of including the various price-shock terms in our basic price equations.[12] The most interesting of the regression estimates themselves—those for the U.S. and oil price shocks—are contained in a series of tables in the appendix to this chapter. In all instances—for each country and for each of the price shocks—we used

---

11. Darby in chapter 8 of this volume contains a more complete theoretical discussion of the impact of oil prices on the overall price level.

12. As measures of the relative price of oil, we used the ratio of the dollar price of Venezuelan crude to either the U.S. CPI or GNP deflator. As measures of commodity prices, we used the ratio of the London *Economist*'s dollar-based index of commodity to either the U.S. CPI or GNP deflator. For each country, we calculated separate rest-of-world indices of the CPIs or deflators as nominal-income weighted averages of the indices for the seven foreign countries.

Table 14.3   The Effects of Foreign Price Shocks on Domestic Price Levels

Country	GNP/GDP Deflator				CPI/Cost of Living			
	Relative Price of Oil	World Commodity Price Index	U.S. Deflator	Rest-of-World Deflator	Relative Price of Oil	World Commodity Price Index	U.S. CPI	Rest-of-World CPI
CA	†	†,§	...	...	...	...	...	...
FR	...	...	...	†,§	†,§	...	...	†,§
GE	§	...	...	...	†,§	...	...	...
IT	...	†	...	...	†,§	†,§	...	§
JA	†,§	...	§	†	†,§	...	†,§	†,§
NE	...	...	...	...	...	...	...	...
UK	†,§	...	§	†	...	...	†	†
US	†	†	...	†	†,§	...	...	...
Number of Countries for Which Foreign Shock is Significant								
First order	4	3	...	3	4	1	2	3
Second order	3	1	2	1	4	1	1	3

Note. Variables are as defined in text.

†Significant F statistics at 10% or better in equation with a correction for first-order autocorrelation.

§Significant F statistics at 10% or better in equation with a correction for second-order autocorrelation.

two measures of the domestic price level: the CPI or other cost of living index as well as the GNP or GDP deflator that we used in the regressions summarized above. Again we estimated these equations via GLS.

In virtually every case, we again had to use a second-order autoregressive model of the disturbances before we found no evidence of significant autocorrelation. That in and of itself is a finding of some interest since a possible explanation for the findings reported above is that foreign price shocks were omitted from the regressions. Such shocks conceivably could be responsible for the apparent random walk process we have uncovered.

Our finding of little difference in the error process after inclusion of the price shocks in the regressions, however, does not support that hypothesis. Either something else is responsible, or our price-shock measures are highly imperfect proxies for the true shocks. The latter, however, does not seem to be the case—at least with respect to oil and other commodity price shocks. Estimating the basic equations over shorter periods in which such shocks might be considered of little importance produced in general, no substantial changes in our estimates of the error process.

Now let us consider the test results, first those for the U.S. and rest-of-world price variables. Here the evidence is quite mixed. Only for Japan and the U.K. are both of the U.S. price variables significantly greater than zero at a level of 10% or better. Rest-of-world prices are significant for France, Japan, and the U.K. in both the deflator and the CPI regressions, and for Italy in the CPI regression. Some evidence of price arbitrage therefore exists, but even on the most favorable interpretation of the evidence it is weak and hardly universal. Canada, Germany, and the Netherlands (relative to both measures of rest-of-world prices) show little or no such effects, and Italy an inconsistent effect. In most instances, moreover, the bulk of the effects show up after a lag of two quarters or more.

Commodity prices in general do not fare well at all in the test of price-shock effects. The London *Economist* index of commodity prices is only significant in four of the sixteen comparisons.

The variable that appears to have the most persistent influence is the relative price of oil. With the deflator as the measure of the price level, the oil price variable is significant at a level of 10% or better in five countries: Canada, Germany, Japan, the U.K., and the U.S. In one other, France, the effect was nearly significant. Using the CPI, we found significant effects for Japan again as well as for France and Italy.

Table 14.4 contains alternative estimates of the magnitude of these effects on both measures of the price level for all of the countries other than the Netherlands. We omitted the Netherlands because its coefficients were consistently negative, a problem to which we return below.

These estimates are for two periods, 1973I to 1974IV and 1973I to

**Table 14.4   Contribution of Changes in Relative Oil Prices
to Domestic Price Levels**

| | GNP/GDP Deflator | | | |
| | 1973I–74IV | | 1973I–76IV | |
Country	GLS1	GLS2	GLS1	GLS2
CA	28.8	29.2	15.5	15.7
FR	51.9	23.5	25.0	11.2
GE	17.9	14.9	11.1	9.2
IT	21.9	−4.6	12.5	−2.7
JA	25.9	31.0	18.2	21.8
UK	7.3	4.0	3.3	1.8
US	24.5	4.1	14.2	2.4
	CPI/Cost of Living			
CA	17.0	−38.4	9.0	−20.4
FR	58.1	52.2	30.1	27.0
GE	9.3	−10.0	5.7	6.1
IT	28.1	10.4	14.2	5.1
JA	34.5	43.0	23.3	29.0
UK	−8.8	−21.5	−3.5	−8.6
US	27.6	12.5	16.4	7.4

Note. The above figures are the ratio of (1) the product of the change in logarithm of the relative price of oil over the appropriate period and the sum of the oil price coefficients in the relevant regression to (2) the change in the logarithm of the relevant domestic price index. The symbol GLS1 denotes a regression with a correction for first-order autocorrelation; GLS2, a regression with a correction of second-order autocorrelation.

1976IV, and for both the CPI and deflator measures of the price level. To derive them we first multiplied the ratio of the annualized change in the logarithm of the relative price of oil by the sum of the oil price coefficients in the relevant regression. We then divided that product by the annualized change in the logarithm of the price level.

With relatively few exceptions, the ratios for the deflator fall in a range of roughly 5% to 30%. These ratios moreover tend to decrease with the length of the time period and the complexity of the error model used in the underlying regressions. The median ratio for the period ending in 1974IV is 24.5% in the regressions with a first-order correction and 14.9% in those with a second-order regression. For the longer period, the median ratios are 14.2% and 9.2% from the two types of regressions respectively.

The median ratios for the CPI exhibit the same general pattern: 27.6% and 10.4% for the period ending 1974IV and 14.2% and 6.1% for the period ending 1976IV in the two types of regressions.

Comparison of these estimates with those reported in a recent study by Phillip Cagan (1980) of manufacturing industries in the United States may prove interesting. Cagan estimates that approximately 15% of the 17.0% annual average rate of increase of manufacturing prices in 1972–74, or about 2.6 percentage points, can be accounted for in terms of increases in oil prices. Our own estimates are for the shorter 1973–74 period and for price indices that place less weight on traded goods. Their range is from approximately equal to Cagan's to considerably below.[13]

The estimate derived from the regressions with a first-order correction are 24.5% of the increase in the deflator and 27.6% of the increase in the CPI, or 2.1 and 2.5 percentage points respectively. Those derived from the regressions with a second-order correction are a good deal lower: 4.1% of the deflator increase (0.3 percentage points) and 12.5% of the CPI increase (or 1.12 percentage points).

There are, however, a number of problems with our results that lead us to question how seriously they can be taken. The most obvious is the negative coefficients obtained in a considerable number of cases: Canada, Italy, Germany, and the U.K. for at least one price variable and one type of regression, and the Netherlands, as we have already stated, for both price variables and both types of regressions.

For the deflator, which is based upon value added production, negative effects are possible but over periods of several years somewhat implausible. For the CPI, which is an index of prices in consumption, negative estimates for countries that do not produce petroleum make little sense.

That difference in what the two price indices measure raises an additional question. Even if we ignore the greater incidence of negative sums of coefficients with the CPI on the grounds that the use of the second-order correction may be unduly influencing the results, the CPI fares no better than the deflator. We would have expected exactly the opposite. Indeed that was the main reason we reestimated the price equations using the CPI in place of the deflator, the price variable we used in developing the basic model.

Equally disturbing is the lack of consistency in results for the two indices. Only for Japan do we obtain significant positive effects with both price measures and both types of regressions.

A further problem, as Michael Darby has pointed out in chapter 8, is that in a number of countries the removal of price controls occurred more or less coincidentally with the rise in oil prices. Separating these effects from those of oil prices on the price level is virtually impossible.

14.5 Summary and Conclusions

Starting with a conventional money demand function, a Lucas-type aggregate supply function, and a general form of the public's expected

---

13. There is a further difference between Cagan's (1980) and our estimates. What Cagan is measuring is impact effects. Our estimates, in contrast, implicitly allow for subsequent adjustment of the relative prices of other products.

money function, we have derived a reduced-form price equation that we have estimated with quarterly data for the United States and seven other industrial countries for a near twenty-year period beginning in the late 1950s. We have then gone on to use these equations to test a variety of hypotheses about the international inflation process during these years.

The equations themselves fit the data fairly well. Moreover, the parameter estimates we obtain are both reasonably consistent across countries and tolerably close to our prior expectations of magnitude and, in the case of the monetary shocks, temporal pattern. We therefore have confidence in using the equations as a basis for testing competing hypotheses.

The principal conclusion that emerges from this exercise is that movements in domestic money in all eight countries serve as the key link in the process leading to changes in the domestic rates of inflation. The factors that produced changes in the domestic money shocks, however, differed among countries. In the seven foreign countries, international factors— the balance of payments or United States money, in some instances both—had some influence in the expected money equations; in the United States, the reserve-currency country, they did not.

Foreign rates of inflation, as measured by either United States inflation or a rest-of-world inflation index, however, had a direct impact on domestic rates of inflation in relatively few of the comparisons we made. To the extent that inflation was actually transmitted from one country to another, it appears to have been via channels much closer to a specie-flow type of mechanism than to the price-arbitrage mechanism.[14]

These findings therefore point to the short-run possibility of monetary control. Other evidence, namely that foreign factors by no means predominate in terms of explainability in the expected money equations, add to this impression.

The other factor that may have had an influence upon domestic inflation rates in these countries is increases in the relative price of oil. The extent of the influence, though, is not easily ascertainable from our comparisons. Viewed in terms of the results most favorable to the hypothesis, the regressions with the corrections for first-order autocorrelation, the oil price impact accounted for a substantial, but in most countries far from major, proportion of the inflation over the 1973–74 period. Viewed on the basis of the regressions with the second-order correction, the effects are in general of considerably less magnitude and may in fact be largely spurious.

---

14. The two are not competing hypotheses. Both channels of transmission in principle can operate at the same time. The key question is the quantitative importance of the one vis-à-vis the other within the relevant time period.

It is also important to note that our results are for measured price indices. Aggregation as well as measurement error may obscure the effects of price arbitrage in individual markets.

The other major area requiring some additional discussion is the demand for money. We find that in all of these countries the rate of inflation rather than level of prices is uniquely determined. This is consistent with a number of other pieces of evidence. Our study using time series of cross-state data, the Huffman and Lothian (1980) paper on the United Kingdom, and several studies based upon time-series data for the United States are all examples.[15]

The cause of these stochastic shifts, however, so far has not been determined. Measurement error in either prices, real income, or money is a possibility. Omitted variables in the money demand function—the change in "financial sophistication" used by Friedman and Schwartz (1982) or the similar variable used by Bordo and Jonung in their long-term time-series study—is another. Further investigation of this question is clearly of considerable importance. Our results suggest, however, that the explanation will have to be applicable to more countries than just the United States.

Acknowledgments

The authors would like to acknowledge the able research assistance of Connie McCarthy and the helpful comments of Michael R. Darby, Anna J. Schwartz, Alan C. Stockman, and the members of the monetary workshops at Columbia University and of the Graduate School of Business at New York University.

15. See the studies cited above in footnote 9.

Appendix

International Price Behavior and the Demand for Money

Table 14.5A   **Price Equation with Dependent Variable** log PD − log(M2/N), **1957III to 1976IV**
(absolute value of *t* statistic in parentheses)

	CA	FR	GE	IT	JA	NE	UK	US
Coefficient								
Constant	2.774	5.834	5.087	11.837	5.307	1.706	−0.109	−0.967
	(3.829)	(6.484)	(9.830)	(39.380)	(29.060)	(2.763)	(0.099)	(1.409)
$ResM2_t$	−0.148	0.485	−0.722	−0.731	−0.552	−0.233	−0.904	−0.927
	(0.378)	(0.655)	(2.331)	(2.126)	(1.321)	(0.898)	(2.751)	(2.311)
$ResM2_{t-1}$	−1.032	−0.103	−0.619	−0.644	−0.595	−0.389	−0.861	−1.963
	(2.697)	(0.152)	(1.989)	(1.847)	(1.405)	(1.521)	(2.612)	(5.239)
$ResM2_{t-2}$	−1.117	0.030	−0.366	−0.554	−0.934	−0.553	−1.119	−2.158
	(3.035)	(0.046)	(1.203)	(1.627)	(2.212)	(2.184)	(3.279)	(6.056)
$ResM2_{t-3}$	−0.991	0.113	−0.696	−0.590	−0.791	−0.294	−1.292	−1.889
	(3.022)	(0.169)	(2.254)	(1.708)	(2.209)	(1.240)	(4.085)	(5.411)

ResM2$_{t-4}$	−0.765 (2.050)	−0.037 (0.054)	−0.428 (1.336)	−0.504 (1.450)	−0.593 (1.441)	−0.023 (0.094)	−1.254 (3.876)	−1.704 (4.721)
ResM2$_{t-5}$	−1.345 (3.678)	0.479 (0.674)	−0.790 (2.189)	−0.538 (1.548)	−0.410 (1.007)	−0.071 (0.286)	−1.226 (3.692)	−1.580 (4.291)
ResM2$_{t-6}$	−0.934 (2.581)	−0.299 (0.377)	−1.274 (3.579)	−0.121 (0.347)	−0.554 (1.392)	−0.123 (0.454)	−1.025 (3.116)	−1.496 (4.325)
log(y^P/N)$_{t-1}$	−1.185 (16.332)	−1.375 (17.870)	−1.386 (31.148)	−1.810 (94.312)	−1.213 (165.900)	−1.029 (18.355)	−0.836 (5.735)	−0.785 (11.556)
log R_L	0.077 (1.513)	0.479 (6.460)	0.023 (0.463)	0.137 (6.701)	0.828 (17.128)	0.104 (2.394)	0.026 (0.475)	−0.008 (0.201)
log y^t_{t-7}	0.119 (0.759)	−0.784 (2.123)	0.878 (4.203)	1.008 (5.543)	0.131 (2.386)	1.247 (6.673)	−0.566 (1.397)	0.090 (1.278)
$\bar{R}^2$	0.982	0.952	0.981	0.996	0.999	0.968	0.849	0.988
S.E.E.	0.0306	0.0661	0.0354	0.0287	0.0202	0.0332	0.0513	0.0143
D-W	0.32	0.21	0.41	0.30	0.34	0.45	0.26	0.32

Note. Variables are defined as in table 14.1.

Table 14.5B Price Equation with Dependent Variable log PD − log(M2/N), 1957III to 1976IV (absolute value of t statistic in parentheses)

Coefficient	CA	FR	GE	IT	JA	NE	UK	US
Constant	3.178 (3.856)	0.703 (0.619)	3.640 (3.553)	12.477 (12.279)	3.895 (7.717)	0.731 (0.639)	−3.800 (1.817)	−1.371 (2.389)
$ResM2_t$	−0.465 (2.658)	−0.983 (5.693)	−0.841 (7.751)	−0.716 (4.336)	−0.944 (5.160)	−0.841 (8.059)	−0.968 (8.644)	−0.942 (6.815)
$ResM2_{t-1}$	−1.063 (4.940)	−1.145 (4.698)	−0.560 (3.944)	−0.571 (2.669)	−1.086 (4.508)	−0.818 (6.490)	−0.804 (5.663)	−1.698 (10.111)
$ResM2_{t-2}$	−0.842 (3.889)	−0.874 (3.451)	−0.411 (2.685)	−0.474 (2.043)	−1.138 (4.832)	−0.818 (6.288)	−0.703 (4.679)	−1.759 (9.690)
$ResM2_{t-3}$	−0.886 (4.584)	−0.584 (2.272)	−0.492 (3.073)	−0.339 (1.444)	−1.058 (5.275)	−0.605 (4.747)	−0.931 (6.412)	−1.464 (8.107)
$ResM2_{t-4}$	−0.688 (3.256)	−0.485 (1.871)	−0.344 (2.205)	−0.214 (0.931)	−0.920 (4.045)	−0.515 (3.625)	−0.757 (5.074)	−1.113 (6.079)

ResM2$_{t-5}$	−0.948	−0.291	−0.220	−0.240	−0.473	−0.335	−0.660	−0.857
	(4.550)	(1.152)	(1.398)	(1.145)	(2.145)	(2.441)	(4.549)	(4.985)
ResM2$_{t-6}$	−0.337	−0.198	−0.223	0.028	−0.235	−0.287	−0.368	−0.522
	(2.032)	(1.104)	(1.689)	(0.177)	(1.357)	(2.588)	(3.041)	(3.933)
log$(y^P/N)_{t-1}$	−1.232	−0.928	−1.234	−1.863	−1.181	−0.953	−0.318	−0.738
	(13.405)	(7.828)	(11.239)	(25.891)	(34.760)	(7.678)	(1.037)	(11.426)
log R_L	0.086	0.128	0.0003	0.106	0.441	0.005	−0.098	−0.009
	(2.096)	(2.389)	(0.011)	(3.316)	(6.281)	(0.131)	(1.735)	(0.479)
log y^t_{-1}	0.105	−0.068	0.220	0.454	0.158	0.151	0.097	0.174
	(0.735)	(0.667)	(1.660)	(3.221)	(2.241)	(1.134)	(0.545)	(2.575)
Rho1	0.9102	0.9884	0.9714	0.9410	0.9694	0.9704	0.9767	0.9508
$\bar{R}^2$	0.804	0.554	0.692	0.912	0.954	0.672	0.540	0.814
S.E.E.	0.0148	0.0154	0.0130	0.0137	0.0093	0.0139	0.0193	0.0058
D-W	1.77	0.52	0.71	1.34	1.36	1.63	1.28	0.80

Note. Variables are defined as in table 14.1.

Table 14.6A   **Price Equation with Dependent Variable** $\log PD - \log(M2/N)$, **1957III to 1976IV**
(absolute value of t statistics in parentheses)

Coefficient	CA	FR	GE	IT	JA	NE	UK
Constant	2.361	4.193	5.788	12.854	5.768	−1.520	6.287
	(1.246)	(2.349)	(3.602)	(10.681)	(13.300)	(0.586)	(2.483)
ResM2_t	−0.671	−1.011	−0.846	−0.732	−0.887	−0.867	−0.852
	(5.928)	(5.766)	(8.060)	(5.455)	(4.102)	(8.322)	(10.078)
ResM2_{t-1}	−0.824	−1.284	−0.556	−0.653	−1.223	−0.882	−0.714
	(5.681)	(5.312)	(4.185)	(3.736)	(4.357)	(6.972)	(6.727)
ResM2_{t-2}	−0.790	−1.128	−0.435	−0.776	−1.290	−0.983	−0.679
	(5.528)	(4.559)	(3.048)	(4.113)	(4.656)	(7.548)	(6.133)
ResM2_{t-3}	−0.859	−0.887	−0.556	−0.679	−1.094	−0.724	−0.677
	(6.762)	(3.523)	(3.704)	(3.604)	(4.641)	(5.649)	(6.417)
ResM2_{t-4}	−0.736	−0.791	−0.344	−0.494	−1.237	−0.649	−0.540
	(5.249)	(3.104)	(2.358)	(2.694)	(4.609)	(4.551)	(4.897)
ResM2_{t-5}	−0.557	−0.591	−0.295	−0.267	−0.712	−0.516	−0.400
	(4.068)	(2.352)	(1.988)	(1.601)	(2.759)	(3.732)	(3.779)
ResM2_{t-6}	−0.236	−0.386	−0.223	−0.093	−0.516	−0.349	−0.201
	(2.151)	(2.178)	(1.779)	(0.711)	(2.511)	(3.150)	(2.300)

$\log(y^P/N)_{t-1}$	−1.173 (5.108)	−1.325 (6.852)	−1.453 (8.408)	1.887 (21.114)	−1.327 (36.887)	−0.684 (2.381)	−1.812 (4.745)
$\log R_L$	−0.010 (0.370)	0.047 (0.729)	0.041 (1.381)	0.127 (4.253)	0.421 (4.494)	0.042 (1.116)	−0.019 (0.420)
$\log y^f_{t-1}$	0.076 (0.801)	−0.106 (1.066)	0.054 (0.425)	0.145 (1.268)	0.110 (1.438)	−0.064 (0.476)	0.038 (0.292)
$\log USPC_t$	0.882 (2.187)	0.566 (0.842)	−0.179 (0.373)	0.174 (0.403)	0.655 (1.341)	−0.082 (0.149)	−1.574 (2.711)
$\log USPC_{t-1}$	0.064 (0.139)	0.644 (0.878)	−0.192 (0.344)	0.908 (1.726)	−0.168 (0.273)	−0.527 (0.832)	0.295 (0.440)
$\log USPC_{t-2}$	−0.178 (0.390)	0.328 (0.426)	−0.088 (0.139)	−0.365 (0.702)	0.236 (0.390)	−0.749 (1.158)	0.745 (1.126)
$\log USPC_{t-3}$	−0.774 (2.074)	−0.869 (1.442)	0.462 (0.982)	−0.813 (1.929)	−0.181 (0.384)	0.918 (1.764)	1.388 (2.418)
Rho1	0.9889	0.9893	0.9678	0.8936	0.8451	0.9801	0.9799
$\bar{R}^2$	0.734	0.558	0.779	0.973	0.990	0.695	0.673
S.E.E.	0.0099	0.0146	0.0119	0.0107	0.0104	0.0137	0.0138
D-W	0.80	0.62	0.98	1.10	1.62	1.61	0.75

Note. USPC is the U.S. consumer price index; the other variables are as defined in table 14.1.

Table 14.6B Price Equation with Dependent Variable $\log PD - \log(M2/N)$, 1957III to 1976IV (absolute value of t statistic in parentheses)

Coefficient	CA	FR	GE	IT	JA	NE	UK
Constant	-1.107	-3.179	2.989	13.045	5.649	-1.831	1.527
	(1.686)	(0.912)	(1.847)	(13.368)	(14.337)	(0.624)	(0.640)
$ResM2_t$	-0.917	-0.885	-0.867	-0.920	-1.065	-0.928	-0.751
	(14.814)	(9.358)	(10.591)	(8.243)	(4.990)	(9.057)	(12.521)
$ResM2_{t-1}$	-1.128	-1.023	-0.592	-0.844	-1.411	-0.928	-0.594
	(10.390)	(6.038)	(4.027)	(4.392)	(4.377)	(6.725)	(6.105)
$ResM2_{t-2}$	-1.058	-0.970	-0.453	-0.919	-1.340	-1.020	-0.562
	(7.974)	(4.779)	(2.456)	(3.760)	(4.057)	(6.906)	(4.610)
$ResM2_{t-3}$	-1.016	-0.783	-0.555	-0.773	-1.130	-0.757	-0.544
	(7.669)	(3.568)	(2.785)	(2.969)	(3.815)	(5.122)	(4.308)
$ResM2_{t-4}$	-0.817	-0.601	-0.300	-0.528	-1.316	-0.683	-0.402
	(6.153)	(2.782)	(1.582)	(2.174)	(4.105)	(4.261)	(3.189)
$ResM2_{t-5}$	-0.481	-0.310	-0.259	-0.299	-0.691	-0.537	-0.261
	(4.323)	(1.651)	(1.680)	(1.570)	(2.324)	(3.590)	(2.485)
$ResM2_{t-6}$	-0.107	-0.619	-0.187	-0.111	-0.442	-0.371	-0.092
	(1.688)	(1.646)	(2.036)	(1.022)	(2.197)	(3.382)	(1.392)

	(1)	(2)	(3)	(4)	(5)	(6)	(7)
$\log y^P_{t-1}$	-0.746 (9.522)	-0.547 (1.477)	-1.166 (6.691)	-1.911 (26.612)	-1.331 (39.526)	-0.649 (1.998)	-1.099 (3.056)
$\log R_L$	-0.008 (0.512)	0.046 (1.440)	0.001 (0.034)	0.064 (2.699)	0.355 (3.654)	0.045 (1.258)	-0.023 (0.717)
$\log y^f_{t-7}$	-0.075 (1.837)	0.021 (0.523)	-0.105 (1.455)	0.019 (0.240)	0.045 (0.618)	-0.125 (0.972)	-0.084 (1.169)
$\log \text{USPC}_t$	0.479 (1.991)	0.694 (1.955)	0.360 (0.984)	0.014 (0.040)	0.634 (1.318)	-0.101 (0.191)	-0.606 (1.444)
$\log \text{USPC}_{t-1}$	-0.536 (2.809)	-0.082 (0.244)	-0.550 (1.708)	0.506 (1.612)	-0.054 (0.106)	-0.568 (1.016)	0.003 (0.009)
$\log \text{USPC}_{t-2}$	-0.503 (2.652)	-0.180 (0.543)	-0.634 (1.834)	-0.448 (1.454)	0.269 (0.539)	-0.822 (1.459)	0.374 (1.105)
$\log \text{USPC}_{t-3}$	0.054 (0.221)	-0.663 (1.893)	0.522 (1.322)	-0.043 (0.118)	-0.308 (0.691)	1.026 (1.995)	0.561 (1.286)
Rho1	1.7243	1.8789	1.6919	1.5458	1.1470	1.2111	1.7379
Rho2	-0.8915	-0.9007	-0.7642	-0.6913	-0.3370	-0.2419	-0.7994
$\bar{R}^2$	0.984	0.734	0.904	0.985	0.992	0.702	0.826
S.E.E.	0.0057	0.0086	0.0089	0.0086	0.0100	0.0134	0.0098
D-W	2.02	2.04	2.48	2.09	2.09	2.01	2.11

Note. USPC is the U.S. consumer price index; the other variables are as defined in table 14.1.

Table 14.7A Price Equation with Dependent Variable log PD − log(M2/N), 1957III to 1976IV (absolute value of t statistic in parentheses)

Coefficient	CA	FR	GE	IT	JA	NE	UK
Constant	0.100	3.694	3.969	9.980	5.473	−6.822	6.855
	(0.065)	(1.905)	(2.152)	(6.369)	(11.137)	(2.647)	(2.289)
ResM2$_t$	−0.442	−1.059	−0.797	−0.736	−0.870	−0.876	−1.029
	(2.470)	(6.001)	(6.867)	(4.494)	(4.715)	(8.852)	(9.930)
ResM2$_{t-1}$	−1.037	−1.270	−0.495	−0.552	−1.009	−0.872	−0.830
	(4.720)	(5.061)	(3.418)	(2.675)	(4.146)	(7.217)	(6.482)
ResM2$_{t-2}$	−0.829	−0.992	−0.400	−0.487	−1.085	−0.894	−0.730
	(3.866)	(3.812)	(2.629)	(2.206)	(4.579)	(7.128)	(5.406)
ResM2$_{t-3}$	−0.845	−0.666	−0.482	−0.432	−1.039	−0.675	−0.932
	(4.366)	(2.538)	(3.005)	(1.923)	(5.270)	(5.462)	(7.197)
ResM2$_{t-4}$	−0.702	−0.574	−0.316	−0.363	−0.875	−0.580	−0.735
	(3.098)	(2.175)	(2.025)	(1.625)	(3.891)	(4.148)	(5.442)
ResM2$_{t-5}$	−0.920	−0.430	−0.242	−0.392	−0.364	−0.405	−0.622
	(4.046)	(1.657)	(1.518)	(1.911)	(1.615)	(3.047)	(4.739)
ResM2$_{t-6}$	−0.303	−0.273	−0.241	−0.081	−0.173	−0.332	−0.314
	(1.712)	(1.458)	(1.780)	(0.514)	(0.983)	(3.065)	(2.876)

$\log(y^P/N)_{t-1}$	-0.865 (4.711)	-1.253 (6.012)	-1.266 (6.381)	-1.681 (14.497)	-1.316 (33.231)	-0.108 (0.381)	-1.919 (4.267)
$\log R_L$	0.072 (1.712)	0.106 (1.821)	0.007 (0.223)	0.125 (3.584)	0.367 (4.789)	0.004 (0.132)	-0.080 (1.451)
$\log y^f_{t-7}$	0.129 (0.927)	-0.074 (0.722)	0.269 (1.997)	0.476 (3.480)	0.130 (1.825)	0.091 (0.713)	0.272 (1.615)
$\log USPD_t$	0.441 (0.828)	-0.007 (0.012)	-0.741 (1.702)	0.473 (1.094)	0.636 (2.002)	-0.743 (1.715)	-0.823 (1.306)
$\log USPD_{t-1}$	-0.859 (1.400)	0.679 (1.163)	-0.038 (0.075)	0.568 (1.152)	-0.155 (0.442)	-0.666 (1.374)	0.458 (0.650)
$\log USPD_{t-2}$	0.710 (1.224)	0.111 (0.192)	1.024 (2.070)	-0.328 (0.664)	0.067 (0.198)	-0.046 (0.096)	0.022 (0.032)
$\log USPD_{t-3}$	-0.616 (1.219)	-0.328 (0.664)	-0.187 (0.425)	-0.977 (2.272)	-0.237 (0.708)	0.728 (1.813)	1.366 (2.158)
Rho1	0.8455	0.9869	0.9694	0.8934	0.8906	0.9664	0.9604
$\bar{R}^2$	0.901	0.568	0.711	0.960	0.989	0.730	0.646
S.E.E.	0.0145	0.0153	0.0128	0.0129	0.0089	0.0128	0.0170
D-W	1.78	0.55	0.80	1.56	1.42	1.80	1.73

Note. USPD is the U.S. GNP deflator; the other variables are as defined in table 14.1.

Table 14.7B Price Equation with Dependent Variable $\log PD - \log(M2/N)$, 1957III to 1976IV (absolute value of t statistic in parentheses)

Coefficient	CA	FR	GE	IT	JA	NE	UK
Constant	−0.212 (0.144)	5.649 (2.566)	1.445 (0.878)	9.759 (6.359)	5.449 (11.509)	−6.860 (2.548)	5.908 (1.908)
ResM2_t	−0.473 (2.662)	−0.955 (9.871)	−0.920 (12.342)	−0.798 (4.972)	−0.978 (4.968)	−0.888 (9.984)	−1.044 (10.055)
ResM2_{t-1}	−1.052 (4.452)	−1.075 (6.094)	−0.704 (5.003)	−0.549 (2.241)	−1.038 (3.569)	−0.879 (6.969)	−0.850 (6.146)
ResM2_{t-2}	−0.822 (3.488)	−0.857 (3.994)	−0.625 (3.436)	−0.464 (1.613)	−1.048 (3.616)	−0.899 (6.779)	−0.757 (5.016)
ResM2_{t-3}	−0.832 (3.817)	−0.571 (2.464)	−0.632 (3.249)	−0.307 (1.032)	−1.051 (4.186)	−0.682 (5.182)	−0.942 (6.382)
ResM2_{t-4}	−0.685 (2.745)	−0.451 (1.996)	−0.409 (2.215)	−0.170 (0.595)	−1.061 (3.817)	−0.585 (3.984)	−0.749 (4.915)
ResM2_{t-5}	−0.894 (3.616)	−0.256 (1.294)	−0.227 (1.532)	−0.191 (0.800)	−0.318 (1.165)	−0.404 (2.927)	−0.617 (4.291)
ResM2_{t-6}	−0.285 (1.603)	−0.126 (1.158)	−0.179 (2.109)	0.035 (0.237)	−0.063 (0.336)	−0.333 (3.078)	−0.292 (2.608)

$\log y^P_{t-1}$	-0.828	-1.465	-1.000	-1.668	-1.326	-0.105	-1.771
	(4.742)	(6.300)	(5.652)	(14.723)	(34.331)	(0.354)	(3.807)
$\log R_L$	0.067	-0.077	0.004	0.105	0.307	0.002	-0.067
	(1.566)	(2.437)	(0.245)	(2.934)	(3.730)	(0.067)	(1.162)
$\log y^t_{t-1}$	0.085	0.026	0.045	0.216	0.106	0.087	0.195
	(0.644)	(0.643)	(0.718)	(1.725)	(1.446)	(0.684)	(1.224)
$\log \text{USPD}_t$	0.225	0.062	0.062	0.385	0.317	-0.678	-0.710
	(0.424)	(0.230)	(0.220)	(0.924)	(0.946)	(1.572)	(1.141)
$\log \text{USPD}_{t-1}$	-0.793	0.500	-0.164	0.310	0.170	-0.719	0.292
	(1.390)	(2.104)	(0.710)	(0.792)	(0.513)	(1.549)	(0.452)
$\log \text{USPD}_{t-2}$	0.674	0.227	0.332	-0.224	0.180	-0.090	0.008
	(1.257)	(1.001)	(1.416)	(0.569)	(0.557)	(0.200)	(0.013)
$\log \text{USPD}_{t-3}$	-0.452	-0.110	-0.533	-0.724	-0.330	0.763	1.306
	(0.888)	(0.425)	(1.934)	(1.756)	(0.946)	(1.893)	(2.055)
Rho1	0.9969	1.8884	1.7950	1.2988	1.1178	1.0656	1.1463
Rho2	-0.1755	-0.9312	-0.8740	-0.4301	-0.2634	-0.1049	-0.1996
$\bar{R}^2$	0.916	0.831	0.915	0.966	0.991	0.731	0.656
S.E.E.	0.0143	0.0085	0.0082	0.0123	0.0092	0.0127	0.0168
D-W	2.08	1.99	2.63	2.18	2.04	2.00	2.18

Note. USPD is the U.S. GNP deflator; the other variables are as defined in table 14.1.

Table 14.8A Price Equation with Dependent Variable log PC − log(M2/N), 1957III to 1976IV (absolute value of t statistic in parentheses)

Coefficient	CA	FR	GE	IT	JA	NE	UK	US
Constant	3.595	0.758	6.039	13.764	3.230	2.494	−2.450	−0.734
	(2.966)	(0.698)	(6.785)	(10.959)	(5.620)	(2.197)	(1.220)	(0.998)
$ResM2_t$	−0.672	−1.085	−0.829	−0.744	−0.770	−0.852	−0.824	−1.029
	(5.416)	(5.929)	(8.086)	(5.778)	(3.516)	(8.007)	(7.982)	(6.917)
$ResM2_{t-1}$	−0.880	−1.279	−0.541	−0.650	−1.012	−0.862	−0.733	−1.741
	(5.606)	(5.244)	(3.954)	(3.811)	(3.542)	(6.717)	(5.547)	(9.589)
$ResM2_{t-2}$	−0.930	−1.137	−0.416	−0.784	−1.065	−0.956	−0.717	−1.762
	(5.847)	(4.545)	(2.768)	(4.179)	(3.782)	(7.308)	(5.044)	(8.944)
$ResM2_{t-3}$	−0.976	−0.935	−0.538	−0.704	−0.977	−0.690	−0.749	−1.648
	(6.924)	(3.699)	(3.401)	(3.652)	(4.055)	(5.435)	(5.514)	(8.446)
$ResM2_{t-4}$	−0.806	−0.765	−0.308	−0.544	−0.923	−0.623	−0.663	−1.381
	(5.098)	(3.001)	(2.003)	(2.876)	(3.362)	(4.347)	(4.797)	(7.082)
$ResM2_{t-5}$	−0.619	−0.545	−0.269	−0.311	−0.497	−0.479	−0.520	−1.056
	(4.066)	(2.215)	(1.790)	(1.825)	(1.852)	(3.439)	(3.954)	(5.744)
$ResM2_{t-6}$	−0.301	−0.381	−0.201	−0.078	−0.329	−0.332	−0.247	−0.585
	(2.540)	(2.191)	(1.606)	(0.604)	(1.586)	(2.875)	(2.262)	(4.076)

$\log(y^P/N)_{t-1}$	-1.320	-0.955	-1.482	-1.957	-1.150	-1.126	-0.506	-0.824
	(9.103)	(8.311)	(15.478)	(21.524)	(32.398)	(9.087)	(1.704)	(9.756)
$\log R_L$	0.002	0.076	0.043	0.115	0.359	0.055	-0.054	-0.032
	(0.054)	(1.362)	(1.548)	(3.883)	(3.022)	(1.513)	(1.002)	(1.463)
$\log y^f_{t-7}$	0.104	-0.081	0.043	0.180	0.108	-0.048	-0.127	0.153
	(0.995)	(0.830)	(0.346)	(1.604)	(1.287)	(0.350)	(0.749)	(2.058)
$\log OIL_t$	0.004	0.017	-0.007	0.030	0.043	0.005	-0.018	0.018
	(0.314)	(1.022)	(0.547)	(2.437)	(3.041)	(0.338)	(0.919)	(2.545)
$\log OIL_{t-1}$	0.015	0.022	-0.002	0.011	0.018	-0.029	-0.014	0.009
	(1.314)	(1.362)	(0.202)	(0.915)	(1.622)	(2.062)	(0.801)	(1.519)
$\log OIL_{t-2}$	0.003	0.028	0.003	0.014	0.030	-0.020	-0.007	0.010
	(0.295)	(1.727)	(0.231)	(1.258)	(2.719)	(1.430)	(0.396)	(1.575)
$\log OIL_{t-3}$	0.003	0.033	0.016	0.015	0.004	-0.007	0.021	0.004
	(0.229)	(1.905)	(1.172)	(1.305)	(0.324)	(0.421)	(1.003)	(0.521)
Rho1	0.9937	0.9876	0.9637	0.9833	0.9561	0.9660	0.9832	0.9685
$\bar{R}^2$	0.667	0.565	0.793	0.878	0.950	0.733	0.493	0.769
S.E.	0.0106	0.0146	0.0119	0.0106	0.0108	0.0138	0.0171	0.0614
D-W	0.79	0.55	0.99	0.92	1.37	1.64	0.54	0.65

Note. OIL is the relative price of oil index; the other variables are as defined in table 14.1. PC is the consumer price index.

Table 14.8B   Price Equation with Dependent Variable log PC − log(M2/N), 1957III to 1976IV (absolute value of t statistic in parentheses)

Coefficient	CA	FR	GE	IT	JA	NE	UK	US
Constant	2.796	0.173	5.863	12.929	2.774	2.505	−1.155	−0.095
	(7.622)	(0.161)	(8.693)	(30.057)	(5.549)	(2.340)	(1.123)	(0.392)
ResM2$_t$	−0.927	−0.934	−0.871	−0.875	−1.006	−0.919	−0.727	−0.962
	(12.418)	(9.312)	(10.439)	(8.252)	(5.042)	(8.747)	(12.650)	(13.116)
ResM2$_{t-1}$	−1.182	−1.022	−0.615	−0.786	−1.240	−0.916	−0.591	−1.552
	(8.959)	(5.960)	(4.187)	(4.261)	(3.869)	(6.507)	(6.113)	(11.532)
ResM2$_{t-2}$	−1.110	−0.943	−0.500	−0.870	−1.084	−1.003	−0.593	−1.472
	(7.029)	(4.642)	(2.679)	(3.677)	(3.159)	(6.716)	(4.811)	(8.392)
ResM2$_{t-3}$	−1.034	−0.767	−0.596	−0.721	−0.950	−0.725	−0.578	−1.263
	(6.650)	(3.525)	(2.926)	(2.840)	(3.022)	(4.891)	(4.566)	(6.907)
ResM2$_{t-4}$	−0.828	−0.565	−0.351	−0.496	−0.881	−0.667	−0.445	−0.880
	(5.302)	(2.638)	(1.829)	(2.082)	(2.609)	(4.107)	(3.596)	(5.068)
ResM2$_{t-5}$	−0.526	−0.305	−0.273	−0.252	−0.288	−0.512	−0.286	−0.531
	(3.989)	(1.648)	(1.718)	(1.354)	(0.941)	(3.381)	(2.843)	(3.853)
ResM2$_{t-6}$	−0.147	−0.189	−0.172	−0.045	−0.107	−0.371	−0.094	−0.188
	(1.939)	(1.901)	(1.750)	(0.442)	(0.554)	(3.250)	(1.479)	(2.375)

	(1)	(2)	(3)	(4)	(5)	(6)	(7)	(8)
$\log(y^P/N)_{t-1}$	-1.206 (28.786)	-0.900 (7.871)	-1.469 (20.079)	-1.902 (64.910)	-1.155 (40.114)	-1.126 (9.658)	-0.690 (4.565)	-0.892 (32.717)
$\log R_L$	0.013 (0.684)	0.051 (1.691)	0.023 (1.213)	0.069 (2.865)	0.168 (1.419)	0.061 (1.707)	-0.005 (0.160)	-0.014 (1.494)
$\log y^f_{t-7}$	-0.094 (1.854)	0.028 (0.731)	-0.103 (1.293)	0.090 (1.189)	0.029 (0.407)	-0.132 (0.972)	-0.094 (1.329)	-0.024 (0.552)
$\log OIL_t$	-0.007 (1.137)	0.018 (2.034)	-0.004 (0.389)	0.019 (2.423)	0.055 (4.525)	0.011 (0.691)	0.005 (0.540)	0.004 (1.272)
$\log OIL_{t-1}$	-0.020 (2.820)	0.019 (1.549)	-0.009 (0.826)	-0.001 (0.155)	0.023 (2.230)	-0.030 (2.112)	-0.015 (1.120)	0.002 (0.510)
$\log OIL_{t-2}$	-0.023 (3.477)	0.026 (2.185)	-0.003 (0.318)	0.002 (0.226)	0.032 (3.036)	-0.019 (1.323)	-0.016 (1.237)	0.005 (1.457)
$\log OIL_{t-3}$	-0.006 (0.929)	0.028 (2.818)	0.007 (0.690)	0.006 (0.795)	0.010 (0.847)	-0.008 (0.515)	-0.018 (1.515)	0.008 (2.701)
Rho1	1.7477	1.8879	1.5988	1.5661	1.4562	1.1918	1.8294	1.7757
Rho2	-0.8802	-0.9139	-0.6712	-0.7201	-0.5321	-0.2420	-0.8946	-0.8968
$\bar{R}^2$	0.964	0.776	0.896	0.988	0.964	0.753	0.839	0.965
S.E.E.	0.0069	0.0080	0.0094	0.0082	0.0097	0.0135	0.0097	0.0033
D-W	1.95	1.98	2.45	2.00	2.16	2.07	2.08	1.98

Note. OIL is the relative price of oil index; the other variables are as defined in table 14.1. PC is the consumer price index.

Table 14.9A Price Equation with Dependent Variable log PD − log(M2/N), 1957III to 1976IV (absolute value of t statistic in parentheses)

	CA	FR	GE	IT	JA	NE	UK	US
Coefficient								
Constant	3.256 (2.569)	1.253 (1.149)	4.008 (4.080)	12.684 (8.254)	3.894 (9.268)	−0.082 (0.096)	−3.474 (1.832)	−0.948 (1.336)
$ResM2_t$	−0.557 (3.291)	−1.804 (5.780)	−0.846 (7.606)	−0.732 (4.371)	−0.830 (4.681)	−0.857 (8.137)	−1.001 (9.190)	−0.928 (6.848)
$ResM2_{t-1}$	−1.172 (5.477)	−1.258 (5.033)	−0.536 (3.612)	−0.608 (2.734)	−0.944 (4.085)	−0.825 (6.500)	−0.793 (5.690)	−1.670 (10.090)
$ResM2_{t-2}$	−0.972 (4.479)	−1.019 (3.977)	−0.379 (2.323)	−0.542 (2.214)	−0.964 (4.235)	−0.818 (6.341)	−0.645 (4.302)	−1.742 (9.702)
$ResM2_{t-3}$	−1.001 (5.203)	−0.756 (2.908)	−0.467 (2.719)	−0.426 (1.691)	−0.917 (4.712)	−0.592 (4.733)	−0.852 (5.947)	−1.495 (8.405)
$ResM2_{t-4}$	−0.773 (3.588)	−0.602 (2.304)	−0.255 (1.532)	−0.313 (1.270)	−0.722 (3.256)	−0.522 (3.703)	−0.707 (4.848)	−1.129 (6.358)
$ResM2_{t-5}$	−1.009 (4.869)	−0.408 (1.616)	−0.178 (1.090)	−0.346 (1.555)	−0.285 (1.313)	−0.339 (2.474)	−0.602 (4.340)	−0.885 (5.279)
$ResM2_{t-6}$	−0.348 (2.161)	−0.276 (1.549)	−0.175 (1.291)	−0.034 (0.200)	−0.085 (0.508)	−0.307 (2.695)	−0.324 (2.810)	−0.568 (4.337)

$\log y^P_{t-1}$	−1.261 (8.415)	−1.003 (8.699)	−1.272 (12.027)	−1.886 (16.978)	−1.203 (50.200)	−0.853 (9.396)	−0.369 (1.324)	−0.793 (9.690)
$\log R_L$	0.043 (1.023)	0.088 (1.524)	0.015 (0.490)	0.084 (2.173)	0.346 (3.591)	0.017 (0.487)	−0.097 (1.700)	−0.014 (0.695)
$\log y^t_{t-7}$	0.092 (0.646)	−0.091 (0.911)	0.219 (1.621)	0.425 (2.910)	0.159 (2.380)	0.172 (1.271)	0.001 (0.005)	0.130 (1.900)
$\log \text{OIL}_t$	0.034 (2.084)	0.011 (0.608)	−0.019 (1.299)	0.003 (0.211)	0.026 (2.261)	−0.002 (0.160)	−0.030 (1.485)	0.011 (1.715)
$\log \text{OIL}_{t-1}$	0.014 (0.909)	0.012 (0.724)	0.005 (0.354)	0.020 (1.310)	0.020 (2.294)	−0.026 (1.907)	−0.031 (1.663)	0.007 (1.290)
$\log \text{OIL}_{t-2}$	0.031 (2.068)	0.030 (1.809)	0.003 (0.193)	0.010 (0.646)	0.021 (2.369)	−0.016 (1.160)	0.051 (2.701)	0.009 (1.663)
$\log \text{OIL}_{t-3}$	−0.029 (1.818)	0.027 (1.502)	0.031 (2.129)	0.018 (1.184)	−0.006 (0.559)	−0.025 (1.611)	0.027 (1.194)	0.005 (0.853)
Rho1	0.9729	0.9357	0.9656	0.9788	0.9357	0.9326	0.9731	0.9747
$\bar{R}^2$	0.627	0.980	0.718	0.819	0.980	0.778	0.601	0.767
S.E.E.	0.0143	0.0087	0.0130	0.0138	0.0087	0.0135	0.0180	0.0056
D-W	1.81	1.35	0.72	1.40	1.35	1.68	1.26	0.88

Note. OIL is the relative price of oil index; the other variables are as defined in table 14.1.

Table 14.9B   Price Equation with Dependent Variable log PD − log(M2/N), 1957III to 1976IV (absolute value of t statistic in parentheses)

Coefficient	CA	FR	GE	IT	JA	NE	UK	US
Constant	3.287	0.987	4.309	11.624	3.840	−0.197	−0.089	−0.588
	(2.605)	(0.970)	(7.333)	(15.256)	(8.972)	(0.250)	(0.070)	(2.029)
ResM2$_t$	−0.583	−0.883	−0.967	−0.844	−0.931	−0.901	−1.026	−0.915
	(3.498)	(8.344)	(13.446)	(5.135)	(4.975)	(8.570)	(10.514)	(9.896)
ResM2$_{t-1}$	−1.195	−0.953	−0.726	−0.628	−0.925	−0.859	−0.820	−1.582
	(5.375)	(5.263)	(5.497)	(2.339)	(3.432)	(6.175)	(5.111)	(9.471)
ResM2$_{t-2}$	−0.976	−0.767	−0.598	−0.505	−0.899	−0.844	−0.777	−1.603
	(4.276)	(3.573)	(3.449)	(1.527)	(3.310)	(5.763)	(3.854)	(7.418)
ResM2$_{t-3}$	−1.004	−0.528	−0.643	−0.268	−0.913	−0.605	−0.929	−1.297
	(4.884)	(2.298)	(3.360)	(0.766)	(3.820)	(4.179)	(4.502)	(5.768)
ResM2$_{t-4}$	−0.792	−0.360	−0.394	−0.076	−0.859	−0.538	−0.744	−0.825
	(3.494)	(1.593)	(2.176)	(0.228)	(3.237)	(3.385)	(3.665)	(3.851)
ResM2$_{t-5}$	−1.022	−0.138	−0.233	−0.113	−0.157	−0.350	−0.530	−0.555
	(4.714)	(0.707)	(1.597)	(0.418)	(0.618)	(2.348)	(3.156)	(3.229)
ResM2$_{t-6}$	−0.344	−0.075	−0.156	0.071	0.044	−0.324	−0.213	−0.307
	(2.144)	(0.712)	(1.835)	(0.444)	(0.247)	(2.847)	(1.973)	(3.079)

$\log(y^P/N)_{t-1}$	-1.265 (8.465)	-0.978 (9.071)	-1.309 (20.510)	-1.807 (34.305)	-1.205 (53.507)	-0.839 (10.098)	-0.836 (4.642)	-0.829 (25.684)
$\log R_L$	0.042 (0.995)	0.068 (2.142)	0.002 (0.143)	0.072 (1.868)	0.311 (2.865)	0.021 (0.604)	0.036 (0.678)	-0.004 (0.289)
$\log y^f_{t-7}$	0.051 (0.373)	0.016 (0.400)	0.070 (1.085)	0.163 (1.301)	0.145 (2.086)	0.153 (1.143)	0.012 (0.095)	-0.055 (1.020)
$\log OIL_t$	0.035 (2.154)	0.008 (0.864)	-0.009 (1.027)	-0.010 (0.776)	0.023 (1.945)	0.004 (0.264)	0.010 (0.674)	0.0002 (0.071)
$\log OIL_{t-1}$	0.013 (0.815)	0.0002 (0.002)	0.003 (0.307)	0.001 (0.100)	0.027 (3.060)	-0.027 (2.064)	-0.027 (1.560)	-0.002 (0.461)
$\log OIL_{t-2}$	0.030 (2.037)	0.019 (1.508)	-0.001 (0.094)	-0.007 (0.512)	0.019 (2.139)	-0.018 (1.332)	0.046 (2.757)	0.002 (0.574)
$\log OIL_{t-3}$	-0.028 (1.748)	0.009 (0.069)	0.023 (2.718)	0.005 (0.362)	-0.003 (0.253)	-0.030 (1.980)	-0.021 (1.152)	0.005 (1.277)
Rho1 Rho2	-1.0846 -0.1170	1.8716 -0.9007	1.7546 -0.8320	1.4179 -0.5375	1.1518 -0.2386	1.1210 -0.2124	1.5894 -0.6864	1.6683 -0.7950
$\bar R^2$	0.628	0.800	0.914	0.956	0.982	0.806	0.789	0.948
S.E.E.	0.0143	0.0084	0.0082	0.0120	0.0090	0.0133	0.0153	0.0040
D-W	2.03	1.86	2.60	2.29	2.11	2.20	2.72	2.51

Note. OIL is the relative price of oil index; the other variables are as defined in table 14.1.

References

Al-Khuri, S., and S. M. Nsouli. 1978. The Speed of Adjustment of the actual to the desired money stock: A comparative study. *European Economic Review* 11: 181–206.

Barro, H. J. 1978. Unanticipated money, output, and the price level in the United States. *Journal of Political Economy* 86: 549–80.

Blinder, A. S., and S. Fischer. 1978. Inventories, rational expectations, and the business cycle. MIT working paper, June.

Bordo, M. D., and L. Jonung. 1981. The long run behavior of the income velocity of money in five advanced countries, 1870–1975: An institutional approach. *Economic Inquiry* 19 (January): 96–116.

Boughton, J. M. 1979. Demand for money in major OECD countries. *OECD Economic Outlook Occasional Studies*, January, pp. 35–57.

Brunner, K., and A. H. Meltzer, eds. 1978. *Carnegie-Rochester conference Series on public policy: A supplement to the Journal of Monetary Economics*, vol. 8. Amsterdam: North-Holland.

Cagan, P. 1980. Imported inflation, 1973–74, and the accommodation issue. *Journal of Money, Credit and Banking* 12, no. 1 (February): 1–16.

Carr, J., and M. Darby. 1981. The role of money supply shocks in the short-run demand for money. *Journal of Monetary Economics* 8 (September): 183–99.

Coats, W. L., Jr. 1979. Modeling the short-run demand for money with exogenous supply. Board of Governors of the Federal Reserve System, unpublished, June.

Darby, M. R. 1972. The allocation of transitory income among consumers' assets. *American Economic Review* 62 (December): 928–41.

Dewald, W., and M. Marchon. 1978. A modified Federal Reserve of St. Louis spending equation for Canada, France, Germany, Italy, the United Kingdom, and the United States. *Kredit und Kapital*, vol. 11, no. 2.

Frenkel, J. A., and C. A. Rodriguez. 1975. Portfolio equilibrium and the balance of payments: A monetary approach. *American Economic Review* 64, no. 4: 674–88.

Friedman, M., and A. J. Schwartz. 1963. *A monetary history of the United States, 1867–1960*. Princeton: Princeton University Press.

———. 1982. *Monetary trends in the United States and the United Kingdom: Their relation to income, prices, and interest rates, 1867–1975*. Chicago: University of Chicago Press.

Gandolfi, A. E., and J. R. Lothian. 1976. The demand for money from the great depression to the present. *American Economic Review* 66: 46–51.

Gordon, R. J. 1980. A consistent characterization of a near-century of price behavior. *American Economic Review* 70, no. 2: 243–49.

Griliches, Z. 1961. A note on serial correlation bias in estimates of distributed lags. *Econometrica* 29 (January): 65–73.

Hafer, R. W., and S. E. Hein. 1980. The dynamics and estimation of short-run money. *Federal Reserve Bank of St. Louis Review*, March, pp. 26–35.

Huffman, W. E., and J. R. Lothian. 1980. Money in the U.K., 1833–1880. *Journal of Money, Credit and Banking* 12, no. 2: 155–74.

Laidler, D. 1977. The demand for money: Theories and evidence. 2d ed. New York: Dun-Donnelly.

———. 1980. The demand for money in the United States—yet again. In K. Brunner and A. H. Meltzer, eds., *Carnegie-Rochester conference series on public policy on the state of macro-economics*, vol. 12. Amsterdam: North-Holland, pp. 219–72.

Lothian, J. R. 1976. The demand for high-powered money. *American Economic Review*, 66 (March): 56–68.

Lucas, R. E., Jr. 1973. Some international evidence on output-inflation tradeoffs. *American Economic Review* 63 (June): 326–34.

Martino, A. 1980. Another Italian economic miracle? Unpublished, Mont Pelerin Society meeting, Stanford.

15   Movements in Purchasing Power Parity: The Short and Long Runs

Michael R. Darby

Purchasing power parity is a customary starting point for explanations of price changes in a country maintaining a pegged exchange rate with a reserve country whose price changes are taken as given. Alternatively, movements in the exchange rate may be explained by relative changes in the price levels of two floating countries. One might argue that much of the difference between the monetary approach to the balance of payments and exchange rates and other approaches is to be found in the empirical question of whether purchasing power parity holds well enough for the problem being analyzed.

"Does purchasing power parity work?" has been a controversial empirical issue for decades, suggestive of a root conceptual problem. This chapter argues that the controversy over purchasing power parity (PPP) indeed arises from murky concepts rather than differences in data. A framework is proposed to identify those problems for which PPP "works" and those for which it does not. It is shown that in a stochastic framework, growth rates may coverge to the PPP relations even though the levels of the variables become unpredictable. This occurs because uncorrelated "permanent" shifts in PPP cumulate for the levels but average out for growth rates.

The empirical results do not really speak to the issue—so prominent in part III above—of whether a nonreserve country can exercise short-run monetary control under pegged exchange rates. The results do show, however, that even if short-run monetary control is possible, harmonization of money growth rates is not sufficient to maintain a pegged exchange rate and a balance-of-payments feedback rule is required.

An earlier version of this chapter appeared as "Does Purchasing Power Parity Work?" in the *Proceedings of Fifth West Coast Academic/Federal Reserve Economic Research Seminar* (San Francicso: Federal Reserve Bank of San Francicso, 1982).

The argument is presented in four sections: Section 15.1 analyzes the implications of alternative concepts of PPP. Section 15.2 examines the theoretical basis for supposing that the parity value takes a random walk. Section 15.3 reports estimated stochastic processes for the observed purchasing power ratio and discusses the implications of these estimates for alternative concepts of PPP. The chapter is concluded by a discussion of the implications of the results for monetary policies consistent with maintenance of a pegged exchange rate.

15.1 Concepts of Purchasing Power Parity

People who ask whether purchasing power parity works normally examine either of two distinct concepts:[1] the level concept and the growth concept. The level concept refers to the ability to predict the price level conditional upon the exchange rate and foreign price level or else the exchange rate conditional upon the two price levels. The growth concept refers to predictions of the inflation rate given the growth rates of the exchange rate and the foreign price level or to predictions of the growth rate of the exchange rate given the two inflation rates. It is generally unappreciated that the properties of the prediction errors of these two concepts may differ sharply.

The difference between the two concepts may be seen by reference to a simple discrete stochastic model. Define the purchasing power ratio (PPR) as the ratio of the domestic price level to the product of the exchange rate and the foreign price level, or, measuring the variables in logarithms,

(15.1) $\psi_t \equiv P_t - E_t - P_t^*$.

Suppose further that the stochastic process governing the log PPR is a martingale so that

(15.2) $\psi_t = \psi_{t-1} + \epsilon_t$,

---

1. I treat the level—as well as growth rate—concept in relative purchasing power rather than absolute terms. Some writers require that all prices be the same across countries, but this absolute purchasing power parity is generally conceded to fail without necessarily reducing the usefulness of the parity idea. A third concept of purchasing power parity is sometimes assumed in theoretical modeling—that a parity value exists for any moment (although it might change unpredictably in the next period) so that $dP/dX = dE/dX + dP^*/dX$ holds. If this third concept holds as in Stockman (1980), nonreserve central banks have no monetary control under pegged exchange rates. That issue is examined in part III of this volume. Most of the literature (and this paper) is concerned with the unconditional *predictive* power of PPP, but, despite popular opinion to the contrary, this can tell us little about the theoretical implications of the monetary approach, only about its predictive power. No attempt is made here to review the huge literature on purchasing power parity, but see the May 1978 issue of the *Journal of International Economics* for a number of recent perspectives.

where ϵ_t is white noise with mean zero and variance σ^2. For the moment the random walk process (15.2) is only for illustrative purposes although previous estimates by Frenkel (1980a, b), Roll (1979), and Stockman (1978b) suggest it is not too far from the truth.

In this case the best prediction of ψ_{t+n} given the information available at time t is simply ψ_t. The prediction error is

$$(15.3) \qquad \psi_{t+n} - \psi_t = \sum_{i=1}^{n} \epsilon_{t+i}.$$

This has mean zero and variance $n\sigma^2$. Thus the variance of the prediction error increases with the forecast period and goes to infinity for long-run predictions $(n \to \infty)$.

But suppose we were interested in the growth concept of PPP. The relevant identity is now

$$(15.4) \qquad \Gamma_n \psi_t \equiv \Gamma_n P_t - \Gamma_n E_t - \Gamma_n P_t,$$

where the growth-rate operator Γ_n computes the average growth rate over n periods $(\Gamma_n X_t \equiv (X_t - X_{t-n})/n)$. The average growth rate of ψ_t from t to $t+n$ is

$$(15.5) \qquad \Gamma_n \psi_{t+n} = \frac{1}{n} \sum_{i=1}^{n} \epsilon_{t+i}.$$

By inspection, the optimal prediction and the mean of the prediction error (15.5) are zero. The variance of the prediction error is σ^2/n, which decreases with the forecast period and goes to zero for long-run predictions $(n \to \infty)$. Note that only for one-period predictions are the error variances the same for the level and growth concepts of PPP.

It seems paradoxical that the longer the period over which we are predicting, the less accurate are our predictions of the price level and the more accurate are our predictions of the average inflation rate, both conditional upon the behavior of the exchange-rate converted foreign price level. This occurs because errors shift the price level in a permanent and cumulative fashion in the level case, but these uncorrelated shifts average out in the growth case.

15.2   Need the Purchasing Power Parity Ratio Take a Random Walk?

Some authors—most notably Roll (1979)—have asserted that under conditions such that the interest arbitrage relations holds, the logarithm of the PPR, ψ_t, must follow a random walk. There is some evidence that those conditions do not obtain for national interest rates, where risks of currency controls and default in the forward contract arise.[2] Nonetheless let us suppose a strong form of the efficient-market-interest-arbitrage approach holds and show that it is not strictly necessary for ψ_t to take a random walk.

The interest relation for continuously compounded nominal interest rates i_t and i_t^* is

(15.6) $i_t = \xi_t(\Delta E_{t+1}) + i_t^*$,

where ξ_t denotes expected values conditional upon information at time t. Also, assume a simple Fischer relation holds:

(15.7) $i_t = r_t + \xi_t(\Delta P_{t+1})$,

(15.8) $i_t^* = r_t^* + \xi_t(\Delta P_{t+1}^*)$,

where r_t and r^* are the respective real interest rates.[3] Substituting equations (15.7) and (15.8) in (15.6) and rearranging terms yields

(15.9) $\xi_t(\Delta P_{t+1}) - \xi_t(\Delta E_{t+1}) - \xi_t(\Delta P_{t+1}^*)$
$$= r_t^* - r_t.$$

Note that the left-hand side is simply $\xi_t(\Delta\psi_{t+1})$, the expected change in the log PPR. This can differ from zero if the real interest rates differ. If shocks do occur which affect investment or saving in the countries and if it is costly to adjust the international allocation of capital instantaneously, then such shocks can cause temporary self-reversing movements in the log PPR which do not present any profit opportunities on either the financial or real side. That is, even if assets were perfect substitutes, nontrivial investment functions would permit movements in relative real interest rates.

Thus the form of the stochastic process governing the evolution of the PPR is an empirical question. This process may be a random walk, but there are good theoretical reasons to expect a more complicated process. In particular a random walk with an overlaid self-reversing moving average process is suggested by the above analysis. Doubtless other, possibly stationary processes could be justified by relaxation of some of

2. Interest arbitrage clearly does apply in the Eurocurrency markets where there is no differential control and default risk, but Eurocurrency rates do vary relative to the respective domestic interest rates. As discussed in chapter 10 above, since central banks seem to exercise monetary control under pegged exchange rates, we may infer that different national assets are not perfect substitutes. This latter finding implies, of course, that interest arbitrage won't hold with respect to the various national interest rates. See Dooley and Isard (1980) for an excellent treatment of these issues.

3. This abstracts from the effects of income taxes on nominal interest rates discussed in Darby (1975). To consider taxes, we would also have to consider differential taxation of interest and exchange gains, which would greatly complicate the analysis.

the assumptions. Let us turn to some estimated processes and see in what, if any, senses PPP works.

15.3   Estimated Stochastic Processes for the Purchasing Power Ratio

This section reports estimates of the stochastic process governing the log PPR for our standard seven countries: the United Kingdom, Canada, France, Germany, Italy, Japan, and the Netherlands. They will adequately serve to illustrate the senses in which PPP does and does not work. We define ψ_t, the logarithm of the ratio of the domestic price level to the exchange-rate converted U.S. price level, in three alternative ways according to whether wholesale price indices, consumer price indices, or implicit price deflators for GNP (sometimes GDP) are used. Since parts II and III of this volume imply that central bank intervention to maintain pegged rates can move the log PPR independently of fundamental forces, it is desirable to confine the analysis to the period after the breakdown of the Bretton Woods system. To obtain a sufficiently long post–Bretton Woods sample for estimating ARIMA processes, data for July 1971 through December 1978 were taken from the International Monetary Fund as detailed in the appendix to this chapter.

In every case ψ_t appeared to be nonstationary so that there is no *fixed*, long-run parity level of the PPR. A similar finding was made by Stockman (1978*b*) and is implicit in Frenkel's (1980*a*) inability to reject the hypothesis that the PPR follows a random walk.[4] The estimated ARIMA processes are reported in table 15.1. All are of the form ARIMA(0,1,q)— that is, moving average processes MA(q) applied to $\Delta\psi_t$, the first difference in the log PPR:[5]

$$(15.10) \qquad \Delta\psi_t = \mu + \epsilon_t - \sum_{i=1}^{q} \theta_i \epsilon_{t-i}.$$

The drift term μ is admitted to allow for the possibility of trend movements in relative price levels. These may occur because of trends in movements of the relative prices of individual commodities weighted differently in the two national price levels.[6] Random shifts in relative prices are the most obvious explanation for permanent shifts in the log

---

4. Frenkel preferred the model AR(1) with an autoregressive parameter in the neighborhood of 0.9, in which case ψ_t is (barely) stationary and slowly tends toward a long-run value. If this is so, ARIMA(p,1,q) models will be overdifferenced; tests for this are reported below, but it is very difficult to distinguish a very slow autoregressive adjustment to a long-run parity value from a random walk for ψ_t.

5. At most q moving average parameters were fitted, since some series appeared to be MA(0) or MA(1) plus a seasonal component (usually quarterly or semiannual) which was also fitted.

6. See Stockman (1978*a*, 1980). Balassa (1964), and Samuelson (1964) provide different explanations for a trend.

Table 15.1   **Estimated ARIMA Processes for ψ_t, the Logarithm of the Purchasing Power Ratio [All Fitted Processes Are ARIMA $(0,1,q)$]**

Statistics	Price Index Definition		
	WPI	CPI	Deflator
	United Kingdom		
q	1	1	0
μ	0.0020(0.0033)	0.0026(0.0977)	0.0067(0.0087)
MA parameters	$\theta_1 = -0.4009(0.0997)$	$\theta_1 = -0.4689(0.0977)$	...
$\hat{\sigma}$	0.0223	0.0192	0.0459
$Q(12)$ [d.f.]	8.80 [11]	6.50 [11]	11.00 [12]
	Canada		
q	1	9	1
μ	0.0001(0.0014)	$-0.0006(0.0008)$	0.0002(0.0051)
MA parameters	$\theta_1 = -0.2075(0.1059)$	$\theta_1 = -0.1784(0.1001)$	$\theta_1 = -0.5187(0.1791)$
	...	$\theta_9 = 0.4086(0.1150)$	...
$\hat{\sigma}$	0.0107	0.0095	0.0186
$Q(12)$ [d.f.]	7.90 [11]	11.70 [10]	13.0 [11]
	France		
q	6	6	
μ	0.0019(0.0019)	0.0043(0.0027)	NA
MA parameters	$\theta_2 = 0.1150(0.1071)$	$\theta_1 = -0.2820(0.0894)$	
	$\theta_6 = 0.1694(0.1100)$	$\theta_3 = -0.2249(0.1012)$	
	...	$\theta_6 = 0.3389(0.1074)$	
$\hat{\sigma}$	0.0246	0.0221	
$Q(12)$ [d.f.]	13.90 [10]	7.30 [9]	
	Germany		
q	6	6	0
μ	0.0032(0.0019)	0.0050(0.0025)	0.0163(0.0092)
MA parameters	$\theta_6 = 0.3757(0.1046)$	$\theta_1 = -0.2706(0.1022)$	...
	...	$\theta_6 = 0.3550(0.1132)$	...
$\hat{\sigma}$	0.0275	0.0252	0.0495
$Q12)$ [d.f.]	9.40 [11]	2.90 [10]	14.9 [12]
	Italy		
q	4	7	4
μ	0.0018(0.0015)	0.0020(0.0027)	0.0040(0.0035)
MA parameters	$\theta_4 = 0.2718(0.1055)$	$\theta_1 = -0.2725(0.1049)$	$\theta_4 = 0.6427(0.2336)$
		$\theta_7 = -0.2359(0.1093)$	...
$\hat{\sigma}$	0.0190	0.0177	0.0349
$Q(12)$ [d.f.]	6.40 [11]	10.70 [10]	11.6 [11]

Table 15.1 (continued)

Statistics	Price Index Definition		
	WPI	CPI	Deflator
		Japan	
q	0	0	0
μ	0.0050(0.0025)	0.0088(0.0026)	0.0253(0.0076)
MA parameters	...	...	...
$\hat{\sigma}$	0.0235	0.0248	0.0403
$Q(12)$ [d.f.]	9.00 [12]	11.40 [12]	18.7 [12]
		Netherlands	
q	6	6	NA
μ	0.0033(0.0017)	0.0065(0.0025)	
MA parameters	$\theta_6 =$ 0.3770(0.1055)	$\theta_1 = -0.2880(0.1028)$	
	...	$\theta_6 =$ 0.2834(0.1153)	
$\hat{\sigma}$	0.0254	0.0233	
$Q(12)$ [d.f.]	9.40 [11]	6.00 [10]	

Notes. Standard errors appear in parentheses.

WPI and CPI data are monthly. Deflator data are quarterly. All estimations are for the period July 1971–December 1978, except some of the deflators were not yet available for the whole period; for these cases (*deflator only*) the estimation ends as follows: United Kingdom and Japan in September 1978, Italy in December 1977. The estimated standard error $\hat{\sigma}$ of the white noise process is the single-period standard error of forecast computed by the conditional method.

$Q(12)$ is the Box-Ljung variant of the Box-Pierce statistic for the "portmanteau lack of fit test." It is approximately distributed as χ^2(d.f.), where the degrees of freedom are indicated in square brackets following the value of Q. To reject the model at the 5% significance level, Q must exceed 21.0 for 12 d.f., 19.7 for 11 d.f., 18.3 for 10 d.f., and 16.9 for 9 d.f.; thus all the models pass this overall lack of fit test.

Estimation (backcasting method) was performed using BMDQ2T (a preliminary version of BMDP2T) on the UCLA computer.

PPR, so trends should be allowed also. If only trends were at work, then ψ_t would be nonstationary but the ARIMA(0,1,q) process would be noninvertible due to overdifferencing as discussed further below. The correct model to estimate would have the form

$$(15.11) \qquad \psi_t = \alpha + \mu t + u_t.$$

We shall see that this deterministic but trended parity ($\alpha + \mu t$) does not appear to hold. Besides, with the exceptions of Japan, Netherlands, and perhaps Germany, the estimated values of μ in table 15.1 are all insignificant.

Of the forty processes estimated and reported in table 15.1, only five are strict random walks ($q = 0$). The rest of the cases may be viewed as a random walk to which one or more moving-average terms have been added. As suggested by Muth (1960), for the $q = 1$ cases we can view

$(1 - \theta_1)\epsilon_t$ as the permanent shift in the parity value of the log PPR and $\theta_1 \epsilon_t$ as the transitory change in log PR during the (one-period) adjustment process. If $0 < \theta_1 < 1$, then the initial change in ψ_t is greater than the change in the parity value so that a partially self-reversing correction occurs the following period. If, however, $-1 < \theta_1 < 0$, then the initial change in the log PPR is less than the change in the parity value and two periods are taken for full adjustment. For $q > 1$, similar albeit more complicated adjustment patterns are indicated for the first $q + 1$ quarters until the permanent shift

$$\left(1 - \sum_{i=1}^{q} \theta_i\right)\epsilon_t$$

in the parity value is reflected in the log PPR.

If there were no permanent shifts in the parity value of ψ_t, then

$$\sum_{i=1}^{q} \theta_i$$

would be 1. Table 15.2 reports t statistics of the form

(15.12)
$$t = \frac{\sum_{i=1}^{q} \theta_i - 1}{\text{s.e. of } \sum_{i=1}^{q} \theta_i}.$$

Plosser and Schwert (1977) have pointed out that under the null hypothesis ($\Sigma \theta_i = 1$), the moving-average process is strictly noninvertible. In their examination of the case $q = 1$ and $\theta_1 = 1$, they showed that $\hat{\theta}_1$ was biased downward and their Monte Carlo experiments suggested that for sample sizes such as these a t greater than 3 or even 4 would be required to safely reject the null hypothesis at the 5% level of significance. Since this criterion is met in every case except for the Italian deflator definition, the hypothesis that there is a constant or deterministically trended parity value for the log PPR appears to be generally rejected. Note, however, that time-series tests for weak but persistent adjustment processes are prone to reject them; so it is perhaps appropriate to view the estimated processes as casting PPP in the worst light consistent with the data. It would be possible to impose a deterministically trended parity or force in more positive moving-average terms, either of which would reduce estimated prediction errors over substantial lengths of time.

The basic hypothesis of sections 15.1 and 15.2—that the log PPR takes a random walk with perhaps a moving-average adjustment process added—appears to be consistent with the data. On this hypothesis there is no parity value[7] toward which the log PPR tends in the long run. The

---

7. This applies to either a constant or a deterministic time trend which could be used for making predictions.

Table 15.2   Test t Statistics for Stationarity of $\psi_t - \mu t$

Country	t Statistics[†]		
	WPI	CPI	Deflator
United Kingdom	−14.05	−15.03	−4.77[§]
Canada	−11.40	−5.03	−8.48
France	−5.02	−5.74	NA
Germany	−5.97	−5.53	−6.19[§]
Italy	−6.90	−4.43	−1.53
Japan	−10.60[§]	−11.18[§]	−6.47[§]
Netherlands	−5.91	−5.95	NA

[†]The t statistics (15.12) are for the null hypothesis $\Sigma_i \theta_i = 1$, which would imply that $\psi_t - \mu t$ is stationary (there is a deterministic parity value of log PPR) and that the moving-average process is noninvertible. These t ratios are biased downward under the null hypothesis, but judging from Monte Carlo experiments reported in Plosser and Schwert (1977), $t < -4$ should be sufficient to reject the null hypothesis at the 5% significance level or better.

[§]In those cases in which an ARIMA(0,1,0) process (random walk) was reported as the optimal process in table 15.1, an alternative model ARIMA(0,1,1) was fitted and the t statistic for $\theta_1 = 1$ is reported with a §.

further ahead we make predictions of ψ_t, the greater is the variance. On the other hand, the longer the period over which we predict the average growth rate of ψ_t, the smaller is the variance. This paradoxical result is illustrated in table 15.3, which reports the standard errors of prediction implied for the models of table 15.1 for periods ranging from one observation to six years in the future. For ease in interpretation and comparison, the average growth rates per period $\Gamma_n \psi_t$ have all been converted to annual rates. Thus the prediction error for the one-year-ahead level and the corresponding annualized growth rate are the same. Over shorter periods, the prediction error of the annualized growth rates is greater than that of the corresponding level. Over longer periods the standard errors of the growth rates fall toward zero while those of the levels rise toward infinity. As was illustrated for the random walk case in section 15.1, these progressions toward zero and ∞, respectively, progress roughly with $1/\sqrt{n}$ and $\sqrt{n}$, respectively.[8] Thus at twenty-four years the level standard errors will be about double and the growth standard errors about half of those indicated for six years.

To interpret table 15.3, note that the growth rates are in decimal form so that the Canadian CPI-PPR six-year average growth rate has a standard error of 1.06% per annum. On the other hand, the corresponding British standard error is 3.98% per annum, nearly four times greater. These standard errors pretty well bracket the range for growth rates, with

8. For non–random walk cases, the early prediction errors are reduced by knowledge of past shocks, but this knowledge soon becomes unimportant. Nonetheless, the square-root rule is only approximate for these cases.

Table 15.3   **Standard Errors of Prediction for ψ_t and Annualized $\Gamma_n \psi_t$**

Periods†		WPI		CPI		Deflator	
n		Level ψ_t	Growth $12\Gamma_n\psi_t$	Level ψ_t	Growth $12\Gamma_n\psi_t$	Level ψ_t	Growth $4\Gamma_n\psi_t$
				United Kingdom			
1	[−]	0.0223	0.2676	0.0192	0.2304	. . .	. . .
3	[1]	0.0494	0.1976	0.0443	0.1772	0.0459	0.1836
12	[4]	0.1058	0.1058	0.0957	0.0957	0.0917	0.0917
24	[8]	0.1512	0.0756	0.1369	0.0685	0.1297	0.0649
48	[16]	0.2149	0.0537	0.1947	0.0487	0.1834	0.0459
72	[24]	0.2636	0.0439	0.2389	0.0398	0.2247	0.0375
				Canada			
1	[−]	0.0107	0.1284	0.0095	0.1140	. . .	. . .
3	[1]	0.0212	0.0848	0.0185	0.0740	0.0186	0.0744
12	[4]	0.0443	0.0443	0.0352	0.0352	0.0547	0.0547
24	[8]	0.0630	0.0315	0.0424	0.0212	0.0808	0.0404
48	[16]	0.0894	0.0224	0.0540	0.0135	0.1166	0.0292
72	[24]	0.1096	0.0183	0.0635	0.0106	0.1437	0.0240
				France			
1	[−]	0.0246	0.2952	0.0221	0.2652	NA	NA
3	[1]	0.0411	0.1644	0.0464	0.1856		
12	[4]	0.0701	0.0701	0.0989	0.0989		
24	[8]	0.0923	0.0462	0.1339	0.0670		
48	[16]	0.1254	0.0314	0.1851	0.0463		
72	[24]	0.1515	0.0253	0.2249	0.0375		
				Germany			
1	[−]	0.0275	0.3300	0.0252	0.3024	. . .	. . .
3	[1]	0.0477	0.1908	0.0518	0.2072	0.0495	0.1980
12	[4]	0.0792	0.0792	0.0942	0.0942	0.0991	0.0991
24	[8]	0.0985	0.0493	0.1230	0.0615	0.1401	0.0701
48	[16]	0.1287	0.0322	0.1662	0.0416	0.1982	0.0486
72	[24]	0.1531	0.0255	0.2003	0.0334	0.2427	0.0405
				Italy			
1	[−]	0.0190	0.2280	0.0177	0.2124	. . .	. . .
3	[1]	0.0329	0.1316	0.0360	0.1440	0.0349	0.1396
12	[4]	0.0543	0.0543	0.0820	0.0820	0.0698	0.0698
24	[8]	0.0722	0.0361	0.1225	0.0613	0.0711	0.0356
48	[16]	0.0987	0.0247	0.1778	0.0445	0.0735	0.0184
72	[24]	0.1195	0.0199	0.2195	0.0366	0.0758	0.0126

Table 15.3 (continued)

Periods†	WPI		CPI		Deflator	
n	Level ψ_t	Growth $12\Gamma_n\psi_t$	Level ψ_t	Growth $12\Gamma_n\psi_t$	Level ψ_t	Growth $4\Gamma_n\psi_t$
			Japan			
1 [−]	0.0235	0.2820	0.0248	0.2976	. . .	. . .
3 [1]	0.0408	0.1632	0.0430	0.1720	0.0403	0.1612
12 [4]	0.0816	0.0816	0.0860	0.0860	0.0806	0.0806
24 [8]	0.1154	0.0577	0.1216	0.0608	0.1140	0.0570
48 [16]	0.1632	0.0408	0.1719	0.0430	0.1613	0.0403
72 [24]	0.1998	0.0333	0.2105	0.0351	0.1975	0.0329
			Netherlands			
1 [−]	0.0254	0.3048	0.0233	0.2796	NA	NA
3 [1]	0.0439	0.1756	0.0484	0.1936		
12 [4]	0.0726	0.0726	0.0912	0.0912		
24 [8]	0.0900	0.0450	0.1219	0.0610		
48 [16]	0.1172	0.0293	0.1672	0.0418		
72 [24]	0.1392	0.0232	0.2026	0.0338		

Note. Growth rates are reported on an annualized basis.
†The number of periods for the deflator is in square brackets.

the WPI definitions (with the exception of Britain and Canada) having smaller standard errors than the CPI definitions and the ranking of the deflator definitions mixed. The standard errors on the levels refer to the log PPR, so they indicate approximate proportionate errors. That is, two-thirds of the time after six years, the actual level of the CPI-definition Canadian PPR will be within 6.6% ($e^{0.0635} − 1 = 0.0656$) of the predicted level.

In view of table 15.3, can we say that PPP works? In an absolute sense, most of the average growth rate standard errors seem large even at six years, and it would take generation-long averages to halve these. The level standard errors are similarly large and growing. This would seem to suggest that PPP does not work. This answer appears too easy for a number of reasons: (1) Statistically, the standard errors in table 15.3 may be biased upward by omission of statistically insignificant but cumulatively important weak adjustment factors. Further, some observers would argue that the standard errors may be inflated by greater instability in ψ_t in the early post–Bretton Woods years than in recent years. (2) If one country is inflating much more rapidly than the other, the standard error will be a small fraction of the predicted change or average growth rate of the exchange rate. Only when relative price levels are fairly similar are the other factors important by comparison. (3) Finally, the other factors causing permanent movements in the log PPR are unpredictable (see Roll 1979); so PPP provides the best—although perhaps a poor—*predictor* of differences in real interest rates.[9]

The large standard errors of table 15.3 certainly do indicate the importance of efforts aimed at explaining movements in the value of the PPR relative to a deterministic PPP. It is not possible from these results, however, to infer whether these movements imply the absence of effective price arbitrage or merely period-to-period movements in the arbitrage parity values.

15.4 Conclusions and Implications for Monetary Policy

The key implication of these results for monetary policy is that it is not possible to maintain a pegged exchange rate or achieve an exchange-rate growth goal by manipulating monetary growth according to relative price levels. The fact that there are permanent shifts in the parity value of the purchasing power ratio implies that a policy targeted on a deterministic parity will result in deviations from the actual parity which become arbitrarily large as time progresses. Therefore, to maintain a pegged rate system, even if short-run sterilization policies are effective, a current and/or lagged balance-of-payments feedback rule must be used so that the domestic price level will fluctuate relative to the foreign price level according to the movements in the parity value. Similarly an exchange-rate growth goal can be achieved only if a feedback rule based on either actual exchange-rate growth or exchange intervention is followed. If two countries both follow either constant inflation-rate or money-growth rules, the level of their exchange rate (although not its growth rate) becomes increasingly unpredictable the further into the future one considers.

Nelson and Plosser (1980) have recently presented evidence that a large number of macroeconomic series are stationary and invertible in the first differences and therefore do not follow deterministic models such as equation (11). For all of those series, we have a result analogous to that in this paper: The variance of the levels increases without limit and the variance of the average growth rate goes to zero as the prediction interval goes to infinity. Consider, for example, the implications of random permanent shifts in the trend growth path of the money demand function, as well as transitory shifts.[10] Then even given the growth path of nominal

---

9. See section 15.2 above.

10. Lothian and Gandolfi in chapter 14 above fitted a second-order autoregressive process on the levels rather than fitting a process to the first differences as suggested by Nelson and Plosser and done for the log PPR in this chapter. As noted in chapter 14, given the estimated parameters, the fitted processes are de facto first-order autoregressive processes on the first differences.

money over a long period, we can only predict the future price level with great undertainty although the average inflation rate is almost perfectly predictable.

Permanent shifts—whether in the real demand for money or the purchasing power ratio—imply an opportunity for economists to explain the shifts by underlying real factors.[11] But they do place important restrictions on the evolution of the factors causing the permanent changes. As to purchasing power parity, while it may be the best predictor, it is not a very good one. There is much room for economic explanations of the permanent shifts in the purchasing power ratio. Does purchasing power parity work? For what?

Acknowledgments

The author acknowledges comments from Deborah Allen, Dan Friedman, Michael Melvin, and Charles Plosser. Michael T. Melvin and Andrew A. Vogel provided able research assistance. Pigott and Sweeney (1980) in an unpublished paper have independently arrived at similar conclusions by a rather more complicated and (I believe) problematic route.

Appendix

All data series were taken from the International Financial Statistics tape of the International Monetary Fund, dated April 1979. The actual series used are listed.

EXCHANGE RATES

Country	IMF Code	Description
United Kingdom	112_AF	market rate/par or central rate (£/$US)
Canada	156_AF	market rate/par or central rate ($Can/$US)
France	132_AF	market rate/par or central rate (FF/$US)
Germany	134_AF	market rate/par or central rate (DM/$US)
Italy	136_AF	market rate/par or central rate (L/$US)
Japan	158_AF	market rate/par or central rate (¥/$US)
Netherlands	138_AF	market rate/par or central rate (Dfl/$US)

11. For example, shifts in the real demand for money may be explained by real income taking a random walk and by random occurrence of institutional innovations. Or permanent changes in purchasing power parity may reflect changes in commercial policy and changes in the relative prices of goods with differing weights in the price indices.

WHOLESALE PRICE INDICES

Country	IMF Code	Description
United States	111_63	wholesale prices, 1975 = 100
United Kingdom	112_63	wholesale prices, 1975 = 100
Canada	156_63	wholesale prices, 1975 = 100
France	132_63	wholesale prices, 1975 = 100
Germany	134_63	wholesale prices, 1975 = 100
Italy	136_63	wholesale prices, 1975 = 100
Japan	158_63	wholesale prices, 1975 = 100
Netherlands	138_63	wholesale prices, 1975 = 100

CONSUMER PRICE INDICES

Country	IMF Code	Description
United States	111_64	consumer prices, 1975 = 100
United Kingdom	112_64	consumer prices, 1975 = 100
Canada	156_64	consumer prices, 1975 = 100
France	132_64	consumer prices, 1975 = 100
Germany	134_64	consumer prices, 1975 = 100
Italy	136_64	consumer prices, 1975 = 100
Japan	158_64	consumer prices, 1975 = 100
Netherlands	138_64	consumer prices, 1975 = 100

IMPLICIT PRICE DEFLATORS

These series are the ratio of the nominal to real product series for each country as follows:

Country	IMF Code	Description
United States	111_99A	GNP (billions of $US)
	111_99A.R	GNP, 1975 prices (billions of $US), seasonally adjusted
United Kingdom[12]	112_99A	GNP (£)
	112_99B	GDP: 1975 prices (£)

12. For the United Kingdom, the IMF tape contains no nominal GDP or real GNP data. Judging from the ARIMA process reported in table 15.1, the difference is close enough to proportionate to present no problem in this case.

Canada	156_99A	GNP ($Can)
	156_99A.R	GNP: 1975 prices ($Can), SA
Germany	134_99A	GNP (DM)
	134_99A.R	GNP: 1975 prices (DM), SA
Italy	136_99B	GDP (L)
	136_99B.R	GDP: 1975 prices (L), SA
Japan	158_99A	GNP (¥)
	158_99A.R	GNP: 1975 prices (¥), SA

References

Balassa, B. 1964. The purchasing power parity doctrine: A reappraisal. *Journal of Political Economy* 72 (December): 584–96.

Darby, M. R. 1975. The financial and tax effects of monetary policy on interest rates. *Economic Inquiry* 13 (June): 266–76.

Dooley, M. P., and P. Isard. 1980. Capital controls, political risk, and deviations from interest-rate parity. *Journal of Political Economy* 88 (April): 370–84.

Frenkel, J. A. 1980a. Flexible exchange rates in the 1970's. NBER Working Paper, no. 450, February.

———. 1980b. Exchange rates, prices, and money: Lessons from the 1920's. *American Economic Review* 70 (May): 235–42.

Muth, J. F. 1960. Optimal properties of exponentially weighted forecasts. *Journal of the American Statistical Association* 55 (June): 299–306.

Nelson, C. R., and C. I. Plosser. 1980. Trends and random walks in macroeconomic time series. University of Rochester Center for Research in Government Policy and Business Working Paper no. GPB80-11, August.

Pigott, C., and R. J. Sweeney. 1980. Purchasing power parity and exchange rate dynamics: Some empirical results. Unpublished paper, circa April.

Plosser, C. I., and G. W. Schwert. 1977. Estimation of a non-invertible moving average process: The case of overdifferencing. *Journal of Econometrics* 6 (September): 199–224.

Roll, R. 1979. Violations of purchasing power parity and their implications for efficient international commodity markets. In M. Sarnat and G. Szego, eds., *International finance and trade*, vol. 1. Cambridge, Mass.: Ballinger.

Samuelson, P. A. 1964. Theoretical notes on trade problems. *Review of Economics and Statistics* 46 (May): 145–54.

Stockman, A. C. 1978*a*. International relative prices under fixed and flexible exchange rate systems. UCLA Department of Economics Discussion Paper no. 130, September.

————. 1978*b*. Evidence on the time-series behavior of deviations from purchasing power parity and implications for exchange-rate theories. UCLA Department of Economics, unpublished paper, November.

————. 1980. A theory of exchange rate determination. *Journal of Political Economy* 88 (August): 673–98.

16   The United States as an Exogenous Source of World Inflation under the Bretton Woods System

Michael R. Darby

The evolution of the American price level under the Bretton Woods system was essentially independent of international influences. America was a source but scarcely a victim of inflationary trends in the rest of the world. This indictment follows from the special role of the United States as provider of a fiat reserve currency. This is not the role suggested by the "gold-exchange standard," but it is the role the United States in fact appears to have pursued.

The essential independence from foreign influences of a fiat reserve country is demonstrated in section 16.1. In particular, it is shown that the world inflation trends are determined by the reserve country alone and that world money and world reserves adjust passively without causal significance. Section 16.2 examines the evidence on the empirical question as to whether the United States acted as a fiat or commodity reserve country. Neither balance-of-payments deficits nor decreases in the gold stock induced any reduction in the American money supply, so the fiat reserve interpretation is supported. Domestic monetary policy is seen in section 16.3 to be the dominant determinant of American inflation, especially over longer periods. Other domestic and foreign influences have played decidedly minor roles which are trivial in explaining inflationary trends. Conclusions and implications complete the chapter.

16.1   A Model of a Fiat-Reserve-Currency System

This section proposes a simple model of a fiat-reserve-currency system as a stylized description of the Bretton Woods System. Since our primary concern is inflationary trends, it is assumed that we are dealing with a time period sufficiently long that the monetary approach to the balance of payments with exogenously given purchasing power parities is applicable. As will be obvious, the essential nature of a fiat reserve country as an independent exogenous source of world inflation would not be altered by allowing for the nonreserve countries to affect their parities via commercial policies or to pursue partial sterilization policies.[1]

The reserve country is defined by the fact that other countries peg the exchange rates E_i between their currencies and that of the reserve country. The reserve country in turn is on a fiat standard and makes no effort to peg its exchange value relative to any commodity or other currency. For our purposes let the "world" consist of a currency bloc of n countries, the nth of which is the reserve currency. Floating exchange rates insulate this world from other worlds built around other reserve currencies; so they can be ignored for now. Each of the first $n - 1$ countries holds reserves R_i in the form of bonds issued by country n. In the long-run equilibrium being considered, real income y_i grows at a constant rate $\overline{\Gamma y_i}$ fixed by supply conditions, where Γ is the growth rate operator.

The model contains $n - 1$ purchasing power parity conditions ($\Gamma E_i = 0$):

(16.1) $$\Gamma P_i = \Gamma P_n, \qquad i = 1, \ldots, n - 1.$$

Money demand is determined according to the Cambridge equation with constant trend fluidity growth $\overline{\Gamma \phi_i}$:[2]

(16.2) $$\Gamma M_i^D = \overline{\Gamma \phi_i} + \overline{\Gamma y_i} + \Gamma P_i, \qquad i = 1, \ldots, n.$$

Money market equilibrium holds in the long run:

(16.3) $$\Gamma M_i^D = \Gamma M_i^S, \qquad i = 1, \ldots, n.$$

The money multiplier in each country is assumed to grow at a constant rate $\overline{\Gamma \mu_i}$. High-powered money H_i is the sum of domestic credit D_i fixed by the local monetary authority and reserves R_i:

(16.4) $$\Gamma M_i^S = \overline{\Gamma \mu_i} + \frac{D_i}{H_i} \overline{\Gamma D_i} + \frac{R_i}{H_i} \Gamma R_i, \qquad i = 1, \ldots, n.$$

Equation counting yields $4n - 1$ equations to solve for the $4n$ endogenous variables (the ΓP_i, ΓM_i^D, ΓM_i^S, and ΓR_i). The missing equation is obtained by noting that a fiat reserve currency producer has no need for reserves since it only exchanges one unit of its money for another. So its reserves can be fixed as zero[3] ($H_i = D_i$ or $\overline{\Gamma H_i} = \overline{\Gamma D_i}$):

(16.5) $$\Gamma R_n = 0.$$

---

1. The short-run importance of such policies is examined at length in parts II and III of this volume.
2. Fluidity (the inverse of income velocity) is of course a function of interest rates and real income as well as payments practices and institutions. As their long-run growth rates are unaffected, we can assume constant fluidity growth without loss of generality.
3. Or any other constant.

Note the recursive structure of this model: Equations (16.2) through (16.4) for country n plus (16.5) completely determine the equilibrium values for the reserve country. Given this equilibrium value of $\Gamma P_n = \overline{\Gamma \mu_n} + \overline{\Gamma H_n} - \overline{\Gamma \phi_n} - \overline{\Gamma y_n}$ and the $n - 1$ purchasing power parity conditions, all the other inflation rates $\Gamma P_1, \ldots, \Gamma P_{n-1}$, are determined. This in turn determines the money supply growth in each nonreserve country which finally determines the growth in each country's reserves given its chosen trend domestic credit growth. This simple recursive structure differs sharply from the world money supply and demand approach, which builds up world real money demand and world nominal money supply aggregates (in reserve currency units) and then solves for the world inflation rate as the difference in their growth rates.[4] The flaw in this approach is that even if there is a stable multiplier between the world money supply on the one hand and world domestic credit plus reserves on the other, world-reserves growth adjusts passively so as to equate the world inflation rate thus determined with the equilibrium ΓP_n determined in the reserve country. The crucial point is that nonreserve countries hold the reserve country's interest-bearing bonds—not its money—as reserves and those holdings have no natural constraint.[5]

The essential exogeneity of the reserve country as a source of world inflation rests on two assumptions: (1) The reserve country's nominal money supply growth $(\Gamma \mu_n + \Gamma H_n)$ does not respond to changes in its own reserves or in the reserves of other central banks. (2) The growth-rate of the reserve country's real money demand $(\Gamma \phi_n + \Gamma y_n)$ is independent of foreign influences. The empirical validity of those assumptions is the subject of sections 16.2 and 16.3.

16.2 Was the United States on a Fiat Standard?

The previous section showed that the essential thing about a fiat reserve country is that its nominal money stock is independent of international reserve flows. That is a statement about the behavior of its central

---

4. See, for example, Heller (1976, 1979) and the papers in Meiselman and Laffer (1975) and Parkin and Zis (1976a, b).

5. In the real world, nonreserve countries may also hold reserves as gold, SDRs, and IMF reserve position, but as indicated by Heller (1979, p. 236) the dominant source of variation in reserve growth is in fact variations in holdings of foreign exchange (and its valuation after 1971). Heller's evidence that changes in reserves have a small lagged coefficient in explaining changes in money and ultimately prices (particularly for industrialized countries) is consistent with the complete contemporaneous sterilization and lagged response which figured so prominently in parts II and III of this volume; in that case a stimulative American monetary policy results in exaggerated reserve flows as detailed in chapter 10. For further discussion, see Darby (1980).

bank—to be specific, the behavior of the Federal Reserve System. For present purposes, convertibility between money and gold, or between money and milk, is an entirely separate *relative* price program so long as the Fed does not adjust its monetary policy to maintain the pegged exchange rate between the dollar and the commodity, whether gold or milk. The question at the head of this section can thus be restated as: Did gold flows or the balance of payments enter as a significant variable in the reaction function describing the Fed's monetary policy?

The Federal Reserve Act required the Fed to hold gold certificates issued by the Treasury as reserves against Federal Reserve Notes and the Fed's deposit liabilities, the required reserve ratios being 40 and 35% respectively. After the gold price was raised from $20.67 to $35.00 per ounce in 1933–34, the Fed pursued a policy of partial if not total sterilization so that free gold holdings rose dramatically.[6] Monetization of World War II deficits reduced the free gold holdings, but Congress in 1945 reduced the gold reserve requirements on Federal Reserve Notes and deposits to 25% each when it appeared that they might impose a real limit on the Fed's monetary policy. Then beginning around the mid-1950s—about the time the GNP deflator rose significantly above its devaluation-adjusted 1929 level—total and free gold holdings began a steady decline. In March 1965, the reserve requirement against Fed deposits was eliminated, again lest monetary policy be constrained by a shortage of free gold. On 17 March 1968, the United States stopped sales and purchases of gold at $35.00 per ounce with everyone except other central banks who agreed to trade gold only among themselves thus eliminating the pegged dollar price of gold for private firms and individuals. The next day the final reserve requirement against Federal Reserve Notes was eliminated. Finally, on 15 August 1971, the United States suspended convertibility of dollars into gold even for foreign central banks.

This thumbnail sketch certainly at least raises the possibility that the ties of the dollar to gold had no real effect on monetary policy, but were merely so much political window dressing to be disposed of whenever burdensome. To proceed further, we need to work with an empirical specification of the Fed's reaction function. The reaction function (R4) contained in the Mark III International Transmission Model is a logical starting point. It is reproduced here for convenience using simplified notation:[7]

---

6. Free gold is the excess of the Fed's holdings of gold certificates over the required amount. Sterilization is discussed in detail in chapter 10.

7. See chapters 5 and 6 above for a discussion of this model. The standard errors appear below the estimated coefficients, and the t statistics are below the standard errors; Durbin's h cannot be computed in this case. Note that $4\Delta \log M = \Gamma M$ for one-quarter observations.

(16.6)

$$\Delta \log M = 0.004 + 0.00025t$$
$$ (0.003) \ (0.00005)$$
$$ 1.59 \quad 5.06$$
$$ + 0.004 \, \hat{g} + 0.002(\hat{g}_{-1} + \hat{g}_{-2}) + 0.029(\hat{g}_{-3} + \hat{g}_{-4})$$
$$ (0.029) \quad (0.021) (0.020)$$
$$ 0.14 \quad\quad 0.08 1.46$$
$$ - 0.058(\log P_{-1} - \log P_{-3}) - 0.237(\log P_{-3} - \log P_{-5})$$
$$ (0.090) (0.100)$$
$$ - 0.64 - 2.38$$
$$ - 0.117 u_{-1} + 0.539 u_{-2} \ - 0.432 u_{-3} \ - 0.055 u_{-4}$$
$$ (0.193) \quad\quad (0.363) \quad\quad (0.367) \quad\quad (0.195)$$
$$ - 0.60 \quad\quad\ 1.49 \quad\quad\quad - 1.18 \quad\quad - 0.28$$
$$ + 0.461\Delta \log M_{-1} - 0.230\Delta \log M_{-2},$$
$$ (0.12) (0.12)$$
$$ 3.98 - 1.98$$
$$ \bar{R}^2 = 0.56, \quad \text{S.E.E.} = 0.0046, \quad \text{D-W} = 2.05,$$

where M is nominal money, t a time index, $\hat{g}$ the innovation in real government spending, P the price level, and u the unemployment rate; a negative subscript indicates the number of quarters a variable is lagged. This reaction function allows the Fed to respond to unanticipated changes in government spending, inflation, and unemployment.

To the basic functional form (16.6), we add three scaled balance-of-payments terms such as those included in the nonreserve reaction functions in the Mark III Model[8] and obtain

(16.7)

$$\Delta \log M = \eta_1 + \eta_2 t + \eta_3 \hat{g} + \eta_4(\hat{g}_{-1} + \hat{g}_{-2})$$
$$ + \eta_5(\hat{g}_{-3} + \hat{g}_{-4}) + \eta_6(\log P_{-1} - \log P_{-3})$$
$$ + \eta_7(\log P_{-3} - \log P_{-5}) + \eta_8 u_{-1} + \eta_9 u_{-2} + \eta_{10} u_{-3}$$
$$ + \eta_{11} u_{-4} + \eta_{12}\Delta \log M_{-1} + \eta_{13}\Delta \log M_{-2}$$
$$ + \eta_{14}(B/Y)\text{DUMMY} + \eta_{15}[(B/Y)_{-1} + (B/Y)_{-2}]\text{DUMMY}$$
$$ + \eta_{16}[(B/Y)_{-3} + (B/Y)_{-4}]\text{DUMMY} + \epsilon,$$

where (B/Y) is the balance of payments (surplus positive) as a ratio to nominal GNP. The DUMMY variable is included to allow for the possibility that the Fed was concerned about the balance of payments only until private gold sales and gold reserve requirements were eliminated or, alternatively, only until convertibility was suspended in 1971; this is detailed below but can be ignored for the moment. The fiat-reserve-

---

8. At least some of these terms were significantly positive in the nonreserve reaction functions reported in chapter 6.

country hypothesis implies that $\eta_{14} = \eta_{15} = \eta_{16} = 0$; the alternative hypothesis is that the balance-of-payments effect is positive.

It is unclear exactly what concept of the balance of payments is appropriate, so we tried three: (*a*) the change in gold certificates held by the Fed and thus available to satisfy reserve requirements, (*b*) the change in the total gold stock including intervention account balance, and (*c*) the balance of payments on the official reserve transaction basis. The gold stock data are described in an appendix to this chapter. We also tried three variants of the DUMMY variable as well: one with value 1 through 1968I and 0 thereafter, a second with value 1 through 1971I and 0 thereafter, and a third with value 1 throughout. Whatever the period or balance-of-payments definition, the results were qualitatively the same as summarized in table 16.1: One cannot reject the hypothesis that $\eta_{14} = \eta_{15} = \eta_{16} = 0$ or, alternatively, that $\eta_{14} = 0$ in favor of the alternative hypothesis that the balance of payments has a positive effect. Indeed, in the sample period the partial correlation was if anything negative. Inclusion of the (B/Y) terms had no significant effect on the other coefficients in the basic equation. These results correspond to the fact that the residuals of the basic reaction function (16.6) displayed no pattern of significant correlation with the residuals of any of the other behavioral equations in the Mark III Model as reported at the end of section 6.2.

An original working hypothesis of the International Transmission Project was that, contrary to popular opinion, the gold reserve requirement

Table 16.1   **Tests for Significance of Balance-of-Payments Variables in American Money Reaction Function (16.7)**

Balance-of-Payments Definition	Period of Effect[+]	t Statistic for Current (B/Y) Coefficient	F Statistic for All (B/Y) Coefficients[§]
Scaled change in gold certificates	1957I–68I	−1.356	0.742
	1957I–71II	−1.198	1.133
	1957I–76IV	−1.758	1.732
Scaled change in total U.S. gold stock	1957I–68I	−1.319	0.928
	1957I–71II	−1.172	1.662
	1957I–76IV	−1.818	2.363
Scaled official reserve transactions balance	1957I–68I	−0.892	1.463
	1957I–71II	−1.356	0.661
	1957I–76IV	−1.982	1.538

[+]The period of effect indicates the period for which the variable DUMMY in equation (16.7) has the value 1; otherwise DUMMY = 0. All regressions are estimated over the period 1957I–76IV using the principal components 2SLS technique and instrument list described in chapter 6 above.

[§]The 5% significance level of $F(3/64)$ is 2.75.

had been a significant constraint on U.S. monetary policy in the 1950s and in the 1960s until sometime around the Vietnam War, when a behavioral shift occurred and inflation got started. Extensive experimentation with alternative forms of the American money reaction function, some including various measures of the magnitude of the Vietnam War, yielded results similar to table 16.1. This ultimately forced us to conclude that such a position could not be supported by the data and that throughout the period the Fed behaved as if on a purely fiat standard.

The evidence thus indicates that the evolution of the American nominal money supply in the postwar period has not been significantly affected by international factors. Two caveats must be entered however: (1) The time trend is very powerful, accounting for an increase in steady-state money growth from 0.2% per annum at the end of 1956 to 6.0% per annum at the end of 1976.[9] A multitude of slowly changing factors, some perhaps international, may be proxied by t. (2) Foreign factors may have affected the U.S. inflation and unemployment rates and hence indirectly nominal money growth. Note, however, that unemployment effects are self-reversing and a factor increasing inflation would, with a lag, induce a partially offsetting decrease in nominal money growth.[10] Further, the simulated behavior of the American variables was nearly identical in the U.S. money-shock experiments reported in section 7.2 despite widely different responses in the nonreserve countries under pegged and floating exchange rates. Similarly the simulated effects on American nominal money of the oil-price shock was minimal—cumulating to about -1% over seven quarters as reported in chapter 8.

16.3   Have International Factors Significantly Affected Trends in American Real Money Demand?

There is no question but that foreign developments have had a statistically significant effect on the real quantity of money demanded in the United States: Real export shocks have a statistically significant effect on both real income and nominal interest rates, the major determinants of money demand, and real American exports depend on foreign income and the real price of oil.[11] The level of real income may be significantly reduced by increases in the real price of oil, but the evidence on this

---

9. This steady-state growth assumes that all variables equal their expected values: $\hat{g} = \hat{g}_{-1} = \hat{g}_{-2} = \hat{g}_{-3} = \hat{g}_{-4} = 0$, $\log P_{-1} - \log P_{-3} = \log M_{-1} - \log M_{-3} - \frac{1}{2}\mu$, $\log P_{-3} - \log P_{-5} = \log M_{-3} - \log M_{-5} - \frac{1}{2}\mu$, $u_{-1} = u_{-2} = u_{-3} = u_{-4} = \bar{u}$, where μ is the steady-state growth rate of real money (see section 16.3) and $\bar{u}$, the natural rate of unemployment, is 0.0475 in 1956 and 0.0575 in 1976. The precise values of the natural unemployment rate are not important to these calculations, and the 4¾ and 5¾% figures are my approximations of the mean estimates in the literature.

10. That is, the sum of the coefficients of the u is -0.065 and the sum of the implied coefficients for a quarterly change in the price level is -0.590.

11. See tables 6.2, 6.3, 6.9, and 6.10 above in chapter 6.

is mixed.[12] The question addressed here is whether these effects have been quantitatively significant as determinants of American inflationary trends.

Both international and domestic factors can have either permanent or transitory effects on real money demand. Transitory effects are those which are temporary and self-reversing, such as the increase in real money demand associated with an unexpected increase in nominal money supply or with any other factor which *temporarily* increases real income, lowers nominal interest rates, or both. Permanent factors permanently shift the growth path of money demand up or down; examples would be the introduction of a money substitute or a permanent decrease in real income due to a permanent adverse shift in the terms of trade (OPEC).[13] By their very self-reversing nature, transitory money demand effects play practically no role in explaining inflationary trends while permanent shifts average out in their effects on inflationary trends, although not on the price level.[14]

In this section we address the empirical question of how important are factors other than nominal money growth in determining American inflation. The answer should differ with the length of period over which we are measuring the inflation rate for reasons outlined above and discussed at length in chapter 15: The longer the period of observation, the less important will be nonmonetary factors as determinants of inflation. A simple but robust measure can be obtained by running the following regression:

$$(16.8) \qquad \Gamma_j P = \sum_{i=0}^{16/j} k_i \Gamma_j M_{-ij} - \mu + \nu ,$$

where Γ_j is the j-quarter growth rate operator $[\Gamma_j X \equiv 4(\log X - \log X_{-j})/j]$, μ is the trend annual growth rate in the real quantity of money demanded, and the disturbance ν represents the effect on inflation of all nonmonetary factors. The four-year distributed lag on money growth appears sufficient from the previous work of others to allow for most of the effects of variations in nominal money growth on the growth rate of

---

12. See chapter 8.
13. See, for example, the discussions in chapters 14 and 8.
14. That is, the evolution of real money demand can be described by

$$\Delta \log m_t = \mu + \epsilon_t - \sum_{i=1}^{q} \theta_i \epsilon_{t-i},$$

where μ is the trend growth rate of real money demanded m and ϵ_t is white noise process. The permanent effect of the factors represented by ϵ_t is

$$\left(1 - \sum_{i=1}^{q} \theta_i\right)\epsilon_t.$$

If the moving average terms (the θ_i) sum to 1, then all factors affecting money demand are transitory and the disturbance u_t in $\log m_t = \log m_0 + \mu t + u_t$ is stationary. See chapter 15 for a detailed analysis of this problem as applied to purchasing power ratios.

real money demand.[15] Regressions of the form (16.8) were estimated for $j = 1, 4, 8$, and 16 using American nominal money (M_1) data for 1954IV through 1978IV.[16] The results are reported in table 16.2. We see that while nominal money growth explains most of the variance of the inflation rate for quarterly observations, nonmonetary factors are also important (and serially correlated). For annual or biennial observations, however, the standard error drops to 1.2% per annum and the serial correlation largely disappears. Looking at longer-run trends as evidenced by quadrennial observations, money growth explains 97% of the variance of the inflation rate with the remaining standard error of estimate only 0.4% per annum. These results indicate that (domestic and international) nonmonetary factors affecting real money demand may play a substantial role in short-run inflationary developments, but long-run inflation trends are dominated by movements in the average growth rate of the nominal quantity of money supplied.[17] These results complement the more formal statistical analyses of previous chapters by placing an upper bound on the potential influence of all factors other than nominal money supply as determinants of American inflation.

16.4   Conclusions and Implications

The empirical results in section 16.2 demonstrated that the Federal Reserve System did not display any significant response to the balance of payments or gold flows in determining the American money supply. Indeed the point estimates of the response generally had the wrong sign for our sample period. We conclude that the United States was de facto on a fiat standard from 1957 through the present, even in those years in which the price of gold was being pegged at $35 per ounce.

---

15. Note that there are sixteen lag terms when $j = 1$ and only one lag term when $j = 16$. This is obviously not a model which will maximize the explanatory power of nominal money growth for the inflation rate, but should provide a good lower bound for the $\bar{R}^2$ and upper bound for the standard error of estimate. Except for the quadrennial regressions, the contemporaneous money growth $(i = 0)$ term was insignificant; so reverse causation does not appear to inflate the reported $\bar{R}^2$ values.

16. This was the longest post-Accord period available for all the regressions at the time the regressions were run.

17. Similar, albeit not quite as strong, results are obtained using high-powered money H (currency held by the public + reserves) or M_2 (M_1 + time deposits at commercial banks excluding large negotiable CDs):

Observation Length	$\bar{R}^2$ for H	$\bar{R}^2$ for M_2
¼ year	0.5053	0.6600
1 year	0.6550	0.7770
2 years	0.6912	0.7783
4 years	0.9348	0.8596

Apparently for short observation lengths, variations in money-multiplier growth adversely affect the predictive power of H while for longer observation lengths, variations in the growth of time deposits do the same for M_2.

Table 16.2   **Summary Statistics for Prediction of Inflation Rate by**

$$\Gamma_j P = \sum_{i=0}^{16/j} k_i \Gamma_j M_{-ij} - \mu$$

Observation Length	S.E.E.	$\bar{R}^2$	D-W
¼ year ($j=1$)	0.0165	0.6264	1.00
1 year ($j=4$)	0.0119	0.7802	1.48
2 years ($j=8$)	0.0121	0.7586	1.74
4 years ($j=16$)	0.0040	0.9699	2.83

Note. P is the GNP deflator; M is the M_1 (currency + demand deposits) money stock; all regressions are run for 1959:1 through 1978:4 on data from 1954:4 through 1978:4.

Section 16.1 had shown that a fiat reserve country would autonomously determine world inflationary trends unless foreign factors had a significant effect on the growth rate of the real quantity of money demanded in the reserve country. So section 16.3 examined the extent that fluctuations in U.S. real money demand other than those explained by time and nominal money growth affected the rate of inflation. These nonmonetary factors played an important supporting role in determining short-run variations in the inflation rate, but were negligible for inflationary trends over a period of four years.

This chapter illuminates the meaning of some of the earlier results in this volume: There is plenty of room for significant effects of foreign variables estimated earlier to play an important role in determining the inflation rate in any particular quarter or year. But because the induced shifts in the real quantity of money demanded are in part temporary and otherwise average out over longer periods of time, United States inflation was a very nearly independent or exogenous source of trends in world inflation under the Bretton Woods system. Foreign influences had no significant effect on the evolution of American monetary policy, and that was very nearly the only factor determining the trends in American inflation.

Acknowledgments

This chapter integrates new material with results published previously in Darby (1980, 1981). The author acknowledges helpful comments from Malcolm Fisher, James Lothian, and members of the UCLA Workshop in Monetary Economics.

Appendix

Two alternative series for the American gold stock were compiled. The first of these is the Treasury gold stock at the end of the quarter. This concept, listed in table 16.3, is the value of the gold certificates issued by the Treasury and held by the Federal Reserve System. It excludes the intervention-transactions holdings of the Exchange Stabilization Fund even though those holdings could be converted into gold certificates by the stroke of a bookkeeper's pen as was done for $1 billion of gold in the first quarter of 1970. Thus the second concept, the total gold stock of the U.S. monetary authorities, adds the Exchange Stabilization Fund hold-

Table 16.3 **United States Treasury Gold Stock, End of Quarter**
Official Values in Billions of Dollars

| Year | Quarter | | | |
	1	2	3	4
1954	...	...	...	21.7125
1955	21.7192	21.6776	21.6837	21.6904
1956	21.7157	21.7991	21.8843	21.9495
1957	22.3058	22.6229	22.6355	22.7810
1958	22.3941	21.3562	20.8735	20.5343
1959	20.4417	19.7046	19.4907	19.4559
1960	19.4078	19.3222	18.6846	17.7666
1961	17.3882	17.5502	17.3760	16.8890
1962	16.6084	16.4352	16.0674	15.9781
1963	15.8775	15.7333	15.5816	15.5130
1964	15.4607	15.4617	15.4631	15.3877
1965	14.5635	13.9341	13.8576	13.7332
1966	13.6335	13.4335	13.2583	13.1591
1967	13.1074	13.1097	13.0061	11.9816
1968	10.4840	10.3669	10.367	10.367
1969	10.367	10.367	10.367	10.367
1970	11.367	11.367	11.117	10.732
1971	10.732	10.332	10.132	10.132
1972	9.588	10.410	10.410	10.410
1973	10.410	10.410	10.410	11.567
1974	11.567	11.567	11.567	11.652
1975	11.620	11.620	11.599	11.599
1976	11.599	11.598	11.598	11.598

Sources. "Gold Assets and Liabilities of the Treasury," in the *Treasury Bulletin*, December issues, 1955–76, and January 1979.

Note. Increase in 1972:2 and 1973:4 are due to devaluations only. Increase in 1970:1 is due to a $1 billion transfer from the Exchange Stabilization Fund. Gold is priced at $35 per ounce through 1972:1, $38 per ounce from 1972:2 through 1973:3, and $42.22 thereafter.

Table 16.4   **United States Total Gold Stock,**
Including Exchange Stabilization Fund,
End of Quarter Official Values in Billions of Dollars

	Quarter			
Year	1	2	3	4
1954	. . .	. . .	. . .	21.793
1955	21.763	21.730	21.745	21.753
1956	21.765	21.868	21.032	22.058
1957	22.406	22.732	22.759	22.857
1958	22.487	21.412	20.929	20.582
1959	20.486	19.746	19.579	19.507
1960	19.457	19.363	18.725	17.804
1961	17.433	17.603	17.457	16.947
1962	16.643	16.527	16.081	16.057
1963	15.946	15.830	15.634	15.596
1964	15.550	15.623	15.643	15.471
1965	14.639	14.049	13.925	13.806
1966	13.738	13.529	13.356	13.235
1967	13.184	13.169	13.077	12.065
1968	10.703	10.681	10.755	10.892
1969	10.836	11.153	11.164	11.859
1970	11.903	11.889	11.494	11.072
1971	10.963	10.507	10.207	10.206
1972	9.662	10.490	10.487	10.487
1973	10.487	10.487	10.487	11.652
1974	11.652	11.652	11.652	11.652
1975	11.620	11.620	11.599	11.599
1976	11.599	11.598	11.598	11.598

Sources. Tables (variously titled "Analysis of Changes in U.S. Gold Stock . . ." and "U.S. Gold Stock Holdings . . .") in the *Federal Reserve Bulletin*, January issues, 1956–77.
Note. Increase in 1972:2 and 1973:4 are due to devaluations only.

ings to the first concept (see table 16.4). Both series are affected by devaluations from $35 to $38 per ounce in 1972II and from $38 to $42.22 in 1973IV, but these took place after the end of convertibility of the dollar into gold.

References

Darby, M. R. 1980. The monetary approach to the balance of payments: Two specious assumptions. *Economic Inquiry* 18 (April): 321–26.

————. 1981. The international economy as a source of and restraint on United States inflation. In W. A. Gale, ed., *Inflation: Causes, consequents, and control.* Cambridge: Oelgeschlager, Gunn & Hain.

Heller, H. R. 1976. International reserves and world-wide inflation. *International Monetary Fund Staff Papers* 23 (March): 61–87

————. 1979. Further evidence on the relationship between international reserves and world inflation. In M. Boskin, ed., *Economics and human welfare: Essays in honor of Tibor Scitovsky.* New York: Academic Press.

Meiselman, D. I., and A. B. Laffer, eds. 1975. *The phenomenon of world-wide inflation.* Washington: American Enterprise Institute.

Parkin, M., and G. Zis, eds. 1976a. *Inflation in the world economy.* Toronto: University of Toronto Press.

————. 1976b. *Inflation in open economics.* Toronto: University of Toronto Press.

PART

V Conclusions

17 Conclusions on the International Transmission of Inflation

Michael R. Darby and James R. Lothian

> Science is organized knowledge.
>
> Herbert Spencer
>
> It is better to know nothing than to
> know what ain't so.
>
> Josh Billings

The goal of empirical research in any science is to maximize the number of assumptions which can be securely included in the body of theory. While empirical research can never establish the truth of any statement about the world, conformity of the world to a particular hypothesis in repeated and varied trials does give us confidence to incorporate the hypothesis into the set of assumptions we use to make scientific predictions. In cases in which data or measurement tools are lacking, a hypothesis may gain wide currency on the basis not of solid empirical successes but of logical, aesthetic, or even political grounds. One example in economics would be the Phillips curve, another much of the Keynesian revolution. Because of awesome data problems, international finance has been particularly prone to intellectual fads in which particular assumptions achieve dominance on the basis more of the intellectual force of their proponents than of strength of supporting empirical evidence.

With many contending and inconsistent hypotheses in the field, once the data are available it merely takes hard work to find that some hypotheses are very unlikely to be true given the observations. Thus the greatest contribution of this project must be the creation of the consistent set of data on which the rest of our research is based. We have explored the conformity of this data set to the implications of certain popular hypotheses relevant to the international transmission of inflation. These tests, besides their intrinsic interest, served as a quality check on the data by highlighting any questionable observations.

Our conclusions from the tests reported in this volume can be organized around four related issues: monetary versus other explanations of inflation, the channels of international transmission of inflation, sterilization and monetary control, and alternative monetary arrangements. These are presented in sections 17.1 to 17.4, respectively. We write finis by proposing a number of topics for future research suggested by our analyses of the data.

17.1   Money versus Special Factors

Two very different views of what caused the inflation of the second half of the 1960s and the 1970s have been widely propounded. On the one hand, there are those who stress the role of special factors: the monopoly power of the business sector and of trade unions, the substantial rise in commodity prices in 1973, and, most important, the OPEC–induced increases in the price of petroleum in 1974–75.[1] On the other hand are those observers who regard inflation in general as a monetary phenomenon and this particular episode as just another member of the species. According to most proponents of this view, the United States played a key role in the process, its excessive monetary growth being exported abroad via the fixed exchange-rate system formally in existence until 1973.[2]

In broad outline, both explanations are consistent enough with the facts that neither can be ruled out. The relative prices of agricultural commodities did increase markedly immediately prior to and during the peak inflation years. So also did the relative price of oil. Increases in monopoly power might have accounted for inflation up until that point. At least there was general concern in government and among a relatively large segment of economists that they did. Moreover, inflation abated for a time once commodity prices fell in relative terms and oil prices ceased rising so rapidly.

By the same token, monetary growth in the United States accelerated substantially after 1965. Fixed exchange rates via a variety of channels would normally have been expected to spread that inflationary American monetary impulse to other countries. Moreover, monetary growth in

---

1. The clearest statement of the special-factor view was made by Kaldor (1976). See also, Bruno and Sachs (1979), Fried and Schultze (1975) on oil, and Perry (1975, 1980) on wage push. Laidler and Parkin (1975) and Gordon (1977) have provided particularly useful critical assessments of this view.

2. Laidler and Parkin (1975), Meiselman (1975), and Johnson (1976) provide clear statements of the monetary approach to worldwide inflation, but as we demonstrate in this chapter there is considerable room for disagreement among economists who agree that inflation is an essentially monetary phenomenon. Further, many economists who stress "special factors" assume that the central bank accommodates those factors by money growth.

most other industrial countries followed the same general pattern as monetary growth in the United States.

To students of economic history and the history of economic thought, the current debate about the causes of inflation provides just another illustration of the Ecclesiastes dictum "There is no new thing under the sun." In Britain during the bullionist controversy at the start of the nineteenth century and then again several decades later during the currency-school banking-school debate almost the exact same arguments were being voiced as today. The same is true for the widespread discussions of inflation in America at the start of this century.

So similar, in fact, have the views of the various participants on each side of this recurrent debate been that proponents of one position at one time almost appear to be responding directly to proponents of the other position during earlier and later periods. Consider Irving Fisher's (1920) discussion of explanations of inflation that rely purely on movements in relative prices as an example: "Obviously no explanation of a general rise of prices is sufficient which merely explains one price in terms of another" (p. 14). He soon added, "[n]or will special causes working on selected commodities prove to be general enough to explain the concerted behavior of commodities" (p. 16). Fisher concluded instead that the available empirical evidence indicated that "the chief disturber of the peace, so far as the purchasing power of money is concerned, has invariably, or at any rate almost invariably, been money itself, not the goods which money purchases" (p. 35).

Though Fisher was writing in 1920, his argument could easily have been a response to Thomas Tooke and William Newmarch, who more than sixty years before had concluded that "in every instance of a variation of Prices, a full explanation of the change is apparently afforded by circumstances affecting the Supply or Demand" (1857, reprinted in 1928, p. 233), or indeed to the modern-day advocates of that position.

Our own evidence lends very little support to the most recent reincarnation of the special-factor explanation of inflation. In spite of this hypothesis's broad popular appeal and rather widespread support in economic policy circles, we find that at best it can account for only a minor fraction of the inflation in the first half of the 1970s. Monetary factors, we find, explain the bulk.

Both the trade-union and monopoly-power versions of the cost-push or special-factor hypothesis would suggest that nominal money growth either lags behind price changes as central banks react to the unemployment resulting from wage and price increases or is unrelated to price changes. Cassese and Lothian in chapter 4 report just the opposite with lagged money growth significantly affecting prices but not vice versa. We conclude—as have others—that a viable special-factor hypothesis must rely on increases in the price of oil and other commodities.

Darby in chapter 8 reviews the theoretical underpinnings of the special-factor hypothesis as applied to oil before going on to test and otherwise evaluate its validity. The gist of the conclusions he reaches in the theoretical analysis is that for the special-factor hypothesis to make sense either of two things would have had to have happened: real income would have to have fallen or monetary growth have been increased in response to oil-price shocks.

To assess the importance of the first of these two avenues of influence, Darby incorporates oil-price terms into the real-income equations of the Mark III Model. Since these equations did not perform even tolerably well for three of the eight countries in the sample at the outset, he focuses upon the remaining five. In only three of these five cases are the oil-price terms taken as a group significant. These three countries—the Netherlands, the United Kingdom, and the United States—all had general price controls, however, that were removed more or less coincidentally with the increase in oil prices. Canada and Germany, the other two countries that Darby considers and for which he could uncover no significant effect, did not have controls during the relevant period. Given the tendency for price controls to affect the time pattern of changes in the real and price components of nominal income as well as the time pattern of movements in velocity, Darby concludes that the estimated reductions in real income may well be spurious.

So that he can also allow for the indirect effects of the oil-price increase on nominal money supplies and on real exports while assessing its direct influence on real incomes and hence price levels, Darby performs a simulation experiment with the Mark IV Simulation Model. Unfortunately, these results are not at all conclusive. For several countries, the simulations are distorted by theoretically perverse effects. In the remaining instances, the problem of price controls coupled with the differences in behavior among countries makes it impossible to say anything definitive about "the" influence of oil prices on the price level: The price level might be increased by anywhere from 0 to 5%. However, if we translate this into the effect on the 1971–75 inflation rate, this amounts to only a 0 to 1% per annum oil component as compared to the 3.5% per annum average increase in inflation over the previous quinquennium. Thus, while it is possible that the oil-price increase had a significant role in increasing inflation, it certainly was not a dominant one.

Incorporating oil-price terms directly into their price equation in chapter 14, Gandolfi and Lothian take a more direct approach than Darby but reach conclusions qualitatively similar to his. In almost all of the eight countries, they are able to uncover a significant effect in at least one formulation of their equation. However, the significance of such effects in a given country is not at all consistent among equations. It varies both by the model of the error structure and by the measure of the price level that they use. Even if one ignores these differences and focuses upon the equation most favorable to the oil-price hypothesis, the estimated effects in most countries are still not terribly large.

In another set of tests, Gandolfi and Lothian incorporate the relative price of basic commodities as an additional variable in their price equations. The results of this exercise are unambiguous. In their regressions with a correction for second-order serial correlation, the commodity price variable enters significantly only two times: for Canada with the GNP deflator but not the CPI used as the measure of the price level and for Italy with the CPI but not the GNP deflator.

The other question that is highly relevant to the debate over monetary versus special factors, and which is logically antecedent to our discussion of channels of transmission, is the role of the United States as the reserve-currency country. Darby deals with this issue explicitly in chapter 16 from both the theoretical and empirical perspectives. Schwartz in her historical overview of the period in chapter 2 describes the principal events in the international monetary arena and the part the United States played both during the Bretton Woods years and afterward. Also of interest are Cassese and Lothian's analysis of movements in American and foreign money and Gandolfi and Lothian's estimates of expected money functions.

Darby's theoretical model in chapter 16 illustrates the importance of the reserve-currency country in a world of fixed exchange rates. In the model, the reserve-currency country's money supply (rather than the world money supply, which some others have stressed) is the ultimate determinant of the price level in the rest of the world as well as in the reserve-currency country. This exogeneity of the United States as a source of world inflation rests on two assumptions: that growth in its nominal money supply is independent of changes in its and other countries' reserves and that growth in its real money demand is similarly independent of foreign influences.

Darby evaluates this second assumption by estimating a simple distributed lag relation between inflation in the United States and growth in M1 over the previous sixteen quarters. He finds that as the data are averaged over progressively longer periods the explainability of the relation progressively increases to the point where, when he uses four-year averages, he can account for 97% of the variation in inflation. From this exercise, he concludes that if foreign influences were important, they only operated in the shorter term, affecting the transition to a new equilibrium rate of inflation, but not the equilibrium itself.

To examine the validity of the first assumption, Darby reestimates the Federal Reserve's reaction function and includes various measures of the balance of payments. He finds that he cannot reject the hypothesis that these variables had no influence, over either the full sample period or the several subperiods that he examines. In contrast, in chapter 6 he and Stockman show that balance-of-payments variables do enter significantly in the money-supply reaction functions of the other seven countries' monetary authorities.

These findings moreover square with evidence that Cassese and Lothian present in chapter 4 and that Gandolfi and Lothian give in chapter 14. Using bivariate causality tests, Cassese and Lothian find no significant effect—positive or negative—of the lagged balance of payments on growth in American high-powered money. They do, however, find a significant negative effect running in the opposite direction.

Gandolfi and Lothian's estimates of the expected money functions that underlie their price equations tell a similar story: In each of the seven foreign countries, monetary growth in the United States or the domestic balance of payments—sometimes both—has a significant effect on monetary growth; in the United States, the balance of payments is not significant.

Schwartz's review in chapter 2 of the institutional framework of the Bretton Woods system supports the results of the econometric analysis. Securities denominated in U.S. dollars were the dominant source of increase in international reserves under Bretton Woods, and these outflows had no direct effect on the American money supply. The Federal Reserve System's response to continuing balance-of-payments deficits appeared to go little beyond public statements of concern and cosmetic operations.

We turn next to a detailed examination of the channels of international transmission which explicates how a homegrown American inflation was exported to the industrialized West.

17.2   Channels of Transmission

The international linkages among national macroeconomies follow four main channels: goods substitution, bonds substitution, currency substitution, and absorption effects. The previous chapters have disclosed evidence that all of these channels have been operative, but not so strongly as argued by respective proponents. In this section we examine these arguments and the empirical evidence. Section 17.3 then presents evidence on the extent to which central bank sterilization policies frustrated or delayed the international transmission of inflation under the Bretton Woods system.

17.2.1   Goods Substitution

There are two distinct traditions in the literature as to the nature of the linkages operating through tradable goods. The first, which we associate with David Hume, views internationally traded goods as substitutes, but not perfect substitutes. Thus their relative prices may change temporarily as part of the adjustment process initiated by a monetary disturbance.[3] The second view, associated by Whitman (1975) with the "global monetarists" like Laffer (1975) and usually termed price arbitrage, assumes that internationally traded goods indeed are perfect substitutes with prices continuously and rigidly linked. Further consideration of factor competition between tradable and nontradable goods results in the "law of one price level," which states that purchasing power parity holds continuously, and not just in long-run equilibrium as in Humean analyses.[4] Thus the empirical question to be answered is to what extent are goods substitutable internationally, or as Isard (1977) wryly put it, "How far can we push the 'Law of One Price'?"

In this volume we have reported a variety of evidence to support the conclusion of such authors as Isard (1977), Kravis and Lipsey (1977, 1978), and Richardson (1978) that goods are substitutable internationally, but far from perfectly so. This evidence can be arranged on a spectrum from direct to most roundabout. The latter, which infers that goods (and assets) are imperfect substitutes from the ability of non-reserve countries to exercise independent monetary policies under pegged exchange rates, is presented at length in section 17.3. The remainder of the evidence is considered here.

The most direct evidence is found in the relatively weak price effects found in the export- and import-price equations estimated by Darby and Stockman in chapter 6.[5] Generally, the relative-price effect on the balance of trade is not large although it does increase over time. Experiments with the Mark IV International Simulation Model confirm that Humean movements in relative price levels are implied by monetary shocks whether originating in the United States or abroad.[6]

An only slightly less direct sort of evidence is provided by Cassese and Lothian in chapter 4. They use bivariate Granger tests to analyze two

3. Dietrich Fausten (1979) has persuasively distinguished the Humean tradition from the law of one price level discussed below. Either the law of one price level or interest arbitrage (discussed in the next subsection) together with ancillary assumptions can be used to establish the result that the nominal quantity of money demanded in a small economy maintaining pegged exchange rates is determined by foreign factors. Hence the conclusion, if money supply equals money demand, that reserve changes must supply the money not supplied via domestic credit and "the balance of payments is essentially a monetary phenomenon" (Frenkel and Johnson 1976, p. 21).

4. The relevant concept of purchasing power parity is a ceteris paribus one: The purchasing power ratio (real exchange rate) is unaffected in short-run and long-run equilibrium by a monetary disturbance. As discussed in note 1 to chapter 15 above, this equilibrium value may shift randomly due to such factors as *permanent* shifts in relative prices.

5. See tables 6.10 and 6.13.

6. We refer here only to the Humean effect on relative price levels, since for neither the United Kingdom nor Canada does Darby simulate the working of a specie-flow mechanism. For those countries sterilization prevented any substantial impact on domestic nominal money of an American money shock.

relations: domestic versus foreign inflation and domestic money growth versus domestic inflation. In the inflation comparisons, they use two different measures of foreign inflation. For the United States as well as the seven nonreserve countries, they use the percentage change in a nominal-income weighted index of the remaining seven countries' GNP (or GDP) deflators; for the seven nonreserve countries alone, they use the percentage change in the United States deflator. In both instances, the lagged foreign inflation rate was significant in fewer than half the countries.

For their tests of the domestic money-price relations, they used three measures of money—M1, M2, and high-powered money—and the consumer price index as well as the deflator. For all eight countries, they find a much more consistent effect running from lagged values of money to current inflation than the other way around. Furthermore, these relations exhibit no tendency to reverse themselves during the shorter fixed rate sample period ending in the third quarter of 1971. Cassese and Lothian's results thus stand at odds with the assumption of continuous price arbitrage with money supplies adjusting with a lag to changes in nominal money demand induced by foreign price shocks.

In chapter 14, Gandolfi and Lothian use their reduced-form price equation to conduct tests of the price arbitrage mechanism similar to those discussed in section 17.1 for oil and commodity prices. Like Cassese and Lothian, they use both the price level in the United States and a weighted average of the price levels in the seven countries other than the one being analyzed as alternative measures of foreign prices. In the great bulk of the comparisons these measures are not statistically significant. Moreover, in their regressions with the second-order correction, the United States price variable is only significant in both the CPI and GNP relations in Japan and the rest-of-world price index only significant in both the relations in France. They conclude: "Some evidence of price arbitrage, therefore, exists but even on the most favorable interpretation of the evidence it is weak and hardly universal." Similarly weak results with a preliminary version of the Mark III Model were reported in Darby (1979).

Darby examines the predictive power of purchasing power parity under floating exchange rates in chapter 15. His results do not speak to the issue of whether goods are perfect substitutes since changes in the parity value may occur due to permanent changes of relative prices.[7] The major implication for examining historical data is that as the period of

---

7. See Stockman (1980). However, Kravis, Heston, and Summers (1978) attempt to make international purchasing power comparisons based on standardized baskets and find these to differ from exchange-rate converted nominal income ratios.

observation is increased, the level of the purchasing power ratio becomes less predictable while its growth rate becomes more predictable.[8]

17.2.2 Asset Flows and Monetary Linkages

We have already suggested that the substitutability of goods may transmit inflation from country to country not only by direct price arbitrage but also by inducing changes in the money supply. The money supply changes are supposed to result from the effect of the trade balance on the balance of payments. Asset flows may provide important balance-of-payments effects even if the trade balance responds only weakly to a monetary disturbance. The extent to which the balance of payments affects the nominal supply of money is discussed at length in section 17.3.[9]

Recent presentations of the monetary approach to the balance of payments have come to stress "interest arbitrage" rather than price arbitrage on Dornbusch's (1976b, p. 1162) "assumption that exchange rates and asset markets adjust fast relative to goods markets." The essential idea is that assets are perfect substitutes internationally so that the interest rate in any nonreserve country must equal the interest rate in the reserve country plus the expected depreciation in the exchange rate. So long as the expected depreciation is independent of domestic monetary policy and the balance of payments, this interest parity relation fixes the domestic interest rate and hence the domestic nominal money supply, price level, and so forth as effectively as did the law of one price level in the early versions of the monetary approach.

This airtight conclusion breaks down if assets (bonds in the macroeconomic paradigm) are not perfect substitutes internationally because of nondiversifiable risk.[10] In this case capital flows will change the equilibrium domestic interest rate for a given foreign interest rate plus expected depreciation. This is the essence of the portfolio-balance approach pioneered by Branson (1968, 1970) and advanced by Dan Lee and Michael Melvin in chapters 12 and 13 of this volume.[11] With imperfect

8. Thus Darby shows that convergence of exchange-rate-adjusted inflation rates over longer periods of observation—such as noted by Gailliot (1970) and Lawrence (1979)—are consistent with the equilibrium value of the purchasing power ratio following a random walk. However, it is very difficult to distinguish statistically a random walk from a very slow adjustment process as argued by Frenkel (1980b, c).

9. To anticipate section 17.3 a bit, we find that the balance of payments generally does affect nominal money growth in nonreserve countries, but only very weakly at first.

10. This risk may be with regard to exchange-rate changes or to capital controls since exchange-rate crises were international events which would affect many countries simultaneously.

11. Even if assets were imperfect substitutes internationally, induced changes in the expected exchange-rate depreciation may limit the ability of a nonreserve central bank to choose nominal money growth rates much different from those consistent with interest-rate "parity." See chapter 15 above and section 7.3 below for details.

asset substitutability there may be movements in relative interest rates analogous to the movements in relative price levels during the adjustment period. Again, the balance-of-payments effect of the induced capital flows may induce the gradual changes in money supply which ultimately reestablish equilibrium. In this way, the portfolio-balance approach is the asset market analogue to the Humean relative price adjustment mechanism.

The evidence in this volume is generally consistent with the view that reserve flows induced by a portfolio-balance mechanism were an important channel of international transmission under the Bretton Woods system. However, the strength of this channel is not overwhelming, and, if we use the simulations as a guide, the actual transmission of effects through this mechanism appears to have been both fairly weak and rather drawn out over time. Besides the evidence of exercise of monetary control examined in section 17.3 below, our evidence is of several types: the tests and other assessments of the interest arbitrage mechanism by Cassese and Lothian and by Darby and Stockman and Darby's simulation results with the Mark IV Model.

Cassese and Lothian report in chapter 4 that for all seven nonreserve countries lagged American interest rates were a significant determinant of the domestic interest rates during the pegged rate period. With the exception of Canada, where the effect was largely in the current quarter, these effects were typically distributed over a number of quarters. Arbitrage therefore appears to have been rather limited in the short run in most countries, contrary to the implications of perfect asset substitutability, but more powerful in the long run.

Darby and Stockman on the basis of their estimates of capital-flows equations concur in chapter 6. With the exception of Japan and the United Kingdom, for which the estimated equations were exceedingly poor, they find a negative but weak relation between capital flows and either the level or first difference of the domestic versus foreign interest-rate differential adjusted for expected changes in the exchange rate. The chapter 7 simulation experiments confirm this impression. For Germany substantial capital flows result in *partial* contemporaneous harmonization of domestic money growth to an American monetary shock, but a domestic money shock does not induce large offsetting reserve flows. For the Netherlands, balance-of-trade effects seem quite as important as capital flows. However, in neither Canada nor the United Kingdom are the simulated effects of the increase in the nominal stock of money in the United States at all substantial. An important reason that the simulated capital flows are so weak and easily sterilized is the small estimated liquidity effect of money shocks on domestic interest rates.[12]

---

12. Recall from chapter 10 that the capital flows induced by a difference between domestic nominal money and its international "parity" value depend upon the *product* of

17.2.3   Other Channels of Transmission

The two remaining channels of transmission to be discussed are currency substitution and Keynesian absorption effects. Evidence on both channels comes from the simultaneous model, the estimates of the model presented in chapter 6, and the results of the simulation experiments described in chapter 7.

The theoretical rationale for currency substitution is that monetary assets denominated in the domestic currency are substitutes in demand with those denominated in the foreign currency. In the extreme case in which both are near-perfect substitutes, German money holders, for example, will be indifferent between deposits in dollars and in DM, so that any contraction in the supply of DM deposits will induce German money holders to increase their deposits denominated in dollars by an equivalent amount in terms of DM. As the supply cf money in German DM declines, therefore, its velocity rises to offset decreases with the end result that income flows in Germany are left unaltered. This Radcliff-esque view is contradicted by the existence of stable money demand functions, but it may well be that foreign moneys are substitutes in demand for domestic money.

One test of this proposition has been to include a foreign—usually United States—(uncovered) interest-rate variable in the domestic money demand function. Miles (1978) follows this procedure for Canada, justifying the inclusion of the variable within the context of a model similar to that used by Chetty (1969) in his investigation of the substitutability of monetary assets within the United States. Other studies of this type are Hamburger (1977) and Brittain (1981). An alternative procedure, which Brittain also follows, is to examine the cross-correlations of the residuals from simple regressions of velocity on time. The authors of all of these studies find support, to varying degrees, for the currency substitution hypothesis. Bordo and Choudhri (1982) note that the differential cost of holding foreign instead of domestic money is the expected change in the exchange rate, but this variable does not enter the Canadian demand for money. Further, their reexamination of Miles's work shows that his finding of currency substitution was spurious.

These tests are generally ill suited to differentiate between currency substitution and the more general concept of asset substitution. Indeed we would argue that foreign bonds (and domestic bonds!) are generally more important substitutes for domestic money than are foreign moneys. The return to a domestic holder of a foreign bond is the foreign interest

---

the interest-rate coefficient in the capital-flows equation and the derivative of the interest rate with respect to money. Thus, if the liquidity effect is small or nil, so will be the capital flows. Large liquidity effects are not consistent with a shock-absorber money demand function which distinguishes between unexpected and expected money growth; see Carr and Darby (1981).

rate plus the expected depreciation in the exchange rate.[13] This more general concept has been examined in this volume.

Darby and Stockman include a foreign interest rate plus expected depreciation term in each country's money demand function in the Mark III Model. For the nonreserve countries they use the three-month U.S. treasury bill rate; for the United States they use the three-month U.K. treasury bill rate.[14] Only for Japan and the United Kingdom is the foreign interest rate statistically significant. In both instances, moreover, the magnitude of the estimated coefficients is exceedingly small. One possible explanation for the disparity between our results and those reported in some other studies may be simultaneous equations bias since our results are obtained in the context of a simultaneous model and the others using single-equation approaches. We conclude that foreign asset substitution for domestic money is not an important channel of economic transmission among countries.

The traditional Keynesian absorption channel links one country's increase in real income to increased demand for imports and hence increased exports and real income in other countries. On the one hand, regressions of an extended Barro real-income equation (reported in chapters 6 and 9) find that the distributed lag coefficients on real export shocks are insignificant as a group for all countries at the 5% level and for all countries except the United States and Germany at the 10% level. These results suggest that the absorption channel is empirically irrelevant. On the other hand, absorption effects are the dominant channel of transmission in the simulation experiments for two countries, Canada and the United Kingdom. Their domestic money shocks, as already mentioned, were unaffected by the increase in the money stock in the United States. Increases in their exports, however, affected real income and, in the case of the United Kingdom, interest rates.[15] Whether the importance of the absorption channel and unimportance of monetary channels for these countries will survive further study is an interesting question.

17.2.4 Summary

Neither goods nor assets appear to be perfect substitutes, but both the trade balance and capital flows are responsive to movements in foreign prices and (expected-exchange-rate-change-adjusted) interest rates rela-

13. Including this variable and the domestic interest rate in the money demand function is equivalent to Bordo and Choudhri's approach to currency substitution under their assumption that bonds (but not moneys) are perfect substitutes internationally.

14. The expected changes in the exchange rates are proxied by the predictions of behavioral equations described in section 5.3.

15. Although the distributed lag coefficients on export shocks were insignificant as a group, individual coefficients passed the t statistic criterion for inclusion in the simulation model.

tive to their domestic counterparts, with the response increasing over time. Only weak evidence was found in support of either asset-substitution effects on money demand or absorption effects on real income.

17.3   Sterilization and Monetary Control

Monetary control by nonreserve central banks under pegged exchange rates implies an ability to move domestic interest rates and prices relative to their international parity values. So evidence of monetary control reinforces the direct evidence of imperfectly substitutable assets and goods. The exercise of monetary control is complete or partial according to whether induced reserve flows are completely or partially sterilized. If sterilization is complete, then the central bank chooses the money supply without regard to the induced variations in its reserve assets. Where only partial (or no) sterilization is practiced, the induced reserve flows move the money supply to a point intermediate between that otherwise desired by the central bank and that consistent with the international parity values.

In this section we will assess our evidence on three aspects of this larger issue: the prevalence and magnitude of sterilization among our sample of nonreserve countries, whether short-run monetary control was in fact exercised by these countries under pegged exchange rates, and the implications for dynamic stability of their exercise of short-run monetary control. Finally, we draw out the implications of this evidence for the effects of central bank intervention in the foreign exchange markets under floating exchange rates.

17.3.1   The Prevalence and Magnitude of Sterilization

Complete sterilization occurs if the contemporaneous scaled balance of payments (B/H) does not enter into the nonreserve central bank's money supply function.[16] No sterilization occurs if the contemporaneous scaled balance of payment enters that reaction function with a coefficient of 1 so that the money growth rate is $(B + \Delta D)/H$, where the scaled-domestic-credit change $\Delta D/H$ is determined independently of the balance of payments. Partial sterilization occurs if central bank behavior falls between these extremes.

Traditional presentations of the monetary approach such as Johnson (1976, pp. 152–53) have made the extreme assumption that nonreserve central banks do not sterilize the balance of payments at all. This assumption appears to be made primarily for analytical convenience, since it

---

16. To put it another way, the scaled balance of payments B/H enters the scaled-change-in-domestic-credit ($\Delta D/H$) reaction function with a coefficient of -1.

permits analysis to proceed conditioned upon an exogenously determined domestic credit. Mussa (1976, p. 192) makes it clear, for example, that a (partial) sterilization policy will merely result in exaggerated movements in the balance of payments under the other assumptions of the monetary approach. To the extent that proponents of the monetary approach have not taken this assumption seriously, it is hoped that the generalized monetary approach model presented in chapter 10 will demonstrate by example that sterilization presents no real analytical or expositional inconvenience.

In the past, at least, some monetary approachers have taken the no-sterilization assumption to be a true statement of how the world operates. The reasoning of Genberg (1976, p. 322) is typical: The nominal money supply is determined by the international parity values of prices and interest rates; so complete sterilization is impossible. Further, partial sterilization results in exaggerated movements in the balance of payments with no effect on the money supply; this is not attractive to a central bank, and so the policy will not be attempted. There are two empirical statements here: (1) Nonreserve central banks have no monetary control. (2) They are aware of that lack of control and averse to exaggerated movements in the balance of payments. Thus sterilization is an empirical, not a theoretical, question.

Nonreserve central bank behavior is quite strictly limited if they are to eschew sterilization. They must formulate their policy in terms of their holdings of assets denominated in domestic currency and forswear any goals as to domestic interest rates or money supply. Herring and Marston (1977) and Hilliard (1979) conducted exemplary studies indicating that the German and British central banks, respectively, indeed did follow active policies of sterilization. Obstfeld (1980a) confirmed Herring and Marston's results for Germany. Connolly and Taylor (1979) used a very simple monetary model, but still found significant evidence of sterilization for the ten developed countries they examined, even over periods as long as two years.[17] In work using preliminary versions of our data bank and single-equation methods, John Price (1978) also found evidence of substantial sterilization for five nonreserve countries.

Three separate investigations of the existence of sterilization policies have been reported above in chapters 4, 6, and 11. Although the approaches are diverse, the conclusions are identical: Partial or complete sterilization appears to have been a universal practice at least for this set of developed nonreserve countries.

Cassese and Lothian use bivariate causality tests in chapter 4 to examine the relation between changes in foreign reserves and changes in

---

17. The large standard errors for their seventeen developing countries precluded any definite conclusion for them, but all the point estimates indicated only slightly less active sterilization.

domestic credit. They find that generally the balance of payments Granger-causes changes in domestic credit, but only for the U.K. and Canada is there evidence of a relation going the other way. Since these tests are limited to the two variables and do not speak directly to the contemporaneous relation, we do not view them as more than suggestive.

Darby and Stockman estimate a uniformly specified nominal money reaction function for all nonreserve countries in the simultaneous-equation environment of the quarterly Mark III International Transmission Model. Their results for the pegged exchange-rate period are summarized in tables 6.7 and 6.8 above. The reaction function for Italy had little explanatory value, but for the other six countries, only for Germany and perhaps Japan could the hypothesis of complete contemporaneous sterilization be rejected.[18] Stated differently, between 87% and all of the contemporaneous effect of the balance of payments on money growth was eliminated by sterilization policies of the nonreserve central banks. However, lagged responses to the balance of payments ultimately induced a positive relation in all six countries.[19] Thus, while quarterly data indicate either complete or partial sterilization, only partial sterilization would be observed in annual data.

Laskar investigates a number of variants of the Mark III reaction functions in section 11.3 above. Aside from differences in estimation technique, the major innovation in Laskar's specification is the inclusion of the lagged scaled reserves *stock*. This variable enters positively and eliminates most of the explanatory power of the lagged balance-of-payments terms, but the results are qualitatively the same as those in chapter 6 except that the Netherlands replaces Japan as one of the two countries for which complete contemporaneous sterilization can be rejected.[20] In other variants of the reaction functions, Laskar found indications that in Japan payments surpluses were completely sterilized but deficits only partially so and that in the United Kingdom, Canada, and France speculative capital flows were partially sterilized while other components of the balance of payments were completely sterilized.

It is clear that money-supply reaction functions are a fertile area for

18. The contemporaneous balance-of-payments effect on money growth was significantly negative (!) for Italy, but little can be made of this given the poor fit of the regression.

19. In Italy, even the lagged response was negative.

20. The inclusion of scaled lagged reserves is preferable to four quarters of lagged balances of payments if a slow partial adjustment process is operative. Heller and Knight (1978), Heller and Kahn (1978), Bilson and Frenkel (1979), and Frenkel (1980*a*) have made recent contributions to the literature on the demand for reserves by central banks. Bilson and Frenkel have presented evidence supporting the slow partial adjustment mechanism for reserves. Note, however, that a slow partial adjustment of actual toward desired reserves could be accomplished entirely via changes in domestic credit with no effects on the money supply; this would correspond to the workings of the monetary approach to the balance of payments. So it is difficult to go directly from the reserves literature to the proper form for the money-supply reaction function.

future research, but the work reported here in conjunction with earlier work strongly indicates that partial or complete sterilization is standard operating procedure among nonreserve developed countries maintaining pegged exchange rates. Besides the implications for monetary control to be discussed immediately below, this implies that changes in domestic credit are simultaneously determined with the balance of payments. Therefore the standard single-equation estimates explaining the balance of payments by changes in domestic credit and money demand variables tell us little about the validity of the monetary approach to the balance of payments.[21]

17.3.2 Short-Run Monetary Control

The most striking conclusion of the monetary approach to the balance of payments was that nonreserve central banks are impotent with respect to their domestic money supplies and interest rates but can attain any desired balance of payments via their actions. Either or both of two assumptions have traditionally been offered to justify this conclusion: goods are perfect substitutes internationally, and assets are perfect substitutes internationally.[22] Darby in chapter 10 adds a third condition which would imply a lack of monetary control: expectations of depreciation which are too responsive to variations in the balance of payments.[23] In recent papers, Stockman (1979) and Obstfeld (1980b, c, d) have emphasized that even if assets are not perfect substitutes, it is sufficient that consumers completely discount future taxes for them to act as if government holdings of foreign bonds were their own. In this case a government exchange of foreign for domestic bonds will induce an exactly offsetting shift in private demands so that monetary control is again lost.

Since any one of these four conditions—and there are doubtless others—preclude monetary control, it is difficult to conclusively reject the impotence of nonreserve central banks with respect to their money supplies. Nonetheless, the hypothesis is a scientific one and so tests can be derived. Two types of tests have led us to the conclusion that nonreserve central banks did indeed exercise monetary control under pegged exchange rates: First, we have direct evidence on the two major conditions which indicates that neither goods nor assets are perfect substitutes internationally; this evidence was discussed in section 17.2 above. Second, we have evidence that the actual growth in the money supply is indeed determined, at least in part, by domestic policy goals.

21. See section 10.2 above and Darby (1980) on this.
22. As noted in chapter 10, these assumptions must be coupled with supporting assumptions that the *contemporaneous* effect of money on prices is positive and on the interest rate negative, respectively.
23. The last is a stability condition explaining perhaps how a central bank might induce overwhelming speculative capital flows; it is not applicable to explaining loss of control in the absence of such a speculative crisis.

One way to see whether nonreserve central banks in fact exercised monetary control is to specify and estimate a structural model and then determine the implications of the estimates. The Mark III International Transmission Model described in chapters 5 and 6 is our major effort of this sort. A simplified version (the Mark IV Simulation Model) was used in chapter 7 to determine how the significant channels of international transmission interact, particularly with respect to monetary control. Four nonreserve countries (United Kingdom, Canada, Germany, and the Netherlands) were examined in some detail, and only Germany displayed any evidence of the balance of payments limiting short-run monetary control. For Germany an immediate, albeit partial, response of domestic nominal money to increased U.S. money was observed, but the balance of payments only slightly offset an upward shift in the domestic money-supply reaction function. Thus the model estimates do indeed imply substantial short-run monetary control.

Daniel Laskar in chapter 11 deals with a set of smaller single-country models in the tradition of Kouri and Porter (1974), Argy and Kouri (1974), and Herring and Marston (1977). Although his estimation techniques allow for possible endogeneity of the balance of *trade*, Laskar's analysis of monetary control assumes that the only significant loss of control would occur via offsetting capital flows. The offset coefficient (the fraction of an increase in domestic credit offset by contemporaneous capital flows) is significantly less than one at the 5% level for all countries except Canada, for which the difference is significant at the 10% level. While some of the offset coefficients are nonetheless quite high,[24] Laskar measures the independence of monetary policy by a scalar A which takes account of the extent to which induced capital flows are themselves sterilized. This A indicates the fraction of a shift in the money-supply reaction function which will actually be reflected in money growth given the central bank's reaction to the induced balance of payments. Laskar's estimates of A are all significantly different from 0, and none are significantly different from 1. Thus a high degree of monetary independence is estimated for all seven nonreserve countries.

The results of both the Mark III International Transmission Model and Laskar's smaller models may be criticized as being due to some omitted channels such as that suggested by Stockman (1979) and Obstfeld (1980*b*, *c*, *d*) as described above.[25] A set of relatively model-free tests were performed, however, that confirm the results obtained from the structural models. These tests rely on the fact that in the absence of short-run

---

24. For example, the German offset coefficient of about 0.9 is as high as any of the estimates listed in Obstfeld's (1980*a*, p. 3) summary of the German evidence and higher than any of the simultaneous equation estimates, including Obstfeld's own.

25. A residual cross-correlation check for such omitted channels for the Mark III Model is reported in section 6.2. No pattern of significant correlations was found.

monetary control, movements in money-supply reaction function variables other than the current balance of payments will be uncorrelated with actual movements in the money supply. If unemployment increases, the central bank might want to increase money growth but the induced balance-of-payments deficit will dissuade it from doing so. As reported in chapter 10, the growth of the money supply is indeed dependent on these domestic policy variables in all the countries, except perhaps the Netherlands.

Taken as a whole, the evidence from this volume and the work of others can be summarized as follows: The central banks of developed nonreserve countries can exercise independent monetary control in the short run under pegged exchange rates. Induced changes in the balance of payments will deter them somewhat from deviating from the reserve country's policy, but domestic goals appear to be generally dominant in determining actual money growth.

17.3.3   The Dynamic Stability of the Bretton Woods System

The idealized Bretton Woods system survived only some fifteen years from the general restoration of dollar convertibility to the breakdown of 1971. We can now assess the weaknesses in the adjustment process which led to this dynamic instability and then consider briefly alternative means of achieving equilibrium.

The adjustment process can be described by the following salient features: (1) The evolution of American monetary and inflationary trends was determined by domestic factors with international forces playing only a transient role. (2) The proximate determinant of inflation in the nonreserve countries is to be found in their own past money-supply growth. (3) Changes in American money growth do not cause overwhelming capital flows abroad; trade-flow effects build up only as the resulting inflation shifts relative price levels. (4) These balance-of-payments flows have little or no contemporaneous effects on nonreserve money growth, although the cumulative lagged effect may be substantial.

The essence of the process is lagged adjustment to lagged adjustment to lagged adjustment. The long cumulative lag from an increase in American money growth to an increase in nonreserve inflation can explain the failure of the Bretton Woods system. Table 17.1 illustrates that the initial increase in American inflation in 1966–70 occasioned very little concurrent rise in inflation in the nonreserve countries. The cumulative effect was to shift relative price levels by some 8% since even as nonreserve money growth rates finally began to rise in response to growing balance-of-payments surpluses, their inflation rates would respond only with a lag. The large surpluses of the late 1960s and early 1970s ultimately produced sufficient money growth to surpass American inflation in 1971–75 and offset about half of the 8% change in relative price levels in

Table 17.1   **Increase in Average Continuously Compounded**
                    Inflation Rates over 1956–65 Average

		Nonreserve Countries	
Period	United States	Unad-justed	Adjusted for Exchange-Rate Changes
1966–70	2.4%	0.6%	0.9%
1971–75	4.8%	5.6%	8.7%
1966–75	3.6%	3.1%	4.8%

Source. Table 1.1.

1966–70.[26] However, the surpluses ultimately became sufficiently large to induce a speculative capital flows which destroyed the Bretton Woods system. Furthermore, a full adjustment would have required an even sharper increase in the average nonreserve inflation rate during the catch-up period.

What lessons can be drawn? First, the asset-flows channel was too weak to induce large immediate balance-of-payments effects. This may reflect more the weakness of the liquidity effect on interest rates than the unresponsiveness of asset flows to movements in interest rates.[27] Second, Humean relative-price movements do characterize the adjustment process. Third, sterilization policies did result in exaggerated balance-of-payments flows—some speculative—which ultimately caused a very rapid increase in nonreserve money growth.

Besides this adjustment process, three other means were available to reconcile short-run monetary independence with long-run equilibrium: harmonization of inflation targets, progressive changes in trade and capital barriers, and revaluations. The first of these may be viewed as an alternative means of harmonizing foreign and American inflation rates while the latter two are means of avoiding that harmonization.

If the inflation targets of the Federal Reserve System and the nonreserve central banks were in harmony, the lagged adjustment process just described might be equal to the relatively small stress implied by

26. All of the inflation rates in table 17.1 are measured relative to the corresponding 1956–65 average inflation rates. This implicitly assumes that the 1.1 to 1.6% per annum higher nonreserve inflation rates in the earlier period reflect stable trends in purchasing power parity. If we were to insist that purchasing power parity has no trend, the 42% change in exchange-rate-adjusted relative price levels from 1955 to 1975 is difficult to explain.

McKinnon (1980) argues that the comparatively rapid nonreserve money growth and inflation rates in 1970–76 contradict the view that American monetary policy caused the world inflation. He obviously overlooks that lagged adjustment in the late 1960s requires overshooting of the corresponding American rates in the catch-up period. Such catch-up periods are characteristic of dynamic models in which variables lag behind changes in the growth rates of their long-run equilibrium values.

27. See note 12 above.

random, once-and-for-all shifts in purchasing power parities. Unfortunately the strong upward trend captured in the American money-supply reaction function was not reflected in any of the nonreserve reaction functions except the Netherlands.[28] Indeed, the average nonreserve inflation rates were 3.25%, 3.96%, and 4.25% in the three quinquennia ending with 1966–70, and the final increase can be attributed to the incipient effects of increased U.S. inflation. So while the trend in American money growth brought it closer to those countries (Britain and, later, Italy) which would prefer faster money growth, it simultaneously moved it away from countries such as Germany which would prefer a lower rate of inflation. Thus the incompatible money-supply rules pursued by the reserve and nonreserve central banks put the lagged balance-of-payments adjustment system to a test beyond its powers.

Given inconsistent money-supply rules and a weak balance-of-payments adjustment mechanism, only two means were available for reconciling the cumulating inconsistencies in price levels: changes in trade and capital controls or revaluation. Of course the former may be thought of as a covert and costly version of the latter. As recounted in chapter 2, these methods were used, usually sequentially, only *in extremis*.[29] The relaxation of controls at the time of revaluations is the apparent explanation for the generally much larger coefficients on foreign prices than exchange rates in both export and import-supply equations in the Mark III Model.[30]

In summary, the balance-of-payments adjustment mechanism was too slow and too weak to reconcile money growth in the face of inconsistent central bank inflation goals. Repeated revaluations and fluctuations in controls were a politically unacceptable alternative, and thus was born the floating regime which has evolved since 1971.

17.3.4   Intervention under Floating Exchange Rates

The short sample period permits little by way of direct evidence on the operation of the floating exchange-rate system. But our evidence on monetary control under pegged exchange rates does permit us to draw

---

28. The strong upward trend in American money growth is discussed in sections 6.2 and 16.2. It accounts for an increase of about 5.7 percentage points in the annualized American money growth rate between 1956 and 1976. For five of the nonreserve countries reported in table 6.7 the coefficient of the time trend was either insignificant or negative. Taking account of implied changes in inflation (but not the balance of payments), the Italian trend would increase money growth by far more (some 19 percentage points) while the Netherlands effect is similar in magnitude (about 7 percentage points).

29. In the simple monetary approach models—e.g. Dornbusch (1976a)—devaluations (appreciations) are means to induce domestic inflations (deflations) since international parities hold continuously. On the present Humean view, such revaluations are means of short-circuiting the adjustment process so that appreciations are used to avoid faster money growth and increased inflation.

30. See tables 6.10 and 6.13.

inferences about the efficacy of the widespread practice of central bank intervention. Monetary control is possible only if shifts in the central bank's portfolio between foreign and domestic assets can affect the exchange rate consistent with a given domestic money supply and foreign variables. Otherwise, the balance of payments would increase without limit if the nonreserve central bank chose a money supply inconsistent with the parity values of interest rates and prices. Thus our evidence on short-run monetary control directly implies that (sterilized) foreign exchange intervention can affect the exchange rate for a given money supply. This analysis is pursued by Dan Lee in chapter 12 along lines initiated by Branson, Halttunen, and Masson (1977), Girton and Henderson (1976), and Henderson (1977, 1979). Conversely, Taylor (1981) has found that central banks have been consistent money losers under floating exchange rates. While Taylor stresses the destabilizing nature of central bank intervention, central banks must have had an effect in order to have destabilized. So Taylor's evidence supports the feasibility of monetary control under pegged exchange rates.

17.4 Monetary Policy and the International Monetary System

The results summarized above have important implications for two related issues: the control of inflation and the relative economic merits of various international monetary arrangements. Discussion of either question, however, is to a large extent conditional upon the answer to the other. Accordingly, we first focus very briefly on the inflation issue and then go on to consider it further within the context of our discussion of monetary standards and exchange-rate regimes.

To us, the results reported in this volume establish beyond a shadow of a doubt the essential monetary nature of the inflation experienced both in the United States and in the seven foreign countries that we and our colleagues have investigated. Special factors—oil prices, in particular—may have had some impact on the price levels in these countries, but that impact was neither continual nor substantial. Controlling inflation therefore reduces to the problem of controlling the nominal stock of money in each of these countries. Therefore the fact that inflation was not controlled is attributable to the failure of policymakers in these countries to exercise control over the nominal stocks of money. In the United States, the reserve country, that failure was largely a domestic matter: The Federal Reserve because of either ineptness or, as we consider more likely, political pressure to pursue other goals, steadily increased the longer-term rate of monetary growth over this period. In the nonreserve countries, the inability to control monetary growth over the longer term was an inherent feature of the Bretton Woods system of pegged exchange rates.[31] As we point out below, however, policymakers in some countries seemed to view that constraint differently from those in others, some apparently being content to see their domestic money stock increase with that of the United States.

Experience in the four years after our sample period ended is instructive in both regards. From the start of 1977 to the end of 1980, rates of inflation diverged fairly markedly among the countries in our sample. Japan and, to a somewhat lesser but still noticeable extent, Germany and the Netherlands have consistently had much lower rates of inflation than the United States. Two countries, Canada and France, have had approximately the same pattern of inflation as the United States while two others, Italy and the United Kingdom, have experienced considerably higher inflation. These figures are presented in table 17.2.

The experience suggests that in at least three of the seven nonreserve countries—Germany, Japan, and the Netherlands—policy in the United States was of paramount importance during our sample period. When they severed the fixed exchange-rate link, all three were able to contain inflation to a much greater extent than did the United States. Presumably, therefore, had they begun to float their exchange rates earlier, they would have avoided much of the increase in their inflation rates in 1971–75. The domestic political impetus to higher monetary growth would not have been strong.

In Italy and the United Kingdom, that most likely would not have been the case.[32] The subsequent behavior of inflation in both suggests that the high rates of monetary expansion and ensuing inflation would have occurred even in the absence of American monetary stimulus.

Canada and France are less clear-cut cases. The fact that both—Canada particularly so—have had broadly similar patterns of inflation to that of the United States since the early 1960s regardless of the exchange-rate system deprives us of a meaningful counterfactual experiment. But given the attempts of both to revalue their exchange rates vis-à-vis the United States dollar even before the formal break with Bretton Woods, we are inclined to view them also as heavily influenced by policy in the United States during our sample period.[33]

Comparison of the experience under floating rates with the experience under Bretton Woods and in its immediate aftermath suggests therefore

31. We interpret the Bretton Woods system here as prohibiting regular changes in valuations for these countries.

32. In Britain, in particular, the impetus to inflate appears to have been strong during our sample period: Darby and Stockman find that unemployment entered the Bank of England's reaction function while inflation did not.

33. The Canadian versus U.S. dollar exchange rate declined with only minor interruption in twelve quarters prior to the formal demise of fixed rates in February 1973. The franc-dollar rate underwent a similar quarterly decline beginning six quarters later in mid-1971.

Table 17.2   **Average Continuously Compounded Growth Rates
of Consumer Prices, 1977 through 1980**

	Periods[†]				
Country	1977–80	1977	1978	1979	1980
United States	9.85%	6.53%	8.71%	12.48%	11.68%
Japan	5.11%	4.70%	3.45%	5.49%	6.79%
Germany	4.12%	3.29%	2.63%	5.24%	5.31%
Netherlands	5.02%	5.09%	3.76%	4.71%	6.53%
Canada	9.28%	9.07%	8.10%	9.32%	10.62%
France	10.45%	8.60%	9.27%	11.16%	12.77%
Italy	15.15%	13.10%	10.96%	17.19%	19.36%
United Kingdom	12.37%	11.46%	8.05%	15.90%	14.08%

Source. Economics Department, Citibank, N.A.

[†]All inflation rates are computed from the quarter immediately preceding to the quarter ending the designated period. The price index used is the CPI or other index of retail prices.

that fixed exchange rates are only viable if the domestic economic policy goals of the various countries involved are in harmony over the longer run. Conversely, floating rates provide those countries with the degree of freedom necessary to pursue different goals.

In this respect, the breakdown of Bretton Woods is almost a mirror image of the collapse of the gold standard in the early 1930s. In the thirties, many countries abandoned the fixed-rate gold standard because they did not want to import a further contraction in output from the United States. In the seventies, many countries abandoned the fixed-rate dollar standard because they did not want to import American inflation.[34] In both instances, the moves away from fixed and toward flexible rates successfully provided the countries making these changes with insulation from foreign disturbances. That fact, in and of itself, provides an additional bit of evidence corroborating our findings.[35]

34. An additional inflation-related factor, as Klein (1978) points out, may have been the decrease in the predictability of the longer-term United States inflation rate during these years that accompanied the increase in the average rate of inflation.

35. Writing shortly after the fact, Irving Fisher (1935) used the differences in the behavior of output abroad relative to that in the United States under the two different international monetary standards as a test of the hypothesis that the Depression was in the main engendered by money. In the seventies, the differences in the patterns of inflation under fixed and floating rate regimes provide an additional test in favor of the hypotheses we have advanced to explain inflation during our sample period.

Interestingly, Fisher's analysis is based, in modern terms, on a "Lucas" (price-level innovation) aggregate-supply curve and either "a law of one price level" or a Humean specie-flow mechanism for countries linked by fixed exchange rates. (It is unclear in this presentation whether Fisher contemplates a price arbitrage or monetary transmission, but the latter is used in Fisher 1920 cited here.) It appears from his charts that somewhat better explanatory power would have been obtained by concentrating on money flows and a

Why monetary growth in the United States increased and why some other countries were apparently content to accept if not add to the inflationary consequences of that monetary growth are the ultimate questions. Attempting to answer them would draw us far afield from this study. The burgeoning literature in the field of public choice and the related studies of regulation point to directions in which to search. Both suggest that political considerations that make inflation desirable to government policymakers and other officials are the root cause. How to quantify those returns from inflationary monetary policies, how to juxtapose them in a quantifiable way against the costs, not to mention what role ideas play in the process, are all crucial questions that at this juncture appear to us unanswerable.

The Federal Reserve System has operated under a legislative mandate as well as more subtle political pressure to weigh a variety of goals in formulating monetary policy. It is our judgment that this process is inconsistent with achieving price stability. Indeed we see no effective means of controlling inflation in the absence of the birth of a political consensus in support of an effective monetary constitution. Such a constitution might enforce single-minded pursuit of price stability by establishing a prespecified growth path for money and requiring the Federal Reserve System to continuously maintain money within 1% of that path; adoption of a fixed gold or other commodity standard would also serve.[36] In any case, it is important that the standard—whether fiat or commodity—be understandable and proof against well-meaning tinkering. Otherwise this monetary constitution—like other constitutional provisions and monetary standards in the past—might fail with no explicit repeal until long after the fact.

Had the Federal Reserve System been constrained by such a rule in the postwar period, we believe that the United States—and many other countries—would have been spared much of the economic loss that high and variable inflation and the periodic half-hearted attempts to check it have brought. As Leijonhufvud (1980) has persuasively argued, an appropriate monetary reform or transitional procedure could minimize or eliminate the transitional unemployment costs of ending the inflation

---

"Barro" (money-supply innovation) real-income equation, but the movements are large enough that either chain works.

A more recent statement of this hypothesis together with supporting empirical evidence virtually identical to Fisher's is Choudhri and Kochin (1980). Lothian (1981) contains a similar discussion of the interwar U.K. evidence.

36. We do not wish to suggest that a commodity standard would serve equally well in the short run. Shifts in gold's relative price might be a potent source of short-run instability and occur due to both monetary and nonmonetary factors. Nonetheless, over long periods of time the *average* inflation rate converges to 0 under a gold standard with a constant mint ratio.

within the context of a believable political consensus enforcing the new monetary constitution.[37]

For the United States, fixing an exchange rate with another country is not a viable basis for a monetary constitution. Other countries do have this option as well as the options open to the United States.[38] As the Bretton Woods system indicated, this option fails as a control on inflation if the reserve country itself lacks an effective monetary constitution or if there is insufficient feedback of reserve flows on the domestic money supply.

17.5 Areas for Future Research

At the end of a project like that described in this volume, researchers find it hard to be satisfied with what has been accomplished rather than troubled by all the questions which would have been studied had there been but time, money, and energy enough. The knowledge that any science develops in small increments and no one person or group can make more than a marginal contribution rings hollow against the wish to have done more. By way of exorcism for these futile wishes, we like our predecessors list the issues that we think particularly deserve further study.

The most obvious next step would be to extend our data bank and link it directly with currently available national data sources. Lothian is currently making efforts along these lines. When the extended data set becomes available, it will be possible to reestimate both the Mark III and Mark IV Models and a number of other relations applicable to the floating rate period. In particular, data for 1979–80 may permit much sharper estimates of the effects of changes in the real price of oil.

Daniel Laskar's work introduced a number of sophisticated approaches to the formulation of money-supply reaction functions. Those are well worth developing and applying to other data sets.

Stockman (1979) and Obstfeld (1980b, c, d) have shown that monetary control under pegged exchange rates need not obtain even if bonds are imperfect substitutes internationally. Although some of our tests apparently reject their ultrarationality postulate, it would be interesting

---

37. Feldstein (1979) has recently observed that these unemployment costs must be weighed against the very large present value of the benefits. Since the costs of inflation tend to grow with real income, their present value is much larger than might appear from previous estimates of relatively small annual cost. Since he analyzes a permanent reduction in inflation, Feldstein too must implicitly anticipate a monetary constitution which would prevent repetition of our past mistakes.

38. With the understanding, of course, that choosing a monetary constitution is simultaneously choosing an exchange-rate regime.

to see whether private-capital-flow functions do indeed shift in a partial if incomplete manner in response to sterilized foreign exchange operations.

Substitution in demand for domestic money by foreign money and foreign assets did not appear to be important in the tests we conducted. Some other economists have reported conflicting results. Further work is required to reconcile these differences.

The behavior of exchange rates in the floating period remains largely unexplained. However, Dan Lee's integration of the information set used in forming inflationary and exchange-rate expectations seems to be a valuable starting point. This approach is pursued to some extent in the expectational functions of the Mark III and Mark IV Models, but much remains to be done. Such an approach suggests that with consistent expectations in the bond and foreign exchange markets, a money shock will initially affect the exchange rate by an amount equal to the integral of the induced deviations between the domestic and foreign real interest rates.

Except for the United States, the Barroesque real-income equation did relatively poor and added little if anything to the explanatory power of short distributed lags on the actual changes in aggregate-demand variables. An errors-in-the-variables argument is capable of explaining the results numerically, but the weak evidence suggests the value of further research.

Finally, we propose an examination of the political economy of alternative monetary systems. This work has already begun, but is only at the earliest stage of development at present.[39] Given the probability that action to change the existing system will be taken in the near future whether in ignorance or not, the potential value of research here is great indeed.

Besides these major areas for further research, a number of additional topics have been suggested in the individual chapters. Furthermore, it is all too likely that the most important leads eluded our notice. We only hope that, if that be the case, our readers will correct our oversight as well as our other errors.

Acknowledgments

The authors have benefited in drafting this chapter from conversations with the other contributors to this volume but are solely responsible for opinions expressed here.

---

39. Willett and Mullen (1982) contribute not only new insights but a careful review of this literature.

References

Argy, V., and P. J. K. Kouri. 1974. Sterilization policies and the volatility in international reserves. In R. Z. Aliber, ed., *National monetary policies and the international financial system*. Chicago: University of Chicago Press.

Bilson, J. F. O., and J. A. Frenkel. 1979. Dynamic adjustment and the demand for international reserves. NBER Working Paper, no. 407, November.

Bordo, M. D., and E. U. Choudhri. 1982. Currency substitution and the demand for money: Some evidence for Canada. *Journal of Money, Credit and Banking* 14 (February): 48–57.

Branson, W. H. 1968. *Financial capital flows in the U.S. balance of payments*. Amsterdam: North-Holland.

———. 1970. Monetary policy and the new view of international capital movements. *Brookings Papers on Economic Activity*, no. 2, pp. 235–62.

Branson, W. H., and H. Halttunen; and P. Masson. 1977. Exchange rates in the short run. *European Economic Review* 10 (December): 303–24.

Brittain, B. 1981. International currency substitution and the apparent instability of velocity in some Western European economies and in the United States. *Journal of Money, Credit and Banking* 13 (May): 135–55.

Bruno, M., and J. Sachs. 1979. Supply versus demand approaches to the problem of stagflation. NBER Working Paper, no. 382, August.

Carr, J., and M. R. Darby. 1981. The role of money supply shocks in the short-run demand for money. *Journal of Monetary Economics* 8 (September): 183–99.

Chetty, V. K. 1969. On measuring the nearness of near monies. *American Economic Review* 59 (June): 270–81.

Choudhri, E. U., and L. A. Kochin. 1980. The exchange rate and the international transmission of business cycle disturbances: Some evidence from the Great Depression. *Journal of Money, Credit and Banking* 12 (November): 565–74.

Connolly, M., and D. Taylor. 1979. Exchange rate changes and neutralization: A test of the monetary approach applied to developed and developing countries. *Economica* 46 (August): 281–94.

Darby, M. R. 1979. The NBER International Transmission Model: The Mark II disequilibrium version, estimates, and lessons. In *Proceedings of 1978 West Coast Academic/Federal Reserve Economic Research Seminar*. San Francisco: Federal Reserve Bank of San Francisco.

———. 1980. The monetary approach to the balance of payments: Two specious assumptions. *Economic Inquiry* 18 (April): 321–26.

Dornbusch, R. 1976a. Devaluation, money, and non-traded goods. In J. A. Frenkel and H. G. Johnson, eds., *The monetary approach to the balance of payments*. Toronto: University of Toronto Press.

————. 1976b. Expectations and exchange rate dynamics. *Journal of Political Economy* 84 (December): 1161–76.

Fausten, D. K. 1979. The Humean origin of the contemporary monetary approach to the balance of payments. *Quarterly Journal of Economics* 93 (November): 655–73.

Feldstein, M. S. 1979. The welfare cost of permanent inflation and the optimal short-run economic policy. *Journal of Political Economy* 87 (August): 749–68.

Fisher, I. 1920. *Stabilizing the dollar: A plan to stabilize the general price level without fixing individual prices*. New York: Macmillan.

————. 1935. Are booms and depressions transmitted internationally through monetary standards? *Bulletin of the International Statistical Institute* 28: 1–29.

Frenkel, J. A. 1980a. The demand for international reserves under pegged and flexible exchange rate regimes and aspects of the economics of managed float. In D. Bigman and T. Taya, eds., *The functioning of floating exchange rates: Theory, evidence, and policy implications*. Cambridge, Mass.: Ballinger.

————. 1980b. Flexible exchange rates in the 1970's. NBER Working Paper, no. 450, February.

————. 1980c. The collapse of purchasing power parities during the 1970's. NBER Working Paper, no. 569, October.

Frenkel, J. A., and H. G. Johnson. 1976. The monetary approach to the balance of payments: Essential concepts and historical origins. In J. A. Frenkel and H. G. Johnson, eds., *The monetary approach to the balance of payments*. Toronto: University of Toronto Press.

Fried, E. R., and C. L. Schultze, eds. 1975. *Higher oil prices and the world economy: The adjustment problem*. Washington: Brookings Institution.

Gaillot, H. J. 1970. Purchasing power parity as an explanation of long-term changes in exchange rates. *Journal of Money, Credit and Banking* 2 (August): 348–57.

Genberg, A. H. 1976. Aspects of the monetary approach to balance-of-payments theory: An empirical study of Sweden. In J. A. Frenkel and H. G. Johnson, eds., *The monetary approach to the balance of payments*. Toronto: University of Toronto Press.

Girton, L., and D. W. Henderson. 1976. Financial capital movements and central bank behavior in a two-country, short-run portfolio balance model. *Journal of Monetary Economics* 2 (January): 33–61.

Gordon, R. J. 1977. World inflation and monetary accommodation in eight countries. *Brookings Papers on Economic Activity*, no. 2, pp. 409–68.

Hamburger, M. J. 1977. The demand for money in an open economy: Germany and the United Kingdom. *Journal of Monetary Economics* 3 (January): 25–40.

Heller, H. R., and M. S. Khan. 1978. The demand for international reserves under fixed and floating exchange rates. *International Monetary Fund Staff Papers* 25 (December): 623–49.

Heller, H. R., and M. Knight. 1978. *Reserve-currency preferences of central banks*, Essays in International Finance no. 131. Princeton: International Finance Section, Department of Economics, Princeton University.

Henderson, D. W. 1977. Modeling the interdependence of national money and capital markets. *American Economic Review* 67 (February): 190–99.

———. 1979. The dynamic effects of exchange market intervention policy: Two extreme views and a synthesis. Board of Governors of the Federal Reserve System, International Finance Discussion Paper no. 142, June.

Herring, R. J., and R. C. Marston. 1977. *National monetary policies and international financial markets*. Amsterdam: North-Holland.

Hilliard, B. C. 1979. Exchange flows and the gilt-edged security market: A causality study. Bank of England, Discussion Paper no. 2, February.

Isard, P. 1977. How far can we push the "law of one price?" *American Economic Review* 67 (December): 942–48.

Johnson, H. 1976. The monetary approach to balance-of-payments theory. In J. A. Frenkel and H. G. Johnson, eds., *The monetary approach to the balance of payments*. Toronto: University of Toronto Press.

Kaldor, N. 1976. Inflation and recession in the world economy. *Economic Journal* 86 (December): 703–14.

Klein, B. 1978. Competing monies, European Monetary Union, and the dollar. In M. Fratianni and T. Peeters, eds, *One money for Europe*. New York: Praeger.

Kouri, P. J. K., and M. G. Porter. 1974. International capital flows and portfolio equilibrium. *Journal of Political Economy* 82 (May/June): 443–67.

Kravis, I. B., A. W. Heston; and R. Summers. 1978. Real GDP per capita for more than one hundred countries. *Economic Journal* 88 (June): 215–42.

Kravis, I. B., and R. E. Lipsey. 1977. Export prices and the transmission of inflation. *American Economic Review* 67 (February): 155–63.

———. 1978. Price behavior in the light of balance of payments theories. *Journal of International Economics* 8 (May): 193–246.

Laffer, A. B. 1975. The phenomenon of worldwide inflation: A study in international market integration. In D. I. Meiselman and A. B. Laffer, eds., *The phenomenon of worldwide inflation*. Washington: American Enterprise Institute for Public Policy Research.

Laidler, D. E. W., and J. M. Parkin. 1975. Inflation: A survey. *Economic Journal* 85 (December): 741–809.

Lawrence, R. Z. 1979. Within and between-country variances in inflation rates. *Journal of Monetary Economics* 5 (January): 145–52.

Leijonhufvud, A. 1980. Theories of stagflation. *Revue de l'Association Francaise de Finance* 2 (December): 185–201.

Lothian, J. R. 1981. Comments on "monetarist interpretations of the Great Depression." In K. Brunner, ed., *The Great Depression revisited*. Boston: Martinus Nijhoff.

McKinnon, R. I. 1980. Review of *Inflation, exchange rates, and the world economy: Lectures on international monetary economics*, by W. M. Corden. *Journal of Political Economy* 88 (October): 1058–61.

Meiselman, D. I. 1975. Worldwide inflation: A monetarist view. In D. I. Meiselman and A. B. Laffer, eds., *The phenomenon of worldwide inflation*. Washington: American Enterprise Institute for Public Policy Research.

Miles, M. A. 1978. Currency substitution, flexible exchange rates, and monetary interdependence. *American Economic Review* 68 (June): 428–36.

Mussa, M. 1976. Tariffs and the balance of payments: A monetary approach. In J. A. Frenkel and H. G. Johnson, eds., *The monetary approach to the balance of payments*. Toronto: University of Toronto Press.

———. 1979. Empirical regularities in the behavior of exchange rates and theories of the foreign exchange market. In K. Brunner and A. H. Meltzer, eds., *Policies for employment, prices, and exchange rates*. Carnegie-Rochester Conference Series on Public Policy, vol. 11. Amsterdam: North-Holland.

Obstfeld, M. 1980*a*. Sterilization and the offsetting capital movements: Evidence from West Germany, 1960–1970. NBER Working Paper, no. 494, June.

———. 1980*b*. The capitalization of income streams and the effects of open-market policy under fixed exchange rates. NBER Working Paper, no. 528, August.

———. 1980*c*. Capital mobility and devaluation in an optimizing model with rational expectations. NBER Working Paper, no. 557, October.

———. 1980*d*. Macroeconomic policy, exchange-rate dynamics, and optimal asset accumulation. NBER Working Paper, no. 599. December.

Perry, G. L. 1975. Determinants of wage inflation around the world. *Brookings Papers on Economic Activity*, no. 2, pp. 403–35.

————. 1980. Inflation in theory and practice. *Brookings Papers on Economic Activity*, no. 1, pp. 207–41.

Price, W. J. 1978. Time series analysis of money supply reaction functions: International evidence. Ph.D. dissertation, UCLA.

Richardson, J. D. 1978. Some empirical evidence on commodity arbitrage and the law of one price. *Journal of International Economics* 8 (May): 341–51.

Stockman, A. C. 1979. Monetary control and sterilization under pegged exchange rates. University of Rochester, Department of Economics, Xerox, August.

————. 1980. A theory of exchange rate determination. *Journal of Political Economy* 88 (August): 673–98.

Taylor, D. 1981. Official intervention in the foreign exchange market; or, Bet against the central bank. Department of Economics, UCLA, unpublished, March.

Tooke, T., and W. Newmarch. 1928 (originally published 1857). *A history of prices and of the state of the circulation from 1792 to 1856*, vol. 6. London: P. S. King & Son.

Whitman, M. v. n. 1975. Global monetarism and the monetary approach to the balance of payments. *Brookings Papers on Economic Activity*, no. 3, pp. 491–536.

Willett, T. D., and J. Mullen. 1982. The discipline debate and inflationary biases under alternative exchange-rate systems. In R. Lombra and W. Witte, eds., *The political economy of domestic and international monetary relations*. Ames: Iowa State University Press.

Data Appendix

James R. Lothian with the assistance of
Anthony Cassese and Laura Nowak

Note: For most series, we provide both seasonally adjusted and original (non–seasonally adjusted) data, denoted respectively by the letters S and N in the sixth place of the variable's name.

Laura Nowak is an assistant professor at Fordham University, Lincoln Center.

Sources and Notes on Time Series for Canada

The primary source for the Canadian data was the computer tapes of Statistics Canada, the CANSIM data base, from Data Resources Incorporated. Most of these series are also published in the Bank of Canada *Review*. Table and series numbers from that publication are listed below.

I. INTERNATIONAL VARIABLES

A. *Balance of Payments*

    CABPQNCC   Balance of Payments. Unit: Billions of Canadian Dollars at
    CABPQSCC   Quarterly Rates.

Source: From our own estimates based on official international reserve asset data (II.D below).

Description: The official settlements balance of payments was derived as a one-quarter change in official reserve asset holdings with an increase denoted by a positive value corresponding to an overall surplus on international accounts.

B. *Exports*

 1. Total Exports

    CAEXQNTL   Total Exports. Unit: Billions of Canadian Dollars at
    CAEXQSTL   Annual Rates.

Source: From Bank of Canada *Review*, table 70, entitled "Canadian Balance of International Payments: Current Account," series *D50525*, various issues.

Description: The balance-of-payments current account total of receipts from exports of merchandise, services, and transfers. The data were originally in millions of Canadian dollars at quarterly rates.

 2. Exports of Goods

    CAEXQNGO   Exports of Goods. Unit: Billions of Canadian Dollars at
    CAEXQSGO   Annual Rates.

Source: Same as I.B.1., series *D50501*.

Description: The balance-of-payments current account total of receipts from exports of merchandise. The data were originally in millions of Canadian dollars at quarterly rates.

C. *Imports*
1. Total Imports
     CAIMQNTL   Total Imports. Unit: Billions of Canadian Dollars at
     CAIMQSTL   Annual Rates.
Source: Same as I.B.1., series *D50550.*
Description: The balance-of-payments current account total payments for imports of merchandise, services, and transfers. The data were originally in millions of Canadian dollars at quarterly rates.
2. Imports of Goods
     CAIMQNGO   Imports of Goods. Unit: Billions of Canadian Dollars at
     CAIMQSGO   Annual Rates.
Source: Same as I.B.1., series *D50526.*
Description: The balance-of-payments current account total of receipts from imports of merchandise. The data were originally in millions of Canadian dollars at quarterly rates.
D. *Net Capital Outflows*
     CAKPQNCC   Net Capital Outflows. Unit: Billions of Canadian Dollars at
     CAKPQSCC   Annual Rates.
Source: From Bank of Canada *Review*, table 68, entitled, "Canadian Balance of Payments: Summary," series *D50689.*
Description: The balance of total—short- and long-term—capital transactions including the balancing item, with net capital exports defined positive.

Note that these figures are for net *total* capital outflows; i.e. they include capital outflows from and inflows to the government sector. There appear to be no data on short-term capital inflows, at least as the capital account is presented in the Bank of Canada *Review* in its more disaggregated form in table 71. It would be possible, however, to exclude long-term government capital flows on the basis of this table. The data were originally in millions of Canadian dollars at quarterly rates.

E. *Exchange Rate*
     CAXRQNSP   Exchange Rate. Unit: Canadian Dollars per U.S. Dollar.
Source: From Bank of Canada *Review*, table 65, entitled "Exchange Rates," series *B3400.*
Description: The data are quarterly averages of the monthly averages of daily (noon) spot rates in the Canadian interbank market.

II. FINANCIAL VARIABLES
A. *Narrow Money Stock*
     CAM1QNCC   Narrow Money Stock (M1). Unit: Billions of Canadian
     CAM1QSCC   Dollars, Quarter's Average.
Source: From Bank of Canada *Review*, table 14, entitled "Currency outside Banks and Chartered Bank Deposits," series *B2001* and *B459.*
Description: M1, currency held by the (nonbank) public (B2001) plus adjusted Canadian dollars demand deposits of chartered bank (B459).

Currency consists of Bank of Canada notes and coin in circulation. Holdings of notes are calculated by the Bank of Canada by subtracting from the total amount outstanding the amount held by the chartered banks. The amount of coin in circulation outside banks is total coin outstanding, as reported by the Royal Mint, less coin held by chartered banks and the Bank of Canada. The underlying note data are weekly, and the underlying coin data monthly. The data were originally monthly averages of Wednesday figures in millions of Canadian dollars.

B. *Broader Money Stock (M2)*

CAM2QNQA   Broader Money Stock (M2). Unit: Billions of Canadian
CAM2QSQA   Dollars, Quarter's Average.

Source: Same as II.A., series *B2001, B451, B455, B459.*

Description: M2, the sum of M1 (B2001 plus B459) plus Canadian dollar-denominated personal savings deposits at chartered banks (B451) and Canadian dollar-denominated nonpersonal term and notice deposits of chartered banks (B455). The data were originally monthly averages of Wednesday figures in millions of Canadian dollars.

C. *High-Powered Money*

CAMHQNCC   High-Powered Money. Unit: Billions of Canadian Dollars,
CAMHQSCC   Quarter's Average.

Source: From Bank of Canada *Review*, table 4, entitled "Bank of Canada: Weekly Series," series *B52* and *B53*; *Review*, table 14, series *B2001*; and unpublished statistics of the Bank of Canada.

Description: The sum of currency held by the public (B2001), notes held by chartered banks (B52), coin held by chartered banks, and deposits of chartered banks at the Bank of Canada (B53).

Notes held by chartered banks and chartered bank deposits at the Bank of Canada are monthly averages of weekly data published by the Bank of Canada that we converted to a quarterly basis. Coin held by chartered banks is unpublished monthly data that we obtained directly from the Bank and converted to quarterly averages. The data were originally in millions of Canadian dollars.

D. *Official International Reserve Assets*

CAFHQNSD   Official International Reserve Assets. Unit: Billions of
CAFHQSSD   Canadian Dollars, End-of-Quarter.

Source: From Bank of Canada *Review*, table 67, entitled "Canada's Official International Reserves," series *B3801, B3802, B3803*, and *B3804.*

Description: Official holdings of convertible currencies, gold, and SDRs.

The Canadian holdings of convertible foreign currencies are broken down in the source tables into holdings of U.S. dollars (B3801) and holdings of other foreign currencies (B3802). Both are given in billions of U.S. dollars and are on a monthly basis. They are aggregates of the separate holdings of the Exchange Fund Account, the Receiver General for Canada, and the Bank of Canada.

Canadian holdings of gold and of SDRs (B3803 and B3804, respectively) are denominated in U.S. dollars. Note that prior to May 1972 gold was valued at slightly less than the official price in the reported data. The reason given for the undervaluation was to reflect potential transportation costs of international gold movements. Beginning in May 1972 gold was revalued to the official price, which raised the U.S. dollar value of gold holdings approximately $2.5 billion.

E. *Interest Rates*

1. Short-Term

CARSQNTB   Short-Term Interest Rate. Unit: Decimal Rate per Annum.

Source: From Bank of Canada *Review*, table 20, entitled "Selected Canadian and International Interest Rates," series *B14007.*

Description: Three-month treasury bill rate, average yield of the weekly tender on the Thursday following the last Wednesday of each month. Monthly observations coverted to quarterly data, were originally expressed in per cent per annum.

  2. Long-Term

    CARLQNCC   Long-Term Interest Rate. Unit: Decimal Rate per Annum.

Source: Same as II.E.1., series *B14013*.

Description: Average yields on government of Canada securities with maturities of ten years or more. Average yields are calculated from Wednesday mid-market closing prices of the last Wednesday of each month. Monthly observations, converted to quarterly data, were originally expressed in percent per annum.

III. NONFINANCIAL DOMESTIC VARIABLES

A. *National Product*

  1. Nominal Gross National Product

    CAYNQNCA   Gross National Product in Current Market Prices. Unit:

    CAYNQSCA   Billions of Canadian Dollars at Annual Rates.

Source: For 1955–74 from Statistics Canada, *National Income and Expenditure Accounts, vol. 2, The Quarterly Estimates, 1947–1974*, table 2, February 1976; for 1975–76 from Statistics Canada, *National Income and Expenditure Accounts*, table 2, various issues.

Description: This measures the final expenditures on goods and services in current market prices, equivalent to the total income and product of residents including net factor income from abroad. The data was originally in millions of Canadian dollars at quarterly rates.

  2. Real Gross National Product

    CAYRQN70   Gross National Product in 1970 Market Prices. Unit: Bil-

    CAYRQS70   lions of Canadian Dollars at Annual Rates.

Source: Same as III.A.1., table 10.

Description: This measures final expenditures on goods and services in 1970 market prices, equivalent to the total income and product of residents including net factor income from abroad. The data were originally in millions of Canadian dollars at quarterly rates and in 1971 market prices.

B. *Prices*

  1. Implicit Price Deflator

    CAPDQN70   GNP Implicit Price Deflator. Unit: 1970 = 1.00.

    CAPDQS70

Source: See III.A.1. and III.A.2. above.

Description: Derived as the ratio of nominal GNP to real GNP described above.

  2. Consumer Prices

    CAPCQN70   Consumer Price Index. Unit: 1970 = 1.00.

    CAPCQS70

Source: Bank of Canada *Review*, table 62, entitled "Consumer Price Index," series *D616101*.

Description: A general index of consumer prices covering all items. The data are quarterly averages of monthly averages. The data were originally in percent form with 1971 = 100.

C. *Industrial Production*

    CAIPQS70   Index of Industrial Production. Unit: 1970 = 1.00.

Source: Bank of Canada *Review*, table 64, entitled "Other Economic Indicators," series *D100657*.

Description: A general index of industrial production including mining, manufacturing, and utilities but excluding construction.

The Canadian industrial production data contain a break in 1975. The earlier series with a 1961 base covers the period 1947:1 to 1975:3. The later series with a 1971 base begins in 1971. To combine the two we adjusted the first series by multiplying by the average of the ratios of the overlapping observations in 1975. We then rebased the series to 1970 = 1.00. The data were originally given in seasonally adjusted monthly form.

D. *Government Accounts*
 1. Government Expenditure
     CAGXQNEX   Federal Government Expenditure. Unit: Billions of Cana-
     CAGXQSEX   dian Dollars at Annual Rates.
Source: For 1955–74 from Statistics Canada, *National Income and Expenditure Accounts*, vol. 2, *The Quarterly Estimates, 1947–1974*, table 6; for 1975–76 from Statistics Canada, *National Income and Expenditure Accounts*, table 6, various issues.
Description: The total current expenditure by the federal government including capital consumption allowance. The data were originally in millions of Canadian dollars at quarterly rates.
 2. Government Deficit
     CAGDQNDF   Federal Government Deficit. Unit: Billions of Canadian
     CAGDQSDF   Dollars at Annual Rates.
Source: Same as III.D.1.
Description: The federal government deficit defined as a negative value. The data were originally in millions of Canadian dollars at quarterly rates.
E. *Population*
     CAPPQNIN   Population. Unit: Billions of Persons.
Source: From United Nations *Demographic Yearbooks*, various issues, and International Monetary Fund *International Financial Statistics*, 1977 Supplement.
Description: Total population estimated by straight-line interpolation from mid-year estimates.
F. *Unemployment Rate*
     CAURQN14   Unemployment Rate. Unit: Decimal Rate.
     CAURQS14
Source: Bank of Canada *Review*, table 57, entitled "Labour Force Status of Population," series *D767289*, various issues.
Description: Ratio of unemployed persons to civilian labor force fifteen years of age and over. The data were originally in percent form.

List of Tables for Canada (Quarterly Data)

CANADA_CABPQNCC

1955	1	-0.027870	0.033924	0.039779	-0.017923
1956	1	-0.016824	-0.003309	-0.012490	0.004605
1957	1	-0.018272	-0.004202	0.003799	-0.021938
1958	1	0.004128	0.006741	0.018866	0.012669
1959	1	-0.030418	0.012440	-0.009007	-0.064087
1960	1	-0.005525	-0.029812	0.036642	0.024612
1961	1	0.100459	0.057730	0.062154	0.152600
1962	1	-0.279141	-0.125103	0.722593	0.307132
1963	1	0.038203	0.078745	-0.184167	0.087354
1964	1	-0.070441	-0.026299	0.069087	0.121947
1965	1	-0.072413	-0.111175	0.052390	0.093076
1966	1	-0.128312	-0.142338	-0.141369	-0.036655
1967	1	-0.026178	-0.027777	0.004675	0.087053
1968	1	0.042366	0.286975	-0.053475	0.137156
1969	1	0.159041	-0.094207	-0.167165	0.050998
1970	1	0.187247	0.616521	0.236970	0.053055
1971	1	-0.005265	0.122407	0.260907	0.318916
1972	1	0.262309	0.257089	0.136200	-0.076759
1973	1	-0.059394	-0.072529	-0.248713	0.026465
1974	1	0.196462	0.059069	-0.237512	-0.177666
1975	1	-0.030877	-0.367719	-0.174453	0.090659
1976	1	0.335527	-0.019894	-0.275907	-0.169808

CANADA_CABPQSCC

1955	1	-0.015005	0.024890	0.030033	-0.012082
1956	1	-0.003742	-0.012427	-0.022412	0.011095
1957	1	-0.007290	-0.009746	-0.008722	-0.015462
1958	1	0.013440	0.008081	0.003740	0.008449
1959	1	-0.012685	0.024133	-0.032359	-0.085434
1960	1	0.031507	-0.014768	0.013306	-0.023922
1961	1	0.160977	0.077526	0.037692	0.080734
1962	1	-0.202496	-0.100367	0.703959	0.210666
1963	1	0.126689	0.109914	-0.202606	-0.014440
1964	1	0.013453	0.005748	0.060228	0.023532
1965	1	-0.003002	-0.083093	0.053583	0.015300
1966	1	-0.089151	-0.118804	-0.124865	-0.098348
1967	1	-0.004237	-0.020886	0.032891	0.048267
1968	1	0.049477	0.275716	-0.015800	0.114814
1969	1	0.164258	-0.125992	-0.127152	0.048740
1970	1	0.184377	0.576425	0.277624	0.062619
1971	1	-0.014004	0.073363	0.310340	0.338166
1972	1	0.231849	0.212165	0.203670	-0.056993
1973	1	-0.120147	-0.108471	-0.155903	0.045611
1974	1	0.096492	0.037912	-0.116244	-0.166430
1975	1	-0.161227	-0.377629	-0.032504	0.095447
1976	1	0.188959	-0.023495	-0.124856	-0.171365

CANADA_CAEXQNTL

1955	1	4.9560	5.8320	6.4120	6.1600
1956	1	5.4800	6.6200	7.0040	6.6760
1957	1	5.7560	6.4160	7.1640	6.6160
1958	1	5.5800	6.5280	6.7160	6.7880
1959	1	5.4760	7.0120	7.2240	7.4000
1960	1	6.4880	6.9320	7.7920	7.2400
1961	1	6.5320	7.6520	8.6600	8.3560
1962	1	7.0760	8.5080	9.1520	8.9600
1963	1	7.5760	9.1800	10.0320	10.2720
1964	1	8.7400	11.0920	11.8560	11.1840
1965	1	9.3040	11.2960	12.6280	12.5000
1966	1	11.1240	13.2760	14.7040	14.2240
1967	1	12.9080	15.6920	15.8960	15.4000
1968	1	14.6760	17.5760	17.9360	17.9040
1969	1	17.0800	19.5440	19.4960	20.2400
1970	1	19.4360	22.7680	22.0480	21.9200
1971	1	19.8560	23.5000	23.4080	23.7120
1972	1	21.2560	26.4280	24.4760	28.0000
1973	1	27.1480	32.3840	30.3600	35.1280
1974	1	33.6040	41.0080	40.8320	42.8960
1975	1	36.3120	43.5640	40.7320	43.4080
1976	1	40.6760	49.0080	47.1320	47.7720

CANADA_CAEXQSTL

1955	1	5.6451	5.7613	5.9213	5.9935
1956	1	6.2545	6.5227	6.4908	6.4790
1957	1	6.5688	6.3224	6.6542	6.4067
1958	1	6.3581	6.4513	6.2356	6.5671
1959	1	6.2308	6.9483	6.7024	7.1478
1960	1	7.3942	6.8719	7.2220	6.9893
1961	1	7.4631	7.5813	8.0097	8.0725
1962	1	8.1129	8.4134	8.4469	8.6703
1963	1	8.7153	9.0421	9.2586	9.9621
1964	1	10.0775	10.8477	10.9811	10.8968
1965	1	10.6807	10.9846	11.7492	12.2697
1966	1	12.6516	12.8317	13.7884	14.0635
1967	1	14.5045	15.0771	15.0660	15.2951
1968	1	16.3124	16.7860	17.2135	17.8014
1969	1	18.8160	18.5796	18.9458	20.0707
1970	1	21.2897	21.5728	21.6775	21.6257
1971	1	21.6688	22.2438	23.2217	23.2453
1972	1	23.1922	24.9781	24.4470	27.3087
1973	1	29.6417	30.5732	30.4445	34.1574
1974	1	36.7273	38.6620	41.0446	41.6601
1975	1	39.6945	41.0657	40.9451	42.1548
1976	1	44.4805	46.2050	47.3501	46.3995

CANADA_CAEXQNGO

1955	1	3.8680	4.3920	4.5080	4.5600
1956	1	4.2040	5.0480	4.9880	5.1080
1957	1	4.3960	4.8520	5.2120	5.1160
1958	1	4.3400	5.1120	4.8800	5.2280
1959	1	4.2400	5.4200	5.1440	5.8000
1960	1	5.1240	5.2840	5.5920	5.5680
1961	1	5.0640	5.7880	6.2280	6.4760
1962	1	5.6000	6.4960	6.5280	6.9240
1963	1	5.9440	7.1040	7.2240	8.0560
1964	1	6.9200	8.7920	8.7280	8.5120
1965	1	7.3040	8.7640	9.0520	9.8600
1966	1	8.8920	10.4080	10.7800	11.2240
1967	1	10.3840	12.0120	10.7640	12.1920
1968	1	12.0680	14.1280	13.2840	14.6680
1969	1	14.0160	15.4560	14.3160	16.3680
1970	1	15.8320	18.0800	16.2760	17.4960
1971	1	16.3280	18.6960	17.4400	19.0440
1972	1	17.6760	21.4720	18.3360	23.0320
1973	1	22.7200	26.4680	23.3120	29.3440
1974	1	28.5000	33.6920	32.2360	35.9360
1975	1	30.3440	35.5560	31.4960	35.9920
1976	1	34.3200	40.3840	37.1560	40.0400

CANADA_CAEXQSGO

1955	1	4.2928	4.2858	4.3629	4.3755
1956	1	4.6783	4.9102	4.8497	4.8837
1957	1	4.8952	4.7179	5.0880	4.8713
1958	1	4.8255	4.9880	4.7687	4.9665
1959	1	4.7018	5.3074	5.0315	5.4962
1960	1	5.6792	5.1804	5.4711	5.2770
1961	1	5.6103	5.6724	6.0840	6.1539
1962	1	6.2101	6.3484	6.3677	6.6046
1963	1	6.6017	6.9030	7.0567	7.7124
1964	1	7.6918	8.4658	8.5872	8.1816
1965	1	8.0690	8.3878	8.9798	9.5319
1966	1	9.7112	9.9128	10.8222	10.8930
1967	1	11.1924	11.3975	10.9484	11.8567
1968	1	12.8579	13.3579	13.6889	14.2640
1969	1	14.8054	14.5776	14.9051	15.8926
1970	1	16.6405	17.0219	17.0938	16.9186
1971	1	17.1324	17.6038	18.4069	18.3215
1972	1	18.5865	20.2059	19.4114	22.0590
1973	1	23.9651	24.9046	24.6891	28.0238
1974	1	30.1647	31.6796	34.1358	34.2683
1975	1	32.1828	33.4510	33.2816	34.3206
1976	1	36.4504	38.0128	39.1936	38.1987

CANADA_CAIMQNTL

1955	1	5.6560	6.4640	6.7160	7.1520
1956	1	6.9120	8.3600	7.8280	8.0400
1957	1	7.4720	8.6040	7.9800	7.5680
1958	1	6.7000	7.8120	7.4920	7.9080
1959	1	7.1240	8.7760	8.4400	8.4960
1960	1	7.6920	8.7720	8.2120	8.3800
1961	1	7.7480	8.7800	8.7880	9.3080
1962	1	8.3000	9.9160	9.2640	9.3320
1963	1	8.4640	9.9720	9.9080	10.6640
1964	1	10.0520	11.6760	10.9920	11.7200
1965	1	10.9840	12.7840	12.5080	13.9920
1966	1	12.7040	14.9040	14.6760	15.9720
1967	1	14.2280	16.9520	15.2520	15.9240
1968	1	15.6120	17.7000	16.9840	18.8680
1969	1	18.4040	21.4200	19.7320	21.1200
1970	1	19.5960	22.5120	20.6280	19.7720
1971	1	19.5160	23.2440	22.5040	24.4760
1972	1	23.0440	26.9520	24.7640	28.0680
1973	1	28.6480	32.0920	29.9080	35.3400
1974	1	36.0880	42.2040	41.5760	46.6440
1975	1	44.1880	48.6240	44.2280	48.4920
1976	1	48.7920	53.9080	48.1200	52.7000

CANADA_CAIMQSTL

1955	1	6.1315	6.0481	6.6787	7.1259
1956	1	7.4981	7.8228	7.7841	8.0034
1957	1	8.1145	8.0500	7.9405	7.5206
1958	1	7.2775	7.3210	7.4571	7.8381
1959	1	7.7396	8.2392	8.4122	8.3919
1960	1	8.3502	8.2606	8.1946	8.2497
1961	1	8.4019	8.2839	8.7945	9.1338
1962	1	8.9798	9.3779	9.2986	9.1270
1963	1	9.1405	9.4446	9.9801	10.3964
1964	1	10.8442	11.0575	11.1139	11.4083
1965	1	11.8261	12.0913	12.7009	13.6228
1966	1	13.6367	14.0650	14.9690	15.5727
1967	1	15.2246	15.9491	15.6185	15.5619
1968	1	16.6637	16.5941	17.4497	18.4932
1969	1	19.5829	20.0258	20.3488	20.7411
1970	1	20.7639	21.0259	21.3726	19.4107
1971	1	20.5776	21.7410	23.4237	23.9836
1972	1	24.1721	25.2799	25.8796	27.4659
1973	1	29.8636	30.2005	31.3781	34.5455
1974	1	37.3862	39.8436	43.7603	45.5547
1975	1	45.5784	46.0052	46.6373	47.3258
1976	1	50.2229	51.0907	50.7297	51.4243

CANADA_CAIMQNGO

1955	1	3.8840	4.6000	4.6520	5.0360
1956	1	4.9800	6.1680	5.4040	5.7080
1957	1	5.3120	6.0720	5.4000	5.1680
1958	1	4.6160	5.4440	4.8080	5.3960
1959	1	4.8720	6.2040	5.5200	5.6920
1960	1	5.2960	6.0320	5.2640	5.5680
1961	1	5.0400	5.9120	5.6760	6.2360
1962	1	5.5920	6.6560	6.2360	6.3280
1963	1	5.6480	6.8080	6.6200	7.2400
1964	1	6.7800	8.1880	7.3080	7.8720
1965	1	7.4640	8.8720	8.4040	9.7680
1966	1	8.8520	10.6040	9.8880	11.0640
1967	1	9.9240	11.9000	10.3640	10.9000
1968	1	11.0160	12.5600	11.4360	13.6360
1969	1	13.0640	14.9440	13.2480	15.0280
1970	1	13.2480	15.5360	13.2880	13.4040
1971	1	13.3960	16.2560	14.7840	16.8200
1972	1	16.4520	19.5320	17.1200	19.9840
1973	1	20.5960	23.5280	20.9360	25.8440
1974	1	26.3160	31.5680	30.8760	34.8120
1975	1	32.5640	36.5320	31.8640	34.9840
1976	1	35.9720	39.4640	34.3000	37.8080

CANADA_CAIMQSGO

1955	1	4.1671	4.2184	4.7568	5.0357
1956	1	5.3494	5.6494	5.5350	5.6998
1957	1	5.7128	5.5509	5.5529	5.1406
1958	1	4.9675	4.9853	4.9506	5.3425
1959	1	5.2504	5.6957	5.6929	5.5964
1960	1	5.7190	5.5689	5.4138	5.4492
1961	1	5.4549	5.4780	5.8305	6.0794
1962	1	6.0566	6.1922	6.3974	6.1524
1963	1	6.1199	6.3408	6.8066	7.0184
1964	1	7.3453	7.6209	7.5453	7.6216
1965	1	8.0654	8.2391	8.7391	9.4497
1966	1	9.5154	9.8366	10.3625	10.6832
1967	1	10.6279	11.0191	10.9274	10.5279
1968	1	11.7549	11.6049	12.1053	13.2068
1969	1	13.8879	13.7629	14.0744	14.6251
1970	1	13.9890	14.2928	14.1704	13.0778
1971	1	14.0618	14.9719	15.7914	16.4470
1972	1	17.1696	18.0355	18.2966	19.5789
1973	1	21.3641	21.8040	22.3827	25.3487
1974	1	27.1355	29.3839	33.0201	34.1211
1975	1	33.4725	34.1255	34.0392	34.2759
1976	1	36.9440	36.9351	36.5883	37.0490

CANADA_CAKPQNCC

1955	1	0.44400	0.85600	0.37200	0.90000
1956	1	1.35600	1.87600	0.94400	1.50400
1957	1	1.69600	2.25600	0.64000	0.79200
1958	1	1.32000	1.54000	0.72000	1.40400
1959	1	1.50400	1.95600	1.28400	1.16000
1960	1	1.24400	1.57200	0.66000	1.30000
1961	1	1.70400	1.44000	0.15600	1.58000
1962	1	-0.22400	-1.08800	2.88400	2.36400
1963	1	1.20000	1.26000	-0.35600	0.56000
1964	1	1.18000	0.87200	-0.20400	1.30400
1965	1	1.40400	1.45600	0.76000	1.53200
1966	1	1.01600	1.02800	-0.47600	1.64400
1967	1	1.19200	0.86800	-0.57600	0.59200
1968	1	-2.21600	2.43200	-0.54800	2.11600
1969	1	1.16800	1.33200	0.09200	1.33600
1970	1	1.60800	2.64800	-0.76400	-1.79600
1971	1	-0.34800	-0.46800	-0.64800	2.84800
1972	1	1.84400	1.48800	-0.01200	-0.90000
1973	1	1.04400	-1.03200	-2.23200	-0.03200
1974	1	3.53600	0.62800	-1.12000	3.02000
1975	1	7.38000	2.63600	2.97600	5.25200
1976	1	9.63600	4.99600	-0.27600	4.48000

CANADA_CAKPQSCC

1955	1	0.27987	0.38554	0.87400	1.02961
1956	1	1.19373	1.41517	1.43487	1.62880
1957	1	1.54122	1.80458	1.12379	0.90120
1958	1	1.17208	1.11495	1.19389	1.47445
1959	1	1.37064	1.57566	1.76010	1.14632
1960	1	1.14407	1.23927	1.14792	1.20231
1961	1	1.61633	1.14988	0.69480	1.39098
1962	1	-0.32704	-1.33773	3.48917	2.10265
1963	1	1.06136	1.03514	0.34232	0.21673
1964	1	1.01538	0.65709	0.56689	0.91584
1965	1	1.22437	1.21462	1.61523	1.09033
1966	1	0.85284	0.74624	0.42007	1.19072
1967	1	1.08275	0.47580	0.36349	0.19604
1968	1	-2.33526	1.94586	0.41225	1.87540
1969	1	0.91773	0.78181	1.10847	1.30237
1970	1	1.05766	2.14477	0.34178	-1.61949
1971	1	-1.32627	-0.87896	0.67163	3.17484
1972	1	0.29939	1.29816	1.57086	-0.50350
1973	1	-1.08627	-0.98326	-0.32942	0.34020
1974	1	0.90663	0.90380	1.05351	3.32965
1975	1	4.41926	3.03179	5.36845	5.49105
1976	1	6.50755	5.45294	2.21514	4.65559

CANADA_CAXRQNSP

1955	1	0.97572	0.98548	0.98582	0.99808
1956	1	0.99881	0.99129	0.98023	0.96603
1957	1	0.95836	0.95618	0.95269	0.96815
1958	1	0.98102	0.96642	0.96715	0.96788
1959	1	0.97054	0.96175	0.95447	0.94970
1960	1	0.95188	0.97443	0.97353	0.97923
1961	1	0.98994	0.99396	1.03212	1.03623
1962	1	1.04771	1.07333	1.07777	1.07627
1963	1	1.07757	1.07743	1.08079	1.07827
1964	1	1.08023	1.08088	1.07868	1.07460
1965	1	1.07691	1.08031	1.07944	1.07528
1966	1	1.07573	1.07674	1.07540	1.08149
1967	1	1.08071	1.08163	1.07630	1.07620
1968	1	1.08560	1.07828	1.07306	1.07295
1969	1	1.07460	1.07757	1.07899	1.07596
1970	1	1.07285	1.06133	1.02309	1.01961
1971	1	1.00848	1.01252	1.01578	1.00246
1972	1	1.00302	0.98788	0.98299	0.98882
1973	1	0.99708	0.99980	1.00379	0.99969
1974	1	0.98003	0.96527	0.98071	0.98607
1975	1	0.99853	1.02186	1.03074	1.01751
1976	1	0.99540	0.97900	0.97750	0.99230

CANADA_CAM1QNCC

1955	1	4.4117	4.5503	4.7820	4.8233
1956	1	4.5830	4.6517	4.7607	4.7557
1957	1	4.4990	4.5440	4.6200	4.7470
1958	1	4.6540	4.8780	5.2267	5.4353
1959	1	5.1420	5.0990	5.2123	5.2347
1960	1	5.0310	5.1487	5.2910	5.4850
1961	1	5.3347	5.3427	5.5803	5.7877
1962	1	5.5317	5.5893	5.6653	5.9947
1963	1	5.7777	5.9957	6.0870	6.2530
1964	1	6.1227	6.2750	6.3690	6.5730
1965	1	6.4157	6.6417	6.8657	7.0293
1966	1	6.8957	7.0600	7.2783	7.5910
1967	1	7.5697	7.7903	8.0267	8.2407
1968	1	7.8787	7.9243	8.4747	8.7307
1969	1	8.5717	8.8300	8.9457	9.1177
1970	1	8.7213	8.8857	9.2210	9.4423
1971	1	9.3987	9.9287	10.5147	11.0847
1972	1	10.8653	11.2273	11.9453	12.6017
1973	1	12.4727	13.0510	13.7713	14.0800
1974	1	13.9030	14.7367	14.8407	15.0760
1975	1	15.2720	15.9837	17.0583	18.3026
1976	1	17.3040	17.5657	18.3780	18.6520

CANADA_CAM1QSCC

1955	1	4.5362	4.6038	4.7170	4.7055
1956	1	4.7092	4.7091	4.6965	4.6396
1957	1	4.6176	4.6033	4.5615	4.6305
1958	1	4.7684	4.9448	5.1684	5.3002
1959	1	5.2586	5.1695	5.1661	5.1008
1960	1	5.1387	5.2157	5.2560	5.3447
1961	1	5.4442	5.4020	5.5563	5.6423
1962	1	5.6421	5.6395	5.6489	5.8518
1963	1	5.8895	6.0390	6.0735	6.1121
1964	1	6.2380	6.3162	6.3510	6.4343
1965	1	6.5331	6.6861	6.8407	6.8856
1966	1	7.0206	7.1125	7.2450	7.4346
1967	1	7.7094	7.8559	7.9820	8.0668
1968	1	8.0309	7.9955	8.4206	8.5405
1969	1	8.7460	8.9151	8.8792	8.9161
1970	1	8.9072	8.9743	9.1416	9.2356
1971	1	9.6061	10.0282	10.4088	10.8583
1972	1	11.1017	11.3385	11.8177	12.3545
1973	1	12.7396	13.1833	13.6165	13.8139
1974	1	14.1935	14.8890	14.6716	14.7931
1975	1	15.5896	16.1510	16.8584	17.9680
1976	1	17.6604	17.7454	18.1652	18.3132

CANADA_CAM2QNQA

1953	1	9.1603	9.3597	9.4463	9.3483
1954	1	9.2643	9.4973	9.8020	9.9933
1955	1	10.2047	10.6440	11.0480	11.0090
1956	1	10.7530	10.9777	11.1663	11.2067
1957	1	10.9960	11.1483	11.3120	11.4003
1958	1	11.4020	11.8867	12.5603	12.9117
1959	1	12.6930	12.8323	12.9967	12.8003
1960	1	12.5317	12.7617	13.0223	13.2817
1961	1	13.3140	13.6423	14.1060	14.3810
1962	1	14.1843	14.5810	14.6617	14.9290
1963	1	14.9277	15.4597	15.7027	15.9153
1964	1	15.8640	16.3183	16.6096	16.9840
1965	1	17.2050	18.0470	18.7383	19.1043
1966	1	19.0107	19.5517	20.0520	20.4250
1967	1	20.7170	21.5677	22.6670	23.7510
1968	1	23.3790	24.5273	26.0233	26.6137
1969	1	27.0816	27.5650	27.6760	27.9063
1970	1	27.4137	28.5820	29.7473	30.5430
1971	1	31.0100	32.5767	34.1947	35.2987
1972	1	36.2523	38.8243	40.2727	41.1207
1973	1	41.4557	43.3657	45.1560	47.4803
1974	1	49.4777	52.1783	54.6667	56.6367
1975	1	58.5517	60.9037	64.2123	66.5370
1976	1	67.8683	72.4363	75.0930	77.4063
1977	1	79.0656	83.8056	86.6286	

CANADA_CAM2QSQA

1953	1	9.2988	9.3639	9.3309	9.3192
1954	1	9.4056	9.5024	9.6842	9.9565
1955	1	10.3607	10.6560	10.9179	10.9564
1956	1	10.9180	11.0005	11.0359	11.1406
1957	1	11.1659	11.1796	11.1849	11.3216
1958	1	11.5760	11.9250	12.4272	12.8156
1959	1	12.8826	12.8706	12.8719	12.7041
1960	1	12.7126	12.7897	12.9104	13.1872
1961	1	13.5025	13.6518	14.0030	14.2866
1962	1	14.3799	14.5725	14.5678	14.8380
1963	1	15.1316	15.4381	15.6075	15.8250
1964	1	16.0761	16.2989	16.5027	16.8893
1965	1	17.4318	18.0423	18.6010	19.0026
1966	1	19.2495	19.5733	19.8905	20.3071
1967	1	20.9806	21.6089	22.4697	23.6136
1968	1	23.6793	24.5782	25.7896	26.4573
1969	1	27.4506	27.6015	27.4205	27.7627
1970	1	27.7966	28.5828	29.4868	30.3996
1971	1	31.4543	32.5351	33.9113	35.1619
1972	1	36.7508	38.7552	39.9575	40.9754
1973	1	42.0108	43.2787	44.8088	47.3305
1974	1	50.1224	52.0740	54.2498	56.4529
1975	1	59.3278	60.7810	63.7050	66.3178
1976	1	68.7927	72.3045	74.4535	77.1573
1977	1	80.1719	83.6505	85.8567	

CANADA_CAMHQNCC

1955	1	2.1987	2.2341	2.3196	2.3526
1956	1	2.3247	2.3721	2.4286	2.4697
1957	1	2.3846	2.4398	2.4927	2.5188
1958	1	2.4882	2.5658	2.6825	2.7440
1959	1	2.6895	2.7447	2.7887	2.7800
1960	1	2.7087	2.7515	2.8063	2.8320
1961	1	2.7932	2.8445	2.9196	2.9740
1962	1	2.9576	3.0454	3.1041	3.0964
1963	1	3.0591	3.1343	3.2109	3.2582
1964	1	3.2376	3.3015	3.3997	3.4522
1965	1	3.4542	3.5608	3.7133	3.8027
1966	1	3.7704	3.8548	3.9689	4.0555
1967	1	4.0561	4.2194	4.3195	4.2931
1968	1	4.1225	4.2043	4.3571	4.5108
1969	1	4.5912	4.7068	4.8538	4.9026
1970	1	4.9245	4.9458	5.0696	5.1561
1971	1	5.2857	5.4736	5.7540	5.9213
1972	1	6.1411	6.3159	6.5314	6.7559
1973	1	6.9420	7.2093	7.6027	7.8232
1974	1	7.9297	8.2050	8.5650	8.8706
1975	1	9.2637	9.5952	9.9996	10.3026
1976	1	10.5068	10.7070	11.1111	11.3332

CANADA_CAMHQSCC

1955	1	2.2350	2.2484	2.2938	2.3260
1956	1	2.3635	2.3870	2.4015	2.4420
1957	1	2.4247	2.4542	2.4655	2.4907
1958	1	2.5302	2.5795	2.6540	2.7144
1959	1	2.7344	2.7578	2.7601	2.7514
1960	1	2.7532	2.7629	2.7785	2.8050
1961	1	2.8372	2.8550	2.8917	2.9477
1962	1	3.0018	3.0564	3.0753	3.0701
1963	1	3.1026	3.1465	3.1813	3.2308
1964	1	3.2827	3.3153	3.3681	3.4231
1965	1	3.5015	3.5766	3.6788	3.7712
1966	1	3.8201	3.8730	3.9327	4.0236
1967	1	4.1050	4.2400	4.2819	4.2633
1968	1	4.1653	4.2251	4.3217	4.4855
1969	1	4.6286	4.7304	4.8188	4.8808
1970	1	4.9539	4.9715	5.0370	5.1377
1971	1	5.3088	5.5019	5.7211	5.9033
1972	1	6.1622	6.3478	6.4965	6.7377
1973	1	6.9622	7.2450	7.5658	7.8011
1974	1	7.9506	8.2471	8.5248	8.8437
1975	1	9.2868	9.6466	9.9531	10.2702
1976	1	10.5324	10.7654	11.0587	11.2988

CANADA_CAFHQNSD

1954	1				1.87217
1955	1	1.84430	1.87823	1.91801	1.90008
1956	1	1.88326	1.87995	1.86746	1.87206
1957	1	1.85379	1.84959	1.85339	1.83145
1958	1	1.83558	1.84232	1.86119	1.87385
1959	1	1.84344	1.85588	1.84687	1.78278
1960	1	1.77726	1.74745	1.78409	1.80870
1961	1	1.90916	1.96689	2.02904	2.18164
1962	1	1.90250	1.77740	2.49999	2.80712
1963	1	2.84533	2.92407	2.73990	2.82726
1964	1	2.75682	2.73052	2.79961	2.92155
1965	1	2.84914	2.73796	2.79035	2.88343
1966	1	2.75512	2.61278	2.47141	2.43476
1967	1	2.40858	2.38080	2.38548	2.47253
1968	1	2.51490	2.80187	2.74839	2.88555
1969	1	3.04459	2.95039	2.78322	2.83422
1970	1	2.22276	2.85126	3.13472	3.24596
1971	1	3.42735	3.59931	3.87828	4.20404
1972	1	4.58307	4.82713	4.95727	4.87859
1973	1	4.81648	4.74496	4.49501	4.48656
1974	1	4.69016	4.75665	4.51801	4.33334
1975	1	4.28597	3.91835	3.75921	3.85599
1976	1	4.20490	4.20999	3.93528	3.76055

CANADA_CAFHQSSD

1954	1				1.86850
1955	1	1.85432	1.87963	1.90996	1.89641
1956	1	1.89370	1.88108	1.85907	1.86984
1957	1	1.86268	1.85190	1.84412	1.82997
1958	1	1.84257	1.84796	1.85111	1.86901
1959	1	1.84961	1.86804	1.83838	1.76816
1960	1	1.78609	1.76336	1.78125	1.78062
1961	1	1.92105	1.99051	2.03407	2.13283
1962	1	1.91437	1.80241	2.51776	2.72992
1963	1	2.86008	2.96959	2.76787	2.74657
1964	1	2.76583	2.76846	2.83347	2.84750
1965	1	2.85476	2.76254	2.82401	2.83229
1966	1	2.75476	2.62144	2.49742	2.40905
1967	1	2.41152	2.37469	2.40225	2.46417
1968	1	2.52100	2.78405	2.75709	2.89009
1969	1	3.05872	2.92420	2.78227	2.85116
1970	1	2.23045	2.82778	3.12741	3.27253
1971	1	3.43463	3.56939	3.87161	4.24818
1972	1	4.57216	4.78658	4.96758	4.93796
1973	1	4.78232	4.69302	4.53032	4.55317
1974	1	4.62962	4.69327	4.57874	4.40760
1975	1	4.21260	3.85850	3.82185	3.92950
1976	1	4.12266	4.14189	4.00720	3.83469

CANADA_CARSQNTB

1955	1	0.010333	0.013300	0.016533	0.024467
1956	1	0.025767	0.027100	0.029033	0.035100
1957	1	0.037200	0.037733	0.038800	0.036667
1958	1	0.027933	0.016133	0.015433	0.030667
1959	1	0.038833	0.049233	0.054333	0.050000
1960	1	0.040733	0.031133	0.022100	0.034100
1961	1	0.031200	0.029967	0.024667	0.026633
1962	1	0.031333	0.040133	0.051367	0.039267
1963	1	0.036500	0.033633	0.035667	0.036667
1964	1	0.038433	0.036233	0.037333	0.037967
1965	1	0.037000	0.038667	0.040867	0.042833
1966	1	0.047933	0.050633	0.050233	0.051000
1967	1	0.044633	0.041733	0.044733	0.054533
1968	1	0.066900	0.068333	0.057233	0.058233
1969	1	0.064633	0.068900	0.076933	0.077233
1970	1	0.074600	0.063533	0.055333	0.046167
1971	1	0.039667	0.031333	0.038433	0.033067
1972	1	0.034600	0.036233	0.035267	0.036333
1973	1	0.041167	0.051867	0.061400	0.064367
1974	1	0.062667	0.083400	0.090500	0.076400
1975	1	0.063300	0.069033	0.079067	0.084400
1976	1	0.087700	0.089700	0.090400	0.087900

CANADA_CARLQNCC

1955	1	0.030700	0.030567	0.031000	0.033200
1956	1	0.033300	0.034867	0.037567	0.039267
1957	1	0.040300	0.041800	0.043533	0.038900
1958	1	0.038633	0.038633	0.042167	0.045033
1959	1	0.047400	0.049400	0.052667	0.053500
1960	1	0.054300	0.051733	0.049033	0.052333
1961	1	0.051667	0.051133	0.049833	0.049200
1962	1	0.049233	0.050267	0.054067	0.050967
1963	1	0.050833	0.049667	0.051700	0.051300
1964	1	0.051967	0.052167	0.052200	0.051000
1965	1	0.050167	0.051100	0.053167	0.053900
1966	1	0.055333	0.056233	0.058100	0.057933
1967	1	0.055733	0.057167	0.060200	0.064367
1968	1	0.067233	0.067367	0.065067	0.070167
1969	1	0.071933	0.074233	0.076200	0.081000
1970	1	0.081233	0.081200	0.079300	0.074767
1971	1	0.067600	0.072167	0.072033	0.066100
1972	1	0.069567	0.073533	0.074633	0.071533
1973	1	0.072233	0.076167	0.077567	0.076467
1974	1	0.078933	0.090600	0.097133	0.089467
1975	1	0.083133	0.088767	0.094833	0.094667
1976	1	0.093167	0.093367	0.092567	0.087933

CANADA_CAYNQNCA

1947	1	11.216	12.660	16.004	14.012
1948	1	12.740	14.088	19.196	16.012
1949	1	14.368	15.816	19.900	17.116
1950	1	15.580	17.084	21.980	19.320
1951	1	18.464	20.788	25.732	21.576
1952	1	20.780	23.316	29.712	24.544
1953	1	22.736	24.656	30.440	25.500
1954	1	23.068	25.028	29.004	26.572
1955	1	24.388	27.188	33.224	29.312
1956	1	27.672	30.360	37.356	32.844
1957	1	30.336	32.588	37.696	33.432
1958	1	30.732	33.848	38.968	35.560
1959	1	33.032	35.688	41.192	37.472
1960	1	35.320	36.780	42.800	38.536
1961	1	35.476	38.728	43.256	41.124
1962	1	38.692	40.992	48.148	43.876
1963	1	40.876	43.904	51.324	47.808
1964	1	45.320	48.652	55.376	51.772
1965	1	49.428	53.360	61.028	57.640
1966	1	55.708	60.408	68.196	63.000
1967	1	60.320	65.648	71.716	67.952
1968	1	64.808	70.656	79.284	75.596
1969	1	72.340	78.240	85.940	82.740
1970	1	78.716	84.884	90.992	88.148
1971	1	83.372	92.400	101.908	98.780
1972	1	93.552	103.300	111.400	110.424
1973	1	107.696	119.004	132.580	131.048
1974	1	127.712	139.228	160.424	151.100
1975	1	141.664	154.044	179.680	169.140
1976	1	165.224	179.280	202.672	190.800

CANADA_CAYNQSCA

1947	1	12.832	13.311	13.584	14.070
1948	1	14.552	14.797	16.300	16.134
1949	1	16.354	16.594	16.887	17.357
1950	1	17.648	17.890	18.646	19.718
1951	1	20.820	21.718	21.836	22.135
1952	1	23.355	24.267	25.291	25.221
1953	1	25.488	25.594	26.014	26.186
1954	1	25.786	25.918	24.962	27.171
1955	1	27.195	28.069	28.873	29.806
1956	1	30.757	31.226	32.833	33.218
1957	1	33.541	33.478	33.435	33.674
1958	1	33.783	34.786	34.825	35.672
1959	1	36.126	36.751	36.993	37.464
1960	1	38.481	37.961	38.548	38.460
1961	1	38.499	40.087	38.998	41.024
1962	1	41.897	42.410	43.518	43.787
1963	1	44.174	45.289	46.556	47.773
1964	1	48.899	49.915	50.497	51.829
1965	1	53.179	54.481	55.937	57.791
1966	1	59.790	61.377	62.877	63.175
1967	1	64.595	66.454	66.488	68.053
1968	1	69.348	71.267	73.920	75.512
1969	1	77.415	78.686	80.513	82.436
1970	1	84.263	85.186	85.566	87.634
1971	1	89.216	92.801	95.835	98.091
1972	1	100.173	103.995	104.407	109.716
1973	1	115.340	120.343	123.526	130.384
1974	1	136.855	141.346	148.680	150.558
1975	1	151.786	156.960	165.864	168.607
1976	1	177.133	183.059	186.603	190.339

CANADA_CAYRQN70

1947	1	25.263	27.581	33.080	28.458
1948	1	25.065	27.306	35.422	29.431
1949	1	26.178	28.888	35.941	30.703
1950	1	28.093	30.478	39.699	32.645
1951	1	30.373	32.680	42.347	32.060
1952	1	30.823	34.685	47.567	36.667
1953	1	33.979	37.004	48.563	37.904
1954	1	34.177	37.314	45.174	38.850
1955	1	35.810	40.118	51.871	42.394
1956	1	40.955	44.298	52.635	46.682
1957	1	43.216	45.953	52.890	46.849
1958	1	43.061	46.698	54.290	49.226
1959	1	45.310	48.513	56.012	50.781
1960	1	47.737	49.269	57.629	51.774
1961	1	47.609	51.859	57.962	54.833
1962	1	51.661	54.352	63.189	57.540
1963	1	53.600	57.047	66.439	61.336
1964	1	58.253	61.770	69.498	64.888
1965	1	61.689	65.807	74.062	69.801
1966	1	66.675	71.034	79.541	72.965
1967	1	69.254	74.124	80.701	75.830
1968	1	71.902	77.719	85.990	81.825
1969	1	77.149	81.945	89.906	85.346
1970	1	79.592	84.822	91.441	86.885
1971	1	82.352	88.859	97.832	93.365
1972	1	87.688	95.482	101.442	99.519
1973	1	94.532	101.403	108.255	106.494
1974	1	99.720	105.056	109.806	107.541
1975	1	100.174	106.227	109.538	110.500
1976	1	105.506	111.811	118.631	114.156

CANADA_CAYRQS70

1947	1	28.907	29.038	27.839	28.819
1948	1	28.657	28.782	29.733	29.905
1949	1	29.890	30.505	30.017	31.392
1950	1	32.033	32.219	32.977	33.616
1951	1	34.586	34.528	35.072	33.186
1952	1	35.056	36.555	39.432	38.055
1953	1	38.542	38.829	40.538	39.268
1954	1	38.594	38.954	38.150	40.060
1955	1	40.182	41.624	44.525	43.365
1956	1	45.629	45.774	45.853	47.446
1957	1	47.762	47.371	46.687	47.313
1958	1	47.276	48.128	48.352	49.502
1959	1	49.478	50.020	50.219	50.870
1960	1	51.950	50.847	51.853	51.812
1961	1	51.609	53.557	52.311	54.850
1962	1	55.840	56.055	57.255	57.560
1963	1	57.763	58.693	60.475	61.357
1964	1	62.640	63.319	63.584	64.925
1965	1	66.177	67.214	68.105	69.814
1966	1	71.425	72.287	73.510	72.907
1967	1	74.113	75.217	74.895	75.679
1968	1	76.900	78.687	80.101	81.549
1969	1	82.472	82.775	84.097	84.922
1970	1	84.992	85.516	85.937	86.281
1971	1	87.807	89.427	92.420	92.523
1972	1	93.299	95.957	96.336	98.417
1973	1	100.344	101.815	103.264	105.161
1974	1	105.596	105.464	105.065	106.094
1975	1	105.880	106.663	104.966	108.980
1976	1	111.404	112.286	113.747	112.559

CANADA_CAPDQN70

1947	1	0.44398	0.45901	0.48380	0.49238
1948	1	0.50828	0.51593	0.54193	0.54405
1949	1	0.54886	0.54749	0.55368	0.55747
1950	1	0.55458	0.56054	0.55367	0.59181
1951	1	0.60790	0.63610	0.60764	0.67299
1952	1	0.67417	0.67222	0.62464	0.66938
1953	1	0.66911	0.66631	0.62681	0.67276
1954	1	0.67495	0.67074	0.64205	0.68397
1955	1	0.68105	0.67771	0.64052	0.69142
1956	1	0.67567	0.68536	0.70972	0.70356
1957	1	0.70196	0.70915	0.71272	0.71361
1958	1	0.71369	0.72483	0.71777	0.72238
1959	1	0.72903	0.73564	0.73541	0.73791
1960	1	0.73989	0.74652	0.74268	0.74432
1961	1	0.74515	0.74679	0.74628	0.74998
1962	1	0.74896	0.75419	0.76196	0.76253
1963	1	0.76261	0.76961	0.77250	0.77945
1964	1	0.77798	0.78763	0.79680	0.79787
1965	1	0.80125	0.81086	0.82401	0.82578
1966	1	0.83551	0.85041	0.85737	0.86343
1967	1	0.87100	0.88565	0.88867	0.89611
1968	1	0.90133	0.90912	0.92202	0.92387
1969	1	0.93767	0.95478	0.95589	0.96947
1970	1	0.98900	1.00072	0.99508	1.01453
1971	1	1.01238	1.03985	1.04167	1.05800
1972	1	1.06687	1.08188	1.09817	1.10958
1973	1	1.13925	1.17357	1.22470	1.23056
1974	1	1.28070	1.32528	1.46098	1.40504
1975	1	1.41418	1.45014	1.64034	1.53068
1976	1	1.56602	1.60343	1.70842	1.67139

CANADA_CAPDQS70

1947	1	0.44414	0.46091	0.48345	0.49074
1948	1	0.50829	0.51712	0.54347	0.54172
1949	1	0.54803	0.54730	0.55903	0.55386
1950	1	0.55255	0.55843	0.56397	0.58628
1951	1	0.60405	0.63167	0.62466	0.66444
1952	1	0.66860	0.66604	0.64636	0.65904
1953	1	0.66288	0.66022	0.64955	0.66170
1954	1	0.66890	0.66569	0.66293	0.67335
1955	1	0.67627	0.67392	0.65669	0.68264
1956	1	0.67279	0.68247	0.72193	0.69719
1957	1	0.70095	0.70672	0.71971	0.71011
1958	1	0.71388	0.72257	0.72118	0.72109
1959	1	0.72989	0.73343	0.73685	0.73789
1960	1	0.74093	0.74450	0.74329	0.74439
1961	1	0.74656	0.74520	0.74620	0.74992
1962	1	0.75067	0.75317	0.76109	0.76241
1963	1	0.76479	0.76877	0.77096	0.77958
1964	1	0.78044	0.78657	0.79505	0.79831
1965	1	0.80379	0.80946	0.82219	0.82683
1966	1	0.83782	0.84840	0.85598	0.86504
1967	1	0.87275	0.88311	0.88803	0.89786
1968	1	0.90288	0.90580	0.92246	0.92529
1969	1	0.93924	0.95111	0.95659	0.97055
1970	1	0.99126	0.99716	0.99459	1.01585
1971	1	1.01541	1.03789	1.03756	1.05975
1972	1	1.07192	1.08279	1.08744	1.11283
1973	1	1.14672	1.17893	1.20434	1.23588
1974	1	1.29170	1.33578	1.42763	1.41338
1975	1	1.42817	1.46535	1.59631	1.54073
1976	1	1.58308	1.62240	1.65911	1.68322

CANADA_CAPCQN70

1955	1	0.69355	0.69287	0.69458	0.69732
1956	1	0.69527	0.69801	0.70898	0.71721
1957	1	0.71858	0.72304	0.73126	0.73538
1958	1	0.73846	0.74669	0.74669	0.75286
1959	1	0.75046	0.74806	0.75458	0.76418
1960	1	0.75903	0.76109	0.76349	0.77309
1961	1	0.77035	0.76966	0.77000	0.77343
1962	1	0.77446	0.77755	0.78235	0.78612
1963	1	0.78783	0.79092	0.79709	0.79914
1964	1	0.80223	0.80600	0.81114	0.81251
1965	1	0.81869	0.82520	0.83171	0.83583
1966	1	0.84680	0.85605	0.86394	0.86840
1967	1	0.87251	0.88485	0.89891	0.90165
1968	1	0.91194	0.92051	0.93113	0.93971
1969	1	0.94691	0.96473	0.97639	0.98222
1970	1	0.99147	1.00039	1.00519	1.00347
1971	1	1.00861	1.02267	1.03776	1.04496
1972	1	1.05730	1.06655	1.08781	1.09878
1973	1	1.11901	1.14438	1.17694	1.19820
1974	1	1.22700	1.26780	1.30585	1.34185
1975	1	1.37099	1.40082	1.44847	1.47829
1976	1	1.49783	1.52046	1.54275	1.56538

CANADA_CAPCQS70

1955	1	0.69490	0.69475	0.69378	0.69495
1956	1	0.69650	0.69990	0.70838	0.71460
1957	1	0.71978	0.72496	0.73102	0.73244
1958	1	0.73959	0.74865	0.74682	0.74968
1959	1	0.75153	0.74981	0.75508	0.76095
1960	1	0.75996	0.76274	0.76402	0.77018
1961	1	0.77120	0.77106	0.77028	0.77122
1962	1	0.77522	0.77867	0.78205	0.78495
1963	1	0.78851	0.79159	0.79628	0.79894
1964	1	0.80290	0.80632	0.80981	0.81309
1965	1	0.81943	0.82518	0.83006	0.83681
1966	1	0.84780	0.85573	0.86201	0.86969
1967	1	0.87370	0.88430	0.89681	0.90298
1968	1	0.91350	0.91978	0.92878	0.94118
1969	1	0.94861	0.96407	0.97370	0.98373
1970	1	0.99339	0.99992	1.00207	1.00505
1971	1	1.01057	1.02250	1.03436	1.04626
1972	1	1.05954	1.06677	1.08410	1.09968
1973	1	1.12148	1.14512	1.17307	1.19829
1974	1	1.22994	1.26910	1.30180	1.34100
1975	1	1.37455	1.40248	1.44445	1.47641
1976	1	1.50207	1.52229	1.53876	1.56284

CANADA_CAIPQS70

1947	1	0.27203	0.27659	0.28343	0.28457
1948	1	0.28742	0.29256	0.29427	0.29997
1949	1	0.30168	0.30282	0.30567	0.30739
1950	1	0.31024	0.31765	0.33248	0.34788
1951	1	0.35757	0.36270	0.35700	0.35187
1952	1	0.35928	0.36727	0.37582	0.38894
1953	1	0.39920	0.40205	0.40148	0.39578
1954	1	0.39920	0.39407	0.39578	0.40433
1955	1	0.42144	0.43570	0.44996	0.46136
1956	1	0.47049	0.48646	0.49501	0.50356
1957	1	0.50413	0.50014	0.49729	0.48703
1958	1	0.48703	0.49444	0.49558	0.50356
1959	1	0.52124	0.53322	0.54006	0.55090
1960	1	0.55945	0.54577	0.54177	0.54577
1961	1	0.54748	0.56401	0.57827	0.59025
1962	1	0.60051	0.61534	0.62789	0.62846
1963	1	0.63758	0.65184	0.65868	0.68549
1964	1	0.70545	0.72084	0.72655	0.74309
1965	1	0.76190	0.77046	0.78700	0.81665
1966	1	0.82920	0.83262	0.82692	0.84859
1967	1	0.84916	0.85999	0.86912	0.87767
1968	1	0.88452	0.91759	0.93356	0.95865
1969	1	0.97918	0.98147	0.98375	0.99230
1970	1	1.00941	0.99458	0.99800	0.99800
1971	1	1.02609	1.04442	1.07191	1.08460
1972	1	1.09940	1.12126	1.12760	1.17695
1973	1	1.21079	1.22947	1.23159	1.25943
1974	1	1.28129	1.27988	1.26754	1.24851
1975	1	1.21361	1.20691	1.20127	1.21643
1976	1	1.25274	1.27318	1.27001	1.27283
1977	1	1.29609			

CANADA_CAGXQNEX

1955	1	5.2360	4.3360	4.4440	4.5600
1956	1	5.2000	4.6480	4.8120	5.0000
1957	1	5.5880	4.8560	5.0600	5.3160
1958	1	6.1800	5.6360	5.4720	6.1480
1959	1	6.5080	6.0040	5.8120	6.1360
1960	1	6.9440	6.2240	6.3920	6.5120
1961	1	7.2360	6.7680	6.7120	6.8160
1962	1	7.8880	7.0360	6.8120	7.1280
1963	1	7.7720	7.3560	7.0480	7.3160
1964	1	8.2800	7.6520	7.4320	7.8400
1965	1	8.7280	7.9800	7.8680	8.2240
1966	1	9.3320	8.9720	9.0640	9.9240
1967	1	10.3640	10.8120	10.3560	10.5720
1968	1	11.6760	11.6520	11.5320	12.0560
1969	1	13.2640	12.8320	12.8040	13.0320
1970	1	14.7840	14.9080	14.6280	14.8680
1971	1	17.0160	16.3080	16.3520	17.8120
1972	1	19.6080	19.5960	19.2120	19.5960
1973	1	22.3640	21.2440	20.7120	22.4800
1974	1	27.6480	26.8440	27.4840	29.5760
1975	1	35.2840	33.5360	33.6480	34.9440
1976	1	39.0440	36.8800	36.6760	39.7600

CANADA_CAGXQSEX

1955	1	4.7470	4.5589	4.6023	4.6496
1956	1	4.7211	4.8739	4.9908	5.0969
1957	1	5.0859	5.0686	5.2566	5.4194
1958	1	5.6431	5.8487	5.6921	6.2764
1959	1	5.9591	6.1936	6.0546	6.2711
1960	1	6.3784	6.3795	6.6727	6.6627
1961	1	6.6606	6.9031	7.0207	6.9726
1962	1	7.2801	7.1458	7.1357	7.2951
1963	1	7.1819	7.4528	7.3884	7.4814
1964	1	7.6749	7.7302	7.7872	8.0172
1965	1	8.1167	8.0441	8.2256	8.4091
1966	1	8.7225	9.0196	9.4360	10.1684
1967	1	9.7335	10.8292	10.7450	10.8585
1968	1	11.0068	11.6272	11.9381	12.4252
1969	1	12.5181	12.7616	13.2601	13.4741
1970	1	13.9181	14.8101	15.1782	15.4167
1971	1	15.9428	16.2044	17.0237	18.5069
1972	1	18.2520	19.5209	20.0670	20.3610
1973	1	20.7141	21.2225	21.6978	23.3170
1974	1	25.5254	26.8979	28.8458	30.6034
1975	1	32.5397	33.6697	35.3465	36.0963
1976	1	35.9826	37.0853	38.5262	41.0275

CANADA_CAGDQNDF

1955	1	-0.91600	0.65600	0.48400	0.58400
1956	1	-0.24400	1.21200	0.66400	0.76000
1957	1	-0.02400	0.88000	0.27600	-0.13200
1958	1	-1.43200	-0.56000	-0.36800	-0.70800
1959	1	-1.47200	-0.04800	-0.02400	0.18800
1960	1	-1.12800	0.50400	-0.24400	-0.04800
1961	1	-1.47200	-0.07200	-0.23600	0.14000
1962	1	-1.82000	-0.08400	-0.27600	0.15200
1963	1	-1.40800	-0.15200	-0.12400	0.54000
1964	1	-1.01200	0.85600	0.60800	0.92800
1965	1	-0.80800	1.14000	0.51200	1.33200
1966	1	-0.61200	0.86800	0.20400	0.46400
1967	1	-0.59200	-0.07600	-0.26000	0.59200
1968	1	-0.84400	-0.03600	-0.11600	0.95200
1969	1	-0.50000	1.65600	0.76000	2.16800
1970	1	-0.67200	0.64000	0.20000	0.89600
1971	1	-2.09200	0.60000	0.50000	0.41200
1972	1	-2.53200	-0.71200	-0.19600	1.17600
1973	1	-1.06000	-0.16800	0.69600	2.08000
1974	1	-1.98800	2.19200	2.09200	2.03600
1975	1	-6.40400	-4.23600	-2.53600	-1.02800
1976	1	-6.18400	-3.23600	-0.78000	-1.31600

CANADA_CAGDQSDF

1955	1	-0.15455	0.17069	0.36313	0.42475
1956	1	0.51816	0.74149	0.53365	0.58337
1957	1	0.75353	0.42420	0.13873	-0.34505
1958	1	-0.62414	-0.99427	-0.51488	-0.98426
1959	1	-0.60168	-0.47236	-0.17543	-0.16233
1960	1	-0.18976	0.09355	-0.40233	-0.47651
1961	1	-0.45354	-0.49043	-0.38999	-0.34842
1962	1	-0.74540	-0.51135	-0.41308	-0.39337
1963	1	-0.28483	-0.59909	-0.23609	-0.03213
1964	1	0.10944	0.41175	0.52797	0.33290
1965	1	0.28726	0.71540	0.46036	0.71987
1966	1	0.44818	0.46867	0.19315	-0.20872
1967	1	0.47497	-0.44227	-0.26118	-0.16265
1968	1	0.29122	-0.37805	-0.14399	0.10011
1969	1	0.75563	1.34809	0.65140	1.21902
1970	1	0.74172	0.37788	-0.01737	-0.19668
1971	1	-0.44960	0.39171	0.14866	-0.88565
1972	1	-0.59518	-0.83456	-0.72120	-0.36390
1973	1	1.20175	-0.16933	-0.04002	0.32087
1974	1	0.56011	2.32361	1.15995	0.09131
1975	1	-3.61075	-4.01890	-3.61262	-3.08842
1976	1	-3.22367	-3.00184	-1.91616	-3.43026

CANADA_CAPPQNIN

1954	1		0.015330	0.015431	0.015533
1955	1	0.015635	0.015740	0.015834	0.015928
1956	1	0.016023	0.016120	0.016258	0.016396
1957	1	0.016536	0.016680	0.016789	0.016898
1958	1	0.017008	0.017120	0.017219	0.017318
1959	1	0.017418	0.017520	0.017616	0.017713
1960	1	0.017811	0.017910	0.017999	0.018089
1961	1	0.018179	0.018270	0.018354	0.018439
1962	1	0.018524	0.018610	0.018697	0.018784
1963	1	0.018871	0.018960	0.019052	0.019144
1964	1	0.019236	0.019330	0.019417	0.019504
1965	1	0.019591	0.019680	0.019772	0.019864
1966	1	0.019956	0.020050	0.020139	0.020229
1967	1	0.020319	0.020410	0.020489	0.020569
1968	1	0.020649	0.020730	0.020804	0.020879
1969	1	0.020954	0.021030	0.021102	0.021174
1970	1	0.021247	0.021320	0.021390	0.021459
1971	1	0.021529	0.021600	0.021662	0.021724
1972	1	0.021787	0.021850	0.021920	0.021989
1973	1	0.022059	0.022130	0.022217	0.022304
1974	1	0.022391	0.022480	0.022567	0.022654
1975	1	0.022741	0.022830	0.022907	0.022984
1976	1	0.023062	0.023140	0.023218	0.023296

CANADA_CAURQN14

1955	1	0.074333	0.044000	0.025667	0.032333
1956	1	0.058000	0.033333	0.019333	0.026667
1957	1	0.061000	0.040333	0.031667	0.053000
1958	1	0.101333	0.069667	0.048333	0.063333
1959	1	0.093000	0.057333	0.037667	0.051667
1960	1	0.093667	0.067000	0.051000	0.068000
1961	1	0.110000	0.073667	0.049000	0.054667
1962	1	0.087667	0.056333	0.041667	0.052667
1963	1	0.083667	0.055667	0.039333	0.044667
1964	1	0.069000	0.047000	0.034000	0.038333
1965	1	0.057667	0.041667	0.028667	0.030000
1966	1	0.049667	0.035000	0.029000	0.031333
1967	1	0.053000	0.041667	0.031000	0.039000
1968	1	0.063000	0.050333	0.039000	0.041667
1969	1	0.058667	0.049000	0.037333	0.043333
1970	1	0.064333	0.062667	0.052333	0.057333
1971	1	0.079667	0.067667	0.052667	0.056667
1972	1	0.074667	0.064000	0.054667	0.059333
1973	1	0.072667	0.056000	0.046333	0.050333
1974	1	0.067000	0.054000	0.045000	0.052000
1975	1	0.085333	0.073333	0.060333	0.064000
1976	1	0.078660	0.070330	0.067660	0.069660

CANADA_CAURQS14

1955	1	0.047645	0.045600	0.041660	0.037412
1956	1	0.037371	0.034558	0.031096	0.030695
1957	1	0.039661	0.041797	0.050070	0.060460
1958	1	0.066832	0.072127	0.074624	0.071676
1959	1	0.062352	0.059292	0.056583	0.058114
1960	1	0.063848	0.069142	0.074591	0.076480
1961	1	0.075976	0.075819	0.069965	0.061598
1962	1	0.061346	0.057625	0.058257	0.059706
1963	1	0.059145	0.056650	0.053830	0.051040
1964	1	0.049304	0.047405	0.045741	0.044171
1965	1	0.041614	0.041691	0.037917	0.034716
1966	1	0.036385	0.034573	0.037843	0.036261
1967	1	0.039493	0.040754	0.039784	0.044918
1968	1	0.047956	0.048712	0.049348	0.047489
1969	1	0.045635	0.047215	0.046444	0.048731
1970	1	0.051117	0.060295	0.064176	0.063689
1971	1	0.064195	0.065464	0.063657	0.062552
1972	1	0.060527	0.062326	0.065588	0.065143
1973	1	0.059028	0.054905	0.055231	0.055226
1974	1	0.054400	0.053152	0.053458	0.057098
1975	1	0.069288	0.072242	0.071443	0.070578
1976	1	0.063771	0.069239	0.080106	0.077010

Sources and Notes on Time Series for France

Of the eight countries in our sample, the most troublesome was France. Many series lacked quarterly and sometimes even consistent annual observations, particularly for the earlier years of the period. Balance-of-payments statistics, nominal income, and the consumer price index are all examples. Numerous other series, including real income, several monetary totals, and the industrial production index, contained breaks in definitions of variables, or reporting procedures changed. Hence we have had to resort to a good deal of interpolation and in some instances to substitute completely a proxy series.

A further difficulty is inadequate documentation of series in official sources. This problem is particularly acute in settling on the choice of a series or subseries where more than one series appears to represent the same theoretical construct.

We acknowledge the help of Professor André Fourçans of the Ecole supérieure des sciences économiques et commerciales and of Thomas Huertas of Citibank, N.A., in providing information about the data. Both also supplied us with data they had collected for their own analyses of the French economy. Jacques Melitz of the Institut national de la statistique et des études économiques (INSEE) provided detailed descriptions of various monetary totals he used in his study of the demand for money in France ("Inflationary Expectations and the French Demand for Money, 1959–70," *Manchester School* 7 [March 1976]: 17–41).

I. INTERNATIONAL VARIABLES

A. *Balance of Payments*

    FRBPQNFF   Balance of Payments. Unit: Billions of Francs at Quarterly
    FRBPQSFF   Rates.

Source: See description of source for official international reserve assets, II.D. below.

Description: The series is the official settlements balance as provided by the change in net foreign reserves. Quarterly data for balance of payments do not exist in any continuous form prior to 1967, and the earlier yearly data differ among the various possible sources: French government agencies, the OECD, the IMF, and the BIS. We were unable to determine which among these variant annual series was closest in construction to the quarterly series, hence made no attempt to interpolate quarterly observations between annual observations.

B. *Exports*

FREXQNFF   Merchandise Exports. Unit: Billions of Francs at Annual
FREXQSFF   Rates.

Source: For 1955I to 1961IV, *Bulletin mensuel statistiques (BMS)*, various monthly issues, table entitled "Commerce extérieur"; 1962I to 1969IV, *BMS*, March 1971, "Séries rétrospectives, commerce extérieur"; 1970I to 1976IV, *BMS*, various issues, table entitled "Commerce extérieur."

Description: Merchandise trade exports inclusive of trade in industrial gold adjusted for breaks in the monthly data in 1962I with the subsequent issuance of new French trade data on an F.O.B. basis and inclusive of military transactions. To allow for the break, we adjusted the earlier data by the mean of the ratios of the overlapping series in the year the break occurred. Data are quarterly averages of monthly figures converted to annual rates.

C. *Imports*

FRIMQNFF   Merchandise Imports. Unit: Billions of Francs at Annual
FRIMQSFF   Rates.

Source: Same as described for exports, I.B. above.

Description: Same as described for exports above.

D. *Exchange Rate*

FRXRQNFF   Spot Exchange Rate. Unit: Francs per Dollar.

Source: For 1955I to 1956IV, International Monetary Fund, computer tapes; 1957I to 1976IV, *International Financial Statistics (IFS)*, various issues, line 1 of table for France.

Description: Data prior to 1957I are quarterly averages of end of month figures as given on IMF's computer tapes. After 1957I, the figures are quarterly averages of monthly averages of daily figures.

II. FINANCIAL VARIABLES

The most readily available monetary data for France in official French publications are those that appear periodically in INSEE's *Bulletin mensuel de statistiques (BMS)* in the tables entitled "Statistiques rétrospectives, finances." These tables provide monthly data for periods ranging from four or five years to a decade or more. One problem, however, is that the data in general are not continuous from one version of the tables to the next. Two breaks in particular occur in all of the monetary data: a break in 1958:12, after which data for the Saar are excluded, and a break in 1969:12 with the redefinition of the banking sector. A second even more troublesome problem is that in one instance—currency figures—the description of the data is totally misleading. The term "billets en circulation" is used at various times to describe two different things: total notes outstanding of the Banque de France, whether held by banks or the nonbank public, and notes held by the nonbank public alone.

Accordingly, we have relied on a variety of other sources in attempting to derive homogeneous and theoretically satisfactory monetary series for our full sample period. These included the *Rapport annuel* of the Banque de France, publications of the Conseil national du crédit (CNC), chiefly the *Annexes* to their *Rapport annuel*, the regular tables in the *BMS* that give monthly monetary data one year at a time, and the OECD's *Main Economic Indicators*. Since the monetary data currently published by INSEE in their regular monthly tables and extended back to December 1969 in the "Statistiques rétrospectives" in the March 1976 issue of the *BMS*, appeared to be the theoretically best set available, we constructed estimates for the earlier period that are consistent with those data.

A. *Narrow Money Stock*

FRM1QSFF   Money Stock, M1. Unit: Billions of Francs.

Source: *Coin*: 1955:1–76:12, *BMS*, various issues, tables of monetary data entitled "Finances: Monnaie, crédit, disponibilitiés monétaires et quasi monétaires." *Notes*: 1955–59, same publication and tables as for coin; 1959–69, CNC, *Annexes* to various issues of the *Rapport annuel*, tables entitled "Disponibilités monétaires et quasi monétaires," and OECD, *Main Economic Indicators*, various editions; 1969–74, *BMS*, March 1976, section entitled "Statistiques rétrospectives: Monnaie, crédit, épargne"; 1975, 1976, monetary tables in various issues of the *BMS*. *Demand Deposits*: 1955–59, monetary tables in various monthly issues of the *BMS*, 1959–74, *BMS*, "Statistiques rétrospectives: Monnaie, crédit, épargne," August 1967 (for 1959–65), July 1971 (for 1966–69), and March 1976 (for 1969–74), 1975, 1976, monetary tables in various monthly issues of the *BMS*.

Description: *Currency held by the public*: There are two sources of inconsistency between the note series contained in the current and in the earlier versions of the money supply data that INSEE publishes. One is that the current version excludes notes held by banks while earlier versions do not. The other is that the division between banks and the nonbank public has changed between the earlier sets of data and the latest one.

To solve the first problems we used an alternative note series compiled by the CNC for the period 1959 through 1969 that excluded notes held in banks. This series, like the INSEE data, however, was defined on the basis of the earlier classification of financial institutions. It consisted of monthly estimates of the CNC for the period 1959:1–69:12. Where the CNC figures were not available, we derived monthly figures from the OECD's published money supply series by subtracting appropriate estimates of demand deposits and coin. These estimates were checked against end-of-year estimates of the CNC and end-of-quarter data provided by André Fourçans. In all instances they corresponded completely.

We then had two separate series for notes held by the public: the currently published version extending from 1969:12 forward and this earlier version from 1959:1 to 1969:12, the first defined according to the earlier classification of financial institutions and the second according to the current classification. To combine the two we used the ratio of the overlapping observations to adjust the earlier version of the series to the same basis as the later.

Note data prior to 1959:1 included notes held by banks. In addition, prior to 1958:12, they also included a small number of notes held in the Saar region. A further complication was that in the publications we had available, for 1955–57 notes were aggregated with coin.

The coin data also posed some problems. For our entire sample period, the only figures available were for total coin outstanding. Any plausible method of adjustment would have resulted in only a minute percentage difference either in the currency components of M1 or in M1 itself. Accordingly, we simply added the unadjusted figures for coin to both note series—the series for total notes outstanding for the period 1955:1 to 1959:1 in France and the Saar and the series for notes held by the public which we had put together for the period from 1959:1 on. We then adjusted the earlier series to conform to the later on the basis of the overlapping observations in 1959:1.

Demand Deposits: To derive a homogeneous series for demand deposits, we had to make adjustments to the underlying data similar to those we made for currency. To account for the break in 1969:12 caused by the changed classification of financial institutions, we adjusted the demand deposit data for the period 1958:12 to 1969:11 to conform to the latest version of the deposit data, which, like the note data, begin in 1969:12. The adjustment factor was derived from a regression of the later on the earlier version of the two series in the period of overlap from 1969:12 to 1972:12.

To correct for the discontinuity in the data caused by exclusion of the Saar in 1958:12, we multiplied the series for earlier dates by the ratio in 1958:12 of our newly derived deposit series to the series for deposits including those held in the Saar.

The narrow money stock M1, is the sum of the two series described above. The data are quarterly averages of monthly observations given in billions of francs. Since we used seasonally adjusted data in much of our interpolation of the separate deposit and currency series, the final M1 series is only available on a seasonally adjusted basis.

B. *Broader Money Stock*

1. FRM2QSFF   Money Stock, M2. Unit: Billions of Francs.

Source: for 1957I to 1965IV, *BMS*, August 1966, "Statistiques rétrospectives: Monnaie, crédit, épargne," column entitled "Comptes speciaux"; 1966–70, *BMS*, July 1971, same table, column entitled "Comptes sur livrets dans les banques"; 1969:12–74:12 (new basis of defining banks), *BMS*, July 1975, same table, section entitled "Comptes sur livrets dan les banques"; 1975–76, *BMS*, monthly issues, table entitled "Finances monnaie, crédit, masse monétaire."

Description: The broader definition of money used in official publications is the "masse monétaire," the sum of what we have called M1 and total "disponibilités quasi monétaires." These include the public's holdings of the following five types of obligations: (1) term deposits and CD–like bonds of commercial banks (dépôts à terme et bons de caisse dan les banques), (2) term deposits at the Treasury (dépôts à terme au Trésor), (3) bonds of the Caisse national du crédit agricole (bons de la C.N.C.A., part détenu par le public), (4) special time deposits at commercial banks that are tied in with mortgage loans (épargne logement), and (5) passbook time deposits of commercial banks (comptes sur livrets dans les banques).

According to Jacques Melitz (see the appendix to his "Inflationary Expectations and the French Demand for Money" cited above) a definition of money similar to M2 in the U.S. would include only this last category of deposits. The others, excluding the épargne logement, are all term deposits in the true sense of the word—subject to withdrawal only after a certain set period has elapsed, ranging from one month for dépôts à terme to three years for bons de la C.N.C.A. A compte d'épargne-logement, while in some respects more akin to a conventional passbook account, has certain other features—a minimum holding period and interest tie-in with mortgage loans—that raise questions about its comparability with ordinary time deposits.

We have therefore decided to exclude the épargne logement from our definition of M2 and, like Melitz, only include comptes sur livrets of commercial banks. The data for these deposits begin in 1957:1, prior to which no such category of deposits existed. There is one break in 1969:12 due to the reclassification of financial institutions already mentioned. To correct for it we adjusted the pre-1969:12 data on the basis of the mean of the ratios of the overlapping monthly observations from 1969:12 to 1970:12. Our final series is a sum of quarterly averages of the separately seasonally adjusted M1 and comptes sur livrets series.

   2. FRM2QSSD   Money Stock, M2, Plus Savings Deposits. Unit: Billions of Francs.

Source: For 1955–69, CNC, *Annexe au rapport anneul*, yearly issues, tables and columns entitled "Dépôts dans les caisses d'épargne, montant des dépôts. Total"; 1970–75, same source as above, tables and columns entitled "Placements auprès des caisses d'épargne. Total"; 1976, CNC, *Statistiques mensuelles*, various issues, table and lines entitled "Placement liquides au court terme. Placements auprès de caisses d'épargne."

Description: We constructed an alternative measure of the broader money stock in France that Melitz also uses in his work. It is M2 as defined above plus "dépôts traditionnels dans les caisses d'épargne," savings deposits at the caisses d'épargne, which are a type of savings bank. The data are quarterly averages of monthly observations in seasonally adjusted form.

C. *High-Powered Money*
    FRMHQNFF   High-powered Money. Unit: Billions of Francs, NSA, SA.
    FRMHQSFF

Source: For coin outstanding, see sources for II.A., M1, above; notes outstanding, Banque de France, *Rapport annuel*, Balance Sheet; deposits of banks at the Banque de France, *Rapport annuel*; private deposits at the Banque de France and at the Treasury, *BMS*, various issues, tables entitled the "masse monétaire".

Description: The series is the sum of notes and coin outstanding, deposits of the public and banks at the Banque de France, and deposits of the public at the Treasury. The coin series is the same as the one already described in the discussion of M1, above, II.A.

For notes outstanding, which are available on a weekly basis, we used the figures for the Thursday closest to the end of each month, whether that Thursday actually fell in the month in question or not. For December we used the end-of-year figures. Deposits of banks at the Banque de France are figures for the Thursday closest to the end of the month. Prior to 1962:4, the only data available were combined data for French and foreign financial institutions. After that date, figures for French banks were given separately. Accordingly we reduced the series prior to 1962:4 by multiplying by the average share of deposits of French financial institutions in the overlap period. Private deposits at the Banque de France and at the Treasury are monthly figures.

The final series is a quarterly average of these monthly observations in billions of francs.

D. *Official International Reserve Assets*
   FRFHQNFF   Official International Reserve Assets. Unit: Billions of
   FRFHQSFF   Francs.
Source: Various monthly issues, *BMS*, tables entitled "Finances: Monnaie-crédit," now marked "Contreparties des disponibilités monétaires et quasi moné-taires. Or et devises (net)."
Description: Net foreign assets of the monetary authorities, given on a monthly basis in the source and converted to quarterly averages.
E. *Interest Rates*
  1. Short-Term
     FRRSQNST   Short-Term Money Market Rate on Private Bills. Unit:
                    Decimals.
Source: *BMS*, various monthly issues, table entitled "Bourse" under the heading "Taux de l'argent au jour et jour: Effets privés."
Description: The data are quarterly averages of monthly averages of daily figures of the day-to-day money market rate on private bills, in decimal form.
  2. Long-Term
     FRRLQNLT   Long-Term Secondary Market Yield on Government
                    Bonds. Unit: Decimals.
Source: *BMS*, various monthly issues, table entitled "Bourse" under the heading "Exprunt de l^{re} catégorie avec crédit d'impôt et sans lot-public et semi-public."
Description: The series is the secondary market yield on longer-term government (central government and nationalized industries) bonds. Beginning in 1974:1, there is an unexplained break in the series. To maintain consistency of the data we adjusted the series beginning 1974:1 by multiplying by the ratio of the two series that month. The data are quarterly averages of end-of-month figures in decimal form.
III. NONFINANCIAL DOMESTIC VARIABLES
A. *National Product*
   French data for income are available on a quarterly basis for any extended period only for what the French term "produit intérieur brut." The series, however, is not a measure of gross domestic product as conventionally defined. It excludes government services and certain other types of nonindustrial produc-tion. Since these data are all that exist, we use them as our income measure. We have considerable doubts about their accuracy. Viewed graphically, both series show so little variation about their trends—excluding the quarters surrounding the student revolt in May 1968—that they appear to have been generated primar-ily by linear interpolation between annual estimates.
  1. *Nominal Income*
     FRYNQSFF   Nominal Income. Unit: Billions of Francs at Annual Rates.
Source: for 1958I to 1972IV, Les collections de l'INSEE, *Comptes trimestriels*, methods statistiques et séries rétrospectives, 40-C, tables 192, 500; 1973I to 1976IV, tables 16.1.1, 16.1.2, INSEE, *Tendances de la conjoncture*, various issues.
Description: Data in current prices are available only from 1958I to 1976IV. For the period prior to 1958, we constructed an implicit deflator (1970 = 1.00) from the regression relation between the consumer price index and the implicit deflator for the period 1958 to 1972. We then used this new series for the deflator to

estimate nominal income from real income. The series was available only in seasonally adjusted form at the source.

2. *Real Income*

FRYRQS70   Real Income, 1970 Prices, 1951I to 1976IV. Unit: Billions of Francs at Annual Rates.

Source: See source for nominal income, III.A.1. above.

Description: Two separate series were published by INSEE. The first, for the period 1949I to 1959IV, was in 1956 prices; the second, for the period 1959I to 1976IV, was in 1963 prices. To link the two, we rebased the first series in 1963 prices and then rebased the new combined series in 1970 prices. The underlying data were available only in seasonally adjusted form in the original source.

B. *Prices*

1. Implicit Price Deflator

FRPDQS70   Implicit Deflator. Unit: 1970 = 1.00.

Source: Same as for nominal and real income, III.A.1 and III.A.2 above.

Description: For the period 1951I to 1957IV, the deflator is estimated from the logarithmic relation between the deflator and the consumer price index over the period 1958I to 1972IV (described in III.A.1 above). For the period 1958I to 1976IV, it is the ratio of nominal to real income based in 1970 prices.

2. Consumer Price Index

FRPCQS70   Consumer Price Index. Unit: 1970 = 1.00.

Source: *BMS*, table entitled "Indice national des prix à la consommation des familles de condition modeste," various issues.

Description: Prior to 1962, there are no published CPI data for France as a whole on anything other than a yearly basis. Throughout our sample period there are, however, monthly data for a Paris CPI, and for the period 1957–61, end-of-quarter data for a CPI for a sample of provincial cities.

The derivation of the series for the whole of France for the full period involved three steps. To obtain a monthly index for the period through 1957, we estimated the relation between the yearly provincial and Parisian indices for the years 1949–56 and used this relation, together with the monthly Parisian index to obtain a monthly provincial index.

For the period 1957–63 we estimated the relation between the quarterly provincial index and the Parisian index for the last month of the quarter and used it together with the monthly Parisian index to estimate the monthly provincial index.

Using equal weights, we combined the monthly Parisian and estimated a monthly provincial index for each period. The result was two separate national indices: a 1949 based series for the period through 1957 and a 1956–57 based index for the period 1957–63. We linked these indexes and the two published indexes for all of France, the 1962 based index for 1962–70 and the 1970 based index for 1970–76, by multiplying by means of the ratios of overlapping observations in the relevant overlapping year to arrive at a continuous 1970 based series for our full period. Data are quarterly averages of monthly figures.

C. *Industrial Production*

FRIPQS70   Industrial Production Index. Unit: 1970 = 1.00.

Source: For 1950I to 1973IV, *BMS*, "Statistiques rétrospectives production industrielle," October 1961, September 1966, and June 1974; 1974I to 1976IV,

BMS, various monthly issues, table entitled "Indices mensuels de la production industrielle."

Description: The final series is the index of industrial production, 1970 = 1.00, including construction and public works projects, without adjustment for working days. Data are quarterly averages of monthly figures.

There is a bewildering array of French industrial production indexes: monthly, quarterly, and annual series, in ascending order of inclusiveness, all on a variety of base years, some with and some without adjustment for working days, and some exclusive or inclusive of construction and public works projects.

To construct a homogeneous series for our full period, we linked the following three monthly indexes: 1952 = 100 for 1950–61, 1959 = 100 for 1956–69, and 1970 = 100 for 1963–76.

D. *Government Accounts*
  1. Government Expenditure
     FRGXQNFF   Government Expenditures. Unit: Billions of Francs at
     FRGXQSFF   Annual Rates.
Source: For 1955I to 1976IV, CNC, *Statistiques er études financières*, table now marked "Totaux généraux, dépenses."
Description: Data are quarterly flows at annual rates in billions of francs, converted from the cumulated monthly flows given in the source.
  2. Government Deficit
     FRGDQNFF   Government Deficit. Unit: Billions of Francs at Annual
     FRGDQSFF   Rates.
Source: Same as described in III.D.1 above, table 3, entitled "La Trésorerie et la dette publique," currently worded "Soldes de l'exécution de lois de finances."
Description: These figures are for the total deficit on a cash-flow basis, quarterly, converted from cumulated monthly flows to annual rates in billions of francs.

E. *Population*
     FRPPQNIN   Population. Unit: Billions of Persons.
Source: For 1954IV to 1976IV, United Nations *Demographic Yearbook*, various issues.
Description: The data including armed forces are linear interpolations of mid-year estimates.

F. *Labor Force Statistics*
  1. Labor Force
     FRLFQSFF   Total Labor Force. Unit: Billions of Persons.
Source: 1955–58, *Yearbook of Labor Statistics*, 1957, 1960; 1959–74, INSEE, *Tendances de la conjoncture*, table entitled "Population Active"; 1975–76, estimated as described below.
Description: The data for 1955 to 1974 are quarterly data interpolated linearly by us from published annual figures. For 1975–76, we derived estimates by regressing labor force on unemployed for the period 1959–74 and applying the relation to the figures for unemployed in 1975 and 1976. No seasonal adjustment was required.
  2. Number Unemployed
     FRUNQNFF   Number Unemployed. Unit: Billions of Persons.
     FRUNQSFF
Source: For 1955–58, *Yearbook of Labor Statistics*, 1957, 1960 monthly figures;

1959–76, INSEE, *Tendances de la conjoncture.* "Demands d'emplois non satis-
faites" end-of-quarter figures.

Description: Data are end-of-quarter figures of the number of unemployed.

3. Unemployment Rate
   FRURQNFF   Unemployment Rate. Unit: Decimals.
   FRURQSFF

Source: As described in III.E.1 and III.E.2 above.

Description: The ratio of the number unemployed to the labor force in decimals
as defined above.

List of Tables for France (Quarterly Data)

FRANCE_FRBPQNFF

1954	1		0.2200	0.3000	0.8400
1955	1	0.8800	0.8000	1.1500	0.1700
1956	1	-0.5100	-0.6300	-0.6000	-1.3300
1957	1	-1.1400	-1.1600	-0.6300	-1.1100
1958	1	0.1000	-0.0900	1.1100	-0.9800
1959	1	2.7300	2.5000	1.3000	0.7000
1960	1	0.6900	0.9400	1.3200	0.3700
1961	1	1.6900	1.8100	0.0800	1.2100
1962	1	1.6200	2.8000	-0.0500	0.4200
1963	1	1.9100	1.2700	0.2600	0.7200
1964	1	0.4200	1.4300	0.5300	1.4200
1965	1	1.3900	0.9700	0.4600	0.5100
1966	1	0.5400	1.4300	0.6500	-0.7900
1967	1	-0.0200	-0.1900	0.3700	1.0800
1968	1	-0.3300	-8.7100	-5.4500	-1.3800
1969	1	-2.4600	-8.8700	-0.6000	2.6700
1970	1	4.0200	4.8000	2.9100	1.9800
1971	1	1.9400	2.8700	9.6700	3.3000
1972	1	0.5600	4.7100	1.7300	-0.4900
1973	1	3.3000	-0.9600	-9.7600	-0.0100
1974	1	-6.3200	0.5400	1.8700	1.4700
1975	1	2.2000	5.1200	-1.5900	6.5000
1976	1	-10.1500	1.5700	0.3200	-0.1000

FRANCE_FRBPQSFF

1954	1		0.24710	0.07522	1.00242
1955	1	0.91654	0.81288	0.92992	0.38275
1956	1	-0.52081	-0.65452	-0.78802	-1.03675
1957	1	-1.22337	-1.24786	-0.76639	-0.70593
1958	1	-0.07975	-0.28122	1.09346	-0.40685
1959	1	2.47618	2.16859	1.45964	1.19453
1960	1	0.37076	0.48383	1.68418	0.78382
1961	1	1.38450	1.26136	0.58893	1.53687
1962	1	1.32972	2.23287	0.54702	0.60935
1963	1	1.69460	0.73761	0.84355	0.82609
1964	1	0.20843	1.05538	1.05937	1.39397
1965	1	1.12492	0.89359	0.92713	0.29527
1966	1	0.12934	1.80574	1.02860	-1.25571
1967	1	-0.48810	0.52991	0.67304	0.42453
1968	1	-0.80149	-7.69280	-5.42507	-2.02992
1969	1	-2.71838	-7.96283	-0.80565	2.29770
1970	1	3.90999	5.36278	2.62225	1.88066
1971	1	2.16964	2.70569	9.50715	3.55934
1972	1	0.97547	3.84773	1.84720	-0.14457
1973	1	4.08912	-2.55947	-9.31086	0.41042
1974	1	-5.40106	-1.50316	2.70765	1.63774
1975	1	3.42178	2.76845	-0.60123	6.58694
1976	1	-8.81193	-0.82766	1.28392	-0.04288

FRANCE_FREXQNFF

1955	1	16.363	17.246	15.054	19.170
1956	1	15.493	17.011	15.706	17.855
1957	1	19.176	18.741	17.230	21.885
1958	1	21.851	20.934	19.747	25.257
1959	1	23.902	28.697	26.818	33.744
1960	1	36.405	33.928	31.084	36.791
1961	1	35.829	36.676	34.099	38.850
1962	1	37.584	36.236	32.800	42.620
1963	1	37.756	42.088	37.764	44.392
1964	1	45.156	45.440	40.044	49.140
1965	1	47.008	50.348	47.196	56.012
1966	1	53.072	56.304	50.160	57.348
1967	1	55.420	58.400	47.836	62.372
1968	1	64.584	53.208	64.200	72.008
1969	1	72.320	78.284	71.156	92.232
1970	1	95.710	104.617	91.965	110.079
1971	1	109.372	116.364	108.016	127.660
1972	1	125.000	139.240	118.756	150.956
1973	1	151.880	158.144	149.644	182.300
1974	1	207.908	234.660	210.748	239.168
1975	1	230.916	237.012	202.428	238.208
1976	1	253.404	283.060	251.628	304.876

FRANCE_FREXQSFF

1955	1	16.045	17.042	16.815	17.877
1956	1	15.177	16.812	17.553	16.679
1957	1	18.697	18.585	19.218	20.527
1958	1	21.189	20.816	21.992	23.768
1959	1	23.079	28.617	29.776	31.825
1960	1	35.198	33.753	34.457	34.758
1961	1	34.731	36.380	37.720	36.750
1962	1	36.605	35.778	36.227	40.359
1963	1	36.932	41.385	41.693	41.984
1964	1	44.501	44.350	44.328	46.411
1965	1	46.542	48.872	52.443	52.772
1966	1	52.769	54.377	55.969	53.950
1967	1	55.189	56.232	53.509	58.724
1968	1	64.270	51.123	71.955	67.899
1969	1	71.844	75.197	79.667	87.243
1970	1	94.854	100.599	102.558	104.650
1971	1	108.186	111.904	119.814	122.244
1972	1	123.376	133.673	131.291	145.516
1973	1	149.755	151.172	165.440	176.578
1974	1	204.764	223.488	233.128	232.648
1975	1	227.222	224.812	224.461	232.100
1976	1	249.164	268.087	279.219	297.349

FRANCE_FRIMQNFF

1955	1	15.839	19.448	15.310	17.659
1956	1	16.562	18.767	17.214	18.889
1957	1	21.422	21.407	18.564	19.911
1958	1	22.768	22.895	18.980	19.890
1959	1	21.262	23.235	20.177	25.584
1960	1	28.718	27.949	25.931	28.710
1961	1	29.512	31.178	26.299	31.424
1962	1	32.740	34.220	31.284	36.124
1963	1	37.468	41.732	36.216	44.688
1964	1	47.620	49.012	40.944	47.596
1965	1	46.748	48.988	42.520	52.084
1966	1	53.848	56.108	49.572	58.520
1967	1	60.416	57.660	50.052	60.448
1968	1	63.240	56.828	61.636	75.768
1969	1	77.324	86.128	77.248	94.336
1970	1	94.785	103.441	91.623	108.504
1971	1	105.720	112.780	103.660	121.408
1972	1	126.384	130.284	113.576	141.380
1973	1	147.652	156.788	144.704	173.824
1974	1	225.420	257.208	231.736	242.296
1975	1	228.096	218.412	197.496	241.868
1976	1	267.980	290.248	280.176	336.372

FRANCE_FRIMQSFF

1955	1	15.468	17.903	16.838	18.047
1956	1	16.120	17.289	18.998	19.291
1957	1	20.696	19.843	20.522	20.321
1958	1	21.843	21.340	21.078	20.195
1959	1	20.305	21.802	22.464	25.770
1960	1	27.499	26.257	29.043	28.591
1961	1	28.392	29.370	29.520	31.000
1962	1	31.657	32.282	35.220	35.365
1963	1	36.293	39.533	40.783	43.526
1964	1	46.144	46.597	46.204	46.109
1965	1	45.222	46.901	47.925	50.193
1966	1	52.141	53.983	55.797	56.082
1967	1	58.708	55.677	56.110	57.727
1968	1	61.796	54.889	68.817	72.305
1969	1	75.912	83.059	85.937	90.201
1970	1	93.341	99.392	101.691	104.310
1971	1	104.065	107.977	114.798	117.602
1972	1	123.918	124.580	125.483	137.967
1973	1	143.989	150.089	159.586	170.250
1974	1	219.119	246.581	255.248	237.702
1975	1	221.390	209.655	217.355	237.157
1976	1	260.224	278.804	307.968	329.938

FRANCE_FRXRQNFF

1955	1	3.49950	3.49950	3.49983	3.50000
1956	1	3.50000	3.50000	3.49983	3.49967
1957	1	3.50000	3.50000	3.58833	4.12733
1958	1	4.20000	4.20000	4.19233	4.43267
1959	1	4.90300	4.90233	4.90567	4.90700
1960	1	4.90910	4.90348	4.90100	4.90485
1961	1	4.90140	4.90124	4.91096	4.90999
1962	1	4.90116	4.90076	4.90076	4.90084
1963	1	4.90076	4.90076	4.90084	4.90124
1964	1	4.90124	4.90108	4.90100	4.90092
1965	1	4.90132	4.90172	4.90132	4.90212
1966	1	4.90180	4.90132	4.90912	4.94422
1967	1	4.94894	4.92446	4.90493	4.90396
1968	1	4.92304	4.94983	4.97364	4.96493
1969	1	4.95426	4.96936	5.29840	5.57756
1970	1	5.54764	5.52538	5.52069	5.52171
1971	1	5.51775	5.52364	5.51694	5.48344
1972	1	5.10067	5.02200	5.00433	5.05000
1973	1	4.79333	4.42933	4.18667	4.40667
1974	1	4.93533	4.87533	4.78400	4.64510
1975	1	4.28257	4.08153	4.35723	4.42427
1976	1	4.52273	4.70260	4.90740	4.98580
1977	1	4.97653			

FRANCE_FRM1QSFF

1955	1	49.694	50.839	51.875	54.072
1956	1	56.898	58.562	59.957	60.308
1957	1	60.810	62.351	63.966	65.242
1958	1	66.072	66.874	67.029	68.526
1959	1	69.867	71.549	73.456	75.914
1960	1	76.756	79.319	82.362	85.979
1961	1	90.392	93.510	96.319	100.259
1962	1	104.717	109.460	114.579	119.514
1963	1	125.068	129.631	134.266	138.296
1964	1	141.973	144.089	147.303	150.301
1965	1	153.997	157.895	161.506	165.881
1966	1	170.165	173.588	176.680	179.112
1967	1	183.609	187.234	186.940	187.747
1968	1	190.055	194.211	201.684	206.829
1969	1	207.889	209.708	209.809	206.475
1970	1	205.127	207.355	211.443	220.346
1971	1	231.356	236.186	244.313	248.070
1972	1	256.896	264.453	278.620	284.449
1973	1	287.886	297.145	301.423	305.616
1974	1	314.888	330.581	328.477	347.559
1975	1	352.227	355.283	376.469	400.346
1976	1	406.241	422.147	430.554	442.881

FRANCE_FRM2QSFF

1955	1	49.694	50.839	51.875	54.072
1956	1	56.898	58.562	59.957	60.308
1957	1	60.814	62.388	64.054	65.401
1958	1	66.305	67.165	67.388	68.963
1959	1	70.443	72.253	74.318	76.919
1960	1	77.934	80.647	83.870	87.689
1961	1	92.283	95.590	98.565	102.712
1962	1	107.405	112.344	117.757	123.024
1963	1	128.920	133.797	138.721	143.060
1964	1	147.138	149.589	153.127	156.477
1965	1	160.438	164.715	168.661	173.256
1966	1	178.151	182.327	186.130	189.142
1967	1	194.323	198.623	201.312	205.756
1968	1	210.824	216.638	224.900	230.677
1969	1	232.880	235.691	236.899	233.326
1970	1	231.812	234.270	239.066	249.196
1971	1	261.802	268.617	278.575	284.231
1972	1	295.064	305.268	322.079	331.227
1973	1	337.119	349.785	356.499	362.428
1974	1	372.664	389.439	389.020	410.039
1975	1	418.869	426.764	454.057	485.647
1976	1	499.706	520.188	533.278	548.649

FRANCE_FRM2QSSD

1955	1	62.393	64.221	66.001	69.018
1956	1	72.605	74.885	76.844	77.599
1957	1	78.580	80.641	82.662	84.398
1958	1	85.872	87.379	88.289	90.692
1959	1	93.044	95.715	98.781	102.457
1960	1	104.346	107.885	112.001	116.744
1961	1	122.013	126.138	130.099	135.150
1962	1	140.552	146.631	153.340	160.082
1963	1	167.469	173.699	180.008	185.721
1964	1	192.285	196.795	202.294	207.550
1965	1	213.218	219.190	225.001	231.287
1966	1	238.312	244.768	250.726	255.741
1967	1	263.019	269.576	274.814	281.549
1968	1	288.815	296.751	306.620	314.031
1969	1	317.570	322.207	326.744	328.012
1970	1	330.896	336.514	345.089	359.294
1971	1	376.379	388.120	402.500	412.679
1972	1	427.933	442.702	464.675	479.406
1973	1	490.552	508.823	521.556	533.400
1974	1	550.513	574.640	583.197	611.646
1975	1	631.115	651.137	690.748	737.201
1976	1	766.417	799.927	825.995	853.354

FRANCE_FRMHQNFF

1951	1	17.327	18.122	19.252	19.978
1952	1	20.743	20.955	21.483	22.043
1953	1	22.373	23.005	23.745	23.905
1954	1	24.249	24.833	25.521	26.259
1955	1	26.897	27.314	28.265	29.334
1956	1	30.159	30.502	31.827	32.220
1957	1	32.669	34.104	36.288	36.883
1958	1	36.736	37.927	38.483	38.820
1959	1	37.235	36.735	37.800	37.691
1960	1	37.975	38.864	40.733	41.604
1961	1	42.481	43.746	46.147	47.388
1962	1	47.630	49.220	51.598	53.309
1963	1	53.803	55.425	58.722	59.886
1964	1	59.625	61.245	63.542	63.860
1965	1	64.025	66.215	68.534	68.950
1966	1	69.180	70.499	72.436	72.753
1967	1	72.774	74.830	77.429	78.635
1968	1	76.815	79.714	81.554	82.912
1969	1	83.587	83.967	84.048	81.230
1970	1	79.662	81.008	85.591	86.684
1971	1	87.288	88.490	99.996	102.131
1972	1	97.816	98.344	111.900	120.660
1973	1	124.656	131.099	141.127	135.457
1974	1	150.534	149.708	156.902	140.047
1975	1	132.016	130.399	121.557	117.808
1976	1	115.087	119.561	124.739	129.083

FRANCE_FRMHQSFF

1951	1	17.397	18.183	19.157	19.933
1952	1	20.820	21.027	21.386	21.992
1953	1	22.437	23.101	23.640	23.839
1954	1	24.315	24.966	25.384	26.172
1955	1	26.991	27.489	28.081	29.196
1956	1	30.320	30.735	31.558	32.035
1957	1	32.903	34.399	35.918	36.636
1958	1	37.062	38.290	38.024	38.548
1959	1	37.612	37.086	37.337	37.407
1960	1	38.381	39.242	40.226	41.282
1961	1	42.948	44.164	45.571	47.023
1962	1	48.176	49.667	50.933	52.923
1963	1	54.467	55.854	57.971	59.482
1964	1	60.395	61.650	62.733	63.472
1965	1	64.857	66.597	67.676	68.584
1966	1	70.043	70.883	71.542	72.386
1967	1	73.648	75.295	76.442	78.194
1968	1	77.712	80.437	80.366	82.298
1969	1	84.598	85.120	82.563	80.450
1970	1	80.725	82.471	83.767	85.763
1971	1	88.564	90.367	97.428	101.215
1972	1	99.388	100.329	108.776	119.929
1973	1	126.860	133.176	137.209	135.051
1974	1	153.461	151.040	152.936	139.995
1975	1	134.719	130.828	118.749	117.985
1976	1	117.453	119.624	121.975	129.449

FRANCE_FRFHQNFF

1954	1	2.3567	2.6767	2.8233	3.4333
1955	1	4.3767	5.3233	6.3567	6.7967
1956	1	6.4400	5.9600	5.1367	4.2367
1957	1	3.0033	1.7467	0.7333	-0.0933
1958	1	-0.2500	-0.5667	0.6500	0.5167
1959	1	1.7233	4.2900	6.3100	7.0167
1960	1	7.5033	8.6500	9.7667	10.4233
1961	1	11.4733	13.2500	14.3233	14.7800
1962	1	16.1633	18.8300	19.1667	20.2533
1963	1	21.3433	22.7733	23.3167	23.9967
1964	1	24.4800	25.5367	26.5033	27.4067
1965	1	29.0400	30.0500	30.6500	31.1567
1966	1	31.6167	32.8867	34.1200	33.4967
1967	1	33.1867	33.0267	33.2600	34.2533
1968	1	34.1567	31.1600	21.6500	18.6700
1969	1	17.6333	9.7800	6.8400	7.8333
1970	1	12.5467	16.8533	20.3033	22.1333
1971	1	24.5000	26.9033	36.7100	38.8000
1972	1	41.1233	42.8967	47.4300	47.4400
1973	1	48.6333	51.0433	44.7333	38.8000
1974	1	33.1567	33.9000	35.4567	36.7867
1975	1	38.8167	42.8133	42.1600	47.6300
1976	1	46.1833	40.9267	41.3100	41.1233

FRANCE_FRFHQSFF

1954	1	2.4106	2.6685	2.8023	3.4039
1955	1	4.4426	5.3125	6.3122	6.7822
1956	1	6.5329	5.9394	5.0416	4.2479
1957	1	3.1493	1.6984	0.5741	-0.0421
1958	1	-0.0419	-0.6544	0.4209	0.6201
1959	1	1.9912	4.1459	6.0344	7.1761
1960	1	7.8044	8.4504	9.4843	10.6153
1961	1	11.7785	13.0115	14.0696	14.9894
1962	1	16.4313	18.5811	18.9680	20.4488
1963	1	21.5594	22.5524	23.1604	24.1760
1964	1	24.6221	25.3585	26.4221	27.5561
1965	1	29.0642	29.9379	30.6456	31.3258
1966	1	31.4548	32.8374	34.2256	33.6905
1967	1	32.8481	33.0331	33.4222	34.4832
1968	1	33.6926	31.2539	21.7934	18.8806
1969	1	17.1692	10.0011	6.7856	8.0539
1970	1	12.2345	17.1214	20.0184	22.3036
1971	1	24.5179	27.1225	36.1687	38.9337
1972	1	41.5046	42.9716	46.8059	47.4590
1973	1	49.2740	51.0164	44.1192	38.7288
1974	1	33.9275	33.7352	35.0227	36.5723
1975	1	39.6280	42.5911	41.8698	47.3080
1976	1	47.0132	40.6770	41.1018	40.7183

FRANCE_FRRSQNST

1951	1	0.024400	0.025767	0.025900	0.031833
1952	1	0.036467	0.036933	0.038700	0.039633
1953	1	0.040000	0.040700	0.042167	0.038867
1954	1	0.035433	0.035533	0.037933	0.034833
1955	1	0.032667	0.032300	0.031200	0.030233
1956	1	0.030200	0.030667	0.030767	0.035767
1957	1	0.038467	0.051933	0.071767	0.051767
1958	1	0.054600	0.081100	0.067600	0.056100
1959	1	0.043267	0.038933	0.040833	0.039867
1960	1	0.040633	0.042067	0.042433	0.038167
1961	1	0.036467	0.037900	0.035800	0.035667
1962	1	0.035733	0.038333	0.035333	0.035067
1963	1	0.034233	0.041967	0.041633	0.041467
1964	1	0.044800	0.053733	0.047567	0.041967
1965	1	0.041100	0.041933	0.040700	0.043267
1966	1	0.042400	0.046533	0.048067	0.054500
1967	1	0.052167	0.047033	0.045200	0.046367
1968	1	0.049467	0.055133	0.062267	0.081533
1969	1	0.080333	0.089200	0.091533	0.097800
1970	1	0.097933	0.090900	0.082767	0.075267
1971	1	0.060767	0.059400	0.057667	0.055800
1972	1	0.050900	0.046467	0.038100	0.062700
1973	1	0.074767	0.075433	0.088300	0.110300
1974	1	0.126633	0.127633	0.137267	0.124667
1975	1	0.101833	0.077267	0.071300	0.066500
1976	1	0.070667	0.075467	0.089900	0.106166

FRANCE_FRRLQNLT

1955	1	0.055967	0.053333	0.052533	0.054967
1956	1	0.058733	0.058467	0.062367	0.067167
1957	1	0.071567	0.072333	0.077700	0.076067
1958	1	0.080633	0.079233	0.073467	0.071367
1959	1	0.067100	0.063767	0.060633	0.059800
1960	1	0.057933	0.057600	0.055767	0.055233
1961	1	0.055933	0.054933	0.054433	0.055467
1962	1	0.055867	0.054700	0.053400	0.053400
1963	1	0.053533	0.053100	0.052967	0.053933
1964	1	0.054367	0.054733	0.054200	0.054667
1965	1	0.060200	0.062900	0.061767	0.063233
1966	1	0.063667	0.065300	0.066567	0.067633
1967	1	0.067167	0.067000	0.066733	0.067367
1968	1	0.067733	0.069067	0.069233	0.072000
1969	1	0.076267	0.077267	0.077500	0.077500
1970	1	0.087033	0.085367	0.083567	0.082633
1971	1	0.080767	0.081133	0.081067	0.081200
1972	1	0.079833	0.076267	0.075733	0.077833
1973	1	0.081967	0.083333	0.088467	0.091433
1974	1	0.099653	0.104608	0.108545	0.106291
1975	1	0.102035	0.098066	0.096573	0.098828
1976	1	0.097208	0.097716	0.100924	0.104576

FRANCE_FRYNQSFF

1951	1	115.04	123.66	129.46	136.66
1952	1	144.82	140.99	141.80	142.68
1953	1	142.79	146.64	144.56	146.36
1954	1	148.57	151.94	154.05	155.92
1955	1	159.07	163.53	165.42	167.98
1956	1	167.39	172.98	176.07	181.49
1957	1	182.16	184.42	194.67	201.98
1958	1	217.12	227.50	227.30	227.48
1959	1	229.64	235.81	243.66	254.83
1960	1	259.64	266.84	274.19	279.01
1961	1	285.71	287.70	297.23	304.02
1962	1	316.07	325.49	330.68	338.20
1963	1	338.98	363.02	373.97	385.49
1964	1	397.28	405.75	408.02	415.72
1965	1	421.60	434.35	443.18	451.95
1966	1	461.08	473.54	478.46	488.72
1967	1	501.02	507.98	520.20	529.10
1968	1	545.58	509.84	581.57	604.54
1969	1	618.35	640.10	653.66	662.04
1970	1	685.85	713.92	721.03	746.55
1971	1	760.21	784.50	809.37	834.32
1972	1	862.80	874.40	904.80	938.00
1973	1	968.80	996.00	1024.40	1068.80
1974	1	1109.60	1149.20	1201.60	1188.80
1975	1	1211.60	1261.20	1280.80	1344.80
1976	1	1404.80	1464.00	1510.40	1545.20

FRANCE_FRYRQS70

1951	1	255.267	259.197	262.046	263.660
1952	1	269.822	263.583	263.807	266.440
1953	1	268.973	274.718	272.255	279.560
1954	1	282.811	287.568	291.290	293.174
1955	1	300.015	306.363	310.185	311.807
1956	1	310.703	318.641	322.672	332.973
1957	1	336.618	339.274	346.633	345.714
1958	1	351.096	355.072	350.500	350.008
1959	1	348.919	357.457	362.262	375.196
1960	1	380.494	387.094	396.963	403.407
1961	1	408.316	410.079	418.850	422.536
1962	1	435.102	442.561	451.529	455.340
1963	1	447.678	472.467	481.638	492.291
1964	1	504.473	511.373	511.497	517.189
1965	1	519.999	532.248	540.511	550.055
1966	1	557.017	566.301	568.904	575.959
1967	1	588.255	592.641	601.516	607.768
1968	1	624.030	581.760	643.081	656.637
1969	1	660.519	676.569	682.504	685.174
1970	1	696.796	715.313	719.139	736.106
1971	1	737.993	750.745	762.575	777.505
1972	1	793.487	792.129	805.793	823.346
1973	1	836.166	843.941	850.162	862.085
1974	1	874.008	880.747	885.413	851.199
1975	1	837.721	847.570	844.460	872.453
1976	1	891.634	903.038	911.332	907.704

FRANCE_FRPDQS70

1951	1	0.45068	0.47708	0.49403	0.51830
1952	1	0.53671	0.53490	0.53751	0.53549
1953	1	0.53088	0.53379	0.53098	0.52352
1954	1	0.52532	0.52837	0.52885	0.53184
1955	1	0.53021	0.53377	0.53330	0.53872
1956	1	0.53874	0.54287	0.54567	0.54507
1957	1	0.54114	0.54356	0.56161	0.58425
1958	1	0.61839	0.64072	0.64850	0.64993
1959	1	0.65814	0.65968	0.67261	0.67919
1960	1	0.68237	0.68935	0.69072	0.69164
1961	1	0.69972	0.70158	0.70964	0.71952
1962	1	0.72642	0.73547	0.73236	0.74274
1963	1	0.75719	0.76836	0.77646	0.78305
1964	1	0.78751	0.79346	0.79769	0.80381
1965	1	0.81077	0.81606	0.81993	0.82164
1966	1	0.82777	0.83619	0.84103	0.84853
1967	1	0.85170	0.85715	0.86481	0.87057
1968	1	0.87429	0.87638	0.90435	0.92066
1969	1	0.93616	0.94610	0.95774	0.96624
1970	1	0.98429	0.99806	1.00263	1.01419
1971	1	1.03010	1.04496	1.06136	1.07307
1972	1	1.08735	1.10386	1.12287	1.13925
1973	1	1.15862	1.18018	1.20495	1.23978
1974	1	1.26955	1.30480	1.35711	1.39662
1975	1	1.44630	1.48802	1.51671	1.54140
1976	1	1.57553	1.62119	1.65735	1.70232

FRANCE_FRPCQS70

1951	1	0.43188	0.45851	0.47564	0.50024
1952	1	0.51892	0.51709	0.51974	0.51769
1953	1	0.51300	0.51596	0.51310	0.50553
1954	1	0.50735	0.51046	0.51094	0.51398
1955	1	0.51232	0.51594	0.51546	0.52097
1956	1	0.52099	0.52518	0.52803	0.52743
1957	1	0.52343	0.52589	0.54426	0.56734
1958	1	0.59910	0.61768	0.62621	0.62665
1959	1	0.64177	0.64711	0.65375	0.66147
1960	1	0.66781	0.67359	0.68080	0.68302
1961	1	0.68234	0.68497	0.69277	0.70606
1962	1	0.71534	0.72353	0.72927	0.73668
1963	1	0.74801	0.75729	0.76811	0.77623
1964	1	0.77997	0.78359	0.78916	0.79407
1965	1	0.79916	0.80888	0.81059	0.81446
1966	1	0.82006	0.82709	0.83244	0.83722
1967	1	0.84295	0.84738	0.85396	0.86509
1968	1	0.87582	0.88275	0.89449	0.91111
1969	1	0.92579	0.93906	0.95083	0.96385
1970	1	0.97842	0.99341	1.00579	1.01591
1971	1	1.02994	1.04606	1.06055	1.07535
1972	1	1.08860	1.10394	1.12529	1.14879
1973	1	1.15916	1.18211	1.21103	1.24470
1974	1	1.29014	1.34200	1.38807	1.43062
1975	1	1.47116	1.50534	1.53883	1.57279
1976	1	1.61186	1.64672	1.68619	1.73030

FRANCE_FRIPQS70

1950	1	0.36531	0.37611	0.39105	0.39642
1951	1	0.40328	0.40815	0.41851	0.41658
1952	1	0.42224	0.41032	0.41586	0.41199
1953	1	0.40870	0.41914	0.41709	0.43566
1954	1	0.43455	0.44513	0.45303	0.46088
1955	1	0.46551	0.47107	0.48066	0.48923
1956	1	0.46960	0.50340	0.52374	0.51862
1957	1	0.52997	0.53316	0.55492	0.55327
1958	1	0.56582	0.56145	0.56647	0.55279
1959	1	0.54729	0.56517	0.57434	0.58877
1960	1	0.59011	0.60072	0.62205	0.62128
1961	1	0.63305	0.63074	0.65431	0.64878
1962	1	0.66740	0.66960	0.69223	0.68582
1963	1	0.65229	0.71668	0.72931	0.73801
1964	1	0.76506	0.76139	0.76150	0.77044
1965	1	0.76538	0.78925	0.79944	0.81357
1966	1	0.81527	0.83343	0.84822	0.84118
1967	1	0.84446	0.85567	0.86405	0.86516
1968	1	0.88463	0.78747	0.90734	0.93143
1969	1	0.92460	0.96623	0.96865	0.95907
1970	1	0.98452	1.01028	1.00489	1.00694
1971	1	0.99131	1.00463	1.02820	1.04916
1972	1	1.05333	1.06918	1.07802	1.10122
1973	1	1.12997	1.10990	1.14191	1.13275
1974	1	1.16555	1.15549	1.17407	1.10516
1975	1	1.07366	1.06080	1.03925	1.08740
1976	1	1.12723	1.13514	1.13905	1.16136

FRANCE_FRGXQNFF

1955	1	35.360	39.160	43.840	50.560
1956	1	45.920	43.960	46.800	59.600
1957	1	49.800	45.400	53.920	63.880
1958	1	53.800	52.680	61.440	70.560
1959	1	60.320	68.480	61.640	78.720
1960	1	63.840	70.440	66.600	81.000
1961	1	67.600	72.840	70.400	92.760
1962	1	79.080	82.680	77.640	102.200
1963	1	91.400	96.560	96.280	106.760
1964	1	99.560	100.600	90.360	115.200
1965	1	105.000	112.320	100.000	111.960
1966	1	118.560	123.000	104.560	119.800
1967	1	137.320	138.760	121.760	123.160
1968	1	150.400	131.600	157.120	125.960
1969	1	178.880	172.040	164.440	180.000
1970	1	185.080	176.440	175.760	201.160
1971	1	235.240	206.160	194.000	253.160
1972	1	245.080	225.880	212.520	275.640
1973	1	278.680	262.440	237.840	311.240
1974	1	318.880	287.080	299.640	351.200
1975	1	374.160	396.880	416.920	419.400
1976	1	444.960	437.440	426.400	474.120

FRANCE_FRGXQSFF

1955	1	36.967	42.933	44.576	44.041
1956	1	48.126	47.910	47.776	51.936
1957	1	52.315	48.975	55.462	55.653
1958	1	56.811	55.912	63.919	61.512
1959	1	63.932	71.405	64.961	68.761
1960	1	67.855	72.073	71.119	71.212
1961	1	71.482	73.458	76.052	82.384
1962	1	82.712	82.520	84.385	92.375
1963	1	94.037	95.448	105.012	98.793
1964	1	100.523	98.336	98.705	109.838
1965	1	103.568	108.782	109.535	109.738
1966	1	114.248	118.766	114.584	119.981
1967	1	129.585	134.526	133.568	124.563
1968	1	139.535	129.204	172.252	127.201
1969	1	164.122	171.614	180.928	179.100
1970	1	169.392	178.472	194.769	195.805
1971	1	216.317	210.823	215.890	241.951
1972	1	227.149	232.423	236.320	260.395
1973	1	260.936	270.682	262.398	293.181
1974	1	301.616	295.535	327.530	331.296
1975	1	356.799	408.017	450.597	398.116
1976	1	425.280	449.829	457.765	452.427

FRANCE_FRGDQNFF

1955	1	-0.880	-1.120	-9.840	-12.280
1956	1	-7.120	-4.040	-12.720	-16.360
1957	1	-5.600	-2.360	-16.360	-11.520
1958	1	0.680	-1.960	-14.960	-11.360
1959	1	-4.280	-5.160	-7.640	-8.040
1960	1	0.160	-2.080	-9.040	-5.480
1961	1	2.600	1.040	-7.240	-13.920
1962	1	-1.400	-2.480	-8.800	-11.680
1963	1	-6.120	-5.800	-18.800	-21.200
1964	1	-0.800	1.960	-3.960	-3.520
1965	1	1.200	-1.400	-4.560	5.320
1966	1	-3.960	-1.760	-6.200	3.840
1967	1	-10.680	-6.960	-16.920	9.240
1968	1	-14.120	13.960	-34.760	25.000
1969	1	-12.960	-6.200	-18.640	24.280
1970	1	0.040	19.160	-20.520	16.080
1971	1	-25.600	6.480	-13.160	18.400
1972	1	-4.200	4.280	-4.840	21.800
1973	1	-11.360	3.080	-8.240	45.200
1974	1	6.720	36.920	-70.480	44.080
1975	1	-14.200	-22.800	-148.600	13.560
1976	1	-76.080	23.160	-82.000	63.400

FRANCE_FRGDQSFF

1955	1	-5.1155	-6.4772	-4.8429	-7.6506
1956	1	-11.5105	-9.1642	-7.7472	-11.8691
1957	1	-10.1558	-7.1283	-11.3521	-7.3000
1958	1	-4.0353	-6.2497	-10.0598	-7.3430
1959	1	-9.1434	-8.9579	-2.9457	-4.2078
1960	1	-4.6585	-5.5394	-4.6892	-1.6732
1961	1	-2.0671	-2.2539	-3.1478	-10.2745
1962	1	-5.8036	-5.6060	-4.7191	-8.7660
1963	1	-10.0390	-8.4843	-14.5391	-19.9425
1964	1	-3.7135	-0.1393	0.8849	-5.0437
1965	1	-0.0077	-3.0645	1.3659	0.2321
1966	1	-3.0929	-3.2348	1.3775	-5.2977
1967	1	-7.2789	-9.1130	-7.0489	-3.9100
1968	1	-8.0136	10.3889	-22.4061	8.6951
1969	1	-4.8284	-11.3948	-3.7367	5.7342
1970	1	8.8024	13.2244	-3.3956	-3.8642
1971	1	-17.1183	-1.4617	9.1716	-4.2077
1972	1	3.2182	-6.5250	25.9293	-5.7240
1973	1	-4.0098	-13.1389	34.7345	10.4590
1974	1	14.2734	15.9025	-16.0690	2.1289
1975	1	-5.2804	-49.0846	-84.0787	-34.4623
1976	1	-66.3293	-5.8291	-12.2548	11.5533

FRANCE_FRPPQNIN

1954	1		0.043060	0.043152	0.043244
1955	1	0.043337	0.043430	0.043532	0.043634
1956	1	0.043737	0.043840	0.043957	0.044074
1957	1	0.044191	0.044310	0.044429	0.044549
1958	1	0.044669	0.044790	0.044902	0.045014
1959	1	0.045127	0.045240	0.045349	0.045459
1960	1	0.045569	0.045680	0.045799	0.045919
1961	1	0.046039	0.046160	0.046368	0.046577
1962	1	0.046787	0.047000	0.047203	0.047407
1963	1	0.047612	0.047820	0.047942	0.048064
1964	1	0.048186	0.048310	0.048422	0.048534
1965	1	0.048647	0.048760	0.048860	0.048959
1966	1	0.049059	0.049160	0.049257	0.049354
1967	1	0.049452	0.049550	0.049640	0.049729
1968	1	0.049819	0.049910	0.050012	0.050114
1969	1	0.050217	0.050320	0.050432	0.050544
1970	1	0.050657	0.050770	0.050889	0.051009
1971	1	0.051129	0.051250	0.051362	0.051474
1972	1	0.051587	0.051700	0.051807	0.051914
1973	1	0.052022	0.052130	0.052225	0.052319
1974	1	0.052414	0.052510	0.052610	0.052709
1975	1	0.052809	0.052910	0.052912	0.052915
1976	1	0.052917	0.052920	0.052922	0.052925

FRANCE_FRLFQSFF

1955	1	0.019280	0.019310	0.019337	0.019364
1956	1	0.019395	0.019425	0.019453	0.019480
1957	1	0.019510	0.019540	0.019583	0.019624
1958	1	0.019668	0.019712	0.019754	0.019794
1959	1	0.019837	0.019828	0.019817	0.019804
1960	1	0.019793	0.019782	0.019772	0.019760
1961	1	0.019751	0.019787	0.019825	0.019862
1962	1	0.019901	0.019937	0.019974	0.020012
1963	1	0.020052	0.020013	0.019977	0.019941
1964	1	0.019907	0.019943	0.019981	0.020020
1965	1	0.020061	0.020106	0.020153	0.020201
1966	1	0.020251	0.020299	0.020348	0.020399
1967	1	0.020451	0.020455	0.020461	0.020468
1968	1	0.020475	0.020514	0.020553	0.020593
1969	1	0.020634	0.020704	0.020775	0.020847
1970	1	0.020918	0.020979	0.021039	0.021101
1971	1	0.021163	0.021211	0.021258	0.021309
1972	1	0.021359	0.021419	0.021470	0.021528
1973	1	0.021592	0.021652	0.021689	0.021742
1974	1	0.021809	0.021873	0.021901	0.021950
1975	1	0.022184	0.022171	0.022442	0.022518
1976	1	0.022455	0.022294	0.022452	0.022508

FRANCE_FRUNQNFF

1955	1	0.000266	0.000226	0.000168	0.000171
1956	1	0.000191	0.000134	0.000094	0.000087
1957	1	0.000100	0.000074	0.000056	0.000063
1958	1	0.000081	0.000073	0.000063	0.000090
1959	1	0.000169	0.000150	0.000109	0.000135
1960	1	0.000174	0.000141	0.000103	0.000116
1961	1	0.000149	0.000117	0.000088	0.000102
1962	1	0.000122	0.000100	0.000086	0.000093
1963	1	0.000120	0.000101	0.000077	0.000091
1964	1	0.000111	0.000097	0.000076	0.000106
1965	1	0.000156	0.000142	0.000119	0.000147
1966	1	0.000171	0.000145	0.000121	0.000154
1967	1	0.000194	0.000189	0.000168	0.000217
1968	1	0.000264	0.000243	0.000251	0.000258
1969	1	0.000246	0.000193	0.000204	0.000233
1970	1	0.000250	0.000227	0.000270	0.000322
1971	1	0.000331	0.000289	0.000341	0.000398
1972	1	0.000389	0.000327	0.000386	0.000413
1973	1	0.000378	0.000329	0.000419	0.000461
1974	1	0.000439	0.000379	0.000534	0.000723
1975	1	0.000754	0.000738	0.000945	0.001010
1976	1	0.000938	0.000813	0.000955	0.001005

FRANCE_FRUNQSFF

1955	1	0.000218	0.000222	0.000206	0.000181
1956	1	0.000156	0.000131	0.000116	0.000093
1957	1	0.000081	0.000072	0.000070	0.000067
1958	1	0.000066	0.000070	0.000079	0.000096
1959	1	0.000136	0.000146	0.000139	0.000143
1960	1	0.000141	0.000137	0.000131	0.000123
1961	1	0.000121	0.000114	0.000111	0.000107
1962	1	0.000100	0.000098	0.000109	0.000097
1963	1	0.000099	0.000099	0.000096	0.000093
1964	1	0.000092	0.000095	0.000095	0.000108
1965	1	0.000131	0.000141	0.000145	0.000148
1966	1	0.000145	0.000147	0.000144	0.000152
1967	1	0.000168	0.000195	0.000193	0.000211
1968	1	0.000234	0.000258	0.000277	0.000246
1969	1	0.000223	0.000211	0.000218	0.000219
1970	1	0.000231	0.000254	0.000280	0.000298
1971	1	0.000312	0.000330	0.000346	0.000363
1972	1	0.000372	0.000379	0.000386	0.000375
1973	1	0.000366	0.000385	0.000414	0.000416
1974	1	0.000429	0.000444	0.000524	0.000654
1975	1	0.000740	0.000864	0.000923	0.000914
1976	1	0.000922	0.000952	0.000932	0.000910

FRANCE_FRURQNFF

1955	1	0.013820	0.011730	0.008690	0.008820
1956	1	0.009830	0.006920	0.004810	0.004490
1957	1	0.005100	0.003800	0.002870	0.003210
1958	1	0.004110	0.003680	0.003170	0.004540
1959	1	0.008509	0.007590	0.005521	0.006801
1960	1	0.008806	0.007117	0.005210	0.005890
1961	1	0.007539	0.005908	0.004434	0.005140
1962	1	0.006136	0.005026	0.004330	0.004672
1963	1	0.005990	0.005032	0.003844	0.004543
1964	1	0.005587	0.004854	0.003818	0.005290
1965	1	0.007792	0.007052	0.005895	0.007292
1966	1	0.008460	0.007168	0.005951	0.007530
1967	1	0.009477	0.009225	0.008220	0.010602
1968	1	0.012894	0.011846	0.012217	0.012543
1969	1	0.011932	0.009322	0.009819	0.011186
1970	1	0.011932	0.010816	0.012823	0.015279
1971	1	0.015641	0.013620	0.016044	0.018673
1972	1	0.018195	0.015260	0.017980	0.019186
1973	1	0.017495	0.015224	0.019321	0.021177
1974	1	0.020129	0.017326	0.024384	0.032934
1975	1	0.034000	0.033300	0.042100	0.044800
1976	1	0.041800	0.036500	0.042500	0.044600

FRANCE_FRURQSFF

1955	1	0.011328	0.011497	0.010667	0.009353
1956	1	0.008046	0.006757	0.005944	0.004771
1957	1	0.004158	0.003696	0.003580	0.003420
1958	1	0.003332	0.003569	0.003991	0.004835
1959	1	0.006879	0.007353	0.006993	0.007225
1960	1	0.007118	0.006901	0.006606	0.006218
1961	1	0.006119	0.005742	0.005603	0.005396
1962	1	0.005001	0.004905	0.005447	0.004862
1963	1	0.004919	0.004925	0.004810	0.004687
1964	1	0.004625	0.004774	0.004736	0.005393
1965	1	0.006527	0.006998	0.007188	0.007339
1966	1	0.007183	0.007239	0.007062	0.007449
1967	1	0.008205	0.009537	0.009421	0.010301
1968	1	0.011407	0.012585	0.013500	0.011958
1969	1	0.010807	0.010174	0.010489	0.010485
1970	1	0.011043	0.012107	0.013305	0.014118
1971	1	0.014748	0.015566	0.016282	0.017058
1972	1	0.017428	0.017681	0.017956	0.017411
1973	1	0.016956	0.017765	0.019082	0.019164
1974	1	0.019682	0.020255	0.023902	0.029833
1975	1	0.033383	0.038902	0.041137	0.040628
1976	1	0.041098	0.042606	0.041507	0.040468

Sources and Notes on Time Series for Germany

All economic data were provided by Dr. Manfred J. M. Neumann of the Institut für Banken und Industrie, Geld und Kredit, except the following series: (1) Consumer Price Index; (2) Industrial Production Index; (3) Population. The sources from which Dr. Neumann originally obtained the data are noted below.

All time series are on a quarterly basis and cover the period from 1955I to 1976IV, except where noted otherwise. We made the seasonal adjustment using the Census X-11 program.

I. INTERNATIONAL VARIABLES

A. *Balance of Payments*

GEBPQNDR   Balance of Payments. Unit: Billions of Deutsche Marks
GEBPQSDR   (DM) at Quarterly Rates.

Source: Deutsches Institut fur Wirtschaftsforschung (DIW).

Description: The overall balance of payments was derived by adding the balance on current account, the balance on private capital account, and the balance of unclassifiable transactions. The figures were originally in millions of DM. Compatible data can be obtained from the Deutsches Bundesbank, *Monthly Report*, table IX.1, "Important Items in the Balance of Payments."

B. *Exports*

1. Total Exports

GEEXQNTL   Total Exports. Unit: Billions of DM at Annual Rates.
GEEXQSTL

Source: From statistics of DIW.

Description: The balance-of-payments current account total of receipts from exchanges of goods and services as well as transfers from abroad. A break in the series occurs in 1960 prior to which the data exclude Berlin and the Saar. To allow for this break we multiplied the observations for the years 1955 to 1959 by the mean of the ratios of total exports including Berlin and the Saar to total exports excluding those areas for the four quarters of 1960, the only overlap period provided. The data were originally in millions of DM at quarterly rates.

2. Exports of Goods
   GEEXQNGO   Exports of Goods. Unit: Billions of DM at Annual Rates.
   GEEXQSGO
Source: From statistics of the Statistisches Bundesamt (SB).
Description: Balance-of-payments current account receipts from the sale of goods only. The data were originally in millions of DM at quarterly rates.
3. Exports of Services and Transfers
   GEEXQNST   Exports of Services and Transfers. Unit: Billions of DM at
   GEEXQSST   Annual Rates.
Source: From I.B.1 and I.B.2 above.
Description: This series was derived by subtracting exports of goods from total exports and measures current account receipts from services and transfers from abroad, including income from investments abroad.
C. *Imports*
1. Total Imports
   GEIMQNTL   Total Imports. Unit: Billions of DM at Annual Rates.
   GEIMQSTL
Source: From statistics of DIW.
Description: The balance-of-payments current account total of payments for goods and services as well as transfers abroad. A break in the series occurred in 1960 as described for total exports (I.B.1). Accordingly we adjusted the data using a method similar to that used for total exports. The data were originally in millions of DM at quarterly rates.
2. Imports of Goods
   GEIMQNGO   Imports of Goods. Unit: Billions of DM at Annual Rates.
   GEIMQSGO
Source: From statistics of SB.
Description: The balance-of-payments current account payments for goods only. The data were originally in millions of DM at quarterly rates.
3. Imports of Services and Transfers
   GEIMQNST   Imports of Services and Transfers. Unit: Billions of DM at
   GEIMQSST   Annual Rates.
Source: From I.C.1 and I.C.2 above.
Description: This series was derived by subtracting imports of goods from total imports and measures current account payments for services and transfers abroad, including e.g. interest payments.
D. *Net Private Capital Outflows*
   GEKPQNDR   Net Private Capital Outflows. Unit: Billions of DM at
   GEKPQSDR   Annual Rates.
Source: From the Deutsche Bundesbank, *Monthly Report*, table IX.5, "Capital Transactions."
Description: The balance of total—short- and long-term—private capital transactions plus the balance of unclassifiable transactions, exclusive of official capital transactions; net capital exports defined positive. The data were originally in millions of DM at quarterly rates.
E. *Exchange Rate*
   GEXRQNDM   Spot Exchange Rate. Unit: DM per Dollar.
Source: From Deutsche Bundesbank, *Monthly Report*, table IX.9, "Averages of

Official Foreign Exchange Quotations," various issues.
Description: The middle spot exchange rate of the U.S. dollar. Figures are averages of daily quotations of the last month of each quarter on the Frankfurt currency exchange.

II. FINANCIAL VARIABLES

A. *Narrow Money Stock (M1)*
　　GEM1QNDR　　Narrow Money Stock. Unit: Billions of DM, End-of-
　　GEM1QSDR　　Quarter.
Source: From the Deutsche Bundesbank, *Monthly Report*, table I.1, "Money Stock and Its Determinants."
Description: Defined as currency held by the (nonbank) public plus demand deposits of the (nonbank) public:

1. Currency Holdings of Nonbank Public
   The original data contain several breaks. The first break occurred in the last quarter of 1959 when the number of reporting banks increased and hence the estimates of currency holdings of nonbanks were reduced. The second break occurred in the beginning of 1960. Prior to that, the figures for currency held by the public were underestimated because banks' holdings of foreign, in addition to domestic, currency were subtracted from total currency in circulation. An overlap exists for the four quarters of 1960, and the mean of the ratios was used to adjust the data from 1955 to 1959. A third break occurred in the final quarter of 1968 due to changes in statistical classifications. The series prior to 1968 was adjusted by the mean of the ratios of the overlap, 1968I to 1968IV.

2. Demand Deposits of Domestic Nonbank Public
   Two breaks occurred in the deposit series also. The first occurred beginning in 1960 with the inclusion of the Saar. The second break occurred at the beginning of 1968 with the inclusion of additional reporting banks. An overlap exists for the four quarters of 1968. To adjust the pre-1968 data we used the mean of the ratios of the later to the earlier data in the overlap period. The data were originally in millions of DM.

B. *Broader Money Stock (M2)*
　　GEM2QNDR　　Broader Money Stock. Unit: Billions of DM, End-of-
　　GEM2QSDR　　Quarter.
Source: From the Deutsche Bundesbank, *Monthly Report*, tables I.1 and I.2.
Description: The broader definition of money M2 is the sum of the narrowly defined money stock and time deposits at domestic banks with maturities of less than four years. The original time deposit data contain several breaks. The first break occurred in the last quarter of 1959 with the inclusion of an additional number of reporting banks. The second break occurred in 1960 with the inclusion of data for the Saar. The earlier period was adjusted by the mean of the ratio of the later series to the earlier for the 1960 overlap. The third break occurred in the last quarter of 1968 to adjust for changes in statistical classifications (adjusted by the mean of the ratios). The data were originally in millions of DM.

C. *High-powered Money*
　　GEMHQNDR　　High-powered Money. Unit: Billions of DM, End-of-
　　GEMHQSDR　　Quarter.
Source: From the Deutsches Bundesbank, *Monthly Report*, table I.1.

Description: Currency in circulation plus total deposits of banks at the Deutsche Bundesbank. Several breaks occur in this series which we adjusted by using the mean of the ratios of data for the period of overlap: The first break occurred with the inclusion of data on Berlin in 1956I; the second break occurred with the inclusion of data for the Saar beginning in 1959III; the third is due to the exclusion of data for the working balances of the Federal Post Office beginning in 1970I. A fourth break is due to the exclusion of deposits of credit institutions at the Bundesbank that were not held on giroaccount, i.e. as current account deposits, beginning in 1972I.

D. *Official International Reserve Assets*

   GEFHQNDR   Official International Reserve Assets. Unit: Billions of
   GEFHQSDR   DM, End-of-Quarter.

Source: From the Deutsche Bundesbank, *Monthly Report*, table IX.6.a., "Monetary Reserves."

Description: The sum of gold holdings, convertible currency holdings, and special drawing rights.

   1. Gold Holdings

      The Deutsche mark value of gold holdings of the Bundesbank. The series includes data for the Berlin branch of the Bundesbank from 1957III and for the Saarland branch from 1959III; an adjustment was not possible in the absence of an overlap in the data.

   2. Convertible Currencies

      The Deutsche mark value of the Bundesbank's balances with foreign banks and money market investments abroad, foreign notes and coin and foreign checks, valued at par prior to May 1971 and adjusted for exchange-rate movements thereafter. The series includes data for the Berlin branch of the Bundesbank from 1957III and for the Saarland from 1959III. Another break in the series occurs beginning in 1958III after which the original data exclude both credits to international institutions and consolidation loans. These breaks were adjusted for by the mean of the ratio of the overlap.

   3. Special Drawing Rights

      Total SDRs, measured in Deutsche marks, held by the Deutsche Bundesbank.

The data were originally in millions of DM.

E. *Interest Rates*

   1. Short-Term

      GERSQN3M   Short-Term Interest Rate. Unit: Decimal Rate per Annum.

Source: From the Deutsche Bundesbank *Monthly Report*, table V.5, "Money Market Rates."

Description: This three-month money market rate is from daily quotations reported by Frankfurt banks on three-month loans. The rates are not fixed or quoted officially. For the period from 1955I to 1964IV the rate is a simple average of the minimum and maximum rates quoted during the last month of the respective quarter. For the period from 1965I to 1966IV the rate is an average of weekly figures of the last month of the respective quarter. For the period from 1967I to 1976IV the rate is a daily average of figures quoted for the last month of the respective quarter. The data were originally in percent per annum.

2. Long-Term

   GERLQNNM   Long-Term Interest Rate. Unit: Decimal Rate per Annum.
Source: From the Deutsche Bundesbank *Monthly Report*, table VI.6, "Yields on Domestic Securities."
Description: To obtain a continuous series 1955I to 1976IV we combined a series for 1955I to 1959II for yields of mortgage bonds with a series for the period 1959III to 1976IV for yields of newly issued bonds and adjusted by the mean of the ratios.

a. Mortgage bonds in circulation

   The average yield on tax-free bonds paying a fixed coupon of 5.5% per annum from 1955I to 1959II

b. Newly issued bonds in circulation

   The average yield on fully taxed fixed-interest bearer bonds with maximum maturities according to terms of issue of over four years, with the exception of convertible bonds and, from January 1973 on, bank bonds with unscheduled redemption. The yields are weighted by the amounts sold. The figures are averages of the yields on the four bank-week return dates of the last month of the quarter, including the yield on the last day of the preceding month.

III. NONFINANCIAL DOMESTIC VARIABLES

A. *National Product*

Source: From statistics of DIW.

1. Nominal Gross Product

a. GEYNQNGN   Gross National Product in Current Market Prices. Unit:
   GEYNQSGN   Billions of DM at Annual Rates.

Description: The value of final expenditures on goods and services, produced domestically, in current market prices, equivalent to total income and product of residents including net factor income from abroad. The original series contains a break in 1960 after which data on Berlin and the Saar are included. In each case, we adjusted the pre-1960 data by the mean of the ratios for the overlap period, 1960I to 1960IV. The data were originally at quarterly rates.

b. GEYNQNGD   Gross Domestic Product in Current Market Prices. Unit:
   GEYNQSGD   Billions of DM at Annual Rates.

Description: The value of final expenditures on goods and services, produced domestically, in current market prices, equivalent to total income and product of the geographic region excluding net factor income from abroad. A break in the series was adjusted as described in III.A.1.a above. The data were originally at quarterly rates.

2. Real Gross Product

a. GEYRQNN7   Gross National Product in 1970 Market Prices. Unit: Bil-
   GEYRQSN7   lions of DM at Annual Rates.

Description: The value of final expenditures on goods and services, produced domestically, in 1970 market prices, equivalent to total income and product of residents including net factor income from abroad. A break in the series was adjusted as described in III.A.1.a. above. The data were originally in 1962 prices at quarterly rates.

b. GEYRQND7   Gross Domestic Product in 1970 Market Prices. Unit: Bil-
   GEYRQSD7   lions of DM at Annual Rates.

Description: The value of final expenditures on goods and services, produced domestically, in 1970 market prices, equivalent to total income and product of the geographic region excluding net factor income from abroad. Since we could obtain no figures for real GDP, we deflated nominal GDP by the GNP price deflator to arrive at our estimates of real GDP.

B. *Prices*

1. Implicit Price Deflator
   GEPDQNN7   GNP Implicit Price Deflator. Unit: 1970 = 1.00.
   GEPDQNN7

Source: From statistics of DIW.

Description: The implicit deflator for Gross National Product with base: 1970 = 1.00. The original series contains a break in 1960 after which data on Berlin and the Saar are included. The break was adjusted by the mean of the ratios for the overlap period, 1960I to 1960IV. The data were originally in percent form with 1962 = 100.

2. Consumer Prices
   GEPCQN70   Consumer Price Index. Unit: 1970 = 1.00.
   GEPCQS70

Source: From statistics of SB.

Description: A general index of consumer prices covering all items. Figures are quarterly averages of monthly averages. The data were originally in percent form with 1967 = 100.

C. *Industrial Production*
   GEIPQS70   Index of Industrial Production. Unit: 1970 = 1.00.

Source: From SB, *Wirtschafts und Statistik*, "Index der industriellen Nettoproduktion." Various issues.

Description: A general index of industrial production including the mining, manufacturing, construction, and utility industries. Figures are quarterly averages of monthly averages. The data were originally in percent form with 1962 = 100.

D. *Government Accounts*

1. Government Expenditure
   GEGXQNFG   Federal Government Expenditure. Unit: Billions of DM at
   GEGXQSFG   Annual Rates.

Source: From the Deutsche Bundesbank *Monthly Report*, table VII.9, "Federal Finance on a Cash Basis."

Description: Cash payments out of the federal accounts at the Deutsche Bundesbank, including current payment commitments toward pension and unemployment insurance funds. A break in this series occurs in 1964, but we were unable to obtain any information on the reason for the change. We adjusted the earlier data for the break by multiplying by the mean of the ratios for the overlap period, 1964I to 1964IV. The data were originally in millions of DM at quarterly rates.

2. Government Deficit
   GEGDQNFG   Federal Government Deficit. Unit: Billions of DM at
   GEGDQSFG   Annual Rates.

Source: Same as III.D.1 above.

Description: Net cash payments out of the federal accounts at the Deutsche Bundesbank. A break in this series occurs in 1964 analogous to that described for government expenditures. The deficit is defined negative. The data were originally in millions of DM at quarterly rates.

E. *Population*
    GEPPQNIN   Population. Unit: Billions of Persons.
Source: From UN, *Demographic Yearbook*, various issues.
Description: Total population was estimated by straight-line interpolation of mid-year estimates. The data were originally in millions of persons.

F. *Labor Force Statistics*
Source: The source for all labor force statistics was the Bundesanstalt für Arbeit.
  1. Employment
    GEEMQNER   Employed Persons. Unit: Billions of Persons.
    GEEMQSER
Description: The number of wage and salary earners working in Germany regardless of nationality or country of residency. All data are based on estimates by the Bundesanstalt from annual and semiannual reports. Two breaks occur in this series: the first to include information on Berlin and the Saar in 1960; the second in 1962 due to changes in the method of estimation and revisions of the data. The breaks were adjusted by multiplying by the mean of the ratios for the overlap periods. The data were originally in thousands of persons.
  2. Unemployment
    GEUNQNER   Unemployed Persons. Unit: Billions of Persons.
    GEUNQSER
Description: The number of persons seeking work as wage and salary earners. A break in the series occurs in 1963 with the inclusion of information on Berlin. This was adjusted by the mean of the ratios. The data were originally in thousands of persons.
  3. Labor Force
    GELFQNDR   Total Labor Force. Unit: Billions of Persons.
    GELFQSDR
Description: Derived as the sum of employed (III.F.1) and unemployed (III.F.2) wage and salary earners.
  4. Unemployment Rate
    GEURQNDR   Unemployment Rate. Unit: Decimal Rate per Annum.
    GEURQSDR
Description: Derived as the ratio of unemployed persons (III.F.2) to the total labor force (III.F.3).

List of Tables for Germany (Quarterly Data)

GERMANY_GEBPQNDR

1955	1	0.2862	0.5924	1.1696	1.0234
1956	1	0.5504	1.5555	2.3731	1.7964
1957	1	0.8733	1.6299	4.2355	0.0657
1958	1	0.3511	1.6245	1.5999	1.5490
1959	1	-2.2395	0.4585	1.2641	2.7669
1960	1	1.8380	4.2180	3.6970	3.1900
1961	1	1.4650	3.4990	0.3960	2.4740
1962	1	-0.4270	2.6000	-0.2380	3.8780
1963	1	0.9210	1.8250	1.7410	4.7700
1964	1	1.4810	1.1670	1.0700	2.6070
1965	1	0.9190	1.0240	1.1560	1.5400
1966	1	0.7570	2.1630	2.2200	4.9680
1967	1	2.1020	1.2030	1.9790	2.3410
1968	1	2.7210	2.5670	2.3050	5.3440
1969	1	-5.5520	8.8440	9.8350	-14.2610
1970	1	2.9230	8.2320	11.0730	10.3560
1971	1	9.8130	5.3870	4.9780	6.3380
1972	1	5.6450	12.6090	7.7650	2.8780
1973	1	22.3280	6.3900	13.0920	-0.2200
1974	1	2.7919	6.0750	-1.8750	6.6851
1975	1	9.0919	-1.7770	1.6730	2.7400
1976	1	12.4950	-1.5030	6.4540	4.4970

GERMANY_GEBPQSDR

1955	1	1.1376	0.5274	0.5589	0.8014
1956	1	1.4800	1.4468	1.7875	1.5073
1957	1	1.9199	1.4313	3.6993	-0.3021
1958	1	1.5314	1.2655	1.2265	1.0469
1959	1	-0.9531	-0.0589	1.1417	2.0573
1960	1	3.1823	3.6015	3.8784	2.2252
1961	1	2.7751	2.9366	0.7899	1.3046
1962	1	0.7656	2.2007	0.2781	2.5628
1963	1	1.9547	1.6517	2.2845	3.3747
1964	1	2.3597	1.2207	1.5190	1.3120
1965	1	1.6189	1.1978	1.4884	0.4440
1966	1	1.4405	2.1321	2.4428	4.3221
1967	1	2.7443	0.7829	2.1665	2.1799
1968	1	3.3072	1.7623	2.4151	5.7127
1969	1	-5.0102	7.5981	9.9187	-13.2923
1970	1	3.1329	6.9293	10.8321	12.1235
1971	1	9.5242	4.0001	4.8543	8.5393
1972	1	4.4687	11.7644	7.7701	5.2058
1973	1	20.1514	6.2981	13.4628	1.9554
1974	1	-0.5882	7.2285	-1.5119	8.7326
1975	1	4.8319	0.2376	2.2303	4.4548
1976	1	7.8331	0.9220	7.2357	5.7360

GERMANY_GEEXQNTL

1955	1	30.091	31.462	32.617	36.550
1956	1	33.807	39.256	40.482	43.657
1957	1	43.910	46.183	48.059	48.961
1958	1	46.183	46.436	48.853	51.415
1959	1	48.528	53.616	54.734	60.471
1960	1	59.600	60.240	61.640	69.200
1961	1	63.560	65.440	64.520	67.120
1962	1	64.920	67.520	68.560	72.480
1963	1	66.360	73.440	76.080	82.080
1964	1	78.560	82.880	80.880	89.320
1965	1	86.480	87.240	89.760	100.000
1966	1	93.800	99.120	103.680	112.560
1967	1	103.960	109.600	106.920	120.000
1968	1	114.840	114.440	124.000	142.040
1969	1	125.440	141.760	145.640	154.560
1970	1	143.760	157.480	157.840	175.240
1971	1	170.400	170.960	175.000	180.560
1972	1	175.840	185.240	185.080	214.440
1973	1	210.880	222.160	226.800	249.600
1974	1	277.920	294.640	304.760	317.960
1975	1	281.040	291.920	287.680	315.240
1976	1	312.440	327.640	337.120	360.680

GERMANY_GEEXQSTL

1955	1	30.954	31.636	32.632	35.343
1956	1	34.792	39.464	40.530	42.188
1957	1	45.156	46.469	48.163	47.251
1958	1	47.471	46.738	49.051	49.558
1959	1	49.804	54.022	55.055	58.173
1960	1	61.204	60.616	62.160	66.494
1961	1	65.270	65.747	65.254	64.399
1962	1	66.681	67.772	69.466	69.482
1963	1	68.093	73.814	77.153	78.483
1964	1	80.707	83.338	82.157	85.149
1965	1	88.862	87.871	91.357	94.896
1966	1	96.571	99.963	105.561	106.500
1967	1	107.323	110.517	108.771	113.469
1968	1	118.825	115.249	125.896	134.748
1969	1	129.708	142.456	147.848	147.196
1970	1	148.234	158.015	160.203	167.740
1971	1	175.006	171.269	177.809	173.386
1972	1	180.101	185.351	188.114	206.516
1973	1	215.505	222.196	230.719	240.241
1974	1	284.229	294.684	309.730	306.026
1975	1	287.807	291.919	292.163	303.190
1976	1	320.324	327.851	341.868	347.048

GERMANY_GEEXQNGO

1955	1	23.544	24.764	25.132	29.428
1956	1	26.132	31.792	30.644	34.876
1957	1	33.540	35.444	36.036	38.852
1958	1	34.540	35.804	37.412	40.236
1959	1	35.636	40.244	41.232	47.624
1960	1	45.684	46.040	46.132	53.928
1961	1	48.996	51.280	50.332	53.304
1962	1	50.592	52.820	52.000	56.488
1963	1	51.636	58.052	58.560	64.988
1964	1	62.260	64.872	61.900	70.648
1965	1	69.508	69.564	69.012	78.520
1966	1	75.828	78.496	79.560	88.628
1967	1	83.108	87.604	82.752	94.716
1968	1	93.348	91.376	98.684	114.796
1969	1	102.432	114.004	114.192	123.600
1970	1	114.840	124.732	123.332	138.204
1971	1	132.564	134.976	135.368	141.132
1972	1	140.832	146.544	140.552	168.160
1973	1	166.964	174.512	173.768	198.340
1974	1	218.724	228.764	229.896	244.928
1975	1	210.724	222.936	212.072	240.624
1976	1	241.524	251.360	254.468	277.340

GERMANY_GEEXQSGO

1955	1	24.484	24.998	25.627	27.566
1956	1	27.194	32.092	31.236	32.682
1957	1	34.876	35.806	36.728	36.418
1958	1	35.884	36.167	38.156	37.761
1959	1	36.940	40.640	42.087	44.780
1960	1	47.286	46.349	47.201	50.881
1961	1	50.543	51.437	51.709	50.434
1962	1	51.996	52.822	53.610	53.626
1963	1	52.788	58.028	60.540	61.767
1964	1	63.457	64.801	64.189	67.160
1965	1	70.603	69.564	71.797	74.415
1966	1	77.035	78.584	82.800	83.813
1967	1	84.618	87.738	85.971	89.462
1968	1	95.427	91.418	102.144	108.740
1969	1	104.822	113.880	117.962	117.506
1970	1	117.347	124.441	127.200	132.241
1971	1	134.709	134.597	139.715	135.622
1972	1	142.446	145.982	145.303	162.227
1973	1	167.984	173.876	180.165	191.205
1974	1	219.772	227.963	238.641	236.024
1975	1	211.602	222.306	220.282	231.497
1976	1	242.658	250.880	264.135	266.711

GERMANY_GEEXQNST

1955	1	6.5472	6.6982	7.4848	7.1216
1956	1	7.6754	7.4636	9.8383	8.7814
1957	1	10.3700	10.7391	12.0232	10.1093
1958	1	11.6431	10.6316	11.4410	11.1788
1959	1	12.8923	13.3716	13.5021	12.8469
1960	1	13.9160	14.2000	15.5080	15.2720
1961	1	14.5640	14.1600	14.1880	13.8160
1962	1	14.3280	14.7000	16.5600	15.9920
1963	1	14.7240	15.3880	17.5200	17.0920
1964	1	16.3000	18.0081	18.9800	18.6721
1965	1	16.9720	17.6760	20.7480	21.4800
1966	1	17.9720	20.6240	24.1200	23.9320
1967	1	20.8521	21.9960	24.1680	25.2841
1968	1	21.4921	23.0640	25.3160	27.2440
1969	1	23.0081	27.7560	31.4481	30.9600
1970	1	28.9200	32.7480	34.5081	37.0360
1971	1	37.8361	35.9841	39.6320	39.4280
1972	1	35.0081	38.6960	44.5281	46.2800
1973	1	43.9160	47.6480	53.0320	51.2600
1974	1	59.1960	65.8760	74.8640	73.0320
1975	1	70.3160	68.9840	75.6080	74.6160
1976	1	70.9160	76.2800	82.6520	83.3400

GERMANY_GEEXQSST

1955	1	6.4484	6.8423	7.0465	7.5580
1956	1	7.5489	7.6075	9.3033	9.3060
1957	1	10.1753	10.9324	11.4347	10.6637
1958	1	11.4391	10.7849	10.9633	11.6937
1959	1	12.7051	13.5604	13.0091	13.2526
1960	1	13.8602	14.3967	14.9689	15.5091
1961	1	14.7152	14.3995	13.6489	13.8039
1962	1	14.7395	15.0113	15.8164	15.7622
1963	1	15.4090	15.8008	16.5983	16.6373
1964	1	17.3429	18.5663	17.8766	17.9754
1965	1	18.3191	18.2478	19.5015	20.4798
1966	1	19.6233	21.2695	22.6654	22.7009
1967	1	22.9342	22.5793	22.7655	23.9777
1968	1	23.6543	23.5670	23.9242	25.9140
1969	1	25.2480	28.2086	29.8550	29.5861
1970	1	31.5232	33.2129	32.8196	35.6277
1971	1	40.9226	36.4580	37.7254	38.2190
1972	1	37.4721	39.3163	42.3427	45.1468
1973	1	46.6379	48.5081	50.4246	50.1994
1974	1	62.5259	67.1715	71.1207	71.7731
1975	1	74.0620	70.2638	71.9185	73.4543
1976	1	74.4996	77.7237	78.6473	82.0844

GERMANY_GEIMQNTL

1955	1	27.720	28.878	29.240	31.049
1956	1	30.688	34.379	33.655	35.573
1957	1	38.758	39.300	38.866	39.843
1958	1	40.639	38.902	40.422	42.195
1959	1	41.327	45.742	47.298	50.591
1960	1	51.920	54.800	55.240	59.160
1961	1	54.040	58.080	60.160	62.200
1962	1	59.680	64.160	66.360	68.640
1963	1	63.360	70.960	73.400	69.880
1964	1	70.400	76.240	79.840	85.080
1965	1	82.480	91.320	95.040	96.800
1966	1	92.880	96.200	97.000	97.280
1967	1	87.600	93.600	95.240	100.360
1968	1	97.480	101.640	111.360	114.400
1969	1	114.920	127.560	132.200	133.560
1970	1	135.760	146.760	150.160	156.960
1971	1	153.840	160.360	164.920	168.920
1972	1	162.280	174.080	176.640	188.920
1973	1	190.760	196.600	203.040	220.160
1974	1	233.560	260.320	279.000	263.120
1975	1	245.040	270.560	275.680	283.600
1976	1	286.720	305.800	324.160	329.520

GERMANY_GEIMQSTL

1955	1	27.709	28.611	29.665	30.879
1956	1	30.709	34.098	34.095	35.323
1957	1	38.864	39.051	39.278	39.440
1958	1	40.946	38.720	40.708	41.594
1959	1	41.915	45.621	47.407	49.607
1960	1	53.203	54.603	55.121	57.810
1961	1	55.887	57.762	59.822	60.644
1962	1	62.183	63.675	65.771	66.985
1963	1	66.151	70.471	72.554	68.190
1964	1	73.675	75.674	78.822	83.109
1965	1	86.234	90.732	93.798	94.557
1966	1	97.085	95.580	95.671	95.274
1967	1	91.301	93.030	93.934	98.540
1968	1	101.333	100.924	109.954	112.661
1969	1	118.992	126.577	130.830	131.764
1970	1	140.056	145.540	148.954	155.120
1971	1	158.113	159.080	163.803	167.057
1972	1	166.533	172.776	175.330	186.981
1973	1	195.798	195.276	201.008	218.189
1974	1	239.921	258.787	275.260	261.260
1975	1	251.943	269.136	271.156	282.007
1976	1	294.994	304.382	318.189	328.041

GERMANY_GEIMQNGO

1955	1	22.028	23.520	25.168	27.184
1956	1	24.480	27.824	28.516	31.036
1957	1	30.668	30.884	31.916	34.072
1958	1	31.784	29.992	31.876	34.524
1959	1	30.872	35.064	36.384	40.972
1960	1	40.184	42.544	41.540	46.624
1961	1	41.320	44.448	43.452	48.232
1962	1	48.120	49.068	48.124	52.680
1963	1	48.632	53.328	53.508	53.640
1964	1	52.704	56.980	59.160	66.512
1965	1	65.116	69.748	70.824	76.104
1966	1	72.444	72.992	70.528	74.716
1967	1	65.784	69.848	67.572	77.528
1968	1	75.976	77.660	82.072	89.008
1969	1	91.352	98.332	98.248	103.960
1970	1	103.028	111.268	106.276	117.852
1971	1	117.916	122.044	116.732	123.784
1972	1	122.780	130.848	122.184	139.164
1973	1	143.416	146.692	134.044	157.516
1974	1	165.640	180.768	182.996	189.524
1975	1	168.504	186.104	178.992	203.652
1976	1	207.368	220.676	220.620	237.888

GERMANY_GEIMQSGO

1955	1	22.874	23.777	25.253	25.852
1956	1	25.438	28.101	28.649	29.506
1957	1	31.857	31.132	32.182	32.350
1958	1	33.014	30.142	32.286	32.768
1959	1	32.021	35.128	37.045	38.822
1960	1	41.743	42.434	42.409	44.240
1961	1	42.927	44.175	44.426	45.845
1962	1	49.987	48.686	49.124	50.313
1963	1	50.303	53.022	54.529	51.301
1964	1	54.466	56.672	60.268	63.727
1965	1	67.059	69.475	72.232	72.952
1966	1	74.419	72.679	72.047	71.846
1967	1	67.260	69.455	69.206	74.818
1968	1	77.410	76.897	84.343	86.347
1969	1	92.674	96.871	101.407	101.398
1970	1	103.998	109.081	110.272	115.397
1971	1	118.477	119.269	121.705	121.305
1972	1	123.093	127.679	127.821	136.157
1973	1	143.747	143.321	140.194	153.831
1974	1	166.132	177.075	190.981	184.772
1975	1	169.270	182.784	186.236	198.340
1976	1	208.589	217.163	228.977	231.670

GERMANY_GEIMQNST

1955	1	5.692	5.358	4.072	3.865
1956	1	6.208	6.555	5.139	4.537
1957	1	8.090	8.416	6.950	5.771
1958	1	8.855	8.910	8.546	7.671
1959	1	10.455	10.678	10.914	9.619
1960	1	11.736	12.256	13.700	12.536
1961	1	12.720	13.632	16.708	13.968
1962	1	11.560	15.092	18.236	15.960
1963	1	14.728	17.632	19.892	16.240
1964	1	17.696	19.260	20.680	18.568
1965	1	17.364	21.572	24.216	20.696
1966	1	20.436	23.208	26.472	22.564
1967	1	21.816	23.752	27.668	22.832
1968	1	21.504	23.980	29.288	25.392
1969	1	23.568	29.228	33.952	29.600
1970	1	32.732	35.492	43.884	39.108
1971	1	35.924	38.316	48.188	45.136
1972	1	39.500	43.232	54.456	49.756
1973	1	47.344	49.908	68.996	62.644
1974	1	67.920	79.552	96.004	73.596
1975	1	76.536	84.456	96.688	79.948
1976	1	79.352	85.124	103.540	91.632

GERMANY_GEIMQSST

1955	1	4.8864	4.7316	4.4766	4.8420
1956	1	5.3535	5.8396	5.5737	5.6101
1957	1	7.0712	7.6231	7.3427	6.9557
1958	1	7.9417	8.2733	8.6935	8.9352
1959	1	9.7346	10.1981	10.6426	10.7883
1960	1	11.4466	11.9779	12.8476	13.6572
1961	1	12.9702	13.4942	15.2481	14.8777
1962	1	12.2648	14.9643	16.3564	16.8290
1963	1	16.0272	17.4262	17.7053	17.0392
1964	1	19.5417	18.9617	18.3253	19.5215
1965	1	19.2061	21.2688	21.4235	21.7006
1966	1	22.6542	22.9762	23.3305	23.6439
1967	1	24.1187	23.7366	24.2944	23.7977
1968	1	23.7618	24.2163	25.6224	26.3273
1969	1	25.9568	29.8729	29.6743	30.3818
1970	1	36.0764	36.6166	38.2870	39.9386
1971	1	39.5246	39.8164	41.9434	46.0490
1972	1	43.4244	45.0163	47.2528	51.0324
1973	1	51.9719	51.7839	59.8053	64.7000
1974	1	74.5119	81.9904	83.1562	76.7642
1975	1	83.7088	86.4973	83.8359	83.9169
1976	1	86.6111	86.8438	89.8837	96.4840

GERMANY_GEKPQNDR

1955	1	-1.2240	-0.2120	1.3040	-1.4040
1956	1	-0.9160	1.3480	2.6680	-0.8960
1957	1	-1.6560	-0.3600	7.7520	-8.8520
1958	1	-4.1360	-1.0320	-2.0280	-3.0200
1959	1	-16.1560	-6.0360	-2.3760	1.1920
1960	1	-0.3280	11.4320	8.3880	2.7200
1961	1	-3.6600	6.6360	-2.7760	4.9760
1962	1	-6.9480	7.0400	-3.1520	11.6720
1963	1	0.6840	4.8200	4.2840	6.8800
1964	1	-2.2360	-1.9720	3.2400	6.1880
1965	1	-0.3240	8.1760	9.9040	2.9600
1966	1	2.1080	5.7320	2.2000	4.5920
1967	1	-7.9520	-11.1880	-3.7640	-10.2760
1968	1	-6.4760	-2.5320	-3.4200	-6.2640
1969	1	-32.7280	21.1760	25.9000	-78.0439
1970	1	3.6920	22.2080	36.6120	23.1440
1971	1	22.6920	10.9480	9.8320	13.7120
1972	1	9.0200	39.2760	22.6200	-14.0080
1973	1	69.1920	0.0	28.6080	-30.3200
1974	1	-33.1920	-10.0200	-33.2600	-28.1000
1975	1	0.3680	-28.4680	-5.3080	-20.6800
1976	1	24.2600	-27.8520	12.8560	-13.1720

GERMANY_GEKPQSDR

1955	1	0.4534	-0.6307	-0.8630	-0.7149
1956	1	1.1477	0.7467	0.4991	-0.4646
1957	1	1.0596	-1.3832	5.5835	-8.7291
1958	1	-0.5537	-2.7659	-3.8696	-3.4688
1959	1	-11.6219	-8.5554	-3.5910	-0.1251
1960	1	5.0420	8.3722	7.8786	0.5076
1961	1	2.0694	3.6734	-2.9469	2.1229
1962	1	-1.2504	4.6032	-3.3754	8.6118
1963	1	5.9813	3.1332	3.7569	3.8536
1964	1	2.6683	-2.9049	1.8020	4.0777
1965	1	4.0651	7.6004	7.4211	1.7447
1966	1	7.4914	3.6963	-1.3181	5.2896
1967	1	-1.5413	-15.4835	-7.9774	-7.6433
1968	1	0.9621	-9.1259	-8.3262	-1.3712
1969	1	-24.9122	12.6411	20.4816	-70.8030
1970	1	10.9178	12.8800	30.0316	33.4021
1971	1	28.2162	1.2661	3.2617	26.2519
1972	1	10.8800	31.7314	16.0221	-0.0424
1973	1	66.5333	-4.0796	22.1407	-15.4924
1974	1	-40.8988	-9.3384	-40.5480	-12.6648
1975	1	-11.0713	-24.2945	-12.8969	-5.3030
1976	1	10.9765	-22.1119	5.6499	1.1720

GERMANY_GEXRQNDM

1955	1	4.20400	4.21320	4.21490	4.21530
1956	1	4.21600	4.20040	4.19150	4.19730
1957	1	4.20190	4.20080	4.20110	4.20170
1958	1	4.20160	4.19080	4.18870	4.18180
1959	1	4.18170	4.17820	4.18380	4.17090
1960	1	4.17000	4.17000	4.17000	4.17100
1961	1	3.99660	3.97310	3.99660	3.99900
1962	1	3.99800	3.99330	4.00040	3.99560
1963	1	3.99630	3.98060	3.98050	3.97370
1964	1	3.97380	3.97350	3.97540	3.97600
1965	1	3.97690	3.99910	4.01060	4.00090
1966	1	4.01370	4.00590	3.98850	3.97300
1967	1	3.97370	3.98030	4.00150	3.98520
1968	1	3.98910	3.99580	3.97440	3.99420
1969	1	4.01910	4.00140	3.96650	3.68520
1970	1	3.67420	3.63240	3.63140	3.64460
1971	1	3.63140	3.51300	3.36170	3.27050
1972	1	3.17000	3.17110	3.19230	3.19810
1973	1	2.82690	2.57850	2.42360	2.65490
1974	1	2.62130	2.52580	2.66160	2.45800
1975	1	2.31650	2.34050	2.61590	2.62380
1976	1	2.56010	2.57630	2.49210	2.38510

GERMANY_GEM1QNDR

1955	1	27.645	28.610	29.454	31.718
1956	1	30.587	31.219	31.694	34.109
1957	1	32.498	34.128	35.860	38.043
1958	1	37.321	38.615	39.901	42.902
1959	1	42.431	44.163	45.507	47.534
1960	1	46.260	47.633	48.270	50.941
1961	1	49.327	51.812	53.758	58.556
1962	1	55.184	57.704	59.096	63.136
1963	1	58.969	61.973	63.389	67.583
1964	1	64.232	67.643	68.334	72.886
1965	1	69.978	74.031	74.237	78.351
1966	1	74.031	77.719	76.671	79.429
1967	1	75.657	78.787	80.209	87.690
1968	1	80.953	85.298	86.749	93.182
1969	1	87.211	92.412	93.949	99.041
1970	1	93.089	98.188	98.781	107.807
1971	1	101.514	109.695	111.994	121.015
1972	1	116.765	125.516	127.839	138.787
1973	1	132.920	132.903	128.737	141.493
1974	1	132.536	140.377	141.110	157.920
1975	1	148.954	160.211	163.957	182.758
1976	1	166.294	179.601	176.413	186.334

GERMANY_GEM1QSDR

1955	1	28.252	28.875	29.585	30.651
1956	1	31.246	31.509	31.835	32.982
1957	1	33.174	34.447	36.009	36.814
1958	1	38.089	38.969	40.048	41.535
1959	1	43.322	44.546	45.669	45.995
1960	1	47.311	48.006	48.443	49.230
1961	1	50.567	52.149	53.975	56.508
1962	1	56.722	57.978	59.359	60.873
1963	1	60.759	62.127	63.714	65.147
1964	1	66.283	67.686	68.731	70.238
1965	1	72.299	73.979	74.718	75.456
1966	1	76.561	77.643	77.179	76.407
1967	1	78.330	78.723	80.760	84.213
1968	1	83.912	85.274	87.356	89.360
1969	1	90.459	92.399	94.723	94.830
1970	1	96.548	98.168	99.808	103.085
1971	1	105.178	109.636	113.563	115.449
1972	1	120.853	125.463	130.061	132.079
1973	1	137.482	132.887	131.309	134.342
1974	1	137.086	140.412	144.106	149.732
1975	1	154.119	160.263	167.515	173.159
1976	1	172.138	179.658	180.236	176.522

GERMANY_GEM2QNDR

1955	1	38.794	39.910	40.523	42.316
1956	1	40.904	42.020	43.720	46.942
1957	1	46.607	48.761	51.851	54.256
1958	1	54.276	55.471	57.266	59.876
1959	1	59.282	61.150	63.282	66.204
1960	1	65.588	67.089	68.129	71.150
1961	1	70.569	73.757	75.530	80.490
1962	1	78.204	81.183	82.086	86.679
1963	1	82.752	85.874	87.441	92.586
1964	1	89.082	92.726	93.176	98.849
1965	1	95.724	99.472	99.137	104.894
1966	1	101.104	105.487	106.162	110.996
1967	1	108.130	111.728	113.782	124.755
1968	1	120.121	126.359	129.813	142.043
1969	1	136.942	145.108	150.206	156.487
1970	1	148.471	158.588	159.932	172.971
1971	1	168.980	179.036	181.418	198.088
1972	1	191.658	204.181	210.007	231.819
1973	1	230.882	241.274	246.559	263.851
1974	1	255.425	261.809	257.637	279.091
1975	1	259.766	254.460	253.708	283.678
1976	1	260.065	274.010	275.504	297.662

GERMANY_GEM2QSDR

1955	1	39.444	40.334	40.533	41.211
1956	1	41.567	42.462	43.735	45.758
1957	1	47.310	49.267	51.867	52.962
1958	1	55.045	56.000	57.304	58.515
1959	1	60.095	61.644	63.395	64.692
1960	1	66.553	67.500	68.362	69.430
1961	1	71.739	74.061	75.936	78.376
1962	1	79.679	81.377	82.669	84.229
1963	1	84.472	85.973	88.183	89.824
1964	1	91.032	92.785	94.075	95.756
1965	1	97.874	99.543	100.185	101.463
1966	1	103.422	105.605	107.353	107.182
1967	1	110.724	111.876	115.083	120.321
1968	1	123.121	126.523	131.342	136.849
1969	1	140.493	145.219	152.081	150.723
1970	1	152.258	158.690	162.064	166.641
1971	1	173.021	179.178	184.165	190.829
1972	1	195.635	204.683	213.664	223.034
1973	1	234.998	242.389	251.498	253.296
1974	1	259.322	263.757	263.196	267.376
1975	1	263.402	256.778	259.542	271.296
1976	1	263.554	276.758	282.055	284.271

GERMANY_GEMHQNDR

1955	1	15.894	16.439	17.097	18.766
1956	1	18.098	18.352	18.818	20.272
1957	1	19.351	21.202	22.031	23.706
1958	1	22.943	23.430	23.535	26.349
1959	1	24.727	25.259	25.688	28.862
1960	1	29.143	31.141	32.583	33.908
1961	1	31.922	31.861	32.503	35.101
1962	1	32.585	33.317	33.828	36.938
1963	1	33.502	36.218	36.396	39.628
1964	1	37.582	38.398	40.096	43.448
1965	1	41.796	43.546	43.817	46.371
1966	1	44.432	45.738	46.449	48.897
1967	1	44.425	46.202	43.428	47.648
1968	1	44.914	47.193	46.323	52.140
1969	1	47.818	52.490	55.095	53.871
1970	1	53.265	56.636	61.634	65.735
1971	1	64.706	71.862	73.520	75.768
1972	1	71.254	81.064	88.511	95.333
1973	1	104.210	99.898	101.323	102.888
1974	1	101.378	102.274	95.354	101.906
1975	1	98.645	100.226	97.268	105.141
1976	1	101.266	108.797	109.453	114.086

GERMANY_GEMHQSDR

1955	1	16.239	16.617	17.305	17.978
1956	1	18.484	18.546	19.069	19.410
1957	1	19.750	21.434	22.338	22.691
1958	1	23.406	23.701	23.863	25.214
1959	1	25.214	25.581	26.036	27.589
1960	1	29.743	31.561	33.009	32.376
1961	1	32.608	32.330	32.873	33.506
1962	1	33.329	33.809	34.173	35.276
1963	1	34.292	36.730	36.743	37.872
1964	1	38.529	38.809	40.548	41.539
1965	1	42.913	43.842	44.406	44.307
1966	1	45.781	45.823	47.129	46.735
1967	1	45.915	46.175	43.958	45.596
1968	1	46.636	47.038	46.685	50.051
1969	1	49.803	52.273	55.196	51.946
1970	1	55.574	56.321	61.431	63.867
1971	1	67.266	71.400	73.215	74.067
1972	1	73.636	80.336	88.618	93.445
1973	1	106.959	98.772	102.308	100.813
1974	1	103.421	100.983	96.995	99.773
1975	1	100.138	98.959	99.425	102.840
1976	1	102.501	107.427	112.213	111.357

GERMANY_GEFHQNDR

1955	1	7.1032	7.5250	7.9534	8.4162
1956	1	8.8616	9.8463	11.0973	12.0791
1957	1	13.0975	14.4932	18.3370	17.2070
1958	1	17.0240	17.7360	19.6340	20.2740
1959	1	17.7960	17.6510	16.9030	19.2830
1960	1	19.8860	23.1470	26.4940	28.1910
1961	1	28.3150	27.1090	25.4600	25.8140
1962	1	24.0010	24.5740	25.5380	25.4190
1963	1	25.4180	26.4240	27.1090	28.0320
1964	1	28.0900	28.2680	27.8650	27.5010
1965	1	27.0570	25.1920	25.2880	25.4820
1966	1	24.4710	24.4800	25.2690	26.6800
1967	1	26.6290	26.4040	26.8260	27.0000
1968	1	27.6680	26.4710	27.3590	29.3830
1969	1	22.9040	29.9490	37.5520	20.3930
1970	1	23.2040	28.2000	36.0400	43.6450
1971	1	51.3210	54.8850	55.9200	53.9890
1972	1	58.0810	67.8280	71.8690	69.0040
1973	1	85.8600	85.0040	92.8030	84.2880
1974	1	83.4170	85.3850	75.6870	67.9840
1975	1	73.1320	68.5560	65.5520	69.7590
1976	1	76.6690	72.0880	77.5670	70.8010

GERMANY_GEFHQSDR

1955	1	7.3289	7.5688	7.7659	8.3087
1956	1	9.1447	9.9055	10.8624	11.8795
1957	1	13.5204	14.6032	17.9918	16.8572
1958	1	17.5641	17.8796	19.3593	19.7831
1959	1	18.3206	17.8199	16.7245	18.7898
1960	1	20.4155	23.3327	26.3438	27.4911
1961	1	28.9543	27.2955	25.3568	25.2927
1962	1	24.4070	24.7178	25.4814	24.9902
1963	1	25.7317	26.6056	27.0447	27.6250
1964	1	28.3444	28.4887	27.8195	27.1138
1965	1	27.2453	25.4483	25.2089	25.1123
1966	1	24.6890	24.7528	25.0654	26.3064
1967	1	27.0490	26.6437	26.4176	26.7061
1968	1	28.3419	26.5704	26.7133	29.3082
1969	1	23.6007	29.8249	36.4662	20.5631
1970	1	23.9255	27.8966	34.8315	44.6154
1971	1	52.7158	53.8653	54.1656	55.9142
1972	1	58.9163	66.3146	70.1338	72.0698
1973	1	85.7837	83.1153	91.3939	88.4270
1974	1	82.0835	83.8948	74.9863	71.3319
1975	1	71.3664	67.5981	65.1715	73.1926
1976	1	74.4921	71.1496	77.3625	74.1194

GERMANY_GERSQN3M

1955	1	3.4400	3.5000	4.3800	6.3800
1956	1	4.8800	6.8100	6.5000	6.8100
1957	1	5.0000	5.1900	4.5000	4.5000
1958	1	3.9400	3.6900	3.1300	3.5000
1959	1	3.0000	2.8800	3.0600	4.7500
1960	1	4.7500	5.0000	5.6300	5.0600
1961	1	3.6900	3.1300	3.0600	3.8100
1962	1	3.0600	3.1300	3.1900	4.3800
1963	1	3.5600	3.8800	3.7500	4.0600
1964	1	3.5000	3.7500	4.1300	5.3100
1965	1	4.3000	4.8000	5.3600	6.5600
1966	1	5.6900	6.8100	6.8000	7.5700
1967	1	5.0400	3.9800	3.4300	4.0700
1968	1	3.5200	3.7200	3.5400	4.2200
1969	1	4.2100	5.5000	6.9400	8.8300
1970	1	9.5600	9.5600	9.2500	8.2000
1971	1	7.4600	6.8000	7.5900	6.6300
1972	1	4.8000	4.6500	5.3200	8.6000
1973	1	8.7700	13.6200	14.2500	13.2000
1974	1	11.2000	9.4600	9.6900	8.6000
1975	1	5.7100	4.8800	3.9300	4.2100
1976	1	3.7400	4.1400	4.5600	4.9300

GERMANY_GERLQNNM

1955	1	0.060259	0.060259	0.059143	0.060259
1956	1	0.060259	0.061375	0.063607	0.063607
1957	1	0.066955	0.066955	0.064723	0.063607
1958	1	0.061375	0.060259	0.056912	0.056912
1959	1	0.053000	0.053000	0.054000	0.060000
1960	1	0.064000	0.067000	0.069000	0.060000
1961	1	0.060000	0.055000	0.060000	0.062000
1962	1	0.060000	0.061000	0.061000	0.061000
1963	1	0.061000	0.060000	0.061000	0.061000
1964	1	0.059000	0.062000	0.062000	0.063000
1965	1	0.064000	0.071000	0.074000	0.076000
1966	1	0.076000	0.080000	0.085000	0.076000
1967	1	0.073000	0.067000	0.068000	0.068000
1968	1	0.068000	0.065000	0.063000	0.063000
1969	1	0.063000	0.068000	0.071000	0.071000
1970	1	0.082000	0.084000	0.085000	0.083000
1971	1	0.077000	0.081000	0.082000	0.078000
1972	1	0.074000	0.081000	0.081000	0.085000
1973	1	0.085000	0.098000	0.096000	0.095000
1974	1	0.103000	0.105000	0.103000	0.097000
1975	1	0.087000	0.082000	0.087000	0.082000
1976	1	0.078000	0.081000	0.080000	0.072000

GERMANY_GEYNQNGN

1955	1	170.33	185.11	201.51	213.57
1956	1	193.27	208.22	218.33	231.83
1957	1	213.57	225.67	240.03	248.82
1958	1	230.47	240.41	256.47	267.85
1959	1	241.77	264.37	278.81	297.76
1960	1	274.88	293.92	309.44	330.96
1961	1	312.92	323.88	335.88	357.72
1962	1	335.32	354.28	364.20	386.60
1963	1	348.00	375.20	394.88	417.92
1964	1	385.60	412.80	425.32	459.88
1965	1	423.68	456.72	468.32	492.88
1966	1	461.80	490.60	495.64	514.76
1967	1	462.60	491.00	493.80	534.60
1968	1	490.16	526.24	547.96	595.64
1969	1	540.64	591.76	614.04	674.36
1970	1	608.08	683.92	692.88	757.52
1971	1	699.04	754.56	767.72	826.28
1972	1	768.04	823.96	825.44	918.16
1973	1	857.76	925.44	912.52	1014.28
1974	1	920.04	991.56	987.84	1088.56
1975	1	957.68	1031.52	1026.20	1159.00
1976	1	1048.24	1125.76	1115.68	1250.72

GERMANY_GEYNQSGN

1955	1	180.92	188.14	197.12	203.02
1956	1	205.15	211.60	213.73	220.43
1957	1	226.38	229.30	235.32	236.71
1958	1	243.79	244.16	251.92	255.03
1959	1	255.05	268.32	274.57	283.47
1960	1	289.64	297.87	305.48	315.00
1961	1	329.59	327.58	332.48	340.22
1962	1	353.32	357.60	361.16	367.69
1963	1	366.73	378.09	392.12	397.33
1964	1	406.84	415.11	422.92	437.09
1965	1	447.32	458.57	466.42	467.99
1966	1	487.95	492.03	494.42	488.25
1967	1	488.98	492.01	493.50	506.35
1968	1	518.37	526.82	548.67	563.75
1969	1	571.42	591.83	616.40	637.96
1970	1	641.85	683.08	697.97	716.20
1971	1	736.57	752.66	776.45	780.19
1972	1	808.09	821.18	838.25	864.84
1973	1	901.81	922.31	930.10	951.98
1974	1	967.63	988.60	1009.70	1017.99
1975	1	1008.29	1028.92	1050.77	1080.85
1976	1	1104.72	1123.52	1142.76	1164.92

GERMANY_GEYNQNGD

1955	1	170.54	185.76	202.29	214.87
1956	1	193.36	208.75	218.95	232.93
1957	1	213.68	226.17	240.58	249.80
1958	1	230.55	240.53	256.68	268.24
1959	1	241.47	264.72	279.33	298.76
1960	1	274.52	294.12	309.80	331.76
1961	1	312.76	324.88	336.96	359.20
1962	1	335.84	354.76	364.76	388.28
1963	1	348.68	376.28	395.12	419.00
1964	1	386.76	414.20	425.72	461.88
1965	1	424.48	459.96	469.32	494.32
1966	1	463.00	492.16	496.92	516.32
1967	1	463.44	492.28	495.80	535.92
1968	1	490.28	526.96	548.76	596.16
1969	1	541.80	591.92	614.08	674.92
1970	1	610.12	684.36	694.84	758.52
1971	1	696.32	754.40	770.04	829.40
1972	1	767.40	824.24	828.04	918.84
1973	1	857.72	927.00	913.00	1015.00
1974	1	920.40	995.88	992.80	1089.56
1975	1	956.96	1038.36	1027.40	1159.36
1976	1	1048.20	1127.36	1115.60	1254.84

GERMANY_GEYNQSGD

1955	1	181.61	188.74	197.85	203.86
1956	1	205.82	212.05	214.30	221.04
1957	1	227.16	229.66	235.80	237.18
1958	1	244.64	244.09	252.06	254.94
1959	1	255.54	268.43	274.99	284.00
1960	1	290.12	297.79	305.74	315.42
1961	1	330.20	328.30	333.48	341.38
1962	1	354.49	357.75	361.76	369.11
1963	1	367.91	378.79	392.53	398.20
1964	1	408.47	416.04	423.59	438.82
1965	1	448.58	461.34	467.67	469.17
1966	1	489.66	493.18	495.86	489.52
1967	1	490.31	493.08	495.44	507.42
1968	1	518.96	527.52	549.15	564.06
1969	1	573.21	592.14	615.82	638.32
1970	1	644.78	683.68	699.08	717.00
1971	1	734.77	752.54	777.69	783.15
1972	1	808.78	821.10	839.75	865.77
1973	1	903.35	922.94	929.44	953.38
1974	1	969.63	991.34	1013.87	1019.99
1975	1	1009.05	1033.76	1051.27	1082.50
1976	1	1106.30	1122.72	1142.03	1170.26

GERMANY_GEYRQNN7

1955	1	274.038	301.231	321.003	338.842
1956	1	303.096	328.938	337.567	355.518
1957	1	328.522	345.540	356.913	369.435
1958	1	335.638	351.300	373.663	391.927
1959	1	352.967	381.946	399.906	423.740
1960	1	392.525	415.085	433.266	458.190
1961	1	428.763	439.913	449.044	473.448
1962	1	440.152	459.583	470.094	493.297
1963	1	441.475	471.175	495.841	518.729
1964	1	477.193	506.877	520.029	551.494
1965	1	506.720	542.026	551.793	569.881
1966	1	532.850	560.877	564.345	575.427
1967	1	520.086	551.968	559.296	597.605
1968	1	550.449	585.729	607.136	648.521
1969	1	591.826	639.559	659.451	698.035
1970	1	627.420	690.848	688.288	732.474
1971	1	671.111	703.069	707.584	739.019
1972	1	690.079	725.506	719.365	780.554
1973	1	733.303	766.099	755.017	810.591
1974	1	747.422	775.754	765.023	793.385
1975	1	708.494	738.087	733.957	802.663
1976	1	745.679	786.846	777.825	839.528

GERMANY_GEYRQSN7

1955	1	291.553	303.616	315.830	322.359
1956	1	322.172	331.722	332.219	338.333
1957	1	348.469	348.859	351.486	351.846
1958	1	354.888	355.135	368.385	373.556
1959	1	371.943	386.554	394.750	404.004
1960	1	412.830	420.161	428.111	436.953
1961	1	450.681	444.853	444.147	451.599
1962	1	462.839	463.954	465.276	470.796
1963	1	464.587	474.788	490.892	495.263
1964	1	502.974	509.588	515.076	526.800
1965	1	534.549	544.002	547.038	544.248
1966	1	562.441	562.252	560.192	549.318
1967	1	548.774	553.118	556.006	570.045
1968	1	580.437	586.872	604.514	618.579
1969	1	622.826	640.685	658.242	665.885
1970	1	658.506	691.565	689.289	699.111
1971	1	701.943	703.290	711.088	705.531
1972	1	719.695	725.198	725.287	744.950
1973	1	763.231	765.443	763.419	772.497
1974	1	777.523	774.932	775.025	754.860
1975	1	737.251	737.337	744.306	762.594
1976	1	776.375	786.320	788.706	797.245

GERMANY_GEYRQND7

1955	1	274.381	302.282	322.248	340.901
1956	1	303.248	329.775	338.525	357.195
1957	1	328.687	346.299	357.725	370.883
1958	1	335.745	351.477	373.975	392.497
1959	1	352.524	382.445	400.655	425.163
1960	1	392.011	415.368	433.770	459.298
1961	1	428.544	441.271	450.489	475.406
1962	1	440.835	460.206	470.817	495.441
1963	1	442.337	472.531	496.142	520.069
1964	1	478.629	508.597	520.518	553.892
1965	1	507.677	545.871	552.971	571.546
1966	1	534.235	562.661	565.802	577.171
1967	1	521.031	553.407	561.561	599.081
1968	1	550.584	586.531	608.022	649.087
1969	1	593.096	639.732	659.494	698.615
1970	1	629.525	691.292	690.235	733.441
1971	1	668.500	702.920	709.722	741.810
1972	1	689.504	725.752	721.631	781.132
1973	1	733.269	767.391	755.415	811.166
1974	1	747.714	779.134	768.865	794.114
1975	1	707.961	742.982	734.815	802.912
1976	1	745.651	787.965	777.769	842.293

GERMANY_GEYRQSD7

1955	1	292.578	304.673	317.028	323.707
1956	1	323.041	332.563	333.137	339.311
1957	1	349.378	349.618	352.253	352.640
1958	1	355.685	355.300	368.661	373.548
1959	1	372.116	387.034	395.450	404.888
1960	1	412.867	420.395	428.601	437.614
1961	1	450.938	446.121	445.643	453.155
1962	1	463.954	464.346	466.209	472.556
1963	1	465.848	475.785	491.530	496.276
1964	1	504.869	510.822	515.965	528.815
1965	1	535.995	547.333	548.554	545.591
1966	1	564.388	563.570	561.839	550.789
1967	1	550.227	554.267	558.234	571.307
1968	1	581.065	587.543	605.128	618.992
1969	1	624.747	640.833	657.799	666.300
1970	1	661.477	691.952	690.631	699.894
1971	1	700.192	702.933	712.556	708.119
1972	1	720.322	724.897	726.914	745.587
1973	1	764.614	765.750	763.283	773.312
1974	1	779.297	776.904	778.629	755.934
1975	1	738.024	740.657	745.104	763.224
1976	1	777.760	785.622	788.672	800.300

GERMANY_GEPDQNN7

1955	1	0.62155	0.61451	0.62774	0.63029
1956	1	0.63764	0.63300	0.64676	0.65210
1957	1	0.65009	0.65311	0.67252	0.67353
1958	1	0.68667	0.68435	0.68637	0.68343
1959	1	0.68497	0.69217	0.69719	0.70269
1960	1	0.70029	0.70810	0.71420	0.72232
1961	1	0.72982	0.73624	0.74799	0.75556
1962	1	0.76183	0.77087	0.77474	0.78371
1963	1	0.78827	0.79631	0.79638	0.80566
1964	1	0.80806	0.81440	0.81788	0.83388
1965	1	0.83612	0.84262	0.84872	0.86488
1966	1	0.86666	0.87470	0.87826	0.89457
1967	1	0.88947	0.88954	0.88290	0.89457
1968	1	0.89047	0.89844	0.90253	0.91846
1969	1	0.91351	0.92526	0.93114	0.96608
1970	1	0.96917	0.98997	1.00667	1.03419
1971	1	1.04161	1.07324	1.08499	1.11808
1972	1	1.11297	1.13570	1.14746	1.17629
1973	1	1.16972	1.20799	1.20861	1.25128
1974	1	1.23095	1.27819	1.29125	1.37204
1975	1	1.35171	1.39756	1.39818	1.44394
1976	1	1.40575	1.43072	1.43436	1.48979

GERMANY_GEPDQSN7

1955	1	0.62043	0.61957	0.62468	0.62933
1956	1	0.63672	0.63774	0.64389	0.65112
1957	1	0.64957	0.65705	0.67007	0.67249
1958	1	0.68671	0.68727	0.68446	0.68253
1959	1	0.68539	0.69390	0.69599	0.70186
1960	1	0.70097	0.70884	0.71376	0.72146
1961	1	0.73053	0.73632	0.74845	0.75429
1962	1	0.76250	0.77068	0.77602	0.78186
1963	1	0.78883	0.79605	0.79854	0.80300
1964	1	0.80862	0.81416	0.82090	0.83017
1965	1	0.83684	0.84252	0.85245	0.86005
1966	1	0.86769	0.87486	0.88243	0.88866
1967	1	0.89102	0.88992	0.88706	0.88797
1968	1	0.89278	0.89869	0.90674	0.91108
1969	1	0.91680	0.92537	0.93512	0.95783
1970	1	0.97396	0.98946	1.01103	1.02436
1971	1	1.04849	1.07190	1.08998	1.10597
1972	1	1.12240	1.13319	1.15374	1.16140
1973	1	1.18156	1.20482	1.21629	1.23298
1974	1	1.24512	1.27448	1.30088	1.34932
1975	1	1.36854	1.39369	1.40959	1.41805
1976	1	1.42411	1.42679	1.44661	1.46201

GERMANY_GEPCQN70

1949	1	0.69272	0.68046	0.66513	0.66513
1950	1	0.64061	0.62835	0.62835	0.63755
1951	1	0.65594	0.68352	0.68965	0.70498
1952	1	0.70498	0.69272	0.68965	0.69272
1953	1	0.68965	0.68965	0.68659	0.68046
1954	1	0.68352	0.68965	0.68965	0.68965
1955	1	0.68965	0.68965	0.69272	0.70498
1956	1	0.71111	0.71724	0.71724	0.72337
1957	1	0.72644	0.72644	0.72950	0.73563
1958	1	0.74483	0.75096	0.74483	0.74176
1959	1	0.74483	0.74789	0.75709	0.76322
1960	1	0.76322	0.76322	0.76322	0.76322
1961	1	0.77241	0.78161	0.78774	0.78774
1962	1	0.80306	0.81226	0.81226	0.80919
1963	1	0.83678	0.83985	0.83065	0.83678
1964	1	0.84598	0.84598	0.84598	0.85211
1965	1	0.85824	0.87356	0.88276	0.88582
1966	1	0.89808	0.91034	0.91034	0.91341
1967	1	0.91954	0.91954	0.91954	0.91954
1968	1	0.93793	0.93793	0.93180	0.94406
1969	1	0.95939	0.96552	0.96552	0.97471
1970	1	0.99004	0.99923	1.00230	1.00843
1971	1	1.02988	1.05134	1.06054	1.07280
1972	1	1.09119	1.10651	1.12490	1.14329
1973	1	1.16782	1.18927	1.19847	1.22299
1974	1	1.25364	1.27509	1.28429	1.30268
1975	1	1.32720	1.35172	1.36398	1.37624
1976	1	1.36889	1.38728	1.39310	1.39739

GERMANY_GEPCQS70

1949	1	0.69155	0.68090	0.66780	0.66315
1950	1	0.63959	0.62881	0.63059	0.63585
1951	1	0.65512	0.68388	0.69158	0.70362
1952	1	0.70437	0.69269	0.69128	0.69183
1953	1	0.68916	0.68940	0.68800	0.67993
1954	1	0.68301	0.68922	0.69103	0.68936
1955	1	0.68908	0.68908	0.69403	0.70497
1956	1	0.71043	0.71651	0.71858	0.72356
1957	1	0.72565	0.72567	0.73070	0.73612
1958	1	0.74398	0.75019	0.74548	0.74296
1959	1	0.74400	0.74676	0.75736	0.76535
1960	1	0.76226	0.76151	0.76345	0.76606
1961	1	0.77127	0.77920	0.78837	0.79098
1962	1	0.80178	0.80927	0.81323	0.81268
1963	1	0.83541	0.83638	0.83201	0.84019
1964	1	0.84470	0.84246	0.84749	0.85536
1965	1	0.85687	0.87019	0.88442	0.88891
1966	1	0.89656	0.90713	0.91201	0.91670
1967	1	0.91759	0.91641	0.92141	0.92301
1968	1	0.93559	0.93466	0.93395	0.94781
1969	1	0.95668	0.96204	0.96799	0.97850
1970	1	0.98735	0.99546	1.00497	1.01218
1971	1	1.02740	1.04720	1.06339	1.07651
1972	1	1.08898	1.10214	1.12780	1.14689
1973	1	1.16583	1.18483	1.20130	1.22643
1974	1	1.25186	1.27062	1.28712	1.30596
1975	1	1.32555	1.34736	1.36668	1.37953
1976	1	1.36733	1.38297	1.39567	1.40069

GERMANY_GEIPQS70

1948	1	0.10130	0.10624	0.13094	0.14824
1949	1	0.17048	0.17542	0.18530	0.19024
1950	1	0.20259	0.21495	0.23718	0.25448
1951	1	0.26436	0.27177	0.26683	0.27177
1952	1	0.27918	0.27918	0.28660	0.29895
1953	1	0.29648	0.30883	0.32119	0.32860
1954	1	0.33107	0.34589	0.35824	0.37060
1955	1	0.38048	0.39530	0.41507	0.42495
1956	1	0.42248	0.43236	0.44472	0.44472
1957	1	0.45213	0.45954	0.46201	0.46695
1958	1	0.47684	0.47189	0.47931	0.48178
1959	1	0.48425	0.49907	0.51390	0.53613
1960	1	0.54601	0.56331	0.57566	0.58802
1961	1	0.60778	0.60037	0.60778	0.60778
1962	1	0.61766	0.63002	0.63743	0.64484
1963	1	0.62755	0.64237	0.65966	0.67449
1964	1	0.68190	0.70167	0.70908	0.72637
1965	1	0.73873	0.74367	0.74614	0.74861
1966	1	0.76837	0.76837	0.75602	0.73873
1967	1	0.72390	0.72143	0.74120	0.77826
1968	1	0.77826	0.81037	0.85238	0.88449
1969	1	0.90673	0.93391	0.95120	0.98085
1970	1	0.99320	1.01050	1.00062	0.99567
1971	1	1.02532	1.02779	1.01544	0.99814
1972	1	1.03026	1.04509	1.04509	1.08462
1973	1	1.12909	1.13403	1.12909	1.15380
1974	1	1.13403	1.12909	1.11179	1.08462
1975	1	1.05991	1.03273	1.02532	1.07968
1976	1	1.09944	1.11921	1.11674	1.13403

GERMANY_GEGXQNFG

1955	1	24.332	23.079	23.673	24.151
1956	1	24.943	25.372	27.609	31.468
1957	1	29.617	31.545	33.773	33.014
1958	1	32.633	30.063	31.099	32.818
1959	1	44.411	35.882	37.701	37.733
1960	1	39.592	36.259	39.022	48.371
1961	1	34.581	41.805	45.174	52.435
1962	1	43.046	46.676	51.142	60.125
1963	1	45.990	49.568	55.403	68.189
1964	1	49.748	53.348	55.688	71.012
1965	1	54.880	60.464	64.812	72.640
1966	1	59.980	62.520	70.032	76.504
1967	1	66.148	68.592	74.976	89.744
1968	1	64.332	67.992	75.476	91.804
1969	1	66.364	70.152	82.920	104.252
1970	1	70.300	78.488	88.680	110.576
1971	1	80.792	90.524	97.284	121.240
1972	1	93.012	98.840	103.720	141.392
1973	1	107.860	110.192	119.380	157.156
1974	1	119.252	124.000	134.196	175.348
1975	1	144.084	157.128	158.244	197.168
1976	1	153.868	159.016	168.588	205.136

GERMANY_GEGXQSFG

1955	1	24.421	23.837	23.700	23.346
1956	1	24.932	26.265	27.668	30.445
1957	1	29.405	32.838	33.993	31.681
1958	1	32.410	31.497	31.369	31.110
1959	1	44.356	37.855	38.193	34.940
1960	1	40.263	38.490	39.502	43.747
1961	1	36.002	44.536	45.825	46.064
1962	1	46.284	49.705	51.763	51.843
1963	1	50.656	52.763	55.959	58.135
1964	1	55.571	56.914	55.985	60.355
1965	1	61.509	64.814	65.013	61.465
1966	1	67.391	67.454	70.036	64.422
1967	1	74.522	74.549	74.802	75.070
1968	1	72.826	74.281	75.317	76.225
1969	1	75.517	76.716	83.158	86.008
1970	1	80.117	85.711	89.599	90.990
1971	1	91.645	98.628	99.125	99.894
1972	1	104.570	107.261	106.656	116.900
1973	1	120.002	119.148	123.611	130.551
1974	1	131.428	133.770	139.486	146.269
1975	1	157.805	169.336	164.535	165.048
1976	1	168.111	171.114	175.285	172.144

GERMANY_GEGDQNFG

1955	1	-0.2346	0.6711	2.2233	2.6898
1956	1	2.1170	1.8332	0.7366	-1.6041
1957	1	-0.3628	-2.0542	-3.2818	-0.9548
1958	1	-1.2822	0.3574	0.2537	0.0791
1959	1	-8.6751	-2.0106	-1.6832	-0.8593
1960	1	-2.5316	1.4431	0.8293	-3.4591
1961	1	4.9514	0.0818	-0.9112	-3.2382
1962	1	1.6586	-0.4665	-2.2015	-3.2000
1963	1	1.3204	-0.6465	-2.9326	-6.3127
1964	1	4.0200	-0.0480	1.9800	-10.3520
1965	1	2.5200	-3.0040	-0.7960	-7.1080
1966	1	2.8080	1.7920	-4.8600	-9.8320
1967	1	-3.4280	-5.1320	-7.4440	-17.1000
1968	1	-0.5600	-2.0920	-0.7000	-12.2680
1969	1	9.4360	6.6400	0.8960	-10.2560
1970	1	9.8600	0.6400	0.5160	-13.2680
1971	1	9.9880	0.0480	-2.1640	-13.3200
1972	1	5.9240	-0.9600	-0.3400	-19.1960
1973	1	4.7880	1.1320	2.1640	-19.4840
1974	1	3.6760	-6.7800	-6.7480	-30.5560
1975	1	-25.5120	-42.4200	-25.4320	-42.8280
1976	1	-24.1680	-27.3520	-27.4560	-41.6760

GERMANY_GEGDQSFG

1955	1	-0.2834	0.5139	2.2499	2.8014
1956	1	2.1946	1.6163	0.7319	-1.5354
1957	1	-0.0557	-2.4602	-3.3664	-0.7023
1958	1	-0.9489	-0.2316	0.1376	0.6386
1959	1	-8.4837	-2.7961	-1.8114	0.2504
1960	1	-2.7950	0.4969	0.7960	-1.7029
1961	1	4.0264	-0.9132	-1.0564	-0.4022
1962	1	-0.3311	-1.3298	-2.5114	0.7020
1963	1	-1.5974	-1.5280	-3.3709	-1.4408
1964	1	0.4440	-1.1764	1.4780	-4.5973
1965	1	-1.4769	-4.5581	-1.4704	-0.1965
1966	1	-1.7638	-0.2604	-5.5585	-1.7562
1967	1	-8.7266	-7.6282	-8.0701	-7.8686
1968	1	-6.7915	-4.8284	-1.2300	-2.0152
1969	1	2.2063	4.0553	0.0289	1.1049
1970	1	1.7394	-1.6672	-0.8366	-1.1053
1971	1	1.3747	-1.8414	-4.2370	-0.7652
1972	1	-2.6138	-2.4580	-3.1402	-6.7491
1973	1	-3.1906	-0.0037	-1.3660	-7.3620
1974	1	-3.5591	-7.7605	-10.6709	-18.8829
1975	1	-32.1742	-43.2393	-29.5164	-31.5670
1976	1	-30.5655	-27.9924	-31.5747	-30.7730

GERMANY_GEPPQNIN

1954	1		0.051870	0.051994	0.052119
1955	1	0.052244	0.052370	0.052527	0.052684
1956	1	0.052841	0.053000	0.053161	0.053323
1957	1	0.053486	0.053650	0.053807	0.053964
1958	1	0.054121	0.054280	0.054429	0.054579
1959	1	0.054729	0.054880	0.055014	0.055149
1960	1	0.055284	0.055420	0.055621	0.055823
1961	1	0.056025	0.056230	0.056409	0.056588
1962	1	0.056768	0.056950	0.057114	0.057279
1963	1	0.057443	0.057610	0.057779	0.057948
1964	1	0.058118	0.058290	0.058476	0.058663
1965	1	0.058851	0.059040	0.059199	0.059359
1966	1	0.059519	0.059680	0.059727	0.059775
1967	1	0.059822	0.059870	0.059945	0.060020
1968	1	0.060095	0.060170	0.060337	0.060504
1969	1	0.060671	0.060840	0.060792	0.060745
1970	1	0.060697	0.060650	0.060809	0.060969
1971	1	0.061129	0.061290	0.061385	0.061480
1972	1	0.061575	0.061670	0.061745	0.061820
1973	1	0.061895	0.061970	0.061987	0.062005
1974	1	0.062022	0.062040	0.061987	0.061935
1975	1	0.061882	0.061830	0.061747	0.061665
1976	1	0.061582	0.061500	0.061418	0.061336

GERMANY_GEEMQNER

1955	1	0.016677	0.017754	0.018062	0.017633
1956	1	0.017782	0.018655	0.018875	0.018261
1957	1	0.018729	0.019191	0.019238	0.018446
1958	1	0.018582	0.019476	0.019633	0.019029
1959	1	0.019371	0.019870	0.020065	0.019783
1960	1	0.019747	0.020294	0.020509	0.020020
1961	1	0.020389	0.020810	0.020888	0.020832
1962	1	0.020693	0.021100	0.021240	0.021094
1963	1	0.020866	0.021373	0.021540	0.021357
1964	1	0.021087	0.021588	0.021674	0.021582
1965	1	0.021428	0.021851	0.021965	0.021785
1966	1	0.021614	0.021946	0.021931	0.021568
1967	1	0.020983	0.021059	0.021181	0.020992
1968	1	0.020793	0.021057	0.021384	0.021495
1969	1	0.021399	0.021657	0.021942	0.022013
1970	1	0.021875	0.022197	0.022466	0.022445
1971	1	0.022231	0.022401	0.022598	0.022426
1972	1	0.022201	0.022382	0.022607	0.022548
1973	1	0.022424	0.022540	0.022705	0.022587
1974	1	0.022275	0.022225	0.022205	0.021903
1975	1	0.021491	0.021411	0.021427	0.021351
1976	1	0.022885	0.023025	0.023051	0.022708

GERMANY_GEEMQSER

1955	1	0.016951	0.017445	0.017731	0.018002
1956	1	0.018063	0.018336	0.018540	0.018630
1957	1	0.019009	0.018883	0.018912	0.018801
1958	1	0.018830	0.019198	0.019330	0.019345
1959	1	0.019613	0.019622	0.019789	0.020050
1960	1	0.019979	0.020081	0.020269	0.020208
1961	1	0.020635	0.020626	0.020675	0.020962
1962	1	0.020944	0.020944	0.021048	0.021168
1963	1	0.021128	0.021237	0.021359	0.021396
1964	1	0.021352	0.021474	0.021498	0.021595
1965	1	0.021693	0.021762	0.021788	0.021781
1966	1	0.021866	0.021885	0.021758	0.021549
1967	1	0.021210	0.021028	0.021021	0.020956
1968	1	0.021003	0.021051	0.021225	0.021447
1969	1	0.021601	0.021667	0.021785	0.021959
1970	1	0.022067	0.022218	0.022310	0.022394
1971	1	0.022411	0.022423	0.022450	0.022383
1972	1	0.022363	0.022399	0.022473	0.022521
1973	1	0.022564	0.022542	0.022590	0.022583
1974	1	0.022388	0.022210	0.022113	0.021919
1975	1	0.021579	0.021381	0.021353	0.021381
1976	1	0.022966	0.022984	0.022980	0.022746

GERMANY_GEUNQNER

1955	1	0.001514	0.000701	0.000533	0.001126
1956	1	0.001097	0.000516	0.000443	0.001173
1957	1	0.000756	0.000489	0.000396	0.001306
1958	1	0.001193	0.000432	0.000353	0.001003
1959	1	0.000639	0.000279	0.000201	0.000477
1960	1	0.000277	0.000144	0.000121	0.000293
1961	1	0.000176	0.000107	0.000102	0.000240
1962	1	0.000205	0.000095	0.000089	0.000236
1963	1	0.000216	0.000112	0.000105	0.000252
1964	1	0.000227	0.000112	0.000100	0.000202
1965	1	0.000201	0.000095	0.000085	0.000178
1966	1	0.000141	0.000101	0.000113	0.000372
1967	1	0.000576	0.000401	0.000341	0.000526
1968	1	0.000460	0.000227	0.000175	0.000266
1969	1	0.000243	0.000111	0.000101	0.000192
1970	1	0.000198	0.000095	0.000097	0.000175
1971	1	0.000207	0.000135	0.000147	0.000270
1972	1	0.000268	0.000190	0.000195	0.000279
1973	1	0.000287	0.000201	0.000219	0.000486
1974	1	0.000562	0.000451	0.000557	0.000946
1975	1	0.001114	0.001002	0.001005	0.001223
1976	1	0.001190	0.000921	0.000899	0.001090

GERMANY_GEUNQSER

1955	1	0.001209	0.001103	0.000968	0.000720
1956	1	0.000877	0.000816	0.000803	0.000743
1957	1	0.000610	0.000778	0.000718	0.000816
1958	1	0.000984	0.000686	0.000633	0.000624
1959	1	0.000531	0.000444	0.000354	0.000298
1960	1	0.000231	0.000229	0.000207	0.000187
1961	1	0.000144	0.000168	0.000171	0.000157
1962	1	0.000165	0.000147	0.000147	0.000160
1963	1	0.000170	0.000171	0.000171	0.000177
1964	1	0.000174	0.000168	0.000161	0.000146
1965	1	0.000153	0.000138	0.000134	0.000133
1966	1	0.000106	0.000143	0.000175	0.000284
1967	1	0.000433	0.000558	0.000516	0.000410
1968	1	0.000346	0.000312	0.000258	0.000210
1969	1	0.000185	0.000151	0.000144	0.000153
1970	1	0.000153	0.000128	0.000134	0.000140
1971	1	0.000163	0.000179	0.000197	0.000219
1972	1	0.000216	0.000245	0.000252	0.000229
1973	1	0.000237	0.000251	0.000274	0.000408
1974	1	0.000473	0.000548	0.000680	0.000810
1975	1	0.000949	0.001193	0.001206	0.001064
1976	1	0.001017	0.001086	0.001074	0.000955

GERMANY_GELFQNDR

1955	1	0.018191	0.018456	0.018595	0.018759
1956	1	0.018879	0.019171	0.019318	0.019433
1957	1	0.019485	0.019680	0.019635	0.019753
1958	1	0.019775	0.019908	0.019987	0.020031
1959	1	0.020010	0.020149	0.020266	0.020260
1960	1	0.020024	0.020438	0.020630	0.020313
1961	1	0.020565	0.020917	0.020990	0.021072
1962	1	0.020898	0.021195	0.021329	0.021330
1963	1	0.021082	0.021485	0.021645	0.021609
1964	1	0.021314	0.021700	0.021774	0.021784
1965	1	0.021629	0.021946	0.022050	0.021963
1966	1	0.021755	0.022047	0.022044	0.021940
1967	1	0.021559	0.021460	0.021522	0.021518
1968	1	0.021253	0.021284	0.021559	0.021761
1969	1	0.021642	0.021768	0.022043	0.022205
1970	1	0.022073	0.022292	0.022563	0.022620
1971	1	0.022438	0.022536	0.022745	0.022696
1972	1	0.022469	0.022572	0.022802	0.022827
1973	1	0.022711	0.022741	0.022924	0.023073
1974	1	0.022837	0.022676	0.022762	0.022849
1975	1	0.022605	0.022413	0.022432	0.022574
1976	1	0.024075	0.023946	0.023950	0.023798

GERMANY_GELFQSDR

1955	1	0.018259	0.018410	0.018573	0.018758
1956	1	0.018949	0.019128	0.019291	0.019428
1957	1	0.019564	0.019638	0.019598	0.019743
1958	1	0.019871	0.019864	0.019940	0.020014
1959	1	0.020131	0.020099	0.020206	0.020234
1960	1	0.020172	0.020383	0.020555	0.020278
1961	1	0.020745	0.020852	0.020903	0.021032
1962	1	0.021100	0.021127	0.021232	0.021287
1963	1	0.021292	0.021419	0.021543	0.021564
1964	1	0.021519	0.021648	0.021671	0.021732
1965	1	0.021824	0.021911	0.021952	0.021900
1966	1	0.021932	0.022037	0.021954	0.021862
1967	1	0.021716	0.021476	0.021441	0.021426
1968	1	0.021393	0.021325	0.021477	0.021658
1969	1	0.021776	0.021827	0.021956	0.022098
1970	1	0.022199	0.022365	0.022473	0.022514
1971	1	0.022554	0.022613	0.022664	0.022595
1972	1	0.022562	0.022649	0.022744	0.022733
1973	1	0.022773	0.022812	0.022896	0.022990
1974	1	0.022863	0.022739	0.022766	0.022778
1975	1	0.022600	0.022467	0.022457	0.022513
1976	1	0.024051	0.023998	0.023989	0.023736

GERMANY_GEURQNDR

1955	1	0.083236	0.037988	0.028668	0.060049
1956	1	0.058127	0.026908	0.022912	0.060349
1957	1	0.038799	0.024844	0.020184	0.066134
1958	1	0.060340	0.021693	0.017674	0.050053
1959	1	0.031915	0.013844	0.009937	0.023548
1960	1	0.013822	0.007061	0.005847	0.014421
1961	1	0.008536	0.005097	0.004874	0.011397
1962	1	0.009791	0.004471	0.004191	0.011057
1963	1	0.010246	0.005213	0.004851	0.011662
1964	1	0.010650	0.005161	0.004593	0.009273
1965	1	0.009293	0.004329	0.003855	0.008105
1966	1	0.006481	0.004581	0.005126	0.016955
1967	1	0.026717	0.018686	0.015844	0.024445
1968	1	0.021644	0.010665	0.008117	0.012224
1969	1	0.011228	0.005099	0.004582	0.008647
1970	1	0.008970	0.004262	0.004299	0.007737
1971	1	0.009225	0.005990	0.006463	0.011896
1972	1	0.011928	0.008418	0.008552	0.012222
1973	1	0.012637	0.008839	0.009553	0.021064
1974	1	0.024609	0.019889	0.024471	0.041402
1975	1	0.049281	0.044706	0.044802	0.054177
1976	1	0.049429	0.038462	0.037537	0.045802

GERMANY_GEURQSDR

1955	1	0.066009	0.060050	0.052165	0.038493
1956	1	0.046164	0.042787	0.041679	0.038341
1957	1	0.031118	0.039726	0.036695	0.041354
1958	1	0.049439	0.034637	0.031804	0.031147
1959	1	0.026401	0.022176	0.017569	0.014705
1960	1	0.011468	0.011266	0.010083	0.009190
1961	1	0.006985	0.008080	0.008206	0.007473
1962	1	0.007856	0.006983	0.006925	0.007514
1963	1	0.008001	0.008009	0.007921	0.008209
1964	1	0.008136	0.007737	0.007413	0.006734
1965	1	0.007020	0.006287	0.006127	0.006069
1966	1	0.004862	0.006473	0.007980	0.013020
1967	1	0.020015	0.025862	0.024098	0.019172
1968	1	0.016230	0.014566	0.012033	0.009697
1969	1	0.008508	0.006889	0.006580	0.006938
1970	1	0.006879	0.005706	0.005981	0.006239
1971	1	0.007225	0.007898	0.008679	0.009692
1972	1	0.009571	0.010821	0.011086	0.010082
1973	1	0.010439	0.010998	0.011952	0.017726
1974	1	0.020763	0.024055	0.029861	0.035414
1975	1	0.042186	0.053013	0.053758	0.046999
1976	1	0.042496	0.045202	0.044792	0.039986

Sources and Notes on Time Series for Italy

The major sources of data were the monthly publications *Bollettino* of the Banca d'Italia (BI), the Italian central bank, and the *Bollettino mensile di statistica* of ISTAT, the Italian Central Institute of Statistics. Thomas Huertas of Citibank, N.A, provided valuable advice on the sources and definitions of the Italian data. Laura Marrone of the Ufficio italiano di cambi, the Italian foreign exchange office in New York, provided us with official publications which were not otherwise readily available. Professor Vincenzo Siesto of the Pro Deo University, Rome, Italy, provided us with his estimates of quarterly national accounts data.

All time series are on a quarterly basis and cover the period 1955I to 1976IV, except where noted otherwise. We made seasonal adjustment, where necessary, using the Census X-11 program.

I. INTERNATIONAL VARIABLES

A. *Balance of Payments*

ITBPQNVL Balance of Payments. Units: Billions of Lire at Quarterly
ITBPQSVL   Rates.

Source: For 1955–60, estimated from data on official international reserve assets in BI, *Bollettino*, table A6, various monthly issues; for 1961–76, ibid., table F2, "Bilancia dei pagamenti valutaria," various monthly issues beginning with January–March 1963, vol. 18, no. 1.

Description: The official settlements balance of payments on a cash basis. For the period 1955I to 1960IV, we estimated the official settlements balance as the first difference in official international reserve assets (see II.D. below).

B. *Exports*

1. Total Exports
ITEXQNTL Total Exports. Unit: Billions of Lire at Annual Rates.
ITEXQSTL

Source: For 1955–60, our own estimates based on Siesto's national accounts data, table 6, part A.1; for 1961–76, from BI, *Bollettino*, table F2, "Bilancia dei pagamenti valutaria," various monthly issues beginning with January–March 1963, vol. 18, no. 1.

Description: This measures current account receipts from exports of goods and services, and transfers on a valuation basis. For the period 1955I to 1960IV, we estimated, by regression, the relation between the current account exports given by the Banca d'Italia data, and the exports of goods and services national accounts data provided by Siesto in his table 6, part A.1, for the overlap period 1961I to 1975IV. We then estimated current account total exports for the period 1955I to 1960IV, using the estimated relation and the Seisto data. The data were originally at quarterly rates.

2. Exports of Goods

ITEXQNGO   Exports of Goods. Unit: Billions of Lire at Annual Rates.
ITEXQSGO

Source: Same as I.B.1, Total Exports, above.

Description: This measures current account exports of goods on a valuation basis. For 1955–60 we applied a method similar to that described in I.B.1 above, except that we estimated a relation between exports of goods from the BI source and the Siesto data for total exports. The data were originally at quarterly rates.

3. Exports of Services and Transfers

ITEXQNST   Exports of Services and Transfers. Unit: Billions of Lire at
ITEXQSST   Annual Rates.

Source: Same as I.B.1, Total Exports, above.

Description: Derived by subtracting exports of goods from total exports. The data were originally at quarterly rates.

C. *Imports*

1. Total Imports

ITIMQNTL   Total Imports. Unit: Billions of Lire at Annual Rates.
ITIMQSTL

Source: For 1955–60, our own estimates based on Siesto's national accounts data, table 6, part A.1; for the period 1961I to 1976IV, Banca d'Italia, *Bollettino*, table F2, "Bilancia dei pagamenti valutaria," various monthly issues beginning with January–March 1963, vol. 18, no. 1.

Description: Current account receipts from imports of goods and services and transfers on a valuation basis. For the period 1955I to 1960IV, we estimated, by regression, the relation between the current account imports given by the Banca d'Italia data and the imports of goods and services national accounts data provided by Siesto in his table 6, part A.1, for the overlap period 1961I to 1975IV. We then estimated current account total imports for the period 1955I to 1960IV, using the estimated relation and the Siesto data. The data were originally at quarterly rates.

2. Imports of Goods

ITIMQNGO   Imports of Goods. Unit: Billions of Lire at Annual Rates.
ITIMQSGO

Source: Same as I.C.1, Total Imports, above.

Description: This measures current account imports of goods on a valuation basis. For 1955–60, we applied a method similar to that described in I.C.1 above, except that we estimated a relation between imports of goods from the BI source and the Siesto data for total imports. The data were originally at quarterly rates.

3. Imports of Services and Transfers

ITIMQNST   Imports of Services and Transfers. Unit: Billions of Lire at
ITIMQSST   Annual Rates.

Source: Same as I.C.1, Total Imports, above.

Description: Derived by subtracting imports of goods from total imports. The data were originally at quarterly rates.

D. *Net Private Capital Outflows*

    ITKPQNEP   Net Private Capital Outflows. Units: Billions of Lire at
    ITKPQSEP   Annual Rates.

Source: For 1955–60, our own estimates are based on annual data from International Monetary Fund (IMF), *International Financial Statistics*, various issues; for 1961I to 1976IV, BI, *Bollettino*, table F2, "Bilancia dei pagamenti valutaria: Capitali privati," various monthly issues through July–September 1977.

Description: The balance of total—short- and long-term— private capital transactions on a valuation basis, excluding unclassifiable transactions, with net capital exports defined positive. An attempt was made to estimate this series by regression (as described in I.B.1 and I.C.1 above), using as a related series, net capital transactions from Siesto's estimates of national account data, table 6.C.S. However, the regression was a very poor fit, and we therefore chose to use the IMF annual data to represent the annual flow for each quarter of the respective year. The data from the *Bollettino* were originally at monthly rates.

E. *Exchange Rate*

    ITXRQNLR   Exchange Rate. Unit: Lire per U.S. Dollar.

Source: For period 1955 to 1977, BI, *Bollettino*, table F1, "Corso dei cambi, tasso medio di deprezzamento della lira," various monthly issues from January–March 1956 to July–September 1977.

Description: The series is the quarterly average of daily quotations on the Rome and Milan exchanges for the spot exchange rate.

II. FINANCIAL VARIABLES

A. *Narrow Money Stock*

    ITM1QNDR   Money Stock—M1. Unit: Billions of Lire, End-of-Quarter.
    ITM1QSDR

Source: For 1955I to 1957IV, IMF, *International Financial Statistics*; 1958I to 1976IV, BI, *Bollettino*, table H1, "Attivita liquide del pubblico," various monthly issues from January–March 1959 to July–September 1977.

Description: M1, currency plus demand deposits of the (nonbank) public, including the public's deposits at commercial banks, the Italian Treasury, the Banca d'Italia, and the Italian Post Office. For 1955I–57IV we could find no complete data in Italian sources. Since IMF data corresponded almost exactly with the official Italian series in later years, we used the IMF figures without adjustment for the earlier period. These data appear to be unpublished estimates of the Banca d'Italia made available directly to the IMF, since IMF publications list the Banca d'Italia as their ultimate source. Data in the OEEC publication, *General Statistics*, for any overlap period did not conform to official Italian data.

B. *Broader Money Stock*

    ITM2QNQE   Money Stock—M2. Unit: Billions of Lire, End-of-Quarter.
    ITM2QSQE

Source: Same as described in II.A, narrow money stock.

Description: We derived a broader definition of money by adding time deposits of the public at commercial banks and the Italian Post Office to the narrow definition of money (II.A.1). The estimates of time deposits for the period 1955I to 1957IV obtained from the IMF conformed exactly with the data from the official Italian sources. The OEEC publication, referred to in II.A.1, also had data on time deposits, but these figures did not conform to the official Italian statistics for any overlap period.

C. *High-powered Money*

ITMHQNDR   High-powered Money. Unit: Billions of Lire, End-of-
ITMHQSDR   Quarter.

Source: For 1955I to 1957IV, source as described in II.A; 1958I to 1976IV, BI, *Bollettino*, table A6, various monthly issues from January–March 1959 to July–September 1977.

Description: The series is the sum of currency outstanding, including vault cash, and the public's deposits at the Banca d'Italia and the Treasury plus the deposits of commercial banks at the Banca d'Italia and the Treasury. For the period 1955I to 1957IV, the same procedure was used as described in II.A.

D. *Official International Reserve Assets*

ITFHQNDR   Official International Reserve Assets. Unit: Billions of
ITFHQSDR   Lire, End-of-Quarter.

Source: For 1955I to 1959IV, IMF, *International Financial Statistics*, various issues; 1960I to 1976IV, BI, *Bollettino*, table A6, "Banca d'Italia e Ufficio italiano dei cambi: Situzaione consolidata," various monthly issues from January–March 1961 to July–September 1977.

Description: The series is the sum of official gold, convertible currency holdings, and special drawing rights. The *Bollettino* provided data only for the period 1960 to 1976 on a quarterly basis and annually for 1955 to 1959. We obtained quarterly data for the earlier period 1955I–59IV from the IMF. Since these figures were given in U.S. dollars, we converted them to lire at the market rate of exchange. The converted figures for the fourth quarter proved to be completely compatible with the end-of-year figures given in the *Bollettino* in lire. Hence, to complete the series for the remaining three quarters of each year, we used the converted values of the IMF data without adjustment.

E. *Interest Rates*

1. Short-Term

No short-term interest rate which covers the full period under study exists in any consistent and continuous form. Monthly data for a money market rate beginning in 1974 are published by Morgan Guaranty Trust Co. in *World Financial Markets*.

2. Long-Term

a. ITRLQNGV   Market Yield on Long-term Government Bonds. Unit:
    Decimal Rate per Annum.

Source: 1955I to 1976IV, BI, *Bollettino*, table E7, "Indice e rendimento netto dei valori mobiliari," column entitled "Titoli di stato, totale," various monthly issues from January–March 1956 to July–September 1977.

Description: The data are quarterly averages of monthly figures of the market yield on long-term government bonds. The data were originally in percent per annum.

b. ITRLQNCP   Market Yield on Long-term Corporate Bonds. Unit: Dec-
    imal Rate per Annum.

Source: Same as II.E.2.a, column entitled "Obbligazioni impresse."

Description: The data are quarterly averages of monthly figures of the market yield. The data were originally in percent per annum.

III. NONFINANCIAL DOMESTIC VARIABLES

A. *National Product*

1. Nominal Gross Domestic Product

ITYNQNGD   Gross Domestic Product in Current Prices. Unit: Billions of
ITYNQSGD   Lire at Annual Rates.

Source: For 1955–75, from Siesto, *Italian National Accounts*, table 1.A.1; for 1976, our own estimates.

Description: This measures the final expenditures on goods and services in current market prices, equivalent to the total income and product of the geographic region less net factor income from abroad. For 1976 we estimated nominal GDP by multiplying real GDP (described below, III.A.2) by the implicit price deflator. The figures were originally at quarterly rates.

2. Real Gross Domestic Product

ITYRQND7   Gross Domestic Product in 1970 Prices. Unit: Billions of
ITYRQSD7   Lire at Annual Rates.

Source: For 1955–75, from Siesto, *Italian National Accounts*, table 1.B.1; for 1976, from ISTAT *Bollettino mensile di statistica*, table 16.1, "Bilancio economico nazionale."

Description: This measures the final expenditures on goods and services in 1970 market prices, equivalent to the total income and product of the geographic region less net factor income from abroad. The figures were originally at quarterly rates.

B. *Prices*

1. Implicit Price Deflator

ITPDQND7   GDP Implicit Price Deflator. Unit: 1970 = 1.00.
ITPDQSD7

Source: For 1955–75, from Siesto, *Italian National Accounts*, Tables 1.A.1 and 1.B.1; for 1976, from our own estimates.

Description: For the period 1955–75, the implicit price index was derived as the ratio of nominal to real GDP. For 1976, we estimated the values based on a regression of the implicit index on the consumer price index for 1955–75.

2. Consumer Prices

ITPCQN70   Consumer Price Index. Unit: 1970 = 1.00.
ITPCQS70

Source: From ISTAT, *Bollettino mensile di statistica*, table 13.1, "Numeri indici dei prezzi all'ingrosso."

Description: A general index of consumer prices covering all items. The data are quarterly averages of monthly figures. The figures were originally in percent.

C. *Industrial Production*

ITIPQN70   Index of Industrial Production. Unit: 1970 = 1.00.
ITIPQS70

Source: From ISTAT, *Bollettino mensile di statistica*, table 7.1, "Numeri indici della produzione industriale."

Description: A general index of industrial production including the mining, manufacturing, and utility industries but excluding construction. The data are quarterly averages of monthly figures. The figures were originally in percent.

D. *Government Accounts*

1. Government Expenditure

ITGXQNFD   Federal Government Expenditure. Unit: Billions of Lire at
ITGXQSFD   Annual Rates.

Source: From ISTAT, *Bollettino mensile di statistica*, table 15.1, "Movimento di cassa del Tesoro."

Description: Expenditure of the federal government exclusive of deficit of local governments. The data were originally at monthly rates.

2. Government Deficit

ITGDQNFD   Federal Government Deficit. Unit: Billions of Lire at
ITGDQSFD   Annual Rates.

Source: Same as III.D.1 above.

Description: Deficit of the federal government exclusive of deficit of local governments. The deficit is defined as a negative value. The data were originally at monthly rates.

E. *Population*

ITPPQNIN   Population. Unit: Billions of Persons.

Source: From UN, *Demographic Yearbook*, various issues.

Description: Straight-line interpolation of mid-year estimates of population. The figures were originally in millions of persons.

F. *Labor Force Statistics*

The source of all labor force statistics was the *Bollettino mensile di statistica*, table 4.1, "Popoliozione e forze di lavoro." For the period 1955–58, only annual estimates were available, thereafter quarterly estimates.

1. Employment

ITEMQNSE   Employment. Unit: Billions of Persons.
ITEMQSSE

Description: Employed wage and salary workers including self-employed.

2. Unemployment

ITUNQNSE   Unemployment. Unit: Billions of Persons.
ITUNQSSE

Description: Unemployed wage and salary workers and self-employed including new entrants.

3. Labor Force

ITLFQNSE   Total Labor Force. Units: Billions of Persons.
ITLFQSSE

Description: Total civilian employed and unemployed wage and salary workers. For 1955–58, annual estimates were used as the basis for a linear interpolation of the quarterly figures. The figures were originally in thousands of persons.

4. Unemployment Rate

ITURQNDR   Unemployment Rate. Unit: Decimal Rate.
ITURQSDR

Description: This series was derived as the ratio of unemployment to total labor force.

List of Tables for Italy (Quarterly Data)

ITALY_ITBPQNVL

1955	1	-25.60	19.30	84.90	-11.80
1956	1	8.70	13.80	84.40	-39.30
1957	1	-20.00	41.90	70.60	78.70
1958	1	8.60	32.50	235.50	155.80
1959	1	104.50	166.90	237.90	28.10
1960	1	-73.80	39.10	116.20	-3.10
1961	1	-59.80	100.60	243.10	76.80
1962	1	-58.70	-10.60	209.40	-108.70
1963	1	-167.30	-257.30	-70.30	-282.80
1964	1	-272.70	141.60	313.90	300.90
1965	1	42.60	277.20	497.30	179.30
1966	1	48.50	124.90	340.30	-79.00
1967	1	-180.10	41.80	361.60	-21.10
1968	1	-71.10	97.60	385.60	-20.10
1969	1	-226.90	-334.30	-201.50	-106.70
1970	1	-473.40	113.60	209.50	372.80
1971	1	180.00	75.30	549.80	-315.80
1972	1	-102.90	-223.40	50.40	-471.30
1973	1	-507.50	-415.80	704.60	2.80
1974	1	-1349.70	-1606.60	220.70	-852.70
1975	1	-113.40	-191.30	-173.40	-863.60
1976	1	-1395.40	-1007.80	629.50	746.00
1977	1	-1542.70			

ITALY_ITBPQSVL

1955	1	14.07	26.27	3.21	20.98
1956	1	51.89	21.54	-1.33	-8.11
1957	1	30.82	49.02	-21.84	106.95
1958	1	72.50	36.94	134.44	180.65
1959	1	183.62	171.25	122.11	53.61
1960	1	18.52	46.22	-18.76	26.04
1961	1	46.86	109.37	86.68	111.16
1962	1	64.46	-2.71	31.37	-68.70
1963	1	-26.39	-250.40	-272.37	-233.93
1964	1	-116.86	148.29	88.87	359.17
1965	1	210.73	283.80	254.53	244.58
1966	1	220.96	135.24	94.65	-25.17
1967	1	0.90	56.44	121.54	13.03
1968	1	113.08	128.98	143.55	-5.19
1969	1	-37.88	-280.61	-457.67	-104.22
1970	1	-287.23	214.36	-82.97	352.32
1971	1	383.36	229.33	203.44	-353.02
1972	1	116.16	-9.80	-357.01	-527.75
1973	1	-260.64	-153.25	240.30	-73.05
1974	1	-1073.13	-1305.55	-282.94	-965.51
1975	1	210.91	125.53	-702.27	-1000.69
1976	1	-1039.01	-688.00	89.37	604.14
1977	1	-1174.95			

ITALY_ITEXQNTL

1954	1	1617.7	1573.5	1742.8	1741.8
1955	1	1669.9	1838.5	2016.9	2004.3
1956	1	2012.3	2062.8	2265.9	2306.9
1957	1	2332.5	2511.2	2627.4	2644.1
1958	1	2380.0	2507.0	2494.0	2525.2
1959	1	2370.7	2454.5	2878.8	3083.3
1960	1	3145.2	3353.4	3405.1	3397.3
1961	1	3216.4	3593.2	4198.0	3844.8
1962	1	3857.2	4119.2	4844.8	4280.8
1963	1	4058.8	4556.0	5208.8	4710.4
1964	1	4454.0	5054.0	5954.8	5638.0
1965	1	5264.4	6084.8	7233.2	6602.8
1966	1	6391.2	6912.0	8245.6	7154.4
1967	1	6881.6	7591.2	8458.0	7542.8
1968	1	8125.2	8440.4	9463.6	9349.2
1969	1	9154.8	10236.4	11458.4	10281.6
1970	1	10206.8	11243.2	12602.4	12281.2
1971	1	11268.8	12343.6	14355.2	13660.4
1972	1	13600.0	14120.4	15603.6	13432.4
1973	1	15840.4	15862.8	19948.4	19807.6
1974	1	20734.0	23714.0	28440.8	28012.0
1975	1	27251.6	29055.2	30444.8	29596.4
1976	1	31220.4	36005.2	42770.8	41143.6
1977	1	43785.6			

ITALY_ITEXQSTL

1954	1	1672.3	1604.3	1673.8	1721.9
1955	1	1729.8	1870.3	1941.4	1976.3
1956	1	2091.0	2092.8	2185.6	2269.3
1957	1	2430.0	2544.0	2535.7	2595.2
1958	1	2489.9	2539.1	2396.7	2480.6
1959	1	2491.5	2490.7	2737.4	3041.6
1960	1	3328.8	3410.9	3187.3	3378.7
1961	1	3430.2	3659.1	3869.5	3851.2
1962	1	4153.7	4192.8	4407.3	4314.3
1963	1	4406.0	4635.0	4694.5	4767.1
1964	1	4860.9	5135.3	5344.1	5725.7
1965	1	5744.6	6171.6	6504.8	6706.9
1966	1	6962.2	6990.1	7450.2	7276.5
1967	1	7451.7	7667.6	7689.5	7661.0
1968	1	8763.4	8509.4	8659.1	9480.2
1969	1	9828.5	10318.6	10547.5	10385.7
1970	1	10934.6	11344.4	11628.0	12399.2
1971	1	12025.4	12487.8	13258.1	13781.7
1972	1	14487.4	14292.3	14424.4	13575.0
1973	1	16815.4	16049.6	18479.9	20047.8
1974	1	21947.8	23953.9	26398.9	28429.6
1975	1	28743.7	29317.7	28318.8	30063.1
1976	1	32872.3	36300.4	39842.9	41790.5
1977	1	46059.6			

ITALY_ITEXQNGO

1954	1	973.3	944.7	1054.5	1053.9
1955	1	1007.2	1117.0	1234.0	1225.7
1956	1	1231.0	1264.2	1398.7	1425.9
1957	1	1443.0	1562.3	1640.2	1651.4
1958	1	1474.6	1559.5	1550.8	1571.6
1959	1	1468.4	1524.3	1809.7	1948.4
1960	1	1990.6	2132.7	2168.1	2162.7
1961	1	2230.8	2343.6	2506.8	2546.0
1962	1	2732.8	2734.0	2875.6	2808.8
1963	1	2829.2	2946.0	3014.4	3118.8
1964	1	3134.4	3328.0	3681.2	3801.2
1965	1	3886.8	4022.0	4371.6	4464.0
1966	1	4606.0	4535.2	4940.4	4925.6
1967	1	4903.6	5150.0	5176.0	5198.4
1968	1	5867.6	5758.8	6144.4	6545.6
1969	1	6648.0	6921.6	7352.0	7111.6
1970	1	7240.4	7716.8	8325.2	8709.2
1971	1	8108.8	8687.2	9429.2	9500.4
1972	1	9883.2	9939.6	10322.4	9597.6
1973	1	12020.8	11322.0	13574.0	14706.4
1974	1	15360.8	17672.0	21319.6	21458.8
1975	1	20786.0	22475.6	22900.8	23767.6
1976	1	24429.6	28449.6	32555.6	32666.4
1977	1	35481.2			

ITALY_ITEXQSGO

1954	1	1007.8	964.2	1010.3	1042.2
1955	1	1044.2	1137.2	1186.0	1209.1
1956	1	1279.4	1282.0	1350.3	1403.8
1957	1	1500.5	1578.2	1591.7	1624.5
1958	1	1531.4	1569.8	1512.1	1548.6
1959	1	1518.1	1531.7	1769.8	1926.8
1960	1	2047.4	2141.1	2122.8	2149.1
1961	1	2281.7	2353.1	2455.1	2540.7
1962	1	2781.3	2749.1	2816.7	2807.5
1963	1	2868.6	2971.2	2951.9	3115.6
1964	1	3172.5	3364.7	3606.9	3791.7
1965	1	3929.0	4072.9	4287.9	4446.5
1966	1	4655.4	4592.1	4849.1	4907.0
1967	1	4953.9	5215.1	5080.4	5170.1
1968	1	5951.2	5816.9	6027.9	6505.9
1969	1	6764.6	6983.4	7203.4	7056.0
1970	1	7401.9	7780.3	8130.5	8645.1
1971	1	8309.9	8773.8	9168.5	9420.8
1972	1	10185.8	10026.9	10000.7	9523.0
1973	1	12439.5	11408.1	13109.6	14602.0
1974	1	15963.4	17763.4	20544.8	21333.0
1975	1	21659.3	22566.9	22020.1	23639.8
1976	1	25524.0	28535.4	31260.0	32510.2
1977	1	37115.9			

ITALY_ITEXQNST

1954	1	644.4	628.8	688.3	687.9
1955	1	662.8	721.6	782.9	778.6
1956	1	781.3	798.5	867.2	880.9
1957	1	889.5	948.9	987.2	992.7
1958	1	905.4	947.5	943.2	953.5
1959	1	902.3	930.1	1069.1	1134.9
1960	1	1154.7	1220.7	1237.0	1234.5
1961	1	985.6	1249.6	1691.2	1298.8
1962	1	1124.4	1385.2	1969.2	1472.0
1963	1	1229.6	1610.0	2194.4	1591.6
1964	1	1319.6	1726.0	2273.6	1836.8
1965	1	1377.6	2062.8	2861.6	2138.8
1966	1	1785.2	2376.8	3305.2	2228.8
1967	1	1978.0	2441.2	3282.0	2344.4
1968	1	2257.6	2681.6	3319.2	2803.6
1969	1	2506.8	3314.8	4106.4	3170.0
1970	1	2966.4	3526.4	4277.2	3572.0
1971	1	3160.0	3656.4	4926.0	4160.0
1972	1	3716.8	4180.8	5281.2	3834.8
1973	1	3819.6	4540.8	6374.4	5101.2
1974	1	5373.2	6042.0	7121.2	6553.2
1975	1	6465.6	6579.6	7544.0	5828.8
1976	1	6790.8	7555.6	10215.2	8477.2
1977	1	8304.4			

ITALY_ITEXQSST

1954	1	663.36	639.57	664.25	681.05
1955	1	683.62	732.33	756.93	768.94
1956	1	809.06	808.30	838.50	868.14
1957	1	926.53	960.73	947.39	976.53
1958	1	956.47	961.99	886.12	940.41
1959	1	975.36	950.29	968.55	1127.81
1960	1	1291.34	1254.80	1070.69	1244.52
1961	1	1145.49	1289.12	1399.98	1331.02
1962	1	1359.58	1427.54	1572.18	1532.76
1963	1	1536.32	1652.06	1709.94	1681.47
1964	1	1680.04	1762.11	1750.11	1966.62
1965	1	1755.54	2095.01	2204.51	2305.40
1966	1	2255.93	2401.00	2569.02	2408.42
1967	1	2461.18	2456.90	2588.84	2523.19
1968	1	2762.98	2696.80	2659.69	2995.91
1969	1	3018.34	3340.12	3339.21	3357.30
1970	1	3524.20	3572.90	3504.98	3773.03
1971	1	3700.88	3730.59	4051.19	4405.52
1972	1	4286.21	4295.16	4346.81	4097.16
1973	1	4327.35	4681.07	5267.41	5490.30
1974	1	5998.71	6230.22	5912.62	7101.28
1975	1	7130.46	6773.37	6305.42	6326.48
1976	1	7435.46	7770.68	8579.34	9188.64
1977	1	9065.45			

ITALY_ITIMQNTL

1954	1	1675.6	1626.4	1452.8	1659.6
1955	1	1762.2	1849.0	1760.9	1879.1
1956	1	2062.5	2164.0	2067.1	2267.5
1957	1	2505.9	2573.2	2323.6	2619.6
1958	1	2167.8	2246.3	2171.9	2307.0
1959	1	2111.8	2297.8	2239.2	2615.4
1960	1	3141.8	3248.3	3223.8	3418.5
1961	1	3436.4	3482.8	3376.4	3650.0
1962	1	3922.0	4091.2	4023.2	4735.6
1963	1	4647.6	5217.6	5260.8	5551.6
1964	1	5508.8	5028.8	4830.0	5078.0
1965	1	4958.0	5111.6	5217.2	5730.4
1966	1	5732.4	6200.4	6568.0	6673.6
1967	1	6716.4	7001.6	6686.4	7000.0
1968	1	7443.2	7346.8	7415.2	8211.6
1969	1	8126.4	9464.8	9734.0	10002.4
1970	1	10845.6	11492.0	11961.2	12273.6
1971	1	11579.2	12482.4	12133.2	13451.2
1972	1	12622.8	13536.8	15745.2	16022.0
1973	1	17002.0	19095.6	21204.0	23497.2
1974	1	28871.2	32583.2	29176.0	33598.0
1975	1	28656.0	30342.0	29752.8	33137.6
1976	1	36813.6	40428.8	39645.2	40768.8
1977	1	51788.0			

ITALY_ITIMQSTL

1954	1	1619.1	1573.6	1548.8	1668.7
1955	1	1704.1	1792.5	1874.0	1883.3
1956	1	2001.6	2102.9	2191.3	2266.6
1957	1	2439.1	2510.3	2452.0	2610.6
1958	1	2117.8	2198.2	2282.6	2294.6
1959	1	2066.6	2256.6	2346.2	2594.2
1960	1	3084.3	3194.8	3368.1	3389.4
1961	1	3375.7	3435.5	3515.9	3613.3
1962	1	3862.5	4045.6	4174.7	4675.2
1963	1	4593.3	5180.6	5427.0	5462.4
1964	1	5482.1	4999.7	4952.2	4994.1
1965	1	4957.3	5087.0	5319.4	5633.8
1966	1	5771.9	6152.3	6664.9	6579.1
1967	1	6791.7	6930.9	6751.9	6918.1
1968	1	7571.4	7238.4	7466.7	8135.9
1969	1	8284.6	9329.9	9753.7	9919.7
1970	1	11100.0	11325.2	11920.8	12231.5
1971	1	11832.7	12327.5	12025.4	13478.2
1972	1	12893.1	13317.2	15619.0	16153.2
1973	1	17281.2	18719.2	21104.5	23827.7
1974	1	29204.2	31731.7	29216.1	34313.7
1975	1	28759.0	29430.0	29961.8	33980.2
1976	1	36774.7	39070.1	40149.8	41773.5
1977	1	51653.3			

ITALY_ITIMQNGO

1954	1	1498.1	1455.8	1306.1	1484.4
1955	1	1572.5	1646.9	1571.4	1672.6
1956	1	1829.3	1915.8	1833.2	2003.7
1957	1	2205.9	2262.8	2051.4	2302.1
1958	1	1919.0	1985.7	1922.5	2037.3
1959	1	1871.3	2029.5	1979.7	2298.5
1960	1	2741.6	2830.9	2810.4	2973.3
1961	1	3103.2	3077.6	2960.8	3211.6
1962	1	3472.4	3590.4	3496.0	4152.4
1963	1	4101.6	4560.4	4573.2	4917.2
1964	1	4830.4	4317.6	4084.0	4442.4
1965	1	4270.4	4281.6	4392.4	4880.4
1966	1	4922.4	5192.4	5596.0	5786.8
1967	1	5704.4	5942.0	5617.6	5963.2
1968	1	6214.4	5972.0	6083.2	6834.0
1969	1	6796.0	7758.4	8020.8	8223.2
1970	1	8613.6	9202.0	9663.2	9961.6
1971	1	9386.8	9906.8	9715.2	10907.6
1972	1	10320.0	11038.8	12665.6	13034.4
1973	1	13616.0	15577.6	16973.6	18851.2
1974	1	23304.0	27165.6	23953.6	27376.8
1975	1	23084.8	25022.8	24795.6	27110.8
1976	1	30545.2	34290.0	33734.4	35103.6
1977	1	44595.2			

ITALY_ITIMQSGO

1954	1	1449.3	1410.2	1389.1	1492.5
1955	1	1522.1	1598.3	1668.8	1676.8
1956	1	1776.0	1863.4	1940.4	2005.2
1957	1	2144.4	2209.8	2163.3	2300.0
1958	1	1867.0	1946.1	2021.9	2034.2
1959	1	1817.8	1997.3	2080.1	2289.3
1960	1	2663.7	2792.6	2952.0	2956.5
1961	1	3010.2	3049.8	3108.0	3178.5
1962	1	3373.8	3574.9	3663.4	4082.2
1963	1	4000.9	4570.8	4767.0	4797.8
1964	1	4753.2	4341.3	4228.9	4319.2
1965	1	4231.4	4315.6	4515.5	4735.8
1966	1	4923.2	5220.5	5712.7	5629.4
1967	1	5744.6	5955.4	5694.4	5820.8
1968	1	6308.7	5947.7	6138.2	6700.1
1969	1	6923.0	7714.5	8046.6	8087.6
1970	1	8817.2	9120.7	9638.4	9870.1
1971	1	9608.4	9799.3	9635.4	10898.5
1972	1	10576.6	10830.3	12563.2	13149.4
1973	1	13909.6	15168.7	16878.3	19184.6
1974	1	23729.2	26207.6	23932.4	28123.9
1975	1	23357.0	23996.3	24888.0	28002.3
1976	1	30785.1	32743.5	34014.1	36275.4
1977	1	44865.2			

ITALY_ITIMQNST

1954	1	177.47	170.58	146.70	175.22
1955	1	189.70	202.11	189.53	206.45
1956	1	233.19	248.23	233.86	263.71
1957	1	299.98	310.35	272.18	317.54
1958	1	248.79	260.53	249.41	269.67
1959	1	240.47	268.29	259.46	316.89
1960	1	400.17	417.37	413.40	445.11
1961	1	333.20	405.20	415.60	438.40
1962	1	449.60	500.80	527.20	583.20
1963	1	546.00	657.20	687.60	634.40
1964	1	678.40	711.20	746.00	635.60
1965	1	687.60	830.00	824.80	850.00
1966	1	810.00	1008.00	972.00	886.80
1967	1	1012.00	1059.60	1068.80	1036.80
1968	1	1228.80	1374.80	1332.00	1377.60
1969	1	1330.40	1706.40	1713.20	1779.20
1970	1	2232.00	2290.00	2298.00	2312.00
1971	1	2192.40	2575.60	2418.00	2543.60
1972	1	2302.80	2498.00	3079.60	2987.60
1973	1	3385.98	3518.00	4230.41	4646.00
1974	1	5567.19	5417.61	5222.39	6221.19
1975	1	5571.20	5319.20	4957.20	6026.80
1976	1	6268.41	6138.80	5910.81	5665.20
1977	1	7192.78			

ITALY_ITIMQSST

1954	1	170.27	163.61	159.04	175.89
1955	1	182.85	194.10	204.82	205.84
1956	1	227.31	238.45	250.79	261.53
1957	1	295.89	298.91	288.82	312.93
1958	1	248.89	251.67	261.28	264.69
1959	1	243.47	260.34	268.26	309.66
1960	1	411.43	405.34	420.50	437.79
1961	1	344.95	394.55	414.63	436.55
1962	1	468.59	485.81	518.04	589.95
1963	1	571.19	633.04	669.09	651.52
1964	1	711.39	677.69	723.25	664.90
1965	1	714.85	785.83	801.38	898.59
1966	1	836.93	947.35	952.17	941.48
1967	1	1036.59	994.62	1057.03	1094.19
1968	1	1255.27	1292.16	1328.78	1437.97
1969	1	1355.33	1619.58	1714.03	1829.84
1970	1	2276.05	2199.43	2300.57	2350.88
1971	1	2219.65	2518.26	2426.07	2551.69
1972	1	2312.94	2479.50	3116.51	2959.01
1973	1	3357.98	3542.72	4329.49	4554.81
1974	1	5454.76	5499.96	5408.20	6081.98
1975	1	5376.70	5434.72	5186.87	5877.20
1976	1	6001.16	6273.22	6250.63	5487.96
1977	1	6887.04			

ITALY_ITKPQNEP

1955	1	57.20	57.20	57.20	57.20
1956	1	144.70	144.70	144.70	144.70
1957	1	66.50	66.50	66.50	66.50
1958	1	108.80	108.80	108.80	108.80
1959	1	163.40	163.40	163.40	163.40
1960	1	200.80	200.80	200.80	200.80
1961	1	540.20	540.20	96.40	76.40
1962	1	-214.80	-87.20	-62.80	-188.40
1963	1	-112.40	-354.40	-42.80	-348.00
1964	1	-12.00	518.00	1.60	573.20
1965	1	-116.80	132.40	-95.60	-178.80
1966	1	-357.20	-219.60	-330.80	-688.80
1967	1	-726.00	-504.00	-376.00	-579.20
1968	1	-963.20	-627.20	-607.60	-1092.00
1969	1	-1866.80	-1932.80	-2392.00	-1298.40
1970	1	-1095.60	-284.40	-162.00	1023.60
1971	1	832.00	614.80	-236.40	-930.80
1972	1	-705.20	-891.20	-119.60	291.20
1973	1	-298.80	921.60	2349.20	4114.80
1974	1	2804.80	3402.00	1276.80	1474.40
1975	1	1328.40	421.20	-665.60	-93.60
1976	1	-724.80	198.80	-156.40	1290.80
1977	1	1484.40			

ITALY_ITKPQSEP

1955	1	37.02	52.83	58.73	80.84
1956	1	123.92	139.04	147.91	169.49
1957	1	44.30	58.14	70.65	98.47
1958	1	82.61	90.96	122.33	141.24
1959	1	141.54	131.75	181.92	201.52
1960	1	180.96	164.43	208.10	249.12
1961	1	533.69	495.50	80.95	140.36
1962	1	-200.55	-145.51	-99.29	-120.75
1963	1	-59.10	-433.13	-102.71	-275.61
1964	1	73.32	432.68	-84.98	641.09
1965	1	5.00	41.33	-199.14	-124.29
1966	1	-210.79	-315.88	-412.94	-679.79
1967	1	-560.08	-605.85	-406.86	-629.92
1968	1	-801.03	-718.26	-579.70	-1200.77
1969	1	-1729.30	-1987.45	-2320.78	-1470.11
1970	1	-973.82	-299.19	-48.68	779.22
1971	1	951.43	627.02	-80.97	-1228.15
1972	1	-601.52	-865.08	86.35	-42.23
1973	1	-212.55	930.48	2621.10	3767.76
1974	1	2860.46	3371.26	1637.67	1110.40
1975	1	1362.96	327.08	-209.97	-454.40
1976	1	-733.25	67.51	359.12	938.08
1977	1	1429.34			

ITALY_ITXRQNLR

1955	1	624.847	624.870	624.860	624.810
1956	1	624.876	624.847	624.830	624.903
1957	1	624.890	624.866	624.883	624.843
1958	1	624.823	624.803	624.773	624.680
1959	1	621.283	620.600	620.600	620.677
1960	1	620.906	620.653	620.603	620.683
1961	1	621.787	620.800	620.613	620.617
1962	1	620.866	620.690	620.610	620.833
1963	1	620.967	621.337	621.453	622.430
1964	1	622.846	624.896	624.863	624.827
1965	1	624.837	624.793	624.740	624.797
1966	1	624.823	624.417	623.680	624.390
1967	1	625.017	624.627	623.493	623.133
1968	1	624.550	623.383	622.007	623.420
1969	1	626.097	627.437	628.603	626.967
1970	1	629.200	628.977	627.183	622.920
1971	1	623.037	623.156	618.613	608.613
1972	1	586.400	582.033	581.376	583.950
1973	1	577.810	591.610	572.693	588.183
1974	1	645.533	638.437	653.443	664.190
1975	1	637.723	628.617	664.570	680.023
1976	1	763.513	861.747	839.563	862.717
1977	1	882.623	886.197		

ITALY_ITM1QNDR

1955	1	4019.0	4058.0	4273.0	4585.0
1956	1	4396.0	4458.0	4630.0	4976.0
1957	1	4707.0	4759.0	4881.0	5266.0
1958	1	5015.4	5118.1	5358.7	5687.9
1959	1	5695.8	5900.1	5998.9	6512.3
1960	1	6285.3	6507.6	6909.9	7395.3
1961	1	7238.3	7465.8	7786.5	8585.1
1962	1	8449.0	8777.2	9186.8	10094.0
1963	1	10098.9	10416.8	10746.8	11464.5
1964	1	10972.4	11133.7	11291.5	12317.2
1965	1	12022.3	12571.0	13049.0	14330.1
1966	1	13989.6	14500.0	14989.7	16222.6
1967	1	15922.7	16531.2	16853.9	17876.2
1968	1	17952.7	18722.0	19215.4	20365.9
1969	1	20649.8	21495.3	22110.8	23724.5
1970	1	24576.3	26054.7	27211.1	29940.6
1971	1	30601.7	32099.4	34788.5	35585.4
1972	1	36486.5	37939.0	38824.5	41881.4
1973	1	42981.1	46074.8	47711.8	51451.1
1974	1	52544.3	54402.3	54682.4	57471.2
1975	1	56090.2	56651.8	59331.2	64326.4
1976	1	67680.1	69859.9	71444.0	77337.2
1977	1	80257.6			

ITALY_ITM1QSDR

1955	1	4097.2	4152.4	4296.4	4379.0
1956	1	4481.2	4558.2	4657.9	4755.2
1957	1	4796.8	4860.3	4913.6	5037.9
1958	1	5108.2	5218.5	5400.8	5447.0
1959	1	5796.7	6008.1	6049.6	6247.2
1960	1	6388.8	6618.5	6975.0	7102.4
1961	1	7349.6	7587.0	7864.0	8255.2
1962	1	8571.2	8909.3	9288.7	9711.2
1963	1	10241.8	10560.5	10871.8	11042.7
1964	1	11126.2	11265.8	11427.7	11884.4
1965	1	12190.0	12693.2	13202.4	13867.8
1966	1	14175.6	14607.2	15157.6	15760.9
1967	1	16110.4	16617.9	17038.6	17432.0
1968	1	18135.3	18784.5	19422.2	19927.0
1969	1	20826.2	21533.4	22357.1	23258.7
1970	1	24767.2	26065.7	27526.5	29390.1
1971	1	30816.3	32088.5	35224.8	34925.4
1972	1	36734.0	37922.2	39327.7	41120.5
1973	1	43209.6	46085.6	48367.3	50533.7
1974	1	52705.6	54477.2	55465.6	56501.1
1975	1	56098.3	56798.3	60242.6	63257.4
1976	1	67551.1	70105.6	72575.4	76057.8
1977	1	80016.0			

ITALY_ITM2QNQE

1955	1	6176.0	6245.0	6567.0	7049.0
1956	1	6957.0	7093.0	7367.0	7879.0
1957	1	7721.0	7833.0	8068.0	8653.0
1958	1	8784.9	8980.5	9380.6	10013.7
1959	1	10184.8	10494.1	10725.7	11545.9
1960	1	11439.5	11770.3	12350.2	13161.6
1961	1	13182.6	13546.1	14087.3	15345.4
1962	1	15444.0	15934.8	16643.0	18087.0
1963	1	18329.7	18785.4	19351.4	20590.9
1964	1	20184.3	20370.5	20714.8	22379.8
1965	1	22299.6	23009.7	23826.8	25985.8
1966	1	25911.7	26637.4	27546.6	29655.4
1967	1	29553.1	30422.1	31097.4	32774.3
1968	1	33272.4	34300.5	35155.2	37006.2
1969	1	37617.6	38567.5	39497.7	41575.5
1970	1	42384.7	43507.1	44440.7	47399.1
1971	1	48109.5	49999.3	53339.7	55230.4
1972	1	56984.3	59146.2	60799.6	65112.8
1973	1	67176.2	70937.9	73425.5	79561.1
1974	1	82972.0	86020.6	87564.6	93376.8
1975	1	97348.2	101776.1	106829.8	115554.4
1976	1	121613.6	124910.1	128648.2	139712.2
1977	1	146311.6			

ITALY_ITM2QSQE

1955	1	6219.1	6344.3	6617.8	6844.8
1956	1	7002.5	7202.9	7427.6	7654.0
1957	1	7767.1	7950.0	8138.1	8412.5
1958	1	8832.6	9106.6	9469.1	9740.7
1959	1	10234.1	10636.6	10831.3	11236.2
1960	1	11490.4	11925.1	12481.5	12803.3
1961	1	13240.1	13723.7	14245.3	14920.9
1962	1	15511.4	16137.8	16846.1	17578.2
1963	1	18407.9	19017.6	19598.4	20015.6
1964	1	20270.8	20601.6	20986.4	21772.2
1965	1	22399.1	23239.9	24128.3	25331.4
1966	1	26024.2	26861.2	27871.0	28993.2
1967	1	29662.0	30630.0	31439.4	32133.6
1968	1	33375.7	34481.4	35518.1	36378.6
1969	1	37709.3	38714.6	39905.7	40939.0
1970	1	42473.1	43610.4	44923.7	46731.2
1971	1	48173.4	50060.0	53985.4	54479.9
1972	1	57013.9	59170.6	61603.1	64289.3
1973	1	67087.6	70954.2	74493.2	78630.9
1974	1	82659.9	86069.4	88936.0	92385.1
1975	1	96725.8	101893.4	108622.3	114385.6
1976	1	120617.7	125118.4	130868.7	138329.6
1977	1	144975.2			

ITALY_ITMHQNDR

1955	1	1761.2	1773.7	1826.0	1938.5
1956	1	1889.1	1880.9	2000.6	2080.8
1957	1	2028.7	2072.8	2171.0	2276.4
1958	1	2474.4	2580.5	2747.3	2829.3
1959	1	2797.6	2895.1	3011.7	3117.7
1960	1	3152.6	3134.3	3269.2	3396.3
1961	1	3249.8	3197.8	3460.7	3744.7
1962	1	3595.7	3571.7	3719.2	4266.4
1963	1	4504.4	4617.8	4776.8	4960.4
1964	1	4845.2	5001.0	5049.3	5440.9
1965	1	5312.1	5460.1	5606.3	6069.8
1966	1	5936.4	6114.9	6309.8	6565.0
1967	1	6426.2	6727.6	6770.4	7233.7
1968	1	7027.6	7373.7	7379.0	7787.7
1969	1	7697.6	8001.7	8179.2	8819.5
1970	1	8992.1	9343.3	9402.6	10277.6
1971	1	10769.4	11271.6	11268.9	11924.2
1972	1	11960.2	12575.9	12503.8	13311.0
1973	1	13300.5	14017.2	14595.1	15580.0
1974	1	16413.3	17634.4	17591.3	18415.8
1975	1	19247.0	21591.6	23867.0	26072.2
1976	1	27761.6	29262.8	29961.3	32106.3
1977	1	33310.5			

ITALY_ITMHQSDR

1955	1	1779.6	1805.8	1820.7	1891.0
1956	1	1909.1	1914.1	1994.3	2032.1
1957	1	2048.2	2110.1	2162.8	2225.1
1958	1	2496.6	2627.5	2738.9	2764.4
1959	1	2818.2	2951.3	3008.8	3039.7
1960	1	3172.1	3197.5	3277.0	3302.6
1961	1	3264.9	3263.9	3482.3	3630.5
1962	1	3612.5	3640.9	3754.9	4128.9
1963	1	4530.3	4693.2	4834.3	4798.9
1964	1	4883.6	5062.1	5113.4	5271.1
1965	1	5367.5	5501.7	5679.8	5890.6
1966	1	6009.8	6138.6	6393.4	6384.8
1967	1	6509.0	6731.6	6866.8	7056.0
1968	1	7106.0	7360.0	7492.8	7621.9
1969	1	7766.4	7965.1	8319.6	8656.0
1970	1	9055.9	9282.6	9567.1	10116.6
1971	1	10836.9	11176.7	11457.0	11770.0
1972	1	12039.1	12454.2	12679.6	13179.8
1973	1	13398.7	13865.3	14765.7	15463.3
1974	1	16541.2	17445.8	17744.8	18326.6
1975	1	19388.7	21361.2	24045.2	25985.5
1976	1	27947.9	28955.9	30164.6	32025.2
1977	1	33520.5			

ITALY_ITFHQNDR

1955	1	531.20	550.50	635.40	623.60
1956	1	632.30	646.10	730.50	691.20
1957	1	671.20	713.10	783.70	862.40
1958	1	871.00	903.50	1139.00	1294.80
1959	1	1399.30	1566.20	1804.10	1832.20
1960	1	1758.40	1797.50	1913.70	1910.60
1961	1	1884.60	1996.70	2188.60	2221.37
1962	1	2147.10	2093.63	2139.83	2219.23
1963	1	2186.40	2186.07	2222.17	1973.10
1964	1	1816.70	1862.63	2017.23	2270.47
1965	1	2234.33	2240.57	2257.47	2329.27
1966	1	2281.77	2368.87	2346.97	2262.73
1967	1	2230.53	2377.70	2578.47	2383.43
1968	1	2333.80	2340.33	2525.90	2410.23
1969	1	2341.60	2397.73	2568.23	2416.40
1970	1	2532.77	2442.43	2740.60	3181.93
1971	1	3595.56	3611.66	3914.40	3741.17
1972	1	3628.10	3540.23	3526.97	3246.50
1973	1	3211.13	2995.60	3250.17	3198.87
1974	1	3213.57	2835.87	3940.53	3846.73
1975	1	3815.80	3570.53	3264.13	2762.80
1976	1	2923.83	3459.53	3621.97	8836.86

ITALY_ITFHQSDR

1955	1	551.14	571.34	601.01	614.35
1956	1	655.58	670.29	692.21	680.45
1957	1	694.98	738.97	745.64	847.45
1958	1	901.14	933.38	1090.01	1270.39
1959	1	1444.69	1612.70	1737.85	1795.54
1960	1	1812.13	1844.14	1852.01	1874.64
1961	1	1936.71	2042.58	2126.37	2182.42
1962	1	2201.67	2134.73	2086.82	2182.66
1963	1	2238.52	2220.89	2175.72	1941.44
1964	1	1860.41	1885.25	1976.35	2240.18
1965	1	2289.71	2261.11	2208.66	2305.62
1966	1	2340.40	2387.40	2287.44	2252.04
1967	1	2281.90	2400.03	2505.88	2382.78
1968	1	2374.71	2373.34	2447.24	2419.23
1969	1	2366.05	2445.88	2487.40	2426.34
1970	1	2543.40	2506.84	2656.67	3189.78
1971	1	3585.91	3747.32	3784.64	3739.04
1972	1	3608.62	3708.08	3394.47	3235.99
1973	1	3185.92	3181.36	3107.02	3170.21
1974	1	3191.16	3045.74	3748.95	3791.70
1975	1	3782.35	3889.11	3090.28	2707.91
1976	1	2898.59	3798.11	3416.39	8645.64

ITALY_ITRLQNGV

1955	1	0.063267	0.063267	0.063600	0.065267
1956	1	0.066067	0.067667	0.066767	0.062067
1957	1	0.070667	0.071200	0.072167	0.073567
1958	1	0.066467	0.063467	0.058700	0.058033
1959	1	0.054400	0.052533	0.055367	0.054167
1960	1	0.053033	0.052233	0.051400	0.053067
1961	1	0.050433	0.049533	0.049867	0.049400
1962	1	0.048267	0.050367	0.052867	0.050833
1963	1	0.048600	0.051067	0.052867	0.055533
1964	1	0.056667	0.059533	0.058400	0.056933
1965	1	0.053500	0.054633	0.054767	0.054100
1966	1	0.052400	0.055067	0.055567	0.056267
1967	1	0.055467	0.056133	0.056033	0.056067
1968	1	0.056033	0.056367	0.056467	0.056367
1969	1	0.056100	0.056400	0.057467	0.062533
1970	1	0.069733	0.077467	0.081100	0.080533
1971	1	0.071133	0.070433	0.071500	0.068467
1972	1	0.067467	0.064933	0.064600	0.066100
1973	1	0.066933	0.067867	0.068767	0.070233
1974	1	0.072000	0.085900	0.100167	0.106500
1975	1	0.103233	0.101833	0.100333	0.097100
1976	1	0.103733	0.125367	0.130600	0.142117
1977	1	0.149200	0.152367	0.148300	

ITALY_ITRLQNCP

1955	1	0.063533	0.063200	0.062900	0.063800
1956	1	0.062900	0.064033	0.065167	0.067233
1957	1	0.064600	0.065800	0.066567	0.069133
1958	1	0.066833	0.066600	0.065033	0.063667
1959	1	0.058367	0.046767	0.042367	0.042167
1960	1	0.038367	0.041833	0.043733	0.049967
1961	1	0.042067	0.044867	0.052033	0.051967
1962	1	0.054567	0.059700	0.060467	0.061600
1963	1	0.059600	0.061000	0.063367	0.067767
1964	1	0.072200	0.081733	0.080633	0.076200
1965	1	0.073700	0.072467	0.072267	0.069400
1966	1	0.065900	0.066133	0.066367	0.066200
1967	1	0.066067	0.068000	0.067367	0.068400
1968	1	0.068400	0.069633	0.069067	0.069367
1969	1	0.068100	0.069067	0.072967	0.078867
1970	1	0.083867	0.095600	0.103467	0.098167
1971	1	0.087033	0.087233	0.087800	0.082167
1972	1	0.079167	0.075300	0.076533	0.077800
1973	1	0.076900	0.077800	0.077267	0.079400
1974	1	0.080667	0.102267	0.118467	0.132800
1975	1	0.114533	0.116233	0.114900	0.116933
1976	1	0.124600	0.145433	0.145833	0.151483
1977	1	0.156100	0.156533	0.154133	

ITALY_ITYNQNGD

1954	1	11306.0	12888.8	14610.8	15494.4
1955	1	12445.2	14565.2	16352.0	16601.6
1956	1	13572.4	15551.2	17716.4	18416.0
1957	1	15174.4	17003.2	18744.4	19186.0
1958	1	16051.6	18216.8	20196.4	20731.2
1959	1	17056.0	19133.6	21518.4	22132.0
1960	1	18914.8	20779.6	23017.6	23816.0
1961	1	21067.2	23208.4	25808.0	26388.4
1962	1	23306.0	26178.8	28754.0	30229.2
1963	1	26357.2	29844.0	33027.2	34983.6
1964	1	30447.2	32805.6	35271.2	37240.0
1965	1	32178.8	35599.2	38467.6	39874.4
1966	1	34588.4	38517.6	41710.0	43268.0
1967	1	38338.4	42526.4	45865.6	47337.6
1968	1	42025.6	46244.8	49078.4	50463.2
1969	1	45309.2	51024.0	54838.8	55592.0
1970	1	51684.0	55981.2	60069.2	64013.6
1971	1	56938.8	60874.4	64566.8	69844.0
1972	1	63120.0	67023.2	69860.0	76316.7
1973	1	69492.7	77583.2	85087.6	96408.4
1974	1	88120.4	96062.0	101235.2	111538.4
1975	1	100736.0	108356.7	114349.6	125989.6
1976	1	118594.0	129477.0	133498.0	146591.0

ITALY_ITYNQSGD

1954	1	12965.4	13231.2	13628.0	14330.7
1955	1	14259.9	14947.3	15262.1	15367.4
1956	1	15520.1	15954.7	16553.1	17076.3
1957	1	17287.4	17440.2	17542.7	17833.9
1958	1	18190.2	18680.7	18939.6	19332.6
1959	1	19208.6	19607.9	20239.1	20694.6
1960	1	21176.0	21272.6	21726.4	22317.1
1961	1	23452.3	23731.8	24465.4	24748.1
1962	1	25830.6	26734.2	27368.7	28362.0
1963	1	29119.0	30425.7	31549.2	32831.2
1964	1	33571.4	33381.8	33771.0	34998.5
1965	1	35406.2	36156.1	36885.3	37564.6
1966	1	37977.6	39029.3	40049.3	40880.0
1967	1	41975.6	43000.4	44146.1	44811.1
1968	1	45842.5	46705.1	47424.2	47784.1
1969	1	49173.1	51558.3	53270.8	52545.1
1970	1	55803.9	56646.9	58713.8	60300.0
1971	1	61187.0	61715.4	63496.7	65541.7
1972	1	67564.1	68060.2	69060.2	71417.1
1973	1	74140.1	78833.2	84483.7	90039.3
1974	1	93832.9	97575.4	100830.1	104073.3
1975	1	107138.9	109987.8	114121.7	117492.2
1976	1	126074.6	131384.1	133317.1	136706.3

ITALY_ITYRQND7

1954	1	21209.2	23442.0	25376.0	26936.8
1955	1	22490.4	25402.0	27323.6	28160.0
1956	1	23817.6	26384.4	28281.6	29524.4
1957	1	25245.6	27938.4	29844.0	30476.0
1958	1	26289.2	28990.0	31300.8	32384.0
1959	1	27981.2	31242.8	33307.6	34304.4
1960	1	30012.0	33158.8	35436.0	36621.2
1961	1	32809.2	35945.2	38487.2	39054.4
1962	1	35146.4	37991.2	40310.4	41860.0
1963	1	36657.2	40264.8	42620.0	44390.0
1964	1	38811.6	41504.0	43026.0	44906.4
1965	1	39446.8	42901.2	44811.6	46408.4
1966	1	41306.8	45555.6	48024.8	48696.8
1967	1	44497.2	48642.4	50738.0	52590.4
1968	1	47322.4	51936.0	54252.4	55373.2
1969	1	50430.4	55815.2	57488.8	56993.6
1970	1	53172.0	57116.0	59356.0	62104.0
1971	1	54416.0	58052.0	59592.0	63284.0
1972	1	56848.0	59964.0	60816.0	65128.0
1973	1	58176.0	64108.0	65532.0	71484.0
1974	1	64268.0	67964.0	66716.0	69264.0
1975	1	60252.0	64296.0	64224.0	69408.0
1976	1	63884.0	68232.0	68856.0	74036.0

ITALY_ITYRQSD7

1954	1	23573.6	23768.9	24278.2	25210.7
1955	1	24983.8	25756.1	26140.1	26377.6
1956	1	26434.3	26739.1	27062.0	27699.8
1957	1	27971.8	28290.7	28572.8	28657.7
1958	1	29049.3	29332.2	29988.6	30536.6
1959	1	30807.7	31595.9	31952.9	32413.9
1960	1	32928.6	33516.8	34062.9	34644.3
1961	1	35878.0	36317.1	37099.0	36952.8
1962	1	38325.1	38366.5	38963.3	39608.6
1963	1	39882.0	40626.3	41299.6	42015.8
1964	1	42160.0	41806.5	41774.8	42561.3
1965	1	42787.9	43124.0	43553.7	44101.9
1966	1	44731.4	45689.0	46702.4	46418.4
1967	1	48098.7	48694.1	49385.8	50228.6
1968	1	51057.9	51931.7	52920.5	52893.4
1969	1	54272.4	55824.3	56269.8	54334.4
1970	1	57092.0	57141.8	58384.5	59022.2
1971	1	58276.3	58106.3	58929.9	59942.5
1972	1	60765.2	59984.1	60453.7	61559.9
1973	1	62067.3	64036.9	65396.6	67539.4
1974	1	68521.8	67695.8	66749.8	65512.9
1975	1	64199.1	63886.2	64331.9	65735.0
1976	1	67007.7	67426.2	68318.8	60565.5
1977	1	72692.4	68251.3	74195.5	

ITALY_ITPDQND7

1954	1	0.53307	0.54982	0.57577	0.57521
1955	1	0.55336	0.57339	0.59846	0.58955
1956	1	0.56985	0.58941	0.62643	0.62376
1957	1	0.60107	0.60860	0.62808	0.62954
1958	1	0.61058	0.62838	0.64524	0.64017
1959	1	0.60955	0.61242	0.64605	0.64516
1960	1	0.63024	0.62667	0.64955	0.65033
1961	1	0.64211	0.64566	0.67056	0.67568
1962	1	0.66311	0.68908	0.71331	0.72215
1963	1	0.71902	0.74119	0.77492	0.78810
1964	1	0.78449	0.79042	0.81976	0.82928
1965	1	0.81575	0.82979	0.85843	0.85921
1966	1	0.83735	0.84551	0.86851	0.88852
1967	1	0.86159	0.87427	0.90397	0.90012
1968	1	0.88807	0.89042	0.90463	0.91133
1969	1	0.89845	0.91416	0.95390	0.97541
1970	1	0.97202	0.98013	1.01202	1.03075
1971	1	1.04636	1.04862	1.08348	1.10366
1972	1	1.11033	1.11772	1.14871	1.17180
1973	1	1.19453	1.21019	1.29841	1.34867
1974	1	1.37114	1.41342	1.51740	1.61034
1975	1	1.67191	1.68528	1.78048	1.81520
1976	1	1.85640	1.89760	1.93880	1.98000

ITALY_ITPDQSD7

1954	1	0.55042	0.55540	0.56030	0.56748
1955	1	0.57104	0.57910	0.58299	0.58146
1956	1	0.58729	0.59556	0.61099	0.61520
1957	1	0.61799	0.61556	0.61354	0.62102
1958	1	0.62571	0.63640	0.63140	0.63168
1959	1	0.62271	0.62069	0.63338	0.63682
1960	1	0.64218	0.63530	0.63776	0.64243
1961	1	0.65283	0.65445	0.65923	0.66796
1962	1	0.67320	0.69803	0.70214	0.71410
1963	1	0.72957	0.74999	0.76388	0.77911
1964	1	0.79597	0.79910	0.80889	0.81987
1965	1	0.82726	0.83851	0.84793	0.84942
1966	1	0.84857	0.85417	0.85872	0.87852
1967	1	0.87222	0.88301	0.89486	0.89022
1968	1	0.89773	0.89932	0.89643	0.90198
1969	1	0.90636	0.92348	0.94639	0.96596
1970	1	0.97838	0.99102	1.00469	1.02112
1971	1	1.05126	1.06129	1.07636	1.09340
1972	1	1.11344	1.13308	1.14109	1.16112
1973	1	1.19615	1.22825	1.29002	1.33636
1974	1	1.37129	1.43645	1.50726	1.59541
1975	1	1.67130	1.71366	1.76872	1.79802
1976	1	1.85531	1.93017	1.92589	1.96120

ITALY_ITPCQN70

1955	1	0.62032	0.62032	0.62032	0.62820
1956	1	0.63805	0.64395	0.64395	0.64592
1957	1	0.64888	0.64573	0.65026	0.65892
1958	1	0.66404	0.67349	0.67369	0.66719
1959	1	0.66365	0.66286	0.66306	0.67507
1960	1	0.67999	0.67901	0.68295	0.68531
1961	1	0.69023	0.69299	0.69653	0.70343
1962	1	0.71367	0.72430	0.73198	0.74360
1963	1	0.76881	0.77905	0.78299	0.80012
1964	1	0.81213	0.82178	0.83517	0.84699
1965	1	0.85723	0.86215	0.87062	0.87771
1966	1	0.88184	0.88460	0.88657	0.89425
1967	1	0.90711	0.91270	0.91976	0.92300
1968	1	0.92535	0.92800	0.92624	0.93036
1969	1	0.93712	0.94654	0.95742	0.96684
1970	1	0.98185	0.99479	1.00244	1.01803
1971	1	1.03100	1.04233	1.05167	1.06667
1972	1	1.08000	1.09467	1.11433	1.14367
1973	1	1.17533	1.21567	1.24367	1.27700
1974	1	1.34533	1.41500	1.49967	1.59233
1975	1	1.64867	1.69367	1.72600	1.77600
1976	1	1.85000	1.96700	2.02200	2.15133

ITALY_ITPCQS70

1955	1	0.61872	0.62000	0.62180	0.62856
1956	1	0.63656	0.64359	0.64546	0.64618
1957	1	0.64751	0.64547	0.65160	0.65911
1958	1	0.66271	0.67342	0.67495	0.66726
1959	1	0.66244	0.66284	0.66416	0.67522
1960	1	0.67873	0.67887	0.68428	0.68546
1961	1	0.68885	0.69278	0.69799	0.70368
1962	1	0.71205	0.72416	0.73356	0.74380
1963	1	0.76711	0.77896	0.78451	0.80036
1964	1	0.81041	0.82180	0.83663	0.84714
1965	1	0.85562	0.86228	0.87183	0.87789
1966	1	0.88041	0.88476	0.88748	0.89454
1967	1	0.90598	0.91251	0.92069	0.92346
1968	1	0.92434	0.92748	0.92727	0.93084
1969	1	0.93625	0.94572	0.95873	0.96720
1970	1	0.98106	0.99379	1.00396	1.01827
1971	1	1.03024	1.04122	1.05353	1.06657
1972	1	1.07930	1.09353	1.11639	1.14335
1973	1	1.17478	1.21440	1.24610	1.27607
1974	1	1.34528	1.41335	1.50261	1.59083
1975	1	1.64908	1.69161	1.72961	1.77360
1976	1	1.85082	1.96473	2.02629	2.14801

ITALY_ITIPQN70

1955	1	0.32276	0.33781	0.33029	0.35099
1956	1	0.34252	0.36322	0.35287	0.38110
1957	1	0.38053	0.39390	0.38392	0.40039
1958	1	0.39088	0.39992	0.39408	0.42335
1959	1	0.41902	0.43822	0.43530	0.49072
1960	1	0.49722	0.51641	0.50615	0.53834
1961	1	0.54737	0.55377	0.54793	0.61258
1962	1	0.62180	0.61907	0.59630	0.66565
1963	1	0.65521	0.68682	0.65652	0.72493
1964	1	0.70404	0.68494	0.64711	0.70640
1965	1	0.69256	0.71910	0.69812	0.77038
1966	1	0.77166	0.81378	0.78373	0.85027
1967	1	0.86235	0.89696	0.82425	0.89964
1968	1	0.90930	0.93908	0.87952	0.97799
1969	1	0.97316	1.02011	0.92889	0.90769
1970	1	1.02172	1.05016	0.97155	1.05741
1971	1	0.99667	0.99833	0.93867	1.06100
1972	1	1.05800	1.04033	0.95533	1.11633
1973	1	1.06433	1.15100	1.10533	1.25400
1974	1	1.23767	1.26033	1.12433	1.15600
1975	1	1.09133	1.10767	0.99800	1.14267
1976	1	1.17500	1.23600	1.14433	1.32000

ITALY_ITIPQS70

1955	1	0.32636	0.33325	0.33899	0.34322
1956	1	0.34602	0.35843	0.36259	0.37247
1957	1	0.38369	0.38916	0.39517	0.39118
1958	1	0.39276	0.39589	0.40670	0.41335
1959	1	0.41907	0.43489	0.45079	0.47839
1960	1	0.49544	0.51316	0.52660	0.52352
1961	1	0.54393	0.55073	0.57237	0.59437
1962	1	0.61723	0.61542	0.62468	0.64504
1963	1	0.65045	0.68189	0.68852	0.70264
1964	1	0.70025	0.67723	0.67946	0.68612
1965	1	0.68950	0.70779	0.73362	0.75082
1966	1	0.76889	0.79625	0.82524	0.83176
1967	1	0.85884	0.87336	0.87047	0.88141
1968	1	0.90560	0.91093	0.93244	0.95787
1969	1	0.96750	0.98975	0.98786	0.88661
1970	1	1.01465	1.02091	1.03528	1.02985
1971	1	0.98861	0.97344	1.00049	1.03113
1972	1	1.04940	1.01569	1.01849	1.08446
1973	1	1.05518	1.12354	1.17949	1.21785
1974	1	1.22808	1.22745	1.20168	1.12300
1975	1	1.08373	1.07614	1.06819	1.10998
1976	1	1.16797	1.19891	1.22545	1.28286

ITALY_ITGXQNFD

1955	1	2742.8	2069.2	1921.2	3053.2
1956	1	2703.2	2614.0	2298.4	2919.2
1957	1	2975.6	2775.2	1818.4	3414.8
1958	1	3032.8	3060.0	2276.8	4295.2
1959	1	3822.0	3103.6	3776.8	3709.2
1960	1	3800.0	3995.6	2645.6	4255.6
1961	1	4310.0	3814.4	2804.8	4798.0
1962	1	5144.4	5098.8	3286.4	5431.2
1963	1	6539.2	4802.8	3822.8	5907.6
1964	1	5992.8	5734.0	3980.0	6881.2
1965	1	6445.2	7988.8	8857.6	7575.2
1966	1	3945.2	8452.8	7516.8	14113.6
1967	1	4837.6	9586.4	8700.0	8877.2
1968	1	7988.4	11054.8	10876.4	10745.2
1969	1	6210.8	12143.6	12142.0	9274.0
1970	1	7254.8	9433.6	13914.0	14788.4
1971	1	10352.8	12908.4	16218.8	17305.2
1972	1	9945.2	17897.2	16621.2	16628.4
1973	1	13880.0	21899.6	22098.8	26358.0
1974	1	12658.8	24935.2	23124.0	37018.8
1975	1	27585.2	33534.8	19234.8	42179.2
1976	1	33359.6	39988.8	44148.8	47678.4

ITALY_ITGXQSFD

1955	1	2518.0	2108.8	2508.9	2616.5
1956	1	2496.9	2645.6	3014.5	2497.4
1957	1	2779.6	2754.6	2418.1	2926.9
1958	1	2843.3	2982.7	3086.3	3686.1
1959	1	3585.1	2980.6	5204.4	3201.4
1960	1	3530.4	3833.9	3644.1	3703.2
1961	1	3985.0	3662.5	3809.1	4210.3
1962	1	4771.8	4940.5	4278.7	4780.0
1963	1	6288.3	4617.3	4742.2	5172.6
1964	1	6130.0	5460.4	4595.1	6056.4
1965	1	7128.5	7447.0	9609.7	6692.3
1966	1	4728.9	7784.5	7594.2	12699.5
1967	1	6198.3	8742.8	8352.8	8096.0
1968	1	10630.7	10189.6	9973.9	9950.3
1969	1	8376.5	11341.9	10896.8	8585.3
1970	1	9832.2	8939.5	12378.2	13565.7
1971	1	14178.7	12173.1	14744.0	15529.6
1972	1	13598.6	16752.3	15735.2	14525.7
1973	1	18712.7	20355.1	21886.0	22587.0
1974	1	16629.2	23150.8	23801.7	31243.1
1975	1	35399.9	31266.4	20214.8	35394.0
1976	1	42166.4	37414.9	46915.8	39695.7

ITALY_ITGDQNFD

1955	1	-178.0	-412.8	-4.0	664.8
1956	1	-475.6	-112.4	156.0	108.8
1957	1	-12.8	-249.2	-451.2	372.4
1958	1	219.2	-270.4	-281.2	-65.6
1959	1	622.4	-327.2	-372.4	-720.8
1960	1	-282.8	-404.4	-422.4	-60.0
1961	1	559.2	-1060.0	-650.8	433.2
1962	1	286.4	-743.6	-518.0	223.2
1963	1	1392.4	-712.4	-482.4	485.2
1964	1	-327.6	-1310.0	-566.0	74.0
1965	1	1805.2	-546.8	1319.6	339.2
1966	1	-1402.4	-820.0	-114.4	-292.4
1967	1	-2482.4	862.8	-486.8	-1807.6
1968	1	-2176.4	134.8	1701.2	-702.4
1969	1	-2428.0	-932.0	1437.6	-2777.2
1970	1	420.4	-2017.6	2449.2	-154.8
1971	1	293.6	-660.4	3068.0	-638.4
1972	1	-2498.0	3641.2	3223.6	-617.2
1973	1	1331.6	3440.8	3431.2	8296.0
1974	1	-24.8	5490.0	3884.0	4374.8
1975	1	8102.0	3108.0	-5833.2	1913.2
1976	1	2449.2	7948.4	8368.0	11121.6

ITALY_ITGDQSFD

1955	1	-278.8	-242.8	108.8	501.9
1956	1	-607.9	67.3	269.8	-24.1
1957	1	-194.9	-65.1	-311.5	278.2
1958	1	-61.7	-51.0	-89.2	-165.3
1959	1	248.6	-54.5	-126.4	-827.5
1960	1	-790.9	-17.8	-130.0	-243.8
1961	1	-4.8	-569.3	-352.9	192.1
1962	1	-330.8	-100.5	-296.2	-112.2
1963	1	896.1	-9.8	-422.8	112.7
1964	1	-593.7	-631.0	-751.7	-305.8
1965	1	1948.4	-49.7	841.5	49.4
1966	1	-850.6	-507.6	-977.9	-359.1
1967	1	-1617.8	1032.3	-1753.8	-1562.8
1968	1	-1182.0	297.3	11.8	-137.5
1969	1	-1330.5	-841.5	-536.5	-1907.2
1970	1	1502.3	-2023.4	444.4	810.6
1971	1	1430.6	-974.4	1406.5	325.3
1972	1	-1520.9	2952.3	2385.5	-6.7
1973	1	2211.9	2273.4	3575.8	8599.9
1974	1	523.9	4028.7	5006.8	4224.2
1975	1	8448.6	1489.0	-4119.3	1561.8
1976	1	2583.4	6320.5	10355.9	10602.1

ITALY_ITPPQNIN

1954	1		0.047900	0.047975	0.048050
1955	1	0.048125	0.048200	0.048267	0.048335
1956	1	0.048402	0.048470	0.048537	0.048605
1957	1	0.048672	0.048740	0.048815	0.048890
1958	1	0.048965	0.049040	0.049120	0.049200
1959	1	0.049280	0.049360	0.049430	0.049500
1960	1	0.049570	0.049640	0.049705	0.049770
1961	1	0.049835	0.049900	0.049985	0.050070
1962	1	0.050155	0.050240	0.050340	0.050439
1963	1	0.050539	0.050640	0.050870	0.051102
1964	1	0.051334	0.051570	0.051662	0.051755
1965	1	0.051847	0.051940	0.052025	0.052110
1966	1	0.052195	0.052280	0.052360	0.052440
1967	1	0.052520	0.052600	0.052677	0.052755
1968	1	0.052832	0.052910	0.052990	0.053070
1969	1	0.053150	0.053230	0.053337	0.053444
1970	1	0.053552	0.053660	0.053747	0.053835
1971	1	0.053922	0.054010	0.054110	0.054209
1972	1	0.054309	0.054410	0.054534	0.054659
1973	1	0.054784	0.054910	0.055034	0.055159
1974	1	0.055284	0.055410	0.055510	0.055609
1975	1	0.055709	0.055810	0.055905	0.056000
1976	1	0.056095	0.056190	0.056285	0.056381

ITALY_ITEMQNSE

1955	1	0.018365	0.018270	0.018175	0.018081
1956	1	0.017987	0.017894	0.018045	0.018198
1957	1	0.018352	0.018508	0.018694	0.018882
1958	1	0.019015	0.019149	0.019285	0.019421
1959	1	0.018940	0.019476	0.019994	0.019847
1960	1	0.019165	0.019906	0.020485	0.020319
1961	1	0.019657	0.020475	0.020652	0.019815
1962	1	0.019641	0.019896	0.020338	0.020197
1963	1	0.019249	0.019619	0.019869	0.019799
1964	1	0.019409	0.019454	0.019646	0.019397
1965	1	0.018696	0.018852	0.019290	0.019176
1966	1	0.018291	0.018603	0.018884	0.018769
1967	1	0.018596	0.018764	0.019058	0.018963
1968	1	0.018548	0.018898	0.018988	0.018767
1969	1	0.018353	0.018664	0.018724	0.018705
1970	1	0.018389	0.018626	0.018909	0.018845
1971	1	0.018476	0.018793	0.018827	0.018490
1972	1	0.018184	0.018205	0.018508	0.018426
1973	1	0.018084	0.018264	0.018813	0.018838
1974	1	0.018706	0.018762	0.019048	0.019076
1975	1	0.018946	0.018769	0.019149	0.019118
1976	1	0.018661	0.018922	0.019603	0.019320

ITALY_ITEMQSSE

1955	1	0.018399	0.018312	0.018136	0.018028
1956	1	0.018048	0.017936	0.017984	0.018127
1957	1	0.018472	0.018547	0.018586	0.018784
1958	1	0.019233	0.019175	0.019111	0.019304
1959	1	0.019250	0.019493	0.019751	0.019708
1960	1	0.019564	0.019913	0.020187	0.020169
1961	1	0.020109	0.020490	0.020327	0.019661
1962	1	0.020100	0.019924	0.020016	0.020038
1963	1	0.019670	0.019672	0.019568	0.019636
1964	1	0.019801	0.019525	0.019365	0.019240
1965	1	0.019042	0.018927	0.019028	0.019033
1966	1	0.018610	0.018663	0.018645	0.018646
1967	1	0.018902	0.018805	0.018835	0.018856
1968	1	0.018840	0.018918	0.018783	0.018676
1969	1	0.018625	0.018676	0.018532	0.018622
1970	1	0.018644	0.018648	0.018718	0.018762
1971	1	0.018712	0.018840	0.018635	0.018405
1972	1	0.018390	0.018285	0.018316	0.018333
1973	1	0.018268	0.018378	0.018611	0.018733
1974	1	0.018884	0.018906	0.018837	0.018961
1975	1	0.019121	0.018930	0.018932	0.019000
1976	1	0.018831	0.019089	0.019380	0.019200

ITALY_ITUNQNSE

1955	1	0.001409	0.001491	0.001577	0.001668
1956	1	0.001765	0.001867	0.001813	0.001762
1957	1	0.001711	0.001662	0.001529	0.001406
1958	1	0.001389	0.001372	0.001356	0.001340
1959	1	0.001583	0.001086	0.000866	0.000974
1960	1	0.001179	0.000772	0.000629	0.000705
1961	1	0.001093	0.000626	0.000541	0.000621
1962	1	0.000883	0.000596	0.000462	0.000500
1963	1	0.000802	0.000426	0.000387	0.000398
1964	1	0.000715	0.000483	0.000469	0.000531
1965	1	0.000826	0.000666	0.000695	0.000668
1966	1	0.000998	0.000656	0.000710	0.000673
1967	1	0.000865	0.000619	0.000576	0.000660
1968	1	0.000800	0.000630	0.000649	0.000656
1969	1	0.000782	0.000595	0.000620	0.000621
1970	1	0.000680	0.000532	0.000614	0.000602
1971	1	0.000671	0.000558	0.000583	0.000615
1972	1	0.000734	0.000619	0.000721	0.000709
1973	1	0.000747	0.000735	0.000606	0.000586
1974	1	0.000600	0.000484	0.000551	0.000605
1975	1	0.000603	0.000667	0.000648	0.000699
1976	1	0.000681	0.000693	0.000776	0.000777

ITALY_ITUNQSSE

1955	1	0.001354	0.001476	0.001626	0.001718
1956	1	0.001670	0.001855	0.001894	0.001821
1957	1	0.001571	0.001670	0.001638	0.001464
1958	1	0.001217	0.001404	0.001504	0.001405
1959	1	0.001318	0.001133	0.000999	0.001032
1960	1	0.000932	0.000823	0.000751	0.000757
1961	1	0.000830	0.000678	0.000659	0.000677
1962	1	0.000653	0.000654	0.000562	0.000553
1963	1	0.000589	0.000471	0.000461	0.000444
1964	1	0.000528	0.000537	0.000544	0.000591
1965	1	0.000622	0.000741	0.000786	0.000733
1966	1	0.000774	0.000729	0.000784	0.000722
1967	1	0.000693	0.000687	0.000623	0.000692
1968	1	0.000663	0.000697	0.000691	0.000675
1969	1	0.000666	0.000658	0.000650	0.000631
1970	1	0.000594	0.000584	0.000636	0.000607
1971	1	0.000598	0.000611	0.000596	0.000616
1972	1	0.000668	0.000670	0.000734	0.000704
1973	1	0.000694	0.000787	0.000614	0.000578
1974	1	0.000570	0.000511	0.000558	0.000592
1975	1	0.000581	0.000701	0.000655	0.000682
1976	1	0.000661	0.000725	0.000785	0.000756

ITALY_ITLFQNSE

1955	1	0.019774	0.019761	0.019752	0.019749
1956	1	0.019752	0.019761	0.019858	0.019960
1957	1	0.020063	0.020170	0.020223	0.020288
1958	1	0.020404	0.020521	0.020641	0.020761
1959	1	0.020523	0.020562	0.020860	0.020821
1960	1	0.020344	0.020678	0.021114	0.021024
1961	1	0.020750	0.021101	0.021193	0.020436
1962	1	0.020524	0.020492	0.020800	0.020697
1963	1	0.020051	0.020045	0.020256	0.020197
1964	1	0.020124	0.019937	0.020115	0.019928
1965	1	0.019522	0.019518	0.019985	0.019844
1966	1	0.019289	0.019259	0.019594	0.019442
1967	1	0.019461	0.019383	0.019634	0.019623
1968	1	0.019348	0.019528	0.019637	0.019423
1969	1	0.019135	0.019259	0.019344	0.019326
1970	1	0.019069	0.019158	0.019523	0.019447
1971	1	0.019147	0.019351	0.019410	0.019105
1972	1	0.018918	0.018824	0.019229	0.019135
1973	1	0.018831	0.018999	0.019419	0.019424
1974	1	0.019306	0.019246	0.019599	0.019681
1975	1	0.019549	0.019436	0.019797	0.019817
1976	1	0.019342	0.019615	0.020379	0.020097

ITALY_ITLFQSSE

1955	1	0.019785	0.019775	0.019739	0.019729
1956	1	0.019772	0.019783	0.019833	0.019925
1957	1	0.020111	0.020202	0.020170	0.020232
1958	1	0.020501	0.020561	0.020544	0.020687
1959	1	0.020676	0.020609	0.020718	0.020729
1960	1	0.020548	0.020732	0.020932	0.020920
1961	1	0.020991	0.021167	0.020986	0.020327
1962	1	0.020774	0.020572	0.020584	0.020582
1963	1	0.020285	0.020145	0.020045	0.020076
1964	1	0.020344	0.020057	0.019908	0.019803
1965	1	0.019724	0.019643	0.019784	0.019722
1966	1	0.019483	0.019373	0.019406	0.019331
1967	1	0.019655	0.019479	0.019454	0.019522
1968	1	0.019542	0.019602	0.019467	0.019336
1969	1	0.019322	0.019323	0.019178	0.019249
1970	1	0.019249	0.019223	0.019353	0.019373
1971	1	0.019315	0.019436	0.019234	0.019029
1972	1	0.019072	0.018930	0.019052	0.019048
1973	1	0.018973	0.019134	0.019233	0.019322
1974	1	0.019450	0.019400	0.019409	0.019565
1975	1	0.019695	0.019606	0.019601	0.019694
1976	1	0.019488	0.019791	0.020177	0.019969

ITALY_ITURQNDR

1955	1	0.071255	0.075452	0.079840	0.084460
1956	1	0.089358	0.094479	0.091298	0.088277
1957	1	0.085281	0.082400	0.075607	0.069302
1958	1	0.068075	0.066858	0.065694	0.064544
1959	1	0.077133	0.052816	0.041515	0.046780
1960	1	0.057953	0.037334	0.029791	0.033533
1961	1	0.052675	0.029667	0.025527	0.030388
1962	1	0.043023	0.029085	0.022212	0.024158
1963	1	0.039998	0.021252	0.019105	0.019706
1964	1	0.035530	0.024226	0.023316	0.026646
1965	1	0.042311	0.034122	0.034776	0.033663
1966	1	0.051739	0.034062	0.036236	0.034616
1967	1	0.044448	0.031935	0.029337	0.033634
1968	1	0.041348	0.032261	0.033050	0.033774
1969	1	0.040868	0.030895	0.032051	0.032133
1970	1	0.035660	0.027769	0.031450	0.030956
1971	1	0.035045	0.028836	0.030036	0.032191
1972	1	0.038799	0.032884	0.037495	0.037053
1973	1	0.039669	0.038686	0.031207	0.030169
1974	1	0.031078	0.025148	0.028114	0.030740
1975	1	0.030846	0.034318	0.032732	0.035273
1976	1	0.035208	0.035330	0.038078	0.038662

ITALY_ITURQSDR

1955	1	0.068330	0.074703	0.082444	0.087131
1956	1	0.084307	0.093849	0.095571	0.091466
1957	1	0.078006	0.082753	0.081223	0.072373
1958	1	0.059328	0.068385	0.073241	0.067848
1959	1	0.063818	0.055044	0.048264	0.049698
1960	1	0.045522	0.039711	0.035902	0.036064
1961	1	0.039759	0.032036	0.031422	0.033167
1962	1	0.031669	0.031785	0.027293	0.026764
1963	1	0.029216	0.023384	0.023013	0.022064
1964	1	0.026116	0.026763	0.027339	0.029803
1965	1	0.031683	0.037742	0.039728	0.037088
1966	1	0.039868	0.037653	0.040442	0.037296
1967	1	0.035367	0.035304	0.032077	0.035386
1968	1	0.033986	0.035589	0.035563	0.034858
1969	1	0.034509	0.034069	0.033929	0.032723
1970	1	0.030909	0.030405	0.032894	0.031306
1971	1	0.030956	0.031458	0.031012	0.032399
1972	1	0.034998	0.035414	0.038579	0.037000
1973	1	0.036512	0.041207	0.031962	0.029927
1974	1	0.029188	0.026411	0.028803	0.030316
1975	1	0.029354	0.035815	0.033472	0.034670
1976	1	0.033749	0.036746	0.038954	0.037914

Sources and Notes on Time Series for Japan

The main sources for Japanese data are the publications of the Bank of Japan (*Economic Statistics Monthly* and *Economic Statistics Annual*) and Japanese Economic Planning Agency (EPA) (*Annual Reports on Business Cycle Indicators*). Most series are complete in these sources. Where this was not the case, we were able to enlist the assistance of Ryuji Tahara of the Research Department of the Sanwa Bank Limited for locating additional sources.

For almost all series we have made our own seasonal adjustment, since the Japanese government sources do not provide continuous seasonally adjusted series for our full period from 1955 on. Adjusted series are published for periods of twenty years at a time by the EPA in *Annual Report on Business Cycle Indicators*. The EPA should be the source for adjusted data subsequent to 1976.

I. INTERNATIONAL VARIABLES

Full presentations of the Japanese balance-of-payments statistics in the Economic Planning Agency's *Annual Report on Business Cycle Indicators* begin in the first quarter of 1965 on a monthly basis. Prior to that, some (but not all) quarterly and monthly data in the Bank of Japan publications for the period beginning in the first quarter of 1961 appear to be consistent with the later EPA series. The measure of the official settlements balance that is given pre-1965 is for changes in international reserves alone. Given the break in the data, we decided to use this measure throughout. Similarly, prior to 1961, data for the capital account were also incomplete. We have therefore only included merchandise trade series in the data base, since we could obtain these series on a temporally consistent basis.

A. *Balance of Payments*

JABPQNJJ   Balance of Payments, 1955I–76IV. Unit: Billions of Yen at
JABPQSJJ   Quarterly Rates.

Source: For 1955 and 1956, Bank of Japan, *Economic Statistics Annual*, 1956 and 1957 issues, table 133, "Gold and Foreign Exchange." For 1957–75, Economic Planning Agency's *Annual Report on Business Cycle Indicators*, August 1976, p. 36. For 1976, Bank of Japan, *Economic Statistics Annual*, 1976 issue, table 124, "Gold and Foreign Exchange." Data for SDRs, which begin in 1970, come from monthly issues of the IMF's *International Financial Statistics*, February 1971–October 1977 issues.

Description: We have used the change in end-of-quarter international reserves as a proxy for the official settlements balance. The reserve data are as described below in II.D.

B. *Exports*

| JAEXQNJJ | Exports, 1955I–76IV. Unit: Billions of Yen at Annual |
| JAEXQSJJ | Rates. |

Source: Bank of Japan, *Economic Statistics Monthly*, table entitled "Exports and Imports by Principal Country." Data were collected from the March and September issues starting with the March 1956 issue.

Description: The only quarterly export data available for our full period are for merchandise exports on a customs (transactions) basis. These figures are for quarterly flows expressed at annual rates. We converted the monthly flow data in dollars at the market exchange rate to quarterly flows at annual rates.

C. *Imports*

| JAIMQNJJ | Imports, 1955I–76IV. Unit: Billions of Yen at Annual |
| JAIMQSJJ | Rates. |

Source: Bank of Japan, *Economic Statistics Monthly*, table entitled "Exports and Imports by Principal Country." Data were collected from the March and September issues starting with the March 1957 issue.

Description: Merchandise imports on a customs basis were also the only quarterly import series available for the full period. The series was derived in the same way as the export series listed immediately above.

D. *Net Capital Outflows*

| JAKPQNJJ | Net Capital Outflows, 1955I–76IV. Unit: Billions of Yen at |
| JAKPQSJJ | Annual Rates. |

Source: Bank of Japan, *Economic Statistics Monthly* and *Economic Statistics Annual*, tables entitled "Statement of Receipts and Payments of Foreign Exchange" and "Balance of Payments."

Description: The monthly figures are a sum of long- and short-term capital movements. The data, originally in U.S. dollars, which we converted to yen at prevailing exchange rates, are for total—private and government sector—capital movements, since no breakdown is published.

E. *Exchange Rate*

| JAXRQNSP | Exchange Rate, 1955I–76IV. Unit: Yen per Dollar. |

Source: Bank of Japan, *Economic Statistics Monthly*, table entitled "Foreign Exchange Rates," column marked "Interbank Rates."

Description: Spot exchange rate, a quarterly average of end-of-month data.

II. FINANCIAL VARIABLES

A. *Narrow Money Stock*

| JAM1QNJJ | Narrow Money Stock, 1955I–76IV. Unit: Billions of Yen at |
| JAM1QSJJ | Quarterly Rates. |

Source: Bank of Japan, *Economic Statistics Monthly*, table entitled "Factors for Money Supply" in the earlier issues and "Money Supply and Related Data" in the later issues.

Description: M1, the sum of currency held by the public and demand deposits. The figures for currency represent the amount of the issues of bank notes and subsidiary coin less the amount of vault cash held by all banks excluding trust accounts, mutual loan and savings banks, credit associations, the Norinchukin Bank, and the Shoko Chukin Bank. Those for deposits represent the total amount of demand deposits (current deposits, ordinary deposits, deposits at notice, and special deposits) in private and public accounts minus the checks and bills held by all banks. Prior to June 1967 the series is called deposit currency instead of deposit money and the two series do not correspond exactly. We adjusted the earlier series by the ratio of the overlapping observations to correspond with the later one. Both currency and deposits were originally given monthly. We computed quarterly averages.

B. *Broader Money Stock*

> JAM2QNJJ   Broader Money Stock, 1955I–76IV. Unit: Billions of Yen
> JAM2QSJJ   at Quarterly Rates.

Source: Data for the year 1955 were interpolated by regression from time and savings data presented in Kokichi Asakura and Chiaki Nishiyama, eds, *A Monetary Analysis and History of the Japanese Economy, 1868–1970*, Center for Modern Economics, Rikkyo University, 1974, chapter 2, section 2, table entitled "Components of Monetary Statistics," columns enitled "All Banks Group" and "Mutual Loan and Savings Bank Group." For the period 1956–75, the source was the *Annual Report on Business Cycle Indicators* (EPA), August 1976, p. 45. Data for 1976 are from Bank of Japan, *Economic Statistics Monthly*, table 3, entitled "Money Supply and Related Data."

Description: M2, the sum of M1 and time and savings deposits of private and public holders at banks plus installments of mutual loan and savings banks. The time and savings deposit data are quarterly averages of monthly data.

C. *High-powered Money*

> JAMHQNJJ   High-powered Money, 1955I–76IV. Unit: Billions of Yen
> JAMHQSJJ   at Quarterly Rates.

Source: Financial institution deposits (from Bank of Japan, *Economic Statistics Monthly*, table entitled "Accounts of the Bank of Japan") plus vault cash (table entitled "Money Supply and Related Data" in the same publication) plus currency held by the public (source as in II.A. above).

Description: Prior to 1967, the vault cash figures were given in the form of first differences in the source. To arrive at figures for levels, we cumulated these changes back in time for the level in 1967.

D. *Official International Reserves Assets*

> JAFHQNJJ   Official International Reserves, 1954IV–76IV. Unit: Billions of Yen at Quarterly Rates.
> JAFHQSJJ   lions of Yen at Quarterly Rates.

Source: For gold and foreign exchange, 1955, IMF, *International Financial Statistics*, Official Gold and Foreign Exchange Holdings (includes Government and Bank of Japan Holdings); 1956, Bank of Japan, *Economic Statistics Annual*, table 133, entitled "Gold and Foreign Exchange"; 1957–75, *Annual Report on Business Cycle Indicators (EPA)*, August 1976, p. 36; 1976, Bank of Japan, *Economic Statistics Annual*, 1976 issue, table 124, entitled "Gold and Foreign Exchange." SDRs, which began in 1970, IMF, *International Financial Statistics*, February 1971–October 1977 issues.

Description: This series is the sum of official holdings of gold and foreign exchange and SDRs. The sources provided figures in thousands of dollars, which were converted to billions of yen at prevailing rates of exchange. Gold holdings reflect the transfers to reserves of a portion ($70 million) of gold formerly in the custody of occupation forces. The remainder of the gold is held by the bank but not reported in published reserves.

E. *Interest Rates*

1. Short-Term Rate

JARSQNLD   Short-Term Rate, 1955I–76IV. Unit: Decimals.

Source: Bank of Japan, *Economic Statistics Annual*, table entitled "Interest Rates on Loans and Deposits of All Banks," in percent, column "All Banks."

Description: Average contracted interest rate on loans and discounts in all banks. Since June 1975, the figures in foreign currency loans such as those extended to overseas borrowers by domestic offices were excluded from the averages of agreed interest rates on loans and discounts. To adjust the figures before that month, we multiplied by the ratio of the overlapping observations.

2. Long-Term Rate

JARLQNJJ   Long-Term Rate, 1955I–76IV. Unit: Decimals.

Source: Bank of Japan, *Economic Statistics Annual, 1975*, table 94, entitled "Rate of Yields to Subscribers and Issue Conditions of Public and Corporate Bonds," column "Guaranteed Bonds by Government (Public Corp. Bonds)" in percent.

Description: Seven- or ten-year public corporation bond yields.

III. NONFINANCIAL DOMESTIC VARIABLES

A. *National Product*

1. Nominal GNP

JAYNQSJJ   Nominal GNP, 1955I–76IV. Unit: Billions of Yen at Annual Rates.

Source: The Japanese Economic Planning Agency provided unpublished estimates of seasonally adjusted GNP on an expenditure basis on current prices directly to the International Indicator Project at the National Bureau of Economic Research. Recent figures are listed in Bank of Japan, *Economic Statistics Annual*, table entitled "Gross National Product and Expenditure."

Description: Data are in billions of yen at current prices and expressed at annual rates.

2. Real GNP

JAYRQS70   Real GNP, 1955I–76IV. Unit: Billions of Yen at Annual Rates in 1970 Prices.

Source: The Japanese Economic Planning Agency provided unpublished estimates of seasonally adjusted GNP in 1970 prices directly to the International Indicator Project at the National Bureau of Economic Research. Recent figures are listed in Bank of Japan, *Economic Statistics Annual*, table entitled "National Income Statistics, Gross National Expenditure at Constant Prices."

Description: Data are in billions of yen at 1970 prices and expressed at annual rates.

B. *Prices*

1. Implicit Price Deflator

JAPDQS70   Implicit Price Deflator, 1955I–76IV. Unit: 1970 = 1.00.

Source: Same as Real GNP and Nominal GNP above.

Description: The ratio of nominal to real GNP.

2. *Consumer Price Index*
   JAPCQN70   Consumer Price Index, 1955I–76IV. Unit: 1970 = 1.00.
   JAPCQS70

Source: For 1955I–65IV, Bank of Japan, *Economic Statistics Monthly*, various issues, series entitled "Cities with Population of 50000 or More" (formerly called "All Cities Index"); 1966I–76IV, same source, various issues, series entitled "All Japan."

Description: Prior to 1966, our series is the index for "Cities with Population of 50000 or More," formerly called the "All Cities Index." After that date, it is the "All Japan" index. Since the two series were almost identical for the period of overlap after 1966, we made no adjustment to the earlier data. The base of the combined indexes is 1970 = 1.00.

C. *Industrial Production*
   JAIPQN70   Industrial Production Index, 1955I–76IV. Unit: Decimals,
   JAIPQS70   1970 = 1.00.

Source: For 1955I to 1976IV, Bank of Japan, *Economic Statistics Monthly*, various issues, tables entitled "Indexes of Industrial Production" and "Key Statistics."

Description: The series is the index of industrial production for all industries with base 1970 = 1.00.

D. *Government Accounts*
   We could find no complete government account data on a national income account basis. Accordingly, we substituted data from the accounts of the Japanese treasury.

1. Government Expenditures
   JAGXQNEX   Government Expenditures, 1955I to 1976IV. Unit: Billions
   JAGXQSEX   of Yen at Annual Rates.

Source: For 1955I to 1976IV, Bank of Japan, *Economic Statistics Monthly*, various issues, table entitled "Statement of Receipts and Payments of Treasury Accounts: Transactions with the Public of Government Current Deposits Payments."

Description: The final series is expressed as quarterly averages of monthly figures converted to annual rates.

2. Government Deficit
   JAGDQNJJ   Government Deficit, 1955I to 1976IV. Unit: Billions of Yen
   JAGDQSJJ   at Annual Rates.

Source: Same as described in III.D.1 above.

Description: The data are the excess of payments over receipts of the Treasury accounts, converted to annual rates.

E. *Population*
   JAPPQNIN   Population, 1955I to 1976IV. Unit: Billions of Persons.

Source: 1954–76, United Nations, *Demographic Yearbook*, various issues, and IMF, *International Financial Statistics*, vol. 30, no. 5.

Description: Straight-line interpolation of annual data. Data for 1954 to 1965 include the population of Okinawa. All data exclude diplomatic personnel outside the country and allied military and civilian personnel and their dependents stationed in Japan.

F. *Labor Force Statistics*
1. Labor Force
   JALFQNJJ   Total Labor Force, 1955I–76IV. Unit: Billions of Persons.
   JALFQSJJ
Source: For 1955I to 1976IV, Bank of Japan, *Economic Statistics Monthly*, table entitled "Labor Force Survey."
Description: Data are quarterly averages of monthly estimates of the Japanese labor force, in billions of persons, based on survey data covering 75,000 persons in approximately 30,000 households. The survey period is one week ending on the last day of a month, and the total figures for the entire country are estimated from these data.
2. Number Unemployed
   JAUNQNTH   Number Unemployed, 1955I–76IV. Unit: Billions of Per-
   JAUNQSTH   sons.
Source: Same as described in III.F.1 above.
Description: Quarterly averages of monthly figures of the number of unemployed in billions of persons.
3. Unemployment Rate
   JAURQNUR   Unemployment Rate, 1955I–76IV. Unit: Decimals.
   JAURQSUR
Source: Same as described above in III.F.1 and III.F.2.
Description: The ratio of the number of unemployed to the quarterly average of number of persons in the labor force expressed in decimal form.

List of Tables for Japan (Quarterly Data)

634   Data Appendix

JAPAN_JABPQNJJ

1955	1	13.51	5.40	40.18	50.86
1956	1	25.19	25.91	-9.12	15.83
1957	1	-43.06	-96.56	-47.14	6.24
1958	1	33.47	-99.08	29.15	-6.24
1959	1	22.43	49.54	25.77	38.77
1960	1	31.98	20.49	44.21	70.21
1961	1	59.54	36.34	-55.81	-87.74
1962	1	-21.32	25.56	24.98	33.90
1963	1	31.64	16.27	11.29	-2.92
1964	1	-14.31	-21.98	-14.63	2.54
1965	1	14.72	3.14	-24.42	19.67
1966	1	27.28	-13.41	-10.77	-10.85
1967	1	11.88	9.13	-6.83	-11.87
1968	1	-1.22	-24.68	86.56	178.90
1969	1	115.29	-2.50	-12.22	73.75
1970	1	91.64	50.51	-115.56	166.57
1971	1	349.82	660.83	1449.06	905.65
1972	1	227.13	-88.55	-32.61	575.16
1973	1	-355.46	-885.66	-254.85	-353.17
1974	1	-191.90	253.58	208.99	133.71
1975	1	14.19	230.52	-145.11	-258.14
1976	1	186.16	333.67	115.62	172.62

JAPAN_JABPQSJJ

1955	1	12.33	23.32	45.92	29.13
1956	1	23.58	42.23	-2.40	-3.89
1957	1	-45.96	-82.89	-38.78	-10.34
1958	1	28.84	-88.87	38.52	-17.92
1959	1	16.01	55.39	35.88	32.11
1960	1	24.74	22.17	54.03	67.81
1961	1	52.30	35.19	-46.52	-88.11
1962	1	-28.30	23.73	33.55	34.09
1963	1	24.08	16.39	18.62	-3.38
1964	1	-22.57	-19.24	-7.41	0.13
1965	1	3.92	11.53	-16.86	13.03
1966	1	13.83	1.43	-1.70	-23.68
1967	1	-2.63	28.90	6.93	-38.22
1968	1	-11.10	7.76	92.77	135.40
1969	1	119.67	45.76	-17.66	4.89
1970	1	117.33	122.78	-150.39	85.30
1971	1	401.72	735.97	1395.59	823.44
1972	1	303.47	-31.06	-103.48	525.15
1973	1	-270.47	-876.18	-313.22	-364.96
1974	1	-112.40	212.88	164.83	171.63
1975	1	77.83	137.46	-161.33	-190.48
1976	1	238.97	210.39	113.98	259.46

JAPAN_JAEXQNJJ

1955	1	225.61	229.01	235.79	256.40
1956	1	285.14	293.99	290.14	317.41
1957	1	326.37	339.20	365.16	305.94
1958	1	357.29	334.11	332.33	351.85
1959	1	349.97	392.92	426.58	477.21
1960	1	444.28	462.52	478.34	488.86
1961	1	537.86	510.09	511.32	496.42
1962	1	528.29	517.80	613.08	612.86
1963	1	609.82	646.31	625.89	706.17
1964	1	662.15	747.97	828.30	924.92
1965	1	932.16	998.81	1050.46	1030.47
1966	1	1174.64	1132.30	1205.83	1224.29
1967	1	1221.34	1244.61	1254.59	1319.36
1968	1	1376.99	1464.16	1508.04	1633.38
1969	1	1756.08	1819.43	1890.81	2006.83
1970	1	2217.95	2206.85	2303.24	2428.16
1971	1	2536.53	2728.09	2834.29	2716.19
1972	1	2724.62	2754.79	2817.65	2933.83
1973	1	3073.14	3003.55	3307.93	3446.77
1974	1	4347.29	4775.68	5782.13	6303.77
1975	1	6109.57	5675.50	5323.42	5629.78
1976	1	4427.94	6384.40	6959.21	7154.70

JAPAN_JAEXQSJJ

1955	1	223.39	227.91	240.94	254.18
1956	1	283.17	292.72	296.08	313.49
1957	1	326.00	337.89	371.42	301.28
1958	1	358.63	333.66	336.02	346.61
1959	1	351.56	394.97	427.33	471.67
1960	1	446.02	467.25	475.96	484.29
1961	1	540.19	516.58	506.48	492.52
1962	1	531.79	523.63	606.25	608.49
1963	1	615.62	652.29	617.95	701.46
1964	1	671.41	750.32	820.31	917.90
1965	1	947.88	996.36	1044.52	1024.25
1966	1	1191.25	1125.83	1203.93	1222.07
1967	1	1228.79	1238.97	1255.79	1320.77
1968	1	1377.54	1458.31	1512.74	1637.19
1969	1	1751.78	1812.89	1899.16	2010.76
1970	1	2209.54	2205.16	2304.50	2442.01
1971	1	2517.09	2740.47	2823.83	2735.20
1972	1	2698.21	2782.12	2794.39	2957.66
1973	1	3038.45	3047.94	3273.50	3466.69
1974	1	4297.80	4867.75	5706.80	6336.36
1975	1	6033.90	5807.43	5249.21	5644.44
1976	1	4374.25	6546.67	6858.76	7160.52

JAPAN_JAIMQNJJ

1955	1	251.02	313.33	293.30	292.59
1956	1	314.72	367.58	398.08	438.87
1957	1	472.28	623.56	560.25	440.61
1958	1	388.31	365.98	364.07	337.82
1959	1	346.21	430.43	451.55	428.79
1960	1	476.64	511.53	545.81	504.69
1961	1	578.32	632.89	710.41	729.02
1962	1	684.51	698.03	673.47	645.28
1963	1	645.52	821.54	848.60	907.47
1964	1	945.48	977.76	942.69	982.68
1965	1	901.25	1012.42	964.47	964.75
1966	1	963.18	1153.40	1109.78	1221.72
1967	1	1246.30	1353.76	1297.79	1467.22
1968	1	1458.19	1531.48	1578.25	1613.54
1969	1	1605.43	1602.87	1752.78	1901.97
1970	1	2010.22	2114.20	2353.46	2330.71
1971	1	2258.49	2366.07	2423.55	1991.83
1972	1	2060.39	2266.69	2132.34	2598.78
1973	1	2642.35	2977.24	3454.68	4026.68
1974	1	4659.18	5962.12	6689.25	6441.65
1975	1	5848.40	5527.92	5901.80	6205.02
1976	1	5807.95	6129.31	6625.23	6658.07

JAPAN_JAIMQSJJ

1955	1	266.79	289.48	286.65	306.86
1956	1	334.08	340.73	388.01	460.71
1957	1	498.53	583.69	542.35	463.37
1958	1	407.53	346.08	350.58	355.37
1959	1	359.96	412.98	433.08	448.70
1960	1	494.39	493.91	525.44	523.95
1961	1	597.31	614.66	689.15	747.77
1962	1	708.33	676.92	660.80	654.11
1963	1	669.23	795.04	841.76	909.89
1964	1	984.27	941.74	944.83	978.55
1965	1	936.19	976.62	972.41	956.34
1966	1	995.17	1120.49	1119.78	1207.79
1967	1	1278.63	1331.07	1302.81	1448.27
1968	1	1490.31	1523.41	1569.21	1596.01
1969	1	1636.21	1610.79	1725.08	1883.66
1970	1	2053.20	2135.52	2295.62	2311.98
1971	1	2319.44	2389.34	2351.18	1975.61
1972	1	2129.55	2284.78	2064.01	2571.56
1973	1	2746.51	2997.81	3345.34	3964.82
1974	1	4860.46	6012.13	6482.26	6310.47
1975	1	6117.17	5586.09	5718.17	6057.71
1976	1	6086.66	6202.40	6411.25	6496.75

JAPAN_JAKPQNJJ

1955	1	8.687	10.490	8.702	11.178
1956	1	11.375	14.611	15.008	14.328
1957	1	17.982	20.426	16.418	17.583
1958	1	16.069	16.388	14.482	16.717
1959	1	17.124	18.702	27.080	22.249
1960	1	20.820	14.833	12.919	5.087
1961	1	48.251	34.662	2.559	7.332
1962	1	31.361	25.098	-2.989	-1.080
1963	1	18.103	22.188	18.568	20.005
1964	1	44.392	30.583	-9.530	-7.846
1965	1	5.679	-19.328	-37.471	-14.941
1966	1	-11.465	-14.498	-49.903	-20.179
1967	1	-6.127	0.459	-17.631	-13.490
1968	1	0.479	-4.594	4.580	-4.048
1969	1	5.008	7.541	-5.430	-4.414
1970	1	-30.159	-37.550	-8.491	-27.299
1971	1	-7.514	99.706	190.114	-119.466
1972	1	7.291	-95.613	-72.665	-92.921
1973	1	-116.046	-145.892	-143.980	-261.788
1974	1	-72.431	-83.131	-8.730	-42.220
1975	1	19.261	-72.592	-11.795	-76.252
1976	1	-7.245	37.963	-4.928	-292.315

JAPAN_JAKPQSJJ

1955	1	8.926	9.086	9.643	11.422
1956	1	11.509	13.374	15.856	14.746
1957	1	17.734	19.307	17.347	18.702
1958	1	14.837	14.787	16.363	18.980
1959	1	14.194	15.978	30.829	25.945
1960	1	15.650	10.717	18.865	10.479
1961	1	40.506	29.096	11.034	14.057
1962	1	21.027	18.602	8.021	5.779
1963	1	6.114	15.294	31.671	25.707
1964	1	32.129	24.085	4.150	-3.631
1965	1	-5.742	-24.836	-24.960	-11.794
1966	1	-21.026	-19.093	-39.763	-18.092
1967	1	-12.415	-2.981	-12.407	-11.513
1968	1	-0.098	-8.536	3.218	-0.269
1969	1	9.598	3.660	-14.108	1.960
1970	1	-21.154	-42.049	-23.235	-16.354
1971	1	0.948	96.982	170.355	-102.724
1972	1	11.402	-95.656	-96.316	-68.469
1973	1	-119.660	-142.809	-171.026	-228.796
1974	1	-83.493	-78.524	-38.573	-0.794
1975	1	2.165	-67.827	-43.864	-28.249
1976	1	-28.160	42.648	-37.927	-241.059

JAPAN_JAXRQNSP

1954	1				360.000
1955	1	359.842	359.842	359.842	359.842
1956	1	359.842	359.842	359.842	359.842
1957	1	359.842	359.842	359.842	359.842
1958	1	359.842	359.842	359.842	359.842
1959	1	359.842	359.842	359.928	360.230
1960	1	360.533	360.664	358.980	359.454
1961	1	358.937	361.533	362.056	362.056
1962	1	361.921	361.986	360.968	358.423
1963	1	358.543	362.054	362.788	362.524
1964	1	362.498	362.573	362.228	360.662
1965	1	360.027	362.220	362.273	361.396
1966	1	361.680	362.450	362.507	362.523
1967	1	362.277	361.923	362.017	361.990
1968	1	361.980	361.940	359.396	357.867
1969	1	357.843	358.573	358.866	357.757
1970	1	357.590	358.683	358.270	357.617
1971	1	357.447	357.377	343.527	323.917
1972	1	306.283	304.517	301.100	301.400
1973	1	278.993	265.250	264.817	275.610
1974	1	287.533	281.917	299.667	300.300
1975	1	292.750	293.667	299.317	303.317
1976	1	301.880	298.920	289.870	294.080

JAPAN_JAM1QNJJ

1955	1	1721.4	1740.9	1762.5	1918.0
1956	1	1951.8	2039.7	2112.4	2303.4
1957	1	2351.7	2348.4	2241.3	2422.9
1958	1	2397.1	2453.5	2479.8	2731.6
1959	1	2729.1	2856.2	2864.4	3152.9
1960	1	3219.7	3337.6	3390.5	3765.1
1961	1	3947.6	4267.6	4245.7	4498.6
1962	1	4464.4	4625.1	4673.8	5164.8
1963	1	5684.7	6256.4	6463.1	7055.9
1964	1	7122.9	7385.7	7419.3	8000.8
1965	1	8263.6	8499.0	8655.2	9469.0
1966	1	9639.9	9955.7	10167.2	10814.6
1967	1	10911.7	11420.6	11404.8	12332.4
1968	1	12417.2	13129.1	13106.7	14074.3
1969	1	14313.8	15309.9	15699.0	17124.1
1970	1	17184.9	18449.3	18410.6	19840.0
1971	1	20672.2	22584.6	23699.2	25774.8
1972	1	26124.0	27643.2	27709.8	31726.8
1973	1	32950.9	36067.8	35795.4	37985.3
1974	1	38369.8	40980.3	40024.1	42197.8
1975	1	42490.3	44600.4	44319.4	46793.7
1976	1	48468.2	50961.7	50501.9	53634.7

JAPAN_JAM1QSJJ

1955	1	1708.5	1743.1	1821.4	1868.6
1956	1	1937.5	2041.8	2182.0	2244.3
1957	1	2336.3	2349.0	2313.1	2361.0
1958	1	2386.4	2451.3	2557.2	2666.3
1959	1	2720.9	2847.8	2948.4	3083.1
1960	1	3214.8	3320.0	3483.1	3688.9
1961	1	3947.2	4236.9	4353.7	4421.3
1962	1	4465.8	4587.2	4786.3	5078.6
1963	1	5685.8	6206.2	6610.5	6944.5
1964	1	7128.8	7332.0	7582.7	7869.1
1965	1	8280.9	8442.3	8839.5	9306.5
1966	1	9670.7	9888.2	10378.0	10621.3
1967	1	10969.5	11331.8	11634.0	12113.8
1968	1	12504.6	13007.8	13364.9	13833.0
1969	1	14434.9	15143.8	16011.4	16843.3
1970	1	17339.7	18220.8	18784.3	19523.3
1971	1	20865.8	22267.0	24200.5	25388.8
1972	1	26358.1	27209.1	28319.5	31272.0
1973	1	33229.3	35443.0	36622.2	37524.8
1974	1	38663.1	40212.7	40964.1	41693.9
1975	1	42832.6	43732.8	45383.2	46266.7
1976	1	48841.5	49948.0	51716.8	53115.7

JAPAN_JAM2QNJJ

1955	1	3563.9	3692.5	3837.4	4124.6
1956	1	4212.0	4410.6	4622.2	4958.0
1957	1	5178.6	5380.4	5458.3	5757.4
1958	1	5896.8	6127.3	6382.9	6844.3
1959	1	7049.1	7412.6	7621.4	8192.0
1960	1	8517.6	8870.1	9241.0	9902.8
1961	1	10376.8	10973.6	11291.2	11933.5
1962	1	12266.8	12806.7	13328.0	14296.4
1963	1	15038.1	15895.4	16636.9	17778.6
1964	1	18352.8	19057.2	19579.6	20607.9
1965	1	21315.5	22052.5	22841.8	24290.2
1966	1	25042.0	25973.2	26983.2	28282.6
1967	1	29037.0	30108.0	31080.0	32736.3
1968	1	33459.3	34833.4	35783.4	37641.4
1969	1	38695.6	40596.6	42207.0	44705.9
1970	1	45747.0	48132.6	49609.7	52190.5
1971	1	54130.5	57440.2	60730.6	64642.9
1972	1	66841.6	70789.4	74075.2	80056.1
1973	1	83476.2	88835.4	91424.4	95109.7
1974	1	96841.8	100476.9	101935.2	105744.9
1975	1	107852.0	112146.4	115517.1	121035.7
1976	1	124727.4	129924.7	133083.1	138279.5

JAPAN_JAM2QSJJ

1955	1	3565.0	3696.9	3876.5	4077.5
1956	1	4213.3	4415.1	4670.5	4901.8
1957	1	5178.5	5385.4	5516.1	5694.4
1958	1	5895.0	6130.3	6452.4	6772.1
1959	1	7045.2	7414.9	7702.7	8110.1
1960	1	8513.6	8869.6	9336.9	9808.0
1961	1	10372.9	10973.4	11400.1	11827.3
1962	1	12261.9	12806.2	13450.8	14172.9
1963	1	15032.1	15901.6	16778.9	17627.0
1964	1	18347.8	19072.3	19736.6	20427.4
1965	1	21319.4	22077.0	23008.4	24077.0
1966	1	25063.7	26000.2	27163.2	28028.2
1967	1	29099.8	30122.2	31263.4	32447.8
1968	1	33574.1	34823.0	35971.1	37315.0
1969	1	38880.5	40542.1	42411.8	44335.0
1970	1	46005.2	48022.9	49842.9	51776.8
1971	1	54465.7	57257.0	61017.6	64172.9
1972	1	67250.1	70525.5	74425.5	79532.1
1973	1	83948.8	88479.7	91875.9	94529.9
1974	1	97338.2	100078.1	102442.2	105133.8
1975	1	108362.1	111712.1	116096.5	120348.9
1976	1	125293.5	129434.9	133738.4	137514.2

JAPAN_JAMHQNJJ

1955	1	562.2	553.5	555.1	615.6
1956	1	602.8	610.5	627.0	705.4
1957	1	701.0	701.9	689.3	763.1
1958	1	728.9	725.9	727.3	807.4
1959	1	799.5	815.7	840.8	974.9
1960	1	954.7	986.8	1010.0	1169.8
1961	1	1168.8	1222.7	1265.9	1488.9
1962	1	1449.0	1488.9	1505.8	1633.6
1963	1	1625.6	1707.7	1706.5	1853.2
1964	1	1938.0	1981.4	2079.1	2272.2
1965	1	2225.4	2260.0	2263.2	2466.1
1966	1	2520.6	2584.9	2606.3	2812.7
1967	1	2878.0	2932.5	3036.6	3330.7
1968	1	3373.3	3484.8	3563.7	3892.4
1969	1	3947.0	4069.5	4211.6	4656.1
1970	1	4788.0	4908.5	5026.2	5460.4
1971	1	5580.0	5677.5	5882.6	6341.3
1972	1	6413.8	6599.6	6984.1	7879.5
1973	1	8290.5	8996.5	9490.0	10813.2
1974	1	10845.4	11548.9	11917.6	12684.5
1975	1	12748.1	13018.5	13254.4	13648.5
1976	1	13248.5	13512.6	13675.3	14532.4

JAPAN_JAMHQSJJ

1955	1	560.5	562.6	576.9	586.4
1956	1	601.0	620.5	651.4	670.6
1957	1	699.2	713.2	715.5	725.4
1958	1	728.4	737.5	755.2	766.6
1959	1	799.9	828.1	872.3	926.3
1960	1	956.7	1000.5	1046.3	1113.6
1961	1	1172.4	1238.0	1308.3	1421.1
1962	1	1453.6	1505.4	1552.2	1566.3
1963	1	1629.3	1724.6	1753.5	1782.1
1964	1	1940.0	1999.2	2131.9	2200.9
1965	1	2224.1	2280.1	2316.1	2393.8
1966	1	2515.7	2606.1	2665.2	2735.7
1967	1	2871.6	2956.4	3102.8	3242.4
1968	1	3364.3	3513.4	3638.5	3786.2
1969	1	3937.6	4105.8	4295.4	4529.5
1970	1	4779.6	4954.7	5119.0	5312.6
1971	1	5581.3	5730.2	5982.6	6174.1
1972	1	6430.7	6656.1	7089.6	7651.4
1973	1	8333.8	9063.0	9616.8	10518.4
1974	1	10930.0	11618.6	12056.2	12336.3
1975	1	12887.1	13089.8	13397.5	13306.1
1976	1	13405.1	13581.2	13817.8	14160.1

JAPAN_JAFHQNJJ

1954	1				367.92
1955	1	381.43	386.83	427.01	477.87
1956	1	503.06	528.97	519.85	535.68
1957	1	492.62	396.06	348.93	355.16
1958	1	388.63	289.55	318.70	312.46
1959	1	334.89	384.43	410.20	448.97
1960	1	480.95	501.44	545.65	615.86
1961	1	675.40	711.74	655.93	568.19
1962	1	546.86	572.42	597.40	631.30
1963	1	662.95	679.21	690.51	687.59
1964	1	673.28	651.30	636.68	639.21
1965	1	653.93	657.07	632.65	652.32
1966	1	679.60	666.18	655.41	644.57
1967	1	656.45	665.58	658.75	646.88
1968	1	645.65	620.97	707.53	886.44
1969	1	1001.72	999.22	987.00	1060.75
1970	1	1152.39	1202.90	1087.35	1253.92
1971	1	1603.74	2264.58	3713.64	4619.29
1972	1	4846.41	4757.86	4725.26	5300.42
1973	1	4944.95	4059.30	3804.44	3451.28
1974	1	3259.38	3512.96	3721.95	3855.65
1975	1	3869.84	4100.37	3955.26	3697.12
1976	1	3883.29	4216.96	4332.58	4505.20

JAPAN_JAFHQSJJ

1954	1				358.78
1955	1	370.84	394.76	441.50	466.59
1956	1	490.04	538.09	536.73	524.60
1957	1	481.29	400.70	359.45	349.52
1958	1	381.21	291.08	326.68	309.56
1959	1	330.35	383.76	417.77	447.84
1960	1	477.34	497.93	551.72	617.68
1961	1	673.60	704.85	659.98	571.53
1962	1	546.28	566.84	599.99	635.61
1963	1	661.04	674.17	693.93	691.69
1964	1	669.27	648.12	641.47	642.13
1965	1	646.25	656.96	640.01	653.50
1966	1	667.74	668.53	666.22	644.24
1967	1	641.61	669.88	672.74	643.52
1968	1	630.78	626.58	723.53	877.31
1969	1	980.53	1011.17	1010.29	1041.56
1970	1	1133.79	1221.87	1109.12	1225.35
1971	1	1587.70	2303.46	3769.74	4500.64
1972	1	4842.02	4833.05	4754.80	5184.73
1973	1	4976.71	4097.77	3810.68	3393.59
1974	1	3296.81	3523.00	3709.82	3823.64
1975	1	3925.21	4078.63	3937.01	3687.16
1976	1	3947.86	4174.94	4306.63	4513.84

JAPAN_JARSQNLD

1955	1	0.090000	0.089800	0.088800	0.087800
1956	1	0.086000	0.084300	0.083400	0.082500
1957	1	0.082267	0.082867	0.085033	0.086167
1958	1	0.086300	0.086300	0.084767	0.083033
1959	1	0.082300	0.081067	0.080633	0.080767
1960	1	0.081900	0.082200	0.081867	0.080933
1961	1	0.079900	0.078933	0.079500	0.081533
1962	1	0.082100	0.082233	0.082367	0.081733
1963	1	0.079600	0.078067	0.077000	0.076767
1964	1	0.076900	0.079233	0.079900	0.079900
1965	1	0.079633	0.078767	0.077300	0.076367
1966	1	0.075633	0.075100	0.074500	0.073900
1967	1	0.073367	0.073000	0.072867	0.073367
1968	1	0.074433	0.075200	0.074800	0.073867
1969	1	0.073633	0.073567	0.073627	0.075407
1970	1	0.076223	0.076480	0.076827	0.076973
1971	1	0.076747	0.076377	0.075713	0.074887
1972	1	0.073400	0.071857	0.069057	0.067500
1973	1	0.067097	0.068890	0.073200	0.078263
1974	1	0.086860	0.091873	0.092497	0.093303
1975	1	0.093943	0.092913	0.090137	0.086803
1976	1	0.084365	0.083464	0.083005	0.082716

JAPAN_JARLQNJJ

1955	1	0.074340	0.074340	0.078310	0.077570
1956	1	0.076090	0.072150	0.071430	0.070000
1957	1	0.070000	0.070000	0.072690	0.072690
1958	1	0.072690	0.072690	0.072690	0.072690
1959	1	0.072690	0.072690	0.072690	0.072690
1960	1	0.072690	0.072690	0.072690	0.072690
1961	1	0.072690	0.070530	0.070530	0.070530
1962	1	0.070530	0.070530	0.070530	0.070530
1963	1	0.070530	0.070530	0.070530	0.070530
1964	1	0.070530	0.070530	0.070530	0.070530
1965	1	0.070530	0.070530	0.070530	0.070530
1966	1	0.070530	0.070530	0.070530	0.070530
1967	1	0.070530	0.070530	0.070530	0.070530
1968	1	0.071100	0.071390	0.071390	0.071390
1969	1	0.071390	0.071390	0.071390	0.071390
1970	1	0.071390	0.074340	0.074340	0.074340
1971	1	0.074340	0.074340	0.073680	0.072360
1972	1	0.072360	0.070530	0.068680	0.068680
1973	1	0.068680	0.070490	0.072950	0.075750
1974	1	0.083370	0.083370	0.083370	0.087930
1975	1	0.087930	0.087930	0.086950	0.084760
1976	1	0.082270	0.082270	0.082270	0.082270

JAPAN_JAYNQSJJ

1955	1	8104.8	8288.2	8731.6	9098.0
1956	1	9310.6	9541.5	9670.0	10142.6
1957	1	10455.7	11157.6	11359.2	11266.4
1958	1	11168.6	11331.3	11635.6	12012.7
1959	1	12144.5	12660.6	13370.2	13582.0
1960	1	14774.0	14865.5	15695.8	16490.1
1961	1	17671.8	18573.8	19239.6	20668.6
1962	1	20665.7	21087.8	21312.5	21586.8
1963	1	22555.8	23739.7	25013.9	26253.2
1964	1	27359.5	28403.8	29357.8	30056.6
1965	1	30727.9	31459.4	32239.9	33005.3
1966	1	34330.7	36264.8	37674.2	38918.0
1967	1	41003.5	42005.4	44286.4	46308.9
1968	1	48335.0	49975.9	52027.5	55283.7
1969	1	55629.2	58761.1	60152.4	63470.5
1970	1	66567.5	69664.7	72245.7	73911.9
1971	1	76129.9	77737.2	80585.6	82216.9
1972	1	85582.5	87203.4	92005.4	96564.6
1973	1	102819.4	108310.4	112674.1	117933.0
1974	1	122920.7	129431.5	135304.3	139341.1
1975	1	140191.6	143076.1	147246.2	151038.9
1976	1	157073.4	163580.5	167105.0	169950.4

JAPAN_JAYRQS70

1955	1	16141.3	16447.5	17059.8	17704.3
1956	1	17812.9	17959.6	17993.3	18546.3
1957	1	18823.3	19396.7	19756.9	19873.3
1958	1	19927.4	20414.0	20797.1	21184.4
1959	1	21292.2	22181.3	23080.6	23088.6
1960	1	24723.7	24538.4	25505.0	26672.7
1961	1	27842.5	28623.0	29175.1	30427.6
1962	1	30398.9	30983.2	31322.5	31523.5
1963	1	32468.4	33628.6	34762.9	36223.9
1964	1	37621.3	38496.9	39197.0	39799.5
1965	1	39798.6	40475.1	41454.5	41491.1
1966	1	42771.5	44236.7	45588.9	46654.8
1967	1	48438.7	49517.9	51505.7	52957.4
1968	1	54930.1	56071.5	57857.4	60655.2
1969	1	60883.0	63387.0	63645.6	66319.1
1970	1	68038.2	70062.4	71859.1	72438.9
1971	1	73991.4	74957.2	76698.0	77756.0
1972	1	80053.0	80725.9	83521.5	86291.7
1973	1	89209.7	91229.0	91150.8	91253.4
1974	1	88184.7	89302.7	90333.9	90743.8
1975	1	90274.1	91082.2	92552.0	93908.7
1976	1	96055.7	97473.6	97861.9	98693.0

JAPAN_JAPDQS70

1955	1	0.50211	0.50392	0.51182	0.51388
1956	1	0.52269	0.53128	0.53742	0.54688
1957	1	0.55546	0.57523	0.57495	0.56691
1958	1	0.56047	0.55507	0.55948	0.56705
1959	1	0.57037	0.57078	0.57928	0.58826
1960	1	0.59757	0.60580	0.61540	0.61824
1961	1	0.63471	0.64891	0.65945	0.67927
1962	1	0.67982	0.68062	0.68042	0.68478
1963	1	0.69470	0.70594	0.71956	0.72475
1964	1	0.72724	0.73782	0.74898	0.75520
1965	1	0.77209	0.77725	0.77772	0.79548
1966	1	0.80266	0.81979	0.82639	0.83417
1967	1	0.84650	0.84829	0.85983	0.87446
1968	1	0.87994	0.89129	0.89924	0.91144
1969	1	0.91371	0.92702	0.94512	0.95705
1970	1	0.97838	0.99432	1.00538	1.02033
1971	1	1.02890	1.03709	1.05069	1.05737
1972	1	1.06907	1.08024	1.10158	1.11905
1973	1	1.15256	1.18724	1.23613	1.29237
1974	1	1.39390	1.44936	1.49782	1.53554
1975	1	1.55295	1.57084	1.59096	1.60836
1976	1	1.63523	1.67820	1.70756	1.72201

JAPAN_JAPCQN70

1955	1	0.52859	0.52681	0.52280	0.52043
1956	1	0.52280	0.52844	0.52577	0.53141
1957	1	0.54210	0.54744	0.54937	0.54741
1958	1	0.54046	0.54152	0.54592	0.54644
1959	1	0.54381	0.54574	0.55155	0.55665
1960	1	0.55981	0.56509	0.57652	0.57476
1961	1	0.58524	0.58923	0.60213	0.62282
1962	1	0.63042	0.63877	0.64390	0.65035
1963	1	0.67427	0.69002	0.69591	0.69629
1964	1	0.69724	0.71223	0.71812	0.73330
1965	1	0.74830	0.77431	0.77564	0.78209
1966	1	0.79288	0.80307	0.80358	0.81147
1967	1	0.82676	0.82625	0.82956	0.85656
1968	1	0.87031	0.87235	0.87897	0.89578
1969	1	0.90011	0.91641	0.93704	0.94850
1970	1	0.97372	0.98594	0.99766	1.02924
1971	1	1.03933	1.05700	1.06700	1.08067
1972	1	1.08400	1.10567	1.11500	1.12967
1973	1	1.16100	1.22167	1.25833	1.31533
1974	1	1.44533	1.51333	1.57000	1.63867
1975	1	1.66367	1.72067	1.73600	1.77667
1976	1	1.79400	1.85000	1.87000	1.91667

JAPAN_JAPCQS70

1955	1	0.52834	0.52652	0.52280	0.52078
1956	1	0.52276	0.52829	0.52559	0.53151
1957	1	0.54238	0.54759	0.54876	0.54736
1958	1	0.54087	0.54208	0.54505	0.54612
1959	1	0.54435	0.54655	0.55049	0.55646
1960	1	0.56016	0.56584	0.57561	0.57478
1961	1	0.58554	0.58938	0.60148	0.62354
1962	1	0.63055	0.63788	0.64390	0.65142
1963	1	0.67458	0.68782	0.69662	0.69793
1964	1	0.69725	0.70923	0.71980	0.73486
1965	1	0.74784	0.77111	0.77827	0.78323
1966	1	0.79160	0.80067	0.80686	0.81174
1967	1	0.82477	0.82500	0.83315	0.85589
1968	1	0.86796	0.87216	0.88250	0.89427
1969	1	0.89827	0.91657	0.94020	0.94646
1970	1	0.97324	0.98533	1.00024	1.02749
1971	1	1.04023	1.05480	1.06952	1.07925
1972	1	1.08632	1.10157	1.11791	1.12835
1973	1	1.16457	1.21566	1.26229	1.31317
1974	1	1.45112	1.50466	1.57572	1.63524
1975	1	1.67095	1.71033	1.74335	1.77157
1976	1	1.80237	1.83893	1.87840	1.91010

JAPAN_JAIPQN70

1955	1	0.11026	0.11690	0.12161	0.12636
1956	1	0.12594	0.14047	0.14610	0.15334
1957	1	0.16772	0.17714	0.17251	0.16934
1958	1	0.17168	0.16677	0.16958	0.17995
1959	1	0.19243	0.20557	0.21503	0.23352
1960	1	0.25237	0.26061	0.26746	0.28733
1961	1	0.25237	0.26061	0.26746	0.28733
1962	1	0.35036	0.34662	0.33746	0.34351
1963	1	0.35356	0.36486	0.37910	0.40329
1964	1	0.43168	0.43879	0.44244	0.46113
1965	1	0.46726	0.45855	0.45810	0.46878
1966	1	0.49280	0.50241	0.52189	0.55757
1967	1	0.59155	0.60481	0.63223	0.67901
1968	1	0.68966	0.71791	0.74246	0.79881
1969	1	0.79650	0.83895	0.86952	0.94023
1970	1	0.94826	0.99365	1.01604	1.04213
1971	1	1.03102	1.02283	1.04577	1.05000
1972	1	1.04267	1.07367	1.10633	1.17967
1973	1	1.22400	1.27433	1.28567	1.34933
1974	1	1.27567	1.26400	1.22000	1.17400
1975	1	1.02767	1.08767	1.12300	1.15167
1976	1	1.15500	1.24700	1.27600	1.31033

JAPAN_JAIPQS70

1955	1	0.11015	0.11496	0.12224	0.12804
1956	1	0.12564	0.13829	0.14706	0.15519
1957	1	0.16686	0.17488	0.17399	0.17099
1958	1	0.17028	0.16517	0.17146	0.18135
1959	1	0.19003	0.20435	0.21797	0.23479
1960	1	0.24858	0.25961	0.27164	0.28860
1961	1	0.24801	0.25997	0.27200	0.28828
1962	1	0.34411	0.34597	0.34333	0.34460
1963	1	0.34696	0.36461	0.38565	0.40387
1964	1	0.42404	0.43930	0.44955	0.46060
1965	1	0.45997	0.46010	0.46479	0.46615
1966	1	0.48721	0.50497	0.52855	0.55208
1967	1	0.58787	0.60807	0.63932	0.66983
1968	1	0.68889	0.72189	0.74903	0.78635
1969	1	0.79920	0.84311	0.87524	0.92516
1970	1	0.95414	0.99802	1.02100	1.02535
1971	1	1.03981	1.02650	1.04916	1.03347
1972	1	1.05362	1.07717	1.10751	1.16087
1973	1	1.24136	1.27676	1.28451	1.32712
1974	1	1.29894	1.26439	1.21733	1.15328
1975	1	1.05062	1.08635	1.11934	1.13065
1976	1	1.18338	1.24513	1.27038	1.28676

JAPAN_JAGXQNEX

1955	1	2113.6	2615.2	3043.0	4018.9
1956	1	2548.1	2845.9	2801.9	3835.3
1957	1	2554.1	3034.9	3063.7	4371.2
1958	1	2817.5	3234.4	3175.4	4544.8
1959	1	3028.1	3531.0	3302.8	4885.2
1960	1	3208.9	3906.2	3926.4	5538.5
1961	1	3838.4	4691.5	4370.9	6576.5
1962	1	4601.6	5743.9	5306.4	7867.0
1963	1	5258.0	6707.2	5444.0	8673.2
1964	1	6321.6	7724.8	6789.2	10369.6
1965	1	7341.6	8500.8	7931.2	11337.2
1966	1	8727.6	10149.6	9318.4	12363.2
1967	1	9708.0	10732.4	10690.8	15086.8
1968	1	11903.6	12808.8	12420.8	17768.8
1969	1	13828.8	14896.8	13566.8	19608.0
1970	1	16511.6	17093.6	15485.2	22299.6
1971	1	21044.8	23584.4	27127.6	27842.0
1972	1	23868.8	24660.0	25455.2	32282.8
1973	1	31491.6	31590.0	25455.2	36166.4
1974	1	35191.6	38750.0	35210.8	46576.0
1975	1	39492.4	46316.8	37206.4	57313.2
1976	1	44552.0	54232.0	40404.0	55826.8

JAPAN_JAGXQSEX

1955	1	2559.2	2759.9	3250.7	3117.1
1956	1	3081.2	2997.1	3003.7	2976.5
1957	1	3079.5	3183.7	3306.3	3395.4
1958	1	3385.5	3369.9	3459.5	3533.5
1959	1	3626.3	3647.7	3635.5	3804.4
1960	1	3831.9	3995.9	4365.6	4324.4
1961	1	4566.2	4757.1	4899.8	5156.8
1962	1	5442.0	5784.4	5981.5	6208.7
1963	1	6162.5	6728.9	6145.9	6908.4
1964	1	7312.4	7752.7	7649.5	8351.5
1965	1	8352.4	8564.7	8910.1	9227.2
1966	1	9758.6	10278.0	10452.1	10161.3
1967	1	10667.3	10910.0	12005.1	12512.9
1968	1	12860.2	13062.8	13962.4	14879.6
1969	1	14712.1	15210.7	15247.9	16627.2
1970	1	17307.7	17401.1	17432.7	19175.6
1971	1	21757.9	23866.2	30604.6	24290.3
1972	1	24432.3	24676.2	28961.4	28366.1
1973	1	32186.8	31144.3	29317.6	31846.8
1974	1	36087.9	37547.7	41305.9	40831.9
1975	1	40727.6	44318.3	44271.0	50030.0
1976	1	46073.7	51625.9	48412.1	48527.7

JAPAN_JAGDQNJJ

1955	1	410.2	-191.8	-254.5	-1129.7
1956	1	469.5	37.7	137.1	-566.2
1957	1	1045.0	710.9	405.0	-811.8
1958	1	734.8	-229.7	-92.1	-1382.6
1959	1	700.6	-290.2	94.6	-1388.2
1960	1	1050.8	-128.4	174.3	-1311.2
1961	1	1283.8	155.7	1071.6	-1066.9
1962	1	1828.8	-382.8	228.0	-2177.0
1963	1	1547.5	-918.8	920.8	-2095.6
1964	1	1893.2	-994.8	457.2	-3167.6
1965	1	2078.8	-748.8	477.6	-629.6
1966	1	2048.8	-537.6	-740.4	-1836.8
1967	1	2607.2	290.8	770.0	-3136.8
1968	1	2533.6	-369.2	687.2	-4424.0
1969	1	2717.6	-745.6	1610.0	-4289.6
1970	1	2901.2	-244.4	2851.2	-4747.6
1971	1	2719.2	-4603.6	-5037.2	-5768.0
1972	1	3296.0	827.2	2268.8	-5062.4
1973	1	28.0	3371.2	6676.0	-785.6
1974	1	5343.2	-2167.2	4355.2	-11365.2
1975	1	2965.2	-5656.0	2292.4	-9205.6
1976	1	4069.2	-5672.8	4889.6	-5750.4

JAPAN_JAGDQSJJ

1955	1	-349.20	-298.32	-314.55	-195.00
1956	1	-305.34	-54.79	56.27	402.66
1957	1	233.57	647.78	279.62	229.65
1958	1	-144.09	-246.24	-285.40	-231.82
1959	1	-279.65	-241.75	-184.55	-89.90
1960	1	-78.23	19.85	-215.53	167.74
1961	1	-31.96	423.91	554.23	636.95
1962	1	281.93	6.86	-393.43	-259.26
1963	1	-214.59	-459.60	242.07	31.01
1964	1	-63.05	-529.05	-239.43	-841.32
1965	1	-24.25	-341.26	-246.72	1957.32
1966	1	-221.82	-186.29	-1527.41	1039.22
1967	1	164.80	623.28	-168.58	138.06
1968	1	-188.96	-4.27	-352.62	-836.18
1969	1	-249.83	-319.54	428.64	-418.46
1970	1	-240.86	237.86	1537.77	-738.15
1971	1	-458.29	-3952.43	-6773.61	-1415.02
1972	1	-26.61	1787.70	-14.85	-297.72
1973	1	-3569.96	4887.70	3581.44	4568.93
1974	1	1384.21	-82.56	521.06	-5499.60
1975	1	-1342.18	-3025.96	-2228.21	-2859.21
1976	1	-484.91	-2771.39	50.20	872.20

JAPAN_JAPPQNIN

1954	1		0.088760	0.089023	0.089288
1955	1	0.089552	0.089820	0.090054	0.090288
1956	1	0.090523	0.090760	0.090959	0.091159
1957	1	0.091358	0.091560	0.091766	0.091973
1958	1	0.092181	0.092390	0.092614	0.092838
1959	1	0.093063	0.093290	0.093492	0.093694
1960	1	0.093896	0.094100	0.094311	0.094523
1961	1	0.094736	0.094950	0.095169	0.095388
1962	1	0.095608	0.095830	0.096074	0.096318
1963	1	0.096563	0.096810	0.097064	0.097318
1964	1	0.097573	0.097830	0.098091	0.098353
1965	1	0.098615	0.098880	0.099106	0.099333
1966	1	0.099561	0.099790	0.100049	0.100308
1967	1	0.100568	0.100830	0.101111	0.101392
1968	1	0.101675	0.101960	0.102261	0.102562
1969	1	0.102865	0.103170	0.103461	0.103752
1970	1	0.104045	0.104340	0.104653	0.104967
1971	1	0.105282	0.105600	0.105938	0.106277
1972	1	0.106616	0.106960	0.107305	0.107651
1973	1	0.107999	0.108350	0.108678	0.109007
1974	1	0.109337	0.109670	0.109988	0.110307
1975	1	0.110627	0.110950	0.111401	0.111854
1976	1	0.112309	0.112770	0.113228	0.113689

JAPAN_JALFQNJJ

1955	1	0.038477	0.043170	0.042663	0.042900
1956	1	0.040340	0.044233	0.043597	0.043480
1957	1	0.041583	0.044437	0.044457	0.044370
1958	1	0.041827	0.045127	0.044597	0.044440
1959	1	0.041990	0.045477	0.045043	0.044607
1960	1	0.042710	0.046100	0.046173	0.045627
1961	1	0.043440	0.046240	0.046193	0.046107
1962	1	0.044007	0.047147	0.047023	0.046387
1963	1	0.044110	0.047530	0.047517	0.046940
1964	1	0.045033	0.048190	0.047870	0.047303
1965	1	0.045683	0.048790	0.048840	0.048163
1966	1	0.046857	0.050003	0.049783	0.048990
1967	1	0.047550	0.051140	0.050837	0.050270
1968	1	0.048460	0.051740	0.051557	0.050683
1969	1	0.049050	0.052067	0.051897	0.050900
1970	1	0.049763	0.052537	0.052450	0.051377
1971	1	0.050440	0.052750	0.052397	0.051577
1972	1	0.050443	0.052423	0.052440	0.051983
1973	1	0.051803	0.053467	0.053533	0.053163
1974	1	0.051613	0.053587	0.053173	0.052280
1975	1	0.051203	0.053403	0.053520	0.052943
1976	1	0.052483	0.054253	0.054503	0.053893

JAPAN_JALFQSJJ

1955	1	0.040731	0.041906	0.042085	0.042494
1956	1	0.042585	0.042978	0.043009	0.043091
1957	1	0.043795	0.043218	0.043838	0.044020
1958	1	0.043983	0.043965	0.043936	0.044128
1959	1	0.044092	0.044375	0.044336	0.044330
1960	1	0.044777	0.045037	0.045428	0.045384
1961	1	0.045483	0.045193	0.045419	0.045909
1962	1	0.046019	0.046103	0.046228	0.046247
1963	1	0.046087	0.046472	0.046711	0.046866
1964	1	0.046980	0.047097	0.047065	0.047301
1965	1	0.047591	0.047664	0.048040	0.048223
1966	1	0.048723	0.048857	0.048988	0.049102
1967	1	0.049366	0.049994	0.050045	0.050427
1968	1	0.050215	0.050610	0.050781	0.050875
1969	1	0.050712	0.050983	0.051146	0.051118
1970	1	0.051308	0.051524	0.051733	0.051606
1971	1	0.051862	0.051817	0.051715	0.051803
1972	1	0.051765	0.051554	0.051798	0.052193
1973	1	0.053049	0.052657	0.052916	0.053354
1974	1	0.052813	0.052821	0.052564	0.052459
1975	1	0.052380	0.052664	0.052907	0.053118
1976	1	0.053658	0.053517	0.053890	0.054068

JAPAN_JAUNQNTH

1955	1	0.000710	0.000680	0.000700	0.000620
1956	1	0.000830	0.000630	0.000567	0.000533
1957	1	0.000667	0.000500	0.000483	0.000453
1958	1	0.000650	0.000550	0.000560	0.000503
1959	1	0.000767	0.000567	0.000540	0.000437
1960	1	0.000593	0.000433	0.000387	0.000313
1961	1	0.000483	0.000357	0.000327	0.000383
1962	1	0.000513	0.000383	0.000357	0.000350
1963	1	0.000573	0.000363	0.000347	0.000320
1964	1	0.000497	0.000337	0.000330	0.000297
1965	1	0.000460	0.000380	0.000377	0.000353
1966	1	0.000587	0.000410	0.000387	0.000360
1967	1	0.000583	0.000427	0.000403	0.000500
1968	1	0.000767	0.000567	0.000573	0.000467
1969	1	0.000693	0.000590	0.000550	0.000470
1970	1	0.000653	0.000557	0.000593	0.000570
1971	1	0.000727	0.000617	0.000603	0.000610
1972	1	0.000873	0.000703	0.000697	0.000630
1973	1	0.000800	0.000700	0.000617	0.000540
1974	1	0.000820	0.000647	0.000677	0.000813
1975	1	0.001063	0.000937	0.000933	0.001020
1976	1	0.001257	0.001083	0.001010	0.000963

JAPAN_JAUNQSTH

1955	1	0.000588	0.000699	0.000737	0.000715
1956	1	0.000685	0.000648	0.000597	0.000618
1957	1	0.000547	0.000515	0.000510	0.000530
1958	1	0.000528	0.000569	0.000592	0.000594
1959	1	0.000616	0.000587	0.000575	0.000520
1960	1	0.000469	0.000452	0.000415	0.000374
1961	1	0.000377	0.000374	0.000355	0.000458
1962	1	0.000395	0.000405	0.000391	0.000418
1963	1	0.000438	0.000385	0.000382	0.000382
1964	1	0.000378	0.000358	0.000364	0.000353
1965	1	0.000350	0.000404	0.000414	0.000420
1966	1	0.000450	0.000435	0.000422	0.000427
1967	1	0.000454	0.000449	0.000436	0.000588
1968	1	0.000608	0.000592	0.000614	0.000543
1969	1	0.000560	0.000613	0.000583	0.000541
1970	1	0.000539	0.000572	0.000627	0.000648
1971	1	0.000609	0.000630	0.000638	0.000684
1972	1	0.000739	0.000716	0.000744	0.000695
1973	1	0.000680	0.000714	0.000663	0.000587
1974	1	0.000701	0.000660	0.000732	0.000876
1975	1	0.000910	0.000957	0.001014	0.001090
1976	1	0.001078	0.001106	0.001100	0.001025

JAPAN_JAURQNUR

1955	1	0.018387	0.015764	0.016408	0.014429
1956	1	0.020481	0.014269	0.012999	0.012280
1957	1	0.015980	0.011268	0.010873	0.010211
1958	1	0.015469	0.012192	0.012557	0.011338
1959	1	0.018211	0.012464	0.011984	0.009809
1960	1	0.013858	0.009408	0.008377	0.006878
1961	1	0.011115	0.007717	0.007072	0.008318
1962	1	0.011639	0.008141	0.007585	0.007553
1963	1	0.012939	0.007648	0.007296	0.006832
1964	1	0.011005	0.006991	0.006894	0.006284
1965	1	0.010049	0.007792	0.007712	0.007347
1966	1	0.012483	0.008202	0.007770	0.007350
1967	1	0.012185	0.008350	0.007936	0.009962
1968	1	0.015810	0.010961	0.011119	0.009212
1969	1	0.014126	0.011333	0.010598	0.009236
1970	1	0.013128	0.010602	0.011314	0.011089
1971	1	0.014393	0.011695	0.011514	0.011834
1972	1	0.017307	0.013422	0.013287	0.012121
1973	1	0.015442	0.013097	0.011519	0.010163
1974	1	0.015875	0.012070	0.012727	0.015612
1975	1	0.020760	0.017547	0.017441	0.019268
1976	1	0.024000	0.020000	0.018000	0.018000

JAPAN_JAURQSUR

1955	1	0.014594	0.016663	0.017559	0.016835
1956	1	0.016206	0.015101	0.013911	0.014399
1957	1	0.012573	0.011942	0.011659	0.012069
1958	1	0.012052	0.012964	0.013517	0.013500
1959	1	0.014043	0.013274	0.013006	0.011764
1960	1	0.010537	0.010076	0.009182	0.008272
1961	1	0.008343	0.008316	0.007837	0.010002
1962	1	0.008643	0.008828	0.008481	0.009053
1963	1	0.009556	0.008318	0.008206	0.008176
1964	1	0.008096	0.007631	0.007768	0.007496
1965	1	0.007403	0.008519	0.008650	0.008737
1966	1	0.009273	0.008930	0.008650	0.008694
1967	1	0.009179	0.009032	0.008746	0.011684
1968	1	0.012142	0.011741	0.012146	0.010681
1969	1	0.011071	0.012058	0.011443	0.010578
1970	1	0.010536	0.011141	0.012153	0.012554
1971	1	0.011748	0.012201	0.012371	0.013202
1972	1	0.014309	0.013925	0.014388	0.013299
1973	1	0.012853	0.013590	0.012564	0.010985
1974	1	0.013300	0.012493	0.013997	0.016692
1975	1	0.017447	0.018159	0.019292	0.020434
1976	1	0.020218	0.020691	0.019977	0.018994

Sources and Notes on Time Series for the Netherlands

The sources for most series were publications of the Dutch central bank, De Nederlandsche Bank (DNB). Assistance in choosing series and in collecting data not available in central bank publications was provided by Professor Pieter Korteweg of Erasmus Universiteit, Rotterdam. Additional assistance in obtaining data for some series in the early part of our sample period was provided by Dr. W. J. de Ridder of the Nederlandsche Middenstandsbank, Amsterdam, and an associate, Mr. L. I. W. Soutendijk of the New York office of the Middenstandsbank. The notes below list the sources for each series in more detail.

All series are on a quarterly basis and cover the period from 1955I to 1976IV, except where noted otherwise. We made the seasonal adjustment, where necessary, using the Census X-11 program.

I. INTERNATIONAL VARIABLES

A. *Balance of Payments*

NEBPQNSB   Balance of Payments. Unit: Billions of Guilders at Quar-
NEBPQSSB   terly Rates.

Source: For 1955–69, from unpublished statistics of De Nederlandsche Bank (DNB); for 1970–76, DNB, *Quarterly Statistics*, table 6.1, "Balance of Payments, on a Cash Basis," June 1972, March 1974, December 1974, March 1976, and June 1977 issues.

Description: The official settlements balance of payments where a net increase in official reserves represents a surplus and is indicates as a positive value. These reserves include: gold, foreign exchange (including those expressed in terms of gold), special drawing rights, and the reserve position in the International Monetary Fund. For 1955–57, the unpublished data were semiannual flows. The quarterly observations for this period were estimated as one-half the corresponding semiannual figures. The data were originally in millions of guilders.

B. *Exports*

NEEXQSTL   Export, Current Account Total. Unit: Billions of Guilders at Annual Rates, in Seasonally Adjusted Form Only.

Source: Unpublished statistics of the Dutch Central Planning Bureau.

Description: This measures current account total exports of goods and services, and primary (investment and personal earned) income at current prices. The data were originally in millions of guilders and in seasonally adjusted form.

C. *Imports*

    NEIMQSTL   Imports, Current Account Total. Unit: Billions of Guilders at Annual Rates, in Seasonally Adjusted Form Only.

Source: Unpublished statistics of the Dutch Central Planning Bureau.

Description: This measures total current account imports of goods and services, and primary (investment and personal earned) income at current prices.

D. *Net Private Capital Outflows*

    NEKPQNEP   Net Private Capital Outflows. Unit: Billions of Guilders at
    NEKPQSEP   Annual Rates.

Source: For 1955–59, from unpublished statistics of DNB; for 1970–76, DNB, *Quarterly Statistics*, table 6.3, "External Capital Transactions," June 1972, March 1974, December 1974, March 1976, and June 1977 issues.

Description: This measures net private capital transfers, plus net long-term private capital outflows, plus short-term private capital outflows where net private capital *exports* are defined positive. The data were originally in millions of guilders at quarterly rates.

E. *Exchange Rate*

    NEXRQNGL   Spot Exchange Rate. Unit: Guilders per Dollar.

Source: For 1955–70, from unpublished statistics of DNB; for 1971–76, DNB, *Quarterly Statistics*, table 9.4, "Foreign Exchange Rates at Amsterdam," March 1975, June 1976, and June 1977 issues.

Description: This measures the middle spot exchange rate of the U.S. dollar. The figures are average of high and low daily quotations on the Amsterdam Exchange for each week of the quarter.

II. FINANCIAL VARIABLES

A. *Narrow Money Stock (M1)*

    NEM1QNDR   Narrow Money Stock. Unit: Billions of Guilders, End-of-
    NEM1QSDR   Quarter.

Source: For 1955I–56III, from unpublished statistics of the DNB; for 1956IV–71IV, from DNB, *Monetary Statistics Yearly and Quarterly*, table 3.1, "Money Stock and Savings Deposits," October 1973; for 1972–76, from DNB, *Quarterly Statistics*, table 3.1, "Money Stock and Savings Deposits," June 1977.

Description: This measures M1, the sum of currency and demand deposits of the nonbank public. The data are end of last month of each quarter. The figures were originally in millions of guilders.

B. *Broader Money Stock (M2)*

    NEM2QNDR   Broader Money Stock. Unit: Billions of Guilders, End-of-
    NEM2QSDR   Quarter.

Source: Same as II.A., Narrow Money Stock, above.

Description: This measures M2, the sum of M1 and the public's time and liquid savings deposits at Dutch money-creating institutions. The data are end of last month of each quarter. The figures were originally in millions of guilders.

C. *High-powered Money*

    NEMHQNDR   High-powered Money. Unit: Billions of Guilders, End-of-
    NEMHQSDR   Quarter.

Source: For 1955I–56III, from unpublished statistics of the DNB; for 1965IV–71IV, from DNB, *Monetary Statistics, Yearly and Quarterly*, table 2.1, "Balance Sheets of Money-creating Institutions," October 1973; for 1972–76, from DNB, *Quarterly Statistics*, table 2.1, "Balance Sheets of Money-creating Institutions," June 1977.

Description: This measures currency outstanding plus deposits at the central bank of the (nonbank) public as well as deposits of money-creating institutions. Currency outstanding is the sum of currency held by the nonbank public and bank vault cash. The data are end of last month of each quarter. The figures were originally in millions of guilders.

D. *Official International Reserve Assets*

NEFHQNTL   Official International Reserve Assets. Unit: Billions of
NEFHQSTL   Guilders, End-of-Quarter.

Source: For 1955I–56III, from unpublished statistics of DNB; for 1956IV–1976IV, from DNB, *Monetary Statistics, Yearly and Quarterly*, table 1.1, "Summary Balance Sheets of the Netherlands Bank," October 1973; for 1972–76, from DNB, *Quarterly Statistics*, table 1.1, "Summary Balance Sheets of the Netherlands Bank," June 1976, June 1977.

Description: This measures the gross holdings of gold, convertible currency, and special drawings rights of Dutch central bank. The data are aggregates as of end of last month of each quarter. The figures were originally in millions of guilders.

E. *Interest Rates*

1. Short-Term

NERSQN3T   Short-Term Interest Rate. Unit: Decimal Rate per Annum.

Source: For 1955–70, from unpublished statistics of DNB; for 1971–76, DNB, *Quarterly Statistics*, table 9.2, "Market Interest Rates," June 1976, June 1977.

Description: This measures the three-month Dutch Treasury paper rate, calculated on a true yield to maturity basis. The data are quarterly averages of monthly averages of daily quotations of bill brokers. The figures were originally in percent per annum.

2. Long-Term

NERLQNGB   Long-Term Interest Rate. Unit: Decimal Rate per Annum.

Source: Same as II.E.1, Short-term Interest Rate, above.

Description: This measures the yield on 3¼% Netherlands government bonds of 1948, which had an average remaining life of 12¼ years as of 1 April, 1976. The data are quarterly averages of monthly averages of daily figures. The figures were originally in percent per annum.

III. NONFINANCIAL DOMESTIC VARIABLES

A. *National Product*

1. Nominal Gross Product

NEYNQSNP   Gross National Product in Current Market Prices. Unit:
             Billions of Guilders at Annual Rates.

Source: From unpublished statistics of the Dutch Central Planning Bureau.

Description: This measures the purchases of final goods and services, produced domestically, at current market prices, equivalent to the total income and product of residents, inclusive of net factor income from abroad. The figures were originally in millions of guilders and in seasonally adjusted form.

2. Real Gross Product
    NEYRQSN7   Gross National Product in 1970 Market Prices. Unit: Billions of Guilders at Annual Rates.

Source: Same as for III.A.1, Nominal Gross Product, above.

Description: This measures the purchases of final goods and services, produced domestically, in 1970 market prices, equivalent to the income and product of residents, inclusive of net factor income from abroad. The figures were originally in millions of guilders and in seasonally adjusted form.

B. *Prices*
1. Implicit Price Deflator
    NEPDQSN7   GNP Implicit Price Deflator. Unit: 1970 = 1.00.

Source: From unpublished statistics of the Dutch Central Planning Bureau.

Description: Derived as the ratio of nominal GNP (III.A.1) to real GNP (III.A.2).

2. Consumer Prices
    NEPCQN70   Consumer Price Index. Unit: 1970 = 1.00.
    NEPCQS70

Source: For 1955–72, Dutch Central Bureau of Statistics (CBS), *Maandstatistiek van de Binnenlandse Handel*, various issues; for 1973–76, CBS, *Maandstatistiek van de Prijzen*, various issues.

Description: This represents a general index of retail consumer prices covering most items but excluding social security premiums and indirect taxes. The data are quarterly averages of monthly figures. The original figures are on four different base years: 1951, 1959/60, 1964, 1969.

C. *Industrial Production*
    NEIPQN70   Industrial Production Index. Unit: 1970 = 1.00.
    NEIPQS70

Source: Central Bureau of Statistics, *Maandstatistiek van de Industrie*, various issues.

Description: A general index of industrial production including the mining, manufacturing, and utility industries but excluding the construction industry. The data are quarterly averages of monthly averages of daily figures. The original figures are on five different base years: 1947, 1953, 1958, 1963, and 1970.

D. *Government Accounts*
1. Government Expenditures
    NEGXQNFD   Government Expenditures. Unit: Billions of Guilders at
    NEGXQSFD   Annual Rates.

Source: For 1955–71, from DNB, *Monetary Statistics, Yearly and Quarterly*, table 5.1, "Government Finance, on a Cash Basis," October 1973; for 1972–76, from DNB, *Quarterly Statistics*, table 5.1, "Government Finance, on a Cash Basis," March 1975, June 1976, June 1977 issues.

Description: This represents current cash payments out of the central government's account at DNB. The data were originally in millions of guilders at quarterly rates.

2. Government Deficit
    NEGDQNFD   Government Deficit. Unit: Billions of Guilders at Annual
    NEGSQSFD   Rates.

Source: Same as III.D.1, Government Expenditure, above.

Description: Government expenditures less government receipts of the central government's account at DNB inclusive of transactions with government enterprises, social insurance funds, and the Bank for Netherlands Municipalities. The deficit is defined as a negative value. The data were originally in millions of guilders at quarterly rates.

E. *Population*

   NEPPQNIN   Population. Unit: Billions of Persons.

Source: From the UN, *Demographic Yearbook*, various issues.

Description: Straight-line interpolation of mid-year estimates of total population. The data were originally in millions of persons.

F. *Unemployment Rate*

   NEURQSSE   Unemployment Rate. Unit: Decimal Rate per Annum.

Source: For 1955I to 1975IV, from unpublished statistics of the Dutch Central Planning Bureau, which made the seasonal adjustment; for 1976I to 1976IV, our own estimates based on International Labour Office, *Yearbook of Labour Statistics*, 1977, and Federal Reserve Bank of St. Louis, *International Economic Conditions*, 6 March 1978.

Description: To estimate the figures for 1976 we used an estimate of employment, for the year 1970, from the *Yearbook of Labor Statistics, 1977* and applied to it the employment index on the base 1970 from the *International Economic Conditions* to obtain an estimated employment series for the period 1972IV to 1976IV. We divided the estimated level of employment by one minus the unemployment rate to obtain estimates of the labor force for 1972IV to 1975IV. We then regressed (in double-log form) estimated labor force on estimated employment for this period. We used the estimated relation to obtain 1976 quarterly estimates of the labor force from the employment estimates. Dividing estimated employment by estimated labor force for 1976 resulted in estimates of the unemployment rate.

List of Tables for the Netherlands (Quarterly Data)

NETHER_NEBPQNSB

1955	1	-0.08850	-0.08850	0.09700	0.09700
1956	1	-0.22000	-0.22000	-0.23300	-0.23300
1957	1	-0.14050	-0.14050	0.20350	0.20350
1958	1	0.80100	0.13800	0.47500	0.48900
1959	1	0.57600	-0.22300	0.18600	0.07700
1960	1	0.46800	0.15700	0.13400	0.23900
1961	1	-0.24500	0.10000	0.39100	-0.00300
1962	1	-0.09800	0.31800	-0.12000	-0.15100
1963	1	0.05300	0.26400	0.04900	0.25000
1964	1	-0.21900	-0.10300	0.62600	0.60000
1965	1	-0.03100	-0.00800	0.31400	-0.00800
1966	1	-0.14400	-0.13200	0.25200	0.17600
1967	1	-0.08000	0.20200	0.02000	0.47500
1968	1	-0.22400	-0.26900	0.06500	-0.18000
1969	1	-0.20200	-0.45900	-0.09300	0.98400
1970	1	0.49800	0.05100	1.11000	0.90000
1971	1	1.11000	-0.20800	0.37600	-0.38700
1972	1	1.76700	0.08800	1.53100	-0.35500
1973	1	2.79300	-2.96500	0.04700	2.16300
1974	1	0.18700	-1.22300	3.06200	0.63600
1975	1	0.47600	-0.94400	0.64100	0.72000
1976	1	0.60200	-3.11900	0.57800	2.61400
1977	1	-0.64000			

NETHER_NEBPQSSB

1955	1	-0.10664	0.01358	0.05825	0.06551
1956	1	-0.26607	-0.09643	-0.27756	-0.25233
1957	1	-0.22289	0.01147	0.15605	0.18701
1958	1	0.70330	0.30687	0.41205	0.48302
1959	1	0.48429	-0.06385	0.11520	0.06966
1960	1	0.41646	0.28107	0.05738	0.22186
1961	1	-0.23652	0.18098	0.31507	-0.05557
1962	1	-0.01017	0.36796	-0.21627	-0.22246
1963	1	0.18978	0.31648	-0.07598	0.16120
1964	1	-0.05245	-0.03901	0.49184	0.48330
1965	1	0.14562	0.08423	0.17552	-0.15291
1966	1	0.03255	-0.02134	0.13356	0.00783
1967	1	0.06156	0.35536	-0.08889	0.31320
1968	1	-0.16042	-0.05695	-0.02906	-0.31542
1969	1	-0.28011	-0.09975	-0.24356	0.91183
1970	1	0.22115	0.65123	0.87095	0.81999
1971	1	0.67714	0.72479	-0.06370	-0.48814
1972	1	1.25458	1.31848	0.92453	-0.55160
1973	1	2.25672	-1.44344	-0.70489	1.78460
1974	1	-0.26680	0.49736	2.26183	-0.00624
1975	1	0.17150	0.91407	-0.20812	-0.13359
1976	1	0.47264	-1.23339	-0.31421	1.71149
1977	1	-0.70197			

NETHER_NEEXQSTL

1955	1	13.692	14.616	15.876	16.172
1956	1	15.916	16.216	16.756	16.168
1957	1	18.964	17.940	17.596	17.564
1958	1	17.068	18.416	18.412	18.864
1959	1	18.904	20.284	20.156	21.196
1960	1	22.108	22.580	22.452	23.444
1961	1	23.216	23.452	22.596	22.840
1962	1	23.684	24.140	24.508	25.100
1963	1	24.756	26.068	27.408	28.080
1964	1	28.936	29.644	30.624	31.788
1965	1	32.624	32.492	33.688	34.232
1966	1	33.668	34.988	35.708	35.952
1967	1	35.840	37.220	38.228	39.696
1968	1	39.948	40.504	42.264	45.676
1969	1	46.324	49.132	48.964	53.860
1970	1	54.844	58.640	58.212	63.476
1971	1	65.664	65.624	69.408	68.264
1972	1	70.236	72.656	75.400	81.068
1973	1	86.640	88.644	88.784	97.292
1974	1	109.432	119.576	120.152	117.880
1975	1	115.296	116.026	114.530	121.758
1976	1	124.428	126.324	130.604	139.956
1977	1	133.968			

NETHER_NEIMQSTL

1955	1	13.520	13.840	14.820	15.064
1956	1	16.140	17.032	17.156	17.568
1957	1	19.816	19.192	18.336	16.872
1958	1	15.984	16.540	16.920	17.072
1959	1	17.048	18.196	18.416	19.524
1960	1	20.332	21.088	21.508	22.568
1961	1	22.196	22.268	22.244	22.588
1962	1	24.052	23.180	23.996	23.664
1963	1	24.232	25.868	27.128	27.952
1964	1	29.628	31.608	30.700	31.284
1965	1	30.980	32.080	32.996	35.876
1966	1	36.268	34.604	36.096	35.304
1967	1	36.436	36.676	38.040	39.500
1968	1	39.380	39.508	43.196	44.000
1969	1	45.404	48.508	49.624	52.992
1970	1	56.032	60.360	60.912	64.560
1971	1	66.448	66.740	69.140	67.472
1972	1	67.456	67.196	69.852	75.856
1973	1	79.424	81.448	87.652	89.636
1974	1	103.276	113.148	115.964	113.252
1975	1	112.896	110.428	108.896	117.180
1976	1	112.652	125.860	124.972	132.868
1977	1	130.244			

NETHER_NEKPQNEP

1955	1	-0.00400	-0.00400	0.04600	0.04600
1956	1	-0.34600	-0.34600	-0.25200	-0.25200
1957	1	0.77600	0.77600	0.24800	0.24800
1958	1	1.86400	-0.07600	0.51200	0.58800
1959	1	-0.43600	-0.68400	-0.40400	-1.59200
1960	1	0.78800	1.40400	0.00800	-0.22400
1961	1	-0.62400	0.48000	-0.41200	-0.54000
1962	1	0.72000	0.68800	-0.34000	-1.41600
1963	1	0.58000	1.06800	0.02400	-1.41600
1964	1	-0.19600	-0.20800	1.47600	1.53600
1965	1	0.55200	-0.04400	0.24800	-0.80000
1966	1	-0.17600	0.68400	-0.02800	0.24000
1967	1	0.14800	-1.04800	0.83600	-0.08000
1968	1	-0.54800	-1.02400	1.13200	-0.02800
1969	1	0.42000	-3.30800	1.47600	1.54800
1970	1	1.10000	2.88400	5.37200	1.84400
1971	1	4.21600	2.30800	2.56800	1.91200
1972	1	-0.18800	-0.31600	-2.19200	-4.10000
1973	1	-2.73200	-5.48400	-3.79200	-4.39600
1974	1	-0.68400	-3.12000	0.51200	-3.78800
1975	1	-1.97600	-2.96800	-0.30000	-3.04800
1976	1	-4.53600	-7.62400	-6.66000	-6.19200
1977	1	-0.44400			

NETHER_NEKPQSEP

1955	1	-0.22010	-0.07915	0.17449	0.20497
1956	1	-0.55405	-0.41749	-0.16023	-0.03919
1957	1	0.55814	0.66960	0.32406	0.52540
1958	1	1.66924	-0.28589	0.58727	0.97839
1959	1	-0.63635	-1.01943	-0.30289	-1.10979
1960	1	0.60868	0.94259	0.09859	0.39251
1961	1	-0.84287	-0.02199	-0.34069	0.10670
1962	1	0.51066	0.22972	-0.34176	-0.78042
1963	1	0.35162	0.79132	-0.09477	-0.90273
1964	1	-0.38263	-0.22606	1.16878	1.92303
1965	1	0.40656	0.23075	-0.25257	-0.57358
1966	1	-0.25070	1.22797	-0.71764	0.32941
1967	1	0.17820	-0.32924	-0.05900	0.04145
1968	1	-0.51899	-0.21251	0.13149	0.13305
1969	1	0.47790	-2.55856	0.47139	1.84024
1970	1	1.04281	3.57175	4.46083	2.22346
1971	1	4.03470	2.95872	1.66672	2.52069
1972	1	-0.64906	0.42630	-3.09217	-3.40569
1973	1	-3.33288	-4.65768	-4.75213	-3.54880
1974	1	-1.50755	-2.13771	-0.50494	-2.89150
1975	1	-2.89980	-1.86708	-1.43386	-2.02334
1976	1	-5.58885	-6.41000	-7.87553	-5.14773
1977	1	-1.47151			

NETHER_NEXRQNGL

1955	1	3.79667	3.80333	3.82000	3.81667
1956	1	3.83000	3.83000	3.83000	3.83000
1957	1	3.83000	3.82333	3.83000	3.79333
1958	1	3.79000	3.79000	3.78333	3.77000
1959	1	3.77333	3.77000	3.77333	3.77333
1960	1	3.77000	3.77000	3.77000	3.77333
1961	1	3.72000	3.59000	3.60000	3.60333
1962	1	3.61333	3.63000	3.59667	3.60000
1963	1	3.60000	3.59667	3.60667	3.60000
1964	1	3.61000	3.61333	3.61333	3.59333
1965	1	3.59000	3.60333	3.60000	3.60333
1966	1	3.62000	3.62667	3.61333	3.62000
1967	1	3.61000	3.60333	3.60000	3.60000
1968	1	3.60667	3.62000	3.62667	3.62667
1969	1	3.62667	3.63667	3.62667	3.60667
1970	1	3.63333	3.62667	3.60333	3.60000
1971	1	3.59667	3.57000	3.48667	3.32333
1972	1	3.19667	3.20667	3.20667	3.23333
1973	1	3.04667	2.86000	2.63333	2.66333
1974	1	2.84000	2.64333	2.67000	2.60333
1975	1	2.41333	2.41000	2.62333	2.66667
1976	1	2.67333	2.71880	2.63380	2.51200

NETHER_NEM1QNDR

1955	1	8.7240	9.1630	9.3540	9.5840
1956	1	9.2930	9.4290	9.3580	9.2270
1957	1	8.9840	9.3090	9.0240	9.0500
1958	1	9.0690	9.5650	9.6500	10.1370
1959	1	10.2420	10.5380	10.4620	10.5880
1960	1	10.4920	11.1550	11.1480	11.3030
1961	1	11.5450	12.0290	11.9380	12.1680
1962	1	11.8880	12.5990	12.6630	13.0860
1963	1	12.9720	13.8590	13.9760	14.2870
1964	1	14.2770	15.0670	15.1150	15.4410
1965	1	15.6490	16.7900	16.8680	16.9920
1966	1	16.8740	18.4110	17.8200	18.1580
1967	1	18.1290	19.7900	19.3700	19.2880
1968	1	19.5440	21.4580	20.9580	21.4860
1969	1	21.3700	23.3440	22.5570	23.2210
1970	1	23.4120	25.6730	25.5360	25.9500
1971	1	27.1250	30.1030	29.9400	29.8520
1972	1	32.2760	35.6870	36.1110	35.1240
1973	1	37.4720	39.0460	36.1000	35.1390
1974	1	36.0500	39.7360	38.4910	39.4300
1975	1	40.4990	47.3910	46.9120	47.1930
1976	1	49.0370	52.8410	48.7290	50.3950
1977	1	52.4140			

NETHER_NEM1QSDR

1955	1	8.8864	9.0323	9.3597	9.5466
1956	1	9.4585	9.2952	9.3682	9.1926
1957	1	9.1368	9.1746	9.0410	9.0192
1958	1	9.2179	9.4218	9.6753	10.1018
1959	1	10.4123	10.3733	10.4949	10.5450
1960	1	10.6784	10.9768	11.1775	11.2508
1961	1	11.7701	11.8313	11.9554	12.1160
1962	1	12.1380	12.3816	12.6619	13.0490
1963	1	13.2635	13.5918	13.9635	14.2762
1964	1	14.6149	14.7339	15.0904	15.4770
1965	1	16.0376	16.3486	16.8488	17.0816
1966	1	17.3129	17.8409	17.8214	18.3016
1967	1	18.6184	19.0874	19.4059	19.4834
1968	1	20.0779	20.6217	21.0125	21.7840
1969	1	21.9133	22.3903	22.6183	23.6456
1970	1	23.9314	24.5972	25.6013	26.5494
1971	1	27.6306	28.8082	30.0309	30.6496
1972	1	32.8080	34.0847	36.2483	36.1756
1973	1	38.0363	37.1866	36.3292	36.2251
1974	1	36.5836	37.7259	38.8587	40.6364
1975	1	41.1125	44.8767	47.5040	48.5789
1976	1	49.8131	49.9706	49.4044	51.8491
1977	1	53.2654			

NETHER_NEM2QNDR

Year					
1955	1	10.2070	10.5700	10.8480	11.2550
1956	1	11.2700	11.3460	11.2140	10.9120
1957	1	10.8980	11.0800	10.7810	10.9230
1958	1	11.3780	11.6330	11.8410	12.3820
1959	1	12.8460	13.0950	13.1030	13.3830
1960	1	13.7050	14.1310	14.5340	14.5670
1961	1	15.1970	15.4880	15.4630	15.4340
1962	1	15.6250	16.3940	16.3810	16.6010
1963	1	16.9780	17.5640	17.9380	18.2570
1964	1	18.5370	18.7960	19.4080	19.9810
1965	1	20.8380	21.5430	21.9550	21.4490
1966	1	21.3550	22.7200	22.4590	22.7280
1967	1	23.0860	24.5970	24.8980	25.0650
1968	1	26.1320	28.0370	28.0370	28.5910
1969	1	28.9310	31.1730	30.6800	31.3520
1970	1	32.1010	34.5700	34.6080	34.5180
1971	1	35.2580	37.3270	37.2420	37.9960
1972	1	40.0420	43.0110	42.9190	43.7590
1973	1	47.0570	49.8040	51.4740	52.6050
1974	1	56.2460	62.1890	63.5620	63.8910
1975	1	65.5900	69.2660	66.1350	67.4630
1976	1	70.7780	77.0400	80.2420	81.5470
1977	1	87.2010			

NETHER_NEM2QSDR

Year					
1955	1	10.2139	10.4636	10.9155	11.2984
1956	1	11.2670	11.2359	11.2882	10.9548
1957	1	10.8821	10.9821	10.8498	10.9736
1958	1	11.3498	11.5377	11.9095	12.4467
1959	1	12.8105	12.9966	13.1609	13.4575
1960	1	13.6805	14.0285	14.5759	14.6427
1961	1	15.1966	15.3846	15.4715	15.5161
1962	1	15.6509	16.2908	16.3519	16.6948
1963	1	17.0397	17.4450	17.8754	18.3684
1964	1	18.6454	18.6402	19.3146	20.1235
1965	1	21.0106	21.3022	21.8396	21.6332
1966	1	21.5830	22.3745	22.3515	22.9571
1967	1	23.3910	24.1021	24.8203	25.3478
1968	1	26.5195	27.3580	27.9966	28.9603
1969	1	29.3572	30.3360	30.6825	31.8075
1970	1	32.5330	33.6088	34.6219	35.0866
1971	1	35.6852	36.2783	37.2375	38.6941
1972	1	40.4869	41.8040	42.8690	44.6431
1973	1	47.5485	48.4159	51.3524	53.7480
1974	1	56.8000	60.4753	63.3512	65.3370
1975	1	66.2247	67.3817	65.8512	69.0469
1976	1	71.4414	74.9541	79.8750	83.4773
1977	1	88.0202			

NETHER_NEMHQNDR

Year					
1955	1	4.2973	4.4062	4.5271	4.6946
1956	1	4.6559	4.8052	4.7867	4.7650
1957	1	4.5840	4.6620	4.7180	4.7720
1958	1	4.7610	4.9200	5.0450	5.3540
1959	1	5.3110	5.2360	5.1230	5.4120
1960	1	5.1550	5.5210	5.6840	5.8950
1961	1	5.9380	6.3570	6.1080	6.0410
1962	1	6.1170	6.5600	6.3630	6.4860
1963	1	6.6340	6.6880	6.6980	6.7530
1964	1	6.8820	7.1590	7.3030	7.5860
1965	1	7.4760	7.9920	8.0480	8.2480
1966	1	8.1660	8.9300	8.6350	8.8360
1967	1	8.6040	9.5280	8.9460	9.0960
1968	1	8.8480	9.5360	9.1150	9.2670
1969	1	9.3610	9.9290	9.6800	9.8670
1970	1	9.8540	10.3470	10.5610	10.6610
1971	1	10.7690	11.1480	10.8290	11.0110
1972	1	12.0650	12.3230	12.6330	12.0260
1973	1	14.5730	13.3230	12.5580	12.6260
1974	1	12.6570	13.8000	13.4260	13.6060
1975	1	13.7090	15.4980	14.9180	15.2680
1976	1	15.5940	16.8320	16.3140	16.7700
1977	1	16.8440			

NETHER_NEMHQSDR

1955	1	4.3634	4.4011	4.5178	4.6423
1956	1	4.7225	4.7992	4.7820	4.7113
1957	1	4.6465	4.6522	4.7195	4.7208
1958	1	4.8258	4.8966	5.0528	5.3078
1959	1	5.3860	5.1862	5.1401	5.3817
1960	1	5.2273	5.4447	5.7074	5.8839
1961	1	6.0190	6.2492	6.1335	6.0457
1962	1	6.2004	6.4392	6.3831	6.5016
1963	1	6.7309	6.5555	6.7195	6.7661
1964	1	6.9934	7.0104	7.3287	7.5899
1965	1	7.6199	7.8055	8.0874	8.2412
1966	1	8.3479	8.6919	8.6912	8.8288
1967	1	8.8081	9.2463	9.0182	9.1025
1968	1	9.0393	9.2518	9.1928	9.3021
1969	1	9.5141	9.6563	9.7572	9.9417
1970	1	9.9524	10.0900	10.6449	10.7721
1971	1	10.8301	10.8826	10.9151	11.1483
1972	1	12.1281	11.9937	12.7523	12.1882
1973	1	14.6844	12.9061	12.6901	12.8017
1974	1	12.8115	13.2887	13.5895	13.7868
1975	1	13.9420	14.8621	15.1019	15.4607
1976	1	15.9250	16.0913	16.5165	16.9821
1977	1	17.2315			

NETHER_NEFHQNTL

1955	1	4.8031	4.8107	4.7046	4.8381
1956	1	4.8680	4.5984	4.3039	4.0590
1957	1	3.9380	3.8540	3.4900	3.9960
1958	1	4.6840	4.9060	5.0710	5.4540
1959	1	5.3890	5.1980	5.2280	5.1300
1960	1	5.2910	5.5350	5.9070	6.6270
1961	1	6.0540	6.1720	6.2350	6.1860
1962	1	6.2960	6.4700	6.4190	6.2810
1963	1	6.3060	6.6210	6.6560	6.8540
1964	1	6.6290	6.4590	7.0980	7.5350
1965	1	7.4710	7.2650	7.4670	7.4520
1966	1	7.2540	6.9690	7.2470	7.3920
1967	1	7.2800	7.6520	7.6830	8.2280
1968	1	7.5670	7.2050	7.2390	7.1080
1969	1	7.0570	7.0860	7.2350	7.5410
1970	1	7.9520	7.7580	8.9230	9.7340
1971	1	10.8440	10.7220	10.6530	10.2370
1972	1	12.0555	12.4330	14.1014	13.6913
1973	1	16.1026	15.1153	13.7359	17.7827
1974	1	16.0858	14.6869	17.7139	17.2609
1975	1	16.9760	16.0680	17.3560	17.6472
1976	1	18.0891	14.9802	15.2284	17.0370
1977	1	16.4464			

NETHER_NEFHQSTL

1955	1	4.6930	4.8049	4.8149	4.8443
1956	1	4.7585	4.5984	4.3973	4.0614
1957	1	3.8542	3.8622	3.5542	3.9930
1958	1	4.5984	4.9282	5.1367	5.4474
1959	1	5.3135	5.2279	5.2678	5.1165
1960	1	5.2498	5.5673	5.9218	6.6012
1961	1	6.0429	6.2072	6.2310	6.1451
1962	1	6.3123	6.5168	6.3997	6.2239
1963	1	6.3335	6.6894	6.6286	6.7657
1964	1	6.6679	6.5484	7.0612	7.4142
1965	1	7.5193	7.3911	7.4204	7.3189
1966	1	7.3014	7.0991	7.2014	7.2683
1967	1	7.3045	7.8037	7.6344	8.1241
1968	1	7.5585	7.3329	7.2040	7.0705
1969	1	6.9901	7.2145	7.1938	7.5781
1970	1	7.7991	7.9058	8.8692	9.8634
1971	1	10.5209	11.0123	10.5439	10.4088
1972	1	11.6339	12.8644	13.9234	13.8857
1973	1	15.4817	15.8122	13.5501	17.8630
1974	1	15.4818	15.4861	17.5383	17.1103
1975	1	16.3635	17.0898	17.2357	17.2746
1976	1	17.5108	15.9992	15.1349	16.5905
1977	1	15.9647			

NETHER_NERSQN3T

1955	1	0.009333	0.011633	0.008733	0.009267
1956	1	0.014300	0.019467	0.029967	0.034133
1957	1	0.036800	0.037367	0.045733	0.049400
1958	1	0.039733	0.031067	0.027767	0.025600
1959	1	0.018567	0.017167	0.017200	0.022300
1960	1	0.024967	0.023933	0.021167	0.017133
1961	1	0.011800	0.008400	0.009133	0.016100
1962	1	0.014067	0.023500	0.018033	0.019700
1963	1	0.018600	0.019567	0.019500	0.021400
1964	1	0.025600	0.033800	0.039967	0.038633
1965	1	0.034167	0.039833	0.041667	0.042800
1966	1	0.044933	0.049033	0.049833	0.050967
1967	1	0.048867	0.046500	0.046167	0.046200
1968	1	0.044000	0.045500	0.045900	0.046600
1969	1	0.051000	0.056233	0.060000	0.061200
1970	1	0.061800	0.061800	0.061800	0.060600
1971	1	0.051833	0.040500	0.043367	0.042467
1972	1	0.030867	0.019433	0.009833	0.027933
1973	1	0.023967	0.026567	0.059500	0.058767
1974	1	0.065967	0.071933	0.077967	0.072133
1975	1	0.066400	0.039867	0.029433	0.047800
1976	1	0.034333	0.042433	0.089600	0.074367
1977	1	0.053133			

NETHER_NERLQNGB

1955	1	0.032400	0.031867	0.032567	0.033600
1956	1	0.034133	0.037533	0.039833	0.041967
1957	1	0.043200	0.043633	0.047233	0.049100
1958	1	0.045267	0.041833	0.042233	0.043433
1959	1	0.041300	0.040433	0.041100	0.041900
1960	1	0.042867	0.042767	0.041500	0.041033
1961	1	0.039633	0.037900	0.039033	0.039967
1962	1	0.039867	0.042700	0.043433	0.042400
1963	1	0.041500	0.041100	0.041400	0.044967
1964	1	0.046667	0.047600	0.050667	0.051867
1965	1	0.048533	0.051333	0.052800	0.055900
1966	1	0.058367	0.062033	0.064300	0.064800
1967	1	0.059333	0.058667	0.060700	0.061300
1968	1	0.061200	0.061967	0.063333	0.062400
1969	1	0.065533	0.068333	0.071567	0.076333
1970	1	0.076300	0.079733	0.079767	0.077300
1971	1	0.071567	0.069900	0.069167	0.071233
1972	1	0.066833	0.068800	0.064900	0.066167
1973	1	0.067933	0.068200	0.077833	0.078467
1974	1	0.084367	0.089067	0.093433	0.088067
1975	1	0.080767	0.076067	0.081500	0.080033
1976	1	0.072700	0.078933	0.090000	0.082367
1977	1	0.076800			

NETHER_NEYNQSNP

1955	1	28.691	29.902	30.272	31.239
1956	1	31.167	32.116	32.356	33.505
1957	1	34.826	34.762	35.407	35.097
1958	1	34.809	35.871	35.444	36.250
1959	1	36.752	37.389	38.519	39.609
1960	1	41.038	42.343	42.448	43.391
1961	1	44.407	44.927	44.540	45.413
1962	1	46.237	47.931	48.184	49.660
1963	1	50.094	51.072	52.837	55.025
1964	1	59.258	60.030	62.090	64.522
1965	1	66.188	66.978	69.325	71.734
1966	1	72.230	74.454	74.302	76.735
1967	1	78.756	80.722	83.062	84.844
1968	1	87.047	88.612	90.113	95.845
1969	1	98.307	101.454	103.215	106.482
1970	1	109.492	113.264	117.956	119.224
1971	1	124.750	126.822	133.890	133.938
1972	1	140.012	145.580	147.124	156.204
1973	1	161.832	163.808	167.343	172.936
1974	1	177.593	183.649	191.620	195.299
1975	1	195.385	198.812	204.016	213.076
1976	1	224.028	232.298	239.520	246.227

NETHER_NEYRQSN7

1955	1	55.862	57.284	58.074	59.460
1956	1	58.828	59.730	60.246	61.876
1957	1	63.032	62.178	61.270	60.400
1958	1	59.974	61.026	61.420	62.140
1959	1	62.470	63.470	64.256	65.404
1960	1	67.084	69.054	69.466	70.476
1961	1	71.126	71.096	71.016	72.042
1962	1	72.476	73.570	74.640	74.914
1963	1	73.462	76.258	78.012	79.308
1964	1	82.160	82.446	83.424	85.410
1965	1	86.632	86.506	87.956	89.586
1966	1	88.412	90.006	90.360	91.062
1967	1	93.356	94.350	95.122	97.052
1968	1	98.874	99.668	100.628	104.710
1969	1	105.524	107.348	107.376	111.152
1970	1	112.256	114.442	116.104	117.134
1971	1	119.054	119.146	121.610	119.630
1972	1	122.264	124.404	124.304	128.028
1973	1	130.834	129.712	129.676	132.418
1974	1	133.424	135.408	135.666	135.422
1975	1	131.740	130.738	129.946	136.214
1976	1	140.594	142.238	144.281	145.342

NETHER_NEPDQSN7

1955	1	0.51360	0.52200	0.52127	0.52538
1956	1	0.52980	0.53769	0.53707	0.54149
1957	1	0.55251	0.55907	0.57788	0.58108
1958	1	0.58040	0.58780	0.57708	0.58336
1959	1	0.58831	0.58908	0.59946	0.60561
1960	1	0.61174	0.61319	0.61106	0.61568
1961	1	0.62434	0.63192	0.62718	0.63037
1962	1	0.63796	0.65150	0.64555	0.66289
1963	1	0.68190	0.66973	0.67729	0.69381
1964	1	0.72125	0.72811	0.74427	0.75544
1965	1	0.76401	0.77426	0.78818	0.80073
1966	1	0.81697	0.82721	0.82229	0.84267
1967	1	0.84361	0.85556	0.87322	0.87421
1968	1	0.88038	0.88907	0.89551	0.91534
1969	1	0.93161	0.94509	0.96125	0.95798
1970	1	0.97538	0.98971	1.01595	1.01784
1971	1	1.04784	1.06443	1.10098	1.11960
1972	1	1.14516	1.17022	1.18358	1.22008
1973	1	1.23693	1.26286	1.29047	1.30599
1974	1	1.33104	1.35626	1.41244	1.44215
1975	1	1.48311	1.52069	1.57001	1.56427
1976	1	1.59340	1.63320	1.66010	1.69410

NETHER_NEPCQN70

1955	1	0.57591	0.57232	0.57053	0.56515
1956	1	0.57053	0.57591	0.58129	0.58668
1957	1	0.61718	0.62973	0.66023	0.66382
1958	1	0.66203	0.65844	0.64947	0.64947
1959	1	0.65306	0.64947	0.67279	0.67638
1960	1	0.67638	0.67997	0.68535	0.68356
1961	1	0.68081	0.69420	0.68973	0.68973
1962	1	0.69197	0.72322	0.68527	0.68527
1963	1	0.71206	0.72098	0.70536	0.71875
1964	1	0.73661	0.76563	0.76563	0.77009
1965	1	0.77232	0.80804	0.79018	0.79018
1966	1	0.81474	0.84599	0.83036	0.83036
1967	1	0.84592	0.85599	0.86506	0.87034
1968	1	0.87941	0.88847	0.89325	0.90408
1969	1	0.94587	0.96047	0.95720	0.96627
1970	1	0.97835	0.99346	1.00831	1.01989
1971	1	1.04482	1.07123	1.08378	1.10407
1972	1	1.12757	1.15526	1.16364	1.19326
1973	1	1.21193	1.24960	1.25959	1.28889
1974	1	1.31979	1.35972	1.38387	1.42895
1975	1	1.45954	1.50010	1.52973	1.56450
1976	1	1.59000	1.64300	1.65400	1.69600
1977	1	1.70800			

NETHER_NEPCQS70

1955	1	0.57485	0.57246	0.56862	0.56780
1956	1	0.56969	0.57604	0.57938	0.58904
1957	1	0.61673	0.62984	0.65807	0.66596
1958	1	0.66221	0.65832	0.64740	0.65116
1959	1	0.65426	0.64800	0.67132	0.67849
1960	1	0.67801	0.67647	0.68504	0.68651
1961	1	0.68257	0.68813	0.69084	0.69404
1962	1	0.69344	0.71461	0.68752	0.69075
1963	1	0.71346	0.71037	0.70865	0.72559
1964	1	0.73746	0.75371	0.76957	0.77772
1965	1	0.77276	0.79614	0.79379	0.79791
1966	1	0.81461	0.83515	0.83345	0.83784
1967	1	0.84538	0.84681	0.86760	0.87760
1968	1	0.87796	0.88099	0.89552	0.91043
1969	1	0.94405	0.95403	0.95943	0.97173
1970	1	0.97684	0.98752	1.01085	1.02420
1971	1	1.04415	1.06490	1.08693	1.10737
1972	1	1.12774	1.14854	1.16737	1.19535
1973	1	1.21317	1.24235	1.26401	1.28991
1974	1	1.32195	1.35168	1.38927	1.42904
1975	1	1.46246	1.49127	1.53601	1.56393
1976	1	1.59337	1.63359	1.66075	1.69514
1977	1	1.71176			

NETHER_NEIPQN70

1955	1	0.31943	0.34128	0.34128	0.35861
1956	1	0.36596	0.38857	0.37418	0.39782
1957	1	0.38549	0.39680	0.38446	0.38549
1958	1	0.37007	0.39268	0.38960	0.40708
1959	1	0.38960	0.43277	0.42661	0.45231
1960	1	0.45847	0.49548	0.47595	0.50782
1961	1	0.49034	0.49856	0.47595	0.51564
1962	1	0.49146	0.49908	0.49273	0.54225
1963	1	0.49273	0.52701	0.52447	0.58289
1964	1	0.57273	0.59051	0.54987	0.63750
1965	1	0.60067	0.62480	0.58035	0.67178
1966	1	0.64004	0.66924	0.61591	0.71242
1967	1	0.66986	0.68767	0.64313	0.75715
1968	1	0.73755	0.76250	0.70905	0.85692
1969	1	0.83376	0.84801	0.79278	0.95312
1970	1	0.94243	0.92996	0.85870	1.01725
1971	1	1.02082	0.99410	0.91036	1.08852
1972	1	1.10277	1.08139	0.97806	1.19363
1973	1	1.19541	1.14909	1.07667	1.28333
1974	1	1.24333	1.23333	1.11000	1.27667
1975	1	1.19333	1.14333	1.01000	1.27000
1976	1	1.26333	1.24000	1.13333	1.35667

NETHER_NEIPQS70

1955	1	0.32534	0.33429	0.34617	0.35446
1956	1	0.37288	0.38063	0.37953	0.39310
1957	1	0.39286	0.38862	0.39049	0.38023
1958	1	0.37709	0.38489	0.39658	0.40034
1959	1	0.39660	0.42494	0.43594	0.44240
1960	1	0.46625	0.48799	0.48837	0.49398
1961	1	0.49760	0.49228	0.49177	0.49790
1962	1	0.49784	0.49377	0.51303	0.51999
1963	1	0.49829	0.52161	0.55099	0.55516
1964	1	0.57863	0.58388	0.58256	0.60461
1965	1	0.60540	0.61650	0.62072	0.63487
1966	1	0.64270	0.65965	0.66430	0.67209
1967	1	0.66858	0.67841	0.69860	0.71372
1968	1	0.73066	0.75427	0.77408	0.80875
1969	1	0.81866	0.84128	0.87025	0.90014
1970	1	0.91784	0.92550	0.94684	0.96059
1971	1	0.98872	0.99149	1.00719	1.02670
1972	1	1.06534	1.08022	1.08433	1.12353
1973	1	1.15494	1.14844	1.19544	1.20473
1974	1	1.20286	1.23339	1.23314	1.19542
1975	1	1.15663	1.14379	1.12190	1.18737
1976	1	1.22617	1.24059	1.25854	1.26783

NETHER_NEGXQNFD

1955	1	1.8720	1.8720	1.8720	1.8720
1956	1	1.9597	1.9597	1.9597	1.9597
1957	1	1.8760	2.0580	2.0400	2.2820
1958	1	1.9940	2.0220	2.2640	2.7670
1959	1	1.8190	1.9970	2.2980	2.8020
1960	1	2.1240	2.1830	2.5780	3.0840
1961	1	2.5550	2.3710	2.8860	3.6150
1962	1	2.5680	2.7060	3.0680	3.9130
1963	1	2.6760	3.0510	3.2450	4.3910
1964	1	3.0550	3.5000	3.8770	5.0570
1965	1	3.9040	4.2860	4.3640	5.9840
1966	1	4.0410	5.1640	5.1240	6.2130
1967	1	4.9090	6.3300	5.4970	6.6130
1968	1	5.8120	6.6440	6.4880	7.4640
1969	1	6.2320	7.4210	7.5240	8.3150
1970	1	7.1110	7.9310	8.4600	9.5020
1971	1	8.6470	9.4400	9.6600	11.2490
1972	1	9.9890	10.9100	10.4960	12.6830
1973	1	11.0990	12.3110	12.7170	13.7200
1974	1	12.8910	14.3760	14.9320	16.3660
1975	1	15.3390	18.1250	18.3950	20.4390
1976	1	19.1770	21.1360	21.3940	24.0050
1977	1	20.7470			

NETHER_NEGXQSFD

1955	1	1.9422	1.9174	1.8856	1.7483
1956	1	2.0384	2.0204	1.9708	1.8076
1957	1	1.9671	2.1488	2.0437	2.0646
1958	1	2.1160	2.1458	2.2645	2.4386
1959	1	1.9607	2.1600	2.2938	2.4043
1960	1	2.3324	2.3898	2.5827	2.5804
1961	1	2.8620	2.6061	2.9007	2.9821
1962	1	2.9194	2.9533	3.1115	3.2003
1963	1	3.0797	3.2821	3.3155	3.5991
1964	1	3.5380	3.6863	3.9944	4.1863
1965	1	4.5204	4.4191	4.5060	5.0576
1966	1	4.6358	5.2267	5.2909	5.3714
1967	1	5.5649	6.3297	5.6457	5.8529
1968	1	6.5003	6.5983	6.6302	6.7298
1969	1	6.8755	7.3707	7.6385	7.6080
1970	1	7.7484	7.8993	8.5473	8.7789
1971	1	9.3357	9.4300	9.7159	10.4789
1972	1	10.7225	10.8852	10.5412	11.9006
1973	1	11.8602	12.2482	12.7749	12.9321
1974	1	13.7654	14.2394	15.0107	15.4759
1975	1	16.3772	17.9026	18.4965	19.3525
1976	1	20.4939	20.8409	21.5171	22.7359
1977	1	22.1840			

NETHER_NEGDQNFD

1955	1	-0.08475	-0.08475	-0.08475	-0.08475
1956	1	0.01875	0.01875	0.01875	0.01875
1957	1	-0.04700	-0.27000	0.36100	0.30700
1958	1	-0.20200	-0.27300	-0.01900	0.0
1959	1	-0.07300	-0.11000	0.22400	0.14600
1960	1	-0.02300	-0.21300	0.22800	0.35700
1961	1	-0.02100	-0.28000	0.11600	-0.09200
1962	1	-0.01400	-0.29200	0.24500	-0.46900
1963	1	-0.14500	-0.16000	0.28700	-0.28700
1964	1	-0.17100	-0.33700	0.22000	-0.44200
1965	1	0.09000	-0.79300	0.05400	-0.39300
1966	1	-0.05500	-1.27300	-0.12900	-0.14900
1967	1	-0.47900	-1.74200	-0.08600	0.26400
1968	1	-0.74500	-1.95400	0.04400	0.36500
1969	1	-0.91700	-2.12900	0.22600	0.62300
1970	1	-0.78000	-1.58900	0.45300	0.68700
1971	1	-1.08000	-2.34300	0.97700	0.78700
1972	1	-0.81500	-1.90000	1.53300	1.38600
1973	1	-0.69300	-2.43000	1.02500	2.66900
1974	1	-1.07200	-3.56600	2.49100	1.16600
1975	1	-2.24200	-4.91100	0.53300	0.27500
1976	1	-3.58500	-4.32000	-0.12900	-0.40000
1977	1	-3.76300			

NETHER_NEGDQSFD

1955	1	-0.03647	0.01531	-0.15404	-0.16779
1956	1	0.07020	0.12654	-0.05917	-0.06834
1957	1	0.00637	-0.14299	0.26502	0.21405
1958	1	-0.14600	-0.11993	-0.14356	-0.08943
1959	1	-0.01716	0.06974	0.05786	0.08207
1960	1	0.02615	-0.01653	0.01944	0.33532
1961	1	0.00973	-0.06779	-0.12863	-0.07226
1962	1	-0.01834	-0.04287	-0.02620	-0.43506
1963	1	-0.19877	0.17137	-0.00748	-0.28567
1964	1	-0.27726	0.12946	-0.09210	-0.54796
1965	1	-0.04386	-0.14002	-0.28761	-0.67327
1966	1	-0.17451	-0.39971	-0.52586	-0.64615
1967	1	-0.53099	-0.64280	-0.57511	-0.45515
1968	1	-0.68469	-0.63784	-0.58161	-0.55209
1969	1	-0.71445	-0.61669	-0.56520	-0.45807
1970	1	-0.44083	0.11790	-0.50352	-0.56480
1971	1	-0.61105	-0.40625	-0.17532	-0.63127
1972	1	-0.23388	0.31519	0.15573	-0.21987
1973	1	0.04393	0.03513	-0.58007	0.89773
1974	1	-0.17695	-0.90899	0.71430	-0.76448
1975	1	-1.18283	-2.14233	-1.37154	-1.74526
1976	1	-2.42397	-1.48109	-2.12189	-2.44269
1977	1	-2.53884			

NETHER_NEPPQNIN

1954	1		0.010620	0.010652	0.010685
1955	1	0.010717	0.010750	0.010785	0.010820
1956	1	0.010855	0.010890	0.010922	0.010955
1957	1	0.010987	0.011020	0.011062	0.011105
1958	1	0.011147	0.011190	0.011230	0.011270
1959	1	0.011310	0.011350	0.011382	0.011415
1960	1	0.011447	0.011480	0.011520	0.011560
1961	1	0.011600	0.011640	0.011680	0.011720
1962	1	0.011760	0.011800	0.011842	0.011885
1963	1	0.011927	0.011970	0.012007	0.012045
1964	1	0.012082	0.012120	0.012162	0.012205
1965	1	0.012247	0.012290	0.012330	0.012370
1966	1	0.012410	0.012450	0.012487	0.012525
1967	1	0.012562	0.012600	0.012630	0.012660
1968	1	0.012690	0.012720	0.012757	0.012795
1969	1	0.012832	0.012870	0.012910	0.012950
1970	1	0.012990	0.013030	0.013070	0.013110
1971	1	0.013150	0.013190	0.013225	0.013260
1972	1	0.013295	0.013330	0.013357	0.013385
1973	1	0.013412	0.013440	0.013465	0.013490
1974	1	0.013515	0.013540	0.013567	0.013595
1975	1	0.013622	0.013650	0.013680	0.013710
1976	1	0.013740	0.013770	0.013800	0.013830

NETHER_NEURQSSE

1955	1	0.014810	0.013530	0.012760	0.011990
1956	1	0.011710	0.009720	0.009460	0.008950
1957	1	0.009410	0.011310	0.013470	0.016840
1958	1	0.021850	0.026660	0.024520	0.023080
1959	1	0.021150	0.019400	0.017890	0.016190
1960	1	0.013540	0.012530	0.010850	0.010360
1961	1	0.008930	0.008440	0.008170	0.008120
1962	1	0.007610	0.007810	0.008230	0.008430
1963	1	0.009070	0.007930	0.007460	0.007200
1964	1	0.007150	0.006910	0.007100	0.007300
1965	1	0.007730	0.008160	0.007930	0.007910
1966	1	0.008970	0.008950	0.009810	0.012400
1967	1	0.017150	0.019730	0.020380	0.020780
1968	1	0.019260	0.018960	0.018020	0.016060
1969	1	0.014300	0.014240	0.014200	0.013350
1970	1	0.012670	0.011780	0.011360	0.011330
1971	1	0.012140	0.012920	0.014590	0.017930
1972	1	0.021890	0.023760	0.025010	0.025210
1973	1	0.023730	0.024760	0.024530	0.024300
1974	1	0.026070	0.027920	0.030840	0.033580
1975	1	0.036980	0.041990	0.045310	0.046160
1976	1	0.047230	0.048650	0.050410	0.053240

Sources and Notes on Time Series for the United Kingdom

Most data were obtained directly from the publications of the Bank of England (BOE) and the British Central Statistical Office (CSO). Assistance in obtaining other British publications not readily available was provided by Elizabeth Rumbold of the British Information Service in New York.

All the time series are on a quarterly basis in seasonally unadjusted and adjusted form and cover the period from 1955I to 1976IV, except where noted otherwise. We made the seasonal adjustment using the Census X-11 program available on the TROLL system.

I. INTERNATIONAL VARIABLES

A. *Balance of Payments*

    UKBPQNCF   Balance of Payments. Unit: Billions of Pounds at Quarterly
    UKBPQSCF   Rates.

Source: For 1955–57, from BOE, *Statistical Abstract I (1970)*, table 19, "Balance of Payments," and CSO, *United Kingdom Balance of Payments*, table 1, "General Balance of Payments," Cmnd. 122 and 273. For the period 1958I to 1976IV, the sources for this series are the BOE publications: *Statistical Abstract I (1970)*, table 19, "Balance of Payments"; *Statistical Abstract II (1975)*, table 20, "Balance of Payments"; *Quarterly Bulletin*, table 19, June 1976, and table 25, June 1977, "Balance of Payments."

Description: The definition we used is a measure of the overall balance of payments, including both current account and capital account transactions, referred to in official British sources as "total currency flow." The difference between this total and the balance of official reserve transactions published in official United States publications is that the British definition includes only a portion of United Kingdom liabilities to foreign monetary institutions. We were unable to obtain complete and consistent quarterly data for these additional liabilities and thus used the total currency flow measure. The following procedure was used to estimate the official settlements balance of payments for the period 1955I to 1957IV:

1) Annual data for these years indicated that for the years 1955 and 1957 official settlements took the form solely of drawings on or additions to official re-

serves. Thus quarterly estimates were obtained by taking the first difference in the official (stock of) reserves, e.g. $BP_{1955I} = FH_{1955I} - FH_{1954IV}$.

2) For 1956 official settlements not only took the form of drawings on or additions to official reserves but also included some official borrowings. Work done by Peter B. Kenen, *British Monetary Policy and the Balance of Payments: 1951–1957*, Harvard University Press (Cambridge, Mass.), 1960, directed us to the CSO publications, listed above, which detailed on a semiannual basis the data we required. The sum of these half-year figures corresponds exactly with our annual series. Moreover the reserve part of official financing for the first half of 1956 corresponds with the sum of the first two quarters for 1956 of the series of first differences in official reserves. Hence we estimated the balance-of-payments figures for 1956I to 1956IV as quarterly changes in official reserves plus one-half of the appropriate semiannual official borrowing figure.

B. *Exports*

1. Total Exports

    UKEXQNCA   Total Exports. Unit: Billions of Pounds at Annual Rates.
    UKEXQSCA

Source: For 1955–59, from our own estimates. For 1960–76, the British Central Statistical Office (CSO) publications: *Economic Trends*, "Balance of Payments: Current Account," and *Financial Statistics*, table 84, "Balance of Payments: Current Account," various issues.

Description: Total current account receipts from exports of goods and services and transfers on a transactions basis. For the period 1955I to 1959IV, complete current account data are available only at annual dates. Quarterly U.K. data on goods exports (f.o.b.) were obtained from *International Financial Statistics* (IFS) for the period 1955 to 1973. We used the IMF U.K. data on goods exports as a regressor for the British data on total exports for the period 1960I to 1973IV and applied the estimated relation to the IMF data to obtain total current account exports for 1955I to 1959IV. The quarterly data were originally in millions of pounds at quarterly rates.

2. Exports of Goods

    UKEXQNGO   Exports of Goods. Unit: Billions of Pounds at Annual
    UKEXQSGO   Rates.

Source: Same as I.B.1, Total Exports, above.

Description: The current account exports of goods (f.o.b.). For the period 1955I to 1959IV, complete current account data are available only at annual dates. Quarterly U.K. data of goods exports (f.o.b.) were obtained from the IMF publication IFS for the period 1955–73. We used the IMF data on goods exports as a regressor for the British data on goods exports for the period 1960I to 1973IV and applied the estimated relation to the IMF data to obtain exports of goods for 1955I to 1959IV. The quarterly data were originally in millions of pounds at annual rates.

3. Exports of Services and Transfers

    UKEXQNST   Exports of Services and Transfers. Unit: Billions of Pounds
    UKEXQSST   at Annual Rates.

Source: Same as I.B.1, Total Exports, above.

Description: Derived by subtracting exports of goods from total exports, as described above.

C. *Imports*

1. Total Imports

UKIMQNCA   Total Imports. Unit: Billions of Pounds at Annual Rates.
UKIMQSCA

Source: For 1955–59, from our own estimates. For 1960–76, from CSO publications: *Economic Trends*, "Balance of Payments: Current Account," and *Financial Statistics*, table 84, "Balance of Payments: Current Account."

Description: Total current account receipts from imports of goods and services and transfers on a transactions basis. For the period 1955I to 1959IV, complete current account data are available only at annual dates. Quarterly U.K. data on goods imports (f.o.b.) were obtained from the IMF publication IFS for the period 1955 to 1973. We used the IMF data on goods imports as a regressor for the British data on total imports for the period 1960I to 1973IV and applied the estimated relation to the IMF data to obtain the total current account imports for 1955I to 1959IV. The quarterly data were originally in millions of pounds at quarterly rates.

2. Imports of Goods

UKIMQNGO   Imports of Goods. Unit: Billions of Pounds at Annual
UKIMQSGO   Rates.

Source: Same as I.C.1, Total Imports, above.

Description: The current account imports of goods (f.o.b.). For the period 1955I to 1959IV, complete current account data are available only at annual dates. Quarterly U.K. data on goods imports (f.o.b.) were obtained from the IMF publication for the period 1955 to 1973. We used the IMF data on goods imports as a regressor for the British data on imports of goods for the period 1960I to 1973IV and applied the estimated relation to the IMF data to obtain imports of goods for 1955I to 1959IV. The quarterly data were originally in millions of pounds at quarterly rates.

3. Imports of Services and Transfers

UKIMQNST   Imports of Services and Transfers. Unit: Billions of Pounds
UKIMQSST   at Annual Rates.

Source: Same as I.C.1, Total Imports, above.

Description: Derived by subtracting imports of goods from total imports as defined above.

D. *Exchange Rate*

UKXRQNLB   Exchange Rate. Unit: Pounds per Dollar.

Source: From BOE, *Quarterly Bulletin*, table 28, "Exchange Rates."

Description: The spot exchange rate of the U.S. dollar is the middle market rate as recorded by the Bank of England during the late afternoon. The data are averages of highs and lows of rates recorded on the last working day of each month and are in pounds.

II. FINANCIAL VARIABLES

A. *Narrow Money Stock (M1)*

UKM1QSDR   Narrow Money Stock. Unit: Billions of Pounds, End-of-
              Quarter.

Source: For 1955 to 1962, from our own estimates. For 1963–76, Bank of England, *Statistical Abstract II*, table 12/1, and subsequent issues of the Bank of England *Quarterly Bulletin* (table 11/1).

Description: M1, currency held by the (nonbank) public plus demand deposits adjusted.

The official U.K. money stock series begins in 1963 on an end-of-quarter basis and in late 1971 on a mid-month basis. Prior to those dates, however, there are monthly estimates of currency held by the public and of current account (demand) deposits and deposit account (time) deposits of the three major classes of U.K. domestic banks: London Clearing, Scottish, and Northern Irish (see Bank of England, *Statistical Abstract I*, tables 4 and 9(1) thru 9(3)). Since the official mid-month series provided no overlap with the earlier data, we used the official quarterly series and extended it back in time.

We first obtained monthly figures for adjusted current account deposits for all three categories of banks for the period 1955I to 1969IV. For the London Clearing banks we used the estimate of float implicit in the official figures for total deposits of this set of banks; i.e. adjusted current accounts equal gross current accounts less the difference between total gross deposits and total net (adjusted) deposits. For the Scottish banks similar estimates of float are available only from October 1960 on; for the Northern Irish there are no such estimates. Hence to estimate float for the period prior to October 1960 for the Scottish banks we assumed that the ratio of float to current accounts was the same for Scottish and London Clearing banks; for the Northern Irish we assumed that the ratio was the same as for the Scottish.

To the sum of the monthly adjusted current accounts of all three classes of banks we added the official monthly estimates of currency. We took quarterly averages of the seasonally adjusted monthly figures centered in the last month of each quarter. The result is our proxy series for M1, which we correlated with the official M1 series over the period of overlap, 1963I to 1969IV. We applied the estimated relation to the proxy to extend the official series back to 1955.

The official series itself also contained a number of breaks for which we had to allow: in 1967IV, 1972I, and 1973I due to inclusion of additional banks and in 1971IV and 1975II due to changes in reporting techniques. In each instance official sources contained figures compiled on both the old and new basis for each quarter in which a break occurred. Hence we used the ratio of the new to the old figures to adjust earlier data for these discontinuities. The data were originally in millions of pounds.

B. *Broader Money Stock (M2)*
    UKM2QSUK   Broader Money Stock. Unit: Billions of Pounds End-of-Quarter.
Source: For 1955–62, from our own estimates. For 1963–76, from Bank of England, *Statistical Abstracts I, II*, table 12(1), entitled "Money Stock: Amounts Outstanding," and corresponding tables in subsequent issues of the *Quarterly Bulletin*.
Description: Official sources provide figures for two broader definitions of money—termed M3 and sterling M3. The first definition is equal to M1 plus the sum of U.K. private and public sector sterling time deposits and U.K. residents' deposits in other currencies, including in each instance CDs. Sterling M3 excludes residents' deposits in other currencies.

To arrive at a broader definition of money, we used the second series, but first obtained estimates of central government deposits from sterling M3. From 1975II on, the figures we used were taken directly from the Bank of England *Quarterly Bulletin*, table 6(1), column entitled "U.K. Residents' Deposits, Central Government, Sterling." Prior to that the official figures only give total central government deposits and do not distinguish between deposits denominated in sterling and deposits denominated in other currencies.

Since the published sterling M3 series contained the same series of breaks as the published M1 described above, we adjusted those figures in the same way as the M1 figures to obtain a continuous series. From this we subtracted our estimates of central government deposits and seasonally adjusted the result, which we designate M2.

To extend this M2 series back in time we first constructed a monthly proxy series for the period 1955I to 1969IV—currency held by the public plus the sum of total deposits of London Clearing, Scottish, and Northern Irish banks, adjusted for float in the same way as current accounts were for M1. We regressed official M2 on the seasonally adjusted quarterly average (centered in the last month of the quarter) of the proxy series for the overlap period 1963I to 1969IV and used the resultant equation to estimate an M2 series for 1955I to 1962IV. The data were originally in millions of pounds.

C *High-powered Money*

UKMHQNQE   High-powered Money. Unit: Billions of Pounds, End-of-
UKMHQSQE   Quarter.

Source: For currency in circulation, from BOE, *Statistical Abstracts I, II*, table 4, and *Quarterly Bulletin*, table 10, "Currency in Circulation."

For the period 1955I to 1963IV, we used various weekly issues of the London *Economist* to obtain Bank of England balance sheet data; for 1964I to 1976IV, from BOE, *Statistical Abstracts I, II*, table 5, and *Quarterly Bulletins*, table 1, "Bank of England" balance sheet.

Description: Our definition of high-powered money is the total monetary liabilities of the monetary authorities to both banks and nonbanks. To construct such a series we added total currency outstanding to the sum of the following three categories of deposits at the Bank of England: special deposits (of banks), bankers' deposits, and other accounts. The data were originally in millions of pounds.

D. *Official International Reserve Assets*

UKFHQNQE   Official International Reserve Assets. Unit: Billions of
UKFHQSQE   Pounds, End-of-Quarter.

Source: For 1955–70, from BOE, *Statistical Abstracts I, II*, table entitled "Reserves and Related Items." For 1971–76, from BOE, *Quarterly Bulletin*, table 23, "Reserves and Related Items," various issues.

Description: This measures the gold and convertible currency holdings and SDRs of the Bank of England. The data were originally in millions of pounds.

E. *Interest Rates*

1. Short-Term

UKRSQN3T   Short-Term Interest Rate. Unit: Decimal Rate per Annum.

Source: For 1955–69, from BOE, *Statistical Abstract I*, table 28, "Exchange Rates and Comparative Interest Rate"; for 1970–73, from BOE, *Statistical Abstract II*, table 28; for 1974–76, from BOE, *Quarterly Bulletin*, table 28, various issues.

Description: The average rate of discount for 91-day U.K. Treasury bills after the weekly redemption derived from a representative London discount market selling rate expressed as a yield per annum. The data were originally in percent per annum.

2. Long-Term

UKRLQN25   Long-Term Interest Rate. Unit: Decimal Rate per Annum.

Source: For 1955–73, from CSO, *Annual Abstract of Statistics*, table entitled "Security Prices and Yields," 1965, 1966, 1967, 1968, 1971, 1974 issues; for 1974–76, from CSO, *Financial Statistics*, table entitled "British Government Securities," October 1976, July 1977 issues.

Description: The average flat yield on 2½% consols. The data are averages of working days based on the mean of the middle opening and closing prices excluding gross accrued interest and ignoring taxes. The data were originally in percent per annum.

III. NONFINANCIAL DOMESTIC VARIABLES

A. *National Product*

1. Nominal Gross Domestic Product

UKYNQNGD   Gross Domestic Product at Current Prices. Unit: Billions of
UKYNQSGD   Pounds at Annual Rates.

Source: From CSO, *Economic Trends*, table enitled "Expenditure on the Gross Domestic Product," annual supplement, 1977.

Description: This measures the final expenditures on goods and services at current factor costs, equivalent to the total income and product of the geographic region less net factor income from abroad. The figures were originally in millions of pounds at quarterly rates.

2. Real Gross Domestic Product

UKYRQND7   Gross Domestic Product at 1970 Prices. Unit: Billions of
UKYRQSD7   Pounds at Annual Rates.

Source: Same as III.A.1, Nominal GDP, above.

Description: This measures the final expenditures on goods and services at 1970 factor costs, equivalent to the total income and product of the geographic region less net factor income from abroad. The figures were originally in millions of pounds at quarterly rates.

B. *Prices*

1. Implicit Price Deflator

UKPDQND7   GDP Implicit Price Deflator. Unit: 1970 = 1.00.
UKPDQSD7

Source: Same as III.A.1, Nominal GDP, above.

Description: Derived by computing the ratio of nominal to real GDP, described above.

2. Consumer Prices

UKPCQN70   Consumer Price Index. Unit: 1970 = 1.00.
UKPCQS70

Source: From CSO, *Economic Trends*, table entitled "Prices," annual supplement, 1977.

Description: A general index of retail prices including all items. The data were originally in percentage form.

C. *Industrial Production*

UKIPQS70   Industrial Production Index. Unit: 1970 = 1.00.

Source: From CSO, *Economic Trends*, table entitled "Index of Industrial Production," annual supplement 1977.

Description: A general index of industrial production including the mining, manufacturing, utility, and construction industries. The data were originally in seasonally adjusted and percentage form.

D. *Government Accounts*
 1. Government Expenditure
    UKGXQNCG   Central Government Expenditure. Unit: Billions of
    UKGXQSCG   Pounds at Annual Rates.

Source: For 1955–58, from our own estimates; for 1959–62, from CSO, *Economic Trends*, table F, October issues for 1966, 1968, 1970, and 1972; for 1963–71, from BOE, *Statistical Abstract II* (1975), table 1, "Central Government: Current and Capital Accounts"; for 1972–76, from CSO, *Financial Statistics*, table entitled "Central Government," October 1976 and July 1977.

Description: Expenditure of the central government including current and capital transactions. For the period 1955I to 1958IV, the total expenditures of the central government were estimated from the current account expenditures of the central government. We first regressed (in double-log form) total expenditures on current expenditures for the period 1959–76. We then used this relation to estimate total expenditures based on data for current expenditures for 1955–58. The data were originally in millions of pounds at quarterly rates.

 2. Government Deficit
    UKGDQNBR   Central Government Deficit. Unit: Billions of Pounds at
    UKGDQSBR   Annual Rates.

Source: For 1955I–59I, from our own estimates; for 1959II–62IV, from BOE, *Quarterly Bulletin*, table 1, "Exchequer," various issues beginning March 1961 to March 1965; for 1963–69, from BOE, *Statistical Abstract II* (1975), table 2, "Central Government: Borrowing Requirement"; for 1970–76, from BOE, *Quarterly Bulletin*, table 7, "Central Government: Borrowing Requirement."

Description: The central government's borrowing requirement including the borrowing requirement of the government of Northern Ireland, with the deficit defined as a negative value.

For the period 1955I to 1959I, data on the central government deficit are not available from British sources. Quarterly data for 1955I to 1963IV on the central government deficit were obtained from the IMF publication *International Financial Statistics*: December 1956, December 1958, and supplement 1967/68 issues. We regressed the British data on the IMF data for the period 1959II to 1963IV and obtained the central government deficit from the estimated relation using the IMF data. The data were originally in millions of pounds at quarterly rates.

E. *Population*
    UKPPQNIN   Population. Unit: Billions of Persons.

Source: UN, *Demographic Yearbook*, various issues.

Description: This series is a straight-line interpolation of mid-year estimates of population. The data were originally in millions of persons.

F. *Labor Force Statistics*
All labor force statistics were obtained from the following publications of CSO:
(i) *British Labor Statistics, Historical Abstract*, table 118, "Total Working Popula-

tion," (ii) *Monthly Digest of Statistics*, table III, "Labour: Distribution of Working Population," (iii) *Economic Trends*, "National Employment and Unemployment."

1. Labor Force
   UKLFQNCV   Civilian Labor Force; Unit: Billions of Persons.
   UKLFQSCV

Description: The total civilian employed and "wholly" unemployed exclusive of individuals in Her Majesty's Service. The data were originally in thousands of persons.

2. Employment
   UKEMQNCV   Civilian Employment. Unit: Billions of Persons.
   UKEMQSCV

Description: Total civilian employment inclusive of employers and self-employed. The data were originally in thousands of persons.

3. Unemployment
   UKUNQNWH   Unemployment. Unit: Billions of Persons.
   UKUNQSWH

Description: Defined as the number "wholly" unemployed, i.e. only those seeking full-time employment. The data were originally in thousands of persons.

4. Unemployment Rate
   UKURQNDR   Unemployment Rate. Unit: Decimal Rate per Annum.
   UKURQSDR

Description: Derived by computing the ratio of "wholly" unemployed to the civilian labor force. The data are in decimal form.

List of Tables for the United Kingdom (Quarterly Data)

UK_UKBPQNCF

1955	1	-0.03300	0.00400	-0.11900	-0.08100
1956	1	-0.05800	-0.05800	-0.02150	-0.02150
1957	1	0.02700	0.02400	-0.18900	0.15100
1958	1	0.17700	0.11400	0.01700	-0.01800
1959	1	0.09600	0.07000	0.04500	-0.19300
1960	1	0.03100	0.05800	0.13300	0.10300
1961	1	-0.26600	-0.20500	0.03800	0.09400
1962	1	0.13700	0.08400	-0.03600	0.00700
1963	1	-0.08600	0.05000	0.00600	-0.02800
1964	1	0.00100	0.01200	-0.12600	-0.58200
1965	1	-0.16600	-0.16600	-0.19600	0.17500
1966	1	0.04800	-0.16300	-0.48800	0.05600
1967	1	0.50900	-0.01200	-0.50600	-0.66200
1968	1	-0.51900	-0.52100	-0.02400	-0.34600
1969	1	0.27200	0.08200	-0.04700	0.43600
1970	1	0.91500	0.22700	-0.20200	0.34700
1971	1	0.97300	0.63400	0.66800	0.95300
1972	1	0.05700	-1.04500	-0.07900	-0.19800
1973	1	0.06900	0.37700	-0.25800	0.02200
1974	1	-0.03900	-0.32400	-0.00600	-0.99700
1975	1	-0.32600	-0.57200	-0.21300	-0.35400
1976	1	-0.67800	-1.95500	-0.86200	-0.13300
1977	1	-4.20372			

UK_UKBPQSCF

1954	1				0.84400
1955	1	-0.06086	-0.02056	-0.08568	-0.06090
1956	1	-0.08685	-0.08077	0.00569	0.00543
1957	1	-0.00522	0.00785	-0.17479	0.18415
1958	1	0.14683	0.10612	0.01390	0.01981
1959	1	0.07044	0.06956	0.02959	-0.16042
1960	1	0.01896	0.05776	0.11229	0.13000
1961	1	-0.26848	-0.21263	0.02828	0.11187
1962	1	0.13556	0.06521	-0.01858	0.01684
1963	1	-0.10319	0.01591	0.07271	-0.02683
1964	1	-0.05281	-0.02588	-0.01074	-0.58242
1965	1	-0.26908	-0.19930	-0.03426	0.17303
1966	1	-0.10997	-0.17772	-0.28976	0.04958
1967	1	0.29897	-0.00275	-0.27297	-0.68070
1968	1	-0.77845	-0.47096	0.23053	-0.39901
1969	1	-0.01314	0.19693	0.18707	0.35177
1970	1	0.63010	0.40111	-0.00266	0.22192
1971	1	0.72010	0.86272	0.79408	0.82428
1972	1	-0.15812	-0.78552	-0.02196	-0.32747
1973	1	-0.11206	0.68368	-0.28977	-0.08745
1974	1	-0.19531	-0.00099	-0.07685	-1.10434
1975	1	-0.47390	-0.22584	-0.31279	-0.45467
1976	1	-0.82213	-1.60875	-0.96512	-0.23302

UK_UKEXQNCA

1955	1	5.0044	4.3822	4.9093	5.2706
1956	1	5.2706	5.5176	4.9727	5.6694
1957	1	5.7327	5.7517	5.4100	5.7137
1958	1	5.6252	5.2960	5.3593	5.6062
1959	1	5.3277	5.6631	5.2960	6.0424
1960	1	5.9680	5.9200	5.8240	6.0400
1961	1	6.1760	6.1880	6.1480	6.1200
1962	1	6.2440	6.5360	6.2360	6.3520
1963	1	6.5880	6.8040	6.7240	6.9320
1964	1	7.2040	7.3440	6.9960	7.3080
1965	1	7.4240	7.8600	7.8080	8.0440
1966	1	8.1480	8.0520	8.1560	8.5800
1967	1	8.5080	8.6200	8.4520	8.3600
1968	1	9.8800	10.1040	10.4480	10.4760
1969	1	10.7280	11.7240	11.7760	12.0280
1970	1	12.3440	13.2400	12.7120	14.0600
1971	1	13.2760	15.1040	14.9360	14.9840
1972	1	14.5600	15.8120	14.3920	17.2760
1973	1	17.8000	20.1520	20.6000	22.9680
1974	1	23.9640	26.8600	27.1200	28.1680
1975	1	28.2160	30.1480	30.3440	33.3120
1976	1	34.7560	38.6320	40.0840	43.5440
1977	1	44.2600	47.7440		

UK_UKEXQSCA

1955	1	4.9268	4.3798	5.1238	5.1345
1956	1	5.1944	5.5213	5.1787	5.5183
1957	1	5.6666	5.7552	5.6180	5.5611
1958	1	5.5781	5.3009	5.5331	5.4755
1959	1	5.2935	5.6666	5.4313	5.9370
1960	1	5.9378	5.9109	5.9362	5.9838
1961	1	6.1474	6.1458	6.2547	6.1035
1962	1	6.2164	6.4561	6.3441	6.3658
1963	1	6.5508	6.7053	6.8449	6.9512
1964	1	7.1682	7.2323	7.1235	7.3183
1965	1	7.3970	7.7484	7.9378	8.0422
1966	1	8.1446	7.9413	8.2587	8.5869
1967	1	8.5339	8.4890	8.5320	8.3721
1968	1	9.9652	9.9090	10.5254	10.5049
1969	1	10.8760	11.4337	11.8786	12.0434
1970	1	12.5846	12.8413	12.8591	14.0477
1971	1	13.5742	14.6062	15.1687	14.9108
1972	1	14.9090	15.2918	14.6467	17.1464
1973	1	18.2104	19.5357	20.9780	22.7518
1974	1	24.4836	26.1201	27.5867	27.8968
1975	1	28.7811	29.3933	30.8331	32.9860
1976	1	35.4271	37.7277	40.6682	43.1488
1977	1	45.0924	46.6561		

UK_UKEXQNGO

1955	1	3.1587	2.7685	3.0990	3.3255
1956	1	3.3255	3.4802	3.1388	3.5752
1957	1	3.6148	3.6267	3.4128	3.6030
1958	1	3.5475	3.3413	3.3810	3.5356
1959	1	3.3640	3.5400	3.3240	3.8000
1960	1	3.8760	3.7760	3.4520	3.8080
1961	1	3.9480	3.9480	3.6720	3.9640
1962	1	3.9480	4.1440	3.7680	4.1160
1963	1	4.2280	4.3480	4.0680	4.5040
1964	1	4.6160	4.6800	4.2280	4.7480
1965	1	4.6920	4.9680	4.7400	5.2520
1966	1	5.3200	5.0240	5.0080	5.7520
1967	1	5.5720	5.5640	4.9480	4.8800
1968	1	6.3320	6.2600	6.2840	6.8560
1969	1	6.6760	7.4320	7.1800	7.7880
1970	1	7.8640	8.2960	7.3680	8.9560
1971	1	8.1320	9.5080	9.0520	9.5520
1972	1	8.9520	9.8120	7.9360	11.0600
1973	1	11.0360	11.9560	11.9160	13.5520
1974	1	14.4280	16.9480	16.7680	18.0080
1975	1	18.0400	19.3840	18.6720	21.7480
1976	1	22.8680	25.2880	24.7800	28.7280
1977	1	30.2080	32.3560		

UK UKEXQSGO

1955	1	3.1245	2.7277	3.2535	3.2550
1956	1	3.2898	3.4275	3.2987	3.4983
1957	1	3.5740	3.5675	3.5983	3.5234
1958	1	3.5003	3.2858	3.5748	3.4588
1959	1	3.3103	3.4796	3.5235	3.7206
1960	1	3.8059	3.7080	3.6651	3.7346
1961	1	3.8712	3.8675	3.9102	3.8875
1962	1	3.8718	4.0522	4.0189	4.0332
1963	1	4.1481	4.2541	4.3396	4.4010
1964	1	4.5406	4.5810	4.5085	4.6273
1965	1	4.6253	4.8711	5.0444	5.1042
1966	1	5.2697	4.9259	5.3055	5.5935
1967	1	5.5447	5.4459	5.2257	4.7379
1968	1	6.3576	6.0938	6.6191	6.6584
1969	1	6.7544	7.1883	7.5701	7.5429
1970	1	8.0202	7.9813	7.7651	8.6812
1971	1	8.3118	9.1257	9.5490	9.2557
1972	1	9.1540	9.4173	8.3569	10.7573
1973	1	11.2417	11.4903	12.5361	13.2276
1974	1	14.6274	16.3301	17.5892	17.6679
1975	1	18.2039	18.6983	19.5785	21.3819
1976	1	23.0292	24.4069	25.9549	28.2924
1977	1	30.4004	31.2091		

UK_UKEXQNST

1955	1	1.8458	1.6137	1.8103	1.9452
1956	1	1.9452	2.0374	1.8339	2.0942
1957	1	2.1179	2.1249	1.9972	2.1108
1958	1	2.0777	1.9546	1.9783	2.0705
1959	1	1.9636	2.1231	1.9720	2.2424
1960	1	2.0920	2.1440	2.3720	2.2320
1961	1	2.2280	2.2400	2.4760	2.1560
1962	1	2.2960	2.3920	2.4680	2.2360
1963	1	2.3600	2.4560	2.6560	2.4280
1964	1	2.5880	2.6640	2.7680	2.5600
1965	1	2.7320	2.8920	3.0680	2.7920
1966	1	2.8280	3.0280	3.1480	2.8280
1967	1	2.9360	3.0560	3.5040	3.4800
1968	1	3.5480	3.8440	4.1640	3.6200
1969	1	4.0520	4.2920	4.5960	4.2400
1970	1	4.4800	4.9440	5.3440	5.1040
1971	1	5.1440	5.5960	5.8840	5.4320
1972	1	5.6080	6.0000	6.4560	6.2160
1973	1	6.7640	8.1960	8.6840	9.4160
1974	1	9.5360	9.9120	10.3520	10.1600
1975	1	10.1760	10.7640	11.6720	11.5640
1976	1	11.8880	13.3440	15.3040	14.8160
1977	1	14.0520	15.3880		

UK_UKEXQSST

1955	1	1.8149	1.6116	1.8863	1.8990
1956	1	1.9197	2.0361	1.9011	2.0439
1957	1	2.1059	2.1228	2.0487	2.0650
1958	1	2.0850	1.9563	1.9914	2.0450
1959	1	1.9848	2.1308	1.9426	2.2450
1960	1	2.1258	2.1548	2.2893	2.2738
1961	1	2.2684	2.2464	2.3585	2.2300
1962	1	2.3378	2.3894	2.3342	2.3399
1963	1	2.4002	2.4428	2.5088	2.5520
1964	1	2.6343	2.6414	2.6174	2.6863
1965	1	2.7897	2.8636	2.9026	2.9193
1966	1	2.8979	3.0018	2.9724	2.9486
1967	1	3.0223	3.0276	3.3048	3.6223
1968	1	3.6636	3.8058	3.9254	3.7631
1969	1	4.1950	4.2415	4.3357	4.4057
1970	1	4.6414	4.8798	5.0512	5.2941
1971	1	5.3288	5.5214	5.5813	5.6114
1972	1	5.8038	5.9336	6.1456	6.3805
1973	1	6.9966	8.1396	8.2828	9.6013
1974	1	9.8716	9.8833	9.8816	10.3036
1975	1	10.5457	10.7668	11.1452	11.6765
1976	1	12.3437	13.3644	14.6169	14.9278
1977	1	14.6043	15.4241		

UK_UKIMQNCA

1955	1	5.3950	4.8340	5.2668	5.3576
1956	1	5.2882	5.3256	5.0317	5.2401
1957	1	5.7848	5.6300	5.4484	5.3523
1958	1	5.1012	4.9516	5.1546	5.3790
1959	1	5.1238	5.3522	5.3522	5.8510
1960	1	6.0680	6.1200	6.3200	6.3320
1961	1	6.2560	6.2440	6.1520	6.1160
1962	1	6.1080	6.2120	6.3640	6.3120
1963	1	6.2520	6.5240	6.8960	6.9480
1964	1	7.3800	7.5960	7.6600	7.6400
1965	1	7.4720	7.8440	8.0600	7.8640
1966	1	8.1360	8.1280	8.4440	7.8120
1967	1	8.4160	8.7720	8.6800	9.2720
1968	1	10.3960	10.3440	10.7040	10.6120
1969	1	10.7880	11.1040	11.1920	11.4120
1970	1	11.3920	12.5760	12.4240	13.1840
1971	1	13.0200	13.7000	13.4120	13.9360
1972	1	14.6240	14.8920	14.9480	17.1560
1973	1	19.2120	20.1680	21.5320	24.2960
1974	1	27.8760	30.3960	30.4440	31.6560
1975	1	30.9040	31.5640	32.6760	33.6800
1976	1	35.5600	40.2120	41.6280	45.3236
1977	1	46.6320	48.8480		

UK_UKIMQSCA

1955	1	5.2753	4.8866	5.3345	5.3453
1956	1	5.1818	5.3827	5.0946	5.2152
1957	1	5.6923	5.6828	5.5131	5.3138
1958	1	5.0409	4.9948	5.2065	5.3275
1959	1	5.0915	5.3948	5.3855	5.7929
1960	1	6.0604	6.1628	6.3259	6.2841
1961	1	6.2758	6.2718	6.1260	6.0978
1962	1	6.1471	6.2158	6.3129	6.3299
1963	1	6.2958	6.5105	6.8185	7.0104
1964	1	7.4270	7.5496	7.5766	7.7576
1965	1	7.4799	7.7858	7.9873	8.0166
1966	1	8.1072	8.0545	8.4001	7.9751
1967	1	8.3522	8.6881	8.6736	9.4392
1968	1	10.3208	10.2186	10.7629	10.7541
1969	1	10.7102	10.9557	11.3303	11.4865
1970	1	11.3265	12.3933	12.6493	13.2107
1971	1	12.9368	13.5015	13.7122	13.9179
1972	1	14.5267	14.6791	15.3049	17.1251
1973	1	19.0696	19.8961	22.0353	24.2267
1974	1	27.7280	30.0008	31.0518	31.5764
1975	1	30.8597	31.1034	33.2617	33.5550
1976	1	35.6824	39.5547	42.2990	45.1433
1977	1	46.9161	47.9727		

UK_UKIMQNGO

1955	1	3.5175	3.1512	3.4338	3.4930
1956	1	3.4477	3.4721	3.2803	3.4163
1957	1	3.7720	3.6709	3.5523	3.4896
1958	1	3.3257	3.2280	3.3605	3.5070
1959	1	3.4360	3.5480	3.5440	3.8240
1960	1	4.1080	4.1160	4.0320	4.1680
1961	1	4.2240	4.1120	3.7920	3.9240
1962	1	4.1160	4.0880	4.0080	4.1560
1963	1	4.1960	4.3080	4.3440	4.6320
1964	1	5.0720	5.0640	4.9080	5.2280
1965	1	4.9920	5.1560	5.0760	5.3200
1966	1	5.5360	5.3360	5.3720	5.1240
1967	1	5.8400	5.8960	5.4480	6.0000
1968	1	7.1440	7.0080	7.0240	7.2240
1969	1	7.3800	7.4840	7.1880	7.6480
1970	1	7.7400	8.4800	7.8120	8.5520
1971	1	8.6960	8.9640	8.3960	9.0680
1972	1	9.8240	9.9200	9.2440	11.6160
1973	1	13.1440	13.5000	14.2520	16.9760
1974	1	20.0160	22.2600	21.7520	22.9000
1975	1	22.1680	22.1040	22.5200	23.8640
1976	1	25.2160	28.9440	29.1800	32.6080
1977	1	34.1000	35.2760		

UK_UKIMQSGO

1955	1	3.4481	3.1623	3.4910	3.4916
1956	1	3.3822	3.4843	3.3356	3.4125
1957	1	3.7029	3.6800	3.6181	3.4840
1958	1	3.2625	3.2322	3.4324	3.4990
1959	1	3.3684	3.5468	3.6303	3.8143
1960	1	4.0248	4.1055	4.1405	4.1615
1961	1	4.1351	4.0908	3.9024	3.9221
1962	1	4.0287	4.0556	4.1317	4.1600
1963	1	4.1020	4.2730	4.4728	4.6507
1964	1	4.9528	5.0116	5.0552	5.2799
1965	1	4.8464	5.1022	5.2311	5.4005
1966	1	5.3514	5.2670	5.5543	5.2178
1967	1	5.6255	5.8083	5.6528	6.1052
1968	1	6.8911	6.8692	7.3343	7.3257
1969	1	7.1258	7.3185	7.5528	7.7026
1970	1	7.4960	8.2819	8.2486	8.5610
1971	1	8.4373	8.7643	8.8790	9.0369
1972	1	9.5529	9.7183	9.7534	11.5586
1973	1	12.8127	13.2535	14.9693	16.8625
1974	1	19.6133	21.8859	22.6909	22.7386
1975	1	21.8783	21.6889	23.3944	23.6680
1976	1	25.0461	28.3490	30.2246	32.3325
1977	1	33.9840	34.4876		

UK_UKIMQNST

1955	1	1.8775	1.6828	1.8330	1.8646
1956	1	1.8404	1.8534	1.7514	1.8237
1957	1	2.0128	1.9591	1.8961	1.8627
1958	1	1.7755	1.7236	1.7941	1.8720
1959	1	1.6878	1.8042	1.8082	2.0270
1960	1	1.9600	2.0040	2.2880	2.1640
1961	1	2.0320	2.1320	2.3600	2.1920
1962	1	1.9920	2.1240	2.3560	2.1560
1963	1	2.0560	2.2160	2.5520	2.3160
1964	1	2.3080	2.5320	2.7520	2.4120
1965	1	2.4800	2.6880	2.9840	2.5440
1966	1	2.6000	2.7920	3.0720	2.6880
1967	1	2.5760	2.8760	3.2320	3.2720
1968	1	3.2520	3.3360	3.6800	3.3880
1969	1	3.4080	3.6200	4.0040	3.7640
1970	1	3.6520	4.0960	4.6120	4.6320
1971	1	4.3240	4.7360	5.0160	4.8680
1972	1	4.8000	4.9720	5.7040	5.5400
1973	1	6.0680	6.6680	7.2800	7.3200
1974	1	7.8600	8.1360	8.6920	8.7560
1975	1	8.7360	9.4600	10.1560	9.8160
1976	1	10.3440	11.2680	12.4480	12.7156
1977	1	12.5320	13.5720		

UK_UKIMQSST

1955	1	1.8331	1.7211	1.8445	1.8496
1956	1	1.8068	1.8961	1.7571	1.7994
1957	1	1.9985	2.0032	1.8884	1.8274
1958	1	1.7888	1.7651	1.7641	1.8284
1959	1	1.7310	1.8507	1.7481	1.9794
1960	1	2.0437	2.0581	2.1705	2.1258
1961	1	2.1482	2.1838	2.2014	2.1797
1962	1	2.1223	2.1635	2.1720	2.1732
1963	1	2.1970	2.2430	2.3377	2.3598
1964	1	2.4678	2.5484	2.5180	2.4725
1965	1	2.6457	2.6994	2.7341	2.6133
1966	1	2.7631	2.8054	2.8246	2.7546
1967	1	2.7293	2.8939	2.9863	3.3370
1968	1	3.4378	3.3591	3.4233	3.4361
1969	1	3.5913	3.6486	3.7465	3.8087
1970	1	3.8289	4.1268	4.3429	4.6867
1971	1	4.5030	4.7691	4.7511	4.9304
1972	1	4.9698	4.9950	5.4381	5.6162
1973	1	6.2461	6.6947	6.9706	7.4228
1974	1	8.0720	8.1488	8.3547	8.8723
1975	1	8.9708	9.4541	9.7918	9.9182
1976	1	10.6548	11.2269	12.0288	12.8205
1977	1	12.9316	13.5121		

UK_UKKPQNDR

1955	1	0.35978	0.42070	0.28771	0.15858
1956	1	0.09225	-0.03802	0.19401	-0.10641
1957	1	0.22014	0.10416	-0.22942	-0.14241
1958	1	-0.35100	-0.16600	-0.28100	-0.10800
1959	1	-0.04400	0.46200	0.05700	0.38300
1960	1	0.17900	0.37800	0.67300	0.56300
1961	1	-0.19400	-0.14500	-0.03000	0.22200
1962	1	0.02900	-0.15200	0.12400	0.15900
1963	1	-0.42200	-0.15800	0.21000	0.20800
1964	1	0.28900	0.33200	0.66200	-0.09400
1965	1	-0.02200	-0.12600	0.16800	0.07500
1966	1	0.18000	-0.13500	-0.12800	-0.54000
1967	1	0.49700	0.11600	-0.21800	0.37400
1968	1	0.11700	-0.45300	0.18000	-0.22200
1969	1	0.45600	-0.50200	-0.76700	0.10400
1970	1	0.12300	-0.31300	-0.44600	-0.20100
1971	1	0.92500	-0.57400	-0.69200	0.46900
1972	1	0.27700	-1.72900	0.50900	0.18600
1973	1	1.64500	0.52500	0.57800	1.81800
1974	1	4.11300	3.34800	3.55400	3.12700
1975	1	2.67400	0.90800	2.05100	0.68600
1976	1	0.47000	-0.13500	0.84200	1.72700

UK_UKKPQSDR

1955	1	0.35712	0.40619	0.32049	0.13699
1956	1	0.09965	-0.05526	0.22577	-0.13956
1957	1	0.24408	0.09235	-0.20671	-0.20046
1958	1	-0.29612	-0.16989	-0.26800	-0.20326
1959	1	0.04542	0.48138	0.04554	0.25543
1960	1	0.29936	0.42345	0.63213	0.42088
1961	1	-0.06268	-0.06623	-0.11405	0.10020
1962	1	0.14976	-0.05891	0.01533	0.08133
1963	1	-0.33933	-0.06217	0.08670	0.20739
1964	1	0.29933	0.41495	0.56844	-0.03710
1965	1	-0.09965	-0.03823	0.10587	0.18812
1966	1	-0.00702	-0.03312	-0.10852	-0.44154
1967	1	0.21983	0.25091	-0.12092	0.45855
1968	1	-0.27761	-0.26986	0.40143	-0.22781
1969	1	-0.01981	-0.24945	-0.47309	0.06172
1970	1	-0.46251	0.00509	-0.06830	-0.29512
1971	1	0.26457	-0.19613	-0.30137	0.39829
1972	1	-0.46608	-1.29712	0.89737	0.10209
1973	1	0.90043	1.00602	0.89581	1.75266
1974	1	3.38530	3.85732	3.81957	3.04785
1975	1	1.99816	1.42794	2.27153	0.60443
1976	1	-0.18639	0.39719	1.04699	1.62646

UK_UKM2QSUK

1955	1	8.6469	8.5029	8.3953	8.3122
1956	1	8.2602	8.2102	8.2824	8.3501
1957	1	8.2857	8.4487	8.4634	8.3685
1958	1	8.2791	8.2289	8.0602	8.4979
1959	1	8.7874	8.9037	9.2954	9.5536
1960	1	9.5271	9.4980	9.4817	9.4470
1961	1	9.6750	9.8891	9.6923	9.6397
1962	1	9.7259	9.7895	9.9351	10.0997
1963	1	10.7172	10.9138	11.0689	11.3576
1964	1	11.4711	11.6437	11.8785	11.9890
1965	1	12.1469	12.4208	12.5935	12.9004
1966	1	13.2117	13.2218	13.3819	13.3289
1967	1	13.5728	13.8649	14.3448	14.5623
1968	1	14.7835	15.1626	15.3061	15.5239
1969	1	15.6855	15.4157	15.6153	15.8663
1970	1	15.9351	16.4781	16.9503	17.3499
1971	1	17.9712	18.3006	18.8125	19.8112
1972	1	20.8024	22.3026	23.2271	24.5908
1973	1	26.0652	27.4272	29.4859	31.1133
1974	1	32.2076	32.5864	32.9380	34.4311
1975	1	32.9556	35.6892	36.4018	36.5714
1976	1	37.4084	38.4848	39.7620	40.1446

UK_UKMHQNQE

1955	1	2.2961	2.3786	2.3714	2.4027
1956	1	2.4010	2.4713	2.4922	2.5118
1957	1	2.4868	2.5700	2.5913	2.6212
1958	1	2.5930	2.6437	2.6472	2.6782
1959	1	2.6518	2.7221	2.7576	2.7843
1960	1	2.7841	2.9235	3.0188	3.0591
1961	1	3.0497	3.1493	3.2093	3.2465
1962	1	3.2211	3.1617	3.1200	3.0540
1963	1	2.9927	3.0660	3.0916	3.1386
1964	1	3.1364	3.2538	3.2815	3.3192
1965	1	3.3574	3.5196	3.5642	3.6252
1966	1	3.6498	3.7669	3.8594	3.8841
1967	1	3.8493	3.9274	3.9754	4.0797
1968	1	4.0736	4.1758	4.2097	4.2689
1969	1	4.2861	4.3501	4.3241	4.3837
1970	1	4.3285	4.4906	4.6335	4.8463
1971	1	5.1457	5.1233	4.8700	4.8197
1972	1	4.8327	5.1103	5.0940	5.5603
1973	1	6.0877	6.4250	6.7707	7.2150
1974	1	7.1190	6.9857	7.3613	7.7130
1975	1	7.7893	8.1213	8.2410	8.3747
1976	1	8.5510	9.0937	9.4210	10.0277
1977	1	9.3740			

UK_UKMHQSQE

1955	1	2.32615	2.36487	2.36459	2.39251
1956	1	2.43242	2.45758	2.48436	2.50093
1957	1	2.51980	2.55669	2.58165	2.60950
1958	1	2.62831	2.63114	2.63557	2.66629
1959	1	2.68856	2.71008	2.74377	2.77252
1960	1	2.82297	2.91068	3.00271	3.04757
1961	1	3.09203	3.13394	3.19226	3.23687
1962	1	3.26517	3.14338	3.10505	3.04702
1963	1	3.03211	3.04603	3.07888	3.13296
1964	1	3.17544	3.23176	3.27079	3.31265
1965	1	3.39645	3.49717	3.55515	3.61700
1966	1	3.68796	3.74527	3.85461	3.87210
1967	1	3.88429	3.90736	3.97620	4.06801
1968	1	4.10023	4.15476	4.22082	4.25804
1969	1	4.30267	4.32534	4.34802	4.37733
1970	1	4.32908	4.46471	4.67418	4.83604
1971	1	5.13308	5.10205	4.91906	4.80343
1972	1	4.81400	5.10238	5.14308	5.52788
1973	1	6.07347	6.42925	6.82219	7.15566
1974	1	7.12326	7.00190	7.39944	7.62900
1975	1	7.82527	8.14783	8.26239	8.27096
1976	1	8.61601	9.12774	9.42747	9.90071
1977	1	9.46488			

UK_UKFHQNQE

1955	1	0.95667	0.94167	0.84533	0.78000
1956	1	0.81133	0.85233	0.81533	0.76067
1957	1	0.81933	0.84467	0.72433	0.81733
1958	1	0.97900	1.09567	1.11700	1.11833
1959	1	1.13633	1.13233	1.13767	0.99933
1960	1	0.99200	1.04133	1.10933	1.14800
1961	1	1.09100	0.96767	1.25833	1.22433
1962	1	1.23200	1.17533	1.00733	1.01833
1963	1	1.00700	0.99700	0.97667	0.96467
1964	1	0.95233	0.96933	0.90200	0.82833
1965	1	0.83867	0.98833	0.97767	1.07267
1966	1	1.27867	1.17800	1.13467	1.13167
1967	1	1.17067	1.02133	0.98800	1.16367
1968	1	1.14767	1.13367	1.12367	1.02300
1969	1	1.03000	1.01867	1.01833	1.05667
1970	1	1.12667	1.16033	1.13300	1.19900
1971	1	1.37933	1.52967	2.08767	2.50900
1972	1	2.71167	2.56733	2.25867	2.15100
1973	1	2.03167	2.29733	2.35736	2.71945
1974	1	2.65859	2.77381	2.99543	2.93554
1975	1	2.85638	2.71838	2.65842	2.81328
1976	1	3.67986	3.02305	2.96288	3.24658
1977	1	5.34327			

UK_UKFHQSQE

1955	1	0.93729	0.90763	0.85377	0.81817
1956	1	0.79614	0.82389	0.82047	0.79543
1957	1	0.80696	0.82064	0.72538	0.84859
1958	1	0.96919	1.07298	1.11301	1.14985
1959	1	1.13176	1.11646	1.13198	1.01604
1960	1	0.99262	1.03274	1.10354	1.15842
1961	1	1.09525	0.96015	1.25546	1.23088
1962	1	1.23846	1.16158	1.01023	1.02603
1963	1	1.00793	0.98039	0.98659	0.97609
1964	1	0.94497	0.95203	0.91680	0.84131
1965	1	0.82369	0.97387	0.99673	1.09126
1966	1	1.24661	1.16614	1.15895	1.15019
1967	1	1.13589	1.01644	1.00832	1.18073
1968	1	1.11231	1.13343	1.14481	1.03369
1969	1	1.00216	1.02026	1.03366	1.06424
1970	1	1.10466	1.15917	1.14960	1.20147
1971	1	1.36171	1.52578	2.11758	2.50446
1972	1	2.68557	2.56312	2.29464	2.14048
1973	1	2.00715	2.29909	2.40335	2.70800
1974	1	2.60556	2.78214	3.07219	2.92854
1975	1	2.76981	2.73424	2.74200	2.81425
1976	1	3.53364	3.05207	3.06139	3.25373
1977	1	5.09959			

UK_UKRSQN3T

1955	1	0.033000	0.039300	0.040167	0.040800
1956	1	0.048200	0.050367	0.050333	0.049600
1957	1	0.042667	0.038933	0.048600	0.064800
1958	1	0.058867	0.047633	0.038467	0.033467
1959	1	0.032300	0.033033	0.034000	0.034500
1960	1	0.045000	0.048833	0.054500	0.045933
1961	1	0.042967	0.044300	0.063433	0.054867
1962	1	0.050167	0.038967	0.037167	0.037300
1963	1	0.035133	0.036333	0.036667	0.036733
1964	1	0.040600	0.043233	0.045800	0.058633
1965	1	0.064167	0.060000	0.055000	0.053767
1966	1	0.054900	0.056033	0.066467	0.065233
1967	1	0.058033	0.052533	0.052833	0.068033
1968	1	0.074067	0.072333	0.068867	0.067700
1969	1	0.074500	0.079000	0.078900	0.078000
1970	1	0.075100	0.069100	0.068800	0.068700
1971	1	0.067600	0.056733	0.053933	0.044567
1972	1	0.043700	0.047533	0.061167	0.074933
1973	1	0.081700	0.073600	0.112000	0.121667
1974	1	0.122700	0.116000	0.114133	0.112167
1975	1	0.099733	0.095767	0.106700	0.112867
1976	1	0.089367	0.108900	0.116967	0.144733
1977	1	0.106900			

UK_UKRLQN25

1955	1	0.039333	0.040800	0.043333	0.043567
1956	1	0.045967	0.046700	0.048167	0.048733
1957	1	0.046033	0.048167	0.051567	0.054433
1958	1	0.051933	0.049867	0.049033	0.048500
1959	1	0.047567	0.048433	0.047900	0.049167
1960	1	0.051967	0.054100	0.055733	0.055300
1961	1	0.058200	0.060567	0.065167	0.064667
1962	1	0.063333	0.061767	0.058167	0.056567
1963	1	0.058033	0.055433	0.053933	0.056200
1964	1	0.059133	0.060400	0.060367	0.061300
1965	1	0.063000	0.065533	0.064833	0.063367
1966	1	0.065333	0.067800	0.071100	0.067833
1967	1	0.064667	0.065100	0.068200	0.070067
1968	1	0.071333	0.073000	0.074733	0.076867
1969	1	0.084200	0.091067	0.091533	0.088733
1970	1	0.086033	0.092300	0.092800	0.095867
1971	1	0.093767	0.092400	0.090533	0.085933
1972	1	0.084533	0.089800	0.094633	0.096267
1973	1	0.099467	0.103167	0.112700	0.118600
1974	1	0.133733	0.144833	0.153067	0.166400
1975	1	0.149633	0.148333	0.140867	0.148500
1976	1	0.137567	0.139000	0.141766	0.151566
1977	1	0.133300	0.126030		

UK_UKYNQNGD

1955	1	16.052	16.184	17.268	18.072
1956	1	17.216	18.348	18.124	19.468
1957	1	18.436	19.356	19.388	20.380
1958	1	19.528	20.048	20.236	21.004
1959	1	19.756	21.336	21.188	22.664
1960	1	21.440	22.548	22.532	23.940
1961	1	23.112	23.896	24.828	24.956
1962	1	23.720	25.572	25.396	26.320
1963	1	24.828	27.108	26.840	28.676
1964	1	27.268	29.232	29.236	30.992
1965	1	29.444	31.048	31.536	32.820
1966	1	31.336	32.948	33.264	34.784
1967	1	33.380	34.808	35.244	36.076
1968	1	35.460	36.724	37.848	39.528
1969	1	36.820	38.980	39.668	41.884
1970	1	39.748	42.600	43.760	47.364
1971	1	44.376	47.784	50.716	53.728
1972	1	50.596	53.584	55.468	60.184
1973	1	60.076	61.452	64.108	68.332
1974	1	63.884	68.492	78.176	84.056
1975	1	84.548	89.300	94.212	104.252
1976	1	102.392	104.712	109.828	119.388
1977	1	113.952	119.488		

UK_UKYNQSGD

1955	1	16.546	16.104	17.429	17.473
1956	1	17.753	18.250	18.292	18.824
1957	1	19.026	19.234	19.565	19.716
1958	1	20.172	19.896	20.407	20.347
1959	1	20.423	21.147	21.342	21.987
1960	1	22.196	22.303	22.683	23.246
1961	1	23.965	23.594	24.992	24.237
1962	1	24.623	25.233	25.551	25.564
1963	1	25.773	26.783	26.971	27.850
1964	1	28.289	28.944	29.344	30.081
1965	1	30.516	30.841	31.601	31.829
1966	1	32.452	32.843	33.263	33.699
1967	1	34.579	34.784	35.189	34.889
1968	1	36.787	36.764	37.748	38.141
1969	1	38.267	39.070	39.555	40.329
1970	1	41.324	42.792	43.633	45.518
1971	1	46.096	48.133	50.578	51.578
1972	1	52.402	54.176	55.348	57.724
1973	1	61.988	62.358	64.041	65.497
1974	1	65.675	69.680	78.226	80.467
1975	1	86.756	90.961	94.400	99.718
1976	1	104.994	106.672	110.110	114.181
1977	1	116.820	121.702		

UK_UKYRQND7

1955	1	28.2880	28.4080	29.4520	30.2640
1956	1	28.4600	30.0040	29.2880	30.8400
1957	1	29.5040	30.7080	29.8600	30.8120
1958	1	29.4080	29.7640	30.2320	31.0640
1959	1	29.4040	30.9000	31.2760	33.0160
1960	1	31.2800	32.4640	32.4560	34.1480
1961	1	32.5440	34.0200	33.8920	34.5640
1962	1	32.3120	34.6280	34.2040	35.1800
1963	1	32.8600	35.8560	35.6560	37.3920
1964	1	35.7600	37.7240	37.4120	39.1120
1965	1	36.6800	38.6480	38.7280	39.9080
1966	1	37.6680	38.9920	39.4160	40.8200
1967	1	39.0520	40.3280	40.5040	41.1640
1968	1	39.9360	41.3320	42.0280	43.5880
1969	1	40.2520	41.9840	42.6800	44.7160
1970	1	41.2760	43.2640	43.2960	45.6360
1971	1	41.8320	44.1000	45.1360	46.9680
1972	1	42.7640	44.9360	45.0000	48.1560
1973	1	47.1120	47.6120	48.0920	49.9120
1974	1	44.7480	47.5040	49.0120	50.4320
1975	1	46.1360	46.1920	46.5240	49.5720
1976	1	47.1520	46.9920	48.2920	51.1400
1977	1	46.2000	47.0800		

UK_UKYRQSD7

1955	1	29.0775	28.2090	29.6379	29.4840
1956	1	29.2523	29.8098	29.4620	30.0316
1957	1	30.3401	30.5178	30.0332	29.9801
1958	1	30.2653	29.5953	30.3831	30.2037
1959	1	30.3057	30.7304	31.3926	32.0888
1960	1	32.3012	32.2793	32.5256	33.1899
1961	1	33.6797	33.7857	33.9449	33.5906
1962	1	33.4983	34.3500	34.2484	34.1933
1963	1	34.0863	35.5621	35.6924	36.3481
1964	1	37.0714	37.4625	37.4293	38.0131
1965	1	37.9805	38.4672	38.7245	38.7424
1966	1	38.9792	38.9200	39.3697	39.5566
1967	1	40.4392	40.3400	40.4288	39.7830
1968	1	41.4306	41.4115	41.9269	41.9983
1969	1	41.8714	42.0810	42.5968	42.9555
1970	1	43.0292	43.3864	43.2293	43.7287
1971	1	43.6812	44.2473	45.0782	44.9465
1972	1	44.6344	45.1720	44.9363	46.0423
1973	1	49.1005	47.9835	48.0310	47.6771
1974	1	46.5211	48.0443	48.9506	48.0995
1975	1	47.8947	46.8509	46.4662	47.2162
1976	1	48.8996	47.7681	48.2116	48.6834
1977	1	47.8946	47.9057		

UK_UKPDQND7

1955	1	0.56745	0.56970	0.58631	0.59715
1956	1	0.60492	0.61152	0.61882	0.63126
1957	1	0.62486	0.63032	0.64930	0.66143
1958	1	0.66404	0.67357	0.66936	0.67615
1959	1	0.67188	0.69049	0.67745	0.68646
1960	1	0.68542	0.69455	0.69423	0.70107
1961	1	0.71018	0.70241	0.73256	0.72202
1962	1	0.73409	0.73848	0.74249	0.74815
1963	1	0.75557	0.75602	0.75275	0.76690
1964	1	0.76253	0.77489	0.78146	0.79239
1965	1	0.80273	0.80335	0.81429	0.82239
1966	1	0.83190	0.84499	0.84392	0.85213
1967	1	0.85476	0.86312	0.87014	0.87640
1968	1	0.88792	0.88851	0.90054	0.90686
1969	1	0.91474	0.92845	0.92943	0.93667
1970	1	0.96298	0.98465	1.01072	1.03786
1971	1	1.06081	1.08354	1.12363	1.14393
1972	1	1.18314	1.19245	1.23262	1.24977
1973	1	1.27517	1.29068	1.33303	1.36905
1974	1	1.42764	1.44182	1.59504	1.66672
1975	1	1.83258	1.93324	2.02502	2.10304
1976	1	2.17153	2.22829	2.27425	2.33453
1977	1	2.46649	2.53798		

UK_UKPDQSD7

1955	1	0.56921	0.57207	0.58535	0.59378
1956	1	0.60716	0.61320	0.61837	0.62788
1957	1	0.62750	0.63063	0.64978	0.65830
1958	1	0.66689	0.67242	0.67065	0.67394
1959	1	0.67415	0.68822	0.67946	0.68529
1960	1	0.68670	0.69186	0.69675	0.70076
1961	1	0.71018	0.70005	0.73542	0.72215
1962	1	0.73284	0.73710	0.74504	0.74839
1963	1	0.75364	0.75553	0.75496	0.76692
1964	1	0.76071	0.77470	0.78354	0.79204
1965	1	0.80133	0.80323	0.81600	0.82202
1966	1	0.83083	0.84502	0.84489	0.85224
1967	1	0.85382	0.86319	0.87055	0.87685
1968	1	0.88703	0.88882	0.90033	0.90778
1969	1	0.91340	0.92961	0.92853	0.93780
1970	1	0.96104	0.98705	1.00892	1.03955
1971	1	1.05770	1.08725	1.12138	1.14607
1972	1	1.17866	1.19701	1.23044	1.25283
1973	1	1.26901	1.29533	1.33155	1.37348
1974	1	1.41988	1.44497	1.59506	1.67359
1975	1	1.82202	1.93407	2.02734	2.11352
1976	1	2.15870	2.22582	2.27861	2.34755
1977	1	2.45134	2.53340		

UK_UKPCQN70

1955	1	0.57800	0.58400	0.59200	0.60600
1956	1	0.61000	0.62200	0.62000	0.62600
1957	1	0.63300	0.63700	0.64600	0.65400
1958	1	0.65600	0.66600	0.65800	0.66700
1959	1	0.67000	0.66400	0.66200	0.66700
1960	1	0.66700	0.67100	0.67200	0.67900
1961	1	0.68200	0.69100	0.70000	0.70800
1962	1	0.71500	0.73000	0.72700	0.72600
1963	1	0.73700	0.74100	0.73600	0.74200
1964	1	0.74800	0.76200	0.76800	0.77500
1965	1	0.78200	0.80200	0.80500	0.81000
1966	1	0.81600	0.83200	0.83500	0.84100
1967	1	0.84600	0.85300	0.84900	0.85900
1968	1	0.87100	0.89200	0.89700	0.90700
1969	1	0.92500	0.94000	0.94200	0.95400
1970	1	0.97100	0.99500	1.00600	1.02700
1971	1	1.05500	1.09300	1.10800	1.12200
1972	1	1.13900	1.16000	1.18000	1.20800
1973	1	1.23000	1.26900	1.28800	1.33200
1974	1	1.38800	1.47000	1.50700	1.57500
1975	1	1.67000	1.82700	1.90700	1.97300
1976	1	2.04500	2.11900	2.16800	2.26800
1977	1	2.38200	2.48800	2.52700	

UK_UKPCQS70

1955	1	0.57858	0.58276	0.59373	0.60500
1956	1	0.61045	0.62074	0.62190	0.62497
1957	1	0.63329	0.63580	0.64806	0.65298
1958	1	0.65595	0.66515	0.65986	0.66601
1959	1	0.67005	0.66306	0.66370	0.66623
1960	1	0.66718	0.66989	0.67342	0.67848
1961	1	0.68273	0.68917	0.70124	0.70795
1962	1	0.71619	0.72745	0.72790	0.72651
1963	1	0.73875	0.73758	0.73676	0.74309
1964	1	0.74992	0.75792	0.76886	0.77647
1965	1	0.78400	0.79735	0.80606	0.81177
1966	1	0.81791	0.82698	0.83633	0.84299
1967	1	0.84777	0.84769	0.85054	0.86125
1968	1	0.87259	0.88626	0.89881	0.90954
1969	1	0.92660	0.93380	0.94389	0.95685
1970	1	0.97282	0.98812	1.00790	1.03031
1971	1	1.05741	1.08475	1.11000	1.12595
1972	1	1.14239	1.15012	1.18202	1.21279
1973	1	1.23441	1.25691	1.29038	1.33768
1974	1	1.39370	1.45487	1.50964	1.58235
1975	1	1.67730	1.80732	1.91019	1.98264
1976	1	2.05447	2.09579	2.17084	2.27969
1977	1	2.39336	2.46055	2.52991	

UK_UKIPQS70

1955	1	0.65300	0.65900	0.66500	0.67700
1956	1	0.66900	0.67200	0.66600	0.66800
1957	1	0.67800	0.68100	0.68800	0.67800
1958	1	0.68100	0.67200	0.66900	0.67900
1959	1	0.68400	0.70100	0.70900	0.74100
1960	1	0.75500	0.75400	0.75600	0.76600
1961	1	0.76100	0.77300	0.77100	0.76500
1962	1	0.76600	0.77800	0.78400	0.77100
1963	1	0.75300	0.79000	0.81300	0.83100
1964	1	0.85600	0.85600	0.86200	0.88500
1965	1	0.89000	0.88700	0.88700	0.90100
1966	1	0.90900	0.91000	0.91200	0.89300
1967	1	0.90500	0.91400	0.91500	0.93400
1968	1	0.96100	0.97100	0.97800	0.98000
1969	1	0.99000	1.00700	1.00200	0.99600
1970	1	0.99400	0.99800	1.00200	1.00600
1971	1	0.99900	1.00800	1.00200	1.00300
1972	1	0.97000	1.03000	1.03600	1.06300
1973	1	1.09700	1.09500	1.10700	1.09900
1974	1	1.04000	1.08900	1.09100	1.05700
1975	1	1.04800	1.01000	1.00000	1.00900
1976	1	1.01500	1.02600	1.01800	1.03300
1977	1	1.03600	1.02000		

UK_UKGXQNCG

1955	1	5.7908	5.5690	5.7389	6.0505
1956	1	6.0788	6.0316	6.0836	6.3812
1957	1	6.4852	6.2111	6.3056	6.5987
1958	1	6.8399	6.6082	6.7595	6.9629
1959	1	7.1001	7.1475	7.1143	7.4315
1960	1	7.5520	6.9760	7.4360	7.9560
1961	1	8.0440	7.3280	8.1680	8.5240
1962	1	8.7760	7.7160	8.3960	8.9240
1963	1	8.8320	8.1800	9.3240	9.3120
1964	1	9.9280	8.8600	10.0720	10.3080
1965	1	10.8040	10.6560	11.3920	11.3440
1966	1	12.1360	11.2040	12.6080	12.6440
1967	1	13.9160	12.5760	14.6640	14.3000
1968	1	16.7200	14.0720	15.4240	15.7600
1969	1	15.8640	14.1280	16.9400	16.8920
1970	1	17.1480	15.9000	18.4880	18.5240
1971	1	19.3360	18.2320	20.1960	21.4600
1972	1	22.5920	20.5920	22.4120	24.2000
1973	1	26.9400	24.0320	23.7960	27.4760
1974	1	31.1600	29.0440	35.0720	36.1000
1975	1	42.3560	42.3600	45.1600	44.0960
1976	1	53.1000	48.5560	51.1960	49.3280
1977	1	55.4800			

UK_UKGXQSCG

1955	1	5.6714	5.6876	5.8366	5.9553
1956	1	5.9460	6.1680	6.1862	6.2797
1957	1	6.3305	6.3728	6.4095	6.4866
1958	1	6.6541	6.8281	6.8568	6.8316
1959	1	6.8803	7.4582	7.1901	7.2738
1960	1	7.2942	7.3617	7.4688	7.7797
1961	1	7.7485	7.8124	8.1476	8.3366
1962	1	8.4464	8.2835	8.3126	8.7577
1963	1	8.4921	8.8107	9.1772	9.1806
1964	1	9.5393	9.5507	9.8681	10.2189
1965	1	10.3573	11.4938	11.1458	11.2621
1966	1	11.6228	12.1115	12.3161	12.5432
1967	1	13.3281	13.6357	14.3097	14.1418
1968	1	16.0437	15.2887	15.0461	15.5416
1969	1	15.2477	15.3321	16.5797	16.6183
1970	1	16.4861	17.1837	18.2009	18.2308
1971	1	18.5439	19.5894	19.9966	21.2320
1972	1	21.5613	21.9488	22.3073	24.1716
1973	1	25.5375	25.4181	23.7521	27.7667
1974	1	29.3504	30.5197	35.0244	36.8793
1975	1	39.7049	44.3637	44.9760	45.4331
1976	1	49.6732	50.7430	50.8780	51.0394
1977	1	51.8607			

UK_UKGDQNBR

1955	1	2.0163	-1.0184	-1.0575	-1.1961
1956	1	2.4214	-0.8194	-1.2139	-1.5017
1957	1	2.3397	-0.8052	-1.1748	-1.5372
1958	1	2.5102	-0.9936	-1.0149	-1.1357
1959	1	2.9651	-1.1113	-1.3007	-1.7494
1960	1	2.5324	-1.1854	-2.1117	-2.0541
1961	1	2.7794	-0.2837	-0.3620	-1.7494
1962	1	2.3224	-1.4489	-0.8931	-1.6342
1963	1	3.4320	-1.0880	-1.2200	-1.7360
1964	1	2.5320	-0.9280	-1.3760	-1.9640
1965	1	2.9800	-1.9400	-1.3440	-2.1360
1966	1	3.3720	-1.9520	-1.7640	-1.9880
1967	1	2.5040	-1.6920	-2.2360	-3.1960
1968	1	1.7560	-1.6120	-1.4360	-1.7440
1969	1	5.8880	0.9200	-1.2280	-1.9920
1970	1	5.9120	0.4800	-1.1120	-2.6000
1971	1	3.1480	-0.1000	-2.0280	-3.5560
1972	1	3.3480	-1.6520	-2.8120	-5.2680
1973	1	1.8080	-4.5680	-2.5800	-3.9440
1974	1	2.4360	-3.9400	-3.4320	-9.0280
1975	1	-3.9480	-9.4240	-9.1520	-10.9800
1976	1	-5.6400	-8.8320	-6.6200	-6.0520
1977	1	-1.8760			

UK_UKGDQSBR

1955	1	-0.64586	-0.41683	-0.14413	-0.03161
1956	1	-0.27337	-0.20023	-0.29980	-0.31645
1957	1	-0.40794	-0.15842	-0.26169	-0.31470
1958	1	-0.29826	-0.32126	-0.11892	0.14604
1959	1	0.09189	-0.41028	-0.44097	-0.38857
1960	1	-0.41484	-0.44766	-1.29108	-0.62958
1961	1	-0.22031	0.46992	0.44871	-0.27662
1962	1	-0.74924	-0.65890	-0.08282	-0.12006
1963	1	0.26118	-0.24278	-0.38772	-0.19043
1964	1	-0.76266	-0.02429	-0.50086	-0.39762
1965	1	-0.40454	-1.05345	-0.39522	-0.48919
1966	1	-0.13781	-1.13753	-0.72184	-0.18543
1967	1	-1.17437	-0.98876	-1.08157	-1.20611
1968	1	-2.10185	-1.03148	-0.17540	0.42222
1969	1	1.88486	1.39629	0.08929	0.34630
1970	1	1.74420	0.98798	0.14977	-0.13050
1971	1	-1.14750	0.56423	-0.94595	-1.02392
1972	1	-0.96209	-0.79180	-1.97382	-2.76179
1973	1	-2.37017	-3.56680	-1.98424	-1.49589
1974	1	-1.56854	-2.83685	-3.02026	-6.67582
1975	1	-7.75681	-8.28785	-8.85413	-8.71704
1976	1	-9.28248	-7.69923	-6.38669	-3.82612
1977	1	-5.40490			

UK_UKPPQNIN

1954	1		0.050770	0.050815	0.050860
1955	1	0.050905	0.050950	0.051007	0.051065
1956	1	0.051122	0.051180	0.051242	0.051305
1957	1	0.051367	0.051430	0.051485	0.051540
1958	1	0.051595	0.051650	0.051727	0.051805
1959	1	0.051882	0.051960	0.052062	0.052164
1960	1	0.052267	0.052370	0.052480	0.052589
1961	1	0.052699	0.052810	0.052937	0.053064
1962	1	0.053192	0.053320	0.053400	0.053480
1963	1	0.053560	0.053640	0.053692	0.053745
1964	1	0.053797	0.053850	0.053932	0.054015
1965	1	0.054097	0.054180	0.054260	0.054340
1966	1	0.054420	0.054500	0.054575	0.054650
1967	1	0.054725	0.054800	0.054862	0.054925
1968	1	0.054987	0.055050	0.055105	0.055160
1969	1	0.055215	0.055270	0.055305	0.055340
1970	1	0.055375	0.055410	0.055460	0.055510
1971	1	0.055560	0.055610	0.055657	0.055705
1972	1	0.055752	0.055800	0.055832	0.055865
1973	1	0.055897	0.055930	0.055940	0.055950
1974	1	0.055960	0.055970	0.055967	0.055965
1975	1	0.055963	0.055960	0.055952	0.055945
1976	1	0.055937	0.055930	0.055923	0.055915

UK_UKLFQNCV

1955	1	0.023660	0.023699	0.023852	0.023903
1956	1	0.023910	0.023962	0.024062	0.024031
1957	1	0.024054	0.024111	0.024111	0.024097
1958	1	0.024013	0.024064	0.024078	0.024104
1959	1	0.024174	0.024199	0.024383	0.024429
1960	1	0.024573	0.024583	0.024685	0.024837
1961	1	0.024927	0.024872	0.025024	0.024966
1962	1	0.025131	0.025180	0.025275	0.025240
1963	1	0.025209	0.025292	0.025365	0.025435
1964	1	0.025349	0.025427	0.025602	0.025628
1965	1	0.025566	0.025626	0.025721	0.025804
1966	1	0.025704	0.025751	0.025874	0.025728
1967	1	0.025015	0.025087	0.025240	0.025111
1968	1	0.024959	0.024987	0.025103	0.025071
1969	1	0.024989	0.025013	0.025111	0.025052
1970	1	0.025010	0.024921	0.024998	0.024949
1971	1	0.024696	0.024756	0.024758	0.024783
1972	1	0.024927	0.024863	0.025091	0.025127
1973	1	0.025269	0.025217	0.025309	0.025224
1974	1	0.025166	0.025257	0.025500	0.025502
1975	1	0.025327	0.025459	0.025751	0.025751
1976	1	0.025600	0.025757	0.025933	0.025876
1977	1	0.025727			

UK_UKLFQSCV

1955	1	0.023685	0.023705	0.023823	0.023901
1956	1	0.023933	0.023970	0.024034	0.024031
1957	1	0.024070	0.024121	0.024087	0.024098
1958	1	0.024018	0.024081	0.024058	0.024104
1959	1	0.024170	0.024223	0.024365	0.024427
1960	1	0.024564	0.024615	0.024664	0.024830
1961	1	0.024923	0.024909	0.024997	0.024951
1962	1	0.025140	0.025218	0.025241	0.025214
1963	1	0.025239	0.025330	0.025320	0.025398
1964	1	0.025401	0.025467	0.025544	0.025581
1965	1	0.025637	0.025670	0.025650	0.025752
1966	1	0.025786	0.025799	0.025794	0.025677
1967	1	0.025094	0.025139	0.025158	0.025065
1968	1	0.025034	0.025037	0.025027	0.025029
1969	1	0.025053	0.025062	0.025041	0.025017
1970	1	0.025061	0.024969	0.024935	0.024922
1971	1	0.024733	0.024808	0.024695	0.024757
1972	1	0.024965	0.024918	0.025020	0.025099
1973	1	0.025319	0.025275	0.025225	0.025190
1974	1	0.025235	0.025315	0.025401	0.025461
1975	1	0.025417	0.025516	0.025641	0.025701
1976	1	0.025710	0.025811	0.025818	0.025821
1977	1	0.025850			

UK_UKEMQNCV

1955	1	0.023374	0.023489	0.023642	0.023667
1956	1	0.023639	0.023747	0.023813	0.023732
1957	1	0.023681	0.023835	0.023822	0.023743
1958	1	0.023571	0.023658	0.023626	0.023586
1959	1	0.023634	0.023779	0.023957	0.023986
1960	1	0.024137	0.024257	0.024360	0.024481
1961	1	0.024571	0.024585	0.024699	0.024575
1962	1	0.024681	0.024774	0.024803	0.024680
1963	1	0.024530	0.024796	0.024863	0.024949
1964	1	0.024898	0.025078	0.025238	0.025261
1965	1	0.025190	0.025327	0.025389	0.025454
1966	1	0.025368	0.025470	0.025521	0.025225
1967	1	0.024451	0.024584	0.024677	0.024515
1968	1	0.024351	0.024445	0.024533	0.024493
1969	1	0.024385	0.024495	0.024534	0.024450
1970	1	0.024373	0.024366	0.024382	0.024308
1971	1	0.023958	0.024032	0.023903	0.023872
1972	1	0.023960	0.024057	0.024200	0.024345
1973	1	0.024552	0.024641	0.024731	0.024710
1974	1	0.024548	0.024715	0.024850	0.024776
1975	1	0.024524	0.024593	0.024605	0.024550
1976	1	0.024315	0.024425	0.024477	0.024505
1977	1	0.024343			

UK_UKEMQSCV

1955	1	0.023448	0.023462	0.023587	0.023677
1956	1	0.023710	0.023720	0.023759	0.023745
1957	1	0.023745	0.023809	0.023773	0.023759
1958	1	0.023624	0.023637	0.023581	0.023606
1959	1	0.023675	0.023763	0.023914	0.024007
1960	1	0.024172	0.024248	0.024313	0.024500
1961	1	0.024608	0.024580	0.024648	0.024585
1962	1	0.024730	0.024771	0.024747	0.024678
1963	1	0.024597	0.024794	0.024798	0.024934
1964	1	0.024987	0.025077	0.025162	0.025236
1965	1	0.025297	0.025329	0.025302	0.025424
1966	1	0.025486	0.025474	0.025428	0.025196
1967	1	0.024564	0.024591	0.024585	0.024488
1968	1	0.024461	0.024447	0.024450	0.024469
1969	1	0.024486	0.024493	0.024464	0.024428
1970	1	0.024464	0.024358	0.024326	0.024288
1971	1	0.024038	0.024024	0.023854	0.023849
1972	1	0.024042	0.024048	0.024150	0.024317
1973	1	0.024643	0.024635	0.024674	0.024674
1974	1	0.024651	0.024711	0.024787	0.024732
1975	1	0.024638	0.024592	0.024537	0.024498
1976	1	0.024439	0.024423	0.024406	0.024450
1977	1	0.024473			

UK_UKUNQNWH

1955	1	0.000286	0.000210	0.000210	0.000236
1956	1	0.000271	0.000215	0.000249	0.000299
1957	1	0.000373	0.000276	0.000289	0.000354
1958	1	0.000442	0.000406	0.000452	0.000518
1959	1	0.000540	0.000420	0.000426	0.000443
1960	1	0.000436	0.000326	0.000325	0.000356
1961	1	0.000356	0.000287	0.000325	0.000391
1962	1	0.000450	0.000406	0.000472	0.000560
1963	1	0.000679	0.000496	0.000502	0.000486
1964	1	0.000451	0.000349	0.000364	0.000367
1965	1	0.000376	0.000299	0.000332	0.000350
1966	1	0.000336	0.000281	0.000353	0.000503
1967	1	0.000564	0.000503	0.000563	0.000596
1968	1	0.000608	0.000542	0.000570	0.000578
1969	1	0.000604	0.000518	0.000577	0.000602
1970	1	0.000637	0.000555	0.000616	0.000641
1971	1	0.000738	0.000724	0.000855	0.000911
1972	1	0.000967	0.000806	0.000891	0.000782
1973	1	0.000717	0.000576	0.000578	0.000514
1974	1	0.000618	0.000542	0.000650	0.000726
1975	1	0.000803	0.000866	0.001146	0.001201
1976	1	0.001285	0.001332	0.001456	0.001371
1977	1	0.001384			

UK_UKUNQSWH

1955	1	0.000246	0.000238	0.000229	0.000227
1956	1	0.000234	0.000244	0.000270	0.000286
1957	1	0.000325	0.000312	0.000312	0.000338
1958	1	0.000388	0.000458	0.000485	0.000492
1959	1	0.000480	0.000473	0.000455	0.000419
1960	1	0.000391	0.000367	0.000345	0.000336
1961	1	0.000322	0.000323	0.000342	0.000369
1962	1	0.000409	0.000458	0.000493	0.000529
1963	1	0.000620	0.000561	0.000520	0.000459
1964	1	0.000414	0.000396	0.000374	0.000347
1965	1	0.000347	0.000339	0.000339	0.000332
1966	1	0.000312	0.000317	0.000358	0.000479
1967	1	0.000526	0.000564	0.000568	0.000573
1968	1	0.000569	0.000601	0.000572	0.000560
1969	1	0.000568	0.000570	0.000576	0.000589
1970	1	0.000601	0.000607	0.000610	0.000631
1971	1	0.000700	0.000789	0.000841	0.000899
1972	1	0.000924	0.000875	0.000870	0.000772
1973	1	0.000692	0.000623	0.000560	0.000508
1974	1	0.000603	0.000584	0.000625	0.000718
1975	1	0.000791	0.000928	0.001098	0.001188
1976	1	0.001274	0.001423	0.001393	0.001356
1977	1	0.001376			

UK_UKURQNDR

1955	1	0.012088	0.008861	0.008804	0.009873
1956	1	0.011334	0.008973	0.010348	0.012442
1957	1	0.015507	0.011447	0.011986	0.014691
1958	1	0.018407	0.016872	0.018772	0.021490
1959	1	0.022338	0.017356	0.017471	0.018134
1960	1	0.017743	0.013261	0.013166	0.014333
1961	1	0.014282	0.011539	0.012988	0.015661
1962	1	0.017906	0.016124	0.018675	0.022187
1963	1	0.026935	0.019611	0.019791	0.019108
1964	1	0.017792	0.013726	0.014218	0.014320
1965	1	0.014707	0.011668	0.012908	0.013564
1966	1	0.013072	0.010912	0.013643	0.019551
1967	1	0.022546	0.020050	0.022306	0.023735
1968	1	0.024360	0.021691	0.022706	0.023055
1969	1	0.024171	0.020709	0.022978	0.024030
1970	1	0.025470	0.022270	0.024642	0.025692
1971	1	0.029883	0.029245	0.034534	0.036759
1972	1	0.038793	0.032418	0.035511	0.031122
1973	1	0.028375	0.022842	0.022838	0.020377
1974	1	0.024557	0.021459	0.025490	0.028468
1975	1	0.031705	0.034015	0.044503	0.046639
1976	1	0.050195	0.051714	0.056145	0.052983
1977	1	0.053796			

UK_UKURQSDR

1955	1	0.010402	0.010042	0.009602	0.009482
1956	1	0.009791	0.010161	0.011249	0.011925
1957	1	0.013491	0.012938	0.012963	0.014024
1958	1	0.016178	0.019024	0.020176	0.020431
1959	1	0.019849	0.019525	0.018667	0.017169
1960	1	0.015917	0.014902	0.013979	0.013544
1961	1	0.012906	0.012965	0.013700	0.014794
1962	1	0.016261	0.018150	0.019544	0.020976
1963	1	0.024565	0.022127	0.020550	0.018089
1964	1	0.016280	0.015526	0.014645	0.013577
1965	1	0.013524	0.013189	0.013207	0.012902
1966	1	0.012069	0.012293	0.013883	0.018677
1967	1	0.020927	0.022424	0.022588	0.022847
1968	1	0.022700	0.024032	0.022885	0.022371
1969	1	0.022641	0.022747	0.022988	0.023535
1970	1	0.023974	0.024299	0.024472	0.025310
1971	1	0.028298	0.031792	0.034039	0.036309
1972	1	0.037027	0.035131	0.034761	0.030744
1973	1	0.027339	0.024702	0.022173	0.020136
1974	1	0.023891	0.023141	0.024583	0.028151
1975	1	0.031075	0.036593	0.042713	0.046148
1976	1	0.049449	0.055510	0.053799	0.052422
1977	1	0.053130			

Sources and Notes on Time Series for the United States

All time series are quarterly and generally cover the period from 1947I to 1976IV inclusive, except where noted otherwise. Some series were available from the source only in seasonally adjusted form, calculated from Census X-11 program. In all other series we copied unadjusted data and made the seasonal adjustment, also using the Census X-11 program.

I. INTERNATIONAL VARIABLES

A. *Balance of Payments*

USBPQNDR   Balance of Payments, 1955I to 1976IV. Unit: Billions of
USBPQSDR   Dollars of Quarterly Rates, NSA. SA.

Source: For 1955I to 1959IV, U.S. Department of Commerce, *Survey of Current Business* (SCB), September 1970, table 1, "U.S. International Transactions Quarterly, 1955–59," pp. 50–51, line 46 (net transactions in U.S. official reserve assets), and our estimates of the official portion of liquid and nonliquid liabilities to foreign official agencies based on data from U.S. Treasury, *Treasury Bulletin* (TB), CM-1-2, "Short-term Liability by Type of Liability," various issues (see description of estimation procedure below). For 1960I to 1961IV, SCB, June 1973, table 2, "U.S. International Transactions," pp. 28–29, lines 55–57 (U.S. liquid and nonliquid liabilities to foreign official agencies) and line 58 (net transactions in U.S. official reserve assets). For 1962I to 1963IV, SCB, June 1974, table 2, "U.S. International Transactions," pp. 34–35, lines 55–58 (same entries as data for 1960–61). For 1964I to 1966IV, SCB, June 1975, table 2, "U.S. International Transactions," pp. 30–31, lines 55–58 (same entries as data for 1960–63). For 1967 I to 1974IV, SCB, June 1976, table 1, "U.S. International Transactions," pp. 32–33, line 34 (net U.S. official reserve assets) and lines 52, 56, 57 (U.S. liquid and nonliquid liabilities to foreign official agencies). For 1975I to 1976IV, SCB, March 1977, table 1, "U.S. International Transactions," p. 44, lines 34, 52, 57 (same entries as data for 1967–74).

Description: The balance of payments reported here measures the official reserve transactions balance where a net increase in official reserves represents a surplus and is indicated as a positive value. In the source, the signs are reversed. The basic approach in constructing the series was to combine net transactions in U.S. official reserve assets and U.S. liquid and nonliquid liabilities to foreign official agencies.

The format for the statement of international transactions has undergone substantial changes over several years, as indicated by the changes in line numbers in the source. No published breakdown of U.S. liquid and nonliquid liabilities to foreign official agencies is available for the period 1955I to 1959IV. Lines 59 and 60 of the September 1970 issue of SCB report U.S. Treasury marketable or convertible bonds and notes, and deposits and money market paper held in the U.S., respectively, as liabilities to all foreigners inclusive of foreign official agencies, foreign commercial banks, other foreign residents, and international and regional organizations. Therefore we estimated the official portion of liquid and nonliquid liabilities by first regressing U.S. liquid and nonliquid liabilities to foreign official agencies (lines 55–57 of table 1, SCB, June 1973, June 1974, and June 1975) on bank-reported short-term liabilities to foreign official agencies (from TB, table CM-1-2, various monthly issues) for the period 1960I to 1974IV. We then estimated the official portion of U.S. liquid and nonliquid liabilities for 1955I to 1959IV using the regression coefficients and the bank-reported data from TB for that same period. The estimates were then added to net transactions in U.S. official reserve assets (line 46 of table 1, SCB, September 1970) to obtain the official settlements balance of payments for 1955I to 1959IV.

Only seasonally unadjusted data were copied from the sources listed above. We made the seasonal adjustment. The data were originally in millions of U.S. dollars.

B. *Exports*

1. Total Exports

   USEXQNTL Total Exports, 1955I to 1976IV. Unit: Billions of Dollars at
   USEXQSTL Annual Rates.

Source: For 1955I to 1959IV, SCB, September 1970, table 2, "U.S. International Transactions," line 1; 1960I to 1976IV, SCB, June issues, 1973, 1975, 1976, 1977, table 2, line 1.

Description: The balance-of-payments current account total of receipts from the sale of goods and services abroad as well as transfers from abroad on a transactions basis excluding transfers under military grants. The data were converted from quarterly rates to annual rates.

2. Exports of Goods

   USEXQNGO Exports of Goods, 1955I to 1976IV. Unit: Billions of Dol-
   USEXQSGO lars at Annual Rates.

Source: For 1955I to 1959IV, SCB, September 1970; 1960I to 1976IV, SCB, June issues, 1973, 1975, 1976, 1977: table 2, "U.S. International Transactions," line 2.

Description: Current account receipts from the sale of goods abroad excluding exports of goods under U.S. military contracts. The data were converted from quarterly rates to annual rates.

3. Exports of Services and Transfers

   USEXQNST Exports of Services and Transfers, 1955I to 1976IV. Unit:
   USEXQSST Billions of Dollars at Annual Rates.

Source: SCB, issues as in B.1 and B.2 above, table 2, line 1 minus 2.

Description: Derived by subtracting exports of goods from total exports and thus excludes transfers under military grants. Data were converted from quarterly rates to annual rates.

C. *Imports*

1. Total Imports

USIMQNTL   Total Imports, 1955I to 1976IV. Unit: Billions of Dollars at
USIMQSTL   Annual Rates.

Source: SCB, issues as in B.1 above, table 2, "U.S. International Transactions," line 15. Data were converted from quarterly rates to annual rates.

Description: The balance-of-payments current account total of payments for goods and services abroad as well as transfers to foreigners.

2. Imports of Goods

USIMQNGO   Imports of Goods, 1955I to 1976IV. Unit: Billions of Dol-
USIMQSGO   lars at Annual Rates.

Source: SCB, issues as in B.2 above, table 2, line 16.

Description: Current account payments for the purchase of goods excluding imports of goods included under direct defense expenditures. Data were converted from quarterly rates to annual rates.

3. Imports of Services and Transfers

USIMQNST   Imports of Services and Transfers, 1955I to 1976IV. Unit:
USIMQSST   Billions of Dollars at Annual Rates.

Source: SCB, issues as in B.1 and B.2 above, line 15 minus line 16.

Description: Derived by subtracting imports of goods from total imports and thus excludes direct defense expenditures on imports of goods. Data were converted from quarterly rates to annual rates.

D. *Net Private Capital Outflows*

USKPQNDR   Net Private Capital Outflows, 1955 I to 1976IV. Unit: Bil-
USKPQSDR   lions of Dollars at Annual Rates.

Source: For 1955I to 1959IV, SCB, September 1970, table 1, "U.S. International Transactions," lines 32, 52–56; 1960I to 1975III, SCB, June issues, 1973–75, March 1976, table 2, lines 38, 49–54; 1975IV to 1976IV, SCB, June 1976, 1977, table 2, lines 43, 59, 62–65.

Description: The balance of short- and long-term private (nonofficial) capital transactions, with net capital exports defined positive. Data were converted from quarterly rates to annual rates.

II. FINANCIAL VARIABLES

A. *Narrow Money Stock*

USM1QSQE   Money Stock—M1, 1955I to 1976IV. Unit: Billions of Dol-
USM1QSAE   lars.

Source: For 1955I to 1958IV, Board of Governors of Federal Reserve System, *Banking and Monetary Statistics, 1941–1970*, Washington, D.C., 1976, table 1.1; 1959I to 1973IV, Statistical Release of the Federal Reserve System, dated 22 February 1977; 1974I to 1976IV, Statistical Release of Federal Reserve System, dated 21 April 1977.

Description: Money stock—M1, currency in the hands of the (nonbank) public and demand deposits of the (nonbank) public, seasonally adjusted at the source. The two series are quarterly averages of monthly averages of daily figures centered on quarter's end (USM1QSQE) and quarter's average (USM1QSAE).

B. *Broader Money Stock*

    USM2QSQE   Money Stock—M2, 1955I to 1976IV. Unit: Billions of Dol-
    USM2QSAE   lars.

Source: Same as described in II.A above.

Description: Money stock—M2, the sum of M1 plus time deposits at commercial banks other than certificates of deposit, seasonally adjusted at the source. The two series are quarterly averages of monthly averages of daily figures centered on quarter's end (USM2QSQE) and quarter's average (USM2QSAE).

C. *High-powered Money*

    USMHQSQE   High-powered Money, 1955I to 1976IV. Unit: Billions of
    USMHQSAE   Dollars.

Source: For currency held by the public, same as II.A above; commercial bank vault cash, unpublished monthly Federal Reserve figures; member bank reserves at Federal Reserve Banks: 1955I to 1970IV, *Banking and Monetary Statistics, 1944–1970*, table 10.1; 1971I to 1976IV, *Federal Reserve Bulletin*, monthly issues, p. A-5; for nonmember bank clearing accounts: from Board of Governors of Federal Reserve System, *Annual Report*, annual issues 1954–77, table 1, "Detailed Statement of Condition of all Federal Reserve Banks Combined as of December 31."

Description: The series is the sum of currency held by the public, commercial bank vault cash, member bank reserves at Federal Reserve Banks, and nonmember bank clearing accounts. Currency held by the public is seasonally adjusted at the source. The seasonal adjustments on member bank reserves and vault cash were made by us. The 31 December nonmember clearing accounts data were interpolated along a straight line to mid-month dates. The final series is a quarterly average of monthly figures which, except for the latter component, are averages of daily figures, centered on quarter's end (USMHQSQE) and quarter's average (USMHQSAE).

D. *Official International Reserve Assets*

    USFHQNQE   Official International Reserve Assets, 1955I to 1976IV.
    USFHQSQE   Unit: Billions of Dollars.

Source: For 1955I to 1970IV, *Banking and Monetary Statistics, 1941–1970*, table 14.1, "U.S. Reserve Assets, End of Month"; 1971I to 1976IV, *Federal Reserve Bulletin*, January issues, 1972–77, table entitled "U.S. Reserve Assets."

Description: The series is the sum of gross holdings of gold, convertible currencies and, beginning in 1970, special drawing rights. The data are quarterly averages of end-of-month figures centered on quarter's end.

E. *Interest Rates*

 1. Short-Term

 a. USRSQN3T   Three-Month Treasury Bill Market Yield. Unit: Decimals.

Source: For 1947I to 1970IV, *Banking and Monetary Statistics, 1941–1970*, table 12.7, "Yields on Short-term U.S. Government Taxable Securities"; 1971I to 1976IV, January issues, 1972–77 of *Federal Reserve Bulletin*, table entitled "Money Market Rates."

Description: The series is a quarterly average of monthly averages of daily figures for three-month treasury bills.

 b. USRSQNFF   Federal Funds Effective Market Yield, 1955I to 1976IV.
                   Unit: Decimals.

Source: For 1955I to 1970IV, *Banking and Monetary Statistics, 1941–1970*, table 12.6, "Effective Rate on Federal Funds," 1971I to 1976IV, same as cited above in II.E.1.a above.

Description: The series is a quarterly average of monthly averages of daily figures of the effective market yield on federal funds.

2. Long-Term
   a. USRLQNGV   Market Yield on Long-Term U.S. Government Bonds. Unit: Decimals.

Source: For 1947I to 1970IV, *Banking and Monetary Statistics, 1941–1970*, table 12.12, "Bond Yields by Type of Security"; 1971I to 1976IV, U.S. Treasury Department, *Treasury Bulletin*, March 1978, table AY-1, "Average Yields of Long-term Treasury, Corporate, and Municipal Bonds."

Description: The series is a quarterly average of monthly averages of daily figures of the market yield on long-term U.S. government bonds.

   b. USRLQN3A   Market Yield on Triple A Corporate Bonds, Moody's Rating. Unit: Decimals.

Source: For 1947I to 1976IV, Moody's Investors Service, Moody's Industrial Manual, 1977, vol. 1, p. A36, "Moody's Average of Yields on Aaa Corporate Bonds."

Description: The series is a quarterly average of monthly averages of daily figures of the market yield on Triple A corporate bonds, Moody's Rating.

III. NONFINANCIAL DOMESTIC VARIABLES

A. *National Income*
 1. Nominal Gross Product
   a. USYNQSGN   Nominal Gross National Product. Unit: Billions of Dollars at Annual Rates.

Source: For 1947I to 1972IV, U.S. Department of Commerce, *The National Income and Product Accounts of the United States, 1929–74: Statistical Tables*, table 1.7, line 1; 1973I to 1975III, SCB, July 1976, table 1; 1975IV to 1976IV, SCB, May 1977, table 3, line 1.

Description: Gross national product at current market prices. The data are seasonally adjusted at the source.

   b. USYNQSGD   Nominal Gross Domestic Product. Unit: Billions of Dollars at Annual Rates.

Source: Same as described in III.A.1.a above, line 2.

Description: Gross domestic product at current market prices. The data are seasonally adjusted at the source.

 2. Real Gross Product
   a. USYRQSNO   Real Gross National Product. Unit: Billions of 1970 Dollars at Annual Rates.

Source: For 1947I to 1972IV, *The National Income and Product Accounts of the United States, 1929–1974: Statistical Tables*, table 1.8, line 1; 1973I to 1975III, SCB, July 1976, table 1; 1975IV to 1976IV, SCB, May 1977, table 3.

Description: Gross national product at 1970 market prices, seasonally adjusted at the source. Data were converted by us from 1972 base to 1970 base.

   b. USYRQSDO   Real Gross Domestic Product. Unit: Billions of 1970 Dollars at Annual Rates.

Source: Same as described in III.A.2.a above, line 2.

Description: The series is gross domestic product at 1970 market series, seasonally adjusted at the source. The data were converted by us from the 1972 base to 1970.

B. *Prices*

1. Implicit Price Deflator

a. USPDQSNO   Gross National Product Implicit Price Deflator. Unit: 1970 = 1.00.

Source: For 1947I to 1972IV, same as described in III.A., table 7.5, line 1; 1973I to 1975III, same as described in III.A above, table 7.5, line 1; 1975IV to 1976IV, same as described in III.A. above, table 22.

Description: Gross national product implicit price deflator, seasonally adjusted at the source, was converted by us from a 1972 base to the 1970 base.

b. USPDQSDO   Gross Domestic Product Implicit Price Deflator. Unit: 1970 = 1.00.

Source: For 1947I to 1972IV, same as described in III.A above, line 2; 1973I to 1975III, same as described in III.A above, table 7.5, line 2; 1975 IV to 1976IV, same as described in III.A above, table 22.

Description: Gross domestic product implicit price deflator, seasonally adjusted at the source, was converted from a 1972 base to the 1970 base.

2. Consumer Price Index

USPCQN70   Consumer Price Index. Unit: 1970 = 1.00.

USPCQS70

Source: For 1947I to 1976IV, U.S. Department of Commerce, *Business Conditions Digest*, March 1977, series 320, "Index of Consumer Prices, All Items," and table B1, "Price Movements."

Description: A general index of all consumer items. The final series is a quarterly average of monthly data, seasonally adjusted at the source, converted by us from a 1967 to the 1970 base.

C. *Industrial Production*

USIPQS70   Industrial Production Index. Unit: 1970 = 1.00.

Source: For 1947I to 1975IV, Board of Governors of Federal Reserve System, *Industrial Production: 1976 Revision*, table A-5; 1976I to 1976IV, Statistical Release of Federal Reserve System, "Industrial Production Indexes 1976," dated September 1977.

Description: A general index of industrial production including mining, manufacturing, utility, and construction industries. The data are quarterly averages of monthly data, seasonally adjusted at the source, converted by us from a 1967 base to 1970.

D. *Government Accounts*

1. Government Expenditure

USGXQSFD   Government Expenditure, 1955I to 1976IV. Unit: Billions of Dollars at Annual Rates.

Source: For 1955I to 1972IV, *The National Income and Product Accounts of the United States, 1929–74*, table 3.2, line 20; 1973I to 1975III, SCB, July 1976, table 3.2; 1975IV to 1976IV, May 1977, table 12.

Description: Expenditure of federal government inclusive of grants-in-aid to state and local governments. Data are seasonally adjusted at the source.

2. Government Deficit

USGDQSFD   Government Deficit, 1955I to 1976IV. Unit: Billions of Dollars at Annual Rates.

Source: For 1955I to 1972IV, same as described in III.D.1 above, line 43; 1973I to 1975III, same as described in III.D.1 above; 1975IV to 1976IV, same as described in III.D.1 above.

Description: Federal government deficit, defined negative, inclusive of expenditures of grants-in-aid to state and local governments. Data are seasonally adjusted at the source.

E. *Population*

1. USPPQNNB   Population. Unit: Billions of Persons.

Source: For 1947I to 1973IV, U.S. Department of Commerce, *The National Income and Product Accounts of the United States, 1929–74*, table 2.1, line 33; 1974I to 1977II, U.S. Department of Commerce, SCB, July 1977, table 2.1, line 33.

Description: The data are mid-quarter estimates taken from source in quarterly form and include armed forces.

2. USPPQNIN   Population, 1954IV to 1976IV. Unit: Billions of Persons.

Source: For 1954IV to 1976IV, United Nations, *Demographic Yearbook*, various issues.

Description: The data are straight-line interpolations of mid-year estimates and include armed forces.

F. *Labor Force Statistics*

1. USEMQSCV   Civilian Employment, 1955I to 1976IV. Unit: Billions of Persons.

Source: For 1955I to 1976IV, U.S. Department of Commerce, *Business Conditions Digest (BCD)*, April 1977, Historical Series 442, "Total Civilian Employment, Labor Force Survey," and table C1 (1976), "Civilian Labor Force and Major Components."

Description: The series is total civilian employment including part-time and self-employed regardless of nationality and is seasonally adjusted at the source.

2. USUNQSCV   Civilian Unemployment, 1955I to 1976IV. Unit: Billions of Persons.

Source: For 1955I to 1976IV, BCD, April 1977, Historical Series 37, "Number of Persons Unemployed, Labor Force Survey," and table C1 (1976) as cited above in III.F.1.

Description: The series is civilian unemployment including part-time job seekers and is seasonally adjusted at the source.

3. USLFQSCV   Total Labor Force, 1955I to 1976IV. Unit: Billions of Persons.

Source: For 1955I to 1976IV, BCD, April 1977, Historical Series 441, "Total Civilian Labor Force, Labor Force Survey," and table C1 as cited above in F.1 above.

Description: The series is total civilian labor force which includes civilian employed and unemployed persons sixteen years of age and older and is seasonally adjusted at the source.

4. USURQSCV   Unemployment Rate, 1955I to 1976IV. Unit: Decimals.

Source: Same as described in III.F.2 and III.F.3 above.

Description: The series is the ratio of civilian unemployment to the civilian labor force and these components were seasonally adjusted at the source.

List of Tables for the United States (Quarterly Data)

US_USBPQNDR

1955	1	0.1767	0.1305	0.0770	0.2945
1956	1	0.3038	0.3934	0.6335	0.9148
1957	1	0.2061	0.8536	0.2346	0.3613
1958	1	-0.0357	-0.9990	-0.0435	-0.0097
1959	1	-0.1457	-0.1797	0.3484	-0.1372
1960	1	-0.0190	-0.6770	-1.1560	-1.5510
1961	1	-0.4230	0.6150	-0.7140	-0.8260
1962	1	0.1110	-0.4120	-1.2660	-1.0830
1963	1	-0.3410	-0.9960	-0.4520	-0.1450
1964	1	0.4790	-0.5540	-0.6760	-0.7830
1965	1	0.0400	0.0690	-0.2780	-1.1210
1966	1	-1.3640	-0.3920	-0.7930	-0.5300
1967	1	-1.2790	-0.7100	-0.0200	-1.4090
1968	1	0.0910	1.5500	-0.0290	0.0280
1969	1	1.6920	1.2090	-1.0010	0.8390
1970	1	-1.9750	-2.0670	-2.6110	-3.1860
1971	1	-4.7180	-6.4620	-12.7030	-5.8700
1972	1	-2.5060	-0.7410	-5.5900	-1.5710
1973	1	-9.9940	0.7690	0.9040	2.9660
1974	1	1.3480	-4.1320	-1.7280	-4.3110
1975	1	-2.6330	-1.8840	2.3190	-2.3610
1976	1	-1.6870	-1.7300	-0.8460	-6.3010

US_USBPQSDR

1955	1	0.2039	0.2220	0.1230	0.1313
1956	1	0.3267	0.4965	0.6538	0.7845
1957	1	0.2107	0.9604	0.2233	0.2997
1958	1	-0.0657	-0.9134	-0.0787	0.0385
1959	1	-0.2487	-0.1223	0.3102	0.0266
1960	1	-0.2141	-0.6463	-1.1770	-1.2873
1961	1	-0.7226	0.6366	-0.7022	-0.5091
1962	1	-0.2557	-0.3954	-1.2304	-0.7588
1963	1	-0.7057	-1.0079	-0.3881	0.1317
1964	1	0.1994	-0.6275	-0.6059	-0.5408
1965	1	-0.1179	-0.1333	-0.1651	-0.8776
1966	1	-1.4597	-0.7345	-0.5498	-0.3400
1967	1	-1.3448	-1.1758	0.4121	-1.2775
1968	1	-0.0375	0.9474	0.7638	0.0005
1969	1	1.4791	0.4700	0.1633	0.6780
1970	1	-2.3044	-2.8784	-1.1313	-3.5518
1971	1	-5.0971	-7.1084	-11.3466	-6.2443
1972	1	-2.8904	-1.0816	-4.6891	-1.8174
1973	1	-10.3063	0.8307	0.9884	3.1003
1974	1	1.1084	-3.7008	-2.4499	-3.8264
1975	1	-2.7912	-1.1242	0.8746	-1.5138
1976	1	-1.8318	-0.7965	-2.6288	-5.2494

US_USEXQNTL

1955	1	18.956	19.684	19.392	21.760
1956	1	21.660	24.056	23.048	26.324
1957	1	26.968	27.948	25.272	26.424
1958	1	22.340	23.764	22.312	24.452
1959	1	21.776	23.344	23.748	25.740
1960	1	25.580	28.020	26.816	29.544
1961	1	27.988	28.560	27.404	31.140
1962	1	28.612	31.984	29.088	32.364
1963	1	29.608	33.572	30.944	36.376
1964	1	36.096	37.196	35.508	40.524
1965	1.	34.740	42.004	38.280	42.988
1966	1	40.660	43.220	41.328	45.892
1967	1	44.356	46.212	43.512	48.164
1968	1	46.376	51.460	49.752	52.148
1969	1	46.180	57.804	54.572	60.240
1970	1	59.984	64.984	60.448	64.516
1971	1	64.332	68.412	64.604	65.112
1972	1	68.580	70.908	69.460	81.712
1973	1	89.216	99.484	99.576	120.336
1974	1	133.808	146.628	140.296	158.480
1975	1	147.976	146.696	139.848	158.936
1976	1	155.288	164.976	160.740	175.800

US_USEXQSTL

1955	1	19.225	19.220	20.320	20.976
1956	1	22.023	23.503	24.107	25.335
1957	1	27.522	27.305	26.390	25.380
1958	1	22.856	23.258	23.255	23.419
1959	1	22.366	22.840	24.763	24.568
1960	1	26.366	27.367	28.019	28.152
1961	1	28.887	27.813	28.755	29.635
1962	1	29.510	31.093	30.647	30.759
1963	1	30.506	32.620	32.676	34.540
1964	1	37.172	36.158	37.459	38.557
1965	1	35.702	40.920	40.199	41.062
1966	1	41.749	42.155	43.141	44.076
1967	1	45.550	45.023	45.176	46.565
1968	1	47.621	49.979	51.518	50.765
1969	1	47.276	56.014	56.512	58.964
1970	1	61.093	62.887	62.803	63.362
1971	1	65.053	66.214	67.530	63.954
1972	1	68.807	68.838	73.064	79.963
1973	1	89.056	96.998	105.221	117.131
1974	1	133.245	143.633	148.567	153.500
1975	1	147.318	144.180	148.218	153.402
1976	1	154.646	162.480	170.348	169.303

US_USEXQNGO

1955	1	14.008	14.400	13.736	15.552
1956	1	16.004	17.872	16.612	19.736
1957	1	20.600	20.828	18.016	18.804
1958	1	16.372	16.936	15.408	16.940
1959	1	15.388	16.484	16.408	17.552
1960	1	18.656	20.232	18.944	20.768
1961	1	20.248	19.880	18.876	21.428
1962	1	20.228	21.652	19.840	21.004
1963	1	20.076	23.088	21.088	24.836
1964	1	24.824	25.436	23.948	27.796
1965	1	22.588	28.368	25.532	29.356
1966	1	28.364	29.604	28.020	31.252
1967	1	30.552	31.864	28.760	31.488
1968	1	31.760	34.576	33.240	34.928
1969	1	29.772	39.460	35.744	40.680
1970	1	40.988	44.596	40.564	43.728
1971	1	44.124	45.364	43.420	40.368
1972	1	44.064	48.296	46.476	55.088
1973	1	62.440	70.568	68.880	83.752
1974	1	91.068	101.180	92.632	108.360
1975	1	109.048	107.400	98.552	113.352
1976	1	109.148	117.552	109.700	122.368

US_USEXQSGO

1955	1	13.982	13.915	14.712	15.071
1956	1	16.025	17.277	17.747	19.107
1957	1	20.710	20.130	19.195	18.186
1958	1	16.491	16.416	16.350	16.360
1959	1	15.543	16.009	17.350	16.936
1960	1	18.888	19.662	19.991	20.046
1961	1	20.524	19.297	19.921	20.701
1962	1	20.494	20.996	20.980	20.266
1963	1	20.348	22.383	22.317	23.936
1964	1	25.194	24.628	25.363	26.801
1965	1	22.900	27.502	26.970	28.379
1966	1	28.729	28.713	29.523	30.297
1967	1	30.939	30.885	30.201	30.672
1968	1	32.168	33.376	34.907	34.203
1969	1	30.078	37.966	37.583	40.059
1970	1	41.213	42.775	42.854	43.201
1971	1	44.109	43.406	46.208	39.926
1972	1	43.733	46.218	49.846	54.356
1973	1	61.674	67.641	74.301	82.334
1974	1	89.675	97.275	100.271	106.016
1975	1	107.395	103.433	106.891	110.541
1976	1	107.510	113.355	119.065	119.077

US_USEXQNST

1955	1	4.9480	5.2840	5.6560	6.2080
1956	1	5.6560	6.1840	6.4360	6.5880
1957	1	6.3680	7.1200	7.2560	7.6200
1958	1	5.9680	6.8280	6.9040	7.5120
1959	1	6.3880	6.8600	7.3400	8.1880
1960	1	6.9240	7.7880	7.8720	8.7760
1961	1	7.7400	8.6800	8.5280	9.7120
1962	1	8.3840	10.3320	9.2480	11.3600
1963	1	9.5320	10.4840	9.8560	11.5400
1964	1	11.2720	11.7600	11.5600	12.7280
1965	1	12.1520	13.6360	12.7480	13.6320
1966	1	12.2960	13.6160	13.3080	14.6400
1967	1	13.8040	14.3480	14.7520	16.6760
1968	1	14.6160	16.8840	16.5120	17.2200
1969	1	16.4080	18.3440	18.8280	19.5600
1970	1	18.9960	20.3879	19.8840	20.7880
1971	1	20.2080	23.0480	21.1839	24.7440
1972	1	24.5159	22.6120	22.9839	26.6240
1973	1	26.7759	28.9159	30.6960	36.5840
1974	1	42.7400	45.4480	47.6640	50.1200
1975	1	38.9280	39.2960	41.2960	45.5840
1976	1	46.1400	47.4240	51.0400	53.4320

US_USEXQSST

1955	1	5.3316	5.3148	5.5919	5.8159
1956	1	6.1043	6.2188	6.3670	6.1561
1957	1	6.8964	7.1486	7.1930	7.0952
1958	1	6.4847	6.8403	6.8722	6.9613
1959	1	6.9676	6.8455	7.3516	7.5585
1960	1	7.5615	7.7343	7.9474	8.0882
1961	1	8.4338	8.5768	8.6707	8.9810
1962	1	9.0763	10.1548	9.4662	10.5625
1963	1	10.2409	10.2600	10.1275	10.8133
1964	1	12.0012	11.4915	11.8850	12.0230
1965	1	12.8345	13.3372	13.0568	12.9917
1966	1	12.9044	13.3409	13.5565	14.0556
1967	1	14.4364	14.0768	14.9537	16.1012
1968	1	15.2331	16.5982	16.6958	16.6951
1969	1	16.9858	18.1072	19.0552	18.9883
1970	1	19.5054	20.2221	20.1921	20.1903
1971	1	20.5326	23.0140	21.5999	23.9889
1972	1	24.6905	22.7660	23.4666	25.7728
1973	1	26.7672	29.3882	31.2862	35.3224
1974	1	42.6622	46.4673	48.3829	48.3981
1975	1	38.8396	40.3428	41.7392	44.0321
1976	1	46.0866	48.7531	51.4583	51.6574

US_USIMQNTL

1955	1	16.412	17.844	18.472	18.452
1956	1	19.348	19.732	20.248	19.180
1957	1	20.272	21.148	21.220	20.368
1958	1	19.600	20.988	21.292	21.564
1959	1	21.412	23.704	24.668	23.584
1960	1	23.132	24.368	24.272	21.816
1961	1	21.364	22.796	24.584	24.024
1962	1	23.788	25.716	26.328	25.864
1963	1	24.168	26.756	28.512	27.296
1964	1	26.392	28.736	30.232	29.836
1965	1	27.672	33.088	34.276	34.412
1966	1	34.416	37.856	41.052	39.716
1967	1	39.076	41.000	42.252	42.556
1968	1	44.168	48.004	51.680	49.568
1969	1	44.248	56.772	57.588	56.280
1970	1	55.356	60.492	62.220	60.112
1971	1	59.372	68.364	70.992	64.756
1972	1	73.480	78.064	80.368	82.564
1973	1	87.828	99.164	100.748	105.256
1974	1	117.168	146.664	151.856	149.060
1975	1	131.592	125.960	133.784	136.856
1976	1	145.148	157.904	167.920	168.228

US_USIMQSTL

1955	1	16.947	17.462	18.023	18.721
1956	1	20.009	19.306	19.742	19.449
1957	1	21.001	20.698	20.646	20.647
1958	1	20.350	20.566	20.644	21.855
1959	1	22.292	23.261	23.838	23.865
1960	1	24.175	23.957	23.363	22.046
1961	1	22.400	22.456	23.593	24.229
1962	1	25.012	25.383	25.217	26.030
1963	1	25.456	26.439	27.316	27.404
1964	1	27.815	28.420	28.981	29.951
1965	1	29.100	32.762	32.872	34.580
1966	1	36.109	37.498	39.370	39.996
1967	1	40.926	40.582	40.512	42.937
1968	1	46.307	47.338	49.578	50.147
1969	1	46.446	55.699	55.332	57.090
1970	1	58.187	58.943	60.006	61.133
1971	1	62.383	66.220	68.829	65.880
1972	1	77.083	75.391	78.325	83.918
1973	1	91.755	95.958	98.559	106.600
1974	1	121.975	142.594	148.773	150.433
1975	1	136.635	123.076	131.135	137.551
1976	1	150.735	154.704	164.527	168.692

US_USIMQNGO

1955	1	11.104	11.232	11.296	12.476
1956	1	13.020	12.692	12.620	12.880
1957	1	13.188	13.376	13.060	13.540
1958	1	12.556	12.664	12.496	14.092
1959	1	14.388	15.540	15.404	15.908
1960	1	15.344	15.468	14.240	13.980
1961	1	13.636	13.872	14.764	15.876
1962	1	15.808	16.384	15.920	16.928
1963	1	15.792	16.976	17.308	18.116
1964	1	17.464	18.400	18.716	20.220
1965	1	18.440	21.972	21.972	23.652
1966	1	23.652	25.080	26.160	27.080
1967	1	26.456	26.344	25.664	29.000
1968	1	30.736	32.808	33.884	34.536
1969	1	29.320	38.968	36.660	38.280
1970	1	37.896	40.136	39.344	42.088
1971	1	41.884	47.900	47.380	45.152
1972	1	53.432	54.572	54.836	60.348
1973	1	64.712	70.520	69.112	77.652
1974	1	88.404	106.072	107.712	112.528
1975	1	99.760	92.336	96.712	103.424
1976	1	112.436	121.268	127.616	134.344

US_USIMQSGO

1955	1	11.092	11.233	11.578	12.180
1956	1	13.032	12.675	12.930	12.576
1957	1	13.237	13.323	13.365	13.234
1958	1	12.642	12.584	12.758	13.792
1959	1	14.536	15.408	15.694	15.569
1960	1	15.566	15.322	14.464	13.674
1961	1	13.886	13.745	14.953	15.505
1962	1	16.154	16.261	16.072	16.507
1963	1	16.175	16.878	17.447	17.638
1964	1	17.903	18.314	18.857	19.701
1965	1	18.860	21.892	22.136	23.092
1966	1	24.133	24.979	26.355	26.527
1967	1	26.936	26.192	25.857	28.479
1968	1	31.344	32.439	34.180	34.020
1969	1	29.954	38.292	37.019	37.837
1970	1	38.801	39.148	39.825	41.775
1971	1	42.850	46.483	48.123	44.898
1972	1	54.560	52.846	55.887	60.046
1973	1	65.758	68.530	70.534	77.113
1974	1	89.499	103.659	109.855	111.550
1975	1	100.686	90.752	98.553	102.198
1976	1	113.500	119.515	129.936	132.497

US_USIMQNST

1955	1	5.3080	6.6120	7.1760	5.9760
1956	1	6.3280	7.0400	7.6280	6.3000
1957	1	7.0840	7.7720	8.1600	6.8280
1958	1	7.0440	8.3240	8.7960	7.4720
1959	1	7.0240	8.1640	9.2640	7.6760
1960	1	7.7880	8.9000	10.0320	7.8360
1961	1	7.7280	8.9240	9.8200	8.1480
1962	1	7.9800	9.3320	10.4080	8.9360
1963	1	8.3760	9.7800	11.2040	9.1800
1964	1	8.9280	10.3360	11.5160	9.6160
1965	1	9.2320	11.1160	12.3040	10.7600
1966	1	10.7640	12.7760	14.8920	12.6360
1967	1	12.6200	14.6560	16.5880	13.5560
1968	1	13.4320	15.1960	17.7960	15.0320
1969	1	14.9280	17.8040	20.9280	18.0000
1970	1	17.4600	20.3560	22.8760	18.0240
1971	1	17.4880	20.4640	23.6120	19.6040
1972	1	20.0480	23.4920	25.5320	22.2160
1973	1	23.1160	28.6440	31.6360	27.6040
1974	1	28.7640	40.5920	44.1440	36.5320
1975	1	31.8320	33.6240	37.0720	33.4320
1976	1	32.7120	36.6360	40.3040	33.8840

US_USIMQSST

1955	1	5.7277	6.2646	6.4795	6.5531
1956	1	6.8434	6.6784	6.8763	6.8933
1957	1	7.6756	7.4045	7.3237	7.4470
1958	1	7.6654	7.9680	7.8492	8.1214
1959	1	7.6846	7.8515	8.2216	8.3002
1960	1	8.5859	8.5902	8.8535	8.4457
1961	1	8.5631	8.6460	8.6289	8.7563
1962	1	8.8768	9.0634	9.1255	9.5774
1963	1	9.3399	9.5104	9.8240	9.8040
1964	1	9.9746	10.0674	10.0883	10.2592
1965	1	10.3102	10.8528	10.7621	11.4813
1966	1	12.0129	12.4960	13.0096	13.4875
1967	1	14.0786	14.3511	14.4732	14.4804
1968	1	14.9864	14.8800	15.5108	16.0891
1969	1	16.6522	17.3947	18.2558	19.3113
1970	1	19.4725	19.7895	20.0220	19.3775
1971	1	19.4907	19.7813	20.7655	21.0885
1972	1	22.3111	22.6285	22.5760	23.8371
1973	1	25.6734	27.5928	28.1076	29.4536
1974	1	31.9071	39.2042	39.3459	38.7367
1975	1	35.2960	32.5961	33.0799	35.2729
1976	1	36.2869	35.6159	35.9542	35.6416

US_USKPQNDR

1955	1	-0.6028	-0.4542	0.9841	-2.9618
1956	1	-0.3031	-2.3095	-1.2780	-4.0711
1957	1	-3.2724	-5.2743	-1.6145	-1.5813
1958	1	-2.5331	-4.1201	-2.1660	-2.7053
1959	1	0.8147	0.2946	1.4265	-1.4352
1960	1	0.0120	-1.3960	-3.4240	-8.1120
1961	1	-3.5800	-0.6960	-1.7800	-3.8520
1962	1	-0.5960	-2.5280	-3.9000	-5.1640
1963	1	-2.8200	-5.3160	-0.4720	-5.6520
1964	1	-4.4880	-5.6160	-2.6080	-7.2520
1965	1	-4.2680	-3.5040	0.3640	-6.7600
1966	1	-0.8000	-1.9560	3.5840	-2.8800
1967	1	-5.6720	-1.4440	3.2400	-4.7880
1968	1	4.0320	9.1480	4.2880	1.2160
1969	1	13.4720	12.0200	5.8080	1.2400
1970	1	-10.7560	-5.4320	-3.3920	-12.0280
1971	1	-17.4000	-10.0200	-20.0360	-10.6160
1972	1	-7.4160	11.6720	-2.3680	5.5680
1973	1	-22.7440	4.6960	9.8720	1.2960
1974	1	-9.1680	-14.0880	2.5280	-22.6960
1975	1	-29.1360	-19.7080	5.3480	-26.6800
1976	1	-33.0920	-27.1480	-3.2720	-23.6240

US_USKPQSDR

1955	1	-1.2518	0.3308	-0.2618	-1.8359
1956	1	-0.9576	-1.5816	-2.4784	-2.8912
1957	1	-3.9460	-4.6891	-2.7233	-0.2874
1958	1	-3.2297	-3.7582	-3.1825	-1.2225
1959	1	0.0783	0.4064	0.4904	0.2489
1960	1	-0.7745	-1.4009	-4.4503	-6.2329
1961	1	-4.3608	-0.6999	-3.0429	-1.8287
1962	1	-1.2799	-2.3983	-5.6157	-2.9488
1963	1	-3.3809	-4.9935	-2.7116	-3.2975
1964	1	-4.7455	-5.2438	-5.4624	-4.5110
1965	1	-4.2210	-3.4836	-2.7689	-3.5851
1966	1	-0.4838	-2.6010	0.5696	0.5369
1967	1	-5.0298	-2.8390	0.5507	-1.4677
1968	1	5.3286	6.7980	2.1285	4.0649
1969	1	15.8336	8.6741	3.9350	3.4592
1970	1	-6.8484	-9.7170	-5.3805	-10.5680
1971	1	-11.8359	-14.1937	-23.6719	-9.3471
1972	1	-0.2238	8.3232	-8.7113	7.2337
1973	1	-14.4164	3.0566	-0.0492	3.9201
1974	1	-0.0902	-14.0437	-10.5006	-19.2135
1975	1	-19.7843	-17.9346	-10.2604	-22.3748
1976	1	-23.7121	-24.4049	-20.1517	-18.7837

US_USM1QSQE

1947	1	110.367	112.000	112.833	113.267
1948	1	112.700	112.100	112.200	111.500
1949	1	111.233	111.333	110.933	111.233
1950	1	112.600	114.133	115.300	116.267
1951	1	117.500	118.633	120.333	122.600
1952	1	123.833	124.933	126.267	127.267
1953	1	127.900	128.533	128.667	128.833
1954	1	128.967	129.967	131.033	132.467
1955	1	133.800	134.600	135.000	135.200
1956	1	135.733	135.933	136.067	136.800
1957	1	136.867	136.967	136.800	135.900
1958	1	136.567	138.100	139.567	141.400
1959	1	142.967	144.333	144.167	143.467
1960	1	142.900	142.933	144.200	144.267
1961	1	145.233	146.333	147.300	148.667
1962	1	149.467	149.800	149.600	150.967
1963	1	152.233	153.967	155.200	156.767
1964	1	157.700	159.700	162.200	163.833
1965	1	164.867	166.400	168.600	171.433
1966	1	174.267	175.333	175.367	175.567
1967	1	177.933	181.367	184.900	187.367
1968	1	190.000	194.300	197.833	202.067
1969	1	204.833	206.733	207.633	209.300
1970	1	211.067	213.700	217.033	219.600
1971	1	224.133	229.667	232.367	234.233
1972	1	239.533	243.600	249.200	255.100
1973	1	258.200	263.600	265.767	270.300
1974	1	274.133	277.533	280.133	282.567
1975	1	283.667	290.067	293.333	295.233
1976	1	298.900	303.900	307.667	311.967

US_USM1QSAE

1947	1	109.833	111.633	112.600	113.100
1948	1	113.067	112.133	112.233	111.800
1949	1	111.200	111.367	111.033	111.033
1950	1	112.033	113.667	114.933	115.933
1951	1	117.133	118.200	119.700	121.900
1952	1	123.500	124.533	125.800	127.067
1953	1	127.567	128.433	128.633	128.733
1954	1	129.100	129.400	130.633	131.967
1955	1	133.500	134.300	134.867	135.100
1956	1	135.567	135.933	135.967	136.600
1957	1	136.867	136.933	136.967	136.233
1958	1	136.067	137.633	139.000	140.700
1959	1	142.600	143.800	144.533	143.633
1960	1	143.000	142.767	143.933	144.233
1961	1	144.833	146.033	146.867	148.300
1962	1	149.167	149.833	149.533	150.433
1963	1	151.833	153.333	154.800	156.400
1964	1	157.333	158.833	161.433	163.400
1965	1	164.500	165.800	167.700	170.500
1966	1	173.333	175.467	175.267	175.467
1967	1	177.167	179.733	183.867	186.600
1968	1	189.100	192.767	196.667	200.667
1969	1	204.067	206.167	207.333	208.533
1970	1	210.367	213.133	215.833	218.667
1971	1	222.400	227.967	231.767	233.267
1972	1	237.600	242.300	247.300	252.933
1973	1	257.700	261.633	265.200	268.667
1974	1	272.833	276.400	279.333	282.267
1975	1	282.767	287.733	292.800	294.600
1976	1	296.733	302.833	305.967	310.800

US_USM2QSQE

1947	1	143.967	145.900	147.533	148.633
1948	1	148.400	147.867	148.100	147.533
1949	1	147.367	147.700	147.333	147.633
1950	1	149.233	151.000	151.900	152.933
1951	1	154.133	155.600	157.967	160.800
1952	1	162.733	164.433	166.533	168.400
1953	1	169.767	171.167	172.200	173.333
1954	1	174.600	176.833	178.967	180.800
1955	1	182.633	183.767	184.533	185.133
1956	1	185.833	186.600	187.500	188.900
1957	1	190.467	191.833	192.933	193.233
1958	1	196.967	201.267	204.333	207.033
1959	1	209.233	211.233	211.300	210.933
1960	1	209.967	210.933	214.567	217.200
1961	1	220.233	223.400	226.133	229.033
1962	1	233.433	236.467	238.567	243.033
1963	1	247.167	251.367	255.167	259.267
1964	1	262.067	266.467	271.900	277.233
1965	1	282.633	287.333	293.900	301.400
1966	1	307.400	312.033	315.200	318.200
1967	1	325.400	335.000	343.800	350.000
1968	1	356.333	363.733	372.533	382.500
1969	1	387.900	391.033	390.600	392.467
1970	1	394.833	402.833	414.000	423.900
1971	1	440.433	454.200	461.833	472.233
1972	1	486.400	498.100	511.867	525.133
1973	1	535.333	547.533	557.567	571.267
1974	1	584.367	594.067	603.400	612.567
1975	1	622.667	641.100	653.000	665.567
1976	1	683.800	699.700	717.533	739.633
1977	1	757.133	774.633		

US_USM2QSAE

1947	1	143.300	145.433	146.967	148.300
1948	1	148.700	147.867	148.100	147.767
1949	1	147.300	147.667	147.433	147.433
1950	1	148.567	150.500	151.633	152.533
1951	1	153.767	155.000	157.133	159.900
1952	1	162.167	163.833	165.800	167.900
1953	1	169.200	170.800	171.833	172.933
1954	1	174.300	175.867	178.300	180.167
1955	1	182.167	183.367	184.267	184.967
1956	1	185.533	186.400	187.167	188.367
1957	1	190.000	191.367	192.667	193.233
1958	1	195.167	199.967	203.467	205.867
1959	1	208.767	210.533	211.633	211.033
1960	1	210.100	210.333	213.433	216.367
1961	1	219.167	222.367	225.200	228.000
1962	1	231.800	235.767	237.667	241.433
1963	1	245.867	250.000	253.833	258.200
1964	1	261.033	264.733	270.100	275.400
1965	1	280.967	285.567	291.467	299.000
1966	1	305.433	311.033	314.133	316.967
1967	1	322.866	331.300	341.167	348.167
1968	1	354.167	361.167	369.300	379.433
1969	1	386.433	390.467	390.567	391.833
1970	1	393.167	400.167	410.300	420.200
1971	1	434.633	450.367	459.367	468.100
1972	1	481.900	494.067	507.300	520.500
1973	1	532.600	543.367	554.033	566.467
1974	1	580.267	590.833	600.267	610.033
1975	1	618.733	634.167	650.200	660.733
1976	1	677.033	694.833	710.633	732.833
1977	1	751.033	768.333		

US_USMHQSQE

1947	1	44.574	44.919	45.524	45.346
1948	1	45.180	45.613	46.969	47.550
1949	1	47.169	45.850	43.983	43.267
1950	1	43.331	43.590	43.835	44.348
1951	1	46.540	47.087	47.890	48.378
1952	1	48.720	49.352	50.020	50.451
1953	1	50.397	50.316	50.030	49.944
1954	1	49.707	49.663	48.759	48.988
1955	1	48.957	49.175	49.330	49.381
1956	1	49.532	49.658	49.828	50.034
1957	1	50.002	50.142	50.128	50.048
1958	1	49.809	49.727	49.910	50.038
1959	1	50.305	50.637	50.726	50.374
1960	1	50.142	50.166	49.951	49.200
1961	1	48.943	48.887	49.524	50.232
1962	1	50.606	51.016	51.246	51.135
1963	1	51.744	52.313	52.789	53.669
1964	1	54.255	55.004	55.828	56.560
1965	1	57.291	57.892	58.669	59.653
1966	1	60.558	61.439	62.293	62.895
1967	1	63.730	64.230	65.331	66.486
1968	1	68.066	69.009	70.332	71.732
1969	1	72.604	73.652	74.030	75.414
1970	1	76.221	77.223	78.528	79.744
1971	1	81.724	83.167	84.302	85.737
1972	1	87.808	89.202	90.537	90.124
1973	1	92.046	93.911	96.226	98.643
1974	1	101.145	103.669	105.156	106.780
1975	1	107.167	108.065	109.042	110.907
1976	1	112.801	114.285	115.727	118.398

US_USMHQSAE

1947	1	44.541	44.779	45.337	45.448
1948	1	45.206	45.399	46.262	47.797
1949	1	47.199	46.446	44.591	43.350
1950	1	43.274	43.538	43.731	44.027
1951	1	45.852	46.965	47.556	48.287
1952	1	48.680	48.999	49.898	50.362
1953	1	50.422	50.411	50.072	49.900
1954	1	49.843	49.773	48.884	49.022
1955	1	48.891	49.097	49.282	49.372
1956	1	49.498	49.615	49.794	49.973
1957	1	49.949	50.095	50.167	50.065
1958	1	50.028	49.587	49.895	49.927
1959	1	50.266	50.525	50.740	50.429
1960	1	50.268	50.131	50.075	49.526
1961	1	48.928	48.884	49.210	50.070
1962	1	50.437	50.923	51.168	51.152
1963	1	51.534	52.108	52.662	53.377
1964	1	54.045	54.749	55.546	56.352
1965	1	56.996	57.711	58.350	59.343
1966	1	60.238	61.139	62.071	62.670
1967	1	63.545	63.944	64.943	66.080
1968	1	67.587	68.687	69.834	71.340
1969	1	72.326	73.491	73.677	75.005
1970	1	75.849	76.974	78.117	79.179
1971	1	81.183	82.652	83.944	85.128
1972	1	87.181	88.838	89.874	90.316
1973	1	91.403	93.230	95.429	97.851
1974	1	100.302	103.002	104.695	106.371
1975	1	106.997	107.757	108.654	110.347
1976	1	111.945	114.059	115.022	117.490

US_USFHQNQE

1955	1	21.7583	21.7303	21.7413	21.7530
1956	1	21.7713	21.8690	21.9987	22.1803
1957	1	22.4087	22.7310	22.7697	22.8513
1958	1	22.4217	21.4537	20.9173	20.5873
1959	1	20.4547	19.8817	19.5980	19.5393
1960	1	19.4436	19.3153	18.7377	17.7440
1961	1	17.4933	17.7000	17.5327	17.0580
1962	1	16.8610	16.8257	16.4857	16.1580
1963	1	16.0490	15.9097	15.8077	15.8117
1964	1	15.9487	15.8637	15.8207	15.9330
1965	1	15.0777	14.6010	14.8773	14.5743
1966	1	14.2250	14.3223	14.5487	14.2577
1967	1	13.5627	13.7797	14.3540	14.5487
1968	1	13.6450	13.4877	13.5657	14.3793
1969	1	14.3990	14.4817	14.6817	14.5837
1970	1	14.7817	13.7980	13.4510	12.8767
1971	1	12.7070	12.0197	14.5580	11.8077
1972	1	11.7753	12.8243	12.7690	12.7063
1973	1	12.4500	12.4467	12.9047	13.8430
1974	1	13.8437	13.9043	14.1357	14.0317
1975	1	14.0480	14.0247	14.1573	14.2267
1976	1	14.5503	14.9680	14.9257	14.6090

US_USFHQSQE

1955	1	21.7319	21.7495	21.7850	21.7231
1956	1	21.7343	21.8912	22.0428	22.1579
1957	1	22.3658	22.7484	22.8047	22.8512
1958	1	22.3888	21.4454	20.9323	20.6181
1959	1	20.4436	19.8432	19.5874	19.6044
1960	1	19.4540	19.2493	18.7082	17.8226
1961	1	17.5187	17.6304	17.4927	17.1239
1962	1	16.9020	16.7821	16.4319	16.1832
1963	1	16.1065	15.9182	15.7341	15.7742
1964	1	16.0367	15.9388	15.7172	15.8212
1965	1	15.2021	14.7187	14.7661	14.4049
1966	1	14.3811	14.4684	14.4271	14.0695
1967	1	13.7144	13.9314	14.2326	14.3689
1968	1	13.7813	13.6331	13.4414	14.2417
1969	1	14.5333	14.6011	14.5490	14.4823
1970	1	14.9223	13.8747	13.3279	12.8124
1971	1	12.8362	12.0598	14.4277	11.7591
1972	1	11.8997	12.8538	12.6622	12.6503
1973	1	12.5880	12.4571	12.8176	13.7872
1974	1	13.9706	13.9145	14.0655	13.9868
1975	1	14.1346	14.0428	14.0975	14.2055
1976	1	14.5997	15.0028	14.8602	14.6016

US_USRSQN3T

1947	1	0.003800	0.003800	0.007367	0.009067
1948	1	0.009900	0.010000	0.010500	0.011400
1949	1	0.011700	0.011700	0.010433	0.010767
1950	1	0.011033	0.011533	0.012200	0.013367
1951	1	0.013667	0.014900	0.016033	0.016100
1952	1	0.015667	0.016467	0.017833	0.018933
1953	1	0.019800	0.021533	0.019567	0.014733
1954	1	0.010600	0.007867	0.008833	0.010167
1955	1	0.012267	0.014833	0.018567	0.023400
1956	1	0.023267	0.025667	0.025833	0.030333
1957	1	0.031000	0.031367	0.033533	0.033033
1958	1	0.017600	0.009567	0.016800	0.026900
1959	1	0.027733	0.030000	0.035400	0.042300
1960	1	0.038733	0.029933	0.023600	0.023067
1961	1	0.023500	0.023033	0.023033	0.024600
1962	1	0.027233	0.027133	0.028400	0.028133
1963	1	0.029067	0.029367	0.032933	0.034967
1964	1	0.035300	0.034767	0.034967	0.036833
1965	1	0.038900	0.038733	0.038667	0.041667
1966	1	0.046100	0.045867	0.050433	0.052100
1967	1	0.045133	0.036600	0.043000	0.047533
1968	1	0.050500	0.055200	0.051967	0.055867
1969	1	0.060933	0.061967	0.070233	0.073533
1970	1	0.072100	0.066767	0.063300	0.053533
1971	1	0.038400	0.042500	0.050100	0.042300
1972	1	0.034367	0.037700	0.042200	0.048633
1973	1	0.057000	0.066033	0.083233	0.075000
1974	1	0.076167	0.081533	0.081900	0.073600
1975	1	0.057500	0.053933	0.063300	0.056267
1976	1	0.049167	0.051567	0.051500	0.046733

US_USRSQNFF

1955	1	0.013367	0.014933	0.019200	0.023567
1956	1	0.024800	0.026933	0.028100	0.029267
1957	1	0.029633	0.030000	0.032433	0.032333
1958	1	0.018633	0.009400	0.013233	0.021633
1959	1	0.025600	0.030833	0.035667	0.039900
1960	1	0.039333	0.036967	0.029367	0.022967
1961	1	0.020033	0.017367	0.016800	0.024033
1962	1	0.024033	0.025533	0.028467	0.029233
1963	1	0.029633	0.029633	0.033300	0.034533
1964	1	0.034633	0.034900	0.034567	0.035767
1965	1	0.039733	0.040767	0.040733	0.041667
1966	1	0.045567	0.049133	0.054100	0.055667
1967	1	0.048233	0.039900	0.038933	0.041700
1968	1	0.047900	0.059833	0.059433	0.059167
1969	1	0.065767	0.083267	0.089833	0.089400
1970	1	0.085733	0.078800	0.067033	0.055667
1971	1	0.038567	0.045633	0.054767	0.047500
1972	1	0.035400	0.043000	0.047400	0.051433
1973	1	0.065367	0.078167	0.105600	0.099967
1974	1	0.093233	0.112500	0.120900	0.093467
1975	1	0.063033	0.054200	0.061600	0.054133
1976	1	0.048267	0.051967	0.052833	0.048767

US_USRLQNGV

1947	1	0.022033	0.022000	0.022433	0.023400
1948	1	0.024467	0.024233	0.024467	0.024433
1949	1	0.023967	0.023800	0.022433	0.022033
1950	1	0.022367	0.023133	0.023433	0.023833
1951	1	0.024200	0.026133	0.025867	0.026567
1952	1	0.027167	0.026067	0.026733	0.027333
1953	1	0.028400	0.030700	0.030067	0.028267
1954	1	0.026133	0.025233	0.024900	0.025667
1955	1	0.027467	0.028167	0.029267	0.028900
1956	1	0.028867	0.029900	0.031267	0.033000
1957	1	0.032733	0.034333	0.036300	0.035333
1958	1	0.032567	0.031533	0.035700	0.037533
1959	1	0.039167	0.040600	0.041567	0.041667
1960	1	0.042233	0.041067	0.038300	0.039067
1961	1	0.038267	0.038033	0.039733	0.040067
1962	1	0.040600	0.038900	0.039800	0.038767
1963	1	0.039133	0.039800	0.040133	0.041067
1964	1	0.041567	0.041633	0.041433	0.041400
1965	1	0.041500	0.041433	0.041967	0.043500
1966	1	0.045567	0.045833	0.047800	0.046967
1967	1	0.044400	0.047100	0.049333	0.053300
1968	1	0.052433	0.053033	0.050733	0.054200
1969	1	0.058833	0.059133	0.061367	0.065333
1970	1	0.065633	0.068200	0.066500	0.062667
1971	1	0.058233	0.058833	0.057500	0.055200
1972	1	0.056500	0.056567	0.056267	0.056100
1973	1	0.061000	0.062267	0.065967	0.063000
1974	1	0.066367	0.070500	0.072700	0.069733
1975	1	0.067033	0.069733	0.070933	0.072233
1976	1	0.069100	0.068867	0.067900	0.065500

US_USRLQN3A

1947	1	0.025567	0.025367	0.025733	0.027767
1948	1	0.028467	0.027667	0.028300	0.028233
1949	1	0.027067	0.027067	0.026300	0.025967
1950	1	0.025767	0.026100	0.026333	0.026700
1951	1	0.027000	0.029000	0.028867	0.029533
1952	1	0.029567	0.029333	0.029467	0.029867
1953	1	0.030700	0.033233	0.032700	0.031333
1954	1	0.029567	0.028767	0.028833	0.028867
1955	1	0.029600	0.030333	0.031000	0.031167
1956	1	0.030967	0.032600	0.034233	0.036767
1957	1	0.037000	0.037733	0.040700	0.039967
1958	1	0.036067	0.035800	0.038700	0.040933
1959	1	0.041300	0.043533	0.044733	0.045700
1960	1	0.045533	0.044533	0.043133	0.043200
1961	1	0.042700	0.042833	0.044367	0.044100
1962	1	0.044100	0.042967	0.043367	0.042567
1963	1	0.041967	0.042200	0.042867	0.043333
1964	1	0.043700	0.044067	0.044100	0.044300
1965	1	0.044200	0.044433	0.044967	0.046133
1966	1	0.048133	0.050033	0.053200	0.053833
1967	1	0.051200	0.052633	0.056167	0.060267
1968	1	0.061267	0.062533	0.060767	0.062433
1969	1	0.067000	0.068867	0.070633	0.074667
1970	1	0.078933	0.081400	0.082200	0.079067
1971	1	0.072167	0.074733	0.075567	0.073000
1972	1	0.072333	0.072767	0.072067	0.071367
1973	1	0.072200	0.073067	0.075867	0.076500
1974	1	0.078967	0.083633	0.089867	0.090167
1975	1	0.087067	0.088733	0.089133	0.088100
1976	1	0.085567	0.085333	0.084633	0.081833

US_USYNQSGN

1946	1	197.40	205.00	215.30	220.40
1947	1	224.90	229.10	233.30	243.60
1948	1	249.60	257.10	264.00	265.50
1949	1	260.10	256.60	258.60	256.50
1950	1	267.40	276.90	294.50	305.90
1951	1	319.90	327.70	334.40	338.50
1952	1	341.10	341.30	347.00	359.20
1953	1	365.40	368.80	367.80	362.60
1954	1	362.00	361.80	366.20	375.00
1955	1	387.50	395.40	404.00	410.20
1956	1	411.90	417.40	422.40	430.90
1957	1	438.90	441.00	448.20	442.80
1958	1	435.80	439.90	453.10	466.30
1959	1	476.00	489.90	486.50	493.50
1960	1	506.60	506.50	506.20	504.60
1961	1	507.10	518.20	527.20	540.70
1962	1	553.00	562.10	567.80	572.30
1963	1	580.20	587.90	600.50	610.40
1964	1	622.40	632.40	642.10	646.00
1965	1	665.40	678.70	695.10	713.30
1966	1	733.70	747.60	759.00	771.70
1967	1	777.50	785.80	803.10	818.70
1968	1	837.30	861.80	880.00	894.70
1969	1	913.00	929.00	946.90	953.30
1970	1	964.20	976.50	992.60	996.30
1971	1	1034.00	1056.20	1072.40	1091.20
1972	1	1127.00	1156.70	1181.40	1219.40
1973	1	1265.30	1288.40	1317.50	1355.10
1974	1	1372.70	1399.40	1431.60	1449.20
1975	1	1446.20	1482.30	1548.70	1588.20
1976	1	1636.20	1675.20	1709.80	1745.10

US_USYNQSGD

1947	1	224.00	228.10	232.40	242.60
1948	1	248.50	255.90	262.80	264.20
1949	1	258.90	255.50	257.50	255.50
1950	1	266.20	275.60	293.00	304.50
1951	1	318.70	326.20	332.80	336.80
1952	1	339.70	339.90	345.50	357.80
1953	1	363.80	367.10	366.30	361.00
1954	1	360.30	360.10	364.40	373.00
1955	1	385.50	393.50	402.00	408.20
1956	1	409.60	415.20	420.10	429.10
1957	1	436.70	438.50	445.70	441.00
1958	1	433.70	437.70	450.90	463.90
1959	1	473.70	487.60	484.10	490.80
1960	1	504.20	504.10	503.70	501.90
1961	1	504.10	515.30	524.00	537.40
1962	1	549.90	558.60	564.30	568.20
1963	1	576.50	584.40	596.80	606.50
1964	1	618.00	628.20	637.60	641.80
1965	1	660.40	673.70	690.40	709.20
1966	1	729.50	743.30	754.90	767.40
1967	1	773.50	781.80	798.30	813.50
1968	1	832.90	856.70	875.20	890.10
1969	1	908.20	924.50	942.50	949.20
1970	1	959.50	972.20	987.80	991.70
1971	1	1028.50	1049.00	1066.60	1083.20
1972	1	1120.70	1150.10	1174.10	1211.30
1973	1	1256.50	1279.60	1308.80	1345.10
1974	1	1355.50	1387.00	1417.80	1434.40
1975	1	1436.70	1471.70	1537.40	1577.10
1976	1	1623.20	1662.80	1696.10	1730.40
1977	1	1777.70			

US_USYRQSN0

1947	1	423.92	427.17	427.49	432.83
1948	1	436.11	444.03	448.40	453.14
1949	1	448.54	446.63	450.63	446.88
1950	1	467.30	479.86	495.51	506.67
1951	1	513.74	523.60	534.12	535.06
1952	1	540.19	540.98	546.60	559.55
1953	1	568.43	572.26	568.77	563.31
1954	1	553.99	553.31	561.26	571.97
1955	1	585.75	594.55	603.31	609.38
1956	1	606.68	609.76	610.14	617.34
1957	1	621.59	622.06	626.41	618.20
1958	1	606.12	610.52	625.23	641.50
1959	1	649.28	663.58	656.54	663.54
1960	1	676.47	675.06	672.11	668.72
1961	1	672.91	684.36	693.24	709.87
1962	1	720.02	729.37	734.78	736.12
1963	1	743.25	752.59	766.46	773.80
1964	1	786.72	796.60	804.39	807.61
1965	1	825.09	837.26	851.74	869.85
1966	1	885.74	892.03	900.34	907.04
1967	1	908.48	914.79	925.96	933.23
1968	1	942.32	958.79	970.06	972.66
1969	1	981.92	986.35	989.83	984.36
1970	1	980.87	981.36	988.52	978.86
1971	1	1000.73	1008.01	1014.99	1023.77
1972	1	1042.58	1062.64	1076.24	1098.26
1973	1	1123.54	1124.81	1129.49	1135.31
1974	1	1124.18	1115.25	1108.15	1088.84
1975	1	1060.85	1075.41	1104.81	1113.85
1976	1	1138.60	1151.10	1162.29	1169.75

US_USYRQSD0

1947	1	423.12	425.59	426.65	431.51
1948	1	434.40	442.26	447.42	451.49
1949	1	447.45	444.94	449.27	445.78
1950	1	466.23	478.12	494.23	505.24
1951	1	512.98	522.29	532.86	533.66
1952	1	539.19	539.50	545.55	558.22
1953	1	566.62	570.78	566.65	561.30
1954	1	553.62	551.46	559.92	570.26
1955	1	583.52	592.68	601.52	607.81
1956	1	603.99	607.35	607.72	615.86
1957	1	619.96	619.63	624.01	616.49
1958	1	603.52	608.16	622.71	638.74
1959	1	647.35	661.41	653.75	660.85
1960	1	673.93	672.81	669.34	665.98
1961	1	669.87	681.78	690.30	705.92
1962	1	716.16	725.43	730.75	731.66
1963	1	739.22	748.30	762.05	770.13
1964	1	781.48	792.18	799.62	802.69
1965	1	819.23	832.34	847.25	865.67
1966	1	881.04	887.16	896.32	902.95
1967	1	904.31	910.52	921.52	927.36
1968	1	937.78	954.00	965.20	967.63
1969	1	976.85	981.68	985.90	980.57
1970	1	975.78	976.74	983.77	974.91
1971	1	996.09	1001.09	1009.46	1016.75
1972	1	1037.04	1056.76	1070.21	1092.14
1973	1	1116.38	1118.43	1123.54	1129.25
1974	1	1115.45	1111.36	1104.11	1083.80
1975	1	1057.57	1071.26	1100.68	1109.98
1976	1	1133.70	1146.47	1158.07	1164.96
1977	1	1180.29			

US_USPDQSN0

1947	1	0.53052	0.53632	0.54574	0.56281
1948	1	0.57234	0.57901	0.58875	0.58591
1949	1	0.57989	0.57452	0.57387	0.57398
1950	1	0.57223	0.57704	0.59434	0.60375
1951	1	0.62268	0.62586	0.62608	0.63264
1952	1	0.63144	0.63089	0.63483	0.64195
1953	1	0.64282	0.64447	0.64665	0.64370
1954	1	0.65344	0.65388	0.65246	0.65563
1955	1	0.66154	0.66504	0.66964	0.67314
1956	1	0.67894	0.68453	0.69230	0.69799
1957	1	0.70609	0.70893	0.71550	0.71627
1958	1	0.71900	0.72054	0.72470	0.72688
1959	1	0.73312	0.73827	0.74100	0.74374
1960	1	0.74888	0.75031	0.75315	0.75458
1961	1	0.75359	0.75720	0.76049	0.76169
1962	1	0.76804	0.77067	0.77275	0.77745
1963	1	0.78063	0.78117	0.78347	0.78884
1964	1	0.79113	0.79387	0.79825	0.79989
1965	1	0.80646	0.81062	0.81609	0.82003
1966	1	0.82835	0.83809	0.84302	0.85079
1967	1	0.85582	0.85900	0.86731	0.87727
1968	1	0.88855	0.89884	0.90716	0.91985
1969	1	0.92981	0.94185	0.95663	0.96845
1970	1	0.98301	0.99505	1.00413	1.01781
1971	1	1.03325	1.04780	1.05656	1.06586
1972	1	1.08097	1.08852	1.09771	1.11030
1973	1	1.12617	1.14544	1.16645	1.19360
1974	1	1.22107	1.25478	1.29189	1.33096
1975	1	1.36325	1.37835	1.40178	1.42586
1976	1	1.43702	1.45530	1.47106	1.49186
1977	1	1.51287			

US_USPDQSD0

1947	1	0.52940	0.53596	0.54471	0.56221
1948	1	0.57205	0.57862	0.58737	0.58518
1949	1	0.57862	0.57424	0.57315	0.57315
1950	1	0.57096	0.57643	0.59284	0.60268
1951	1	0.62127	0.62456	0.62456	0.63112
1952	1	0.63002	0.63002	0.63331	0.64096
1953	1	0.64206	0.64315	0.64643	0.64315
1954	1	0.65081	0.65299	0.65081	0.65409
1955	1	0.66065	0.66393	0.66831	0.67159
1956	1	0.67815	0.68362	0.69128	0.69675
1957	1	0.70440	0.70768	0.71425	0.71534
1958	1	0.71862	0.71972	0.72409	0.72628
1959	1	0.73175	0.73722	0.74050	0.74269
1960	1	0.74815	0.74925	0.75253	0.75362
1961	1	0.75253	0.75581	0.75909	0.76128
1962	1	0.76784	0.77003	0.77222	0.77659
1963	1	0.77987	0.78097	0.78316	0.78753
1964	1	0.79081	0.79300	0.79737	0.79956
1965	1	0.80613	0.80941	0.81488	0.81925
1966	1	0.82800	0.83785	0.84222	0.84988
1967	1	0.85535	0.85863	0.86628	0.87722
1968	1	0.88816	0.89800	0.90675	0.91988
1969	1	0.92972	0.94176	0.95597	0.96801
1970	1	0.98332	0.99535	1.00410	1.01723
1971	1	1.03254	1.04785	1.05660	1.06535
1972	1	1.08067	1.08832	1.09707	1.10911
1973	1	1.12551	1.14411	1.16489	1.19114
1974	1	1.21520	1.24802	1.28411	1.32349
1975	1	1.35849	1.37380	1.39677	1.42084
1976	1	1.43177	1.45037	1.46459	1.48537
1977	1	1.50615			

US_USPCQN70

1947	1	0.55714	0.56517	0.58122	0.59726
1948	1	0.60644	0.61647	0.63022	0.62420
1949	1	0.61503	0.61446	0.61245	0.61073
1950	1	0.60586	0.61073	0.62478	0.63739
1951	1	0.66032	0.66691	0.66949	0.67894
1952	1	0.67894	0.68124	0.68812	0.68840
1953	1	0.68439	0.68726	0.69270	0.69356
1954	1	0.69299	0.69241	0.69270	0.68955
1955	1	0.68869	0.68869	0.69098	0.69213
1956	1	0.69069	0.69585	0.70474	0.70990
1957	1	0.71420	0.72136	0.72910	0.73168
1958	1	0.73913	0.74486	0.74572	0.74572
1959	1	0.74572	0.74801	0.75260	0.75661
1960	1	0.75632	0.76148	0.76292	0.76750
1961	1	0.76779	0.76808	0.77209	0.77295
1962	1	0.77467	0.77811	0.78126	0.78298
1963	1	0.78412	0.78613	0.79186	0.79387
1964	1	0.79588	0.79759	0.80046	0.80361
1965	1	0.80505	0.81078	0.81450	0.81794
1966	1	0.82453	0.83285	0.84087	0.84718
1967	1	0.84890	0.85463	0.86380	0.87096
1968	1	0.88013	0.88988	0.90106	0.91195
1969	1	0.92226	0.93831	0.95178	0.96497
1970	1	0.97930	0.99506	1.00624	1.01942
1971	1	1.02716	1.03891	1.04922	1.05496
1972	1	1.06327	1.07187	1.08161	1.09135
1973	1	1.10654	1.13090	1.15584	1.18278
1974	1	1.21602	1.25041	1.28853	1.32608
1975	1	1.35015	1.37136	1.40059	1.42294
1976	1	1.43670	1.45447	1.47768	1.49431

US_USPCQS70

1947	1	0.56015	0.56655	0.57861	0.59541
1948	1	0.60954	0.61790	0.62764	0.62235
1949	1	0.61781	0.61590	0.61021	0.60906
1950	1	0.60825	0.61200	0.62290	0.63577
1951	1	0.66248	0.66822	0.66773	0.67747
1952	1	0.68084	0.68239	0.68656	0.68711
1953	1	0.68602	0.68841	0.69107	0.69255
1954	1	0.69453	0.69339	0.69110	0.68878
1955	1	0.69014	0.68944	0.68950	0.69158
1956	1	0.69203	0.69636	0.70349	0.70939
1957	1	0.71549	0.72168	0.72807	0.73114
1958	1	0.74036	0.74512	0.74486	0.74513
1959	1	0.74686	0.74825	0.75188	0.75602
1960	1	0.75728	0.76187	0.76220	0.76690
1961	1	0.76864	0.76857	0.77135	0.77238
1962	1	0.77543	0.77868	0.78042	0.78255
1963	1	0.78487	0.78659	0.79104	0.79352
1964	1	0.79664	0.79797	0.79960	0.80335
1965	1	0.80586	0.81103	0.81369	0.81765
1966	1	0.82547	0.83298	0.84002	0.84697
1967	1	0.84989	0.85462	0.86300	0.87075
1968	1	0.88126	0.88973	0.90019	0.91191
1969	1	0.92338	0.93805	0.95089	0.96502
1970	1	0.98054	0.99461	1.00527	1.01969
1971	1	1.02832	1.03844	1.04828	1.05516
1972	1	1.06438	1.07162	1.08064	1.09136
1973	1	1.10749	1.13120	1.15483	1.18223
1974	1	1.21705	1.25130	1.28745	1.32486
1975	1	1.35125	1.37289	1.39952	1.42101
1976	1	1.43795	1.45645	1.47655	1.49190

US_USIPQS70

1947	1	0.36246	0.36338	0.36369	0.37359
1948	1	0.37761	0.38163	0.38503	0.38101
1949	1	0.36864	0.35689	0.35782	0.35627
1950	1	0.37514	0.40637	0.43915	0.44627
1951	1	0.45554	0.45678	0.44627	0.44936
1952	1	0.45987	0.45307	0.46637	0.49946
1953	1	0.50998	0.51678	0.51616	0.49266
1954	1	0.47719	0.47534	0.47750	0.49080
1955	1	0.51771	0.53966	0.54801	0.56131
1956	1	0.56317	0.56100	0.55791	0.57801
1957	1	0.58358	0.57616	0.57832	0.55420
1958	1	0.52296	0.51400	0.54121	0.56564
1959	1	0.59038	0.61884	0.59379	0.59626
1960	1	0.63275	0.61884	0.60863	0.59379
1961	1	0.58513	0.60832	0.62780	0.64976
1962	1	0.65935	0.66584	0.67265	0.67821
1963	1	0.69120	0.70945	0.71409	0.72615
1964	1	0.73605	0.75337	0.76543	0.77656
1965	1	0.80625	0.82481	0.84212	0.85944
1966	1	0.88356	0.90243	0.91635	0.92501
1967	1	0.91944	0.91635	0.92470	0.95037
1968	1	0.96707	0.98253	0.99181	1.00449
1969	1	1.02211	1.02706	1.04036	1.03634
1970	1	1.01036	1.00510	1.00294	0.98160
1971	1	1.00232	1.01191	1.01748	1.03448
1972	1	1.07129	1.09634	1.11891	1.15541
1973	1	1.18324	1.19994	1.21200	1.21942
1974	1	1.20458	1.21571	1.22252	1.15572
1975	1	1.05026	1.05984	1.11799	1.14458
1976	1	1.17860	1.20025	1.21479	1.22252

US_USGXQSFD

1946	1	10.675	8.875	8.025	8.000
1947	1	7.175	7.300	8.050	7.325
1948	1	7.750	8.250	9.175	9.750
1949	1	10.000	10.425	10.600	10.350
1950	1	11.800	9.750	9.125	10.100
1951	1	11.900	13.625	15.300	16.975
1952	1	16.525	17.525	18.600	18.400
1953	1	19.075	19.550	19.150	19.350
1954	1	18.375	17.400	17.175	16.900
1955	1	16.975	16.675	17.225	17.250
1956	1	17.350	17.950	18.100	18.550
1957	1	19.525	19.950	19.950	20.250
1958	1	20.875	21.950	22.900	23.250
1959	1	22.625	22.475	22.875	22.975
1960	1	22.550	23.075	23.550	23.925
1961	1	24.725	25.425	25.700	26.100
1962	1	27.250	27.300	27.675	28.200
1963	1	28.375	28.050	28.525	29.200
1964	1	29.575	29.700	29.400	29.500
1965	1	29.550	30.100	31.525	32.625
1966	1	33.950	35.000	36.725	37.950
1967	1	39.975	40.225	41.275	42.225
1968	1	43.450	45.250	45.650	46.200
1969	1	46.075	46.800	47.350	48.225
1970	1	48.575	51.875	51.325	52.400
1971	1	53.375	55.225	55.550	56.475
1972	1	58.975	61.050	59.650	65.050
1973	1	65.425	65.550	66.150	67.875
1974	1	70.175	73.350	76.625	79.550
1975	1	84.250	88.575	90.925	94.000
1976	1	95.075	94.675	97.775	101.400

US_USGDQSFD

1946	1	-1.9250	0.6750	2.2500	2.5500
1947	1	3.7000	3.4000	2.5000	3.8000
1948	1	3.4000	2.6250	1.4500	0.8250
1949	1	0.1500	-0.7750	-1.0250	-1.0250
1950	1	-1.1750	1.9500	4.1500	4.3250
1951	1	4.5750	2.1000	0.2500	-0.4250
1952	1	0.0500	-0.9250	-1.8750	-0.9250
1953	1	-1.1250	-1.5500	-1.4500	-2.9500
1954	1	-2.6500	-1.6750	-1.2750	-0.4750
1955	1	0.4500	1.2250	1.2000	1.6250
1956	1	1.6500	1.4500	1.3000	1.5750
1957	1	1.1500	0.7000	0.7000	-0.3250
1958	1	-1.8750	-2.9750	-3.0250	-2.5000
1959	1	-0.7250	0.4000	-0.4500	-0.3750
1960	1	1.9250	1.0500	0.3500	-0.2750
1961	1	-1.0750	-1.2750	-0.9750	-0.5500
1962	1	-1.4000	-1.0250	-0.8000	-1.0250
1963	1	-0.4750	0.4750	0.3000	-0.0500
1964	1	-0.7500	-1.6750	-0.6000	-0.2500
1965	1	1.1500	0.9750	-0.7500	-0.8500
1966	1	0.1500	0.3250	-0.8000	-1.4750
1967	1	-3.2000	-3.3000	-3.4000	-3.2500
1968	1	-2.4250	-3.0000	-0.5750	0.1750
1969	1	2.8000	3.0000	1.6750	1.0500
1970	1	-0.2750	-3.2000	-3.6500	-5.0250
1971	1	-4.6250	-5.9500	-5.8500	-5.5500
1972	1	-3.3500	-5.0000	-2.7000	-6.2250
1973	1	-2.4250	-1.6500	-1.3000	-1.3250
1974	1	-1.0250	-1.9000	-2.2500	-6.3250
1975	1	-12.4500	-24.9750	-16.5000	-17.3500
1976	1	-15.9500	-13.5250	-14.3500	-14.8250

US_USPPQNNB

1947	1	0.143200	0.143800	0.144500	0.145100
1948	1	0.145800	0.146300	0.147000	0.147700
1949	1	0.148300	0.148900	0.149500	0.150200
1950	1	0.150900	0.151400	0.152000	0.152700
1951	1	0.153300	0.153900	0.154700	0.155400
1952	1	0.156000	0.156600	0.157300	0.158000
1953	1	0.158600	0.159200	0.160000	0.160700
1954	1	0.161400	0.162000	0.162800	0.163600
1955	1	0.164300	0.164900	0.165700	0.166500
1956	1	0.167200	0.167900	0.168700	0.169500
1957	1	0.170200	0.170900	0.171700	0.172500
1958	1	0.173100	0.173800	0.174500	0.175300
1959	1	0.176000	0.176700	0.177500	0.178300
1960	1	0.179700	0.180300	0.181100	0.181900
1961	1	0.182600	0.183300	0.184100	0.184900
1962	1	0.185600	0.186200	0.186900	0.187700
1963	1	0.188300	0.188900	0.189600	0.190400
1964	1	0.191000	0.191600	0.192300	0.192900
1965	1	0.193500	0.194000	0.194600	0.195300
1966	1	0.195800	0.196300	0.196900	0.197500
1967	1	0.198000	0.198500	0.199000	0.199600
1968	1	0.200000	0.200400	0.201000	0.201500
1969	1	0.202000	0.202400	0.203000	0.203600
1970	1	0.204100	0.204600	0.205200	0.205800
1971	1	0.206300	0.206800	0.207300	0.207900
1972	1	0.208300	0.208600	0.209100	0.209500
1973	1	0.209900	0.210200	0.210600	0.211000
1974	1	0.211400	0.211700	0.212100	0.212600
1975	1	0.212900	0.213300	0.213800	0.214300
1976	1	0.214600	0.214900	0.215400	0.215800
1977	1	0.216200	0.216600		

US_USPPQNIN

1954	1		0.163030	0.163749	0.164470
1955	1	0.165195	0.165930	0.166666	0.167405
1956	1	0.168147	0.168900	0.169663	0.170429
1957	1	0.171199	0.171980	0.172699	0.173421
1958	1	0.174146	0.174880	0.175611	0.176346
1959	1	0.177083	0.177830	0.178537	0.179246
1960	1	0.179959	0.180680	0.181444	0.182210
1961	1	0.182980	0.183760	0.184440	0.185122
1962	1	0.185807	0.186500	0.187170	0.187843
1963	1	0.188518	0.189200	0.189868	0.190538
1964	1	0.191210	0.191890	0.192489	0.193089
1965	1	0.193692	0.194300	0.194862	0.195425
1966	1	0.195990	0.196560	0.197094	0.197630
1967	1	0.198167	0.198710	0.199207	0.199706
1968	1	0.200206	0.200710	0.201200	0.201691
1969	1	0.202183	0.202680	0.203227	0.203775
1970	1	0.204325	0.204880	0.205419	0.205960
1971	1	0.206503	0.207050	0.207495	0.207942
1972	1	0.208389	0.208840	0.209229	0.209618
1973	1	0.210008	0.210400	0.210771	0.211143
1974	1	0.211515	0.211890	0.212323	0.212757
1975	1	0.213192	0.213630	0.214001	0.214373
1976	1	0.214745	0.215120	0.215494	0.215868

US_USEMQSCV

1948	1	0.057976	0.058296	0.058646	0.058515
1949	1	0.058142	0.057490	0.057390	0.057708
1950	1	0.057705	0.058761	0.059458	0.059643
1951	1	0.059899	0.059899	0.059954	0.060114
1952	1	0.060277	0.060108	0.060094	0.060611
1953	1	0.061831	0.061306	0.061151	0.060536
1954	1	0.060291	0.059962	0.059926	0.060248
1955	1	0.060815	0.061643	0.062753	0.063311
1956	1	0.063561	0.063765	0.063950	0.063894
1957	1	0.064098	0.064076	0.064207	0.063879
1958	1	0.062950	0.062745	0.062979	0.063498
1959	1	0.063940	0.064772	0.064875	0.064927
1960	1	0.065213	0.066061	0.066024	0.065840
1961	1	0.065738	0.065605	0.065667	0.065967
1962	1	0.066380	0.066577	0.066881	0.066969
1963	1	0.067149	0.067635	0.067996	0.068258
1964	1	0.068614	0.069402	0.069480	0.069710
1965	1	0.070188	0.070897	0.071369	0.071827
1966	1	0.072173	0.072594	0.073088	0.073657
1967	1	0.073572	0.074001	0.074714	0.075216
1968	1	0.075103	0.075950	0.076101	0.076499
1969	1	0.077166	0.077605	0.078153	0.078575
1970	1	0.078796	0.078622	0.078580	0.078543
1971	1	0.078508	0.078749	0.079265	0.079895
1972	1	0.080843	0.081449	0.081966	0.082466
1973	1	0.083297	0.084183	0.084625	0.085521
1974	1	0.085944	0.086043	0.086139	0.085577
1975	1	0.084392	0.084406	0.085028	0.085247
1976	1	0.086514	0.087501	0.087804	0.088133

US_USUNQSCV

1948	1	0.002254	0.002239	0.002288	0.002324
1949	1	0.002825	0.003581	0.004118	0.004325
1950	1	0.003946	0.003459	0.002898	0.002618
1951	1	0.002182	0.001923	0.001983	0.002111
1952	1	0.001914	0.001853	0.002005	0.001750
1953	1	0.001707	0.001642	0.001715	0.002334
1954	1	0.003338	0.003689	0.003813	0.003421
1955	1	0.003015	0.002832	0.002698	0.002790
1956	1	0.002679	0.002798	0.002763	0.002741
1957	1	0.002642	0.002722	0.002829	0.003317
1958	1	0.004223	0.004994	0.004975	0.004316
1959	1	0.003945	0.003493	0.003630	0.003855
1960	1	0.003557	0.003652	0.003889	0.004400
1961	1	0.004785	0.004927	0.004762	0.004348
1962	1	0.003958	0.003871	0.003931	0.003911
1963	1	0.004128	0.004083	0.003962	0.004038
1964	1	0.003970	0.003832	0.003658	0.003643
1965	1	0.003604	0.003471	0.003257	0.003082
1966	1	0.002898	0.002883	0.002858	0.002827
1967	1	0.002924	0.002939	0.002949	0.003076
1968	1	0.002919	0.002796	0.002779	0.002696
1969	1	0.002707	0.002762	0.002921	0.002930
1970	1	0.003430	0.003908	0.004295	0.004859
1971	1	0.004934	0.004932	0.005060	0.005085
1972	1	0.004941	0.004886	0.004874	0.004653
1973	1	0.004311	0.004315	0.004282	0.004307
1974	1	0.004556	0.004653	0.005136	0.006083
1975	1	0.007473	0.008126	0.007998	0.007855
1976	1	0.007130	0.007043	0.007457	0.007578

US_USLFQSCV

1948	1	0.060230	0.060535	0.060934	0.060839
1949	1	0.060967	0.061071	0.061508	0.062033
1950	1	0.061651	0.062220	0.062355	0.062261
1951	1	0.062082	0.061822	0.061938	0.062225
1952	1	0.062191	0.061960	0.062099	0.062361
1953	1	0.063539	0.062948	0.062867	0.062870
1954	1	0.063629	0.063651	0.063739	0.063669
1955	1	0.063829	0.064476	0.065451	0.066101
1956	1	0.066239	0.066563	0.066713	0.066634
1957	1	0.066740	0.066798	0.067035	0.067196
1958	1	0.067173	0.067739	0.067954	0.067814
1959	1	0.067884	0.068265	0.068505	0.068783
1960	1	0.068770	0.069713	0.069912	0.070239
1961	1	0.070523	0.070532	0.070429	0.070315
1962	1	0.070337	0.070448	0.070812	0.070881
1963	1	0.071277	0.071718	0.071958	0.072296
1964	1	0.072584	0.073234	0.073138	0.073353
1965	1	0.073792	0.074369	0.074626	0.074909
1966	1	0.075072	0.075477	0.075946	0.076483
1967	1	0.076496	0.076940	0.077663	0.078292
1968	1	0.078021	0.078746	0.078880	0.079195
1969	1	0.079874	0.080367	0.081074	0.081505
1970	1	0.082226	0.082531	0.082875	0.083403
1971	1	0.083442	0.083681	0.084324	0.084979
1972	1	0.085784	0.086335	0.086840	0.087119
1973	1	0.087608	0.088498	0.088907	0.089828
1974	1	0.090500	0.090697	0.091274	0.091661
1975	1	0.091865	0.092531	0.093026	0.093103
1976	1	0.093644	0.094544	0.095261	0.095711

US_USURQSCV

1948	1	0.037416	0.036987	0.037557	0.038200
1949	1	0.046331	0.058635	0.066946	0.069710
1950	1	0.064005	0.055590	0.046477	0.042044
1951	1	0.035156	0.031113	0.032023	0.033925
1952	1	0.030771	0.029900	0.032286	0.028063
1953	1	0.026872	0.026083	0.027287	0.037133
1954	1	0.052452	0.057953	0.059819	0.053725
1955	1	0.047229	0.043927	0.041220	0.042215
1956	1	0.040439	0.042026	0.041410	0.041128
1957	1	0.039597	0.040746	0.042196	0.049354
1958	1	0.062869	0.073719	0.073212	0.063643
1959	1	0.058111	0.051168	0.052993	0.056057
1960	1	0.051726	0.052379	0.055622	0.062634
1961	1	0.067854	0.069856	0.067613	0.061836
1962	1	0.056269	0.054949	0.055509	0.055182
1963	1	0.057915	0.056929	0.055059	0.055848
1964	1	0.054701	0.052326	0.050019	0.049659
1965	1	0.048840	0.046679	0.043644	0.041148
1966	1	0.038606	0.038201	0.037632	0.036957
1967	1	0.038224	0.038193	0.037972	0.039286
1968	1	0.037408	0.035498	0.035230	0.034047
1969	1	0.033896	0.034370	0.036031	0.035945
1970	1	0.041707	0.047358	0.051829	0.058261
1971	1	0.059127	0.058942	0.060002	0.059833
1972	1	0.057598	0.056594	0.056126	0.053412
1973	1	0.049204	0.048762	0.048166	0.047948
1974	1	0.050342	0.051303	0.056261	0.066365
1975	1	0.081346	0.087812	0.085973	0.084373
1976	1	0.076141	0.074494	0.078280	0.079176

Author Index

Subject Index

Adaptive expectations, 363
Aggregate demand function, 241 n. 15, 242–44, 274–75; Barro's approach, 9; elasticity of, 243, 243 n. 17; employment effects and, 243 n. 18; and oil price shocks, 240
Aggregate supply function: autocorrelation in output movements, 422; Lucas approach, 9, 11, 241, 274, 286, 362
Arbitrage channels. *See* Goods substitution; Interest arbitrage; Law of one price level; Price arbitrage
ARIMA models, 97, 164 n. 5, 249 n. 24, 273, 276, 277 n. 11, 283; PPR stochastic process, 466–73
Asset substitution, 3, 116; interest arbitrage, 501; and monetary control, 301, 311; portfolio balance approach, 501–2
Autocorrelation, 284 n. 17

Balance of payments (BOP): of the U.S., 21, 50–51; and sterilization, 295–97. *See also* Monetary control; Sterilization
Bank for International Settlements, 26
Bonds, nonmarketable, 23, 23n
Box-Jenkins techniques, 67. *See also* ARIMA models
Bretton Woods system, 14, 43–44, 201; collapse, 26–32, 510–11, 515; and dollar exchange standard, 19–26; dollar reserves in, role of, 14, 20, 25–26, 498; gold convertibility, 24; gold reserves, 14, 18, 21–23, 29; and the IMF, 14, 24; monetary

policy, U.S., 24–25; preconvertibility, 18–19

Canada: capital flows equation, 402; central bank behavior and the BOP, 77–78; data, 5, 51, 53–54, 527–48; floating rate regime, 19; interest rate arbitrage, tests of, 76; monetary control, 80, 306–11, 342–43; monetary growth sources, 78; money shock simulation, 170–86; oil prices and real income, 250–69; prediction error of PPP, 470–72; price and foreign shocks, 434–37; price arbitrage, tests of, 75; real income and demand changes, 276–82; sterilization coefficient, 337–38
Capital, 235 n. 4; capital-labor ratio, world, 248; growth in the U.S., 248 n. 22; marginal product of, 236n; rental price of, 234 n. 2
Capital flows, 121, 317; and OPEC, 95; and transitory income, 95; of the U.S., 26. *See also* Capital flows equation
Capital flows equation: expectational variables in, 330–36; government restrictions in, 397; IAPM formulations, 397–400; IMF data estimates, 406–15; Kouri-Porter type, 321–22; in Mark III models, 94–95, 119, 149–51, 502; multicollinearity problem, 383–84, 395–96; offset coefficient, 315, 321–22, 326–36; OLS vs. 2SLS estimates, 402–3; portfolio approach models, 380–89; return differentials in, 389–91, 412–13; risk prox-